# THE BROOKLYN BOTANIC GARDEN

# GARDENER'S DESK REFERENCE

# THE

# BROOKLYN

# BOTANIC

# GARDEN

HENRY HOLT AND COMPANY    NEW YORK

# GARDENER'S

# DESK

# REFERENCE

**JANET MARINELLI**, GENERAL EDITOR

Principal Illustrations by Stephen K-M. Tim

Henry Holt and Company, Inc.
*Publishers since 1866*
115 West 18th Street
New York, New York 10011

Henry Holt ® is a registered trademark of Henry Holt and Company, Inc.

Published in Canada by Fitzhenry & Whiteside Ltd.
195 Allstate Parkway, Markham, Ontario L3R 4T8

Library of Congress Cataloging-in-Publication Data
Brooklyn Botanic Garden's gardener's desk reference / Janet Marinelli,
general editor.—1st ed.
p.     cm.
Includes bibliographical references and index.
ISBN 0-8050-5095-7 (hb : alk. paper)
1. Gardening—Handbooks, manuals, etc. 2. Botany—Handbooks,
manuals, etc.  I. Marinelli, Janet.  II. Brooklyn Botanic Garden.
SB450.96.B76 1998
635.9—dc21                                                98-6314

Henry Holt books are available for special promotions
and premiums. For details contact: Director, Special Markets.

First Edition 1998

DESIGNED BY KATE NICHOLS

Printed in the United States of America
All first editions are printed on acid-free paper.

1   3   5   7   9   10   8   6   4   2

# TABLE OF CONTENTS

FOREWORD     vii

PREFACE     ix

CONTRIBUTORS     xi

**1.** WHO THEY WERE     3

**2.** GARDENER'S ATLAS     14

**3.** BOTANY FOR GARDENERS     39
*Plant Names*
*Plant Classification*
*Plant Structures and Their Functions*
*Plant Reproduction*

**4.** PLANT CONSERVATION     112
*Plant Diversity*
*Vanishing Plants*

**5.** ECOLOGY FOR GARDENERS     142

**6.** NATURAL GARDENING     180

**7.** KITCHEN GARDENING     232
*Vegetables*
*Herbs*
*Fruits*

**8.** ORNAMENTAL GARDENING     288
*Plants for Every Purpose and Every Region*
*Gardening Techniques*

**9.** SAFE PEST CONTROL  538

**10.** INDOOR GARDENING  569

**11.** CITY GARDENING  598

**12.** GARDEN TOOLS  611

**13.** THE HORTICULTURAL TRAVELER  621

**14.** POISONOUS PLANTS  641

**15.** PLANTS IN LITERATURE AND LORE  671

**16.** PLANT TRIVIA  685

ESSENTIAL RESOURCES  697
WEIGHTS, MEASURES, AND CONVERSIONS  733
GLOSSARY  739
INDEX  761

# FOREWORD

The Brooklyn Botanic Garden's pioneering publications have helped generations of gardeners find answers to their plant predicaments. Today, with the publication of the *Gardener's Desk Reference,* we add a new landmark volume to your library, one that presents a treasure trove of information for the horticulturally inclined in one concise book.

As with all our publications, we have relied heavily on the expertise of our talented staff, who have experience growing more than 12,000 different kinds of plants from all over the world on BBG's 52 acres. We have also gathered together regional contributors from across the country to ensure that this reference is of great value to plant enthusiasts throughout North America.

Such a monumental undertaking would have been impossible without the vision and tenacity of General Editor Janet Marinelli, our Director of Publishing, and the guiding hand of Dr. Stephen K-M. Tim, Vice President for Science, Library, and Publications at the Brooklyn Botanic Garden. Together with their team of experts they have produced a reference that should serve your gardening needs well into the twenty-first century.

—Judith D. Zuk, President
Brooklyn Botanic Garden

# PREFACE

What's a good shrub rose for my coastal California garden? What's chewing holes in my hostas? Can you recommend a spectacular shade-tolerant shrub that can grow in a container in my small city garden? How can I force daffodils to bloom in my living room? How do I espalier my flowering quince? What is a good bonsai for growing indoors? Where's the best place to have my soil tested? Why is it important to grow open-pollinated vegetables? What's the difference between a sepal and a tepal? For decades, experts at the Brooklyn Botanic Garden have been answering these and countless other questions.

In 1919, BBG established a Plant Information Service to serve as a horticultural hot line for gardening enthusiasts, the first of its kind at an American botanic garden. In 1945, the Garden began publishing the country's first gardening handbooks. Over the years, the handbook series has grown into an entire library, while the horticulturists who staff the hot line have amassed banks of file cabinets bulging with information on every conceivable plant-related topic. A few years ago we decided to condense this vast storehouse of knowledge and practical expertise into one concise, user-friendly reference.

There's enough information in this volume to serve any plant enthusiast—beginner and professional alike—over a lifetime. New gardeners across the continent will find thousands of plant recommendations, from choice flowering trees to disease-resistant turf grasses, compiled by a team of veteran landscape designers and horticulturists from every region. Among the many helpful features for professionals is the exhaustive list of names and addresses of the International Registration Authorities for cultivated plants.

Plant enthusiasts could find much of the information in this book in other sources, if they were willing to spend hours scouring library shelves and surfing the World Wide Web. One of this volume's chief virtues is having this far-flung material compiled, condensed, and published under one cover. To help readers find the information they are looking for in the quickest and most efficient manner, the *Desk Reference* is divided into some twenty different sections—from "Botany for Gardeners" and "Ornamental Gardening" to "Kitchen Gardening" and an encyclopedia of poisonous plants. In one indispensable section alone ("Weights, Measures, and Conversions"), gardeners will find charts, tables, and simple explanations that help solve such pesky problems as calculating how much potting soil is needed to fill a certain size pot or how much fertilizer should be applied to a given plot of land. In fact, hundreds of useful sidebars, graphs, tables, lists, maps, and illustrations are sprinkled throughout the book to make it more accessible and attractive.

Because the love of plants inevitably leads gardeners into other, related pursuits—notably travel—we've included a whole section on the world's biggest flower shows and most spectacular public gardens, as well as ecotourism destinations featuring some of Earth's most remarkable flora. Last but not least is one of the most comprehensive glossaries of plant-related terms ever published. Because a work of this scope could never be the definitive treatment of any single subject, lists of recommended resources for further information—both print and electronic—are appended at the end of each topic section.

In some important ways the *Desk Reference* breaks new ground. To do justice to North America's breathtaking diversity of climates and plant communities, from temperate rain forest to desert and from alpine to subtropical, all plant lists are organized by region, and each and every species or cultivar has been recommended by an experienced landscaper who has been tested by years of gardening in the area. Environmentally appropriate garden designs for every region are included. Indeed, this volume is unique among major horticultural references in its view of gardens as essential ecosystems. Chapters such as "Ecology for Gardeners," "Plant Conservation," and "Natural Gardening" go a long way toward making gardeners aware of their increasingly critical role as participants in the living landscape.

We at the Brooklyn Botanic Garden would like to thank Henry Holt and Company for giving us this opportunity to continue our tradition of producing pioneering publications for those who love plants. Our hope is that this *Desk Reference* will help gardeners everywhere to celebrate our glorious past, reap greater pleasure in the present, and articulate a bold new vision for the future.

—Janet Marinelli
General Editor

# CONTRIBUTORS

GENERAL EDITOR

**Janet Marinelli,** Director of Publishing, Brooklyn Botanic Garden

REGIONAL CONTRIBUTORS

Midwest and Northern Plains: **C. Colston Burrell,** President, Native Landscape Design and Restoration, Ltd., Minneapolis, Minnesota

California: **Robyn Sherrill,** landscape architect, Novato, California

Southeast: **Ken Moore,** Assistant Director, North Carolina Botanical Garden

Northeast: **Robert Newgarden,** Curator of Plant Family Collection and Herb Garden, Brooklyn Botanic Garden

Western Deserts: **Judith Phillips,** landscape designer, Veguita, New Mexico

Pacific Northwest: **Andy Rice,** landscape architect, Lake Oswego, Oregon

South Florida: **Georgia Tasker,** garden writer, *Miami Herald*

Texas and the Southern Plains: **Sally Waskowski,** landscape designer and author of *Native Texas Plants*

Rocky Mountain Region: **Gayle Weinstein,** landscape designer and owner, Eletes Consultants, Denver, Colorado

WRITERS

**Paul Dunphy,** freelance garden writer

**Anne Garland,** Publications Department, Brooklyn Botanic Garden

**Judy Glattstein,** freelance garden writer and author of *Waterscaping: Plants and Ideas for Natural and Created Water Gardens*

**Carol Goodstein,** Publications Department, Brooklyn Botanic Garden

**Beth Hanson,** Publications Department, Brooklyn Botanic Garden

**Betsy Kissam,** Publications Department, Brooklyn Botanic Garden

**Paul Prince,** freelance writer

**Lee Reich,** freelance garden writer and horticultural consultant and author of *Uncommon Fruits Worthy of Attention*

**Carole Turner,** freelance garden writer

TECHNICAL EDITORS

**Scott R. Canning,** Curator of Warm Temperate Plants, Brooklyn Botanic Garden

**Dr. Steven E. Clemants,** Director of Science, Brooklyn Botanic Garden

**Sheila Daar,** Executive Director, Bio-Integral Resource Center

**Dr. Thomas Delendick,** Research Associate, Brooklyn Botanic Garden

**Dr. Bryan E. Dutton,** Research Taxonomist, Brooklyn Botanic Garden

**Jacqueline Fazio,** Director of Horticulture, Brooklyn Botanic Garden

**Mark Fisher,** Foreman of Conservatories, Brooklyn Botanic Garden

**Robert M. Hays,** Propagator, Brooklyn Botanic Garden

**Robert Hyland,** Vice President, Horticulture, Education, and Operations, Brooklyn Botanic Garden

**Patricia Jasaitis,** Coordinator, Urban Composting Project, Brooklyn Botanic Garden

**Dr. John Kartesz,** Biota of North American Program, North Carolina Botanical Garden

**Robert A. Mahler,** Curator of Bonsai, Brooklyn Botanic Garden

**Elvin McDonald,** Garden Editor, *Traditional Home* magazine

**Wayne Morris,** Arborist, Brooklyn Botanic Garden

**Dr. Peter Nelson,** Professor Emeritus of Biology, Brooklyn College

**Dr. John M. Randall,** Wildland Weeds Management and Research Project, The Nature Conservancy

**Daniel K. Ryniec,** Curator of Lilac Collection and Osborne Garden, Brooklyn Botanic Garden

**Stephen Scanniello,** Rosarian, Brooklyn Botanic Garden

**Elizabeth Scholtz,** Director Emeritus, Brooklyn Botanic Garden

**Dr. Stephen K-M. Tim,** Vice President, Science, Library, and Publications, Brooklyn Botanic Garden

# THE BROOKLYN BOTANIC GARDEN

# GARDENER'S DESK REFERENCE

# 1

# WHO THEY
# WERE

From antiquity to the present day, countless people have contributed to our knowledge of plants and gardening. It would be impossible to list each and every one, but here are some of the most influential people throughout history who have made significant contributions in botany, horticulture, landscaping, and related fields.

### Adanson, Michel *(1727–1806)*
A French naturalist and plant systematist, Adanson spent four years in Senegal, West Africa, and became one of the first scientists to learn the flora and fauna of the tropics and recognize how different they were from those of temperate regions. Adanson formally organized all plant genera into families and published an opus on his work, called *Familles des Plantes.* This publication presented a new concept of plant relationships and introduced a new approach to naming plants, although his nomenclature system was considered too radical to replace the binomial system of Linnaeus.

### Bailey, Liberty Hyde, Jr. *(1858–1954)*
An American horticulturist, Bailey began his career working under Asa Gray as assistant curator of the herbarium at Harvard University, where he was also in charge of nomenclature for the gardens, greenhouses, and herbaria. He later became a professor of horticulture and landscape gardening at Michigan State (Agricultural) College, and in 1888 he moved on to Cornell University. Bailey was the founder and president of the American Society for Horticultural Science and of the Botanical Society of America. He also founded and developed the Bailey Hortorium of the New York State College of Agriculture, which publishes the quarterly *Baileya.* Liberty Hyde Bailey is best remembered for *Hortus,* the comprehensive,

widely used encyclopedia of plants that he compiled with his daughter Ethel.

## Banks, Joseph (1743–1820)

An English botanist, plant collector, and explorer in the late eighteenth century, Banks had a great deal of family wealth, which he used to fund his many expeditions. He had resolved as a boy to become a botanist, and his first trip was to Labrador and Newfoundland to study the plants there. Beginning in 1769, he made a three-year voyage to the South Pacific with Captain James Cook, accompanied by botanist Daniel Solander (1736–1782). Another voyage was planned with Cook in 1772, but the trip fell through, and Banks went to Iceland instead. Banks was active in shaping the science policy of eighteenth- and nineteenth-century England. He advocated the study of science and natural history, particularly botany and horticulture, and helped in founding the Horticultural Society of London (now the Royal Horticultural Society), of which he was president for forty-two years. He also played a part in establishing the Royal Botanic Gardens at Kew, bringing seeds and plants from all around the world to help expand its horticultural collections.

## Barton, Benjamin Smith (1766–1815)

The first professor of botany at the University of Pennsylvania, Barton had Meriwether Lewis among his students. He promoted the idea of a comprehensive flora of North America, but never succeeded in writing it. However, he did publish *Elements of Botany,* the first botanical textbook in the United States.

## Bartram, John (1699–1777)

A Quaker farmer born in Pennsylvania, Bartram has been called "the father of American botany." Linnaeus himself dubbed him "the greatest natural botanist of his time." Together with his son William (1739–1823), Bartram made many expeditions collecting seeds, bulbs, roots, cuttings, and plants of native American species, which he then shipped to England. In 1765, he was appointed royal botanist in the American colonies by King George III. Bartram established a botanical garden in Philadelphia, Pennsylvania.

## Bosenberg, Henry F. (dates unknown)

The first person to obtain a United States plant patent, on August 18, 1931. Plant Patent No. 1 covered the climbing rose New Dawn, which blooms successively throughout the season instead of in June only.

## Bridgeman, Thomas (dates unknown)

An American who published the first gardener's manual in 1835. Called the *Young Gardener's Assistant,* the manual contained a catalog of vegetable and flower seeds with practical instructions for cultivation.

## Britton, Nathaniel Lord (1859–1934)

Britton was an American botanist who established the New York Botanical Garden, inspired by the Royal Botanic Gardens at Kew, England. He was responsible for developing the NYBG's comprehensive botanical library and reference herbarium. He also wrote several floras, including *Illustrated Flora of the Northern United States and Canada,* the first fully illustrated flora on any part of North America, written with Judge Addison Brown from 1896 to 1898.

## Brown, Lancelot "Capability" (1715–1783)

An English landscape gardener who created parks for the gentry and nobility in the late eighteenth century, Brown was eventually appointed Master Gardener to King George III. He was nicknamed "Capability Brown" because he would tell his clients that their property had "great capabilities." Brown helped advance a revolution in English garden design, which had been very formal. He removed knot gardens, formal parterres, gravel walks, and topiaries, and replaced them with meandering paths and streams, gently rolling hills, and serpentine lakes. He softened formal elements and eliminated straight lines and geometric shapes. His ideal landscape was somewhere between utilitarian and wild. He believed in tastefully improving on nature. Brown was an architect as well as a landscape gardener; the mansions and other buildings he designed were usually practical as well as ornamental. Among the many famous English gardens he designed are Stowe, Castle Ashby, Coombe Abbey, and Milton Abbey.

## Budding, Edwin B. *(dates unknown)*

The Englishman who invented the lawn mower in the 1830s, revolutionizing the gardens of the nineteenth century. Before that time, lawns had frequently been kept trimmed by goats and other livestock, or by gardeners wielding scythes.

## Burbank, Luther *(1849–1926)*

An American naturalist and plant breeder, Burbank had a flair for observing minute differences between plants, and was able to develop and extend these through techniques like hybridizing and grafting. He began his botanical work in 1870 on a small farm in Massachusetts, where he developed the Burbank potato. In 1875, he moved to California and began developing new varieties of fruit. In his fifty years there, he introduced sixty varieties of plum and ten varieties of berry. Burbank also bred many new ornamental plants, such as the fire poppy, the Burbank rose, the Shasta daisy, and the ostrich-plume clematis. He never quite accepted, however, that plant variations were determined genetically at the time of seed fertilization, but believed instead in the inheritance of acquired characteristics.

## Camerarius, Rudolph Jacob *(1665–1721)*

A German botanist and university professor, Camerarius wrote to another professor in 1694 to report that pistillate flowers failed to produce seed in the absence of staminate flowers. His conclusion was that the anthers with their pollen were the male organs, and that the style and ovary were the female parts of the flower. Although he was not the first to make this observation, his subsequent scientific experiments confirmed it, and he is now credited with the discovery of sexuality in plants.

## Candolle, Augustin Pyramus de *(1778–1841)*

A French plant taxonomist who introduced new and significant principles of plant classification; his system of classification is largely in use to this day. De Candolle's family had fled to Switzerland from religious persecution in France, but in 1798 he returned to France to pursue his botanical studies. In 1813, he invented the word "taxonomy" to describe the science of classification, and he proposed that morphology is the basis of taxonomy. He also developed a theory of symmetry in the structure of plants, especially the floral organs. De Candolle created the Conservatoire Botanique and Botanical Garden in Geneva, Switzerland. He also wrote most of the first seven volumes of the *Prodromus Systematis Naturalis Regni Veg-*

*etabilis,* the only comprehensive flora of the world. The remaining volumes were completed by his son Alphonse (1806–1893).

## Church, Thomas Dolliver *(1902–1978)*

An American landscape architect who studied at the University of California, Berkeley, and at Harvard in the late 1920s. In the 1930s, he was famous for creating the so-called California garden, characterized by formality and native plantings, and influenced by Cubism. He recognized that the era of the grand estate garden in America was coming to an end, and believed that gardens should have a more human scale. Church promoted the concept of the garden as an "outdoor room" in his book *Gardens Are for People,* published in 1955. He designed landscapes for the University of California at Berkeley and Santa Cruz, Stanford University, Longwood Gardens, and more than two thousand private residences. One of his most famous gardens is the El Novillero garden in Sonoma, California, which he designed in 1947.

## Clements, Frederic E. *(1874–1945)*

An American plant ecologist, Clements was a leading promoter of what came to be known as "dynamic ecology." As head of the botany department at the University of Minnesota, he put his students to work doing hands-on experiments measuring the factors in the environments of living organisms and studying the behavior of plants under controlled conditions. Clements crisscrossed the continent studying the vegetation associations of North America and wrote books dealing with plant succession and climax communities, classification of plant communities, climatic cycles, and methods for determining what plants are native to an area after disturbance has taken place.

## Colden, Jane *(1724–?)*

The first woman botanist to distinguish herself in America. By the age of thirty-four, in 1758, she had described four hundred plants according to the Linnaean method, using English terms.

## Curtis, William *(1746–1799)*

An apothecary in London who sold his practice in 1771 to establish a botanic garden, Curtis is best known as the founder of the first popular garden periodical, *The Botanical Magazine,* launched in 1775. The magazine was immediately successful and has continued to the present day. Curtis was also Demonstrator of Botany to the Society of Apothecaries at the Chelsea Physic Garden.

## Dioscorides, Pedanius *(A.D. 20–?)*

Born in ancient Turkey, Dioscorides was a founder of botany and the author of *De Materia Media,* a famous herbal that was used for over a thousand years. He traveled widely in search of plants, mostly to seek out their usefulness for medicinal purposes. The five volumes of his herbal included six hundred plants and nearly a thousand drugs, all described objectively, accurately, and without superstition (uncommon for that time).

## Downing, Andrew Jackson *(1815–1852)*

An American nurseryman, landscape designer, and writer who has been called "the father of American landscape gardening," Downing admired the English School of Landscape Gardening, from which he formed an American approach. His landscapes had a naturalistic look, with serpentine lines, soft grasslands, and wooded copses, and were well adapted to American middle-class homes of the mid-nineteenth century. Downing also drew early plans for the gardens of the White House and the Smithsonian Institution. He began a partnership with Calvert Vaux in 1849. Downing wrote the influential book, *The Theory and Practice of Landscape Gardening,* and was a founding editor of *The Horticulturist* (or *Journal of Rural Art & Rural Taste*).

## Farrand, Beatrix Jones *(1872–1959)*

Farrand was a leading landscape architect in America and admirer of Gertrude Jekyll. She was from an old New York family and did most of her work on the East Coast, where she designed the Abby Aldrich Rockefeller Garden in Maine, as well as gardens for the Rockefellers, the Morgans, the White House, Yale and Princeton Universities, and the New York Botanical Garden. Overall, she worked as a consultant and designer on more than two hundred gardens. She was also a founding member and the first woman to be elected a charter fellow of the American Society of Landscape Architects in 1899, at age twenty-seven. In 1927, Farrand became a consulting landscape gardener to Yale University. She and her husband, Max Farrand, also moved to San Marino, California, in 1927, but she was unable to get much work there and ended up commuting back and forth to the East Coast to continue her work. She did, however, become a consultant to the Santa Barbara Botanic Garden from 1938 until her death.

## Fernald, Merritt Lyndon *(1873–1950)*

An American botanist who served as curator of the Gray Herbarium at Harvard University from 1935 to 1937, and director of the herbarium for the next ten years, Fernald wrote the eighth edition of *Gray's Manual of Botany* in 1950, based on his vast field work. He was also a pioneering botanical explorer in Labrador and Newfoundland, and in the Coastal Plain of Virginia.

## Fortune, Robert *(1812–1880)*

Fortune was an English botanical explorer who traveled to China and brought back plants such as the popular bleeding heart (*Dicentra spectabilis*), balloon flower (*Platycodon grandiflorus*), Chinese anemone (*Anemone hupehensis*), doublefile viburnum (*Viburnum plicatum*), and weigela (*Weigela florida*). He was very successful at sending living plants from China to England using the Wardian case (a new invention at the time), a glass box that kept plants moist by preventing the evaporation of moisture.

## Fraser, John *(1750–1811)*

A Scottish plant collector, Fraser traveled in Newfoundland and much of the southeastern United States in the late 1700s. His son, John, accompanied him on his travels, and together they introduced plants like mountain rosebay (*Rhododendron catawbiense*), Fraser magnolia (*Magnolia fraseri*), and Fraser fir (*Abies fraseri*) to Europe. He was very successful at transporting living plants across the sea to Europe, probably by packing them in sphagnum moss found in the boreal bogs he explored. Fraser was appointed botanical collector by the czar of Russia in 1797.

## Goethe, Johann Wolfgang von *(1749–1832)*

A German poet who also wrote on scientific subjects (often incorrectly), Goethe coined the word "morphology" to represent the systematic study of the structure of living things, and his writing laid the groundwork for the next two hundred years of plant morphology research.

## Gray, Asa *(1810–1888)*

An American botanist and plant taxonomist, Asa Gray is known as the founder of systematic botany in the United States. In 1835, he was appointed Curator and Librarian of the New

York Lyceum of Natural History, where he wrote the first of a series of botanical textbooks called *Elements of Botany.* He collaborated with John Torrey on the *Flora of North America* from 1838 to 1843. Gray then became a professor of natural history and the head of the botanic garden at Harvard University, where he created the Gray Herbarium and Library. In 1848, he wrote the *Manual of the Botany of the Northern United States* (also known as *Gray's Manual of Botany*). Gray was a pioneer in plant geography, and he made a great impact with his hypothesis that the similar floras in eastern Asia and eastern North America are the relicts of preglacial flora that once encircled the globe. This theory had practical ramifications, as it drew the conclusion that plants from Japan and other Asian countries are compatible with the climate of eastern North America. Collectors were soon bringing these plants back to the United States in great numbers.

### Hales, Stephen *(1677–1761)*

An English chemist and plant physiologist, Hales was most interested in the respiration of plants and animals. He conducted elaborate experiments on the absorption of water and air by growing plants, eventually demonstrating that it is the leaves that absorb air. He also recognized that air contributes to the nourishment of plants, and that light plays a vital role in plant growth. For these studies he came to be considered the founder of plant physiology.

### Hall, George Rogers *(1820–1899)*

An American physician and plant collector living in Japan who sent numerous plant samples back to the United States, including Japanese honeysuckle (*Lonicera japonica*), which was to become an invasive weed in the East and Southeast, transforming the woodlands by over-whelming the native vegetation. He also brought the first Japanese yew (*Taxus cuspidata*) to North America; it is also showing signs of invasiveness, particularly in southern New England.

### Hogg, Thomas *(1820–1892)*

An American plant collector (English by birth) and U.S. consul to Japan, Hogg sent many plants home from Japan, including the infamous kudzu vine (*Pueraria lobata*), which has escaped from cultivation in the South to become one of the most invasive weeds in this country.

### Hooke, Robert *(1635–1703)*

An English scientist who invented the compound microscope, among other things. Hooke also coined the word "cell" for the smallest living part of a plant, which he discovered as he was studying the porous structure of cork.

### Hooker, Joseph Dalton *(1817–1911)*

An English plant taxonomist and botanical explorer, Hooker traveled to Antarctica, India, Nepal, Syria, Palestine, Morocco, and the western United States, and wrote floras about many of these places. He was appointed assistant director of the Royal Botanic Gardens, Kew, and eventually succeeded his father, William Jackson Hooker (1785–1865), as director. He was responsible for establishing Kew as an international center of scientific research, and the Kew Herbarium is still arranged according to a plant classification system he devised along with George Bentham.

### Hosack, David *(1769–1835)*

An American doctor, Hosack collected and studied plants of the eastern United States. With his own money, he founded the first botanic garden in the United States—the Elgin Botanical Garden in New York City, now the site of Rockefeller Center. Here Hosack grew more than a thousand kinds of American plants.

## Jekyll, Gertrude (1843–1932)

Born in England, Jekyll was trained as an artist and later became a famous gardener and garden designer. She is now considered the most important single influence on twentieth-century gardeners in England and the United States. Jekyll had studied painting, metal work, stenciling, and needlecrafts, but as her eyesight began to fail her in her forties, she turned to gardening and photography. Using her skills as an artist, she concentrated on the use of flowers and color in her garden designs. She used flowers in woodlands, water gardens, and herbaceous borders, often arranging them in careful gradations of color. Although she did not invent the herbaceous border, she perfected it in her landscapes. Jekyll collaborated with the English architect Edwin Lutyens (1869–1944) on about fifty design projects, including her own house and garden in Surrey, where she gardened for fifty years. She was also an editor for William Robinson's weekly *The Garden,* and she wrote about a thousand magazine articles for *The Garden, Gardening Illustrated,* and *Country Life.* Jekyll was the author of ten books, including *Wood and Garden, Home and Garden,* and *Colour in the Flower Garden.*

## Jensen, Jens (1860–1951)

A Danish-born American landscape architect, Jensen began his career as a gardener in Chicago in 1886. He developed the "prairie style," best known for its informal lines, massing of plants, and broad lawns and woodlands. He studied Midwestern native plants and used them exten-sively in his designs. Jensen was a friend and colleague of famed architect Frank Lloyd Wright.

## Landreth, David and Cuthbert (dates unknown)

American brothers who published the first horticultural magazine, *Floral Magazine and Botanical Repository,* in Philadelphia in May 1832. Publication of the magazine stopped after eighty pages and thirty-one color lithographs had been issued.

## Le Nôtre, André (1613–1700)

Le Nôtre has been called "the most copied and celebrated landscape designer in western history." As royal landscape gardener to Louis XIV, the French landscape architect is most famous for designing the gardens at Versailles, beginning in 1661. Versailles is sometimes referred to as "the queen of geometrical gardens" because of its extreme formality, a hallmark of Le Nôtre's work. He also created Vaux-le-Vicomte in 1657, with now-classic details—a strong central axis, framed vistas, and formal parterres—on a monumental scale. Through his designs, Le Nôtre changed the course of European landscape design for the next hundred years.

## Linnaeus, Carolus (1707–1778)

This Swedish naturalist established the rules of binomial nomenclature, the Latin plant-naming system used globally to this day. In 1741, Linnaeus became a professor of medicine and botany in Sweden. In 1753, he published *Species Plantarum,* which became an internationally accepted starting point for modern botanical nomenclature. Before Linnaeus introduced his system of naming, plants had been given long, cumbersome, descriptive names in Latin. The Linnaean system assigned each plant two complementary names, one for genus and one for species. In setting up this system, he created botanical Latin, a technical language distinct from classical or medieval Latin. In later years, Linnaeus went by the name Carl von Linné.

## Mapes, James Jay *(dates unknown)*

An American who developed the first artificial fertilizer after experimenting on his twenty-acre farm in Newark, New Jersey. He received a patent in 1859 for his superphosphate of lime made from charred bone (waste products of sugar refineries), sulfate of ammonia, and Peruvian guano.

## Marx, Roberto Burle *(1909–1994)*

A Brazilian landscape architect and plant collector famous for his use of native tropical plants. He studied art before taking up landscape architecture as a career, and his artistic background is reflected in his Cubist, geometric designs. Marx was also known for his exploration of problems of urban regeneration.

## Michaux, André *(1746–1803)*

A French botanical explorer, Michaux was botanist to King Louis XVI and royally appointed botanist in North America, assigned to bring American trees back to France to replenish forests cut for timber. He and his son François (1770–?) explored Canada, New England, and the Northeast in search of new plants. He is remembered for his discovery of Oconee bells (*Shortia galacifolia*) and yellow-wood (*Cladrastis kentukea*), while his son is famous for his book *Sylva of North America.* André Michaux also brought new plants to the United States from the Orient, including camellia (*Camellia japonica*), sweet olive (*Osmanthus fragrans*), mimosa (*Albizia julibrissin*), crape myrtle (*Lagerstroemia indica*), and maidenhair tree (*Gingko biloba*).

## Nuttall, Thomas *(1786–1859)*

Nuttall was a printer from Philadelphia who became a botanist, ornithologist, and plant explorer. In his search for new plants, he was one of the first to travel west as far as the Missouri River (then unknown territory) and even across the Rocky Mountains to the Columbia River. During his travels, he became familiar with all the plant life from the Great Lakes to the Gulf of Mexico, and he subsequently wrote the *Genera of North American Plants,* which was unequaled for many years. Among the new plants he discovered were mountain dogwood (*Cornus nuttallii*) and eastern flowering dogwood (*Cornus florida*). He spent his later years as the curator of the botanical garden at Harvard University.

## Olcott, Ralph Thrall *(1861–1932)*

Olcott cofounded the country's first horticultural trade journal, *National Nurseryman,* with Charles L. Yates in 1892. He went on to found *American Nurseryman* magazine in 1916, a trade journal that still exists to this day.

## Olmsted, Frederick Law *(1822–1903)*

The Connecticut-born Olmsted is considered the founder of landscape architecture, although he thought of himself as an "environmental planner." He was a partner of Calvert Vaux until 1878; together they designed Central Park in New York City. Olmsted is still remembered most for his design of Central Park and other large urban parks, such as those in Brooklyn; Boston; Detroit; Louisville, Kentucky; Rochester, Minnesota; Chicago; Buffalo, New York; and Montreal. He also designed the landscape of the Biltmore estate of the Vanderbilts in North Carolina, as well as those of numerous residences, hospitals, railway stations, cemeteries, campuses, and residential communities. As a footnote, Olmsted proposed a series of national and state park systems to be established as reserves. Yosemite and Yellowstone National Parks were two results of that proposal.

## Pliny (Gaius Plinius Caecilius Secundus, the Elder) *(A.D. 23–79)*

Pliny was a Roman scientific encyclopedist, author of *Naturalis Historia,* a multivolume compilation derived from a wide range of authors. Although they were full of superstition and error, his books helped maintain curiosity and wonder about the natural world. For modern scientists, his work has been valuable in preserving information about the technical arts of antiquity. Pliny's encyclopedia includes volumes on the varieties, uses, and products of trees; submarine vegetation; insect pests and parasitic plants; use of manures; seed propagation; transplanting; grafting and pruning; diseases and medication of trees; and vegetable gardening.

## Prince, William *(dates unknown)*

Prince's family established the first U.S. commercial nursery in Flushing, New York, in 1737. The nursery was called Linnaean Botanic Gardens, and it remained in business for over a century.

## Pursh, Frederick *(1774–1820)*

A German who immigrated to America in 1799, Pursh wrote the first comprehensive flora of the United States, *Flora Americae Septentrionalis,* which was published in 1814.

## Ray, John *(1628–1705)*

An English naturalist and prolific author on botanical, zoological, theological, and literary subjects, Ray traveled throughout Europe in search of plant specimens. In 1669, he wrote a three-volume encyclopedia of plant life, in which he described 18,600 different plant species and attempted to create an early system of plant nomenclature. His was the first attempt to produce order from unsystematic plant descriptions, and it laid the groundwork for the Linnaean system of binomial nomenclature that later superseded it. For his work, Ray has been called the "father of natural history" and the "Aristotle of England."

## Repton, Humphrey *(1752–1818)*

An English landscape gardener trained as an artist, Repton used his skills to prepare before-and-after sketches and watercolors for his wealthy clients. He was greatly inspired by the work of Capability Brown, although he worked on a smaller scale and felt that parkland should be separated from the house by a terrace, garden, fence, or other device. Repton also had a more eclectic style than Brown; he mixed formal and informal elements, copied styles from every period and nation, and experimented heavily with exotic plants. Interest in plant collecting was increasing at the time, and he gladly indulged his clients' interest in exotics.

## Robinson, William *(1839–1935)*

An Anglo-Irish journalist, critic, and landscape designer, Robinson was the publisher of the weekly *The Garden* and a strong influence on

Gertrude Jekyll. He was fascinated with "natural" design based on plants and their changing form, and he felt that the "wild woodland garden" was the ideal. Robinson was also very interested in the English kitchen garden and in rock gardening. Among his influential books were *The English Flower Garden* and *Alpine Flowers for English Gardens.*

## Sackville-West, Vita *(1892–1962)*

A noted English garden designer, Sackville-West was influenced by Gertrude Jekyll's practices. She designed many large private gardens in England, including the garden of Sissinghurst Castle in Kent, on which she collaborated with her husband, Harold Nicolson (1886–1968). The geometric plan uses walls and hedges to define a series of garden rooms, which are bound together by paths and rectangular lawns.

## Sargent, Charles Sprague *(1841–1927)*

A student of Asa Gray, Sargent was appointed in 1873 as the first director of the Arnold Arboretum at Harvard University, and he served in that role until his death at the age of eighty-six. He began with an inventory of plants already growing in the Boston area, and proceeded to introduce others from around the United States and abroad, especially eastern Asia. Later, he employed Ernest "Chinese" Wilson to go on plant-collecting expeditions for the arboretum, and the Arnold soon gained an international reputation as a center of plant introduction and distribution.

## Steele, Fletcher *(1885–1971)*

A landscape architect from New York, Steele addressed small suburban residential gardens in his how-to manual *Design for the Small Garden.*

He is known for his criticism of the American yard, especially the ubiquitous front lawn and the middle-class aversion to elements creating privacy in the garden.

## Theophrastus *(B.C. 370–285)*

Born in ancient Greece, Theophrastus is usually considered the founder of botany. He was the first to invent botanical terms, thus making scientific botany possible. He was a pupil of Plato and also of Aristotle, for whom he was chief assistant. He became head of the Peripatetic School at Athens, where he and his students made numerous botanical observations. He was also a prolific writer; unfortunately, of his two hundred or so scientific volumes, only two botanical works survive. The first, *Historia Plantarum,* deals with the description and classification of plants (he was the first to attempt plant classification). The other, *De Causis Plantarum,* deals with plant physiology. Theophrastus observed the difference between monocotyledons and dicotyledons, as well as the relationship between flowers and fruit. Also, he believed that plant distribution depended on soil and climate. In his books, he described over 550 plant species.

## Thunberg, Carl Pieter *(1743–1828)*

Thunberg was a Swedish physician and botanical explorer who traveled to Japan in 1775 with the Dutch East India Company to collect Japanese plants for Holland. At that time, Japan was virtually closed to foreigners, yet he was able to bring back large collections of new plants, mostly in the form of dried specimens. In 1784, he wrote *Flora Japonica.* Thunberg also collected over three thousand species of plants in South Africa, including more than a thousand new to science.

## Torrey, John *(1796–1873)*

A pioneer taxonomic botanist in the United States, Torrey was a mentor to Asa Gray. Together they wrote the *Flora of North America,* which updated all the work of previous botanists. Torrey founded the first botanical organization in the western hemisphere, the Torrey Botanical Society. He also founded two North American herbaria: the Torrey Herbarium and the U.S. National Herbarium. He did extensive botanical exploration of the southwestern and western states, and a genus of evergreen tree was named *Torreya* in his honor. He was commissioned state botanist of New York, and helped found the New York Lyceum of Natural History.

## Tradescant, John, Jr. *(1608–1662)*

Both Tradescant and his father, John Tradescant the elder (?–1638), were gardeners for noblemen and royalty in England in the seventeenth century. Father and son traveled frequently to obtain new and unusual plants for their clients, and also established a museum of the curiosities they brought back. They introduced many Eurasian and North American natives to England, including tulip tree (*Liriodendron tulipifera*), red maple (*Acer rubrum*), horse chestnut (*Aesculus hippocastanum*), mock orange (*Philadelphus coronarius*), and Virginia creeper (*Parthenocissus quinquefolia*). The genus *Tradescantia* was named in their honor.

## Vaux, Calvert *(1824–1895)*

An English-born American architect and landscape architect who was partner first with Andrew Jackson Downing, then with Frederick Law Olmsted, Vaux designed New York City's Central Park with Olmsted.

## Von Siebold, Philipp *(1796–1866)*

A German-born physician and plant collector who became infatuated with all things Japanese, Von Siebold eventually moved to Japan and began introducing native Japanese plants to Europe, including Japanese wisteria (*Wisteria floribunda*), Siebold forsythia (*Forsythia suspensa* var. *sieboldii*), Japanese flowering crabapple (*Malus floribunda*), Peegee hydrangea (*Hydrangea paniculata* 'Grandiflora'), and Japanese maple (*Acer palmatum*). In 1835, he cowrote the second *Flora Japonica* with J. G. Zuccarini.

## Wilson, Ernest Henry "Chinese" *(1876–1930)*

Wilson was a young English botanist who made numerous collecting expeditions to China, both for the Veitch family nursery in England and for the Arnold Arboretum in the United States. He brought back countless plants for introduction into western gardens, including paperbark maple (*Acer griseum*), beautybush (*Kolkwitzia amabilis*), bridal-wreath spirea (*Spiraea veitchii*), and kiwi fruit (*Actinidia* species).

# 2

# GARDENER'S ATLAS

Plant geography is the study of the distribution of plants and what causes them to grow where they do. For example, the region just east of the Rocky Mountains is home to the shortgrass prairie (or was, before it was converted to farmland). What is a shortgrass prairie, and what kinds of plants occur there? Why does the shortgrass prairie grow in one particular area of the western United States but not in the Northeast or in southern Florida? Is shortgrass prairie found in any other part of the world? Plant geography attempts to answer these kinds of questions by examining species range and migration, climate, soil conditions, plant hardiness, and many other factors—and for this reason it is a useful (but, unfortunately, rarely utilized) science for gardeners interested in finding the plants that are best adapted to their areas.

## Floristic Provinces

For almost two hundred years, botanists involved in the comparative study of the vegetation of different countries have divided the world into floristic units. The widely respected classification system of Russian botanist Armen Takhtajan, for example, divides the world into several floristic ranks. The highest rank is the *kingdom* or *realm*. Kingdoms are characterized by endemic families and by very high rates of generic and species endemism; in other words, there are plant families and many genera and species that occur nowhere else in the world. A kingdom is divided into *regions*, which have high rates of species and generic endemism. Certain plant families also predominate in various regions. The floristic region that Takhtajan calls the North American Atlantic Region, for

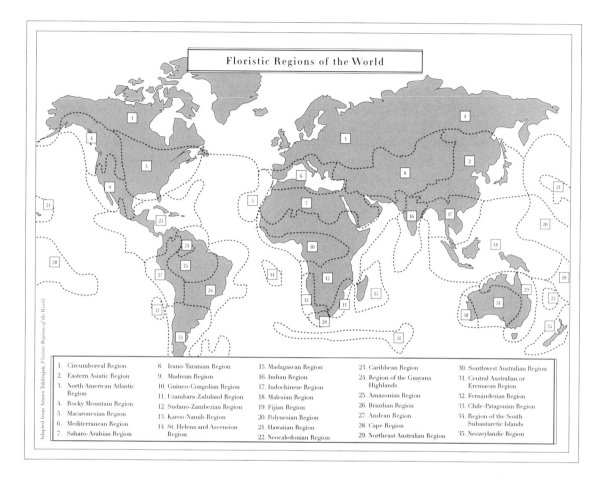

Floristic Regions of the World

Adapted from Armen Takhtajan, *Floristic Regions of the World*

| | | | |
|---|---|---|---|
| 1. Circumboreal Region | 8. Irano-Turanian Region | 15. Madagascan Region | 23. Caribbean Region | 30. Southwest Australian Region |
| 2. Eastern Asiatic Region | 9. Madrean Region | 16. Indian Region | 24. Region of the Guayana Highlands | 31. Central Australian or Eremaean Region |
| 3. North American Atlantic Region | 10. Guineo-Congolian Region | 17. Indochinese Region | 25. Amazonian Region | 32. Fernándezian Region |
| 4. Rocky Mountain Region | 11. Uzambara-Zululand Region | 18. Malesian Region | 26. Brazilian Region | 33. Chile-Patagonian Region |
| 5. Macaronesian Region | 12. Sudano-Zambezian Region | 19. Fijian Region | 27. Andean Region | 34. Region of the South Subantarctic Islands |
| 6. Mediterranean Region | 13. Karoo-Namib Region | 20. Polynesian Region | 28. Cape Region | 35. Neozeylandic Region |
| 7. Saharo-Arabian Region | 14. St. Helena and Ascension Region | 21. Hawaiian Region | 29. Northeast Australian Region | |
| | | 22. Neocaledonian Region | | |

example, stretches across eastern North America from the Atlantic Ocean to the Rocky Mountains, and from the Gulf of Mexico to southern Canada. In this region there is only one endemic family (Leitneriaceae, the corkwood family, with a single species, *Leitneria floridana,* a shrub that occurs in wet woods from southern Florida west to Missouri and Texas), but almost a hundred endemic or nearly endemic genera of vascular plants. Another characteristic of the region is the abundance and variety of species of various genera in the aster family, including *Aster, Solidago, Helianthus, Rudbeckia,* and *Silphium.*

Regions in turn are subdivided into *provinces.* Floristic provinces may include some endemic genera, although fewer than regions do. Species endemism is characteristic, but again occurs at a lower frequency than in regions. Floristic provinces also are characterized by distinct assemblages of species, such as prairies, deciduous forests, and coastal plain pine forests in the North American Atlantic Region. The growing conditions—the climate, soils, and other environmental conditions—are generally similar throughout a floristic province. Takhtajan recognizes 153 floristic provinces worldwide.

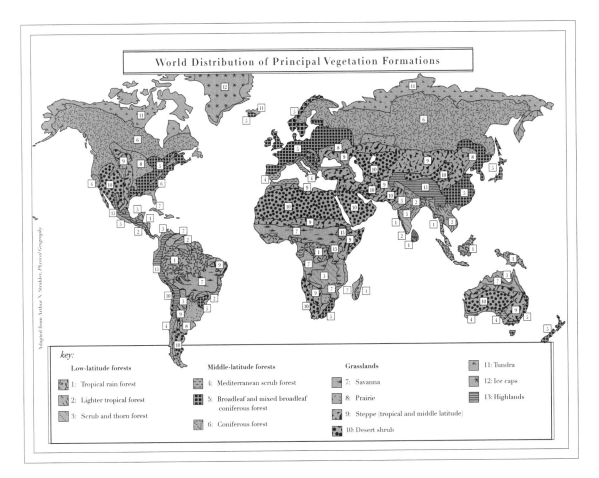

World Distribution of Principal Vegetation Formations

Adapted from Arthur N. Strahler, *Physical Geography*

key:

**Low-latitude forests**

1: Tropical rain forest

2: Lighter tropical forest

3: Scrub and thorn forest

**Middle-latitude forests**

4: Mediterranean scrub forest

5: Broadleaf and mixed broadleaf coniferous forest

6: Coniferous forest

**Grasslands**

7: Savanna

8: Prairie

9: Steppe (tropical and middle latitude)

10: Desert shrub

11: Tundra

12: Ice caps

13: Highlands

In Takhtajan's classification system, the lowest floristic rank is the *district,* which is characteristized mainly by endemism at the subspecies level.

Other botanists and ecologists have devised classification systems with greater stress on the principal vegetation types, also known as *formations*—prairies, eastern deciduous forests, western coniferous forests, and desert in North America, for example. Formations comprise more or less distinct vegetation subtypes, also known as *associations,* such as the tallgrass, shortgrass, and mixed grass prairies of the Midwest and plains states.

Similar formations are often found around the world. For example, in spite of the large number of endemic genera in both areas, there is a remarkable similarity between the flora of the deciduous forests of eastern North America and those of eastern Asia, or between California chaparral and other sclerophyllous shrub communities in the Mediterranean floristic region.

It is essential for natural gardeners interested in re-creating native plant communities to be aware of the vegetation types indigenous to their areas. Knowledge of native vegetation types and related ones around the world is also helpful for gardeners choosing plants for more traditional mixes of native and nonnative species and cultivars, because plants from a similar environment often will be better adapted to conditions in a particular area than those from very different vegetation formations.

## Floristic Provinces of North America

North America stretches from semitropical to tundra, from one extreme to another in climate, precipitation, and soil type. Each region is marked by differences in maximum and minimum summer and winter temperatures, seasonal rainfall, latitude and altitude, soil composition and pH, groundwater levels and soil water-holding capacity. All these variations give rise to equally varied plant communities.

There is no single "correct" map of the floristic provinces of North America. In *North American Terrestrial Vegetation,* botanists Michael G. Barbour and W. D. Billings divide the continent into seventeen vegetation formations:

- Ice
- Arctic Tundra
- Taiga or Coniferous Boreal Forests
- Pacific Coastal/Cascadian Forests
- Palouse Prairies of the Intermountain Region
- Intermountain Deserts, Shrub Steppes, Woodlands, and Forests
- Californian Forests and Alpine Vegetation
- Californian Grasslands, Chaparral, and Woodlands
- Mojave and Sonoran Deserts
- Rocky Mountain Forests and Alpine Vegetation
- Central Prairies and Plains
- Mixed Deciduous Forests
- Chihuahuan Deserts and Woodlands
- Appalachian Forests
- Piedmont Oak-Pine Forests

- Coastal Plain Forests, Bogs, Swamps, Marshes, and Strand
- Tropical Forests

Gardening books that include information on floristic provinces usually use the classification system devised by botanists Henry Gleason and Arthur Cronquist in *The Natural Geography of Plants,* which divides the United States and Canada into the following ten floristic provinces. (For more on the various vegetation associations in each of these provinces, see "Ecology for Gardeners," page 142.)

- **Arctic or Tundra Province.** Found around the world in Arctic latitudes. In North America, it is found in parts of Alaska, northern Canada, and above the timberline in the mountains of the West and New England. Plants include moss campion (*Silene acaulis*), mountain heaths (*Phyllodoce* species), and cassiopes (*Cassiope* species).
- **Northern Conifer Province.** Also called the Taiga or Boreal Forest. Stretches from Labrador and Maine westward and northwestward to Minnesota and Alaska. Rainfall is plentiful—frequently over 40 inches per year—and winters are cold with plenty of snow. Summer temperatures are cool. In the dense shade cast by evergreens, the forest soil is moist and usually acidic. Plants include tamarack (*Larix laricina*), balsam fir (*Abies balsamea*), and black spruce (*Picea mariana*).
- **Eastern Deciduous Forest Province.** Found from Maine to Minnesota and southward across the eastern states to northern Georgia, northern Louisiana, and eastern Texas, this province includes many forest associations in which different species predominate. Soil is usually rich and fertile. Rainfall is about 25 to 35 inches per year. Plants include sugar maple (*Acer saccharum*), American beech (*Fagus grandi-*

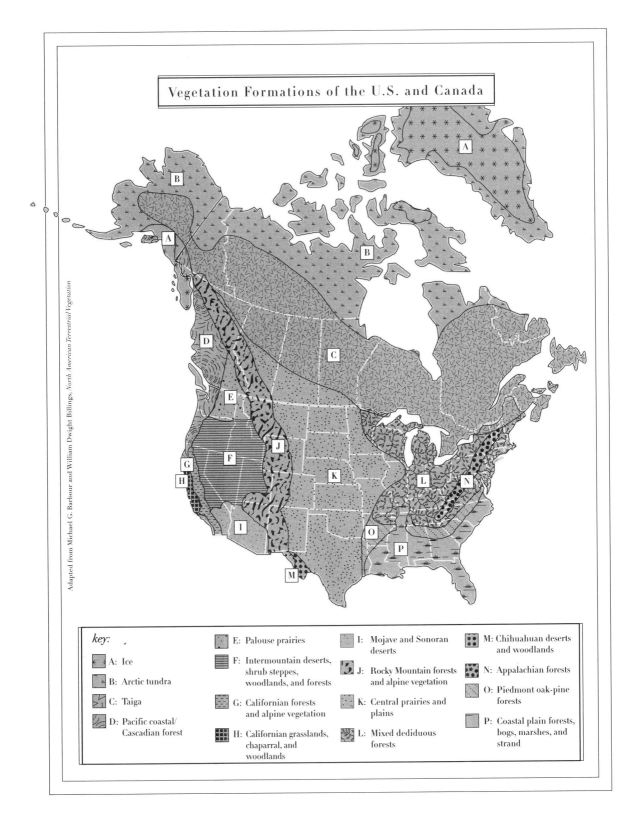

# Vegetation Formations of the U.S. and Canada

key:

A: Ice

B: Arctic tundra

C: Taiga

D: Pacific coastal/ Cascadian forest

E: Palouse prairies

F: Intermountain deserts, shrub steppes, woodlands, and forests

G: Californian forests and alpine vegetation

H: Californian grasslands, chaparral, and woodlands

I: Mojave and Sonoran deserts

J: Rocky Mountain forests and alpine vegetation

K: Central prairies and plains

L: Mixed dediduous forests

M: Chihuahuan deserts and woodlands

N: Appalachian forests

O: Piedmont oak-pine forests

P: Coastal plain forests, bogs, marshes, and strand

Adapted from Michael G. Barbour and William Dwight Billings, *North American Terrestrial Vegetation*

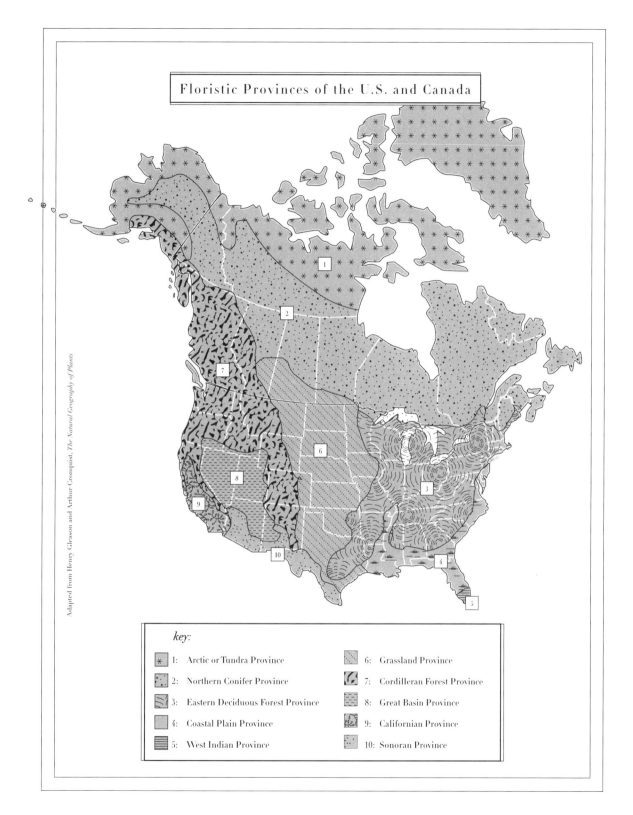

# Floristic Provinces of the U.S. and Canada

*Adapted from Henry Gleason and Arthur Cronquist, The Natural Geography of Plants*

**key:**

1: Arctic or Tundra Province
2: Northern Conifer Province
3: Eastern Deciduous Forest Province
4: Coastal Plain Province
5: West Indian Province
6: Grassland Province
7: Cordilleran Forest Province
8: Great Basin Province
9: Californian Province
10: Sonoran Province

*folia*), basswood (*Tilia americana*), oaks (*Quercus* species), and hickories (*Carya* species).

• **Coastal Plain Province.** Found on the coastal plain of the Atlantic and Gulf states, from New Jersey south to Florida and west to Texas. Soil is usually sandy, moist, and acidic. This province is characterized by wet forests, savannahs, pine barrens, and swamps. Forests are open and sunny, with many spring- and summer-blooming wildflowers. Winters are mild, and summers are hot and humid with plentiful rainfall. Plants include bald cypress (*Taxodium distichum*), live oak (*Quercus virginiana*), and longleaf pine (*Pinus palustris*).

• **West Indian Province.** Found at the tip of southern Florida and the Florida Keys, and throughout the West Indies, this province includes pinelands, swamp forests, mangrove swamps, and sawgrass prairies known as the Everglades, dotted with islands of hardwoods, called hammocks. Summers are hot and humid; winters are mild. Plants include black mangrove (*Avicennia nitida*), gumbo limbo (*Bursera simaruba*), orchids, and various palms.

• **Grassland Province.** Found east of the Rocky Mountains from Alberta, Canada, southward to Texas and eastward to Iowa and parts of Illinois. Much of this province of prairies and plains is now farmland. Grassland associations are characterized by the height of the grasses, determined by annual rainfall. For example, low-rainfall areas (10 inches or less per year) have shortgrass prairies, with grasses less than 2 feet tall. Farther east, the tallgrass prairie receives 25 to 29 inches of rain annually and grows up to 5 feet or more. The grasslands have a variety of soils. Winters are extremely cold, summers very hot and dry. Grassland plants include buffalo grass (*Buchloe dactyloides*), grama grass (*Bouteloua curtipendula*), Indiangrass (*Sorghastrum nutans*), and big bluestem (*Andropogon gerardii*).

• **Cordilleran Forest Province.** Found in the mountains of the western states and Canada, from Alaska to California and New Mexico. This province has moderate summer temperatures and cold winters with deep snow. Coniferous forests create deep shade with moist, rich, acidic soils. Three distinct vegetation associations are found in the province: the forests of the Pacific Northwest, those of the Sierras, and those of the Rocky Mountains. Near the coast are rain forests with moist, rich soil. Inland plateaus in the Rocky Mountain region have dry forests, and moist to dry forests are found in the Sierra Nevada range. The three vegetation associations have unique assemblages of species, but a few trees, including Douglas fir (*Pseudotsuga menziesii*) and lodgepole pine (*Pinus contorta*), are found throughout the province.

• **Great Basin Province.** A cold-desert region encompassing most of Utah and Nevada and parts of adjacent states, with low annual rainfall and extreme temperature fluctuations. The province is characterized by small mountain ranges and low, arid valleys with lakes that go dry in periods of drought. Most precipitation comes in the form of winter snow. Plants include sagebrush (*Artemisia tridentata*), greasewood (*Sarcobatus vermiculatus*), and saltbushes (*Atriplex* species).

• **Californian Province.** Found in California and extending into southwestern Oregon and northern Baja California, this province reaches from the coastal ranges to the westernmost slopes of the Sierras. Chaparral, a plant community dominated by shrubs, low trees, and some grasses, as well as oak woodlands and grasslands (which were once plentiful but have been converted to farmland or rangeland), are the major vegetation associations of the Californian Province. Southern areas have hot, dry summers and cool, moist winters; northern areas are colder with less rain. Many of the native plants are drought-tolerant, including California live oak (*Quercus agrifolia*), digger pine (*Pinus sabiniana*), manzanitas (*Arctostaphylos* species), and madrone (*Arbutus menziesii*).

• **Sonoran Province.** Hot deserts and valleys from Southern California to Texas and southward into Mexico. Characterized by low annual rainfall (average 10 inches) and extreme temperature fluctuations. In the Sonoran desert, there are long rainy spells in winter and thunderstorms in late summer. Most plants bloom in early spring. The Mojave desert is mostly low-elevation with warmer temperatures all year and rain in winter. Plants bloom in spring and early summer. The Chihuahuan desert has high valleys and low plains. Rain is unpredictable but comes mostly in summer. Plants of the Sonoran Province include creosote bush (*Larrea tridentata*), giant saguaro cactus (*Carnegiea gigantea*), mesquite (*Prosopis pubescens*), prickly pears (*Opuntia* species), and yuccas (*Yucca* species).

## Factors in Plant Distribution

Although plant communities around the world are classified by their similarities to one another, it is important to pay attention to the differences as well. Local environmental factors are critical in plant distribution. Two separate regions may both be classified as "coniferous forest" because the resident trees are primarily coniferous, but while one area may have dry soil that supports a variety of pines, the other may have moist soil that produces fir, spruce, or cedar. Most vegetation maps are greatly simplified. Smaller plant communities exist even in the vegetation associations within larger floristic provinces or formations.

To analyze your own region or site to find out which plants would grow best there, first look at the broadly defined vegetation formations and associations. Then narrow your focus to the following environmental factors that may have an effect on your growing conditions.

## Climate

Climate refers to the average weather conditions in an area over a period of years. It includes trends in temperature, precipitation, and prevailing winds. Most gardening is done in either temperate or tropical climates, defined as follows:

• **Temperate climates.** Mostly warm and moist, with seasonal fluctuations. Mean temperature of the warmest month is greater than 50°F. Annual precipitation is greater than 30 inches. Vegetation is luxuriant. The temperate region includes the so-called Mediterranean climates, characterized by hot, dry summers and mild, wet winters.

• **Tropical climates.** Warm and humid, with little seasonal variation. Mean temperature of coldest month is greater than 64°F. Rainfall is heavy. Frost and snow are nonexistent.

### Climatic Regions of the United States

The climate of the United States has been broken down a bit further, into four zones based on vegetation: cool, temperate, hot and arid, and hot and humid. Each zone has its own characteristic weather patterns and implications for plants, but the conditions are not identical throughout each zone, and there are areas of overlap where the zones merge with one another.

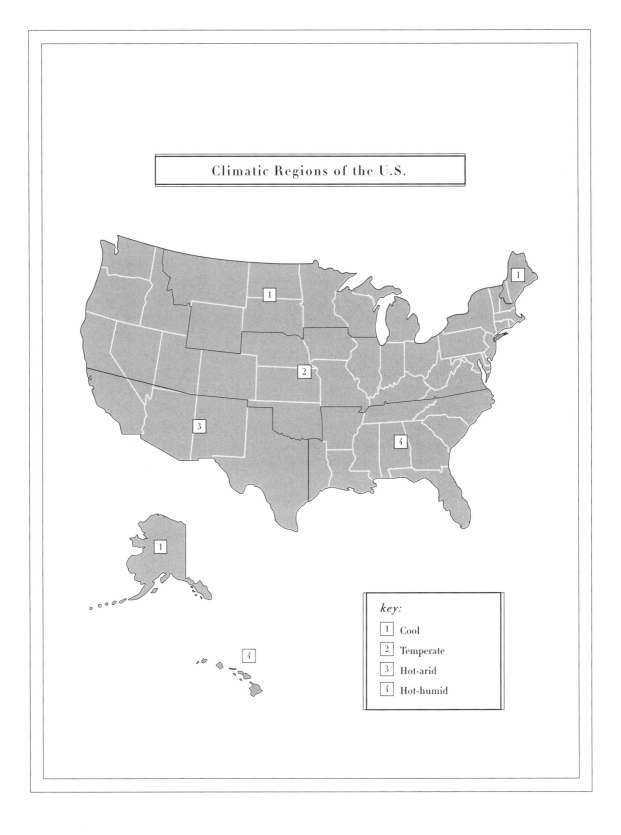

# Climatic Regions of the U.S.

key:

1 Cool
2 Temperate
3 Hot-arid
4 Hot-humid

- **Cool zone.** Has a wide range of temperatures, from −30° to 100°F. It is characterized by hot summers and cold winters, with persistent northwest or southeast winds all year.
- **Temperate zone.** Has an equal number of extreme hot and cold periods, along with high humidity and high rainfall. Seasonal winds come from the northwest and south.
- **Hot and arid zone.** The sky is usually clear and the atmosphere dry. There are long periods of extreme heat, but daily temperatures can fluctuate greatly.
- **Hot and humid zone.** Has consistently high temperatures and humidity. Wind speed and direction vary greatly throughout the year.

## Climatic Conditions by Continent

- **North America.** Nearly all the land falls within middle and northern latitudes. There are moderate summer and winter temperatures along the northwestern coasts, in contrast to the extreme highs and lows found in the interior region from the Great Lakes north and northwest. Annual precipitation is over 40 inches from southern Alaska to northern California west of the mountains; just east of this area, precipitation is less than 20 inches annually. On the coast of British Columbia, rainfall is over 100 inches per year, but in the desert areas of the Southwest, it can be less than 5 inches per year. There is a narrow region of maritime climate along the Atlantic coast. From the Southeast to Newfoundland, average annual precipitation is more than 40 inches. From southern Florida into the Caribbean, the climate is subtropical. In Mexico and Central America, the climate is subtropical to temperate, depending on elevation. Rainfall in these subtropical areas is abundant but spotty.

- **South America.** Most of the continent is within the tropical latitudes. The southern end of South America is narrow and therefore not subject to the extreme highs and lows of a continental climate. The western coastal regions northward to the equator are usually cool due to the Antarctic current. On the east side of the continent, the Brazilian current has a warming effect on coastal regions, except southern Argentina. Northern countries have dry and wet seasons related to the trade winds. In the Amazon River basin, high rainfall is related to equatorial low pressure and to trade winds. Desert areas on the west coast from the equator to Santiago, Chile, are due to the cold Humboldt or Peruvian current. Southern Chile has extremely wet winters and relatively dry summers.
- **Europe.** The east-west direction of the mountain ranges in Europe causes conditions to change more gradually than in the Americas. Rainfall is heaviest on the western coast (60 inches per year) and diminishes to less than 20 inches in eastern Russia. In Scandinavia, however, the mountains cause a rain shadow that results in less than 20 inches of annual rain to eastern Sweden, while western Norway receives over 60 inches. Rainfall is abundant and evenly distributed throughout the year in much of Europe, except along the Mediterranean, where summers are extremely dry and winters wet. Temperatures are rarely extreme in Europe, except in Scandinavia.
- **Asia.** The size of Asia creates an opportunity for continental conditions: very cold winters northeast of the Himalayas and hot summers from west to east in the latitude of northern India. In winter, air circulation is outward over the land, with light precipitation. In summer, air flows in from the oceans, producing abundant rain, especially over India. Lighter rainfall occurs in summer over Japan

and eastern Asia, and does not extend far into China. While southeast Asia has heavy to excessive rainfall, the rest of the continent is fairly dry (less than 10 inches per year). North of the Himalayas, the low plains are extremely cold in winter and hot in summer. In southwestern Asia, winter temperatures are generally low, especially at high elevations, and summer temperatures are excessively high at low elevations.

• **Africa.** Africa lies mostly within the tropical latitudes. Along the southwestern coast, the cool Benguela current moves northward; on the eastern coast are the warm tropical currents of the Indian Ocean. In the tropical areas, low pressure brings abundant rainfall. In areas north and south of the tropics, barometric pressure is usually high and the climate is dry. Except in the Atlas Mountains of northern Africa, the desert conditions of the Sahara extend from west to east coast, and from the Mediterranean coast in the north to the latitudes of southern Arabia. South of the desert there is increased rainfall; in the eastern and western areas of the Guinea coast, annual rainfall is as high as 80 inches. The climate becomes arid in southwest Africa.

• **Australia.** In winter, a high-pressure belt crosses the interior regions, and all except the southernmost parts of the continent are dry. In summer, the pressure belt has moved south of the continent, and the southern and western areas remain dry. Total annual precipitation is less than 20 inches, except in the southwest corner and a narrow area circling from southeast to northwest. In one large south-central area, the annual precipitation is less than 10 inches. In the south, cyclones occur in winter. Summer brings heavy monsoon rain in the north. Only a small section of the continent, at high elevations in the south, experiences far below freezing temperatures. In the arid interior, maximum temperatures are some of the hottest on earth.

## High and Low Temperatures

Temperature is primarily determined by solar radiation, which in turn is determined by latitude. However, there are many modifying factors, such as prevailing winds, ocean currents, topography, and precipitation. If one of these factors changes, it will have an effect on temperature. For example, on a garden scale, if you block the sun but not the wind, the site will be cooler. Conversely, if you block the wind but not the sun, it will be warmer. Plants themselves can be used to control temperature by providing shade or acting as windbreaks.

Plant hardiness, the factor used most widely by gardeners to determine a plant's suitability for a particular area, is usually measured by the lowest temperature a plant can withstand (see page 30–31). However, fluctuations in temperature can be even more important than the temperature itself. A hardy woody plant can survive low temperatures if they arrive gradually in the fall and are fairly consistent through the winter. But if the temperature drops abruptly, as with a sudden early frost, the plant's tender tissues may be destroyed by expanding ice crystals. Plant damage can also be caused by a sudden late-winter warm spell in cold regions. At this time of year, evergreens are especially vulnerable: by late winter, their leaves contain little moisture. A sunny day can cause this last remaining moisture to evaporate, and the roots will not be able to replace it if the soil is still frozen.

Many plants, such as birches, actually require a cold winter for dormancy, and will not thrive in areas where the winters are mild. There are

## MONTHLY MEAN, AVERAGE MAXIMUM, AND AVERAGE MINIMUM TEMPERATURES (F) FOR SELECTED CITIES IN THE US (DATA FROM 1964–1993)

| | Jan | Feb | Mar | Apr | May | Jun | Jul | Aug | Sep | Oct | Nov | Dec |
|---|---|---|---|---|---|---|---|---|---|---|---|---|
| Birmingham, AL | 44.8 | 47.0 | 54.8 | 62.7 | 70.5 | 77.6 | 80.1 | 79.6 | 75.0 | 64.2 | 53.4 | 46.2 |
| | 54.1 | 56.9 | 65.7 | 74.1 | 81.4 | 88.2 | 90.1 | 89.7 | 85.4 | 75.6 | 64.2 | 55.6 |
| | 35.5 | 37.0 | 44.0 | 51.3 | 59.5 | 67.0 | 70.1 | 69.5 | 64.5 | 52.7 | 42.6 | 36.7 |
| Mobile, AL | 51.5 | 54.2 | 60.1 | 67.1 | 74.2 | 80.3 | 81.8 | 81.5 | 78.0 | 68.8 | 59.0 | 53.0 |
| | 60.4 | 63.3 | 69.2 | 76.2 | 83.2 | 88.9 | 90.1 | 89.8 | 86.4 | 78.5 | 68.7 | 61.9 |
| | 42.5 | 45.1 | 51.0 | 57.9 | 65.1 | 71.6 | 73.5 | 73.2 | 69.5 | 59.0 | 49.2 | 44.0 |
| Anchorage, AK | 13.9 | 17.8 | 24.6 | 35.4 | 46.4 | 54.4 | 58.1 | 56.0 | 47.9 | 34.7 | 21.5 | 15.4 |
| | 21.0 | 25.6 | 32.9 | 43.2 | 54.7 | 62.2 | 65.4 | 63.2 | 55.0 | 41.0 | 27.8 | 21.9 |
| | 6.8 | 9.9 | 16.2 | 27.5 | 38.1 | 46.5 | 50.8 | 48.7 | 40.7 | 28.4 | 15.3 | 8.9 |
| Fairbanks, AK | −10.1 | −3.4 | 10.1 | 30.4 | 48.0 | 59.3 | 61.3 | 55.6 | 44.5 | 25.6 | 3.1 | −7.7 |
| | −1.2 | 7.7 | 23.5 | 41.6 | 59.1 | 70.5 | 71.9 | 65.7 | 54.0 | 33.1 | 11.3 | 0.6 |
| | −19.0 | −14.5 | −3.4 | 19.2 | 36.8 | 48.0 | 50.7 | 45.6 | 35.0 | 18.1 | −5.1 | −16.0 |
| Juneau, AK | 24.1 | 28.0 | 32.5 | 39.5 | 47.1 | 53.3 | 56.0 | 54.8 | 49.4 | 42.0 | 32.8 | 27.7 |
| | 29.5 | 33.7 | 38.6 | 46.9 | 55.2 | 61.6 | 63.9 | 62.6 | 55.9 | 47.0 | 37.4 | 32.2 |
| | 18.8 | 22.3 | 26.4 | 32.0 | 39.0 | 45.0 | 48.0 | 47.0 | 42.8 | 37.0 | 28.2 | 23.1 |
| Flagstaff, AZ | 28.1 | 31.1 | 35.8 | 42.9 | 50.4 | 59.4 | 65.8 | 63.9 | 57.4 | 47.1 | 36.8 | 29.7 |
| | 41.5 | 44.2 | 49.3 | 57.9 | 66.8 | 77.4 | 81.1 | 78.6 | 73.3 | 63.0 | 51.4 | 43.2 |
| | 14.7 | 17.9 | 22.3 | 27.8 | 33.9 | 41.3 | 50.4 | 49.2 | 41.5 | 31.2 | 22.1 | 16.1 |
| Tucson, AZ | 50.6 | 53.6 | 58.0 | 64.9 | 73.0 | 82.4 | 86.1 | 84.1 | 80.1 | 69.7 | 58.3 | 51.5 |
| | 64.4 | 67.8 | 73.0 | 81.1 | 89.7 | 99.1 | 99.3 | 96.8 | 94.1 | 84.9 | 73.1 | 65.3 |
| | 36.8 | 39.3 | 43.0 | 48.8 | 56.3 | 65.7 | 72.9 | 71.4 | 66.1 | 54.5 | 43.5 | 37.7 |
| Little Rock, AR | 41.3 | 44.7 | 53.1 | 62.4 | 70.2 | 78.3 | 81.6 | 80.6 | 74.2 | 63.6 | 51.8 | 43.7 |
| | 50.0 | 53.9 | 62.9 | 72.5 | 80.0 | 88.0 | 91.2 | 90.4 | 84.4 | 74.4 | 61.6 | 52.3 |
| | 32.5 | 35.4 | 43.2 | 52.3 | 60.3 | 68.5 | 71.9 | 70.8 | 63.9 | 52.8 | 42.1 | 35.0 |
| Los Angeles, CA | 55.5 | 56.6 | 57.4 | 60.0 | 62.4 | 65.3 | 68.6 | 69.7 | 69.0 | 65.9 | 61.0 | 56.9 |
| | 64.6 | 65.2 | 65.3 | 67.5 | 69.2 | 71.7 | 75.0 | 76.1 | 76.1 | 73.8 | 70.5 | 66.3 |
| | 46.4 | 48.0 | 49.5 | 52.4 | 55.6 | 58.9 | 62.2 | 63.2 | 61.9 | 57.9 | 51.5 | 47.4 |
| Sacramento, CA | 45.3 | 50.4 | 53.5 | 58.6 | 64.9 | 71.0 | 75.4 | 74.4 | 71.5 | 63.9 | 53.0 | 45.6 |
| | 53.0 | 59.7 | 64.2 | 71.4 | 79.6 | 87.0 | 92.8 | 91.3 | 87.5 | 77.7 | 63.5 | 53.3 |
| | 37.5 | 41.0 | 42.9 | 45.7 | 50.2 | 55.0 | 57.9 | 57.4 | 55.5 | 50.1 | 42.6 | 37.9 |
| San Francisco, CA | 48.4 | 51.4 | 53.2 | 55.2 | 57.8 | 60.8 | 62.1 | 62.6 | 63.3 | 60.5 | 54.6 | 49.4 |
| | 55.7 | 59.1 | 61.1 | 63.5 | 66.2 | 69.6 | 70.9 | 71.3 | 73.0 | 70.1 | 63.3 | 56.6 |
| | 41.1 | 43.7 | 45.3 | 46.8 | 49.4 | 51.9 | 53.2 | 53.8 | 53.5 | 50.9 | 45.9 | 42.2 |
| Denver, CO | 30.1 | 33.0 | 38.9 | 47.7 | 56.8 | 66.8 | 72.8 | 71.3 | 62.8 | 51.5 | 39.4 | 32.1 |
| | 42.8 | 45.4 | 51.5 | 60.5 | 69.6 | 80.7 | 86.7 | 85.0 | 77.0 | 65.5 | 52.4 | 44.8 |
| | 17.4 | 20.5 | 26.3 | 34.9 | 44.1 | 52.9 | 58.9 | 57.6 | 48.5 | 37.5 | 26.4 | 19.4 |
| Hartford, CT | 26.6 | 27.9 | 37.2 | 48.2 | 59.3 | 67.9 | 73.2 | 71.0 | 63.5 | 53.0 | 42.1 | 30.4 |
| | 34.8 | 36.4 | 46.1 | 58.5 | 70.4 | 78.7 | 83.7 | 81.4 | 74.1 | 63.7 | 50.7 | 38.2 |
| | 18.5 | 19.3 | 28.2 | 37.9 | 48.1 | 57.1 | 62.6 | 60.6 | 52.8 | 42.2 | 33.4 | 22.6 |

*(continued on next page)*

| | Jan | Feb | Mar | Apr | May | Jun | Jul | Aug | Sep | Oct | Nov | Dec |
|---|---|---|---|---|---|---|---|---|---|---|---|---|
| Washington, DC | 35.7 | 38.0 | 46.3 | 56.3 | 66.1 | 74.7 | 79.0 | 77.3 | 70.7 | 59.5 | 48.9 | 38.8 |
| | 43.3 | 46.4 | 55.4 | 66.6 | 75.9 | 84.0 | 87.9 | 86.0 | 79.5 | 68.8 | 57.6 | 46.3 |
| | 28.1 | 29.6 | 37.1 | 46.1 | 56.3 | 65.3 | 70.1 | 68.7 | 61.8 | 50.1 | 40.2 | 31.2 |
| Jacksonville, FL | 54.5 | 56.4 | 61.8 | 67.4 | 73.7 | 78.7 | 80.7 | 80.3 | 77.4 | 69.0 | 60.8 | 54.9 |
| | 63.8 | 65.9 | 71.5 | 77.1 | 82.9 | 87.2 | 89.1 | 88.5 | 84.8 | 77.0 | 69.9 | 64.2 |
| | 45.1 | 46.9 | 52.0 | 57.8 | 64.5 | 70.2 | 72.3 | 72.2 | 69.9 | 60.9 | 51.7 | 45.6 |
| Miami, FL | 67.3 | 68.2 | 71.5 | 74.9 | 78.3 | 81.3 | 82.6 | 82.9 | 81.8 | 78.2 | 73.1 | 68.9 |
| | 75.6 | 76.7 | 79.5 | 82.6 | 85.5 | 88.1 | 89.4 | 89.8 | 88.3 | 84.8 | 80.3 | 76.9 |
| | 59.0 | 59.7 | 63.4 | 67.2 | 71.0 | 74.4 | 75.7 | 76.0 | 75.3 | 71.5 | 65.9 | 60.9 |
| Orlando, FL | 60.5 | 62.2 | 66.8 | 71.8 | 77.2 | 81.2 | 82.4 | 82.6 | 81.0 | 74.8 | 67.6 | 62.1 |
| | 71.6 | 73.4 | 78.0 | 83.1 | 88.1 | 90.9 | 91.8 | 91.6 | 89.6 | 84.0 | 77.8 | 72.8 |
| | 49.5 | 50.9 | 55.5 | 60.4 | 66.3 | 71.5 | 73.0 | 73.5 | 72.4 | 65.6 | 57.4 | 51.3 |
| Tampa, FL | 60.9 | 62.2 | 66.7 | 71.4 | 77.0 | 80.8 | 82.0 | 82.1 | 80.7 | 74.7 | 67.3 | 62.0 |
| | 70.3 | 71.7 | 76.2 | 81.1 | 86.4 | 89.2 | 89.8 | 90.0 | 88.7 | 83.3 | 76.7 | 71.5 |
| | 51.4 | 52.7 | 57.2 | 61.7 | 67.5 | 72.4 | 74.1 | 74.2 | 72.6 | 66.0 | 57.9 | 52.6 |
| Atlanta, GA | 43.0 | 45.7 | 52.8 | 61.3 | 69.6 | 76.5 | 78.8 | 78.0 | 73.2 | 62.8 | 52.3 | 44.8 |
| | 51.5 | 54.9 | 62.7 | 71.6 | 79.5 | 86.0 | 87.8 | 86.8 | 82.1 | 72.3 | 61.6 | 53.2 |
| | 34.6 | 36.5 | 42.9 | 51.1 | 59.6 | 67.0 | 69.7 | 69.1 | 64.2 | 53.2 | 43.0 | 36.3 |
| Savannah, GA | 51.3 | 53.3 | 59.4 | 66.1 | 73.6 | 79.4 | 81.7 | 81.0 | 77.0 | 67.8 | 58.8 | 52.3 |
| | 60.8 | 63.1 | 69.3 | 76.1 | 83.1 | 88.4 | 90.4 | 89.4 | 85.1 | 77.1 | 68.8 | 62.0 |
| | 41.7 | 43.6 | 49.5 | 56.1 | 64.0 | 70.3 | 72.9 | 72.6 | 68.9 | 58.6 | 48.8 | 42.6 |
| Honolulu, HI | 72.6 | 72.7 | 73.8 | 75.3 | 76.8 | 78.8 | 79.8 | 80.6 | 80.4 | 79.0 | 76.7 | 74.1 |
| | 79.7 | 79.9 | 80.7 | 82.0 | 83.7 | 85.6 | 86.5 | 87.3 | 87.4 | 85.9 | 83.3 | 80.7 |
| | 65.5 | 65.4 | 66.9 | 68.5 | 70.0 | 72.0 | 73.1 | 73.9 | 73.4 | 72.1 | 70.0 | 67.4 |
| Boise, ID | 29.4 | 35.4 | 42.4 | 49.8 | 57.7 | 65.6 | 74.2 | 72.4 | 62.7 | 52.3 | 40.2 | 31.5 |
| | 36.7 | 43.5 | 52.5 | 61.8 | 70.8 | 79.4 | 89.9 | 87.8 | 76.9 | 64.8 | 49.2 | 38.7 |
| | 22.1 | 27.3 | 32.3 | 37.8 | 44.6 | 51.7 | 58.4 | 56.9 | 48.4 | 39.8 | 31.1 | 24.2 |
| Chicago, IL | 21.4 | 25.8 | 36.6 | 48.5 | 59.2 | 68.3 | 73.2 | 71.8 | 64.3 | 52.5 | 39.8 | 27.0 |
| | 29.3 | 33.7 | 45.2 | 58.5 | 70.3 | 79.5 | 83.6 | 82.0 | 74.7 | 63.0 | 48.0 | 34.4 |
| | 13.5 | 17.9 | 28.0 | 38.5 | 48.0 | 57.2 | 62.7 | 61.7 | 53.9 | 42.1 | 31.5 | 19.5 |
| Indianapolis, IN | 28.0 | 30.7 | 40.4 | 52.0 | 62.5 | 71.8 | 75.8 | 73.6 | 66.8 | 55.3 | 42.2 | 31.8 |
| | 35.8 | 38.8 | 49.3 | 61.8 | 72.6 | 81.7 | 85.7 | 83.6 | 77.2 | 65.4 | 50.4 | 39.0 |
| | 20.3 | 22.6 | 31.5 | 42.2 | 52.4 | 61.8 | 65.8 | 63.6 | 56.5 | 45.1 | 33.9 | 24.5 |
| Des Moines, IA | 20.8 | 24.9 | 36.7 | 50.6 | 61.7 | 71.2 | 76.2 | 73.8 | 65.3 | 53.8 | 38.4 | 25.9 |
| | 29.5 | 33.8 | 45.9 | 60.9 | 71.9 | 81.2 | 86.5 | 84.1 | 75.9 | 64.4 | 47.5 | 34.1 |
| | 12.0 | 16.0 | 27.4 | 40.3 | 51.4 | 61.2 | 65.8 | 63.5 | 54.8 | 43.2 | 29.2 | 17.8 |
| Lexington, KY | 33.1 | 35.2 | 44.2 | 54.3 | 64.1 | 72.7 | 76.3 | 74.8 | 68.8 | 57.2 | 45.0 | 36.0 |
| | 41.1 | 43.8 | 53.7 | 64.5 | 74.2 | 82.6 | 86.0 | 84.7 | 79.1 | 67.5 | 53.7 | 43.8 |
| | 25.1 | 26.5 | 34.6 | 44.1 | 54.0 | 62.7 | 66.5 | 65.0 | 58.6 | 46.9 | 36.2 | 28.1 |
| New Orleans, LA | 53.3 | 56.0 | 61.8 | 68.7 | 75.3 | 80.7 | 82.3 | 82.1 | 78.7 | 70.3 | 60.9 | 55.4 |
| | 62.1 | 65.2 | 71.1 | 78.0 | 84.3 | 89.5 | 90.6 | 90.3 | 86.7 | 79.7 | 70.3 | 64.4 |
| | 44.5 | 46.8 | 52.5 | 59.3 | 66.2 | 71.9 | 74.0 | 73.8 | 70.7 | 60.9 | 51.4 | 46.3 |
| Shreveport, LA | 47.0 | 50.5 | 58.0 | 66.0 | 73.2 | 80.3 | 83.1 | 82.7 | 77.1 | 66.9 | 56.1 | 49.1 |
| | 56.1 | 60.3 | 68.3 | 76.4 | 83.1 | 90.2 | 93.0 | 92.9 | 87.4 | 78.1 | 66.5 | 58.4 |
| | 37.9 | 40.7 | 47.6 | 55.6 | 63.2 | 70.3 | 73.1 | 72.4 | 66.8 | 55.8 | 45.7 | 39.7 |

| | Jan | Feb | Mar | Apr | May | Jun | Jul | Aug | Sep | Oct | Nov | Dec |
|---|---|---|---|---|---|---|---|---|---|---|---|---|
| Portland, ME | 22.3 | 23.5 | 32.4 | 42.9 | 53.3 | 62.4 | 68.3 | 66.8 | 59.5 | 49.3 | 38.7 | 26.9 |
| | 30.8 | 32.3 | 40.3 | 51.3 | 62.3 | 71.7 | 77.5 | 75.7 | 68.5 | 58.1 | 46.3 | 34.7 |
| | 13.7 | 14.8 | 24.5 | 34.5 | 44.3 | 53.1 | 59.1 | 57.8 | 50.4 | 40.5 | 31.0 | 19.0 |
| Boston, MA | 28.8 | 29.4 | 37.1 | 47.2 | 57.9 | 67.2 | 72.7 | 71.0 | 64.1 | 54.0 | 43.7 | 32.8 |
| | 36.3 | 37.1 | 44.6 | 55.2 | 66.5 | 75.9 | 81.1 | 78.9 | 72.1 | 62.0 | 50.8 | 39.8 |
| | 21.3 | 21.8 | 29.6 | 39.1 | 49.3 | 58.4 | 64.3 | 63.0 | 56.1 | 46.1 | 36.5 | 25.7 |
| Detroit, MI | 23.4 | 25.8 | 35.5 | 47.5 | 58.7 | 67.7 | 72.3 | 70.7 | 63.3 | 51.3 | 40.1 | 28.6 |
| | 30.6 | 33.5 | 44.2 | 57.8 | 69.9 | 78.8 | 83.2 | 81.4 | 73.8 | 61.5 | 47.9 | 35.4 |
| | 16.1 | 18.0 | 26.8 | 37.1 | 47.5 | 56.5 | 61.4 | 60.0 | 52.7 | 41.1 | 32.2 | 21.8 |
| Sault Ste. Marie, MI | 14.1 | 13.9 | 23.6 | 37.9 | 49.6 | 58.5 | 63.8 | 63.0 | 55.5 | 45.0 | 32.5 | 20.4 |
| | 22.0 | 22.8 | 32.2 | 46.8 | 60.2 | 69.9 | 75.0 | 73.0 | 64.5 | 52.8 | 38.5 | 27.0 |
| | 6.2 | 5.0 | 14.9 | 29.0 | 38.9 | 47.1 | 52.6 | 52.9 | 46.4 | 37.3 | 26.5 | 13.7 |
| Duluth, MN | 8.5 | 12.6 | 24.2 | 38.3 | 49.5 | 58.6 | 65.2 | 63.7 | 55.0 | 44.2 | 28.6 | 14.5 |
| | 17.3 | 21.7 | 32.6 | 47.2 | 59.7 | 69.1 | 75.5 | 73.4 | 64.0 | 52.5 | 35.4 | 22.2 |
| | −0.3 | 3.5 | 15.8 | 29.4 | 39.3 | 48.1 | 54.9 | 54.0 | 45.9 | 35.8 | 21.7 | 6.8 |
| Minneapolis, MN | 13.2 | 17.3 | 30.1 | 46.0 | 58.3 | 67.9 | 73.2 | 70.6 | 61.4 | 49.5 | 32.8 | 19.2 |
| | 21.8 | 25.9 | 38.4 | 55.8 | 68.5 | 77.8 | 83.2 | 80.5 | 71.3 | 59.0 | 40.4 | 26.7 |
| | 4.6 | 8.6 | 21.8 | 36.3 | 48.0 | 58.0 | 63.1 | 60.7 | 51.5 | 40.1 | 25.2 | 11.7 |
| Jackson, MS | 47.4 | 50.5 | 57.3 | 65.1 | 72.5 | 79.6 | 81.9 | 81.4 | 76.8 | 66.0 | 55.7 | 49.1 |
| | 57.9 | 61.6 | 68.9 | 76.9 | 84.0 | 90.8 | 92.6 | 82.4 | 88.4 | 79.3 | 68.1 | 59.8 |
| | 36.8 | 39.4 | 45.7 | 53.2 | 61.0 | 68.3 | 71.2 | 70.4 | 65.1 | 52.7 | 43.2 | 38.4 |
| St. Louis, MO | 31.3 | 34.7 | 44.5 | 56.1 | 65.9 | 75.2 | 79.5 | 77.6 | 70.1 | 58.8 | 45.4 | 35.0 |
| | 39.5 | 43.3 | 53.8 | 65.8 | 75.6 | 84.5 | 88.8 | 87.0 | 79.8 | 68.5 | 53.9 | 42.8 |
| | 23.0 | 26.1 | 35.1 | 46.4 | 56.3 | 65.8 | 70.2 | 68.1 | 60.4 | 49.0 | 36.8 | 27.3 |
| Billings, MT | 23.0 | 27.9 | 34.9 | 45.7 | 55.5 | 64.0 | 72.4 | 70.7 | 59.7 | 49.4 | 35.3 | 27.4 |
| | 32.3 | 37.7 | 45.2 | 57.3 | 67.5 | 76.5 | 86.6 | 84.9 | 72.6 | 61.1 | 44.7 | 36.4 |
| | 13.6 | 18.0 | 24.5 | 34.0 | 43.6 | 51.5 | 58.2 | 56.5 | 46.8 | 37.7 | 25.8 | 18.4 |
| Omaha, NE | 20.5 | 25.5 | 37.0 | 49.5 | 60.6 | 71.3 | 75.8 | 73.7 | 64.6 | 53.3 | 37.8 | 25.4 |
| | 29.5 | 34.6 | 46.7 | 60.2 | 70.8 | 81.5 | 85.6 | 83.7 | 74.8 | 63.9 | 46.9 | 34.0 |
| | 11.4 | 16.5 | 27.2 | 38.8 | 50.3 | 61.0 | 66.0 | 63.7 | 54.3 | 42.7 | 28.6 | 16.8 |
| Las Vegas, NV | 44.6 | 49.9 | 55.8 | 64.6 | 73.9 | 83.5 | 89.8 | 87.7 | 80.0 | 67.3 | 53.5 | 45.7 |
| | 56.5 | 62.4 | 68.9 | 78.5 | 88.3 | 98.6 | 104.5 | 102.2 | 94.8 | 81.7 | 66.6 | 57.7 |
| | 32.7 | 37.4 | 42.7 | 50.6 | 59.4 | 68.3 | 75.0 | 73.2 | 65.1 | 53.0 | 40.4 | 33.6 |
| Reno, NV | 32.0 | 36.8 | 41.5 | 47.8 | 55.1 | 62.9 | 70.3 | 68.7 | 60.9 | 51.1 | 40.9 | 33.3 |
| | 43.7 | 49.3 | 55.0 | 62.8 | 70.6 | 80.0 | 89.5 | 87.8 | 79.4 | 68.2 | 55.3 | 45.3 |
| | 20.2 | 24.4 | 28.0 | 32.7 | 39.6 | 45.7 | 51.1 | 49.5 | 42.4 | 34.0 | 26.5 | 21.3 |
| Albuquerque, NM | 34.6 | 39.8 | 46.5 | 55.0 | 63.9 | 73.6 | 77.4 | 75.3 | 68.4 | 56.8 | 43.9 | 35.3 |
| | 47.0 | 53.1 | 60.9 | 70.1 | 79.1 | 89.1 | 91.3 | 88.7 | 82.2 | 71.1 | 57.4 | 47.5 |
| | 22.2 | 26.5 | 32.1 | 39.9 | 48.7 | 58.0 | 63.5 | 61.9 | 54.7 | 42.6 | 30.4 | 23.1 |
| Buffalo, NY | 25.0 | 24.7 | 32.6 | 43.8 | 55.1 | 64.8 | 70.5 | 69.0 | 62.4 | 51.5 | 40.0 | 29.5 |
| | 31.4 | 31.6 | 39.9 | 52.0 | 63.7 | 72.7 | 78.3 | 77.0 | 70.5 | 59.1 | 46.3 | 35.4 |
| | 18.5 | 17.7 | 25.3 | 35.5 | 46.4 | 56.9 | 62.6 | 60.9 | 54.3 | 44.0 | 33.8 | 23.6 |
| New York City, NY | 32.2 | 33.1 | 41.2 | 51.5 | 62.2 | 71.1 | 76.3 | 74.8 | 68.1 | 57.7 | 47.0 | 36.0 |
| | 38.5 | 40.0 | 48.7 | 60.0 | 71.2 | 79.8 | 84.8 | 83.1 | 76.3 | 65.6 | 53.5 | 42.0 |
| | 25.8 | 26.2 | 33.6 | 43.1 | 53.2 | 62.3 | 67.8 | 66.6 | 59.8 | 49.8 | 40.4 | 29.9 |

(continued on next page)

| | Jan | Feb | Mar | Apr | May | Jun | Jul | Aug | Sep | Oct | Nov | Dec |
|---|---|---|---|---|---|---|---|---|---|---|---|---|
| Greensboro, NC | 38.3 | 40.6 | 48.2 | 57.8 | 66.5 | 74.1 | 77.4 | 76.0 | 69.9 | 58.7 | 48.6 | 40.1 |
| | 48.2 | 51.4 | 59.7 | 70.0 | 78.1 | 85.0 | 87.6 | 86.0 | 80.4 | 70.5 | 59.9 | 50.2 |
| | 28.4 | 29.8 | 36.7 | 45.5 | 54.9 | 63.2 | 67.2 | 66.0 | 59.4 | 46.8 | 37.2 | 30.0 |
| Fargo, ND | 5.5 | 10.2 | 24.6 | 42.5 | 55.2 | 64.8 | 70.1 | 68.1 | 58.0 | 45.5 | 27.4 | 12.7 |
| | 15.0 | 19.7 | 33.7 | 53.2 | 67.3 | 76.1 | 81.9 | 80.2 | 69.7 | 56.4 | 36.0 | 21.4 |
| | −4.0 | 0.7 | 15.5 | 31.8 | 43.1 | 53.5 | 58.3 | 56.0 | 46.2 | 34.6 | 18.7 | 4.0 |
| Cleveland, OH | 27.1 | 27.8 | 36.2 | 47.3 | 58.4 | 67.8 | 72.3 | 70.7 | 64.6 | 53.6 | 41.7 | 31.3 |
| | 34.0 | 35.1 | 44.0 | 56.0 | 67.4 | 76.7 | 80.8 | 79.1 | 73.2 | 61.9 | 48.6 | 37.5 |
| | 20.2 | 20.5 | 28.3 | 38.5 | 49.3 | 59.0 | 63.7 | 62.2 | 55.9 | 45.2 | 34.8 | 25.0 |
| Columbus, OH | 29.0 | 30.8 | 40.2 | 51.2 | 61.9 | 70.7 | 74.8 | 72.8 | 66.4 | 54.7 | 42.4 | 32.4 |
| | 36.5 | 38.8 | 49.2 | 61.4 | 72.5 | 81.2 | 85.2 | 83.2 | 77.1 | 65.0 | 50.6 | 39.5 |
| | 21.4 | 22.7 | 31.1 | 40.9 | 51.3 | 60.2 | 64.3 | 62.4 | 55.8 | 44.4 | 34.2 | 25.3 |
| Portland, OR | 39.0 | 43.3 | 46.7 | 51.2 | 57.3 | 61.4 | 66.6 | 66.6 | 63.0 | 54.5 | 45.8 | 40.6 |
| | 44.7 | 50.5 | 55.3 | 60.8 | 67.4 | 71.4 | 78.0 | 77.9 | 74.6 | 63.8 | 52.4 | 46.0 |
| | 33.2 | 36.0 | 38.1 | 41.6 | 47.1 | 51.3 | 55.2 | 55.3 | 51.5 | 45.1 | 39.1 | 35.2 |
| Philadelphia, PA | 32.8 | 33.8 | 41.9 | 52.4 | 63.2 | 71.8 | 76.7 | 74.9 | 68.4 | 57.3 | 46.3 | 36.2 |
| | 39.9 | 41.4 | 50.3 | 61.8 | 72.8 | 81.2 | 85.5 | 83.3 | 77.0 | 66.1 | 54.1 | 43.1 |
| | 25.6 | 26.2 | 33.4 | 42.9 | 53.5 | 62.5 | 67.9 | 66.4 | 59.8 | 48.5 | 38.5 | 29.2 |
| Pittsburgh, PA | 30.0 | 31.1 | 39.9 | 51.0 | 61.7 | 70.1 | 74.3 | 72.5 | 66.2 | 54.7 | 43.1 | 33.3 |
| | 37.6 | 39.3 | 49.0 | 61.1 | 72.3 | 80.4 | 84.3 | 82.4 | 76.3 | 64.4 | 50.9 | 40.3 |
| | 22.4 | 22.9 | 30.8 | 40.8 | 51.1 | 59.8 | 64.2 | 62.5 | 56.1 | 44.9 | 35.3 | 26.3 |
| Columbia, SC | 45.9 | 48.0 | 55.2 | 63.3 | 71.7 | 78.4 | 80.9 | 79.8 | 75.0 | 64.2 | 54.4 | 47.1 |
| | 56.1 | 58.8 | 66.5 | 75.2 | 83.2 | 89.2 | 91.1 | 89.7 | 85.0 | 75.7 | 65.9 | 57.5 |
| | 35.7 | 37.1 | 43.8 | 51.4 | 60.1 | 67.6 | 70.7 | 70.0 | 64.9 | 52.6 | 42.9 | 36.7 |
| Rapid City, SD | 22.9 | 25.5 | 33.4 | 45.0 | 55.1 | 64.6 | 72.2 | 70.8 | 60.6 | 49.2 | 35.7 | 26.3 |
| | 34.5 | 36.9 | 44.9 | 57.0 | 66.9 | 76.6 | 85.4 | 84.4 | 74.2 | 62.1 | 47.3 | 37.5 |
| | 11.3 | 14.1 | 21.9 | 33.1 | 43.3 | 52.6 | 59.0 | 57.3 | 47.1 | 36.3 | 24.1 | 15.1 |
| Memphis, TN | 40.9 | 44.1 | 52.5 | 62.3 | 70.6 | 78.4 | 81.5 | 80.2 | 74.3 | 63.5 | 51.8 | 43.5 |
| | 48.9 | 52.6 | 61.5 | 71.6 | 79.8 | 87.4 | 90.3 | 89.1 | 83.6 | 73.6 | 60.9 | 51.5 |
| | 32.9 | 35.6 | 43.5 | 52.9 | 61.3 | 69.3 | 72.7 | 71.3 | 64.9 | 53.3 | 42.7 | 35.6 |
| Dallas, TX | 45.1 | 48.8 | 56.9 | 65.2 | 72.7 | 80.9 | 84.6 | 84.7 | 77.8 | 67.6 | 56.0 | 47.5 |
| | 55.4 | 59.4 | 68.0 | 75.9 | 82.7 | 91.1 | 95.0 | 95.3 | 88.2 | 78.5 | 66.5 | 57.6 |
| | 34.8 | 38.1 | 45.8 | 54.8 | 62.7 | 70.7 | 74.2 | 74.0 | 67.3 | 56.6 | 45.4 | 37.3 |
| El Paso, TX | 44.5 | 49.3 | 55.6 | 63.8 | 72.1 | 80.8 | 82.0 | 80.3 | 74.8 | 64.5 | 52.3 | 45.0 |
| | 57.2 | 62.6 | 69.3 | 77.8 | 86.1 | 94.7 | 94.1 | 92.1 | 87.0 | 77.9 | 65.7 | 57.5 |
| | 31.9 | 35.9 | 41.8 | 49.7 | 58.1 | 66.8 | 69.8 | 68.4 | 62.5 | 51.1 | 38.9 | 32.6 |
| Houston, TX | 50.9 | 54.6 | 61.8 | 68.3 | 74.9 | 80.8 | 83.2 | 82.9 | 78.5 | 70.0 | 60.4 | 54.0 |
| | 61.0 | 65.5 | 72.7 | 78.9 | 84.8 | 90.7 | 93.4 | 93.3 | 88.6 | 81.5 | 71.5 | 64.7 |
| | 40.8 | 43.7 | 50.8 | 57.8 | 65.0 | 71.0 | 73.0 | 72.5 | 68.4 | 58.4 | 49.3 | 43.3 |
| San Antonio, TX | 51.6 | 55.2 | 62.2 | 69.3 | 75.5 | 81.6 | 84.0 | 84.2 | 79.4 | 70.9 | 60.5 | 53.5 |
| | 62.1 | 66.1 | 73.4 | 80.0 | 85.5 | 91.6 | 94.4 | 94.9 | 89.6 | 81.8 | 71.1 | 64.0 |
| | 41.1 | 44.2 | 50.9 | 58.6 | 65.5 | 71.6 | 73.6 | 73.5 | 69.2 | 59.9 | 49.8 | 43.1 |
| Salt Lake City, UT | 28.0 | 33.3 | 41.1 | 49.4 | 58.4 | 68.4 | 77.3 | 75.5 | 65.3 | 53.2 | 40.4 | 31.2 |
| | 36.1 | 41.7 | 50.7 | 60.3 | 70.5 | 81.8 | 91.2 | 89.1 | 78.6 | 65.1 | 50.0 | 39.1 |
| | 19.9 | 24.9 | 31.5 | 38.5 | 46.3 | 54.9 | 63.3 | 61.9 | 51.9 | 41.3 | 30.8 | 23.3 |

| | Jan | Feb | Mar | Apr | May | Jun | Jul | Aug | Sep | Oct | Nov | Dec |
|---|---|---|---|---|---|---|---|---|---|---|---|---|
| Burlington, VT | 17.9 | 18.6 | 29.6 | 43.0 | 55.5 | 64.8 | 69.8 | 67.4 | 59.5 | 48.5 | 36.7 | 23.4 |
| | 26.5 | 27.5 | 38.0 | 52.2 | 65.8 | 74.9 | 79.9 | 77.2 | 68.9 | 57.2 | 43.5 | 30.7 |
| | 9.3 | 9.7 | 21.2 | 33.7 | 45.2 | 54.7 | 59.7 | 57.7 | 50.1 | 39.8 | 29.9 | 16.0 |
| Norfolk, VA | 41.2 | 42.2 | 48.9 | 57.5 | 66.8 | 74.7 | 78.8 | 77.6 | 72.5 | 62.1 | 52.3 | 43.7 |
| | 49.0 | 50.5 | 57.8 | 66.9 | 75.8 | 83.3 | 87.0 | 85.1 | 79.8 | 69.9 | 60.3 | 51.4 |
| | 33.3 | 33.9 | 40.0 | 48.1 | 57.7 | 66.1 | 70.6 | 70.0 | 65.1 | 54.3 | 44.2 | 35.9 |
| Roanoke, VA | 35.9 | 38.3 | 46.1 | 56.6 | 64.7 | 72.1 | 76.3 | 74.8 | 67.8 | 57.1 | 47.1 | 38.4 |
| | 45.1 | 48.3 | 56.8 | 67.7 | 76.2 | 83.5 | 87.2 | 85.6 | 78.7 | 68.6 | 57.4 | 47.5 |
| | 26.7 | 28.4 | 35.4 | 45.5 | 53.1 | 60.6 | 65.3 | 64.0 | 56.9 | 45.6 | 36.7 | 29.2 |
| Seattle, WA | 41.7 | 44.6 | 46.8 | 51.1 | 57.0 | 61.5 | 65.6 | 65.6 | 61.4 | 54.1 | 46.7 | 42.4 |
| | 46.2 | 50.3 | 53.4 | 58.6 | 65.0 | 69.5 | 74.6 | 74.2 | 69.2 | 60.3 | 51.5 | 46.7 |
| | 37.1 | 38.9 | 40.2 | 43.6 | 49.0 | 53.4 | 56.6 | 57.0 | 53.6 | 47.9 | 41.8 | 38.1 |
| Spokane, WA | 26.8 | 31.8 | 39.5 | 47.6 | 55.6 | 62.4 | 69.8 | 68.6 | 59.4 | 48.5 | 36.5 | 29.7 |
| | 32.6 | 38.9 | 48.4 | 58.5 | 67.3 | 74.5 | 83.9 | 82.7 | 72.3 | 59.3 | 43.0 | 35.0 |
| | 20.9 | 24.7 | 30.5 | 36.7 | 43.8 | 50.3 | 55.7 | 54.5 | 46.4 | 37.7 | 30.0 | 24.4 |
| Green Bay, WI | 16.0 | 18.3 | 29.4 | 43.5 | 55.2 | 65.2 | 70.3 | 67.9 | 60.0 | 48.6 | 34.5 | 21.8 |
| | 24.0 | 26.6 | 37.4 | 52.7 | 66.0 | 75.6 | 80.8 | 78.2 | 69.8 | 57.6 | 41.5 | 28.8 |
| | 8.0 | 9.9 | 21.3 | 34.2 | 44.3 | 54.7 | 59.7 | 57.7 | 50.2 | 39.6 | 27.4 | 14.8 |
| Casper, WY | 22.7 | 26.7 | 33.0 | 43.0 | 52.5 | 62.6 | 70.8 | 69.1 | 58.4 | 47.1 | 33.1 | 25.4 |
| | 33.0 | 37.3 | 44.5 | 55.9 | 66.2 | 77.7 | 87.0 | 85.3 | 74.0 | 60.9 | 43.9 | 35.3 |
| | 12.4 | 16.1 | 21.4 | 30.0 | 38.8 | 47.5 | 54.5 | 52.9 | 42.7 | 33.3 | 22.2 | 15.5 |

*Data from *Weather of U.S. Cities* (Gale Research, 1996)

also plants that enjoy heat and humidity but cannot tolerate a hot, arid climate.

## Frost and Freezing

There are several degrees of frost severity, ranging from light frost (32°F) to hard freeze (24°F or below), when the ground actually freezes solid. Frosts and freezes can cause several problems for plants. Extremely tender plants cannot survive even a light frost. On the other hand, hardy, nonwoody plants can generally withstand all but the most severe frosts, unless freezing temperatures come on so quickly that the plant has not had a chance to acclimate. The chart beginning on page 32 lists the first and last frost dates for selected cities in the United States.

Frost heave is another potential problem. This occurs when water in the soil freezes and expands, pushing plants out of the ground and exposing the roots to the sun or drying winds. Frost heave is especially likely with clay soils that are poorly drained to below the frost line.

Moisture in the air protects against freezing temperatures. In coastal areas, the seawater warms the atmosphere and moderates winter temperatures. However, if temperatures do drop to freezing, the moisture clinging to the plants can turn to ice and do great damage.

## Precipitation

Precipitation is not necessarily rain. It also refers to snow, sleet, fog, or hail. The amount and type of precipitation are influenced by temperature, humidity, and elevation. Generally,

## HARDINESS ZONES

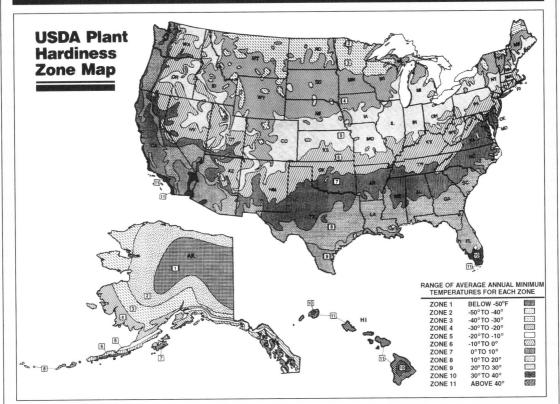

**USDA Plant Hardiness Zone Map**

| RANGE OF AVERAGE ANNUAL MINIMUM TEMPERATURES FOR EACH ZONE | |
| --- | --- |
| ZONE 1 | BELOW -50°F |
| ZONE 2 | -50° TO -40° |
| ZONE 3 | -40° TO -30° |
| ZONE 4 | -30° TO -20° |
| ZONE 5 | -20° TO -10° |
| ZONE 6 | -10° TO 0° |
| ZONE 7 | 0° TO 10° |
| ZONE 8 | 10° TO 20° |
| ZONE 9 | 20° TO 30° |
| ZONE 10 | 30° TO 40° |
| ZONE 11 | ABOVE 40° |

A plant's "hardiness" generally refers to its ability to survive throughout the winter. For example, crape myrtle (*Lagerstroemia indica*) is considered hardy in Georgia but cannot withstand the bitterly cold winters of Minnesota. Hardiness zone maps were first developed to help gardeners and horticulturists determine which plants would survive the minimum temperatures of a particular area. However, hardiness zones provide only a starting point. There are many other factors that come into play, including soil composition, rainfall, humidity, and exposure. Every zone also has microclimates that vary slightly from the norm. A microclimate may be warmer or colder than the surrounding area, depending on exposure, wind, elevation, and precipitation. Taking advantage of microclimates enables gardeners to grow plants that technically should not survive in their hardiness zone.

Zone maps have gradually improved throughout the years, and they can be a helpful guide to choosing plants if used with caution. The first zone map, published in 1927 in Alfred Rehder's *Manual of Cultivated Trees and Shrubs,* divided the country into eight zones according to 5°F differences in the lowest mean temperature of the coldest month. In 1938, Donald Wyman of the Arnold Arboretum at Harvard University updated this rough map, basing his zones on average annual minimum temperatures. His Arnold Arboretum hardiness zone map was revised in 1951, 1967, and 1971.

However, the Arnold map still had flaws. The zones were not based on uniform temperature ranges. Some zones had 15°F ranges, while others were based on 5° or 10°F ranges. In 1960, the United States Department of Agriculture resolved this problem by publishing its own hardiness zone map based on uniform 10°F ranges in average annual minimum temperature. Even though the Arnold map and the USDA map were based on the same climatic data, the zones were drawn differently because of the USDA's uniform temperature ranges. Today, the Arnold Arboretum map is considered obsolete.

The USDA hardiness zone map is now widely used in nursery catalogs, garden books, and magazines. Wherever a hardiness zone is mentioned, it usually refers to the USDA zones. The latest version of the map, published in 1990, has eleven color-coded zones, each divided into A and B regions based on 5°F differences; the A region is 5°F cooler than the B region.

In 1954, Sunset Publishing Corporation, in its first *Western Garden Book*, devised its own climate zones for the West, believing that the USDA map was too limited to be useful in the region, with its wide variety of growing conditions. The twenty-four Sunset zones, which cover Arizona, California, Colorado, Idaho, Montana, Nevada, New Mexico, Oregon, Utah, Washington, and Wyoming, are based not only on minimum winter temperatures but also on summer highs, length of the growing season, humidity, rainfall, latitude, elevation, ocean influence, continental air influence, and topography. The zones are numbered from 1 (the harshest growing conditions) to 24 (the mildest conditions).

In 1997, the company published its first *National Garden Book*, applying the same range of climatic criteria to those parts of the United States and Canada lying east of the Continental Divide. The result is twenty-one new climate zones—zones 25 to 45—additions to the list of twenty-four zones already established for the West.

The Sunset zones for eastern North America, like those for the West, are laid out in a number of regional maps. For more information, consult Sunset's *Western Garden Book* and *National Garden Book* (see Further Reading, page 38).

---

tropical regions get the most rain because of the high heat and humidity. Arid deserts, on the other hand, have the heat but not the humidity needed for condensation. In polar regions, the air is dry and cold, and there is little precipitation. At high elevations, cold temperatures and humidity combine to produce snow.

In the United States, the distribution of precipitation is influenced by the mountain ranges. As warm, moist air comes off the Pacific Ocean, it rises against the mountains and is cooled. As it cools, it releases its moisture as precipitation, which falls on the windward side of the mountains, creating dry conditions on the other side. Smaller mountains or hills create

the opposite effect: the slope is low enough that the wind is able to carry precipitation over the top to the leeward side, while the windward side remains dry.

For woody plants, the amount of precipitation per year is critical to growth. For herbaceous plants, the season in which precipitation occurs is most important. The charts on pages 34–35 and 36 show both annual and seasonal precipitation for the United States.

### Evaporation

Plants are greatly affected by evaporation. Evaporation is influenced by wind and relative

## FIRST AND LAST FROST DATES AND LENGTH OF GROWING SEASONS (IN DAYS)

| | Mean Date of First Frost in Fall | Mean Date of Last Frost in Spring | Mean Length of Growing Season |
|---|---|---|---|
| Birmingham, AL | Nov. 14 | Mar. 19 | 241 |
| Mobile, AL | Dec. 12 | Feb. 17 | 298 |
| Anchorage, AK | Sept. 13 | May 18 | 118 |
| Fairbanks, AK | Aug. 29 | May 24 | 97 |
| Juneau, AK | Oct. 19 | Apr. 27 | 176 |
| Flagstaff, AZ | Oct. 2 | June 8 | 116 |
| Tucson, AZ | Nov. 23 | Mar. 6 | 261 |
| Little Rock, AR | Nov. 15 | Mar. 16 | 244 |
| Sacramento, CA | Dec. 11 | Jan. 24 | 321 |
| Denver, CO | Oct. 14 | May 2 | 165 |
| Hartford, CT | Oct. 19 | Apr. 22 | 180 |
| Washington, DC | Oct. 28 | Apr. 10 | 200 |
| Jacksonville, FL | Dec. 16 | Feb. 6 | 313 |
| Orlando, FL | Dec. 17 | Jan. 31 | 319 |
| Tampa, FL | Dec. 26 | Jan. 10 | 349 |
| Atlanta, GA | Nov. 19 | Mar. 20 | 244 |
| Savannah, GA | Dec. 9 | Feb. 21 | 291 |
| Boise, ID | Oct. 16 | Apr. 29 | 171 |
| Chicago, IL | Oct. 28 | Apr. 19 | 192 |
| Indianapolis, IN | Oct. 27 | Apr. 17 | 193 |
| Des Moines, IA | Oct. 19 | Apr. 20 | 183 |
| Lexington, KY | Oct. 28 | Apr. 13 | 198 |
| New Orleans, LA | Dec. 12 | Feb. 13 | 302 |
| Shreveport, LA | Nov. 27 | Mar. 1 | 272 |
| Portland, ME | Oct. 15 | Apr. 29 | 169 |
| Boston, MA | Oct. 25 | Apr. 16 | 192 |
| Detroit, MI | Oct. 23 | Apr. 25 | 181 |
| Sault Ste. Marie, MI | Oct. 3 | May 18 | 138 |
| Duluth, MN | Sept. 24 | May 22 | 125 |
| Minneapolis, MN | Oct. 13 | Apr. 30 | 166 |
| Jackson, MS | Nov. 13 | Mar. 10 | 248 |
| St. Louis, MO | Nov. 8 | Apr. 2 | 220 |
| Billings, MT | Sept. 24 | May 15 | 132 |
| Omaha, NE | Oct. 20 | Apr. 14 | 189 |
| Las Vegas, NV | Nov. 13 | Mar. 13 | 245 |

| | Mean Date of First Frost in Fall | Mean Date of Last Frost in Spring | Mean Length of Growing Season |
|---|---|---|---|
| Reno, NV | Oct. 2 | May 14 | 141 |
| Albuquerque, NM | Oct. 29 | Apr. 16 | 196 |
| Buffalo, NY | Oct. 25 | Apr. 30 | 179 |
| New York City, NY | Nov. 12 | Apr. 7 | 219 |
| Charlotte, NC | Nov. 15 | Mar. 21 | 239 |
| Fargo, ND | Sept. 27 | May 13 | 137 |
| Cleveland, OH | Nov. 2 | Apr. 21 | 195 |
| Columbus, OH | Oct. 30 | Apr. 17 | 196 |
| Portland, OR | Dec. 1 | Feb. 25 | 279 |
| Philadelphia, PA | Nov. 17 | Mar. 30 | 232 |
| Pittsburgh, PA | Oct. 23 | Apr. 20 | 187 |
| Columbia, SC | Nov. 21 | Mar. 14 | 252 |
| Rapid City, SD | Oct. 4 | May 7 | 150 |
| Memphis, TN | Nov. 12 | Mar. 20 | 237 |
| Dallas, TX | Nov. 22 | Mar. 18 | 249 |
| Houston, TX | Dec. 11 | Feb. 5 | 309 |
| Salt Lake City, UT | Nov. 1 | Apr. 12 | 202 |
| Burlington, VT | Oct. 3 | May 8 | 148 |
| Norfolk, VA | Nov. 27 | Mar. 18 | 254 |
| Roanoke, VA | Oct. 24 | Apr. 20 | 187 |
| Seattle, WA | Dec. 1 | Feb. 23 | 281 |
| Spokane, WA | Oct. 12 | Apr. 20 | 175 |
| Green Bay, WI | Oct. 13 | May 6 | 161 |
| Casper, WY | Sept. 25 | May 18 | 130 |

humidity. High or constant winds can cause a drying effect on soil and plant tissues, as well as erosion of soil and physical damage to plants. Seaside or hillside gardens may be especially susceptible to damage from wind unless they are protected by a windbreak on the windward side. Lack of humidity also causes plants to dry out. The higher the relative humidity, the better for plants because transpiration, the loss of moisture from plant tissues, is reduced. Humidity also prevents temperatures from fluctuating too quickly. Cold, dry, windy places are extremely hard on plants; species native to such areas have adapted by evolving characteristics such as woolly or leathery leaves, which help retain moisture in plant tissues.

## Soil

Soil is the layer of mineral and organic material on the Earth's surface that provides a medium for the growth of plants. Its formation involves a handful of broad factors. Weathering breaks bedrock into smaller and smaller fragments. Plants and other organisms move in, grow, and die, adding organic matter that becomes part of

33

## MEAN MONTHLY AND ANNUAL PRECIPITATION (INCHES) IN SELECTED CITIES OF THE U.S. (DATA FROM 1964–1993)

| | Jan | Feb | Mar | Apr | May | Jun | Jul | Aug | Sept | Oct | Nov | Dec | Annual |
|---|---|---|---|---|---|---|---|---|---|---|---|---|---|
| Birmingham, AL | 4.94 | 4.81 | 5.97 | 4.70 | 4.25 | 3.95 | 5.27 | 4.18 | 3.53 | 2.74 | 3.79 | 5.02 | 53.15 |
| Mobile, AL | 4.87 | 5.15 | 6.59 | 5.04 | 4.84 | 5.53 | 7.42 | 6.66 | 5.54 | 3.20 | 3.85 | 5.12 | 63.82 |
| Anchorage, AK | .83 | .79 | .61 | .54 | .64 | 1.08 | 1.87 | 2.55 | 2.69 | 1.80 | 1.06 | 1.07 | 15.52 |
| Fairbanks, AK | .71 | .46 | .41 | .28 | .66 | 1.38 | 1.84 | 2.11 | 1.06 | .87 | .70 | .70 | 11.18 |
| Juneau, AK | 4.23 | 3.66 | 3.44 | 2.79 | 3.46 | 3.06 | 4.24 | 5.23 | 6.97 | 7.89 | 5.62 | 4.63 | 55.21 |
| Flagstaff, AZ | 2.06 | 2.07 | 2.11 | 1.31 | .71 | .51 | 2.73 | 2.89 | 1.78 | 1.56 | 1.53 | 1.95 | 21.20 |
| Tucson, AZ | .90 | .83 | .74 | .34 | .21 | .25 | 2.20 | 2.22 | 1.31 | .72 | .74 | 1.03 | 11.49 |
| Little Rock, AR | 4.51 | 3.89 | 4.70 | 5.18 | 5.01 | 3.64 | 3.42 | 3.30 | 3.36 | 3.10 | 4.42 | 4.30 | 48.82 |
| Los Angeles, CA | 2.56 | 2.81 | 2.05 | .82 | .11 | .04 | .02 | .08 | .24 | .35 | 1.37 | 1.98 | 12.43 |
| Sacramento, CA | 3.59 | 3.00 | 2.53 | 1.30 | .44 | .13 | .03 | .05 | .28 | .99 | 2.20 | 2.89 | 17.43 |
| San Francisco, CA | 4.14 | 3.34 | 2.94 | 1.30 | .32 | .12 | .02 | .04 | .18 | .95 | 2.10 | 3.54 | 18.99 |
| Denver, CO | .48 | .57 | 1.16 | 1.95 | 2.41 | 1.51 | 1.74 | 1.45 | 1.09 | 1.02 | .72 | .63 | 14.72 |
| Hartford, CT | 3.50 | 3.17 | 3.74 | 3.76 | 3.71 | 3.59 | 3.57 | 3.91 | 3.62 | 3.24 | 3.83 | 3.71 | 43.35 |
| Washington, DC | 2.74 | 2.52 | 3.35 | 2.81 | 3.88 | 3.30 | 3.98 | 4.24 | 3.31 | 2.98 | 3.05 | 3.10 | 39.26 |
| Jacksonville, FL | 2.95 | 3.19 | 3.45 | 2.81 | 3.84 | 5.78 | 6.68 | 6.60 | 7.20 | 4.43 | 1.98 | 2.71 | 51.62 |
| Miami, FL | 2.02 | 1.92 | 2.35 | 3.57 | 5.96 | 8.58 | 6.63 | 7.38 | 8.40 | 6.88 | 2.99 | 1.75 | 58.43 |
| Orlando, FL | 2.23 | 2.70 | 3.53 | 2.62 | 3.40 | 6.98 | 7.83 | 6.68 | 6.74 | 3.36 | 1.88 | 1.91 | 49.84 |
| Tampa, FL | 2.22 | 2.77 | 3.03 | 2.00 | 3.04 | 6.76 | 7.62 | 7.92 | 6.48 | 2.61 | 1.64 | 2.01 | 48.10 |
| Atlanta, GA | 4.72 | 4.69 | 5.55 | 4.01 | 3.71 | 3.79 | 4.82 | 3.95 | 3.31 | 2.66 | 3.32 | 4.41 | 48.94 |
| Savannah, GA | 2.98 | 3.13 | 3.60 | 2.95 | 3.40 | 5.53 | 6.65 | 7.09 | 5.58 | 2.77 | 2.06 | 2.80 | 48.55 |
| Honolulu, HI | 3.76 | 2.50 | 2.68 | 1.32 | .96 | .38 | .56 | .59 | .76 | 2.02 | 2.66 | 3.57 | 21.77 |
| Boise, ID | 1.44 | 1.25 | 1.32 | 1.21 | 1.20 | .89 | .29 | .26 | .58 | .92 | 1.35 | 1.32 | 12.03 |
| Chicago, IL | 1.62 | 1.37 | 2.74 | 3.58 | 3.22 | 3.76 | 3.68 | 4.12 | 3.69 | 2.54 | 2.87 | 2.29 | 35.49 |
| Indianapolis, IN | 2.85 | 2.52 | 3.78 | 3.67 | 3.93 | 4.00 | 3.97 | 3.33 | 3.14 | 2.72 | 3.30 | 2.95 | 40.18 |
| Des Moines, IA | 1.11 | 1.14 | 2.03 | 2.97 | 4.19 | 4.64 | 3.53 | 3.82 | 3.39 | 2.44 | 1.68 | 1.23 | 32.17 |
| Lexington, KY | 3.94 | 3.24 | 4.44 | 3.63 | 3.90 | 4.09 | 4.53 | 3.54 | 2.89 | 2.45 | 3.27 | 3.72 | 43.62 |
| New Orleans, LA | 5.03 | 5.17 | 5.30 | 4.88 | 4.79 | 5.33 | 6.71 | 6.02 | 5.33 | 3.07 | 4.45 | 5.09 | 61.16 |
| Shreveport, LA | 4.16 | 3.73 | 4.15 | 4.63 | 4.64 | 3.62 | 3.51 | 2.61 | 2.91 | 3.16 | 3.99 | 4.47 | 45.58 |
| Portland, ME | 3.86 | 3.66 | 3.95 | 3.65 | 3.43 | 3.27 | 3.12 | 3.07 | 3.21 | 3.39 | 4.12 | 3.96 | 42.70 |
| Boston, MA | 3.62 | 3.38 | 3.86 | 3.61 | 3.22 | 3.15 | 3.15 | 3.60 | 3.19 | 3.29 | 3.91 | 3.65 | 41.62 |
| Detroit, MI | 1.87 | 1.72 | 2.48 | 3.00 | 2.92 | 3.63 | 3.11 | 3.38 | 2.90 | 2.22 | 2.65 | 2.65 | 32.52 |
| Sault Ste. Marie, MI | 2.10 | 1.49 | 1.91 | 2.24 | 2.72 | 2.99 | 2.71 | 3.03 | 3.65 | 3.07 | 3.18 | 2.44 | 31.53 |
| Duluth, MN | 1.11 | .90 | 1.64 | 2.20 | 3.13 | 4.03 | 3.73 | 3.54 | 3.45 | 2.20 | 1.73 | 1.12 | 28.77 |
| Minneapolis, MN | .83 | .85 | 1.60 | 2.17 | 3.38 | 4.17 | 3.55 | 3.40 | 2.89 | 2.01 | 1.45 | .94 | 27.26 |
| Jackson, MS | 4.95 | 4.77 | 5.54 | 5.39 | 4.64 | 3.75 | 4.52 | 3.60 | 2.87 | 2.52 | 4.06 | 5.47 | 52.09 |
| St. Louis, MO | 2.14 | 2.28 | 3.35 | 3.68 | 4.08 | 4.04 | 3.45 | 2.96 | 3.19 | 2.73 | 2.85 | 2.36 | 37.11 |
| Billings, MT | .72 | .62 | 1.07 | 1.61 | 2.24 | 2.34 | 1.02 | .89 | 1.32 | 1.12 | .74 | .68 | 14.39 |
| Omaha, NE | .71 | .79 | 2.18 | 2.68 | 4.30 | 4.16 | 3.78 | 3.65 | 3.54 | 2.25 | 1.30 | .86 | 30.21 |
| Las Vegas, NV | .53 | .48 | .51 | .22 | .18 | .08 | .41 | .48 | .30 | .24 | .37 | .40 | 4.21 |
| Reno, NV | 1.29 | 1.06 | .76 | .45 | .63 | .38 | .27 | .26 | .31 | .42 | .69 | 1.02 | 7.55 |
| Albuquerque, NM | .40 | .39 | .45 | .54 | .64 | .60 | 1.41 | 1.42 | .93 | .83 | .46 | .47 | 8.53 |
| Buffalo, NY | 3.06 | 2.69 | 2.79 | 2.75 | 2.95 | 2.92 | 2.96 | 3.23 | 3.13 | 3.09 | 3.34 | 3.32 | 36.23 |

| | Jan | Feb | Mar | Apr | May | Jun | Jul | Aug | Sept | Oct | Nov | Dec | Annual |
|---|---|---|---|---|---|---|---|---|---|---|---|---|---|
| New York City, NY | 3.43 | 3.34 | 3.88 | 3.54 | 3.64 | 3.46 | 4.27 | 4.35 | 3.73 | 3.50 | 3.52 | 3.48 | 44.14 |
| Greensboro, NC | 3.29 | 3.30 | 3.80 | 3.29 | 3.67 | 3.62 | 4.60 | 4.13 | 3.54 | 3.09 | 2.88 | 3.23 | 42.42 |
| Fargo, ND | .64 | .59 | .92 | 1.92 | 2.45 | 3.42 | 3.09 | 2.74 | 1.94 | 1.50 | .87 | .66 | 20.74 |
| Cleveland, OH | 2.49 | 2.34 | 2.90 | 2.86 | 3.22 | 3.37 | 3.44 | 3.06 | 3.22 | 2.63 | 2.78 | 2.56 | 34.87 |
| Columbus, OH | 2.84 | 2.45 | 3.90 | 3.14 | 3.70 | 3.71 | 3.91 | 3.20 | 2.63 | 2.25 | 2.80 | 2.62 | 37.16 |
| Portland, OR | 5.39 | 3.94 | 3.64 | 2.40 | 2.14 | 1.57 | .60 | .91 | 1.64 | 3.07 | 5.40 | 5.88 | 36.59 |
| Philadelphia, PA | 3.21 | 3.02 | 3.53 | 3.34 | 3.45 | 3.55 | 4.16 | 4.41 | 3.39 | 2.76 | 3.11 | 3.20 | 41.14 |
| Pittsburgh, PA | 2.84 | 2.46 | 3.27 | 3.07 | 3.39 | 3.75 | 3.99 | 3.21 | 2.69 | 2.46 | 2.47 | 2.78 | 36.39 |
| Columbia, SC | 3.47 | 3.83 | 3.98 | 3.18 | 3.28 | 4.14 | 5.59 | 5.67 | 3.78 | 2.60 | 2.86 | 3.19 | 45.58 |
| Rapid City, SD | .41 | .47 | 1.00 | 1.91 | 3.06 | 3.21 | 2.27 | 1.61 | 1.25 | 1.02 | .61 | .51 | 17.33 |
| Memphis, TN | 4.82 | 4.37 | 5.20 | 5.16 | 4.37 | 3.69 | 3.41 | 3.21 | 3.00 | 2.89 | 4.45 | 4.81 | 49.40 |
| Dallas, TX | 1.83 | 2.10 | 2.43 | 3.75 | 4.79 | 3.04 | 2.19 | 2.18 | 2.87 | 3.08 | 2.27 | 2.05 | 32.57 |
| El Paso, TX | .45 | .41 | .33 | .25 | .37 | .63 | 1.67 | 1.54 | 1.31 | .80 | .44 | .56 | 8.75 |
| Houston, TX | 3.79 | 3.16 | 2.86 | 3.48 | 4.92 | 4.81 | 3.96 | 3.91 | 4.40 | 3.91 | 4.01 | 4.00 | 47.20 |
| San Antonio, TX | 1.66 | 1.74 | 1.70 | 2.89 | 3.66 | 3.10 | 2.06 | 2.32 | 3.11 | 2.55 | 1.96 | 1.76 | 28.52 |
| Salt Lake City, UT | 1.28 | 1.32 | 1.84 | 1.98 | 1.82 | .87 | .63 | .86 | .95 | 1.43 | 1.37 | 1.34 | 15.69 |
| Burlington, VT | 1.82 | 1.66 | 2.16 | 2.53 | 3.02 | 3.45 | 3.62 | 3.54 | 3.39 | 2.96 | 2.79 | 2.07 | 33.01 |
| Norfolk, VA | 3.37 | 3.34 | 3.76 | 3.25 | 3.68 | 3.98 | 5.54 | 5.35 | 3.83 | 3.13 | 2.66 | 3.19 | 45.06 |
| Roanoke, VA | 2.72 | 3.15 | 3.66 | 3.30 | 3.95 | 3.37 | 3.72 | 4.04 | 3.34 | 3.41 | 2.99 | 3.09 | 40.75 |
| Seattle, WA | 5.54 | 3.79 | 3.62 | 2.45 | 1.65 | 1.48 | .77 | 1.06 | 1.69 | 3.09 | 5.32 | 5.62 | 36.08 |
| Spokane, WA | 2.05 | 1.57 | 1.36 | 1.10 | 1.36 | 1.27 | .57 | .62 | .81 | 1.20 | 2.06 | 2.21 | 16.17 |
| Green Bay, WI | 1.29 | 1.25 | 1.94 | 2.57 | 3.09 | 3.40 | 3.14 | 3.05 | 3.20 | 2.15 | 2.03 | 1.43 | 28.54 |
| Casper, WY | .53 | .57 | .94 | 1.50 | 2.12 | 1.39 | 1.10 | .67 | .89 | .91 | .76 | .58 | 11.96 |

*Data from *Weather of U.S. Cities* (Gale Research, 1996)

the developing soil. The whole process is aided or slowed down by climatic conditions, particularly temperature and precipitation. Topography is a factor in the erosion of the surface material, and all these activities take place over long periods of time.

## Soil Profile

Worldwide, soils vary tremendously, from blowing sand dunes to thick, muddy riverbanks. Scientists have classified approximately 15,000 soil types. Soils are differentiated and classified by their profiles. A profile is a vertical cross-section of soil from the surface down to the bedrock (at least 5 feet deep). Each layer of soil material in the profile is called a *horizon*.

Horizons can be composed primarily of organic matter, clay, deposits of lime or salts, sand, hardpan, or other materials. By studying their soil profile, gardeners can learn a great deal about the texture and structure of their soil, as well as the depth of the crucial upper layers of dead and decaying organic materials.

## Soil Formation

Five major processes are involved in the formation of soil: podzolization, laterization, calcification, gleyization, and invertization. Regional climate determines which of these process predominates, and so it is possible to generalize about the broad character of the soil of a particular region—as well as its vegetation type—

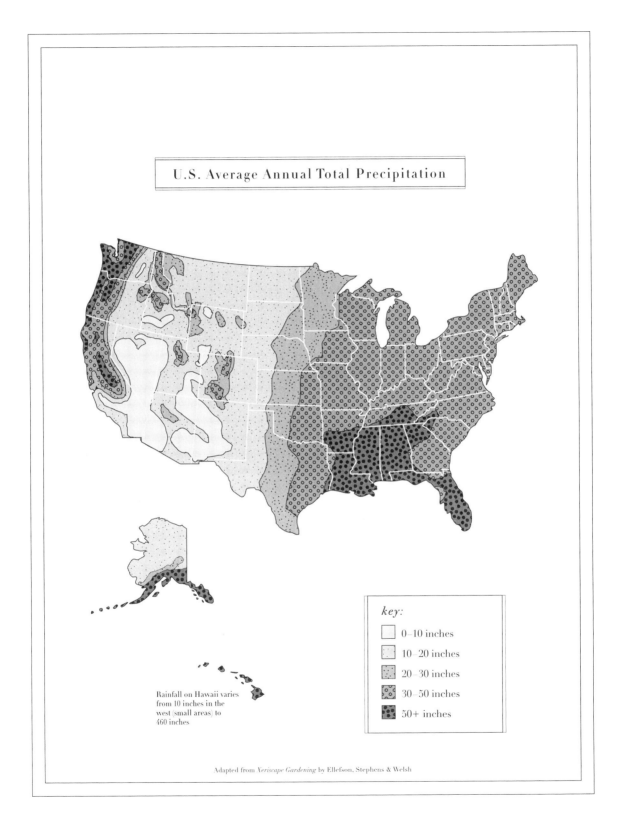

# U.S. Average Annual Total Precipitation

Rainfall on Hawaii varies
from 10 inches in the
west (small areas) to
460 inches

*key:*

☐ 0–10 inches

☐ 10–20 inches

☐ 20–30 inches

☐ 30–50 inches

☐ 50+ inches

Adapted from *Xeriscape Gardening* by Ellefson, Stephens & Welsh

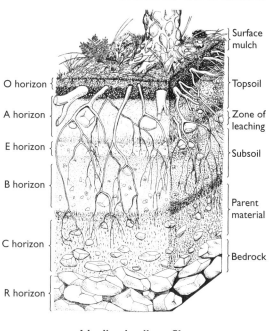

O horizon

A horizon

E horizon

B horizon

C horizon

R horizon

Surface
mulch

Topsoil

Zone of
leaching

Subsoil

Parent
material

Bedrock

**Idealized soil profile**

*A soil profile consists of a series of vertical layers, from sur-
face down to bedrock. Each layer is called a horizon and is
designated by a letter.*

based on the process most central to the development of soil in the area.

• **Podzolization.** Also called spodsolization, this process occurs in moist climates with
variation in seasonal temperatures. Winter temperatures slow the decomposition of organic
matter in the upper soil layers. The typical vegetation is deciduous and coniferous forest.

• **Laterization.** Also called oxisolation, this
process occurs in warm, moist climates. Nutrients like calcium, magnesium, and potassium
leach down through the soil away from plant
roots and into the groundwater; this leaves an
abundance of hydrogen ions behind, making
soils formed by laterization very acidic. Typical
vegetation is subtropical and tropical forest.

• **Calcification.** This process occurs in
semiarid to arid regions where evaporation
from the soil exceeds precipitation. Calcium,
sodium, magnesium, and potassium ions are
drawn to and accumulate near the surface of the
soil because of the evaporation of water; as a
result of the repeated drawing of salts toward
the soil surface, calcium carbonate accumulates,
and calcified soils usually are neutral to slightly
alkaline. In very dry climates, salts accumulate
in excessive concentrations near the surface,
resulting in salinization, which can destroy
agriculturally productive soils. Plains, prairies,
and desert regions are typical in areas where calcification occurs.

• **Gleyization.** This process occurs in areas
of standing water or where drainage is poor.
Because of poor drainage, the soils typically are
waterlogged and therefore low in oxygen. The
breakdown of organic matter is incomplete, and
so it may accumulate as peat. Gleyization
occurs in coastal wetlands and in the permafrost
regions of northern tundra areas.

• **Invertization.** This process occurs in
regions where there are distinct wet seasons followed by periods of extended evaporation and
drying and in soils with a high clay content near
the surface. During the prolonged dry periods,
the surface clay begins to crack, allowing upper
and lower soil layers to mix. Invertization
occurs in prairie and other grassland areas.

### Soil Classification

Soil taxonomy is similar to that of plants (see
"Plant Classification," page 50). The first scien-
tific classification of soils was proposed by V. V.
Dokuchaiev and finalized in 1900. In 1912,
George Nelson Coffey classified the soils of the
United States into five categories: arid soils,
dark-colored prairie soils, light-colored prairie

soils, black swamp soils, and organic soils. Today, soils are classified in the following manner:

Order
   Suborder
      Great Group
         Subgroup
            Family
               Series

This can be compared to the system of plant classification, which is broken down as follows:

Division
   Class
      Subclass
         Order
            Family
               Genus
                  Species

The U.S. Comprehensive Soil Classification System recognizes ten soil orders:

- **Alfisols.** These soils are formed by podzolization, where humus is restricted to the upper surface. They are the gray-brown soils of wooded areas.
- **Aridisols.** These soils are dry for extended periods, are low in humus, and may display some calcification. They are typically desert soils.
- **Entisols.** These soils are subject to erosion, and do not have distinct horizons. They are commonly found on floodplains.
- **Histosols.** These soils usually are formed by gleyization and are high in organic matter. They are commonly found in bogs.
- **Inceptisols.** These soils are formed by podzolization and substantial erosion. Thus, they are typically shallow.
- **Mollisols.** These soils result from podzolization and some calcification. They typically are dark and rich in nutrients and found in semihumid prairie areas.
- **Oxisols.** These highly weathered and often red, yellow, or gray soils result from laterization. They are found in tropical and subtropical regions, including Florida.
- **Spodosols.** These soils are the result of podzolization. They are light gray in color and common in eastern North America.
- **Utisols.** Also formed from podzolization, these are intensely leached and weathered soils containing a large proportion of clay. They are found in warm climates of the southeastern United States.
- **Vertisols.** These dark clay soils that exhibit deep, wide cracks when dry are formed by invertization and found, for example, in Texas.

## Further Reading

Akin, Wallace E. *Global Patterns: Climate, Vegetation and Soils.* Norman, Okla.: University of Oklahoma Press, 1991.

Barbour, Michael G., and William Dwight Billings, eds. *North American Terrestrial Vegetation.* New York: Cambridge University Press, 1988.

Gleason, Henry, and Arthur Cronquist. *The Natural Geography of Plants.* New York: Columbia University Press, 1964.

The Editors of Sunset Books and *Sunset* magazine. *Sunset National Garden Book.* Menlo Park, Calif.: Sunset Books, 1997.

The Editors of Sunset Books and *Sunset* magazine. *Sunset Western Garden Book.* Menlo Park, Calif.: Sunset Books, 1995.

Takhtajan, Armen. *Floristic Regions of the World.* Berkeley, Calif.: University of California Press, 1986.

# 3

# BOTANY FOR GARDENERS

## PLANT NAMES

*"What's in a name? That which we call a rose
By any other name would smell as sweet."*

—WILLIAM SHAKESPEARE,
*Romeo and Juliet*

By any other name a rose might smell as sweet, but if there were no internationally uniform system for naming plants, botanists, horticulturists, and gardeners would never be able to tell each other about it. For this reason, there is an *International Code of Botanical Nomenclature,* a system of rules governing the naming of plants.

### Taxon

*Taxonomy* is the science of plant classification. The word "taxon" (plural, taxa) refers to any taxonomic entity, regardless of rank. In other words, the plant family Ericaceae is a taxon, the genus *Vaccinium* is a taxon, and the species *Vaccinium angustifolium* is a taxon.

### Genus and Species

The basic category of plants is the *species.* Every species on Earth has one, and only one, correct scientific name by which it is known throughout the world. This species name is called a binomial because, in fact, it is two words: the genus and the specific epithet. The binomial system we use today was founded by the Swedish botanist Linnaeus over two hundred years ago. Because there has been a standard method of naming plants and rules for the creation and application of new names, we can not only communicate more effectively but also read works from Linnaeus's day and easily understand which species the author was referring to.

The following is the scientific name for the potato:

*Solanum tuberosum* Linnaeus

*Solanum,* the first part of the scientific name for potato, is the genus. It comes from the classical Latin name for this large and varied group that includes bittersweet nightshade, potato, and Jerusalem cherry. In fact, the genus name is often based on the original Latin or Greek name for the plant. It also may be derived from a number of other sources, including the name of a botanist or an anagram. The name of the genus is written in italics.

The specific epithet is *"tuberosum."* It should almost always be in lower case; occasionally, if it is a proper noun (for example, someone's name), it can have an initial capital letter (this is optional under the code). The specific epithet is usually an adjective that modifies the genus. In this case, *tuberosum* indicates that potato is a tuberous species in the genus *Solanum.* Like the genus, the species is always written in italics.

"Linnaeus" refers to the author of the scientific name for potato. In other words, Linnaeus was the first person to use the binomial *Solanum tuberosum* for the potato plant. If the species were first classified in a different genus or at a different rank (if, for example, it were once considered a subspecies of another species) and were reclassified in its current genus and rank at a later time, the original author's name would be placed in parentheses, followed by the author of the current binomial. For example,

*Petroselinum crispum* (Miller) A. W. Hill indicates that the botanist Philip Miller first named parsley using the epithet *"crispum."* Its original name was *Apium crispum* Miller. Later, this species was transferred by a botanist named Arthur Hill to the genus *Petroselinum.* In the interest of brevity, in many gardening books the author's name is omitted.

## Subspecies, Variety, or Form

Often, a species exhibits some variation, such as different flower color, leaf shape, or height. If this variation is sufficient to warrant naming a new species, then a new species is named, but if the variation is minor or there is a broad range of overlap, a subspecies, variety, or form may be named. When one of these ranks is recognized, its name is formed by using the species name followed by "subsp.," "var.," or "f.," an additional epithet, and the name of the author of the subspecies, variety, or form. Which of these three ranks is used depends upon the type and magnitude of the differences between it and the other members of the species.

*Subspecies* is usually used to designate a group of populations that are approaching species status, and given time it is expected that the subspecies will evolve into a species. A subspecies is usually geographically distinct and has other characteristics that distinguish it from the species; however, the degree of separation is insufficient to call it a species. This is admittedly subjective and is one of the reasons why botanists change the names of plants. An alternative view held by many botanists is that subspecies is a rank between species and variety. In other words, subspecies are groups of varieties.

An example of a subspecies is

*Chimaphila umbellata* subsp. *cisatlantica* S. F. Blake

This is the scientific name for the eastern North American variant of pipsissewa. This plant is larger, with longer leaves and racemose inflorescences (the flower stalks occur along a branch), compared to the typical European subspecies, which has umbellate inflorescences (the flower stalks all come from a common point).

Variety has traditionally been used in the same manner as subspecies, to distinguish taxa that are approaching species but have not yet reached species status. Variety is also used to distinguish groups of populations with ecological differences. Variety and subspecies are often used interchangeably.

A form is usually used to designate a minor variation within a population or a region. For instance, albino forms of species are often designated as f. *alba*.

## Cultivar

The names of cultivated variants are created in a similar manner. If a plant has been selected for some purpose—color, shape, growth characteristics, or other properties—and this selection can be propagated, it can be given a cultivar name. This name is created by taking the binomial species name and appending a non-Latin, nonitalicized name placed in single quotation marks. (It is no longer acceptable to use "cv." before the cultivar name.) When a new cultivated plant is derived by hybridizing two species, the name is derived from the genus only, followed by the cultivar epithet in single quotes. Some examples include:

*Clematis alpina* 'Ruby'
*Magnolia* 'Elizabeth'

In other words, *Clematis alpina* 'Ruby' is a selection of the species *Clematis alpina*. *Magnolia* 'Elizabeth' is a magnolia hybrid resulting from the crossing of at least two *Magnolia* species.

## Some Common Specific Epithets

In many cases, the specific epithet is the Latin word that describes some important characteristic of the plant—flower color, for example, or leaf shape. Familiarity with these Latin terms helps in understanding a plant's name and its characteristics. These are some common examples:

*alba:* white
*aqua:* water
*arbor:* tree
*aurantiacus:* orange
*bi-:* two-
*californicus:* from California
*campanulate:* bell-shaped
*canadensis:* from Canada
*caroliniana:* from the Carolinas
*communis:* common
*concolor:* of the same color
*discolor:* of another color
*ebeneus:* ebony black
*eburneus:* ivory white
*ellipticus:* oval
*erythrinus:* red
*fallax:* deceptive
*filiformis:* thread-shaped

*flavescens:* yellowish

*floridus:* abounding in flowers

*foetida:* stinking

*frutescens:* becoming shrubby

*funestrus:* deadly

*hispida:* covered with coarse, erect hairs

*inodoratus:* without an odor

*laciniatus:* slashed into narrow divisions

*lanceolate:* with a narrow elliptic or ovate, pointed shape

*linearis:* with a very narrow shape

*luteus:* yellow

*magnus:* great, big

*maritima:* maritime, by the sea

*multi-:* many-

*nigra:* black

*novaeanglia:* from New England

*novacaesarea:* from New Jersey

*noveboracum:* from New York

*ob-:* reversed-

*officinalis:* used in medicine

*ovatus:* ovate (oval, but widest below the middle)

*pensylvanica:* from Pennsylvania

*radicans:* rooting, putting out aerial roots

*rubra:* red

*sanguinia:* blood

*tomentosa:* thickly and evenly covered with short, curled, and matted hairs

*urceolate:* urn-shaped

*vacillans:* swinging to and fro

*velutinus:* velvety

*virginiana:* from Virginia

*viridis:* green

*vulgaris:* common

# The Rules for Naming Plants

## International Code of Botanical Nomenclature

Over the past 250 years, the botanical community has developed an elaborate system of rules for the proper naming of plants. Members of this community meet every six years to discuss changes to the published code of botanical nomenclature. The latest edition, the *International Code of Botanical Nomenclature* (Tokyo Code), was published in 1994.

The rules of botanical nomenclature are based on six broad principles:

1. **Independence** Plant names and the rules that govern them are independent of animal and bacteria names or rules. This means that it is permissible for a plant to have a name that is also used for an animal. For example, *Pieris* is both a genus in the Ericaceae (heath family) and the genus of cabbage white butterfly (*Pieris rapae*).

2. **Types** Names are based on their types. Every plant name is tied to a particular herbarium specimen called a type. A *type* is a specimen that a botanist designates as typical of what he or she believes a new species to be. Another botanist may not be able to understand the classification proposed by the first botanist but can always examine the type specimen and use that as a guide to applying the name. If the group is reorganized (say, two species are recognized where formerly only one was recognized), then the original name will refer to only one of the new species—that is, the new species that contains the type for that name. There are also many examples of names that have

had to be changed because the type, after it had been examined, was found to belong to a different species. For instance, the small-headed aster of eastern North America had been called *Aster vimineus,* but the type of this name was shown to be a specimen of the goblet aster, *Aster lateriflorus.* Therefore, *Aster vimineus* can no longer be used for the small-headed aster, which is now called *Aster racemosa.*

3. **Priority** The earliest name that is in accordance with the rules is the correct one. Botanists are notorious for their detailed knowledge of precisely when a book or paper was published. In some cases, a name has priority because it predates another by only a few days.

4. **Uniqueness** There is only one correct name for any taxon. There are, however, examples of taxa that are treated by different authors as species or subspecies. But for any particular rank there is only one correct name. While any one author can recognize a taxon as a species or subspecies, the author cannot recognize a taxon as both a species and subspecies.

5. **Latin** Names are treated as Latin. While many names are derived from languages other than Latin, they are treated as Latin. In other words, Latin rules of grammar are applied to these words. A specific epithet is usually an adjective modifying the genus (a noun) and must agree in number, gender, and so on.

6. **Retroactivity** The rules are retroactive. Many names that were correct when published are made incorrect by retroactive changes in the rules.

## International Code of Nomenclature for Cultivated Plants

During the past fifty years, a systematized set of rules for the naming of cultivated plants has been developed. The latest edition of the *International Code of Nomenclature for Cultivated Plants* was published in 1995. These rules apply to the cultivar portion of the name (the part in single quotes) and not the Latin portion. They have been developed around the following twelve principles:

1. **The Need for Rules** A system for the naming of cultivated plants is essential for understanding and communication.

2. **Only the Cultivated Groups Are Governed** These rules only govern the naming of cultivated plants; the Latin portion of the name is governed by the *Botanical Code.*

3. **The Importance of Standards** Preservation of standards (such as herbarium specimens, photos, and descriptive information) is important for stabilizing the naming of cultivated plants.

4. **Precedence** The first cultivar name used is the correct one.

5. **Uniqueness** For any particular group, there is only one correct name.

6. **Universality** The cultivar names must not be trademarks or otherwise restricted in use.

7. **Legal Terms Take Precedence** This code does not regulate the use of terms for cultivated plants defined under national and international legislation but rather recognizes that these legal terms take precedence.

8. **Unacceptability of Trade Designations** Trade designations cannot be used as replacements for cultivar names.

9. **Common Names Are Not Regulated**
Common names are not regulated by the code.

10. **Registration** Cultivar names should be registered.

11. **Free Assent** The rules have no force of law. The code is enforced only by the free assent of the users.

12. **Retroactivity** The rules are retroactive.

## Registration Authorities for Cultivated Plants

Most cultivated plants have one or more societies or individuals who register the cultivar names. These international registration authorities (IRAs) check to make sure that the name is in accordance with the *International Code of Botanical Nomenclature* and the *International Code of Nomenclature for Cultivated Plants.* They often publish lists of the cultivars for their group and make them available upon request. On the opposite page is a list of the current registration authorities or their North American representative (for a complete listing see *International Code of Nomenclature for Cultivated Plants,* in "Further Reading" on this page).

## Why Plant Names Change

It may seem as if botanists take perverse pleasure in changing long-established names, but they are simply following the international rules that have been in force for nearly a hundred years. There are many reasons why names change; the following are some of the major ones:

• Change in circumscription. If, after research on a particular group, it is determined that the group (typically a genus or a species)

needs to be reclassified, it will often need a new name. For example, if a genus is split into several genera, only some of the species can retain the original genus name. *Chrysanthemum* is one genus that has been reclassified as several distinct genera. As a result, the botanical name of the ox-eye daisy changed from *Chrysanthemum leucanthemum* to *Leucanthemum vulgare.*

• The discovery of an earlier name. If an earlier name is found, it takes priority. An example of a plant whose botanical name changed several times as botanists discovered earlier epithets is wheat, *Triticum aestivum.* Recent changes in the rules make this type of change less likely in the future.

• Type. If, after examining the type, botanists determine that it belongs to a different species, its name must change. For an example, see the discussion of the small-headed aster of eastern North America on page 43.

## Further Reading

Greuter, W., et al., eds. *International Code of Botanical Nomenclature* (Tokyo Code). Königstein, Germany: Koeltz Scientific Books, 1994.

Healey, B. J. *A Gardener's Guide to Plant Names.* New York: Charles Scribner's Sons, 1972.

Jaeger, E. C. *A Source-Book of Biological Names and Terms.* Springfield, Ill.: Charles C Thomas, 1944.

Mabberley, D. J. *The Plant-Book.* Cambridge, England: Cambridge University Press, 1996.

Stearn, W. T. *Botanical Latin.* 4th ed. Portland, Ore.: Timber Press, 1992.

Stearn, W. T. *Stearn's Dictionary of Plant Names for Gardeners.* London: Cassell Publishers Limited, 1972.

Trehane, P., et al., eds. *International Code of Nomenclature for Cultivated Plants.* Wimbourne, U.K.: Quarterjack Publishing, 1995.

# INTERNATIONAL REGISTRATION AUTHORITIES

## GENERAL

Bulbous, cormous, and tuberous-rooted plants, excluding *Dahlia, Lilium,* and *Narcissus:*

Dr. Johan van Scheepen, Royal General Bulbgrowers' Association (KAVB), Postbus 175, NL-2180 AD Hillegom, The Netherlands. E-mail: kavb@bulbgrowing.nl, fax: (31) 252 51 9714.

Hardy Herbaceous Perennials, excluding those genera or other groups for which other IRAs have been appointed:

International Stauden Union (ISU), Attn.: Dr. Josef Sieber, Institut für Stauden und Gehölze, Versuchanstalt für Gartenbau Weihenstephan, Murstrasse 22, D-85356 Freising, Germany. Fax: (49) 816 18 3616.

Woody Plant Genera, excluding those genera or other groups for which other IRAs have been appointed:

The American Association of Botanical Gardens and Arboreta, Attn.: Dr. Steven Clemants, Brooklyn Botanic Garden, 1000 Washington Ave., Brooklyn, NY 11225. E-mail: steveclemants@bbg.org, fax: (718) 941-4774.

## REGIONAL

Australian Plant Genera, excluding those genera or groups for which other IRAs have been appointed:

Australian Cultivar Registration Authority, Attn: Iain Dawson, Australian National Botanic Gardens, GPO Box 1777, Canberra, ACT 2602, Australia. E-mail: idawson@anbg.gov.au, fax: (61) 6 250 9599.

## TAXONOMIC

*Acacia*

Australian Cultivar Registration Authority, Attn.: Iain Dawson, Australian National Botanic Gardens, GPO Box 1777, Canberra, ACT 2602, Australia. E-mail: idawson@anbg.gov.au, fax: (61) 6 250 9599.

*Aloe*

A. J. Bezuidenhout, South African Aloe Breeders Assoc., P.O. Box 59904, Karen Park, 0118, Pretoria, Republic of South Africa.

*Amelanchier*

Dr. Richard St. Pierre, Dept. of Horticulture Science, Univ. of Saskatchewan, Saskatoon, Saskatchewan S7N 0W0, Canada. Fax: (306) 966-8106.

*Andromeda*

The Heather Society of Great Britain, Attn.: A. W. Jones, Otters Court, West Camel, Somerset BA22 7QF, United Kingdom.

Araceae

The International Aroid Society, Attn.: John Banta, Route 2, Box 144, Alva, FL 33920.

*Begonia*

The American Begonia Society, Attn.: Carrie Karegeannes, 3916 Lake Blvd., Annandale, VA 22003.

*Bougainvillea*

Dr. Brijendra Singh, Div. of Floriculture & Landscaping, Indian Agricultural Research Institute (IARI), New Delhi, 110012, India. E-mail: guest@bic-iari.ren.nic.in, fax: (91) 11 576 6420.

Bromeliaceae

The Bromeliad Society International, Attn.: Ellen Baskerville, Marie Selby Botanical Gardens, 811 South Palm Ave., Sarasota, FL 34236. E-mail: mizellen@worldnet.att.net, fax: (941) 951-1474.

*Bruckenthalia*

The Heather Society of Great Britain, Attn.: A. W. Jones, Otters Court, West Camel, Somerset BA22 7QF, United Kingdom.

*(continued on next page)*

*Buxus*
The American Boxwood Society, Attn.: Lynn R. Batdorf, U.S. National Arboretum, 3501 New York Ave. NE, Washington, DC 20002. E-mail: nalb@ars-grin.gov, fax: (202) 245-4575.

*Callistephus*
Prof. Dr. K. Zimmer & Renate Noack, Institut für Zierpflanzenbau, Herrenhäuser Strasse 2, D-30419 Hannover-Herrenhausen, Germany. Fax: (49) 511 76 22654.

*Calluna*
The Heather Society of Great Britain, Attn.: A. W. Jones, Otters Court, West Camel, Somerset BA22 7QF, United Kingdom.

*Camellia,* North American representative
The American Camellia Society, Attn.: Edith Mazzei, Concord, 1486 Yosemite Circle, CA 94521.

*Catharanthus*
Wim Snoeijer, Gorlaeus Laboratories, P.O. Box 9502, Einsteinweg 55, 2300 RA Leiden, The Netherlands. Fax: (31) 71 527 4511.

*Chaenomeles*
Dr. Stephen A. Spongberg, Arnold Arboretum, Jamaica Plain, MA 02130. E-mail: spongberg@arnarb.harvard.edu, fax: (617) 524-1418.

*Clematis*
The Royal Horticultural Society, Attn.: V. A. Matthews, 7350 SW-173rd St., Miami, FL 33157-4835. E-mail: atragene@herald.infi.net, fax: (305) 233-1483.

Conifers, North American representative
The American Conifer Society, Attn.: Susan Martin, U.S. National Arboretum, 3501 New York Ave. NE, Washington, DC 20002. Fax: (202) 245-4575.

*Coprosma*
The Royal New Zealand Institute of Horticulture Inc., Attn.: L. J. Metcalf, "Greenwood," Stringers Creek, RD1, Richmond, Nelson, New Zealand.

*Cornus*
Dr. Stephen A. Spongberg, Arnold Arboretum, Jamaica Plain, MA 02130. E-mail: spongberg@arnarb.harvard.edu, fax: (617) 524-1418.

*Cotoneaster*
Allen Coombes, Sir Harold Hillier Gardens and Arboretum, Jermyns Lane, Ampfield, Romsey, Hampshire SO51 0QA, United Kingdom. E-mail: hillarb@compuserve.com, fax: (44) 1794 368027.

Cyperaceae
The Hardy Plant Society, Attn.: Dr. Alan C. Leslie, Monksilver, 72 Boxgrove Rd., Guildford, Surrey GU1 1UD, United Kingdom. Fax: (44) 1483 211750.

*Daboecia*
The Heather Society of Great Britain, Attn.: A. W. Jones, Otters Court, West Camel, Somerset BA22 7QF, United Kingdom.

*Dahlia*
Ronald Hedge, Royal Horticultural Society's Garden, Wisley, Woking, Surrey GU23 6QB, United Kingdom. Fax: (44) 1483 211750.

*Delphinium* (perennials only)
Dr. Alan C. Leslie, Royal Horticultural Society's Garden, Wisley, Woking, Surrey, GU23 6QB, United Kingdom. Fax: (44) 1483 211750.

*Dianthus,* North American representative
American Dianthus Society, Attn.: R. B. Lee, P.O. Box 22232, Santa Fe, NM 87502. E-mail: randbean@nets.com.

*Erica*
The Heather Society of Great Britain, Attn.: A. W. Jones, Otters Court, West Camel, Somerset BA22 7QF, United Kingdom.

*Erodium*
David Victor, The Old Stables, Church Lane, Hockliffe, Leighton Buzzard, Bedfordshire LU7 9NL, United Kingdom. E-mail: david@victor.u-net.com, fax: (44) 1525 210070.

*Escallonia*
Dr. Elizabeth McClintock, 1551 9th Ave., San Francisco, CA 94122.

*Fagus*
Dr. Stephen A. Spongberg, Arnold Arboretum, Jamaica Plain, MA 02130. E-mail: spongberg@arnarb.harvard.edu, fax: (617) 524-1418.

*Forsythia*
Dr. Stephen A. Spongberg, Arnold Arboretum, Jamaica Plain, MA 02130. E-mail: spongberg@arnarb.harvard.edu, fax: (617) 524-1418.

*Fuchsia*
The American Fuchsia Society, Attn.: Delight A. Logan, 8710 South Sheridan Ave., Reedley, CA 93654.

*Gentiana*
Ian Christie, Downfield, Westmuir, Kirriemuir, Angus DD8 5LP, United Kingdom. Fax: (44) 1575 572977.

*Geranium*
David Victor, The Old Stables, Church Lane, Hockliffe, Leighton Buzzard, Bedfordshire LU7 9NL, United Kingdom. E-mail: david@victor.u-net.com, fax: (44) 1525 210070.

Gesnericeae (excluding *Saintpaulia*)
The American Gloxinia and Gesneriad Society Inc., Attn.: Judy Becker, 432 Undermountain Rd., Route 41, Salisbury, CT 06068.

*Gladiolus* (excluding species and early-flowering cultivars)
The North American Gladiolus Council, Attn.: Samuel N. Fisher, 11734 Road 33½, Madera, CA 93638.

*Gleditsia*
Dr. Stephen A. Spongberg, Arnold Arboretum, Jamaica Plain, MA 02130. E-mail: spongberg@arnarb.harvard.edu, fax: (617) 524-1418.

*Hebe*
The Royal New Zealand Institute of Horticulture Inc., Attn.: L. J. Metcalf, "Greenwood," Stringers Creek, RD1, Richmond, Nelson, New Zealand.

*Hedera*
The American Ivy Society, Attn.: Dr. Sabine M. Sulgrove, 2624 Centre Creek Cir., Spring Valley, OH 45370. E-mail: ivylady@erinet.com, fax: (937) 862-4700.

*Hemerocallis*
The American Hemerocallis Society, Attn.: Binion Amerson, 13339 Castleton Circle, Dallas, TX 75234-5111. E-mail: aba@daylilies.com, fax: (972) 241-4124.

*Hibiscus rosa-sinensis*
The Australian Hibiscus Society, Attn.: Christopher Noble, 61 Cockatoo Ct., Caboolture, Queensland 4510, Australia.

*Hosta*
The American Hosta Society, Attn.: David H. Stevenson, Univ. of Minnesota Landscape Arboretum, P.O. Box 39, 3675 Arboretum Dr., Chanhassen, MN 55317. E-mail: steve021@maroon.tc.umn.edu, fax: (612) 443-2521.

*Hydrangea*
Dr. Elizabeth McClintock, 1551 9th Ave., San Francisco, CA 94122.

*Ilex*
The Holly Society of America, Attn.: Michael R. Pontti, 10520 Cedar Ave., Fairfax, VA 22030. E-mail: ponttim@gunet.georgetown.edu, fax: (202) 245-4575.

*Iris* (excluding bulbous species)
The American Iris Society, Attn.: Keith Keppel, P.O. Box 18145, Salem, OR 97305.

*(continued on next page)*

*Jovibarba*
  The Sempervivum Society, Attn.: Peter J. Mitchell, 11 Wingle Tye Rd., Burgess Hill, West Sussex RH15 9HR, United Kingdom. Fax: (44) 1444 236848.

Juncaceae
  The Hardy Plant Society, Attn.: Dr. Alan C. Leslie, Monksilver, 72 Boxgrove Rd., Guildford, Surrey GU1 1UD, United Kingdom. Fax: (44) 1483 211750.

*Kalmia*
  Dr. Richard A. Jaynes, Broken Arrow Nursery, 13 Broken Arrow Rd., Hamden, CT 06518.

*Lagerstroemia*
  The United States National Arboretum, 3501 New York Ave. NE, Washington, DC 20002. Fax: (202) 245-4575.

*Lantana*
  Dr. Stephen A. Spongberg, Arnold Arboretum, Jamaica Plain, MA 02130. E-mail: spongberg@arnarb.harvard.edu, fax: (617) 524-1418.

*Leptospermum*
  The Royal New Zealand Institute of Horticulture Inc., Attn.: L. J. Metcalf, "Greenwood," Stringers Creek, RD1, Richmond, Nelson, New Zealand.

*Lilium*
  Dr. Alan C. Leslie, Royal Horticultural Society's Garden, Wisley, Woking, Surrey, GU23 6QB, United Kingdom. Fax: (44) 1483 211750.

*Magnolia*
  The Magnolia Society, Attn.: Dorothy J. Callaway, Sweetbay Farm, 4260 Enon Rd., Coolidge, GA 31738. Fax: (912) 227-0578.

*Malus* (ornamental cultivars only)
  Dr. Stephen A. Spongberg, Arnold Arboretum, Jamaica Plain, MA 02130. E-mail: spongberg@arnarb.harvard.edu, fax: (617) 524-1418.

*Mangifera indica*
  Dr. S. N. Pandey, Div. of Fruits & Horticultural Tech., Indian Agricultural Research Institute (IARI), New Delhi, 110012, India.

*Narcissus,* North American representative
  The American Daffodil Society, Attn.: Mary Lou Gripshover, 1686 Grey Fox Trails, Milford, OH 45150. E-mail: daffmlg@aol.com, fax: (513) 248-0898.

*Nelumbo*
  The International Water Lily Society, Attn.: Philip R. Swindells, Vale Lodge, Ropley, Harrogate, North Yorkshire HG3 3AY, United Kingdom. E-mail: 101647.2525@compuserve.com, fax: (44) 1423 684861.

*Nymphaea*
  The International Water Lily Society, Attn.: Philip R. Swindells, Vale Lodge, Ropley, Harrogate, North Yorkshire HG3 3AY, United Kingdom. E-mail: 101647.2525@compuserve.com, fax: (44) 1423 684861.

Orchidaceae
  The Royal Horticultural Society, Attn.: Peter F. Hunt, P.O. Box 1072, Frome, Somerset BA11 5NY, United Kingdom. E-mail: orcreg@rhs.org.uk, fax: (44) 137 3301501.

*Paeonia*
  The American Peony Society, Attn.: Greta Kessenich, 250 Interlachen Rd., Hopkins, MN 55343.

*Pelargonium*
  The Australian Geranium Society, Attn.: J. D. Llewellyn, "Nyndee," 56 Torokina Ave., St. Ives, New South Wales, 2075, Australia.

*Penstemon*
  The American Penstemon Society, Attn.: Dr. Dale T. Lindgren, Univ. of Nebraska, West Central Research and Extension Center, Route 4, Box 46A, North Platte, NE 69101. E-mail: wrcr013@unlum.unl.edu

*Petunia*

Prof. Dr. K. Zimmer & Renate Noack, Institut für Zierpflanzenbau, Herrenhäuser Strasse 2, D-30419 Hannover-Herrenhausen, Germany. Fax: (49) 511 76 22 654.

*Philadelphus*

Dr. Stephen A. Spongberg, Arnold Arboretum, Jamaica Plain, MA 02130. E-mail: spongberg@arnarb.harvard.edu, fax: (617) 524-1418.

*Phormium*

The Royal New Zealand Institute of Horticulture Inc., Attn.: L. J. Metcalf, "Greenwood," Stringers Creek, RD1, Richmond, Nelson, New Zealand.

*Pieris*

Dr. Stephen A. Spongberg, Arnold Arboretum, Jamaica Plain, MA 02130. E-mail: spongberg@arnarb.harvard.edu, fax: (617) 524-1418.

*Pittosporum*

The Royal New Zealand Institute of Horticulture Inc., Attn.: L. J. Metcalf, "Greenwood," Stringers Creek, RD1, Richmond, Nelson, New Zealand.

*Plumeria*

The Plumeria Society of America Inc., Attn.: John P. Oliver, P.O. Box 22791, Houston, TX 77227-2791.

Poaceae (excluding turf, silage, and cereal crops)

The Hardy Plant Society, Attn.: Dr. Alan C. Leslie, Monksilver, 72 Boxgrove Rd., Guildford, Surrey GU1 1UD, United Kingdom. Fax: (44) 1483 211750.

*Populus*

J. B. Ball, Secretary, International Poplar Commission, Food and Agriculture Organization of the United Nations (FAO), Viale delle Terme di Caracalla, 00100 Rome, Italy. E-mail: james.ball@fao.org fax: (39) 6 522 5137.

*Potentilla fruticosa*

Dr. Campbell G. Davidson, Agriculture Canada Research Station, Unit 100-101, Route 100, Morden, Manitoba R6M 1Y5, Canada. E-mail: cdavidson@em.agr.ca, fax: (204) 822-6841.

Proteaceae

M. S. Joubert, Directorate of Plant Quality Control, Dept. of Agriculture, Private Bag X258, Pretoria 0001, Republic of South Africa. Fax: (27) 12 319 6055.

*Pyracantha*

The United States National Arboretum, 3501 New York Ave. NE, Washington, DC 20002. Fax: (202) 245-4575.

*Rhododendron*, North American representative

The American Rhododendron Society, Attn.: J. W. Murray, 21 Squire Terr., Colts Neck, NJ 07722.

*Rosa*

Michael C. Kromer, American Rose Society, P.O. Box 30,000, Shreveport, LA 71130-0030. E-mail: arg@ars-hg.org, fax: (318) 938-5405.

*Rosularia*

The Sempervivum Society, Attn.: Peter J. Mitchell, 11 Wingle Tye Rd., Burgess Hill, West Sussex RH15 9HR, United Kingdom. Fax: (44) 1444 236848.

*Saintpaulia*

The African Violet Society of America Inc., Attn.: Iris Keating, 149 Loretto Ct., Claremont, CA 91711.

*Saxifraga*

The Saxifrage Society, Attn.: Dr. John Whiteman, 63 Elthorne Ave., Hanwell, London W7 2JZ, United Kingdom.

*Sempervivum*

The Sempervivum Society, Attn.: Peter J. Mitchell, 11 Wingle Tye Rd., Burgess Hill, West Sussex RH15 9HR, United Kingdom. Fax: (44) 1444 236848.

*(continued on next page)*

*Syringa*
> Freek Vrugtman, Royal Botanical Gardens, Box 399, Hamilton, Ontario L8N 3H8, Canada. fax: (905) 577-0375.

*Tagetes*
> Prof. Dr. K. Zimmer & Renate Noack, Institut für Zierpflanzenbau, Herrenhäuser Strasse 2, D-30419 Hannover-Herrenhausen, Germany. Fax: (49) 511 76 22 654.

*Ulmus*
> Dr. Stephen A. Spongberg, Arnold Arboretum, Jamaica Plain, MA 02130. E-mail: spongberg@arnarb.harvard.edu, fax: (617) 524-1418.

*Viburnum*
> The United States National Arboretum, 3501 New York Ave. NE, Washington, DC 20002. Fax: (202) 245-4575.

*Weigela*
> Dr. Stephen A. Spongberg, Arnold Arboretum, Jamaica Plain, MA 02130. E-mail: spongberg@arnarb.harvard.edu, fax: (617) 524-1418.

# PLANT CLASSIFICATION

Plant classification is an attempt to organize the hundreds of thousands of species of plants into a meaningful scheme that allows us to make assumptions about the life history, biology, and chemical constituents of various groups. The *International Code of Botanical Nomenclature,* the rules that govern the naming of plants, currently recognizes seven ranks. Each of these ranks is included in one (and only one) higher rank and has one or more members of subordinate rank.

For example, the complete classification of corn, with the names of each of the seven ranks of corn, is as follows:

Kingdom: Plantae
  Division: Magnoliophyta
    Class: Liliopsida
      Order: Cyperales
        Family: Poaceae
          Genus: *Zea*
            Species: *Zea mays*

The way corn is classified at each of these seven ranks indicates something about the plant. The kingdom Plantae indicates that corn is a plant and probably photosynthesizes using chlorophyll. The division Magnoliophyta indicates that it is a flowering plant. The class Liliopsida indicates that corn is a monocot—that is, it has one cotyledon (the first leaf formed on a seedling), and leaves with parallel veins, and its flower parts occur in multiples of three (three or six petals, three or six stamens, and so on). The order Cyperales indicates that the seeds store starch and the flowers lack petals and sepals. The family Poaceae indicates that it has a unique type of inflorescence (see the family description on page 60), round stems, and a distinctive internal anatomy. And so on, down to the species level.

The highest rank for living organisms is the kingdom. For many centuries, living organisms were grouped into one of two kingdoms: plant or animal. Only in the past several decades have new classifications arisen; with new discoveries and new understanding of life, this undoubtedly will continue to change. Today, the most widely accepted classification recognizes five kingdoms: Monera, Protista, Fungi, Plantae, and Animalia.

## A Summary of the Classification of Life, Particularly Plants

KINGDOM: Monera

Bacteria and blue-green algae.

These organisms are prokaryotic, meaning that their cells lack nuclei and other organelles. They are the most common, diverse, and oldest organisms on Earth.

All of the following kingdoms have eukaryotic cells (with nuclei and other cellular organelles):

KINGDOM: Protista

Primarily unicellular organisms that do not fit into the next three kingdoms, Protista include such diverse organisms as *Amoeba* (which causes amoeboid dysentery), *Laminaria* (kelp), and *Physarium* (slime mold).

This group is a catch-all for any unicellular (rarely multicellular) eukaryotic organism. Some protista are more closely related to plants (they photosynthesize), others to animals (they move and eat other organisms); still others are unrelated to any other kingdom. Protista is a large, diverse, and important group that undoubtedly will be divided into numerous kingdoms in the future.

All of the following organisms are multicellular:

KINGDOM: Fungi

Spore-bearing, nongreen organisms.

The cell walls of most species consist of chitin, a complex carbohydrate found in the exoskeleton of insects and crustaceans. Fungi cannot manufacture their own food; they are either saprophytes (living on dead organisms, causing them to decay) or parasites (living on other live organisms, causing disease).

KINGDOM: Animalia

Mobile, nongreen organisms without cell walls.

Animals have muscles, which they use to move. They usually live by consuming other living organisms.

KINGDOM: Plantae

Photosynthetic organisms with a cellulose cell wall.

The plant kingdom is very diverse and is split into several divisions (the equivalent of phyla in animals). Some of the more important divisions of plants are the following:

DIVISION: Bryophyta

Mosses, Liverworts, and Hornworts

Bryophytes are nonvascular plants with free-living gametophytes (the sperm- and egg-producing stage in a plant life cycle) on which the sporophyte (the spore-producing stage in a plant life cycle) grows (see "Plant Reproduction," page 94). They were the first land plants and developed an ability to withstand periodic desiccation as well as a central strand of dead cells in the stems for conducting water to the leaves.

All of the following plants have vascular tissue (the portion of a stem that conducts water from the roots to the leaves and usually assists in or acts as the support for the plant). The gametophytic stage is reduced and the sporophyte is the dominant phase of the life cycle:

DIVISION: Lycophyta

Ground Pine

The Lycophyta have vascular tissue in their roots and leaves, and the sporangia (the spore-producing organ) is intimately associated with the leaves.

DIVISION: Polypodiophyta

Ferns

The ferns have larger and more complex leaves than the Lycophyta but do not produce seeds. There are an estimated 10,000 species of ferns growing around the world.

All of the following plants have seeds, structures that enclose the gametophyte completely. The gametophyte is no longer free-living.

DIVISION: Cycadophyta

Cycads

The cycads have large, fernlike leaves and rather simple cones. The sperm of cycads and ginkgo are motile, like those found in ferns, and have the largest number of flagella (the whiplike structures that propel the sperm cell of any plant)—an estimated 10,000 to 12,000 flagella per sperm. There are ten genera and about a hundred species of cycads. Many are important ornamental plants, including *Cycas circinalis* (sago palm) and *Dioon edule* (Chestnut dioon).

DIVISION: Ginkgophyta

Ginkgo

*Ginkgo biloba* (maidenhair tree) is the only member of this division. First known in the West only in fossils, it was discovered growing in and around temples in Japan and China by nineteenth-century explorers. Ginkgo has flagellated sperm, like the cycads, but its leaves are smaller and not divided into leaflets, and its wood is more like that of the conifers. *Ginkgo biloba* is grown as a street tree. The outer seed coat gives off a noxious odor, making male plants, which produce no seeds, more desirable for landscaping.

DIVISION: Pinophyta

Conifers

The conifers do not have motile sperm; the sperm cell in this group is deposited directly next to the egg and does not swim to it. The conifers have undivided, scale- or needlelike leaves, and complex cones. There are six families and about 500 species worldwide. The most economically important family is the Pinaceae or pine family.

DIVISION: Magnoliophyta

Flowering Plants

Flowering plants are the most recent and successful group of plants. At least 300,000 species have been described, and it is widely assumed that thousands more have not yet been discovered. Flowering plants are easily characterized by several attributes that virtually all members of the division share: flowers, double fertilization, and vessels. The flower is a complex reproductive organ that is discussed in detail beginning on page 104. Double fertilization is a process in which two sperm nuclei are required; one fertilizes the egg and the other fuses with two other nuclei in the gametophyte to form the endosperm, which provides nutrition for developing seedlings. Vessels are large, open-ended cells in the vascular tissue of the plant that efficiently conduct water and nutrients.

CLASS: Magnoliopsida

## Dicots

As their name suggests, dicotyledons have two cotyledons (the first leaves formed on a seedling). They are further characterized by having net-veined leaves, and flowers with sepals (the outer parts of the flower), petals (the inner showy parts), and stamens (the male parts of a flower where the pollen is shed), often in multiples of four or five (for example, four or five sepals, four or five petals, and eight or ten stamens). Dicots are much more diverse than monocots, and it is generally believed that the monocots (which have a single cotyledon) are derived from them. The dicots are usually divided into 5 subclasses, 64 orders, and 315 families.

SUBCLASS: Magnoliidae

This is considered the most primitive group of flowering plants. Members of the Magnoliidae have retained many primitive anatomical and morphological characteristics, including flowers with an indefinite number of petals, sepals, and stamens arranged in a spiral. Though the Magnoliidae is the most primitive group of flowering plants, no one individual is considered the most primitive plant; all living species show some advanced characteristics. There are 8 orders, 39 families, and about 12,000 species in this subclass. Among the more important families are these:

FAMILY: Lauraceae

## The Laurel Family

Members of the laurel family are aromatic trees or shrubs. The small flowers have sepals that are poorly differentiated from the petals (both sepals and petals in this case may be known as tepals) and numerous stamens (the male parts of the flower where the pollen is shed). One characteristic of the family is that the anthers (the top part of the stamen where the pollen is produced) have small flaps, which flip open to let the pollen out. There are about 2,200 species in the laurel family, mostly in the tropics. Several species are the source of spices, including *Cinnamomum verum* (cinnamon) and *C. camphora* (camphor tree), *Laurus nobilis* (bay leaf), and *Sassafras albidum* (sassafras). A few are grown as ornamentals, such as camphor tree and laurel.

FAMILY: Ranunculaceae

## The Buttercup Family

Members of the buttercup family are mostly herbs (sometimes shrubs or vines) with leaves that are divided into separate leaflets or are deeply dissected into narrow lobes. The flowers have often been considered primitive because of the indefinite number of petals, stamens, and pistils. There are 1,750 species in this family, primarily in the northern temperate and boreal regions of the world. A number of genera include important ornamental plants, including *Anemone* (windflower), *Aquilegia* (columbine), *Clematis* (virgin's bower), *Delphinium* (larkspur), and *Ranunculus* (buttercup, crowfoot).

SUBCLASS: Hamamelidae

Unlike most other plant groups, the Hamamelidae have evolved toward wind pollination. Many of the more primitive families are pollinated by insects; however, as the Hamamelidae became more advanced, they evolved structures more conducive to wind pollination. There are 11 orders, 26 families, and about 3,400 species in this subclass. Among the more important families are the following:

FAMILY: Betulaceae

The Birch Family

Members of the birch family are trees or shrubs with minute flowers in pendulous inflorescences called catkins. Each catkin has either male or female flowers, and female catkins bear small, winged fruit. There are about 60 species in this familiar family, primarily in the Northern Hemisphere. The family includes several genera with important ornamental species, including *Alnus* (alder), *Betula* (birch), and *Carpinus* (hornbeam), and another, *Corylus,* is the source of filberts. The pollen of most genera can cause allergic reactions in humans. *Betula nana* (dwarf birch), found north of the Arctic Circle, grows farther north than any other woody plant.

FAMILY: Fagaceae

The Oak Family

Members of the oak family are trees or shrubs with unisexual flowers that lack petals or sepals. The male flowers are found on pendulous inflorescences known as catkins; the female flowers occur singly or in small clusters. At the bottom of the fruit is a protective structure consisting of a cluster of overlapping bracts, called an involucre (for example, the cap of an acorn). There are 1,050 species in this family, usually found in northern temperate regions or tropical mountains. The pollen of most genera can cause allergic reactions in humans. Several important timber and ornamental trees come from the oak family, including members of the following genera: *Castanea* (chestnut), *Fagus* (beech), and *Quercus* (oak).

FAMILY: Juglandaceae

The Walnut Family

Members of the walnut family are trees with large leaves divided into several leaflets, flowers that lack petals and sepals, and catkins (pendulous inflorescences). There are 59 species, primarily in the northern temperate regions of the world. The nuts of several genera are edible, including *Carya* (pecans, hickory nuts) and *Juglans* (walnuts, butternuts). Some, such as *Carya, Juglans,* and *Pterocarya* (wingnut), are grown as ornamentals.

SUBCLASS: Caryophyllidae

Members of the Caryophyllidae share a number of technical characteristics, including the presence of a class of pigments known as betalains, which often make leaves red and turn the beet root beet red. There are 3 orders, 14 families, and about 11,000 species in this subclass. Among the more important families are these:

FAMILY: Cactaceae

The Cactus Family

Cacti are succulent herbs or small trees that lack leaves. Instead, the stems take on the role of photosynthesis, and are covered in spines. Cactus flowers are showy, and the outer parts of the flower are green and sepal-like but progressively become more petal-like and colorful toward the center of the flower. The family includes 1,650 species found only in the Western Hemisphere, particularly in hot areas. Members of the spurge family from Africa look very much like cacti and grow in similar habitats. Many cacti are ornamental, including *Cereus* (hedge cactus), *Mammillaria* (pincushion cacti), *Opuntia* (prickly pear, cholla), and *Schlumbergera* (Christmas cacti). Because cacti are slow-growing, they have often been collected from the wild, a practice that has had a severe impact on wild populations.

FAMILY: Caryophyllaceae

The Pink Family

Members of the pink family are herbs with simple leaves (not divided into separate leaflets) found in pairs at each node of the stem, and an ovary with a single locule (cavity) and in which the seeds are attached to a central column. The family includes 2,070 species around the world, particularly in the Northern Hemisphere. Many Caryophyllaceae are ornamental, including members of the genera *Arenaria* (sandwort), *Cerastium* (mouse-ear, chickweed), *Dianthus* (carnation, pink, sweet William), *Gypsophila* (baby's breath), and *Saponaria* (soapwort, bouncing Bet).

SUBCLASS: Dilleniidae

Members of the Dilleniidae have a number of technical characteristics that distinguish them from the Rosidae, to which this subclass is closely allied. Both show some advancement beyond the Magnoliidae—for example, their flowers tend to have a more definite number of sepals, petals, and stamens—but they are not as advanced as the Asteridae. Unlike the Rosidae, most members of this subclass have simple leaves (not divided into separate leaflets), the flower petals are often partly or entirely fused to each other, and many flowers have parietal placentation (the seeds are attached to the outer wall of the ovary). There are 13 orders, 78 families, and about 25,000 species in this subclass. Among the more important families are the following:

FAMILY: Brassicaceae

The Mustard Family

Mustards are herbs, often with acrid sap. Their flowers have four sepals (the outer parts of the flower), four petals (the inner showy parts), and four or six stamens (the male parts of a flower that shed pollen). The mustard fruit is distinctive because the ovary is partitioned into two cavities by a false septum (the partition is not part of the ovary wall as in other fruit with two or more cavities); these fruit are called siliques (if they are longer than wide) or silicles (if they are wider than long). A good example of a silicle is *Lunaria annua* (penny flower). The "penny flower" that is used in dried flower arrangements is the false septum; the ovary wall and seeds have usually fallen off at this stage. There are 3,000 species in this family, mostly in the Northern Hemisphere. Members include sources of food and condiments such as *Armoracia rusticana* (horseradish), *Brassica nigra* (black mustard), *Brassica oleracea* (broccoli, cabbage, cauliflower, Brussels sprouts), *Brassica rapa* (turnip), *Nasturtium officinale* (watercress), and *Raphanus sativus* (radish). Others, such as *Iberis amara* (candytuft), are used ornamentally.

FAMILY: Cucurbitaceae

The Cucumber Family

Members of the cucumber family are herbaceous (rarely slightly woody) vines with leaves that are palmately lobed (the lobes radiate out from a common point) or palmately compound (divided into several leaflets attached at a common point) and tendrils at the base of the leaf stalk. There are 735 species in this family, usually in the tropics. Many Cucurbitaceae are food plants, including *Citrulus lanatus* (watermelon), *Cucumis melo* (cantaloupe, honeydew, muskmelon), and *Cucurbita argyrosperma* (gourds, pumpkins, squashes). Others are used ornamentally, including *Ecballium ela-*

*terium* (squirting cucumber) and *Luffa aegyptiaca* (loofah, vegetable sponge).

FAMILY: Ericaceae

The Heath Family

Members of the heath family are shrubs (occasionally trees or herbs), with alternate, simple leaves (the leaves are undivided and attached singly at each node), flowers with parts in multiples of four or five (four or five sepals, four or five petals, and eight or ten stamens), and a peculiar way of shedding pollen (the anther, the sac that contains the pollen, opens via pores or slender tubes at its tip). The family includes 3,350 species around the world, particularly on acidic soils. The fruit of *Vaccinium* (blueberries) is eaten, and other genera include important ornamental plants, particularly *Erica* (heaths) and *Rhododendron* (rhododendrons and azaleas).

SUBCLASS: Rosidae

Members of the Rosidae share a number of technical characteristics that distinguish them from the Dilleniidae, to which this subclass is otherwise allied. The Rosidae differ from the Dilleniidae in having leaves that are usually divided into separated leaflets and petals that are not fused into a tube. Most members have axile placentation (the seeds are attached to the central common wall of the ovary). There are 18 orders, 114 families, and about 58,000 species in the subclass. Among the most important families are the following:

FAMILY: Apiaceae

The Carrot Family

Members of the carrot family are aromatic herbs with leaves that are divided into separate leaflets or are deeply dissected into narrow lobes, an umbel (an inflorescence shaped like the spokes of an umbrella), and a distinctive fruit known as a schizocarp, which separates into two fruitlets, each of which falls separately. The family includes 3,100 species worldwide, including many sources of foods and spices, such as *Anethum graveolens* (dill), *Apium graveolens* (celery), *Carum carvi* (caraway), *Coriandrum sativum* (coriander), *Daucus carota* (carrot), *Petroselinum crispum* (parsley), and *Pastinaca sativa* (parsnip). Others are highly poisonous, such as *Cicuta* (water hemlock) and *Conium* (poison hemlock). *Conium* is the hemlock of antiquity used by Socrates.

FAMILY: Euphorbiaceae

The Spurge Family

The spurges are highly variable, including trees, shrubs, vines, and herbs. They exude milky sap when cut and have leaves that are attached singly at each node. The flowers, which lack sepals and petals, are often clustered into inflorescences that mimic flowers (called cyathea); the "flower" of a poinsettia (*Euphorbia pulcherrima*) is actually a cyathea. There are 7,750 species in this family, found around the world but mostly in the tropics. Many species are sources of food or other commercial products, including *Hevea brasiliensis* (rubber), *Manihot esculenta* (arrowroot starch, cassava, tapioca), and *Ricinus communis* (castor oil). Other genera include plants used ornamentally, including *Acalypha* (chenille plant, copperleaf), *Codiaeum* (croton), *Euphorbia* (crown of thorns, poinsettia), and *Jatropha* (coral plant, physic-nut).

FAMILY: Fabaceae

The Pea Family

This is one of the largest plant families in the world. Also known as legumes, these plants are highly variable, including trees, shrubs, and herbs, usually with leaves that are attached singly along the stem and divided into separate leaflets. In the largest subfamilies, the flowers are papilionoid—that is, they have a large petal above called a standard, two lateral petals called wings, and two petals below that are fused together called a keel (the pea flower, for example, is papilionoid). The most characteristic feature of the family is the fruit, called a legume, a dehiscent fruit with one cavity, and seeds attached along one side; the fruit splits open along the other side. The family includes 16,400 species worldwide, many of them food plants such as *Cicer arietinum* (chickpeas), *Glycine max* (soybeans), *Phaseolus vulgaris* (kidney beans, string beans, navy beans), and *Pisum sativum* (peas). Among the numerous genera with species used ornamentally are *Albizia* (mimosa), *Cercis* (redbud), *Erythrina* (cockspur coral tree, cherokee bean), *Lathyrus* (sweet pea), and *Wisteria.* Many legumes are associated with a bacterium (*Rhizobium*) that lives in root nodules; the bacteria change atmospheric nitrogen into a form that can be used by the plant, thus providing a form of natural fertilizer.

FAMILY: Melastomataceae

The Melastome Family

Members of the melastome family are small trees, shrubs, herbs, or vines with a pair of leaves attached at each node. Each leaf has three to nine prominent veins that run more or less parallel to the midvein up to the tip of the leaf. This vein pattern makes a melastome leaf easily recognizable. The family has 4,750 species, which are widespread in the tropics and subtropics. Only a few are used

by humans—for example, the ornamental *Tibouchina urvilleana* (glorybush).

FAMILY: Rosaceae

The Rose Family

Members of the rose family are highly variable, including trees, shrubs, vines, and herbs. The leaves are attached singly at each node and may or may not be divided into separate leaflets. Many members of the rose family have a hypanthium (a cup formed by the fusion of the sepals, petals, and stamens). There are 3,100 species worldwide. Many genera are grown for fruit, including *Fragaria* (strawberry), *Malus* (apple), *Prunus* (almond, apricot, cherry, nectarine, peach, plum, prune), *Pyrus* (pear), and *Rubus* (blackberry, raspberry). Others, such as *Crataegus* (hawthorn), *Pyracantha* (firethorn), *Rosa* (rose), and *Spiraea,* are grown as ornamentals.

SUBCLASS: Asteridae

This subclass is easily distinguished by the petals, which are fused into a tube, and the stamens (the male parts of the flower that shed pollen), which are attached to the inner wall of this tube. There are 11 orders, 49 families, and nearly 60,000 species in the subclass.

FAMILY: Asteraceae

The Aster Family

Members of the Asteraceae are highly variable, but all have a distinctive "composite" inflorescence in which numerous, very small flowers are clustered together in such a way as to mimic a more typical flower. The white petals of a daisy as well as the yellow center are actually separate flowers; what we call a flower is in fact an inflorescence. The aster family is one of the largest, with 21,000 species worldwide, including numerous genera with important ornamental plants, such as *Aster, Calendula* (common marigold), *Dahlia, Dendranthema* (chrysanthemum), *Helianthus* (sunflower), *Senecio* (dusty miller, Mexican flame vine), *Tagetes* (French marigold, African marigold), and *Zinnia.* A few are used as food plants, including *Cichorium endivia* (endive), *Cichorium intybus* (chicory), *Cynara scolymus* (globe artichoke), and *Lactuca sativa* (lettuce).

FAMILY: Gesneriaceae
The Gesneriad Family

Members of the gesneriad family are usually herbs with paired leaves at each node and showy flowers. They are closely related to the figwort family but differ in having parietal placentation (the seeds line the outer wall of the ovary). The family includes 2,400 species, usually found in the tropics. Among the many genera with plants used ornamentally are *Saintpaulia* (African violet) and *Sinningia* (gloxinia).

FAMILY: Lamiaceae
The Mint Family

Mints are aromatic herbs with square stems and paired leaves at each node. The flowers often have two lobes that resemble lips, hence the older family name Labiatae. There are 5,600 mints around the world. Members of many genera are used as condiments and sources of perfume, including *Lavandula* (lavender), *Mentha* (peppermint, spearmint), *Ocimum* (basil), and *Thymus* (thyme). Others are grown as ornamentals, including *Solenostemon scutellarioides* (coleus), *Salvia* species (sage), and *Scutellaria* species (skullcap).

FAMILY: Rubiaceae
The Madder Family

Members of the madder family have a suite of characteristics that distinguish them from related families (particularly the gesneriad family). They have two leaves attached at each node. The flowers have an inferior ovary (the sepals, petals, and stamens are attached at the top of the ovary), and regular corolla (without a pronounced upper or lower lip). The madder family includes 10,700 species that are widespread throughout the tropics, with a few genera in temperate regions. Only a few species are important economically, particularly *Cinchona officinalis* (quinine), *Coffea arabica* (Arabian coffee), and *Coffea canephora* (robusta coffee).

FAMILY: Scrophulariaceae
The Figwort Family

Members of the figwort family are mostly herbs, seldom shrubs or small trees, with flowers that have five sepals (outer parts), five petals (inner showy parts), and five stamens (male parts of the flower that shed pollen). The ovary has two cavities and axile placentation (the seeds are attached to the central common wall of the ovary), and the ovary usually develops into a capsule (a dry fruit that splits open to release its seeds). The family has 4,500 species around the world. With the exception of ornamentals such as *Chelone glabra* (turtlehead) and sources of drugs such as *Digitalis purpurea* (foxglove), they are of little economic importance.

FAMILY: Solanaceae
The Nightshade Family

Members of the nightshade family are herbs or shrubs with leaves attached singly at each node. The flowers have five sepals (the outer parts), five petals (the inner showy parts) fused into a tube, five stamens (the male parts of the flower that shed pollen), and an ovary with two cavities. The family includes 2,600 species worldwide. Many genera are important food plants, such as *Capsicum* (cayenne pepper, red and green peppers), *Lycopersicon* (tomato), and *Solanum* (eggplant, potato). Many others are grown as ornamentals, including *Datura* (thorn apple, angel's trumpet), *Petunia, Physalis* (ground cherry, Chinese lantern), and *Solanum* (nightshade, potato vine).

## CLASS: Liliopsida
### Monocots

Monocots have one cotyledon (the first leaf produced on a seedling). They have leaves with parallel veins, and flower parts in multiples of three (three or six sepals, three or six petals, and three or six stamens). Monocots are generally thought to have evolved from an aquatic dicot such as the water lily. They are usually divided into 5 subclasses, 19 orders, and 65 families.

### SUBCLASS: Alismatidae

Members of the subclass Alismatidae exhibit more primitive characteristics than any other monocot, including an indefinite number of sepals, petals, stamens, and pistils arranged in a spiral. They are also predominantly aquatic. There are 4 orders, 16 families, and about 500 species in this subclass.

### SUBCLASS: Arecidae

Members of the subclass Arecidae have numerous small flowers, and the inflorescences have a prominent bract called a spathe at their base. The leaves are usually large and do not always exhibit the parallel venation typical of the monocots. The subclass includes 4 orders, 5 families, and about 5,600 species.

### FAMILY: Araceae
#### The Arum Family

Members of the arum family are herbs with a very distinctive inflorescence in which the flowers are crowded onto a structure known as a spadix (a thickened stalk covered with flowers). The spadix is surrounded by a showy bract known as a spathe. The classic aroid inflorescence is the jack-in-the-pulpit; the "jack" is the spadix, and the "pulpit" is the spathe. The family encompasses 2,950 species worldwide, including many common ornamental plants such as *Anthurium, Caladium, Dieffenbachia* (dumb cane), *Philodendron,* and *Spathiphyllum* (spatheflower). Others are very important food sources, including *Alocasia macrorrhiza* (giant taro) and *Colocasia esculenta* (taro).

### FAMILY: Arecaceae
#### The Palm Family

Palms are slender, usually unbranched trees or shrubs with a cluster of extremely large, compound leaves (divided into numerous separate leaflets) at the top. There are 2,675 palm species worldwide, including food plants, such as *Cocos nucifera* (coconut palm) and *Phoenix dactylifera* (date palm), and ornamental plants such as *Roystonea regia* (royal palm) and *Washingtonia filifera* (California fan palm).

### SUBCLASS: Commelinidae

Members of the Commelinidae often have flowers that lack sepals and petals. They also lack nectar and nectaries, and the seeds store starch. The subclass includes 7 orders, 16 families, and about 15,000 species.

FAMILY: Poaceae

The Grass Family

Grasses are herbs with round stems, long, narrow leaves, and flowers that lack sepals or petals. Each flower has two bracts at its base (the lemma and palea); the lemma, palea, and flower together are called a floret. The florets in turn are grouped into a cluster with another two bracts (glumes) at its base; this cluster of florets and glumes is called a spikelet. The grass family includes 7,950 species worldwide. The family is arguably the most important on Earth. It is the source

---

## THE 25 MOST DIVERSE PLANT FAMILIES

Of the 380 flowering plant families, the following have the highest numbers of species:

1. Asteraceae—Aster family (1,317 genera, 21,000 species)
2. Orchidaceae—Orchid family (795 genera, 17,500 species)
3. Fabaceae—Pea family (657 genera, 16,400 species)
4. Rubiaceae—Madder family (637 genera, 10,700 species)
5. Poaceae—Grass family (737 genera, 7,950 species)
6. Euphorbiaceae—Spurge family (326 genera, 7,750 species)
7. Lamiaceae—Mint family (224 genera, 5,600 species)
8. Melastomataceae—Melastome family (215 genera, 4,750 species)
9. Liliaceae—Lily family (294 genera, 4,550 species)
10. Scrophulariaceae—Figwort family (222 genera, 4,500 species)
11. Acanthaceae—Acanthus family (357 genera, 4,350 species)
12. Myrtaceae—Myrtle family (121 genera, 3,850 species)
13. Cyperaceae—Sedge family (115 genera, 3,600 species)
14. Ericaceae—Heath family (103 genera, 3,350 species)
15. Apiaceae—Carrot family (420 genera, 3,100 species)
16. Rosaceae—Rose family (107 genera, 3,100 species)
17. Brassicaceae—Mustard family (390 genera, 3,000 species)
18. Araceae—Arum family (106 genera, 2,950 species)
19. Asclepiadaceae—Milkweed family (348 genera, 2,900 species)
20. Arecaceae—Palm family (207 genera, 2,675 species)
21. Solanaceae—Potato family (90 genera, 2,600 species)
22. Boraginaceae—Borage family (156 genera, 2,500 species)
23. Gesneriaceae—Gesneriad family (146 genera, 2,400 species)
24. Lauraceae—Laurel family (45 genera, 2,200 species)
25. Bromeliaceae—Bromeliad family (46 genera, 2,110 species)

---

of major food crops around which human civilization arose, including *Avena sativa* (oats), *Hordeum vulgare* (barley), *Oryza sativa* (rice), *Secale cereale* (rye), *Triticum aestivum* (wheat), and *Zea mays* (corn). The grass family is also the most abundant and widespread family on the planet, with representatives on all continents, including Antarctica.

## SUBCLASS: Zingiberidae

The Zingiberidae have flowers in which the sepals (outer parts) are well differentiated from the petals (inner showy parts). They also have nectar and nectaries, as well as seeds that store starch. The subclass includes 2 orders, 9 families, and 3,800 species.

## SUBCLASS: Liliidae

The Liliidae have sepals that are poorly differentiated from the petals (both sepals and petals in this case may be known as tepals) and seeds that store oil, not starch. The subclass includes 2 orders, 19 families, and about 25,000 species.

## FAMILY: Iridaceae
### The Iris Family

Irises and related plants are perennial herbs with equitant leaves (leaves that are oriented with one of their edges toward the stem). The flowers have three sepals and three petals that generally are poorly differentiated (both sepals and petals in this case are called tepals), three stamens (the male parts of the flower where pollen is shed), and an inferior ovary (the tepals and stamens are attached at the top of the ovary). There are 1,850 species in the iris family worldwide. Many of the genera are ornamental, including *Crocus* (also the source of saffron), *Freesia, Gladiolus, Iris* (flag, fleur-de-lis), and *Tigridia* (tiger-flower).

## FAMILY: Liliaceae
### The Lily Family

Members of the lily family are herbs with simple leaves that are usually attached singly at the nodes, and flowers with three sepals and three petals that generally are poorly differentiated (both sepals and petals in this case are called tepals) and six stamens (the male parts of the flower that shed pollen). The family is very diverse, and recent studies suggest that it should be separated into a large number of families. The lily family as here defined has 4,550 species worldwide. It includes a few food plants, such as species in the genera *Allium* (onion, garlic, chives) and *Asparagus*. It is best known, however, for the numerous ornamental genera, including *Amaryllis, Convallaria* (lily of the valley), *Hemerocallis* (daylily), *Hosta, Lilium* (lily), *Narcissus* (narcissus, daffodil), *Trillium,* and *Tulipa* (tulip).

## FAMILY: Orchidaceae
### The Orchid Family

Orchids are herbs with simple, often xerophytic leaves (adapted to dry conditions) and unique flowers. The flowers have three sepals and three petals that generally are poorly differentiated (both sepals and petals in this case are called tepals), and one of the inner tepals is modified into a "lip." The stamens (the male parts of the flower that shed pollen) are fused with the style and stigma (the female parts) to form a "column," and the ovary is inferior (the tepals and column are attached at the top of the ovary). The orchid family is one of the most successful and diverse on Earth, with 17,500 species worldwide. *Vanilla planifolia* is the source of vanilla flavoring. Many genera are grown ornamentally, including *Cattleya* (corsage

## THE RAREST PLANT FAMILY

A number of plant families include only a single species, but the family with the fewest individuals may be the Saccifoliaceae, with a single species, *Saccifolium bandeirae*, native only to the summit of an isolated mountain in southern Venezuela.

orchid), *Epidendrum* (buttonhole orchid), *Paphiopedilum* (slipper orchid), and *Vanda*. Most orchids are pollinated by one species of insect; in some cases the flower mimics the smell or shape of the insect in order to attract it and facilitate pollination.

## Phylogeny

Ever since Darwin, biologists have attempted to arrange living organisms into classifications that reflect their evolutionary relationships, putting those with a common ancestor near each other, as in a family tree. The study of the evolution of organisms and how they are related to each other through evolution is called *phylogeny*. The result of phylogenetic research is a phylogenetic tree (called a *dendrogram*), which can be used to create a classification. Phylogenies can be developed for groups of families, genera, or species.

Because they cannot go back and watch evolution occur, scientists can only guess at what occurred. But there are ways they make their guesses more educated. One method is called *cladistics*. In cladistics it is assumed that evolution has occurred, and that the evolutionary history of living organisms can be portrayed as branching trees. The method involves analyz-

ing each of the characteristics of the group under study and determining which characteristics have changed, and the sequence of change. The branching diagram is formed by grouping together species with similar characteristics, and particularly special kinds of similar characteristics called *synapomorphies* (shared derived characteristics). The result of a cladistic study is a *cladogram*. As often happens in life, cladograms are never so simple. Plants often evolved similar structures at different times and in different ways. These similarities should not be used in grouping plants based on evolution. In order to weed out this extraneous information, phylogenists assume that the shortest tree is the best—shortest meaning the tree with the fewest character changes.

An example of a cladogram is shown below. This cladogram portrays the divisions of seed plants. Point A represents the hypothetical common ancestor of all seed plants. Each additional node (B, C, and D) represents the hypothetical ancestor for each group above (B is the hypo-

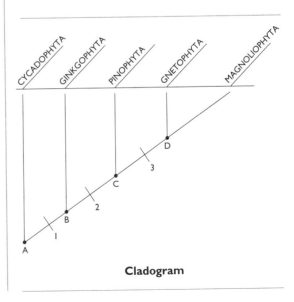

**Cladogram**

thetical ancestor for Ginkgophyta, Pinophyta, Gnetophyta, and Magnoliophyta; C is the hypothetical ancestor of Pinophyta, Gnetophyta, and Magnoliophyta; and D is the hypothetical ancestor of Gnetophyta and Magnoliophyta). Between each node some evolutionary change has occurred represented by a synapomorphy. For example, between B and C (step 2) the means of fertilization changed; it no longer was necessary for the sperm to swim to the egg and so the sperm lost its flagella. At step 3 the means of fertilization changed again and double fertilization occurred, in which one sperm nucleus fertilizes the egg and a second nucleus fertilizes a different cell in the female gametophyte.

These branching diagrams, in addition to being useful for classifying organisms, are also very valuable for studying the structure of the organisms and for predicting attributes of poorly known organisms. It is known that *Taxus brevifolia* (the Pacific yew) has an important medical compound, taxol. By knowing how this species of *Taxus* is related to other yews, it is possible to predict which other yews also contain taxol.

# Keys

Keys are devices used to identify plants. A typical key provides the user with a series of two or more botanical statements, called *leads.* A lead may have more than one statement; the first is the most important, but additional statements are added if the first statement is difficult to use or will only be seen at one time of the year (for example, flowers or fruit). You select the lead that best describes the plant at hand, then follow this lead to additional ones. With each subsequent lead, the choice of representative plants is narrowed down, until ultimately you are left with the one plant that matches the series of leads. Typically there are several sets of keys: one to identify the plant family, another to identify the genus, and a third to identify the species. There also may be separate keys based on flowers, fruits, or leaves.

There are two common types of keys: indented and bracketed. In indented keys, each set of leads is indented, with subordinate leads indented immediately below. In bracketed keys, each set of leads is placed side by side.

## Keys to the Species of Rhododendron in the New York Metropolitan Region

The following are examples of an indented and a bracketed key to the same group of species.

### An Indented Key

1. Leaves evergreen
    2. Leaves densely hairy below, the hairs orange or white; the flower deeply cleft and appearing to have separate petals ............................*Rhododendron groenlandicum*
    2. Leaves hairless; the flower with five petals fused into a shallowly lobed tube ............................*Rhododendron maximum*
1. Leaves deciduous
    3. Flowers with three petals fused together and two petals not fused, flowers pink ............................*Rhododendron canadense*
    3. Flowers with all the petals fused together, flowers white to pink ..............
        4. Flowers appearing after the leaves have expanded (essentially when all of the leaves have unfolded, and the vegetative bud scales are absent)............................*Rhododendron viscosum*

4. Flowers appearing before or with the leaves (when at least some of the leaves are still folded or the vegetative bud scales are still present)

    5. Floral bud scales hairless; flower stalks without both short and long hairs, usually only with long hairs; leaves hairless or with a few scattered one-celled hairs ..................*Rhododendron periclymenoides*

    5. Floral bud scales densely covered with one-celled hairs; flower stalks with both short and long hairs; leaves moderately to densely covered with one-celled hairs on the lower side...............*Rhododendron prinophyllum*

**A Bracketed Key**

1. Leaves evergreen ........................................2
1. Leaves deciduous......................................3

2. Leaves densely hairy below, the hairs orange or white; the flower deeply cleft and appearing to have separate petals...........................*Rhododendron groenlandicum*
2. Leaves hairless; the flower with five petals fused into a shallowly lobed tube ...............*Rhododendron maximum*

3. Flowers with three petals fused together and two petals not fused, flowers pink ..............*Rhododendron canadense*
3. Flowers with all the petals fused together, flowers white to pink ..............................4

4. Flowers appearing after the leaves have expanded (essentially when all of the leaves have unfolded, and the vegetative bud scales are absent) .................*Rhododendron viscosum*

4. Flowers appearing before or with the leaves (when at least some of the leaves are still folded or the vegetative bud scales are still present) ....................................................5

5. Floral bud scales hairless; flower stalks without both short and long hairs, usually only with long hairs; leaves hairless or with a few scattered one-celled hairs ............................*Rhododendron periclymenoides*
5. Floral bud scales densely covered with one-celled hairs; flower stalks with both short and long hairs; leaves moderately to densely covered with one-celled hairs on the lower side......................*Rhododendron prinophyllum*

## Further Reading

Cardillo, F. M. *Classification of Plants.* URL = http://www.mancol.edu/science/biology/plants_new/intro/plntlist.html

Cronquist, A. *An Integrated System of Classification of Flowering Plants.* New York: Columbia University Press, 1981.

Cronquist, A. *The Evolution and Classification of Flowering Plants.* 2nd ed. Bronx, N.Y.: The New York Botanical Garden, 1988.

Lampinen, R., S. Liu, A. R. Brach, and K. McCree. *Internet Directory for Botany: Vascular Plant Families.* URL = http://www.helsinki.fi/kmus/botvasc.html

Maddison, D. R., and W. P. Maddison. *The Tree of Life.* URL = http://phylogeny.arizona.edu/tree/life.html

Mabberley, D. J. *The Plant Book.* Cambridge, England: Cambridge University Press, 1987.

Speer, B. R. *Green Plant Phylogeny Research Coordination Group.* URL = http://ucjeps.berkley.edu/bryolab/greenplantpage.html

The Royal (Dick) School of Veterinary Studies. *Taxonomic Hierarchy.* URL = http://www.vet.ac.uk/tol/kingdoms.htm

Zomlefer, W. B. *Guide to Flowering Plant Families.* Chapel Hill: The University of North Carolina Press, 1989.

# PLANT STRUCTURES AND THEIR FUNCTIONS

Any discussion of the structures of plants and their functions can be organized around either the structures or the functions. This section is organized around the various structures. Modern plant morphology (the study of form) recognizes a continuum between leaves and stems and between stems and roots. In some plants it is not easy to distinguish precisely between, say, a leaf and a stem. In this section, the discussion of plant structure and function is somewhat generalized and simplified.

There are several good reasons to be familiar with plant structures and their functions. Gardeners are bound to come across many of the terms discussed below in gardening books, certainly in botany books. And understanding the diversity of forms in plants inevitably leads to a greater appreciation of the plants in the garden.

## Grouping Plants by Form and Function

Plants are grouped together according to their form or function in a variety of ways. One of the most obvious takes into account the overall form of the plant. Habit is one way of discussing overall form.

## Habit

Gardeners traditionally have grouped plants into broad categories on the basis of their overall appearance, or habit. The following is a list of the more common habits of plants:

- **Trees:** Woody plants with a single or few trunks near the base.
- **Shrubs:** Woody plants that branch near the base and therefore have several trunks.
- **Lianas:** Woody plants that climb on other plants and use them for support. They may climb via tendrils, hooks, pads, aerial roots, or other mechanisms.
- **Herbs:** Nonwoody plants. There are several types of herbs, including the following:

  **Forbs:** Broad-leaved herbs.
  **Graminoids:** Grasslike herbs, with very narrow leaves.
  **Ferns:** Herbs with broad but highly dissected leaves and no flowers.
  **Herbaceous vines:** Nonwoody plants that climb on other plants.

## Raunkiaer's Classification System

The famous Danish botanist Raunkiaer noted that the traditional classification of plants into trees, shrubs, herbs, and other categories based on habit does not take into account much of the ecology or lifestyle of the plants. He devised an alternative system, based on lifestyle and the position of buds (the points on a stem from which new shoots grow in the spring), with the following categories:

- **Phanerophyte:** Woody or herbaceous evergreen perennial, taller than 20 inches, whose shoots do not die back. In other words, these plants are trees and large shrubs.

- **Chamaephyte:** Woody or herbaceous evergreen perennial from 10 to 20 inches tall or whose shoots die back periodically. These plants are small shrubs covered by snow in the winter.

- **Hemicryptophyte:** Perennial (or biennial) herbaceous plant in which the stems die back to a remnant shoot system that lies on the ground. These are herbaceous plants with runners along the ground.

- **Geophyte:** Perennial (or biennial) herbaceous plant in which the stems die back to a remnant shoot system with storage organs that are imbedded in the soil. These are the plants gardeners call bulbs (including corms, rhizomes, and tubers as well as true bulbs).

- **Therophyte:** Annual; plant that dies after seed production and completes its entire life cycle within one year.

- **Liana:** Plant that germinates on the ground and maintains soil contact while using another plant for support. Grapevines are typical lianas.

- **Hemi-epiphyte:** Plant that germinates on other plants and then establishes soil contact; or plant that germinates on the ground but later loses contact with the soil. Hemi-epiphytes use other plants for support, at least during part of their life. The strangler fig is an interesting hemi-epiphyte: it starts life as an epiphyte, growing on other trees; as it matures, it sends down roots to the ground, and slowly, over many years, the fig encloses and "strangles" the tree that was its nursery.

- **Epiphyte:** Plant that germinates and roots on other plants, never coming in contact with the soil. Many orchids and bromeliads are epiphytes.

- **Errant vascular hydrophyte:** Free-moving water plant. These are the floating aquatic plants.

- **Vascular semiparasite:** Green plant growing attached to other living, green plants. Many plants, such as eastern North American native gerardia (*Agalinis purpurea*), photosynthesize but also supplement their nutrients by parasitizing other plants.

---

## THE TALL AND THE SMALL

### THE TALLEST PLANTS

Three trees can lay claim to being the tallest trees in the world: the Douglas fir (*Pseudotsuga menziesii*) that grows in the Pacific Northwest, the coast redwood (*Sequoia sempervirens*) of coastal California and Oregon, and a eucalyptus from Australia (*Eucalyptus regnans*). The tallest living tree is a coast redwood measured at 367 feet. The tallest Douglas fir is 329 feet, but there is good historical evidence that they reached 393 feet or higher. The tallest *Eucalyptus regnans* has been measured at 326 feet tall, but there is historical evidence that suggests they reached 400 and perhaps 500 feet in the recent past.

### THE SMALLEST PLANTS

The world's smallest plant is water meal (*Wolffia globosa*), a floating aquatic herb that, when mature, is not much larger than the period at the end of this sentence.

- **Vascular parasite:** Nongreen plant growing on living, green plants. Indian pipe (*Monotropa uniflora*) is a good example of a vascular parasite.

## Mode of Nutrition

Plants can be classified according to how they get their nutrition.

- **Heterotrophic:** Heterotrophic plants depend on other organisms for nourishment. Vascular parasites, such as Indian pipe (*Monotropa uniflora*), fit into this category. Vascular semiparasites, such as gerardia (*Agalinis purpurea*), are dependent to some extent on other organisms but also photosynthesize.
- **Autotrophic:** Autotrophic plants produce their own nourishment via photosynthesis. The vast majority of plants fall into this category; only vascular parasites and vascular saprophytes do not produce any of their own nutrients.

## Plant Longevity

Another way of looking at plants is based on longevity—how many years the plant lives.

- **Annual:** A plant that completes its life cycle within a single year.
- **Biennial:** A plant that completes its life cycle in two years.
- **Perennial:** A plant that lives more than two years.

## Life Stages

Within broad categories such as annual and perennial, individual plants exhibit a variety of forms and functions during their life span. These stages in the life of a plant can be classified as follows:

- **Seed:** A period in the life of a plant in which no growth is taking place.
- **Prereproductive:** The period in the life of a plant after germination but before reproduction. This phase can be separated into several stages: seedling, juvenile, and virginile.
  - **Seedling:** A young plant that is partly dependent on substances of the maternal plant stored in the seed (especially the first leaves, called cotyledons). The plant always has embryological structures, including cotyledons, a primary root (the embryological root), and a primary shoot (the embryological stem).
  - **Juvenile:** Juvenile plants are structurally simple but have progressed beyond the seedling stage. They no longer have cotyledons and often exhibit the mature forms of leaves, shoots, and roots. A tree sapling is an example of a juvenile plant.
  - **Virginile:** Virginile plants begin to show the main features of mature plants but are not reproductive. In other words, these are mature plants that have not started to flower.
- **Reproductive:** A mature plant that forms flowers and fruits. This long period can be separated into three subcategories: young, mature, and old.
  - **Young:** Young reproductive plants exhibit more new growth than death of old parts.
  - **Mature:** Mature plants exhibit a balance between growth and death of parts. These plants usually have the greatest yearly seed production and biomass increase (increase in weight). In other words, they are at their peak.
  - **Old:** In old plants, the death of parts prevails over the production of new

parts. Reproductive activity is diminished.

• **Postreproductive:** In a postreproductive plant, flowering and fruit production practically stops, and overall vegetative structure becomes simplified. Juvenile leaves reappear and the plant's growth rate decreases.

• **Senile:** A plant that has reached its final stage before death.

## Growth, Architecture, and Branching

Plants are often grouped according to their branching structure. The growth and branching of plants has been compared to foraging behavior in animals. In other words, plants

### THE TORTOISE AND HARE OF THE PLANT WORLD

#### FAST PLANTS

This is a group of plants that can go from seed to fruit in one month. For this reason, they are often used in studies of plant development and genetics. The most often studied fast plant is *Arabidopsis thaliana* (thale cress), a small mustard native to the north temperate parts of the world.

#### THE OLDEST PLANTS

Among the oldest plants on Earth are the bristlecone pines (*Pinus longaeva*). Some individuals are known to be over 4,000 years old and others are estimated to be 5,000 years old. Some creosote plants (*Larrea tridentata*) are even older. The creosote is clonal and some clones are estimated to be 11,700 years old, but the individual stems live for much shorter periods of time.

grow in ways that enable them to seek out the best food and habitat. Several aspects of growth are particularly notable.

• **Phototropic:** Growing toward light. Since light is the major source of energy for plants, they often grow toward light to increase their light-gathering ability. Some plants, such as the tulip tree (*Liriodendron tulipifera*), however, grow away from gravity rather than toward light. Because the tulip tree does not bend toward light, its stem is very straight.

• **Geotropic:** Growing toward gravity. Roots often grow geotropically to reach the water table.

• **Plagiotropic:** Characterized by horizontal growth. The lateral branches of a tree are often plagiotropic. Pin oaks (*Quercus palustris*) have plagiotropic mid branches; in fact, the lower branches decline at a slight angle, a characteristic that can be used to identify the species.

• **Orthotropic:** Characterized by vertical growth. The main shoot of a tree is often orthotropic. Many of the upper branches of the American elm (*Ulmus americana*) are orthotropic, giving the tree its characteristic vase shape.

• **Dichotomous:** Characterized by a type of branching in which the stem tip divides into two equal parts, as in highbush blueberry (*Vaccinium corymbosum*).

## Plant Parts

There are three basic structures on plants and various modifications of them. The three structures are stems, leaves, and roots. A stem is formed from the epicotyl, the portion of the embryo above the cotyledons (the seed leaves); it has a shoot apex, the growing tip, around which leaves develop. Leaves are formed from small stubs formed on the side of the growing

Abnormal growth, caused by disease, genetics, or human manipulation, is far from unusual in the plant world. These are three common forms.

• **Fasciation:** A stem or root that is abnormally flattened or sometimes develops into a hollow tube (ring fasciation). Cockscomb (*Celosia cristata*) is a fasciated form of the species *Celosia argentea*. In this case, the inflorescence has become abnormally flattened and resembles a cockscomb.

• **Chimera:** A structure or tissue that is formed from two genetically different sources. Some chimeras are the result of grafts in which a branch is formed from tissue from the root stock and the grafted stem growing together. *Vinca minor* 'Variegata' is an example of a chimera.

• **Galls:** A structure formed in response to insect, nematode, mite, or fungal infestations. The galls often are home to the invader for a portion of its life cycle. Oak trees often have a large number of ball-shaped galls formed by wasps. They appear to be so normal a part of the plant at times that botanists in the past have mistaken them for a type of fruit.

the only parts of flowering plants that cannot be traced back to a stem, leaf, or root. They are derived from the male and female parts of more primitive plants.

## Roots

Roots are plant parts that can bear other roots and stems but never leaves. They have a characteristic structure, including a growing tip, or root apex, that does not produce leaves but is surrounded by a cap of cells, the root cap. They also have a characteristic internal structure.

Roots have several functions. They anchor a plant to a site, absorb water and nutrients from the soil, store nutrients, and support bacteria or fungal hyphae, which work with the root to the benefit of both organisms.

### Root Systems

Roots are formed in two ways during the development of the plant. Primary root systems are roots and their branches derived from the hypocotyl, the portion of the embryo below the seed leaves (cotyledons). They are the first root structures formed. In monocots, the primary root system does not develop well; instead, an adventitious root system forms, in which roots arise from stem or leaf tissue. At the bottom of a corn plant, for example, are a number of these adventitious roots growing out of, and acting as a prop for, the stem.

### Root Types and Modifications

There are many different types of roots, based partly on structure and partly on the major function of the root.

• **Aerial roots:** Roots formed and remaining above ground. They often have functions

tip, and generally develop into flattened structures. Roots, on the other hand, are formed from the hypocotyl, the portion of the embryo below the cotyledons.

Flowers are thought to be elaborate structures formed from leaves highly modified to promote pollination. The sepals, petals, stamens, and pistils are thought to have evolved from leaves. The fruit is a further development of parts of the flower—generally the pistil, the female portion of the flower—to promote dispersal. Like flowers, fruits are thought to have been derived from leaves. Seeds and pollen are

other than absorption. For instance, poison ivy (*Toxicodendron radicans*) has aerial roots that attach the vine to the trunk of a tree.

- **Fibrous roots:** Threadlike, numerous roots, such as those of many grasses. They are usually adventitious in origin.
- **Haustoria:** The areas of a parasitic plant that attach to its host, through which the parasite absorbs nutrients. These may be derived from roots or stems. Dodder (*Cuscuta* species),

the yellow or orange parasitic plants that look like string, form haustoria on their stems that penetrate the host plant's stems.

- **Nodules and mycorrhizae:** Connections between a plant and either bacteria or fungi. Many members of the bean family form root nodules. These nodules contain a bacterium that converts atmospheric nitrogen into a form the plant can use. Alfalfa (*Medicago sativa*) is one so-called nitrogen-fixing plant. One reason

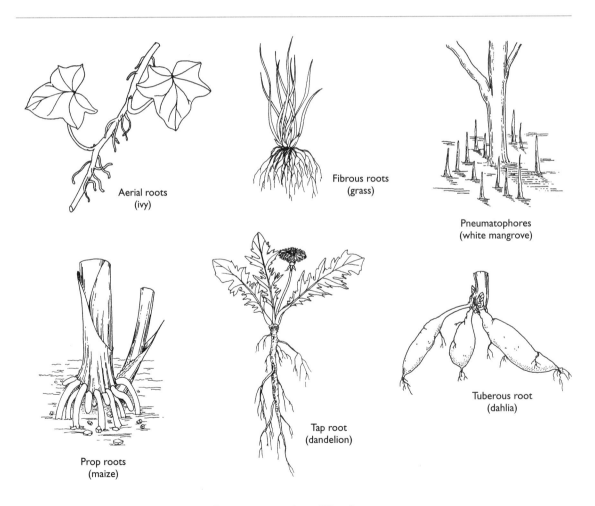

Aerial roots (ivy)

Fibrous roots (grass)

Pneumatophores (white mangrove)

Prop roots (maize)

Tap root (dandelion)

Tuberous root (dahlia)

**Root types and modifications**

farmers plant alfalfa as part of their crop rotation is to fertilize the soil with nitrogen. Mycorrhizae are fungi that are connected to a plant via haustoria. The fungi gain some nutrients from the parent plant, and they benefit the parent plant by absorbing nutrients more efficiently. Some plants, such as rhododendrons and native orchids, are dependent on the mycorrhizae and will not grow without them.

• **Pneumatophores:** Roots found on plants in swampy areas in which there is not enough oxygen in the water for the root to survive. These roots grow toward the water surface and then bend over, forming a knob above the water. Pneumatophores are almost hollow, allowing air to pass to the living tissue of the root. The knees of cypress (*Taxodium distichum*) are examples of pneumatophores.

• **Prop root:** A root that acts as support for the parent plant. Mangroves (*Rhizophora* species) have extensive prop roots that keep the plants above salt water.

• **Root hairs:** Small, hairlike projections from the epidermis or outermost layer of a root. Most absorption of water and nutrients occurs via root hairs.

• **Tap root:** Primary roots that have more or less enlarged and grown downward. The carrot is a typical tap-rooted plant.

• **Tuberous root:** A swollen root in which nutrients (usually starch) are stored for the parent plant. Dahlias and *Dioscorea* (yams) are examples of plants with tuberous roots.

## Stem

Stems are formed from the epicotyl, the portion of an embryo above the seed leaves (cotyledons). They usually have leaves, and their growing tip or shoot apex has small stubs on its side, which develop into leaves. The stem has several functions. It acts as a support for the leaves, and transports nutrients to the leaves and food to the roots. In some plants, such as cacti, the stems also photosynthesize and store food.

Stems comprise several parts. In the middle is the pith, a region of undifferentiated cells that, together with the cortex, form a base for the other layers to grow in. Surrounding the pith is either a ring or a series of bundles containing the cells that transport fluids. This is known as the vascular tissue. Outside of this is a layer of cells known as the cortex and then the epidermis, the skin of the stem, which is modified into bark in woody plants.

### Vascular System

The vascular system is made up of xylem, which transports water and nutrients from the roots to the leaves, and phloem, which transports food to the roots and the stem.

In herbaceous plants the xylem and phloem are found in bundles running vertically through the stem. In woody plants, however, the stem structure is more elaborate. The xylem and phloem form rings. The xylem is formed yearly as a ring on the inside of the growth layer (called the cambium) and becomes wood. Each yearly ring is called a growth ring. The phloem is formed in rings on the outside of the cambium and is periodically sloughed off as bark.

### Bark

Bark is the external skin of a woody stem. It can vary in appearance, but its main functions are to protect the growing stem and at the same time allow air to pass into the living portions of the stem. Because the stem is constantly growing in circumference, the bark is often shed periodically.

## CORK TREE

One of the most economically important barks is that of *Quercus suber*, an oak tree native to the western shores of the Mediterranean Sea, which is used to create cork. When the tree is 20 years old (about 9 inches in diameter) the bark is stripped from the stem, boiled, scraped, and dried. Subsequently, the bark grows faster and the bark can be stripped at 10-year intervals. Because cork comes from wild trees and when removed properly does them no harm, it is an environmentally friendly industry. Many of the cork groves are considered national treasures.

Many trees and shrubs can be identified solely by their bark. The following is a short list of some bark types:

- **Smooth:** Without hair, glands, or roughness. Beech trees (*Fagus* species) have smooth bark.
- **Ridged:** With prominent, longitudinal ribs. Chestnut oak (*Quercus muehlenbergii*) has deep ridges.
- **Furrowed:** With longitudinal grooves. The American elm (*Ulmus americana*) has furrowed bark.
- **Plated:** With shallow, circular depressions. The bark of the red pine (*Pinus resinosa*) is plated.
- **Fibrous:** With threadlike strands. Grapevines have fibrous bark.

### Stem Modifications

Stems of some plants occur in a modified form to accommodate additional functions. The following are some modified stem forms:

- **Corm:** An underground, vertical stem that is swollen. A corm looks very much like a bulb but is composed of stem tissue, as opposed to a bulb, which is made up of leaf tissue. Gladioli, crocuses, and freesias are corms.
- **Phylloclade:** A flattened, green stem with small, scalelike leaves. Phylloclades look like leaves and even function as leaves. But morphologically, they are stems. One plant with phylloclades is *Ruscus hypoglossum,* the "laurel" of Caesar.
- **Rhizome:** A horizontal stem found underground. A rhizome can be distinguished from a root by the presence of nodes on the rhizome ends. Ginger (*Zingiber officinale*) is a rhizome.
- **Runner:** A thin, horizontal stem found above ground with a rosette of leaves at the end. A runner is very similar to a stolon (see below). Both structures allow the plant to move within its environment. Strawberries (*Fragaria* species) have runners.
- **Spine:** A modified stem (or leaf stipule, or root) that is sharp. The term *thorn* is a synonym. A prickle is similar, but is produced from the epidermis of the stem, leaf, or root. *Opuntia* and other cacti have spines.
- **Stolon:** A horizontally growing stem at ground level with leaves along its length (not just a rosette at the end, as in a runner) and adventitious roots that form at the nodes. Stolons are similar to runners (see above). White clover (*Trifolium repens*) has stolons.
- **Tendril and hook:** Modified stems or leaves that grasp other plants and act like grappling hooks. Tendrils and hooks, which are found on vines, assist the vine in supporting itself. The Virginia creeper is unusual because it has small pads at the ends of its tendrils. These pads attach themselves to walls and tree trunks instead of twining around the trunk.
- **Tuber:** An underground, swollen stem. A

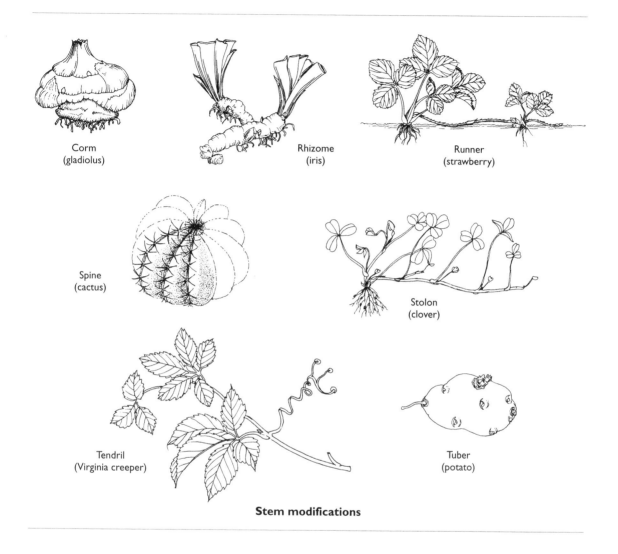

**Corm**
(gladiolus)

**Rhizome**
(iris)

**Runner**
(strawberry)

**Spine**
(cactus)

**Stolon**
(clover)

**Tendril**
(Virginia creeper)

**Tuber**
(potato)

**Stem modifications**

tuber is usually a swollen rhizome. The potato is the classic tuber.

## Leaves

The leaf is the third basic organ of plants (the others are roots and stems). The leaf is usually defined by its position—that is, it originates as a small projection at the apex or tip of the stem; it is attached to the stem; and in temperate plants there nearly always is a vegetative bud near where it is attached to the stem.

The basic role of the leaf is photosynthesis. Photosynthesis is the process in which energy from sunlight is combined with carbon dioxide and water to produce sugar and oxygen. The structure of the leaf is tailored to this process. Leaves are generally flat to provide as much surface area as possible for the absorption of sunlight. Leaves also have small openings on their lower surface, called *stomata,* which allow the carbon dioxide in and the oxygen out. What is more, the leaf is supplied with a system of veins that link up with the veins in the roots and stems. These veins supply the water for photosynthesis and other nutrients needed by the photosynthesizing cells, and they carry the sugars formed via photosynthesis to other parts of the plant, where they feed the living cells of the roots and stems or are stored for future use.

## Parts of the Leaf

The leaf consists of two main parts: the lamina and the petiole.

- **Lamina:** The flat portion of a leaf, also called the leaf blade.
- **Petiole:** The stalk to which the lamina is attached. There are several types of petiole.
  - **Phyllode:** A broadened, leaflike petiole. In this case, the leaf has lost its lamina during evolution and the petiole has taken its place in photosynthesis. Some acacias have phyllodes.
  - **Pulvinus:** A swollen area at the base of a petiole. The pulvinus often acts to lower the leaf when it is wilted. It is also the part of the sensitive plant (*Mimosa pudica*) that makes the leaves close up when touched.
  - **Sheath:** A broadened petiole base that surrounds the stem. Most grasses have leaf sheaths.

Other leaf parts include:

- **Stipule:** A leaflike growth at the base of the petiole. The presence of stipules is characteristic of a number of species. Often, they protect the buds and developing leaves and then fall off. Some can be large and conspicuous. They are typically paired in dicots, when they are present, and absent in monocots.

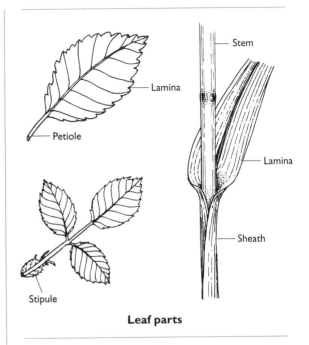

**Leaf parts**

- **Buds:** Small shoots with scalelike leaves that, when given the proper conditions, burst out in growth. Although not technically leaves, buds are nearly always found associated with the base of a leaf petiole.

## Leaf Division

Leaves can consist of a single blade or can be divided into two or more blades. The way these divisions are arranged is characteristic of individual species.

- **Simple leaf:** A leaf with only one lamina.
- **Compound leaf:** A leaf with two or more lamina (called *leaflets*). It is often difficult to distinguish a leaflet from a simple leaf; they look for all intents and purposes the same. It is important to keep in mind that a leaf is defined by its development and position, not just by its appearance. In general, compound leaves can be recognized by the absence of a bud at the base of

Simple

Palmate

Pinnate

Tripinnate

Ternate

Trifoliate

**Leaf division**

the leaflet. There are several different types of compound leaves, including:

- **Palmate:** Leaves with the leaflets attached to a common point like the fingers of a human hand.
- **Pinnate/bipinnate/tripinnate:** Leaves with the leaflets aligned along a central stalk (called a *rachis*) like the tines of a comb. Pinnately compound leaves may have only a single rachis or the rachis may branch once, in which case it is called *bipinnate;* twice, in which case it is called *tripinnate;* or three times, in which case it is called *quadripinnate.* These leaves can be further classified into *paripinnate,* in which all the leaflets are more or less paired, and there is no single terminal leaflet, and *imparipinnate,* in which there is a single terminal leaflet.
- **Ternate/biternate:** Leaves with three leaflets and in which the terminal leaf is not stalked. In other words, this is a palmately compound leaf with three leaflets. It follows that biternate leaves are doubly ternate, with the ternate divisions again ternately divided.
- **Trifoliate:** Leaves with three leaflets and in which the terminal leaflet is stalked. In other words, this is a pinnately compound leaf with three leaflets.

## Evergreen vs. Deciduous

One way that plants have become adapted to their climates is by either retaining their leaves year-round or shedding them as a difficult season approaches. In cold-winter temperate areas, for example, many plants drop their leaves in autumn because the loss of energy that went into creating the leaves and the loss of energy that might be manufactured by photosynthesis in winter is outweighed by even greater energy that would be needed to support the leaves during the cold months and the potential threat of leaf death due to freezing. In plants that retain most of their leaves year-round, even through difficult seasons, the leaves have acquired certain characteristics that enable them to survive the extremes.

Evergreen plants retain their leaves for more than one year. This does not mean that the leaves are retained forever but rather that the plant is always green. Individual leaves of most evergreen plants are shed after a few years.

Deciduous plants deliberately drop their leaves at the onset of a difficult season—winter in temperate and boreal areas and the dry season in desert areas of the world.

## Leaf Texture

The texture of the leaf is often an reflection of the duration of the leaf. Evergreen leaves are usually coriaceous, while deciduous leaves are usually membranaceous or chartaceous.

- **Membranaceous:** Thin and flexible.
- **Chartaceous:** Thin and papery.
- **Coriaceous:** Thick and leathery.

## Leaf Shape

When describing leaf shapes, botanists use a variety of terms often taken from Latin. These terms can be used for describing any flat shape on a plant—not only the leaf, but also the stipule, sepal, petal, and so on. These terms take into account the length-to-width ratio, the curving of the margin or edge, and the position of the widest point. For additional preci-

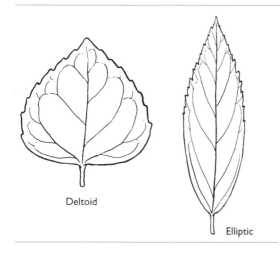

Deltoid

Elliptic

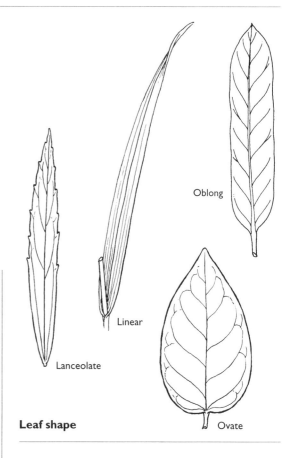

Oblong

Linear

Lanceolate

Ovate

**Leaf shape**

sion, words like "narrowly," "widely," and "depressed" are often used to qualify the terms. The following are some of the more common leaf shapes:

• **Deltoid (deltate):** About the same length as width. Shaped like a triangle in which all sides are the same length. Cottonwood (*Populus grandidentata*) has deltoid leaves.

• **Elliptic:** One and a half to two times longer than wide. Shaped like a narrow oval. The margins are symmetrically curved, and the leaf is widest at the middle. Chestnuts (*Castanea* species) have elliptic leaves.

• **Lanceolate:** Three to six times longer than wide. Shaped like the tip of a lance. The margins are symmetrically curved, and the leaf is widest toward the base. Willows (*Salix* species) have lanceolate leaves.

• **Linear:** More than twelve times longer than wide. Long and narrow with more or less parallel margins. Most grasses have linear leaves.

• **Oblong:** One and a half to two times longer than wide. Similar to elliptic but the margins are parallel, not curved. Willow oak (*Quercus phellos*) has oblong leaves.

• **Ovate:** One and a half to two times longer than wide. Shaped like an egg. The margins are symmetrically curved, and the leaf is widest below the middle. Beaked hazelnut (*Corylus cornuta*) has ovate leaves.

## Leaf Base

The base of the leaf blade can have a wide variety of shapes. The following are a few common leaf-base shapes:

• **Acute:** Tapering to a sharp point with convex sides.

• **Auriculate:** A base with rounded projections that have a concave inner margin.

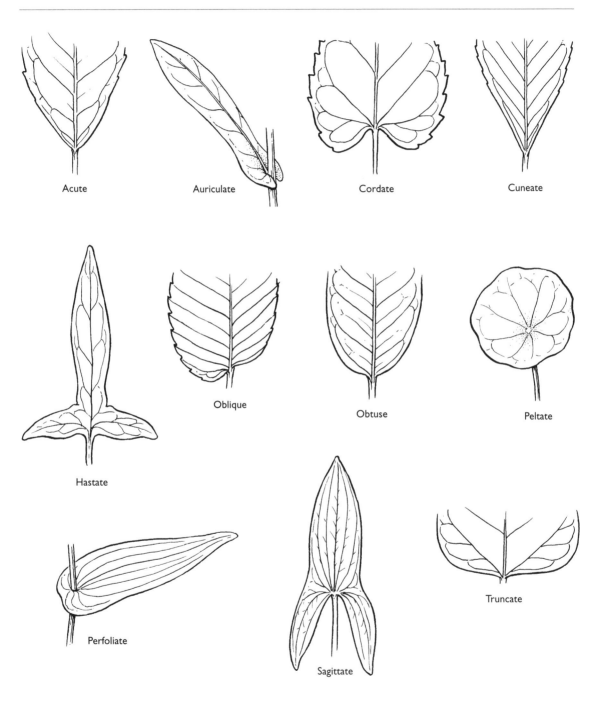

Acute

Auriculate

Cordate

Cuneate

Hastate

Oblique

Obtuse

Peltate

Perfoliate

Sagittate

Truncate

**Leaf base**

- **Cordate:** Heart-shaped; the base has a notch similar to that at the top of a heart.
- **Cuneate:** Tapering to a sharp point. Similar to acute but with straight, not convex, sides.
- **Hastate:** A base with outwardly pointed lobes.
- **Oblique:** A base that is not symmetrical on both sides.
- **Obtuse:** Tapering to a blunt point.
- **Peltate:** Borne on a stalk attached to the lower surface rather than to the base or margin of the leaf. Nasturtiums (*Tropaeolum majus*) have peltate leaves.
- **Perfoliate:** A leaf in which the bases of two opposite leaves are fused around the stem, so that the stem appears to pass through the leaf.
- **Sagittate:** With a downwardly pointed lobe on each side of the base.
- **Truncate:** A base that is squared off at the ends, as if cut off.

## Leaf Margin

The margin or edge of a leaf can have teeth, hairs, or other type of indentation. Some of the more common margin types are the following:

- **Ciliate:** With hairs along the margin.
- **Crenate:** With low, rounded teeth that have no point.
- **Dentate:** With teeth along the margin that are pointed outward from the margin. Similar to serrate, but in serrate the teeth are pointed at least slightly upward toward the tip.
- **Double serrate:** With serrate teeth along the margins of other, larger serrate teeth.
- **Entire:** Without any indentations or teeth.
- **Serrate:** With teeth along the margin that are pointed upward toward the tip of the leaf.
- **Undulate:** With a wavy margin.

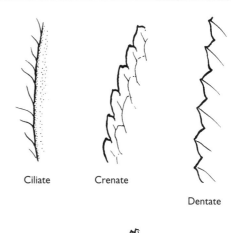

Ciliate     Crenate

Dentate

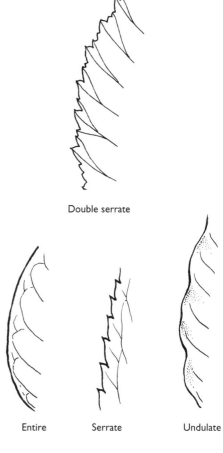

Double serrate

Entire     Serrate     Undulate

**Leaf margin**

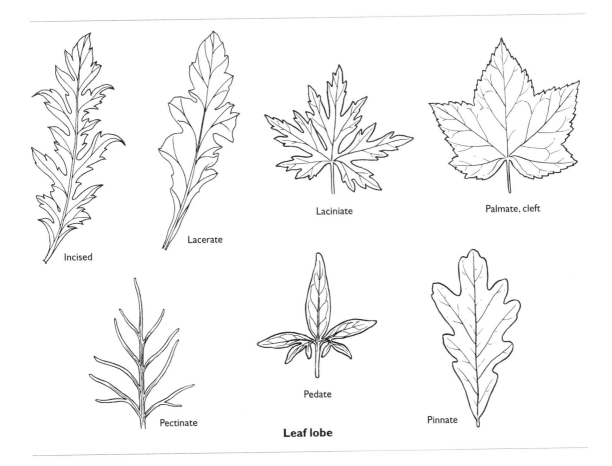

Incised

Lacerate

Laciniate

Palmate, cleft

Pectinate

Pedate

Pinnate

**Leaf lobe**

## Leaf Lobe

Leaves can have shallow indentations (see above) or deeper indentations, forming lobes. It can be difficult to distinguish between deeply incised teeth and shallow lobes. Some of the more common types of lobing:

- **Cleft:** The margin is cut in toward the midvein.
- **Incised:** The leaf is cut sharply and deeply, usually into regularly shaped lobes.
- **Lacerate:** Irregularly lobed with deep incisions that look as if they were torn.
- **Laciniate:** Slashed; similar to incised, but the cuts are sharply angled.
- **Palmate:** Palm-shaped; with several lobes from a single point.

- **Pectinate:** Comb-shaped; the same as pinnatifid but with more numerous, straighter, and narrower lobes.
- **Pedate:** Similar to palmate, but the lateral lobes are further dissected.
- **Pinnate:** Feather-shaped, with the lobes arranged on either side of a central vein.
- **Pinnatifid:** Pinnately lobed half the distance or more to the midrib, but not all the way to the midrib.

## Leaf Apex

The apex or tip of the leaf, like the base, comes in a wide variety of shapes that are characteristic of different species. Some of the more common leaf apex shapes:

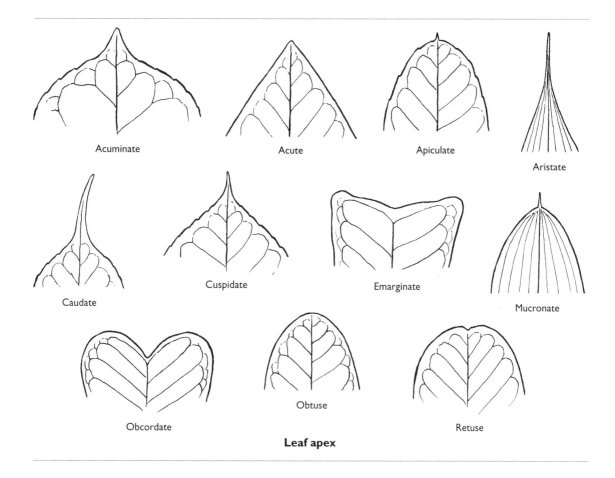

**Leaf apex**

- **Acuminate:** A sharp apex with less than a 90-degree angle and concave sides.
- **Acute:** Similar to acuminate but with straight-to-convex sides.
- **Apiculate:** Similar to mucronate in that it ends in a sharp point but the point includes tissue from the midvein and the lamina.
- **Aristate:** Ending in a hard, bristle-shaped tip.
- **Caudate:** Very acuminate, with a long and thin tip.
- **Cuspidate:** A form of acuminate in which the tip tapers gradually to a point.
- **Emarginate:** Broadly notched at the apex. Similar to retuse, which is only slightly notched.
- **Mucronate:** A sharp point (mucro) formed by a continuation of the midvein.

- **Obcordate:** Heart-shaped; notched at the tip like the top of a heart.
- **Obtuse:** A blunt apex with more than a 90-degree angle.
- **Retuse:** Slightly notched at the apex.

## Leaf Folding

Because the leaves are often fully formed but not expanded, they need to be packed in the bud. The exact form these contorted leaves take is useful in the identification of many species. All leaves show folding during some part of their development, but most eventually become flat or only slightly curled. The folding of mature leaves is called *ptyxis*. These are two common types of ptyxis:

- **Circinate:** The apex of the leaf is curled toward the base. Many ferns exhibit circinate vernation in their "fiddleheads."
- **Revolute:** The margins of the leaf are curled under. An example is labrador tea (*Rhododendron groenlandicum*).

## Leaf Modifications

Leaves seem to be the most malleable plant organ. They have been modified to function in a wide variety of ways. Some of the most common or interesting are as follows:

- **Bract and bracteole:** Bracts are leaves associated with flowers. The colorful parts of a shrimp plant (*Justicia brandegeana*) are bracts. Bracteoles are small bracts found on the pedicel (the stalk supporting the flower). Bracteoles are usually paired in dicots and borne singly in monocots.
- **Prophyll:** The leaves found at the first node of a shoot.
- **Tendril:** See stems.
- **Spine:** See stems.
- **Insect traps:** Leaves modified to trap insects and often absorb nutrients (particularly nitrogen) from the decaying insect carcasses. Plants from very unrelated parts of the plant kingdom have become insectivorous, and have done so by evolving "traps" such as sticky or epiascidiate leaves (see below).
- **Sticky leaves:** This type of trap, exemplified by the sundews (*Drosera* species), catches insects in goo either on the leaf surface or on hairs.
- **Epiascidiate leaves** (container leaves): In this type of trap, exemplified by the pitcher plants (*Sarracenia* species), the leaves form containers in which the insects are caught. Other types of epiascidiate leaves are the bladders of the bladderworts (*Utricularia* species), which suck the unsuspecting insect into the trap, and the Venus's-flytrap (*Dionaea muscipula*), with leaves that snap shut when an insect then lands on them.
- **Emergence, prickle:** A sharp, spiny structure formed on the surface of a leaf (or stem). It is similar to a spine, which is a modified stem, leaf, or root.
- **Food bodies:** Many plants produce food for visiting insects that benefit the plants in some way. This food is found in food bodies, which have a wide variety of names. The most famous are the Beltian bodies found on antplants (*Acacia* species), which attract ants that bite any intruder.
- **Bulb:** An underground, swollen bud. Food is stored in the leaves of the bud. A bulb resembles a corm, but in a corm the food is stored in the stem.
- **Succulent:** Noticeably fleshy; used to store water. This term can also be used for roots and stems.
- **Indeterminate growth:** Most leaves are determinate—that is, once they reach a certain size, they stop growing in length. The leaves of a few plants can continue to grow indefinitely. For example, many grass leaves grow from the base and can continue to grow after the tops of the leaves are cut, making it possible to grow and mow lawns.

## Leaf Arrangement

Leaves can be arranged on a stem in a variety of ways. Some of the more common arrangements are as follows:

- **Alternate:** One leaf per node. Oaks have alternate leaves.
- **Basal:** All the leaves coming from the base. Tulips have basal leaves.

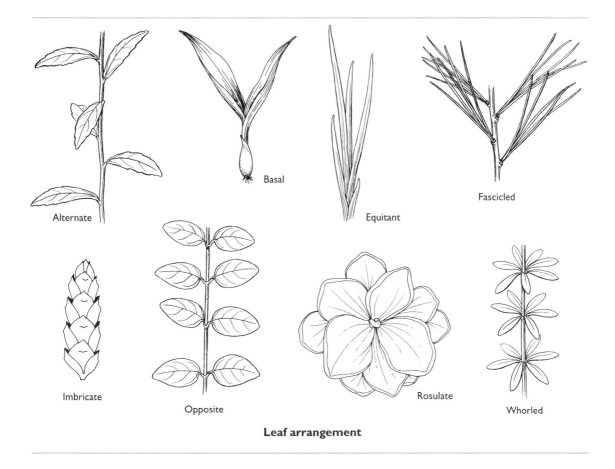

**Leaf arrangement**

- **Equitant:** Overlapping one another into two vertical rows or ranks, forming a fan, as the leaves of irises.
- **Fascicled:** Clustered, as in most species of pine.
- **Imbricate:** Overlapping one another. The leaves of Norfolk Island pine (*Araucaria heterophylla*) are imbricate.
- **Opposite:** Borne across from one another at the same node; paired. Maples have opposite leaves.
- **Rosulate:** Arranged in a basal rosette, with little or no stem. Sedums have rosulate leaves.

- **Whorled:** With three or more leaves at the same node, arranged in whorls. Joe-Pye weed (*Eupatorium maculatum*) has whorled leaves.

## Inflorescences

The inflorescence is the flowering part of the plant.

There are two major classes of inflorescences: *terminal*, in which the inflorescence terminates the shoot, and *axillary*, in which the inflorescence is found in the axil of a leaf.

## Inflorescence Parts

An inflorescence is composed of several different parts:

• **Floret:** The smallest unit of an inflorescence. In grasses, it is composed of a flower and two bracts called the *palea* and the *lemma*.

• **Pedicel:** The portion of stem immediately below a flower (or spikelet in grasses).

• **Peduncle:** The portion of stem above the leaves and below the lowest branching point of the inflorescence. Or, in a single-flowered inflorescence, the portion of stem below the flower and above the leaves.

• **Rachis:** The main stem portion of an inflorescence above the peduncle and below the pedicels.

• **Ray:** The outermost flowers of a composite inflorescence. Rays often look like petals of a flower.

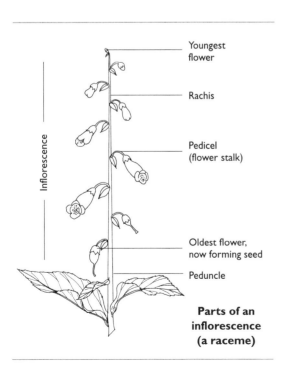

Youngest flower

Rachis

Pedicel (flower stalk)

Inflorescence

Oldest flower, now forming seed

Peduncle

**Parts of an inflorescence (a raceme)**

• **Scape:** A leafless stem arising at ground level and ending at the inflorescence. The term is equivalent to peduncle but only for plants with basal leaves.

• **Spathe:** A large bract beneath and enclosing the inflorescence.

## Types of Inflorescences

Inflorescences are some of the most complex parts of a plant to describe. There are many small differences and exceptions to common definitions. Some of the more common inflorescence types are the following:

• **Capitulum:** An inflorescence in which the flowers are found on a flattened surface called a *receptacle*. This is the type of inflorescence found in the sunflower family (Asteraceae).

• **Catkin:** A pendulous spike of reduced flowers. Catkins are adapted to wind pollination; they dangle down from the branch and blow in the wind, allowing the pollen to be freely dispersed. Oaks and birches have catkins.

• **Cauliflory:** Having inflorescences on the stem of a tree. This is the type of inflorescence found in the native redbud tree (*Cercis canadensis*).

• **Corymb:** A flat-topped raceme; the lower branches of the raceme are long and the upper branches are short so that the overall shape is flat. Bridal-wreath *Spiraea* x *van houtei* is an example of a plant with corymbose inflorescences.

• **Cyme:** An inflorescence that terminates in a flower, and lateral branches arising below this flower also terminate in flowers. Usually, the flower at the end of the central shoot blooms first, with additional flower buds opening in sequence, from inside out. Wild pink (*Silene caroliniana*) bears cymes.

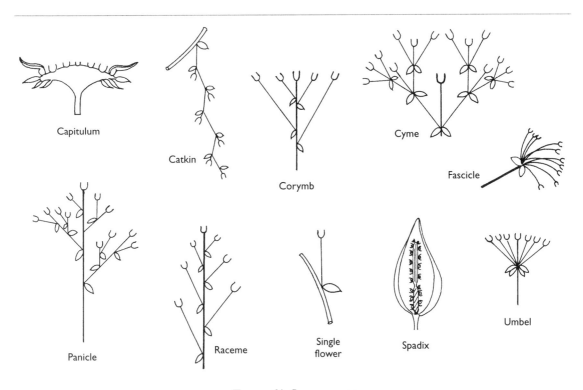

Capitulum

Catkin

Corymb

Cyme

Fascicle

Panicle

Raceme

Single flower

Spadix

Umbel

**Types of inflorescences**

• **Fascicle:** An inflorescence with a very short shoot and long pedicels, so that it appears as if a cluster of flowers arises from a single point. Common cherries (*Prunus domestica*) are borne on fascicles.

• **Panicle:** A raceme in which the lateral branches are themselves branched. Kentucky bluegrass (*Poa pratensis*) has spikelets in panicles.

• **Raceme:** An unbranched, elongated shoot with lateral flowers that mature from the bottom upward. Black cherry (*Prunus serotina*) has racemose inflorescences.

• **Single flower:** An inflorescence composed of a single flower. Tulips have single-flowered inflorescences.

• **Spadix:** A spike with small flowers crowded on a fleshy axis, characteristic of the Araceae (jack-in-the-pulpit family).

• **Spike:** A raceme with unstalked flowers maturing from the bottom upward. Wheat (*Triticum aestivum*) has spike-form inflorescences.

• **Umbel:** A flat-topped inflorescence in which the pedicels all originate from a single point, much like the struts of an umbrella. Queen Anne's lace (*Daucus carota*) has umbelliform inflorescences.

## Flowers

For a general discussion of the structure and function of the flower, see "Plant Reproduction," beginning on page 94.

## Flower Parts

The following are the major flower parts:

- **Androecium:** The male parts of the flower forming a whorl between the gynoecium (the female parts) to the inside and the corolla (the showy parts) to the outside. It includes one to many stamens, each of which typically includes a filament and an anther. Within the anther pollen is produced.

- **Anther:** The part of a stamen where pollen is produced. It typically sits atop a filament.

- **Calyx:** The outermost whorl of modified leaves found in the typical flower. It is the collective term for all the sepals of a single flower and is frequently green and inconspicuous.

- **Corolla:** The usually showy part of the flower, a whorl of modified leaves just inside the calyx. This is the collective term for all the petals of a single flower.

- **Carpel:** The structure that bears and encloses the ovules (egg-containing structures in the ovary).

- **Corona:** An extrafloral set of appendages that protrude from between the corolla and the stamens or from the corolla. The crownlike corona of daffodils is an example.

- **Filament:** The part of the stamen that typically serves as a stalk for the anther.

- **Fruit:** A mature ovary that frequently contains mature ovules or seeds.

- **Gynoecium:** The female parts forming a whorl at the center of the flower. It includes one to many pistils, each of which typically includes a stigma, style, and ovary.

- **Hypanthium:** The cup formed from the receptacle and/or perianth that has fused with the androecium. Not all flowers have a hypanthium. The rose family (Rosaceae) has many species whose flowers have a hypanthium.

- **Ovary:** The typically enlarged, bottom part of the pistil where ovules are produced.

- **Ovule:** The egg-containing structures within the ovary that develop into seeds.

- **Locule:** A chamber within the ovary. A simple ovary has a single locule while a compound ovary has more than one locule. For example, a bicarpellate ovary has two locules. The number of locules is usually the same as the number of carpels.

- **Pedicel:** The "stalk" that supports a single flower in an inflorescence made up of more than one flower.

- **Peduncle:** The "stalk" that supports either a single flower, in plants that produce only a single flower, or an entire inflorescence.

- **Perianth:** The collective term for all the sepals and petals of a single flower.

- **Petal:** A sterile, highly modified leaf that is a single "unit" of the corolla. Petals are usually the showy part of a flower and may include

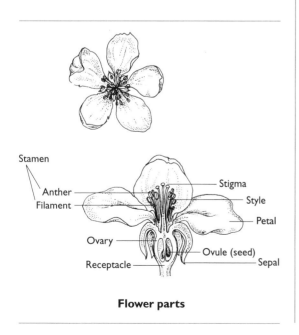

**Flower parts**

special structures, called *nectaries*, for attracting insect pollinators and/or special ultraviolet markings, called *honey guides*, for guiding insects, such as bees, to pollen.

- **Pistil:** A single female reproductive "unit." The pistil typically has three recognizable regions: the stigma, the style, and the ovary.
- **Pollen:** The male gametophyte. Pollen grains give rise to sperm.
- **Rachis:** The central stalk of an inflorescence to which the pedicels of individual flowers are attached.
- **Receptacle:** The region at the top of either the peduncle or pedicel where the floral appendages (for example, sepals, petals, stamens, and pistils) are attached.
- **Sepal:** A sterile, modified leaf that is a single "unit" of the calyx. Sepals are frequently green and inconspicuous.
- **Stamen:** The male reproductive structure made up of an anther and a filament.
- **Staminode:** A whorl of modified leaves just outside the stamens. Staminodes are frequently inconspicuous and stamenlike.
- **Stigma:** Typically, the top portion of a pistil, which receives pollen and provides conditions necessary for their germination.
- **Style:** The typically elongated region of a pistil between the stigma and ovary.
- **Tepal:** The term used for any single "unit" of the perianth when sepals and petals are morphologically similar.

Botanists often rely on reproductive characteristics to classify plants and establish their evolutionary relationships. Because the flower is the structure where reproduction occurs, there is a large body of terminology describing flowers in minute detail. Some of these terms are presented here. Becoming familiar with these terms can help you not only identify plants but also develop a greater understanding of their relationships.

## Flower Sexuality

- **Bisexual:** With both stamens (male parts) and pistils (female parts).
- **Pistillate:** Female flowers—that is, imperfect flowers lacking stamens.
- **Staminate:** Male flowers, that is, imperfect flowers lacking pistils.

## Plant Sexuality

- **Dioecious:** Species having male and female plants (that is, only male flowers on some plants and only female flowers on other plants).
- **Monoecious:** Species having both sexes on the same plant in separate (that is, imperfect) flowers.
- **Polygamous:** Species having both imperfect (pistillate and/or staminate) flowers and perfect flowers on the same plants.
- **Polygamo-dioecious:** Polygamous, but primarily dioecious.
- **Polygamo-monoecious:** Polygamous, but primarily monoecious.

## Numbers of Flower Parts

- **Complete:** Flowers that have all four floral whorls (calyx, corolla, stamens, and pistils).
- **Incomplete:** Flowers that lack one or more of the four floral whorls.
- **Perfect:** Flowers with both stamens (male parts) and pistils (female parts).
- **Imperfect:** Flowers lacking either stamens or pistils.

## Position of Flower Parts

- **Epigynous:** The perianth (sepals and petals) and androecium (male parts) are attached above the base of the ovary. Therefore, the ovary is inferior or half-inferior.
- **Half-inferior:** The ovary is surrounded by, or embedded in, the receptacle (the region at the top of either the peduncle or pedicel where floral appendages are attached). Therefore, the flower is epigynous.
- **Hypogynous:** The perianth (sepals and petals) and androecium (male parts) are attached below the ovary. Therefore, the ovary is superior.
- **Inferior:** The ovary sits primarily below the attachment point of the perianth (sepals and petals) and androecium (male parts). Therefore, the perianth is epigynous.
- **Perigynous:** The perianth (sepals and petals) and androecium (male parts) are fused at the base so that the sepals, petals, and stamens appear to arise from the rim of a floral cup (the hypanthium). This condition is frequently found in plants of the rose family (Rosaceae).
- **Superior:** The ovary sits primarily above the attachment point of the perianth (sepals and petals) and androecium (male parts). Therefore, the perianth is hypogynous.

## Perianth Terminology

The perianth is the collective term for all the sepals and petals of a single flower.
- **Apetalous:** A flower lacking petals. Common in wind-pollinated plants.
- **Banner:** Topmost petal of the flowers of some plants in the pea family.
- **Beard:** A sepal or petal with a dense cluster or line of hairs.
- **Claw:** A very narrow, stalklike base of a sepal or petal.

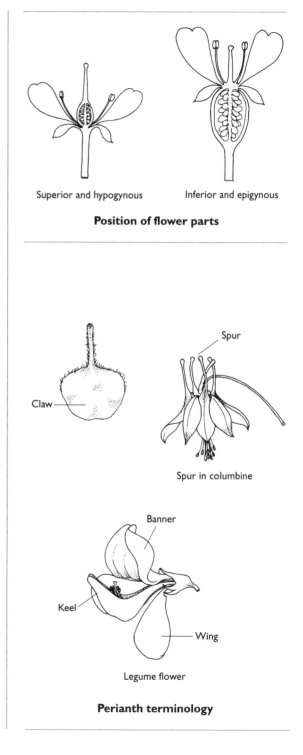

Superior and hypogynous    Inferior and epigynous

**Position of flower parts**

Spur

Claw

Spur in columbine

Banner

Keel

Wing

Legume flower

**Perianth terminology**

• **Cruciform:** A corolla that, when viewed from above, appears cross-shaped.

• **Keel:** The two united lowermost petals of the flowers of some plants in the pea family.

• **Lobe:** Any distinct segment of a divided sepal or petal. Members of the pink family (Caryophyllaceae) have divided petals that appear to have been cut with pinking shears (thus the common family name "pink").

• **Spur:** Any hollow protuberance from a sepal or petal. *Impatiens* species, for example, frequently have spurred sepals.

• **Wing:** One of two lateral petals of the flower of some plants in the pea family.

## Corolla Parts

Corolla is the collective term for all the petals of a single flower. This is usually the showy part of the flower.

• **Limb:** In fused corollas, any extension of the petal beyond its fused base.

• **Throat:** The opening at the top of the tube in fused corollas.

• **Tube:** The tubelike structure where the petals are united at the bottom of fused corollas.

## Corolla Shapes

Corollas can be either actinomorphic (radially symmetrical, meaning that when you look down on the calyx or corolla, you can see an infinite number of bisecting lines or planes that can cut the flower in equal halves) or zygomorphic (bilaterally symmetrical, meaning that when you look down on the calyx or corolla, you can see that only one bisecting line that can cut the flower in equal halves). The following are different actinomorphic forms:

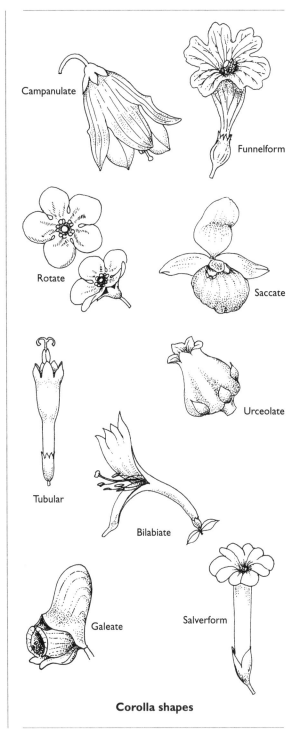

Campanulate
Funnelform
Rotate
Saccate
Tubular
Urceolate
Bilabiate
Galeate
Salverform

**Corolla shapes**

- **Campanulate:** Bell-shaped, as in bell-flowers (*Campanula* species).
- **Funnelform:** Funnel-shaped, as in bindweeds (*Convolvulus* species).
- **Rotate:** Wheel-shaped, as in bluets (*Hedyotis caerulea*).
- **Salverform:** Trumpet-shaped, as in Russian olive (*Elaeagnus angustifolia*).
- **Tubular:** Cylindrical, as in trumpet vine (*Campsis radicans*).
- **Urceolate:** Urn-shaped, as in highbush blueberry (*Vaccinium corymbosum*).

The following are different zygomorphic forms:

- **Bilabiate:** With two lips composed of fused petals, as in snapdragon (*Antirrhinum majus*).
- **Galeate:** With a helmet-shaped appendage on one side. The corollas of monkshoods (*Aconitum* species) are galeate.
- **Saccate:** With an enlarged, pouchlike appendage on one side, as in the lady slipper orchid (*Cypripedium acaule*).

## Fruit

A fruit is the structure that encloses one or more seeds and to some extent assists in the dissemination of the seeds. Many botanists consider a fruit to be a mature ovary, and therefore do not consider cones to be fruits. (For more on cones, see the discussion of gymnosperms in "Plant Reproduction," page 101.) In the more advanced fruits discussed below, a carpel surrounds the seed, which is therefore no longer naked. This type of fruit is found in the angiosperms, or flowering plants (see "Angiosperms," page 104).

## Terms for Describing a Fruit

The fruit is a very complex structure composed of a number of different parts. Some of the more common terms used for describing fruit follow:

- **Carpel:** The unit of an ovary formed from one highly modified leaf. Simple pistils have a single carpel. Compound pistils have several to many carpels (often three or five) fused together.
- **Dehiscent:** Split, allowing the seeds to fall out and be dispersed.
- **Endocarp:** The inner layer of the pericarp (fruit wall). The endocarp can be hard and bony as in peaches or soft as in grapes.
- **Epicarp or exocarp:** The outer layer of the pericarp (fruit wall). The epicarp can be tough and leathery as in citrus or soft as in cherries.
- **Fruitlet:** The part of a fruit that becomes dispersed in schizocarpic fruits. The fruitlet contains one or more seeds surrounded by part

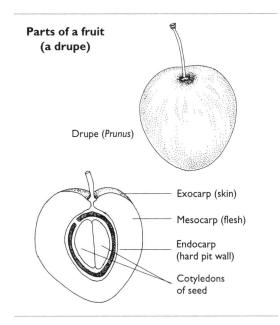

**Parts of a fruit (a drupe)**

Drupe (*Prunus*)

Exocarp (skin)

Mesocarp (flesh)

Endocarp (hard pit wall)

Cotyledons of seed

of the ovary wall. Dill "seeds" are actually fruitlets.

- **Indehiscent:** A fruit that does not split open. For example, a berry.
- **Locule:** A chamber or cavity of a fruit.
- **Mesocarp:** The middle layer of the pericarp (fruit wall).
- **Pericarp:** The fruit wall, often composed of three layers: epicarp, mesocarp, and endocarp.
- **Pit:** The stony endocarp of a peach or other drupe.
- **Sarcocarp:** Any internal fleshy layer of a fruit.
- **Schizocarp:** A fruit that forms from one ovary but breaks into two or more fruitlets, each containing seeds.
- **Seed:** Mature ovules composed of a seed coat, endosperm (starch or oil used to nourish the developing embryo), and embryo.
- **Segment:** A division or portion of a fruit. Usually these correspond to the locules.
- **Septum:** A partition between two fused carpels.
- **Stone:** The hardened endocarp of a peach or other drupe.
- **Valves:** The parts of the pericarp (fruit wall) that are separated at dehiscence.

## General Types of Fruit

One way to understand fruits is to look at how they develop. In the simplest developmental pattern, a single pistil develops into a single fruit. Three fruit types display this pattern: simple, rhexocarpic, and schizocarpic. A simple fruit is dispersed as a whole (for example, a berry); a rhexocarpic fruit splits open and the seeds are shed from the fruit (for example, a capsule); and a schizocarpic fruit splits into separate fruitlets, which are dispersed (for example, a dill fruit splits into two fruitlets).

In addition to this basic type of fruit are compound fruits (also called *aggregate fruits*), which develop from more than one pistil in a single flower (such as raspberries and strawberries), and multiple fruits, which develop from more than one pistil in more than one flower (such as a pineapple; cut open a pineapple and the remnants of each of the many flowers that contributed to the fruit become visible).

Another way to look at fruits is to distinguish between those that are formed solely from the ovary and those that are formed from the ovary as well as other flower parts.

A pericarpium is a fruit formed solely from the ovary. These are some of the more common types of pericarpium:

- **Achene:** A simple, one-seeded fruit in which the pericarp (fruit wall) is attached to the seed. A nut (in some uses of the term) is an achene with a hardened pericarp. A common achene is that of the sunflower (*Helianthus annuus*).
- **Bacca** (also called *berry*): A simple, fleshy fruit that does not dehisce. A common berry is the grape (*Vitis vinifera*). Berries are usually dispersed by animals that eat them. The seeds pass through their bodies and are excreted.
- **Capsule:** A rhexocarpic (dehiscent) fruit formed from more than one carpel. Rhododendrons have capsular fruit. There are several types of capsule, which are distinguished by the type of dehiscence they exhibit: in a septicidal capsule, dehiscence is along the septa (the area where the carpels or locules are fused to each other) separating the carpels. In a loculicidal capsule, dehiscence is via slits formed in the outer wall of the locules (or cavities). In a poricidal capsule, dehiscence is via pores, small holes in the side of the capsule.
- **Drupe:** A simple, fleshy, indehiscent fruit with one or more internal stones. The stones are

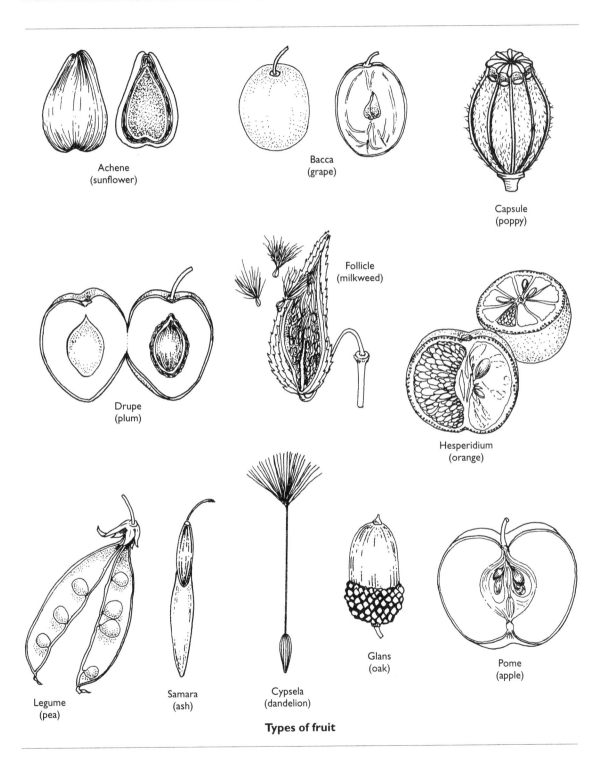

Achene
(sunflower)

Bacca
(grape)

Capsule
(poppy)

Drupe
(plum)

Follicle
(milkweed)

Hesperidium
(orange)

Legume
(pea)

Samara
(ash)

Cypsela
(dandelion)

Glans
(oak)

Pome
(apple)

**Types of fruit**

an adaptation to animal dispersal; they protect the seed during its passage through the animal's digestive tract. Some common examples of drupes are peach (*Prunus persica*) and mango (*Mangifera indica*).

- **Follicle:** A dry, dehiscent fruit that develops from one carpel and opens through only one slit. Magnolias have follicular fruit.
- **Hesperidium:** A fleshy, berrylike fruit with a tough rind, such as orange, lemon, and other citrus. In citrus fruits the juice is formed in each wedge in hairs.
- **Legume:** A dry dehiscent fruit formed from a single carpel, which usually opens along two sides. This type of fruit is found only in the bean family, for example, the bean (*Phaseolus vulgaris*).
- **Samara:** A simple, dry, indehiscent fruit with wings. A typical samara is the fruit of elms (*Ulmus* species). Maples (*Acer* species) are more complex. They are schizocarpic; each winged portion is a fruitlet.

An anthocarp is a fruit formed from the ovary and attached floral parts that have undergone marked development after fertilization in order to aid in the dissemination of the seeds.

Some common types of anthocarp:

- **Anthecium:** A grass fruit in which a single spikelet with fertile florets breaks apart above the glumes (the bracts at the base of the spikelet). There are several other types of grass fruit that will not be covered here.
- **Cypsela:** A fruit with wings or bristles at its tip. A typical cypsela is the fruit of a dandelion (*Taraxacum officinale*).
- **Glans:** A fruit in which the receptacle, pedicel, or peduncle are enlarged. A typical example is the acorn in oaks (*Quercus* species), in which the acorn cap is formed from bracts below the flower.
- **Pome:** A fruit in which the hypanthium

(a cup formed by the fusion of the sepals, petals, and stamens) becomes enlarged and fleshy. The typical pome is the apple (*Malus domestica*).

## Fruit and Seed Dispersal

Fruits and seeds usually move away from the parent plant in some way. The mechanism by which this is done is called *dispersal*. There are six common means of dispersal:

- **Anemochory:** Dispersal by wind. The dandelion (*Taraxacum officinale*), with its fluffy parachutes, is easily dispersed by wind over long distances.
- **Autochory:** Dispersal by physical expulsion, often explosively. The fruit of the jewelweed (*Impatiens capensis*) explodes, shooting its seeds some distance.
- **Endozoochory:** Dispersal through animal ingestion and excretion. Many seeds cannot germinate and grow without first passing through the gut of an animal. The acid washing or physical grinding of the seeds helps them germinate. Bearberry (*Arctostaphylos uva-ursi*) will not germinate without first passing through a bird's digestive tract.
- **Epizoochory:** Dispersal by attachment to fur or feathers. Plants such as burdock (*Arctium minus*) have barbs on their fruit, which become attached to passing animals and fall to the ground when the animals clean themselves.
- **Hydrochory:** Dispersal by water. Seeds of rushes (*Juncus* species) are light and easily carried by water. They also often have tails at each end, which subsequently help them become lodged in mud or other debris.
- **Myrmecochory:** Dispersal by ants. Myrmechochory is a very important but often overlooked form of dispersal. Violets and many other spring wildflowers form small bodies attached to the seed, the sole purpose of which

is to provide food for the ant. The ant takes the whole seed to its nest and then removes the food body. In the process, the seed is dispersed.

## Surface Features

Some features can be found on virtually any part of a plant—namely, surface features. These generally are hairs, called trichomes in botany. To describe the hairiness of a leaf, for example, botanists describe the trichomes, their abundance, and orientation, collectively called the *indumentum*. The following are common terms used to describe plant surfaces:

- **Glabrous:** Without any hairs or other surface covering.
- **Glabrescent:** Becoming glabrous over time. In other words, the hairs fall off as the leaf ages.
- **Pubescent:** Downy. With short soft hairs.
- **Hispid:** With stout, stiff hairs.
- **Hirsute:** With rough, coarse hairs.
- **Tomentose:** Woolly. With long, soft, matted hairs.
- **Villous:** Shaggy. With long, soft, unmatted hairs.
- **Strigose:** With long, stiff, appressed hairs.
- **Stellate:** With stellate hairs (hairs that branch and look like small stars).
- **Viscid:** Sticky.

## Further Reading

Bell, A. D. *Plant Form: An Illustrated Guide to Flowering Plant Morphology.* Oxford, England: Oxford University Press, 1991.

Brenckmann, Francoise. Seeds of Life. URL = http://www.versicolores.ca/SeedsOfLife/

Cork Supply USA. *Cork from Tree to Bottle: A Photo Essay.* URL = http://www.corksupplyusa.com/ce-intro.htm

Harris, J. G., and M. W. Harris. *Plant Identification Terminology.* Spring Lake, Utah: Spring Lake Publishing, 1994.

Lawrence, G. H. M. *Taxonomy of Vascular Plants.* New York: Macmillan Co., 1951.

Miller, Leonard. The Ancient Bristlecone Pine. URL = http://www.sonic.net/bristlecone/intro.html

Russell, Scott. Scott's Botanical Links. URL = http://www.ou.edu/cas/botany-micro/bot-linx/

The Tall Trees Club. The Archive of the Largest and Tallest Trees. URL = http://www.northcoast.com/~mtaylor/trees.htm

University of Wisconsin, Madison. Wisconsin Fast Plants. URL = http://fastplants.cals.wisc.edu/

Wilford, Dianne. Basic Classification of Fruits of Flowering Plants (*Angiosperms*). URL = http://vertigo.derby.ac.uk/BiologicalImaging/Show95/DW.html

# PLANT REPRODUCTION

Plants reproduce in two basic ways: asexually and sexually. These basic modes of reproduction are not necessarily mutually exclusive; the same plant species often uses both strategies.

As the term suggests, asexual reproduction is reproduction without sex, or without syngamy, the fusion of male and female gametes, while sexual reproduction involves syngamy.

## Asexual Reproduction

There are two types of asexual reproduction in plants: vegetative reproduction and apomixis. While the specific processes of each are different, the result is always the same: the creation of clones, offspring that are genetically identical to the parent plant. Asexual reproduction can be advantageous for plants well adapted to their environments; it guarantees that traits that make the plant well suited to its environment will be preserved in future generations.

### Vegetative Reproduction

Plants that produce rhizomes, stolons, tubers, and other modified stems are frequently capable of vegetative reproduction. These modified stems may have buds, and each one of these buds is capable of developing into an independent plant. Gardeners commonly take advantage of this trait to propagate such species by dividing modified stem segments with buds into separate pieces that can grow into new plants. By propagating vegetatively, you can be sure that desirable traits of the parent plant— say, a certain color leaf—will be passed on to the new plants, which will be genetically identical to the parent (see "Propagation," page 474).

### Apomixis

In some plants, embryos can develop without the fusion of male and female gametes. For example, an embryo might arise from an unreduced female gametophyte—that is, from the structure that will produce the female gamete or egg. The female gametophyte is unreduced because the meiocyte, a specialized cell involved in sexual reproduction, fails to undergo meiosis, the process that reduces the chromosome number by half and results in the formation of gametes (see the discussion of sexual reproduction below). The plants that develop after germination from such an embryo are clones, just like the products of vegetative reproduction.

## The Sexual Plant Life Cycle

Unlike asexual reproduction, sexual reproduction is important in providing genetic variability. All plants that reproduce sexually must go through meiosis. Meiosis is a unique kind of cell division during which the paired sets of chromosomes present in sexually mature plants, called sporophytes, are halved. Because they have two sets of chromosomes, one from the male parent and the other from the female, the cells of sporophytes are called *diploid*. During this process, pairs of homologous, or identical, chromosomes, one from each parent, line up together. Crossing-over, or the exchange of genetic material between these homologous chromosomes, may occur at this time. Crossing-over is critical for producing some of the genetic variability in resulting offspring. Meiosis typically produces four haploid cells, each with one set of chromosomes, from a single diploid cell. These haploid cells become gametes—eggs and sperm. Without meiosis, sexually reproducing organisms would not have a mechanism for reducing the total chromosome number by half so that genetic variability can be introduced via crossing-over. Meiosis is a critical step that must occur prior to the fusion of sperm and egg, which restores the diploid chromosome number.

## Alternating Generations

Plants undergo a two-phase cycle of sexual reproduction known as the *alternation of generations*. This sexual life cycle involves alternation of the diploid sporophyte generation with the haploid gametophyte generation. The sporophyte stage begins with fusion of an egg and sperm, which produces a zygote. The diploid zygote develops into a sporophytic plant. This sexually mature plant eventually produces meiocytes, cells that will undergo meiosis, typically resulting in four haploid cells. These haploid cells, in turn, develop into gametophytes, which eventually form sex organs where eggs and sperm are produced.

The sporophyte and gametophyte stages usually are easy to tell apart; one is typically parasitic or dependent upon the other. Which generation is dominant differs in different plants. Generally, the gametophytes of primitive land plants such as mosses are dominant and larger than the sporophytes. In higher, or more advanced plants, the reverse is true.

In other words, the alternation of generations is the alternation between meiocytes undergoing meiosis and the fusion of gametes that produces a zygote.

### The Gametophyte Stage:

The gametophyte generation normally begins with a spore (sexual spore or meiospore) and ends with a gamete. The cells of the gametophyte are usually haploid.

### The Sporophyte Stage:

The sporophyte generation usually begins with a zygote and ends with a meiocyte. The cells of the sporophyte are usually diploid.

## The Life Cycles of Plants

The following are generalized descriptions of the sexual life cycles of the groups of plants traditionally used by gardeners: bryophytes, including mosses; pteridophytes or ferns; gymnosperms, including conifers; and angiosperms or flowering plants.

### Bryophytes

*Bryophytes*, commonly known as mosses, hornworts, and liverworts, exhibit a pronounced alternation of generations during which the conspicuous "leafy" plant is a part of the gametophyte generation and the sporophyte is frequently smaller and dependent upon it. Bryophytes are usually found in moist habitats, but they do occur in drier areas as well. These habitats vary widely, ranging from animal dung and insects (in the tropics) to bare rock. Bryophytes are frequently small and always lack xylem (specialized water-conducting tissue) and phloem (specialized food-transporting tissue). The absence of these vascular tissues sets bryophytes apart from the more advanced ferns, gymnosperms, and angiosperms.

An individual moss plant, for example, consists of an upright or prostrate slender, leafy stalk that may have absorptive rootlike structures called rhizoids. Mosses usually form large colonies. These colonies are found in a variety of habitats such as moist soil, rocks, and wood. Mosses are usually small, but some species in the Southern Hemisphere can grow a foot high.

### Bryophyte Reproduction

The starting point for the sporophyte, as noted previously, is the zygote, which is the product of syngamy, or the fusion of gametes. In mosses, syngamy occurs in a structure called

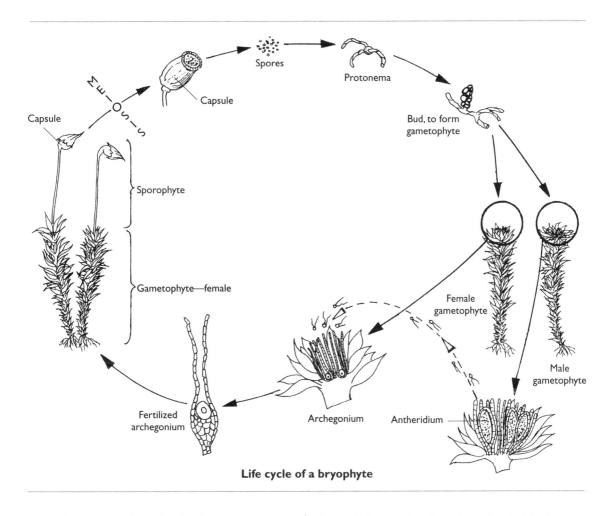

**Life cycle of a bryophyte**

an *archegonium*, where haploid eggs are produced. The zygote grows from, and remains permanently attached to, the archegonium, from which it gets its nutrition. The cells of the developing sporophyte soon become photosynthetic, making it able to, at least partially, synthesize its own nutrients. As the needlelike sporophyte grows, it becomes visible above the tip of the leafy gametophyte plant.

Once the sporophyte has reached its mature length, an enlarged, spore-bearing region called the *capsule* or *sporangium* forms at its tip. The capsule is situated atop a stalk, or seta. At the base of the seta is a foot that is buried in the top of the leafy gametophyte. The seta gets progressively longer as the sporophyte develops, raising the capsule high above the rest of the plant. As the capsule matures, certain cells in the sporangium separate, forming sporocytes. Each of these spore mother cells is capable of undergoing meiosis—having its chromosome number reduced from the diploid condition to the haploid condition—and also a process called *cytokinesis*, in which the remaining contents of the cell are divided. The result is the formation of four spores.

## PROPAGATING MOSSES

Mosses are most commonly used by gardeners in bonsai and terrarium plantings. The easiest way to obtain moss for these purposes is simply to collect samples from habitats similar to those you intend to simulate. Bare soil, tree trunks, and rocks are common moss habitats—as well as common "props" in bonsai and terrarium plantings. You can also cultivate beds of moss by grinding fertile moss plants—those bearing spores—and spreading them over a planting flat containing an even mixture of peat moss and sand covered with cheesecloth. Be certain to keep the flat moist.

Spores, the products of meiosis, are widely distributed in the atmosphere, and those that come to rest in a favorable environment can germinate. The spores of many moss species require light before they can germinate. In many mosses, the spore develops into a prostrate, many-branched, filamentous structure called the *protonema*. The protonema is capable of photosynthesis, as its cells contain chloroplasts. After a period of growth, the protonema forms buds, which become leaf shoots. While the protonema serves as a primitive root system for its shoots, additional rootlike structures called *rhizoids* develop from the bases of the "leaves." Archegonia and the male sex organs, called *antheridia*, are produced at the tips of some branches of mature "leafy" gametophyte plants. Some mosses are monoecious, having both archegonia and antheridia on the same plant (for example, *Funaria*), while others are dioecious, with male and female sex organs on separate, unisexual plants (for example, *Polytrichum*). When there is enough moisture

present, mature antheridia release their sperm, some of which may swim to the archegonia. Raindrops sometimes help the process along by splashing sperm to the archegonia, especially in monoecious species. Once in the vicinity of the mature archegonium, the sperm swim down the neck canal to the egg. The resulting fusion of the gametes produces a zygote.

### Ferns

Numbering just over 10,000 species worldwide, ferns, technically called *pteridophytes*, are more advanced than the bryophytes, in part because they have vascular tissue (xylem and phloem). These plants are capable of growing much larger than the bryophytes (some to more than 80 feet tall), partly as a result of their vascular tissues. They are considered less advanced than the gymnosperms and angiosperms because they do not produce seeds. The typical fern has a horizontal underground stem known as a *rhizome*; the aboveground structures are fronds or leaves. In many ferns, the newly emerging frond is called a *crozier* or *fiddlehead* because it looks like the carved spiral at the end of a violin.

#### Fern Reproduction

Sporophyte development is very rapid in common garden and woodland ferns. The zygote develops an embryonic root, leaf, stem, and foot. The foot apparently aids in absorbing nutrients from the gametophyte. The stem develops slowly, but ultimately produces leaves. The first few leaves of juvenile ferns differ from those of the mature sporophyte. As growth continues, the leaves finally begin to resemble those of the adult species.

When the minute sporophyte has become established, the gametophyte dies. The game-

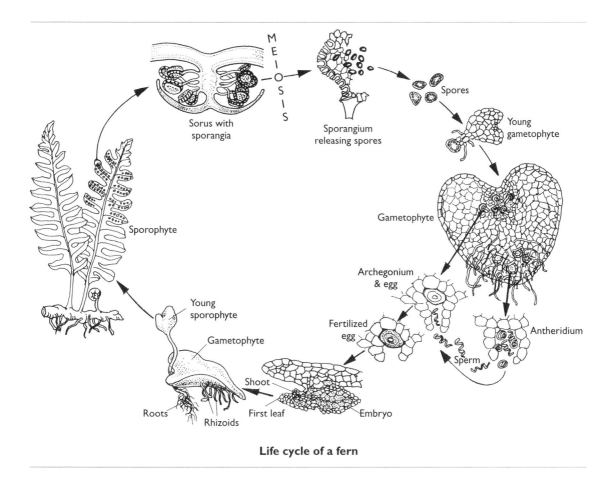

**Life cycle of a fern**

tophyte generation in ferns, as in other seedless vascular plants, is relatively short-lived and simple. The sporophytic phase is dominant in the life cycle. As in all vascular plants, what we recognize as "the plant" is the sporophytic generation, and at maturity it develops sporangia, the spore-producing organs.

In the common ferns, sporangia are borne on the undersides of fronds, or on modified fronds. The first fronds produced in spring are sterile—that is, they lack reproductive structures. The fertile fronds arise later in the season. In some species, such as lady fern (*Athyrium filix-femina*) the sterile and fertile fronds are similar.

In other species—sensitive fern (*Onoclea sensibilis*), for example—the sterile and fertile fronds are very different.

The fertile regions on fronds that bear sporangia are known as *receptacles*, and the group of sporangia on a single receptacle is called a *sorus*. In many species, but by no means in all, the sorus is covered during development by a flap of tissue called an *indusium*. The shape and arrangement of the sori are different in different species.

Spores arise by meiosis from sporocytes. For the most part, immature sori are a pale, whitish color, although there are exceptions, such as

## PROPAGATING FERNS

Becoming acquainted with the life cycles of ferns makes propagating them from spores much less daunting. One of the most important aspects of fern propagation is collecting ripe spores. Ripe sori are plump with little brown, black, yellow, or green spores, depending on the species. (Once the sporangia have released their spores, or dehisced, it is too late to harvest. Once they have dehisced, the sori are frayed, scruffy-looking, and generally a dull cinnamon-brown.) Cleanse the ripe sori-bearing frond in a 5 to 10 percent bleach solution. Separate the spores from the frond and other debris using camera lens tissue or a fine screen.

The spores can be sown in a variety of sterilized media, including garden soil, peat moss, perlite, vermiculite, compost, or combinations of these. Growing containers should also be sterilized, because cleanliness is absolutely critical for the successful germination of spores. Once sown, the spore cultures should be kept in an environment with constant temperatures and controlled light and moisture.

The typically heart-shaped gametophytes will be too small to see without magnification when they first emerge in four to fourteen days. There should be a solid mat of prothalli in two to five months. Thin the gametophytes, or transplant them in clumps to additional, sterilized containers. Depending on the species and growing conditions, gametophytes will produce sporophytes from six to twelve months.

It is also possible, and simpler, to propagate ferns vegetatively via division of rhizomes, bud-bearing fronds, and other techniques. For more on fern propagation, consult *Ferns: Wild Things Make a Comeback in the Garden* (see "Further Reading," page 111).

autumn fern (*Dryopteris erythrosora*), whose sori, which are produced in the fall, are bright red. As the spores inside each sporangium mature, they typically get darker, until they are a deep brown or black. Not all spores mature to a deep brown or black, however. Polypodiums are ripe when they are buttercup yellow, osmundas when they are green.

The sporangia of ferns is typically a thin-walled case, usually on a stalk, and surrounded by a ring of thick-walled cells known as the *annulus*, which aids in opening the sporangium when the spores are mature.

The indusium, if present, ultimately shrivels when the spores have matured, exposing the sporangia. The annulus breaks near the base of one side, tearing the sporangium apart, and arches backward. Then the annulus snaps forward abruptly, catapulting the spores into the air. Ferns produce tremendous numbers of spores, but the special requirements of most species for moisture and shade effectively reduce the number of gametophytes that ultimately develop.

Spores that are deposited by air currents on sufficiently moist soil and rocks germinate within five to six days, and the gametophyte begins to develop. Most fern spores also require light for germination; those of the bracken fern (*Pteridium aquilinum*) are an exception. Early in germination, colorless rhizoidal cells form at the base of the filament of green cells. These rhizoids, or rootlike hairs, absorb and carry water and nutrients to the developing gametophyte.

Eventually, the gametophyte becomes heart-shaped, and in some species may be as big as half an inch in diameter. The fern gametophyte was long ago called the *prothallus* or *prothallium*, because it was known to be the precursor of the fern plant, even before its sexual function was clearly understood.

As well-nourished, bisexual gametophytes mature, they develop antheridia and archegonia, normally on their undersides. The female, egg-producing organs, or archegonia, occur near the notch of the heart-shaped prothallus. The male, sperm-producing organs, or antheridia, occur on the "wings" and opposite the notch. Each archegonium has a chimneylike protuberance that is flared at the top to receive the sperm. Each antheridium is a minute, capsulelike sac where the sperm grow.

The cells inside the neck of a mature archegonium dissolve, creating a moist passageway through which the sperm can swim to the mature eggs. The eggs of several archegonia may be fertilized, but usually only one of the zygotes develops into a juvenile sporophyte.

It is interesting to note that while bisexual prothalli may be capable of fertilizing themselves, experiments have shown that the resulting sporophytes often fail to thrive. This suggests that crossfertilization, the union of sperm and egg from different prothalli, necessary for increasing genetic variability within species, is promoted in at least some ferns.

## Gymnosperms

Gymnosperms are plants with vascular tissue and are considered more advanced than both bryophytes and ferns because, among other things, they produce seeds. The word "gymnosperm" is a combination of two Greek words meaning naked (*gymnos*) seed (*sperma*). The ability to produce seeds has enabled gymnosperms, along with the only other seed-bearing group, the flowering plants, to become the major vegetation on Earth today. Gymnosperms are woody and may be trees, shrubs, or even vines. Examples include the needle-leaved pines, hemlocks, spruces, and firs, the awl- and scaled-leaved junipers, the fernlike-leaved cycads, and the broad-leaved *Ginkgo.*

### Gymnosperm Reproduction
After a number of years of strictly vegetative growth from the seed and seedling stages, young pine trees begin to produce strobili, the sexual reproductive structures that are cone-shaped in many gymnosperms. Pines are monoecious, with microstrobili (strobili that produce male spores) and megastrobili (strobili that produce female spores) on the same plant. However, other gymnosperms, such as cycads and *Ginkgo,* are dioecious, with separate male and female plants. In addition, all gymnosperms are heterosporous, meaning that they produce two types of spores, small male spores called *microspores* and large female spores called *megaspores*—a condition also true of certain ferns, *Selaginella* (the spike mosses), *Isoetes* (the quillworts), and all flowering plants. (The bryophytes and many ferns and fern-allies are homosporous—that is, they produce a single type of spore.)

Microstrobili, or male cones, occur in clusters just below the tips usually of lower branches as the buds unfold at the beginning of the growing season. The minute megastrobili, or female cones, are borne on short side branches of the elongating central stalks of uppermost buds on the higher branches of the same plant. The megastrobili are visible only as these buds elongate in the spring.

A microstrobilus, or male cone, is composed of a central stalk bearing microsporophylls, which are modified leaves, each with two elongated microsporangia on its lower surface. Early in the spring, each of the microsporocytes, or cells capable of producing male spores within each microsporangium, undergo meiosis and produce groups of four haploid micro-

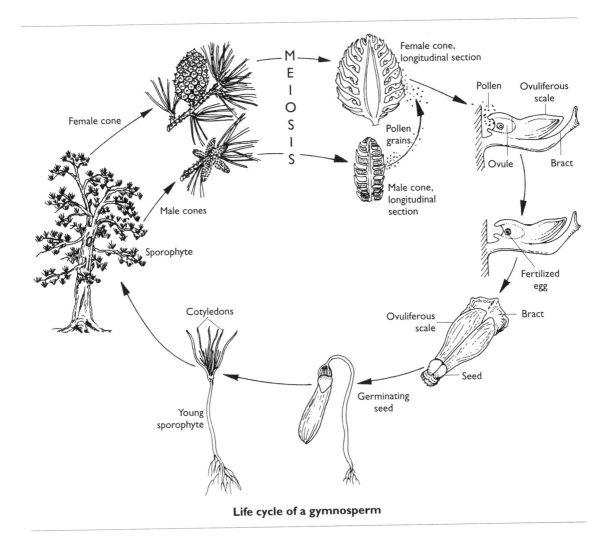

**Life cycle of a gymnosperm**

spores; these separate into individual microspores with winged cell walls. At this stage, each microspore looks like a ball with "mouse ears" attached. The exact time at which meiosis and microspore formation occur varies according to season and latitude.

Megastrobili, or female cones, are structurally more complex and much larger than the rather short-lived microstrobili. A single megastrobilus is composed of a central stalk with bracts. Each of these bracts bears ovule-bearing appendages known as *ovuliferous scales*. Each ovuliferous scale, in turn, bears two megasporangia or ovules. The ovule is covered with a specialized tissue known as the *integument*, which becomes the seed coat following fertilization, and includes a passageway known as the *micropyle*. After pollination, within each ovule a single megasporocyte undergoes meiosis, forming a row of four megaspores. The three megaspores nearest the micropyle deteriorate, leaving one viable megaspore, which develops into a female gametophyte over a period of several months.

The microspores of pines begin developing into male gametophyte-bearing pollen grains before being shed from the microsporangia, usually in the spring. The microsporangia release clouds of minute pollen once they have developed into four-celled gametophytes containing a generative cell, a tube cell, and two sterile or prothallial cells. At the same time, the ovuliferous scales of the current year's megastrobili begin to separate slightly following the elongation of the central stalk. This results in the formation of cracks between adjacent ovuliferous scales through which a sticky substance, called *pollen drops* or *droplet*s, is exuded. Pollination occurs when some of the airborne pollen grains land on these droplets and are drawn down into the ovule through the micropyle.

After pollination, the scales of the megastrobili close and protect the developing ovules. As the female gametophyte matures, two or three archegonia are formed at the end of the ovule where the micropyle is located. It takes more than a year for the female gametophytes in pines to mature.

During this time, the pollen grains adhering to the pollination droplets each form a pollen tube—an outgrowth that slowly "digests" the tissues of the megasporangium or ovule and eventually delivers the sperm to the mature archegonia. The generative cell, one of the cells in a pollen grain, divides, forming a sterile cell and a spermatogenous cell. Before reaching the archegonia, the spermatogenous cell divides to form two sperm. It is at this stage, when it consists of the pollen grain and tube with its two sperm, that the male gametophyte has reached maturity.

Once the pollen tube reaches the now-

## PROPAGATING CONIFERS

Propagating gymnosperms from seed, especially conifers, is relatively easy, but growth can be slow, especially during the first two years.

Sow seeds in outdoor beds or in seed pans set in cold frames. Many conifer seeds require a cold period of several weeks to germinate; expose the seeds to this cold treatment as soon as possible after collecting them. Seeds can be sown in a variety of media, as long as they include materials that will provide adequate drainage and the correct pH. Gardeners have also developed various techniques for the vegetative propagation of conifers, including stem cuttings and layering (see "Propagation," page 474).

For a detailed discussion of propagating gymnosperms, consult *Creative Propagation: A Grower's Guide* (see "Further Reading," page 111).

mature, egg-containing archegonium, the two sperm are released, and one unites with the egg to form a zygote. The second sperm degenerates.

A single female gametophyte normally contains two or three archegonia, the eggs of all of which may be fertilized. However, only a single embryo normally completes development. As the embryo develops, the integument hardens, forming the seed coat. Likewise, the ovuliferous scales harden, and a thin layer of each scale becomes the "wing" of a seed. Each pine seed is an embryonic sporophyte.

The mature, winged seeds are shed from the female cone as its appendages spread apart. In pines, seeds typically are released the autumn of the year after pollination. In some species, female cones do not open until they are exposed to extreme heat, such as that generated by forest fires. If seeds land in a favorable location, they may germinate.

## Angiosperms

There are an estimated 240,000 species of flowering plants, or angiosperms (from the two Greek words *angeion,* meaning vessel, and *sperma,* meaning seed). This makes the angiosperms the largest plant group; it is also the youngest, having first appeared in the fossil record roughly 125 million years ago.

What features have made such diversity possible? While the possession of vascular tissue and the production of seeds, also characteristic of the gymnosperms, have undoubtedly played a part in the success of the flowering plants, it is the flower that may well be the single most important factor responsible for the abundance of species. Many flowering plants have benefited from evolutionary associations with their animal pollinators. This association, better known as *coevolution*, most likely has driven much of this recent and rapid diversification.

### Angiosperm Reproduction

Flowers are where sexual reproduction occurs in angiosperms. The entire sexual reproductive cycle—pollination, fertilization, and seed and fruit production—begins in flowers. Pollination is the transfer of pollen grains from an anther, the structure where these grains are produced, to a stigma, a structure or surface receptive to pollen. If conditions are right, each pollen grain will produce a tube that grows down through the style and into an egg-containing ovule in the ovary, where it deposits two sperm. Fertilization occurs when a sperm unites with the egg.

In angiosperms, a second remarkable event occurs when the second sperm unites with additional material in the ovary. This is called *double fertilization* and results in the production of endosperm (a nutritive tissue). The ovule, with its now-fertilized egg, develops into a seed, while at the same time the ovary develops into a fruit. Fruits are the vehicles that disseminate or disperse seeds away from the parent plant. Once a seed is released from its fruit, and conditions are favorable for its germination, it can grow into a mature plant that produces its own flowers.

Although all angiosperms share this basic life cycle, it is affected in various plants by different factors. For example, some plants are annual, producing their flowers and fruits within a single year and then dying; others are biennial, taking two years to produce flowers and fruits before dying; others are perennial, living and producing flowers and fruits for many years. The young plants of some species—biennials, for example—require a period of exposure to cold in order to flower, a process called *vernalization*. The onset of flowering in some plants is affected by photoperiodism, an alteration in the length of the periods of light and dark to which the plants are exposed. Some species require exposure to longer periods of light before they flower and are called *long-day plants* (for example, wheat and cabbage). Others require a longer exposure to dark and are called *short-day plants* (for example, violets and strawberries).

## The Flower

"Flower" is a general term that usually refers to four basic parts: sepals (collectively called the *calyx*), petals (collectively called the *corolla*), stamens (collectively called the *androecium*), and pistils (collectively called the *gynoecium*). These

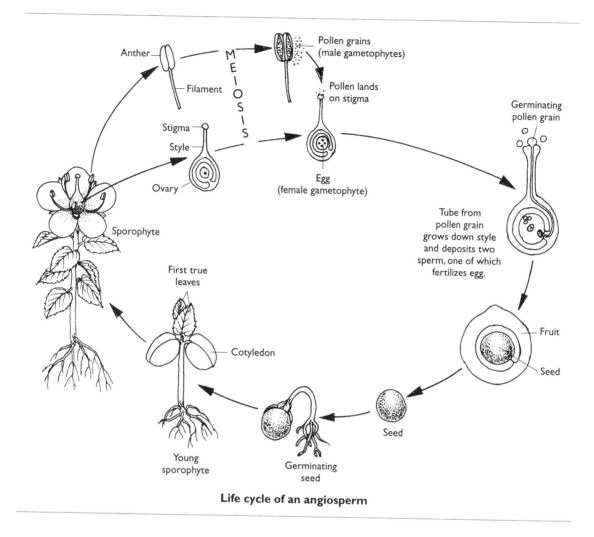

Anther
Filament
Pollen grains (male gametophytes)
M E I O S I S
Pollen lands on stigma
Germinating pollen grain
Stigma
Style
Ovary
Egg (female gametophyte)
Tube from pollen grain grows down style and deposits two sperm, one of which fertilizes egg.
Sporophyte
First true leaves
Fruit
Seed
Cotyledon
Seed
Young sporophyte
Germinating seed

**Life cycle of an angiosperm**

parts are attached to the tip of a specialized branch called a *peduncle*. The tip of the peduncle is called a *receptacle*. (For an illustration of the parts of a flower, see page 86.) The remarkable thing about all of these parts is that they are thought to be derived from leaves. Think of parts of a flower attached to a receptacle as if they were leaves attached to a twig, except that, unlike leaves, the different parts of a flower are separated by very short distances. These distances are so short, in fact, that when you look

down at an open flower, the components (for example, the petals) of any one part (in this case the corolla) appear to be connected to the "twig" (the receptacle) at the same point.

In a typical flower, the calyx, or outermost part of the flower, usually most closely resembles the leaves of the plant on which they occur. In fact, the calyx is frequently green and produces food from sunlight via photosynthesis, just as the leaves do. The calyx protects the developing flower bud in many plants. The corolla, the frequently colored part of the flower, is located just inside the calyx. Showy corollas can attract pollinators such as insects or birds. Wind-pollinated plants frequently have minute corollas or lack corollas entirely.

The androecium is just inside the corolla. The individual stamens, the male reproductive organs that make up the androecium, are composed of an anther (usually a swollen structure) and a filament (a long stalk supporting the anther). With magnification, you can see that the anther is actually made up of sacs. It is in these sacs that pollen grains are produced. Pollen grains are capable of producing sperm, the male sex cells.

In the center of the flower (actually at the top of the receptacle) is the gynoecium. Each individual pistil, or female reproductive organ, of the gynoecium typically looks like a flower vase and has three recognizable parts: a stigma, which will receive pollen grains, at the top of the vase; a style, the "necklike" portion of the vase, which supports and typically elevates the stigma; and an ovary, the swollen part at the bottom. Eggs, the female sex cells, are produced in ovules, which are inside the ovary.

It is important to note that the above is a description of a "typical" flower. In many species, some flower parts may be fused with others, extremely reduced, or completely absent. One example of a flower "missing" parts is the *Anemone,* or windflower, which lacks petals; its sepals have taken on a petal-like appearance (the sepals are colored, not green as in the typical flower). "Perfect" or "imperfect" and "complete" or "incomplete" are terms botanists use to describe the various types of variation in flowers. Perfect flowers possess male (stamens) and female (pistil) parts, while imperfect flowers lack one of these parts. Complete flowers have sepals, petals, stamens, and pistils, while incomplete flowers lack one of these parts. The typical flower described above is both perfect and complete, while anemones are perfect and incomplete. Flowers can be perfect and complete, perfect and incomplete, or imperfect and incomplete, but never imperfect and complete.

For more on the structure of flowers, see "Plant Structures," page 83.

### Pollination

Pollination can occur in two ways: self-pollination—the transfer of pollen from an anther to a stigma in the same flower or to a flower on the same plant—and cross-pollination—the transfer of pollen from one plant to a stigma on a different plant, but of the same species. Self-pollination can be an effective method of pollination, but it has the disadvantage of excluding genetic variability. Cross-pollination, on the other hand, increases genetic variability within species and is promoted by many plants in a variety of ways. In some species, unisexual (male or female) flowers are produced on separate plants. This condition is called *dioecy* and guarantees cross-pollination. Chemical reactions between the pollen and stigmas of the same plant prevent self-pollination in many species, usually by hindering germination of the pollen grains or preventing the growth of pollen tubes. Another, perhaps less effective method for ensuring cross-pollination involves the timing of maturation of stamens and pistils: in some species the anthers release pollen before the stigmas of the same plant are ready to receive it, or the stigma may be isolated from the mature pollen produced by the same plant because its styles have not yet elongated. Pollen is usually able to germinate for only a short period after being released from the anthers, and so these species are much more likely to be pollinated by another plant.

Wind and animals are the major agents of pollination. The flowers of wind-pollinated plants are usually small, greenish, lack fragrance, and have small petals or no petals. Oaks and grasses are examples of wind-pollinated plants. The wind generally does not carry pollen far, and so individual plants frequently grow close to one another to help guarantee pollination. Nevertheless, wind delivery of pollen to stigma is not a particularly precise procedure, and some plants have evolved more accurate pollination mechanisms: they employ animals as pollinators.

Flowers must be able to attract animals if animals are to be efficient pollinators. This has been accomplished through the evolution of flower colors, shapes, sizes, and fragrances that appeal to different animals. Plants use other strategies to lure pollinators to their flowers as well, including the production of sweet nectar and nutritious pollen. However, once an animal visits a flower and comes in contact with its pollen, it needs to visit another flower of the same species for pollination to occur. Inflorescences, more or less organized clusters of two or more flowers, may have evolved in many plants to ensure visits to different flowers. In some plant groups, such as the aster family, flowers have undergone a great deal of modification and are grouped together in "headlike" inflorescences that frequently look like a single flower. The sunflower, for example, is actually made up of hundreds of tiny, separate flowers.

Animal pollination has advantages for both the plants and their pollinators. The plants are able to disperse their pollen accurately and widely. The animal pollinators benefit by having a reliable and easily recognizable food source. The development of this relationship

## THE BIRDS AND THE BEES AND . . .

Birds do it, bees do it, and there are also a number of other mechanisms, called *syndromes*, by which plants are pollinated. The following are some of the common ways in which pollen is successfully transferred from anther to stigma.

- **Anemophily:** Pollination by wind.
- **Cantharophily:** Pollination by beetles.
- **Chiropterogamy:** Pollination by bats.
- **Cleistogamy:** Self-pollination within a closed flower.
- **Entomophily:** Pollination by insects.
- **Hydrophily:** Pollination by water.
- **Malacophily:** Pollination by slugs or snails.
- **Melittophily:** Pollination by bees.
- **Myophily:** Pollination by flies.
- **Myrmecophily:** Pollination by ants.
- **Ornithogamy:** Pollination by birds.
- **Phalaenophily:** Pollination by moths.
- **Psychophily:** Pollination by butterflies.
- **Zoophily:** Pollination by animals.

between plants and animals has been one of the most important factors in the evolution of both groups. This coevolution between plants and their animal pollinators has meant that flowers have become adapted to attract specific animals. For example, yellow flowers are primarily attractive to bees, while red flowers attract birds. Some plants produce nectar deep inside their flowers that can be reached only by hummingbirds (with their long bills) or long-tongued insects such as moths and butterflies. Once flowers have evolved to attract a specific pollinator, they must be able to continue to attract that particular pollinator or the chances for successful pollination will be drastically reduced.

## SOME PLANTS AND THEIR POLLINATORS

For a list of native plants attractive to pollinators, organized by region and season as well as by pollinator, see "Natural Gardening," page 180.

### FLOWERS POLLINATED BY BEETLES

Flowers are dull-colored or white, have sour or fruity odors, and have heavily protected ovules. A couple of examples:
*Calycanthus* species (Sweet shrubs)
*Paeonia* species (Peonies)

### FLOWERS POLLINATED BY BEES

Typically conspicuous and usually bright blue or yellow, never completely red. They frequently have "honey guides"—special patterns or markings that guide the visiting bees to the nectar within. Examples:

*Acer negundo* (box elder)
*Achillea millefolium* (yarrow)
*Aesculus pavia* (red buckeye)
*Caltha palustris* (marsh marigold)
*Coccoloba uvifera* (seagrape)
*Cornus florida* (flowering dogwood)
*Erica tetralix* (cross-leaved heath)
*Eschscholzia californica* (California poppy)
*Geraea canescens* (desert sunflower)
*Geum rivale* (water avens)
*Guaiacum sanctum* (lignum vitae)
*Hamamelis virginiana* (witchhazel)
*Oenothera biennis* (common evening primrose)
*Penstemon palmeri* (Palmer's penstemon)
*Phlox adsurgens* (phlox)
*Phlox paniculata* (fall phlox)
*Phlox subulata* (moss-pink)
*Piscidia piscipula* (Jamaica dogwood)

*Pithecellobium guadalupense* (blackbead)
*Potentilla fruticosa* (shrubby five-fingers)
*Quercus virginiana* (live oak)
*Ribes odoratum* (buffalo currant)
*Ribes sanguineum* (red flowering currant)
*Solidago* species (goldenrods)

### FLOWERS POLLINATED BY BUTTERFLIES AND MOTHS

Similar to bee flowers, mainly because both groups are guided to flowers by a combination of sight and smell. Some species of butterflies, however, are able to perceive red as a distinct color, and the flowers they favor are red and orange. The nectary of a moth or butterfly flower is often located at the base of a long, slender corolla tube or a spur and is usually accessible only to the long sucking mouthparts of these insects. Examples:

*Aloysia gratissima* (bee bush)
*Apocynum androsaemifolium* (spreading dogbane)
*Asclepias subulata* (desert milkweed)
*Asclepias tuberosa* (butterfly weed)
*Bebbia juncea* (Chuckwalla's delight)
*Calliandra eriophylla* (fairyduster)
*Ceanothus americanus* (New Jersey tea)
*Celtis pallida* (desert hackberry)
*Clethra alnifolia* (sweet pepperbush)
*Dalea frutescens* (indigo bush)
*Dalea greggii* (indigo bush)
*Echinacea purpurea* (purple coneflower)
*Eriogonum fasciculatum* (coastal buckwheat)
*Glandularia gooddingii* (verbena)
*Hyptis emoryi* (desert lavender)
*Lotus scoparius* (deerweed)
*Lycium andersonii* (wolfberry)
*Mimulus* species (monkeyflowers)

*Monarda fistulosa* (wild bergamot)
*Prosopis velutina* (velvet mesquite)
*Pycnanthemum muticum* (mountain mint)
*Senna covesii* (desert senna)
*Solidago* species (goldenrods)
*Thymophylla pentachaeta* var. *pentachaeta* (dyssodia)

### FLOWERS POLLINATED BY HUMMINGBIRDS

Typically contain large quantities of thin nectar rich in carbohydrates. Because hummingbirds have a poor sense of smell but an excellent sense of sight, the flowers they visit have little odor and are red or yellow. Examples:

*Anisacanthus thurberi* (desert honeysuckle)
*Aquilegia formosa* (red columbine)
*Astragalus coccineus* (scarlet locoweed)
*Calliandra eriophylla* (fairyduster)
*Castilleja angustifolia* (desert paintbrush)
*Castilleja sessiliflora* (downy paintbrush)
*Chilopsis linearis* (desert willow)
*Cynoglossum grande* (hound's-tongue)
*Delphinium cardinale* (cardinal larkspur)
*Delphinium nudicaule* (orange larkspur)
*Dicentra chrysantha* (golden eardrops)
*Erysimum capitatum* (western wallflower)
*Fouquieria splendens* (ocotillo)
*Justicia californica* (chuparosa)
*Kalmia latifolia* (mountain laurel)
*Lonicera sempervirens* (trumpet honeysuckle)
*Mertensia virginica* (eastern bluebells)
*Mimulus aurantiacus* (orange bush monkeyflower)
*Penstemon eatonii* (Eaton's beardtongue)
*Penstemon palmeri* (Palmer's penstemon)
*Penstemon pseudospectabilis* (Arizona penstemon)
*Phacelia campanularia* (desert bell)
*Sphaeralcea ambigua* (apricot mallow)
*Stanleya pinnata* (Prince's plum)

### FLOWERS POLLINATED BY BATS

Large, sturdy, dull-colored, and "fruity" scented, and contain large amounts of nectar. Bat pollination occurs mostly in tropical areas. Examples:

*Adansonia digitata* (baobab)
*Carnegiea gigantea* (saguaro)
*Kigelia pinnata* (sausage tree)
*Lemaireocereus* species (organ-pipe cacti)

### FLOWERS POLLINATED BY WIND

Usually have exposed stamens (which hold the pollen-bearing anthers) and correspondingly small, reduced, or entirely absent sepals and petals, and they are produced before the leaves. The stamens typically hold large amounts of pollen. The following list includes families of plants that are entirely or predominantly wind-pollinated.

Betulaceae (alders, birches, filberts, hazelnuts)
Cyperaceae (sedges)
Fagaceae (beeches, oaks)
Juglandaceae (hickories, walnuts)
Juncaceae (rushes)
Poaceae (grasses)
Ulmaceae (elms)
Urticaceae (nettles)

### FLOWERS POLLINATED BY WATER

Flowers of water-pollinated plants tend to be rather small and inconspicuous. This type of pollination is thought to be an advanced feature among angiosperms. Examples:

*Callitriche hamulata* (water starwort)
*Ceratophyllum* species (hornwort)
*Halophila* species (sea grass)
*Najas* species (naiad)

## PARTHENOCARPIC FRUITS

Fruits that develop from ovaries with unfertilized eggs are said to be parthenocarpic. Such fruits, which are seedless, are found in navel oranges, bananas, and certain varieties of figs and grapes.

Not all seedless fruits are parthenocarpic. In Thompson seedless grapes, for example, fertilization does occur, but the ovules fail to develop with the fruit. Parthenocarpy can be induced artificially by applying dilute hormone sprays to flowers; seedless tomatoes are often produced in this way. Seedless watermelons are produced by crossing varieties with different chromosome numbers. The hybrid that results from such a cross produces fruit, but the chromosomes cannot pair properly during meiosis, and so fertilization and seed formation do not occur.

## THE GIANT AND THE DIMINUTIVE

The smallest flowering plant: Duckweed (*Wolffia globosa*)—0.6 mm long

The largest flower: Rafflesia (*Rafflesia arnoldii*)—up to 3 feet in diameter

The smallest fruit: Duckweed (*Wolffia* species)—0.3 mm long

The largest fruit: Pumpkin (*Cucurbita pepo*)—as large as 1,000 pounds

The smallest seed: Species of epiphytic orchids of the tropical rain forests—the size of a dust particle

The largest seed: Coco-de-mer palm (*Lodoicea maldivica*)—as large as 12 inches long

## PROPAGATING FLOWERING PLANTS

Given their agricultural, horticultural, and overall economic importance, it is not surprising that the angiosperms have been the major focus of plant propagators, who have developed numerous propagation techniques (see "Propagation," page 474). For more detail on the propagation of flowering plants, consult *Propagation Handbook: Basic Techniques for Gardeners* (see "Further Reading," below).

### The Fruit

Fruits are the vehicles that disseminate (disperse) seeds away from the parent plant. Once a seed is released from its fruit and conditions are favorable for its germination, it can grow into a mature plant that produces its own flowers. It is important to remember that all the stages of this cycle (pollination, fertilization, seed and fruit production) take place in flowers. For more on fruits, see "Plant Structures," page 90.

## Further Reading

Armstrong, W. P. Wayne's Word. URL = http://www.palomar.edu/Wayne/

Bracegirdle, B., and P. H. Miles. *An Atlas of Plant Structure* vol. 1. London: Heinemann Educational Books, 1986.

Bracegirdle, B., and P. H. Miles. *An Atlas of Plant Structure* vol. 2. London: Heinemann Educational Books, 1988.

Bryant, G. *Propagation Handbook: Basic Techniques for Gardeners.* Mechanicsburg, Pa.: Stackpole Books, 1995.

Burrell, C. Colston, ed. *Ferns: Wild Things Make a Comeback in the Garden.* Brooklyn, N.Y.: Brooklyn Botanic Garden, 1994.

Capon, B. *Botany for Gardeners: An Introduction and Guide.* Portland, Ore.: Timber Press, 1990.

Fægri, K., and L. van der Pijl. *The Principles of Pollination Ecology.* 3rd rev. ed. Oxford, England: Pergamon Press, 1979.

Lellinger, D. B. *A Field Manual of the Ferns and Fern-allies of the United States & Canada.* Washington, D.C.: Smithsonian Institution Press, 1985.

Mickel, John. *Ferns for American Gardens.* New York: Macmillan Publishing Company, 1994.

Raven, P. H., R. F. Evert, and S. E. Eichhorn. *Biology of Plants.* 5th ed. New York: Worth Publishers, 1992.

Schenk, George. *Moss Gardening: Including Lichens, Liverworts, and Other Miniatures.* Portland, Ore.: Timber Press, 1997.

Stern, K. R. *Introductory Plant Biology.* 5th ed. Dubuque, Iowa: Wm. C. Brown Publishers, 1991.

Thompson, P. *Creative Propagation: A Grower's Guide.* Portland, Ore.: Timber Press, 1992.

# 4

# PLANT CONSERVATION

## PLANT DIVERSITY

The term "biodiversity" refers to the total variability of life on Earth. It includes the diversity of species, the genetic diversity within species, and the diversity of ecosystems that include various species.

The Convention on Biological Diversity, headquartered in Montreal, went into effect officially on December 29, 1993, providing the first comprehensive framework for conserving biodiversity around the globe. The convention emphasizes the importance of maintaining healthy ecosystems and the sustainable and equitable use of nature's goods and services. So far, more than 160 governments have ratified the convention.

### Basic Levels of Biodiversity

There are three basic levels of biodiversity: genetic diversity, species diversity, and ecosystem diversity. Genetic diversity refers to variation within and variation among populations of species. It is measured in terms of difference between genes or between DNA or amino acid sequences. All species require a diversity of genes spread among their populations if they are to retain their ability to adapt to changing environments. Genetic diversity also is necessary for food production, forestry, and new pharmaceuticals. It is the selection and manipulation of genetic variability in crop plants that provides the raw material for agriculture. Because genetic variation is the material from which new species evolve, it is also key to biodiversity over the long haul.

The species is the basic unit of classification commonly used by biologists; it can be defined as a group of individuals that are capable of breeding with each other (see "Botany for Gardeners," page 39). While for many purposes species are the basic unit of biodiversity, it is important to note that they are made up of populations. The local breeding population is the fundamental unit on which natural selection and evolution operate. Individuals within a population contain genetic information, and it is this genetic diversity that determines the population's evolutionary fate and therefore underlies species diversity.

Species do not exist in isolation but rather in a wide array of ecological groupings. On the largest scale, the Earth's natural vegetation is divided into large areas of forest, grassland, and desert called *plant provinces*, or *biomes*. Each plant province is a plant community on a grand scale containing many smaller communities within its borders. For instance, the great sea of grass that once covered the central United States and south-central Canada included both tall- and shortgrass prairies as well as riverside communities. In the same way, different groups of plants predominate in "cold" and "hot" deserts of the West. What is more, within one of the

warm deserts, such as the Sonoran Desert, the assemblages of plants growing in relatively moist areas like arroyos are different from those found in dry, open, exposed expanses (see "Gardener's Atlas," page 14).

## Distribution of Diversity

Plants occur over most of the Earth's land surface, but the distribution of species is distinctly uneven. Distribution is affected by environmental factors including climate, soils, and topography. Knowing the distribution of species enables scientists to establish criteria and guidelines for their conservation and ecologically sustainable use.

Botanists have collected the most data on plant species found in countries with relatively low diversity. Britain's flora has probably been studied more extensively and better inventoried than that of any other country, while in many tropical countries, only a handful of botanists

---

### SPECIES DIVERSITY BY PLANT GROUP

250,000+ Flowering plants
700 Conifers and allies
12,000 Ferns, horsetails, and allies
22,000 Mosses and liverworts
25,000+ Algae
70,000+ Fungi
18,000+ Lichens

---

### DISTRIBUTION OF HIGHER PLANT SPECIES BY CONTINENT

| | |
|---|---|
| Central & South America | 85,000 |
| Tropical & Subtropical Africa | 40,000–45,000 |
| North Africa | 10,000 |
| Tropical Africa | 21,000 |
| Southern Africa | 21,000 |
| Tropical & Subtropical Asia | 50,000 |
| India | 15,000 |
| Malaysia | 30,000 |
| China | 25,000 |
| North America | 18,000 |
| Europe | 12,500 |

are studying tens of thousands of plants. Often, once a plant has been named or described, it is not seen again for years. Almost nothing is known about the distribution of immense numbers of tropical plants.

## Diversity Hotspots Around the World

In 1988, British ecologist Norman Myers published an article in which he identified international conservation priorities on the basis of "hotspots," or areas exhibiting high degrees of species richness (numbers of species), endemism (taxa that are restricted to a particular area and occur nowhere else), and threats to them. At the time, Myers identified ten hotspots, all tropical forest regions that together contained at least 14 percent of the world's plants. Although tropical forests cover only 7 percent of the Earth's surface, they contain a significant proportion of its biodiversity.

Within the temperate zones of the United States, species richness is highest in California, Texas, Arizona, Oregon, and Florida.

The World Conservation Monitoring Centre, in collaboration with the World Wildlife Fund, has identified 250 sites of high plant-species diversity concentrated in northwestern South America, Central America, tropical Africa, the eastern Mediterranean, and Southeast Asia/Malaysia. Information on the sites is extensively documented in the three-volume set *Centres of Plant Diversity: A Guide and Strategy for Their Conservation* (see "Further Reading," page 122). Criteria for selection is based primarily on species richness and degree of endemism. Other important factors include potential value to humans, diversity of habitats in a particular site, and imminent threat of large-scale devastation.

## Endemic Plants

*Endemism*, the occurrence of species within narrow geographical ranges, is second in impor-

### GLOBALLY RARE HABITAT TYPES

According to the World Wildlife Fund, the following are naturally rare major habitat types:

| Habitat Type | Countries |
| --- | --- |
| Pacific temperate rain forest | United States & Canada |
| Validivian temperate rain forest | Chile |
| Tasmanian temperate rain forest | Australia |
| Chilean matorral | Chile |
| Fynbos | South Africa |
| Mediterranean region shrubland | Crete, Cyprus, Greece, Spain |
| Kwongan heathland | Australia |

# PLANT DIVERSITY BY ECOLOGICAL REGION

According to the World Wildlife Fund, the following ecological regions have the highest number of plant species:

| Ecological Region | Countries |
|---|---|
| Atlantic moist forest complex | Argentina, Brazil, Paraguay |
| Northern Andean moist forest | Colombia, Ecuador, Venezuela |
| Choco-Darien moist forest | Colombia, Ecuador, Panama |
| Napo moist forest of Amazon & Orinoco basins | Colombia, Ecuador, Peru |
| Sumatra, Mentawai, & Nicobar Islands moist forest | Indonesia, India |
| Fynbos | South Africa |
| Kwongan heathland | Australia |

The World Wildlife Fund rates the following ecological regions as being second highest in plant species globally:

| Ecological Region | Countries |
|---|---|
| Central and southern Andean yunga | Bolivia, Colombia, Ecuador, Peru, Venezuela |
| Peninsular Malaysia forests | Malaysia |
| New Guinea lowland moist forest | Indonesia, Papua New Guinea |
| Southern Mexican dry forest | Mexico |
| Madagascar dry forest | Madagascar |
| Mexican pine-oak forest | Mexico, Guatemala |
| Appalachian Mountains & mixed mesophytic forest | United States |
| Southeastern coniferous forest/sand pine scrub & pine rockland (highest herbaceous richness anywhere) | United States |
| Caucasus & northeast Anatolia temperate forest | Georgia, Azerbaijan, Turkey |
| Temperate forest of Sichuan & southern Yunnan | China |
| North American mixed- & tallgrass prairie | United States |
| Sonoran, Baja, & Sinaloan cactus scrub & xeric shrubland | Mexico & United States |
| Chihuahuan, Pueblan cactus scrub, northern & central Mexican cactus scrub & xeric shrubland | Mexico & United States |

According to the World Wildlife Fund, the following is the most species-rich boreal forest region:

Northwest Canadian boreal forest

According to the World Wildlife Fund, the following are the most species-rich Arctic tundra regions:

| | |
|---|---|
| Alaskan North Slope coastal tundra | United States & Canada |
| Chukotsky coastal tundra | Russia |

tance only to species richness as a measure of biodiversity. Endemic plants are native to a particular place and found only there. Centers of endemism are areas where many endemic species occur together. Endemism correlates generally but not exclusively with species rich-ness. The greatest numbers of endemics occur on islands, on mountain peaks, around desert springs, and in other unusual and isolated habitats. Arid zones are particularly rich in endemic succulent plants. Serpentine soils (composed primarily of hydrated magnesium silicate) typ-

## ECOLOGICAL REGIONS WITH THE MOST ENDEMIC PLANTS

According to the World Wildlife Fund, the following ecological regions have the highest percentage of endemic plants:

| Ecological Region | Country |
| --- | --- |
| Madagascar moist forest | Madagascar |
| New Caledonian moist forest | New Caledonia |
| Hawaii moist forest | United States |
| Madagascar dry forest | Madagascar |
| New Caledonia dry forest | New Caledonia |
| Hawaii dry forest | United States |
| Mexican pine-oak forest | Mexico, Guatemala |
| Fynbos | South Africa |
| Kwongan heathland | Australia |

According to the World Wildlife Fund, the following ecological regions have the second-highest percentage of endemic plants:

| Ecological Region | Country |
| --- | --- |
| Atlantic moist forest complex | Argentina, Brazil, Paraguay |
| Northern Andean moist forest complex | Colombia, Ecuador, Venezuela |
| Napo moist forest | Colombia, Ecuador, Peru |
| Guyanese highlands moist forest | Brazil, Guyana, Venezuela |
| Eastern Arc mountain | Kenya, Malawi, Mozambique, Tanzania |
| Congolese coastal forest | Cameroon, Congo, equatorial Guinea, Gabon, Nigeria |
| Southwest Sri Lankan moist forest | Sri Lanka |
| Sulawesi moist forest | Indonesia |
| Southern Mexican dry forest | Mexico |
| Klamath-Siskiyou coniferous forest | United States |
| Cerrado savannah | Bolivia, Brazil |
| Northern Andean paramo | Colombia, Ecuador, Venezuela |
| Spiny woodland | Madagascar |

# PLANT DIVERSITY BY STATE AND PROVINCE

Traditionally, biologists have measured plant-species diversity by counting the number of native or indigenous species in a particular area. Native species are those that have become distributed across the landscape in response to climatic episodes and adaptation to site conditions and related land formations. In North America, natives are generally defined as plants that occurred here just prior to European settlement; this distinction is made because of the large-scale changes in the flora that have resulted since that time and the accompanying introduction of nonnative plants. Scientists do not yet know how such plant introductions will affect biodiversity in the long term.

The following is a list of the estimated numbers of native and introduced species of vascular plants in North America north of Mexico. The data was provided by Dr. John Kartesz of the Biota of North America Program of the North Carolina Botanical Garden. (In a very few cases, the total number of introduced and native species does not equal the total number of species, due to the presence of species in those states whose origin is uncertain.)

| State, Territory, or Province | Introduced Species | Native | Total |
| --- | --- | --- | --- |
| Alabama | 616 | 3000 | 3616 |
| Alaska | 179 | 1368 | 1547 |
| Arizona | 371 | 3600 | 3972 |
| Arkansas | 484 | 2263 | 2747 |
| California | 1122 | 5589 | 6711 |
| Colorado | 382 | 2667 | 3049 |
| Connecticut | 768 | 1914 | 2682 |
| Delaware | 468 | 1756 | 2224 |
| Florida | 979 | 3285 | 4266 |
| Georgia | 587 | 3127 | 3714 |
| Hawaii | 773 | 1504 | 2280 |
| Idaho | 383 | 2451 | 2834 |
| Illinois | 733 | 2379 | 3112 |
| Indiana | 528 | 2151 | 2679 |
| Iowa | 413 | 1685 | 2098 |
| Kansas | 410 | 1807 | 2217 |
| Kentucky | 592 | 2124 | 2716 |
| Louisiana | 703 | 2494 | 3197 |
| Maine | 627 | 1778 | 2405 |
| Maryland | 786 | 2323 | 3109 |
| Massachusetts | 1032 | 2116 | 3148 |
| Michigan | 736 | 2188 | 2924 |
| Minnesota | 403 | 1865 | 2268 |
| Mississippi | 461 | 2407 | 2868 |
| Missouri | 577 | 2190 | 2767 |

(continued on next page)

| State, Territory, or Province | Introduced Species | Native | Total |
|---|---|---|---|
| Montana | 372 | 2247 | 2619 |
| Nebraska | 317 | 1596 | 1913 |
| Nevada | 306 | 2909 | 3215 |
| New Hampshire | 511 | 1686 | 2197 |
| New Jersey | 807 | 2276 | 3083 |
| New Mexico | 333 | 3377 | 3710 |
| New York | 1115 | 2527 | 3642 |
| North Carolina | 701 | 2939 | 3640 |
| North Dakota | 300 | 1219 | 1519 |
| Ohio | 700 | 2148 | 2848 |
| Oklahoma | 355 | 2399 | 2754 |
| Oregon | 682 | 3212 | 3894 |
| Pennsylvania | 1031 | 2372 | 3403 |
| Rhode Island | 489 | 1490 | 1979 |
| South Carolina | 526 | 2638 | 3164 |
| South Dakota | 295 | 1516 | 1811 |
| Tennessee | 552 | 2444 | 2996 |
| Texas | 692 | 4663 | 5356 |
| Utah | 495 | 2976 | 3471 |
| Vermont | 584 | 1723 | 2307 |
| Virginia | 748 | 2730 | 3478 |
| Washington | 568 | 2484 | 3052 |
| West Virginia | 526 | 1914 | 2440 |
| Wisconsin | 526 | 1969 | 2495 |
| Wyoming | 336 | 2302 | 2638 |
| Puerto Rico | 675 | 2453 | 3131 |
| Virgin Islands | 261 | 1028 | 1289 |
| Alberta | 312 | 1676 | 1988 |
| British Columbia | 645 | 2386 | 3031 |
| District of Franklin | 7 | 346 | 353 |
| District of Keewatin | 11 | 536 | 547 |
| District of MacKenzie | 75 | 1035 | 1110 |
| Greenland | 131 | 520 | 651 |
| Labrador | 89 | 767 | 856 |
| Manitoba | 308 | 1407 | 1715 |
| New Brunswick | 455 | 1295 | 1750 |

| State, Territory, or Province | Introduced Species | Native | Total |
|---|---|---|---|
| Newfoundland | 362 | 1068 | 1430 |
| Nova Scotia | 495 | 1255 | 1750 |
| Ontario | 848 | 2356 | 3204 |
| Prince Edward Island | 298 | 794 | 1092 |
| Quebec | 671 | 2065 | 2736 |
| Saskatchewan | 263 | 1309 | 1572 |
| St. Pierre-et-Miquelon | 171 | 531 | 702 |
| Yukon Territory | 102 | 1081 | 1183 |

ically support many endemic species wherever they occur, but particularly in the tropics.

Of the 250,000 vascular plant species, 170,000 are tropical or subtropical endemics. In the United States, states with the highest numbers of endemic plants generally have the highest plant-species richness, except for Hawaii, which has the second highest number of endemics but the fourth lowest number of native plant species. This high degree of endemism is a consequence of Hawaii's isolation, which has enabled unique and complex ecosystems that include large numbers of endemics to evolve. Because the endemics on oceanic islands have evolved in relative isolation over thousands of years, they are particularly vulnerable to change wrought by humans and introduced species.

## Crop Plant Diversity

Crops are domesticated organisms that have arisen by human and natural selection from wild plant species. Earlier in this century, the Russian scientist Nikolai Vavilov, a geneticist and plant geographer, studied extensive collec-tions of cultivated plants in the less developed parts of the world where the indigenous crop varieties had not been replaced by cultivars selected by plant breeders. He arrived at a theory on the centers of genetic diversity of different crops, which he believed were their centers of origin. All of them were located in mountainous regions with an ancient agricultural civilization.

Although subsequent scientists found that Vavilov's centers of crop diversity were not necessarily the crops' centers of origin, the concept of regions of genetic diversity has proved of great significance in the study of the evolution of crop species and in efforts to preserve food-plant diversity.

As crops were moved by humans, species were modified by the environment and by cultural methods; gene pools were diversified; and secondary centers of diversity evolved. The dispersal of genes was accompanied by selection pressures that made the crops resistant to local pests and pathogens and tolerant of different environmental conditions. These distinctive races that became locally adapted to their new environments are known as *landraces*. In the past century or so, "advanced cultivars" that are the products of scientific plant breeding have

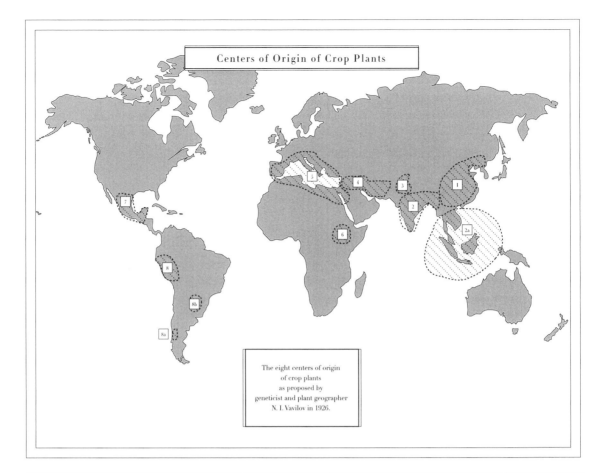

Centers of Origin of Crop Plants

The eight centers of origin
of crop plants
as proposed by
geneticist and plant geographer
N. I. Vavilov in 1926.

## DOMESTICATED CROPS BY PLANT FAMILY

Of the 511 plant families currently recognized, only 173 have domesticated representatives. The following families have large numbers of domesticated species:

| Plant Family | Number of Crops | Area of Origin |
|---|---|---|
| Poaceae (Gramineae) | 379 | Mostly Near East & Africa |
| Leguminosae (Fabaceae) | 337 | Indochina-Indonesia, Mediterranean Coast & adjacent regions, Central America |
| Rosaceae | 158 | Mainly China & Europe-Siberia |
| Solanaceae | 115 | Central America & Peru-Chile |

The following plant families also have made a notable contribution to the total number of plant domesticates:

| | |
|---|---|
| Asteraceae (Compositae) | 86 |
| Cucurbitaceae | 53 |
| Labiatae | 52 |
| Rutaceae | 44 |
| Brassicaceae (Cruciferae) | 43 |
| Apiaceae (Umbelliferae) | 41 |
| Chenopodiaceae | 34 |
| Zingiberaceae | 3 |
| Palmae | 30 |

# AREAS WHERE CROPS WERE DOMESTICATED

The crops in parentheses were probably domesticated independently in different areas.

**NORTH AMERICA**
Sunflower
Tepary bean

**MESOAMERICA**
Maize
Tomato
Sieva bean
Scarlet runner bean
Cotton
Avocado
Papaya
Cacao
(Cassava)
(Sweet potato)
(Common bean)

**LOWLAND SOUTH AMERICA**
Yam
Pineapple
(Cassava)
(Sweet potato)
(Cotton)

**HIGHLAND SOUTH AMERICA**
Potato
Peanut
Lima bean
(Cotton bean)
(Cotton)

**EUROPE**
Oats
Sugarbeet
Rye
Cabbage
(Grapes)
(Olive)

**AFRICA**
African rice
Sorghum
Pearl millet
Yam
Watermelon
Cowpea
Coffee
(Cotton?)
(Sesame?)

**NEAR EAST**
Wheat
Barley
Onion
Pea
Lentil
Chickpea
Fig
Date
Flax
Pear
Pomegranate
(Grapes)
(Olive)
Apple?

**CENTRAL ASIA**
Common millet
Buckwheat
Alfalfa
(Foxtail millet)
(Grapes)
Broad bean?

**INDIA**
Pigeonpea
Eggplant
Cucumber
(Cotton?)
(Sesame?)

**CHINA**
Soybean
Cabbage
Onion
Peach
(Foxtail millet)

**SOUTHEAST ASIA**
Oriental rice
Banana
Citrus
Yam
Mango
Thin sugarcane
Taro
Tea

**SOUTH PACIFIC**
Noble sugarcane
Coconut
Breadfruit

been developed and increasingly have replaced the myriad, locally adapted landraces.

The diversity of many crop plants reached its peak around the end of the nineteenth century. This diversity is now at risk, and the gene pool of many crops is eroding, mainly due to the development of highly uniform cultivars. This uniformity has led to epidemic outbreaks of diseases and the need for constant development of new, disease-resistant varieties. The search for new varieties obliges breeders to search outside the narrow gene pool of modern varieties to older varieties and wild relatives of the crop. Nearly all modern crop varieties contain genetic material recently incorporated from wild species or from more primitive genetic stocks still used and maintained by traditional agricultural peoples.

Many organizations, including the Consultative Group on International Agricultural Research (CGIAR), are actively working to preserve crop diversity (see "Vanishing Plants," below).

## Further Reading

*Centres of Plant Diversity: A Guide and Strategy for Their Conservation.* Published in three volumes jointly by the World Conservation Monitoring Centre and the World Wildlife Fund, 1996.

Dobson, Andrew. *Conservation and Biodiversity.* New York: Scientific American Library, 1996.

Frankel, Otto H., Anthony H. D. Brown, and Jeremy J. Burdon. *The Conservation of Plant Biodiversity.* Cambridge, England; New York: Cambridge University Press, 1995.

Heywood, V. H., executive ed. *Global Biodiversity Assessment.* Cambridge, England; New York: Cambridge University Press, 1995.

Johnson, Nels. *Biodiversity in the Balance.* Washington, D.C.: World Resources Institute, 1995.

Kartesz, J. T. *Biodiversity Network News.* 5(3):6, 1992.

Marinelli, Janet. *Stalking the Wild Amaranth: Gardening in the Age of Extinction.* New York: Henry Holt and Company, 1998.

Noss, Reed F., and Allen Cooperrider. *Saving Nature's Legacy.* Washington, D.C.: Island Press, 1994.

Simon, Noel. *Nature in Danger.* New York: Oxford University Press, 1995.

Soule, M. E., ed. *Conservation Biology.* Sunderland, Mass.: Sinauer Associates, 1986.

# VANISHING PLANTS

Given current statistics regarding the exploding human population and the resulting loss of habitat, scientists estimate that nearly 34,000 vascular plants—more than 12 percent of the world's estimated 270,000 species of ferns, conifers, and flowering plants—are threatened. As the human population continues to grow, requiring more land for agriculture, fuel, timber, and housing, natural habitats inevitably will continue to shrink, putting at risk an increasing number of plant and animal species. By the year 2050, the current world population of 5.7 billion is expected to reach 9.8 billion. The populations of many North African countries are expected to double in the next quarter century; those in Asia, in about 35 years.

Climate change due to global warming, caused by the emissions of carbon dioxide, primarily from the burning of fossil fuels, chlorofluorocarbons, and other gases, is another significant threat to plants. The Inter-Governmental Panel on Climate Change, a network of more than 2,000 scientists and policy experts assembled by the United Nations to advise governments on climate policy, predicts that in the absence of any change in human behavior, the mean global temperature is likely to rise by 1 to 2 degrees Celsius by the year 2030, leading to drastic changes in rainfall and vegetation patterns. According to some studies, the ranges of many plants would be forced to shift northward at an unprecedented rate to keep pace with changing conditions. Many species would fail to survive.

Invasive species pose another serious threat to plant populations. Any time a nonnative plant or seed is transported across oceans or great expanses of land, it has the potential to drive out indigenous species and, in the worst-case scenarios, radically alter native ecosystems in its new location.

Finally, commercial overcollection from the wild of various bulbs, cacti, and orchids threatens to decrease the populations of some wild species to the point of endangerment.

As plant species are lost, any potential benefits they may harbor as medicine or food also vanishes. The World Health Organization estimates that 80 percent of the planet's people still depend on traditional medicine for their primary health care needs. What is more, an estimated 70 percent of the drugs used in modern medicine are modeled on natural compounds. These are derived from approximately 250 plant species. By one estimate, fewer than 0.1 percent of the 250,000 species of vascular plants have been screened for their medicinal properties.

Aside from any direct advantages they may hold for humans, plants also play a fundamental role in the survival of the ecosystems that support all life on the planet. Most ecosystems are naturally diverse. The diverse web of life in a natural forest or prairie has built-in redundancy and therefore resiliency. According to the latest evidence, the ability of natural systems to

rebound from changing environmental conditions such as global warming depends on this species redundancy; in other words, species diversity is an insurance policy that can cushion the shocks to an ecosystem.

The World Conservation Union, or IUCN (formerly named the International Union for the Conservation of Nature), an England-based umbrella organization of over 800 government research institutions and private conservation groups, maintains the most comprehensive database on the world's endangered plants. In the 1960s, the organization first compiled its comprehensive "Red Data Books" to provide information on the distribution of species and to draw attention to rare and endangered taxa. Although the books successfully monitored the status of birds and mammals, plants and invertebrates have been less thoroughly covered until recently.

The number of plant species that the IUCN estimates are in danger may be much higher, because in many tropical countries, where large numbers of plants are threatened, botanists have not yet been yet able to determine the status of many species. In addition, a staggeringly high 91 percent of the listed species are limited in their geographical distribution to a single country.

According to the IUCN definition, "threatened" is a general term to denote species that are endangered, vulnerable, rare, or categorized as "indeterminate," meaning that there is insufficient information to indicate which of the first three categories is appropriate. In determining if a species is threatened, scientists take into account whether it is found in small populations in limited areas; whether it grows in large populations but only in a few remaining areas; whether it occurs over a wide range but is vulnerable to competition from invasive plants;

and whether it is commonly cultivated but nearly extinct in its native habitat.

There is particular concern over threats to tropical rain forests, because they are home to as many as half the world's plants. Clear-cutting for timber is considered to be the biggest threat to rain forests, particularly in South America and Africa. Clear-cutting not only destroys the large canopy trees but also the smaller plants that depend on them for shade and moisture, and it opens up the forest to further encroachment by agricultural settlers who continue the destruction through slash-and-burn farming.

Estimates on the loss of rain forests vary, but all concur that the destruction continues at a rapid rate. According to recent calculations of the U.N. Food and Agriculture Organization, tropical closed forests were being destroyed at a rate of at least 110.5 million hectares (272.9 million acres) per year. In some countries, such as the Philippines, the logging industry has destroyed virtually all of the forests. The Atlantic coastal forest of Brazil is 99 percent gone, and satellite monitoring indicates that the pace of deforestation in the Amazon actually increased 34 percent between 1991 and 1994. The forest of Madagascar has been reduced to about 2 percent of its original cover. All told, about 40 percent of the world's tropical rain forests have been converted to some other type of habitat. The World Resources Institute, an environmental think tank, estimates that at current rates of deforestation, 4 to 8 percent of rain forest species could be extinct by 2015, and 17 to 35 percent by 2040.

## Rare Plants

Rarity and endangerment are not synonymous. Rarity refers to the pattern of distribution and abundance of a species, while endangerment refers to factors that make a species vulnerable to decline and extinction. In other words, just because a plant is rare does not necessarily mean it is endangered. However, rare species are generally more vulnerable to endangerment and extinction than common ones are. Some common species are in jeopardy due to exotic pests or diseases. For example, virtually all adult American chestnut trees (*Castanea dentata*) in the United States have been attacked by a fungus imported from Asia in the early part of the century. Although the roots survive and resprout, the tops are killed by the disease before they can mature, and so the trees cannot reproduce. Commercial exploitation by collection has reduced the numbers of common species such as various cacti, including the saguaro (*Carnegiea gigantea*), and American ginseng (*Panax quinquefolius*).

There are several kinds of rarity: plants may occur only in rare habitats; they may be very localized in a small area; or they may have few individuals. All commonly occurring species are rare somewhere, usually at the peripheries of their geographic ranges. Although scientists are concerned about the increasing extirpation of local populations of many plants and its effect on these species' gene pools, it is important to distinguish between the plants that are rare locally and those that are rare globally, because the latter are in greater immediate danger of extinction.

## Vanishing Plants in the United States

The United States is home to an estimated 18,000 to 22,000 different species of vascular plants. The Center for Plant Conservation

(CPC), an umbrella organization of various botanical gardens working to preserve native plants, estimates that between 4,000 and 5,000 species native to the United States are of "some conservation concern." This includes species officially listed as endangered or threatened by the federal government, as well as others considered rare by botanists. The CPC has identified as many as 700 species that may become extinct in the next ten years, primarily due to the destruction or degradation of natural habitats and the overcollection of unusual plants such as orchids and cacti.

Some North American ecosystems are more endangered than tropical rain forests, particularly old-growth forests of the Pacific Northwest, and stand to lose as great a proportion of their species. Grasslands and savannahs are generally the most endangered terrestrial ecosystems in the United States, primarily due to conversion to agricultural uses, fire suppression, overgrazing, and invasion by exotics. An estimated 2.6 million acres of wetlands in the contiguous United States were lost between the mid-1970s and the mid-1980s. About 54 percent of this loss was due to agricultural conversion. Over half of the estimated 221 million acres of wetlands present in colonial times no longer exist. In California alone, 10 million acres of natural habitat were converted to agricultural or urban uses before 1950. An additional 5 million acres were converted between 1950 and 1980.

A national survey completed by the Center for Plant Conservation found that more than three-quarters of the endangered plant species in the United States occur in just five areas: California, Hawaii, Texas, Florida, and Puerto Rico/Virgin Islands—areas with temperate to tropical climates and varied terrain; 93 percent of all plants listed by the U.S. Fish and Wildlife

Service as endangered occur in those same areas. As a result, the CPC designated these five areas as conservation priority regions in need of intensive conservation efforts.

## Endangered Species Act

In 1973, the U.S. Congress passed the Endangered Species Act, directing the Secretary of the Interior to protect any plant or animal found on the basis of scientific evidence to be threatened with extinction. The decision to list a species as endangered is made upon the recommendation of the U.S. Fish and Wildlife Service when any one of the five following conditions is met:

- The destruction of its habitat is in progress or threatened.
- The species is being overexploited (individuals are being destroyed faster than they can be replaced) for commercial, recreational, scientific, or educational purposes.
- It is suffering losses from disease or predation.
- Existing laws and regulations are inadequate to protect the species.
- There are "other natural or man-made factors affecting its continued existence."

The initial list of plants was established in 1977. A plant is classified as "endangered" if it is in danger of extinction throughout all or a significant portion of its range. It is classified as "threatened" if the species is likely to become endangered within the near future throughout all or a significant portion of its range.

Once a species has been designated endangered or threatened, the act prohibits (with only a few narrow exceptions) anyone from collecting, maliciously endangering, or destroying it on federal land. The act also mandates that a plan be developed and implemented to aid the species's recovery.

## THE MOST IMPERILED PLANTS OF
## THE CONTINENTAL UNITED STATES

The following list of vascular plants occurring in the continental U.S. are ranked "G1" by The Nature Conservancy (TNC), a forty-year-old organization that owns and operates the largest private system of nature sanctuaries in the world. A G1 ranking indicates the highest level of concern for a species. G1 species are those having five or fewer extant natural occurrences anywhere, or 1,000 or fewer mature individuals in their entire natural range.

TNC's State Natural Heritage Inventory programs, established in 1974, typically administered by state agencies, identify rare species and natural communities and their locations within a particular state. The scientific information gathered by the inventory indicates the relative rarity of plant and animal species and aquatic and terrestrial communities, and whether or not they are protected. Once species are identified and ranked, the areas that harbor critically threatened species become the target of TNC's preservation efforts. TNC's international headquarters is located at 1815 North Lynn Street, Arlington, VA 22209; telephone (703) 841-1283.

Note: These rankings are continually updated. This list was current as of August 16, 1996.

### SCIENTIFIC NAME, COMMON NAME—
### DISTRIBUTION

*Abronia macrocarpa*, large-fruited sand verbena—TX

*Acanthomintha duttonii*, San Mateo thornmint—CA

*Agalinis acuta*, sandplain gerardia—CT, MA, MD, NY, RI

*Amsinckia grandiflora*, large-flowered fiddleneck—CA

*Amsonia kearneyana*, Kearney's slimpod—AZ

*Arctomecon humilis*, dwarf bear-poppy—UT

*Arenaria paludicola*, marsh sandwort—CA

*Asimina tetramera*, four-petal pawpaw—FL

*Astragalus albens*, Cushenbury milk-vetch—CA

*Astragalus applegatei*, Applegate's milk-vetch—OR

*Astragalus bibullatus*, Pyne's ground-plum—TN

*Astragalus humillimus*, Mancos milk-vetch—CO, NM

*Astragalus osterhoutii*, Osterhout milk-vetch—CO

*Astrophytum asterias*, star cactus—TX, Mexico

*Baptisia arachnifera*, hairy rattleweed—GA

*Campanula robinsiae*, Brooksville bellflower—FL

*Cardamine micranthera*, small-anthered bitter-cress—NC

*Ceanothus ferrisae*, coyote ceanothus—CA

*Chorizanthe howellii*, Howell's spineflower—CA

*Chorizanthe valida*, Sonoma spineflower—CA

*Chrysopsis floridana*, Florida golden aster—FL

*Clarkia franciscana*, Presidio clarkia—CA

*Clematis morefieldii*, Morefield's leather flower—AL, Tennessee Valley

*Clematis socialis*, Alabama leather flower—AL, Tennesee Valley

*Conradina etonia*, Etonia rosemary—FL

*Conradina glabra*, Apalachicola rosemary—AL, FL

*Cordylanthus palmatus*, palmate-bracted bird's-beak—CA, Mexico

*Crotalaria avonensis*, Avon Park harebells—FL

*Cryptantha crassipes*, Terlingua Creek cat's-eye—TX

*Cupressus abramsiana*, Santa Cruz cypress—CA

*Deeringothamnus pulchellus*, beautiful pawpaw—FL

*Deeringothamnus rugelii*, Rugel's pawpaw—FL

*Dicerandra christmanii*, Garrett's mint—FL

*Dicerandra cornutissima*, long-spurred mint—FL

*Dicerandra frutescens*, scrub mint—FL

*Dicerandra immaculata*, Lakela's mint—FL

*Dodecahema leptoceras*, slender-horned spineflower—CA

*Dudleya traskiae*, Santa Barbara Island dudleya—CA

*Eriophyllum latilobum*, San Mateo woolly-sunflower—CA

*Eryngium cuneifolium*, wedge-leaved button-snakeroot—FL, GA

*Erythronium propullans*, Minnesota trout lily—MN

*Escobaria minima*, Nellie Cory cactus—TX

*Geum radiatum*, spreading avens—NC, Tennessee Valley

*Glaucocarpum suffrutescens*, toad-flax cress—UT

*Harperocallis flava*, Harper's beauty—FL

*Hoffmannseggia tenella*, slender rush-pea—TX

*Ipomopsis sancti-spiritus*, Holy Ghost ipomopsis—NM

*Isoetes louisianensis*, Louisiana quillwort—LA, GA, MS

*Isoetes melanospora*, black-spored quillwort—AL, GA, SC

*Isoetes tegetiformans*, Merlin's grass—NC, GA

*Jacquemontia reclinata*, beach jacquemontia—FL

*Lasthenia burkei*, Burke's goldfields—CA

*Layia carnosa*, beach layia—CA

*Lepidium barnebyanum*, Barneby ridge-cress—UT

*Lesquerella pallida*, white bladderpod—TX

*Lilium occidentale*, western lily—OR, CA

*Malacothamnus clementinus*, San Clemente Island broom—CA

*Manihot walkerae*, Walker's manioc—TX, Mexico

*Nitrophila mohavensis*, Amargosa niterwort—CA, NV

*Rhododendron chapmanii*, Chapman rhododendron—FL

*Rorippa gambellii*, Gambel's watercress—CA

*Sagittaria fasciculata*, bunched arrowhead—NC, SC

*Schoenocrambe barnebyi*, Barneby reed-mustard—UT

*Sclerocactus wrightiae*, Wright fishhook cactus—UT

*Sidalcea pedata*, pedate checker-mallow—CA

*Solidago shortii*, Short's goldenrod—KY

*Stanfordia californica*, California jewelflower—CA

*Stephanomeria malheurensis*, Malheur wire-lettuce—OR

*Streptanthus niger*, Tiburon jewelflower—CA

*Styrax texanus*, Texas snowbells—TX

*Suaeda californica*, California seablite—CA

*Swallenia alexandrae*, Eureka dune grass—CA

*Thalictrum cooleyi*, Cooley's meadowrue—FL, NC

*Thelypodium stenopetalum*, slender-petaled mustard—CA

*Thymophylla tephroleuca*, ashy dogweed—TX

*Torreya taxifolia*, Florida torreya—FL, GA, NC

*Trillium persistens*, persistent trillium—GA, SC

*Tuctoria mucronata*, Solano grass—CA

*Warea amplexifolia*, wide-leaf warea—FL

*Xyris tennesseensis*, Tennessee yellow-eyed grass—AL, GA, TN

*Zizania texana*, Texas wild-rice—TX

*Ziziphus celata*, Florida ziziphus—FL

The Endangered Species Office of the U.S. Fish and Wildlife Service is responsible for identifying threatened and endangered species both in the United States and abroad. However, of the 529 plants listed as threatened or endangered, only three occur outside of U.S. borders. According to the Endangered Species Office, this is because of an informal decision to concentrate on the United States, where they have a better information base and more ability to act within the agency's own jurisdiction.

In the United States, 500, or over half, of the officially listed endangered species are plants. Generally, about fifty new plant species are added annually, the majority of these in the western states, particularly in Hawaii and California.

# THE MOST IMPERILED PLANTS
# OF HAWAII

It is estimated that in the last 100 years about 100 plant species, or 10 percent of Hawaii's 1,093 native species, have become extinct. One-third of the plants listed as endangered by the U.S. Fish and Wildlife Service occur in Hawaii. One hundred eighty-two of Hawaii's taxa have 100 or fewer individual specimens left. The following plants were ranked G1 by The Nature Conservancy's Hawaii Heritage Program as of August 16, 1996. (Common names are not included in this list because Hawaiian plants rarely have them.)

*Abutilon eremitopetalum*
*Abutilon menziesii*
*Adenophorus periens*
*Alsinidendron obovatum*
*Alsinidendron trinerve*
*Argyroxiphium kauense*
*Asplenium rhom-
    boideum*
*Bidens wiebkei*
*Brighamia insignis*
*Brighamia rockii*
*Caesalpinia kavaiensis*
*Canavalia molokaiensis*
*Centaurium sebaeoides*
*Chamaesyce deppeana*
*Chamaesyce halemanui*
*Chamesyce kuwaleana*
*Clermontia lindseyana*
*Clermontia peleana*
*Clermontia pyrularia*
*Colubrina oppositifolia*
*Ctenitis squamigera*
*Cyanea asarifolia*
*Cyanea mannii*
*Cyanea mceldowneyi*
*Cyanea pinnatifida*
*Cyanea procera*
*Cyanea stictophylla*
*Cyanea superba*
*Cyanea truncata*
*Cyanea undulata*

*Cyperus fauriei*
*Cyperus pennatiformis*
*Cyrtandra giffardii*
*Cyrtandra munroi*
*Cyrtandra polyantha*
*Delissea rhytidosperma*
*Diellia erecta*
*Diellia falcata*
*Diellia laciniata*
*Diellia unisora*
*Diplazium molokaiense*
*Dubautia herbstobatae*
*Dubautia latifolia*
*Dubautia pauciflorula*
*Eugenia koolauensis*
*Exocarpos luteolus*
*Flueggea neowawraea*
*Gahnia lanaiensis*
*Gardenia brighamii*
*Geranium arboreum*
*Gouania hillebrandii*
*Gouania meyenii*
*Gouania vitifolia*
*Haplostachys hap-
    lostachya*
*Hedyotis cookiana*
*Hedyotis coriacea*
*Hedyotis degeneri*
*Hedyotis manni*
*Hedyotis parvula*
*Hedyotis st.-johnii*

*Hesperomannia
    arborescens*
*Hesperomannia arbus-
    cula*
*Hesperomannia lydgatei*
*Hibiscadelphus distans*
*Hibiscus brackenridgei*
*Hibiscus clayi*
*Isodendrion hosakae*
*Isodendrion pyrifolium*
*Kokia drynarioides*
*Labordia lydgatei*
*Lipochaeta fauriei*
*Lipochaeta kamolensis*
*Lipochaeta micrantha*
*Lipochaeta tenuifolia*
*Lipochaeta venosa*
*Lipochaeta waimeaensis*
*Lobelia oahuensis*
*Lycopodium nutans*
*Lysimachia filifolia*
*Lysimachia lydgatei*
*Marsilea villosa*
*Melicope adscendens*
*Melicope balloui*
*Melicope haupuensis*
*Melicope knudsenii*
*Melicope lydgatei*
*Melicope mucronulata*
*Melicope ovalis*
*Melicope pallida*

*Melicope quadrangularis*
*Melicope reflexa*
*Munroidendron racemo-
    sum*
*Neraudia angulata*
*Neraudia sericea*
*Nothocestrum breviflo-
    rum*
*Nothocestrum peltatum*
*Phyllostegia mannii*
*Phyllostegia mollis*
*Plantago hawaiensis*
*Poa manni*
*Poa sandvicensis*
*Poa siphonoglossa*
*Portulaca sclerocarpa*
*Pritchardia munroi*
*Pteralyxia kauaiensis*
*Pteris lydgatei*
*Remya kauaiensis*
*Remya mauiensis*
*Remya montgomeryi*
*Rollandia crispa*
*Sanicula mariversa*
*Scaevola coriacea*
*Schiedea adamantis*
*Schiedea apokremnos*
*Schiedea haleakalensis*
*Schiedea kaalae*
*Schiedea lydgatei*
*Silene alexandri*

| | | | |
|---|---|---|---|
| Silene lanceolata | Stenogyne kanehoana | Tetraplasandra gymno- | Viola lanaiensis |
| Silene perlmanii | Tetramolopium arenar- | carpa | Wilkesia hobdyi |
| Solanum sandwicense | ium | Urera kaalae | Xylosma crenata |
| Spermolepis hawaiiensis | Tetramolopium capillare | Vicia menziesii | Zanthoxylum hawaii- |
| Stenogyne bifida | Tetramolopium filiforme | Vigna owahuensis | ense |
| Stenogyne campanulata | Tetramolopium remyi | Viola helenae | |

## National Collection of Endangered Plants

Under the auspices of the Center for Plant Conservation, twenty-five botanical gardens and arboreta around the country are working to preserve endangered native plants ex situ (away from their original habitat or natural environment) by collecting seeds, growing and studying the plants, and banking seeds for the future, in case any of them should become extinct in the wild. Collectively known as the National Collection of Endangered Plants, this seedbank contained seeds, cuttings, and whole plants of 496 species native to the United States as of July 17, 1996, making it one of the largest endangered-plant conservation collections in the world. Many of the species are listed on the federal endangered species list. CPC's own criteria for inclusion require that a plant be diminishing in number, declining at an accelerated rate, and facing imminent threat of extinction.

Information on any plant in the collection may be obtained from CPC's home page on the Internet at www.mobot.org/CPC/.

The following botanical gardens and arboreta form the National Collection of Endangered Plants:

**The Arboretum at Flagstaff**
Transition Zone Horticultural Institute
P.O. Box 670
Flagstaff, AZ 86002

**The Arnold Arboretum of Harvard University**
125 Arborway
Jamaica Plain, MA 02130

**The Berry Botanic Garden**
11505 S.W. Summerville Avenue
Portland, OR 97219

**Bok Tower Gardens**
1151 Tower Boulevard
Lake Wales, FL 33853-3412

**Chicago Botanic Garden**
P.O. Box 400
Glencoe, IL 60022-0400

**Denver Botanic Gardens**
909 York Street
Denver, CO 80206-3799

**Desert Botanical Garden**
1201 N. Galvin Parkway, Papago Park
Phoenix, AZ 85008

**Fairchild Tropical Garden**
10901 Old Cutler Road
Miami, FL 33156

**New England Wild Flower Society**
Garden in the Woods
180 Hemenway Road
Framingham, MA 01701-2699

**The Holden Arboretum**
9500 Sperry Road
Kirland, OH 44094-5172

**Honolulu Botanical Gardens**
50 North Vineyard Boulevard
Honolulu, HI 96817

**Harold L. Lyon Arboretum**
University of Hawaii at Manoa
3860 Manoa Road
Honolulu, HI 96822

Mercer Arboretum and Botanic Gardens
22306 Aldine Westfield Road
Humble, TX 77338

Missouri Botanical Garden
P.O. Box 299
St. Louis, MO 63166

The Morton Arboretum
Route 53
Lisle, IL 60532

National Tropical Botanical Garden
P.O. Box 340
Lawai, HI 96765

The Nebraska Statewide Arboretum
C. Y. Thompson Library, Garden Level
University of Nebraska
Lincoln, NE 68583-0715

The New York Botanical Garden
200 South Street and Southern Boulevard
Bronx, NY 10458-5126

The North Carolina Arboretum
P.O. Box 6617
Asheville, NC 28806

North Carolina Botanical Garden
University of North Carolina at Chapel Hill
Box 3375, Totten Center
Chapel Hill, NC 27599-3375

Rancho Santa Ana Botanic Garden
1500 North College Avenue
Claremont, CA 91711-3157

Red Butte Gardens and Arboretum
University of Utah
18A DeTrobriand Street
Salt Lake City, UT 84113-5044

Regional Parks Botanic Garden
c/o East Bay Regional Parks District
P.O. Box 5381
Oakland, CA 94605-5369

San Antonio Botanical Garden
555 Funston Place
San Antonio, TX 78209

Santa Barbara Botanic Garden
1212 Mission Canyon Road
Santa Barbara, CA 93105

University of California Botanical Garden
Centennial Drive
Berkeley, CA 94720-5045

Waimea Arboretum and Botanical Garden
59-864 Kamehameha Highway
Haleiwa, HI 96712

## Extinct Plants

Extinction of plants is a natural result of changes in climate over thousands of years, of disease, and of competition by stronger plants for light and nutrients. However, the current worldwide rate of extinction is extraordinary. It is estimated that nearly 1,000 of the 270,000 species of vascular plants have gone extinct in the past 100 years and that nearly 60,000 plants will be extinct in the next 50 years—mostly in the tropics.

### NORTH AMERICAN VASCULAR PLANTS PRESUMED EXTINCT

According to The Nature Conservancy, the following species native to North America are presumed to be extinct (this list was current as of August 18, 1996):

Calochortus indecorus
Carex aboriginum
Castilleja cruenta
Mimulus brandegei
Mimulus traskiae
Mimulus whipplei
Monardella pringlei
Orbexilum stipulatum
Phacelia cinera
Potentilla multijuga
Rorippa coloradensis

# U.S. VASCULAR PLANTS RANKED "GH" OR "HISTORIC"

According to The Nature Conservancy, the following species are ranked historic; common names are provided for the plants that have them. Species are classified as historic if, despite extensive field surveys, they have not been sighted in about 50 years. Still, there is some limited hope of finding them in the wild again, particularly in regions with a great deal of inaccessible habitat, such as the western states, Hawaii, and Alaska. (This list was current as of September 24, 1996.)

## BOTANICAL NAME, COMMON NAME—DISTRIBUTION

*Acaena exigua*, liliwai—HI

*Achyranthes atollensis*—HI

*Agalinis calycina*, Leoncita false foxglove—HI

*Arabis hastatula*—OR

*Asplenium leucostegioides*—HI

*Botrychium subbifoliatum*, makou—HI

*Braya pilosa*, hairy rockcress—KW, MK, QC, YT (Canadian provinces), AK

*Calochortus monanthus*, single-flowered mariposa lily—CA

*Clermontia multiflora*—HI

*Cryptantha aperta*, cat's-eye—CO, SK (Canada)

*Cyanea arborea*, tree cyanea—HI

*Cyanea asplenifolia*, spleenwort-leaved cyanea—HI

*Cyanea comata*—HI

*Cyanea giffardii*, Giffard's cyanea—HI

*Cyanea lobata*, lobed cyanea—HI

*Cyanea longissima*—HI

*Cyanea marksii*, Mark's cyanea—HI

*Cyanea obtusa*, blunt-lobe cyanea—HI

*Cyanea pohaku*—HI

*Cyanea profuga*—HI

*Cyanea pycnocarpa*—HI

*Cyanea quercifolia*, oak-leaf cyanea—HI

*Cyanea shipmanii*, Shipman's cyanea—HI

*Cyperus auriculatus*, eared flatsedge—HI

*Cyperus kunthianus*—HI

*Cyperus rockii*—HI

*Cyrtandra crenata*, round-toothed cyrtandra—HI

*Cyrtandra filipes*, slender-stalked cyrtandra—HI

*Cyrtandra gracilis*, slender cyrtandra—HI

*Cyrtandra kohalae*—HI

*Cyrtandra lydgatei*, Lydgate's cyrtandra—HI

*Cyrtandra olona*—HI

*Cyrtandra pruinosa*—HI

*Cyrtandra rivularis*—HI

*Cyrtandra tintinnabula*—HI

*Cyrtandra waiolani*, Waiolan's cyrtandra—HI

*Delissea fallax*—HI

*Delissea laciniata*, cut-leaf delissea—HI

*Delissea lauliiana*—HI

*Delissea parviflora*, small-flowered delissea—HI

*Delissea sinuata*, wavy-leaf delissea—HI

*Deparia kaalaana*—HI

*Diellia mannii*—HI

*Dissanthelium californicum*, California dissanthelium—CA

*Elodea schweinitzii*, Schweinit's waterweed—NJ, NY, PA

*Eragrostis deflexa*, Pacific love grass—HI

*Eragrostis hosakai*, Hosaka love grass—HI

*Eragrostis mauiensis*, Maui love grass—HI

*Erigeron mariposanus*—CA

*Eriogonum truncatum*, Mt. Diablo buckwheat—CA

*Eupatorium droserolepis*, oreganillo—HI

*Haplostachys bryanii*, Bryan's haplostachys—HI

*Haplostachys linearifolia*, linear-leaved haplostachys—HI

*Haplostachys munroi*, Munro's haplostachys—HI

*Haplostachys truncata*, truncate haplostachys—HI

*Hedeoma pilosa*, old blue pennyroyal—TX, NM

*Hedyotis foliosa*, leafy bluet—HI

*Hibiscadelphus bombycinus*, Kawahae hibiscadelphus—HI

(continued on next page)

*Hibiscadelphus wilderianus*—HI

*Kokia lanceolata*, kokiò—HI

*Layia heterotricha*, pale yellow tidy-tips—CA

*Lipochaeta bryanii*, nehe—HI

*Lipochaeta degeneri*, nehe—HI

*Lipochaeta perdita*, nehe—HI

*Lobelia remyi*, Remy's lobelia—HI

*Lupinus sublanatus*, mono lupine—CA, UT

*Lysimachia forbesii*, Forbes' loosestrife—HI

*Malacothamnus davidsonii*, Davidson bush-mallow—CA

*Melicope cruciata*, cross-bearing pelea—HI

*Melicope degeneri*, Degener's pelea—HI

*Melicope haleakalae*, Stone's pelea—HI

*Melicope munroi*, Munro's pelea—HI

*Melicope nealae*, Neal pelea—HI

*Melicope obovata*, obovate pelea—HI

*Melicope paniculata*, alani—HI

*Melicope wailauensis*, pelea—HI

*Micranthemum micranthemoides*, Nuttall's micranthemum—DC, NJ, NY, DE, MD, PA, VA

*Monardella leucocephala*, Merced monardella—CA

*Ochrosia kilaueaensis*, holei—HI

*Orbexilum macrophyllum*, bigleaf scurfpea—NC

*Pediomelum pentaphyllum*, Chihuahua scurfpea—AZ, KS, LA, MT, NE, NM, OK, TX, WY

*Penstemon parviflorus*, Montezuma county beard-tongue—CO, NM

*Peperomia degeneri*, Degener's peperomia—HI

*Perityle inyoensis*, Inyo rock daisy—CA

*Phyllostegia brevidens*, Gray's phyllostegia—HI

*Phyllostegia hillebrandii*, Hillebrand's phyllostegia—HI

*Phyllostegia imminuta*—HI

*Phyllostegia knudsenii*, Knudsen's phyllostegia—HI

*Phyllostegia rockii*, Rock's phyllostegia—HI

*Phyllostegia variabilis*, variable phyllostegia—HI

*Phyllostegia wiameae*—HI

*Phyllostegia wawrana*—HI

*Plagiobothrys glaber*, hairless allocarya—AZ, CA

*Plagiobothrys hystriculus*, bearded allocarya—CA

*Plagiobothrys lamprocarpus*, popcorn flower—OR

*Plagiobothrys lithocaryus*, Mayacamas popcorn-flower—CA

*Polystichum kwakiutlii*—BC (Canada), AK

*Pritchardia lowreyana*—HI

*Priva portoricensis*, velvetbur—PR (Puerto Rico)

*Rollandia parvifolia*, small-flowered rollandia—HI

*Rollandia purpurellifolia*, purple-leaved rollandia—HI

*Rubus aliceae*, Santa Fe raspberry—NM

*Rubus macvaughii*—TX

*Rubus maniseensis*—RI

*Rubus tygartensis*, Tygart Valley blackberry—WV

*Rubus uscetanus*, Tampa blackberry—FL

*Rumex tomentella*, Mogollon dock—NM

*Sanicula kauaiensis*, Kauai sanicle—HI

*Schiedea amplexicaulis*, Maòliòli—HI

*Schiedea implexa*, Sherff schiedea—HI

*Sicyos hillebrandii*, Hillebrand bur-cucumber—HI

*Sida inflexa*, Virginia pine sida—NC, VA

*Silene cryptopetala*, Hawaiian catchfly—HI

*Silene degeneri*, Degener's catchfly—HI

*Solanum conocarpum*, marronbacoba—PR (Puerto Rico)

*Solanum incompletum*, Popolo ku mai—HI

*Stenogyne cinerea*, gray stenogyne—HI

*Stenogyne cranwelliae*—HI

*Stenogyne haliakalae*, Haleakala stenogyne—HI

*Stenogyne oxygona*—HI

*Stenogyne viridis*, green stenogyne—HI

*Tetramolopium conyzoides*—HI

*Tetramolopium tenerrimum*—HI

*Thismia americana*, thismia—IL, WI, IN, MI

*Triphora latifolia*, broad-leaved nodding-caps—FL

*Tropidocarpum capparideum*, caper-fruited tropido-carpum—CA

*Verbena riparia*, riverbank vervain—LA, NJ, NC, VA, MS, MI

*Wikstroemia hanalei*—HI

*Wikstroemia skottsbergiana*, Skottsberg's wikstroemia—HI

*Wikstroemia villosa*, hairy wikstroemia—HI

Plant extinction is extremely difficult to prove. Plants can persist at a site for decades as dormant seed, awaiting return of appropriate conditions for germination and growth. Plants once believed to be extinct have turned up years later in isolated locations. In 1995, The Nature Conservancy declared 17 vascular plants that once occurred in the United States to be extinct. However, after several of these species were found to still exist, that number decreased to the eleven plants listed in the chart "North American Vascular Plants Presumed Extinct," page 130. The organization presumes that nearly 200 full species of vascular plants plus many more subspecies and varieties have gone extinct in North America and Hawaii since European settlement.

## Plants Threatened by Collection

While the main threat to plants is loss of habitat, commercial collection from the wild continues to decrease populations of some species to the point of endangerment. Although the commercial propagation of plants has increased dramatically in recent decades (for example, the vast majority of the more than one billion bulbs sold in the United States each year are now propagated), national and international trade of wild plants continues, usually due to the difficulty of propagating certain species and to a lack of awareness on the part of consumers as to the origin—wild or propagated—of the plants they purchase.

One example of a species that has suffered from wild collection is the saguaro: poachers in the United States and Mexico dig saguaros in the dead of night and sell them for more than

$1,000 apiece to individual collectors. Most cacti, popular among plant collectors and southwestern gardeners, are predominantly grown in nurseries, but approximately 15 percent of the 7.5 million cacti recorded in international trade in 1989 were collected from the wild. Trilliums, popular plants in American woodland gardens, are dug from forested areas of the United States and Canada. World trade in orchids totaled about 9.3 million plants in 1989; over 10 percent of these were likely of wild origin. According to the North American Native Terrestrial Orchid Conference, the predominant threat to orchids, particularly in the United States, is habitat destruction. Most American orchids are terrestrial and difficult to grow in cultivation; the majority are not particularly showy and therefore of little horticultural interest. However, those that are showy are difficult to propagate. For example, lady slipper orchids offered in garden catalogs gen-

### THE SIGNS OF A WILD-COLLECTED PLANT

To avoid encouraging the commercial trade of wild-collected plants, gardeners are advised to pass up any specimen that shows one of the following signs:

- Roots that have been compressed into a pot.
- Soil in the pot that differs from that around the roots.
- Leaves that are skewed and irregular.

Of course, the best way to ensure that the plants you purchase have not been dug up from the wild is to buy only from nurseries who advertise that they propagate the plants they sell.

erally have been wild-collected. All wild orchids in the United States are protected and therefore it is illegal to collect them on federal lands.

Plants that are difficult or slow to propagate are most vulnerable to digging. These include the following:

- Woodland wildflowers, particularly trilliums and other members of the lily family.
- Plants adapted to specialized habitats, such as orchids and bog plants.
- Native terrestrial orchids, which are especially threatened as they have yet to be propagated successfully in commercial quantities.
- Mature specimens of certain cacti.
- Plants that produce few seeds.
- Plants with strict cultural requirements.

## CITES

The first meeting of the Convention on International Trade in Endangered Species of Wild Fauna and Flora, better known by the acronym CITES, was held in Washington, D.C., in 1973. Signed by 21 countries, it took effect in 1975. Today, over 125 nations are party to the convention, which promotes conservation by prohibiting or regulating international trade of plants and animals deemed to be threatened or likely to be threatened by commercial exploitation.

Trade in listed species is controlled by means of a licensing system overseen by the CITES Secretariat based in Lausanne, Switerland. Responsibility for enforcement of the treaty rests with each signatory country. The U.S. agency with jurisdiction over CITES is the U.S. Fish and Wildlife Service. For more information, see "The Horticultural Traveler," page 621.

The CITES list of protected species is updated every two years when all member states meet. The list consists of three appendices, or categories of protection:

- Appendix I includes species threatened with extinction by trade. Trade in wild plants listed in this appendix is essentially prohibited, except for educational and scientific purposes. Even in these instances, two appropriate permits are required, and they are issued only in exceptional circumstances. Nurseries are encouraged to propagate Appendix I plants to reduce the pressure on wild populations.
- Appendix II species are not presently threatened with extinction but are likely to be so in the future unless their trade is regulated. These plants may be traded commercially with appropriate permits provided that this trade is determined not to be detrimental to the species' survival. Propagated plants may be traded with a certificate of artificial propagation. Appendix II includes the majority of CITES-listed plants, such as almost all cacti and orchids, snowdrops (*Galanthus* species), winter daffodils (*Sternbergia* species), cyclamens (*Cyclamen* species), Venus's-flytrap (*Dionaea muscipula*), and ginseng (*Panax quinquefolius*).
- Appendix III includes any species that a signatory to the convention deems is in need of regulation in areas under its jurisdiction.

## The Bulb Trade

In 1994 (the last year surveyed by the National Gardening Association), Americans spent an estimated $503 million on flower bulbs. About 75 percent of these were imported. Ninety percent of the imports came from the Netherlands, and the remaining 10 percent were principally from Great Britain and Israel.

While the vast majority of these bulbs are propagated, nearly all of certain types of bulbs are collected from the wild. According to the American Horticultural Society, more than 4.4 million bulbs imported into the United States from 1990 through 1995 were dug up from their wild habitats in Turkey. These included snowdrops (*Galanthus* species), hardy cyclamen (*Cyclamen hederifolium*), and sternbergias, especially *Sternbergia lutea*. Other bulbs that are sometimes collected from the wild and sold in the United States are winter aconite (*Eranthis hyemalis*) and anemones (*Anemone* species).

Gardeners can easily differentiate between cultivated and wild-collected cyclamen bulbs. Those grown commercially are even and smooth, reflecting the fact that they were raised in a porous growth medium. They are also larger than wild bulbs, which are uneven and roughly shaped.

Although steps have been taken to curtail the collecting of bulbs from the wild, the practice continues. Turkey is by far the largest exporter of wild bulbs. In southeastern Europe and Turkey, for example, the giant snowdrop (*Galanthus elwesii*) is collected in enormous quantities, putting the species at risk. In recent years, Flauna & Flora International, an organization based in Britain that works to conserve endangered plants and animals around the world, as well as representatives of the Dutch bulb industry, have dispatched both Turkish and Western European experts to teach Turkish farmers to grow the bulbs commercially on their own lands and thus avoid resorting to wild-collection.

Farmers in countries such as Hungary and the former Soviet republic of Georgia have been digging up snowdrops within their borders and selling them to Dutch traders. As the wild-bulb populations of these countries are little known to Western botanists, the extent of the damage caused by the uncontrolled digging is unclear.

The World Wildlife Fund, the Garden Club of America, and other groups have been working with the flower-bulb industry to educate gardeners about the probable wild origin of certain plants. In recent years, much progress has been made with the bulb industry in the Netherlands, which in 1990 began phasing in a labeling program: as of 1995, all bulbs exported by Dutch firms, including species bulbs, hybrids, and cultivars, have been bearing the labels "from wild sources" or "from cultivated stock."

Dealers in other European countries and in America have not signed this agreement and therefore are not obligated to comply with the labeling programs. Although some dealers have pledged not to sell wild-collected bulbs, others continue to do so. In December 1994, the U.S. Federal Trade Commission amended the guidelines for the nursery industry. As stipulated in Guide 6, "It is an unfair or deceptive act or practice to sell, offer for sale, or distribute industry products collected from the wild state without disclosing that they were collected from the wild state; provided, however, that plants propagated in nurseries from plants lawfully collected from the wild state may be designated as 'nursery-propagated.' "

In general, bulbs offered at very low prices are likely to have been collected from the wild. *The Good Bulb Guide,* a list of dealers who have pledged not to sell wild bulbs or to inform customers if they do, is available for $1.00 from Faith Campbell, 8208 Dabney Avenue, Springfield, VA 22152.

## Invasive Plants

For centuries, gardeners and farmers have been rearranging the planet's flora, transporting seeds, crops, and prized horticultural specimens to and fro across vast land masses and oceans. Many of the exotic plants we have introduced by intention or accident have been beneficial to us and ecologically benign. But a small percentage have run rampant. Gaining a foothold first in areas disturbed by human activities, they moved into natural areas where they have not only driven out indigenous species but, in the worst cases, radically altered the ecosystems they have invaded.

In 1993, after an extensive review of exotic species, the Congressional Office of Technology Assessment concluded that pest plants and animals have an effect not only on natural areas but also on agriculture, industry, and human health. In its report, *Harmful Non-Indigenous Species in the United States,* the agency noted that from 1906 to 1991, just 79 problem plants and animals caused documented losses of $97 billion, and that a worst-case scenario for a mere 15 potentially high-impact species could cause another $134 billion in future economic losses.

According to *The Flora of North America,* the most comprehensive reference on this continent's plants, one-fifth to one-third of all species growing north of Mexico have come from other continents. The states most affected by the invasion of nonnative plants include Hawaii, where nearly half of the plant species found in the wild are nonnative, and New York, which with 36 percent has the highest percentage of nonnative species among the mainland states.

Invasives reproduce rapidly and can form stands that exclude nearly all other plants. In the process, they damage natural areas, altering ecosystem processes, displacing native species, hybridizing with natives and changing their genetic makeup, and supporting other nonnative plants, animals, and pathogens.

Researchers are working to discover why some nonnatives become invasive while others do not. According to one theory, some probably succeed because they are not held in check by the predators and parasites that controlled their numbers in their original lands; what is more, because they are not under attack, they may be able to redirect to growth and reproduction the energy they would have invested in producing the toxic chemicals or spines to make themselves unpalatable to herbivores and pests. Native plants, by contrast, cannot lower their defenses or they will be attacked by the pests that evolved along with them. Two major studies suggest that the best predictor of invasiveness is whether a plant is known to be invasive in another part of the world.

Recent work has found that species that share some or all of the following characteristics are most likely to be invasive:

• They produce many small seeds and begin reproducing within their first few years.
• Their seeds are dispersed by animals.
• They can reproduce both by seed and vegetative growth.
• They have long flowering and fruiting periods.
• They have no special seed-germination requirements, such as a period of exposure to cold.

Some evidence also indicates the following characteristics may be predictors of a species's invasiveness:

• Self-fertility or self-compatibility, meaning a species can fertilize itself. (Many self-

# THE WORST INVASIVE SPECIES USED HORTICULTURALLY

The following list of invasive nonnative species used horticulturally has been culled from Brooklyn Botanic Garden's *Invasive Plants: Weeds of the Global Garden* (see "Further Reading," page 141) and from the work of Nature Conservancy invasive-weed specialist John Randall. Gardeners should avoid growing those species listed as invasive in their area.

### SPECIES NAME, COMMON NAME—DISTRIBUTION

*Acacia melanoxylon,* Australian blackwood—CA, HI

*Acer ginnala,* Amur maple—IL, Midwest

*Acer platanoides,* Norway maple—DE, MA, MD, MN, NY, PA, RI, VA, WI, WV, Northeast

*Ailanthus altissima,* tree of heaven—AZ, CA, CT, DE, ID, IL, KY, MA, MD, OH, NC, NJ, NY, TN, PA, VA, WI, WV

*Alternanthera philoxeroides,* alligator weed—AR, FL, LA, TX, VA, Gulf Coast

*Ampelopsis brevipedunculata,* porcelain berry—WI and mid-Atlantic states

*Ardisia elliptica,* shoebutton ardisia—FL, Gulf Coast

*Arrhenatherum elatius,* false oat—OR

*Artemisia absinthium,* absinthe—ND

*Artemisia vulgaris,* mugwort—MA, NY, VA

*Arundo donax,* giant reed—CA

*Bassia scoparia,* kochia; summer cypress—ID, TX

*Berberis thunbergii,* Japanese barberry—Northeast, Midwest

*Bischofia javanica,* bishopwood—FL

*Brachypodium sylvaticum,* slender false brome—OR

*Buddleia davidii,* butterfly bush—WA

*Caesalpinia gilliesii,* cat's claw—AZ

*Carduus nutans,* musk thistle—CO, IA, ID, IL, KS, KY, MA, MN, MO, NC, ND, NM, OR, PA, TN, VA, WA, WI, WY

*Carpobrotus chilensis,* sea fig—CA

*Carpobrotus edulis,* iceplant; Hottentot fig—CA

*Casuarina equisetifolia,* Australian pine—FL, HI

*Catharanthus roseus,* Madagascar periwinkle—FL

*Celastrus orbiculatus,* bittersweet—Eastern U.S.

*Centaurea macrocephala,* bighead knapweed—WA

*Cirsium arvense,* Canada thistle—almost entire U.S.

*Cirsium vulgare,* bull thistle—CA, ID, MA, MD, MN, MO, MT, NC, ND, NE, OH, OR, PA, RI, SD, TN, UT, VA, WA, WI, WY

*Clematis terniflora,* yam-leaved clematis—MD, TN

*Coronilla varia,* crown vetch—Northeast, Midwest, Northern Plains

*Cortaderia jubata,* jubata grass—AZ, CA, HI

*Cortaderia selloana,* pampas grass—CA

*Cotoneaster microphyllus, C. pannosus, C. lacteus,* cotoneasters—CA

*Crataegus monogyna,* English hawthorn—OR

*Cupaniopsis anacardiodes,* carrotwood—FL

*Cupressus macrocarpa,* Monterey cypress—HI

*Cynara cardunculus,* artichoke thistle; Cardoon—CA

*Cytisus scoparius,* Scotch broom—CA, ID, MA, OR, WA

*Daucus carota,* Queen Anne's lace—IL, MI around Great Lakes

*Dipsacus fullonum,* common teasel—ID, IL, MD, MO, NM, OH, OR, TN, VA, WA, WI, WV

*Eichhornia crassipes,* water hyacinth—CA, FL, GA, LA, NC, SC, Gulf Coast

*Elaeagnus angustifolia,* Russian olive—Plains, intermountain states

*Elaeagnus umbellata,* autumn olive—Northeast, Midwest

*Eucalyptus globulus,* blue gum—CA, HI

*Euonymus alatus,* winged euonymus—Northeast, Midwest

*Euonymus fortunei,* wintercreeper—AL, IL, MD, MO, TN, VA, WI

*(continued on next page)*

*Festuca arundinacea*, tall fescue—Southeast, CA, Southern Plains

*Festuca ovina*, sheep's fescue—NY

*Ficus carica*, edible fig—CA

*Ficus microcarpa, F. altissima, F. benghalensis*, figs—CA, FL, HI

*Foeniculum vulgare*, fennel—CA, VA, WV

*Glechoma hederacea*, ground ivy—MA, MD, VA, WI, WV

*Grevillea robusta*, silk oak—HI

*Gypsophila paniculata*, baby's breath—CA, MI, OR, WA

*Hedera helix*, English ivy—AL, AZ, CA, GA, IA, MD, NC, OR, TN, WI, WV

*Hedychium gardnerianum*, Kahili ginger—HI

*Hemerocallis fulva*, daylily—MD

*Hibiscus syriacus*, rose of Sharon—AL

*Hypericum perforatum*, common St.-John's-wort—CO, ID, IL, MA, MI, MO, MT, NY, WI, Pacific states

*Imperata cylindrica*, Japanese blood grass—FL

*Ilex aquifolium*, English holly—WA

*Jasminum dichotomum, J. fluminense*, jasmines—FL

*Lantana camara*, lantana—HI, FL

*Leucanthemum vulgare*, ox-eye daisy—NY, OR

*Ligustrum japonicum, L. sinense, L. vulgare*, privets—Southeast, Mid-Atlantic states, OH, VA

*Linaria vulgaris*, common toadflax, butter & eggs—CA, CO, MA, NM, OR, WA, WI, WV, WY

*Lonicera japonica*, Japanese honeysuckle—ME to FL, IL to TX

*Lonicera maackii, L. tatarica, L. morrowii*, bush honeysuckles—Midwest and central southern states

*Lotus corniculatus*, bird's foot trefoil—AK, CA, MN, OR

*Lupinus arboreus*, bush lupine—CA (native south of Tomales Bay)

*Lygodium japonicum*, Japanese climbing fern—FL, LA, TX, Gulf states

*Lysimachia nummularia*, moneywort—IL, IN, MA, MD, MO, VA, WI

*Lythrum salicaria*, purple loosestrife—48 continental states, possibly minus FL

*Lythrum virgatum*, Purple loosestrife—MN, MT, VA, WA (very similar to *L. salicaria* but apparently less widespread)

*Maclura pomifera*, osage orange—AZ, KS, MO, OH, OK

*Marrubium vulgare*, common horehound—AZ, TX

*Melaleuca quinquenervia*, paperbark tree—FL, HI

*Melia azedarach*, chinaberry—FL, GA, SC

*Merremia tuberosa*, Wood rose—FL

*Miscanthus sinensis, M. sacchariflorus*, Amur silver grass—Eastern U.S. from FL to TX, north to MA & NY

*Myoporum laetum*, myoporum—CA

*Nandina domestica*, nandina—FL, possibly east and central Gulf Coast

*Nerium oleander*, common oleander—CA

*Onopordum acanthium*, Scotch thistle—ID, MO, NM, OR, UT, WA, WY

*Passiflora mollissima*, passionflower—HI

*Paulownia tomentosa*, princess tree—IL, MD, NC, PA, TN, WV

*Pennisetum setaceum*, fountain grass—AZ, CA, HI

*Phalaris arundinacea*, reed canary grass—ID, MT, NY, OH, OR, PA

*Phormium tenax*, New Zealand flax—HI

*Pinus pinea*, Stone pine—CA (Santa Cruz Is.), HI

*Polygonum cuspidatum*, Japanese knotweed—CT, MA, MD, NJ, OR, PA, RI, TN, VA, WI

*Populus alba*, white poplar—IL, MA, MD, MO, PA, VA, WI, WV, Northeast

*Portulaca oleracea*, purslane—WI

*Potentilla recta*, sulfur cinquefoil—ID, MI, MT, OR, WA

*Psidium guajava*, common guava—HI

*Quercus acutissima*, sawtooth oak—Southeast

*Rhamnus cathartica*, buckthorn—Northeast to Midwest, KY

*Rhamnus frangula*, alder buckthorn—Northeast to Midwest, KY

*Robinia pseudoacacia,* black locust—CA, IA, IL, MD, MI, NY, OH, PA, VA, WI

*Rosa multiflora,* multiflora rose—Northeast, Midwest

*Sapium sebiferum,* Chinese tallow tree—AL, FL, GA, LA, MS, SC, TX

*Scaevola sericea* var. *taccada,* beach berry—FL

*Schefflera actinophylla,* umbrella tree—FL

*Schinus molle,* pepper tree—CA

*Schinus terebinthifolius,* Brazilian pepper tree—FL, HI, CA

*Spiraea japonica,* Japanese spirea—MD, TN, WA, WV

*Syzygium jambos,* rose apple—HI

*Tamarix ramosissima, T. aphylla, T. parviflora,* tamarisks, salt cedars—Southwest to KS, TX, OK, north to ID, MT

*Tanacetum vulgare,* tansy—ID

*Ulmus pumila,* dwarf elm, Siberian elm—IA, MN, OH, VA, WI

*Verbascum thapsus,* flannel-leaved mullein—CA, CO, HI, MA, MO, OH, OR, PA, TN, WI, WA, WV

*Viburnum opulus,* cranberry bush—Midwest east to PA

*Vinca major,* periwinkle—AZ, CA, NM

*Vinca minor,* periwinkle—Midwest

*Wisteria sinensis,* Chinese wisteria—Southeast

incompatible species are also successful invaders, however.)

• Large native north-south ranges in Europe and Asia. Species with large native ranges appear to be well adapted to a variety of climate and soil conditions and therefore more likely to find suitable habitat in a new area.

• No close relatives (for example, in the same genus) among any native species.

• Introduced on a large scale or repeatedly into a new range.

For a list of invasive plants brought to this continent primarily for horticultural use, see page 137.

## Threats to Crop Plant Diversity

Prior to 1800, when the first seed companies were established, almost all vegetable seeds grown in the United States were imported from Europe. Gardeners saved seeds their crop had produced for use the following year. Families passed down their favorite seed varieties to their children, thus ensuring the crops' survival.

As commercial seed companies flourished, these "open-pollinated" heirloom seeds—pollinated by bees, birds, insects, and the wind—were gradually replaced by hybrids, genetically crossed plant varieties selected primarily for their ability to stand up to mechanical harvesting and cross-country shipping, and for the uniform ripening time of their crops.

As these genetically uniform hybrids have replaced the myriad heirloom varieties, the genetic diversity of many crops has been severely reduced. And because just a few hybrids are so widely grown, they are more vulnerable to pests and disease; a single pest or disease pathogen could endanger an entire crop. Although plant breeders work hard to make the new hybrid cultivars resistant to pests and disease, the evolution of new, resistant strains of pests or diseases is an ongoing threat. The average life span of a new wheat variety, for example, is only five years before a newly evolved fungus attacks it.

Usually, the disease-resistant strain used by

## DECLINE IN CROP PLANT DIVERSITY AT THE VARIETY LEVEL

| Crop | Country | Number of Varieties |
|------|---------|---------------------|
| Rice | Sri Lanka | From 2,000 varieties in 1959 to 5 major varieties today |
| Rice | India | From 30,000 varieties to 75% of production from fewer than 10 varieties |
| Rice | Bangladesh | 62% of varieties descended from one maternal parent |
| Rice | Indonesia | 74% of varieties descended from one maternal parent |
| Wheat | USA | 50% of crop in 9 varieties |
| Potato | USA | 75% of crop in 4 varieties |
| Cotton | USA | 50% of crop in 3 varieties |
| Soybeans | USA | 50% of crop in 6 varieties |

SOURCE: World Conservation Monitoring Centre (1992).

According to the Lancaster, Pennsylvania–based Heirloom Seed Project (a source of heirloom seeds as well as information on vegetables and flowers grown by the Germans who settled in Pennsylvania in the eighteenth and nineteenth centuries), a 1984 U.S. Department of Agriculture inventory of seeds available from catalog sources showed that only 3 percent of the seeds listed in a similar USDA inventory conducted in 1903 were still available commercially. For example, of the 7,000 apple varieties available in the United States in 1900, over 5,000 were lost, and the remaining number was steadily declining.

Several organizations have been established to preserve heirloom varieties of open-pollinated plants, including the following:

**Seed Savers Exchange**
3076 North Winn Road
Decorah, Iowa 52101

**Seeds Blum**
HC 33 Idaho City Stage
Boise, ID 83706

**Native Seed/SEARCH**
2509 North Campbell Avenue
Box 325
Tucson, AZ 85719

**Seeds of Change**
Box 15700
Santa Fe, NM 87506-5700

breeders to decrease crop vulnerability is found in a wild relative of the particular crop. Thus, wild relatives of crops are vital in ensuring world food supplies and must be protected in their native habitats.

Although an estimated 100,000 plant species have been eaten by humans, barely more than 150 species are now under cultivation; only 20 species are now producing the vast majority of the world's food.

The National Seed Storage Laboratory in Fort Collins, Colorado, is the primary seed bank in the United States with the responsibility for preserving seeds of agricultural crops. Its primary focus is to store seeds that will help preserve the genetic diversity, and thus the survival, of crop plants. As part of the National Plant Germplasm System, a network of federal, state, and private organizations and individuals dedicated to the same goal, the laboratory also stores germplasm for other countries and permits free and unrestricted exchanges of its collections to researchers and breeders.

Seed banks are critical in the effort to preserve the genetic diversity of agricultural crops. However, crops must be grown in the field so that they can continue to co-evolve with pests and diseases and develop resistance to them if they are to survive in the long run. For this reason, gardeners can play an important role in preservation of food-plant diversity by both growing open-pollinated heirloom varieties and growing a variety of crops.

## Further Reading

Davis, Stephen D., et al. *Plants in Danger: What Do We Know?* Gland, Switzerland: International Union for Conservation of Nature and Natural Resources, 1986.

Dobson, Andrew P. *Conservation and Biodiversity.* New York: Scientific American Library, New York, 1996.

Heywood, V. H., executive ed. *Global Biodiversity Assessment.* Cambridge, England; New York: Cambridge University Press, 1995.

Marinelli, Janet. *Stalking the Wild Amaranth: Gardening in the Age of Extinction.* New York: Henry Holt and Company, 1998.

Marshall, Nina T. *A Gardener's Guide to Plant Conservation.* Washington, D.C.: World Wildlife Fund and the Garden Club of America, 1993.

Randall, John, and Janet Marinelli, eds. *Invasive Plants: Weeds of the Global Garden.* Brooklyn, N.Y.: Brooklyn Botanic Garden, 1996.

Simon, Noel. *Nature in Danger.* New York: Oxford University Press, 1995.

# 5

# ECOLOGY FOR
# GARDENERS

*Ecology: The science of the relationships among living organisms and between organisms and their environments.*

*Ecosystem: A functioning unit of nature that combines biological communities and the environments with which they interact. Ecosystems vary greatly in size and characteristics.*

The science of ecology had been developing for over a century, yet most people never heard the word until the 1960s and the publication of Rachel Carson's book, *Silent Spring,* which documented how chemical pesticides were spreading insidiously through the food chain and threatening the survival of many bird species. The book brought into sharp focus the ease with which the natural balance of plants, animals, and the environment that constitute life as we know it on this planet can be tipped. From the oil crises of the 1970s to the nuclear fallout from the Chernobyl reactor in the 1980s to the more recent evidence of ozone depletion and climate change on a global scale, we continue to be reminded of the need to protect the biosphere.

Gardeners are mainly concerned with plants, specifically the ones we grow in our gardens. But our gardens, as Rachel Carson showed us, are inextricably linked with the larger landscape. As cities and suburbs spread, gardens and other human-influenced environments predominate. It is our task as tenders of the Earth to ensure that the role our gardens play is a positive one. This requires an understanding of ecological relationships.

The first step in understanding ecological relationships in the garden is understanding those in plant communities in the wild. Have you ever wondered why oaks grow in some woods and not others? Why the East is covered largely with deciduous trees, while in the West conifers dominate? For decades, scientists have been studying vegetation associations, the distinctive mixes of species that predominate in different areas of different regions. Over the past century or so, ecologists have learned that such natural systems are defined by two major kinds of order: structural and functional. A terrestrial ecosystem's structure, or form, depends primarily on its vegetation; the structure of a grassland is very different from that of a forest, for example, because of the form of the predominant plant life. By the same token, the functions of these two plant communities—how they respond to fire, wind damage, and other types of disturbance; how they use and recycle water, nutrients, organic matter, and so on— also differ because the physical environment, the soils, climate, and other conditions that give rise to them are different.

What follows is a basic introduction to the structure and function of the major vegetation associations of North America, and how gardeners in these various regions can use them as models for transforming the garden landscapes that sustain us, without destroying the creatures and natural communities with whom we share the Earth.

## Vegetation Associations of North America

The landscape is a product of forces older than all the generations of our families. The shape of the land today is the result of ancient geological forces and more recent glaciers that retreated about 10,000 years ago. Glaciation gave form to the land, and the erosive forces of wind and rain continue to reshape it. Even though the glaciers penetrated only partway into the United States, the impact was felt all the way to the Gulf of Mexico. Beyond the reach of the glacial ice, plants from the North survived in pockets and intermingled with the southern flora. As the glaciers retreated, plants responded once again to the changes in climate and topography, and the distributions of some species were altered forever.

The first trees to return to the ravaged land released from the glaciers were cold-tolerant conifers that had sought refuge in the south. They proliferated in the virtually inert environment of sand and gravel. As the glaciers retreated farther still, the air and soil warmed, and deciduous forests replaced the conifers. By four to six thousand years ago, the forests, grasslands, deserts, and tundra that the first European settlers saw when they arrived in the New World covered the land. This landscape was made up of regional floras comprising what are referred to today as native plants.

Natives are those species that were found growing on a particular site under a given set of environmental conditions, before plants were massively displaced or introduced by European immigrants to this continent. Native plants give an area its regional identity. Their distribution is determined by physical and biological factors that influence or limit reproduction, growth, or dispersal. The native flora of an area includes trees, shrubs, herbaceous flowering plants, ferns, and mosses. For example, two or three hundred years ago, a blanket of prairie covered much of the Midwest. This sea of grass stretched from western Ohio to the rain shadow of the Rocky Mountains. Boreal conifer forests stretched from the Arctic Circle to the prairie, around the Great Lakes, and into northern New England. Between the prairie and the boreal forests, south and east to the pine savannahs and lush bottomland forests of the Coastal Plain, were deciduous forests.

In *The Natural Geography of Plants,* botanists Henry Gleason and Arthur Cronquist divide the United States and Canada into ten floristic provinces (see "Gardener's Atlas," page 14). The species in these distinct vegetation regions are determined by such regional factors as the high and low temperatures in summer and winter, total annual precipitation, timing and nature of precipitation, elevation, and soil type. Within any floristic province, these same variables are at work on a finer scale as well. The Eastern Deciduous Forest province, for example, stretches from Minnesota south to Texas, and east to Nova Scotia and Georgia. Within this one province, rainfall varies from 50 inches in the Southeast to 27 inches in Minnesota. A garden in Minneapolis is near the border of USDA Hardiness Zone 3, with winter temperatures dipping to −30°F; Georgia gardeners in Zone 8 seldom see temperatures much below freezing. All these factors combine, at the subregional scale, to favor certain associations of plant species with a fairly predictable mix of species. These vegetation associations are sometimes called *habitat types.*

Understanding the habitat types or vegetation associations in your area is the key to being a successful gardener in that region. The habitat type or types are your guide to what sorts of plants will grow best in your garden. Native plants are the most logical choices. However, the major plant associations here have analogous associations in Europe and Asia, the source of many American garden plants, as well as in other parts of the world. If you understand the nature of, for example, a deciduous forest, then you will know how best to grow a woodland plant, regardless of its country of origin. You will also understand how it relates to other species in the woodland community (see also "Natural Gardening," page 180).

The following are the major vegetation associations of the ten floristic provinces described by Gleason and Cronquist. For a list of the dominant plants in each association, see the chart beginning on page 166. The common and scientific names of nondominant plants of each vegetation association are included below; consult the chart for the scientific names of dominant plants.

## Tundra

Tundra is found where the climate is too hostile for trees to grow. The ground stays frozen year-round, except for a thin layer at the surface. There are two major types of tundra. Arctic tundra dominates the far North, above the Arctic Circle. Alpine tundra is found above timberline in the continent's major mountain ranges. Bighorn sheep, marmots, mountain goats, and grizzly bears are common animals of the tundra. Few gardeners toil in the tundra. The climate is too severe and the soil too thin for cultivation. The tundra is, however, a source of specialty plants for gardeners in more temperate regions. See "Cushions and Buns" on page 145.

### Arctic Tundra

The Arctic tundra is a land of vast plains dominated by dwarf shrubs, cushion-forming wildflowers, sedges, grasses, mosses, and lichens. In winter, the ground is covered by a blanket of snow several feet thick. In the dead of winter, the sun never rises above the horizon. By contrast, summer days are warmer and endless. Above the Arctic Circle, the sun never sets in summer. The upper layer of soil thaws, but just a few feet below the surface lies the permafrost, which never melts. Much of the area is covered with standing water, forming shallow marsh associations that support a blanket of sedges. These shallow marshes are critical nurseries for much of North America's waterfowl and shorebirds. In the drier areas, wildflowers bloom in one brief summer burst, along with dwarf willows and shrubs in the heath family (Ericaceae).

## Alpine Tundra

Alpine tundra, found above timberline in the Rocky Mountains, Sierras, and Northern Appalachians, supports a flora similar to that of the Arctic tundra. Cushion- and mat-forming wildflowers grow among a carpet of dwarf shrubs and trees, sedges, grasses, and lichens. The two types of tundra are so much alike because during the last ice age, mountaintops were the only refuge for tundra plants. Above the thick sheets of glacial ice towered the highest peaks, where tundra species flourished. As the glaciers receded, the plants recolonized the North from these lofty precipices.

---

### CUSHIONS AND BUNS

A rock gardener is judged by the quality of his or her buns. That's right: full, tight buns are the sign of a skilled gardener. The more the plants maintain the compact form of their alpine homes, the greater the achievement. Removed from the cool summers of mountaintops and transported into the humid heat of lower elevations, many alpine plants languish. The challenge for the rock gardener is to grow alpines to the perfection of form they would attain in the wild. A well-executed and successfully planted alpine rock garden is a marvel to behold.

---

# Northern Coniferous Forest

The conifer forests of the North, also known as the *boreal forest*, stretch in a vast unbroken arc from Newfoundland and Labrador south to New England, west to the Great Lakes and central Canada, and up to the Yukon and central Alaska. Just to the north is the tundra, where the ground is permanently frozen. In the Northern Coniferous Forest bedrock is close to the surface, and soils are generally thin and highly acidic. In the northern reaches of this region, the bedrock is limestone, but the soils are still acidic due to the buildup of organic matter. Within the trackless northern forests, there are several vegetation associations.

## Taiga

The most extensive association is the taiga or boreal forest, which lies farthest to the north, and blends with the tundra. "Taiga" is a Russian word for conifer forest. Here, the trees are small in stature and the ground is often soggy. In low areas, bogs and muskegs are found, permanent wetlands dominated by ericaceous shrubs and herbs. The farther south you go, the larger the trees become. White spruce and pines dominate the drier sites above the water table. In saturated soils, black spruce, larch, and white cedar are common. In disturbed sites, quaking aspen and alders (*Alnus* species) hold the soil as young conifers become established. The mossy ground layer is carpeted with dense stands of shade-tolerant wildflowers such as twinflower (*Linnaea borealis*) and bunchberry (*Cornus canadensis*).

## Mixed Coniferous/Hardwood Forest

In the southern reaches of the province, conifers form a mixed association with deciduous trees.

## THE BOREAL CHALLENGE

Gardening in the boreal region is a challenge. The growing season is short, and the shade is often dense. Their tall trunks and narrow canopies enable conifers to grow close together, effectively blocking most direct rays from the sun. As an adaptation to year-round shade, plants such as hepaticas (*Hepatica* species), partridgeberry (*Mitchella repens*), and bunchberry (*Cornus canadensis*) bring out the heavy artillery: thick, evergreen leaves. Their persistent leaves enable these plants to photosynthesize all season long.

Another challenge to gardeners is that the evergreen needles of the dominant trees in boreal forests are effective barriers to rain. Much of the precipitation evaporates directly from the tree canopy, without ever reaching the soil. The evergreen leaves of hepatica and other herbaceous species are leathery to help the plants resist drought.

Bloom in coniferous forests is geared less to sunlight patterns than to temperature and moisture. Soil thaws and warms slowly in shade. As the snow melts, marsh marigold (*Caltha palustris*) and other early plants bloom, but the main show is between late spring and summer. Deciduous plants such as orchids, violets (*Viola* species), and bellwort (*Uvularia grandiflora*) flower first, followed by the evergreen species like bunchberry. A few asters bloom in the autumn before winter's snow blankets the ground, resetting the clock and beginning the cycle anew.

The mixed coniferous/hardwood forest association is more diverse than the boreal zone. Along with the near monoculture of spruce, larch, and quaking aspen of the north grow balsam fir, birches, maples, and poplars (*Populus* species) that can survive the milder winters. The ground layer of the forest is more diverse as well. Orchids, twisted stalks and mandarins (*Streptopus* species), asters, and evergreen ground covers such as partridgeberry (*Mitchella repens*) and hepaticas (*Hepatica* species) are common. Most gardeners live in this southern portion of the floristic province.

## Eastern Deciduous Forest

The vast area covered by deciduous forests has a variety of soils, and dramatic topographic variation, from ancient mountains to foothills to gently undulating Piedmont plains. This diverse landscape hosts many plant associations. The age of the association also affects its species composition and structure. For example, the young forests growing in moist soils are composed primarily of mixed oaks, while the mature forests include beech, hemlock, maple, or basswood. Drier sites with leaner soils support associations dominated by oaks. Floodplains have a distinctive association of species that tolerate alternating cycles of flood and drought.

### Oak/Chestnut Forest

The oak/chestnut association, which has virtually vanished from the landscape, was once dominated by an important wildlife food and timber tree, the American chestnut (*Castanea dentata*). The tree has been eliminated as a major component of this forest, which is found on dry, shallow soils and sunny south- and west-facing slopes throughout the eastern half of the Eastern Deciduous Forest province. In 1930, a devastating blight was first recorded in New York, and within thirty years, the chestnut was wiped out. Today, small trees can be found resprouting from old stumps. The trees may live for twenty-five or thirty years, and a few even bear fruit. Scientists continue to search for blight-resistant strains, but the chestnut may never again dominate the canopy of this region of Eastern Deciduous Forest. In this association, the chestnut has been replaced by hickories and oaks.

## Mesophytic Forest

The lush forests of the mixed mesophytic association are often referred to as cove forests, because some of the most magnificent examples grow in the cool, north-facing valleys of the Appalachian Mountains. In coves, the soils are rich, moist loams with ample humus that support a diverse mixture of massive trees, shrubs,

and wildflowers. Tulip tree (*Liriodendron tulipifera*), beech, sugar maple, oaks, and basswood are the dominant canopy species. A wealth of flowering understory trees such as silverbells (*Halesia* species), magnolias, and dogwoods (*Cornus* species) shelter carpets of trilliums, lilies, phlox, lady slipper orchids (*Cypripedium* species), and bleeding heart (*Dicentra eximia*).

The western mesophytic association is a diverse forest type that occupies a transitional zone extending from the western edge of the Cumberland Plateau into the Midwestern states. On its western edge lies the oak-hickory association (see page 148) that forms a dynamic transition into the tallgrass prairie province. On the drier sites, oaks, maples, basswood, and other trees occur in more open-canopied stands.

---

## LIVING COLOR

The growing season in North America's deciduous forests begins and ends with an eruption of color. Spring brings one of the most dazzling wildflower displays seen anywhere in the world. As the days lengthen and the sun begins to prevail, an explosion of growth occurs, and the forest floor is transformed into a wildflower spectacle. Woodland gardeners can re-create this glorious display. But the display may be short-lived. Soon, tree buds break and the burst of leaf growth begins to cast a veil of shade on the forest floor. Many woodland wildflowers are ephemeral; they go dormant soon after blooming, as soon as their seed is ripe. This strategy evolved because when the woods become shaded and dry in summer, foliage is a liability for a small, delicate wildflower.

Ephemeral wildflowers such as spring beauty (*Claytonia virginica*) and Dutchman's-breeches (*Dicentra cucullaria*) have underground food-storage structures such as bulbs and tubers to provide the energy needed for rapid leaf and flower development. Other wildflowers such as trillium, bloodroot (*Sanguinaria canadensis*), and wild geranium (*Geranium maculatum*) spread wide foliage to absorb summer's dim light, instead of going dormant.

Autumn in the deciduous forest is every bit as spectacular as spring. As fall approaches, the trees turn blazing shades of red, orange, and yellow. The nutrients tied up in tree leaves return to the plants below as the colorful foliage that falls to the ground begins to rot. This annual renewal also is essential for providing mulch to protect delicate crowns from drying winter winds. A successful gardener plans for autumn foliage as carefully as for spring blooms, as well as for the textural carpet of greens—ferns, mosses, and the foliage of herbaceous plants—that graces the woodland garden in summer.

## MEADOWS

Meadows are found in breaks in the forest, created either through natural processes or at the hands of humans. Meadows form naturally through changes in the landscape, such as the silting in of beaver ponds and deposition of sandbars in river drainages. Meadows are also found on land that is too wet or too dry to support woody vegetation. Wet meadows are especially common in New England, occurring in swales along the edges of pastures or other open areas. Dry meadows and glades occur on rock outcroppings, mountain slopes, and sandy ridges. Unlike the Midwestern grasslands, a meadow is one stage in the process known as succession (see page 172). It is a temporary stage in the evolution of a forest. Today, most meadows occur on abandoned agricultural land and support a mixture of native and exotic species. Unlike spring-blooming woodlands, eastern meadows slowly build up to a spectacular floral display in late summer. The late-season bloomers include grasses, asters, and goldenrods (*Solidago* species).

### Beech/Maple Forest

In moist, loamy soils of the Piedmont, northern Appalachian, and Great Lakes regions, beech and maple form dominant stands. Due to the dense shade, the diversity of the ground layer is often lower than that of other forests. Evergreen wild gingers (*Hexastylis,* formerly *Asarum,* species), ferns, and sedges (*Carex* species) are common.

### Maple/Basswood Forest

In the Midwest and western Great Lakes region, at the edge of its range, beech disappears and is replaced by basswood as a codominant with sugar maple in mesic forests. Hop hornbeam (*Ostrya virginiana*), pagoda dogwood (*Cornus alternifolia*), serviceberries (*Amelanchier* species), and viburnums are common understory trees and shrubs. Spring wildflowers are often common.

### Oak/Hickory Forest

At the western edge of the Eastern Deciduous Forest province, precipitation drops and the forest forms a transitional zone with open woodlands and savannah. This region of drought-prone soils is dominated by oaks and hickories. Bur, black, and northern pin oak dominate. Shagbark and pignut hickory are present but seldom dominant. In the moister soils, white and northern red oak are also found. Frequent fire has created an edge of fire-tolerant trees growing among stands of prairie grasses. In some areas, the woodlands are confined to the moister ravines, while prairie carpets the uplands. Farther east, in the drier sites of the Piedmont plateau from Virginia south to the Gulf Coast, oaks and hickories also dominate, often in association with loblolly and pitch pines (*Pinus taeda* and *Pinus rigida*).

### Floodplain Forest

The forests along streams and rivers are subject to frequent disturbance wrought by flooding. Silver maples, hackberries (*Celtis* species), green ash, and cottonwood abound. Before the devastation wrought by Dutch elm disease, American elm (*Ulmus americana*) was a dominant tree in these forests. It has been replaced by green ash.

## The Coastal Plain

The Coastal Plain is a flat to gently rolling region that stretches from southern New England south to Florida and west to Texas. This floristic province is characterized by sandy plains, sluggish streams, coastal dunes, and tidal marshes. Barrier islands and mainland beaches are constantly reshaped by the dynamic forces that once sculpted the entire province. Associations of mixed deciduous species and pines cover much of the Coastal Plain. Wildlife abounds throughout the province—bear, deer, turkey, snakes, and forest birds. Gardening can be a challenge due to the heat, humidity, and poor, sandy soils. However, the mild winter climate is a boon to gardeners. The late winter and spring seasons are glorious, with bulbs, flowering trees, and woodland wildflowers in abundance. In summer, gardeners are apt to be more successful growing heat- and humidity-adapted native plants than those pictured in English gardening books.

### Northern Pine Barrens

The dry, acidic soils of coastal New Jersey, eastern Long Island, and Cape Cod support an association similar to that found on the dry ridges of the southern Appalachians. Pitch pine is the dominant tree, but scrub oak is common, as are shrubs such as sweet fern (*Comptonia peregrina*), mountain laurel (*Kalmia latifolia*), and huckleberries (*Gaylussacia* species). In moister soils, inkberry holly (*Ilex glabra*) and sweet pepperbush (*Clethra alnifolia*) are found, as they are on the southern Coastal Plain. Wetlands of sedges (*Carex* species), sundews (*Drosera* species), pitcher plants (*Sarracenia* species), and ferns grow along the shallow bays of streams and in poorly drained depressions.

### Upland Hardwood Forest

Hardwood forests are the mature, or late-successional, forests on many sites in the Coastal Plain. There is considerable variation in species composition and community structure, depending on the availability of moisture and nutrients. In most rich soils, the spring wildflower display in these forests is similar to that in the eastern deciduous forests. Younger, early-successional forest patches include sweet gum, winged elm (*Ulmus alata*), and a mix of other species. In the northern Coastal Plain, oak forests composed of southern red oak, white oak, and a few others are common. Young forests are often mixed with various pines. Older forests of beech (*Fagus grandifolia*) and maple (*Acer saccharum*) grow on undisturbed sites. In the southern Coastal Plain, bullbay magnolia replaces the beech. In peninsular Florida, deciduous and evergreen oaks prevail.

### Xeric Pine Forest

Forests of pine occur over extensive areas of coarse, dry, sandy soils in the fall-line sandhills extending from southern North Carolina through Georgia and parts of Alabama. Longleaf pine and wiregrass are found throughout, mixed with a variety of other pines, oaks, and other deciduous species, depending on the area. Shrubs such as huckleberries (*Gaylussacia* species) and staggerbush (*Lyonia mariana*) intermingle with bracken fern (*Pteridium aquilinum*). Fire plays an important role in keeping the grasses and forbs from being overtaken by shrubs and deciduous trees.

### Mesic Pine Forest

As moisture availability increases, xeric, or dry, sandhill communities grade into pine-dominated flatwoods and savannahs. In the open-canopied savannahs are scattered clumps of longleaf and slash pines with an understory of grasses and herbs. Flatwoods have denser canopies of slash pine and some oaks, with an understory of small trees and a dense tangle of shrubs such as titi (*Cyrilla racemiflora*), sweet pepperbush (*Clethra alnifolia*), and wax myrtle (*Myrica cerifera*). Various palmetto palms (*Sabal* species) are also common. Fire is important to the ecology of this association.

## Savannah and Pocosin

Savannahs and pocosins are dominated by pond and longleaf pine. Grasses, huge drifts of ferns, thickets of wax myrtle, titi, loblolly pine, and sweetbay magnolia (*Magnolia virginiana*) are the common plants. Carnivorous plants also abound in these wetlands. Six species of pitcher plants (*Sarracenia* species) and the Venus's-flytrap (*Dionaea muscipula*) are found here and nowhere else in the world.

## Bottomland Forest

Bottomland forests of maple, tupelo, and cypress are found along water courses in the outer Coastal Plain. Emergent wetland plants such as arrowheads (*Sagittaria* species), pickerel weed (*Pontederia cordata*), iris, and sedges (*Carex* species) grow in open, sunny areas.

## Maritime Communities

The outer dunes and seacoast are pelted by salt spray and storms. Leather-leafed shrubs, grasses, and salt-tolerant wildflowers are the only plants

---

### ONCE AN ANCIENT OCEAN

The Coastal Plain was once at the bottom of the ocean. Some 200 million years ago, North America separated from North Africa, creating the Atlantic Ocean. By this time, the Appalachian Mountains were well formed, and as lofty as the Rocky Mountains are today. As the continents moved apart and the sea floor expanded, the Coastal Plain began to form. Over the next 150 million years, it was built up by the sediments of the eroding Appalachian Mountains. As the Atlantic rose and fell throughout this period in response to global climate and geological changes, the Coastal Plain changed, too. During some periods, it was partially submerged; during others, particularly the last ice age, it was high and dry. For the past 12 to 14 thousand years, the Coastal Plain has occupied roughly its present-day location between the Atlantic Ocean and the Piedmont plateau. Erosion of the now-ancient plain has exposed the ancient sea bottom in some locations.

To this day, sandy soils dominate the province, and shell deposits are common. The shells provide calcium that sweetens the soil in isolated pockets, supporting unique plants that otherwise could not grow in a region generally dominated by more acidic soils. Plants called *disjuncts* are found in the shell-rich soils, hundreds of miles from their nearest relatives in the limestone regions of the Shenandoah Valley, Allegheny Mountains, and Mississippi River Valley. Miterwort (*Mitella diphylla*), dwarf trillium (*Trillium pusillum*), and ferns such as Scott's spleenwort (*Asplenium* x *ebenoides*) are examples. They occur in mixed assemblages with more common Coastal Plain species such as southern maidenhair fern (*Adiantum capillus-veneris*) and mayapple (*Podophyllum peltatum*), which also prefer sweet soil.

tough enough to survive. Poison ivy is abundant in these areas. The coastal saltmarshes are some of the most productive ecosystems in the world. Shorebirds and wading birds feed and nest in the saltmarshes. Many songbirds such as sparrows and wrens find shelter in the dense reeds and grasses. The open waters of these wetlands are important wintering grounds for millions of ducks and geese.

## Subtropical Florida

At the southern tip of the Florida peninsula, through the West Indies, lies a region of subtropical vegetation. This low-elevation land was once beneath the ocean. The soils are sandy and the topography is mostly flat. Many of our winter fruits and vegetables are grown on land drained for agriculture. As a result, the web of subtropical ecosystems is taxed, wildlife is threatened, and water is scarce. Exotic vegetation is overrunning what is left of the native vegetation (see "Invasive Plants," page 136). The endangered Florida panther and the alligator are the symbols of this small but precious part of the continent. Huge populations of wading birds and shorebirds are present, and migrant birds pass through the region in staggering numbers.

### Savannah

In central Florida, the land slopes gradually from Lake Okeechobee down to the sea. The region is covered by a sea of sedge known as sawgrass.

### Hardwood Hammock

In the Everglades of southern Florida, islands of hardwoods rise up above lower-lying plant communities dominated by sawgrass. On these lofty perches, only a foot or two above the water table, tree palmettos, gumbo-limbo, paradise tree, pigeon plum, and coontie thrive. The hammocks are often impenetrable, as the sunny edge promotes lush growth. The center of the hammock may be quite open and shaded by the taller canopy trees.

### Pinelands

Pine savannahs and sandhills occur over most of Florida. The soil is sandy, and lies on a limestone bedrock formed at the bottom of an ancient ocean. As in areas of the Coastal Plain province, these open-canopied communities consist of scattered clumps of longleaf and slash pines with an understory of grasses or a dense tangle of shrubs and saw palmettos. As in other pine communities, fire is important to the ecology of this association.

### Swamp Forests

Cypress swamps are the most common forested wetland in Florida. Most of the old-growth trees have been cut, but a few old stands survive. These trees are often festooned with Spanish moss, a wiry plant that is actually a bromeliad. Tupelo (*Nyssa* species) is a common companion of both bald cypress and pond cypress in these wetlands. Sweetbay magnolias, titi (*Cyrilla racemiflora*), fetterbush (*Leucothoe* species), and sweet pepperbush (*Clethra alnifolia*) are common shrubs. In areas subject to seasonal inundation, willow and water oaks (*Quercus phellos* and *Quercus nigra*) and tupelo form dense stands with shrubs and catbriars (*Smilax* species).

---

## PLANT INVADERS

Exotic plants are those that were introduced into a certain locality by humans. In other words, they are not native there. A small percentage of exotic species have proven invasive, meaning that they grow out of control in their new environments. Invasive species displace local native species, alter the structure of plant communities, change moisture regimes, and alter nutrient cycles (see "Vanishing Plants," page 122). Scientists consider them one of the top three threats to the biodiversity of wildlands.

The plight of the Florida Everglades is a prime example. Paperbark tree (*Melaleuca quinquenervia*) has invaded open marshes, altered the hydrology, and converted them into dense, single-species forests. In forested hammocks it has shaded out and displaced native species. At least 450,000 acres of diverse marshland have been destroyed by this plant. *Melaleuca* is just one of the detrimental exotics that was brought to Florida at least partly for its ornamental appeal. Earleaf acacia (*Acacia auriculiformis*), fig trees (*Ficus* species), Brazilian pepper (*Schinus terebinthifolius*), bishopwood (*Bischofia javanica*), Australian pine (*Casuarina equisetifolia*), and water hyacinth (*Eichhornia crassipes*) are a few of the species that are destroying what is left of Florida's native ecosystems.

Florida, along with California and Hawaii, appears to be the hardest hit by invasive species, but few, if any, regions of the United States and Canada are without nonnative pests. As many as half of the 300 recognized invasive exotic plants throughout the United States were deliberately introduced as ornamentals. Some of them are still sold in nurseries despite their known invasive tendencies. Before you buy any nonnative plant for your garden, check with park and preserve managers or the local chapter of The Nature Conservancy to make sure that the species has not shown any signs of invasiveness in your area. While most exotic plants are innocuous denizens of their adopted shores, invasive species have collided head-on with the local flora.

---

### Mangrove Swamps

Where the land meets the sea, vast mangrove swamps help fend off the force of hurricanes. Three species are found here, depending on the depth of the water. Red mangrove occupies the outermost zone, spreading into the water to claim new ground; as sediment is deposited around its roots, the land slowly impinges on the sea. Behind the red mangrove grows the black mangrove, followed, in turn, by the salt-sensitive white mangrove, which occupies the most sheltered part of the mangrove swamps. As the swamps move out into the sea, the dry land vacated by the mangroves is colonized by hardwood trees.

### Central Prairies and Plains

The great grasslands of the Midwest and Great Plains are defined, both ecologically and aesthetically, by plants that are mostly herbaceous. The midcontinent is a grassland landscape because climatic factors and the influence of fire make the growth of woody plants difficult. Due to the combination of excessive summer heat, persistent winds, and low precipitation, evaporation often equals precipitation. Trees have shallow, widespread root systems and a huge, persistent biomass to support. Where rainfall is sporadic or strongly seasonal, trees are limited to areas where moisture is more predictable, such as along watercourses and coulees, moist valleys in the rolling glacial moraine country, where trees grow sheltered from the harsh environment around them. Wildfire also is essential to the survival of the prairie, keeping it free of trees (see "The Role of Fire," page 154).

Grasses have extensive underground networks of fibrous roots that probe deeply and thoroughly for moisture. In fact, most of the biomass of both grasses and prairie forbs, or native wildflowers, is below the ground. These plants produce foliage and flowers in response to available moisture. In times of plenty, growth is lush and flowers are abundant. During drought cycles, plants may remain in a semidormant condition during the growing season to conserve resources. Soil compaction and grazing by bison also helped shape prairie vegetation. Bison once roamed the Midwest, but the herds were decimated by hunters a century ago, and those that remain are all corralled. Deer, fox, songbirds, and insects are plentiful.

Gardening in the prairie states can be a challenge. The intense winter cold, summer heat, and periodic drought produce stressful conditions for plants. However, winter snows protect them from the worst of the cold, so perennials can survive. In fact, many are adapted to the midcontinental climate; a large number of beautiful perennials such as blazing stars (*Liatris* species), coneflowers (*Echinacea* species), sunflowers (*Helianthus* species), and asters are native to the prairie province. Both perennials and vegetables thrive, especially in the eastern reaches of the prairie region, where there is more precipitation and the soil is richer.

The three broad associations in the prairie province are tallgrass, mixed-grass, and shortgrass prairie. Savannah, an open mixture of trees and prairie plants, is a common ecotone where the forest meets the tallgrass prairie.

## Oak Savannah

Where the prairie meets the forest are open, parklike areas called *savannahs*. In savannahs, small expanses of prairie are interspersed with open groves of trees that shelter shrubs and woodland wildflowers. Grasses, sedges (*Carex* species), and sun-loving wildflowers mingle with woodland plants such as starry Solomon's seal (*Smilacina stellata*) and bellwort (*Uvularia grandiflora*) in unique combinations. The savannah is a fire-dependent community. Extended drought cycles favor prairie plants, as fire burns away trees not adapted to surviving the blister-

### PRAIRIE CLASSIFICATION

Ecologists classify prairies by moisture regime, or the dominant seasonal patterns of rainfall and drought, combined with the soil's ability to hold moisture: *xeric*, or dry; *mesic*, or moist; and *hydric*, or wet. These basic terms relating to moisture are used to describe other plant communities as well, such as forests. Moisture regimes are determined by topography and soil type. In general, dry prairies are found at the highest elevations on gravelly, sandy, or sandy loam soils. Mesic prairies are seldom inundated by water and are on loamy soils with varying degrees of silt and clay. Hydric prairies are often flooded during winter and spring. The underlying soils are heavy clay or highly organic peat. In general, the tallgrass prairie region is composed of hydric and mesic prairies, the mixed-grass prairies are mesic or xeric, and the shortgrass prairie is xeric. The classification is not just a regional one, however. Dry gravel ridges within the tallgrass region may support xeric prairie, and wetlands in the shortgrass prairie region may support hydric plants.

ing heat. The woodland retreats and the prairie makes inroads. During wet cycles, the trees are favored, and in time reseed and advance into the prairie. With them come fire-sensitive shrubs and woodland wildflowers. These drought and wet cycles may last 100 years or more.

## Tallgrass Prairie

The easternmost portion of the prairie province has deep, rich soils and ample rainfall for luxuriant growth. This is the tallgrass prairie association. Bluestems, switchgrass, asters, goldenrods, and milkweeds (*Asclepias* species) are a few of the common plants. In tallgrass prairie there is, on average, less than one tree per acre. Shrubs occur in scattered patches, especially where the soil is moist.

## Mixed-Grass Prairie

Farther west, the mixed-grass prairies have rich soils but more moderate rainfall. With less than 20 inches of rain per year, trees find it very hard to grow. Grasses and perennial forbs dominate. Extreme summer drought and bitterly cold winter temperatures are the rule, not the exception. If conditions become too rigorous during the growing season, plants go dormant to conserve their resources. When the rains return, plants resume growth with few ill effects. This region is peppered with wetlands, especially in the north. These wetlands, called *prairie pot-holes*, are critical habitat for nesting waterfowl, shorebirds, waders, and songbirds.

## Shortgrass Prairie

In the rain shadow of the Rocky Mountains, the shortgrass prairie is the driest midcontinental grassland. On the high plains, the annual rainfall of 15 inches is scarcely more than that in a

### THE ROLE OF FIRE

Fire is an important force of change in the prairie landscape. Historically, fires of varying intensities and durations burned vast tracts of land. During drought years, these raging fires drastically altered the landscape, turning forests to savannahs and savannahs to prairies. Herbaceous plants are resistant to fire because their growing points are below the soil surface, where they are protected from the fire's most intense heat. Woody plants have little ability to withstand a hot fire. Most trees have thin bark, with the actively growing cells, called the *cambium*, close to the surface. The heat of a prairie or woodland fire is intense enough to kill the cambium of most trees. The fire-tolerant bur oak is able to survive because the cambium is protected by a thick layer of corky bark that insulates the living cells from the intense heat. Because of its fire tolerance, bur oak is the dominant tree of the oak savannah.

desert. The plants are adapted to extreme drought and cold. The vegetation is short in stature, and comparatively drought-tolerant grasses outnumber the forbs. There are more annuals in the shortgrass prairie because the open soil between the grasses provides a seedbed for germination. Antelope, badgers, prairie dogs, and shorebirds abound.

## Western Deserts

Deserts are found in areas where evaporation exceeds precipitation. High-incident solar radiation as well as wind add up to a negative water budget, meaning that deserts are always dry. Far from wastelands, however, deserts are teeming with life.

The type of desert and its aridity depend on the timing and amount of precipitation. The nature of desert soil also affects availability of water for plant growth. More rain can infiltrate sandy and gravelly soils than clay soils. If rain comes as deluges, most of the water will not penetrate the soil but rather will run off the surface, and plants will receive little benefit. Many areas have saline or alkaline soils due to the constant evaporation of water, which brings minerals to the surface.

North America's four desert associations— the Great Basin, Mojave Desert, Sonoran Desert, and Chihuahuan Desert—are situated between two enormous mountain ranges, the Sierras and the Rockies. Due to their position between tall mountain ranges and the influence of the cold waters of the Pacific Ocean, the western deserts are subject to dramatic seasonal shifts in storm tracks. In the cold northern Great Basin, most of the sparse annual precipitation falls as snow. The warmer deserts to the south receive their annual precipitation as rain, either in winter or summer.

Gardeners in these regions must acknowledge the limitations of the climate, especially water. Beautiful, water-conserving, and low-maintenance gardens can be created using the desert flora.

## Great Basin

The Great Basin is cold in winter and warm in summer. The elevation varies from high valleys to lofty peaks. The cold and dry landscape is less lush than other deserts, and there are fewer species. Shrubs are common, especially sagebrushes and saltbushes, as well as grasses. Locoweeds (*Oxytropis* species), lupines, and paintbrushes (*Castilleja* species) are common forbs. Pinyon pine (*Pinus edulis*) or Douglas fir

(*Pseudotsuga menziesii*) occur at higher elevations. Pronghorn antelope, jackrabbits, sage grouse, and hawks are common.

## Mojave Desert

To the south of the Great Basin lies the Mojave Desert. This hot, dry desert varies from barren salt flats below sea level to forested peaks. The Mojave receives mainly winter rains. Precipitation is minimal, usually less than 6 inches per year. Yuccas, creosote bush, and beavertail cactus are common. The most conspicuous yucca is the enormous Joshua tree. The soils are generally alkaline or saline. Many of the wildflowers, such as desert marigold (*Baileya multiradiata*) and phacelias, are annuals. The invasive nonnative tamarisks or salt cedars (*Tamarix* species) have taken over most stream- and riverbanks, to the exclusion of most native species. Common Mojave fauna include bighorn sheep, coyotes, mice, sparrows, roadrunners, and lizards.

## Sonoran Desert

The Sonoran Desert is the most diverse and spectacular of the western deserts. This is due in large part to its subtropical climate and biseasonal rainfall. The wettest desert, the Sonoran receives rain from both winter and summer storms. Winter rains are slow and steady, whereas summer storms dump huge amounts of rain in a short time. There not only is a greater diversity of species, but also a greater structural diversity, with trees, shrubs, herbs, and cacti. The cacti vary from diminutive cushions to the towering saguaro. Annuals are common, and if winter rains are sufficient, the desert is blanketed with wildflowers in March and April. Reptiles abound, including the colorful gila monster, as do birds found

## A BARREL OF WATER

Cacti have evolved to survive the rigors of the desert by collecting and storing water. They do not have leaves; leaves lose too much water. Unlike most other plants, they have chlorophyll, and therefore photosynthesize, in their stems. When it rains, the roots absorb water quickly and the plants store the water in the stems. The fleshy stem tissue acts like a sponge. This ready reserve is slowly used by the plant during dry times. Since water is scarce for all creatures, the cactus must protect itself from thirsty animals. That is where the spines come in. Actually modified leaves, the spines provide armor to protect the succulent stems. The spines also help to trap water vapor in the folds of the cactus stem, thus reducing water loss. The flowers of cacti are exquisite. They come in shades of pink, red, orange, and yellow, as well as white.

nowhere else in North America, such as trogons and several species of hummingbirds.

### Chihuahuan Desert

The Chihuahuan Desert reaches its northern limits in Texas and New Mexico; most of the desert lies in Mexico. The mighty Rio Grande cuts through the heart of the desert. The landscape is mountainous, and the valley floors are high. Winters are cold and summers are hot. The Chihuahuan gets most of its precipitation in summer. Precipitation varies between 7 and 12 inches per year. Yuccas, agaves, cacti, and annuals like *Zinnia grandiflora* are common. The areas where precipitation is comparatively high support grasslands. The soils are high in calcium. Pronghorns, badgers, rodents, songbirds, hawks, and reptiles are plentiful.

## Western Coniferous Forest

The Rocky Mountains, Sierra Nevada, and Cascades are blanketed with dense forests of mixed conifers, some of the most magnificent forests in the world. The tall mountain ranges intercept the clouds as they move in from the Pacific Ocean. As a result, there are forests even on the southern mountains amid deserts and grasslands. Only in the cool north, where rainfall is abundant, are there dense forests in the valleys as well. On the mountain slopes, soils are generally shallow and composed of organic duff or peat. In the valleys, alluvial soils from the eroding mountains are deep and rich. Wildlife abounds in the western forests, including elk, moose, bear, squirrels, and birds. Campers are familiar with the thieving jays, often called camp robbers, who never pass up a handout.

Gardeners in this region have cool summers—perfect for growing perennials. The coastal regions have mild winters as well and are a gardening paradise. The herbaceous border so admired in English gardening books, lush with plants from around the globe, is most attainable here.

Three distinct associations are found in the Western Coniferous Forest: the Northwest Coastal Forest, the Sierra Montane Forest, and the Rocky Mountain Montane Forest. Each association has its unique assemblage of species, but trees such as Douglas fir and lodgepole pine are common across the entire province. At higher elevations lie the subalpine zones.

### Northwest Coastal Forest

The Northwest Coastal Forest is dominated by Sitka spruce, western hemlock, western white cedar, and, at its southernmost locations, towering redwoods. The forests of northern California, Oregon, and Washington have been at the center of a controversy for years, as huge stands of old-growth trees have fallen to the saw. The northern Pacific Coast receives over 100 inches of rain a year. The temperate rain forest in this region is lush and productive.

## Sierra Montane Forest

This association carpets the slopes and valleys of the Sierra Nevada chain. The moist, rich soils of valley floors and lower mountain slopes favor incense cedar, Douglas fir, and ponderosa pine. In these areas, the canopy is closed. In sheltered valleys, ancient forests of sequoia are found. These trees may be as much as two thousand years old. The drier slopes are host to many pines, especially lodgepole and sugar pines (*Pinus contorta* and *Pinus lambertiana*), as well as Douglas fir. Here, the trees are more dispersed and the canopy is more open.

## Rocky Mountain Forest

The Rocky Mountain association is dominated by ponderosa pine, lodgepole pine, and Douglas fir. Moist forests in valleys and along streams have closed-canopy forests of Douglas fir, western red cedar, and western hemlock (*Tsuga heterophylla*). The drier slopes have a sparse canopy with a thick shrub layer of redroots (*Ceanothus* species) and ocean spray (*Holodiscus discolor*). In the hotter, drier southern reaches of the mountains, pinyon-juniper woodlands are found. These trees grow in open communities with grasses, bulbs such as mariposa lilies (*Calochortus* species), and annual wildflowers. The soil is generally shallow and rocky.

## Subalpine Forest

In these harsh, high-elevation climates, the trees are often stunted. The soil is thin and rich in organic matter. Engelmann spruce, subalpine fir, and whitebark pine dominate the cooler and wetter subalpine zones. Bristlecone and limber pines (*Pinus aristata* and *Pinus flex-*

---

### ONCE UPON A FOREST

Some 50 million years ago, before the great Ice Age, a lush forest stretched across North America from coast to coast. The northern reaches of the forest were dominated by mixed stands of deciduous and coniferous trees. In these stands grew the ancestors of the common conifers and deciduous trees we know today—oaks, magnolias, spruces, firs. The central and southern regions were subtropical. Ginkgo, ferns, and trees similar to those in present-day Australia were common.

Over the next 45 million years, forces altered the face of the continent. The western mountain ranges slowly began to rise, and in time divided the continent into distinct sections. These mountains changed rainfall patterns, and vast grasslands came to dominate the Midwest, separating the forests of the East and West. The stage was set for divergent evolution. The deciduous trees could not thrive in the cool, arid West, and conifers dominated. The humid East became a great deciduous forest. When the Ice Age began 3 million years ago, plants began migrating in response to warming and cooling trends, but the basic division in vegetation between East and West was already in place. With the final retreat of the ice between 10 and 7 thousand years ago, the die was cast for the distribution of species we see today.

*ilis*) are found in the drier areas. Marmots, chipmunks, Clark's nutcrackers, and finches are often encountered along trails.

## Californian Province

The coastal ranges of California and Oregon, as well as the western slopes of the Sierras, make up this floristic province. The Californian region is distinguished by a Mediterranean climate with warm, dry summers and cool, moist winters. Late winter is emerald green as grasses emerge and annual wildflowers bloom in response to the 15 to 25 inches of precipitation dropped during the rainy season. Drought-tolerant evergreen oaks such as emory oak (*Quercus emoryi*) and coast live oak sprout new leaves at this time. As the summer warms and rain becomes scarce to nonexistent, native grasses go dormant and the landscape turns russet and brown for the rest of the year.

California's ideal climate has attracted millions of people. Coastal regions as well as the foothills of the Sierra have been radically altered by the burgeoning human population. The fertile valleys, too, have been transformed, converted to agricultural crops. As a result, many species of the unique and diverse flora of this province are endangered.

Chaparral, a community dominated by shrubs and small trees interspersed with grasses, oak woodlands, and grasslands, are the major associations of the Californian Floristic Province. They are home to coyotes, foxes, hawks, reptiles, and many songbirds, some of which are endemic to the region, meaning they are found nowhere else—as are an unusually large number of California plants.

### California Grassland

The extensive grasslands of central and southern California were once known as the Pacific Prairie. The association is dominated by cool-season bunch grasses that turn golden during the marked summer dry season. Bulbous plants such as onions (*Allium* species), mariposas (*Calochortus* species), and blue dicks (*Dichelostemma pulchellum*) are common in spring. This vast grassland covered over 5 million hectares, much of which is now grazed or has been converted to farmland. Grazing has disturbed the soil, eliminated many native species, and introduced a vast array of exotic weeds. Fires were once common in the grasslands, controlling the spread of trees. Native Americans set many of the fires to improve the habitat for game animals. Oaks and other trees now invade many areas formerly dominated by grasses.

### Oak Woodland

Oaks cover the low foothills and line the narrow stream valleys. Moving north in the province, pinyons and junipers intermingle with oaks and come to dominate in the higher elevations and colder areas. Blue oak woodland, also called foothills oak woodland, rings the central valley on the slopes of the Coastal and Sierra Ranges. Blue oak is dominant, but digger pine, interior live oak, and black oak are also common. There is no defined shrub layer, and the ground layer is composed of grasses, bulbs, and annuals. Southern oak woodland occurs mainly on the Pacific side of the Coastal Range, but also on the eastern slope in southern California and Mexico. The structure of this community is similar to that of other oak woodlands. The dominant oak is coast live oak, except on eastern slopes in the south, where it is codominant with Engelmann oak.

## Chaparral

Chaparral is a community created by an impenetrable thicket of shrubs. The coastal chaparral is found where the rolling mountain slopes meet the Pacific Ocean, from southern Oregon to Baja. Mountain chaparral is found on the slopes and crests of inland foothills. The coast and mountain chaparral is composed of various shrubs with thick, leathery evergreen leaves, such as manzanitas, which resist drought and salt spray. Many chaparral shrubs rely on fire for renewal and reproduction. The propensity of the chaparral to burn often ends in tragedy for the many Californians who build their homes in the midst of this natural community. Selective, periodic controlled burning is one way to lessen the fire hazard. Reptiles, small mammals, and birds such as the California thrasher are common in chaparral communities.

# Wetland Ecosystems of North America

Wetlands are important ecosystems. They are nature's flood-control systems. They take up excess water unleashed by storms and release it slowly, thereby reducing or eliminating flooding. Without wetlands, floodwaters run quickly over paved areas and into storm sewers or conduits, concentrating in volume and speed as they go; when this water reaches streams and rivers, erosion and flooding occur. Wetlands also filter sediments and break down pollutants. Still another important function of wetlands is groundwater recharge. Wetlands absorb water that eventually returns to the water table. Without wetlands, aquifers would not be replenished.

What is more, wetlands are very productive. The lush wetland vegetation captures the sun's energy and converts it into living plant matter. Much of the vegetation produced in a growing season remains in the wetland, releasing nutrients as it decays. This nutrient-rich water supports a vast array of animals that feed on decaying vegetation. These animals form the foundation of an important food web that includes mink and otter, frogs, turtles, butterflies, dragonflies, and many other creatures. Prairie pothole wetlands are waterfowl factories; Arctic wetlands are essential to shorebirds as well as waterfowl; coastal saltmarshes produce seafood and fish. Without healthy wetlands, we would not have a healthy environment filled with a diversity of beautiful and useful species.

Marshes, bogs, swamps, and saltmarshes are the major wetland types.

## Marshes

Marshes are open, shallow wetlands with standing water for all or part of the year. In general, marshes are treeless, dominated by herbaceous plants. Emergent plants grow in standing water, and sedges, grasses, and water-tolerant forbs grow in the seasonally inundated soils around the margin of the wetland. Emergent plants reproduce by seed during natural drawdown cycles caused by drought. Marshes are classified as shallow or deep, based on the water depth and the persistence of water through the season. Deep marshes have water up to three feet deep. Shallow marshes have six inches or less of standing water.

Marshes are among the most productive wetlands for birds and mammals. Ducks, geese, wading birds such as herons and egrets, rails, terns, and songbirds make their home in marshes. Raptors, including ospreys, bald eagles, northern harriers, and short-eared owls, hunt and nest in or adjacent to marshes. Muskrats, mink, voles, and mice are common. Marshes serve as nurseries for young fish. They also stabilize soil and improve water quality by filtering sediments and absorbing nutrients.

## Peatlands/Bogs

Peatlands form in glacial lake beds in regions where temperatures are too cold for rapid decay of organic matter. The organic matter, called *peat*, accumulates faster than it decomposes, and open wetlands fill with peat over time. Bogs are specialized, acidic peatlands derived mostly from species of sphagnum moss. Bogs are poor in nutrients and generally form in basins with no inlet or outlet for surface water. The lack of fresh water causes the acidity to increase to a level that is toxic to all but specialized plants.

Bogs start as floating mats of vegetation over the open water of a basin. As the mats grow and thicken, the basin begins to fill in with accumulated peat. The older the bog, the drier it becomes, until trees are able to grow. Open bogs are dominated by shrubs in the heath family (Ericaceae) and herbaceous plants. Older bogs are dominated by spruce and larch trees in the dry areas where the mat is thickest, by shrubs in the intermediate zones, and by herbs in the saturated soils.

Bogs are not totally restricted to northern latitudes. They are found in the Appalachian and Rocky Mountains, as well as in the southeastern states. These southern bogs often lie

## MEAT-EATING PLANTS

The greatest concentration of insectivorous plants in North America is found in the southern Coastal Plain, where pitcher plants (*Sarracenia* species), Venus's-flytrap (*Dionaea muscipula*), sundews (*Drosera* species), and bladderworts (*Utricularia* species) all catch and consume insects. The sandy and peaty soils of coastal savannahs and bogs are low in nutrients, especially nitrogen. Insect-eating plants have evolved to catch the food that they need in order to survive. Pitcher plants use a pit-trap method to catch their prey: the insects are lured to the beautiful leaves by sweet excretions. They slip on the edge and fall into a tiny pool of water inside the leaf, where they drown and are digested. The other plant carnivores use active traps to catch their prey. The Venus's-flytrap is the most dramatic, with a snare that snaps shut when an insect walks across the trap. Carnivorous plants are fascinating to grow, but require special care. They need sterile, acidic soil and must be watered with distilled or rainwater. Alkaline and mineral-rich tap or well water will slowly kill them. Many insect-eating plants are collected from the wild for sale, and populations of Venus's-flytrap, for example, are imperiled as a result. Purchase them only from reputable dealers.

over shallow bedrock or hardpan soils that trap water at the surface. They are similar in ecology to northern bogs, but the peaty soils are much shallower.

Bogs are home to an astonishing array of plant and animal life. Bears, lemmings, amphibians, and many songbirds live among shrubs, orchids, ferns, and pitcher plants.

## Swamps

Swamps are wetlands dominated by woody vegetation, with soil that is inundated for all or part of the year. There are three main categories of swamps: shrub swamps, or carrs; deciduous swamps; and coniferous swamps. Shrub swamps grow on the edges of bogs, wet meadows, streams, floodplains, and other wetlands. They are often dominated by a mixture of dogwoods (*Cornus* species) and willows (*Salix* species). A variety of sedges (*Carex* species), grasses, and forbs grows in the dappled shade of the shrubs. Shrub wetlands are important nesting sites for songbirds such as sparrows and warblers, and provide winter shelter for mammals. Shrub carrs dominated by alders (*Alnus* species) are known as *alder thickets*.

Deciduous swamps are found in ancient lake beds and other low-lying areas with poor drainage, seepages, and the oxbows and floodplains of rivers. These seasonally wet areas are critical for floodwater retention and home to a wide variety of plants and animals. Lowland trees such as black ash (*Fraxinus nigra*), red maple (*Acer rubrum*), tupelos (*Nyssa* species), and bald cypress (*Taxodium distichum*) tower above a carpet of marsh marigold (*Caltha palustris*), skunk cabbage (*Symplocarpus foetidus* or *Lysichiton americanus*), orchids, sedges (*Carex* species), and ferns. In southern swamps, red bay (*Persea borbonia*), loblolly bay (*Gordonia lasianthus*), titi (*Cyrilla racemiflora*), and hollies (*Ilex* species) form thickets among the cypress trees.

Coniferous swamps are found in northern areas where winter cold is hard on deciduous trees. In acidic soils, larches (*Larix* species) dominate. Where soils are sweet and nutrient rich, white cedar (*Chamaecyparis thyoides*) is common. The dense year-round shade of coniferous swamps limits the herbaceous vegetation to plants with evergreen leaves such as goldthreads (*Coptis* species), as well as orchids, sedges, and ferns.

## Saltmarshes

Saltmarshes are coastal wetlands found in estuaries and backwaters, behind barrier beaches,

### SEAFOOD NURSERIES

Saltmarshes are virtual seafood factories. The twice-daily influx of tides bathes them with oxygen and nutrient-rich water. Fish, crustaceans, and other marine life spawn in the shallow waters. Crabs, mussels, scallops, and many prized food fish such as striped bass depend on the marshes to shelter their young. Yet these wetlands are some of the most adversely affected by human activity. Not only are they filled or dredged to make room for resorts and marinas, but they also are repositories for upstream pollution. Many saltmarshes are part of estuary systems at the bottom of the watersheds of great rivers. Upstream from the marshes, development and agriculture are common. Erosion dumps soil, fertilizers, and pesticides into streams and rivers. They concentrate as they move downstream toward the saltmarshes, where they are dumped by the slowing currents. The sediment smothers eelgrass and other submergent vegetation, eliminating spawning and hiding places. The pesticides kill plants and animals. The nutrients accelerate the growth of pest plants at the expense of others. The health of saltmarshes depends on careful land management, both upstream and along the coast.

and along bays and inlets. Saltmarshes are subjected to dramatic, twice-daily water-level fluctuations from high and low tides. Grasses dominate saltmarshes, but a variety of sedges (*Carex* species), glassworts (*Salicornia* species), and other forbs are also found. Spartina grasses are a common component of healthy saltmarshes, but pollution and sedimentation have allowed common reed (*Phragmites communis*) to dominate in many situations. This plant forms dense monocultures where it gets a foothold, and it soon crowds out other species. The muck soils are nutrient rich, making saltmarshes very productive. Gulls, terns, and other birds nest and winter in the dense cover of the grasses. Wrens, sparrows, and red-wing blackbirds are common in the drier areas. Rails, ducks, shorebirds, and wading birds frequent the mudflats at low tide. Fish and crustaceans breed in the shallow waters.

## Plant Community Ecology Basics

Plant community ecology is the science that explores the processes that form and influence plant communities and the patterns of distribution within them. For example, plant communities are constantly changing in a process often called *succession*. As young grasslands and forests comprising a certain mix of species mature, new assemblages of species take over, until storms, fires, diseases, or insects disturb them and the process begins anew. Healthy ecosystems are also characterized by biodiversity, a mixture of many different individuals of many different species. In any given plant community, there are dominant, subdominant, and subordinate species. Dominance refers to the one or more species that are most essential to the life and character of the plant community.

Gardens are plant communities, too. Successful gardening requires an understanding of the ecological processes at work on cultivated land. Our models for understanding these processes are local plant communities. Of course, structure and change in the garden are orchestrated by the gardener, not the forces of nature alone. The closer a gardener works with nature, however, the less work and the more successful the garden will be.

## The Physical Structure of Plant Communities

Every native plant community has a recognizable, and somewhat predictable, structure based on the dominant and subordinate vegetation. A forest has a towering canopy of trees that influences what can and cannot grow beneath it. A grassland has a similar structure, but the plants are herbaceous instead of woody, and this vertical structure is re-created above ground each growing season, not over decades and centuries as in a forest.

Plants within a given community also create patterns of distribution on the landscape as a result of environmental factors such as soil, moisture, and light. Different species thrive with different amounts of moisture, for example. In a prairie, shrubs will grow in the wettest areas, grasses and forbs on the slightly higher and drier land. As a result of these factors, plant communities have recognizable vertical and horizontal structure.

Ecological gardeners use the structure of the native plant community as the basis for structuring their gardens. In the eastern forest region, for example, canopy trees lend a grand vertical scale to the garden, creating a cathedral-like enclosure, while understory trees add a more intimate, human-scale "ceiling." Shrubs can become "walls" that divide spaces horizontally and create privacy. The ground layer is where gardeners can create a tapestry of wildflowers, ferns, and grasses in beds and borders. Ecological gardeners know that structuring a garden like the native plant community also helps support birds and butterflies and other wildlife by offering them an array of spaces for feeding, breeding, resting, and nesting.

## Vertical Structure

All plant communities have a vertical structure based on the size and growth pattern of the dominant species. This pattern is called *vertical stratification*, or vertical layering. Vertical structure is most obvious in a forest. The tallest layer is called the *canopy*. It is composed of mature trees that cover the entire forest. The tallest canopy trees may be 100 feet in height or more. The lowest canopy trees grow to about 30 feet. The canopy is interwoven, forming a fairly continuous ceiling over the entire forest. The canopy sets the stage for everything that happens in the layers below it.

The next layer down is called the *understory*. This layer is composed of saplings of canopy tree species as well as smaller flowering trees such as dogwoods, redbud, shadblow, ironwood, and hop hornbeam in the eastern United States. The understory extends from 30 to 12 feet.

The *shrub layer* is the lowest layer of woody vegetation. It occupies the area between 12 and 3 feet above the ground. Shrubs grow in patches where light and space are sufficient. A variety of forest birds, including vireos and some warblers, use the shrub layer for foraging and nesting. Many shrubs produce edible fruits

that enable birds to lay on fat reserves in preparation for migration.

The lowest aboveground layer of the forest, below 3 feet, is called the *ground layer*. Here, wildflowers, ferns, grasses, and sedges grow in often-spectacular assemblages. Plants in the ground layer also partition their environment vertically. The spring ephemerals bloom first, typically raising their foliage only a few inches above the leaf litter. As they are going dormant, the taller ferns, merrybells, and other herbs overtop them.

The age of a plant community affects its structure. Young forests have a well-defined shrub layer and understory. The canopy becomes more distinct as the forest ages. Different forests have different structures. Deciduous forests have the most elaborate structure, as described above. By contrast, coniferous forests, with their dense stands of tall and narrow trees, typically have very little understory, but can have a dense shrub layer and ground layer of herbs and mosses. Pine forests have the most open canopies of the coniferous forests, with scattered understory trees and a well-defined shrub layer. Ground-layer species are scattered in the sunny openings. Oak woodlands have a structure similar to that of the pine woods, except the trees are smaller in stature and the canopies are wider. The ground layer of grasses and annual wildflowers is exceptional during the rainy season.

Shrub communities have mixed layers of different-sized shrubs, with a ground layer of herbs, grasses, and sedges. In communities dominated by herbaceous plants, the vertical structure is no less distinct. The plants resprout from their roots each year. The earliest plants to emerge in the spring are low to the ground. Each successive emerging plant overtops the next, culminating with the tallest grasses and late-blooming composites that end the growing season.

## Horizontal Structure

Light, moisture, slope, and soil have a direct effect on where a plant or group of plants grows in a forest, grassland, desert, or other plant community. Plants form horizontal patterns of distribution in response to these environmental and edaphic, or soil-related, factors, better known to gardeners as *microclimates*. The resulting diversity of associations and species across the landscape is called *horizontal heterogeneity.*

In deciduous forests, oaks are found on the drier sites such as sunny slopes, while maple and basswood grow in the moister soil on east and north slopes. Individual trees are spaced according to their canopy size and shape. In marshes, sedges dominate the wettest areas, shrubs the intermediate regions, and wet meadow or woodland plants the upland zones.

## Ecotones

Ecotones are the transitions between two plant communities. Because they include species from both communities and often their own unique species as well, ecotones are usually the most diverse ecosystems. In the Midwest, the eastern deciduous forest grades into the prairie in an ecotone called oak savannah. In the West, conifer forests grade into pinyon, juniper, or oak woodlands or into shrubby grassland ecotones. Ecotones also occur on a smaller scale, where wind throw has created an opening in the forest, for example, or at the edges of small tracts of woods. Ecotones support not only a variety of plants but also generalist animals such as skunks, deer, robins, and jays, which are not dependent on a single species of plant.

Today, the most common ecotones occur on abandoned agricultural land. These fields are first overtaken by pioneer species, generally a mixture of native and naturalized annuals that colonize open or disturbed ground. As the soil stabilizes and grows richer, an increasing variety of plants parades across the landscape, depending upon soil, moisture, and exposure. In forested regions, canopy trees ultimately become dominant. This new edge of grasses, shrubs, and young trees becomes an ecotone between open field (meadow) and forest.

---

### REESTABLISHING BROKEN CONNECTIONS

Horizontal structure is important to the long-term health of ecosystems. As we have parceled, subdivided, and cleared the land, we have interrupted or destroyed the horizontal connectivity of plant communities. When we do this, we cut off vital links used by wildlife and plants to move freely across the landscape. In effect, we create islands, isolated fragments of vegetation surrounded by cities, suburbs, and farm fields. The health of the plant community, both locally and globally, depends on the connections we have severed. In isolated pockets, plants and animals interbreed, reducing genetic diversity and endangering their survival over the long haul. Isolated patches are also more vulnerable to destruction by pests and diseases. Once plants are eliminated, the island cannot be recolonized by many species, and the diversity of plant life is reduced forever. As gardeners, we have the ability to repair these broken connections. Our gardens, one by one, can reestablish links to parks, nature preserves, and other green spaces, and restore the health of the environment.

## The Biological Structure of Plant Communities

The biological structure of plant communities gives them the character we observe in nature. A deciduous forest dominated by tall, slender oaks looks very different from one composed of wide-spreading beech trees and rich evergreen hemlocks. A prairie dominated by grasses is altogether different from a forest of stately trees. Within different plant communities a vast diversity of species is found. In a tallgrass prairie dominated by three grass species, you may find more than nine different grasses and up to three hundred different forbs. A mixed mesophytic forest may have over thirty different tree species, even though only two or three are codominant. Ecological health depends on diversity. Plant communities are naturally diverse, but our gardens are comparatively barren. A typical garden has one grass, bluegrass turf, a dozen perennial plants, three different shrubs, and one or two different trees. If we are to make our gardens as attractive to wildlife as they are to us, we must understand biological structure and put that knowledge to work. We must learn to appreciate both biological and visual complexity.

### Species Dominance

Dominance refers to the influence of species that contribute the most cover and/or biomass (total mass or weight) to a plant community. In a forest, the dominant species is the tree that contributes the most cover to the canopy. In a prairie it is a grass or a forb. In the tundra, it is a shrub, herb, or lichen. If more than one species make up the dominant cover, then individuals in the suite of species are called *codominants*. Dominant species are often called *visual essence species*, for they are the ones that give a plant community its unique look.

Dominance is determined by density in a plant community—that is, the total number of stems or individual plants within a given area. Ecologists use precise sampling techniques to determine dominance. One common technique is the use of quadrats, or plots of land with fixed dimensions. Within each quadrat, the trees, saplings, shrubs, and herbs are counted and measured. In forests, relative density, relative cover, and relative frequency are weighted to determine dominance. In herbaceous communities, dominance is determined by relative cover and frequency.

### Biodiversity

Biodiversity, a much-used term these days, refers to a healthy mixture of ecosystems, communities within the ecosystems, species within the communities, populations within the species, and individuals within the population. An individual is a single plant of a given species—a barrel cactus, for example. A population is all the barrel cacti in the area. The community is the barrel cacti, along with associated vegetation such as prickly pears, palo verde trees, ocotillo, and mesquite. The ecosystem is the Sonoran Desert. The Sonoran Desert is one of the four associations in the Western Deserts province.

Ecosystem diversity is the broadest aspect of biodiversity. Globally, as well as within North America, the variety of ecosystems contributes to the health and stability of the biosphere. Forests, grasslands, deserts, and other vegetation formations make up the global ecosystem. On a smaller scale, biodiversity is important to the health and resilience of ecosystems as well. For example, food chains are built on the foun-

# DOMINANT SPECIES BY PLANT COMMUNITY

## TUNDRA

There are two tundra associations: alpine and Arctic. The Arctic vegetation in North America is remarkably similar to that of Eurasia. The climate is so severe, and the area so new geologically, that evolution has not produced a distinctive North American Arctic flora. As the name suggests, alpine tundra is found at high mountain elevations.

### Alpine Tundra

Bistorts, *Polygonum* species
Mountain heathers, *Cassiope* species
Mountain heaths, *Phyllodoce* species
Sedges, *Carex* species
Willows, *Salix* species

### Arctic Tundra

Bistorts, *Polygonum* species
Cinquefoils, *Potentilla* species
Cottongrasses, *Eriophorum* species
Lapland rose bay, *Rhododendron lapponicum*
Sweet gale, *Myrica gale*
Willows, *Salix* species

### Tundra Wetlands

Marsh marigold, *Caltha leptosepala*
Sedges, *Carex* species
Willows, *Salix* species

## NORTHERN CONIFEROUS FOREST

The dominant species in this huge province that stretches across the northern reaches of the entire continent are cold-tolerant conifers, though mixed coniferous/deciduous stands are found in the ecotone with the deciduous forests to the south. Many wetlands dominated by either sedges or sphagnum mosses are found throughout the region.

### Mixed Deciduous/Coniferous Forest

Balsam fir, *Abies balsamea*
Paper birch, *Betula papyrifera*
Quaking aspen, *Populus tremuloides*
Sugar maple, *Acer saccharum*
White spruce, *Picea glauca*

### Taiga or Boreal Forest

Black spruce, *Picea mariana*
Eastern white cedar, *Thuja occidentalis*
Larch, *Larix laricina*
Quaking aspen, *Populus tremuloides*
White spruce, *Picea glauca*

### Peatlands

Black spruce, *Picea mariana*
Cottongrasses, *Eriophorum* species
Labrador tea, *Ledum groenlandicum*
Larch, *Larix laricina*
Leatherleaf, *Chamaedaphne calyculata*
Sedges, *Carex* species
Sphagnum mosses, *Sphagnum* species

## EASTERN DECIDUOUS FOREST

This vast province, which stretches from the Atlantic Ocean to the tallgrass prairies of the Midwest, encompasses many associations. Eastern forest associations are determined by climate, soils, and moisture. The common denominator is the dominance of deciduous canopy species. In rare instances, there are codominants that are coniferous, usually pines or hemlock. Meadows occur as scattered breaks in the forest where the soil is too wet or dry to support trees. Old-field meadows occur on abandoned agricultural land.

## Maple-Basswood/Beech-Maple Forest

American beech, *Fagus grandifolia*
Basswood, *Tilia americana*
Canada hemlock, *Tsuga canadensis*
Northern red oak, *Quercus rubra*
Sugar maple, *Acer saccharum*
White oak, *Quercus alba*

## Mixed Mesophytic/Western Mesophytic Forest

American beech, *Fagus grandifolia*
Basswood, *Tilia americana*
Black oak, *Quercus velutina*
Hickories, *Carya* species
Sugar maple, *Acer saccharum*
Tulip tree, *Liriodendron tulipifera*
White oak, *Quercus alba*

## Oak/Hickory Forest
## (Including the former Oak/Chestnut Forest)

American chestnut, *Castanea dentata* (devastated
   by chestnut blight)
Black oak, *Quercus velutina*
Bur oak, *Quercus macrocarpa*
Yellow chestnut oak, *Quercus muehlenbergii*
Hickories, *Carya* species
Northern red oak, *Quercus borealis*
Northern pin oak, *Quercus ellipsoidalis*
White oak, *Quercus alba*

## Floodplain Forest

Cottonwood, *Populus deltoides*
Green ash, *Fraxinus pennsylvanica*
River birch, *Betula nigra*
Silver maple, *Acer saccharinum*
Sycamore, *Platanus occidentalis*

## COASTAL PLAIN

The Coastal Plain of the East and Gulf Coasts is a
vast area with a variety of climates, soils, and moisture regimes. On rich soils, mesic forests of oaks
and other hardwoods dominate, similar to forests
in the Eastern Deciduous Forest province. In sandy
and waterlogged soils, savannahs are found, with
open pine woodlands with well-defined shrub or
grassy ground layers. Bottomlands are dominated
by deciduous trees interspersed with shrubs, wetland sedges, and forbs.

## Northern Pine Barrens

Pitch pine, *Pinus rigida*
Scrub oak, *Quercus ilicifolia*
Shortleaf pine, *Pinus echinata*

## Upland Hardwood Forest

American beech, *Fagus grandifolia*
Bullbay magnolia, *Magnolia grandiflora*
Live oak, *Quercus virginiana*
Loblolly pine, *Pinus taeda*
Red maple, *Acer rubrum*
Southern red oak, *Quercus falcata*
Sweet gum, *Liquidambar styraciflua*
Water oak, *Quercus nigra*
White oak, *Quercus alba*

## Xeric Pine Forest

Blackjack oak, *Quercus marilandica*
Bluejack oak, *Quercus incana*
Slash pine, *Pinus elliottii*
Longleaf pine, *Pinus palustris*
Turkey oak, *Quercus laevis*
Wiregrass, *Aristida stricta*

## Mesic Pine Forest

Loblolly pine, *Pinus taeda*
Longleaf pine, *Pinus palustris*
Saw palmetto, *Serenoa repens*
Scrub oak, *Quercus inopina*
Slash pine, *Pinus elliottii*

## Savannah and Pocosin

Loblolly bay, *Gordonia lasianthus*
Longleaf pine, *Pinus palustris*
Lyonia, *Lyonia lucida*
Pond pine, *Pinus serotina*

*(continued on next page)*

Titi, *Cyrilla racemiflora*
Wax myrtle, *Myrica cerifera*
Zenobia, *Zenobia pulverulenta*

### Bottomland Forest

Atlantic white cedar, *Chamaecyparis thyoides*
Bald cypress, *Taxodium distichum*
Laurel oak, *Quercus laurifolia*
Overcup oak, *Quercus lyrata*
Pond cypress, *Taxodium ascendens*
Red bay, *Persea borbonia*
Red maple, *Acer rubrum*
Swamp tupelo, *Nyssa sylvatica* var. *biflora*
Tupelo, *Nyssa aquatica*
Water hickory, *Carya aquatica*

### Maritime Communities

Beach grass, *Ammophila breviligulata*
Groundsel bush, *Baccharis halimifolia*
Junipers, *Juniperus horizontalis* and *Juniperus virginiana*
Live oak, *Quercus virginiana*
Poison ivy, *Toxicodendron radicans*
Red bay, *Persea borbonia*
Sea oats, *Uniola paniculata*
Wax myrtle, *Myrica cerifera*

## SUBTROPICAL FLORIDA

Subtropical Florida includes varied plant associations such as forested swamps dominated by canopy trees, savannah with open expanses of sawgrass as in the Everglades, islands of trees and shrubs called hammocks, and open pine woodlands on drier sites and ridges.

### Savannah

Palmettos, *Sabal* species
Royal palm, *Roystonea regia*
Sawgrass, *Cladium jamaicensis*
Saw palmetto, *Serenoa repens*
Slash pine, *Pinus elliottii*
Wax myrtle, *Myrica cerifera*

### Hardwood Hammock

Cabbage palmetto, *Sabal palmetto*
Coontie, *Zamia pumila*
Gumbo-limbo, *Bursera simaruba*
Paradise tree, *Simarouba glauca*
Pigeon plum, *Coccoloba diversifolia*
Satin leaf, *Chrysophyllum oliviforme*

### Pineland

Longleaf pine, *Pinus palustris*
Saw palmetto, *Serenoa repens*
Slash pine, *Pinus elliottii*

### Swamp Forests

Cabbage palmetto, *Sabal palmetto*
Cypress, *Taxodium* species
Live oak, *Quercus virginiana*
Red bay, *Persea borbonia*
Strangler fig, *Ficus aurea*
Sweetbay, *Magnolia virginiana*

### Mangrove Swamp

Black mangrove, *Avicennia nitida*
Buttonwood, *Conocarpus erectus*
Gumbo-limbo, *Bursera simaruba*
Red mangrove, *Rhizophora mangle*
White mangrove, *Laguncularia racemosa*

## CENTRAL PRAIRIES AND PLAINS

Moving westward through the Central Prairie Province, rainfall diminishes and the dominant species change from tall grasses such as big bluestem to short grasses such as little bluestem and grama grasses. Composites and legumes are the dominant flowering plant families on the prairies.

### Oak Savannah

Big bluestem, *Andropogon gerardii*
Black oak, *Quercus velutina*
Bur oak, *Quercus macrocarpa*
Little bluestem, *Schizachyrium scoparium*

## Tallgrass Prairie

Asters, *Aster* species
Blazing stars, *Liatris* species
Big bluestem, *Andropogon gerardii*
Bur oak, *Quercus macrocarpa*
Composites and legumes
Goldenrods, *Solidago* species
Indiangrass, *Sorghastrum nutans*
Milkweeds, *Asclepias* species
Prairie clovers, *Dalea (Petalostemum)* species
Rosinweeds, *Silphium* species
Sunflowers, *Helianthus* species
Switchgrass, *Panicum virgatum*

## Mixed-grass Prairie

Asters, *Aster* species
Composites and legumes
Goldenrods, *Solidago* species
Grama grasses, *Bouteloua* species
Little bluestem, *Schizachyrium scoparium*
Western wheatgrass, *Agropyron smithii*

## Shortgrass Prairie

Buffalo grass, *Buchloe dactyloides*
Composites and cacti
Grama grasses, *Bouteloua* species
Locoweeds, *Oxytropis* species
Lupines, *Lupinus* species
Sagebrushes, *Artemisia* species
Western wallflower, *Erysimum asperum*

## WESTERN DESERTS

The deserts of the West are marked by limited rainfall and excessive evaporation, so drought-tolerant vegetation dominates. One plant, creosote bush, is found in all four associations of the desert province.

## Great Basin

Creosote bush, *Larrea tridentata*
Littleleaf horsebrush, *Tetradymia glabrata*
Mormon teas, *Ephedra* species

Plains prickly pear, *Opuntia polyacantha*
Rabbitbrushes, *Chrysothamnus* species
Sagebrushes, *Artemisia tridentata* and others
Saltbushes, *Atriplex* species
Wheatgrasses, *Agropyron* species

## Mojave Desert

Beavertail cactus, *Opuntia basilaris*
Blue yucca, *Yucca baccata*
Creosote bush, *Larrea tridentata*
Joshua tree, *Yucca brevifolia*
Mojave sage, *Salvia mohavensis*
Mojave yucca, *Yucca schidigera*
Parry saltbrush, *Atriplex parryi*
Sagebrushes, *Artemisia* species
Woolly bur sage, *Ambrosia eriocentra*

## Sonoran Desert

Agaves, *Agave deserti* and others
Barrel cactus, *Ferocactus acanthodes*
Bur sages, *Ambrosia* species
Creosote bush, *Larrea tridentata*
Mesquites, *Prosopis* species
Ocotillo, *Fouquieria splendens*
Palo verdes, *Cercidium floridum* and others
Prickly pears, *Opuntia* species
Saguaro, *Carnegiea giganteus*

## Chihuahuan Desert

Creosote bush, *Larrea tridentata*
Desert marigold, *Baileya multiradiata*
Honey mesquite, *Prosopis glandulosa*
Lechuguilla, *Agave lechuguilla*
Mariola, *Parthenium incanum*
Prickly pears, *Opuntia* species
Sotol, *Dasylirion wheeleri*
Tarbush, *Flourensia cernua*
Yuccas, *Yucca elata* and others
Zinnias, *Zinnia* species

*(continued on next page)*

## WESTERN CONIFEROUS FORESTS

Coniferous forests stretch from the Rocky Mountains to the West Coast. Except where disturbance favors aspen, conifers dominate the three major associations tied to the three major mountain ranges: the Coastal Range, the Sierras, and the Rockies.

### Northwest Coastal Forest

Coast redwood, *Sequoia sempervirens*
Douglas fir, *Pseudotsuga menziesii*
Sitka spruce, *Picea sitchensis*
Western red cedar, *Thuja plicata*
Western hemlock, *Tsuga heterophylla*

### Sierra Montane Forest

Douglas fir, *Pseudotsuga menziesii*
Incense cedar, *Calocedrus decurrens*
Ponderosa pine, *Pinus ponderosa*
Sequoia, *Sequoiadendron giganteum*
Western hemlock, *Tsuga heterophylla*
Western red cedar, *Thuja plicata*

### Rocky Mountain Montane Forest

Douglas fir, *Pseudotsuga menziesii*
Lodgepole pine, *Pinus contorta*
Ponderosa pine, *Pinus ponderosa*
Western red cedar, *Thuja plicata*

### Subalpine Forest

Engelmann spruce, *Picea engelmannii*
Subalpine fir, *Abies lasiocarpa*
Whitebark pine, *Pinus albicaulis*

## CALIFORNIAN PROVINCE

In the Californian Province, winters are mild and relatively rainy. Summers are dry and hot, and much of the vegetation goes dormant as the mercury rises. Conifers, evergreen trees and shrubs with leathery leaves, bulbous plants, grasses, and annual forbs are all adapted to surviving summer drought.

### California Grassland

Awn grasses, *Aristida* species
Bluegrass, *Poa scabrella*
Deergrass, *Muhlenbergia rigens*
Junegrass, *Koeleria cristata* (*K. macrantha*)
Needlegrasses, *Stipa* species
Oniongrass, *Melica imperfecta*
Wild ryes, *Elymus* species

### Oak Woodland

#### Moist

California sycamore, *Platanus racemosa*
Canyon live oak, *Quercus chrysolepis*
Coast live oak, *Quercus agrifolia*
Engelmann oak, *Quercus engelmanii*
Fremont cottonwood, *Populus fremontii*
Interior live oak, *Quercus wislizenii*
Pacific madrone, *Arbutus menziesii*

#### Dry

Black oak, *Quercus kelloggii*
Blue oak, *Quercus douglasii*
Digger pine, *Pinus sabiniana*
Valley oak, *Quercus lobata*

### Pinyon Juniper

California juniper, *Juniperus californica*
Parry pinyon, *Pinus quadrifolia*

### Chaparral

Bigleaf mountain mahogany, *Cercocarpus betuloides*
Blueblossom, *Ceanothus thyrsiflorus*
California sagebrush, *Artemisia californica*
Chamise, *Adenostoma fasciculatum*
Deer brush, *Ceanothus integerrimus*
Greenleaf manzanita, *Arctostaphylos patula*
Scrub oak, *Quercus dumosa*

---

## THE BENEFITS OF BIODIVERSITY

Do you ever wonder why you don't see as many birds and butterflies as you used to? You need look only as far as your garden for the answer to this question. The typical North American garden consists of bluegrass or some other turf, a dozen annuals and perennials, and a few shrubs and shade trees. If you are a bird looking for food, visiting the typical garden is like going to a restaurant where there is only one dish on the menu. Nature offers a smorgasbord to animals. The diversity of ecosystems and species within them offers a complete menu for a rich variety of creatures.

Our gardens can do a lot better. Plant thirty or even fifty perennials instead of a dozen. Use many different fruiting shrubs and trees. Choose half a dozen shade trees. Not only will this diversity help wildlife, it will make your garden more interesting. A hidden benefit of diversity is resistance to outbreaks of pests and diseases. It is harder for an epidemic to spread if an infected plant is surrounded by other species that are not susceptible. It is also more likely that some of the plants will be resistant if you have many individuals with diverse genetic makeups, not just a group of the same cultivars or clones. Instead of choosing several plants of *Aster novae angliae* 'Purple Dome', a cultivar of New England aster with a compact habit, for example, opt for a genetically diverse collection of New England aster plants that have been propagated by seed (see "Plant Reproduction," page 94).

---

dation of a healthy, diverse ecosystem of many different native plant species. This is referred to as *species diversity*. Native plants provide food and cover for insects. Insects in turn are a vital food source for many birds and mammals. The greater the diversity of plants, the greater the diversity of other species the ecosystem can support.

Species diversity is a measure of both richness and evenness. Richness refers to the total number of different species in an area or community, while evenness is a measure of the number of individuals of each species. In general, diversity increases with richness and evenness. In other words, the more different species and the more evenly distributed the individuals of each species, the more diverse the community.

On the smallest scale, the genetic diversity of individual species is also critical. Species with the largest number of populations with large numbers of individuals generally have the broadest genetic base. The more diverse its gene pool, the more resilient the species. Species with few populations and few individuals are more likely to lack the genetic diversity necessary to enable them to adapt to environmental change, disease, or other types of stress. In other words, genetic diversity enables a species to adapt and evolve.

## The Functions of Plant Communities

Living systems do not function in isolation. Interactions are the hallmark of healthy ecosystems. Some interactions have positive, others seemingly negative consequences. Not everything that we see as negative is detrimental to the long-term function of ecosystems, however. An animal eats a plant to survive. This is good for the animal, but bad for the plant. Or is it? Some plants respond well to being grazed,

## SUCCESSION AND DISTURBANCE IN THE GARDEN

The twin forces of succession and disturbance are constantly at work in the garden, just as they are in the native landscape. When you plant on bare earth, you are creating a plant community. This community is a human invention, but it will change with time. You not only set in motion the forces of succession but ultimately become the agent of disturbance as well.

In traditional ornamental gardening, the hand of the gardener must always be at work to quell the influence of the dominant native plant community. Consider what happens when you weed your flower border. When you weed, you are thwarting succession. Annual weed seeds exposed by tilling and planting germinate and grow to cover the bare soil. Wildflowers such as goldenrods may blow in as seeds on the wind and find an empty spot in the garden. In forested regions, tree seedlings germinate and start the long process of reforestation. Without constant tending, weeds, unplanted wildflowers, and tree saplings would quickly overtake the garden, turning it into a thicket.

Even in the natural habitat garden, it is often beneficial for the gardener to guide change by thwarting succession, in this case by substituting for natural agents of disturbance such as fire. Meadows remain open grasslands because annual mowing keeps trees out. A meadow would otherwise soon start to become a forest. Prairies are renewed by wildfires that burn off the thatch, clearing the soil and releasing nutrients. Thankfully, most of us do not have wildfires in our gardens. To keep a prairie healthy, however, we must either mow it or do a careful prescribed burn. We must lend mother nature a helping hand. The California chaparral is still another fire-dependent community. One of the reasons wildfires are so devastating in southern California is that regular fires are suppressed. Without regular burning, the large amounts of flammable litter accumulate. When a fire finally does come, it has so much fuel that it spreads out of control, consuming houses as well as native vegetation.

When we build a garden in a woodland, we are acting as agents of disturbance, too. If we thin the canopy or remove a tree, we are initiating what ecologists call *gap phase succession*. We let in more light and alter the dynamics of that piece of forest. When we plant, we disturb the soil, allowing new seeds to germinate. All our actions as gardeners have consequences.

In the interests of both low maintenance and environmental harmony in the garden, it is important to understand and work with natural forces like succession.

while others may die. Death is part of natural renewal. A dead tree feeds insects, provides a home for birds, and ultimately falls to the ground and creates humus. Catastrophic floods and hurricanes can alter the landscape in the blink of an eye. These disturbances set changes in motion that over time alter the nature and composition of plant communities. The landscape as we see it today is the product of all this change, seen and unseen, dramatic and subtle, fast and slow. Ultimately, the system prevails in spite of the individual and local dramas that are played out over time. Without dynamic interaction, there would be no healthy function.

### Disturbance and Succession

*Succession* is the term that scientists use for the vegetation changes in plant communities over time. Succession works at many scales, from the thousands of acres burned in Yellowstone National Park several years ago to the comparatively tiny gap in the canopy left when a tree routinely topples in a forest.

Early ecologists believed that there was a fixed and predictable end point to succession, which they termed the *climax stage*, and that this climax stage was stable and self-perpetuating for long periods of time. They believed that vegetation changes in a plant community are inherent in the community itself, and outside factors such as storms or fire play little or no role in the process. Today, ecologists realize that no self-perpetuating end point is ever really reached, and that periodic disturbance—fire, flooding, damage by insects and diseases, and windstorms, to name a few—plays a critical role in maintaining the diversity of species and habits in a region. Rather than an anomaly that occasionally disrupts climax communities, disturbance is now viewed as the key recurring factor that keeps a mosaic of habitats in different stages of vegetation development in fairly close proximity to one another. This, in turn, assures the presence of a diverse mixture of plants and animals that characterize each phase of the change from, say, bare land to mature forest.

Although *how* vegetation succession or change occurs is more complicated than previously thought, *what* will ultimately happen in most places is still generally predictable. It certainly is true that specific types of vegetation will eventually predominate on most sites in particular floristic provinces.

In the Eastern Deciduous Forest province, vegetation change on abandoned farmland left undisturbed for many years will work something like this, with regional variations: Millions of seeds that lay dormant in the exposed soil germinate, causing an explosion of physio-logically tough, aggressive annuals like horseweed and common ragweed. These plants, called *pioneer species*, dominate the first season. In a few years, biennials (today, many of them nonnatives such as common mullein and Queen Anne's lace) become common, along with a few perennial wildflowers like asters and goldenrods. After five years or so, grasses and wildflowers turn the area into a meadow. Within a few years young maples, ashes, dogwoods, cherries, pines, and cedars, many present as seedlings in the earliest stages, rapidly transform the meadow into "old field," an extremely rich, floriferous blend of pioneer trees, shrubs, and herbaceous species particularly favored by wildlife. Given enough time without major disturbance, perhaps several centuries, a mature or old-growth forest will once again be found on the site.

## Water and Nutrient Cycles

Energy and nutrients are constantly flowing through ecosystems unseen. Water is taken up by plants, transpired through their leaves, and given off to the atmosphere. This invisible process, called *evapotranspiration*, can influence global weather patterns. Eventually, the water falls back to the earth as precipitation. Similarly, the nutrients that sustain every living creature on Earth are transformed and distributed by a perpetual cycle of decay and renewal. The movement of chemical elements among the planet's living organisms and the physical environment is called the *biogeochemical cycle*. Nutrient and water cycles are two of the most important biogeochemical processes.

### Nutrient Cycling

The nutrient cycle is the basis of life. Plants are the foundation of the nutrient cycle. Plants

## RESTORING THE NUTRIENT CYCLE

In the typical garden, the nutrient cycle is interrupted. A primary reason for this is that most gardeners like to keep things neat. Raking and disposing of leaves and lawn clippings eliminates the natural source of nutrients. As a result, fertilizer must be added to the soil to keep the lawn and garden healthy. Fertilizers typically release massive amounts of nutrients to the garden ecosystem at once. The soil cannot store them, nor can plants use them fast enough, and so they leach away. Leached nutrients, especially nitrogen and phosphorous, are a major source of water pollution.

Gardeners can repair the natural nutrient cycling process in their backyard ecosystems. Fallen leaves, lawn clippings, and other potential organic matter can be left in place in many areas of the yard. For a tidier look, leaves can be chopped with a mower or shredder and applied in flowerbeds and around shrubs as a natural mulch. Leaves removed from areas that must be raked can be added to a compost pile. There, along with other garden trimmings and kitchen scraps, they will be transformed into compost rich in humus—nature's soil conditioner and natural, slow-release plant food (see page 441). This not only saves money that otherwise would be spent on fertilizer, but also helps prevent pollution of wetlands and streams.

Another way to restore the natural nutrient cycle is to integrate some beautiful nitrogen-fixing plants—lupines, baptisias, prairie clovers, bush clovers, peas—to beds, borders, and lawn areas. They will increase the soil's fertility while adding aesthetically to garden plantings.

convert the energy of the sun and atmospheric carbon into biomass through a process called *photosynthesis*. Plants are called *primary producers* because they are the starting point, where energy and nutrients enter the system. Animals that eat plants are called *herbivores*. They vary from the krill in the sea to the bison on the prairie. Herbivores are the linchpin of the food chain, which is built upon production and consumption. Herbivorous animals are fed upon by meat-eating predators called *carnivores*. Wolves eat the buffalo that eat the grasses of the prairie. People are also part of the predator/prey system. People also eat the buffalo or, more likely, the cattle that have replaced them on the plains. Carnivores are at the top of the food chain.

Not all biomass is consumed in a living state. When a plant or animal dies, or when a portion of a plant dies, the nutrients are still recycled. When leaves fall from trees in autumn, for example, the nutrients are released by soil insects, fungi, and microbes, which break down this dead living material, called *organic matter*, through a process called *decay*, or *decomposition*. Decomposition of organic matter forms humus, a stable colloidal material that provides a variety of nutrients to plants. Colloids bind nutrients tightly until they are utilized by plants. Some of the nutrients are lost through movement of water down through the soil in a process called *leaching*. As any good gardener knows, the more organic matter and humus in the soil, the less leaching of water and nutrients there is. In such an efficiently operating ecosystem, most nutrients can be taken up by plants and become new biomass—new plant growth—and thus the cycle begins anew.

Nitrogen, an important nutrient for plant

growth, also enters the ecosystem directly from the atmosphere through a process called *fixation*. Nitrogen fixation is the conversion of atmospheric nitrogen into a form usable by plants. Fixation occurs during thunderstorms, when electricity converts nitrogen into a soluble form that dissolves in rainwater, which then falls to the ground. Fixation also occurs in the roots of some higher plants, made possible by bacteria that live symbiotically in thick swellings on the roots called *nodules*. These bacteria absorb nitrogen gas and convert it directly to a form the plants can use. The prairies and deserts are filled with legumes like lupines and prairie clover that fix nitrogen.

### Water Cycling

The movement of water through the environment is called the *water cycle*. Precipitation falls to earth, and moves through the landscape in a variety of different ways. Some of the water is intercepted by the canopy of trees and other vegetation, where it evaporates before it hits the ground. Evaporation also occurs from the ground itself. Most of the water infiltrates into the ground, where it is either taken up by the roots of plants or seeps into the ground and enters the water table. Some of the water runs off the surface into wetlands, streams, ponds, and, today, storm sewers.

A portion of the water that is absorbed by the roots of plants is returned to the atmosphere by the process called *transpiration*. This loss of water through the leaves of plants draws water into the roots and pulls it up the stem or trunk of the plant. Even water that flows to the water table eventually reaches the atmosphere, but it is a longer journey. Groundwater moves with the topography of the land until it reaches the lowest point in the water table—a pond,

stream, or wetland. Water from these wetlands and bodies of water is constantly evaporating as it moves downstream through the watershed and ultimately to the ocean. Evaporation from the world's oceans returns massive amounts of water to the atmosphere, where it joins the water lost via transpiration, and returns to the earth as rain. Thus the cycle is renewed.

Modern cities and suburbs, with their impervious pavement, wreak havoc with the natural water cycle. In natural systems, surface runoff is minimal. By contrast, parking lots, sidewalks, and rooftops often produce torrents of runoff that never infiltrate the ground. There are two serious consequences of reduced infiltration. Flooding is the most dramatic, and destructive. As water runs off roofs and streets,

---

### REDUCING HOME RUNOFF

The roof of a house, as well as sidewalks and driveways, keeps water from infiltrating the ground and contributes to erosion and flooding problems. Even lawn absorbs less water than more diverse types of cover. Gardeners can minimize runoff by designing areas where water is encouraged to infiltrate into the ground. Downspouts can be directed into dry wells instead of down the driveway or over the lawn and into the storm sewer. Lawns and planting beds can be sculpted so that water runs into them instead of away. Patio and walkway stones can be set in sand, unmortared, so that water can percolate down through the cracks and into the soil. Gravel is a good, permeable substitute for asphalt in driveways. These measures not only reduce runoff but also help water plants, ultimately reducing the time spent irrigating the garden.

it collects in storm sewers and is rapidly deposited in streams and rivers. This fast-moving, enormous volume of water causes massive erosion of stream and river banks. Widespread and damaging flooding also occurs, in the worst cases washing away houses and crops. An ecologically sensible regional landscape would be designed to reduce runoff and maximize infiltration from the top of the watershed to the bottom. Since water accumulates in volume and speed as it runs through the system, the key to reducing flooding is to catch the water at the top of the watershed. This can be accomplished in many ways. The most obvious is to reduce or eliminate runoff. Reducing paved areas, using porous pavement that allows infiltration, and running downspouts into the ground are a few solutions. Where this is not possible, storm-water retention basins must be used to trap water. Keeping natural wetlands intact also reduces runoff.

## Plant/Animal Relationships

Plants and animals evolved together, so it is not surprising that there are many complex plant/animal relationships. This process of interdependent evolution of two or more species is called coevolution. Some relationships are beneficial to both parties, while others have a clear benefit for one at the expense, or even death, of the other. Four important plant/animal interactions are explored here: plant/herbivore, plant/pollinator, plant/disperser, and other examples of mutualism.

### Plant/Herbivore Relationships

Herbivory is an interaction in which a plant or portions of the plant are consumed by an animal. At the microscopic scale, herbivory includes the bacteria and fungi that cause dis-

ease as they feed on plant tissue. Microbes that break down dead plant tissue are also specialized herbivores. Browsers and grazers, from aphids and caterpillars to deer and bison, are more familiar herbivores. Even insects and animals that eat seeds are considered herbivores.

Some herbivores consume entire plants, or enough to kill them. Others only eat a portion of the plant, and so the plant can recover. The plant/herbivore relationship traditionally has been seen as lopsided, with the animal as the beneficiary and the plant as the loser. Current research, however, is revealing that herbivory has some potential benefits to plants. One example is canopy grazing by insects, which allows more light to penetrate into the lower layers of the forest. Gypsy moth grazing on

### HERBIVORES AND THEIR FOOD PLANTS

Bison, sheep, and other grazers—Succulent forbs, grasses, grasslike plants
Deer and other ungulate browsers—Leaves and twigs of woody plants such as willows, arborvitaes, yews
Beaver—Tree bark, young shoots, leaves
Rodents—Succulent forbs, grasses, grasslike plants
  Rabbits—Succulent forbs, grasses, bark
  Voles—Roots, bark
Caterpillars—Leaves; in some cases, of specific species
  Monarch butterfly—Milkweeds
  Gypsy moth—Oaks and other hardwoods
Aphids—Plant juices; in some cases, of specific species
Many birds—Seeds and fruits
Locusts—All plants; seeds, leaves, and stems

## IMPERILED POLLINATORS

All is not well in the realm of pollinators. The age-old relationships between plants and pollinators are threatened, especially in urbanized and agricultural regions. Habitat destruction and fragmentation, pesticide abuse, and disease all have taken their toll on pollinators. As more land is cleared for human habitation, bees, butterflies, bats, and birds are left homeless. Our gardens offer little to sustain them. They need a constant source of nectar and pollen throughout the entire season. The few flowering plants most people grow will not suffice.

A related problem is fragmentation of plant communities. Plants must be pollinated in order to set seed for the next generation. Without pollinators, no seed is set and the plants eventually die out, leading to local extinction. Isolated patches of forest, grassland, or desert are particularly vulnerable. A small patch may not sustain enough pollinators, or may be too far from other patches for pollinators to travel. As a result, plants do not reproduce.

Pesticides have also reduced pollinator populations. Bees are often killed by chemicals applied to eliminate other pests. Honeybees are being destroyed by diseases and parasitic mites. The crisis is not just affecting native ecosystems. Fruit trees and many other food crops depend on pollination for production. We stand to lose over three-quarters of our edible crops if we lose pollinators.

What can be done? Encourage pollinators by planting a diverse mixture of adult and larval food plants in your garden. Erect bat houses and birdhouses, as well as beehives. Reduce or eliminate pesticide use. Help restore native plant communities not only in your yard, but also in parks and along roadways, and connect them through corridors to preserves and other natural areas. For more on pollinator-friendly gardening, see "Natural Gardening," page 180.)

canopy trees in some areas of Virginia's Blue Ridge Mountains, for instance, has resulted in more light penetration and therefore a more diverse and productive ground layer.

### Plants and Their Pollinators

Pollination is the transfer of the pollen from one flower to the stigma, or female reproductive organ, of another, which results in fertilization and, ultimately, the formation of seeds (see "Plant Reproduction," page 94). The earliest plants were pollinated by wind, and for some modern plants this is still the most expedient method. Many trees, all grasses, and plants with inconspicuous flowers are designed for wind pollination. Bright, showy flowers evolved for another purpose: to attract a pollinator.

Many plants depend on animals for pollination. Insects, birds, even bats are important for perpetuating plants. The flowers of these plants evolved in concert with their pollinators, and their form reflects the form and habits of their pollinators. Bee-pollinated plants are often irregular in shape, with a lip that acts as a landing pad to facilitate the bee's entry into the flower. Butterfly-pollinated flowers are often broad and flat, like helicopter pads. The flowers of many plants are brightly colored to attract their insect pollinators, and many offer nectar as an enticement. Hummingbirds, with their long beaks, pollinate tubular flowers. Bats require open flowers with room for their wings, such as those of the saguaro cactus. In the tropics, birds and bats take the place of insects as pollinators. Hummingbirds and honeycreepers, for example, have distinctive beaks that have evolved to exploit flowers. Often, a beak may be so specialized that it is only effective on a small group of flowers. (For more on plants and their pollinators, see "Plant Reproduction," page 94.)

The pollinators, in turn, have evolved to take advantage of the flowers. A successful pollinator typically has good color vision, a good memory for finding flowers, and a proboscis, or tongue, for attaining nectar.

Animal pollination has obvious advantages for plants. Many pollinators cover great distances, which ensures genetic diversity through outcrossing, or the transfer of pollen to unrelated individuals. The pollinator benefits as well by gaining access to a source of food. The

relationship of pollinator and plant is an example of mutualism.

### Plants and Their Dispersers

No two plants can occupy the same spot. In order to have room to grow, seeds must be dispersed away from the parent plant. Seed dispersal is accomplished by a variety of means, including wind, water, and animals. Animal dispersal is accomplished by two different methods: ingestion and hitchhiking. Animals consume a wide variety of fruits, and in so doing disperse the seeds in their droppings. Many seeds benefit not only from the dispersal, but the trip through the intestine as well. Digestive acids scarify seeds, helping them to break out of thick seed coats.

Some seeds are armed with hooks and barbs that enable them to lodge in the fur of animals that brush past them. Beggar's ticks and bur marigold are two examples. Eventually, the seeds are rubbed or scratched off, and may find a suitable spot on which to germinate and grow. People are important for dispersing plants, too. The common weed plantain was called "white man's footsteps" by Native Americans because wherever settlers walked, the plantain came in the mud on their shoes.

### Mutualism

Mutualism is an obligate interaction between organisms that requires contributions from both organisms and in which both benefit. There are many examples in nature. Pollination and dispersal, discussed above, are mutualistic because both plant and pollinator or disperser benefit from the relationship. The relationship between mycorrhizal fungi and many higher plants is another common example of mutualism. The bodies of the fungi, called *hyphae*, live on or in the tissues of plants,

---

### SOME ANIMALS AND THE PLANTS THEY DISPERSE

Ants—Many wildflowers, such as trilliums, bloodroot, violets

Birds—Fleshy fruits and grains, such as baneberry, viburnums, mountain ash
  Clark's Nutcracker—Whitebark pine
  Woodpeckers—Poison ivy

Mammals—Fruits, grains, nuts, berries
  Squirrel—Nuts, such as those of oaks, hickories, pines
  Fox—Berries, such as blackberry, grapes
  Humans—Weeds such as plantain, dandelion, lamb's-quarters

Reptiles—Fleshy fruits, especially berries such as strawberry, groundcherry, jack-in-the-pulpit

---

## THE LOVELY LADY SLIPPER

The reason lady slipper orchids are so hard to grow in a garden is that the needs of both the orchid and its fungus must be attended to. The growing conditions in the garden must duplicate exactly those in the orchid's native habitat.

Anyone who tries to cultivate these beautiful plants learns before long that the pink lady slipper (*Cypripedium acaule*) is much harder to grow than the yellow lady slipper (*Cypripedium calceolus*). This is because of the fungus. Yellow lady slippers grow in slightly acidic, rich soils. Their associated mycorrhizal fungus thrives under the same conditions as those in woodland and shade gardens. The pink lady slipper, on the other hand, grows in sterile, acid soil, not the typical garden variety. Plant the pink lady slipper in rich garden soil, and its associated fungus cannot survive. As a result, the pink lady slipper slowly languishes and eventually dies. Most lady slipper orchids are still collected from the wild, harming native populations. Buy them only from nurseries that propagate their plants.

and make nutrients available for the plants to absorb. The plants provide the fungi with amino acids and other complex compounds. One of the most celebrated examples is the orchids. Whereas some plants may support as many as a hundred different fungi, orchids have quite specific mycorrhizal associations (see "The Lovely Lady Slipper," above). Different plant communities have different mycorrhizal associations. The microflora of a grassland is different from that of a forest. These differences, at least in part, may influence the distribution of plant communities.

## Further Reading

Audubon Society Nature Guides. *Atlantic and Gulf Coasts, Deserts, Eastern Forest, Grasslands, Pacific Coast, Western Forests,* and *Wetlands.* New York: Alfred A. Knopf, 1985.

Barbour, M. G., J. H. Burke, and W. D. Pitts. *Terrestrial Plant Ecology.* Menlo Park, Calif.: The Benjamin/Cummings Publishing Company, 1987.

Begon, Michael, John Harper, and Colin Townsend. *Ecology: Individuals, Populations, and Communities.* Boston: Blackwell Science, 1996.

Benyus, Janine M. *The Field Guide to Wildlife Habitats.* Eastern and Western eds. New York: Fireside, 1989.

Buchman, Stephen L., and Gary Paul Nabhan. *Forgotten Pollinators.* Washington, D.C.: Island Press, 1996.

Forman, Richard T. T., and Michel Godron. *Landscape Ecology.* New York: John Wiley and Sons, 1986.

Gleason, H. A., and A. Cronquist. *The Natural Geography of Plants.* New York: Columbia University Press, 1964.

Harris, Larry D. *The Fragmented Forest.* Chicago: The University of Chicago Press, 1984.

Hudson, Wendy E., ed. *Landscape Linkages and Biodiversity.* Washington, D.C.: Island Press, 1991.

Marinelli, Janet. *Stalking the Wild Amaranth: Gardening in the Age of Extinction.* New York: Henry Holt and Company, 1998.

Minckler, Leon S. *Woodland Ecology.* Syracuse, N.Y.: Syracuse University Press, 1980.

Thompson, Janette R. *Prairies, Forests, and Wetlands.* Iowa City: University of Iowa Press, 1992.

Weaver, J. E. *Prairie Plants and Their Environment.* Lincoln: University of Nebraska Press, 1968.

# 6

# NATURAL GARDENING

Natural gardening works with nature. It takes advantage of existing features such as rock outcrops, marshy areas, sand dunes, and woodlands, and highlights them in the landscape. Natural gardeners preserve biodiversity by re-creating native habitats that once existed on the site. They even enhance diversity by adding habitats that did not exist on the site but are found in the area and make the most of the new conditions that have been created by human development—for example, a small wetland garden supported by storm-water runoff from a roof. Even the tiniest yard can include a scaled-down pond, meadow border, or woodland glade.

Strictly speaking, a natural garden includes only plants native to the region and appropriate to the conditions on the site. Purists define a native plant as one that was found within 50 miles of a site two or three hundred years ago, before the native flora was radically altered by European immigrants to the continent. Some experts believe that the 50-mile rule is too rigid, pointing out that plants migrate just as birds and other creatures do. All plants listed in the following sections are native to the regions for which they are recommended. For a more complete listing of plants indigenous to an area, consult local field guides and checklists available from botanical gardens and native plant societies.

Plants introduced from another country are called *nonnatives* or *exotics*. Many exotic plants are now common in home landscapes in North America, while many native plants are virtually unknown. Some plants that appear to be native wildflowers, like Queen Anne's lace (*Daucus carota*), blue chicory (*Cichorium intybus*), and multiflora rose (*Rosa multiflora*), are actually nonnatives that have escaped from cultivation into the wild. Some of these escaped plants, such as purple loosestrife (*Lythrum salicaria*), are so invasive that they threaten native plants or profoundly alter native ecosystems (see "Vanishing Plants," page 122).

Natural gardening is an ecologically sensitive alternative to conventional horticulture. A natural garden may take more time and effort to establish but, properly designed, will require less maintenance in the long run. Natural nutrient and water cycles are restored (see "Ecology for Gardeners," page 142), so use of fertilizers and other chemicals should be minimal and, after plants are established, supplemental watering should be unnecessary. A natural garden is as self-sufficient as possible.

## Natural Landscaping Basics

Nature is more organized than it may seem at first glance. A natural garden is designed around a particular plant community that exists in nature. This is a revolutionary idea to many gardeners who are used to selecting plants for purely ornamental reasons and combining them in ways that bear little resemblance to their original habitats.

A natural garden does not force the site to be something it is not. It is true to the character of the region. The Earth's natural vegetation is divided into large areas of forest, grassland, shrubland, and desert called *floristic provinces* (see "Gardener's Atlas," page 14). Floristic provinces are divided into regional associations of particular species. Much of the Midwest, for example, falls within the floristic province called the Grassland or Central Prairies and Plains province; however, the eastern parts of this area were once covered with tallgrass prairie, whereas in the western part of the

region shortgrass prairie once grew (see "Ecology for Gardeners," page 152).

In other words, in the eastern states a woodland is an appropriate model for a natural garden, as well as a meadow, pond, or streamside planting. A desert or alpine garden would be out of place. Likewise, in Nevada, a bog or seashore garden would be unnatural.

The Earth's natural diversity of vegetation types is further complicated by succession, meaning that the plants presently growing on a previously disturbed site will be replaced over time as the community matures or is changed by further disturbance (see "Ecology for Gardeners," page 172). All of these plant communities, large, small, and successional, are determined by soil types, topography, available water and light, and extremes of temperature—the same factors that gardeners consider when designing a landscape. Natural gardening requires a familiarity not only with regional vegetation patterns but also, like conventional gardening, with the specific conditions on a particular site.

### Choosing Plants and a Plant Community

Choosing a native plant community or communities is of fundamental importance in natural gardening. The basics of the site—soil types, landforms, and microclimates—will dictate which communities are appropriate.

Often, more than one native plant community will be appropriate on any given site. Functional considerations—for example, the need to screen out an eyesore in a neighbor's yard—will usually narrow down the choice, in this case favoring a woodland or tall shrub community over a meadow or prairie.

It is important to keep in mind, however,

that not all plant communities are equally easy to establish, and some are harder to maintain than others. A prairie or meadow typically takes only three or four years to mature, while a forest or woodland can take ten times that long. On the negative side, a meadow needs periodic mowing or controlled burning to keep down exotic weeds and brushy vegetation.

A good way to begin designing a natural planting is to study the key species that occur together in the chosen plant community in the wild. First, note the dominant species—that is, the major plants that form the backbone of the native plant community. In the tallgrass prairie, these are the grasses such as the stately big bluestem, which can reach 6 feet in autumn. In the pinyon-juniper woodlands of the Southwest, the major plants are the species of juniper and pinyon pine, which vary somewhat from state to state. In coastal forests of the Pacific Northwest, the conifers—including redwood and Douglas fir—dominate. (See "Ecology for Gardeners," page 166, for lists of dominant species for the major vegetation associations in North America.)

Next, note which nondominant species are most common in the native plant community—understory trees and shrubs in a forest, for example. Then pay particular attention to other species that may not be present in the same numbers as others but that are nonetheless critical to the community's physical structure. A woodland garden, for example, includes not only tall canopy trees but also smaller trees, shrubs, and herbaceous plants that form several vertical layers (see "Ecology for Gardeners," page 163). Some species are critical to the community's visual character. These may be species with distinctive branching patterns, ornamental flowers, or outstanding fall color.

There are several obvious benefits to using indigenous species in a natural garden: First, they have evolved to become adapted to the particular conditions in an area. Generally, they are less susceptible to pests and diseases than many ornamental exotics are. They have also coevolved with insects and other animals and therefore are critical to the survival of countless other creatures. Growing natives helps to preserve species that might otherwise be lost to development or other disturbance. And many native plants are just as ornamental as their cultivated counterparts.

When purchasing native plants, question the supplier carefully about their origins. Find out if the plants were propagated and grown at the nursery, or collected from the wild and grown to a larger size. Many prized wildflowers, such as woodland orchids, are difficult to propagate and often dug up from the wild and sold, endangering local populations of these species. Some plants are labeled "nursery-grown," but this term is misleading, because it may simply mean that the plants were collected in the wild and grown to a commercially salable size (see "Vanishing Plants," page 122). Buy only plants that are *nursery-propagated.*

Remember birds and wildlife when choosing plants for the natural garden. The best natural gardens strive to create and/or preserve habitats for native birds, butterflies, and larger animals. Investigate their life cycles and migratory habits, and select plants that offer shelter as well as the appropriate food in the season it is needed.

## Designing a Natural Garden

There are many ways to go about creating a natural landscape. City gardeners can simply add to an existing garden a few choice natives that are attractive to wildlife—a flowering climber against a fence, for example, or some woodland shrubs and wildflowers beneath a specimen tree. Suburban gardeners can reduce the size of the lawn and reintroduce pockets of the neighborhood's original plant life on the peripheries of their properties. Rural gardeners may find that they can release an existing native plant community from the grip of invasives and restore its original diversity by replacing the missing species.

Another decision that needs to be made is whether to create either a garden that will be allowed to mature or one that represents a certain stage of succession indefinitely. On a bare lot in a forest association, for example, one way to accommodate growth and change is to plant a grove of young trees and surround them with native grasses and meadow flowers, introducing shade-loving woodland ferns and wildflowers as the trees grow and their canopies intertwine. Or, natural succession can be arrested by planting a meadow with only a few smaller trees such as dogwood or red cedar and mowing periodically to keep woody vegetation from taking over.

Another design consideration is seasonal change. Note the annual succession of bloom in a natural landscape. A spring meadow of pink and purple wildflowers may change to yellows and greens in summer, and shades of purple and gold in fall. To have seasonal complexity, along with the associated wildlife, a natural garden needs a variety of plants in not only a range of heights and shapes but also flowering times.

For a truly natural-looking landscape, it is important to study the patterns of nature. Nature does not line things up in straight rows or plant them in geometric shapes. Observe the way horizontal masses of plants form soft shapes, the way forest paths flow in gentle curves, the way deserts are etched by arroyos.

Note whether a plant grows only at the edges of the woods, or deep in the forest, or both; whether it is usually present only as an individual, in loose colonies, or in dense clumps. The natural growth patterns of individual species, which serve as a useful guide to planting, are generally determined by the way the plants reproduce. Trees, shrubs, and grasses that reproduce mainly by seed appear in random, scattered patterns in the landscape. Those that reproduce vegetatively, by means of suckers or running roots, occur in ever-expanding clumps. Other factors may also influence growth patterns. In the desert, for instance, plants are often spaced relatively far apart because there is intense competition for water and nutrients.

There is plenty of room for artistic expression in the natural garden. As noted above, there is often a choice of plant communities suited to a particular site. And in nature, no two patches of similar vegetation are alike. That means there is a choice of species, particularly nondominant ones, to feature in the plant community. These species can be chosen for their habit or form, seasonal color, interesting bark, and eye-catching contrast—just as in a traditional garden.

## Maintaining a Natural Garden

A natural garden ultimately should be virtually self-sufficient. Natural landscaping will demand some investment of time and energy during the first few years. In a woodland garden, for example, young trees, shrubs, and herbaceous plants will need to be watered until they become established. Mulching will retain moisture and discourage weeds while enriching the soil; after several years, the patch of forest should be producing most of its own mulch as it sheds leaves and needles. Similarly, the first three years are critical for a re-created prairie or meadow; during that time diligent weeding will be necessary to keep down invasive weeds. After the first few seasons, mowing or burning will be essential for long-term weed control and to discourage woody vegetation from turning the grassland into a woodland.

Otherwise, natural processes should be allowed to unfold—leaves to remain on the ground, volunteer seedlings to spring up, dead trees to fall and decay. All these things have their purpose and will contribute to the diversity of life in the natural garden.

## Woodland Gardens

No two woodlands are alike. Although all are characterized by trees—mixed hardwoods or conifers, scrubby oaks or towering redwoods—woodlands come in many heights and densities. Along and north of the U.S.-Canadian border, from coast to coast, is a dense forest of coniferous evergreen trees that cast deep shade. By contrast, on the Coastal Plain of the Atlantic and Gulf states, from New Jersey to Texas, the vegetation consists mostly of an open forest of pines, where the crowns of the trees do not overlap and the ground is carpeted with grasses and flowering herbs. The western Rocky Mountains, including the tablelands of parts of Colorado, Utah, New Mexico, and Arizona, are blanketed with woodlands consisting of widely spaced and often pygmy junipers and pinyon pines (see "Gardener's Atlas," page 14, and "Ecology for Gardeners," page 142).

The structure, shape, density, and overlap of the tree crowns in the canopy greatly influence the amount of shade, the temperature, and the moisture conditions in a woodland. Plants in the lower layers must be adapted to these con-

ditions or they may not survive. Plants adapted to the deep shade of coniferous forests—partridgeberry, for example—may perish in the open sun. Conversely, plants that do best in open, sunny habitats, such as sunflowers, may perish in deep shade. It is important to choose plants suited to the conditions on the site.

A typical deciduous woodland is made up of four vertical layers: canopy (the tallest trees), understory (smaller trees), shrub layer, and ground layer (wildflowers, ferns, and mosses). Plants in the lower layers generally bloom in spring, before the trees leaf out. Over just a few weeks' time, the forest floor is transformed into a sea of wildflowers. In summer, the woodland is a textural carpet of greens—ferns, mosses, and the foliage of herbaceous plants. The fall foliage display, particularly in the Eastern Deciduous Forest province, is every bit as spectacular as the spring wildflower display. Natural gardeners can create memorable color combinations throughout the seasons.

Woodlands also have vertical layers underground. Most plants have a root system that is either near the soil surface or penetrates deeply. Red spruce, for example, tends to have a shallow root system, while its companion species balsam fir and, in the southern Appalachians, fraser fir both have deep taproots. Some plants have a combination of both systems—for example, sugar maple and longleaf pine. In a native forest, shallow, fibrous-rooted plants grow next to plants with deep bulbs, which are next to ones with creeping rhizomes. In this eclectic but well-orchestrated arrangement, competition for root space is minimized and more plants can grow together in a limited space. Gardeners can take their cue from nature and create the most diverse plantings possible by using species with a variety of root systems. In existing forests with very dense

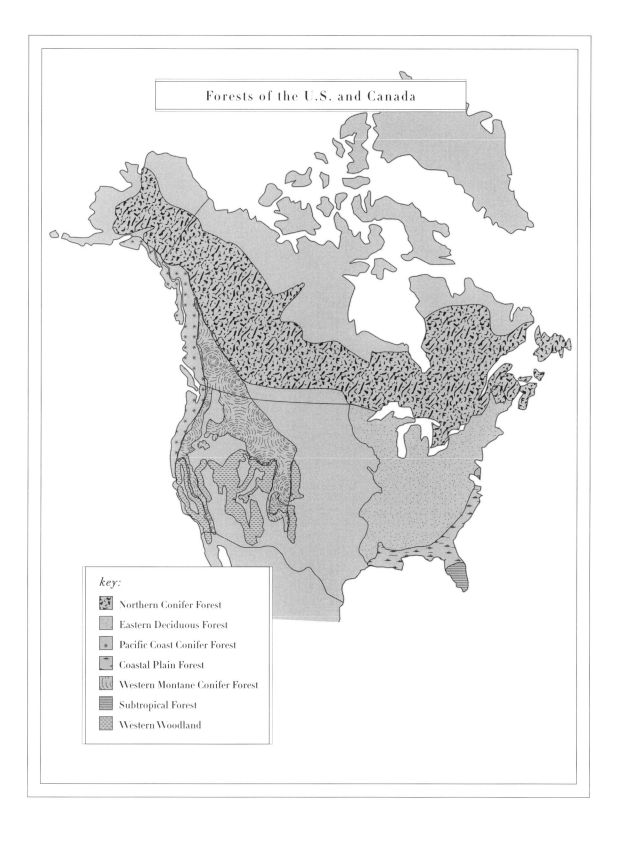

Forests of the U.S. and Canada

key:

Northern Conifer Forest

Eastern Deciduous Forest

Pacific Coast Conifer Forest

Coastal Plain Forest

Western Montane Conifer Forest

Subtropical Forest

Western Woodland

surface root systems, it may be necessary to remove some potential competitors before adding plants.

When planting a woodland garden, first take inventory. What kinds of trees are growing on the site? Deciduous or evergreen? Natives? Invasives? Are they in good condition? How much shade is there? Is there an understory of small trees and shrubs? If there is no woodland on the property, one can be created in miniature by planting small trees, low shrubs, and ground covers to replicate the natural forest layers. To direct movement and protect understory plants, plan to create paths from wood chips or other natural materials.

## Preparing a Woodland Garden

Clearing out invasive species is the first order of business in woodland gardening. In every region of North America there are numerous examples of aggressively spreading shrubs, vines, trees, and herbaceous plants that are wreaking havoc with forest ecosystems. One well-known example is Norway maple (*Acer platanoides*), a tree introduced from Europe during the colonial period. With the help of a tremendous seed supply from urban and suburban plantings, coupled with its shade tolerance, this species has taken over in forests and woodlands in the East. (See "Vanishing Plants," page 137, for a list of invasive species throughout the United States and Canada.) Be cautious about removing any large tree, however; changes in the canopy affect the amount of light in the woodland, and that can dramatically affect the understory plants.

In a natural woodland, everything has its purpose. Dead trees are habitats for woodpeckers or other creatures. Fallen leaves become natural compost. Brush provides shelter for small animals. Do not clear out all the leaves, brush, and dead wood. Remove only invasive species and, if necessary, diseased or injured plants. Many woodland gardens can also benefit from some judicious pruning of canopy trees to admit more light to understory plants and allow air to circulate.

In addition to light and shade, the selection of appropriate plant species should be guided by the drainage and soil characteristics of the site. Instead of trying to change existing conditions, choose species most suited to them. The exception is herbaceous woodland plants, which typically benefit from a rich soil that ensures good air circulation, water and nutrient retention, and drainage. Organic matter is the key. To improve the soil for these plants, use amendments such as leaf mold that closely resemble the natural forest soil, preferably from trees similar to those in the plant community.

## Planting a Woodland Garden

Plant in early spring or late fall. Spring-blooming wildflowers are best planted in fall, except in northern regions where winter snow cover is sparse. After the leaves have dropped in fall, rake them away from the planting areas, put in the wildflowers, and water thoroughly. Pay special attention to spacing when planting trees or shrubs; allow enough room for them to reach their mature size without crowding. Plant wildflowers in natural-looking drifts rather than using them to line paths or encircle tree trunks.

## Maintaining a Woodland Garden

A woodland garden needs to be maintained for about two or three years. Newly installed plants should be kept consistently moist during the

# PLANTS FOR WOODLAND GARDENS

The plants listed below are natives suggested for particular regions. See "Ecology for Gardeners," page 166, for lists of dominant plants in the various vegetation associations within the regions. For best results, choose plants suited to the specific conditions on the site.

## NORTHEAST AND MID-ATLANTIC

### Canopy and Understory

*Acer saccharum*, sugar maple
*Aesculus pavia*, red buckeye
*Amelanchier* species, serviceberries
*Asimina triloba*, pawpaw
*Betula nigra*, river birch
*Betula papyrifera*, paper birch
*Betula populifolia*, white birch
*Cercis canadensis*, eastern redbud
*Chionanthus virginicus*, fringe tree
*Cornus florida*, eastern flowering dogwood
*Crataegus viridis*, hawthorn
*Halesia carolina*, Carolina silverbell
*Hamamelis virginiana*, witchhazel
*Ilex opaca*, American holly
*Juniperus virginiana*, eastern red cedar
*Liriodendron tulipifera*, tulip tree
*Magnolia* species, magnolias
*Quercus* species, oaks

### Shrub Layer

*Aronia arbutifolia*, red chokeberry
*Callicarpa americana*, beautyberry
*Calycanthus floridus*, Carolina allspice, sweet shrub
*Ceanothus americanus*, New Jersey tea
*Clethra acuminata*, cinnamon clethra
*Clethra alnifolia*, sweet pepperbush
*Fothergilla gardenii*, dwarf fothergilla

*Hydrangea quercifolia*, oak-leaf hydrangea
*Ilex* species, hollies
*Itea virginica*, Virginia sweetspire
*Kalmia latifolia*, mountain laurel
*Leucothoe fontanesiana*, drooping leucothoë, doghobble
*Myrica pensylvanica*, bayberry
*Rhododendron* species, native rhododendrons and azaleas
*Viburnum* species, viburnums
*Xanthorhiza simplicissima*, yellowroot

### Ground Layer

*Actaea pachypoda* (*A. alba*), white baneberry, doll's eyes
*Adiantum pedatum*, maidenhair fern
*Aquilegia canadensis*, wild columbine
*Aralia racemosa*, spikenard
*Arisaema triphyllum*, jack-in-the-pulpit
*Asarum* species, wild gingers
*Aster divaricatus*, white wood aster
*Chrysogonum virginianum*, green-and-gold
*Cornus canadensis*, bunchberry
*Cimicifuga racemosa*, black snakeroot, black cohosh
*Cypripedium calceolus* var. *pubescens*, yellow lady slipper
*Dicentra canadensis*, squirrel corn
*Dicentra cucullaria*, Dutchman's-breeches
*Dicentra eximia*, wild bleeding heart
*Dodecatheon meadia*, shooting star
*Dryopteris* species, wood ferns
*Erythronium americanum*, trout lily
*Gentiana clausa*, bottle gentian
*Geranium maculatum*, cranesbill
*Gillenia trifoliata*, Bowman's root, Indian physic
*Heuchera americana*, coral bells
*Hepatica acutiloba*, liverleaf
*Iris cristata*, crested iris

*(continued on next page)*

*Lilium philadelphicum*, wood lily

*Lilium superbum*, Turk's cap lily

*Maianthemum canadense*, wild lily of the valley

*Matteuccia struthiopteris*, ostrich fern

*Mertensia virginica*, Virginia bluebells

*Mitchella repens*, partridgeberry

*Pachysandra procumbens*, Allegheny pachysandra

*Podophyllum peltatum*, mayapple

*Polemonium reptans*, Jacob's ladder

*Polygonatum biflorum* var. *commutatum*, great
 Solomon's seal

*Polystichum acrostichoides*, Christmas fern

*Sanguinaria canadensis*, bloodroot

*Scutellaria incana* (*S. serrata*), showy skullcap

*Smilacina racemosa*, false Solomon's seal

*Stylophorum diphyllum*, celandine poppy

*Tiarella cordifolia*, foamflower

*Trientalis borealis*, starflower

*Trillium* species, trilliums

*Viola rostrata*, long-spurred violet


## SOUTHEAST AND DEEP SOUTH

### Canopy and Understory

*Acer saccharum* subsp. *leucoderme*, chalk maple

*Aesculus pavia*, red buckeye

*Asimina triloba*, pawpaw

*Chionanthus virginicus*, fringe tree

*Cladrastis kentukea*, Kentucky yellowwood

*Cornus florida*, eastern flowering dogwood

*Crataegus apiifolia* (*C. marshallii*), parsley hawthorn

*Franklinia alatamaha*, Franklin tree

*Halesia carolina*, Carolina silverbell

*Ilex cassine*, Dahoon holly

*Ilex vomitoria*, yaupon holly

*Juniperus virginiana*, eastern red cedar

*Magnolia* species, magnolias

*Pinus palustris*, longleaf pine

*Prunus caroliniana*, cherry laurel

*Quercus virginiana*, live oak

*Rhamnus caroliniana*, Carolina buckthorn

*Sabal palmetto*, sabal palm

*Taxodium distichum*, Bald cypress

*Ulmus crassifolia*, Cedar elm


### Shrub Layer

*Aesculus parviflora*, bottlebrush buckeye

*Agarista* (*Leucothoe*) *populifolia*, Florida leucothoe

*Callicarpa americana*, French mulberry

*Calycanthus floridus*, Carolina allspice, sweet shrub

*Clethra alnifolia*, summersweet

*Euonymus americanus*, strawberry bush, hearts-a-
 bustin'

*Hydrangea arborescens*, mountain hydrangea

*Hydrangea quercifolia*, oak-leaf hydrangea

*Illicium floridanum*, starbush, Florida anise

*Itea virginica*, Virginia sweetspire

*Rhapidophyllum hystrix*, needle palm

*Rhododendron* species, native rhododendrons and
 azaleas

*Viburnum dentatum*, arrowwood


### Ground Layer

*Actaea pachypoda* (*A. alba*), white baneberry

*Adiantum capillus-veneris*, Southern maidenhair fern

*Anemone lancifolia*, windflower

*Angelica venenosa*, woodland angelica

*Arisaema dracontium*, green dragon

*Arisaema triphyllum*, jack-in-the-pulpit

*Athyrium asplenioides*, Southern lady fern

*Chamaelirium luteum*, fairy wand

*Chimaphila maculata*, spotted wintergreen

*Chrysogonum virginianum*, green-and-gold

*Cimicifuga racemosa*, black cohosh, black snakeroot

*Dicentra eximia*, eastern wild bleeding heart

*Erythronium americanum*, trout lily

*Gaultheria procumbens*, wintergreen

*Geranium maculatum*, cranesbill, wild geranium

*Hepatica acutiloba*, liverleaf

*Hepatica americana*, liverleaf

*Hexastylis (Asarum) shuttleworthii*, shuttleworth ginger

*Hexastylis (Asarum) virginicum*, wild ginger

*Houstonia caerulea*, bluets, Quaker ladies

*Hydrophyllum virginianum*, Virginia waterleaf

*Jeffersonia diphylla*, twinleaf

*Melanthium virginicum*, bunchflower

*Mertensia virginica*, Virginia bluebells

*Mitchella repens*, partridgeberry

*Osmunda regalis*, royal fern

*Panax trifolius*, dwarf ginseng

*Phlox divaricata*, blue phlox

*Phlox pilosa*, prairie phlox, downy phlox

*Podophyllum peltatum*, mayapple

*Polygonatum biflorum* var. *commutatum*, great Solomon's seal

*Ruellia caroliniensis*, wild petunia

*Shortia galacifolia*, Oconee bells

*Smilacina racemosa*, false Solomon's seal

*Thalictrum (Anemonella) thalictroides*, rue anemone

*Tiarella cordifolia*, foamflower

*Trillium* species, trilliums

*Uvularia* species, bellworts

*Viola* species, violets

*Woodwardia areolata*, netted chain fern

*Zephyranthes atamasco*, rain lily

## MIDWEST

### Canopy and Understory

*Acer saccharum*, sugar maple

*Aesculus pavia*, red buckeye

*Amelanchier* species, serviceberries

*Asimina triloba*, pawpaw

*Betula nigra*, river birch

*Betula papyrifera*, paper birch

*Carpinus caroliniana*, ironwood, American hornbeam, blue beech

*Carya ovata*, shagbark hickory

*Cercis canadensis*, eastern redbud

*Cornus florida*, eastern flowering dogwood

*Hamamelis virginiana*, witchhazel

*Ilex opaca*, American holly

*Juniperus virginiana*, eastern red cedar

*Ostrya virginiana*, hop hornbeam

*Oxydendrum arboreum*, sourwood

*Pinus strobus*, white pine

*Quercus rubra*, northern red oak

*Quercus macrocarpa*, bur oak

*Tilia americana*, linden

### Shrub Layer

*Amelanchier stolonifera*, running serviceberry

*Aronia arbutifolia*, red chokeberry

*Cornus alternifolia*, pagoda dogwood

*Cotinus obovatus*, American smoke tree

*Diervilla lonicera*, bush honeysuckle

*Dirca palustris*, leatherwood, ropebark

*Euonymus americanus*, strawberry bush, hearts-a-bustin'

*Hamamelis virginiana*, witchhazel

*Ilex verticillata*, winterberry holly

*Prunus americana*, American plum

*Rhododendron* species, native rhododendrons and azaleas

*Sambucus canadensis*, elderberry

*Viburnum* species, viburnums

### Ground Layer

*Actaea* species, baneberries

*Adiantum pedatum*, maidenhair fern

*Anemone canadensis*, Canada anemone

*Aquilegia canadensis*, wild columbine

*Aralia racemosa*, spikenard

*Asarum canadense*, wild ginger

*Aster macrophyllus*, bigleaf aster

*Cimicifuga racemosa*, black snakeroot, black cohosh

*Dodecatheon meadia*, shooting star

*Geranium maculatum*, cranesbill

*Hepatica americana*, liverleaf

*(continued on next page)*

*Isopyrum biternatum*, false rue anemone
*Jeffersonia diphylla*, twinleaf
*Matteuccia pensylvanica*, ostrich fern
*Mertensia virginica*, Virginia bluebells
*Mitella diphylla*, bishop's cap
*Osmunda cinnamomea*, cinnamon fern
*Osmunda claytoniana*, interrupted fern
*Osmunda regalis*, royal fern
*Phlox divaricata*, blue phlox
*Thalictrum (Anemonella) thalictroides*, rue anemone
*Tiarella cordifolia*, foamflower
*Uvularia grandiflora*, large-flowered bellwort
*Viola canadensis*, Canada violet

### ROCKY MOUNTAINS

#### Canopy and Understory

*Acer glabrum*, Rocky Mountain maple
*Amelanchier* species, serviceberries
*Betula fontinalis*, water birch
*Juniperus scopulorum*, Rocky Mountain juniper
*Pinus ponderosa*, Ponderosa pine
*Populus fremontii*, valley cottonwood
*Populus tremuloides*, quaking aspen
*Pseudotsuga menziesii*, Douglas fir
*Ptelea trifoliata*, hop tree, water ash
*Quercus gambelii*, gambel oak

#### Shrub Layer

*Ceanothus fendleri*, buckbrush
*Cornus stolonifera*, red osier dogwood
*Jamesia americana*, waxflower
*Physocarpus monogynus*, mountain ninebark
*Prunus virginiana*, western chokecherry
*Ribes aureum*, golden currant
*Rubus deliciosus*, Rocky Mountain raspberry
*Symphoricarpos occidentalis*, snowberry, wolfberry
*Viburnum trilobum*, American cranberry bush

#### Ground Layer

*Actaea rubra*, western red baneberry
*Adiantum pedatum* var. *aleuticum*, Aleutian maiden-
  hair fern
*Anemone canadensis*, Canada anemone
*Anemone (Pulsatilla) patens*, Pasque flower
*Antennaria parvifolia*, pussytoes
*Aquilegia caerulea*, Rocky Mountain columbine
*Arctostaphylos uva-ursi*, kinnikinnick, bearberry
*Camassia quamash*, common camas
*Campanula rotundifolia*, bluebell
*Dryopteris filix-mas*, male fern
*Epilobium angustifolium*, fireweed
*Geranium fremontii*, Fremont geranium
*Gymnocarpium dryopteris*, oak fern
*Gymnocarpium robertianum*, limestone oak fern
*Heuchera sanguinea*, coral bells
*Iris missouriensis*, western blue flag
*Juniperus communis*, common juniper
*Lewisia rediviva*, bitterroot
*Leucocrinum montanua*, sand lily
*Mahonia repens*, Oregon grape, holly grape
*Mertensia lanceolata*, bluebell
*Osmunda claytoniana*, interrupted fern
*Penstemon* species, beardtongues
*Tellima grandiflora*, fringecups

### PACIFIC NORTHWEST

#### Canopy and Understory

*Abies amabilis*, Pacific silver fir
*Acer circinatum*, vine maple
*Acer glabrum* subsp. *douglasii*, Douglas maple
*Alnus rubra*, red alder
*Amelanchier alnifolia*, serviceberry
*Calocedrus decurrens*, western red cedar
*Cornus nuttallii*, Pacific dogwood, mountain dog-
  wood
*Larix occidentalis*, western larch
*Pinus contorta*, lodgepole pine

*Pseudotsuga menziesii*, Douglas fir
*Sorbus sitchensis*, mountain ash
*Taxus brevifolia*, Pacific yew
*Tsuga mertensiana*, mountain hemlock

**Shrub Layer**

*Crataegus douglasii*, Douglas hawthorn
*Gaultheria shallon*, salal
*Lonicera involucrata*, bush honeysuckle
*Mahonia* species, Oregon grapes, holly grapes
*Oemleria cerasiformis*, osoberry
*Paxistima myrsinitis*, Oregon box
*Paxistima myrtifolia*, Oregon boxwood
*Physocarpus capitatus*, Pacific ninebark
*Ribes sanguineum*, red flowering currant
*Rhododendron* species, native rhododendrons and
    azaleas
*Rosa nutkana*, Nootka rose
*Rubus parviflorus*, thimbleberry, salmonberry
*Rubus spectabilis*, salmonberry
*Rubus ursinus*, dewberry
*Sambucus racemosa*, red elderberry
*Spiraea densiflora*, subalpine spirea
*Vaccinium ovatum*, evergreen huckleberry
*Vaccinium parvifolium*, red huckleberry
*Viburnum ellipticum*, oval-leaved viburnum

**Ground Layer**

*Actaea rubra*, baneberry
*Adiantum pedatum*, maidenhair fern
*Aralia californica*, elk clover
*Aruncus dioicus*, goatsbeard
*Asarum caudatum*, western wild ginger
*Blechnum spicant*, deer fern
*Coptis laciniata*, goldthread
*Cornus canadensis*, bunchberry dogwood
*Dicentra formosa*, western bleeding heart
*Disporum hookeri*, fairybells
*Erythronium oregonum*, fawn lily, dogtooth violet

*Erythronium revolutum*, fawn lily, dogtooth violet
*Mahonia nervosa* var. *nervosa*, Cascades Oregon
    grape
*Mitella breweri*, miterwort, bishop's cap
*Oxalis oregana*, Oregon wood sorrel
*Petasites frigidus*, coltsfoot
*Smilacina racemosa*, false Solomon's seal
*Synthyris reniformis*, snow queen
*Tiarella trifoliata*, foamflower
*Trillium ovatum*, western trillium
*Vancouveria hexandra*, inside-out flower
*Vancouveria planipetala*, evergreen vancouveria

### CALIFORNIA

**Canopy and Understory**

*Acer circinatum*, vine maple
*Arbutus menziesii*, Pacific madrone
*Cornus nuttallii*, Pacific dogwood, mountain dog-
    wood
*Corylus cornuta* var. *californica*, western hazelnut
*Prunus virginiana*, western chokecherry
*Quercus agrifolia*, California live oak
*Quercus kelloggii*, California black oak
*Quercus lobata*, valley oak
*Sequoia sempervirens*, redwood

**Shrub Layer**

*Arctostaphylos* species, manzanitas
*Carpenteria californica*, bush anemone
*Euonymus occidentalis*, wahoo, western burning
    bush
*Heteromeles arbutifolia*, toyon
*Mahonia aquifolium*, Oregon grape holly
*Mahonia nevinii*, Nevin's Oregon grape
*Mahonia repens*, creeping Oregon grape
*Rhamnus californicus*, coffeeberry
*Rhododendron* species, native rhododendrons and
    azaleas

*(continued on next page)*

*Ribes sanguineum* var. *glutinosum*, red flowering currant
*Vaccinium ovatum*, evergreen huckleberry

**Ground Layer**

*Aquilegia formosa*, red columbine
*Asarum caudatum*, western wild ginger
*Blechnum spicant*, deer fern
*Clintonia andrewsiana*, red clintonia
*Dicentra formosa*, western bleeding heart
*Dodecatheon* species, shooting stars
*Heuchera maxima*, island alum root
*Iris douglasiana*, Douglas' iris

*Iris innominata*, golden iris
*Osmunda claytoniana*, interrupted fern
*Polystichum munitum*, sword fern
*Sisyrinchium bellum*, California blue-eyed grass
*Sisyrinchium californicum*, golden-eyed grass
*Smilacina racemosa*, false Solomon's seal
*Smilacina stellata*, starry false Solomon's seal
*Solidago californica*, California goldenrod
*Trillium ovatum*, western trillium
*Triteleia laxa*, Ithuriel's spear
*Vancouveria hexandra*, Vancouveria
*Vancouveria planipetala*, inside-out flower
*Viola* species, violets

first growing season. Mulch is the key to the long-term success of a woodland garden. Organic mulches help improve soil structure as they break down over time. Mulch also inhibits the germination of weed seeds and weed growth; reduces the stress on plants by keeping down summer soil temperatures; protects against the winter freeze-thaw cycles that damage plants by keeping soil temperatures relatively constant; and conserves water.

What is more, forest soil gets its nutrients from fallen leaves or needles. An annual application of mulch in the fall, preferably shredded leaf mulch created by running the lawn mower over leaves several times, will protect woodland plants and make synthetic fertilizers unnecessary. A good rule of thumb is to apply 3 to 6 inches of mulch. Never pile it against the tree trunks, where it can encourage fungus buildup and rot the bark.

After the second or third year, maintenance turns into woodland management. To preserve the woodland canopy, nurture healthy young saplings so they can someday replace older trees. Remove invasive plants as soon as they

appear. Finally, watch for signs of damage or decline due to deer, insect pests, or diseases, but intervene only when the problem threatens the health or survival of plants, particularly major canopy trees.

## Wetland Gardens

One definition of a wetland is a site where the soil is saturated at least seven consecutive days a year, and/or where the water table stays within a foot of the soil surface at least seven consecutive days. Otherwise, wetlands differ in many ways. Some are freshwater, others saltwater. Some have currents or tides, others have relatively still water. Wetlands can be marshes, spring-fed seeps, peat bogs, streamsides, or wet meadows. If an area floods during heavy rains but dries out in a day or two, it is not a wetland, and it cannot support moisture-loving plants. On the other hand, an area that is seasonally wet, drying out only during the hot summer months, is a wetland; its saturated soils can sustain moisture-loving species.

Wetlands of the U.S. and Canada

key:
△ Swamps
○ Bogs
□ Marshes

Here "wetland" is used to describe plantings in or around marshes, bogs, ponds, streams, or swamps. Marshes are usually open and sunny. The water is typically shallow, and covered by herbaceous vegetation. A true bog is fed by groundwater and is characterized by highly acidic soils, poor drainage, spaghnum mosses, and peat. A wet meadow is the zone where wetland grades into upland. It regularly undergoes periods of wet and dry. Depending on where in the country the wetland is located, the wet meadow zone may be dominated by herbaceous plants or shrubs and trees. A swamp is a closed-canopy wetland dominated by flood-tolerant trees and shrubs. Streamside, or riparian, wetlands can accommodate plants along their banks or even in the running water. For more on wetland ecology, see "Ecology for Gardeners," page 159.

Certain types of wetland predominate in various regions. Inland marshes, the most widely and evenly distributed, range from the sawgrass marshes of Florida's Everglades to the northern marshes of New England, home to great blue herons, moose, and muskrats. The largest concentration of inland marshes is in the prairie pothole region, extending from the north-central United States into south-central Canada. Peatlands or bogs occur mostly in boreal regions from Minnesota to Maine and northward, with smaller pockets in the Pacific Northwest, western mountains, and Appalachians. Swamps include the tupelo and Spanish moss-laden cypress swamps of the South; the floodplain swamps of the Mississippi Valley; the towering pine pocosins of the Southeast; the red maple swamps of the East; and the black spruce, tamarack, and cedar swamps of the North.

Only freshwater wetlands are described in this section. For information on coastal salt-marshes, see page 161.

## Preparing a Wetland Garden

To create a regionally appropriate wetland garden, start by visiting wetlands in the vicinity and make note of their characteristics. Hydrology is a complex subject, so it might be helpful to speak to a local naturalist or soil conservation official about the site's flooding patterns, soil types, water sources, and so on.

To begin planning to create or restore a wetland, aim to mimic the zones found in similar wetlands in the area. Look to these undisturbed wetlands as a "template" for species that grow under similar conditions. Observe how certain species are grouped together according to water depth. Note the types of species growing and how closely and evenly they are dispersed.

See page 422 for details on constructing a freshwater pool or pond. To improve on an existing wet area, it may be necessary to deepen it or amend the soil. When digging to deepen or enlarge a pond or other wet area, be careful not to break through the layer of dense sand or packed clay a foot or two beneath the surface. This hardpan layer holds the water and keeps it from draining away.

Wetland vegetation continually changes in response both to seasonal flooding and dry spells and to very dry and wet years. During drought years, water levels drop, exposing wetland soils. Exposed to full sun, these moist, organic soils provide ideal conditions for seed germination. As the drought ends and water levels rise, the seedlings grow rapidly. Before planting, it is necessary to re-create this "mud-flat" condition. The seeds of most species require open soil and will not germinate below water.

Before planting, eradicate any existing invasive plant species, preferably by hand or with a weeding tool.

## Planting a Wetland Garden

When choosing plants for a wetland, use only native, noninvasive species. Never use giant reed (*Phragmites australis*), purple loosestrife (*Lythrum salicaria*), or reed canary grass (*Phalaris arundinacea*)—all are highly invasive and can choke out a wetland in a short period of time. Cattails (*Typha* species) can also get out of control. Check all nursery stock carefully and rinse the plants before planting; some may arrive covered with duckweed (*Lemna* species) or other undesirables. Seed is always less expensive than plants, but may be more difficult to get established.

As in a native wetland, plant in visually distinct zones or bands determined by water depth. Plants that are able to tolerate similar depths of water grow in similar zones. As described above, the *wet meadow zone* is found where the wetland intergrades with upland vegetation. Just below the wet meadow zone is the *emergent zone,* dominated by soft-stemmed, herbaceous plants like pickerel weed, arrowheads, and sedges that grow partially in water. Submersed aquatics and floating plants like water lilies and pondweeds are found in deep water. Their leaves are capable of photosynthesizing in water.

Field guides describe the habitats of plants that tolerate damp soils as "moist woodlands," "wet prairies," "bottomlands," or "low-lying meadows." Plants that can grow right in the water are either listed with the aquatic species or described as "growing in ditches or at the water's edge." Upland plants will not grow in a wetland because they do not have the specially adapted cells that allow their roots to "breathe" even when saturated with water.

To begin planting, lay out the grasses and sedges in a large grid directly on the ground with about 3 feet between individual plants.

Group dominant species in large colonies, as they are found in nature. The close observation of natural areas will pay off when it comes time to place wildflowers in the wet meadow zone. Some species, including blue flag iris and turtlehead, grow best on the wetter end of the planting bed. Others, such as redstem aster, occur slightly uphill in somewhat drier soil. Place each plant in the type of soil and setting where it is typically found in nature.

Wetland gardens can be started from seed or with transplants. Seed should be purchased from local sources or collected from nearby wetlands with permission. Some species, particularly sedges, do not establish well from seed. They should be planted as nursery-grown stock during the second or third year after the initial seeding. In zones with standing water, it is also necessary to use live plants or root stocks. And in areas dominated by invasive species or where native species are scarce, plants again are a better choice because they become established quickly. A cover crop of an annual plant such as oats will prevent soil erosion in all planted areas.

Optimal planting time varies by region. In the North, it is best to plant in late spring, after the water recedes. West of the Rockies, plant in the fall. In the southern states, fall and winter are best. Check with a regional nursery about the best time to plant because wetland conditions vary, even within regions.

## Maintaining a Wetland Garden

A wetland garden should require little maintenance once established. Watering and fertilization are unnecessary. Encourage frogs, salamanders, and birds for natural mosquito control. In a pond, certain types of fish will help control algae and other unwanted plant growth.

# PLANTS FOR WETLAND GARDENS

In the regional plant lists below, native species are divided into the following groups: trees, shrubs, perennials, grasses and grasslike plants, ferns, emergents (tolerate persistent flooding; grow at the water's edge), and aquatics (floating and submersed plants). For best results, be familiar with the specific site conditions before choosing plants. For additional (though not necessarily native) candidates for water gardens, see "Plants for Every Purpose and Every Region," page 288.

## NORTHEAST AND MID-ATLANTIC

### Trees

*Asimina triloba*, pawpaw
*Amelanchier laevis*, shadbush
*Betula nigra*, river birch
*Fraxinus nigra*, black ash
*Larix laricina*, tamarack or eastern larch
*Liquidambar styraciflua*, sweet gum
*Nyssa sylvatica*, black or sour gum, tupelo
*Picea mariana*, black spruce
*Quercus palustris*, pin oak
*Thuja occidentalis*, eastern white cedar or eastern arborvitae

### Shrubs

*Cephalanthus occidentalis*, buttonbush
*Cornus amomum*, silky dogwood
*Cornus stolonifera*, red osier dogwood
*Dirca palustris*, leatherwood
*Ledum groenlandicum*, Labrador tea
*Rhododendron arborescens*, sweet azalea
*Rhododendron maximum*, rosebay rhododendron
*Rosa palustris*, swamp rose
*Salix discolor*, pussy willow

*Sambucus canadensis*, American elderberry
*Viburnum dentatum*, arrowwood
*Viburnum trilobum*, American cranberry bush

### Perennials

*Arisaema dracontium*, green dragon
*Arisaema triphyllum*, jack-in-the-pulpit
*Asclepias incarnata*, swamp milkweed
*Calla palustris*, wild calla
*Caltha palustris*, marsh marigold
*Camassia cusickii*, camassia
*Chelone glabra*, white turtlehead
*Coptis trifolia* subsp. *groenlandica*, goldthread
*Dodecatheon meadia*, shooting star
*Eupatorium maculatum*, Joe-Pye weed
*Helianthus angustifolius*, swamp sunflower
*Hibiscus palustris*, marsh mallow
*Lilium canadense*, Canada lily
*Lilium superbum*, Turk's cap lily
*Lobelia siphilitica*, blue lobelia
*Lysimachia terrestris*, swamp candles
*Menyanthes trifoliata*, bog bean
*Mertensia virginica*, Virginia bluebells
*Mimulus guttatus*, monkey musk
*Monarda didyma*, Oswego tea
*Nymphaea odorata*, white water lily
*Orontium aquaticum*, golden club
*Pontederia cordata*, pickerel rush
*Potentilla palustris*, marsh cinquefoil
*Rudbeckia laciniata*, cut-leaf coneflower
*Sagittaria latifolia*, duck potato
*Saururus cernuus*, lizard's tail
*Senecio aureus*, golden ragwort
*Silphium perfoliatum*, cup plant
*Sisyrinchium angustifolium*, blue-eyed grass
*Solidago uliginosa*, marsh goldenrod
*Thalictrum pubescens*, tall meadow rue

*Tradescantia virginiana*, spiderwort

*Triadenum (Hypericum) virginicum*, marsh St.-John's-
wort

*Vernonia noveboracensis*, common ironweed

*Veronicastrum virginicum*, Culver's root

*Xyris iridifolia*, yellow-eyed grass

*Zizia aurea*, golden alexander

### Grasses and Grasslike Plants

*Carex muskingumensis*, palm sedge

*Carex paniculata*, panicled sedge

*Carex pendula*, drooping sedge

*Carex stipata*, tussock sedge

*Eriophorum angustifolium*, narrow-leaved cotton
grass

*Eriophorum latifolium*, broad-leaved cotton grass

*Poa palustris*, fowl meadow grass

*Scirpus tabernaemontani*, bulrush

### Ferns

*Athyrium filix-femina*, lady fern

*Athyrium pycnocarpon*, glade fern

*Dryopteris goldiana*, Goldie's wood fern

*Osmunda claytoniana*, interrupted fern

*Osmunda regalis*, royal fern

*Phegopteris connectilis*, northern beech fern

*Thelypteris palustris*, marsh fern

*Woodwardia virginica*, Virginia chain fern

### Emergents

*Acorus calamus*, sweet flag

*Caltha palustris*, marsh marigold

*Cephalanthus occidentalis*, buttonbush

*Iris versicolor*, blue flag

*Peltandra virginica*, arrow arum

*Pontederia cordata*, pickerel rush

*Sagittaria latifolia*, arrowhead, duck potato

*Saururus cernuus*, lizard's tail

*Symplocarpus foetidus*, skunk cabbage

### Aquatics

*Elodea canadensis*, frogbit

*Nelumbo lutea*, American lotus

*Nuphar advena*, spatterdock, yellow pond lily

*Nymphaea odorata*, white fragrant water lily

*Nymphaea tetragona*, pygmy water lily

*Nymphaea tuberosa*, white water lily

*Orontium aquaticum*, golden club

## SOUTHEAST AND DEEP SOUTH

### Trees

*Betula nigra*, river birch

*Gordonia lasianthus*, loblolly bay

*Liquidambar styraciflua*, sweet gum

*Magnolia virginiana*, sweetbay

*Magnolia virginiana* var. *australis*, evergreen sweetbay

*Pinus taeda*, loblolly pine

*Quercus nigra*, water oak

*Quercus phellos*, willow oak

*Sabal mexicana*, Texas palm

*Sabal palmetto*, cabbage palm

### Shrubs and Vines

*Agarista (Leucothoe) populifolia*, andromeda

*Avicennia germinans*, black mangrove

*Baccharis angustifolia*, false willow

*Cephalanthus occidentalis*, buttonbush

*Cyrilla racemiflora*, titi

*Gelsemium sempervirens*, Carolina jessamine

*Ilex cassine*, Dahoon holly

*Ilex verticillata*, winterberry holly

*Itea virginica*, sweetspire

*Lonicera sempervirens*, coral honeysuckle

*Rhododendron oblongifolium*, sweet azalea

*Rhododendron austrinum*, Florida azalea

*Rosa palustris*, swamp rose

*(continued on next page)*

## Perennials

*Canna flaccida*, swamp canna
*Eupatorium coelestinum*, blue mistflower
*Equisetum hyemale*, horsetail
*Helianthus angustifolius*, swamp sunflower
*Hibiscus coccineus*, Texas star hibiscus
*Hibiscus militaris*, marsh mallow
*Hibiscus laevis*, swamp mallow
*Hymenocallis liriosome*, spider lily
*Iris brevicaulis*, zig-zag iris
*Iris fulva*, red Louisiana iris
*Iris giganticaerulea*, giant Louisiana iris
*Iris hexagona*, blue southern iris
*Iris nelsonii*, Nelson's iris
*Iris virginica*, swamp iris
*Lobelia cardinalis*, cardinal flower
*Monarda fistulosa*, bergamot
*Nelumbo lutea*, yellow lotus
*Nymphaea elegans*, blue water lily
*Nymphaea odorata*, white fragrant water lily
*Peltandra virginica*, arrow-leaf
*Penstemon tenuis*, Gulf coast penstemon
*Phlox divaricata*, Louisiana phlox
*Phlox pilosa*, prairie phlox
*Physostegia angustifolia*, spring-blooming obedient
    plant
*Physostegia virginiana*, fall-blooming obedient plant
*Rudbeckia maxima*, giant coneflower
*Salvia lyrata*, lyreleaf sage
*Sagittaria latifolia*, Delta duck potato
*Saururus cernuus*, lizard's tail
*Thalia dealbata*, powdery thalia
*Typha angustifolia*, cattail
*Viola missouriensis*, Missouri violet
*Viola walteri*, Walter's violet

## Grasses

*Andropogon glomeratus*, bushy bluestem grass
*Chasmanthium latifolium*, inland sea oats
*Rhynchospora colorata*, white-topped sedge

*Muhlenbergia capillaris*, Gulf muhly grass
*Muhlenbergia lindheimeri*, Lindheimer's muhly grass
*Panicum virgatum*, switch grass

## Ferns

*Onoclea sensibilis*, sensitive fern
*Osmunda regalis* var. *spectabilis*, royal fern
*Osmunda cinnamomea*, cinnamon fern
*Polystichum acrostichoides*, Christmas fern
*Thelypteris kunthii*, river fern

## Emergents

*Aletris farinosa*, unicorn root
*Bacopa caroliniana*, blue water hyssop
*Crinum americanum*, swamp lily
*Lygodium palmatum*, creeping fern
*Peltandra virginica*, arrow arum
*Pontederia cordata*, pickerel rush
*Sagittaria latifolia*, arrowhead, duck potato
*Saururus cernuus*, lizard's tail
*Taxodium distichum*, bald cypress

## Aquatics

*Menyanthes trifoliata*, bog bean
*Nelumbo lutea*, American lotus
*Nymphaea mexicana*, Mexican water lily
*Nymphaea odorata*, white fragrant water lily
*Nymphaea tuberosa*, white water lily
*Nymphoides aquatica*, floating heart
*Orontium aquaticum*, golden club

## SOUTH FLORIDA

## Trees

*Ficus aurea*, strangler fig
*Fraxinus caroliniana*, pop ash
*Ilex cassine*, Dahoon holly
*Magnolia virginiana*, sweetbay magnolia
*Persea borbonia*, red bay

*Pinus elliottii* var. *elliottii*, slash pine
*Quercus laurifolia*, laurel oak

## Palms

*Acoelorraphe wrightii*, paurotis palm
*Sabal palmetto*, cabbage or sabal palm
*Serenoa repens*, saw palmetto

## Shrubs

*Cephalanthus occidentalis*, buttonbush
*Ilex glabra*, galberry
*Myrica cerifera*, wax myrtle
*Salix caroliniana*, coastal plains willow
*Sambucus canadensis*, elderberry

## Perennials

*Aletris lutea*, yellow colic root
*Canna flaccida*, golden canna
*Crinum americanum*, swamp or string lily
*Eriocaulon decangulare*, pipewort
*Helenium pinnatifidum*, marsh sneezeweed
*Hydrolea corymbosa*, skyflower
*Hymenocallis palmeri*, alligator lily
*Hypericum cistifolium*, St.-John's-wort
*Iva microcephala*, marsh elder
*Lachnanthes caroliniana*, bloodroot
*Lachnocaulon anceps*, bog-buttons
*Lobelia glandulosa*, glades lobelia
*Nymphoides aquatica*, floating heart
*Peltandra virginica*, green arum
*Pontederia lanceolata*, pickerel weed
*Potamogeton illinoensis*, pondweed
*Pluchea rosea*, marsh fleabane
*Rudbeckia hirta*, black-eyed Susan
*Solidago stricta*, narrowleaf goldenrod
*Teucrium canadense*, wood sage
*Utricularia cornuta*, horned bladderwort
*Utricularia foliosa*, bladderwort
*Utricularia purpurea*, purple bladderwort

## Grasses and Wildflowers

*Coelorachis rugosa*, wrinkled joint-tail
*Coreopsis leavenworthii*, tickseed
*Cyperus tetragonus*, cyperus
*Eragrostis* species, love grass
*Saccharum* (*Erianthus*) *giganteum*, plume grass
*Eustachys glauca*, marsh fingergrass
*Eupatorium coelestinum*, blue mistflower
*Helenium pinnatifidum*, Everglades daisy
*Juncus megacephalus*, juncus
*Muhlenbergia capillaris*, muhly grass
*Panicum hemitomon*, maidencane
*Panicum hians*, gaping panicum
*Rhynchospora colorata*, white-topped sedge
*Schoenus nigricans*, black rush
*Scirpus tabernaemontani*, soft-stem bulrush
*Setaria parviflora*, foxtail
*Solidago stricta*, narrowleaf goldenrod
*Spartina bakeri*, sand cordgrass
*Tripsacum dactyloides*, Fakahatchee grass

## Ferns

*Osmunda regalis* var. *spectabilis*, royal fern
*Thelypteris palustris*, marsh fern
*Woodwardia virginica*, Virginia chain fern

## Vines

*Ampelopsis arborea*, peppervine
*Aster carolinianus*, climbing aster
*Ipomoea sagittata*, Everglades morning glory
*Mikania scandens*, climbing hempweed
*Parthenocissus quinquefolia*, Virginia creeper
*Smilax laurifolia*, catbriar
*Vitis cinerea* var. *floridana*, pigeon grape

## Emergents

*Acer rubrum trilobum*, red maple
*Annona glabra*, pond apple
*Crinum americanum*, swamp lily

*(continued on next page)*

*Eleocharis cellulosa*, spike rush
*Peltandra virginica*, arrow arum
*Pontederia lanceolata*, pickerel weed
*Sagittaria lancifolia*, arrowhead
*Sagittaria latifolia*, arrowhead, duck potato
*Taxodium ascendens*, pond cypress (tolerates
    standing water when mature)
*Thalia geniculata*, alligator flag

### Aquatics

*Nuphar lutea* subsp. *advena*, spatterdock, yellow
    pond lily
*Nymphaea odorata*, white fragrant water lily
*Nymphoides aquatica*, floating heart

## MIDWEST AND GREAT PLAINS

### Trees

*Acer rubrum*, red maple
*Acer saccharinum*, silver maple
*Alnus incana* subsp. *rugosa*, speckled alder
*Asimina triloba*, pawpaw
*Betula nigra*, river birch
*Fraxinus nigra*, black ash
*Larix laricina*, tamarack
*Picea mariana*, black spruce
*Quercus bicolor*, swamp white oak
*Salix nigra*, black willow
*Thuja occidentalis*, white cedar

### Shrubs and Vines

*Andromeda polifolia* var. *glaucophylla*, bog rosemary
*Chamaedaphne calyculata*, leatherleaf
*Ledum groenlandicum*, Labrador tea
*Myrica gale*, sweet gale
*Potentilla fruticosa*, shrubby cinquefoil
*Spiraea tomentosa*, hardhack
*Spiraea virginiana*, spirea
*Viburnum dentatum*, arrowwood

### Perennials

*Acorus calamus*, sweet flag
*Alisma plantago-aquatica*, water plantain
*Aster puniceus*, purple-stemmed aster
*Aster lanceolatus* var. *lanceolatus*, marsh aster
*Bidens cernua*, nodding bidens
*Eupatorium perfoliatum*, boneset
*Helenium autumnale*, sneezeweed
*Helianthus grosseserratus*, big-toothed sunflower
*Hibiscus moscheutos* subsp. *lasiocarpos*, marsh
    mallow
*Hymenocallis caroliniana*, spider lily
*Iris versicolor*, blue flag iris
*Iris virginica*, Virginia blue flag
*Liatris pycnostachya*, prairie blazing star
*Lobelia cardinalis*, cardinal flower
*Lobelia spicata*, pale-spiked lobelia
*Mimulus ringens*, monkeyflower
*Nuphar lutea* subsp. *variegata*, spadderdock
*Nymphaea odorata*, water lily
*Orontium aquaticum*, golden club
*Parnassia glauca*, grass-of-Parnassus
*Petasites frigidus*, coltsfoot
*Physostegia virginiana*, obedient plant
*Polygonum amphibium*, water smartweed
*Pontederia cordata*, pickerel weed
*Ranunculus flabellaris*, water buttercup
*Sagittaria latifolia*, arrowhead
*Sarracenia purpurea*, purple pitcher plant
*Saururus cernuus*, lizard's tail
*Saxifraga pensylvanica*, swamp saxifrage
*Senecio aureus*, golden ragwort
*Solidago* species, including *S. gigantea, S. ohioensis,*
    and *S. riddellii,* goldenrods
*Symplocarpus foetidus*, skunk cabbage
*Veratrum viride*, false hellebore
*Verbena hastata*, blue vervain
*Vernonia gigantea* subsp. *gigantea*, tall ironweed
*Xyris* species, yellow-eyed grasses
*Zigadenus elegans*, death camas

## Grasses and Grasslike Plants

*Carex comosa*, bottle sedge
*Carex muskingumensis*, palm sedge
*Carex pendula*, drooping sedge
*Eriophorum vaginatum* var. *spissum*, cotton grass
*Scirpus* species, bulrushes
*Sparganium* species, bur reeds
*Zizania aquatica*, wild rice

## Ferns

*Dryopteris cristata*, crested wood fern
*Equisetum* species, horsetails
*Onoclea sensibilis*, sensitive fern
*Osmunda cinnamomea*, cinnamon fern
*Osmunda regalis*, royal fern
*Woodwardia areolata*, netted chain fern

## Emergents

*Acorus calamus*, sweet flag
*Alisma plantago-aquatica*, water plantain
*Andromeda glaucophylla*, bog rosemary
*Calla palustris*, water arum
*Caltha palustris*, marsh marigold
*Iris versicolor*, blue flag
*Iris virginica*, Virginia blue flag
*Pontederia cordata*, pickerel rush
*Sagittaria latifolia*, arrowhead, duck potato
*Saururus cernuus*, lizard's tail
*Scirpus tabernaemontana*, soft-stem bulrush
*Symplocarpus foetidus*, skunk cabbage

## Aquatics

*Elodea canadensis*, frogbit
*Menyanthes trifoliata*, bog bean
*Nuphar advena*, spatterdock, yellow pond lily
*Nelumbo lutea*, American lotus
*Nuphar lutea* subsp. *variegata*, spatterdock
*Nymphaea odorata*, white fragrant water lily
*Nymphaea tuberosa*, white water lily

*Orontium aquaticum*, golden club
*Ranunculus flabellaris*, buttercup, yellow water crowfoot

# PACIFIC NORTHWEST AND ROCKY MOUNTAINS

## Trees

*Acer circinatum*, vine maple
*Acer rubrum*, red maple
*Betula nigra*, river birch
*Betula papyrifera*, paper birch

## Shrubs

*Aronia arbutifolia*, red chokeberry
*Cephalanthus occidentalis*, buttonbush
*Clethra alnifolia*, summersweet, sweet pepperbush
*Cornus alba*, red twig dogwood
*Cornus alternifolia*, pagoda dogwood
*Cornus racemosa*, panicled dogwood
*Cornus stolonifera*, creek dogwood
*Gaultheria shallon*, salal
*Lonicera involucrata*, twinberry
*Magnolia virginiana*, sweetbay
*Rhododendron occidentale*, western azalea
*Rubus spectabilis*, salmonberry
*Salix elaeagnos*, rosemary willow
*Salix scouleriana*, scouler's willow
*Spiraea douglasii*, spirea, hardhack

## Perennials

*Aralia californica*, elk clover
*Aquilegia formosa*, columbine
*Aruncus dioicus*, goatsbeard
*Astilbe biternata*, false goatsbeard
*Cammasia quamash*, camas
*Cardamine pratensis*, lady's smock
*Cimicifuga laciniata*, bugbane
*Corydalis scouleri*, corydalis

*(continued on next page)*

*Dactylorhiza maculata*, spotted ground orchid
*Darlingtonia californica*, pitcher plant
*Darmera peltata*, Indian rhubarb
*Geranium maculatum*, cranesbill
*Heracleum lanatum*, cow parsnip
*Iris missouriensis*, western blue flag
*Maianthemum dilatatum*, false lily of the valley
*Mimulus guttatus*, monkeyflower
*Oplopanax horridus*, devil's club
*Peltiphyllum peltatum*, umbrella plant
*Veratrum californicum*, false hellebore
*Viola macloskeyi*, western sweet white violet
*Vaccinium oxycoccus*, small cranberry

### Grasses and Grasslike Plants

*Carex obnupta*, sedge
*Eleocharis acicularis*, spike rush
*Equisetum* species, horsetails
*Eriophorum viridicarinatum* (*E. latifolium* var. *viridicarinatum*), cotton grass
*Juncus* species, rushes
*Scirpus* species, bulrushes

### Ferns

*Adiantum pedatum*, maidenhair fern
*Athyrium filix-femina*, lady fern
*Blechnum spicant*, deer fern
*Polystichum munitum*, western sword fern
*Woodwardia fimbriata*, chain fern

### Emergents

*Caltha leptosepala*, marsh marigold
*Equisetum hyemale*, horsetail
*Lysichiton americanus*, western skunk cabbage

### Aquatics

*Menyanthes trifoliata*, bog bean
*Nymphaea tetragona*, pygmy water lily
*Nymphaea tuberosa*, white water lily
*Orontium aquaticum*, golden club

## CALIFORNIA

### Trees

*Acer circinatum*, vine maple
*Acer glabrum*, Sierra maple
*Acer macrophyllum*, bigleaf maple
*Alnus rhombifolia*, white alder
*Betula occidentalis*, water birch
*Chilopsis linearis*, desert willow
*Platanus racemosa*, western sycamore
*Quercus lobata*, valley oak
*Populus fremontii*, Fremont cottonwood
*Salix laevigata*, red willow
*Salix lucida* subsp. *lasiandra*, yellow tree willow
*Umbellularia californica*, California bay
*Washingtonia filifera*, California fan palm

### Shrubs and Vines

*Aristolochia californica*, California pipevine
*Calycanthus occidentalis*, western spicebush
*Clematis ligusticifolia*, virgin's bower
*Cornus stolonifera*, American dogwood
*Euonymus occidentalis*, western burning bush
*Lonicera hispidula* var. *vacillans*, honeysuckle
*Myrica californica*, wax myrtle
*Philadelphus lewisii*, mock orange
*Physocarpus capitatus*, ninebark
*Rhamnus purshiana*, cascara sagrada
*Rhododendron macrophyllum*, California rhododendron
*Rhododendron occidentale*, western azalea
*Ribes sanguineum*, red flowering currant
*Rosa californica*, California wild rose
*Rubus spectabilis*, salmonberry
*Salix hindsiana*, sandbar willow
*Styrax officinalis*, California snowdrop bush
*Vaccinium ovatum*, California huckleberry

### Perennials

*Aquilegia formosa*, red columbine
*Aralia californica*, elk clover

*Darlingtonia californica*, pitcher plant
*Darmera peltata*, Indian rhubarb
*Delphinium glaucum*, tower delphinium
*Dicentra formosa*, Pacific bleeding heart
*Dodecatheon dentatum*, shooting star
*Drosera rotundifolia*, sundew
*Epipactis gigantea*, stream orchid
*Heracleum lanatum*, cow parsnip
*Heuchera micrantha*, alum root
*Lobelia cardinalis*, cardinal flower
*Lysichiton americanus*, skunk cabbage
*Maianthemum dilatatum*, false lily of the valley
*Mimulus cardinalis*, scarlet monkeyflower
*Mimulus guttatus*, monkeyflower
*Mimulus primuloides*, primrose monkeyflower
*Mitella ovalis*, bishop's cap
*Oxalis oregana*, redwood sorrel
*Petasites frigidus* var. *palmatus*, western coltsfoot
*Rudbeckia californica*, coneflower
*Sambucus racemosa*, red elderberry
*Sidalcea oregana* subsp. *spicata*, Oregon sidalcea
*Sisyrinchium bellum*, blue-eyed grass
*Smilacina racemosa*, branched Solomon's seal
*Smilacina stellata*, star Solomon's seal
*Spiraea douglasii*, spirea
*Symphoricarpos albus* var. *laevigatus*, snowberry
*Tolmiea menziesii*, tolmiea
*Veratrum californicum*, corn lily

**Grasses and Grasslike Plants**

*Anemopsis californica*, yerba mansa
*Carex tumulicola*, Berkeley sedge
*Deschampsia caespitosa*, hairgrass
*Eriophorum gracile*, slender cotton grass
*Juncus balticus*, Baltic rush
*Parnassia californica*, grass-of-Parnassus
*Typha domingensis*, cattail

**Ferns**

*Adiantum pedatum*, five-finger fern
*Athyrium filix-femina* var. *cyclosorum*, lady fern
*Blechnum spicant*, deer fern
*Polypodium californicum*, California polypody
*Polystichum munitum*, western sword fern
*Woodwardia fimbriata*, chain fern

**Emergents**

*Equisetum hyemale*, horsetail
*Lysichiton americanus*, western skunk cabbage

**Aquatics**

*Menyanthes trifoliata*, bog bean
*Nymphaea tuberosa*, white water lily

Continued removal of invasive species is an important part of wetland garden maintenance. Keep an eye out for invasives and remove them as soon as possible to prevent serious infestations.

## Grassland Gardens

Grasslands cover a third of the Earth's land surface in places too cold, too dry, or too wet for trees. They are usually flat or gently rolling open spaces, with few trees (if any) to block the wind or cast shade. Grassland plants are mostly grasses and forbs (herbaceous plants or wildflowers). Different species dominate in various types of grasslands—dry to wet, cold to hot.

The North American grasslands are some of the continent's most imperiled habitats. At one time, the Central Prairies and Plains province covered 250 million acres of North America, stretching from the Appalachians to the Rocky

Mountains. Very little original prairie remains today, but gardeners in this and other areas where there were once native grassland communities can re-create pocket prairies or meadows on their properties.

A prairie is a grassland, and so is a meadow, an old field, a savannah, and a plain. Most prairies occur in relatively dry areas such as the Midwest and Great Plains, which receive less precipitation than forested regions but more than the western deserts. In the easternmost areas of the Central Prairies and Plains province, where rain is comparatively plentiful, is the tallgrass prairie. In some areas, native prairie can include up to 200 species of grasses and forbs, and grow to be 10 feet tall. Farther west are the drier mixed-grass and shortgrass prairies. Most prairies have no trees, except along riverbanks; the exception is a savannah, a prairie with some scattered trees. Trees usually are unable to become established in a prairie because of regular fires, grazing, and drought, and because they cannot compete with the grass roots.

A meadow is a sere or stage in the transition from disturbed earth to forest. In other words, meadows occur in regions, such as the East and Pacific Northwest, where grasslands are not generally dominant. They will eventually revert back to woodland if left undisturbed for many years. Meadows exist in relatively wet climates (about 45 to 50 inches of rain per year) in areas with humid summers. Like prairies, they require full sun, but afternoon shade may be helpful in very hot climates.

Desert grasslands once extended from the shortgrass prairie in Texas and New Mexico through the Southwest into northern Mexico. Ever since domestic livestock was introduced to the region, however, there has been a marked shift from grassland to shrubland dominated by mesquite and creosote bush, due to overgrazing by livestock, the resulting erosion of the thin topsoil, and fire suppression.

Grassland, called the *Pacific Prairie*, also covered vast areas of California. This prairie, too, has succumbed to damage wrought by ranching. In fact, vegetation changes in the California grassland have been more drastic than in any other North American grassland. The original prairie vegetation had been largely replaced by nonnative Mediterranean species by 1860.

The other major North American grassland is the *Palouse Prairie*, which once extended throughout southwestern Canada, eastern Washington and Oregon, and southwestern Idaho into western Montana. This intermountain grassland was dominated by bunchgrasses, but massive changes have been caused by cultivation, grazing, and plant introductions.

## Preparing a Grassland Garden

There is more to making a prairie or meadow than shaking wildflower seeds out over the lawn. Removing all unwanted vegetation—typically lawn or pasture weeds—is the first task at hand. On small areas of a few thousand feet or less, this is a simple process that requires no chemicals. The quickest way to prepare a lawn for planting is to remove the top three inches of grass and soil using a sod-cutter. This usually results in a nearly weed-free site ready for seeding or transplanting.

Pastures or old fields are more difficult to prepare for planting due to the presence of a variety of perennial weeds. Usually, ridding the site of these persistent plants takes at least one full growing season. One organic method of weed removal is solar sterilization: Wet the area thoroughly in spring to allow weed seeds to sprout, then cover the seedlings with black plastic weighted down at the edges. Leave the plastic in place for a full growing season; the heat of the sun will kill grasses and weed seedlings. After removing the plastic, do not turn or till the soil again before planting. Another method of weed removal is to cultivate the area to a depth of 4 to 5 inches every two weeks—religiously—from early spring through fall, then put down the seeds. For transplants, wait until the following spring and cultivate the area again to a depth of 1 inch, one week after the first spring rain, and plant immediately.

Before choosing the plant or seed mix, it is important to have a good understanding of the grassland communities native to your area. On a sunny, open site in the Midwest, a prairie is a good ecological model for a grassland garden. On old pasture land with scattered mature bur oaks (*Quercus macrocarpa*), a savannah garden would be a logical choice. Most prairie plants that tolerate some shade are also found in the savannah. Switchgrass (*Panicum virgatum*), wild ryes (*Elymus canadensis* and *E. virginicus*), shooting star (*Dodecatheon meadia*), smooth blue aster (*Aster laevis*), and golden alexander (*Zizia aurea*) are savannah and prairie plants that tolerate some shade. A meadow would be suitable at the southern edge of a forest or woodland garden.

The plants must also be suited to the conditions on the particular site. For example, a dry prairie is appropriate on gravelly soils, whereas a wet prairie is suited to a low, poorly drained site with heavy clay soils.

A native grassland changes with the seasons, with different species emerging and disappearing in turn. To grow a grassland garden with a spectacular display of showy flowers, plan for a continuous succession of bloom. It also is necessary to keep the grasses from overwhelming the wildflowers. Plant fewer, less vigorous grasses at the beginning, and mix in as much as 50 percent forbs to make the garden floriferous.

A grassland garden does not require acres of space. In some areas, it can form a transition zone between a woody plant community (like a woodland) and the more formal cultivated landscape. Include room for a mown path through the garden, unless the space is very small; it will be an excellent vantage point from which to observe and enjoy the profusion of flowers as well as the plethora of wildlife that a well-designed grassland attracts.

## Planting a Grassland Garden

A grassland garden can be started with either seeds or transplants. Seed is less costly and will provide greater genetic diversity. However, perennial wildflowers and grasses are slow to grow from seed, and typically do not bloom until the third year. Transplants often bloom the first year, providing an instant prairie or meadow garden.

Numerous wildflower-meadow seed mixes are on the market. No wildflower mix is appropriate for every part of the country. The best are tailored to a particular region and set of site conditions. The ideal mix includes regional native species, grasses as well as forbs. Avoid mixtures that include tall fescue, orchard grass, timothy grass, or bluegrass.

Seeding in late spring or early summer typically produces good results. Fall seeding can also be successful, especially on dry soils, allowing the seeds to germinate in early spring and become established before the heat of summer. Fall seeding is also beneficial in heavy clay soils. Mix the seeds with slightly moist sand or sawdust to help them scatter more evenly. On small areas, less than an acre or two, spread the seed

## PLANTS FOR GRASSLAND GARDENS

The plants listed below are natives suggested for particular regions. For best results, be familiar with the specific site conditions before choosing plants.

### EASTERN MEADOWS

The dominant plant community of the eastern United States is woodland. Due to high levels of precipitation, most natural grasslands in this region are meadows that eventually become woodland.

#### Grasses

*Andropogon gerardii*, big bluestem
*Andropogon virginicus*, broomsedge
*Bouteloua curtipendula*, sideoats grama
*Danthonia spicata*, poverty grass
*Panicum virgatum*, switchgrass
*Schizachyrium scoparium*, little bluestem
*Sorghastrum nutans*, Indiangrass

#### Forbs

*Antennaria plantaginifolia*, pussytoes, ladies' tobacco
*Aquilegia canadensis*, wild columbine
*Asclepias* species, milkweeds, including butterfly weed
*Aster* species, asters
*Baptisia* species, wild indigos
*Ceanothus americanus*, New Jersey tea
*Cunila origanoides*, dittany
*Dodecatheon meadia*, shooting star
*Echinacea purpurea*, purple coneflower
*Eupatorium hyssopifolium*, hyssop-leaved thorough-wort
*Eupatorium maculatum*, Joe-Pye weed
*Eupatorium perfoliatum*, boneset
*Gaillardia pulchella*, blanketflower
*Helianthemum dumosum*, bushy rockrose

*Helenium autumnale*, sneezeweed
*Helianthus angustifolius*, swamp sunflower
*Helianthus annuus*, sunflower
*Helianthus tuberosus*, Jerusalem artichoke
*Hypoxis hirsuta*, stargrass
*Liatris* species, blazing stars
*Lilium canadense*, Canada lily
*Lobelia cardinalis*, cardinal flower
*Lobelia siphilitica*, great blue lobelia
*Lupinus perennis*, wild lupine
*Monarda didyma*, bee balm, Oswego tea
*Monarda fistulosa*, bergamot
*Monarda punctata*, dotted mint
*Oenothera biennis*, evening primrose
*Penstemon digitalis*, beardtongue
*Penstemon smallii*, beardtongue
*Pityopsis falcata*, Atlantic golden aster
*Potentilla canadensis*, dwarf cinquefoil
*Rudbeckia hirta*, black-eyed Susan
*Sisyrinchium angustifolium*, blue-eyed grass
*Solidago* species, goldenrods
*Stokesia laevis*, Stokes' aster
*Tradescantia virginiana*, spiderwort
*Vernonia gigantea* (*V. altissima*), tall ironweed
*Vernonia noveboracensis*, ironweed
*Viola* species, violet

### MIDWEST

The tallgrass prairie was the dominant plant community of the Midwest, in parts of Iowa and Minnesota, and on the eastern edges of Kansas, Nebraska, South Dakota, and North Dakota, and northward into Canada. Where the tallgrass prairie intergrades with the deciduous forests to the east, oak savannah was once found. Both tallgrass prairie and savannah have been all but obliterated.

## Grasses

*Andropogon gerardii*, big bluestem
*Panicum virgatum*, switchgrass
*Sorghastrum nutans*, Indiangrass
*Stipa spartea*, needlegrass

## Forbs

*Allium cernuum*, nodding pink onion
*Amorpha canescens*, leadplant
*Asclepias* species, milkweeds, including butterfly weed
*Aster* species, asters
*Astragalus canadensis*, Canada milk vetch
*Baptisia* species, false indigos
*Callirhoë triangulata*, poppy mallow
*Campanula rotundifolia*, harebell
*Ceanothus americanus*, New Jersey tea
*Chelone glabra*, turtlehead
*Coreopsis* species, coreopsis
*Dalea* (*Petalostemon*) *candidum*, white prairie clover
*Dalea* (*Petalostemon*) *purpurea*, prairie clover
*Desmodium canadense*, Canada tick trefoil
*Dodecatheon meadia*, shooting star
*Echinacea* species, coneflowers
*Epilobium angustifolium*, fireweed
*Eryngium yuccifolium*, rattlesnake master
*Eupatorium maculatum*, Joe-Pye weed
*Eupatorium perfoliatum*, boneset
*Euphorbia corollata*, flowering spurge
*Filipendula rubra*, queen-of-the-prairie
*Gentiana andrewsii*, bottle gentian
*Geum triflorum*, prairie smoke
*Helianthus* species, sunflowers
*Heliopsis helianthoides*, ox-eye sunflower
*Heuchera richardsonii*, alum root
*Iris virginica* var. *shrevei*, blue flag
*Lespedeza capitata*, roundheaded bush clover
*Liatris* species, blazing stars
*Lilium superbum*, Turk's cap lily
*Linum perenne* subsp. *lewisii*, prairie flax

*Lithospermum caroliniense*, hairy puccoon
*Lobelia cardinalis*, cardinal flower
*Lobelia siphilitica*, great blue lobelia
*Lupinus perennis*, wild lupine
*Monarda fistulosa*, bergamot
*Monarda punctata*, dotted mint
*Oenothera macrocarpa* (*O. missouriensis*), sundrops
*Parthenium integrifolium*, wild quinine, prairie dock
*Penstemon digitalis*, smooth penstemon
*Phlox pilosa*, prairie phlox, downy phlox
*Ratibida pinnata*, yellow coneflower
*Rudbeckia hirta*, black-eyed Susan
*Rudbeckia subtomentosa*, sweet black-eyed Susan
*Silphium integrifolium*, rosinweed, prairie dock
*Silphium laciniatum*, compass plant
*Silphium perfoliatum*, cup plant
*Silphium terebinthinaceum*, prairie dock
*Solidago* species, goldenrods
*Tradescantia* species, spiderworts
*Verbena stricta*, hoary vervain
*Vernonia fasciculata*, ironweed
*Vernonia gigantea* (*V. altissima*), tall ironweed
*Veronicastrum virginicum*, Culver's root
*Zizia aptera*, heartleaf golden alexander
*Zizia aurea*, golden alexander

### SHORTGRASS PRAIRIE

Also known as the Great Plains and the High Plains, the shortgrass prairie is the most arid of the midcontinental grasslands. Its western boundary is the Rocky Mountains, while its eastern edge is vaguely defined by a transition zone between it and the mixed-grass prairie, which combines species from both the tall- and shortgrass prairies and occupies most of the Dakotas, much of Nebraska and Kansas, the central part of Oklahoma, and parts of north-central Texas. Forbs are not as plentiful on the shortgrass prairie as on the mixed- and tallgrass prairies. Many of the eastern prairie forbs, such as blazing stars, prairie clovers, and goldenrods, grow

(continued on next page)

here, but they grow smaller and less abundantly than they do to the east. Sagebrush and cacti are also found in the shortgrass prairie.

**Grasses**

*Bouteloua* species, grama grasses
*Buchloe dactyloides*, Buffalo grass
*Scizachyrium scoparium*, little bluestem
*Sorghastrum nutans*, Indian grass
*Stipa comata*, needle-and-thread

**Forbs**

*Amorpha canescens*, leadplant
*Anemone patens*, pasqueflower
*Artemisia* species, sagebrushes
*Asclepias* species, milkweeds, including butterfly weed
*Aster* species, asters
*Balsamorhiza sagittata*, arrowleaf balsam root
*Castilleja coccinea*, Indian paintbrush
*Coreopsis lanceolata*, lanceleaf coreopsis
*Dalea (Petalostemon) purpurea* var. *purpurea*, purple prairie clover
*Echinacea pallida*, pale purple coneflower
*Euphorbia corollata*, flowering spurge
*Eustoma grandiflorum*, prairie gentian
*Gaillardia pulchella*, blanketflower
*Geum triflorum*, prairie smoke
*Helianthus annuus*, common sunflower
*Helianthus occidentalis*, western sunflower
*Lespedeza capitata*, roundheaded bush clover
*Liatris aspera*, rough blazing star
*Lupinus perennis*, lupine
*Lupinus texensis*, Texas bluebonnet
*Melampodium leucanthum*, Blackfoot daisy
*Monarda punctata*, dotted mint
*Oenothera hookeri*, Hooker's evening primrose
*Opuntia polyacantha*, many-spined opuntia
*Oxytropis splendens*, locoweed
*Penstemon* species, beardtongues

*Rudbeckia hirta*, black-eyed Susan
*Solidago rigida*, stiff goldenrod
*Solidago nemoralis*, gray goldenrod
*Tradescantia* species, spiderworts
*Zinnia grandiflora*, little golden zinnia

### INTERMOUNTAIN GRASSLAND

Although sagebrushes now dominate the inter-mountain grassland called the Palouse Prairie, it historically supported purer stands of grass with fewer shrubs.

**Grasses**

*Agropyron spicatum*, bluebunch wheatgrass
*Agropyron smithii*, western wheatgrass
*Festuca idahoensis*, Idaho fescue
*Koeleria cristata*, Junegrass
*Stipa comata*, needle-and-thread

**Forbs**

*Astragalus* species, milk vetches
*Balsamorhiza sagittata*, arrowleaf balsam root
*Calochortus* species, sego lilies
*Camassia* species, camas
*Castilleja* species, paintbrushes
*Gaillardia aristata*, blanketflower
*Penstemon* species, beardtongues
*Solidago* species, goldenrods
*Sphaeralcea coccinea*, scarlet globe mallow
*Stanleya pinnata*, desert plume
*Thermopsis rhombifolia* var. *montana*, golden banner
*Wyethia amplexicaulis*, mule's ears

### DESERT GRASSLANDS

Historically, the desert grasslands were found between the Colorado River in Arizona and the Pecos River in New Mexico and extended from the Rocky Mountains in the north, southward into

Mexico. These grasslands usually are found on gentle slopes, sometimes as unbroken stretches, sometimes interspersed with shrubs and cacti.

**Grasses**

*Bouteloua chondroisiodes*, sprucetop grama
*Bouteloua eriopoda*, black grama
*Bouteloua filiformis*, slender grama
*Hilaria mutica*, tobosa grass
*Muhlenbergia porteri*, bush muhly
*Oryzopsis hymenoides*, Indian ricegrass

**Forbs**

*Abronia* species, sand verbenas
*Aster spinosus*, aster
*Baileya multiradiata*, desert marigold
*Erigeron divergens*, spreading fleabane
*Eriogonum* species, wild buckwheats
*Eschscholzia mexicana*, gold poppy
*Mirabilis longiflora*, sweet four-o'clock
*Mirabilis multiflora*, Colorado four-o'clock
*Penstemon eatonii*, firecracker
*Penstemon palmeri*, Palmer penstemon
*Penstemon parryi*, Parry penstemon
*Penstemon pseudospectabilis*, desert penstemon
*Penstemon spectabilis*, penstemon
*Penstemon subulatus*, penstemon
*Salvia columbariae*, chia
*Zinnia grandiflora*, little golden zinnia, desert zinnia

## CALIFORNIA

The California grasslands occupied the central valleys between the Coast Range to the west and the Sierra Nevada to the east. They also were found in a narrow coastal strip in central to northern California and a broader coastal zone in southern California, now the Los Angeles–San Diego megalopolis.

**Grasses**

*Danthonia californica*, California oatgrass
*Deschampsia caespitosa*, tufted hair grass
*Festuca californica*, California fescue
*Koeleria cristata*, Junegrass
*Melica* species, Melic grasses
*Muhlenbergia rigens*, deer grass
*Stipa pulchra*, purple needlegrass

**Forbs**

*Brodiaea elegans*, elegant brodiaea
*Castilleja californica*, Indian paintbrush
*Clarkia amoena*, farewell to spring
*Collinsia heterophylla*, Chinese houses
*Eschscholtzia californica*, California poppy
*Ipomopsis aggregata*, scarlet gilia
*Iris douglasiana*, Douglas' iris
*Iris tenax*, tough-leaved iris
*Lasthenia chrysostoma*, goldfields
*Lupinus nanus*, lupine
*Madia elegans*, common tarweed
*Nemophila menziesii*, baby blue-eyes
*Oenothera hookeri*, Hooker's evening primrose
*Orthocarpus purpurascens*, common owl's clover
*Phacelia linearis*, threadleaf phacelia
*Sidalcea malviflora*, checkerbloom
*Stanleya pinnata*, desert plume
*Wyethia mollis*, mule's ears

by hand broadcasting. Toss the seeds with a sweeping motion, and rake them lightly into the soil. Then roll the site with a roller to firm the seed into the soil. Cover the seeds with a light, weed-free mulch such as straw—the mulch should just cover the soil surface but not bury it—but do not add fertilizer or manure. Spring and summer seedings should be watered regularly during the first four to six weeks after planting, just enough to keep the soil moist.

Transplants do best when installed in spring or early fall. Early spring-blooming wildflowers are best transplanted in autumn. Mulch with 3 to 4 inches of clean straw to help keep down weeds; once the plants are established, little weeding should be necessary.

## Maintaining a Grassland Garden

During the first growing season, keep the young grassland garden mowed back to a height of 4 to 6 inches to prevent weeds from shading out small, slower-growing grass and wildflower seedlings. In spring of the second year, mow the planting right to the ground. If weeds remain a problem in the second year, you may have to mow again in late spring or early summer.

Once established, prairies and meadows need to be mowed or burned periodically—usually in mid-spring, when the buds of the sugar maple tree are just opening up—to discourage weeds and woody vegetation. However, dry prairies should be burned instead in late fall or very early spring. If burning is legal under local burning ordinances, contact a Cooperative Extension office or botanical garden for detailed instructions on how to do a safe burn. If burning is not an option, mow in mid-spring and rake the clippings to expose the soil surface and encourage soil warming. To preserve overwintering butter-

fly eggs and pupae, it is a good strategy to divide a grassland garden into two or three "management units," and to do rotational burning or mowing of one of the units every year.

## Desert Gardens

The four desert associations of the United States cover parts of eastern Oregon, Idaho, Wyoming, Utah, Colorado, California, Arizona, New Mexico, southwest Texas, and all of Nevada. Taken together, these deserts make up 8 percent of the country's land mass. Deserts have certain conditions in common: intense light, temperature extremes, and lack of water. What little precipitation occurs (under 15 inches per year) may evaporate quickly due to heat, wind, and other factors. Differences are related to elevation: high-elevation deserts are colder and support a very different set of native plants than low-elevation deserts do.

Desert plants have adapted to the harsh conditions by developing specialized characteristics. Most are deep-rooted shrubby perennials, cacti, and other succulents. They frequently have small, fuzzy, or waxy leaves to reduce transpiration. The leaves may also be silver or gray to reflect the intense sunlight. Desert plants are often low-growing—an adaptation to strong winds and limited water; not even trees such as acacias, mesquites, and palo verdes grow very tall. Some desert natives, including ocotillo and palo verde, are drought-deciduous—they simply go dormant in times of drought, then leaf out again within days after a rainstorm. Annual wildflowers bloom and set seed quickly after a rain. Many desert plants will thrive only in their own specific habitats.

A few design considerations for dryland gardens:

• A desert does not have a carpet of plants—typically only about 25 percent of the ground is covered with vegetation—so pay special attention to hardscaping and mulch in the garden. The materials should blend in with the setting and the plants.

• The strong light of the desert creates dramatic shadows. Take advantage of this by positioning architectural plants near walls or in other areas where the afternoon sun will create shadow pictures.

• Create cooling shade by using large trees or shrubs near houses and patios and other seating areas.

• Microclimates are especially important in arid regions. Shady spots support very different plants than sunny spots do.

## Preparing a Desert Garden

In arid regions, the soil is usually dry, alkaline, fast-draining, and low in organic matter. Also, it usually has a high concentration of salt, due to natural mineral breakdown, saline irrigation water, inorganic fertilizers or other amendments, or poor drainage. Salt in the soil makes it even more difficult for plants to obtain water, resulting in "salt burn" and stunted growth. A soil test or information from the local Cooperative Extension can help determine whether the soil is saline or otherwise problematic, and what to do about it. Native species are usually more tolerant of soil problems than exotic plants.

## Planting a Desert Garden

Not all desert plants will thrive in all desert gardens. For instance, a native of the Sonoran Desert may not tolerate the conditions of the Great Basin. Many succulents cannot tolerate

heavy frost or a hard freeze and will not do well in relatively cold high-altitude gardens. Other natives are adapted to windy, hot desert conditions but need regular water; in the wild, these plants are usually found growing along desert washes, or in seeps or wet spots where their roots can reach water. The drought-avoiding annual flowers that spring up in the moist soil after it rains and complete their life cycles before dry weather returns need little extra water and can be planted in dry spots. The true xerophytes, the largest group of desert plants, which have evolved ways to efficiently extract and conserve any available moisture from the soil, can be planted in the more distant areas and left on their own without supplemental irrigation after they are established. Consult a reliable field guide or local botanic garden to determine which desert plants are best for the area and specific microclimates on the site.

It is possible to create different microclimates in a desert garden. Desert winds can be strong, especially in exposed areas unprotected by adjacent houses or other structures. In these areas, there is nothing to stop the wind's desiccating effects. One solution is to create a windbreak by constructing a stone wall or fence, or by planting mixed trees and shrubs. By slowing the air flow, a pocket of higher humidity is created on the leeward side, providing a microclimate for species with slightly higher moisture requirements. Shady microclimates can be created by planting trees on the south and west sides of the house or paved areas. They will support plants very different from those that thrive in spots exposed to the full intensity of the sun.

Some possible areas in a desert garden include a shady patio; islands of desert trees, shrubs, and associated vegetation; exposed open areas with cacti and other water-hoarding species; and a meadow or open field of native

## PLANTS FOR DESERT GARDENS

The plants listed below are natives suggested for particular regions. For best results, be familiar with the specific site conditions before choosing plants.

### GREAT BASIN

(Most of NV and parts of OR, ID, CA, WY, UT, CO, AZ, and NM)

*Agropyron spicatum,* bluebunch wheatgrass
*Artemisia* species, sagebrushes
*Astragalus* species, locoweeds
*Atriplex canescens,* saltbush
*Balsamorhiza sagittata,* arrowleaf balsam root
*Calochortus* species, sego lilies
*Castilleja* species, Indian paintbrushes
*Cercocarpus ledifolius,* mountain mahogany
*Chrysothamnus nauseosus,* chamisa
*Fallugia paradoxa,* Apache plume
*Festuca ovina,* sheep fescue
*Forestiera neomexicana,* desert olive
*Juniperus osteosperma,* Utah juniper
*Juniperus scopulorum,* Rocky Mountain juniper
*Larrea tridentata,* creosote bush
*Lupinus* species, lupines
*Phacelia* species, phacelias
*Pinus edulis,* two-leaved pinyon pine
*Pinus monophylla,* single-leaf pinyon pine
*Quercus gambelii,* gambel oak
*Quercus utahensis,* scrub oak
*Sarcobatus vermiculatus,* greasewood
*Yucca* species, yuccas

### MOJAVE DESERT

(CA and NV)

*Atriplex canescens,* saltbush
*Dalea greggii,* trailing smokebush, prostrate indigo-bush
*Encelia farinosa,* brittlebush
*Larrea tridentata,* creosote bush
*Opuntia bigelovii,* teddy bear cholla
*Prosopis glandulosa,* honey mesquite
*Prosopis pubescens,* mesquite
*Yucca brevifolia,* Joshua tree

### SONORAN DESERT

(CA and AZ)

*Agave americana,* century plant
*Agave murpheyi,* agave
*Baileya multiradiata,* desert marigold
*Calliandra eriophylla,* fairyduster
*Carnegiea gigantea,* saguaro cactus
*Cercidium floridum,* blue palo verde
*Chilopsis linearis,* desert willow
*Dalea greggii,* trailing smokebush, prostrate indigo-bush
*Encelia farinosa,* brittlebush
*Fouquieria splendens,* ocotillo
*Justicia californica,* chuparosa
*Justicia spicigera,* hummingbird bush
*Larrea tridentata,* creosote bush
*Lycium fremontii,* wolfberry
*Oenothera* species, evening primroses
*Opuntia* species, prickly pears
*Penstemon* species, beardtongues
*Prosopis glandulosa* var. *torreyana,* western honey mesquite
*Prosopis juliflora,* velvet mesquite
*Simmondsia chinensis,* jojoba
*Sphaeralcea ambigua,* desert mallow
*Sphaeralcea coccinea,* prairie mallow
*Tecoma stans,* Arizona yellowbell
*Verbena gooddingii,* verbena
*Zinnia grandiflora,* little golden zinnia, desert zinnia

**CHIHUAHUAN DESERT**

(AZ, TX, and NM)

*Bouteloua* species, grama grasses
*Chilopsis linearis*, desert willow
*Chrysothamnus nauseosus*, chamisa
*Dalea greggii*, trailing indigobush
*Eragrostis trichodes*, sand lovegrass
*Fallugia paradoxa*, Apache plume
*Fouquieria splendens*, ocotillo
*Larrea tridentata*, creosote bush
*Leucaena retusa*, golden ball leadtree

*Leucophyllum frutescens*, Texas silverleaf, Texas ranger
*Melampodium leucanthum*, Blackfoot daisy
*Mirabilis multiflora*, wild four-o'clock
*Oryzopsis hymenoides*, Indian ricegrass
*Penstemon* species, beardtongues
*Prosopis* species, mesquites
*Rhus microphylla*, littleleaf sumac
*Rhus trilobata*, threeleaf sumac
*Salvia greggii*, autumn sage
*Zinnia grandiflora*, little golden zinnia, desert zinnia

grasses and wildflowers (see page 212). Lusher expanses of relatively moisture-loving species can grow along natural washes.

Seedlings and container plants for desert gardens should be planted in fall or early spring, never in the extreme heat of summer. Water new transplants as necessary until they are completely established. Sow seed on prepared seedbeds in fall, winter, or early spring. Native desert plants tend to be slow-growing because of the lack of water and nutrients.

## Maintaining a Desert Garden

Desert gardens require little maintenance once established. If the plants have been chosen carefully, watering and fertilizing should be unnecessary. Never water in winter. Mulching may be helpful to moderate soil temperatures and retain moisture.

## Shrubland Gardens

Two of the more common native landscapes in the West are plant communities of shrubs and small, shrubby trees—the chaparral that covers

large areas of California and the shrubby pinyon-juniper woodland of the Southwest and the Great Basin.

California chaparral dominates the foothills from the Sierra Nevada to the Pacific Ocean, and from the Rogue River watershed in Oregon to the San Pedro Martir Mountains of Baja California. Throughout this region, it forms a nearly continuous cover of closely spaced shrubs with intertwining branches. Herbaceous vegetation is generally absent, except after fires, which occur frequently. The chaparral is replaced by grassland in frequently burned areas, especially at low elevations, and by oak woodland on moister slopes. More than a hundred evergreen shrub species are found in the chaparral, but only a fraction of these are widespread.

Pinyon-juniper woodland is dominated by various species of pines and junipers, which, though similar, vary somewhat from state to state. The crowns of the trees rarely touch in these open woodlands, although the roots can range out two to three times farther than the canopies. The understory vegetation varies greatly. Generally, it is similar to that of adjacent grasslands in warm-desert areas, while sagebrushes prevail in the northern and western

Great Basin. Overgrazing by domestic live-stock has increased the density of tree cover, radically changing the character of the pinyon-juniper woodlands.

## Preparing a Shrubland Garden

Gardens patterned after native shrublands can combine attractive small, evergreen trees, flow-ering shrubs, and wildflowers. Like other plant communities, shrublands vary according to the particular habitat. Some species thrive on hot, dry south-facing slopes, others on moister, cooler north slopes. Model your garden after native shrublands in your area with similar con-ditions. Plant drought-tolerant shrubs in hot, open areas, and lusher plantings of moisture-loving species in canyons and on north-facing slopes.

One way to go about re-creating a native shrubland is to group plants together in "islands," as large or small as your garden can accommodate. If the islands are to be viewed from all sides, plant the tallest shrubs or trees at the center and the lower, spreading species near the outer edges. Tuck appropriate grasses and wildflowers between the shrubs and, if you have enough room, plant native grasslands around and between the islands as well (for more on grassland plantings, see page 203).

Be sure to choose species appropriate for the conditions on your site. Some chaparral natives are from cooler coastal areas; if planted inland they may need frequent watering even after they become established. What is more, if they are planted with the tougher species from inland regions, this excessive summer water can kill the inland natives.

## Planting a Shrubland Garden

Many shrubland natives are available as con-tainer-grown plants, which makes creating the garden much easier since seeds of some species have complex dormancy requirements that require several treatments to overcome for suc-cessful germination. Space the shrubs and trees widely enough to allow them to grow to their mature size and to have a large enough soil area from which to draw water and nutrients. The best planting time in these warm-summer regions is in the fall.

Some species, particularly annual wildflow-ers, are easily started from seed. Sow them in summer or fall, just before the rains are about to begin. Keep the area moist while the seeds are germinating.

## Maintaining a Shrubland Garden

In these regions of periodic drought and high seasonal temperatures, it is important to water any new plants frequently during the first sea-son—as much as once or twice a week, depend-ing on the weather. The second season, it is probably safe to water drought-tolerant species once a month.

Keep in mind that chaparral plants, like those from other warm regions, make most of their growth in fall and spring, essentially ceas-ing growth during the hot summer season. Some will even drop many of their leaves once the hot weather sets in. This is their way of cop-ing with the difficult climate. Once they are established, the most drought-tolerant plants can go without water all summer but may look better if given an occasional watering.

Mulch around the plants to conserve water and discourage weeds.

## PLANTS FOR SHRUBLAND GARDENS

### CALIFORNIA CHAPARRAL

The actual species composition of chaparral varies according to moisture, elevation, slope, history of fire on the site, and distance from the coast, so be sure to choose plants accordingly.

**Trees and Shrubs**

*Adenostoma fasciculatum,* chamise
*Arctostaphylos* species, manzanitas
*Baccharis pilularis,* coyote bush
*Carpenteria californica,* bush anemone
*Ceanothus* species, California lilacs
*Prunus ilicifolia,* holly-leaved cherry
*Quercus dumosa,* California scrub oak
*Eriogonum* species, buckwheats
*Fremontodendron californicum,* flannel bush
*Garrya elliptica,* silk-tassel bush
*Heteromeles arbutifolia,* toyon
*Mimulus aurantiacus,* monkeyflower
*Rhamnus californica,* coffeeberry
*Ribes viburnifolium,* Catalina currant
*Salvia clevelandii,* sage

**Forbs**

*Clarkia* species, clarkias
*Collinsia* species, collinsias
*Dodecatheon clevelandii,* shooting star
*Dodecatheon hendersonii,* shooting star
*Eschscholzia californica,* California poppy
*Iris douglasiana,* Douglas' iris
*Lupinus nanus,* lupine
*Romneya coulteri,* Matilija poppy
*Zauschneria californica,* California fuchsia

### PINYON-JUNIPER WOODLAND

Choose the combination of junipers and pinyon pines native to your area, and space the specimens widely apart so that the shrubs and forbs that grow among them can get all the sun they need.

**Trees and Shrubs**

*Artemisia tridentata,* big sagebrush
*Cercocarpus* species, mountain mahogany
*Chrysothamnus nauseosus,* rabbitbrush
*Fendlera rupicola,* Fendler's bush
*Juniperus californica,* California juniper
*Juniperus deppeana,* alligator-bark juniper
*Juniperus monosperma,* single-seed juniper
*Juniperus osteosperma,* Utah juniper
*Opuntia imbricata,* cane cactus
*Pinus cembroides,* Mexican pinyon
*Pinus edulis,* Colorado pinyon
*Pinus monophylla,* single-needle pinyon
*Shepherdia argentea,* silver buffalo berry
*Yucca baccata,* banana yucca
*Yucca glauca,* Great Plains yucca
*Yucca schottii,* Schott's yucca

**Forbs and Cacti**

*Castilleja integra,* Indian paintbrush
*Coryphantha vivipara,* pincushion cactus
*Echinocereus fendleri,* hedgehog cactus
*Echinocereus pectinatus,* Arizona rainbow cactus
*Echinocereus triglochidiatus,* claret cup
*Echinocereus viridiflorus,* green-flowered hedgehog
*Gilia aggregata,* fairy trumpet
*Helianthus annus,* common sunflower
*Liatris punctata,* blazing star
*Penstemon barbatus,* scarlet bugler
*Phlox nana,* canyon phlox
*Thermopsis rhombifolia* var. *montana,* golden banner
*Zinnia grandiflora,* desert zinnia

## PLANTS FOR SEASIDE GARDENS

The plants listed below are natives suggested for seaside gardens in the East and West. For best results, be familiar with your specific site conditions and the plants native to your particular area before choosing plants.

### EAST COAST

*Ammophila breviligulata*, beach grass
*Andropogon virginicus*, broom sedge
*Arctostaphylos uva-ursi*, kinnikinnick, bearberry
*Baccharis halimifolia*, groundsel bush
*Chasmanthium latifolium* (*Uniola latifolia*), sea oats
*Comptonia peregrina*, sweet fern
*Hudsonia tomentosa*, beach heather
*Ilex glabra*, inkberry holly
*Juniperus horizontalis*, creeping juniper
*Juniperus virginiana*, eastern red cedar
*Kosteletzkya virginica*, seashore mallow
*Lathyrus japonicus*, beach pea
*Lathyrus japonicus* subsp. *maritimus*, beach pea
*Myrica cerifera*, wax myrtle
*Myrica pensylvanica*, bayberry
*Opuntia compressa* (*O. humifusa*), prickly pear cactus
*Pinus rigida*, pitch pine
*Prunus maritima*, beach plum
*Quercus marilandica*, blackjack oak
*Quercus stellata*, post oak
*Rhus* species, sumac
*Rosa virginiana*, Virginia rose
*Schizachyrium scoparium* subsp. *littorale* (*Andropogon littoralis*), dune broomgrass
*Shepherdia canadensis*, russet buffaloberry
*Solidago sempervirens*, seaside goldenrod
*Yucca filamentosa*, Adam's needle yucca

### WEST COAST

*Aesculus californica*, buckeye
*Arctostaphylos uva-ursi*, kinnikinnick, bearberry
*Armeria maritima* subsp. *californica*, thrift, sea pink

*Artemisia californica*, California sage
*Artemisia pycnocephala*, coastal sagewort, sand hill sage
*Atriplex californica*, saltbush
*Baccharis pilularis*, coyote bush
*Camissonia cheiranthifolia*, beach evening primrose
*Ceanothus thyrsiflorus*, wild lilac
*Cupressus macrocarpa*, Monterey cypress
*Dendromecon rigida* subsp. *harfordii*, island bush poppy
*Dudleya pulverulenta*, chalk lettuce
*Erigeron glaucus*, seaside daisy
*Eriogonum arborescens*, Santa Cruz Island buckwheat
*Eriogonum giganteum*, St. Catherine's lace
*Eriogonum latifolium* subsp. *grande*, buckwheat
*Eriogonum latifolium* var. *rubescens*, rosy buckwheat
*Eriophyllum stoechadifolium*, lizard's tail
*Erysimum suffrutescens*, or *E. concinnum*, coastal wallflower
*Eschscholzia californica*, California poppy
*Fragaria chiloensis*, coastal strawberry
*Fraxinus velutina*, Velvet ash
*Iris douglasiana*, Douglas' iris
*Juniperus horizontalis*, creeping juniper
*Lavatera assurgentiflora*, tree mallow
*Mimulus aurantiacus*, sticky monkeyflower
*Mimulus longiflorus*, southern bush monkeyflower
*Myrica californica*, California wax myrtle
*Pinus muricata*, bishop pine
*Pinus radiata*, Monterey pine
*Quercus agrifolia*, coast live oak
*Rhamnus californicus*, coffeeberry
*Ribes sanguineum*, red flowering currant
*Salvia apiana*, white sage
*Salvia brandegei*, sage
*Salvia leucophylla*, purple sage
*Sambucus callicarpa*, Pacific coast red elderberry
*Scrophularia californica*, bee plant
*Sisyrinchium bellum*, California blue-eyed grass

## Seaside Gardens

Seaside gardens on both coasts share the problems of constant wind, intense sunlight, salt spray, and occasional flooding by salt water. In addition, the soil may have a high salt content. Plants that grow in coastal regions can tolerate salt in the air, soil, and water; desiccating winds; and porous soil. They have adapted by developing characteristics like narrow, flexible leaves that offer little resistance to the wind; fleshy leaves that store moisture; hard, smooth, or shiny leaf surfaces that reduce transpiration; or tough, woody stems. They also have deep root systems that search out water far below the surface.

Along the East Coast, from Cape Cod down to the Gulf Coast, the shoreline is pure sand. This causes the surface to dry out quickly after rain or watering. A number of native grasses, trees, and shrubs are adapted to the harsh conditions in this area. The West Coast has a much different shoreline and a different group of native plants. Much of California's coast has a Mediterranean climate, with mild, wet winters and dry summers. It is a composite of rocky bluffs, dry chaparral, and dunes. The chaparral vegetation consists of low-growing shrubs, herbaceous perennials, and annuals (see "Shrubland Gardens," page 213). On the dunes, low, shrubby, mounding plants grow in tight groups, kept rounded and compact by the wind.

### Preparing and Planting a Seaside Garden

Some native beach plants may be hard to find at ordinary nurseries, but state agencies often grow these plants for preventing dune erosion; contact the local state university or Cooperative Extension office for more information. Never dig up beach plants from the wild; it is better to try starting them from seeds or cuttings if they are not available elsewhere. If you are buying plants, keep in mind that bare-root specimens may topple over when first planted in a light, sandy soil, so choose container plants if possible. Once beach plants are established, they are difficult to transplant successfully because of their deep root systems.

On the East Coast, plant in early spring or fall. On the West Coast, plant in fall or early winter before the rains.

### Maintaining a Seaside Garden

After planting a seaside garden, water it regularly until the plants are well established, especially if natural rainfall is sparse. Except in dune areas, it may be beneficial to mulch to help retain moisture in the soil. Otherwise, very little maintenance should be needed outside of some routine weeding.

## Gardening for Wildlife

A true natural garden is one that provides for the entire ecosystem—not only the native plants but also the insects, birds, and animals that play a critical part in the cycle of life. When designing your garden, plan for the three basic needs of wildlife: food, water, and shelter.

### Food

Wildlife need a variety of seed-, nectar-, and fruit-producing plants. Trees and shrubs that produce seeds, nuts, and berries are food sources for birds and small mammals. Flowers that produce nectar attract insects and birds. Supplementing plants with feeders will attract even more wildlife, especially in winter.

## Water

Water is essential for attracting wildlife, who need it for drinking and bathing. Every natural garden should have water in some form, whether a large pond or a small garden pool or a birdbath. Place birdbaths close to trees and shrubs so that small creatures can find refuge from predators quickly. Change the water frequently to keep it fresh.

## Shelter

Small birds and animals need shelter from predators and bad weather, as well as a place to nest. Leave some brushy areas undisturbed for this purpose. Preserve or create areas with brush piles, dead trees, hollow logs, brambles, and shrub thickets. Some open space is also necessary so that robins and other birds can search for worms and bugs, and fledglings can test their wings. Birdhouses provide additional shelter. Natural birdhouses can be made from holes in dead trees, weathered fenceposts, or coconut shells and bark tacked to tree trunks.

## Other Considerations

Most creatures live in the zones between two different environments—such as meadow and woods, or mowed area and wild area—so that they can take advantage of both environments. To attract a greater variety of wildlife, create these "edges" in your garden. Make the boundaries irregular to create even more edge space.

Use organic techniques when planting a wildlife garden. Herbicides, pesticides, and other chemicals may end up poisoning the very birds, butterflies, and animals the garden is supposed to attract.

## Gardening for Birds

Some birds eat insects, and some eat mostly seeds. Others eat a wide variety of things. To attract specific birds, consult one of the bird gardening books listed in "Further Reading," page 231. Large drifts of wildflowers are useful to almost all birds because they are home to insects and spiders, and also provide nectar and seeds. Allow the seed pods to form on the perennial wildflowers, and deadhead the annuals to encourage new flowers.

For insect eaters, trees like oaks, willows, poplars, and birches are ideal because they harbor many kinds of insects. Some birds need a patch of bare soil or low grass to peck and scratch for insects and worms, as well as the tiny pebbles they swallow to aid their digestion.

Most seed-eating birds are attracted to a hedgerow or thicket tangled with wild roses, hawthorns, sumacs, berry bushes, wild grapes, and other seed-bearing plants. Grasses and vines are also beneficial because they provide seed and nesting materials.

Migratory birds need different foods at different times. In late summer and fall when they are storing up reserves for the long trip south, they need fruits that are high in fats, such as those of spicebush (*Lindera benzoin*), flowering dogwood (*Cornus florida*), and sassafras (*Sassafras albidum*). In spring and summer, birds migrating north feed on high-energy fruits like those of hawthorns (*Crataegus* species) and viburnums (*Viburnum* species). In cold regions, nonmigratory birds need carbohydrates in winter, provided by plants like winterberry (*Ilex verticillata*), poison ivy (*Toxicodendron radicans*), and sumacs (*Rhus* species). In addition, they benefit from seeds, crumbs, and a source of fat such as suet cake or peanut butter.

Hummingbirds have special requirements. Like other birds, they eat insects and spiders. Unlike most other birds, however, their diet consists primarily of flower nectar. Their tiny size allows them to hover like bees in front of tubular blossoms, probing with their long, needlelike beaks to extract the nectar. Hummingbirds are attracted to bright colors, especially red and orange. They are also very territorial, so plant several patches of their favorite flowers to attract more than one bird. Also, keep a source of very shallow water available to give these tiny birds a place to drink.

## Gardening for Butterflies and Other Insect Pollinators

To successfully attract butterflies to your garden, it is useful to know a few things about the butterfly life cycle. Butterflies need specific host plants on which to lay their eggs. When the eggs hatch, these plants provide food for the caterpillars. Some butterfly species have only one specific host plant; others may have a preferred host but will accept other plants. A famous example is the relationship between the monarch butterfly caterpillar and the milkweed plant (*Asclepias syriaca*). Once caterpillars are fully grown, in about fifteen days, they begin forming a pupal case, which eventually splits open as the adult butterfly emerges. Adult butterflies need plants that are rich in nectar. A good butterfly garden will provide both caterpillar host plants and nectar plants for the adults.

Having butterfly caterpillars around is another good reason not to use pesticides in a natural garden. Most of these caterpillars do little damage to plants, and many are beautiful in their own way. If it is necessary to control pest caterpillars, use nonchemical methods such as handpicking. Also protect butterfly eggs and pupae by leaving things undisturbed in fall. Do not rake up all the leaves and branches, cut down all the perennials and grasses, or turn over the soil in fall; these are places where butterflies may be overwintering.

A butterfly garden should have the following features: plenty of sun, shelter from wind and predators, light-colored rocks, mud puddles, a meadow, and nectar and food sources. The rocks should be placed in a warm spot for butterflies to sun themselves. The puddles are a source of moisture and also of salt. However, butterflies cannot drink from open water and prefer to extract moisture from the damp soil near a puddle or stream.

Butterflies prefer full sun, so the plants you choose should be sun-loving species. Choose flowers with nectar-filled tubular blossoms or large, flat blossoms that serve as landing pads for the butterflies. Be sure to include early- and late-blooming species. Like hummingbirds, butterflies are attracted to bright colors. Their favorites are purple, red, orange, and yellow. Blue and white flowers are less popular.

Many other insects, including bees and moths, play essential roles in pollinating plants (see "Plant Reproduction," page 94, and "Ecology for Gardeners," page 142) and are delightful visitors to the garden, too. See the chart beginning on page 220 for a list of the preferred plants of butterflies, bees, and other pollinators, organized by both region and season. See also "Plants for Every Purpose and Every Region," page 288, for lists of nonnative as well as native species in your region that are attractive to butterflies and other wildlife.

## NATIVE PLANTS ATTRACTIVE TO POLLINATORS, BY REGION AND SEASON

The following list of native plants and their pollinators is organized by region, by pollinator (bee, butterfly, and hummingbird), and by season.

SPRING = March–May
SUMMER = June–August
AUTUMN = September–November
WINTER = December–February

Some plants in this list appear under more than one season because bloom time varies within the region.

### NORTHEAST

**Bee**

*Spring*

*Acer negundo* (box elder—tree)
*Aesculus pavia* (red buckeye—shrub/small tree)
*Caltha palustris* (marsh marigold—perennial)
*Cornus florida* (flowering dogwood—small tree)
*Geum rivale* (water avens—perennial)
*Phlox subulata* (moss-pink—perennial)

*Summer*

*Achillea millefolium* (yarrow—perennial)
*Geum rivale* (water avens—perennial)
*Oenothera biennis* (common evening primrose—biennial/short-lived perennial)
*Phlox paniculata* (fall phlox—perennial)
*Potentilla fruticosa* (shrubby five-fingers—shrub)
*Solidago* species (goldenrods—perennials)

*Autumn*

*Achillea millefolium* (yarrow—perennial)
*Aster dumosus* (long-stalked aster—perennial)

*Hamamelis virginiana* (witchhazel—shrub)
*Oenothera biennis* (common evening primrose—biennial/short-lived perennial)
*Phlox paniculata* (fall phlox—perennial)
*Potentilla fruticosa* (shrubby five-fingers—shrub)
*Solidago* species (goldenrods—perennials)

**Butterfly**

*Spring*

*Apocynum androsaemifolium* (spreading dogbane—perennial)
*Ceanothus americanus* (New Jersey tea—shrub)

*Summer*

*Apocynum androsaemifolium* (spreading dogbane—perennial)
*Asclepias tuberosa* (butterfly weed—perennial)
*Ceanothus americanus* (New Jersey tea—shrub)
*Clethra alnifolia* (sweet pepperbush—shrub)
*Monarda fistulosa* (wild bergamot—perennial)
*Pycnanthemum muticum* (mountain mint—perennial)
*Solidago* species (goldenrods—perennials)

*Autumn*

*Ceanothus americanus* (New Jersey tea—shrub)
*Monarda fistulosa* (wild bergamot—perennial)
*Solidago* species (goldenrods—perennials)

**Hummingbird**

*Spring*

*Aquilegia canadensis* (Canada columbine—perennial)
*Castilleja coccinea* (Indian paintbrush—annual/biennial)

*Ceanothus americanus* (New Jersey tea—shrub)
*Kalmia latifolia* (mountain laurel—shrub/small tree)
*Lonicera canadensis* (fly honeysuckle—shrub)
*Lonicera sempervirens* (trumpet honeysuckle—liana)
*Mertensia virginica* (eastern bluebells—perennial)
*Pedicularis canadensis* (forest lousewort—perennial)
*Penstemon digitalis* (beardtongue—perennial)
*Phlox divaricata* (forest phlox—perennial)
*Polygonatum biflorum* (Solomon's seal—perennial)
*Rhododendron periclymenoides* (pinkster flower—shrub)
*Silene virginica* (fire pink—perennial)
*Symphoricarpus albus* (snowberry—shrub)

### Summer

*Aquilegia canadensis* (Canada columbine—perennial)
*Asclepias tuberosa* (butterfly weed—perennial)
*Castilleja coccinea* (Indian paintbrush—annual/biennial)
*Ceanothus americanus* (New Jersey tea—shrub)
*Cephalanthus occidentalis* (buttonbush—shrub)
*Chelone glabra* (turtlehead—perennial)
*Dicentra eximia* (wild bleeding heart—perennial)
*Impatiens capensis* (spotted touch-me-not—annual)
*Kalmia latifolia* (mountain laurel—shrub/small tree)
*Lilium superbum* (Turk's cap lily—perennial)
*Lobelia cardinalis* (cardinal flower—perennial)
*Lonicera canadensis* (fly honeysuckle—shrub)
*Lonicera involucrata* (bearberry honeysuckle—shrub)
*Lonicera sempervirens* (trumpet honeysuckle—liana)
*Pedicularis canadensis* (forest lousewort—perennial)
*Penstemon digitalis* (beardtongue—perennial)
*Phlox divaricata* (forest phlox—perennial)

*Polygonatum biflorum* (Solomon's seal—perennial)
*Monarda didyma* (bee balm—perennial)
*Monarda fistulosa* (wild bergamot—perennial)
*Rhododendron periclymenoides* (pinkster flower—shrub)
*Rhododendron viscosum* (swamp azalea—shrub)
*Silene virginica* (fire pink—perennial)
*Symphoricarpus albus* (snowberry—shrub)
*Symphoricarpos orbiculatus* (coralberry—shrub)
*Tilia americana* (basswood—tree)

### Autumn

*Ceanothus americanus* (New Jersey tea—shrub)
*Chelone glabra* (turtlehead—perennial)
*Impatiens capensis* (spotted touch-me-not—annual)
*Lilium superbum* (Turk's cap lily—perennial)
*Lobelia cardinalis* (cardinal flower—perennial)
*Lonicera sempervirens* (trumpet honeysuckle—liana)
*Monarda didyma* (bee balm—perennial)
*Monarda fistulosa* (wild bergamot—perennial)
*Rhododendron viscosum* (swamp azalea—shrub)
*Silene virginica* (fire pink—perennial)

## SOUTHEAST

### Bee

### Spring

*Acer negundo* (box elder—tree)
*Achillea millefolium* (yarrow—perennial)
*Aesculus pavia* (red buckeye—shrub/small tree)
*Coreopsis auriculata* (tall tickseed—perennial)
*Cornus florida* (flowering dogwood—small tree)
*Phlox subulata* (moss-pink—perennial)

### Summer

*Achillea millefolium* (yarrow—perennial)
*Coreopsis auriculata* (tall tickseed—perennial)

(continued on next page)

*Oenothera biennis* (common evening primrose—biennial/short-lived perennial)
*Phlox paniculata* (fall phlox—perennial)
*Solidago* species (goldenrods—perennials)

### Autumn

*Achillea millefolium* (yarrow—perennial)
*Aster dumosus* (long-stalked aster—perennial)
*Hamamelis virginiana* (witchhazel—shrub)
*Oenothera biennis* (common evening primrose—biennial/short-lived perennial)
*Phlox paniculata* (fall phlox—perennial)
*Solidago* species (goldenrods—perennials)

### Butterfly

#### Spring

*Apocynum androsaemifolium* (spreading dogbane—perennial)
*Ceanothus americanus* (New Jersey tea—shrub)
*Echinacea purpurea* (purple coneflower—perennial)

#### Summer

*Apocynum androsaemifolium* (spreading dogbane—perennial)
*Asclepias tuberosa* (butterfly weed—perennial)
*Ceanothus americanus* (New Jersey tea—shrub)
*Clethra alnifolia* (sweet pepperbush—shrub)
*Echinacea purpurea* (purple coneflower—perennial)
*Monarda fistulosa* (wild bergamot—perennial)
*Phlox paniculata* (fall phlox—perennial)
*Pycnanthemum muticum* (mountain mint—perennial)
*Solidago* species (goldenrods—perennials)

#### Autumn

*Ceanothus americanus* (New Jersey tea—shrub)
*Clethra alnifolia* (sweet pepperbush—shrub)

*Monarda fistulosa* (wild bergamot—perennial)
*Phlox paniculata* (fall phlox—perennial)
*Solidago* species (goldenrods—perennials)

### Hummingbird

#### Spring

*Aesculus pavia* (red buckeye—shrub/small tree)
*Aquilegia canadensis* (Canada columbine—perennial)
*Castilleja coccinea* (Indian paintbrush—annual/biennial)
*Ceanothus americanus* (New Jersey tea—shrub)
*Cercis canadensis* (redbud—shrub/small tree)
*Erythrina herbacea* (coral bean—perennial)
*Ipomopsis rubra* (standing cypress—biennial)
*Kalmia latifolia* (mountain laurel—shrub/small tree)
*Lonicera canadensis* (fly honeysuckle—shrub)
*Lonicera sempervirens* (trumpet honeysuckle—liana)
*Pedicularis canadensis* (forest lousewort—perennial)
*Penstemon digitalis* (beardtongue—perennial)
*Phlox divaricata* (forest phlox—perennial)
*Polygonatum biflorum* (Solomon's seal—perennial)
*Rhododendron catawbiense* (purple laurel—shrub/small tree)
*Rhododendron periclymenoides* (pinkster flower—shrub)
*Robinia pseudoacacia* (black locust—tree)
*Spigelia marilandica* (Indian pink—perennial)

#### Summer

*Aquilegia canadensis* (Canada columbine—perennial)
*Asclepias tuberosa* (butterfly weed—perennial)
*Campsis radicans* (trumpet creeper—liana)
*Castilleja coccinea* (Indian paintbrush—annual/biennial)
*Ceanothus americanus* (New Jersey tea—shrub)
*Cephalanthus occidentalis* (buttonbush—shrub)

Chelone glabra (turtlehead—perennial)

Dicentra eximia (wild bleeding heart—perennial)

Erythrina herbacea (coral bean—perennial)

Impatiens capensis (spotted touch-me-not—annual)

Ipomopsis rubra (standing cypress—biennial)

Kalmia latifolia (mountain laurel—shrub/small tree)

Lilium superbum (Turk's cap lily—perennial)

Lobelia cardinalis (cardinal flower—perennial)

Lonicera canadensis (fly honeysuckle—shrub)

Lonicera sempervirens (trumpet honeysuckle—liana)

Monarda fistulosa (wild bergamot—perennial)

Pedicularis canadensis (forest lousewort—perennial)

Penstemon digitalis (beardtongue—perennial)

Phlox divaricata (forest phlox—perennial)

Polygonatum biflorum (Solomon's seal—perennial)

Rhododendron catawbiense (purple laurel—shrub/small tree)

Rhododendron periclymenoides (pinkster flower—shrub)

Rhododendron viscosum (swamp azalea—shrub)

Robinia pseudoacacia (black locust—tree)

Silene regia (wild pink—perennial)

Silene rotundifolia (roundleaf catchfly—perennial)

Spigelia marilandica (Indian pink—perennial)


**Autumn**

Campsis radicans (trumpet creeper—liana)

Ceanothus americanus (New Jersey tea—shrub)

Chelone glabra (turtlehead—perennial)

Impatiens capensis (spotted touch-me-not—annual)

Ipomopsis rubra (standing cypress—biennial)

Lilium superbum (Turk's cap lily—perennial)

Lobelia cardinalis (cardinal flower—perennial)

Lonicera sempervirens (trumpet honeysuckle—liana)

Monarda fistulosa (wild bergamot—perennial)

Rhododendron viscosum (swamp azalea—shrub)

Spigelia marilandica (Indian pink—perennial)


## SUBTROPICAL FLORIDA

**Bee**

*Spring*

Coccoloba uvifera (seagrape—tree)

Gaillardia pulchella (blanketflower—annual)

Guaiacum sanctum (lignum vitae—tree)

Piscidia piscipula (Jamaica dogwood—tree)

Pithecellobium guadalupense (blackbead—shrub)

Quercus virginiana (live oak—tree)


*Summer*

Cordia globosa (butterfly sage—shrub)

Lysiloma latisiliquum (wild tamarind—tree)

Serenoa repens (saw palmetto—shrub/palm)

Solidago species (goldenrod—perennials)


*Autumn*

Manilkara bahamensis (wild dilly—tree)

Psychotria nervosa (wild coffee—shrub)

Sophora tomentosa (necklace pod—shrub)


**Butterfly**

*Spring*

Coreopsis leavenworthii (tickseed—perennial)

Hamelia patens (firebush—shrub)

Salvia coccinea (scarlet sage—perennial)

Stachytarpheta jamaicensis (blue porterweed—perennial) .


*Summer*

Gaillardia pulchella (blanketflower—annual)

Hamelia patens (firebush—shrub)

Liatris species (blazing stars—perennials)

Stachytarpheta jamaicensis (blue porterweed—shrub)

(continued on next page)

## Autumn/Winter

*Asclepias tuberosa* (butterfly weed—perennial)
*Cordia globosa* (butterfly sage—perennial)
*Eupatorium odoratum* (thoroughwort—shrub)
*Hamelia patens* (firebush—shrub)
*Salvia coccinea* (scarlet sage—perennial)
*Stachytarpheta jamaicensis* (blue porterweed—
    shrub)

## Hummingbird

### Spring

*Cordia sebestena* (geiger tree—tree)
*Erythrina herbacea* (coral bean—shrub)
*Hamelia patens* (firebush—shrub)
*Salvia coccinea* (scarlet sage—perennial)
*Sophora tomentosa* (necklace pod—shrub)

### Autumn

*Bourreria ovata* (Bahama strongbark—tree)
*Cordia sebestena* (geiger tree—tree)
*Hamelia patens* (firebush—shrub)
*Ipomea microdactyla* (man-in-the-ground—vine)
*Pavonia spicata* (mangrove mallow—shrub)
*Salvia coccinea* (scarlet sage—perennial)
*Sophora tomentosa* (necklace pod—shrub)

### Winter

*Pavonia spicata* (mangrove mallow—shrub)
*Salvia coccinea* (scarlet sage—perennial)
*Sophora tomentosa* (necklace pod—shrub)

## MIDWEST AND NORTHERN PLAINS

## Bee

### Spring

*Acer negundo* (box elder—tree)
*Achillea millefolium* (yarrow—perennial)
*Caltha palustris* (marsh marigold—perennial)
*Geum rivale* (water avens—perennial)
*Ribes odoratum* (buffalo currant—shrub)

### Summer

*Achillea millefolium* (yarrow—perennial)
*Geum rivale* (water avens—perennial)
*Oenothera biennis* (common evening primrose—
    biennial/short-lived perennial)
*Phlox paniculata* (fall phlox—perennial)
*Potentilla fruticosa* (shrubby five-fingers—shrub)
*Solidago* species (goldenrods—perennials)

### Autumn

*Achillea millefolium* (yarrow—perennial)
*Oenothera biennis* (common evening primrose—
    biennial/short-lived perennial)
*Phlox paniculata* (fall phlox—perennial)
*Solidago* species (goldenrods—perennials)

## Butterfly

### Spring

*Apocynum androsaemifolium* (spreading dogbane—
    perennial)
*Asclepias* species (milkweeds—perennials/shrubs)
*Ceanothus americanus* (New Jersey tea—shrub)

### Summer

*Apocynum androsaemifolium* (spreading dogbane—
    perennial)
*Asclepias* species (milkweeds—perennials/shrubs)
*Ceanothus americanus* (New Jersey tea—shrub)
*Echinacea purpurea* (purple coneflower—peren-
    nial)
*Solidago* species (goldenrods—perennials)

### Autumn

*Apocynum androsaemifolium* (spreading dogbane—
    perennial)
*Ceanothus americanus* (New Jersey tea—shrub)
*Solidago* species (goldenrods—perennials)

## Hummingbird

### Spring

*Aesculus glabra* (western buckeye—shrub/small tree)

*Aquilegia canadensis* (Canada columbine—perennial)

*Asclepias tuberosa* (butterfly weed—perennial)

*Castilleja sessiliflora* (downy paintbrush—shrub)

*Ceanothus americanus* (New Jersey tea—shrub)

*Lobelia cardinalis* (cardinal flower—perennial)

*Penstemon digitalis* (beardtongue—perennial)

*Ribes odoratum* (buffalo currant—shrub)

*Stanleya pinnata* (prince's plum—perennial, subshrub or shrub)

*Symphoricarpus albus* (snowberry—shrub)

### Summer

*Aquilegia canadensis* (Canada columbine—perennial)

*Castilleja sessiliflora* (downy paintbrush—shrub)

*Ceanothus americanus* (New Jersey tea—shrub)

*Impatiens capensis* (spotted touch-me-not—annual)

*Lobelia cardinalis* (cardinal flower—perennial)

*Penstemon digitalis* (beardtongue—perennial)

*Stanleya pinnata* (prince's plum—perennial, subshrub or shrub)

*Symphoricarpus albus* (snowberry—shrub)

*Symphoricarpos orbiculatus* (coralberry—shrub)

*Tilia americana* (basswood—tree)

### Autumn

*Castilleja sessiliflora* (downy paintbrush—shrub)

*Ceanothus americanus* (New Jersey tea—shrub)

*Impatiens capensis* (spotted touch-me-not—annual)

## TEXAS AND SOUTHERN PLAINS

### Bee

### Spring

*Acer negundo* (box elder—tree)

*Achillea millefolium* (yarrow—perennial)

*Aesculus pavia* (red buckeye—shrub/small tree)

*Cornus florida* (flowering dogwood—small tree)

*Gaillardia pulchella* (Indian blanketflower—annual)

*Ribes odoratum* (buffalo currant—shrub)

### Summer

*Achillea millefolium* (yarrow—perennial)

*Gaillardia pulchella* (Indian blanketflower—annual)

*Oenothera biennis* (common evening primrose—biennial/short-lived perennial)

*Solidago* species (goldenrods—perennials)

### Autumn

*Achillea millefolium* (yarrow—perennial)

*Oenothera biennis* (common evening primrose—biennial/short-lived perennial)

*Solidago* species (goldenrods—perennials)

### Butterfly

### Spring

*Apocynum androsaemifolium* (spreading dogbane—perennial)

*Ceanothus americanus* (New Jersey tea—shrub)

*Echinacea purpurea* (purple coneflower—perennial)

### Summer

*Apocynum androsaemifolium* (spreading dogbane—perennial)

*Ceanothus americanus* (New Jersey tea—shrub)

*Clethra alnifolia* (sweet pepperbush—shrub)

*Echinacea purpurea* (purple coneflower—perennial)

*Solidago* species (goldenrods—perennials)

*(continued on next page)*

*Autumn*

*Ceanothus americanus* (New Jersey tea—shrub)
*Clethra alnifolia* (sweet pepperbush—shrub)
*Solidago* species (goldenrods—perennials)

## Hummingbird

*Spring*

*Aesculus glabra* (western buckeye—shrub/small tree)
*Aquilegia canadensis* (Canada columbine—perennial)
*Castilleja sessiliflora* (downy paintbrush—shrub)
*Ceanothus americanus* (New Jersey tea—shrub)
*Lonicera sempervirens* (trumpet honeysuckle—liana)
*Lupinus texensis* (Texas bluebonnet—annual)
*Pedicularis canadensis* (forest lousewort—perennial)
*Penstemon digitalis* (beardtongue—perennial)
*Ribes odoratum* (buffalo currant—shrub)

*Summer*

*Aquilegia canadensis* (Canada columbine—perennial)
*Asclepias tuberosa* (butterfly weed—perennial)
*Castilleja sessiliflora* (downy paintbrush—shrub)
*Ceanothus americanus* (New Jersey tea—shrub)
*Lobelia cardinalis* (cardinal flower—perennial)
*Lonicera sempervirens* (trumpet honeysuckle—liana)
*Pedicularis canadensis* (forest lousewort—perennial)
*Penstemon digitalis* (beardtongue—perennial)
*Symphoricarpos orbiculatus* (coralberry—shrub)

*Autumn*

*Castilleja sessiliflora* (downy paintbrush—shrub)
*Ceanothus americanus* (New Jersey tea—shrub)
*Lobelia cardinalis* (cardinal flower—perennial)
*Lonicera sempervirens* (trumpet honeysuckle—liana)

## ROCKY MOUNTAINS

### Bee

*Spring*

*Gaillardia pulchella* (Indian blanketflower—annual)

*Summer*

*Acer negundo* (box elder—tree)
*Gaillardia pulchella* (Indian blanketflower—annual)
*Potentilla fruticosa* (shrubby five-fingers—shrub)

*Autumn*

*Acer negundo* (box elder—tree)

### Butterfly

*Spring*

*Verbena* species (verbenas—annuals/perennials)

*Summer*

*Amorpha canescens* (lead plant—shrub)
*Liatris* species (gayfeathers—perennials)
*Monarda fistulosa* (wild bergamot—perennial)
*Verbena* species (verbenas—annuals/perennials)

*Autumn*

*Liatris* species (gayfeathers—perennials)
*Monarda fistulosa* (wild bergamot—perennial)
*Verbena* species (verbenas—annuals/perennials)

### Hummingbird

*Spring*

*Castilleja chromosa* (desert paintbrush—shrub)
*Castilleja integra* (southwestern paintbrush—shrub)
*Castilleja miniata* (giant red paintbrush—shrub)
*Castilleja sessiliflora* (downy paintbrush—shrub)
*Ipomopsis aggregata* (skyrocket—perennial)
*Penstemon eatonii* (Eaton's beardtongue—perennial)

*Robinia neomexicana* (New Mexico locust—tree)
*Symphoricarpus albus* (snowberry—shrub)

### Summer

*Aquilegia caerulea* (Colorado columbine—perennial)
*Castilleja chromosa* (desert paintbrush—shrub)
*Castilleja integra* (southwestern paintbrush—shrub)
*Castilleja miniata* (giant red paintbrush—shrub)
*Castilleja sessiliflora* (downy paintbrush—shrub)
*Ipomopsis aggregata* (skyrocket—perennial)
*Monarda fistulosa* (wild bergamot—perennial)
*Penstemon barbatus* (golden-beard penstemon—perennial)
*Penstemon eatonii* (Eaton's beardtongue—perennial)
*Penstemon strictus* (porch penstemon—perennial)
*Robinia neomexicana* (New Mexico locust—tree)
*Symphoricarpus albus* (snowberry—shrub)

### Autumn

*Castilleja integra* (southwestern paintbrush—shrub)
*Castilleja miniata* (giant red paintbrush—shrub)
*Castilleja sessiliflora* (downy paintbrush—shrub)
*Ipomopsis aggregata* (skyrocket—perennial)
*Monarda fistulosa* (wild bergamot—perennial)
*Penstemon barbatus* (golden-beard penstemon—perennial)

## WESTERN DESERTS

### Bee

### Spring

*Geraea canescens* (desert sunflower—annual)
*Penstemon palmeri* (Palmer's penstemon—perennial)
*Eschscholzia californica* (California poppy—annual/perennial)

### Summer

*Eschscholzia californica* (California poppy—annual/perennial)
*Penstemon palmeri* (Palmer's penstemon—perennial)

### Autumn

*Eschscholzia californica* (California poppy—annual/perennial)
*Penstemon palmeri* (Palmer's penstemon—perennial)

### Butterfly

### Spring

*Bebbia juncea* (Chuckwalla's delight—shrub)
*Calliandra eriophylla* (fairyduster—shrub)
*Dalea frutescens* (indigobush—shrub)
*Glandularia gooddingii* (verbena—perennial)
*Hyptis emoryi* (desert lavender—shrub)
*Lycium andersonii* (wolfberry—shrub)
*Thymophylla pentachaeta* var. *pentachaeta* (dyssodia—perennial)

### Summer

*Aloysia gratissima* (bee bush—shrub)
*Bebbia juncea* (Chuckwalla's delight—shrub)
*Calliandra eriophylla* (fairyduster—shrub)
*Celtis pallida* (desert hackberry—shrub)
*Hyptis emoryi* (desert lavender—shrub)
*Prosopis velutina* (velvet mesquite—tree)
*Senna covesii* (desert senna—subshrub)
*Thymophylla pentachaeta* var. *pentachaeta* (dyssodia—perennial)

### Autumn

*Asclepias subulata* (desert milkweed—perennial)
*Asclepias tuberosa* (butterfly weed—perennial)
*Bebbia juncea* (Chuckwalla's delight—shrub)

(continued on next page)

*Hyptis emoryi* (desert lavender—shrub)
*Senna covesii* (desert senna—subshrub)

**Winter**

*Calliandra eriophylla* (fairyduster—shrub)
*Dalea greggii* (indigobush—shrub)
*Hyptis emoryi* (desert lavender—shrub)
*Lycium andersonii* (wolfberry—shrub)

**Hummingbird**

*Spring*

*Anisacanthus thurberi* (desert honeysuckle—shrub)
*Astragalus coccineus* (scarlet locoweed—perennial)
*Calliandra eriophylla* (fairyduster—shrub)
*Chilopsis linearis* (desert willow—shrub or tree)
*Fouquieria splendens* (ocotillo—shrub)
*Justicia californica* (chuparosa—shrub)
*Penstemon eatonii* (Eaton's beardtongue—perennial)
*Penstemon palmeri* (Palmer's penstemon—perennial)
*Penstemon pseudospectabilis* (Arizona penstemon—perennial)
*Phacelia campanularia* (desert bell—annual)
*Sphaeralcea ambigua* (apricot mallow—annual)
*Stanleya pinnata* (prince's plum—perennial, subshrub or shrub)

*Summer*

*Anisacanthus thurberi* (desert honeysuckle—shrub)
*Astragalus coccineus* (scarlet locoweed—perennial)
*Castilleja chromosa* (desert paintbrush—shrub)
*Chilopsis linearis* (desert willow—shrub or tree)
*Fouquieria splendens* (ocotillo—shrub)
*Justicia californica* (chuparosa—shrub)
*Penstemon eatonii* (Eaton's beardtongue—perennial)
*Penstemon palmeri* (Palmer's penstemon—perennial)

*Sphaeralcea ambigua* (apricot mallow—annual)
*Stanleya pinnata* (prince's plum—perennial, subshrub or shrub)

**Autumn**

*Anisacanthus thurberi* (desert honeysuckle—shrub)
*Castilleja chromosa* (desert paintbrush—shrub)
*Chilopsis linearis* (desert willow—shrub or tree)
*Penstemon palmeri* (Palmer's penstemon—perennial)
*Stanleya pinnata* (prince's plum—perennial, subshrub or shrub)

**PACIFIC NORTHWEST**

**Bee**

*Spring*

*Achillea millefolium* (yarrow—perennial)
*Ribes sanguineum* (red-flowering currant—shrub)

*Summer*

*Achillea millefolium* (yarrow—perennial)
*Phlox adsurgens* (phlox—perennial)
*Ribes sanguineum* (red-flowering currant—shrub)

*Autumn*

*Achillea millefolium* (yarrow—perennial)

**Butterfly**

*Spring*

*Achillea millefolium* (yarrow—perennial)
*Mimulus* species (monkeyflowers—annuals/perennials)

*Summer*

*Achillea millefolium* (yarrow—perennial)
*Mimulus* species (monkeyflowers—annuals/perennials)

Monarda fistulosa (wild bergamot—perennial)
Solidago species (goldenrods—perennials)

**Autumn**

Achillea millefolium (yarrow—perennial)
Mimulus species (monkeyflowers—annuals/perennials)
Monarda fistulosa (wild bergamot—perennial)
Solidago species (goldenrods—perennials)

**Hummingbird**

*Spring*

Aquilegia formosa (red columbine—perennial)
Castilleja miniata (giant red paintbrush—shrub)
Castilleja sessiliflora (downy paintbrush—shrub)
Cynoglossum grande (hound's-tongue—perennial)
Ipomopsis aggregata (skyrocket—perennial)
Lonicera ciliosa (orange honeysuckle—vine)
Penstemon rupicola (cliff penstemon—subshrub)
Ribes sanguineum (red-flowering currant—shrub)

*Summer*

Aquilegia formosa (red columbine—perennial)
Castilleja miniata (giant red paintbrush—shrub)
Castilleja sessiliflora (downy paintbrush—shrub)
Cynoglossum grande (hound's-tongue—perennial)
Ipomopsis aggregata (skyrocket—perennial)
Lonicera ciliosa (orange honeysuckle—vine)
Lonicera involucrata (bearberry honeysuckle—shrub)
Monarda fistulosa (wild bergamot—perennial)
Penstemon rupicola (cliff penstemon—subshrub)
Ribes sanguineum (red-flowering currant—shrub)
Stachys cooleyae (great hedge nettle—perennial)

*Autumn*

Castilleja miniata (giant red paintbrush—shrub)
Castilleja sessiliflora (downy paintbrush—shrub)
Ipomopsis aggregata (skyrocket—perennial)
Monarda fistulosa (wild bergamot—perennial)

## COASTAL CALIFORNIA

**Bee**

*Spring*

Achillea millefolium (yarrow—perennial)
Ribes sanguineum (red-flowering currant—shrub)

*Summer*

Achillea millefolium (yarrow—perennial)
Ribes sanguineum (red-flowering currant—shrub)

*Autumn*

Achillea millefolium (yarrow—perennial)

**Butterfly**

*Spring*

Asclepias species (milkweeds—perennials/shrubs)
Eriogonum fasciculatum (coastal buckwheat—shrub)
Lotus scoparius (deerweed—perennial)
Mimulus species (monkeyflowers—annuals/perennials/shrubs)

*Summer*

Asclepias species (milkweeds—perennials/shrubs)
Eriogonum fasciculatum (coastal buckwheat—shrub)
Solidago species (goldenrods—perennial)
Lotus scoparius (deerweed—perennial)
Mimulus species (monkeyflowers—annuals/perennials/shrubs)

*Autumn*

Asclepias species (milkweeds—perennials/shrubs)
Eriogonum fasciculatum (coastal buckwheat—shrub)
Mimulus species (monkeyflowers—annuals/perennials/shrubs)
Solidago species (goldenrods—perennials)

*(continued on next page)*

**Hummingbird**

*Spring*

*Delphinium cardinale* (cardinal larkspur—perennial)
*Delphinium nudicaule* (orange larkspur—perennial)
*Dicentra chrysantha* (golden eardrops—perennial)
*Erysimum capitatum* (western wallflower—biennial/perennial)
*Isomeris arborea* (bladderpod—shrub)
*Mimulus aurantiacus* (orange bush monkeyflower—subshrub/shrub)
*Phacelia minor* (California bell—annual)
*Ribes sanguineum* (red-flowering currant—shrub)
*Ribes speciosum* (fuchsia-flowered gooseberry—shrub)
*Silene californica* (California Indian pink—perennial)
*Stachys bullata* (hedge nettle—perennial)

*Summer*

*Delphinium cardinale* (cardinal larkspur—perennial)
*Delphinium nudicaule* (orange larkspur—perennial)

*Dicentra chrysantha* (golden eardrops—perennial)
*Erysimum capitatum* (western wallflower—biennial/perennial)
*Isomeris arborea* (bladderpod—shrub)
*Lonicera involucrata* (bearberry honeysuckle—shrub)
*Mimulus aurantiacus* (orange bush monkeyflower—subshrub/shrub)
*Phacelia minor* (California bell—annual)
*Ribes sanguineum* (red-flowering currant—shrub)
*Silene californica* (California Indian pink—perennial)
*Stachys bullata* (hedge nettle—perennial)

*Autumn*

*Dicentra chrysantha* (golden eardrops—perennial)
*Erysimum capitatum* (western wallflower—biennial/perennial)
*Isomeris arborea* (bladderpod—shrub)
*Mimulus aurantiacus* (orange bush monkeyflower—subshrub/shrub)
*Stachys bullata* (hedge nettle—perennial)

## Gardening for Animals

Some animals, especially deer and rodents, can be a nuisance in the garden. But many are a pleasure to observe, and in a natural garden, there should be room for all creatures. Whether for attracting or for fending off certain animals, it is helpful to know what they eat and where they prefer to live.

Squirrels and chipmunks eat pine cones, acorns, hickory nuts, walnuts, hazelnuts, and other seeds and nuts, as well as bulbs, flower buds, and sometimes bark. As any bird enthusiast knows, they are also fond of birdseed. Cottontail rabbits seem to eat any plant they can get. They prefer brushy, brambly areas; boundaries between forests and meadows; and low, swampy areas. Deer, like rabbits, eat just about any plant

they can reach, especially the buds and tender growing tips. Many lists of "deer-resistant" plants have been published, but little consensus has been reached on that topic. Deer are most prevalent in open, rural areas where there are woods, swampland, brushy areas, or farmland. However, they often range into suburban yards.

Water will attract all animals, but certain creatures must have water for their habitat. Turtles and frogs, for instance, require a very wet environment like a pond. Eastern box turtles will settle for a moist woodland or field, where they eat fruit, snails, worms, insects, and some plants. Snakes live in wet meadows, marshes, and other wetlands, feeding on frogs, toads, worms, rodents, and insects. In the Southeast, Southwest, and West, lizards often visit or live in the garden. Lizards eat spiders, insects, and worms. In the East, salamanders and newts live in moist woodlands under rocks or decaying vegetation, and they also eat insects. Toads are insect eaters that live in drier environments with a source of water close by.

## Further Reading

Burrell, C. Colston, ed. *Woodland Gardens.* Brooklyn, N.Y.: Brooklyn Botanic Garden, 1995.

Burrell, C. Colston, ed. *The Natural Water Garden.* Brooklyn, N.Y.: Brooklyn Botanic Garden, 1997.

Dennis, John V. *The Wildlife Gardener.* New York: Alfred A. Knopf, 1985.

Diekelmann, John, and Robert Schuster. *Natural Landscaping.* New York: McGraw-Hill, 1982.

Druse, Ken, with Margaret Roach. *The Natural Habitat Garden.* New York: Clarkson Potter, 1994.

Kress, Stephen W. *Bird Gardens: Welcoming Wild Birds to Your Yard.* Brooklyn, N.Y.: Brooklyn Botanic Garden, 1998.

Lewis, Alcinda, ed. *Butterfly Gardens.* Brooklyn, N.Y.: Brooklyn Botanic Garden, 1995.

Marinelli, Janet, ed. *The Environmental Gardener.* Brooklyn, N.Y.: Brooklyn Botanic Garden, 1992.

Marinelli, Janet, ed. *Going Native: Biodiversity in Our Own Backyards.* Brooklyn, N.Y.: Brooklyn Botanic Garden, 1994.

Marinelli, Janet. *Stalking the Wild Amaranth: Gardening in the Age of Extinction.* New York: Henry Holt and Company, 1998.

Ottesen, Carole. *The Native Plant Primer.* New York: Harmony Books, 1995.

Sawyers, Claire, ed. *Gardening with Wildflowers and Native Plants.* Brooklyn, N.Y. Brooklyn Botanic Garden, 1989.

Stein, Sara. *Planting Noah's Garden.* Boston: Houghton Mifflin, 1997.

Tekulsky, Mathew. *The Butterfly Garden.* Boston: The Harvard Common Press, 1985.

Tufts, Craig, and Peter Loewer. *The National Wildlife Federation's Guide to Gardening for Wildlife.* Emmaus, Pa.: Rodale Press, 1994.

# 7

# KITCHEN GARDENING

Vegetable gardens feed both the body and the spirit. Planting lettuce or mulching tomatoes engages the hands and frees the mind to follow distant thoughts. Just starting down the path from the kitchen door to the garden gate makes the sense of time shift from workaday to garden standard. A three-minute errand for salad greens easily extends to an absorbing half hour of thinning seedlings or pulling weeds.

Vegetable gardens give back according to what they receive. The basic needs of the garden go beyond an allocation of time. Given abundant sunshine, rich soil, and moisture, as well as attention, even a small space can be productive and beautiful.

## Vegetable Garden Basics

### Siting

Before breaking ground for a garden, evaluate the site's solar exposure. Without at least six hours of full sun each day, most vegetables will not thrive. Even leafy cool weather crops will be stunted. Other conditions in the garden, such as soil and water, can be improved, but a poor solar exposure is beyond correcting.

Full sun means not just six hours of sunlight but six hours through the middle of the day, between, say, 9 or 10 o'clock in the morning and 3 or 4 in the afternoon. Determining the hours of sunlight for a given spot is easy enough during the growing season, but in other seasons making accurate projections about summer sunlight is much more difficult, in part because trees leaf out and cast extensive shade and because the sun's path changes so dramatically from month to month.

As a general rule, try to allow 70 feet between the site and mature trees growing to the southeast, south, and southwest of the garden. Allow about 50 feet between the garden site and any two-story buildings, more for taller buildings.

## Soil Preparation

If the garden site is covered with grass, use a spade to cut the sod into strips. Then, undercut the strips below the level of the grass roots. Peel the strips away and use them to fill in bare spots in the lawn or stack them upside down and let them decay for compost.

Site preparation may involve more than clearing away sod. It may be necessary to chop down trees and remove roots and rocks. Gardening inevitably requires disturbing the ground, but the earth may be just as happy in beds of basil or corn as in stones and sumac.

Once a site is cleared, double digging is an excellent way to initially aerate the soil and at the same time work in organic matter and other amendments. Double digging essentially means loosening the soil to a depth of two shovel blades, or roughly 12 to 18 inches.

Few gardeners are fortunate enough to have a site with ideal soil. The best ground for most vegetables is a sandy loam, with a composition of roughly 15 percent clay, 40 percent sand, and 40 percent silt, with about a 5 percent organic content. But even the most forbidding site can be steadily improved. A heavy clay soil can be lightened by adding small amounts of coarse sand, once or twice a year. Spread a ⅛-inch layer of sand over an entire bed before double digging, and thoroughly work the sand into the soil.

Organic matter, too, lightens and aerates heavy clay, allowing water and air to percolate through. In sandy soil, organic matter helps absorb water and nutrients and hold them in the plant's root zone.

In fact, compost, decayed manure, old leaves, and other organic material enhances the fertility of any garden site. It fosters soil life—bacteria, insects, and earthworms—which work their own magic, loosening the ground, retaining moisture, and helping plant roots take up nutrients that otherwise would be inaccessible. In the process of double digging, add one shovel of organic matter for every three shovels of garden soil dug.

Organic matter continually breaks down in the soil and needs to be replenished. Applying a 2-inch layer of compost to the beds each spring will meet most of the nutritional needs of your vegetables (see "Composting," page 441).

The pH of a garden site is another important factor in vegetable growth. Most vegetables thrive in slightly acid soil with a pH of 6.5 to 6.8. Excessively acid soil can be moderated, or sweetened, by adding dolomitic lime. Alkaline soil can be made more acidic by thoroughly working in composted oak leaves or pine bark mold. Applying sulfur will also acidify the soil. Having a soil sample analyzed by a lab recommended by your Cooperative Extension agent is a good way to start in evaluating the pH and determining whether amendments are needed and in what quantity (see "Soil," page 430).

## Extending the Season

Spring arrives too slowly and fall much too quickly for many gardeners. With various types of plant protection, however, you can increase the temperature around your crops and add at least a week a month to the season—two weeks in the spring and two weeks in the fall. With cold-hardy crops, including many salad greens, the season can often be extended two or three months through the fall and into early winter. Using materials like shade cloth can moderate the midsummer sun and give heat-sensitive crops such as lettuce and spinach another week or ten days before they begin to set seed and lose their agreeable flavor.

The following can provide added warmth:

## Shade Cloth

The harvesting period for heat-sensitive salad greens such as arugula, cilantro, lettuce, and spinach can be extended if the plants are kept for a time from going to seed, or bolting. This can be accomplished by protecting them from intense sun with shade cloth. The material can be supported on a wood frame or draped over a hoop house constructed as described above. Keep the bottom edge of the fabric at least 2 feet off the ground to allow air movement and minimize heat buildup.

Most shade fabric is polypropylene and is available in a range of densities providing from 30 to 90 percent shade. A shade density of 60 percent or less is generally best for salad greens; otherwise they will quickly become leggy.

## Cloches

Cloches, or hot caps, can be set over individual plants, usually in the spring when the crops are small and the weather is cool. One-gallon plastic jugs with the top and bottom removed are among the least expensive, least breakable cloches. (The term *cloche,* the French word for bell, derives from the bell-shaped glass caps used by French vegetable growers during the nineteenth century.) Several cloche designs are available commercially, including a double-walled, teepee-shaped product that is filled with water and absorbs solar energy during the day and releases the warmth at night.

## Cold Frames

A cold frame is a simple four-sided structure, usually made of wood with a sloping top of a transparent material to allow in sunlight and capture warmth. Orienting the cold frame to face south will maximize its thermal benefit. The back of many cold frames is roughly twice as high as the front—say, 16 inches high compared to 7 inches for the front. Tops can be constructed of a wood frame fitted with Plexiglas, clear polyethylene, or glass. An old storm window can sometimes be used. The top should be hinged. It can be fitted with a piston device that expands automatically to raise the top when the inside temperature goes above about 70°F. As the weather cools, the piston retracts and the top closes.

A cold frame can be useful in all seasons.

• Spring. Place a cold frame over a garden bed to raise the soil temperature and improve seed germination and accelerate the growth of seedlings. A cold frame can also be used outside the vegetable garden to start seedlings in flats or to gradually acclimatize seedlings to outdoor conditions after they have been started indoors.

• Summer. Second and third plantings of salad greens can be started in the protective environment of the cold frame. Just be sure to raise or remove the top to keep the seedlings from becoming overheated.

• Fall. Placed over a garden bed, the frame will provide considerable frost protection and added daytime warmth to keep cool-season crops growing.

- Winter. In areas as cold as USDA Zone 5, hardy crops such as leeks, kale, parsley, arugula, and other greens may make some growth with cold-frame protection. Root crops can be stored under a cold frame filled with leaves or straw. Root cuttings and difficult-to-propagate seeds will benefit from the moderated environment of a cold frame and be ready to make growth when spring arrives.

## Hoop Houses

A hoop house or mini greenhouse can be constructed of ⅜-inch diameter plastic tubing covered with 4 or 6 mil polyethylene. For a stronger frame able to withstand some snow load, use metal pipe or plastic tubing 1¼ inch in diameter. Plastic tubing is commonly sold in 10-foot lengths. Each piece can be curved to an arch shape and secured with brackets to a wooden raised-bed frame about 5 feet wide. Space the hoops every 2½ feet along the frame. The hoops can be stabilized with three horizontal lengths of tubing, one running across the top of the hoops and one halfway down each side. Fasten the horizontal members to the hoops with duct tape. The plastic sheeting can be secured to the hoops with spring-loaded wood clamps that resemble large clip clothespins. The clamps can be quickly removed, making it easy to pull back the plastic on warm days.

Set up the frame over a garden bed in late winter to protect early-season crops. Take it apart for the summer and put it up again in the fall to extend the growing season by several weeks or months.

## Row Covers

Lightweight synthetic fabric can rest directly on plants or be supported on thin wire hoops. The fabric is porous enough to allow in air, light, and water but dense enough to trap warmth and keep out most insects. The translucent quality of row covers varies, depending on the material and the density of the weave. Most brands allow at least 80 percent of the available sunlight to pass through. Some brands have a light transmission rate of almost 95 percent. The covers provide a small measure of frost protection, depending on the density of the fabric. However, the material's greater horticultural value is increasing warmth during the day, thus stimulating growth and bringing crops to earlier maturity.

Spread the fabric loosely over a row and secure the edges with boards, stones, soil, or U-shaped metal pins. Lift the edges of the fabric during hot days and remove the material as the season advances to prevent plants from overheating and to allow insects to pollinate the flowers.

# Growing Vegetables in Containers

Container gardening makes it possible to harvest fresh vegetables from a rooftop, patio, deck, or courtyard. Even climbing and vining crops can be raised in large pots fitted with a trellis or pole to support their rambling growth. Unlike those raised in a garden plot, container crops can be moved during the growing season to make the most of changing sunlight. And at the end of the year, some frost-tender crops can be brought indoors, where they can continue to grow.

Containers with a capacity of 5 gallons or more have enough soil to insulate plant roots against daily fluctuations in temperature, and can retain sufficient moisture to make constant watering unnecessary. Light-colored pots absorb less heat than dark ones, and so create a more hospitable environment for plant roots. The best containers are often made of wood or terra cotta, which, unlike plastic, do not heat up quickly in direct sunlight. Also, wood and clay absorb moisture and so provide a damp layer between the soil and the surrounding air. Water seeps through clay and wooden pots and evaporates, cooling the container and the plant. However, because of the moisture loss the pots must be watered more often than, say, plastic containers. However, if weight is a consideration—on a balcony or rooftop, for example— light-colored plastic buckets may be the best choice.

Hanging baskets can also be used to grow any number of plants. Like a trellis, they allow gardeners to take advantage of vertical space.

The ideal planting medium for containers is lighter and more resistant to compaction than garden soil. Most commercial mixes contain a large percentage of peat moss, which is light and absorbs a lot of water for its weight. However, if it dries out, peat moss is difficult and time-consuming to rewet. See box in first column for a recipe for a peat-free potting mix.

Fill a container with the planting medium only to within about 1½ inches of the rim to allow enough space for watering.

Container-grown vegetables need to be fed periodically throughout the season to replace nutrients washed out by frequent irrigation. Various liquid fertilizers are suitable, including seaweed and fish formulas. With attentive watering and feeding, container gardens can be far more productive per square foot than conventional garden plots.

## Encyclopedia of Vegetables

In terms of growing conditions, vegetables can be divided into cool-season and warm-season crops. Not all crops fall neatly into either category. There is a continuum of sensitivity to heat and cold. However, these categories offer general but important distinctions.

**Cool-season crops** can be planted or set out before the last expected spring frost. Often quite sensitive to heat, cool-season crops lose their agreeable flavor and go to seed as the summer advances. Second and third plantings can be made after the heat of the summer has passed, so the crops can be harvested into the fall and winter in many areas.

**Warm-season crops** are vulnerable to cold and cannot be safely sown or transplanted without protection until the risk of frost has passed. In areas north of USDA Zone 7, many warm-season crops must be started indoors and set out as seedlings if they are to be fully productive before the onset of cool weather.

---

### A PEAT-FREE POTTING MIX

Here is one recipe for a potting mix that does not contain peat. One batch yields enough for a 5-gallon container.

9 quarts sifted, well-aged compost
3 quarts sifted garden soil
3 quarts coarse builders sand
3 quarts vermiculite
1 cup greensand
½ cup blood meal
½ cup bonemeal

---

In the following encyclopedia, vegetables are listed in alphabetical order by common name. Each entry includes specific information on propagating, growing, and harvesting, and recommended varieties are listed. Zone numbers refer to the USDA Hardiness Zone Map.

## Cool-Season Vegetables

### Arugula (*Eruca vesicaria* subsp. *sativa*, *E. sativa*)

The blue-green leaves of arugula, also known as roquette, have a peppery flavor that intensifies as the plant matures.

CULTURE: Arugula can be planted as soon as the ground is dry enough to work in the spring. Sow seeds about ¼ inch deep, every 3 to 4 inches in a bed or in rows. For an extended harvest, plant several seeds every two weeks. Thin plants to 6 to 8 inches apart.

HARVESTING: Harvest at about 5 weeks, when leaves are 3 to 4 inches long. Plants that are cut back will resprout.

VARIETIES: Seed is usually sold under the common names, arugula or roquette. 'Sylvetta' is one named variety selected for heat tolerance.

### Asparagus (*Asparagus officinalis*)

Asparagus is a perennial usually started from root sections, or crowns, although it can be started from seed. Plants can be started from seed more cheaply than from crowns but will take one to two more years to produce harvestable spears.

CULTURE: Set crowns 14 to 16 inches apart in a trench 6 to 8 inches deep. Cover with 1 to 2 inches of soil. Gradually fill in the trench, shoveling in a few inches of soil at a time over several weeks the first year as young spears appear, grow, and go to seed. A few spears can be harvested the second year and more in years ahead. Each vigorous mature crown can produce 15 to 20 spears in a season. Keep the rows well mulched. Allow the "ferns" that develop by midsummer to die back naturally in the fall.

HARVESTING: Harvest when the buds, or bracts, at the top of the spear are still tightly closed. Cut the spears at ground level.

VARIETIES: Choose varieties with tolerance to fusarium wilt and rust. 'Jersey Knight' and 'Jersey Giant' are productive, disease-resistant varieties for northern and central states (Zones 4 through 6). 'Jersey Gem' is well suited for the Southeast (Zones 7 and 8). 'Greenwich' and 'Jersey King' grow well on the West Coast (Zones 8 and 9).

### Beets (*Beta vulgaris*)

Beets are both a ready source of summer greens and a good winter-storage crop.

CULTURE: For an early crop, sow seeds in flats indoors or under cover 5 to 6 weeks before the last frost and transplant the seedlings when they are about 4 weeks. Outdoors, start seed 2 to 3 weeks before the last expected frost. Plant at a ½-inch depth, 8 to 10 seeds per foot. Thin plants to stand every 4 inches by removing young beets for salads or light steaming. For a continuous harvest of young beets, sow a 3-foot row every 2 weeks through May in Zones 7 and 8, through June in Zones 4 through 6. For a winter-storage crop, plant seeds about 10 weeks before first expected hard frost.

VARIETIES: 'Red Ace' and 'Big Red' are productive main-crop hybrids. 'Lutz Green Leaf' is an old, open-pollinated variety with good keeping quality. Another heirloom, 'Chioggia', is decorative, with red and white concentric circles.

## Broccoli (*Brassica oleracea,* Botrytis group)

Food scientists have recently confirmed what parents have long asserted, that broccoli is, indeed, good for you.

CULTURE: Easy to grow and a versatile food, broccoli for northern gardens (Zones 4 through 6) is best started indoors in flats 6 to 8 weeks before the last expected frost. Sow seeds about ¼ inch deep. Set out transplants when 5 to 6 weeks old, spaced 16 inches apart. Gardeners in the South, Southwest, and along parts of the West Coast (Zones 7 through 9) can plant broccoli directly in the garden as a fall and winter crop. In late summer, sow seeds about ½ inch deep.

HARVESTING: Harvest heads at any time but before they begin to show any signs of yellow, indicating that the florets are opening.

VARIETIES: Hybrid varieties such as 'Packman' and 'Saga' and the heirloom 'De Cicco' will produce many sideshoots after the main head is harvested. The hybrid 'Emperor' and the heirloom 'Waltham 29' yield large main heads, 6 inches or more across.

## Brussels Sprouts (*Brassica oleracea,* Gemmifera group)

When fall frost takes its toll on northern gardens (Zones 4 through 6), cold-hardy brussels sprouts are often one of the few remaining crops in the field. In fact, their flavor is improved by a hard freeze.

CULTURE: Gardeners in the South and West (Zones 7 through 9) can plant seed in late summer for a fall and winter harvest. For fall harvest in northern gardens, sow seeds in flats or outdoors about the time of the last expected frost. In flats, plant seeds about ¼ inch deep; outdoors, about ½ inch deep. Transplant seedlings or thin rows in 4 to 6 weeks, leaving plants about 20 inches apart.

HARVESTING: Harvest when the sprouts reach a diameter of about 1 inch. Each plant can yield about a quart of sprouts. At the onset of winter, plants can be pulled up and set in a container of sand in a root cellar to prolong the harvest.

VARIETIES: 'Queen Marvel' and 'Prince Marvel' are two new high-yielding hybrids. 'Rubine Red' and 'Long Island' are productive heirloom varieties, with 'Rubine Red' bearing attractive reddish sprouts.

## Cabbage (*Brassica oleracea,* Capitata group)

Cabbage can be a two-season crop, with an early planting maturing before the heat of the summer and a second crop planted to grow into the fall.

CULTURE: Seeds can be sown in flats about 6 to 8 weeks before the last expected frost and transplants set out when they are 5 to 6 weeks old. Space plants about 16 inches apart. For a fall crop in the North (Zones 4 through 6) transplant 4-week-old seedlings to the garden in late June. In the South (Zones 7 through 9), set out transplants in late August.

VARIETIES: Early-maturing varieties include the hybrid 'Discovery' and the heirloom 'Early Jersey Wakefield'. 'Ruby Perfection', a red variety, and 'Savoy King' are good fall choices.

## Carrots (*Daucus carota*)

Carrots can be harvested over many weeks. An early crop can be sown three weeks before the last expected frost. A fall crop for winter storage can be planted in mid to late summer.

CULTURE: Try to sow seed thinly, at a ¾- to 1-inch spacing, ¼ inch deep, in a band 2 inches wide. Carrots are slow to germinate. To keep soil from crusting, cover seed drills with a sprinkling of compost. Thin seedlings when the tops touch. Continue thinning so the crop can mature with ½ inch or so of space between each carrot.

HARVESTING: Carrots can be pulled when the size of a little finger or allowed to become long, stout roots.

VARIETIES: The short, stocky Chantenay types 'Kinko' and 'Chantenay' are best suited for clay soils. Long, tapered imperator types 'A-Plus' and 'Blaze' grow best in light, sandy soil. Nantes types such as 'Touchon' and the hybrid 'Napoli' are long and blunt ended and grow well in medium soil. 'Thumbelina' and 'Parmex' are round varieties.

## Garlic (*Allium sativum*)

At the rate garlic is used in most kitchens, it merits space in the kitchen garden. Garlic is easy to grow provided the varieties are appropriate for the region and planted at the proper time. Varieties can be divided into two categories: softneck, sometimes called artichoke garlic (*A. sativum* var. *sativum*), and hardneck, or top setting, garlic (*A. sativum* var. *ophioscorodon*). Softneck varieties are favored by large commercial growers in California because they tend to be better keepers and produce more weight per plant. However, some softneck types are appropriate for gardens in the East and South. (Check seed catalogs for descriptions.) Hardneck garlic has a stronger "garlic" flavor and produces larger, easier-to-peel cloves.

CULTURE: Plant individual cloves 4 inches apart in the fall (tulip planting time). Mulch bed if the ground freezes to prevent plants from being heaved out of the soil. In the Deep South (Zones 8 and 9), refrigerate garlic for two weeks before planting.

HARVESTING: Lift bulbs in midsummer when the necks have yellowed.

VARIETIES: Softneck types include 'New York White' (for the Northeast), 'Italian Late' (for the West), and 'Chet's Italian' (for the Southeast). Hardnecks include 'German Extra Hardy' (Northeast), 'Spanish Roja' (West), and 'Russian Red' (Southeast).

## Kale (*Brassica oleracea*)

Kale is among the most nutritious of cultivated greens. Small leaves make wonderful salad greens, and large leaves can be steamed lightly before serving. Kale is both tolerant of cold and able to endure considerable heat.

CULTURE: Seeds can be sown in flats 6 to 8 weeks before the last expected frost and transplants set out when 5 to 6 weeks old. Seeds can also be sown directly in the garden at a depth of about ½ inch, 2 weeks before the last frost. Sow about one seed per inch and thin plants to stand about 10 inches apart. In the South and along the West Coast (Zones 7 through 9), kale can be grown in the spring and a second crop planted in late summer for fall and winter harvesting. Kale's flavor is enhanced by frost.

HARVESTING: Harvest as soon as leaves are 2 to 3 inches long.

VARIETIES: 'Winterbor' is a vigorous hybrid with curly, blue-green leaves. 'Dwarfed Blue Curled Scotch Vates' is an heirloom type, smaller but similar in growth. 'Red Russian', also called 'Ragged Jack' or 'Oak Leaf', is another heirloom with dark red stems and leaf veins.

## Leeks *(Allium porrum)*

This mild-flavored member of the onion family can endure cold winters and resume growth in the spring. In northern gardens (Zones 5 and 6), crops planted in late summer can provide greens the following spring when few other vegetables are available. In the South and along the West Coast (Zones 7 through 9), leeks will continue to grow through the winter. A few overwintered leeks left in the garden for the summer will produce tennis-ball-sized flowers that attract many beneficial insects.

CULTURE: Seed can be sown in flats 10 to 12 weeks before the last expected frost. Set out transplants 6 to 8 weeks after germination. Plant them deeply so only an inch or two of leaves stands above ground. Seed can also be planted directly in the garden, at a depth of about ¼ inch, 2 weeks before the last frost. Thin seedlings to stand about 6 inches apart. Stems can be blanched by hilling or by setting a 2-inch diameter tube over them.

VARIETIES: Leeks can be sorted into summer and winter varieties, with summer types usually thinner, lighter green, faster growing, and less cold-hardy. 'King Richard' and the heirloom 'Titan' are summer types. The heirloom 'Blue Solaise' and the hybrids 'Laura' and 'St. Victor' are cold-hardy.

## Lettuce *(Lactuca sativa)*

Lettuce is meant to be quick growing and fresh—attributes rarely found in the versions on supermarket shelves.

CULTURE: Sow seed indoors 6 to 8 weeks before the last expected frost. Transplant 4 to 6 weeks after germination, setting plants about 6 to 8 inches apart. Outdoors, sow seed as soon as the ground can be worked, at a depth of about ¼ inch. Sow a few feet of a row every two weeks until the onset of 80°F days. Plant again when the weather cools in the fall. With protection, lettuce will grow through the winter in many areas.

HARVESTING: Harvest by cutting off individual leaves. Or cut plants to ground level and let them resprout.

VARIETIES: Lettuces are often grouped in four categories based on their shape and growth: loose leaf, romaine, bibb or butterhead, and crisphead, with loose leaf and romaine being the most nutritious and crisphead the least. Many varieties have been bred to withstand hot weather, although all lettuces lose their agreeable flavor in prolonged heat. 'Red Grenoble' and 'Black Seeded Simpson' are dependable loose-leaf types. 'Parris Island Cos' is an upright, vase-shaped romaine, while 'Winter Density' is a romaine with curly, butterhead-type leaves. 'Buttercrunch' is a butterhead type bred for heat tolerance. 'Great Lakes' and 'Minetto' are two old crisphead varieties grown for their texture.

## Onions *(Allium cepa)*

Gardeners often grow onions from sets, but starting from seed offers a much wider selection of varieties, including large, mild onions not available in sets.

CULTURE: Sow seeds in flats 8 to 10 weeks before the last expected frost and set out after the last frost. Or seed directly in the garden as soon as the ground can be worked in the spring, planting 2 seeds per inch, ¼ to ½ inch deep. Thin seedlings to every 2 inches for medium-size onions, every 4 inches for large, sweet types. Weed the bed assiduously. In Zones 6 through 8, large 'Walla Walla' type onions can be planted in late summer for harvesting the following year.

HARVESTING: Harvest when tops have yellowed and toppled over.

VARIETIES: Onions are sensitive to day length, and to develop properly must be adapted to the latitude in which they are planted. Large, mild 'Granex' type hybrid varieties grown in Zones 7 through 9 will become only cocktail-sized onions in northern gardens. 'Copra' (yellow) and 'Mambo' (red) are excellent storing varieties in Zones 5 and 6.

## Parsley (*Petroselinum crispum*)

Parsley's tender leaves belie its tough constitution. It can withstand very cold winters and resume growth in the spring. It can also endure considerable summer heat if attentively watered and mulched.

CULTURE: Seeds can take up to 3 weeks to germinate. Soaking overnight before planting hastens the process. Plant as soon as the ground can be worked in the spring. A second crop sown in late summer or early fall will make slow growth in Zones 7 through 9 and provide a rich source of iron and vitamins A and C in winter salads.

VARIETIES: 'Italian Dark Green' has flat, glossy foliage. 'Triple Curled' and 'Forest Green' are two frilly-leaved varieties.

## Peas (*Pisum sativum*)

The onset of hot weather sends peas into a sharp decline, and so early planting is the key to success.

CULTURE: Plant peas about 3 weeks before the last expected frost (seeds planted earlier tend to rot where spring is damp and cool) so they can be harvested before daytime temperatures settle into the upper 80s. Dusting seed with a bacterial inoculant can increase yields if they are to be planted in ground where peas have not grown for at least 4 years. Set fence, trellis, or small tree branches in place to support the climbing vines, then plant seed at least ½ inch deep every 2 to 3 inches. Sow a fall crop about 2 months before first expected hard frost.

HARVESTING: Harvest shelling peas and snap, or edible pod, peas when pods are rounded and full. Pick snow peas while pods are flat. Picking stimulates plants to set more pods.

VARIETIES: 'Maestro' and 'Knight' are consistently among the earliest shelling varieties. 'Sugar Daddy' is a stringless snap type. 'Oregon Sugar Pod II' is a snow pea with resistance to powdery mildew, pea virus, and common wilt, three troubling pea diseases.

## Potatoes (*Solanum tuberosum*)

The long, moderate summer days of Maine are well suited for potatoes. In hot weather the plants cannot store starch, and so the tubers do not bulk up. Potatoes can be grown in the South (Zones 7 through 9) if planted from January into early March. In the North, plant in April or May, about 4 weeks before the last expected frost.

CULTURE: Sow small whole potatoes or pieces that contain at least one "eye." Plant pieces 6 inches deep and potatoes will form underground. Or plant near the surface and hill or mulch vines as they grow. Space plants every 12 inches.

HARVESTING: Small potatoes can be harvested in about 8 weeks. Dig main crop after vines have withered.

VARIETIES: 'Dark Red Norland' is an early, red-skinned variety. 'Carola' is a buttery, yellow-fleshed, midseason type. 'Green Mountain' and 'Kennebec' are late-season, white-fleshed types.

### Radishes (*Raphanus sativus*)

Children enjoy growing radishes—the seeds germinate so quickly that youthful patience is hardly strained.

CULTURE: Southern gardeners (Zones 7 through 9) can plant radishes as a fall to spring crop. In the North (Zones 4 through 6), seed can be sown in the spring, 2 to 3 weeks before the last expected frost. Plant in a 2-inch band with seeds about ½ inch deep and ½ inch apart. Keeping plants well watered helps prolong radish's mild flavor.

HARVESTING: Begin harvesting in 3 to 4 weeks.

VARIETIES: 'Cherry Belle' has a classic radish shape, with red skin and white flesh. 'Valentine' is an heirloom variety with reverse coloring: white skin and red flesh. 'Icicle' is an elongated variety, white inside and out.

### Spinach (*Spinacia oleracea*)

Spinach can be a fall, winter, and spring crop in southern gardens (Zones 7 through 9), and a four-season crop in parts of Zone 6. In Zone 5, spinach will often overwinter with protection and resume growth in the spring. It goes to seed as the summer advances.

CULTURE: Plant a spring crop 2 to 3 weeks before the last expected frost. Sow seed every inch or so, about ½ inch deep. Thin plants to stand every 3 to 4 inches. To maintain a steady supply of young leaves, plant successive crops every 2 weeks until daytime temperatures settle in the upper 80s.

VARIETIES: 'Tyee' is a bolt-resistant savoy, or curly-leaved hybrid. 'Melody' is a savoy type well suited for spring and fall. 'Giant Nobel' is an heirloom with large, smooth leaves.

### Turnip (*Brassica rapa*)

Turnips are a spring and fall crop even north to Zone 5. Their flavor declines when daytime temperatures settle into the upper 80s.

CULTURE: Plant seed about 4 weeks before the last expected frost. Sow ½ inch deep, 1 seed per inch. Gradually thin plants to every 4 inches. Plant a second crop in midsummer (Zones 5 and 6) or late summer and fall (Zones 7 through 9) for fall or winter harvest.

HARVESTING: First plantings will be ready to harvest in about 5 weeks, when the roots are about 1 inch across. The young greens and roots can be added to salads or soups or steamed. Harvest the rest of the spring-sown crop before the roots exceed 4 inches across.

VARIETIES: 'Tokyo Cross' is an early-maturing hybrid recommended for a spring crop. 'Purple-Top White Globe' is an old, open-pollinated variety that takes about 3 weeks longer to mature than the hybrid.

## Warm-Season Vegetables

### Bush and Pole Beans (*Phaseolus vulgaris*)

For best seed germination and early, vigorous growth, plant beans after the daytime soil temperature has risen above 60°F. Plants that get off to a quick start are much less susceptible to insects and disease.

CULTURE: Sow bush bean seeds about 1 inch deep, every 2 inches. Thin plants to every 6 inches. Allow 24 to 36 inches between rows. Pole bean seeds can be planted 1 inch deep, every 3 inches—thinned to 6 inches—along a 6-foot-high fence or trellis or planted in a circle around single poles or teepees made of 3 or 4 poles. Pole beans take up more space but bear more heavily per square foot than bush beans do. Make successive plantings every 2 to 3 weeks through midsummer.

HARVESTING: Harvest when pods are full but still relatively smooth, before the seeds become large and pronounced. Frequent picking stimulates plants to set more pods.

VARIETIES: 'Jade' is a long-season, green bush type. 'Blue Lake 274', another green bush type, ripens its crop all at once, making it ideal for canning or freezing. 'Sunrae' is a yellow or wax bean bred for earliness. The heirloom 'Kentucky Wonder' climbs to 7 feet on poles or a trellis.

## Sweet Corn (*Zea mays*)

In small gardens corn may require too much space to justify its inclusion. Each stalk yields only 1 or 2, or occasionally 3, mature ears.

CULTURE: For uniform pollination, garden corn is generally planted in a block of 4 rows 30 inches apart, or 2 beds of 3 rows each, or in hills or clusters of 4 to 5 plants—so that no matter what direction the wind is blowing, pollen will be blown from the tassels to the corn silk. A soil temperature above 65°F is very beneficial to germination. At cooler temperatures seed may rot. Sow seed 1 inch deep, every 3 to 4 inches, and thin plants to every 10 to 12 inches.

HARVESTING: Harvest when the outer strands of silk are brown and drying.

VARIETIES: 'Early Sunglow', with yellow kernels, and 'Platinum Lady', with white kernels, are early varieties. 'Honey and Cream' and 'Honey 'n Pearl' are midseason hybrids with yellow and white kernels. The heirloom

'Golden Bantam' is a reliable midseason yellow-kernel type.

## Cucumbers (*Cucumis sativus*)

Vining-type cucumbers are willing climbers and make efficient use of garden space when trained to a trellis. Trellis-grown plants generally produce more and straighter fruit than cucumbers that ramble across the ground.

CULTURE: For an early harvest, begin plants indoors two weeks before the last expected frost and set them out 4 weeks after germination, spaced 12 inches apart. Let the central leader grow to the top of the trellis, then pinch it off to encourage lateral growth.

HARVESTING: Harvest finger-sized cukes as "cornichons" or let them grow larger for slicing in sandwiches or salads. Harvest often. Unpicked plants cease to set fruit.

VARIETIES: 'Sweet Success', 'Streamliner', 'Early Pride', and the heirloom 'Windermoor Wonder' are among the most flavorful salad cukes, along with the Middle Eastern cultivars 'Kidma' and 'Sweet Alphee'. Compact bush-type plants do not send out long vines, and offer an alternative to trellising. 'Salad Bush' and 'Bush Champion' are two productive varieties.

## Eggplant (*Solanum melongena*)

For gardeners in Zone 5 and north, the season often seems 2 weeks too short to ripen large eggplants. Thin, elongated Oriental varieties and "baby" types have a greater chance of maturing than the classic oval fruits.

CULTURE: Sow seeds in flats about 6 weeks before the last expected frost. Keep soil about 85°F until seeds germinate, then allow the temperature to drop to the low 70s. Set out transplants at 8 weeks, spacing them 18 inches apart. Sheltering them for 2 to 3 weeks under a lightweight row cover will hasten their growth.

VARIETIES: 'Little Fingers', 'Bambino', and the white-skinned hybrid 'Osterei' bear small fruit well suited for stir frying or grilling. Gardeners in long-season Zone 6 and south have the luxury of enjoying such classic large varieties as the heirloom 'Black Beauty', with its huge, dark purple fruits.

## Melons (*Cucumis melo* and *Citrullus lanatus*)

Melons are meant to bask in the sun, ripening slowly in simmering heat. Gardeners in Zones 7 through 9 can confidently select cantaloupe (*Cucumis melo*) and watermelon (*Citrullus lanatus*) varieties for size and flavor, while gardeners to the north must carefully calculate days to maturity and acknowledge that ripening melons in any year is a roll of the dice.

CULTURE: In Zones 5 and 6, start seed in warm flats (soil temperature about 85°F) 6 weeks before the last expected frost. Spread out plastic mulch a few days before transplanting to warm the garden soil. Handle transplants carefully to avoid disturbing the roots. Set plants about 30 inches apart and cover with lightweight fabric for a few weeks. Remove when flowers appear to allow bees to pollinate.

HARVESTING: Harvest cantaloupe and the smaller Charentais melons when the skin turns a buff yellow and the stem slips easily from the vine. Pick watermelon when the patch of skin touching the ground turns yellow.

VARIETIES: 'Sweet Granite' and the hybrid 'Sweet 'n Early' are early cantaloupes for northern gardens, although their flavor does not always meet the grower's expectations. Gardeners in Zones 7 through 9 can grow large, slow-ripening varieties such as 'Ambrosia'. The watermelons 'Garden Baby' and 'Fordhook' are small, round, comparatively short-season types. The classic Fourth of July picnic watermelon is the heirloom 'Charleston Gray', with its oblong fruits weighing up to 35 pounds.

## Okra (*Abelmoschus esculentus*)

Okra stands as a horticultural reminder that despite the homogenizing influence of television, the country retains some regional distinctions. A common crop south of Zone 6, this member of the hollyhock family is only beginning to gain a following in the North.

CULTURE: Seeds can be planted in pots or flats about 4 weeks before the last expected frost. Rubbing the tough seedcoat with a file or sandpaper will speed germination. Set out transplants 2 to 3 weeks after the last frost, spaced 18 inches apart.

HARVESTING: Harvest the tapered seed pods when they are 2 inches long. Continue harvesting every day or two and plants will continue to set new pods until cold weather.

VARIETIES: The hybrid 'Annie Oakley II' is often described as the earliest, best variety for northern gardeners. 'Burgundy' and 'Clemson Spineless', which each have deep red pods, and the heirloom 'Perkins' are right at home in many southern gardens.

## Peppers (*Capsicum annuum*)

Beginning gardeners may assume that sweet red peppers or red chili peppers are a different variety from green peppers; but, in fact, the red skin is a sign of maturity. Given time and a reprieve from disease, almost every pepper will trade its green cast for red or orange or yellow or purple, depending on the variety. Bringing peppers to maturity takes several weeks beyond the green stage and requires an early start in gardens north of Zone 7.

CULTURE: Sow seeds in flats or pots of warm potting soil (80°F) 6 weeks before the last expected frost. Set out transplants about 8 weeks after germination, ideally when plants have buds but no open flowers. Space seedlings every 18 inches. As plants mature, tie them loosely to stakes to keep them upright and give them uniform exposure to sunlight.

HARVESTING: Harvest when fruits are green or let them reach their mature color, but check them a few times a week for signs of softness or disease.

VARIETIES: In short-season gardens, small-fruited varieties like 'Jingle Bells' have the best chance of fully ripening. Large, blocky, bell varieties also worth trying are 'North Star', 'Gypsy', and 'Golden Bell'. In areas with longer seasons, try large bells such as 'California Wonder' and 'Big Bertha'. Curved Italian types, known as bull's horn peppers, are widely available in varieties like 'Corno di Toro', 'Red Marconi', and 'Italia'. There are dozens of varieties of chili peppers ranging in flavor from mild to hazardous. 'Habanero', 'Serrano', 'Tabasco', and 'Cayenne' are all capable of turning a mild taco sauce into an unforgettable eating experience.

## Pumpkins (*Cucurbita pepo*)

Breeders have taken new pumpkin varieties in two directions, introducing several palm-sized pumpkins as well as ever more mammoth types. For small gardens or short growing seasons, diminutive pumpkins are quick to mature and can be grown on a trellis. Giant pumpkins need rambling vines and an extensive canopy of leaves to collect enough of the sun's energy to fuel the growth of the big fruit.

CULTURE: About 4 weeks before the last expected frost, start seed indoors in large containers to allow unimpeded root development—gallon plastic jugs work well. Transplants can be set out 5 to 6 weeks after germination. To protect plant roots, slit the container and slide the seedling into the planting hole, rather than lifting it out of the container. Space large, rambling varieties at least 6 feet apart. Small varieties or so-called bush types, which do not set out long rambling vines, can be spaced every 30 inches.

HARVESTING: Harvest when fruits develop uniform color. Protect them from frost.

VARIETIES: Large, rambling varieties include 'Howden', 'Big Max', and the heirloom 'Connecticut Field'. 'Jack Be Little' and 'Baby Bear' are small varieties.

## Squash (*Cucurbita* species)

Squash, or cucurbits, comprise a large botanical group with members ranging from the fast-growing and prolific zucchini to the huge and slow-growing Hubbard types weighing upward of 20 pounds apiece.

CULTURE: All cucurbits are frost-tender and need warm soil to germinate, ideally above 70°F. Instead of waiting for the garden soil to warm, growers in Zones 4 and 5 can start plants indoors 2 weeks before the last expected frost and set plants out when they are 5 to 6 weeks. Summer types—zucchini, yellow squash, and pattypan—can be spaced every 24 inches. Winter squash—acorn, buttercup, butternut, and Hubbard, with its rambling vines—can be spaced 36 inches apart or grown 3 plants to a hill with the hills 5 to 6 feet apart.

HARVESTING: Begin harvesting summer types when squash is 4 or 5 inches long, or across in the case of pattypan varieties. Winter types can be picked when the skin has darkened to a uniform tone. Leave about 1 inch of stem when cutting winter squash. Protect squash from frost.

VARIETIES: The hybrid zucchini 'Tipo' and the older varieties 'Long Cocozelle' and 'Black Beauty' are very productive. 'Yellow Crookneck' is highly regarded for its flavor. Among winter squash, the hybrid 'Table Ace' is a very early and long-keeping acorn type. In areas with a prevalence of squash vine borers, grubs that bore into vines and can kill plants, butternut types are a good choice because the vines are hard and resist borers. 'Waltham' is an old, reliable butternut variety. 'Nicklow's Delight' is a hybrid butternut with smaller, earlier maturing squash and shorter vines.

## Tomatoes (*Lycopersicon esculentum*)

Tomatoes need heat as well as a long season. Moderate weather even well into September will not ripen big-fruited varieties as well as a spate of summer days with temperatures in the 80s. Gardeners along the upper West Coast and to the east in Zones 4 and part of 5, where conditions are not ideal for tomatoes, can use an early start and season-extending techniques discussed above to bring in a respectable harvest.

CULTURE: Tomatoes can be planted indoors about 6 weeks before the last expected frost and transplanted when 8 weeks old. Keep soil about 75°F until seeds sprout, then allow temperatures to drop to the upper 60s. If indoor space is at a premium, start seed in flats and transplant the most promising seedlings to 4-inch containers. Tomato growers have two general choices: determinate or indeterminate types. Determinate plants are compact and ripen most of their fruit within the space of several days. Indeterminate plants ramble and ripen fruits over several weeks. Many tomato growers assert that indeterminate types compensate with flavor for what they consume in garden space. Transplant determinate varieties every 18 to 24 inches, indeterminate varieties every 24 inches if pruned and staked or trellised. Pruning involves removing sideshoots, or suckers, and encouraging the plant to concentrate energy on its fruit. Unpruned, unstaked plants can be spaced every 30 to 36 inches.

HARVESTING: If the skin of a tomato is losing any of its smoothness, pick it right away, even if the shoulders are not yet colored.

VARIETIES: 'Prudens Purple', 'Brandywine', and the hybrid 'Big Beef' are indeterminate types. 'Celebrity' and the hybrid cherry types 'Sweet 100' and 'Sweet Million' are determinate varieties. Popular paste tomatoes include the indeterminate 'San Marzano' and the determinates 'Roma' and 'Viva Italia'.

## Further Reading

Cutler, Karan Davis, ed. *Salad Gardens: Gourmet Greens and Beyond*. Brooklyn, N.Y.: Brooklyn Botanic Garden, 1995.

Cutler, Karan Davis, ed. *Tantalizing Tomatoes: Smart Tips and Tasty Picks for Gardeners Everywhere*. Brooklyn, N.Y.: Brooklyn Botanic Garden, 1997.

Damrosch, Barbara. *The Garden Primer*. New York: Workman Publishing, 1988.

Ogden, Shepherd. *Step by Step Organic Vegetable Gardening.* New York: HarperCollins, 1992.

Raver, Anne, ed. *A New Look at Vegetables.* Brooklyn, N.Y.: Brooklyn Botanic Garden, 1993.

Swain, Roger. *The Practical Gardener.* New York: Henry Holt and Company, 1991.

Turner, Carole, ed. *Kitchen Gardens: Beyond the Vegetable Patch.* Brooklyn, N.Y.: Brooklyn Botanic Garden, 1998.

# HERBS

The word "herb" originated from the Latin *herba.* The word was written "erb" until the early sixteenth century, when the Latin *h* was reattached. The *h* was silent until 1800. Since then, the English have pronounced it *herb,* while Americans still say *erb.*

An herb is broadly defined as a plant with a fleshy stem that dies to the ground in winter. However, most people think of herbs in terms of their secondary definition: a plant that is used especially for medicine, scent, or flavoring. Herbs come in a variety of shapes, colors, and sizes, and many today are grown primarily for their ornamental rather than their utilitarian value. On the other hand, herbs continue to be used for cooking, crafts, dyeing, and making medicines, perfumes, teas, flavorings, and a host of other items.

## Herb Garden Design

There are numerous ways of designing a garden with herbs. They can be grown in a simple plot by themselves, in an informal flower border, among vegetables in a kitchen garden, in a formal knot garden, in containers, in raised beds, or even on a sunny windowsill. In general, herb gardens should be situated close to the house for easy access, especially if the fresh herbs are used in cooking.

Below are some of the more common types of herb garden designs. Some modern designs are descendants of ancient Roman and Greek kitchen gardens, medieval cloister and physic gardens, or Colonial American kitchen gardens. Although informal, free-flowing designs are more popular today, the knot garden and other types of formal design still have their place, especially in smaller spaces.

Theme gardens group herbs by certain characteristics. For instance, historic physic gardens were planted with herbs used for medicinal purposes. Pleasure gardens stimulated the five senses with herbs that were pleasurable to see, smell, taste, and touch; a fountain or other water feature was generally used to provide soothing sounds. There are also tactile gardens, fragrance gardens, children's gardens, native-plant gardens, and other specialized types.

### Knot Gardens

Knot gardens reached their greatest popularity during the sixteenth- and seventeenth-century Renaissance period in England. The "knot" was formed by planting bands of neatly clipped herbs in interlocking, knotlike patterns. In a closed knot, the spaces between the bands are filled with low-growing ground covers. In an open knot, the spaces are filled with mulch, gravel, or some other hardscape material. The variety of patterns is virtually endless.

Knot gardens are particularly effective if they can be viewed from above. They are appropriate for both large and small spaces. A knot can also form the centerpiece of a larger garden.

Knot gardens require constant maintenance to keep an attractive appearance. The plants chosen should ideally be dense, slow-growing, compact varieties that accept formal clipping. They should also have attractive, interesting foliage color and texture. Some suitable plants are thymes, dwarf lavender, germander, dwarf santolina, compact rue, small artemisias, dwarf basil, parsley, dwarf winter savory, hyssop, and rosemary. In larger knot gardens, dwarf conifers and other evergreens (boxwood, holly, yew) will help preserve the framework of the garden through winter.

## Kitchen Gardens in the Cottage Garden Style

Kitchen gardens have been cultivated for thousands of years, from ancient Egypt, Rome, and Greece to Asia, Africa, and the Americas. These gardens were grown for a practical reason: to produce plants for food and other utilitarian purposes.

The design was often practical as well. In seventeenth- to nineteenth-century Europe, kitchen gardens were frequently enclosed within walls to protect against thievery and provide a warmer microclimate for the plants. Others were surrounded by grapevines or espaliered fruit trees, thus maximizing the growing space. In Colonial America, vegetables, flowers, and herbs were all mixed together

in the same bed. In all these cases, the four-square design was a common layout. This design, consisting of four beds in simple geometric shapes (not necessarily square), divided by crisscrossing pathways, provided for ease of cultivation and harvest. A large four-square garden might have a fountain or knot garden at the center of the intersecting paths; four squares might be divided into even smaller beds.

What has been called the cottage garden is simply another version of the four-square design. At one time, every English peasant's cottage had a four-square garden in the front yard to provide fruit, vegetables, and herbs for the family. Each quadrant of the garden was devoted to a different purpose. Today's cottage garden is more like that of Colonial America, with vegetables, flowers, and herbs all mixed together. Herbs are recognized for their ornamental qualities as well as their practical uses, and they lend their flowers and foliage to the overall design rather than being planted in straight rows.

## Raised Beds

There are several benefits to planting herbs in raised beds. Used in culinary herb gardens, raised beds make harvesting easier because they require less bending over. A raised bed also helps provide good drainage, which virtually all herbs require, and warms up more quickly in spring. Raised beds can be built of stone, brick, landscape timbers, cement block, or a variety of other materials. If the wall is wide enough, the gardener can use it as a seat while planting, weeding, and harvesting. Raised beds are frequently rectangular, but they can be any shape as long as the herbs in the center of the bed are accessible.

## Container Gardens

Containers are an ideal place for herbs because they usually have good drainage and seldom stay waterlogged. Many herbs will continue to grow in containers for two or three years if over-wintered indoors in cold climates. Container herb gardens are especially helpful to those with very little gardening space, such as apartment and townhouse dwellers, but even those with large properties may want a few pots of herbs to add interest to outdoor beds.

A single pot of culinary herbs can provide enough clippings for an entire growing season, as long as the container is large enough and planted with a good variety of herbs. With continuous clipping, the plants should not outgrow the pot too quickly. When planting a container, a simple rule of thumb is to position trailing herbs around the edges so that they will spill over the sides of the pot, and plant medium-sized and taller herbs in the center of the pot. The container itself can stand alone as a specimen, act as an accent within a larger garden or a grouping of smaller containers, or enliven a sunny spot by the kitchen door.

For a formal effect, some herbs can be trained or clipped into a standard or topiary in a container. These living sculptures usually occupy a place of honor in the garden, such as the center of a knot garden or the intersection of two paths. Good candidates for topiaries or standards are scented geraniums, rosemary, bay, lavender, hyssop, lemon verbena, and sweet myrtle.

For more on gardening in containers, see pages 235 and 493.

### Herbs for Containers

Because containers tend to dry out quickly, herbs that can tolerate dryness and drought will be most successful. Aggressive herbs like mint and lemon balm should not be mixed with other herbs in a pot, as they tend to crowd out the other plants. A container should always have a drainage hole at the bottom, and should be filled with a lightweight, soilless medium. Mix a slow-release fertilizer into the medium before planting. Water containers daily during hot spells unless rain is sufficient, and fertilize regularly. The following herbs are good candidates for containers.

Artemisia
Basil, sweet
Bay, or true laurel
Bee balm, or Oswego tea
Calendula, or pot marigold
Catmint
Chervil
Chives
Comfrey
Coriander, cilantro, or Chinese parsley
Dill
Feverfew
Geranium, scented
Germander
Hyssop
Lady's mantle
Lemon balm
Lemongrass
Lemon verbena
Mints
Marjoram, pot
Marjoram, sweet
Myrtle, sweet
Oregano, or wild marjoram
Parsley
Perilla, purple
Rosemary
Sage
Santolina

Savory, summer
Sweet cicely
Sweet woodruff
Tarragon, French
Thyme

# Herbs for Special Landscape Treatment

## Shady Areas

Few culinary herbs thrive in shade. Most are Mediterranean natives adapted to a hot, dry climate and thin, alkaline soil. Only a handful of herbs can tolerate full shade, although some do prefer light to partial shade. Most should be planted in shade only if they are being grown for their foliage, since herbs generally do not flower well (or produce many seeds) except in sun. Also, since most herbs need good drainage, it is best to plant them in raised beds or containers if they must be in a cool, moist, shady area. This list includes herbs that prefer some degree of shade.

Angelica
Bay, sweet
Bee balm
Burnet
Calamint
Catnip
Chervil
Comfrey
Crocus, saffron
Geranium, peppermint
Heliotrope
Lady's mantle
Lemon balm
Lovage
Mints

Parsley
Perilla, purple
Sorrel, French
Sweet cicely
Sweet woodruff
Tansy
Valerian
Violet, sweet

## Ground Covers

A few herbs are appropriate as ground covers or herbal lawns. Some can even tolerate light foot traffic.

Chamomile, Roman
Comfrey, ground cover
Lady's bedstraw, or yellow bedstraw
Lady's mantle
Lamb's ears
Pennyroyal, true
Sweet cicely
Sweet woodruff
Tansy, curly
Thyme

## Edges and Hedges

Edging or hedging plants help keep the bed looking neat and unify a planting. They also define the shape of garden beds and pathways. A formal edge is composed of one or two types of herbs, usually compact or clipped tightly. An informal edge has many species that creep, crawl, or flop (for example, thyme). In both types of edges, try to repeat common traits (such as color and texture) throughout.

Basil 'Spicy Globe'
Catmint
Chives

Germander
Hyssop
Lady's mantle
Lavender, dwarf
Parsley, curly
Pinks
Rosemary
Sage
Santolina, compact green
Savory, dwarf winter
Thyme
Violet, sweet

## Growing Herbs

Herbs are generally easy to grow. Most are hardy perennials, but even tender perennials can be overwintered indoors. Many popular herbs are native to hot, dry areas of Mediterranean Europe. These plants do best with 6 to 8 hours of sun each day, well-drained soil, little fertilizing, and some spring pruning for renewal. In areas where the ground freezes in winter, they need mulching or other protection. In arid regions, they require summer watering. Herbs are seldom bothered by pests and diseases. There are exceptions to these rules; for instance, many native American woodland herbs perform well in deep shade.

Herbs can be propagated in a variety of ways. Seed propagation is common, especially for annuals and biennials. However, seed for some plants is difficult to find, and the amount of seed in a packet frequently produces more plants than one can use. Some herbs are easier to grow from cuttings or by root division. It is best to divide herbs in spring so the plants have enough time to reestablish before cold weather arrives. If propagating from cuttings, take 1 to 3 inches of new growth in spring, and root in

sand or vermiculite. Some herbs, such as sweet woodruff and French tarragon, are often propagated from root cuttings rather than stem cuttings. Layering is a propagation technique not commonly used with herbs, but a few (as noted in the Encyclopedia of Herbs, below) are increased in this way. For more on propagation, see page 474.

## Harvesting and Preserving Herbs for Culinary Purposes

### Leaves

For best flavor, most herb leaves should be harvested when the flower buds are just beginning to open. An ideal time to harvest is in the early morning after a number of fair days have passed. A perennial herb can be cut back one- to two-thirds of its height; an annual, to 3 or 4 inches. The leaves should be handled gently and allowed good air circulation to prevent bruising and deterioration. It is important to use fresh herbs quickly because the oils in the leaves are volatile. Cut away unnecessary parts, and wash the leaves in warm water (never hot or cold). Rinse several times, lay the leaves on a towel, and pat dry.

Fresh herbs are best but are not always available. Herbs can be preserved in oil, in vinegars, and by freezing. Another way to preserve some herbs is by drying. To dry, wash leaves quickly after clipping and pat dry. Place in a single layer on a screen; leave the screen in a warm, dry place indoors for four or five days, stirring the leaves once a day. Leaves can also be dried in a 104°F oven, or even in a microwave. Another method is to tie herbs in small bunches and hang them upside down. This method takes about a week, and the results will be less satisfactory than if the leaves are dried on screens.

When dry, leaves should be stored in airtight containers in a cool, dark place. Dried herb leaves are three times stronger than fresh ones, and the flavor should last for at least a year.

## Flowers

Herb blossoms are usually harvested at the moment they come into full bloom. The blossoms should be used fresh, or dried and stored in the same manner as herb leaves.

## Roots

Herb roots have the best flavor in spring and fall, when the plant is inactive. Dig up the roots, scrape them, and wash them thoroughly. If they are to be dried, cut them into pieces and lay on racks in a warm, dry room for about six weeks. Turn the roots twice a week until dry, then place in airtight storage containers. A root is dry when it can be snapped easily. Some herb roots can be used fresh, candied, or cooked and eaten as a vegetable.

## Seeds

The seed heads of most herbs are harvested when the stalks are dry and the seeds ripe. Clip the seed heads into a paper bag or paper-lined basket, and spread out in a warm, dry room for five or six days. When seeds are dry, loosen them gently from their pods or stems, remove chaff, and leave the seeds in the drying room for another week to 10 days, stirring them often. Store dry seeds in airtight jars.

# Encyclopedia of Herbs

In the following encyclopedia, herbs are listed alphabetically by common name. Included is information on plant type (perennial, annual, biennial), cultural needs, and practical uses, as well as miscellaneous facts. For each entry there is also specific information on growing, harvesting, and preserving, if the plant's requirements differ from the general guidelines above. Zone numbers refer to the USDA Hardiness Zone Map on page 30.

### Angelica *(Angelica archangelica)*
Apiaceae (Umbelliferae; parsley or carrot family). Biennial. Zone 4. Native to mountainous areas of northern countries such as Iceland, Greenland, and Scandinavia. Six feet tall (in flower). White flower spike.
CULTURE: Partial shade. Moderately moist soils. Cool temperatures.
PROPAGATION: Seeds short-lived; plant immediately after harvesting.
GARDEN USES: Bold accent, background plant, focal point.
HERBAL USES: Culinary, confectionery, perfumery, medicinal.
HARVESTING: Harvest roots and leaves in second year; seeds in late summer.
OTHER VARIETIES OR SPECIES: *A. atropurpurea* is a native American species.

### Anise *(Pimpinella anisum)*
Apiaceae (Umbelliferae; parsley or carrot family). Annual. Native to Mediterranean regions, Russia, Egypt. Grows 2 feet tall. Sprawling. Finely cut leaves. Small, whitish flowers in flat clusters.
CULTURE: Full sun.
PROPAGATION: Seed.
HERBAL USES: Culinary, flavoring, medicinal.

## Anise Hyssop, Giant Blue Hyssop, or Licorice Mint *(Agastache foeniculum)*

Labiatae (mint family). Tender perennial. Zone 8. Native to eastern Asia, North America. Grows 2½ to 4 feet tall. Anise-scented leaves and flowers. Abundant, long-lasting lavender flowers June to August; attractive to honeybees.

CULTURE: Full sun or partial shade. Withstands extreme heat. May need pruning and/or staking.

PROPAGATION: Seed, cuttings, division. Will self-sow.

GARDEN USES: Back of border.

HERBAL USES: Culinary, beverages.

## Artemisia, or Wormwood *(Artemisia* species)

Asteraceae (Compositae; sunflower family). Perennial. Zones 2 to 9, depending on species. Native to dry areas of Northern Hemisphere. Tough, carefree, fast-growing; 2 to 4 feet tall. Shrublike or spreading. Aromatic gray-green, silver, or blue-green foliage; ornamental, often lacy or feathery. 'Silver King' and 'Silver Queen' can spread aggressively.

CULTURE: May need staking in shade. Cut back woody stems in fall to encourage new growth.

PROPAGATION: Division, cuttings in early spring, layering in late summer.

GARDEN USES: Versatile.

HERBAL USES: Medicinal, crafts, moth deterrent.

## Basil, Sweet *(Ocimum basilicum)*

Lamiaceae (Labiatae; mint family). Annual. Native to India. Cultivated for centuries. Grows 1 to 2 feet tall; upright, bushy form. Rounded or ruffled leaves, spicy scent, light green, yellow-green, or purple. Flowers in white or purple-pink July to August.

CULTURE: Full sun or partial shade. Intolerant of cold, wet soils. Pinch regularly throughout summer.

PROPAGATION: Seed, cuttings.

PESTS: Japanese beetles, slugs.

GARDEN USES: Containers. Miniature basils for edging, window-box plants, or miniature knot gardens.

HERBAL USES: Culinary, perfumery, medicinal, cut flower.

HARVESTING: Needs a few weeks more drying time than some other herbs.

OTHER VARIETIES OR SPECIES: *O. basilicum* 'Dark Opal' (purple leaves); *O. basilicum* 'Spicy Globe' (dwarf form); *O. sanctum* (common name: holy basil).

## Bay, or True Laurel *(Laurus nobilis)*

Lauraceae (laurel family). Evergreen woody tree in Zones 9 and 10; tender perennial in colder areas. True laurel used for victory wreaths in classical Greek and Roman times. Native to Mediterranean regions, where it grows up to 40 feet tall. Reaches 4 to 10 feet elsewhere. Sometimes called sweet bay. Glossy green leaves. Tiny yellow flowers. Purplish black berries.

CULTURE: Filtered light. Protect from direct sun. Rich, moist soil. Cool (45° to 50°F), sunny location indoors over winter in cold climates. Prune off suckers.

PROPAGATION: Stem cuttings in late summer; may take several months to root.

PESTS: Scale (indoors).

GARDEN USES: Containers. Use as an accent, specimen, formal standard, or topiary.

HERBAL USES: Culinary, perfumery, crafts, medicinal.

## Bee Balm, or Oswego Tea *(Monarda didyma)*

Lamiaceae (Labiatae; mint family). Perennial.

Zone 4. Native to Canada, United States. Up to 4 feet tall. Mint-scented leaves. Scarlet flowers attract bees and hummingbirds; other varieties in deep red, violet, pink, and white. Related to mint.

CULTURE: Partial shade. Moist, acidic soil. Withstands heat but not high humidity. Do not plant too close together.

PROPAGATION: Division in early spring (every 3 to 5 years), seed.

PESTS/DISEASES: Powdery mildew, rust.

GARDEN USES: Showy flowers. Middle or back of border, raised beds, containers, naturalized plantings.

HERBAL USES: Tea, flavorings.

OTHER VARIETIES OR SPECIES: *M. citriodora* (lemon bergamot).

## Borage (*Borago officinalis*)

Boraginaceae (borage family). Annual. Native to Mediterranean regions. Grows 1 to 2 feet tall. Coarse, hairy leaves. Star-shaped flowers in blue, purple, and white are attractive to bees.

CULTURE: Sun to partial shade. Slightly moist soil. Cool temperatures.

PROPAGATION: Seed. Self-sowing.

HERBAL USES: Culinary, beverages, medicinal.

## Burnet, Salad (*Sanguisorba minor*, formerly classified as *Poterium sanguisorba*)

Rosaceae (rose family). Perennial. Zone 5. Native to Europe, North Africa, Asia. Grows 2 to 3 feet tall in flower. Mounding. Blue-green foliage; stays green into winter. Small purplish flowers May to June.

CULTURE: Partial shade. Intolerant of wet, compacted soils, especially in winter. Tolerates heat but not humidity.

PROPAGATION: Seed, division.

GARDEN USES: Front of border.

HERBAL USES: Culinary, beverages.

HARVESTING: Leaves are best when young.

## Calamint (*Calamintha nepeta*)

Lamiaceae (Labiatae; mint family). Perennial. Zone 6. Native to Europe. Grows 1 to 2 feet tall. Evergreen in warm climates. Aromatic. Lavender flowers. Related to mint.

CULTURE: Sun to partial shade. Moderate moisture.

HERBAL USES: Medicinal, fragrance.

## Calendula, or Pot Marigold (*Calendula officinalis*)

Asteraceae (Compositae; sunflower family). Annual. Native to Mediterranean regions. Grows to 2 feet tall. Yellow, gold, or orange flowers in early spring.

CULTURE: Full sun, cool temperatures.

PROPAGATION: Seed. Self-sowing.

GARDEN USES: Showy flowers.

HERBAL USES: Culinary, dye, medicinal.

HARVESTING: Cut flowers before last one opens. Dry in the shade.

## Caraway (*Carum carvi*)

Apiaceae (Umbelliferae; parsley or carrot family). Perennial or biennial. Zone 3. Native to Europe, western Asia. Grows to 2 feet tall. Small white flowers. Feathery foliage; more attractive in second year, unsightly after bloom.

CULTURE: Cool temperatures. Difficult to transplant.

PROPAGATION: Seed. Self-sowing.

HERBAL USES: Culinary, beverages.

## Catmint (*Nepeta* x *faassenii* and *N. racemosa*, also known as *N. mussinii*)

Lamiaceae (Labiatae; mint family). Perennial. Zone 4. Native to Eurasia, Africa. *N.* x *faassenii* is a sterile hybrid (*N. racemosa* x *N. nepetella*) that grows to 2 feet tall. *N. racemosa* grows to 1 foot tall. Long-lasting blue flowers. Related to mint.

GARDEN USES: Edging (*N. racemosa*), borders, containers. Showy flowers.

HERBAL USES: Tea.

## Catnip (*Nepeta cataria*)

Lamiaceae (Labiatae; mint family). Perennial. Zone 3. Native to Europe, Asia. Grows 1.5 to 3 feet tall in flower. Gray-green foliage; minty fragrance. Irresistible to cats. White and purple flowers June to August.

CULTURE: Light, sandy soil. Tolerates heat. Easy to grow. Needs regular pruning and deadheading.

PROPAGATION: Division in spring.

HERBAL USES: Tea.

## Chamomile, Wild (*Matricaria recutita*)

Asteraceae (Compositae; sunflower family). Annual. Native to Europe, western Asia to India. Grows 1 to 2 feet tall. Spreads rapidly; weedy. Apple-scented leaves. Yellow-and-white daisylike flowers all summer.

PROPAGATION: Seed. Self-sowing.

GARDEN USES: Hard-to-cover areas.

HERBAL USES: Tea, medicinal.

## Chamomile, Roman (*Chamaemelum nobile,* formerly *Anthemis nobilis*)

Asteraceae (Compositae; sunflower family). Perennial. Zone 4. Native to Europe. Grows 2 to 6 inches tall; 12 inches tall when flowering. Low, sprawling. Fine-textured foliage. Small yellow-and-white daisylike flowers June to August. Fragrant.

CULTURE: Light, dry soil. Few flowers in rich soil. Low maintenance. Mulch in winter.

PROPAGATION: Seed, division, cuttings.

GARDEN USES: Pleasure gardens; fragrant lawn; ground cover; rock gardens.

HERBAL USES: Tea, medicinal.

## Chervil, or French Parsley (*Anthriscus cereifolium*)

Apiaceae (Umbelliferae; parsley or carrot family). Annual. Native to Europe, western Asia. Grows 1 to 2 feet tall. Resembles parsley; finely cut leaves. White flowers in umbels.

CULTURE: Partial shade. Moist soil. Cool temperatures. Remove flowers to encourage leaf growth.

PROPAGATION: Seed in early spring. Self-sowing.

GARDEN USES: Containers, window boxes.

HERBAL USES: Culinary.

## Chicory (*Cichorium intybus*)

Asteraceae (Compositae; sunflower family). Perennial. Zone 3. Native to Europe, Asia. Familiar plant along roadsides. Pale blue flowers along 2- to 3-foot-tall stems.

HERBAL USES: Culinary, beverages.

## Chives (*Allium schoenoprasum*)

Liliaceae (lily family). Perennial. Zone 5. Native to Europe, northern Asia, North America. Grows 12 to 15 inches tall. Grassy, upright clump. Lavender-pink flowers in June.

CULTURE: Moist soil. Tolerates heat. Low maintenance.

PROPAGATION: Seed, division.

GARDEN USES: Edging, low borders, small spaces, containers, raised beds. Interesting seed heads.

HERBAL USES: Culinary.

HARVESTING: Do not dry; preserve by freezing.

OTHER VARIETIES OR SPECIES: *A. tuberosum* (garlic chive).

## Comfrey (*Symphytum officinale*)

Boraginaceae (borage family). Perennial. Zone 5. Native to Europe, western Asia. Grows 2 to 4 feet tall. Large, coarse, dark green leaves. Flowers on arching stems May to June; pink, blue, purple, white, or yellow flowers. Vigorous, sturdy, easy to grow.

CULTURE: Full sun to partial shade. Moderately moist, alkaline soils. Tolerates drought.

PROPAGATION: Division, seed.

GARDEN USES: Ground cover, front of border, containers.

HERBAL USES: Culinary, tea, medicinal.

OTHER VARIETIES OR SPECIES: *S. caucasicum* (small blue comfrey), *S. grandiflorum* (ground cover comfrey), *S. x uplandicum* (Russian comfrey).

## Coriander, Cilantro, or Chinese Parsley
### (*Coriandrum sativum*)

Apiaceae (Umbelliferae; parsley or carrot family). Annual. Native to Europe. Grows 3 feet tall. Finely divided leaves. Small white or mauve flowers in umbels.

CULTURE: Sun to partial shade.

PROPAGATION: Seed.

HERBAL USES: Culinary, confectionery, medicinal.

## Costmary, Alecost, or Bible Leaf
### (*Tanacetum balsamita,* formerly classified as *Chrysanthemum balsamita*)

Asteraceae (Compositae; sunflower family). Perennial. Zone 6. Grows 1 to 1½ feet tall. Coarse texture. Gray-green leaves; fragrant. Yellow, buttonlike flowers in clusters.

PROPAGATION: Division.

HERBAL USES: Culinary, medicinal, tea, beverages, moth preventive.

## Crocus, Saffron, or Autumn Crocus
### (*Crocus sativus*)

Iridaceae (iris family). Perennial corm. Zone 6. Native to Europe, North Africa, Middle East, central Asia. Grows 3 to 6 inches tall. Small lavender flower with bright orange stigma; blooms in autumn.

CULTURE: Full sun to partial shade. Mulch in winter. Plant corms 4 inches deep in late summer.

GARDEN USES: Late-season color.

HERBAL USES: Culinary, dye.

WARNING: Sometimes confused with *Colchicum autumnale,* which is also called autumn crocus and is poisonous.

## Dill (*Anethum graveolens*)

Apiaceae (Umbelliferae; parsley or carrot family). Annual. Native to southwest Asia. Grows to 3 feet tall. Upright. Fine, feathery, light green foliage. Blue-green stems. Yellowish flowers in umbels. Aromatic leaves, flowers, and seeds.

CULTURE: Tolerates heat. May need staking in shade. Short-lived; deteriorates after blooming. Plant every three to four weeks.

PROPAGATION: Seed. Self-sowing.

GARDEN USES: Contrast or accent; formal or informal border.

HERBAL USES: Culinary, fragrance, medicinal.

## Fennel (*Foeniculum vulgare*)

Apiaceae (Umbelliferae; parsley or carrot family). Annual or biennial. Native to Mediterranean regions. Grows 3 to 5 feet tall. Fast, vigorous grower. Fine, feathery foliage. Licorice-scented.

CULTURE: Dry, alkaline soils. Intolerant of wet, compacted soil. Tolerates heat. Resents root disturbance.

PROPAGATION: Division, seed. Self-sowing.

HERBAL USES: Culinary, confectionery, beverages.

OTHER VARIETIES OR SPECIES: *F. dulce* (Florence fennel), *F. vulgare* var. *rubrum* (bronze fennel).

**Feverfew** (*Tanacetum parthenium,* formerly classified as *Chrysanthemum parthenium*)

Asteraceae (Compositae; sunflower family). Perennial. Zone 5. Native to southeastern Europe. Grows 1½ to 3 feet tall. Dense, bushy. Fast grower. Scalloped, dark green leaves. Abundant yellow-and-white flowers July to October. Aromatic.

CULTURE: Intolerant of wet soil.

PROPAGATION: Seed, cuttings. Self-sowing.

GARDEN USES: Formal and informal borders, drifts, masses, raised beds, containers.

HERBAL USES: Crafts, medicinal.

**Garlic** (*Allium sativum*)

Liliaceae (lily family). Annual bulb. Native to high altitudes of southern Europe. Long, narrow leaves. White to pink flowers in umbels.

CULTURE: Cool temperatures.

PROPAGATION: Bulblets (fall).

HERBAL USES: Culinary.

HARVESTING: Lift bulbs in fall. Dry and store in net bag, or braid stalks to form a rope. Hang in cool, dark, well-ventilated area.

**Geranium, Scented** (*Pelargonium* species)

Geraniaceae (geranium family). Tender perennial. Zone 10. Native to tropics, South Africa. Grow 1 to 4 feet tall. Fragrant leaves. Small flowers.

CULTURE: Sun to partial shade. Tolerate heat; flower best in cool temperatures. Overwinter indoors in cold climates.

PESTS/DISEASES: Whiteflies, botrytis, stem rot.

PROPAGATION: Cuttings (late summer).

GARDEN USES: Bedding, containers, tactile, or fragrant garden. Standard or topiary.

HERBAL USES: Fragrance, culinary, confectionery, tea, beverages, perfumery.

OTHER VARIETIES OR SPECIES: *P. crispum* (lemon geranium), *P. denticulatum* 'Filicifolium' (fern-leaf pine-scented geranium), *P.* x *domesticum* 'Clorinda' (eucalyptus-scented geranium), *P. graveolens* (rose-scented geranium), *P. odoratissimum* (apple-scented geranium), *P. tomentosum* (peppermint-scented geranium). Other scented geraniums smell like coconut, chocolate, and cinnamon.

**Germander** (*Teucrium chamaedrys*)

Lamiaceae (Labiatae; mint family). Perennial. Zone 5. Native to Europe, Mediterranean. Grows 1 to 2 feet tall. Upright, dense mound. Scalloped, glossy, dark green leaves. Rosy lavender flowers July to September. Slow growing.

CULTURE: Full sun to partial shade. Tolerates heat. Thin during summer to improve air circulation and prevent fungus. Mulch in winter.

PESTS/DISEASES: Mites, mildew, rust.

PROPAGATION: Cuttings, layering, division.

GARDEN USES: Edging, formal or informal beds, raised beds, containers, knot gardens.

HERBAL USES: Medicinal.

OTHER VARIETIES OR SPECIES: *T. canadense* (American germander, or wood sage), *T. fruticans* (tree germander).

**Heliotrope, True** (*Heliotropium arborescens*)

Boraginaceae (borage family). Tender perennial. Zone 10. Native to Peru. Grows 3 to 5 feet tall. Sweet, vanilla-scented flowers in blue, purple, or white.

CULTURE: Sun to partial shade.

HERBAL USES: Perfumery.

**Horehound** (*Marrubium vulgare*)

Lamiaceae (Labiatae; mint family). Perennial. Zone 3. Native to Europe, North Africa, Asia. Grows 2 to 3 feet tall. Weedy. Crinkled, downy gray leaves; coarse. White flowers.

CULTURE: Sun to partial shade. Dry soil. Protect in winter.

PROPAGATION: Seed, cuttings, division.

GARDEN USES: Contrast, back of border.

HERBAL USES: Confectionery, medicinal, tea.

## Horseradish (*Armoracia rusticana*)

Brassicaceae (Cruciferae; mustard family). Perennial. Zone 5. Native to southeast Europe. Large, coarse plant. Above- and belowground parts grow up to 3 feet in length. Small white flowers. Spreads aggressively.

HERBAL USES: Culinary.

HARVESTING: Dig roots in fall; store in cool, moist sand.

## Hyssop (*Hyssopus officinalis*)

Lamiaceae (Labiatae; mint family). Perennial. Zone 3. Native to southern and eastern Europe. Grows 2 to 2½ feet tall. Small, pointed leaves; fragrant. Spikes of small purple, pink, or white flowers are attractive to bees and butterflies. Blooms abundantly when young. Becomes woody with age.

CULTURE: Intolerant of humidity; develops fungus problems. Cut back in fall or early spring to encourage growth.

PROPAGATION: Cuttings, division, seed.

GARDEN USES: Borders, knot gardens, formal gardens, hedging, containers, window boxes, raised beds.

HERBAL USES: Beverages, tea, medicinal, perfumery.

## Lady's Bedstraw, or Yellow Bedstraw (*Galium verum*)

Rubiaceae (madder family). Perennial. Zone 3. Native to North America, Europe, Asia. Grows 1 to 3 feet tall. Leaves in whorls; fine texture. Tiny yellow flowers June and July. Can spread aggressively.

CULTURE: Moderately moist to moist soil.

GARDEN USES: Ground cover.

HERBAL USES: Dye.

OTHER VARIETIES OR SPECIES: See sweet woodruff.

## Lady's Mantle (*Alchemilla mollis*)

Rosaceae (rose family). Perennial. Zone 3. Native to central Europe. Grows 12 to 20 inches tall. Mounding. Velvety, fan-shaped, gray-green leaves. Frothy sprays of tiny chartreuse flowers June through July.

CULTURE: Partial to full shade. Moist, organic soil. Tolerates low fertility but not dryness. Easy to grow; low maintenance.

PROPAGATION: Seed, division. Self-sowing.

GARDEN USES: Ground cover, containers, woodland borders.

HERBAL USES: Medicinal, dye, crafts.

## Lamb's Ears (*Stachys byzantina*)

Lamiaceae (Labiatae; mint family). Perennial. Zone 3. Native to southwestern Asia, Turkey. Grows 8 to 12 inches tall. Fast-growing, vigorous. Thick, woolly leaves are white, silver, or gray. Rose to lavender flowers in June; stalks to 18 inches tall. Scented leaves, flowers.

CULTURE: Intolerant of wet soil, heat, humidity; develops fungus problems. Deadhead for second bloom.

PROPAGATION: Division.

GARDEN USES: Ground cover, contrast, tactile, or children's gardens.

HERBAL USES: Medicinal.

OTHER VARIETIES OR SPECIES: *S. officinalis* (betony).

## Lavender (*Lavandula* species)

Lamiaceae (Labiatae; mint family). Perennial. Zones 5 to 9, depending on species. Native from Mediterranean to India. Grows 1 to 3 feet tall. Slow-growing. Silvery gray-green foliage. Blooms June to July in purple, blue, lavender-blue, violet, rose, or white. Highly fragrant.

CULTURE: Full sun. Alkaline soils. Intolerant of wet soil, humidity; develops leaf spot. May be grown indoors. Deadhead and cut back in spring to renew.

PROPAGATION: Cuttings, seed.

GARDEN USES: Knot gardens, raised beds, borders, rock gardens, edging (dwarf forms), fragrant gardens.

HERBAL USES: Perfumery, crafts, tea, medicinal.

OTHER VARIETIES OR SPECIES: *L. angustifolia, L. dentata, L.* x *intermedia, L. multifida, L. stoechas.*

## Lemon Balm (*Melissa officinalis*)

Lamiaceae (Labiatae; mint family). Perennial. Zone 4. Native to southern Europe. Grows 2 to 3 feet tall. Fast-growing; weedy; can spread aggressively. Medium green leaves; strongly lemon scented.

CULTURE: Full sun. Intolerant of heavy shade and humidity.

DISEASES: Powdery mildew.

PROPAGATION: Division, layering, cuttings, seed.

GARDEN USES: Erosion control.

HERBAL USES: Culinary, tea, medicinal.

## Lemongrass (*Cymbopogon citratus*)

Poaceae (Gramineae; grass family). Annual. Native to southern India. Long, lance-shaped leaves 3 feet long and ½ inch wide. Strongly lemon scented. Forms a dense clump.

CULTURE: Full sun. Hot, tropical conditions.

PROPAGATION: Division.

GARDEN USES: Containers.

HERBAL USES: Culinary, tea, flavoring, medicinal.

## Lemon Verbena (*Aloysia triphylla,* formerly *Lippia citriodora*)

Verbenaceae (vervain or verbena family). Tender woody perennial. Zone 8. Native to Argentina, Chile. Grows to 2 feet tall. Narrow, shiny leaves. Strongly lemon scented. Flowers white, sometimes tinted purple.

CULTURE: Full sun. Bring indoors with cold weather. Becomes woody with age.

PROPAGATION: Cuttings.

GARDEN USES: Containers.

HERBAL USES: Tea, beverages.

## Licorice (*Glycyrrhiza glabra*)

Fabaceae (Leguminosae; pea family). Tender perennial. Zone 8. Native from Mediterranean to southwestern Asia. Grows 2 to 3 feet tall. Deep-rooted. Long, loose clusters of pale blue to violet flowers.

CULTURE: Sun to partial shade. Rich, moist soil.

HERBAL USES: Confectionery, medicinal, fragrance.

## Lovage (*Levisticum officinale*)

Apiaceae (Umbelliferae; parsley or carrot family). Perennial. Zone 6. Native to Mediterranean. Grows 3 to 6 feet tall. Clump-forming. Large, light green leaves resemble those of celery. White or greenish yellow flowers. Long-lived.

CULTURE: Partial shade. Moderate moisture. Cool temperatures.

PROPAGATION: Seed (late summer).

GARDEN USES: Back of border.

HERBAL USES: Culinary, tea.

## Marjoram, Pot (*Origanum onites*)

Lamiaceae (Labiatae; mint family). Perennial. Zone 8. Native to Mediterranean. Grows to 2 feet tall. Hairy leaves. Red stems. White or mauve flowers. Fragrant.

CULTURE: Alkaline soil. Overwinter indoors in cold climates.

PROPAGATION: Seed, division.

HERBAL USES: Culinary.

OTHER VARIETIES OR SPECIES: See sweet marjoram.

## Marjoram, Sweet *(Origanum majorana)*

Lamiaceae (Labiatae; mint family). Annual. Native to Mediterranean regions, Turkey, North Africa. Grows 12 to 18 inches tall. Upright, shrubby. Mildly fragrant. Tiny, gray-green leaves. White, pink, or purple flowers August to September.

CULTURE: Full sun. Tolerates heat. Overwinter indoors.

PROPAGATION: Cuttings, division.

GARDEN USES: Small spaces, containers, raised beds, window boxes, hanging baskets, rock gardens, front of border.

HERBAL USES: Culinary.

## Mint *(Mentha* species)

Lamiaceae (Labiatae; mint family). Perennial. Zones 3 to 7, depending on species. Native to Eurasia, Africa. Group of herbs that grow 1 to 3 feet tall. Vigorous; often aggressively spreading. Highly fragrant leaves. See "Other Varieties," below.

CULTURE: Filtered light. Moist soil. Keep in bounds in containers or with root barriers sunk in the ground.

DISEASES: Rust, anthracnose, verticillium wilt.

PROPAGATION: Division, layering, cuttings.

GARDEN USES: Raised beds, containers, window boxes, fragrant gardens.

HERBAL USES: Culinary, tea, beverages, medicinal, flavoring, fragrance.

OTHER VARIETIES OR SPECIES: *M.* x *piperita* (peppermint): dark green leaves, reddish-tinged stems. *M. spicata* (spearmint): pointed, crinkly leaves. *M. suaveolens* (apple mint):

rounded, hairy leaves. Variegated types include *M.* x *gracilis* 'Variegata' (ginger mint), *M. suaveolens* 'Variegata' (pineapple mint). Also see bee balm, pennyroyal.

## Mustard *(Brassica juncea* and other species)

Brassicaceae (Cruciferae; mustard family). Annual. Native from Russia to central Asia. Grows 3 to 6 feet tall. Broad, dark green leaves. Yellow flowers. Curly-leaved variety ('Crispifolia') resembles kale.

CULTURE: Cool temperatures.

HERBAL USES: Culinary.

HARVESTING: Pull up plants before seed pods ripen; hang to dry.

## Myrtle, Sweet *(Myrtus communis)*

Myrtaceae (myrtle family). Evergreen in Zone 8 and warmer; tender subshrub elsewhere. Native to Mediterranean, North Africa. Grows to 10 feet tall in warm areas; 3 to 5 feet elsewhere. Branching, erect form. Shiny, fragrant leaves. White or pinkish white flowers, fragrant. Blue or red-black fruit. Cultivated since ancient times.

CULTURE: Full sun. Overwinter indoors in cold climates.

GARDEN USES: Containers, topiary, formal gardens, fragrant gardens.

## Nasturtium, or Indian Cress *(Tropaeolum majus)*

Tropaeolaceae (nasturtium family). Annual. Native to South America. Grows 12 to 15 inches tall. Round green leaves on wiry stems. Bright flowers in red, orange, yellow, pink, and intermediate shades.

CULTURE: Full sun except in very hot areas

GARDEN USES: Edging, window boxes, containers, trailing over rocks, mixed with vegetables or other herbs for color.

HERBAL USES: Culinary.

HARVESTING: Cut seed pods when full grown but still green.

OTHER VARIETIES OR SPECIES: *T. minus* (dwarf nasturtium).

## Oregano, or Wild Marjoram *(Origanum vulgare)*

Lamiaceae (Labiatae; mint family). Perennial. Zone 5. Native to Mediterranean, central Asia. Upright, sprawling. Grows to 2 feet tall. Small pink or white flowers. Pleasantly scented.

CULTURE: Full sun to partial shade. Dry, slightly alkaline soil. Fragrance weak in rich soil.

PESTS/DISEASES: Spider mites, aphids, root rot.

PROPAGATION: Seed, division.

GARDEN USES: Front or mid border, containers, raised beds, window boxes.

HERBAL USES: Culinary.

HARVESTING: Flowering doubles concentration of oil in leaves. Harvest after flowering begins, late in season. Opposite is true for nonflowering oreganos.

OTHER VARIETIES OR SPECIES: *O. vulgare* subsp. *hirtum* (Italian oregano), *O. compactum* (dwarf oregano), *O. dictamnus* (dittany-of-Crete). Also see pot marjoram, sweet marjoram.

## Parsley *(Petroselinum crispum)*

Apiaceae (Umbelliferae; parsley or carrot family). Annual or biennial. Native to Mediterranean regions. Grows 8 to 15 inches tall. Clump or mound. Thick, curly, emerald-green foliage.

CULTURE: Partial shade. Moderately rich, moist soil. Intolerant of heat. Difficult to transplant. Best grown as an annual.

PESTS: Parsley worm, spider mites.

PROPAGATION: Seed.

GARDEN USES: Edging, formal or informal gardens, small knot gardens, containers, hanging baskets, strawberry jars.

HERBAL USES: Culinary, tea, dye, medicinal.

HARVESTING: Does not dry well.

OTHER VARIETIES OR SPECIES: *P. crispum* var. *neapolitanum* (flat leaf or Italian parsley).

## Pennyroyal, American *(Hedeoma pulegioides)*

Lamiaceae (Labiatae; mint family). Annual. Native to North America. Small leaves; mintlike odor.

CULTURE: Partial shade.

PROPAGATION: Seed.

HERBAL USES: Tea, medicinal, mosquito repellent.

HARVESTING: Cut and dry entire plant before flowering.

## Pennyroyal, True *(Mentha pulegium)*

Lamiaceae (Labiatae; mint family). Tender perennial. Zone 7. Native to Europe. Creeping, prostrate. Small, oval leaves. Sharp, minty fragrance.

CULTURE: Filtered sun. Moist soil. Overwinter indoors.

PROPAGATION: Division.

GARDEN USES: Ground cover.

HERBAL USES: Tea, medicinal.

WARNING: Contains substances poisonous to some people. Use with caution.

## Perilla, Purple, or Japanese Basil *(Perilla frutescens* 'Atropurpurea')

Lamiaceae (Labiatae; mint family). Annual. Species is native from the Himalayas to eastern Asia. Grows 1½ to 3 feet tall. Fast growing; can be invasive. Related to common coleus. Dark, reddish purple foliage tinged with bronze. Sometimes confused with 'Dark Opal' basil; leaves are larger, coarser, crinkled.

CULTURE: Sun to partial shade.

PROPAGATION: Seed. Self-sowing.

GARDEN USES: Color contrast.

HERBAL USES: Culinary, tea, flavoring, medicinal.

## Pink, Clove (*Dianthus caryophyllus*)

Caryophyllaceae (pink family). Tender perennial. Zone 8. Native to Mediterranean. Grows 1 to 3 feet tall. Gray-blue foliage. Red, pink, white, or salmon flowers. Clove-scented flowers, leaves.

CULTURE: Sun to partial shade. Protect in winter in cold climates.

PROPAGATION: Seed, cuttings, layering.

GARDEN USES: Low borders, edging.

HERBAL USES: Fragrance (sachets, potpourris), flavoring.

OTHER VARIETIES OR SPECIES: *D. plumarius* (garden pink).

## Rose (*Rosa* species)

Rosaceae (rose family). Woody shrub. Hardiness depends on variety. Not technically herbs but rose hips and petals used for centuries in herbal teas, jellies, etc. Flowers in many colors, shapes, and sizes.

GARDEN USES: Various, depending on variety.

HERBAL USES: Culinary, perfumery, tea, fragrance, crafts, flavoring.

HARVESTING: Hips usually taken from *R. rugosa;* pick when plump and red but not overripe. Remove seeds, dry on a screen in an airy, shaded place. Gather rose petals at the height of bloom.

OTHER VARIETIES OR SPECIES: Roses for fragrance include *R.* x *centifolia* (cabbage rose), *R.* x *damascena* (damask rose), *R. gallica* (French rose).

## Rosemary (*Rosmarinus officinalis*)

Lamiaceae (Labiatae; mint family). Tender perennial. Zone 6. Native to Mediterranean. Upright varieties grow 3 to 6 feet tall; prostrate varieties, 1 to 2 feet tall. Long, thin, dark green leaves. Piney fragrance. Blue, pink, or white flowers in early summer.

CULTURE: Full sun. Alkaline soil. Tolerant of heat and drought. Overwinter indoors in cold climates.

PROPAGATION: Cuttings, seed.

GARDEN USES: Container specimen, bonsai, topiary, standard, hedge.

HERBAL USES: Culinary, medicinal.

HARVESTING: Pick leaves in second year.

## Rue (*Ruta graveolens*)

Rutaceae (rue family). Perennial. Zone 4. Native to Mediterranean, southern Europe to western Asia. Grows 1½ to 3 feet tall. Fine-textured, lacy, blue-green foliage. Small yellow flowers June to August. Odor offensive to some.

CULTURE: Full sun. Intolerant of humidity and wet, highly fertile soils; develops fungus problems. Tolerant of clay.

PROPAGATION: Cuttings, division.

GARDEN USES: Knot gardens.

HERBAL USES: Medicinal, dye, crafts, tea.

WARNING: Can be toxic. Should not be consumed at all by pregnant women. Oil in leaves may cause skin rash.

## Sage (*Salvia officinalis*)

Lamiaceae (Labiatae; mint family). Perennial shrub. Zone 5. Native to Mediterranean, North Africa. Grows 1 to 2½ feet tall. Sprawling, upright form. Gray-green, purple, golden, or variegated foliage. Blue, white, violet, or red flowers May to June. Aromatic. Sturdy; easy to grow. May be short-lived in cold climates.

CULTURE: Full sun. Tolerates heat, humidity,

drought, clay soils. Intolerant of wet winter soils.

PESTS/DISEASES: Spider mites, root rot.

PROPAGATION: Cuttings, division, layering, seed.

GARDEN USES: Accent, specimen, borders, edging (dwarf forms), informal gardens, containers, raised beds, erosion control, rock gardens.

HERBAL USES: Culinary, tea.

OTHER VARIETIES OR SPECIES: *S. azurea* (azure sage), *S. greggii* (autumn sage), *S. leucantha* (Mexican bush sage). Also see clary sage, pineapple sage.

## Sage, Clary (*Salvia sclarea*)

Lamiaceae (Labiatae; mint family). Biennial or perennial. Zone 5. Grows 3 feet tall. Large, scalloped leaves. Whitish flowers with pinkish or lavender bracts. Strongly aromatic.

PROPAGATION: Seed.

GARDEN USES: Back of border.

HERBAL USES: Culinary, flavoring, perfumery.

## Sage, Pineapple (*Salvia rutilans,* probably a form of *S. elegans*)

Lamiaceae (Labiatae; mint family). Tender perennial. Zone 10. Not known in the wild. Grows 3 feet tall. Semiwoody. Somewhat scraggly. Pineapple-scented leaves. Red flowers in late summer.

CULTURE: Overwinter indoors in cold climates.

PROPAGATION: Cuttings.

GARDEN USES: Back of border.

HERBAL USES: Flavoring, beverages, potpourri.

## Santolina (*Santolina* species)

Asteraceae (Compositae; sunflower family). Perennial. Zone 6. Native to southern Europe, Mediterranean. Grows 1 to 2½ feet tall. Controlled habit. Fine, intricate, dense, corallike foliage is dark emerald green or sil-

very gray. Musky fragrance. Yellow button-like flowers June and July.

CULTURE: Full sun. Dry, sandy, alkaline soil. Protect in winter in cold climates. Prune hard in early spring.

PROPAGATION: Cuttings, layering.

GARDEN USES: Contrast, accent, specimen, massing, front to mid border, clipped or natural hedges and edges, rock gardens, containers, raised beds.

HERBAL USES: Crafts (dried flowers).

OTHER VARIETIES OR SPECIES: *S. chamaecyparissus* (lavender cotton), *S. pinnata* (compact green santolina), *S. pinnata* subsp. *neapolitana,* *S. rosmarinifolia* (green santolina).

## Savory, Summer (*Satureja hortensis*)

Lamiaceae (Labiatae; mint family). Annual. Native to southeastern Europe. Grows to 18 inches tall. Fast growing. Small, bronzy-green leaves; spicy fragrance. Tiny white or lavender flowers.

CULTURE: Sun to partial shade. Intolerant of humidity; develops fungus problems.

PROPAGATION: Seed.

GARDEN USES: Containers, window boxes, raised beds, front of border.

HERBAL USES: Culinary, medicinal.

HARVESTING: Cut leaves when plant is in bud. Hang in shade until dry.

## Savory, Winter (*Satureja montana*)

Lamiaceae (Labiatae; mint family). Woody perennial. Zone 6. Native to southern Europe. Grows 8 to 15 inches tall. Shrubby. Dark green, shiny leaves; almost evergreen. Small white or lavender flowers.

CULTURE: Sun to partial shade. Light, sandy soil. Intolerant of humidity; develops fungus problems. Prune frequently; trim out dead wood.

PROPAGATION: Cuttings, seed.

GARDEN USES: Edging (dwarf forms).

HERBAL USES: Culinary, beverages, medicinal.

OTHER VARIETIES OR SPECIES: *S. montana* 'Nana' (dwarf winter savory).

### Sorrel, French *(Rumex scutatus)*

Polygonaceae (buckwheat family). Perennial. Zone 6. Native to Europe, western Asia, North Africa. Grows 1 to 2 feet tall. Weedy. Arrowhead-shaped leaves. Reddish flowers in panicles.

CULTURE: Sun to partial shade.

HERBAL USES: Culinary, medicinal.

HARVESTING: Leaves become bitter with age. Does not dry well.

### Sweet Cicely, or Sweet Chervil *(Myrrhis odorata)*

Apiaceae (Umbelliferae; parsley or carrot family). Perennial. Zone 5. Native to Europe. Grows 2 to 3½ feet tall. Upright, airy. Ferny, lacy foliage. White flower clusters in May. Anise-scented leaves, seeds, and fruit. Shiny black seeds.

CULTURE: Partial shade. Cool, moist, acidic soil. Intolerant of heat, dry soil, waterlogged clay. Requires cold winter for dormancy. Difficult to transplant.

PROPAGATION: Division, seed. Self-sowing.

GARDEN USES: Ground cover.

HERBAL USES: Culinary, flavoring, tea, beverages, medicinal.

### Sweet Flag *(Acorus calamus)*

Araceae (arum family). Perennial. Zone 3. Native to Asia, southeastern United States. Broad leaves to 40 inches long. Produces a 2-inch spike in June, studded with small greenish blossoms. Strong lemony fragrance.

CULTURE: Full sun. Damp soil.

PROPAGATION: Division.

GARDEN USES: Back of border. Best grown in clumps.

HERBAL USES: Fragrance (sachets), flavoring, medicinal.

HARVESTING: Dig rhizomes in fall after plant dies down.

### Sweet Woodruff *(Galium odoratum,* formerly *Asperula odorata)*

Rubiaceae (madder family). Perennial. Zone 5. Native to Europe, North Africa. Grows 6 to 12 inches tall. Delicate, slender leaves in starry whorls. Small, white flowers in loose clusters April to May. Vanilla-scented when crushed or dried.

CULTURE: Shade to partial shade. Moist soil. Cool temperatures. Intolerant of humidity, poor drainage; develops fungus problems.

PROPAGATION: Division, cuttings.

GARDEN USES: Ground cover, woodland gardens, containers, raised beds, wall plantings.

HERBAL USES: Flavoring, beverages, medicinal.

HARVESTING: Pick and dry in spring.

### Tansy *(Tanacetum vulgare)*

Asteraceae (Compositae; sunflower family). Perennial. Zone 4. Native to Europe. Grows 3 to 4 feet tall. Upright, spreading. Fast, vigorous growth; may be invasive. Curly-leaf variety is less aggressive. Coarse, large, fern-like leaves are emerald green. Bitter, pungent fragrance. Yellow, flat flower clusters July to September.

CULTURE: Partial shade. Lush foliage in rich soils. Tolerates heat.

PROPAGATION: Division. Self-sowing.

GARDEN USES: Middle or back of border, ground cover, containers. Curly-leaf variety is more ornamental.

HERBAL USES: Crafts (dried flowers, wreaths), dye, medicinal, insect deterrent

OTHER VARIETIES OR SPECIES: *T. vulgare* var. *crispum* (curly-leaf tansy)

## Tarragon, French *(Artemisia dracunculus)*

Asteraceae (Compositae; sunflower family). Perennial. Zone 4. Native to eastern Europe, northern Asia. Grows 2 feet tall. Shrubby. Narrow, pointed leaves. Tiny greenish white flowers in midsummer. Crushed leaves smell like anise.

CULTURE: Full sun. Moderately rich soil. Requires more watering than other artemisias. For best flavor, replace plants every few years. Protect in winter.

PROPAGATION: Root cuttings, division. Cannot be grown from seed.

HERBAL USES: Culinary.

HARVESTING: Use fresh; flavor lost when dried.

## Thyme, Common *(Thymus vulgaris)*

Lamiaceae (Labiatae; mint family). Perennial. Zone 5. Native to Europe, Asia, Mediterranean. Upright varieties 6 to 18 inches tall; creepers 2 to 8 inches tall. Very aromatic. Green or gray-green leaves. Flowers June to July; color depends on variety.

CULTURE: Full sun. Dry, rocky soil. Tolerates heat, drought. Intolerant of wet, heavy, compacted soils. Protect in winter; use antidesiccant spray on upright varieties.

DISEASES: Root rot.

PROPAGATION: Seed, layering, cuttings, division.

GARDEN USES: Ground cover, edging, formal or informal gardens, small knot gardens, rock gardens, raised beds, window boxes, containers, along walkways.

HERBAL USES: Culinary, medicinal, perfumery.

HARVESTING: Reap sparingly first year and twice a year thereafter.

OTHER VARIETIES OR SPECIES: *T.* x *citriodorus* (lemon thyme), *T. herba-barona* (caraway thyme), *T. hyemalis* (winter thyme), *T. nitidus* (tiny-leaf thyme), *T. praecox* var. *arcticus* (creeping thyme), *T. pseudolanuginosus* (woolly thyme), *T. pulegioides* (oregano-scented thyme), *T. serpyllum* (mother-of-thyme).

## Valerian, or Garden Heliotrope *(Valeriana officinalis)*

Valerianaceae (valerian family). Perennial. Zone 3. Native to central Europe, northern Asia. Grows 3 to 4 feet tall. Weedy, untidy habit. Fragrant white, pink, and lavender flowers in flat heads. Attractive to cats.

CULTURE: Partial shade. Moderately moist soil.

HERBAL USES: Medicinal, fragrance.

OTHER VARIETIES OR SPECIES: *V. edulis* is a native American species.

## Violet, Sweet *(Viola odorata)*

Violaceae (violet family). Perennial. Zone 8. Native to Europe. Low-growing mound to 6 inches tall. Deep violet, single blossoms. Heart-shaped leaves.

CULTURE: Partial shade. Thrives in poor soils.

PROPAGATION: Seed, division.

GARDEN USES: Edging, borders.

HERBAL USES: Culinary, medicinal, perfumery.

## Yarrow *(Achillea millefolium)*

Asteraceae (Compositae; sunflower family). Perennial. Zone 2. Native from Europe to western Asia. Grows 2 feet tall; very aggressive. Finely cut, fernlike foliage. White, pink, or red flowers in flat heads.

CULTURE: Full sun.

PROPAGATION: Division.

HERBAL USES: Tea, medicinal.

WARNING: Large doses of yarrow tea can cause headaches and vertigo.

# Herbs for Special Purposes

## Culinary and Confectionery Herbs

A number of herbs are essential for a well-stocked culinary herb garden, including basil, chives, dill, garlic, lemon balm, marjoram, oregano, parsley, mint, rosemary, sage, savory, and thyme. Serious cooks should add tarragon to the list.

Angelica
Anise
Anise hyssop, or giant blue hyssop
Basil, sweet
Bay, or true laurel
Borage
Burnet, salad
Calendula, or pot marigold
Caraway
Chervil
Chicory
Chives
Coriander, cilantro, or Chinese parsley
Crocus, saffron, or autumn crocus
Dill
Fennel
Garlic
Geranium, rose-scented
Horseradish
Lemon balm
Lemongrass
Licorice
Lovage
Marjoram, pot
Marjoram, sweet
Mustard
Nasturtium
Oregano
Parsley
Perilla, purple

Rosemary
Sage
Savory, summer
Savory, winter
Sorrel, French
Spearmint
Sweet cicely
Tarragon, French
Thyme

## Tea and Other Beverages

To make herbal tea, put a handful of fresh herbs (about ¼ cup) per person into a pot. Pour boiling water over them, and steep for three or four minutes. Strain before pouring into cups. To make tea with dried herbs, use only 1 teaspoon of herbs for each cup. For iced drinks, brew the tea at double strength.

Anise hyssop
Bee balm, or Oswego tea
Catmint
Catnip
Chamomile, German
Chamomile, Roman
Chicory
Comfrey
Costmary, alecost or bible leaf
Fennel
Geranium, rose-scented
Horehound
Hyssop
Lemon balm
Lemongrass
Lemon verbena
Lovage
Mints
Parsley
Pennyroyal, American
Perilla, purple

Rose (hips)
Rue (See WARNING in Encyclopedia of
   Herbs, above)
Sage
Sweet cicely
Thyme, lemon
Yarrow (See WARNING in Encyclopedia of
   Herbs, above)

## Medicinal

Herbs have been used for centuries, often in tea, to alleviate coughs, sore throats, colds, stomach ailments, headaches, rheumatism, and myriad other physical ailments. Today, some herbs are used commercially in medications. Others are reputed to have healing effects but are not endorsed by medical practitioners. All should be used with caution. Refer to "Further Reading" on page 268 for more detailed information.

Angelica
Anise
Artemisias, or wormwoods
Basil, sweet
Bay, or true laurel
Bee balm, or Oswego tea
Borage
Calamint
Calendula, or pot marigold
Caraway
Catnip
Chamomile, Roman
Chives
Comfrey
Coriander, cilantro, or Chinese parsley
Costmary, alecost, or bible leaf
Dill
Fennel
Feverfew
Flag, sweet

Germander
Horehound
Hyssop
Lady's bedstraw, or yellow bedstraw
Lady's mantle
Lamb's ears
Lavender
Lemon balm
Lemongrass
Licorice
Marjoram, sweet
Mint
Oregano, or wild marjoram
Parsley
Pennyroyal, American
Pennyroyal, true
Perilla, purple
Rosemary
Rue (See WARNING in Encyclopedia of
   Herbs, above)
Sage
Savory, summer
Savory, winter
Sorrel, French
Sweet cicely
Sweet woodruff
Tansy
Thyme, common
Valerian
Violet, sweet
Yarrow (See WARNING in Encyclopedia of
   Herbs, above)

## Dyeing and Crafts

This list is but a sampling of herbs used in making handicrafts. Many are used for their fresh or dried flowers or foliage in making wreaths and arrangements. Others add fragrance to sachets and potpourri, or are used to make dye for coloring fabrics and yarns.

Anise hyssop, or giant blue hyssop: crafts
Artemisias, or wormwoods: dried foliage
Bay: wreaths
Calendula, or pot marigold: yellow dye
Crocus, saffron: red-orange dye
Feverfew: dried flowers
Geraniums, scented: potpourri
Lady's bedstraw: red dye from roots, yellow dye from stems
Lady's mantle: green dye, fresh or dried flowers
Lavender: wreaths, dried flowers
Parsley: green dye
Pink, clove: potpourri
Rose: potpourri
Rue: red dye, dried flowers
Sage: wreaths
Sage, pineapple: potpourri
Santolina: dried flowers
Sweet flag: sachets
Tansy: dye, wreaths, dried flowers
Yarrow: dried flowers

Costmary, alecost or bible leaf
Flag, sweet
Geraniums, scented
Heliotrope
Hyssop
Lavender
Lemon balm
Lemongrass
Lemon verbena
Mint
Myrtle, sweet
Oregano
Pinks
Rose
Rosemary
Rue
Sage, pineapple
Santolina
Thyme
Valerian

## Fragrance

Many herbs are known for the fragrant oils in their leaves and flowers, whether they are enjoyed in the garden or distilled for use in perfumes. A fragrant herb garden is attractive to bees and butterflies, and can have a soothing, even therapeutic effect on humans.

Angelica
Anise hyssop, or giant blue hyssop
Basil, sweet
Bay, or true laurel
Bee balm
Calamint
Catnip
Chamomile, German
Chamomile, Roman

## Further Reading

Adams, James. *Landscaping with Herbs.* Portland, Ore.: Timber Press, 1987.

Bown, Deni. *Encyclopedia of Herbs and Their Uses.* London; New York: Dorling Kindersley, 1995.

Bremness, Lesley. *Herbs.* London; New York: Dorling Kindersley, 1994.

Chevallier, Andrew. *The Encyclopedia of Medicinal Plants.* London; New York: Dorling Kindersley, 1996.

Crawford, Hester Mettler, ed. *Herbs and Their Ornamental Uses.* Brooklyn, N.Y.: Brooklyn Botanic Garden, 1990.

Forsell, Mary. *Heirloom Herbs.* New York: Villard, 1990.

Kirkpatrick, Debra. *Using Herbs in the Landscape.* Harrisburg, Pa.: Stackpole Books, 1992.

Lima, Patric. *The Harrowsmith Illustrated Book of Herbs.* Camden East, Ont.: Camden House, 1986.

Lovejoy, Ann, ed. *Herbs and Cooking.* Brooklyn, N.Y.: Brooklyn Botanic Garden, 1990.

Sanecki, Kay. *Planning and Planting Herb Gardens.* London: Ward Lock, 1996.

Tolley, Emelie, and Chris Mead. *Gardening with Herbs.* New York: Clarkson Potter, 1995.

Van Brunt, Elizabeth R., ed. *Culinary Herbs.* Brooklyn, N.Y.: Brooklyn Botanic Garden, 1982.

Wilson, Jim. *Landscaping with Herbs.* Boston: Houghton Mifflin, 1994.

# FRUITS

Fruit growing brings together much of the best that gardening has to offer. It enables gardeners to experience the satisfaction of caring for plants and to enjoy the beauty of blossoms. But there is an added bonus: biting into the luscious, fully ripe, just-picked bounty.

To assure success in raising fruits, first evaluate the site. Check the soil for drainage, and test for nutrient deficiencies and acidity. Look at the exposure at various places around the property with an eye for proper plant selection: Fruits with tender, early blooms do best on slight northern slopes or close enough to the north sides of buildings so that winter shade delays the opening of the blossoms. When choosing places to plant, remember that, with some exceptions, most fruiting plants need at least six hours of direct sunlight every day.

Another key to successful fruit growing is learning about the worst pest problems in the area, then searching out resistant varieties if available. Finally, consider growing a whole range of fruits. Not only will this round out the larder, but there will always be plenty of fruit to harvest even if adverse weather or a problem pest wreaks havoc with one or two kinds of fruits during the season.

## Getting Started

Besides evaluating the conditions on the site, it is important to assess the available space, and just how much of any particular fruit it is possible to harvest given the amount of space. The chart on page 270 lists average yields as well as space requirements of various fruit plants.

## Pollination

Fruiting plants usually need to have their flowers pollinated in order to yield fruit. *Self-fruitful* plants produce fruit when pollinated with their own pollen. *Self-sterile* plants need pollen from a different variety of the same kind of fruit in order to bear. Included in the following list of self-fruitful plants are the few, such as certain figs and persimmons, that actually bear fruit without any pollination. Certain varieties of each type of fruit may be exceptions. Apples and sweet cherries, which have specific pollination requirements, are listed separately.

## SPACING AND YIELDS FOR FRUIT PLANTS

| Fruit | Spacing (ft.) | Yield (lbs.) |
|---|---|---|
| Apple | | |
| Dwarf | 7 | 60 |
| Semidwarf | 12 | 150 |
| Standard | 20 | 300 |
| Apricot | 15 | 150 |
| Blackberry | | |
| Trailing | 10 | 3 |
| Erect, semierect | 5 | 3 |
| Blueberry | | |
| Highbush | 5 | 7 |
| Lowbush | 2 | 1 |
| Rabbiteye | 8 | 15 |
| Cherry | | |
| Sweet | 25 | 300 |
| Tart | 10 | 100 |
| Currant | 6 | 8 |
| Gooseberry | 5 | 8 |
| Grape | 8 | 15 |
| Juneberry | | |
| Bushes | 6 | 20 |
| Trees | 15 | 100 |
| Kiwi | 8 | 150 |
| Nectarine | 15 | 100 |
| Pawpaw | 15 | 50 |
| Peach | 15 | 150 |
| Pear | | |
| Dwarf | 8 | 60 |
| Standard | 15 | 300 |
| Persimmon | 15 | 200 |
| Plum | 10 | 75 |
| Raspberry | 2 | 3 |
| Strawberry | 1 | 2 |

## Self-Fruitful Plants

Apricot
Blackberry
Blueberry (but better yields and larger fruit
    with cross-pollination)
Cherry, tart
Crabapple
Currant
Fig
Gooseberry
Grape, American
Grape, European
Juneberry
Nectarine
Peach
Persimmon
Plum, European
Pomegranate
Quince
Raspberry
Strawberry

## Self-Sterile Plants

Apple
Cherry, sweet
Grape, Muscadine
Kiwi
Pawpaw
Pear
Plum, American hybrid
Plum, Oriental

## Sweet Cherry Pollination Classes

Because most varieties of sweet cherry are self-sterile, crosspollination is needed for fruit set. But not all varieties can pollinate each other. Sweet cherries have been divided into pollination groups; some varieties in each pollination group are listed below on the same line. Varieties within the same group cannot pollinate each other.

- Black Tartarian, Knight's Early Black
- Venus, Merton Bigarreau, Bing, Windsor, Van
- Vernon, Emperor Francis, Lambert
- Chinook, Rainier, Hudson
- Vic, Ulster

## Apple Varieties That Cannot Pollinate Other Varieties

Apples require cross-pollination, but not all apple varieties are capable of supplying good pollen for the job. Listed below are some varieties that *cannot* pollinate other varieties. Any variety with good pollen can pollinate any of these varieties. Because the following varieties cannot reciprocate, it is necessary to have a minimum of three trees—two different varieties with good pollen in addition to one of the varieties listed below—in order for all to bear fruit.

Arkansas
Baldwin
Jonagold
Gravenstein
Mutsu
Rhode Island Greening
Spigold
Stayman Winesap
Summer Rambo
Winesap

## Pome Fruits

The pome fruits include apple and pear as well as some lesser-known fruits, such as quince, medlar, and juneberry. Although apples are the most popular fruit (the word "pome" comes from the Latin word that means both apple and fruit), they are not easy to grow everywhere. They need rigorous, annual pruning and, in the eastern half of the country, have a few pest problems that must be attended to. Nonetheless, apple is a delectable fruit of which there are over 5,000 varieties in a wide range of colors, shapes, and, of course, flavors. There are varieties that are resistant to one or more disease problems.

Pears commonly have few pest problems but, like apples, require annual pruning. Timely harvest is the key to luscious European-type pears. Pick them when their background color yellows and they come off easily when lifted upward with a slight twist, then let ripening finish in a cool room indoors. Wait to harvest Asian pears—these are crisp and often round—until the fruit is thoroughly ripe on the tree.

Prune a mature apple or pear tree by occasionally removing whole limbs that shade the interior and by thinning out fruiting spurs—the short growths on which fruit are borne—when they become old and crowded.

## The Best-Tasting Apples

Taste is, of course, a matter of taste. However, the following varieties have been widely acclaimed for their superior flavor.

Ashmead's Kernel
Calville Blanc d'Hiver
Cornish Gilliflower
Cox's Orange Pippin
Esopus Spitzenburg
Gala
Golden Nugget
Hudson's Golden Gem

Jonagold
Mutsu (also called Crispin)
Spigold
Yellow Newtown

## Disease-Resistant Apples

All of the following varieties show resistance to apple scab, the major disease of apples, as well as to one or more of the other three important diseases: fire blight, powdery mildew, and cedar apple rust. Note that disease-resistant varieties may still be attacked by insect pests. These varieties also may be susceptible to other diseases, some of which, such as sooty mold and fly speck, are merely superficial and simply can be washed off the fruits.

Dayton
Freedom
Jonafree
Liberty
Macfree
McShay
Nova Easygro
Novamac
Novaspy
Prima
Priscilla
Redfree
Sir Prize
Trent
William's Pride

## Apples for Warm Climates

Apple trees, like other temperate-zone trees, need a certain amount of winter cold before they can blossom and grow well each spring. The following varieties are suitable for areas with mild winters, those having less than 600 hours of temperatures between about 32°F and 45°F.

Anna
Beverly Hills Braeburn
Dorsett Gold
Ein Shemer
Gordon
Granny Smith
Lady Williams Wealthy
Winter Banana
White Winter Pearmain

## Apples for the Far North

Beacon
Connell Red
Cortland
Davey
Earliblaze
Fameuse
Fireside
Haralson
Honeycrisp
Honeygold
Keepsake
Macoun
McIntosh
Norland
Northern Spy
Regent
State Fair
Sweet Sixteen
Wealthy

## Pears for the Far North

Flemish Beauty
Golden Spice

Harrow Sweet
Honey Sweet
Luscious
Patten
Summercrisp
Tyson
Worden Seckel

## Crabapples for Good Eating

A crabapple is, by definition, any apple that is smaller than 2¼ inches across. Flavor varies almost as much as that of full-size apples, with some varieties good both fresh and cooked, and others best cooked. The following varieties are large and flavorful enough to warrant planting for eating—and they also are ornamental.

Astrachan Crab
Centennial
Chestnut
Cranberry
Dolgo
Hyslop
John Downie
Kerr
Redflesh
Transcendent
Whitney
Wickson

## Fire Blight–Resistant Pears

Fire blight is a bacterial disease that makes pear leaves look as if they have been singed by fire, and causes shoot tips to curl in a characteristic shepherd's crook. This serious disease limits pear growing in many areas, but varieties differ in susceptibility to fire blight. The following are recommended where fire blight is a problem.

Dr. Jules Guyot
Eldorado
Mac
Magness
Maxine
Moonglow
Old Home
Orient
Pineapple
Seckel
Winter Nelis

## Red-Skinned Pears

For something different. In some cases, these red varieties are unique; in other cases they are red-skinned "sports" (single bud mutations) of well-known varieties. The flavor of red-skinned sports is almost the same as that of the green-skinned varieties from which they were derived.

Cascade
Red Bartlett
Red Clapp's Favorite
Red Comice
Red d'Anjou
Reimer Red
Rosi Red
Sensation
Ubileen

# Stone Fruits

Take special care when selecting a site for stone fruits, for all thrive best basking in abundant sunlight, with their roots in well-drained soil. Plums are somewhat more tolerant of less-than-perfect conditions than the others. Apricots, peaches, and nectarines blossom very early in the spring, so be especially careful to choose a site that does not warm up too early, causing the blossoms to open prematurely and exposing them to damage by frosts. Stone fruits do have their share of potential disease and pest problems; nonetheless, they are worth the trouble because the flavor of a fully ripened, fresh-picked apricot or peach is incomparable to that of anything store-bought.

## Recommended White Peaches

For something different in peaches, try white-fleshed varieties. In addition to their pearly white color, these varieties have unique, honey-sweet flavors.

Champion
Eden
Lady Nancy
LaWhite
Morton
Polly
Scarlet Pearl
Sugar Lady
Tasty Zee
White Lady

## Recommended White-Fleshed Nectarines

Nectarines are simply fuzzless peaches. The following white-fleshed nectarines have a honey-sweet flavor similar to that of their fuzzy counterparts.

ArticGlo
Morton
Rose Princess
Stark CrimsonSnow

## Hardy Apricots

Apricots are finicky fruits. But they are worth growing because a tree-ripened apricot is ambrosial. Besides potential pest problems, apricots have particular climatic requirements. They like winters that stay cold, springs that stay warm, and summers that stay dry. If the site is less than perfect, be sure to choose varieties carefully.

Alfred
Goldcot
Goldrich
Hargrand
Harlayne
Rival
Skaha
Sundrop
Sungold
Traverse

# Strawberries

"Doubtless God could have made a better berry, but doubtless God never did," wrote William Butler in the seventeenth century. Whether or not the strawberry is the best berry is debatable, but it is surely true that the most luscious berries are homegrown and fresh picked.

Strawberries are among the most widely adapted fruits. With careful choice of variety, they can be grown in every state in a wide range of soils. Strawberries also are easy to grow and bear quickly. *Everbearers* bear the same season they are planted, and *Junebearers* yield their first harvest the year after planting.

Strawberry plants each need about a square foot of space, so that there is abundant sunlight and enough air circulation to keep the plants healthy and productive. Strawberry plants spread by runners (horizontal stems that make new plants at nodes), so begin a bed by setting plants at a 2-foot by 3-foot spacing, and allow "daughter" plants to fill in the bare ground. Alternatively, set plants a foot apart and remove all runners as they form. The former system requires fewer plants to begin, but initial yields are higher with the latter system. When planting, shorten the roots to about 4 inches, then fan them out in the planting hole, adjusting the planting depth so that the soil line is just below the top of the crown.

The "straw" in "strawberry" may be derived from the fact that straw mulch has been used commonly for this plant. Mulching between the plants through the growing season conserves water, keeps fruit clean, and eliminates the need for hoeing, which damages the plants' shallow roots. For winter protection, cover the plants with mulch as soon as the soil has frozen to about an inch deep in autumn. Pull back the winter mulch, tucking it between the plants, when growth begins in spring.

Renovate an established bed each year right after harvest by thinning out plants so that they are 8 inches apart, cutting off and raking up their leaves, then fertilizing and watering. Everbearing varieties do not need renovation. Eventually, diseases and weeds make inroads into even a healthy bed, so plan on establishing a new bed at a new location after five to ten years.

## Strawberries for the North and Midwest

Catskill
Dunlap
Earliglow

Fletcher
Honeyoye
Jewel
Midland
Raritan
Sparkle
Surecrop
Tristar

## Strawberries for the Mid-Atlantic Region

Blakemore
Dixieland
Guardian
Marlate
Midway
Pocohontas
Redchief
Sunrise
Suwannee

## Strawberries for the South

Albritton
Blakemore
Cardinal
Chandler
Daybreak
Dixieland
Florida Ninety
Headliner
Suwannee
Sweet Charlie

## Strawberries for the Northwest

Hood
Northwest
Puget Beauty
Quinalt

Shuksan
Sumas
Totem

## Strawberries for California

Aptos
Brighton
Chandler
Sequoia
Shasta
Sweet Charlie

## Blueberries

Blueberries are native American fruits that have been hybridized and widely cultivated only since the early 20th century. There are three important species:

• **Highbush blueberry** (*Vaccinium corymbosum*) grows about 6 feet high and is native mostly to the Eastern Seaboard and parts of Michigan. It is adapted from USDA Zones 4 to 7, except for varieties derived from wild southern types, which tolerate somewhat warmer climates.

• **Rabbiteye blueberry** (*V. ashei*) is native to the Southeast and tolerates heat and drought, but its flavor is inferior to that of the highbush blueberry. Rabbiteye bushes grow into shrubs as tall as 15 feet high, and are hardy as far north as USDA Zone 7.

• In the Northeast, the cold-hardy **lowbush blueberry** (*V. angustifolium*), adapted from USDA Zones 3 to 7, is an important commercial berry. Breeders have combined qualities of highbush and lowbush blueberries into hybrids known as *midhigh* or *halfhigh blueberries*.

With their genes for resistance to cold and their relatively low growth, halfhigh blueberries are adapted to northernmost growing areas.

Blueberries generally suffer few insect and disease problems, but are finicky about their soil. They demand ground that is well drained, very acidic (pH 4 to 5), and high in organic matter. A bucket of acidic peat moss mixed into the planting hole gets a bush off to a good start. Blueberry plants also enjoy a thick, permanent mulch of some organic material, such as sawdust, straw, or wood chips. Birds are the major pest of blueberries; plan on controlling this damage or the whole crop could be devoured.

## Highbush Blueberries for USDA Zones 4 to 7

Berkeley
Bluecrop
Blueray
Bluetta
Collins
Coville
Darrow
Duke
Earliblue
Elliot
Spartan

## Halfhigh Blueberries for the Coldest Regions (USDA Zones 3 to 7)

Friendship
Northblue
Northcountry
Northland
Northsky
Patriot
St. Cloud

## Highbush Blueberries for the South (USDA Zones 7 to 9)

Georgia Gem
Gulf Coast
Misty
O'Neal
Reveille
Sharpblue
Wannabe

## Recommended Rabbiteye Blueberries (USDA Zones 7 to 9)

Bonita Blue
Brightwell
Climax
Powderblue
Premier
Tifblue

## Brambles

Wild brambles, including raspberries and blackberries, have been enjoyed for centuries, but these plants were domesticated only in the last few hundred years. Because brambles are so widely distributed over the world, cultivars suited to just about every site should be available.

Brambles are easy to grow if they are located in an appropriate site and pruned regularly. They require full sun and well-drained soil. Prune by removing two-year-old stems, which die anyway after they fruit, anytime from right after harvest until just before growth resumes again in spring. During winter, also thin out young stems to prevent overcrowding, leaving six to eight stems per plant for brambles grown in "hills," or 6 inches between plants for brambles grown in a hedgerow. No matter what the length of the hedgerow, do not let the bases of the plants spread wider than 12 inches. A final pruning step for red and yellow raspberries is to shorten the canes to about 5 feet.

Blackberries, purple raspberries, and black raspberries require a couple of additional pruning steps. Pinch out the tips of the new canes during summer whenever they reach 3 feet in height. In winter, shorten all the branches that grew as a result of that pinching back to about 18 inches.

So-called everbearing red or yellow raspberry canes bear toward their tips in late summer and fall of their first year of growth, then lower down in the second year. One way to prune these types is to simply mow all canes to the ground each year in early winter. This sacrifices the summer crop but avoids any chance of winter damage and decreases disease problems.

## Cold Hardiness of Brambles, from Most to Least

The following is a general list. Cold-hardiness of specific varieties of each kind of bramble varies.

Raspberries (USDA Zones 3 to 8)
    Red and yellow varieties
    Purple raspberries
    Black raspberries
Blackberries (USDA Zones 5 to 8)
Wineberry (USDA Zones 5 to 8)
Raspberry x Blackberry hybrids, such as 'Tayberry', 'Boysenberry', and 'Loganberry' (adaptation varies, but most are adapted only to USDA Zones 8 and 9)

## Red Raspberries for the East and Midwest

Augustred
Boyne
Canby
Fallred
Heritage
Killarney
Latham
Newburgh
Nova
Redwing
Reveille
Sentinel
Taylor
Titan

## Red Raspberries for the Pacific Northwest

Amity
Canby
Chilcotin
Chilliwack
Heritage
Meeker
Nootka
Puyallup
Skeena
Summit
Sumner
Willamette

## Recommended Black Raspberries

Allen
Blackhawk
Bristol
Haut

Jewel
Munger

## Recommended Purple Raspberries

Amethyst
Brandywine
Lowden
Royalty
Sodus
Success

## Blackberries for the South

Brazos
Cherokee
Cheyenne
Choctaw
Comanche
Flordagrand
Humble
Navaho
Shawnee

## Blackberries for the Northeast and Upper Midwest

Chester
Darrow
Illini Hardy

## Blackberries for the West

Boysen
Chehalem
Lincoln Logan
Logan

## Blackberries for the Midwest and Mid-Atlantic Region

Black Satin
Cherokee
Chester
Cheyenne
Choctaw
Hull Thornless
Shawnee
Smoothstem
Thornfree

## Grapes

Grapes are among the oldest of cultivated fruits. They also are adaptable, and can be grown over a wide range of climates. The three major types of grape are best adapted to different regions:

• **Vinifera, or European wine, grape** (*Vitis vinifera*) thrives best where winters are mild and summers are hot and dry. The meaty flesh and mild, sweet flavor of vinifera grapes, typified by Thompson Seedless, makes them the best grapes for wine and raisins.

• **Fox grapes** (*V. labrusca*) are native to the eastern United States, and are hardier and more pest-resistant than vinifera grapes. The fruit is slip-skin—the flesh pops out of the skin when you eat the fruit—and has a strong "foxy" flavor typified by the variety Concord.

• So-called **American grapes** are hybrids of vinifera and fox grapes, and are widely adapted. Muscadine grapes are native to the Southeast, and have clusters of few, but large, berries with intense flavor.

Grapes bear on shoots growing off canes that grew the previous season and need annual pruning to keep vines productive, manageable, and healthy.

## Grapes for the Northeast and Upper Midwest

Alden
Allwood
Bluebell
Buffalo
Campbell Early
Delaware
Edelweiss
Kay Gray
N.Y. Muscat
Swenson Red

## Grapes for the Lower Midwest

Albania
Beacon
Concord
Delaware
Himrod
Interlaken Seedless
Manito
Valhalla
Villard Blanc

## Grapes for the Deep South

Carlos
Golden Isles
Hunt
Jumbo
Scuppernong
Thomas
Triumph

## Grapes for the Lower West

Beauty Seedless
Early Muscat
Flame Seedless
Malaga
Muscat of Alexandria
Ribier
Thompson Seedless

## Grapes for the Pacific Northwest

Aurore
Einset
Interlaken
Marechal Foch
Reliance
Vanessa

## Figs

Along with grapes, figs are among the oldest of cultivated fruits. Although best adapted to a Mediterranean-type climate with hot, dry summers and cool, moist winters, figs often are grown where winters are frigid. In these regions, dormant plants need to be shielded from winter cold. They can either be grown in pots, then moved to a basement or garage, or swaddled in some insulating material, or their tops can be bent over and buried in the ground.

Depending on the variety, a fig may bear one or two distinct crops per year. The first, called the breba crop, grows from buds on the previous year's wood; the second, or main, crop appears on current growth. Knowing how a fig variety bears fruit influences pruning. Varieties producing good breba crops should not be pruned heavily because the previous season's

wood, which will bear the first crop, will be severely cut back or removed. These varieties do need some pruning, though, to stimulate growth for the following year's crop. Varieties bearing only main crops require heavy pruning in order to stimulate an abundance of new wood, for the late crop only. Varieties bearing two crops each season require an intermediate amount of pruning.

## Figs Bearing Mostly on One-Year-Old Wood

Beall
Flanders
King
Mission
Osborne
Pasquale
Tena
Ventura
Verte

## Figs Bearing Mostly on New Wood

Kadotta (Dottato)
Panachee

## Figs Bearing a Main Crop and a Light Breba Crop

Adriatic (Grosse Verte)
Alma
Blanche
Brown Turkey
Calimyrna
Celeste
DiRedo
Everbearing

Excel
Magnolia
Osborne

## Unusual Fruits

When it comes to planting fruits, there is no reason to stick to the usual: apples, peaches, cherries, and others found readily in the markets. There are many other edible fruits, with a wide spectrum of flavors and textures. Some of these unusual fruits are easier to grow, in many cases requiring little or nothing in terms of pest control or pruning. Some are "dessert" fruits—tasty enough to just pop into your mouth. Others, the culinary types, might be too tart or too astringent to eat out of hand, but bake into fine pies, jellies, and jams. Also included in this group are fruits too bland or too seedy to be considered true dessert fruits. The line between dessert and culinary fruits is not rigid, though, and some fruits may be on one side of the line or the other—or both sides—according to each person's taste buds. The following list does not include tropical and subtropical fruits.

### Unusual Culinary Fruits

Akebia, *Akebia quinata*
Barberry, certain *Berberis* species
Bearberry, *Arctostaphylos uva-ursi*
Blackhaw viburnum, *Viburnum prunifolium*
Buffalo berry, *Shepherdia argentea*
Chokeberry, *Aronia melanocarpa*
Cornelian cherry, *Cornus mas*
Cranberry, *Vaccinium macrocarpon*
Elderberry, *Sambucus canadensis*
Gumi, *Elaeagnus multiflora*
Hackberry, *Celtis occidentalis*

Highbush cranberry, *Viburnum opulus* var. *americanum*
Jostaberry, *Ribes nidigrolaria*
Lingonberry, *Vaccinium vitis-idaea*
Oregon grape holly, *Mahonia aquifolium*
Rowan, *Sorbus* species
Salal, *Gaultheria shallon*
Strawberry tree, *Arbutus unedo*

### Unusual Dessert Fruits

Che, *Cudrania tricuspidata*
Clove currant, *Ribes odoratum*
Honeysuckle, *Lonicera caerulea* var. *edulis*
Huckleberry, *Gaylussacia* species
Juneberry, *Amelanchier* species
Maypop, *Passiflora incarnata*
Medlar, *Mespilus germanica*
Mulberry, *Morus* species
Musk strawberry, *Fragaria moschata*
Nanking cherry, *Prunus tomentosa*
Nannyberry, *Viburnum lentago*
Pawpaw, *Asimina triloba*
Prickly pear, *Opuntia* species
Raisin tree, *Hovenia dulcis*
Wineberry, *Rubus phoenicolasius*

## Edible Landscaping

When landscaping a property with trees, shrubs, and vines, it is not necessary to choose between plants providing either beauty or food. Many trees, shrubs, and vines bear edible fruits or nuts, and are ornamental in their own right. Every quality valued in a landscape plant—whether textured bark, fall foliage color, tidy form, bright flowers, or even decorative fruits—can also be found in some plant that also offers good eating. The following list does not include tropical and subtropical fruits.

## Ornamental Trees Bearing Edible Nuts or Fruits

Black walnut, *Juglans nigra*
Butternut, *Juglans cinerea*
Chestnut, *Castanea* species and hybrids
Cornelian cherry, *Cornus mas*
Crabapple, *Malus* species
Filbert, *Corylus* species
Ginkgo, *Ginkgo biloba*
Hackberry, *Celtis occidentalis*
Hawthorn, *Crataegus* species
Hickory, *Carya* species
Juneberry, *Amelanchier* species
Medlar, *Mespilus germanica*
Mulberry, *Morus* species
Pawpaw, *Asimina triloba*
Persimmon, *Diospyros* species
Pine, *Pinus* species, especially *P. koraiensis* in the North
Quince, *Cydonia oblonga*
Raisin tree, *Hovenia dulcis*
Rowan, *Sorbus* species
Strawberry tree, *Arbutus unedo*
Walnut, *Juglans regia*
Yellowhorn, *Xanthoceras sorbifolium*

## Ornamental Bushes Bearing Edible Fruits or Nuts

Barberry, certain *Berberis* species
Blackhaw viburnum, *Viburnum prunifolium*
Blueberry, *Vaccinium* species
Buffalo berry, *Shepherdia argentea*
Chokeberry, *Aronia melanocarpa*
Clove currant, *Ribes odoratum*
Elderberry, *Sambucus canadensis*
Gumi, *Elaeagnus multiflora*
Huckleberry, *Gaylussacia* species
Highbush cranberry, *Viburnum trilobum*
Honeysuckle, *Lonicera caerulea* var. *edulis*

Juneberry, *Amelanchier* species, especially *A. alnifolia*
Nanking cherry, *Prunus tomentosa*
Nannyberry, *Viburnum lentago*
Oregon grape holly, *Mahonia aquifolium*
Rose, *Rosa* species, especially *R. rugosa* and *R. canina*
Salal, *Gaultheria shallon*

## Ornamental Ground Covers Bearing Edible Fruits

Bearberry, *Arctostaphylos uva-ursi*
Checkerberry or creeping wintergreen, *Gaultheria procumbens*
Cranberry, *Vaccinium macrocarpon*
Lingonberry, *Vaccinium vitis-idaea*
Lowbush blueberry, *Vaccinium angustifolium*
Musk strawberry, *Fragaria moschata*

## Ornamental Fruiting Vines for an Arbor or Pergola

Akebia, *Akebia quinata*
Kiwi and hardy kiwi, *Actinidia* species
Maypop, *Passiflora incarnata*

## Fruit and Nut Plants with Especially Good Fall Color

Blackhaw viburnum, *Viburnum prunifolium*
Blueberry, *Vaccinium* species
Cornelian cherry, *Cornus mas*
Filbert, *Corylus* species
Ginkgo, *Ginkgo biloba*
Juneberry, *Amelanchier* species
Medlar, *Mespilus germanica*
Pawpaw, *Asimina triloba*
Persimmon, *Diospyros* species

## Fruit Plants with Especially Showy Flowers

Apple
Cherry
Cornelian cherry, *Cornus mas*
Elderberry, *Sambucus canadensis*
Hawthorn, *Crataegus* species
Juneberry, *Amelanchier* species
Medlar, *Mespilus germanica*
Nanking cherry, *Prunus tomentosa*
Nectarine
Oregon grape holly, *Mahonia aquifolium*
Peach
Pear
Plum
Quince, *Cydonia oblonga*
Rose

## All-Around Best Fruits for Edible Landscaping

The following is a list, an unavoidably subjective list, of the best plants for edible landscaping. These are plants that not only combine the best in beauty and taste, but also are low maintenance. They all are attractive through much of the year, perhaps dramatically so in some seasons. Generally, these plants will need little or no spraying.

Clove currant, *Ribes odoratum*
Hardy kiwi, *Actinidia* species
Juneberry, *Amelanchier* species
Nanking cherry, *Prunus tomentosa*
Pawpaw, *Asimina triloba*
Persimmon, *Diospyros* species

## Growing Fruits in Containers

Planting fruits in containers allows gardeners to grow fruits in an apartment, and to grow subtropical and tropical sorts even in climates where winters are frigid. Producing fruit—especially high-quality fruit—demands a lot of energy from a plant, so potted fruits need abundant light, at least six hours of direct sunlight each day. Deciduous fruits do not need light while they are dormant, but they do need to be kept cool, ideally below about 45°F. Roots cannot tolerate as much cold as stems can, so in northern areas even deciduous potted fruit plants need to be moved to the protection of an unheated garage or basement in winter. Alternatively, pile mulch up around the pots or bury them up to their rims in the ground.

The fruit plants in the lists that follow are the best adapted to growing in pots. These plants are naturally dwarf, lack taproots, and tolerate the regular root-pruning needed to renew the soil around the roots.

### Temperate-Zone Fruits for Containers

Apple (on dwarfing rootstock such as M9, P22, or M27; or a genetic dwarf such as Garden Delicious)
Apricot (genetic dwarf such as Garden Annie)
Blueberry
Cherry (genetic dwarf such as Garden Bing)
Nectarine (genetic dwarf such as Garden Beauty or Garden Delight)
Peach (genetic dwarf such as Garden Sun or Sensation)
Pear (on dwarfing rootstock such as quince)
Pomegranate
Strawberry

## Tropical and Subtropical Fruits for Containers

Acerola, *Malpighia glabra*

Banana, *Musa acuminata* (a dwarf variety such as Dwarf Cavendish)

Citrus, *Citrus* species

Fig (subtropical, but grows best if allowed to shed its leaves in fall and then experience a period of cool temperatures)

Natal plum, *Carissa grandiflora*

Passionfruit, *Passiflora* species

Pineapple, *Ananas comosus*

## The Right Fruit for the Site

Look at supermarket displays and it seems as if just about every fruit can be grown everywhere. Not so. The most sensible approach to growing fruits—and the one that eases maintenance chores—is to grow those that are well adapted to the site. This is especially important in regions such as arid areas or at specific sites with extreme conditions. Native fruits typically are a good choice because they are naturally adapted to local conditions.

### Fruits for Dry Regions

Date, *Phoenix dactylifera*

Eve's date, *Yucca baccata*

Feijoa, *Feijoa sellowiana*

Fig, *Ficus carica*

Jujube, *Ziziphus jujuba*

Olive, *Olea europaea*

Opuntia, *Opuntia* species

Pomegranate, *Punica granatum*

### Native American Fruits

Blackberry, *Rubus* species

Black raspberry, *Rubus occidentalis*

Blueberry, *Vaccinium angustifolium, V. corymbosum, V. ashei*

Cranberry, *Vaccinium macrocarpon*

Grapes, especially *Vitis labrusca* and *V. rotundifolia*

Hawthorn, *Crataegus* species

Highbush cranberry, *Viburnum trilobum*

Huckleberry, *Gaylussacia* species

Juneberry, *Amelanchier* species

Lingonberry, *Vaccinium vitis-idaea*

Maypop, *Passiflora incarnata*

Mulberry, *Morus* species

Pawpaw, *Asimina triloba*

Persimmon, *Diospyros virginiana*

Plums (American types), *Prunus americana*

## Pests

Like other plants, fruit plants sometimes have pest problems. The severity of such problems—both insects and diseases—depends on both the kind and the variety of fruit, as well as many other factors, such as the weather, the soil, and the region where the fruit is grown. Fortunately, each kind of fruit has just a few major pest problems, if any. Do not be intimidated about growing the fruits on the following lists; the pests with which they are associated are *potential* problems. Disease problems precede insect problems in the lists that follow.

### Major Pests of Apple

Cedar apple rust

Fire blight

Mildew

Scab

Apple maggot

Codling moth

Plum curculio

## Major Pests of Pear

Fire blight
Psylla
Scab

Codling moth

## Major Pests of Stone Fruit (Apricot, Peach, Nectarine, Plum, Cherry)

The various stone fruits share many pests in common. However, not all of the pests on the following list attack all the stone fruits equally, or at all.

---

### TEN WAYS TO CONTROL INSECTS AND DISEASES

There are many ways to deal with a pest problem when it rears its head. Often, a combination of methods works best, especially if the aim is to avoid using synthetic chemical pesticides. For more information on safe and sensible pest control, see page 538. The following are ten general techniques, with examples, for dealing with fruit pests:

1. Reduce stress and give fruit plants a leg up on pest and disease problems with good site selection, soil care, and proper pruning. Examples:
   Choose very well drained soil for peaches.
   Mulch raspberry plants so their shallow roots will not be damaged by tillage, and will be kept cool and moist.
2. Choose resistant species or varieties. Examples:
   Poorman gooseberry for mildew resistance.
   Liberty apple for resistance to scab, mildew, and fire blight.
3. Prune to remove damaged or diseased portions and to increase light and air circulation. Examples:
   Remove fire blight–infected stems of apple or pear trees to control this disease.
   Cut away black knot on plum trees.
4. Trap insects using visual or olfactory lures. Example:
   Use red sticky traps for 90 percent control of apple maggots.
5. Clean up infested or infected leaves and fruits. Example:
   Remove grape mummies at the end of the season to help control black rot.
6. Handpick insect pests off plants. Example:
   Pick Japanese beetles off raspberries, and drop them in a can of soapy water.
7. Use pest barriers such as sticky bands on trunks, and bags on fruits. Example:
   Employ sticky bands on plums to prevent aphid problems by impeding the travel of ants up trunk.
8. Encourage and/or import beneficial insects. Example:
   Release trichogramma wasps to help control codling moth on apple.
9. Apply bacteria, fungi, or viruses that target particular pests. Example:
   Spray *Bacillus thurengiensis* to help control codling moth on apple.
10. Apply relatively nontoxic sprays: plain water, insecticidal soaps, insecticides made from plant extracts, or horticultural oils. Use petrochemical pesticides as a last resort. Example:
    Spray dormant oil to help control scale insects on a number of fruit crops.

## SEVEN WAYS TO FEND OFF BIRDS

1. Hang scare-eye balloons (most effective against flocking birds).
2. Use predator bird decoys, such as owls.
3. Erect a scarecrow.
4. Hang aluminum pie pans near fruit plants.
5. Use shiny Mylar tape stretched between posts so that the tape is just above the plants.
6. Drape black cotton thread over the stems of fruit plants.
7. Put netting around the plants (the only reliable method!).

Bacterial spot
Black knot
Brown rot
Cherry leaf spot
Peach leaf curl

Aphids
Oriental fruit moth
Cherry fruit fly
Peach tree borer
Peach twig borer
Plum curculio

## Major Pests of Grape

Anthracnose
Black rot
Botrytis bunch rot
Downy mildew
Powdery mildew
Pierce's disease
Phylloxera

Grape berry moth

## Major Pests of Blueberry

Botrytis tip blight
Stem canker
Stunt virus

Mummyberry

## Major Pests of Strawberry

Anthracnose
Gray mold
Leather rot
Red stele
Verticillium wilt

Grubs
Mites
Plant bug

## Major Pests of Bramble

Anthracnose
Cane blight
Crown gall
Orange rust
Phytophthera root rot
Raspberry mosaic
Spur blight
Verticillium wilt

Cane borer
Crown borer

## Further Reading

Ellis, Barbara, and Fern Bradley, eds. *The Organic Gardener's Handbook of Natural Insect and Disease Control.* Emmaus, Pa.: Rodale, 1992.

Otto, Stella. *The Backyard Berry Book.* Maple City, Mich.: Ottographics, 1995.

Otto, Stella. *The Backyard Orchardist.* Maple City, Mich.: Ottographics, 1993.

Reich, Lee. *Growing Fruit in Your Backyard.* New York: Macmillan, 1996.

Reich, Lee, ed. *Growing Fruits: Nature's Desserts.* Brooklyn, N.Y.: Brooklyn Botanic Garden, 1996.

Reich, Lee. *The Pruning Book.* Newtown, Ct.: Taunton Press, 1997.

Reich, Lee. *Uncommon Fruits Worthy of Attention: A Gardener's Guide.* Reading, Mass.: Addison-Wesley Publishing Co., 1991.

Westwood, Melvin. *Temperate Zone Pomology.* Portland, Ore.: Timber Press, 1993.

# 8

# ORNAMENTAL GARDENING

## PLANTS FOR EVERY PURPOSE AND EVERY REGION

This section covers recommended plants for the nine main growing regions in the United States: the Northeast, the Southeast, subtropical Florida, the Midwest and Northern Great Plains, Texas and the Southern Plains, the Rocky Mountain region, the Pacific Northwest, coastal California, and the western deserts. The section begins with a description of each region, including its range and climate, growing tips particular to the region, and books for further reading. Next is detailed information on various types of plants—trees, shrubs, perennials, foliage plants, ground covers, vines, annuals, plants to attract butterflies and wildlife, heirloom flowers and flowers for cutting, and plants for winter interest—with extensive lists of recommended plants for each of the nine regions. Many of the recommended plants are native to the region and are marked accordingly. Following the plant lists are separate, detailed sections on lawns, bulbs, easy-care roses, and plants for water gardens.

All hardiness zones refer to the U.S. Department of Agriculture Hardiness Zone Map that can be found on page 30. The plants listed in this section are meant to be starting points. In some cases, the plant choices are conservative so that they will be appropriate for the entire region. Experiment with plants for your area; refer to the books listed under "Further Reading" for more recommendations. Native plant societies or other plant societies are also excellent sources of information on plants that will thrive in your part of the country.

# The Regions

## The Northeast

The Northeast has a cool temperate climate with generally abundant rainfall, humid summers, drier autumns, and winters ranging in temperature from moderate (Zone 7, in and around Long Island) to severe (Zone 3, northern New England and the Adirondacks). Most of the population lives in the milder zones. The plants listed for the Northeast are hardy to Zone 5, except for a handful of hardier plants and a few irresistibly ornamental plants hardy only to Zone 6, which are noted. Some of the most beautiful species native to the Northeast, such as paper birch, balsam fir, sugar maple, and Canadian hemlock, thrive only in the cooler zones and resent the hotter summers of the coastal areas. Gardeners in the warmer zones can also grow many of the plants recommended for the Southeast region.

Soils are mostly fertile, but may be thin, gravelly, rocky, or poorly drained in many places. Rarely disturbed soils tend to be acidic, but garden and urban soils may have elevated pH from concrete leaching and continual liming. The Northeast region is world famous for its autumn foliage color, rivaled only by that of temperate eastern Asia. Leaf color is best in long, dry autumns, and is most dramatic in upland regions, where brilliantly colored birches and sugar maples compose much of the forest canopy.

Horticulture in the Northeast has been enriched by the introduction of ornamental plants from temperate regions around the world—especially Japan and east Asia, with their tremendous species diversity and generally compatible climate. On the other hand, some plants that thrive in British and northern European gardens languish in the northeastern United States, with its muggy summers and relative extremes of hot and cold. Northeastern gardeners get around these problems by using winter mulches and sheltered locations to protect marginally hardy favorites and by planting specimens that do not tolerate heat in the partial shade of trees or on north-facing slopes.

### Recommended Gardening References

Gardening books covering the Northeast exclusively are rare or nonexistent; many gardening references seem to treat the northeastern climate and soils as the norm, and other regions of the country as horticulture "special cases." The following outstanding references, although not written exclusively for the Northeast, are very useful for this region.

Brickell, Christopher, et al., eds. *The American Horticultural Society Encyclopedia of Gardening.* New York: Dorling Kindersley, 1993.

Bush-Brown, James, and Louise Bush-Brown. *America's Garden Book.* Rev. ed. New York: Macmillan, 1996.

Free, Montague. *Gardening.* Rev. ed. New York: Harcourt, Brace and Company, 1947. (Out of print but can be found in libraries.)

Wyman, Donald. *Wyman's Gardening Encyclopedia.* New York: Macmillan, 1986.

## The Southeast

The Southeast region is a geographically large area that extends from Delaware, Maryland, and West Virginia down to northern Florida and west to east Texas and Oklahoma. It includes four major USDA hardiness zones, from 6 to 9, with low winter temperatures ranging from minus 10°F to 20°F, depending on the location. In general, the Southeast is relatively mild, with a growing season of 220 days and rainfall averaging 45 to 50 inches per year. The specific climatic conditions, including rainfall, vary dramatically from the coast to the high-elevation mountains and from north to south. Soils also vary from heavy clay in the upper (Piedmont and mountain) regions to very sandy in the lower-lying coastal and sandhills and barrier island areas. Southern soils tend to be naturally acidic, although some considerable areas in western Virginia and in Kentucky and Tennessee where limestone substrates are common have soils that are naturally alkaline.

The Southeast lends itself to year-round gardening, with mild winter days and sometimes weeks, even in the northern and southern mountain highland areas where the most extreme cold conditions occur. The heat and drought of summers—droughts do not occur every year, but should be anticipated—can be made less stressful by careful planning to include ample mulching, appropriate timing of planting, and judicious selection of plants best adapted to local growing conditions.

The plant lists for the Southeast mainly include plants recommended for use throughout the region. Where plants are appropriate only for certain parts of the Southeast, these exceptions are indicated by the following notations: US (Upper South, Zone 6), MS (Middle South, Zone 7 and parts of Zone 8 in the western edge of Mississippi, southern Arkansas, and central Texas), LS (Lower South, Zone 8 plus coastal North Carolina and part of southern coastal Virginia), and CS (Coastal South, Zone 8 in northern Florida and parts of Zone 9 in coastal Texas, Louisiana, and northeastern Florida).

## Recommended Gardening References

Armitage, Alan M. *Herbaceous Perennial Plants: A Treatise on Their Identification, Culture, and Garden Attributes.* Athens, Ga.: Varsity Press, 1989.

Bender, Steve, and Felder Rushing. *Passalong Plants.* Chapel Hill: The University of North Carolina Press, 1993.

Bir, Richard E. *Growing and Propagating Showy Native Woody Plants.* Chapel Hill: The University of North Carolina Press, 1992.

Chaplin, Lois Trigg. *The Southern Gardener's Book of Lists: The Best Plants for All Your Needs, Wants, and Whims.* Dallas: Taylor Publishing Company, 1994.

Halfacre, R. Gordon. *Landscape Plants of the Southeast.* Raleigh, N.C.: Sparks Press, 1986.

*Southern Living Garden Guide.* Birmingham, Ala.: Oxmoor House, Inc., 1996.

Tripp, Kim E., and J. C. Raulston. *The Year in Trees: Superb Woody Plants for Four-Season Gardens.* Portland, Ore.: Timber Press, 1995.

## Subtropical Florida

Subtropical Florida stretches from Palm Beach County to Key West in the east and from Sarasota through Naples and on to Cape Sabal in the west. Three hardiness zones exist here, with a range of microclimates. The closer to the coasts, the milder the weather. Inland, temperatures can be several degrees cooler in winter—which can be detrimental to tropical plants if they are not in a protected area. Some winters remain warm; others bring cold fronts and even the occasional hard freeze. Most people live on or near the coasts, where the chances of success with tropical plants is greater. Some tender tropicals can be grown in the colder areas as well, if they are given protection from northwest winds, placed on the southeast side of the house, or grown beneath protective tree canopies—particularly native tree canopies. The plants listed for subtropical Florida are for Zones 10A, 10B, and 11 unless noted otherwise.

Soil is generally alkaline in South Florida, except for pockets of acid sand in Dade County and acid sands in northern Broward and Palm Beach Counties. The water, drawn from a limestone aquifer, adds to the alkalinity. Micronutrient deficiencies easily occur in such soils, most often iron, magnesium, and manganese deficiencies.

The tropics influence South Florida with wet and dry seasons: summer is wet, winter is dry, and spring is driest. Consequently, plants must withstand cycles of flood and drought as well as occasional wide temperature swings. That is why plants native to the region should form the garden's backbone, and tropicals its ornaments.

## Recommended Gardening References

Stresau, Fred. *Florida: My Eden.* Port Salerno, Fla.: Florida Classics Library, 1986.

Tasker, Georgia. *Enchanted Ground: Gardening with Nature in the Subtropics.* Kansas City: Andrews & McMeel, 1994.

Watkins, John V., and Thomas J. Sheehan. *Florida Landscape Plants: Native and Exotic.* Gainesville: The University Presses of Florida, 1975.

## The Midwest and Northern Great Plains

The Midwest and Northern Great Plains region covers a vast area of the continent's midsection, from the edge of the eastern deciduous forests, west to the rain shadow of the Rocky Mountains, and from boreal Canada south to Okla-

homa. From season to season, diversity is the rule here. Arctic blasts as cold as minus 45°F can grip the region for weeks on end. Winters in the northern reaches of the region generally have consistent snow cover, while Chicago and parts south do not. In the summer, dry southwesterly breezes gain heat over the Southern Plains, causing temperatures to soar to the 90s or higher well into Canada. Moist Gulf air is often pulled in by large weather systems and the atmosphere drips with humidity.

Most gardeners live in USDA Hardiness Zone 3 and warmer areas. The majority of the plants listed in this section for the Midwest and Northern Great Plains are hardy to Zone 3, but not all. All are hardy to Zone 4 unless otherwise indicated.

## Recommended Gardening References

Barr, Claude A. *Jewels of the Plains.* Minneapolis: University of Minnesota Press, 1983.

Diekelmann, John, and Robert Shuster. *Natural Landscaping.* New York: McGraw-Hill Book Company, 1982.

McKeowan, D. *Complete Guide to Midwest Gardening.* Dallas: Taylor Publishing Co., 1985.

Smith, J. R., and B. S. Smith. *The Prairie Garden.* Madison, Wisc.: University of Wisconsin Press, 1980.

Snyder, Leon C. *Flowers for Northern Gardens.* Minneapolis: University of Minnesota Press, 1983.

Snyder, Leon C. *Gardening in the Upper Midwest.* Minneapolis: University of Minnesota Press, 1985.

Snyder, Leon C. *Native Plants for Northern Gardens.* Chanhassen, Minn.: University of Minnesota Libraries, Minnesota Landscape Arboretum: Andersen Horticultural Library, 1991.

Snyder, Leon C. *Trees and Shrubs for Northern Gardens.* Minneapolis: University of Minnesota Press, 1980.

## Texas and the Southern Plains

Texas and the Southern Plains region covers Central and West Texas and the Texas Panhandle; eastern New Mexico plains; Oklahoma, except for the eastern forested edge; southern Kansas; and southwestern Missouri. Most of the plants recommended for this area grow in conjunction with prairie and the savannah trees and riparian woodlands that abut prairies. Almost all of them can tolerate the shrink-swell action of soils high in clay content. All of them are able to thrive in neutral to alkaline soils, and many actually prefer it. Most of the woody plants on the lists for this region need supplemental watering to survive on the Great Plains; the most drought-tolerant trees and shrubs are noted. The plants listed for this region are for Zones 6, 7, and 8 unless noted otherwise.

Planting times are different in this region from those elsewhere in the country. The best planting time for trees and shrubs is late September to mid-April, as the ground never or rarely freezes and summers are brutal. Planting can be successful in summer, but frequent watering is essential. Watering is best accomplished by an immediate overnight soaking with a dribbling hose and then monthly soakings the first summer or whenever it has not rained for a month, with soakings the second year as needed. By the third year, trees planted in their native habitat (except those more than 3 inches in caliper at the time of planting) should be established and able to live on rainfall alone; however, if you live west of Wichita, Oklahoma City, and Abilene, Texas, trees will probably always require some supplemental water.

Seed for annuals can be planted from September to November. Perennials can be planted any time of year, but spring and fall are best.

Most prefer rich loamy soil with good drainage but lots of humus to hold moisture; however, many prefer rocky soil. Where conditions are particularly hot and windy and the soil has a high clay content, place a stepping stone on the south side of the stem to keep the roots moist and to moderate soil temperature. Most perennials will have stronger, shorter, more upright stems if they are watered only once a month during the summer. Never cut back a plant in the growing season unless it has regrown a rosette of leaves at the base. Fall flowers tend to be taller than spring flowers, because in nature they are competing with prairie grasses that tend to be tall in the autumn. To keep fall flowers short and bushy, cut the plants back in early May. Warm-season grasses can be planted while dormant in the winter, but they can also be planted in the summer.

### Recommended Gardening References

Ajilvsgi, Geyata. *Butterfly Gardening for the South.* Dallas: Taylor Publishing, 1990.

Garrett, Howard. *Plants of the Metroplex.* Austin: University of Texas Press, 1994.

Ogden, Scott. *Gardening Success with Difficult Soils.* Dallas: Taylor Publishing, 1994.

Wasowski, Sally, and Andy Wasowski. *Native Texas Gardens.* Houston: Gulf Publishing, 1991, 1997.

Wasowski, Sally, and Andy Wasowski. *Native Texas Plants.* Houston.: Gulf Publishing, 1997.

Welch, William C. *Perennial Garden Color for Texas and the South.* Dallas: Taylor Publishing, 1989.

## The Rocky Mountain Region

It could be said that the Rocky Mountain region has a cold temperate climate with adequate precipitation for growing trees: this is true for the mountainous areas. It could be said that the Rocky Mountain region is a temperate semiarid region supporting grasslands, but growing trees requires supplemental irrigation: this is true east of the Rockies. It could be said that the Rocky Mountain region is a cold desert supporting dryland shrubs and flowering perennials: this is true for the western part of the range. Actually, the Rocky Mountain region consists of many lands, from grasslands and deserts to forests and tundra.

What these contrasting areas have in common is high elevation, low relative humidity and high evaporation, bright sunshine, strong winds, and warm summer temperatures. High evaporation rates make less rainfall available to plants than in humid areas. Strong winds increase the loss of water, and in winter the winds blow snow in drifts, leaving some areas bare, uninsulated, and exposed to cold temperatures. Sunlight is intense, quickly warming plant tissues even in winter.

Although they occur infrequently, there can be extreme, radical temperature fluctuations in short periods of time. In one 24-hour period in 1949, temperatures in Fort Collins, Colorado, went from 50°F to minus 40°F—a difference of 90 degrees. In 1969 and 1971 Denver temperatures went from 80°F to below zero in the same day. Damage to mature trees and shrubs was devastating.

On the bright side, high elevation and intense sunlight create contrasting microclimates for growing a variety of plants from many climates. Plants requiring full sun in humid areas can be grown in partial shade in this region. Plants from forests requiring cool, moist soil can grow on the north side of buildings, and desert plants can be grown on the south.

Differences in elevation add another dimension. For every 1,000 feet in elevation, there is a 3.5- to 5.5-degree change in temperature. Plants in bloom at 5,000 feet will flower two to three weeks later at 7,000 feet.

For plants to thrive here, they need to adapt to or tolerate cold winters and hot summers, rapid temperature changes, late spring snows, early fall freezes, strong winds, intense sunshine, low relative humidity, high evaporation, and limited water. Some tough, reliable plants that can survive these adversities are available. What is most exciting are the new plants being introduced that thrive under these conditions, and the continued search for even more.

## Recommended Gardening References

Denver Water. *Xeriscape Plant Guide.* Golden, Colo.: Fulcrum Publishing, 1996.

Hyde, Barbara. *The Progress of a Gardener.* Longmont, Colo.: Barbara Hyde, Inc., 1995.

Knopf, Jim. *The Xeriscape Flower Gardener: A Waterwise Guide for the Rocky Mountain Region.* Boulder, Colo.: Johnson Publishers, 1991.

Weinstein, Gayle. *Shrubs for the Rocky Mountain and Plains States.* Denver, Colo.: The Shereth Group, 1996.

Weinstein, Gayle. *Trees for the Rocky Mountain and Plains States.* Denver, Colo.: The Shereth Group, 1996.

## The Pacific Northwest

With proper attention to soils, drainage, summer moisture, and exposure, all plants listed for the Pacific Northwest region should thrive in the valleys west of the Cascade Mountains from the Strait of Georgia south to the Siskiyou Mountains in southern Oregon. With greater attention to watering and exposure, many will thrive east of the Cascades as well. All the plants listed for this region are hardy to Zone 7 unless noted otherwise; gardeners in the eastern area should refer to the sources listed below to verify hardiness below Zone 7. In areas where wind and humidity conditions are often extreme, such as the Columbia River gorge, many plants will benefit by placement in sheltered sites.

Soils vary greatly in the Pacific Northwest region, from slow-draining clay soils to fast-draining sandy soils. All plantings benefit from copious amounts of composted organic material. If possible, incorporate compost with double digging of the entire planting area initially, and then add additional compost as each plant is introduced to its new home.

Native plants are always a good foundation for a garden. These can be supplemented with plants from regions of the world with similar growing conditions. Many plants from the Himalayas, Japan, China, and Korea thrive in the Northwest because these areas have similar climates and habitats. Similarly, the British Isles, parts of Europe, and Patagonia offer many choice plants for Northwest gardeners.

### Recommended Gardening References

Ashmun, Barbara. *200 Tips for Growing Flowers in the Pacific Northwest.* Chicago: Chicago Review Press, 1996.

Grant, John A., and Carol L. Grant. *Trees and Shrubs for Pacific Northwest Gardens.* 2nd ed. rev. by Marvin E. Black et al. Portland, Ore.: Timber Press, 1990.

Kruckeberg, Arthur R. *Gardening with Native Plants of the Pacific Northwest.* Seattle: University of Washington Press, 1996.

Lovejoy, Ann. *The Year in Bloom: Gardening for All Seasons in the Pacific Northwest.* Seattle: Sasquatch Books, 1987.

Sunset Publishing. *Sunset Western Garden Book.* 6th ed. Menlo Park, Calif.: Sunset Publishing Corporation, 1995.

## Coastal California

California's coastal regions begin along the northern part of the state from Crescent City to San Francisco. This area is bordered by the Northern Coast Ranges. The coastline veers inland around San Francisco and San Pablo Bays. Communities bordering this area, which is sandwiched between the waterways to the west and the foothills of the western edge of the Central Valley, are subject to the coastal influence. The central coastal region of California runs from Monterey south to San Luis Obispo. This coastal strip is bordered to the east by the Central Coast Ranges. The southern coastal region includes Santa Barbara and areas south to the Mexican border. The southern coastal region is bordered by the Southern Coast Ranges, southern inland valleys and foothills, and the southernmost Peninsular Ranges.

Coastal California has a Mediterranean climate, which is very different from the climate in the interior of the state. In Mediterranean climates most of the precipitation is in winter and early spring, when temperatures are low and daylight is at a minimum—not an ideal combination for plant growth. In mid to late spring, temperatures quickly rise, day length increases, and water is still available to the plants, so it is during this period that plants put on their greatest amount of growth. Mediterranean climates typically have hot, dry summers; plants originating from this type of climate become dormant during this time of year and require a rest—an important factor to note when growing these types of plants.

Gardeners in this region must be cautious

with summer watering regimes. All plants need some summer water when their roots are becoming established. But once plants are established, reduce the amount of water applied during the summer. It is possible to kill a Mediterranean plant or shorten its life span considerably by overwatering in the summer. On the other hand, plants native to the northern coastal regions of California are accustomed to summer fog—a form of precipitation that occurs during the driest months. Plants in these regions can receive up to 30 inches of moisture from fog drip. When using these plants in the garden, it is important to supply summer water.

Take advantage of winter rains by planting in the fall. The soil temperature is still warm enough in the fall to promote root growth, and the winter rains keep the new root growth well watered. By the time spring arrives, the new plantings will have a more substantial root system that will support maximum foliage growth.

## Recommended Gardening References

Keator, Glenn. *Complete Garden Guide to the Native Perennials of California.* San Francisco: Chronicle Books, 1990.

Keator, Glenn. *Complete Garden Guide to the Native Shrubs of California.* San Francisco: Chronicle Books, 1990.

Perry, Bob. *Landscape Plants for Western Regions.* Claremont, Calif.: Land Design Publishing, 1992.

Power, Nancy Goslee. *The Gardens of California: Four Centuries of Design from Mission to Modern.* New York: Clarkson N. Potter, 1995.

Sunset Publishing. *Sunset Western Garden Book.* 6th ed. Menlo Park, Calif.: Sunset Publishing Corporation, 1995.

## The Western Deserts

The western deserts extend from southwestern Washington, southern Idaho, and southwestern Montana through much of Nevada, Utah, Arizona, and New Mexico as well as western Colorado, eastern California, and southwest Texas into Mexico. While the middle elevations, from 1,000 to 6,000 feet, support the bulk of the native desert plant communities, the mountains rising abruptly several thousand feet above the adjacent desert and the prairie grasslands rolling across the Great Plains also contribute to the plant palette. The nonnative plants recommended for this region come from South America, Australia, North and South Africa, the Middle East, and even places as unlikely as India, Siberia, China, and Japan.

Deserts are stereotypically hot and dry. But while persistent drought and alkaline soils lacking organic matter are common denominators of the western deserts, in temperature range this region is very diverse. The Great Basin (Reno, Nevada) and northern Chihuahuan (Albuquerque, New Mexico) Desert have winter temperatures from the low teens to 0°F, with brief and infrequent drops to −15°F. The Mohave (Las Vegas, Nevada) Desert is somewhat milder, and much of the Sonoran (Phoenix, Arizona) Desert enjoys winter low temperatures in the mid-20s and rarely experiences extreme cold. Conversely, while all the deserts are hot in summer, the coolest desert areas rarely top 110°F, and some summers have only a few days above 100°F, while the warm deserts routinely top 100°F, and occasionally reach 120°F. Throughout the plant lists for this region, asterisks are used to help sort out cold and heat tolerances.

Because water conservation is a critical concern throughout the Southwest, all of the plants recommended for this region are relatively drought-tolerant. Most large trees, by virtue of size alone, are oasis plants requiring considerable water to maintain their extensive canopy of leaves. This is especially true in the Southwest, where rainfall may average less than 10 inches annually and heat and wind evaporate moisture rapidly. The trees listed below are drought-adapted to varying degrees, and the trees for small spaces and flowering trees tend to be more water-conservative than larger trees.

Because desert soils tend to compact easily, when trees are transplanted the soil should be loosened to the depth of the rootball and three to five times its diameter. Use the native soil, without organic amendments, as backfill. Trees requiring organic amendments are poorly adapted to desert conditions, so they are not among those listed for this region. Desert plants are adapted to high levels of oxygen and low levels of carbon dioxide in the soil. Organic soil amendments and mulches release carbon dioxide as they decompose and can undermine desert-plant vigor. Day to night temperatures fluctuate widely in the desert, making the tender bark on young trees susceptible to sunscald—sometimes called "southwest injury" because it occurs on the section of trunk facing southwest. Leaving lower branches unpruned or painting or wrapping the trunks with a protective covering until the bark thickens prevents the problem.

Avoid overwatering; it is easier to bring desert plants back from underwatering than from overwatering. In a climate as harsh as the desert, it is obvious that plants need water during the heat of summer. But the more adapted the plants are to the specific conditions of the garden, the less water they will need to survive once established. Depending on the plants and the garden conditions, plants may need summer watering weekly, every two weeks, or only monthly. Water plants deeply after leaves begin to drop in autumn and just before top growth resumes in spring, because these are the times when new roots develop. While plants do not need as much water during winter, in the warm deserts many plants are actively growing, and even in the coldest desert areas evergreen plants transpire enough moisture to require monthly watering. Desert soils are naturally rich in mineral salts; once a season, water twice as deeply as you normally do to leach excess salts out of the root zone.

Perennials can be more particular about the type and depth of mulches used around them than trees or shrubs are. Wildflowers native to deserts often are longer-lived in inorganic stone mulches than when mulched with bark, compost, or pine needles. Perennials adapted to full sun in areas having more cloud cover often require partial to full shade in the desert. Perennials that will grow in sun or shade will usually require less water in the shade. Dry winter winds in cold-desert areas can burn the foliage of broad-leafed evergreens. Plant vulnerable perennials and shrubs in locations that are sheltered from the wind.

## Recommended Gardening References

Mielke, Judy. *Native Plants for Southwestern Landscapes.* Austin: University of Texas Press, 1993.

Phillips, Judith. *Natural by Design: Plants for Natural Gardens.* 2 vols. Santa Fe: Museum of New Mexico Press, 1995.

The Editors of *Sunset* magazine. *New Western Garden Book.* 40th anniversary ed. Menlo Park, Calif.: Sunset Publishing, 1995.

# Trees

Trees are the most important plant features of a garden. They are the largest and longest-living elements, defining the garden's basic structure and levels of light. The canopy they create contributes to the rhythm of the garden, providing cooling shade in the summer and admitting winter and spring light that allows for the garden's spring flowers.

Large, freestanding woody perennial plants, trees grow from a single trunk (which may branch close to the ground into two or more trunklike branches). They are either deciduous or evergreen. Deciduous trees lose most or all of their leaves in the fall, remain bare in the winter, and leaf out again in the spring. Evergreens hold their leaves for a least a year and are never fully bare. There are two main groups of evergreen trees: broad-leaved evergreens and needled evergreens, or conifers.

## What to Consider in Selecting a Tree

Choosing the right tree for your site is the first and most critical step to ensure that it will thrive. Climate and soil are the chief considerations. Look for a tree that will tolerate the extremes of winter cold and summer heat in your region and will be suited to the soil and light conditions of your particular site. Have your soil pH tested, and if your soil is extremely acid or alkaline, choose a suitable species; since tree roots eventually cover such a large area, it is not practical to amend soil to significantly alter its pH. Observe other soil conditions as well. If the soil is sandy and dries out quickly, choose a drought-tolerant species; if the soil is heavy and puddles of water form after a rain, choose a species that will tolerate these wet conditions.

When selecting a tree, it is also important to take into account its growth rate and ultimate size and shape. The wrong tree can quickly outgrow the space and will require severe pruning and eventually need to be removed. Finally, consider the aesthetic issues. Do you want to create dense or dappled shade? If you want a flowering tree or one with colored foliage, plan how the color will fit into your overall garden. Do you want an early-blooming or late-blooming species? Consider your tree in various seasons. In autumn, many deciduous trees exhibit spectacular foliage color. Bark and interesting branch structure can provide winter interest. Fruiting trees can attract birds and wildlife to your garden.

## Planting and Care

For instructions on planting bare-root, container-grown, and balled-and-burlapped trees, see "Planting and Transplanting," page 447. For pruning tips, see "Pruning," page 503. For information on the special needs of street trees and recommended species, see "City Gardening," page 609.

## Trees for the Northeast

Plants are hardy to Zone 5, unless noted.

### Great All-Around Trees

*Acer rubrum,* red maple (native)
*Acer saccharum,* sugar maple (native)
*Betula nigra,* notably the cultivar 'Heritage', black birch (native)
*Cedrus atlantica,* notably the cultivar 'Glauca', atlas cedar
*Cercidiphyllum japonicum,* Katsura tree
*Fraxinus americana,* white ash (native)

*Ginkgo biloba,* ginkgo

*Gleditsia triacanthos,* honey locust (native)

*Liriodendron tulipifera,* tulip tree (native)

*Metasequoia glyptostroboides,* dawn redwood

*Nyssa sylvatica,* tupelo, black gum, sourwood (native)

*Picea omorika,* serbian spruce

*Pinus bungeana,* lacebark pine

*Pinus strobus,* white pine (native)

*Pseudolarix kaempferi,* golden larch

*Quercus alba,* white oak (native)

*Quercus rubra,* northern red oak (native)

*Rhus typhina,* staghorn sumac (native)

*Sophora japonica,* Japanese pagoda tree, scholar tree

*Tilia tomentosa,* silver linden

*Zelkova serrata,* zelkova, Japanese elm

## Trees for Small Spaces

*Acer buergerianum,* trident maple

*Acer carpinifolium,* notably the cultivar 'Esveld', hornbeam maple

*Acer griseum,* paperbark maple

*Acer palmatum,* notably the cultivars 'Sangokaku', 'Okushimo', 'Shigitatsu Sawa', 'Hessei', 'Bloodgood', Japanese maple

*Acer pensylvanicum,* moosewood, striped maple, snake-bark maple (native)

*Betula pendula,* notably the cultivar 'Gracilis', European white birch

*Betula populifolia,* gray birch, canoe birch (native)

*Chamaecyparis obtusa,* Hinoki false cypress

*Cercis canadensis,* redbud

*Cladrastis kentukea (C. lutea),* yellowwood

*Cornus florida,* flowering dogwood (native)

*Cornus kousa,* Japanese dogwood

*Cotinus obovatus,* American smoke tree

*Crataegus* x *lavallei,* Lavalle hybrid hawthorn

*Halesia tetraptera (H. carolina),* silverbell tree

*Hamamelis* x *intermedia,* hybrid oriental witch-hazel

*Juniperus virginiana,* eastern red cedar (native)

*Maackia amurensis,* Amur Maackia, Amur pea-tree

*Magnolia virginiana,* sweetbay magnolia (native)

*Oxydendrum arboreum,* sourwood, sorrel tree

*Pinus cembra,* Swiss stone pine

*Prunus* x 'Okame', hybrid flowering cherry

*Sassafras albidum,* sassafras (native)

*Stewartia pseudocamellia,* Stewartia

*Styrax japonica,* Japanese snowbell

*Thuja occidentalis,* American arborvitae, white swamp cedar (native)

*Xanthoceras sorbifolium,* yellowhorn

## Flowering Trees

*Amelanchier arborea,* shadbush, serviceberry (native)

*Cornus florida,* flowering dogwood (native)

*Cornus kousa,* Japanese dogwood

*Davidia involucrata,* dove tree, handkerchief tree

*Hamamelis mollis,* Chinese witchhazel

*Magnolia* x *soulangiana,* saucer magnolia

*Malus floribunda,* showy crabapple

*Prunus serrulata,* notably the cultivars 'Kwanzan', 'Ojochin', Japanese flowering cherry

*Prunus subhirtella,* Higan cherry, early Japanese flowering cherry

## Trees for the Southeast

Plants can be used throughout the region in Zones 6–9. Where plants are appropriate only for certain parts of the region, they are noted as follows:

US = Upper South, Zone 6

MS = Middle South, Zone 7 and parts of Zone 8 in the western edge of Mississippi, southern Arkansas, and central Texas

LS = Lower South, Zone 8 plus coastal North Carolina and parts of southern coastal Virginia

CS = Coastal South, Zone 8 in northern Florida and parts of Zone 9 in coastal Texas, Louisiana, and northeastern Florida

## Great All-Around Trees

*Acer leucoderme,* chalk maple (native)

*Acer rubrum,* red maple (native)

*Betula nigra,* river birch (native)

*Cryptomeria japonica,* notably the cultivar 'Elegans', Japanese cedar—MS, LS

*Cunninghamia lanceolata,* China fir—MS, LS

*Fagus grandifolia,* American beech (native)

*Firmiana simplex,* Chinese parasol tree—MS, LS, CS

*Ginkgo biloba,* ginkgo

*Ilex opaca,* American holly (native)

*Ilex* 'Nellie R. Stevens', holly

*Juniperus virginiana,* red cedar (native)

*Liriodendron tulipifera,* tulip poplar (native)

*Liquidambar styraciflua,* notably the cultivar 'Rotundiloba', sweet gum (native)

*Magnolia grandiflora,* southern magnolia (native)

*Magnolia macrophylla,* bigleaf magnolia (native)

*Nyssa sylvatica,* black gum (native)

*Pinus palustris,* longleaf pine (native)—LS, CS

*Pinus strobus,* white pine (native)—US

*Pinus taeda,* loblolly pine (native)—MS, LS, CS

*Pinus virginiana,* Virginia pine (native)—US, MS, LS

*Pistacia chinensis,* Chinese pistache

*Quercus alba,* white oak (native)

*Quercus lyrata,* overcup oak (native)

*Quercus michauxii,* swamp chestnut oak (native)

*Quercus phellos,* willow oak (native)

*Quercus virginiana,* live oak (native)—MS, LS, CS

*Sophora japonica,* Japanese pagoda tree—US, MS

*Taxodium distichum,* swamp cypress (native)

## Trees for Small Spaces for the Southeast

*Acer palmatum,* Japanese maple

*Carpinus caroliniana,* ironwood (native)

*Cercis canadensis,* redbud (native)

*Chionanthus virginicus,* fringe tree (native)

*Clerodendrum trichotomum,* harlequin glory-bower

*Cotinus coggygria,* smoke tree—US, MS, LS

*Crataegus marshallii,* parsley leaf hawthorn (native)

*Cyrilla racemiflora,* titi (native)

*Franklinia alatamaha,* Franklinia (native)

*Ilex decidua,* possumhaw (native)

*Ilex vomitoria,* yaupon holly (native)—MS, LS, CS

*Magnolia grandiflora,* notably the cultivar 'Little Gem', magnolia (native)—MS, LS, CS

*Magnolia virginiana,* sweetbay (native)

*Prunus mume,* Japanese flowering apricot

*Rhus typhina,* notably the cultivar 'Dissecta', cut-leaved sumac (native)—US, MS, LS

## Flowering Trees

*Aesculus pavia,* red buckeye (native)

*Amelanchier* x *grandiflora,* notably the cultivar 'Autumn Brilliance', serviceberry

*Cercis canadensis* var. *texensis,* notably the cultivar 'Oklahoma', redbud (native)

*Cornus florida,* flowering dogwood (native)

*Cornus kousa,* Kousa dogwood—US, MS

*Davidia involucrata,* dove tree, handkerchief tree—US, MS, LS

*Halesia carolina,* Carolina silverbell (native)

*Koelreuteria paniculata,* goldenrain tree

*Lagerstroemia fauriei,* notably the cultivar 'Fantasy', Japanese crape myrtle

*Magnolia stellata,* star magnolia

*Malus* hybrids, flowering crabapples

*Oxydendrum arboreum,* sourwood (native)

*Pinckneya bracteata,* poinsettia tree (native)—MS, LS, CS

*Vitex agnus-castus,* chaste tree

## Trees for Subtropical Florida

The plants recommended for Subtropical Florida are appropriate for Zones 10A, 10B, and 11, unless noted as follows:

*Not for Zone 10A
**Not for Zone 11

### Great All-Around Trees

*Acer rubrum* var. *trilobum,* red maple** (native)

*Bucida buceras,* black olive* (native)

*Bulnesia arborea,* verawood*

*Bursera simaruba,* gumbo limbo* (native)

*Chrysophyllum oliviforme,* satin leaf* (native)

*Citrus* species, citruses

*Coccoloba diversifolia,* pigeon plum* (native)

*Ficus citrifolia,* shortleaf fig* (native)

*Guaiacum officinale,* lignum vitae* (native)

*Ilex cassine,* Dahoon holly** (native)

*Jacaranda mimosifolia,* jacaranda

*Krugiodendron ferreum,* ironwood* (native)

*Lysiloma latisiliquum,* wild tamarind* (native)

*Manilkara zapota,* sapodilla*

*Myrcianthes fragrans,* Simpson's stopper (native)

*Nectandra coriacea,* lancewood (native)

*Pinus elliottii* var. *densa,* slash pine (native)

*Prunus myrtifolia,* West Indian cherry* (native)

*Quercus virginiana,* live oak** (native)

*Simaruba glauca,* paradise tree* (native)

*Tamarindus indica,* tamarind*

### Trees for Small Spaces

*Averrhoa carambola,* carambola*

*Caesalpinia mexicana,* caesalpinia*

*Calliandra haematocephala,* red powder puff

*Capparis cynophallophora,* Jamaica caper* (native)

*Citrus latifolia,* lime*

*Conocarpus erectus,* buttonwood* (native)

*Cordia sebestena,* Geiger tree* (native)

*Crescentia alata,* Mexican calabash*

*Eugenia axillaris,* white stopper* (native)

*Eugenia confusa,* redberry stopper* (native)

*Guaiacum officinale,* lignum vitae* (native)

*Pimenta dioica,* allspice*

*Tabebuia* species, tabebuias*

*Zanthoxylum fagara,* lime prickly ash* (native)

### Flowering Trees

*Bauhinia* x *blakeana,* Hong Kong orchid

*Bulnesia arborea,* verawood*

*Butea monosperma,* flame-of-the-forest*

*Caesalpinia mexicana,* caesalpinia*

*Calliandra haematocephala,* red powder puff

*Cananga odorata,* ylang-ylang*

*Capparis cynophallophora,* Jamaica caper* (native)

*Cassia fistula,* golden shower*

*Cassia javanica,* apple-blossom cassia*

*Chorisia speciosa,* floss-silk*

*Delonix regia,* royal poinciana*

*Guaiacum officinale,* lignum vitae (native)*

*Jacaranda mimosifolia,* jacaranda

*Lagerstroemia speciosa,* Queen's crape myrtle*

*Lonchocarpus violaceus,* lonchocarpus*
*Magnolia virginiana,* sweetbay magnolia**
   (native)
*Peltophorum pterocarpum,* copperpod*
*Pseudobombax ellipticum,* shaving brush tree*
*Tabebuia* species, tabebuias*

## Fruit Trees

*Citrus* species, citruses
*Litchi chinensis,* lychee
*Mangifera indica,* mango*

## Large Palms

*Acoelorraphe wrightii,* paurotis/Everglades palm
   (native)
*Bismarckia nobilis,* Bismarck palm
*Chrysalidocarpus cabadae,* cabada palm*
*Cocos nucifera,* coconut palm*
*Dictyosperma album,* hurricane palm*
*Dypsis decaryi,* triangle palm*
*Howea forsteriana,* kentia palm
*Licuala* species, licuala palms*
*Livistona chinensis,* Chinese fan palm
*Phoenix roebelenii,* pygmy date palm
*Pseudophoenix sargentii,* Sargent's palm* (native)
*Ptychosperma elegans,* solitaire palm*
*Roystonea regia,* Florida royal palm (native)
*Sabal palmetto,* cabbage palm, sabal palm
   (native)
*Serenoa repens,* saw palmetto (native)
*Thrinax parviflora,* thatch palm*
*Thrinax radiata,* thatch palm* (native)
*Veitchia montgomeryana,* Montgomery palm*

## Small Palms

*Chamaedorea elegans,* parlor palm*
*Coccothrinax* species, coccothrinax palms*
*Coccothrinax argentata,* silver palm* (native)

*Rhapis excelsa,* lady palm
*Thrinax morrisii,* Key thatch palm* (native)

## Trees for the Midwest and Northern Great Plains

All plants are hardy to Zone 4 unless otherwise indicated.

### Great All-Around Trees

*Acer rubrum,* red maple (native)
*Acer saccharum,* sugar maple (native)
*Carya ovata,* shagbark hickory (native)
*Celtis occidentalis,* hackberry (native)
*Ginkgo biloba,* ginkgo
*Gleditsia triacanthos,* honey locust (native)
*Fraxinus americana,* notably the cultivar
   'Autumn Blaze', white ash (native)
*Fraxinus pennsylvanica,* green ash (native)
*Gymnocladus dioicus,* Kentucky coffee tree
   (native)
*Juglans nigra,* black walnut (native)
*Quercus alba,* white oak (native)
*Quercus bicolor,* swamp white oak (native)
*Quercus macrocarpa,* bur oak (native)
*Quercus rubra,* red oak (native)
*Tilia americana,* basswood (native)
*Tilia cordata,* little-leaf linden

### Trees for Small Spaces

*Acer spicatum,* mountain maple (native)
*Betula lenta,* sweet birch (native)
*Betula nigra,* river birch (native)
*Betula platyphylla* var. *japonica,* notably the cul-
   tivar 'Whitespire', Japanese white birch
*Carpinus betulus,* notably the cultivar 'Fasti-
   giata', European hornbeam (Zone 5)
*Carpinus caroliniana,* blue beech (native)
*Cotinus obovatus,* American smoke tree (native)

*Ostrya virginiana,* ironwood (native)

*Phellodendron amurense,* Amur cork tree

*Picea glauca,* notably the cultivar 'Black Hills', white spruce (native)

*Pinus strobus,* white pine (native)

*Pinus resinosa,* red pine (native)

*Populus tremuloides,* quaking aspen (native)

*Thuja occidentalis,* arborvitae (native)

## Flowering Trees

*Amelanchier laevis,* serviceberry (native)

*Catalpa speciosa,* northern catalpa (native)

*Cercis canadensis,* redbud northern adapted strain (native)

*Chionanthus virginicus,* fringe tree

*Cornus alternifolia,* pagoda dogwood (native)

*Crataegus crus-galli,* notably the cultivar 'Inermis', thornless cockspur hawthorn (native)

*Crataegus* x *mordenensis* 'Snowbird', hawthorn

*Magnolia* x *loebneri* 'Merrill', magnolia

*Magnolia stellata,* notably the cultivar 'Royal Star', star magnolia

*Malus* 'Red Splendor', red splendor crabapple

*Malus sargentii,* Sargent crabapple

*Prunus americana,* American plum (native)

*Prunus maackii,* Amur chokecherry

*Prunus nigra,* notably the cultivar 'Princess Kay', black plum (native)

*Pyrus ussuriensis* 'Mordak', ussurien pear

*Sorbus alnifolia,* Korean mountain ash

*Sorbus americana,* American mountain ash (native)

*Syringa reticulata,* Japanese tree lilac

*Viburnum lentago,* nannyberry viburnum

## Trees for Texas and the Southern Plains

Plants are appropriate for Zones 6, 7, and 8 unless otherwise noted. Plants marked (6) or (7)

are only marginally adapted to those zones and may not survive in the coldest parts. Similarly, those marked (8) may not survive the hotter, drier areas of Zone 8. The most drought tolerant are indicated with an asterisk (*).

## Great All-Around Trees

*Acer barbatum,* Florida maple (native)

*Acer grandidentatum,* bigtooth maple (native)

*Cercis canadensis* subsp. *texensis,* notably the cultivar 'Oklahoma', Texas redbud (native)

*Chilopsis linearis,* desert willow (native) (Zones (6), 7, 8)

*Cotinus obovatus,* American smoke tree (native)

*Diospyros virginiana,* eastern persimmon (native)

*Frangula caroliniana* (*Rhamnus caroliniana*), Carolina buckthorn or Indian cherry (native)

*Fraxinus americana,* white ash (native)

*Fraxinus texensis,* Texas ash (native) (Zones 7, 8)

*Ginkgo biloba,* ginkgo

*Gymnocladus dioicus,* Kentucky coffee tree (native) (Zones 6, 7, (8))

*Ilex decidua,* possumhaw (native)

*Juglans nigra,* black walnut (native)

*Juniperus ashei,* Ashe juniper* (native)

*Juniperus virginiana,* eastern red cedar* (native)

*Pinus cembroides,* Mexican pinyon pine* (native) (Zones 7, 8)

*Populus deltoides* var. *occidentalis,* plains cottonwood (native) (Zones 6, 7)

*Prosopis glandulosa,* honey mesquite* (native) (Zones 7, 8, 9)

*Quercus macrocarpa,* bur oak (native)

*Quercus muehlenbergii,* chinkapin oak (native) (Zones 7, 8)

*Quercus shumardii,* shumard red oak (native)

*Quercus sinuata* var. *breviloba,* Bigelow oak* (native) (Zones 7, 8)

*Quercus stellata,* post oak (native)

*Rhus lanceolata,* prairie flameleaf sumac*
(native)

*Salix nigra,* black willow (native)

*Taxodium distichum,* bald cypress (native)

*Tilia caroliniana,* Carolina basswood, Carolina
linden (native)

*Ulmus americana,* American elm (native)

*Ulmus crassifolia,* cedar elm (native) (Zones 7,
8, 9)

*Ulmus parvifolia,* lacebark elm*

*Ulmus rubra,* slippery elm (native)

*Viburnum rufidulum,* rusty blackhaw (native)

## Small Flowering Trees

*Acacia wrightii,* Wright acacia* (native) (Zones
7, 8, 9)

*Aesculus arguta,* Texas buckeye (native)

*Cercis canadensis* var. *texensis* (*C. reniformis*),
notably the cultivar 'Oklahoma', Texas redbud (native)

*Cercocarpus montanus* var. *argenteus,* silver mountain mahogany* (native)

*Chilopsis linearis,* desert willow (native) (Zones
(6), 7, 8)

*Cornus drummondii,* roughleaf dogwood (native)

*Cotinus obovatus,* American smoke tree (native)

*Crataegus crus-galli,* cockspur hawthorn (native)

*Crataegus viridis,* green hawthorn (native)

*Diospyros virginiana,* eastern persimmon
(native)

*Frangula caroliniana* (*Rhamnus caroliniana*),
Carolina buckthorn or Indian cherry (native)

*Gleditsia triacanthos,* honey locust (native)

*Hibiscus syriacus,* rose of Sharon

*Ilex decidua,* possumhaw (native)

*Lagerstroemia indica,* crape myrtle (Zones (7), 8)

*Magnolia* x *soulangiana,* saucer magnolia (Zones
6, 7, (8))

*Malus ioensis,* prairie crabapple, blanco crabapple (native)

*Pinus cembroides,* Mexican pinyon pine* (native)
(Zones 7, 8)

*Pinus edulis,* pinyon* (native) (Zones 6, 7)

*Poncirus trifoliata,* trifoliate orange

*Prunus mexicana,* Mexican plum (native)

*Prunus serotina,* black cherry (native)

*Ptelea trifoliata,* wafer ash, hop tree* (native)

*Rhus lanceolata,* prairie flameleaf sumac*
(native)

*Sapindus drummondii,* western soapberry*
(native)

*Sophora affinis,* Texas sophora (native) (Zones 7,
8)

*Ungnadia speciosa,* Mexican buckeye (native)
(Zones (7), 8)

*Viburnum rufidulum,* rusty blackhaw viburnum
(native)

*Vitex agnus-castus,* lavender tree, chaste tree
(Zones 8, 9)

# Trees for the
# Rocky Mountain Region

Plants are appropriate for at least Zones 4 to 7,
with many appropriate for Zones 2 and 3. The
exceptions are noted.

## Great All-Around Trees

*Aesculus octandra,* yellow buckeye (Zones 3–8)

*Betula nigra,* notably the cultivar 'Heritage',
river birch

*Catalpa speciosa,* northern catalpa

*Celtis occidentalis,* common hackberry (Zones
2–9)

*Fraxinus americana,* notably the cultivar
'Autumn Purple', white ash (Zones 3–9)

*Fraxinus pennsylvanica,* notably the cultivars
'Patmore', 'Summit', green ash (Zones 3–9)

*Gleditsia triacanthos,* notably the cultivars 'Iner-

mis', 'Imperial', 'Moraine', 'Shademaster',
thornless common honey locust (Zones 3–9)
*Gymnocladus dioicus,* Kentucky coffee tree
(Zones 3–8)
*Larix decidua,* European larch (Zones 2–6)
*Picea glauca,* notably the cultivar 'Densata',
Black Hills spruce (native) (Zones 2–6)
*Picea pungens* f. *glauca,* Colorado blue spruce
(native) (Zones 2–7)
*Pinus aristata,* bristlecone pine (native)
*Pinus nigra,* Austrian pine
*Pinus ponderosa,* ponderosa pine (native) (Zones
3–7)
*Pinus sylvestris,* Scotch pine (Zones 2–8)
*Pseudotsuga menziesii,* Douglas fir (native)
*Populus* x *acuminata,* lanceleaf cottonwood
(native)
*Populus deltoides* subsp. *monilifera,* notably the
cultivar 'Siouxland', plains cottonwood
(native) (Zones 2–9)
*Quercus alba,* white oak (Zones 3–9)
*Quercus bicolor,* swamp white oak (Zones 3–8)
*Quercus macrocarpa,* bur oak (Zones 2–8)
*Quercus robur,* English oak
*Quercus rubra,* red oak
*Tilia americana,* notably the cultivar 'Red-
mond', American linden (Zones 2–8)
*Tilia cordata,* littleleaf linden (Zones 3–7)
*Tilia tomentosa,* silver linden

### Trees for Small Spaces

*Acer campestre,* hedge maple
*Acer ginnala,* Amur maple (Zones 2–8)
*Acer glabrum,* Rocky Mountain maple (native)
*Acer grandidentatum,* bigtooth maple (native)
*Acer tataricum,* Tatarian maple (Zones 3–8)
*Aesculus glabra,* Ohio buckeye (Zones 3–7)
*Alnus tenuifolia,* thin-leaf alder (native) (Zones
2–7)
*Amelanchier laevis,* Allegheny serviceberry

*Celtis reticulata,* netleaf hackberry (native)
*Cornus alternifolia,* pagoda dogwood
*Juniperus scopulorum,* notably the cultivar
'Wichita Blue', Rocky Mountain juniper
(native) (Zones 3–7)
*Prunus cerasus,* notably the cultivars 'Mont-
morency', 'North Star', pie cherry
*Prunus virginiana* var. *melanocarpa* and *P. vir-
giniana* 'Shubert', western chokecherry
(native) (Zones 2–7)
*Quercus gambelii,* gambel oak (native)

### Flowering Trees

*Aesculus* x *carnea,* red horse chestnut
*Crataegus crus-galli,* notably the cultivar 'Iner-
mis', thornless cockspur hawthorn
*Crataegus mollis,* downy hawthorn
*Malus* 'Beverly', 'Coralburst', 'Donald
Wyman', 'Liset', crabapple
*Prunus cerasifera,* cherry plum
*Prunus maackii,* Amur chokecherry
*Prunus padus,* Mayday tree
*Sorbus americana,* American mountain ash
(Zone 2)
*Syringa reticulata,* Japanese tree lilac
*Viburnum lentago,* nannyberry viburnum (Zones
2–8)

## Trees for the Pacific Northwest

Plants are hardy to at least Zone 7 unless otherwise noted.

### Great All-Around Trees

*Abies concolor,* notably the cultivar 'Candicans',
white fir (native)
*Acer rubrum,* notably the cultivar 'Red Sunset',
red maple
*Betula utilis* var. *jacquemontii,* Himalayan white
birch

*Calocedrus decurrens*, California incense cedar (native)

*Castanea mollissima*, Chinese chestnut

*Cedrus deodara*, deodar cedar

*Cercidiphyllum japonicum*, Katsura tree

*Cornus nuttallii*, Pacific dogwood (native)

*Crataegus* x *lavallei*, Lavalle hawthorn

*Ginkgo biloba*, notably the cultivar 'Autumn Gold', maidenhair tree

*Fagus sylvatica*, notably the cultivar 'Purple Rivers', European beech

*Fraxinus americana*, notably the cultivar 'Autumn Purple', American ash

*Liquidambar styraciflua*, American sweetgum

*Liriodendron tulipifera*, tulip tree

*Metasequoia glyptostroboides*, dawn redwood

*Nyssa sylvatica*, black tupelo

*Pinus strobus*, white pine

*Pseudotsuga menziesii*, Douglas fir (native)

*Pyrus calleryana*, notably the cultivar 'Red Spire', Callery pear

*Quercus coccinea*, scarlet oak

*Quercus garryana*, Oregon white oak (native)

*Quercus robur*, notably the cultivar 'Fastigiata', English oak

*Tsuga heterophylla*, western hemlock (native)

## Trees for Small Spaces

*Acer circinatum*, vine maple (native)

*Acer griseum*, paperbark maple

*Acer japonicum*, notably the cultivar 'Aconitifolium', fernleaf full moon maple

*Acer palmatum*, notably the cultivar 'Seiryu', Japanese maple

*Acer triflorum*, three-flowered maple

*Carpinus cordata*, heartleaf hornbeam

*Crataegus phaenopyrum*, Washington hawthorn

*Eucalyptus pauciflora* subsp. *niphophila*, snowgum eucalyptus

*Halesia carolina*, Carolina silverbell

*Parrotia persica*, Persian ironwood

*Picea pungens*, notably the cultivar 'Hoopsii', Hoops Colorado blue spruce

*Pinus contorta*, shore pine (native)

*Quercus kelloggii*, California black oak (native)

*Tsuga mertensiana*, mountain hemlock (native)

## Flowering Trees

*Amelanchier laevis*, Allegheny serviceberry

*Cercis canadensis*, notably the cultivar 'Forest Pansy', redbud

*Chionanthus retusus*, Chinese fringe tree

x *Chitalpa tashkentensis* 'Morning Cloud', chitalpa

*Clerodendron trichotomum*, harlequin glorybower

*Cornus kousa*, notably the cultivar 'Rosabella', pink-flowered kousa dogwood

*Magnolia liliflora* 'Nigra', lily magnolia

*Magnolia sieboldii*, Oyama magnolia

*Malus floribunda*, Japanese crabapple

*Oxydendrum arboreum*, sorrel tree

*Rhododendron calophytum*, calophytum rhododendron

*Stewartia pseudocamellia*, Japanese stewartia

*Styrax japonica*, Japanese styrax

*Styrax obassia*, fragrant snowbell

# Trees for Coastal California

Plants are appropriate for the coastal regions of California from Crescent City to the border of Mexico—and east to the Coast Ranges, the western edge of Central Valley, and the southern inland valleys and southernmost Peninsular Ranges.

## Great All-Around Trees

*Abies bracteata*, Santa Lucia fir (native)

*Aesculus californica*, California buckeye (native)

*Arbutus* 'Marina', arbutus
*Brachychiton populneus,* bottle tree
*Calocedrus decurrens,* incense cedar (native)
*Diospyros kaki,* persimmon
*Fraxinus oxycarpa,* notably the cultivar 'Raywood', ash
*Geijera parviflora,* Australian willow
*Ginkgo biloba,* ginkgo
*Luma apiculata,* Chilean myrtle
*Lyonothamnus floribundus* subsp. *aspleniifolius,* fernleaf Catalina ironwood (native)
*Metrosideros excelsa,* New Zealand Christmas tree
*Nyssa sylvatica,* tupelo
*Olea europaea,* olive
*Parkinsonia aculeata,* Mexican palo verde
*Pinus sabiniana,* foothill pine (native)
*Quercus agrifolia,* coast live oak (native)
*Quercus kelloggii,* California black oak (native)
*Quercus lobata,* valley oak (native)
*Quercus suber,* cork oak
*Rhus lancea,* African sumac
*Sequoia sempervirens,* coast redwood (native)
*Tristania conferta,* Brisbane box

## Trees for Small Spaces

*Acer circinatum,* vine maple (native)
*Acer palmatum,* Japanese maple
*Arbutus unedo,* strawberry tree
*Arctostaphylos manzanita,* notably the cultivar 'St. Helena', manzanita (native)
*Ceanothus arboreus,* island ceanothus (native)
*Cercis occidentalis,* western redbud (native)
*Citrus* species, citruses
*Dendromecon harfordii,* island bush poppy (native)
*Feijoa sellowiana,* pineapple guava
*Garrya elliptica,* coast silk-tassel (native)
*Laburnum* x *watereri,* golden chain tree
*Leptospermum laevigatum,* Australian tea tree

*Luma apiculata,* Chilean myrtle
*Malus floribunda,* flowering crabapple
*Myrica californica,* wax myrtle (native)
*Sorbus aucuparia,* European mountain ash

## Flowering Trees

*Ceanothus* 'Ray Hartman', ceanothus (native)
*Chilopsis linearis,* desert willow (native)
*Cladrastis kentukea* (*C. lutea*), yellowwood
*Cornus* 'Eddie's White Wonder', dogwood
*Corylus cornuta* var. *californica,* western hazelnut (native)
*Koelreuteria bipinnata,* Chinese flame tree
*Koelreuteria paniculata,* goldenrain tree
*Lagerstroemia indica,* notably the cultivar 'Alba', white crape myrtle
*Leptospermum scoparium,* notably the cultivar 'Helene Strybing', New Zealand tea tree
*Magnolia* x *soulangiana,* saucer magnolia
*Malus hupehensis,* tea crabapple
*Styrax japonica,* Japanese snowbell
*Syringa reticulata,* tree lilac
*Tabebuia chrysotricha,* golden trumpet tree

# Trees for the Western Deserts

The plants are appropriate throughout the region, except those noted as follows:

*Not cold-hardy in cold desert areas
**Favor cooler/moister desert areas

## Great All-Around Trees

*Calocedrus decurrens,* incense cedar (native)
*Cedrus atlantica,* blue atlas cedar**
*Cedrus deodara,* deodar cedar
*Celtis reticulata,* netleaf hackberry (native)
*Ceratonia siliqua,* carob*
*Eucalyptus microtheca,* coolibah*

*Fraxinus angustifolia* (*F. oxycarpa*), claret ash**
*Gymnocladus dioicus,* Kentucky coffee tree**
*Juglans major,* Arizona walnut (native)
*Pinus aristata,* bristlecone pine (native)
*Pinus edulis,* pinyon (native)
*Pinus halepensis,* Aleppo pine*
*Pinus nigra,* Austrian pine**
*Pistacia chinensis,* Chinese pistache
*Quercus emoryi,* Emory oak (native)
*Quercus fusiformis,* escarpment live oak (native)
*Quercus suber,* cork oak*
*Sapindus drummondii,* soapberry (native)
*Ulmus parvifolia,* lacebark elm

## Trees for Small Spaces

*Arbutus texana,* Texas madrone (native)
*Eriobotrya japonica,* loquat*
*Ficus carica,* notably the cultivars 'Brown
    Turkey', 'Texas Everbearing', edible fig*
*Forestiera neomexicana,* desert olive (native)
*Prosopis* species, mesquite* (native)
*Prosopis pubescens,* screwbean mesquite (native)
*Yucca brevifolia,* Joshua tree (native)
*Yucca elata,* soaptree (native)
*Ziziphus jujuba,* Chinese date

## Flowering Trees

*Acacia constricta,* whitethorn* (native)
*Acacia salicina,* cooba, aka weeping wattle*
*Acacia farnesiana*, sweet acacia* (native)
*Acacia stenophyllodes,* shoestring acacia*
*Aesculus californica,* California buckeye (native)
*Cercidium* x 'Desert Museum', hybrid palo
    verde* (hybrid of native species)
*Cercis occidentalis,* western redbud (native)
*Cercis reniformis,* Oklahoma redbud (native)
*Chilopsis linearis,* desert willow (native)
*Chitalpa tashkentensis,* chitalpa
*Crataegus crus-galli,* cockspur hawthorn**

*Crataegus phaenopyrum,* Washington
    hawthorn**
*Koelreuteria paniculata,* goldenrain tree
*Lagerstroemia indica,* crape myrtle
*Leucaena retusa,* goldenball leadtree* (native)
*Parkinsonia aculeata,* Mexican palo verde*
    (native)
*Parkinsonia florida,* blue palo verde* (native)
*Robinia* x *ambigua* 'Purple Robe', locust
*Sambucus mexicana,* Mexican elder (native)
*Sophora japonica,* Japanese scholar tree
*Sophora secundiflora,* Texas mountain laurel*
    (native)
*Vitex agnus-castus,* chaste tree

# Shrubs

Shrubs are the "bones" of the garden, providing the framework for other plants and visually pulling together mixed plantings of trees, perennials, grasses, and ground covers. Shrubs are perennial woody plants, usually with several stems instead of the single trunk of a tree, although some shrubs have a main stem and are therefore treelike—in fact, in a small space the right shrub can serve the function of a tree, providing the garden's canopy and shade. Shrubs can be deciduous (shedding their leaves every year), evergreen, or semievergreen. Some shrubs die back completely in the winter and come back in the spring.

Shrubs offer much to the garden, including shape, color from foliage or flowers, texture, interesting bark or fruit, and often fragrance. Planted together, shrubs can be used as noise or wind barriers, or for screening and privacy. Low-growing shrubs can be used as a ground cover. Shrubs can be mixed for seasonal interest with perennials, bulbs, and other plants, and even make natural supports for sprawling vines. They are invaluable for attracting birds and wildlife.

## Planting and Care

For instructions on planting bare-root, container-grown, and balled-and-burlapped shrubs, see "Planting and Transplanting," page 447. For information on pruning shrubs, see "Pruning," page 503.

## Shrubs for the Northeast

Plants are hardy to Zone 5, unless noted.

### Great All-Around Shrubs

*Callicarpa dichotoma, C. japonica* (Zone 5), *C. americana* (native) (Zone 7), beautyberries

*Clethra barbinervis,* Japanese clethra, Japanese sweet pepperbush

*Cornus stolonifera,* notably the cultivar 'Silver and Gold', red osier dogwood

*Cotoneaster apiculatus,* cranberry cotoneaster

*Cotoneaster horizontalis,* rock spray cotoneaster

*Daphne* x *burkwoodii,* notably the cultivar 'Carol Mackie', daphne

*Erica carnea,* notably the cultivar 'Springwood White', heath

*Hydrangea quercifolia,* oak-leaf hydrangea

*Itea virginica,* sweetspire, Virginia willow (native)

*Juniperus chinensis,* notably the cultivar 'Pfitzeriana', Chinese juniper

*Juniperus horizontalis,* carpet juniper (native)

*Juniperus procumbens,* notably the cultivar 'Nana', juniper

*Juniperus virginiana,* eastern red cedar (native)

*Myrica pensylvanica,* bayberry (native)

*Perovskia atriplicifolia,* perovskia, steppe mint shrub, Russian sage

*Pinus mugo,* dwarf mountain pine

*Rhus aromatica,* fragrant sumac (native)

*Rhus copallina,* shining sumac (native)

*Staphylea* species, bladdernuts

*Vaccinium corymbosum,* highbush blueberry (native)

*Viburnum* x *burkwoodii,* Burkwood viburnum

*Viburnum prunifolium,* black haw, nannyberry (native)

*Viburnum setigerum,* tea viburnum (native)

### Shrubs for Shade

*Acer spicatum,* mountain maple (native)

*Cephalotaxus harringtonia,* plum yew

*Corylopsis pauciflora,* dwarf winter hazel

*Enkianthus campanulatus, E. perulatus,* enkianthus

*Fothergilla* species, fothergillas

*Ilex crenata* and cultivars, Japanese holly

*Ilex glabra,* inkberry (native)

*Ilex* x *meserveae,* meserve hybrid holly

*Kalmia latifolia,* mountain laurel (native)

*Leucothoe fontanesiana,* hobblebush, drooping leucothoe (native)

*Lindera benzoin,* spicebush (native)

*Rhododendron calendulaceum,* flame azalea (native)

*Rhododendron carolinianum,* Carolina rhododendron (Zone 6)

*Rhododendron catawbiense,* catawba rhododendron, mountain rosebay

*Rhododendron maximum,* white laurel, rosebay (native)

*Rhododendron mucronulatum,* Korean azalea

*Rhododendron obtusum,* Japanese azalea

*Rhododendron schlippenbachii,* royal azalea

*Rhododendron viscosum,* swamp azalea, swamp "honeysuckle" (native)

*Rhododendron* 'PJM', hybrid rhododendron

## Flowering Shrubs

*Caryopteris* x *clandonensis,* bluebeard
*Cephalanthus occidentalis,* buttonbush (native)
*Clematis davidiana,* David's bush clematis
*Clematis stans,* Japanese shrub clematis, meadow clematis
*Clethra alnifolia,* sweet pepperbush (native)
*Corylopsis spicata,* common winter hazel
*Forsythia* x *intermedia,* notably the cultivar 'Spring Glory', forsythia
*Kerria japonica* 'Pleniflora', globe kerria
*Lespedeza thunbergii,* bush clover
*Paeonia* species, herbaceous and tree peonies
*Pieris japonica,* Japanese andromeda, Japanese lily-of-the-valley shrub
*Rhododendron calendulaceum,* flame azalea (native)
*Rhododendron carolinianum,* Carolina rhododendron (Zone 6)
*Rhododendron catawbiense,* catawba rhododendron, mountain rosebay (native)
*Rhododendron mucronulatum,* Korean azalea
*Rhododendron obtusum,* Japanese azalea
*Rhododendron schlippenbachii,* royal azalea
*Rhododendron viscosum,* swamp azalea, swamp "honeysuckle" (native)
*Rhododendron* 'PJM', hybrid rhododendron
*Salix gracilistyla,* Japanese pussy willow
*Spiraea prunifolia,* bridal-wreath spirea
*Syringa* x *chinensis, Syringa* x *hyacinthiflora, S. vulgaris,* and Canadian hybrid cultivars, lilacs
*Viburnum carlesii,* Korean spice viburnum
*Vitex agnus-castus,* chaste tree

## Shrubs for the Southeast

Plants can be used throughout the region in Zones 6–9. Where plants are appropriate only for certain parts of the region, they are noted as follows:

US = Upper South, Zone 6
MS = Middle South, Zone 7 and parts of Zone 8 in the western edge of Mississippi, southern Arkansas, and central Texas
LS = Lower South, Zone 8 plus coastal North Carolina and parts of southern coastal Virginia
CS = Coastal South, Zone 8 in northern Florida and parts of Zone 9 in coastal Texas, Louisiana, and northeastern Florida

## Great All-Around Shrubs

*Agarista populifolia,* Florida leucothoe (native)—MS, LS, CS
*Baccharis halimifolia,* sea myrtle (native)
*Callicarpa americana,* beautyberry (native)
*Cephalanthus occidentalis,* buttonbush (native)
*Chimonanthus praecox,* wintersweet
*Daphne odora,* winter daphne—US, MS, LS
*Euonymus americana,* strawberry bush (native)
*Gardenia jasminoides,* gardenia—MS, LS, CS
*Ilex cornuta,* notably the cultivar 'Burfordii', Burford holly—MS, LS, CS
*Lonicera fragrantissima,* winter honeysuckle
*Myrica cerifera,* wax myrtle (native)—MS, LS, CS
*Myrica cerifera* var. *pumila,* dwarf wax myrtle (native)—MS, LS, CS
*Osmanthus* x *fortunei,* fortune's osmanthus
*Pyracantha coccinea,* firethorn—MS, LS, CS
*Rhus* species, sumacs (native)
*Spiraea prunifolia,* bridal-wreath spirea
*Vaccinium corymbosum,* highbush blueberry (native)
*Vaccinium ashei,* rabbiteye blueberry (native)
*Viburnum carlesii,* Korean spice viburnum—US, MS, LS
*Xanthorhiza simplicissima,* yellow-root (native)

## Shrubs for Shade

*Aucuba japonica,* Japanese aucuba—MS, LS, CS
*Calycanthus floridus,* sweet shrub (native)
*Danae racemosa,* Alexandrian laurel—MS, LS, CS
*Fothergilla major,* fothergilla (native)
*Hydrangea macrophylla,* notably the cultivar 'Mariesii', lace-cap hydrangea—MS, LS, CS
*Hydrangea quercifolia,* oak-leaf hydrangea (native)
*Illicium floridanum,* Florida anise (native)—MS, LS, CS
*Itea virginica,* Virginia sweetspire (native)
*Kerria japonica,* Japanese kerria
*Leucothoe fontanesiana,* drooping leucothoe
*Mahonia aquifolium,* Oregon grape—MS, LS, CS
*Pieris japonica,* Japanese andromeda

## Flowering Shrubs

*Abelia chinensis,* Chinese abelia
*Clethra alnifolia,* summersweet (native)
*Camellia japonica,* camellia—MS, LS, CS
*Camellia sasanqua,* sasanqua camellia—MS, LS, CS
*Chaenomeles japonica,* Japanese flowering quince
*Forsythia* x *intermedia,* forsythia
*Fothergilla gardenii,* dwarf fothergilla (native)
*Hibiscus syriacus,* rose of Sharon
*Hydrangea arborescens,* notably the cultivar 'Annabelle', wild hydrangea (native)
*Hydrangea paniculata* 'Grandiflora', peegee hydrangea—US, MS, LS
*Jasminum nudiflorum,* winter jasmine
*Loropetalum chinense,* loropetalum—MS, LS, CS
*Philadelphus coronarius,* mock orange

There are countless popular species, hybrids, and cultivars of azalea. Listed here are only a few of the outstanding deciduous native species:

*Rhododendron austrinum,* Florida azalea (native)
*Rhododendron periclymenoides,* pinxterbloom azalea (native)
*Rhododendron prunifolium,* plum-leaf azalea (native)

*Sambucus canadensis,* elderberry (native)

*Spiraea vanhouttei,* Vanhoutte spirea

*Weigela florida,* weigela

## Shrubs for Subtropical Florida

The plants recommended for Subtropical Florida are appropriate for Zones 10A, 10B, and 11, unless noted as follows:

*Not for Zone 10A
**Not for Zone 11

### Great All-Around Shrubs

*Allamanda schottii* (*A. neriifolia*), allamanda*
*Bougainvillea glabra,* bougainvillea*
*Breynia nivosa,* snowbush*
*Brunfelsia americana, B. grandiflora, B. pauciflora,* lady-of-the-night*
*Byrsonima lucida,* locustberry (native)*
*Callicarpa americana,* American beautyberry (native)
*Calyptranthes pallens,* spicewood (native)*
*Carissa macrocarpa,* natal plum*
*Chrysobalanus icaco,* cocoplum (native)*
*Clerodendrum wallichii,* white clerodendron*
*Cocculus laurifolius,* snailseed**
*Codiaeum* species, crotons*
*Dodonaea viscosa,* varnish leaf (native)
*Murraya paniculata,* orange jasmine
*Pithecellobium keyense,* blackbead (native)

*Psychotria nervosa*, wild coffee (native)*
*Randia aculeata*, white indigo berry (native)
*Raphiolepis indica*, Indian hawthorn
*Scaevola plumieri*, inkberry (native)

## Shrubs for Shade

*Ardisia escallonioides*, marlberry (native)
*Eranthemum pulchellum*, bluesage
*Leea coccinea*, West Indian holly (with protection in 10B)
*Leucophyllum frutescens*, Texas silverleaf**
*Malpighia coccigera*, Singapore holly
*Myrica cerifera*, wax myrtle (native)
*Myrsine guianensis*, myrsine* (native)
*Schefflera arboricola*, dwarf schefflera
*Triphasia trifolia*, limeberry**

## Flowering Shrubs

*Allamanda cathartica*, allamanda*
*Bougainvillea* species, bougainvilleas
*Brugmansia versicolor*, *Brugmansia* x *candida*, angel's trumpet*
*Brunfelsia americana*, *B. grandiflora*, *B. pauciflora*, lady-of-the-night*
*Callicarpa americana*, American beautyberry (native)
*Clerodendrum thomsoniae*, bleeding heart
*Clerodendrum ugandense*, blue clerodendron*
*Clerodendrum wallichii*, white clerodendron*
*Dombeya* species, tropical snowballs
*Duranta repens*, golden dewdrop (native)
*Euphorbia leucocephala*, pascuita*
*Galphimia gracilis*, thryallis*
*Gardenia jasminoides* (*G. thunbergia* rootstock), gardenia
*Hamelia patens*, firebush (native)
*Ixora* hybrids, ixora hybrids
*Jatropha multifida*, jatropha, coral plant
*Lagerstroemia indica*, crape myrtle**

*Pachystachys lutea*, golden shrimp plant
*Plumbago auriculata*, plumbago
*Senna alata*, candlebush*
*Senna ligustrina*, Bahama cassia* (native)
*Sophora tomentosa*, necklace pod (native)
*Tabernaemontana divaricata*, crape jasmine
*Tetrazygia bicolor*, West Indian lilac*

# Shrubs for the Midwest and Northern Great Plains

The plants are hardy to Zone 4 unless otherwise indicated.

## Great All-Around Shrubs

*Cornus stolonifera*, red osier dogwood (native)
*Cotinus coggygria*, smoke bush (Zone 5)
*Daphne* x *burkwoodii*, notably the cultivar 'Carol Mackie', daphne
*Hydrangea paniculata* 'Pee Gee', 'Tardiva', hydrangeas
*Ilex verticillata*, winterberry holly (native)
*Juniperus horizontalis*, creeping juniper (native)
*Pinus mugo*, dwarf mountain pine
*Potentilla fruticosa*, shrubby cinquefoil (native)
*Rhododendron* 'Northern Lights Series', azaleas
*Rhus aromatica*, fragrant sumac (native)
*Rosa* 'Explorer Series', 'Parkland Series', roses
*Salix purpurea* 'Nana', dwarf blue Arctic willow
*Spiraea* x *cinerea* 'Grefsheim', willow spirea
*Spiraea* x *vanhouttei*, bridal-wreath spirea
*Syringa meyeri*, dwarf Korean lilac
*Syringa* x *prestoniae* selections, Preston lilac
*Syringa vulgaris*, common lilac
*Viburnum lantana*, notably the cultivar 'Mohican', viburnum
*Viburnum sargentii*, notably the cultivar 'Onondaga', viburnum
*Viburnum opulus* var. *americanum*, highbush cranberry (native)

## Shrubs for Shade

*Aronia melanocarpa* var. *elata,* glossy black
  chokeberry (native)
*Buxus microphylla* var. *koreana,* Korean boxwood
*Cornus racemosa,* gray dogwood (native)
*Diervilla lonicera,* bush honeysuckle (native)
*Dirca palustris,* leatherwood (native)
*Hamamelis virginiana,* witchhazel (native)
*Hydrangea arborescens,* woodland hydrangea
  (native)
*Mahonia repens,* creeping Oregon grape (native)
*Stephanandra incisa,* notably the cultivar
  'Crispa', cutleaf stephanandra
*Symphoricarpos albus, S. orbiculatus,* snowberry
  and coralberry (native)
*Viburnum acerifolium,* maple-leaf viburnum
  (native)

## Flowering Shrubs

*Amelanchier alnifolia,* notably the cultivar
  'Regent', Juneberry (native)
*Andromeda polifolia,* notably the cultivar
  'Nana', bog rosemary (native)
*Aronia arbutifolia,* notably the cultivar 'Bril-
  liantissima', red chokeberry (native)
*Clethra alnifolia,* summersweet
*Cornus alba* selections, European dogwood
*Deutzia corymbosa,* corymb deutzia
*Deutzia gracilis,* notably the cultivar 'Nikko',
  slender deutzia (Zone 5)
*Forsythia* x *intermedia,* forsythia (some Zone 5)
*Philadelphus coronarius,* sweet mock orange
*Philadelphus* x *virginalis,* notably the cultivar
  'Minnesota Snowflake', virginal mock
  orange
*Physocarpus opulifolius,* ninebark (native)
*Ptelea trifoliata,* hop tree (native)
*Rhododendron* 'PJM', hybrid rhododendron
*Rhus glabra, R. typhina,* sumacs (native)

*Rosa* Shrub Rose Selections, shrub roses
*Sorbaria sorbifolia,* ural spirea
*Spiraea* x *bumalda,* bumald spirea
*Spiraea nipponica,* snowmound spirea
*Syringa* x *chinensis,* Chinese lilac
*Viburnum dentatum,* arrowwood viburnum
  (native)
*Weigela florida,* weigela

## Shrubs for Texas and the Southern Plains

Plants are appropriate for Zones 6, 7, and 8
unless otherwise noted. Plants marked (6) or (7)
are only marginally adapted to those zones and
may not survive in the coldest parts. Similarly,
those marked (8) may not survive the hotter,
drier areas of Zone 8.

## Great All-Around Shrubs

*Callicarpa americana,* American beautyberry
  (native) (Zones 7, 8, 9)
*Dalea formosa,* feather dalea (native)
*Fallugia paradoxa,* Apache plume (native)
*Hesperaloe parviflora,* red yucca (native) (Zones
  7, 8, 9)
*Hydrangea quercifolia,* oak-leaf hydrangea
*Ilex vomitoria,* yaupon holly (native) (Zones (7),
  8, 9)
*Ilex vomitoria* 'Nana', dwarf yaupon holly
  (native) (Zones 8, 9)
*Ilex vomitoria* 'Pendula', weeping yaupon holly
  (native) (Zones (7), 8, 9)
*Ilex vomitoria* 'Will Fleming', upright yaupon
  holly (native) (Zones (7), 8, 9)
*Leucophyllum frutescens* 'White Cloud', 'Green
  Cloud', 'Compacta', cenizo (native) (Zones
  8, 9)
*Lonicera albiflora,* white limestone honeysuckle
  (native) (Zones 7, 8)

*Mahonia swaseyi,* Texas barberry (native)
(Zone 8)

*Mahonia trifoliata,* agarito, algerita (native)
(Zones 7, 8)

*Myrica cerifera,* southern wax myrtle (Zones (7),
8, 9)

*Rhus aromatica,* aromatic sumac (native)

*Rhus virens,* evergreen sumac (native) (Zone 8)

*Rosa* species and cultivars, heirloom and native
roses

*Salvia greggii,* autumn sage (native) (Zones 7,
8, 9)

*Sophora secundiflora,* Texas mountain laurel
(native) (Zone 8)

*Yucca glauca,* plains beargrass, soapweed
(native)


## Flowering Shrubs

*Amorpha fruticosa,* false indigo (native)

*Anisacanthus quadrifidus* var. *wrightii,* flame
acanthus (native) (Zone 8)

*Caesalpinia gilliesii,* bird-of-paradise (Zones
8, 9)

*Chaenomeles speciosa,* Japanese flowering quince

*Chrysothamnus nauseosus,* chamisa, rubber
rabbitbrush (native) (western parts of the
region, Zone 6)

*Cornus drummondii,* roughleaf dogwood (native)

*Dalea formosa,* feather dalea (native)

*Dalea frutescens,* black dalea (native) (Zones
7, 8)

*Euonymus atropurpureus,* wahoo (native) (Zones
7, 8)

*Fallugia paradoxa,* Apache plume (native)

*Forsythia* x *intermedia,* forsythia

*Hydrangea arborescens,* wild hydrangea (northeastern parts of the region)

*Hydrangea macrophylla,* French hydrangea

*Hydrangea quercifolia,* oak-leaf hydrangea

*Itea virginica,* Virginia sweetspire

*Lonicera albiflora,* white limestone honeysuckle
(native) (Zones 7, 8)

*Mimosa borealis,* fragrant mimosa (native)

*Philadelphus texensis,* Texas mock orange
(native) (Zones 7, 8)

*Punica granatum,* pomegranate (not dwarf)
(Zones (7), 8, 9)

*Rhus aromatica,* aromatic sumac (native)

*Rhus glabra,* smooth sumac (native) (Zones
7, 8)

*Ribes odoratum,* buffalo currant (native) (Zones
6, 7, (8))

*Rosa* species, heirloom and native roses

*Salvia greggii,* autumn sage (native) (Zones 7,
8, 9)

*Salvia regla,* mountain sage (native) (Zones
7, 8)

*Spiraea prunifolia,* bridal-wreath spirea

*Syringa vulgaris,* common lilac (Zones 6, 7)


## Shrubs for Shade

*Buxus microphylla* var. *japonica,* Japanese boxwood

*Callicarpa americana,* American beautyberry
(native) (Zones 7, 8, 9)

*Cornus drummondii,* roughleaf dogwood (native)

*Elaeagnus macrophylla,* elaeagnus (Zone 8)

*Euonymus atropurpureus,* wahoo (native) (Zones
7, 8)

*Hydrangea arborescens,* wild hydrangea (northeastern parts of the region)

*Hydrangea quercifolia,* oak-leaf hydrangea

*Hypericum henryi,* St.-John's-wort (Zones (6), 7,
8)

*Ilex cornuta* 'Burfordii', Burford holly (Zones 7,
8)

*Ilex cornuta* 'Burfordii Nana', dwarf Burford
holly (Zones 7, 8)

*Ilex cornuta* 'Rotunda', dwarf Chinese holly
(Zones 7, 8)

*Ilex vomitoria,* yaupon holly (native) (Zones (7),
8, 9)

*Ilex vomitoria* 'Nana', dwarf yaupon holly
(native) (Zones 8, 9)

*Ilex vomitoria* 'Pendula', weeping yaupon holly
(native) (Zones (7), 8, 9)

*Ilex vomitoria* 'William Fleming', upright
yaupon holly (native) (Zones (7), 8, 9)

*Lonicera albiflora,* white limestone honeysuckle
(native) (Zones 7, 8)

*Prunus caroliniana,* Carolina cherry laurel
(Zones 7, 8, 9)

*Rhus aromatica,* aromatic sumac (native)

*Salvia regla,* mountain sage (native) (Zones 7, 8)

*Sophora secundiflora,* Texas mountain laurel
(native) (Zone 8)

*Spiraea prunifolia,* bridal-wreath spirea

## Shrubs for the Rocky Mountain Region

Plants are appropriate for Zones 4 to 7, unless
otherwise noted.

### Great All-Around Shrubs

*Amelanchier alnifolia,* Saskatoon serviceberry
(native) (Zones 2–7)

*Amelanchier stolonifera,* running serviceberry

*Artemisia cana,* silver sagebrush (native) (Zones
3–7)

*Artemisia tridentata,* big sagebrush (native)
(Zones 3–7)

*Betula occidentalis* (*B. fontinalis*), western river
birch (native) (Zones 3–7)

*Caragana frutex,* notably the cultivar 'Globosa',
Russian peashrub (Zones 2–7)

*Cornus racemosa,* gray dogwood

*Cornus stolonifera,* notably the cultivar 'Isanti',
red osier dogwood (native) (Zones 2–8)

*Cornus stolonifera* 'Flaviramea', golden twig
dogwood

*Cotoneaster acutifolia,* Peking cotoneaster

*Cotoneaster divaricata,* spreading cotoneaster

*Hippophae rhamnoides,* sea buckthorn (Zones
3–7)

*Physocarpus opulifolius,* common ninebark
(native) (Zones 2–7)

*Physocarpus monogynus,* mountain ninebark
(native)

*Prunus americana,* American plum (native)
(Zones 2–7)

*Prunus tomentosa,* Nanking cherry (Zones 2–7)

*Rhus glabra* var. *cismontana,* dwarf smooth
sumac (native) (Zones 2–6)

*Rhus trilobata,* three-leaf sumac (native) (Zone 3)

*Rhus typhina* 'Laciniata', cutleaf staghorn
sumac (Zone 3)

*Ribes cereum,* wax currant (native) (Zone 3)

*Salix irrorata,* bluestem willow (native)

*Salix purpurea,* notably the cultivar 'Nana',
purple osier willow

*Shepherdia argentea,* silver buffalo berry (native)
(Zone 2)

*Viburnum dentatum,* arrowwood viburnum
(Zones 3–6)

*Viburnum lantana,* wayfaring tree

*Viburnum* x *rhytidophylloides,* notably the cultivar 'Allegheny', lantanaphyllum viburnum
(Zones 3–6)

*Viburnum opulus* var. *americanum,* notably the
cultivar 'Compactum', American cranberry
bush (Zones 2–7)

### Flowering Shrubs

*Amorpha canescens,* silver leadplant (native)
(Zones 2–6)

*Berberis koreana,* Korean barberry

*Caryopteris* x *clandonensis,* blue mist spirea
(Zone 5)

*Cotoneaster multiflorus,* flowering cotoneaster
(Zones 3–7)

*Hibiscus syriacus,* rose of Sharon (Zone 5)

*Holodiscus dumosus,* rock spirea (native)

*Physocarpus monogynus,* mountain ninebark (native)

*Prunus besseyi,* western sand cherry (native) (Zone 3)

*Prunus tenella,* Russian flowering almond (Zone 2)

*Ribes aureum,* golden currant (native)

*Robinia neomexicana,* New Mexico locust (native)

*Rosa glauca (R. rubrifolia),* redleaf rose

*Rosa rugosa,* rugosa rose (Zone 2)

*Rosa woodsii,* Wood's rose (native) (Zone 2)

*Sambucus canadensis,* notably the cultivars 'Aurea', 'Laciniata', American elderberry

*Syringa meyeri,* dwarf Korean lilac (Zones 3–7)

*Syringa microphylla* 'Superba', littleleaf lilac

*Syringa vulgaris,* common lilac (Zones 3–7)

*Syringa* x *chinensis,* Chinese lilac (Zone 3)

*Viburnum opulus* var. *americanum,* notably the cultivar 'Compactum', American cranberry bush (Zones 2–7)

### Shrubs for Shade

*Amelanchier canadensis,* serviceberry (Zones 3–7)

*Aronia melanocarpa,* black chokeberry (Zones 3–8)

*Jamesia americana,* waxflower (native)

*Lonicera involucrata,* twinberry honeysuckle (native) (Zone 2)

*Mahonia aquifolium,* notably the cultivar 'Compacta', Oregon grape

*Ribes alpinum,* Alpine currant (Zones 2–7)

*Rubus deliciosus,* Boulder raspberry (native)

*Sambucus pubens,* red elderberry (native)

*Symphoricarpos albus,* snowberry (Zones 3–7)

*Symphoricarpos* x *chenaultii,* notably the cultivar 'Hancock', Chenault coralberry

*Viburnum* x *rhytidophylloides,* notably the cultivar 'Allegheny', lantanaphyllum viburnum (Zones 3–8)

## Shrubs for the Pacific Northwest

Plants are hardy to at least Zone 7 unless otherwise noted.

### Great All-Around Shrubs

*Acer palmatum,* notably the cultivars 'Atropurpureum', 'Garnet', 'Waterfall', Japanese maple

*Aesculus parviflora,* bottlebrush buckeye

*Arbutus unedo* 'Compacta', compact strawberry madrone

*Callicarpa bodinieri* 'Profusion', beautyberry

*Cornus stolonifera* 'Isanti', red osier dogwood

*Cryptomeria japonica* 'Elegans', plume cryptomeria

*Lithocarpus densiflorus,* tan oak (native)

*Myrica californica,* Pacific wax myrtle (native)

*Philadelphus lewisii,* wild mock orange (native)

*Picea pungens,* notably the cultivar 'R. H. Montgomery', Colorado blue spruce

*Pinus strobus* 'Nana', dwarf white pine

*Salix purpurea* 'Nana', dwarf purple osier willow

*Viburnum davidii,* David viburnum

### Shrubs for Shade

*Berberis verruculosa,* warty barberry

*Camellia sasanqua,* notably the cultivar 'Yuletide', sasanqua camellia

*Enkianthus campanulatus,* red-vein enkianthus

*Hydrangea sargentiana,* Sargent's hydrangea

*Leucothoe davisiae,* western leucothoe (native)

*Rhododendron schlippenbachii,* royal azalea

*Sarcococca ruscifolia,* fragrant sarcococca

*Skimmia reevesiana,* Reeves skimmia

*Taxus baccata* 'Repandens', spreading English yew

*Tsuga canadensis,* notably the cultivar 'Jeddeloh', Canadian hemlock

*Vaccinium ovatum,* evergreen huckleberry (native)

## Flowering Shrubs

*Abelia* x 'Edward Goucher', Edward Goucher abelia

*Azalea* 'Everest', Everest azalea

*Camellia* x *williamsii,* notably the cultivars 'Donation', 'J. C. Williams', camellia

*Caryopteris* x *clandonensis,* notably the cultivar 'Dark Knight', bluebeard

*Ceanothus thyrsiflorus,* blueblossom (native)

*Cistus* x *corbariensis,* white rockrose

*Cornus alba* 'Elegantissima', variegated tartarian dogwood

*Cornus kousa,* notably the cultivar 'Lustgarten Weeping', kousa dogwood

*Daphne* x *burkwoodii,* notably the cultivar 'Carol Mackie', daphne

*Deutzia gracilis,* notably the cultivar 'Nikko', slender deutzia

*Fothergilla gardenii,* notably the cultivar 'Blue Mist', dwarf fothergilla

*Hydrangea quercifolia,* notably the cultivar 'Snowflake', oak-leaf hydrangea

*Itea virginica,* notably the cultivar 'Henry's Garnet', sweetspire

*Kalmia latifolia,* mountain laurel

*Leucothoe axillaris,* drooping leucothoe

*Mahonia aquifolium,* Oregon grape (native)

*Osmanthus delavayi,* osmanthus

*Pieris japonica,* notably the cultivar 'Valley Valentine', Japanese pieris

*Rhododendron* 'Bow Bells', Bow Bells rhododendron

*Rhododendron* 'Dora Amateis', Dora Amateis rhododendron

*Rhododendron macrophyllum,* Pacific rhododendron (native)

*Rhododendron occidentale,* western azalea (native)

*Rhododendron degronianum* subsp. *yakushimanum,* yaku rhododendron

*Ribes sanguineum,* notably the cultivar 'Elk River Red', winter currant (native)

*Rosa gallica,* notably the cultivar 'Iceberg', rose

*Rosa eglanteria,* sweetbriar rose

*Spiraea betulifolia* var. *lucida,* shiny-leaved spirea (native)

*Spiraea* x *bumalda,* notably the cultivar 'Anthony Waterer', bumald spirea

*Viburnum carlesii,* Korean spice viburnum

*Viburnum plicatum* f. *tomentosum,* notably the cultivar 'Pink Beauty', doublefile viburnum

*Viburnum sargentii,* notably the cultivar 'Onondaga', Sargent viburnum

*Weigela floribunda,* notably the cultivar 'Victoria', purple-leaved weigela

## Shrubs for Coastal California

Plants are appropriate for the coastal regions of California from Crescent City to the border of Mexico—and east to the Coast Ranges, the western edge of Central Valley, and the southern inland valleys and southernmost Peninsular Ranges.

### Great All-Around Shrubs

*Arctostaphylos pajaroensis,* notably the cultivar 'Paradise', pajaro manzanita (native)

*Artemisia,* notably the cultivar 'Powis Castle', wormwood

*Brugmansia,* notably the cultivar 'Betty Marshall', angel's trumpet

*Buddleia fallowiana*, notably the cultivar 'Lochinch', butterfly bush

*Carpenteria californica*, notably the cultivar 'Elizabeth', bush anemone (native)

*Ceanothus*, notably the cultivars 'Frosty Blue', 'Julia Phelps', wild lilac (native)

*Cercis occidentalis*, western redbud (native)

*Cotinus coggygria*, notably the cultivar 'Royal Purple', purple smoke bush

*Eriogonum crocatum*, saffron buckwheat (native)

*Fremontodendron mexicanum*, notably the cultivar 'Pacific Sunset', flannel bush (native)

*Garrya elliptica*, notably the cultivar 'Evie', coast silk-tassel (native)

*Grevillea* cultivars, notably 'Robyn Gordon', grevillea

*Heteromeles arbutifolia*, toyon (native)

*Leptospermum laevigatum*, notably the cultivar 'Reevesii Compacta', tea tree

*Mahonia nevinii*, Nevin's Oregon grape (native)

*Philadelphus lewisii*, notably the cultivar 'Goose Creek', mock orange (native)

*Pittosporum tenuifolium*, pittosporum

*Salvia clevelandii*, notably the cultivar 'Allen Chickering', Cleveland sage (native)

*Styrax officinalis* var. *californicus*, snowdrop bush (native)

*Teucrium chamaedrys*, wall germander

*Teucrium fruticans*, notably the cultivar 'Azureum', bush germander

*Trichostema lanatum*, woolly blue curls (native)

## Shrubs for Shade

*Abutilon* x *hybridum*, notably the cultivars 'Little Imp', 'White Parasol', flowering maple

*Azara microphylla*, boxleaf azara

*Daphne odora*, notably the cultivar 'Leucanthe', winter daphne

*Rhododendron occidentale*, western azalea (native)

*Ribes sanguineum*, red flowering currant (native)

*Ribes viburnifolium*, evergreen currant (native)

*Vaccinium ovatum*, evergreen huckleberry (native)

## Flowering Shrubs

*Alyogyne huegelii*, notably the cultivar 'Mood Indigo', blue hibiscus

*Anisodontea* x *hypomandarum*, Cape mallow

*Caryopteris* x *clandonensis*, blue mist

*Ceanothus* cultivars, notably 'Concha', wild lilac (native)

*Cercis occidentalis*, western redbud (native)

*Cistus* x *skanbergii*, rockrose

*Correa* cultivars, notably 'Ivory Bells', Australian fuchsia

*Eriogonum giganteum*, St. Catherine's lace (native)

*Garrya elliptica*, coast silk-tassel (native)

*Gaultheria shallon*, salal (native)

*Hydrangea macrophylla*, notably the cultivar 'Mariesii', hydrangea

*Lavandula* species, lavenders

*Mimulus aurantiacus*, sticky monkeyflower (native)

*Osmanthus delavayi*, delavay osmanthus

*Perovskia atriplicifolia*, Russian sage

*Physocarpus capitatus*, ninebark (native)

*Tagetes lemmoni*, Mexican bush marigold

*Teucrium fruticans*, notably the cultivar 'Compacta', dwarf bush germander

*Tibouchina urvilleana*, princess flower

*Weigela florida*, pink weigela

# Shrubs for the Western Deserts

The plants are appropriate throughout the region, except those noted as follows:

*Not cold-hardy in cold desert areas

**Favor cooler/moister desert areas

## Great All-Around Shrubs

*Arctostaphylos pungens*, pointleaf manzanita (native)

*Artemisia filifolia*, threadleaf sage, sand sage (native)

*Artemisia tridentata*, bigleaf sage (native)

*Baccharis* x 'Centennial', centennial broom*

*Cercocarpus ledifolius*, curly-leaf mountain mahogany (native)

*Cotoneaster buxifolius*, grayleaf cotoneaster

*Dodonaea viscosa*, hopbush* (native)

*Fallugia paradoxa*, Apache plume (native)

*Larrea tridentata*, creosote bush (native)

*Mahonia haematocarpa* (*Berberis haematocarpa*), algerita (native)

*Nerium oleander*, oleander*

*Pyracantha angustifolia*, notably the cultivar 'Gnome', firethorn

*Rhus microphylla*, littleleaf sumac (native)

*Rhus ovata*, sugarbush* (native)

*Rosmarinus officinalis*, notably the cultivar 'Arp', rosemary (other cultivars may not survive some cold desert winters)

*Simmondsia chinensis*, jojoba* (native)

*Vauquelinia californica*, Arizona rosewood* (native)

## Shrubs for Shade

*Arctostaphylos uva-ursi*, kinnikinnick** (native)

*Cordia boissieri*, Texas olive* (native)

*Elaeagnus pungens*, silverberry

*Ilex vomitoria*, notably the cultivar 'Nana', dwarf yaupon holly*

*Mahonia aquifolium*, notably the cultivar 'Compacta', compact Oregon grape holly**

*Mahonia repens*, creeping Oregon grape** (native)

*Myrica cerifera*, wax myrtle*

*Philadelphus microphyllus*, littleleaf mock orange** (native)

*Rhaphiolepis indica*, India hawthorn

*Salvia greggii*, cherry sage (native)

*Viburnum* x *burkwoodii*, Burkwood viburnum**

## Flowering Shrubs

*Caesalpinia gilliesii*, bird-of-paradise

*Caesalpinia pulcherrima*, red bird-of-paradise* (native)

*Calliandra californica*, Baja red fairyduster* (native)

*Calliandra eriophylla*, pink fairyduster (native)

*Caryopteris* x *clandonensis*, blue mist

*Chamaebatiaria millefolium*, fernbush (native)

*Convolvulus cneorum*, bush morning glory*

*Cowania mexicana*, cliffrose (native)

*Dalea frutescens*, black dalea* (native)

*Ericameria laricifolia*, turpentine bush* (native)

*Fallugia paradoxa*, Apache plume (native)

*Hesperaloe parviflora*, red yucca (native)

*Lavandula angustifolia*, notably the cultivar 'Munstead', English lavender

*Leucophyllum candidum*, notably the cultivar 'Silver Cloud', Texas ranger* (native)

*Leucophyllum laevigatum*, Chihuahuan sage* (native)

*Punica granatum*, pomegranate

*Rosa foetida*, notably the cultivar 'Bicolor', Austrian copper rose**

*Ruellia peninsularis*, Baja ruellia* (native)

*Salvia clevelandii*, notably the cultivar 'Allen Chickering', chaparral sage* (native)

*Santolina chamaecyparissus*, lavender cotton

*Senna nemophila* (*Cassia nemophila*), desert cassia*

*Spartium junceum*, Spanish broom

*Syringa* x *chinensis*, Chinese lilac**

*Tecoma stans*, yellow bells* (native)

*Vitex agnus-castus*, chaste tree

# Perennials

Perennials are ever-lasting or long-lasting plants that are herbaceous, meaning they have stems that are fleshy and usually green, rather than woody like the stems of a shrub or the trunk or branches of a tree. In cold regions, most perennials die back to the ground in fall and winter and reemerge in the spring—often in increased numbers that can be divided and moved to other parts of the garden. Perennials can be used in many ways in the garden: in flower borders, mixed with shrubs and annuals, in and around water gardens, and as ground covers. They provide incomparable flowers and color, foliage texture, form, and sometimes fragrance, and are often indispensable for attracting butterflies and wildlife.

## Planting and Care

For instructions on planting perennials, see "Planting and Transplanting," page 447. For tips on dividing overgrown clumps, see "Propagation," page 474. Information on deadheading and other pruning techniques for perennials can be found in "Pruning," page 501.

## Perennials for the Northeast

Plants are hardy to Zone 5, unless noted.

### Perennials for Sun

*Anemone japonica,* autumn anemone
*Aquilegia caerulea,* blue columbine
*Aquilegia canadensis,* American columbine (native)
*Aquilegia vulgaris,* European crowfoot
*Aster* x *frikartii,* Frikart's aster

*Astilbe* x *arendsii, A. thunbergii, A. chinensis,* notably the cultivar *A. c.* 'Pumila', astilbes
*Calamagrostis* x *acutiflora,* notably the cultivar 'Stricta', feather reed-grass
*Centranthus ruber,* red valerian
*Cimicifuga racemosa,* notably the cultivar 'Atropurpurea', black cohosh, black snake-root (native)
*Coreopsis verticillata,* notably the cultivar 'Moonbeam', coreopsis
*Echinacea purpurea,* purple coneflower (native)
*Echinops ritro,* globe thistle
*Eupatorium coelestinum,* wild ageratum (native)
*Eupatorium maculatum, E. purpureum,* Joe-Pye weeds (native)
*Gaura lindheimeri,* gaura
*Helictotrichon sempervirens,* blue oat grass
*Hemerocallis* species, hybrids, and cultivars, notably the cultivars 'Kwanzo', 'Ed Murray', daylilies
*Hibiscus,* notably the cultivar 'Southern Belle', hibiscus
*Iris ensata,* Japanese iris
*Iris sibirica,* Siberian iris
*Iris germanica,* German iris, bearded iris
*Liatris spicata,* blazing star (native)
*Ligularia* species and hybrids, notably the cultivar 'The Rocket', ligularias
*Lobelia cardinalis,* cardinal flower (native)
*Lobelia siphilitica,* blue lobelia (native)
*Lysimachia clethroides,* gooseneck loosestrife
*Narcissus* species, hybrids, and cultivars, daffodils, narcissi
*Nepeta* x *mussinii,* catmint
*Paeonia* species, hybrids, and cultivars, peonies
*Panicum virgatum* cultivars, switchgrass (native)
*Pennisetum alopecuroides,* fountain grass
*Phlox paniculata,* notably the cultivars 'David', 'Miss Lingard', 'Bright Eyes', summer phlox
*Phlox subulata,* moss pink, moss phlox

*Platycodon grandiflorum,* balloon flower

*Rudbeckia fulgida* 'Goldsturm', coneflower

*Rudbeckia maxima,* great coneflower (native)

*Scabiosa,* notably the cultivar 'Butterfly Blue', pincushion flower

*Sedum spectabile,* notably the cultivars 'Herbst-freude', 'Autumn Joy', sedum

*Sedum* x 'Vera Jameson', hybrid stonecrop

*Stokesia laevis,* Stokes' aster

*Thalictrum rochebrunianum,* purple mist flower, lavender meadow-rue

*Veronica,* notably the cultivar 'Sunny Border Blue', veronica, speedwell

## Perennials for Shade

*Arisaema triphyllum,* jack-in-the-pulpit (native)

*Aruncus dioicus,* notably the cultivar 'Kneiffii', goatsbeard

*Astilbe* x *arendsii, A. thunbergii, A. chinensis* cultivars, notably the cultivar *A. chinensis* 'Pumila', astilbes

*Athyrium filix-femina,* lady fern (native)

*Athyrium nipponicum,* notably the cultivar 'Pictum', Japanese painted fern

*Athyrium pycnocarpon,* silvery glade fern (native)

*Digitalis purpurea, D. lutea,* foxgloves

*Dryopteris erythrosora,* Japanese autumn fern

*Dryopteris filix-mas,* male fern (native)

*Dryopteris marginalis,* marginal shield fern (native)

*Epimedium* species, epimediums

*Filipendula rubra,* queen-of-the-prairie (native)

*Filipendula ulmaria,* queen-of-the-meadow (native)

*Hakonechloa macra,* notably the cultivar 'Aureola', Japanese forest grass

*Helleborus* species, hellebores

*Hosta* species, hybrids, and cultivars, hostas, plantain lilies

*Hyacinthoides hispanica (Scilla hispanica),* English bluebell, Spanish bluebell

*Lilium* species, lilies (native)

*Maianthemum canadense,* wild lily of the valley, Canadian mayflower (native)

*Osmunda cinnamomea,* cinnamon fern (native)

*Osmunda claytonia,* interrupted fern (native)

*Osmunda regalis,* royal fern (native)

*Phlox divaricata,* wild sweet William, blue phlox

*Phlox stolonifera,* creeping phlox

*Polygonatum biflorum* var. *commutatum,* Solomon's seal (native)

*Polystichum acrostichoides,* Christmas fern (native)

*Pulmonaria saccharata,* notably the cultivar 'Mrs. Moon', lungwort

*Sanguinaria canadensis,* bloodroot (native)

*Smilacina racemosa,* false Solomon's seal (native)

## Easy-Care Perennials

*Allium sphaerocephalum, A. aflatunense, A. moly,* ornamental onions

*Amsonia tabernaemontana,* bluestar, amsonia (native)

*Asparagus officinalis,* asparagus

*Aster* x *frikartii,* hybrid fall aster

*Baptisia australis,* false indigo

*Camassia leichtlinii,* camosh, quamash

*Centaurea montana,* bluet

*Ceratostigma plumbaginoides,* leadwort

*Chasmanthium latifolium,* sea oats, spangle grass

*Chrysanthemum maximum,* Yukon daisy

*Colchicum autumnale,* autumn crocus

*Convallaria majalis,* lily of the valley

*Dennstaedtia punctilobula,* hay-scented fern (native)

*Echinacea purpurea,* purple coneflower (native)

*Echinops ritro,* globe thistle

*Eupatorium coelestinum,* wild ageratum (native)

*Eupatorium maculatum, E. purpureum,* Joe-Pye weeds (native)

*Gaura lindheimeri,* gaura

*Helenium autumnale,* sneezeweed (native)

*Hemerocallis* species, hybrids, and cultivars, daylilies

*Hosta* species, hybrids, and cultivars, plantain lily, hosta

*Hypericum patulum,* notably the cultivar 'Hidcote', hypericum

*Iris sibirica,* Siberian iris

*Lamium galeobdolon,* notably the cultivar 'Variegatum', archangel plant

*Liatris spicata,* blazing star (native)

*Liriope muscari,* lilyturf

*Lysimachia punctata,* yellow loosestrife

*Mentha* species, mints

*Miscanthus sinensis,* notably the cultivar 'Gracillimus', maiden grass

*Muscari botryoides,* grape hyacinth

*Narcissus* species, hybrids, and cultivars, daffodils, jonquils, narcissi

*Oenothera tetragona,* sundrops

*Rudbeckia fulgida,* notably the cultivar 'Goldsturm', coneflower (native)

*Sedum acre, S. hispanicum, S. sarmentosum, S. spectabile, S. telephium,* sedums, live-forevers

*Solidago* species, goldenrods (native)

*Yucca filamentosa,* Adam's needle

# Perennials for the Southeast

Plants can be used throughout the region in Zones 6–9. Where plants are appropriate only for certain parts of the region, they are noted as follows:

US = Upper South, Zone 6

MS = Middle South, Zone 7 and parts of Zone 8 in the western edge of Mississippi, southern Arkansas, and central Texas

LS = Lower South, Zone 8 plus coastal North Carolina and parts of southern coastal Virginia

CS = Coastal South, Zone 8 in northern Florida and parts of Zone 9 in coastal Texas, Louisiana, and northeastern Florida

## Perennials for Sun

*Acidanthera bicolor,* acidanthera—MS, LS, CS

*Achillea* species, yarrows

*Asclepias tuberosa,* butterfly weed (native)

*Aster novae-angliae,* New England aster (native)—US, MS, LS

*Baptisia alba, B. leucantha,* wild white indigos (native)

*Baptisia australis,* wild blue indigo (native)

*Belamcanda chinensis,* blackberry lily

*Canna* x *generalis,* canna

*Centranthus ruber,* red valerian

*Coreopsis verticillata,* threadleaf coreopsis (native)

*Dendranthema* x *grandiflorum,* chrysanthemum

*Dianthus plumarius,* cottage pink

*Digitalis purpurea,* foxglove

*Echinacea purpurea,* purple coneflower (native)

*Eupatorium purpureum,* Joe-Pye weed (native)

*Heliopsis helianthoides,* sunflower heliopsis (native)

*Hemerocallis* species, hybrids, and cultivars, daylilies

*Hibiscus moscheutos,* marsh mallow (native)

*Iberis sempervirens,* candytuft

*Iris* x *fulvala,* Louisana hybrid irises

*Iris germanica,* bearded irises

*Iris sibirica,* Siberian iris

*Kniphofia uvaria,* red-hot poker

*Leucanthemum* x *superbum,* Shasta daisy

*Liatris spicata, L. pycnostachya,* gayfeathers (native)

*Monarda didyma,* bee balm (native)

*Monarda punctata,* horsemint (native)

*Patrinia scabiosifolia,* patrinia

*Physostegia virginiana,* obedient plant (native)

*Pycnanthemum incanum,* mountain mint (native)

*Rudbeckia fulgida* var. *sullivantii,* coneflower (native)

*Rudbeckia laciniata,* notably the cultivar 'Herbstone', shining coneflower (native)

*Sedum spectabile,* showy sedum

*Solidago* species, goldenrods (native)

*Thermopsis caroliniana,* Carolina lupine (native)


## Perennials for Shade

*Amsonia tabernaemontana,* bluestar (native)

*Anemone* x *hybrida,* Japanese anemone

*Arum italicum,* Italian arum

*Aquilegia canadensis,* columbine (native)

*Astilbe* species, astilbes

*Athyrium filix-femina,* lady fern

*Begonia grandis,* hardy begonia

*Boltonia asteroides,* notably the cultivar 'Snowbank', boltonia (native)

*Carex* species, sedges

*Chasmanthium latifolium,* river oats (native)

*Chrysogonum virginianum,* green and gold (native)

*Dicentra eximia,* bleeding heart (native)

*Dicentra spectablis,* bleeding heart

*Dryopteris ludoviciana,* Florida shield fern (native)

*Helleborus orientalis,* Lenten rose

*Heuchera sanguinea,* coral bells—US, MS, LS

*Hosta* species, hybrids, and cultivars, hostas

*Lobelia cardinalis,* cardinal flower (native)

*Lobelia siphilitica,* great blue lobelia (native)

*Phlox divaricata,* woodland phlox (native)

*Polygonatum biflorum,* Solomon's seal (native)

*Polystichum acrostichoides,* Christmas fern (native)

*Thelypteris kunthii,* southern shield fern (native)

*Tiarella cordifolia* var. *collina (T. wherryi),* foamflower (native)

*Tradescantia ohiensis,* spiderwort (native)

*Tricyrtis hirta,* toad lily


## Easy-Care Perennials

*Achillea,* notably the cultivar 'Coronation Gold', yarrow

*Aquilegia canadensis,* columbine (native)

*Arum italicum,* Italian arum

*Asclepias tuberosa,* butterfly weed (native)

*Begonia grandis,* hardy begonia

*Belamcanda chinensis,* blackberry lily

*Coreopsis verticillata,* threadleaf coreopsis (native)

*Echinacea purpurea,* purple coneflower (native)

*Gaillardia* x *grandiflora,* notably the cultivar 'Goblin', dwarf blanketflower (native)

*Helleborus orientalis,* Lenten rose

*Hemerocallis* species, hybrids, and cultivars, daylilies

*Heuchera americana,* alum root

*Hosta* species, hybrids, and cultivars, hostas

*Iris kaempferi,* Japanese iris

*Iris pseudacorus,* yellow flag

*Iris sibirica,* Siberian iris

*Kosteletzkya virginica,* seashore mallow (native)

*Lobelia cardinalis,* cardinal flower (native)

*Lobelia siphilitica,* great blue lobelia (native)

*Monarda didyma,* bee balm (native)

*Phlox divaricata,* woodland phlox (native)

*Phlox maculata,* notably the cultivar 'Miss Lingard', thick-leaf phlox (native)

*Pycnanthemum incanum,* mountain mint (native)

*Rudbeckia fulgida* var. *sullivantii,* coneflower (native)

*Sedum spectabile,* notably the cultivar 'Autumn Joy', sedum

*Solidago* species, goldenrods (native)
*Tiarella cordifolia* var. *collina* (*T. wherryi*),
    foamflower (native)—US, MS, LS
*Tradescantia virginiana,* spiderwort (native)

## Perennials for Subtropical Florida

The plants recommended for Subtropical Florida are appropriate for Zones 10A, 10B, and 11, unless noted as follows:

*Not for Zone 10A
**Not for Zone 11

### Perennials for Sun

*Agapanthus africanus,* lily-of-the-Nile
*Agave attenuata,* spineless century plant*
*Alpinia zerumbet,* shell ginger
*Asparagus densiflorus,* asparagus fern
*Catharanthus roseus,* periwinkle*
*Chlorophytum comosum,* spider plant*
*Crinum americanum,* swamp lily, string lily
    (native)
*Crinum asiaticum,* tree lily
*Crinum* x *amabile,* giant spider lily
*Cyperus papyrus,* papyrus
*Dietes vegeta,* African iris**
*Evolvulus glomeratus,* blue daze*
*Flaveria linearis,* yellowtop* (native)
*Helianthus debilis,* beach sunflower** (native)
*Lantana montevidensis,* trailing lantana*
*Lantana depressa,* dwarf lantana* (native)
*Liriope muscari, L. spicata,* liriope, lilyturf**
*Musa* x *paradisiaca,* banana
*Neomarica* species, walking irises*
*Pilea microphylla,* artillery plant*
*Ruellia caroliniensis,* wild petunia (native)
*Solidago* species, goldenrods** (native)
*Strelitzia reginae,* bird-of-paradise

*Tradescantia pallida,* purple queen
*Tradescantia spathacea,* oyster plant
*Tulbaghia violacea,* society garlic
*Zephyranthes* species, rain lilies (native)
*Zephyranthes treatiae,* zephyr lily**

### Perennials for Shade

*Aglaonema modestum,* Chinese evergreen (Zone
    11 only)
*Alocasia* x *amazonica,* Amazon elephant's ear*
*Alpinia purpurata,* red ginger (Zone 11 only)
*Amomum compactum,* round cardamom
*Anthurium* species, anthuriums*
*Aphelandra* species, zebra plants*
*Begonia* species, begonias*
*Calathea* species, calatheas, rattlesnake plants*
*Costus speciosus,* crepe ginger
*Curcuma roscoeana,* pride of Burma
*Dieffenbachia* species, dumbcanes
*Elettaria cardamomum,* cardamom
*Haworthia fasciata,* zebra haworthia*
*Heliconia* species, heliconias*
*Hemerocallis* species, hybrids, and cultivars,
    daylilies**
*Kalanchoe pinnata,* live forever*
*Kalanchoe tomentosa,* pussy ears*
*Peperomia* species, peperomias* (native)
*Polianthes tuberosa,* tuberose (Zone 10A only)
*Tacca* species, bat flowers*
*Tradescantia virginiana,* spiderwort (Zone 10A
    only) (native)
*Trimezia martinicensis,* trimezia (Zone 11 only)
*Viola floridana,* Florida violet** (native)
*Zingiber zerumbet,* pinecone ginger

### Easy-Care Perennials

*Agave attenuata,* spineless century plant
*Aloe* species, aloes

*Amorphophallus* species, voodoo lilies

*Anthurium hookeri, A. salviniae,* bird's-nest anthuriums

*Aechmea* species, *Billbergia pyramidalis, Tillandsia* species (native), bromeliads

*Catharanthus roseus,* periwinkle

*Crinum americanum,* swamp lily (native)

*Euphorbia milii,* crown of thorns

*Kalanchoe blossfeldiana,* kalanchoe

*Lantana depressa,* lantana (native)

*Liriope muscari, L. spicata,* liriopes, lilyturfs

*Musa coccinea,* ornamental red banana

*Pentas lanceolata,* pentas

*Peperomia* species, peperomias

*Sisyrinchium* species, blue-eyed grasses

*Tradescantia virginiana,* spiderwort (native)

## Epiphytes

Many epiphytes in South Florida should be grown in protected areas, such as a shadehouse or greenhouse, or attached to tree limbs.

*Aechmea* species, *Billbergia* species, *Guzmania* species (native), *Neoregelia* species, *Tillandsia* species (native), bromeliads

*Anthurium* species, anthuriums

*Ascocenda, Ascocentrum, Brassia, Catasetum, Cattleya, Cymbidium, Dendrobium, Encyclia* (native), *Epidendrum* (native), *Laelia, Masdevallia, Miltonia, Odontoglossum, Oncidium, Phalaenopsis, Paphiopedilum, Vanda, Zygopetalum,* orchids

*Asplenium nidus,* bird's-nest fern (native)

*Cibotium* species, *Cyathea cooperi,* tree ferns

*Davallia fejeensis,* rabbit's-foot fern

*Epiphyllum* species, orchid cacti

*Freycinetia arborea,* freycinetia

*Medinilla magnifica,* medinilla

*Peperomia obtusifolia,* peperomia

*Philodendron* species, philodendrons

*Platycerium* species, staghorn ferns

*Polypodium* species, polypodium ferns (native)

*Psilotum nudum,* whisk fern (native)

*Schlumbergera* species, holiday cacti

## Perennials for the Midwest and Northern Great Plains

The plants are hardy to Zone 4 unless otherwise indicated.

### Perennials for Sun

*Achillea filipendulina, A. millefolium,* yarrows

*Aconitum* species, hybrids, and cultivars, monkshoods

*Aquilegia* species, hybrids, and cultivars, columbines

*Aster novae-angliae, A. novi-belgii,* asters (native)

*Campanula carpatica, C. lactiflora, C. glomerata,* bellflowers

*Chelone glabra, C. lyonii,* turtleheads (native)

*Coreopsis grandiflora, C. verticillata,* coreopsis (native)

*Delphinium* hybrids, delphiniums

*Dendranthema* x *grandiflora,* chrysanthemum

*Dianthus plumarius,* pinks

*Digitalis* species and hybrids, foxgloves

*Echinacea purpurea,* purple coneflower

*Eupatorium purpureum,* Joe-Pye weed

*Geranium* 'Johnson's Blue', Johnson's blue geranium

*Geranium sanguineum,* bloody cranesbill

*Heliopsis helianthoides,* ox-eye (native)

*Hemerocallis* species, hybrids, and cultivars, daylilies

*Iris germanica, I. sibirica,* bearded iris, Siberian iris

*Lilium* species, lilies

*Lysimachia clethroides,* gooseneck loosestrife

*Nepeta mussinii, N. sibirica,* catmints

*Paeonia* species, hybrids, and cultivars, peonies

*Phlox paniculata,* garden phlox

*Veronica* species, hybrids, and cultivars, veronicas

*Veronicastrum virginicum,* Culver's root (native)

## Perennials for Shade

*Adiantum pedatum,* maidenhair (native)

*Anemone nemorosa, A. ranunculoides,* woodland anemones

*Asarum arifolium, A. europaeum,* wild gingers

*Asarum canadense,* wild ginger (native)

*Aster divaricatus,* white wood aster

*Astilbe* species, hybrids, and cultivars, astilbes

*Athyrium filix-femina,* lady fern (native)

*Athyrium nipponicum* 'Pictum', Japanese painted fern

*Brunnera macrophylla,* siberian bugloss

*Cimicifuga japonica* var. *acerina, C. simplex,* bugbanes

*Cimicifuga racemosa,* black cohosh (native)

*Dicentra eximia, D. formosa,* everblooming bleeding hearts

*Dicentra spectabilis,* old-fashioned bleeding heart

*Dryopteris filix-mas, D. setiferum,* wood ferns

*Dryopteris goldiana, D. marginalis,* wood ferns (native)

*Epimedium grandiflorum, E.* x *youngianum,* barrenworts

*Galanthus elwesii, G. nivalis,* snowdrops

*Matteuccia struthiopteris,* ostrich fern (native)

*Mertensia virginica,* Virginia bluebells (native)

*Phlox divaricata, P. stolonifera,* woodland phlox, creeping phlox (native)

*Primula vulgaris,* primrose

*Sanguinaria canadensis,* bloodroot (native)

*Thalictrum thalictroides,* rue anemone (native)

*Tricyrtis macropoda, T. hirta, T. latifolia,* toadlilies

*Trillium grandiflorum,* white trillium (native)

*Uvularia grandiflora,* great merrybells (native)

## Easy-Care Perennials

*Achillea filipendulina,* fernleaf yarrow

*Amsonia tabernaemontana,* bluestar (native)

*Aster novae-angliae,* New England aster (native)

*Astilbe taquetii,* notably the cultivar 'Superba', astilbe

*Baptisia australis, B. leucantha,* false indigo (native)

*Bergenia cordifolia,* heartleaf bergenia

*Campanula carpatica,* Carpathian bellflower

*Coreopsis verticillata,* whorled coreopsis

*Dicentra spectabilis,* old-fashioned bleeding heart

*Echinacea purpurea,* purple coneflower (native)

*Hemerocallis* species, hybrids, and cultivars, daylilies

*Hosta* species, hybrids, and cultivars, hostas

*Iris sibirica,* Siberian iris

*Mertensia virginica,* Virginia bluebells (native)

*Oenothera macrocarpa,* Ozark sundrops (native)

*Paeonia lactiflora,* peony

*Papaver orientale,* Oriental poppy

*Perovskia atriplicifolia,* Russian sage

*Phlox paniculata,* garden phlox

*Platycodon grandiflorus,* balloon flower

*Rudbeckia fulgida,* orange coneflower (native)

*Sanguinaria canadensis,* bloodroot (native)

*Sedum spectabile,* notably the cultivar 'Autumn Joy', sedum

*Uvularia grandiflora,* great merrybells (native)

*Veronicastrum virginicum,* Culver's root (native)

# Perennials for Texas and the Southern Plains

Plants are appropriate for Zones 6, 7, and 8 unless otherwise noted. Plants marked (6) or (7)

are only marginally adapted to those zones and may not survive in the coldest parts. Similarly, those marked (8) may not survive the hotter, drier areas of Zone 8.

## Perennials for Sun

*Allium stellatum,* prairie onion, wild pink onion (native)

*Amsonia ciliata,* Texas bluestar (native)

*Andropogon glomeratus,* brushy bluestem (native) (Zones 6, 7, 8, 9)

*Asclepias tuberosa,* butterfly weed (native)

*Aster ericoides,* notably the cultivar 'Esther', heath aster (native)

*Aster oblongifolius,* aromatic aster (native)

*Aster praealtus,* tall blue aster (native)

*Baptisia australis,* blue false indigo (native) (Zones 6, 7)

*Berlandiera texana,* Texas greeneyes (native) (Zones 6, 7, 8, 9)

*Bouteloua curtipendula,* sideoats grama (native)

*Callirhoe involucrata,* winecup (native)

*Calylophus hartwegii,* calylophus (native)

*Camassia scilloides,* wild hyacinth (native) (Zones 7, 8)

*Castilleja purpurea,* purple paintbrush (native)

*Cooperia pedunculata,* hill country rain lily (native) (Zones 7, 8)

*Coreopsis lanceolata,* coreopsis (native)

*Echinacea angustifolia,* black sampson (native)

*Echinacea purpurea,* purple coneflower

*Engelmannia pinnatifida,* Engelmann daisy (native)

*Gaura lindheimeri,* gaura (native) (Zones 6, 7, 8, 9)

*Hedyotis nigricans,* prairie bluet (native) (Zones 6, 7, 8, 9)

*Helianthus maximilianii,* Maximilian sunflower (native)

*Hemerocallis* species, hybrids, and cultivars, daylilies

*Iris* species, hybrids, and cultivars, bearded iris, Louisiana hybrids, Dutch iris

*Lantana camara,* Texas lantana (Zones 7, 8, 9)

*Liatris mucronata,* narrowleaf gayfeather (native)

*Monarda fistulosa,* notably the cultivar 'Claire Grace', bergamot, bee balm (native)

*Muhlenbergia capillaris,* Gulf muhly (native) (Zones 7, 8, 9)

*Muhlenbergia lindheimeri,* Lindheimer's muhly (native) (Zones (7), 8)

*Perovskia atriplicifolia,* Russian sage

*Phlox paniculata,* notably the cultivar 'Mt. Fuji', summer phlox, autumn phlox

*Phlox pilosa,* prairie phlox (native) (Zones 7, 8)

*Physostegia virginiana,* fall obedient plant (native)

*Ratibida columnifera,* Mexican hat (native)

*Salvia azurea* var. *grandiflora,* blue sage (native)

*Salvia farinacea,* mealy blue sage (native)

*Salvia leucantha,* Mexican bush sage (Zones 8, 9)

*Salvia penstemonoides,* penstemon sage (native) (Zones (7), 8)

*Schizachyrium scoparium,* little bluestem (native) (Zones 6, 7, 8, 9)

*Scutellaria ovata,* eggleaf skullcap (native) (Zones 7, 8)

*Senna marilandica,* Maryland senna (native)

*Silphium gracile,* rosinweed (native)

*Solidago nemoralis,* gray goldenrod (native)

*Sorghastrum nutans,* Indiangrass (native) (Zones 6, 7, 8, 9)

*Stipa tenuissima,* feathergrass (native)

*Tetraneuris scaposa,* four-nerve daisy, hymenoxys (native)

*Tradescantia occidentalis, T. ohiensis,* spiderworts (native)

*Vernonia baldwinii,* Baldwin ironweed (native)

## Perennials for Shade

*Achillea millefolium,* yarrow
*Aquilegia canadensis,* wild red columbine
  (native)
*Aquilegia chrysantha,* yellow columbine
*Aster pratensis,* Christmas aster (native) (Zones
  8, 9)
*Chasmanthium latifolium,* inland sea oats
  (native)
*Eupatorium coelestinum,* wild ageratum (native)
*Hydrangea macrophylla,* bigleaf hydrangea
*Leucanthemum vulgare,* ox-eye daisy
*Malvaviscus arboreus* var. *drummondii,* Turk's cap
  (native) (Zones 7, 8, 9)
*Melica nitens,* three-flower melic (native)
*Ruellia humilis,* fringeleaf ruellia (native)
*Ruellia nudiflora,* wild petunia (native) (Zones
  8, 9)
*Salvia lyrata,* lyreleaf sage (native) (Zones 6, 7,
  8, 9)
*Salvia roemeriana,* cedar sage (native) (Zones
  (7), 8)
*Sedum spectabile,* notably the cultivars 'Autumn
  Joy', 'Ruby Glow', sedum
*Senecio obovatus,* golden groundsel (native)
  (Zones 7, 8)
*Solidago odora,* fragrant goldenrod (native)
*Solidago ulmifolia,* elmleaf goldenrod (native)
*Teucrium canadense,* American germander, wood
  sage (native)
*Thalictrum dasycarpum,* tall meadow rue
  (native)
*Wedelia acapulcensis* var. *hispida,* zexmenia
  (native) (Zones 8, 9)

## Easy-Care Perennials

*Achillea millefolium,* white yarrow
*Aster oblongifolius,* aromatic aster (native)
*Bouteloua curtipendula,* sideoats grama (native)

*Callirhoe involucrata,* winecup (native)
*Chasmanthium latifolium,* inland seaoats (native)
*Cooperia pedunculata,* hill country rain lily
  (native) (Zones 7, 8)
*Coreopsis lanceolata,* coreopsis (native)
*Echinacea purpurea,* purple coneflower
*Hemerocallis* species, hybrids, and cultivars,
  daylilies
*Hydrangea macrophylla,* bigleaf hydrangea
*Iris* species, hybrids, and cultivars, irises
*Lantana urticoides,* Texas lantana (native)
  (Zones 7, 8, 9)
*Malvaviscus drummondii,* Turk's cap (native)
  (Zones 7, 8, 9)
*Monarda fistulosa,* bergamot (native)
*Phlox paniculata,* summer phlox
*Phlox pilosa,* prairie phlox (native)
*Ruellia nudiflora,* wild petunia (native) (Zones
  8, 9)
*Schizachyrium scoparium,* little bluestem (native)
  (Zones 6, 7, 8, 9)
*Scutellaria ovata,* eggleaf skullcap (native)
  (Zones 7, 8)
*Sedum spectabile,* notably the cultivar 'Autumn
  Joy', sedum
*Silphium gracile,* rosinweed (native)
*Solidago odora,* fragrant goldenrod (native)
*Sorghastrum nutans,* Indiangrass (native) (Zones
  6, 7, 8, 9)
*Thalictrum dasycarpum,* tall meadowrue (native)
*Tradescantia ohiensis,* Ohio spiderwort (native)
*Tradescantia occidentalis,* western spiderwort
  (native)
*Vernonia baldwinii,* Baldwin ironweed (native)

## Perennials for the Rocky Mountain Region

Unless otherwise noted, plants are hardy to
Zone 4 as long as the soil is insulated with snow
or mulch during the winter.

## Perennials for Sun

*Achillea millefolium*, fernleaf yarrow (native)

*Anaphalis margaritacea*, pearly everlasting (native) (Zone 2)

*Antennaria rosea*, pussytoes (native) (Zone 2)

*Aquilegia chrysantha*, golden columbine (Zone 5)

*Armeria maritima*, sea pink

*Campanula carpatica*, bellflower

*Centranthus ruber*, red valerian

*Cerastium tomentosum*, snow-in-summer

*Coreopsis lanceolata*, coreopsis

*Dianthus deltoides*, maiden pinks

*Dictamnus albus*, gas plant

*Echinacea purpurea*, purple coneflower

*Erigeron compositus*, fleabane (native)

*Eriogonum umbellatum*, sulfur flower (native)

*Erysimum asperum*, Western wallflower (native)

*Gaillardia aristata*, blanketflower (native)

*Geranium sanguineum*, bloodred geranium

*Helictotrichon sempervirens*, blue avena

*Liatris punctata*, dotted gayfeather (native)

*Linum lewisii* var. *lewisii*, blue flax (native)

*Malva alcea* 'Fastigiata', mallow (Zone 5)

*Miscanthus sinensis*, eulalia

*Oenothera speciosa*, notably the cultivar 'Siskiyou', Mexican evening primrose (Zone 5)

*Oenothera macrocarpa* (*O. missouriensis*), Texas evening primrose (Zone 5)

*Penstemon pinifolius*, pineleaf penstemon

*Perovskia atriplicifolia*, Russian sage

*Potentilla nevadensis*, Spanish cinquefoil

*Ratibida columnifera*, prairie coneflower (native)

*Rudbeckia hirta*, black-eyed Susan (native)

*Saccharum ravennae*, plume grass

*Santolina chamaecyparissus*, lavender cotton

*Sorghastrum nutans*, Indiangrass (native)

*Stachys byzantina*, lamb's ears

*Thermopsis rhombifolia* var. *montana*, golden banner (native) (Zone 3)

*Tradescantia virginiana*, spiderwort

*Veronica spicata*, notably the cultivars 'Minuet', 'Red Fox', speedwell (Zone 5)

## Perennials for Shade

*Alchemilla mollis*, lady's mantle

*Athyrium filix-femina*, lady fern

*Aquilegia caerulea*, Rocky Mountain columbine (native) (Zone 2)

*Astilbe chinensis* 'Pumila', Chinese astilbe (Zone 5)

*Bergenia cordifolia*, bergenia

*Brunnera macrophylla*, alkanet

*Chasmanthium latifolium*, wild oats

*Dicentra eximia*, fringed bleeding heart

*Dicentra spectabilis*, bleeding heart

*Digitalis* x *mertonensis*, foxglove

*Dryopteris filix-mas*, male fern (native)

*Epimedium* x *rubrum*, barrenwort

*Epimedium* x *versicolor*, notably the cultivar 'Sulphureum', yellow-flowered barrenwort

*Heuchera sanguinea*, coral bells

*Hosta* cultivars, hosta

*Luzula nivea*, wood rush

*Thalictrum rochebrunianum*, notably the cultivar 'Lavender Mist', meadow rue (Zone 5)

*Tiarella cordifolia*, foamflower (Zone 5)

## Easy-Care Perennials

*Alchemilla mollis*, lady's mantle

*Antennaria rosea*, pussytoes (native) (Zone 2)

*Aquilegia chrysantha*, golden columbine

*Armeria maritima*, sea pink, thrift

*Bergenia cordifolia*, bergenia

*Centranthus ruber*, red valerian (Zone 5)

*Coreopsis lanceolata*, coreopsis

*Dicentra eximia,* fringed bleeding heart

*Dictamnus albus* 'Ruber', gas plant

*Erigeron compositus,* fleabane (native)

*Eriogonum umbellatum,* sulfur flower (native)

*Geranium sanguineum,* bloodred geranium

*Helictotrichon sempervirens,* blue avena

*Hemerocallis* species, hybrids, and cultivars, daylilies

*Heuchera sanguinea,* coral bells

*Iris pallida* 'Variegata', variegated iris

*Oenothera macrocarpa (O. missouriensis),* Texas evening primrose

*Potentilla nevadensis,* Spanish cinquefoil (Zone 5)

*Stachys byzantina,* lamb's ears

*Veronica pectinata,* woolly veronica

## Perennials for the Pacific Northwest

Plants are hardy to at least Zone 7 unless otherwise noted.

### Perennials for Sun

*Acanthus spinosa,* spiny-leaved acanthus

*Achillea clypeolata,* notably the cultivar 'Moonshine', yarrow

*Alchemilla mollis,* lady's mantle

*Anemone patens,* pasqueflower

*Aquilegia formosa,* red columbine (native)

*Aster subspicatus,* Douglas' aster (native)

*Coreopsis verticillata,* notably the cultivar 'Moonbeam', threadleaf coreopsis

*Bletilla striata,* bletilla

*Delphinium,* notably the cultivar 'Cliveden Beauty', delphinium

*Erigeron glaucus,* seaside daisy (native)

*Erysimum linifolium,* notably the cultivar 'Bowles Mauve', wallflower

*Eupatorium purpureum,* Joe-Pye weed

*Euphorbia characias* subsp. *wulfenii,* shrubby spurge

*Geranium endressii,* notably the cultivar 'Wargrave Pink', cranesbill

*Helenium autumnale,* autumn sneezeweed

*Hemerocallis,* notably the cultivar 'Tender Love', daylily

*Iris* Pacific Coast hybrids, Pacific Coast iris hybrid

*Kniphofia* x 'Primrose Beauty', primrose beauty torch lily

*Lavatera thuringiaca* 'Rosea', rose lavatera

*Lupinus* Russell hybrids, Russell lupine (native)

*Mimulus lewisii,* Lewis monkeyflower (native)

*Paeonia* x 'Prairie Moon', prairie moon peony

*Papaver orientale,* notably the cultivar 'Karine', Oriental poppy

*Pennisetum alopecuroides,* fountain grass

*Penstemon newberryi,* Newberry penstemon (native)

*Sedum spathulifolium,* notably the cultivar 'Cape Blanco', stonecrop (native)

*Sidalcea campestris,* meadow sidalcea (native)

*Stipa gigantea,* feathergrass

*Veronica spicata,* notably the cultivar 'Blue Charm', speedwell

### Perennials for Shade

*Aceriphyllum rossii,* mapleleaf

*Adiantum pedatum,* maiden fern (native)

*Anemone* x *hybrida,* notably the cultivar 'September Charm', windflower

*Anemone nemorosa,* wood anemone

*Aruncus dioicus,* goatsbeard (native)

*Astilbe* x *arendsii,* notably the cultivar 'Fanal', astilbe

*Carex morrowii* 'Aureo-variegata', golden variegated Japanese sedge

*Cimicifuga laciniata,* cut-leaved bugbane (native)

*Dicentra spectabilis,* Japanese bleeding heart
*Disporum smithii,* fairy lanterns (native)
*Dryopteris campyloptera,* woodfern (native)
*Helleborus niger,* Christmas rose
*Heuchera micrantha,* small-flowered alumroot (native)
*Hosta sieboldiana,* notably the cultivar 'Frances Williams', plantain lily
*Iris tectorum* 'Alba', White Japanese roof iris
*Ligularia dentata,* notably the cultivar 'Desdemona', ligularia
*Mertensia virginica,* Virginia bluebells
*Peltoboykinia tellimoides,* peltoboykinia
*Polemonium reptans,* Jacob's ladder
*Polystichum munitum,* western sword fern (native)
*Primula japonica,* notably the cultivar 'Miller's Crimson', primrose
*Rodgersia aesculifolia,* rodgersia
*Saxifraga cuneifolia,* rockfoil
*Shibataea kumasaca,* shibataea
*Smilacina racemosa,* false Solomon's seal (native)
*Smilacina stellata,* starry Solomon's seal (native)
*Thalictrum rochebrunianum,* meadow rue
*Tiarella cordifolia* var. *collina* (*T. wherryi*), Wherry's foamflower
*Viola glabra,* yellow violet (native)
*Woodwardia fimbriata,* western chain fern (native)

## Easy-Care Perennials

*Achillea millefolium,* yarrow
*Anemone hybrida,* Japanese anemone
*Aster* x *frikartii,* notably the cultivar 'Monch', Frikart's aster
*Astrantia major,* notably the cultivar 'Hadspen Blood', astrantia
*Aurinia saxatilis* (*Alyssum saxatile*), basket of gold

*Bergenia cordifolia,* heartleaf bergenia
*Centranthus ruber,* red valerian
*Coreopsis lanceolata,* notably the cultivar 'Goldfink', tickseed
*Dictamnus albus,* gas plant
*Geranium* 'Johnson's Blue', cranesbill
*Hemerocallis lilio-asphodelus,* lemon daylily
*Lychnis coronaria,* rose campion
*Lysimachia punctata,* loosestrife
*Papaver orientale,* Oriental poppy
*Phlox maculata* 'Alpha', wild sweet William
*Physostegia virginiana,* notably the cultivar 'Vivid', obedient plant
*Polygonatum odoratum,* Solomon's seal
*Thalictrum aquilegiifolium,* meadow rue
*Veronica spicata,* notably the cultivar 'Blue Charm', speedwell

## Perennials for Coastal California

Plants are appropriate for the coastal regions of California from Crescent City to the border of Mexico—and east to the Coast Ranges, the western edge of Central Valley, and the southern inland valleys and southernmost Peninsular Ranges.

### Perennials for Sun

*Achillea,* notably the cultivars 'King George', 'Moonshine', yarrows
*Alstroemeria aurea,* Peruvian lily
*Anigozanthos flavidus,* kangaroo paw
*Armeria maritima,* sea thrift (native)
*Artemisia pycnocephala,* notably the cultivar 'David's Choice', sandhill sage (native)
*Asteriscus maritimus,* gold chip
*Coreopsis verticillata,* notably the cultivar 'Moonbeam', coreopsis

*Dierama pulcherrimum,* angel's wand

*Echium wildpretii,* tower of jewels

*Epilobium canum* (*Zauschneria californica*), California fuchsia (native)

*Erysimum linifolium,* notably the cultivar 'Bowles Mauve', shrubby wallflower

*Euphorbia characias* subsp. *wulfenii,* Mediterranean spurge

*Gypsophila paniculata,* baby's breath

*Helianthus angustifolius,* no common name

*Lithodora diffusa* 'Grace Ward', no common name

*Lychnis coronaria,* crown pink

*Nepeta* x *faassenii,* catmint

*Oenothera macrocarpa,* evening primrose

*Origanum pulchellum,* oregano

*Phlomis fruticosa,* Jerusalem sage

*Romneya coulteri,* matilija poppy (native)

*Salvia chamaedryoides,* no common name

*Senecio cineraria,* dusty miller

*Sidalcea malviflora,* mallow

*Tulbaghia violacea,* notably the cultivar 'Silver Lace', society garlic

*Verbena bonariensis,* verbena

## Perennials for Shade

*Aquilegia caerulea,* Rocky Mountain columbine

*Aquilegia formosa,* western columbine (native)

*Campanula glomerata,* notably the cultivar 'Joan Elliot', clustered bellflower

*Campanula rotundifolia,* bellflower

*Cyclamen hederifolium,* baby cyclamen

*Dicentra formosa,* western bleeding heart (native)

*Dierama pulcherrimum,* fairy wand

*Digitalis grandiflora,* yellow foxglove

*Francoa sonchifolia,* maiden's wreath

*Geranium* 'Johnson's Blue', Johnson's blue geranium

*Helichrysum petiolare,* notably the cultivar 'Limelight', licorice plant

*Helleborus argutifolius,* hellebore

*Heuchera maxima,* coral bells (native)

*Heuchera micrantha,* notably the cultivar 'Palace Purple', alum root

*Iris douglasiana,* Douglas' iris

*Iris* Pacific Coast hybrids, Pacific Coast iris hybrids

*Omphalodes cappadocica,* perennial forget-me-not

*Oxalis oregana,* redwood sorrel

*Polygonatum odoratum,* Solomon's seal

*Smilacina racemosa,* false Solomon's seal (native)

*Tanacetum parthenium,* notably the cultivar 'Aureum', feverfew

## Easy-Care Perennials

*Achillea millefolium,* common yarrow

*Agapanthus* species, lilies-of-the-Nile

*Armeria maritima,* sea pink (native)

*Aster* x *frikartii,* notably the cultivar 'Monch', aster

*Cerastium tomentosum,* snow-in-summer

*Crocosmia* cultivars, notably 'Lucifer', crocosmia

*Echium wildpretii,* tower of jewels

*Erigeron* 'Moerheimii', fleabane

*Erysimum linifolium,* notably the cultivar 'Bowles Mauve', shrubby wallflower

*Gaura lindheimeri,* gaura

*Iris* Pacific Coast hybrids, Pacific Coast iris hybrids (native)

*Kniphofia* species and cultivars, notably 'Little Maid', torch lily

*Leucanthemum maximum,* Shasta daisy

*Linaria purpurea,* toadflax

*Lychnis coronaria,* crown pink

*Nepeta* x *faassenii,* catmint

*Origanum laevigatum,* notably the cultivar 'Hopley's', origanum

*Pelargonium* species, geraniums

*Penstemon* species, penstemons

*Phormium tenax,* New Zealand flax

*Stachys byzantina,* lamb's ears

*Strelitzia reginae,* bird-of-paradise

*Tulbaghia violacea,* society garlic

*Verbena bonariensis,* verbena

## Perennials for the Western Deserts

The plants are appropriate throughout the region, except those noted as follows:

*Not cold hardy in cold desert areas

**Favor cooler/moister desert areas

### Perennials for Sun

*Agastache rupestris,* licorice mint (native)

*Asclepias tuberosa,* butterfly weed (native)

*Callirhoe involucrata,* winecups (native)

*Calylophus hartwegii,* sundrops (native)

*Centranthus ruber,* valerian

*Eriogonum fasciculatum,* flattop buckwheat (native)

*Erysimum linifolium,* notably the cultivar 'Bowles mauve', wallflower

*Euphorbia myrsinites,* blue spurge

*Gaura lindheimeri,* gaura (native)

*Gypsophila repens,* creeping baby's breath

*Iris germanica,* bearded iris

*Kniphofia uvaria,* torch lily

*Liatris punctata,* gayfeather (native)

*Melampodium leucanthum,* Blackfoot daisy (native)

*Mirabilis multiflora,* giant four-o'clock (native)

*Nepeta* x *faassenii,* catmint

*Nierembergia hippomanica,* notably the cultivar 'Purple Robe', cupflower

*Oenothera caespitosa,* white-tufted evening primrose (native)

*Origanum libanoticum,* ornamental oregano

*Penstemon ambiguus,* sand penstemon

*Penstemon parryi,* Parry's penstemon (native)

*Penstemon pinifolius,* pineleaf penstemon (native)

*Penstemon pseudospectabilis,* canyon penstemon (native)

*Phlomis fruticosa,* Jerusalem sage*

*Salvia chamaedryoides,* Mexican blue sage (native)

*Salvia officinalis,* garden sage

*Scutellaria orientalis,* prairie skullcap

*Sedum spectabile,* notably the cultivars 'Autumn Joy', 'Red Chief', sedum

*Tagetes lemmoni,* mountain marigold* (native)

*Verbena canadensis,* notably the cultivar 'Homestead Purple', verbena

*Veronica alpina,* notably the cultivar 'Goodness Grows', speedwell**

*Zephyranthes grandiflora,* pink rain lily

### Perennials for Shade

*Achillea taygetea,* notably the cultivar 'Moonshine', yarrow

*Aquilegia chrysantha,* goldspur columbine (native)

*Bergenia cordifolia,* heartleaf bergenia

*Campanula rotundifolia,* harebells**

*Datura wrightii,* sacred datura (native)

*Epilobium canum* (*Zauschneria californica*), hummingbird trumpet (native)

*Geranium sanguineum,* true geranium

*Heuchera sanguinea,* coral bells (native)

*Iberis sempervirens,* candytuft

*Linum perenne,* blue flax (native)

*Lobelia cardinalis,* cardinal flower (native)

*Lychnis chalcedonica,* Maltese cross

*Rudbeckia fulgida,* notably the cultivar 'Goldsturm', rudbeckia**

*Salvia azurea* var. *grandiflora,* blue sage (native)

*Salvia leucantha,* Mexican sage* (native)

*Stachys byzantina,* lamb's ears

*Stachys coccinea,* scarlet mint (native)

*Verbena peruviana,* Peruvian verbena

### Easy-Care Perennials

*Agastache cana,* bubblegum mint (native)

*Asclepias tuberosa,* butterfly weed (native)

*Callirhoe involucrata,* winecups (native)

*Calylophus hartwegii,* sundrops (native)

*Centranthus ruber,* valerian

*Erysimum linifolium,* notably the cultivar 'Bowles mauve', wallflower

*Gypsophila repens,* creeping baby's breath

*Hymenoxys acaulis,* angelita daisy (native)

*Liatris punctata,* gayfeather (native)

*Melampodium leucanthum,* Blackfoot daisy (native)

*Mirabilis multiflora,* giant four-o'clock (native)

*Oenothera macrocarpa* subsp. *macrocarpa* (O. missouriensis), Missouri evening primrose

*Perovskia atriplicifolia,* Russian sage

*Salvia chamaedryoides,* Mexican blue sage (native)

*Scutellaria orientalis,* prairie skullcap

*Sedum spectabile,* notably the cultivars 'Autumn Joy', 'Red Chief', sedum

*Stachys byzantina,* notably the cultivar 'Silver Carpet', lamb's ears

*Verbena canadensis,* notably the cultivar 'Homestead Purple', verbena

*Zephyranthes* species, rain lilies

*Zinnia grandiflora,* desert zinnia (native)

## Foliage Plants

Plants without flowers or with insignificant flowers can still offer amazing variety and interest to the garden, both in the perennial border and by adding texture and foliage color in shady areas. The foliage of the plants in the regional lists that follow ranges from delicate to bold, colorful to fragrant. These foliage plants are primarily perennials (including some ferns and grasses), plus a few annuals, shrubs, and trees.

## Foliage Plants for the Northeast

Plants are hardy to Zone 5, unless noted.

### Plants with Bold and Dramatic Foliage

*Canna indica* and hybrids, cannas (not winter-hardy)

*Colocasia esculenta,* taro (not winter-hardy)

*Ficus carica,* notably the cultivar 'Brown Turkey', common fig

*Hosta sieboldiana,* hosta

*Macleaya cordata,* plume poppy

*Nelumbo nucifera, N. lutea,* sacred lotus

*Peltandra virginica,* arrow arum (native)

*Petasites japonicus,* butterbur

*Podophyllum peltatum,* mayapple (native)

*Rheum cultorum* (R. rhabarbarum), rhubarb

*Ricinus communis,* castor-oil plant

*Sasa palmata,* bamboo

*Xanthosoma violaceum,* blue taro (not winter-hardy)

### Plants with Colorful or Variegated Foliage

*Acer shirasawanum* 'Aureum', golden maple

*Actinidia kolomikta,* flag actinidia

*Arum italicum* subsp. *italicum,* arum

*Athyrium nipponicum* 'Pictum', Japanese painted fern

*Caladium* species, hybrids, and cultivars, caladiums

*Cornus stolonifera* 'Silver and Gold', red osier dogwood

*Disporum sessile* 'Variegatum', variegated Japanese fairy-bells

*Fagus sylvatica* 'Atropunicea', copper beech

*Hakonechloa macra* 'Albo-aurea', Japanese forest grass

*Hosta* 'Frances Williams', Frances Williams hosta

*Hosta ventricosa* 'Albo-marginata', blue plantain lily

*Iris ensata* 'Variegata', sword-leaved iris

*Kerria japonica* 'Picta', Japanese rose

*Ophiopogon planiscapus* 'Arabicus', 'Black Knight', black mondo grass (Zone 6)

*Pennisetum setaceum* 'Rubrum', fountain grass

*Polygonatum odoratum* 'Variegatum', variegated Japanese Solomon's seal

*Strobilanthes dyerianus* 'Persian shield', Mexican petunia

*Yucca smalliana* 'Bright Edge', *Y. filamentosa* 'Golden Sword', yuccas (native)

## Plants with Delicate Foliage

*Acer palmatum* 'Dissectum', 'Filigree', green cutleaf Japanese maples

*Acer palmatum* 'Garnet', 'Ever Red', 'Crimson Queen', 'Red Filigree Lace', red cutleaf Japanese maples

*Anethum graveolens,* dill

*Aruncus dioicus* 'Kneiffii', cutleaf European goatsbeard

*Asparagus officinalis,* garden asparagus

*Athyrium filix-femina,* lady fern

*Betula pendula* 'Gracilis', cutleaf European birch

*Coreopsis verticillata,* coreopsis

*Cosmos bipinnatus,* cosmos

*Dennstaedtia punctilobula,* hay-scented fern (native)

*Foeniculum vulgare,* fennel

*Myrrhis odorata,* sweet cicely, anise, sweet chervil

*Rhus glabra* 'Laciniata', cutleaf smooth sumac (native)

*Tamarix ramosissima,* tamarisk

## Plants with Fragrant Foliage

*Abies balsamea,* balsam fir (native)

*Artemisia dracunculus,* tarragon

*Comptonia peregrina,* sweet fern (native)

*Dennstaedtia punctilobula,* hay-scented fern (native)

*Foeniculum vulgare,* fennel

*Gaultheria procumbens,* wintergreen (native)

*Juniperus virginiana,* Eastern red cedar (native)

*Lindera benzoin,* spice-bush

*Melissa officinalis,* lemon balm

*Mentha arvensis,* field mint

*Mentha* x *piperita,* peppermint

*Mentha pulegium,* pennyroyal

*Mentha spicata,* spearmint

*Myrica pensylvanica,* bayberry (native)

*Myrrhis odorata,* sweet cicely, anise, sweet chervil

*Ocimum basilicum,* basil

*Pelargonium crispum,* lemon geranium

*Pelargonium tomentosum,* peppermint geranium

*Plectranthus amboinicus,* Spanish thyme, vicks plant

*Pycnanthemum muticum, P. virginianum,* mountain mints (native)

*Rhus aromatica,* fragrant sumac (native)

*Zanthoxylum* species, prickly ashes, toothache trees

# Foliage Plants for the Southeast

Plants can be used throughout the region in Zones 6–9. Where plants are appropriate only for certain parts of the region, they are noted as follows:

US = Upper South, Zone 6

MS = Middle South, Zone 7 and parts of Zone 8 in the western edge of Mississippi, southern Arkansas, and central Texas

LS = Lower South, Zone 8 plus coastal North Carolina and parts of southern coastal Virginia

CS = Coastal South, Zone 8 in northern Florida and parts of Zone 9 in coastal Texas, Louisiana, and northeastern Florida

## Plants with Bold and Dramatic Foliage

*Helleborus* species, hellebores

*Hosta sieboldiana* 'Elegans', hosta

*Hydrangea quercifolia*, oak-leaf hydrangea (native)

*Iris* species, hybrids, and cultivars, irises

*Osmunda cinnamomea, O. regalis,* cinnamon fern and royal fern (native)

*Rhapidophyllum hystrix,* needle palm—MS, LS, CS

## Plants with Colorful or Variegated Foliage

*Artemisia ludoviciana* 'Silver King', Silver King artemisia

*Arum italicum* subsp. *italicum,* arum

*Athyrium nipponicum* var. *pictum,* Japanese painted fern

*Heuchera micrantha* 'Palace Purple', alumroot

*Hosta undulata* 'Albomarginata', hosta

*Liriope muscari* 'Variegata', variegated liriope

*Saxifraga stolonifera,* strawberry begonia

*Stachys byzantina,* lamb's ears

## Plants with Delicate Foliage

*Amsonia hubrichtii,* Arkansas bluestar (native)

*Aquilegia canadensis,* columbine (native)

*Coreopsis verticillata,* threadleaf coreopsis (native)

*Dicentra eximia,* bleeding heart (native)

*Rhus typhina* 'Dissecta', cutleaf sumac (native)

*Thalictrum aquilegiifolium,* columbine meadow rue

*Thelypteris kunthii,* southern shield fern (native)

## Plants with Fragrant Foliage

*Artemisia abrotanum,* southernwood

*Mentha* species, mints

*Pycnanthemum incanum,* mountain mint (native)

*Rosmarinus officinalis,* rosemary

*Salvia elegans,* pineapple sage—LS, CS

# Foliage Plants for Subtropical Florida

The plants recommended for Subtropical Florida are appropriate for Zones 10A, 10B, and 11, unless noted as follows:

*Not for Zone 10A

**Not for Zone 11

## Plants with Bold and Dramatic Foliage

*Acrostichum danaeifolium,* leather fern (native)

*Aechmea mexicana,* Mexican vase*

*Anthurium hookeri, A. salviniae,* bird's-nest anthuriums*

*Dioon edule,* dioon*

*Heliconia caribaea,* heliconia*

*Monstera deliciosa,* Swiss cheese plant*

*Philodendron bipinnatifidum,* philodendron

*Polypodium cambraicum* 'Grandiceps', Welsh polypody*

*Ravenala madagascariensis,* traveler's tree

*Yucca aloifolia,* Spanish bayonet

*Yucca elephantipes,* spineless yucca

*Zamia pumila,* Florida palm

## Plants with Colorful or Variegated Foliage

*Acalypha wilkesiana*, copperleaf*

*Alpinia zerumbet*, notably the cultivar 'Variegata', variegated shell ginger

*Anthurium clarinervium, A. magnificum*, anthuriums*

*Breynia disticha*, snowbush*

*Caladium bicolor*, caladium

*Codiaeum variegatum* var. *pictum*, croton*

*Cordyline terminalis*, ti plant*

*Dieffenbachia maculata*, dumbcane*

*Heliconia stricta* 'Carli's Sharonii', heliconia*

*Musa zebrina*, red banana*

*Schefflera arboricola*, dwarf schefflera

## Plants with Delicate Foliage

*Adiantum capillus-veneris*, maidenhair fern (native)

*Davallia fejeensis*, rabbit's-foot fern*

## Plants with Fragrant Foliage

*Cymbopogon citratus*, lemongrass*

# Foliage Plants for the Midwest and Northern Great Plains

The plants are hardy to Zone 4 unless otherwise indicated.

## Plants with Bold and Dramatic Foliage

*Aralia racemosa*, spikenard (native)

*Bergenia cordifolia*, bergenia

*Darmera peltata*, umbrella leaf

*Diphylleia cymosa*, umbrella leaf

*Hosta* species, hybrids, and cultivars, hostas

*Lysichiton americanus*, western skunk cabbage

*Ligularia dentata, L. stenocephala*, ligularias

*Rodgersia* species, rodgersias

*Symplocarpus foetidus*, skunk cabbage (native)

## Plants with Colorful or Variegated Foliage

*Carex siderosticha* 'Variegata', variegated sedge

*Lamium maculatum*, deadnettle

*Penstemon digitalis* 'Husker Red', penstemon (native)

*Polygonatum odoratum* 'Variegatum', variegated Japanese Solomon's seal

*Pulmonaria* species, hybrids, and cultivars, lungworts

*Uvularia sessilifolia* 'Variegata', variegated wild oats (native)

## Plants with Delicate Foliage

*Carex glauca, C. nigra*, sedges

*Dicentra eximia*, wild bleeding heart

*Epimedium* x *youngianum*, barrenwort

*Thalictrum* species, meadow rues (native)

*Thalictrum thalictroides*, rue anemone (native)

## Plants with Fragrant Foliage

*Acorus calamus*, sweet flag (native)

*Agastache foeniculum*, fragrant hyssop (native)

*Artemisia ludoviciana*, prairie sage (native)

*Geranium macrorrhizum*, bigroot geranium

*Stachys lanata*, lamb's ears

*Thymus* species, thymes

# Foliage Plants for Texas and the Southern Plains

Plants are appropriate for Zones 6, 7, and 8 unless otherwise noted. Plants marked (6) or (7) are only marginally adapted to those zones and may not survive in the coldest parts. Similarly, those marked (8) may not survive the hotter, drier areas of Zone 8.

## Plants with Bold and Dramatic Foliage

*Cucurbita foetidissima,* buffalo gourd (native)
*Dasylirion texanum,* sotol (native) (Zones 7, 8)
*Hesperaloe parviflora,* red yucca (native) (Zones 7, 8, 9)
*Hydrangea quercifolia,* oak-leaf hydrangea
*Nolina texana,* sacahuista (native)
*Opuntia imbricata,* cholla (native) (Zones 6, 7, (8))
*Opuntia phaeacantha,* brownspine prickly pear (native) (Zones 6, 7, 8, 9)
*Ricinus communis,* castor bean (annual)
*Sabal minor,* dwarf palmetto (native) (Zones 8, 9)
*Senna alata* (*Cassia alata*), candlestick plant (annual)
*Yucca glauca,* plains beargrass (native) (Zones 6, 7, 8, 9)
*Yucca gloriosa,* softleaf yucca (Zones 7, 8, 9)

## Plants with Colorful or Variegated Foliage

*Acalypha wilkesiana,* copperleaf (Zone 10)
*Elaeagnus macrophylla,* eleagnus (native) (Zone 8)
*Leucophyllum frutescens,* cenizo (native) (Zones 8, 9)
*Schizachyrium scoparium,* little bluestem (native) (Zones 6, 7, 8, 9)
*Sorghastrum nutans,* Indiangrass (native) (Zones 6, 7, 8, 9)
*Yucca pallida,* paleleaf yucca (native) (Zone 8)

## Plants with Delicate Foliage

*Acacia wrightii,* Wright acacia (native) (Zones 7, 8, 9)
*Chilopsis linearis,* desert willow (native) (Zones (6), 7, 8, 9)

*Helianthus salicifolius,* willowleaf sunflower (native)
*Muhlenbergia, Stipa, Andropogon, Schizachyrium, Grama, Chloris* species, grasses (native) (Zones 6, 7, 8, 9)
*Prosopis glandulosa,* honey mesquite (native) (Zones 7, 8, 9)
*Sophora affinis,* Eve's necklace (native) (Zones 7, 8)

## Plants with Fragrant Foliage

*Artemisia ludoviciana,* Louisiana artemisia (native)
*Aster pratensis,* Christmas aster (native) (Zones 8, 9)
*Monarda fistulosa,* bergamot (native)
*Myrica cerifera,* southern wax myrtle (native) (Zones 8, 9)
*Rhus aromatica,* aromatic sumac (native)
*Salvia coccinea,* scarlet sage (native) (Zones 8, 9)
*Salvia roemeriana,* cedar sage (native) (Zones (7), 8)
*Solidago odora,* fragrant goldenrod (native)
*Vitex agnus-castus,* lavender tree (Zones 8, 9)

# Foliage Plants for the Rocky Mountain Region

Plants are hardy to Zone 4 unless otherwise noted.

## Plants with Bold and Dramatic Foliage

*Arum italicum* subsp. *italicum,* arum
*Bergenia cordifolia,* heartleaf bergenia
*Catalpa speciosa,* catalpa
*Gymnocladus dioicus,* Kentucky coffee tree (Zones 3–8)
*Hosta sieboldiana,* hosta
*Ricinus communis,* castor bean (annual)

## Plants with Colorful or Variegated Foliage

*Acer negundo* 'Flamingo', box elder (Zone 5)

*Cornus alba* 'Argenteo-marginata', variegated dogwood (Zone 2)

*Hippophae rhamnoides,* sea buckthorn (Zones 3–7)

## Plants with Delicate Foliage

*Acer saccharinum* 'Wieri', silver maple (Zones 3–8)

*Artemisia filifolia,* sand sage (native)

*Artemisia frigida,* fringed sage (native) (Zone 2)

*Chamaebatiaria millefolium,* fernbush

*Philadelphus microphyllus,* littleleaf mock orange (native)

## Plants with Fragrant Foliage

*Artemisia abrotanum,* southernwood

*Galium odoratum,* sweet woodruff

*Lavandula angustifolia,* lavender (Zone 5)

*Origanum vulgare,* oregano

*Pinus edulis,* pinyon pine (native)

*Ptelea trifoliata,* hop tree (native)

*Thymus pseudolanuginosus,* woolly thyme

*Thymus vulgaris,* common thyme

# Foliage Plants for the Pacific Northwest

Plants are hardy to at least Zone 7 unless otherwise noted.

## Plants with Bold and Dramatic Foliage

*Astilboides tabularis,* shieldleaf rodgersia

*Cynara cardunculus,* cardoon

*Darmera peltata,* darmera (native)

*Gunnera tinctoria,* Chilean gunnera

*Fatsia japonica,* Japan fatsia

*Hydrangea quercifolia,* oak-leaf hydrangea

*Rheum palmatum* 'Atrosanguineum', ornamental rhubarb

*Viburnum rhytidophyllum* 'Allegheny', leatherleaf viburnum

## Plants with Colorful or Variegated Foliage

*Acer shirasawanum* 'Aureum', fullmoon maple

*Chamaecyparis obtusa* 'Aurea', golden Hinoki false cypress

*Helictotrichon sempervirens,* blue oat grass

*Heuchera micrantha* 'Chocolate Ruffles', 'Palace Purple', 'Plum Pudding', coral bells

*Hosta* 'Gold Standard', plantain lily

*Iris pallida* 'Argentea Variegata', 'Aurea Variegata', variegated sweet irises

*Pulmonaria longifolia* 'Roy Davidson', pulmonaria, lungwort

## Plants with Delicate Foliage

*Corydalis scouleri,* Scouler's corydalis (native)

*Dicentra formosa,* Pacific bleeding heart (native)

*Fargesia dracocephala,* hardy dragon bamboo

*Paeonia tenuifolia,* fern-leaved peony

*Rhus typhina* 'Laciniata', cutleaf staghorn sumac

*Sambucus nigra* 'Aurea', golden elderberry

*Thalictrum minus* 'Adiantifolium', maidenhair meadow rue

## Plants with Fragrant Foliage

*Artemisia* species, artemisias

*Calycanthus floridus,* Carolina allspice

*Ledum groenlandicum,* Labrador tea (native)

*Rosmarinus officinalis* 'Arp', rosemary

*Rhododendron* 'PJM', hybrid rhododendron
*Umbellularia californica,* California bay (native)

## Foliage Plants for Coastal California

Plants are appropriate for the coastal regions of California from Crescent City to the border of Mexico—and east to the Coast Ranges, the western edge of Central Valley, and the southern inland valleys and southernmost Peninsular Ranges.

### Plants with Bold and Dramatic Foliage

*Agave americana,* century plant (native)
*Darmera peltata,* Indian rhubarb (native)
*Dicksonia antarctica,* Tasmanian tree fern
*Mahonia lomariifolia,* Chinese holly grape
*Melianthus major,* honey bush
*Phormium tenax,* New Zealand flax
*Polystichum munitum,* western sword fern (native)
*Woodwardia fimbriata,* giant chain fern (native)
*Yucca whipplei,* Our Lord's candle (native)

### Plants with Colorful or Variegated Foliage

*Bothriochloa barbinodis,* cane bluestem
*Carex elegantissima* 'Variegata', variegated sedge
*Carex glauca,* blue sedge
*Cotinus coggygria* 'Royal Purple', purple smoke bush
*Imperata cylindrica* 'Rubra', Japanese blood grass
*Miscanthus sinensis* 'Zebrinus', zebra grass
*Phormium* 'Maori Maiden', New Zealand flax
*Phormium* 'Yellow Wave', New Zealand flax
*Salix purpurea* 'Nana', purple willow

### Plants with Delicate Foliage

*Adiantum pedatum,* five-finger fern (native)
*Artemisia* 'Powis Castle', artemisia
*Blechnum spicant,* deer fern (native)
*Polypodium californicum,* polypodium (native)

### Plants with Fragrant Foliage

*Aloysia triphylla,* lemon verbena
*Myrtus communis,* true myrtle
*Rosmarinus officinalis* 'Huntington Blue', rosemary
*Tagetes lemmoni,* Mexican bush marigold
*Thymus vulgaris* 'Ray Williams', thyme
*Tulbaghia violacea,* society garlic
*Umbellularia californica,* California bay laurel (native)

## Foliage Plants for the Western Deserts

The plants are appropriate throughout the region, except those noted as follows:

*Not cold-hardy in cold desert areas
**Favor cooler/moister desert areas

### Plants with Bold and Dramatic Foliage

*Agave* species, century plant (native)
*Daslirion wheeleri,* desert spoon (native)
*Euphorbia rigida,* gopher plant
*Glaucium oxylobum,* horned poppy
*Hesperaloe parviflora,* red yucca (native)
*Muhlenbergia rigens,* deergrass* (native)
*Nolina microcarpa,* beargrass (native)
*Salvia sclarea,* clary sage

## Plants with Colorful or Variegated Foliage

*Dodonaea viscosa* 'Purpurea', purple hop bush* (native)

*Foeniculum vulgare* 'Purpureum', bronze fennel

*Helictotrichon sempervirens,* blue avena, blue oat grass

*Yucca rigida,* blue yucca (native)

## Plants with Delicate Foliage

*Muhlenbergia dumosa,* bamboo muhly* (native)

*Nassella tenuissima* (*Stipa tenuissima*), threadgrass (native)

*Orostachys furusei,* duncecaps

*Ruta graveolens,* rue

*Tanacetum densum,* partridge feather

## Plants with Fragrant Foliage

*Agastache* species, bubblegum mint, licorice mint (native)

*Artemisia* x 'Powis Castle', artemisia

*Helichrysum italicum* (*H. angustifolium*), curry plant

*Larrea tridentata,* creosote bush (native)

*Monarda* x 'Marshall's Delight', bee balm**

*Teucrium aroanum,* Greek germander

*Thymus pseudolanuginosus,* woolly thyme

# Ground Covers

A ground cover is any plant that covers an area by spreading over it—either by growing wider or in spreading clumps above ground or by means of underground stems, runners, or stolons. A large variety of plants can serve the purpose, including shrubs, vines, perennials, ferns, annuals, bulbs, grasses, and mosses.

Ground covers serve an invaluable function in the garden, providing texture and color in areas where other plants often cannot thrive. Ground covers are often planted instead of grass in areas where lawns are impossible or impractical, such as under shade trees or on steep slopes. Even in places where lawns could grow, ground covers can serve as a more natural-looking, low-maintenance alternative. They help define an area of the garden or fill in spaces next to walls and around or between rocks or stepping stones. Ground covers with light-colored foliage can help lighten up a dark area of the garden.

Choose ground covers appropriate for your light conditions, climate, and soil. Space plants as recommended, and fill in around plants with a layer of compost or mulch. Consider the plants' growing rates and habits. If you want quick coverage, choose a fast-growing plant, but avoid invasive and weedy plants that quickly spread into other areas where they are impossible to control. To cover large areas in the garden, consider using two or more kinds of plants for contrasting textures and colors, but stick to varieties that grow at similar rates so that one does not overwhelm the other.

## Ground Covers for the Northeast

Plants are hardy to Zone 5, unless noted.

### Ground Covers for Sun

*Aurinia* (*Alyssum*) *saxatilis,* basket of gold

*Erica carnea,* notably the cultivar 'Springwood White', heath

*Houttuynia cordata,* notably the cultivars 'Plena', 'Chameleon', houttuynia

*Juniperus horizontalis,* notably the cultivars 'Bar Harbor', 'Wiltonii', shore juniper, blue rug juniper

*Juniperus procumbens* 'Nana', juniper

*Lamium galeobdolon,* notably the cultivar 'Variegatum', archangel plant

*Phalaris arundinacea,* notably the cultivars 'Picta', 'Variegata', painted ribbongrass

*Rhus aromatica,* fragrant sumac (native)

*Rosa wichuraiana,* notably the cultivars 'Red Meidiland', 'Alba Meidiland', memorial rose

## Ground Covers for Shade

*Aegopodium podagraria,* notably the cultivar 'Variegata', goutweed, bishopwort

*Ajuga reptans,* bugleweed

*Athyrium nipponicum* (*A. goeringianum*) 'Pictum', Japanese painted fern

*Cephalotaxus harringtonia* 'Nana', plum yew

*Dennstaedtia punctilobula,* hay-scented fern (native)

*Disporum sessile* 'Variegatum', variegated Japanese fairy-bells

*Epimedium* species, epimediums

*Galium odoratum* (*Asperula odorata*), sweet woodruff

*Helleborus foetidus,* green hellebore

*Hosta clausa,* running plantain lily

*Liriope spicata,* creeping lilyturf, mayflower

*Mnium* (*Plagiomnium*) *cuspidatum, Thuidium delicatulum,* mosses

*Ophiopogon planiscapus,* notably the cultivars 'Arabicus', 'Black Knight', black mondo grass (native)

*Pachysandra procumbens,* Allegheny spurge (native)

*Pachysandra terminalis,* Japanese pachysandra

*Parthenocissus quinquefolia,* Virginia creeper (native)

*Podophyllum peltatum,* mayapple (native)

*Xanthorhiza simplicissima,* yellowroot

## Ground Covers for the Southeast

Plants can be used throughout the region in Zones 6–9. Where plants are appropriate only for certain parts of the region, they are noted as follows:

US = Upper South, Zone 6

MS = Middle South, Zone 7 and parts of Zone 8 in the western edge of Mississippi, southern Arkansas, and central Texas

LS = Lower South, Zone 8 plus coastal North Carolina and parts of southern coastal Virginia

CS = Coastal South, Zone 8 in northern Florida and parts of Zone 9 in coastal Texas, Louisiana, and northeastern Florida

## Ground Covers for Sun

*Cotoneaster dammeri,* barberry cotoneaster

*Festuca ovina* var. *glauca,* blue fescue—US, MS

*Gelsemium sempervirens,* yellow jessamine (native)

*Hemerocallis* species, hybrids, and cultivars, daylilies

*Hypericum calycinum,* creeping St.-John's-wort—US, MS

*Ilex vomitoria* 'Nana', dwarf yaupon holly (native)

*Juniperus chinensis* 'Sargentii', Sargent juniper

*Juniperus procumbens* 'Nana', dwarf juniper

*Juniperus conferta* 'Blue Pacific', shore juniper

*Juniperus horizontalis* 'Blue Rug', creeping juniper

*Liriope muscari, L. spicata,* liriopes

*Parthenocissus quinquefolia,* Virginia creeper (native)

*Pennisetum* species, fountain grasses

*Phlox subulata,* thrift (native)

*Xanthorhiza simplicissima* yellowroot (native)

## Ground Covers for Shade

*Ajuga reptans,* bugleweed

*Asarum canadense,* deciduous wild ginger (native)—US, MS

*Aspidistra elatior,* cast-iron plant—LS, CS

*Athyrium nipponicum* 'Pictum', Japanese painted fern

*Cyrtomium falcatum,* holly fern—LS, CS

*Helleborus orientalis,* Lenten rose

*Hosta* species, hybrids, and cultivars, hostas

*Liriope muscari, L. spicata,* liriopes

*Ophiopogon planiscapus* 'Arabicus', black mondo grass

*Pachysandra procumbens,* Allegheny spurge (native)—US, MS, LS

*Pachysandra terminalis,* Japanese pachysandra—US, MS, LS

*Rohdea japonica,* rohdea—MS, LS, CS

*Sarcococca hookeriana* var. *humilis,* sarcococca—US, MS

*Saxifraga stolonifera,* strawberry begonia

# Ground Covers for Subtropical Florida

The plants recommended for Subtropical Florida are appropriate for Zones 10A, 10B, and 11, unless noted as follows:

*Not for Zone 10A
**Not for Zone 11

## Ground Covers for Sun

*Aechmea* species, *Billbergia pyramidalis, Vriesea* species, bromeliads

*Borrichia frutescens,* sea ox-eye daisy (native)

*Carissa macrocarpa* 'Horizontalis', dwarf carissa

*Cuphea hyssopifolia,* Mexican heather*

*Euphorbia milii,* crown of thorns*

*Gaillardia pulchella,* blanketflower (native)

*Kalanchoe* species, kalanchoes

*Lantana depressa,* pineland lantana (native)

*Lippia nodiflora,* creeping Charlie (native)

*Okenia hypogaea,* beach peanut*

*Pilea microphylla,* artillery plant

*Portulaca oleracea,* purslane* (native)

*Steirodiscus chrysanthemoides,* African bush daisy*

*Tradescantia pallida* (*Setcreasea pallida*) 'Purple Heart', tradescantia

*Tulbaghia violacea,* society garlic

*Verbena maritima,* beach verbena* (native)

*Zephyranthes* species, rain lilies (native)

## Ground Covers for Shade

*Aechmea* species, *Billbergia* species, *Cryptanthus* species, *Neoregelia* species, *Vriesea* species, bromeliads

*Blechnum serrulatum,* swamp fern (native)

*Chlorophytum comosum,* spider plant*

*Crossopetalum ilicifolium,* quailberry* (native)

*Evolvulus glomeratus,* blue daze

*Nephrolepis exaltata,* Boston fern (native)

*Peperomia* species, peperomias* (native)

*Pilea cadierei,* aluminum plant

*Ruellia brittoniana,* Mexican bluebells*

*Selaginella involens, S. uncinata,* selaginellas

*Zamia pumila,* coontie* (native)

# Ground Covers for the Midwest and Northern Great Plains

The plants are hardy to Zone 4 unless otherwise indicated.

## Ground Covers for Sun

*Antennaria* species, pussytoes (native)

*Arctostaphylos uva-ursi,* bearberry (native)

*Cerastium tomentosum,* snow-in-summer

*Geranium* x *cantabrigiense* 'Biokovo', biokovo geranium

*Geum triflorum,* prairie smoke (native)

*Juniperus horizontalis,* creeping juniper (native)

*Phlox subulata,* creeping phlox (native)

*Rudbeckia fulgida* 'Goldsturm', orange coneflower

*Sedum spurium* and others, stonecrops

*Veronica repens,* creeping veronica

*Waldsteinia fragarioides,* barren strawberry (native)

## Ground Covers for Shade

*Ajuga reptans,* bugleweed

*Asarum europaeum,* European wild ginger

*Aster macrophyllus,* bigleaf aster (native)

*Campanula poscharskyana,* Serbian bellflower

*Convallaria majalis,* lily of the valley

*Epimedium* x *rubrum,* red barrenwort

*Galium odoratum,* sweet woodruff

*Iris cristata,* dwarf crested iris (native)

*Pachysandra procumbens,* Allegheny spurge

*Paxistima canbyi,* paxistima (native)

*Pteridium aquilinum,* bracken fern (native)

*Vancouveria hexandra,* vancouveria

# Ground Covers for Texas and the Southern Plains

Plants are appropriate for Zones 6, 7, and 8 unless otherwise noted. Plants marked (6) or (7) are only marginally adapted to those zones and may not survive in the coldest parts. Similarly, those marked (8) may not survive the hotter, drier areas of Zone 8.

## Ground Covers for Sun

*Acacia angustissima,* fern acacia, prairie acacia (native) (Zones (6), 7, 8, 9)

*Antennaria neglecta,* pussytoes (native) (Zones 5, 6, 7)

*Artemisia ludoviciana,* Louisiana artemisia (native)

*Buchloe dactyloides,* buffalo grass (native)

*Juniperus horizontalis,* notably the cultivars 'Wiltoni', 'Blue Rug', juniper

*Liriope muscari,* monkeygrass

*Phyla nodiflora,* frogfruit (native)

*Quincula lobata,* purple groundcherry (native)

*Trachelospermum asiaticum,* Asian jasmine (Zones 7, 8, 9)

## Ground Covers for Shade

*Ajuga reptans,* ajuga (native)

*Berberis repens,* creeping barberry (Zones 6, 7)

*Calyptocarpus vialis,* horseherb (native) (Zones 8, 9)

*Carex planostachys,* cedar sedge (native)

*Chasmanthium latifolium,* inland sea oats (native)

*Dryopteris marginalis,* marginal wood fern (native) (Zones 6, 7)

*Elymus virginicus,* Virginia wild rye (native)

*Geum canadense,* white avens (native)

*Liriope muscari,* monkeygrass

*Ophiopogon japonicus,* mondo grass (Zones 7, 8, 9)

*Polystichum acrostichoides,* christmas fern (native) (Zones 6, 7, (8))

*Rivina humilis,* pigeonberry, rougeplant (native) (Zones 7, 8, 9)

*Ruellia brittoniana* 'Katie', Katie's ruellia (Zones 8, 9)

*Salvia lyrata,* lyre-leaf sage (native)

*Senecio obovatus,* golden groundsel (native)

*Symphoricarpos orbiculatus,* coralberry, buckbrush (native)

*Thelypteris kunthii,* southern wood fern (native) (Zones 8, 9)

*Viola missouriensis,* Missouri violet (native)

## Ground Covers for the Rocky Mountain Region

Unless otherwise noted, plants are hardy to Zone 4 as long as the soil is insulated with snow or mulch during the winter.

### Ground Covers for Sun

*Cerastium tomentosum,* snow-in-summer
*Duchesnea indica,* mock strawberry
*Juniperus communis* var. *saxatilis,* common juniper (native) (Zones 2–6)
*Juniperus horizontalis,* creeping juniper (native) (Zones 3–9)
*Polygonum affine* 'Border Jewell', buckwheat
*Potentilla neumanniana* (*P. tabernaemontani*), creeping cinquefoil
*Teucrium canadense,* germander
*Thymus citriodorus,* lemon thyme
*Veronica allionii,* Allion speedwell
*Veronica pectinata,* Comb speedwell

### Ground Covers for Shade

*Aegopodium podagraria,* bishop's weed
*Ajuga reptans,* carpet bugle
*Arctostaphylos uva-ursi,* kinnikinnick (native) (Zones 2–7)
*Hypericum calycinum,* St.-John's-wort (Zone 5)
*Galium odoratum,* sweet woodruff
*Glechoma hederacea,* ground ivy
*Lamium galeobdolon,* archangel deadnettle
*Lamium maculatum,* spotted deadnettle (Zone 5)
*Lysimachia nummularia,* moneywort
*Mahonia repens,* creeping Oregon grape (native)
*Waldsteinia fragarioides,* barren strawberry (Zone 5)

## Ground Covers for the Pacific Northwest

Plants are hardy to at least Zone 7 unless otherwise noted.

### Ground Covers for Sun

*Ajuga reptans,* carpet bugle
*Arctostaphylos uva-ursi* 'Massachusetts', Massachusetts kinnikinnick (native)
*Calluna vulgaris,* notably the cultivar 'J. H. Hamilton', heather
*Campanula portenschlagiana,* Dalmatian bell-flower
*Erica cinerea* 'Atrorubens', purple bell heath
*Erica* x *darleyensis,* notably the cultivar 'Furzey', heath
*Euphorbia amygdaloides* 'Purpurea', purple-leaved spurge
*Geranium sanguineum,* bloody cranesbill
*Juniperus procumbens* 'Nana', dwarf Japanese garden juniper
*Mahonia aquifolium* 'Compacta', compact Oregon grape (native)
*Rosa wichuraiana,* memorial rose

### Ground Covers for Shade

*Asarum europaeum,* European wild ginger
*Astilbe chinensis pumila,* dwarf Chinese astilbe
*Convallaria majalis,* lily of the valley
*Coptis laciniata,* cutleaf goldthread (native)
*Cornus canadensis,* bunchberry dogwood
*Cyclamen hederifolium,* cyclamen
*Dicentra formosa,* Pacific bleeding heart (native)
*Epimedium perralderianum,* bishop's hat
*Euphorbia amygdaloides* var. *robbiae,* Robb's spurge
*Gaultheria shallon,* salal (native)
*Hosta lancifolia,* lanceleaf plantain lily
*Liriope muscari,* lily turf

*Mahonia nervosa,* cascade's grape (native)
*Oxalis oregana,* redwood sorrel (native)
*Sarcococca hookeriana* var. *humilis,* small
    Himalayan sarcococca
*Vaccinium vitis-idaea,* lingonberry (native)
*Vancouveria hexandra,* inside-out flower (native)

## Ground Covers for Coastal California

### Ground Covers for Sun

*Arctostaphylos* 'Pacific Mist', manzanita (native)
*Ceanothus maritimus* 'Pt. Sierra', wild lilac
    (native)
*Cerastium tomentosum,* snow-in-summer
*Coreopsis auriculata* 'Nana', no common name
*Dodonaea procumbens,* no common name
*Helianthemum* cultivars, sunrose
*Origanum laevigatum* 'Hopley's', ornamental
    oregano
*Rosmarinus officinalis* 'Prostratus', rosemary
*Scaevola* 'Mauve Clusters', scaevola
*Stachys byzantina* 'Silver Carpet', lamb's ears
*Thymus herba-barona,* caraway thyme
*Thymus serpyllum* 'Minor', elfin thyme
*Verbena canadensis* 'Homestead Purple', verbena

### Ground Covers for Shade

*Ajuga reptans* 'Catlin's Giant', carpet bugle
*Asarum caudatum,* wild ginger (native)
*Blechnum penna-marina,* blechnum
*Campanula poscharskyana,* Serbian bellflower
*Geranium incanum,* carpet geranium
*Lamium maculatum* 'Beacon Silver', deadnettle
*Maianthemum dilatatum,* coltsfoot
*Phlomis russelliana,* no common name
*Sedum spathulifolium,* no common name (native)
*Stachys byzantina* 'Silver Carpet', lamb's ears
*Viola labradorica,* violet

## Ground Covers for the Western Deserts

The plants are appropriate throughout the region, except those noted as follows:

*Not cold-hardy in cold desert area
**Favor cooler/moister desert areas

### Ground Covers for Sun

*Acacia redolens* 'Desert Carpet', acacia*
*Antennaria dioica,* pussytoes (native)
*Aptenia cordifolia,* hearts and flowers*
*Baccharis* x 'Centennial', broom
*Convolvulus sabatius,* ground morning glory*
*Cotoneaster microphyllus,* rockspray
*Dalea greggii,* trailing indigo* (native)
*Delosperma cooperi,* purple iceplant
*Gazania rigens* 'Sungold', trailing gazania*
*Lantana montevidensis,* trailing lantana*
*Marrubium rotundifolium,* roundleaf horehound
*Mirabilis multiflora,* giant four-o'clock (native)
*Oenothera speciosa* (*O. berlandieri*), Mexican
    evening primrose (native)
*Teucrium aroanum,* Greek germander
*Teucrium chamaedrys,* prostrate germander
*Verbena rigida,* rough verbena

### Ground Covers for Shade

*Allium tuberosum,* garlic chives
*Anemopsis californica,* yerba mansa (native)
*Arctostaphylos* 'Emerald Carpet', manzanita
*Campanula poscharskyana,* Serbian bellflower
*Ceratostigma plumbaginoides,* dwarf plumbago
*Delosperma nubigenum,* yellow iceplant
*Festuca glauca,* blue fescue (native)
*Saponaria ocymoides,* soapwort
*Veronica liwanensis,* Turkish speedwell

## Vines

Vines are plants—either woody or herbaceous—that climb, creep, trail, drape, or otherwise need support to grow properly. Some attach themselves to the support by twining or wrapping themselves around it or by use of tendrils or suction cup–like rootlets growing from their stems. Others need to be tied, tacked, or otherwise attached to the support.

Vines are perfect for covering and screening and to create architectural elements in the garden. They can be used to hide an unattractive wall or fence or climb up a trellis to create a natural wall. They can tumble down from a stone wall, climb an arched trellis to form an elegant entrance to the garden or an area of the garden, or ramble over an arbor to form a leafy roof. Vines can wrap around poles, climb deck rails, and drape over boulders. Plants used this way may be evergreen or deciduous, have foliage interest or flowers. Some of the most common plants used for fragrance in the garden are vines.

When choosing a vine for a particular purpose in your garden, it is important know the plant's growth habit. Does it attach itself, or need to be supported? If it attaches by twining itself around an object, you cannot expect it to climb a flat wall. Twiners can strangle and kill other plants. Some vines attach themselves very tenaciously to a surface; if you need to paint a fence or wall regularly, do not cover it with a vine. If the area you are covering is small, select a plant that remains relatively compact to avoid the need for drastic pruning. For an arbor effect, consider whether you want to create dense or dappled shade below, and choose your vine accordingly. Know the plant's light needs as well; the roots of many vines should be in shade even if the foliage needs full sun (in hotter climates, you can place a stone over the roots near the base of the plant to help shade the roots). Choose a trellis to fit the vine. Large, heavy vines require a sturdy support, while compact or light-textured plants look best on more refined trellises.

## Vines for the Northeast

Perennial vines are hardy to Zone 5, unless noted.

### Vines for Sun

*Actinidia kolomikta,* flag actinidia
*Aristolochia macrophylla* (*A. durior*), Dutchman's-pipe (native)
*Campsis radicans,* trumpet creeper (native)
*Celastrus scandens,* American bittersweet (native)
*Dioscorea batatas,* cinnamon vine
*Hydrangea anomala,* climbing hydrangea
*Ipomoea quamoclit,* cypress vine, cardinal creeper (annual)
*Lablab purpureus* (*Dolichos lablab*), hyacinth bean (annual)
*Lathyrus odoratus,* sweetpea (annual)
*Luffa* species, dishcloth gourds (annual)
*Lycopersicon esculentum,* tomato (annual)
*Menispermum canadense,* Canadian moonseed (native)
*Parthenocissus quinquefolia,* Virginia creeper (native)
*Parthenocissus tricuspidata,* Boston ivy
*Polygonum aubertii,* silver fleece vine
*Vitis labrusca,* Labrador grape (native)
*Wisteria sinensis, W. floribunda,* Chinese and Japanese wisteria
*Wisteria frutescens,* American wisterias (native)

## Vines for Shade

*Akebia quinata, A. trifoliata,* akebias
*Apios americana,* groundnut (native)
*Parthenocissus quinquefolia,* Virginia creeper
  (native)
*Parthenocissus tricuspidata,* Boston ivy

## Flowering Vines

*Campsis radicans,* trumpet creeper (native)
*Clematis* x *jackmanii, C. terniflora, C. paniculata,*
  clematis
*Convolvulus tricolor,* dwarf morning glory
  (annual)
*Hydrangea anomala,* climbing hydrangea
*Ipomoea quamoclit,* cypress vine (annual)
*Lonicera* x *heckrottii,* Heckrott hybrid honey-
  suckle
*Lonicera sempervirens,* trumpet honeysuckle
  (native)
*Polygonum aubertii,* silver fleece vine
*Thunbergia alata,* black-eyed Susan vine
*Wisteria* species, wisterias

## Fragrant Vines

*Clematis terniflora, C. paniculata,* sweet autumn
  clematis
*Convolvulus tricolor,* dwarf morning glory
  (annual)
*Lathyrus odoratus,* sweetpea (annual)
*Lonicera caprifolium,* woodbine
*Lonicera flava,* yellow honeysuckle (native)
*Wisteria* species, wisterias

## Vines for the Southeast

The perennial vines can be used throughout the
region in Zones 6–9. Where they are appropriate only for certain parts of the region, they are
noted as follows:

US = Upper South, Zone 6
MS = Middle South, Zone 7 and parts of Zone
  8 in the western edge of Mississippi, south-
  ern Arkansas, and central Texas
LS = Lower South, Zone 8 plus coastal North
  Carolina and parts of southern coastal Vir-
  ginia
CS = Coastal South, Zone 8 in northern
  Florida and parts of Zone 9 in coastal Texas,
  Louisiana, and northeastern Florida

## Vines for Sun

*Actinidia chinensis,* kiwi fruit—LS, CS
*Actinidia kolomikta,* kolomikta vine
*Bignonia capreolata,* cross vine (native)
*Campsis radicans,* trumpet-creeper (native)
*Clematis montana* 'Grandiflora', clematis
*Clematis texensis,* scarlet leather flower (native)
*Clematis armandii,* clematis—MS, LS, CS
*Gelsemium sempervirens,* yellow jessamine (native)
*Ipomoea alba,* moonflower (annual)
*Ipomoea* x *multifida,* cardinal climber (annual)
*Ipomoea quamoclit,* cypress vine (annual)
*Lablab purpureus (Dolichos lablab),* hyacinth
  bean (annual)
*Lathyrus latifolius,* perennial pea
*Lonicera sempervirens,* coral honeysuckle
  (native)
*Luffa cylindrica,* luffa gourd (annual)
*Parthenocissus quinquefolia,* Virginia creeper
  (native)
*Passiflora incarnata,* passionflower (native)
*Rosa banksiae,* Lady Banks rose—MS, LS, CS
*Trachelospermum jasminoides,* Confederate jas-
  mine—LS, CS
*Wisteria frutescens,* American wisteria (native)

## Vines for Shade

*Clematis armandii*, clematis—MS, LS, CS

*Ficus pumila*, creeping fig—LS, CS

*Hydrangea anomala*, climbing hydrangea—US, MS

*Lonicera sempervirens*, coral honeysuckle (native)

*Parthenocissus quinquefolia*, Virginia creeper (native)

*Smilax laurifolia*, smilax (native)—MS, LS, CS

*Trachelospermum jasminoides*, Confederate jasmine—LS, CS

## Flowering Vines

*Actinidia kolomikta*, kolomikta vine

*Bignonia capreolata*, cross vine (native)

*Campsis radicans*, including the cultivar 'Flava', trumpet vine (native)

*Clematis armandii*, clematis—MS, LS, CS

*Clematis* x *henryi*, clematis

*Clematis texensis*, scarlet leather flower (native)

*Cobaea scandens*, cup-and-saucer vine (annual)

*Gelsemium sempervirens*, yellow jessamine (native)

*Hydrangea anomala*, climbing hydrangea—US, MS

*Ipomoea alba*, moonflower (annual)

*Ipomoea purpurea*, morning glory (annual)

*Lonicera sempervirens*, coral honeysuckle (native)

*Luffa cylindrica*, luffa gourd (annual)

*Mina lobata*, mina (annual)

*Thunbergia alata*, black-eyed Susan vine (annual)

*Wisteria frutescens*, American wisteria (native)

## Fragrant Vines

*Actinidia kolomikta*, kolomikta vine

*Clematis armandii*, clematis—MS, LS, CS

*Gelsemium sempervirens*, yellow jessamine (native)

*Ipomoea alba*, moonflower (annual)

*Rosa banksiae* var. *banksiae*, white Lady Banks rose—LS, CS

*Trachelospermum jasminoides*, Confederate jasmine—LS, CS

*Wisteria frutescens*, American wisteria (native)

## Vines for Subtropical Florida

The plants are appropriate for Zones 10A, 10B, and 11, unless noted as follows:

*Not for Zone 10A

**Not for Zone 11

### Vines for Sun

*Aristolochia grandiflora*, pelican flower*

*Bougainvillea* species, bougainvilleas*

*Clerodendrum thomsoniae*, clerodendron

*Congea tomentosa*, shower of orchids*

*Cryptostegia madagascariensis*, Madagascar rubber vine (Zone 10A only)

*Ficus repens*, creeping fig

*Lonicera sempervirens*, coral honeysuckle (native) (Zone 10A only)

*Mandevilla sanderi*, mandevilla

*Mandevilla splendens*, pink mandevilla

*Passiflora caerulea*, blue passionflower

*Passiflora coccinea*, red passionflower*

*Passiflora edulis*, passionfruit

*Petrea volubilis*, queen's wreath*

*Podranea ricasoliana*, pink trumpet vine

*Solandra guttata*, chalice vine

*Stephanotis floribunda*, Madagascar jasmine or bridal bouquet*

*Thunbergia mysorensis*, thunbergia*

## Vines for Shade

*Ficus repens,* creeping fig
*Lonicera sempervirens,* coral honeysuckle (native)
  (Zone 10A only)
*Monstera deliciosa,* Swiss cheese plant*
*Solandra guttata,* chalice vine
*Vanilla planifolia,* vanilla orchid*

## Flowering Vines

*Bougainvillea* species, bougainvilleas*
*Clerodendrum thomsoniae,* clerodendron
*Congea tomentosa,* shower of orchids*
*Hoya* species, wax plants*
*Lonicera sempervirens,* coral honeysuckle (Zone
  10A only) (native)
*Mandevilla splendens,* pink mandevilla
*Monstera deliciosa,* Swiss cheese plant*
*Passiflora caerulea,* blue passionflower
*Passiflora coccinea,* red passionflower*
*Petrea volubilis,* queen's wreath*
*Pyrostegia venusta,* flame vine*
*Quisqualis indica,* Rangoon creeper*
*Thunbergia alata,* black-eyed Susan vine*

## Fragrant Vines

*Stephanotis floribunda,* Madagascar jasmine,
  bridal bouquet*

# Vines for the Midwest and Northern Great Plains

The perennial vines are hardy to Zone 4 unless
otherwise indicated.

## Vines for Sun

*Celastrus scandens,* American bittersweet
  (native)

*Humulus lupulus,* hops
*Parthenocissus tricuspidata,* Boston ivy

## Vines for Shade

*Actinidia arguta,* hardy kiwi
*Actinidia kolomikta,* kolomikta vine
*Aristolochia macrophylla* (*A. durior*),
  Dutchman's-pipe
*Hydrangea petiolaris* (*H. anomala* subsp. *petio-
  laris*), climbing hydrangea (Zone 5)
*Menispermum canadense,* common moonseed
  (native)
*Parthenocissus quinquefolia,* Virginia creeper
  (native)
*Vitis riparia,* riverbank grape (native)

## Flowering Vines

*Campsis radicans,* trumpet vine (native)
*Clematis tangutica,* golden clematis
*Clematis virginiana,* virgin's bower (native)
*Clematis viticella,* clematis
*Ipomoea* species, hybrids, and cultivars, morn-
  ing glories (annual)
*Lablab purpureus* (*Dolichos lablab*), hyacinth
  bean (annual)
*Lonicera* x *brownii* 'Dropmore Scarlet', honey-
  suckle
*Lonicera sempervirens,* scarlet honeysuckle
*Polygonum aubertii,* silver lace vine (Zone 5)

## Fragrant Vines

*Clematis paniculata,* sweet autumn clematis
*Wisteria macrostachya,* southern wisteria

# Vines for Texas and the Southern Plains

The perennial vines are appropriate for Zones 6,
7, and 8 unless otherwise noted. Plants marked

(6) or (7) are only marginally adapted to those zones and may not survive in the coldest parts. Similarly, those marked (8) may not survive the hotter, drier areas of Zone 8.

### Vines for Sun

*Bignonia capreolata,* crossvine (native)

*Campsis radicans,* trumpet vine, trumpet creeper (native)

*Clematis pitcheri,* leather flower (native)

*Clematis terniflora (C. dioscoreifolia),* sweet autumn clematis

*Gelsemium sempervirens,* Carolina jessamine (native)

*Ipomoea alba,* moonflower (annual)

*Ipomoea quamoclit,* cypress vine (annual)

*Ipomoea tricolor,* morning glory (annual)

*Lablab purpureus (Dolichos lablab),* hyacinth bean (annual)

*Lathyrus odoratus,* sweetpea (annual)

*Lonicera albiflora,* white limestone honeysuckle (native) (Zones (6), 7, 8)

*Lonicera sempervirens,* coral honeysuckle (native)

*Parthenocissus quinquefolia,* Virginia creeper (native)

*Parthenocissus tricuspidata,* Boston ivy

*Passiflora caerulea,* Brazilian passionflower (Zones 7, 8, 9)

*Polygonum aubertii,* silver lace vine

*Rosa* varieties, heirloom climbing roses and ramblers

*Rosa setigera,* prairie rose (native)

*Vitis vulpina,* winter grape (native)

*Wisteria sinensis,* Chinese wisteria

### Vines for Shade

*Bignonia capreolata,* crossvine (native)

*Clematis pitcheri,* leather flower (native)

*Gelsemium sempervirens,* Carolina jessamine (native)

*Lonicera albiflora,* white limestone honeysuckle (native) (Zones (6), 7, 8)

*Parthenocissus quinquefolia,* Virginia creeper (native)

*Wisteria frutescens,* American wisteria (native)

### Flowering Vines

*Bignonia capreolata,* crossvine (native)

*Campsis radicans,* trumpet vine, trumpet creeper (native)

*Clematis terniflora (C. paniculata),* sweet autumn clematis

*Clematis pitcheri,* leather flower (native)

*Gelsemium sempervirens,* Carolina jessamine (native)

*Ipomoea alba,* moonflower (annual)

*Ipomoea quamoclit,* cypress vine (annual)

*Ipomoea tricolor,* morning glory (annual)

*Lablab purpureus (Dolichos lablab),* hyacinth bean (annual)

*Lathyrus odoratus,* sweetpea (annual)

*Lonicera albiflora,* white limestone honeysuckle (native) (Zones (6), 7, 8)

*Lonicera sempervirens,* coral honeysuckle (native)

*Passiflora caerulea,* Brazilian passionflower (Zones 7, 8, 9)

*Polygonum aubertii,* silver lace vine

*Rosa* varieties, heirloom climbing roses and ramblers

*Rosa setigera,* prairie rose (native)

*Wisteria sinensis,* chinese wisteria

### Fragrant Vines

*Clematis terniflora,* sweet autumn clematis

*Gelsemium sempervirens,* Carolina jessamine (native)

*Lathyrus odoratus,* sweetpea (annual)

*Rosa* varieties, heirloom climbing roses and ramblers

*Rosa setigera,* prairie rose (native)
*Wisteria frutescens,* American wisteria (native)
*Wisteria sinensis,* Chinese wisteria

## Vines for the Rocky Mountain Region

The perennial vines are hardy to Zone 4 unless otherwise noted.

### Vines for Sun

*Celastrus scandens,* American bittersweet (Zones 3–8)
*Clematis ligusticifolia,* western virgin's bower (native)
*Clematis orientalis,* Oriental clematis
*Clematis vitalba,* traveler's joy
*Lycium barbarum* (*L. halimifolium*), matrimony vine (Zone 3)
*Parthenocissus quinquefolia* var. *engelmannii,* Engelmann ivy (Zone 2)
*Parthenocissus tricuspidata* 'Lowii', Boston ivy
*Vitis vulpina,* grapevine

### Vines for Shade

*Akebia quinata,* five-leaf akebia
*Aristolochia macrophylla* (*A. durior*), Dutchman's-pipe

### Flowering Vines

*Campsis radicans,* trumpet vine
*Campsis* x *tagliabuana* 'Madame Galen', clinging vine (Zone 5)
*Clematis* hybrids 'Jackmanii', 'Niobe', clematis
*Hydrangea petiolaris* (*H. anomala* subsp. *petiolaris*), climbing hydrangea
*Lonicera sempervirens,* trumpet honeysuckle
*Polygonum aubertii,* silver lace vine

### Fragrant Vines

*Clematis terniflora, C. paniculata,* sweet autumn clematis (Zone 5)

## Vines for the Pacific Northwest

The perennial vines are hardy to at least Zone 7 unless otherwise noted.

### Vines for Sun

*Actinidia kolomikta,* actinidia vine
*Akebia quinata,* chocolate vine, five-leaf akebia
*Campsis radicans* 'Flava', yellow trumpet creeper
*Stauntonia hexaphylla,* stauntonia
*Vitis coignetiae,* crimson glory vine
*Vitus vinifera* 'Purpurea', claret vine

### Vines for Shade

*Holboellia coriacea,* holboellia
*Hydrangea anomala,* climbing hydrangea
*Parthenocissus henryana,* silver-vein creeper
*Parthenocissus quinquefolia,* Virginia creeper
*Schizophragma hydrangeoides,* schizophragma

### Flowering Vines

*Clematis montana* var. *rubens,* clematis
*Clematis rehderiana,* clematis
*Clematis viticella,* notably the cultivar 'Rubra', clematis
*Jasminum officinale,* climbing white jasmine
*Rosa banksiae* 'Lutea', climbing Lady Banks rose
*Rosa* 'Handel', Handel rose
*Tropaeolum speciosum,* flame creeper
*Wisteria floribunda* 'Issai Perfect', white Japanese wisteria

## Fragrant Vines

*Clematis armandii*, clematis
*Decumaria sinensis*, decumaria
*Jasminum officinale*, climbing jasmine
*Lonicera periclymenum* 'Serotina', Dutch honey-
  suckle
*Rosa* 'New Dawn', climbing rose

# Vines for Coastal California

Plants are appropriate for the coastal regions of California from Crescent City to the border of Mexico—and east to the Coast Ranges, the western edge of Central Valley, and the southern inland valleys and southernmost Peninsular Ranges.

### Vines for Sun

*Actinidia deliciosa*, kiwi
*Bougainvillea* 'San Diego Red', bougainvillea
*Distictis buccinatoria*, bloodred trumpet vine
*Hydrangea anomala*, climbing hydrangea
*Macfadyena unguis-cati*, cat's claw
*Rosa* 'Royal Sunset', climbing rose
*Solanum jasminoides*, white potato vine
*Vitis californica*, California grape (native)

### Vines for Shade

*Aristolochia californica*, Dutchman's-pipe
  (native)
*Clematis armandii*, evergreen clematis
*Pandorea jasminoides* 'Alba', white bower vine
*Parthenocissus tricuspidata*, Boston ivy

### Flowering Vines

*Clematis* x *jackmanii*, clematis
*Clytostoma callistigioides*, violet trumpet vine

*Distictis buccinatoria*, bloodred trumpet vine
*Hardenbergia comptoniana*, lilac vine
*Ipomoea alba*, moonflower
*Ipomoea tricolor* 'Heavenly Blue', blue morning
  glory
*Passiflora* 'Lavender Lady', passion vine
*Thunbergia alata*, black-eyed Susan vine
*Wisteria floribunda*, Japanese wisteria

### Fragrant Vines

*Clematis armandii*, evergreen clematis
*Jasminum polyanthum*, pink jasmine
*Pandorea pandorana*, wonga-wonga vine
*Stephanotis floribunda*, Madagascar jasmine
*Wisteria venusta*, silky wisteria

# Vines for the Western Deserts

The perennial vines are appropriate throughout the region, except those noted as follows:

\*Not cold-hardy in cold desert areas
\*\*Favor cooler/moister desert areas

### Vines for Sun

*Antigonon leptopus*, coral vine, queen's wreath\*
  (native)
*Bougainvillea spectabilis*, bougainvillea\*
*Campsis radicans*, trumpet vine
*Gelsemium sempervirens*, Carolina jessamine
*Hardenbergia violacea*, lilac vine\*
*Macfadyena unguis-cati*, cat's claw vine
*Passiflora foetida*, passionflower\*
*Parthenocissus inserta*, woodbine (native)
*Phaseolus coccineus*, scarlet runner bean (annual)
*Podranea ricasoliana*, pink trumpet vine\*
*Polygonum aubertii*, silver lace vine
*Rosa banksiae*, Lady Banks rose
*Vitis labrusca*, grape
*Wisteria sinensis*, Chinese wisteria

## Vines for Shade

*Clematis texensis,* scarlet clematis* (native)
*Clytostoma callistigioides* (*Bignonia violacea*),
    lavender trumpet vine*
*Lonicera sempervirens,* coral honeysuckle
*Parthenocissus tricuspidata,* Boston ivy
*Wisteria sinensis,* wisteria

## Flowering Vines

*Antigonon leptopus,* coral vine, queen's wreath*
    (native)
*Bignonia capreolata,* cross vine
*Bougainvillea spectabilis,* bougainvillea*
*Campsis radicans,* trumpet vine
*Clematis montana* var. *rubens,* pink anemone
    clematis**
*Gelsemium sempervirens,* Carolina jessamine
*Hardenbergia violacea,* lilac vine*
*Ipomoea tricolor* 'Heavenly Blue', morning glory
    (annual)
*Macfadyena unguis-cati,* cat's claw vine*
*Maurandella antirrhiniflora,* snapdragon vine
    (native)
*Passiflora foetida,* passionflower*
*Phaseolus coccineus,* scarlet runner bean (annual)
*Podranea ricasoliana,* pink trumpet vine*
*Polygonum aubertii,* silver lace vine
*Wisteria sinensis,* Chinese wisteria

## Fragrant Vines

*Gelsemium sempervirens,* Carolina jessamine
*Lonicera heckrottii,* coral honeysuckle
*Millettia reticulata,* evergreen wisteria*
*Polygonum aubertii,* silver lace vine
*Wisteria sinensis,* Chinese wisteria

# Annuals

Annuals technically are herbaceous plants that bloom from seed the first year and complete their life cycle—from seed to maturity to death—in one growing season. In colder climates, gardeners treat some tender perennials, biennials, tuberous plants, and bulbs as annuals—using them for one season, allowing them to die back, and replacing them the following year. Many annuals self-seed, meaning they produce seeds that develop into new plants on their own the following season.

## Tender, Half-Hardy, and Hardy

Hardy annuals can be grown from seed sown directly outside in the garden where they are to grow. Tender annuals are too tender to be planted outside early enough in spring to give them time to bloom in one season, and therefore need to be started indoors and then transplanted outdoors when soil and nighttime temperatures are warm enough (around 65°F). Half-hardy annuals are slightly hardier than tender annuals, but are often started indoors as well.

## Using Annuals in the Garden

Annuals are inexpensive and easy to grow, and provide an amazing variety of color and blooms throughout the summer, as well as form, foliage color and texture, and often fragrance. They can be used in flower beds, cutting gardens, cottage gardens, and all sorts of containers. Annuals add freshness and flexibility to permanent borders and other plantings, under trees, and mixed with perennials and shrubs. They are ideal for filling in spaces in the garden left after spring-flowering bulbs die back. Some annuals trail or climb; lower-growing annuals can provide carpets of color.

## Planting and Care

Annuals are available as plants in four- or six-packs ready for transplanting. They are also relatively easy to grow from seed. If you are planning to sow annual seeds directly outdoors, it is best to prepare the soil with compost or manure the year before in late summer or fall. Sow hardy annual seeds outdoors when the nights are still cool, and as soon as the days are warm enough for weeds to start germinating. Whether sowing seeds indoors or outdoors, avoid overcrowding and thin out seedlings if necessary. If you are transplanting annuals purchased in flats or started indoors, prepare the soil similarly with compost or other organic matter in late fall or early spring. Plant late in the day or on a cloudy day to keep plants from burning in full sun. Allow proper spacing between plants to discourage disease and pests, and plant in the ground at the same height as the plant was growing in the tray or flat. A layer of mulch around plants will help retain moisture and keep the soil cooler. Throughout the season, regularly deadhead, or cut off spent blooms, to encourage repeat blooming; pinch off flowers and new leaves to help keep foliage annuals full.

## Annuals for the Northeast

### Annuals for Sun

*Abelmoschus esculentus,* ornamental okra
*Ageratum houstonianum,* ageratum
*Antirrhinum majus,* snapdragon
*Arctotis venusta,* African daisy
*Catharanthus roseus* (*Vinca rosea*), Madagascar
    periwinkle

*Dahlia* hybrids, bedding dahlias
*Dianthus chinensis,* China pink
*Emilia coccinea* (*E. javanica*), tassel flower,
    Flora's paintbrush
*Gomphrena globosa,* globe amaranth
*Helichrysum petiolare* 'Limelight', strawflower
*Hunnemannia fumariifolia,* Mexican tulip poppy
*Lobelia erinus,* edging lobelia
*Lunaria annua,* honesty
*Nicotiana langsdorffii,* green-flowering tobacco
*Nicotiana sylvestris,* annual tobacco, flowering
    tobacco
*Nierembergia hippomanica* var. *violacea,* blue cup-
    flower
*Portulaca grandiflora,* moss rose, portulaca
*Salvia farinacea* 'Victoria', mealy-cup sage
*Sanvitalia procumbens,* creeping zinnia
*Tagetes* hybrids, marigolds
*Tweedia caerulea,* tweedia
*Verbena bonariensis,* verbena
*Zinnia* species, zinnias

### Annuals for Shade

*Begonia semperflorens,* wax begonia
*Begonia* x *tuberhybrida,* tuberous begonia (ten-
    der perennial)
*Browallia speciosa,* browallia
*Caladium bicolor,* fancy-leaved caladium
*Catharanthus roseus* (*Vinca rosea*), Madagascar
    periwinkle
*Impatiens* New Guinea hybrids, New Guinea
    hybrid impatiens
*Impatiens walleriana,* impatiens
*Nicotiana langsdorffii,* green-flowering tobacco
*Nicotiana sylvestris,* annual tobacco, flowering
    tobacco
*Solenostemon scutellarioides,* coleus
*Torenia fournieri,* wishbone flower
*Viola* x *wittrockiana,* pansy

# Annuals for the Southeast

## Annuals for Sun

*Amaranthus tricolor,* Joseph's coat
*Catharanthus roseus,* Madagascar periwinkle
*Cleome hassleriana,* cleome
*Cosmos bipinnatus,* cosmos
*Gaillardia pulchella,* blanketflower (native)
*Gomphrena globosa,* globe amaranth
*Mirabilis jalapa,* four-o'clock
*Pelargonium* x *hortorum,* geranium
*Petunia* x *hybrida,* petunia
*Portulaca grandiflora,* rose moss
*Portulaca* species, purslanes
*Ricinus communis,* castor bean
*Rudbeckia hirta,* gloriosa daisy
*Salvia farinacea,* mealy-cup sage
*Salvia leucantha,* Mexican bush sage
*Salvia splendens,* scarlet sage
*Solenostemon scutellarioides,* coleus
*Tagetes erecta,* African marigold
*Tagetes patula,* dwarf French marigold
*Tithonia rotundifolia,* Mexican sunflower
*Verbena peruviana,* Peruvian verbena
*Zinnia elegans,* zinnia

## Annuals for Shade

*Begonia* x *semperflorens-cultorum,* green-leafed
   wax begonia
*Browallia speciosa,* browallia
*Caladium bicolor,* caladium
*Digitalis purpurea,* foxglove
*Gerbera jamesonii,* gerbera daisy
*Impatiens walleriana,* impatiens
*Lobelia erinus,* edging lobelia
*Myosotis* species, forget-me-nots
*Nicotiana alata,* flowering tobacco
*Solenostemon scutellarioides,* coleus
*Viola tricolor,* Johnny-jump-up

# Annuals for Subtropical Florida

## Annuals for Sun

*Ageratum houstonianum,* ageratum
*Antirrhinum* hybrids, snapdragons
*Aster* species, asters
*Celosia* species, celosias
*Dianthus* species, dianthus
*Helianthus annuus,* sunflower
*Kalanchoe blossfeldiana,* kalanchoe
*Lobularia maritima,* alyssum
*Nicotiana* species, nicotianas
*Pelargonium* hybrids, geranium
*Pentas lanceolata,* pentas
*Petunia* x *hybrida,* petunia
*Portulaca grandiflora,* rose moss
*Primula auricula,* auricula
*Verbena* x *hybrida,* verbena
*Viola* species, hybrids, and cultivars, pansies

## Annuals for Shade

*Begonia semperflorens, B. coccinea,* begonias
*Caladium bicolor,* caladium
*Crossandra infundibuliformis,* crossandra
*Gerbera jamesonii,* gerbera daisy
*Impatiens balsamina, I. walleriana,* impatiens

# Annuals for the Midwest and Northern Great Plains

## Annuals for Sun

*Ageratum houstonianum,* garden ageratum
*Brachycome iberidifolia,* swan river daisy
*Canna* x *generalis,* canna
*Cleoma hassleriana,* spider flower
*Heliotropium arborescens,* common heliotrope
*Lavatera trimestris,* lavatera
*Lobelia erinus,* annual lobelia
*Lobularia maritima,* sweet alyssum

*Nierembergia hippomanica* var. *violacea,* purple
  cupflower
*Pelargonium* x *hortorum, P. peltatum,* zonal and
  ivy geraniums
*Petunia* x *hybrida,* petunia
*Portulaca grandiflora,* rose moss
*Salvia* species, salvias
*Sanvitalia procumbens,* creeping zinnia
*Solenostemon scutellarioides,* coleus
*Tagetes erecta, T. patula, T. tenuifolia,* African,
  French, and signet marigolds
*Thymophylla tenuiloba,* Dahlberg daisy
*Tropaeolum majus,* nasturtium
*Verbena bonariensis* (*V. patagonica*), verbena
*Zinnia angustifolia, Z. elegans,* narrow-leaf zin-
  nia and common zinnia

## Annuals for Shade

*Browallia speciosa,* browallia
*Helichrysum petiolare,* licorice plant
*Impatiens walleriana,* impatiens
*Scaevola calendulacea,* scaevola
*Torenia fournieri,* wishbone flower

# Annuals for Texas and the Southern Plains

Some of these plants are biennials or short-lived
perennials; all are sold and used as annuals in
this region.

## Annuals for Sun

*Castilleja indivisa,* Indian paintbrush (native)
*Celosia* species, cockscombs
*Chamaecrista fasciculata,* partridge pea (native)
*Coreopsis tinctoria,* goldenwave, plains coreopsis
  (native)
*Cosmos sulphureus,* notably the cultivar 'Bright
  Lights', cosmos

*Eryngium leavenworthii,* eryngo (native)
*Eustoma grandiflorum,* Texas bluebells, showy
  gentian (native)
*Gaillardia pulchella,* Indian blanket (native)
*Gomphrena globosa,* globe amaranth
*Lantana camara,* tropical lantana (native)
*Lantana montevidensis,* purple trailing lantana
*Lupinus texensis,* Texas bluebonnet (native)
*Melampodium leucanthum,* Blackfoot daisy
  (native)
*Moluccella laevis,* bells of Ireland
*Monarda citriodora,* lemon mint, horsemint
  (native)
*Phlox drummondii,* Drummond phlox (native)
*Portulaca grandiflora,* rose moss
*Ricinus communis,* castor bean
*Rudbeckia nirta,* black-eyed Susan (native)
*Salvia coccinea,* scarlet sage (native)
*Senna alata,* candlestick plant
*Verbena bipinnatifida,* prairie verbena (native)
*Verbena rigida,* vervain, hardy verbena
*Verbena tenuisecta,* moss verbena

## Annuals for Shade

*Impatiens* species, hybrids, and cultivars, impatiens
*Begonia* species, hybrids, and cultivars, begonia
*Caladium* species, hybrids, and cultivars, caladiums

# Annuals for the Rocky Mountain Region

## Annuals for Sun

*Achillea millefolium,* notably the cultivar 'Sum-
  mer Pastels', yarrow
*Antirrhinum majus,* snapdragon
*Cleome hassleriana,* spider flower

*Coreopsis grandiflora,* notably the cultivar 'Early Sunrise', coreopsis

*Cosmos sulphureus,* notably the cultivars 'Bright Lights', 'Sunny Gold', 'Sunny Red', cosmos

*Pelargonium* 'Cornell', ivy geranium

*Hunnemannia fumariifolia,* notably the cultivar 'Sunlite', Mexican poppy

*Lavatera trimestris,* notably the cultivar 'Mont Blanc', rose mallow

*Nicotiana alata,* notably the cultivars 'Domino', 'Nikki', jasmine tobacco

*Nicotiana sylvestris,* flowering tobacco

*Pennisetum setaceum,* fountain grass

*Pennisetum villosum,* feather top

*Ricinus communis,* castor bean

*Rudbeckia hirta,* notably the cultivar 'Irish Eyes', black-eyed Susan (native)

*Salvia farinacea,* notably the cultivars 'Blue Bedder', 'Victoria', mealy-cup sage

*Senecio cineraria,* notably the cultivar 'Silver Queen', dusty miller

*Thymophylla tenuiloba,* Dahlberg daisy

*Tithonia rotundifolia,* torch flower

*Verbena bonariensis,* verbena

*Verbena rigida,* verbena

*Zinnia angustifolia,* notably the cultivar 'Tropic Snow', zinnia

## Annuals for Shade

*Begonia sempervirens,* wax begonia

*Browallia speciosa,* notably the cultivar 'Jingle Bells', browallia

*Catharanthus roseus,* Madagascar periwinkle

*Hypoestes phyllostachya,* polka-dot plant

*Impatiens* species, hybrids, and cultivars, impatiens

*Solenostemon scutellarioides,* coleus

# Annuals for the Pacific Northwest

## Annuals for Sun

*Agrostemma githago,* corn cockle

*Amaranthus caudatus,* love-lies-bleeding

*Anchusa capensis,* anchusa

*Arctotis venusta,* African daisy

*Brachycome iberidifolia,* notably the cultivar 'Amethyst', Swan River daisy

*Brassica oleracea,* ornamental cabbage

*Centaurea americana,* basket flower

*Cleome hassleriana,* spider flower

*Eschscholzia californica,* California poppy (native)

*Helianthus annuus,* notably the cultivar 'Colour Fashion', sunflower

*Ipomoea* species, morning glories

*Lavatera trimestris,* notably the cultivar 'Silver Cup', rose mallow

*Limnanthes douglasii,* meadow foam (native)

*Malcolmia maritima,* Virginia stock

*Mirabilis jalapa,* four-o'clock

*Monarda citriodora,* lemon mint

*Nicotiana sylvestris,* tobacco

*Nierembergia hippomanica,* cupflower

*Papaver rhoeas,* Shirley poppy

*Rhodochiton atrosanguineum,* purple bell vine

*Rudbeckia hirta,* gloriosa daisy

*Tropaeolum majus,* nasturtium

## Annuals for Shade

*Browallia speciosa* 'Blue Bells Improved', amethyst flower

*Impatiens walleriana,* impatiens

*Nemophila maculata,* five-spot nemophila

*Nicotiana alata,* nicotiana

*Solenostemon scutellarioides,* coleus

*Thunbergia alata,* black-eyed Susan vine

## Annuals for Coastal California

### Annuals for Sun

*Antirrhinum majus*, snapdragon
*Calendula officinalis*, pot marigold
*Collinsia bicolor*, purple Chinese-houses (native)
*Eschscholzia californica*, California poppy (native)
*Eustoma grandiflorum*, lisianthus
*Helianthus annuus*, sunflower
*Layia platyglossa*, tidy tips (native)
*Limonium sinuatum*, sea lavender
*Lupinus nanus*, lupine (native)
*Matthiola incana*, stock
*Mentzelia lindleyi*, blazing star (native)
*Nemesia strumosa*, no common name
*Nemophila menziesii*, baby blue-eyes (native)
*Papaver rhoeas*, poppy
*Portulaca grandiflora*, rose moss
*Zinnia angustifolia*, zinnia

### Annuals for Shade

*Clarkia concinna*, red ribbons clarkia (native)
*Heliotropium arborescens*, heliotrope
*Linaria maroccana*, baby snapdragon
*Lobelia erinus*, lobelia
*Mimulus* x *hybridus*, monkeyflower (native)
*Nigella damascena*, love-in-a-mist
*Primula obconica*, primrose
*Viola cornuta*, pansy
*Viola tricolor*, Johnny-jump-up

## Annuals for the Western Deserts

### Annuals for Sun

*Arctotis* hybrids, African daisy
*Baileya multiradiata*, desert marigold (native)
*Catharanthus roseus*, Madagascar periwinkle
*Cleome hassleriana*, spider flower

*Consolida ambigua*, larkspur
*Coreopsis tinctoria*, calliopsis
*Cosmos bipinnatus*, cosmos
*Dimorphotheca sinuata*, African daisy, Cape marigold
*Thymophylla tenuiloba* (*Dyssodia tenuiloba*), Dahlberg daisy, golden fleece
*Eschscholzia californica*, California poppy (native)
*Gazania* hybrids, gazanias
*Gomphrena globosa*, globe amaranth
*Helianthus annuus*, sunflower (native)
*Ipomopsis rubra*, skyrocket
*Linum grandiflorum* 'Rubrum', scarlet flax
*Lobularia maritima*, sweet alyssum
*Phacelia campanularia*, California bluebells (native)
*Portulaca grandiflora*, rose moss
*Salvia coccinea*, scarlet sage
*Sanvitalia procumbens*, creeping zinnia
*Tagetes tenuifolia* 'Lemon Gem', signet marigold
*Tithonia rotundifolia*, Mexican sunflower
*Verbascum bombyciferum* 'Arctic Summer', mullein

### Annuals for Shade

*Begonia semperflorens* hybrids, notably the 'Ambassador' and 'Cocktail' series, fibrous-rooted wax begonias
*Viola* hybrids, notably the 'Imperial' series, pansies

# Plants to Attract Butterflies and Wildlife

For detailed information on gardening for wildlife, including lists of indigenous species, see "Natural Gardening," page 180. The plants listed in this section are not necessarily native, and can be used in more formal or ornamental plantings.

## The Northeast

Plants are hardy to Zone 5, unless noted.

### Butterfly Plants

*Allium* species, onions, leeks, chives, garlics (some native)

*Asclepias incarnata, A. syriaca, A. tuberosa,* milkweeds (native)

*Aster novae-angliae,* New England aster (native)

*Aster* x *frikartii,* Frikart aster

*Betula* species, birches (native)

*Brassica* species, mustards, cabbages, broccoli, Brussels sprouts

*Caryopteris* species, bluebeards

*Ceanothus americanus,* New Jersey tea (native)

*Celtis occidentalis,* hackberry (native)

*Cephalanthus occidentalis,* buttonbush (native)

*Echinops* species, globe thistles

*Eupatorium* species, Joe-Pye weeds (native)

*Liatris spicata* and related species, blazing stars (native)

*Medicago sativa,* alfalfa

*Populus tremuloides,* quaking aspen (native)

*Prunus serotina,* black cherry (native)

*Prunus virginiana,* chokecherry (native)

*Rudbeckia fulgida* 'Goldsturm', black-eyed Susan

*Salix discolor,* American pussy willow (native)

*Scabiosa atropurpurea,* pincushion flower, sweet scabious

*Scabiosa* 'Butterfly Blue', pincushion flower

*Trifolium* species, clovers (native)

*Verbena* species, verbenas

*Vicia* species, vetches

*Viola* species, violets (native)

*Vitex agnus-castus,* chaste tree

*Zinnia* species, zinnias

### Wildlife Plants

*Aronia* species, chokeberries (native)

*Campsis radicans,* trumpet creeper (native)

*Carya* species, hickories, pecans (native)

*Celastrus scandens,* American bittersweet (native)

*Corylus americana, C. avellana,* hazelnuts

*Crataegus* species, hawthorns (native)

*Datura stramonium,* jimsonweed (native)

*Fagus grandifolia,* beech (native)

*Ilex opaca, I. decidua, I. ambigua,* hollies (native)

*Juniperus virginiana,* eastern red cedar (native)

*Lobelia cardinalis,* cardinal flower (native)

*Magnolia virginiana,* sweetbay (native)

*Monarda didyma, M. fistulosa,* bee balms (native)

*Myrica pensylvanica,* bayberry (native)

*Pinus strobus,* white pine (native)

*Prunus maritima,* beach plum (native)

*Prunus serotina,* black cherry (native)

*Prunus virginiana,* chokecherry (native)

*Quercus* species, oaks (native)

*Rhus aromatica, R. copallina, R. glabra, R. typhina,* sumacs (native)

*Rubus* species, blackberry, raspberry, briar (native)

*Solidago* species, goldenrods (native)

*Symplocos paniculata,* Asiatic sweetleaf

*Typha latifolia,* broad-leaved cattail (native)

*Vaccinium* species, blueberries (native)

*Vernonia noveboracensis,* New York ironweed (native)

*Viburnum acerifolium, V. cassinoides, V. dentatum, V. prunifolium,* viburnums (native)

*Vitis* species, grapes (native)

*Zizania aquatica,* wild rice (native)

## The Southeast

Plants can be used throughout the region in Zones 6–9. Where plants are appropriate only for certain parts of the region, they are noted as follows:

US = Upper South, Zone 6

MS = Middle South, Zone 7 and parts of Zone 8 in the western edge of Mississippi, southern Arkansas, and central Texas

LS = Lower South, Zone 8 plus coastal North Carolina and parts of southern coastal Virginia

CS = Coastal South, Zone 8 in northern Florida and parts of Zone 9 in coastal Texas, Louisiana, and northeastern Florida

### Butterfly Plants

*Abelia* x *grandiflora,* glossy abelia

*Achillea* species, yarrows

*Anethum graveolens,* dill

*Aralia spinosa,* devil's walkingstick (native)

*Asclepias* species, milkweeds (native)

*Asimina triloba,* pawpaw (native)

*Aster novae-angliae,* New England aster (native)—US, MS, LS

*Centranthus ruber,* red valerian

*Cephalanthus occidentalis,* buttonbush (native)

*Clethra alnifolia,* summersweet (native)

*Cosmos sulphureus,* Klondike cosmos (annual)

*Echinacea purpurea,* purple coneflower (native)

*Eupatorium coelestinum,* hardy ageratum (native)

*Eupatorium purpureum,* Joe-Pye weed (native)

*Foeniculum vulgare,* common fennel

*Gomphrena globosa,* globe amaranth (annual)

*Impatiens walleriana,* impatiens (annual)

*Lantana camara,* lantana (treat as annual in US, MS)

*Liatris* species, gayfeathers (native)

*Petroselinum crispum,* parsley

*Rudbeckia* species, rudbeckias (native)

*Salix* species, willows (native)

*Salvia* species, salvias (annual)

*Sassafras albidum,* sassafras (native)

*Sedum spectabile,* showy sedum

*Solidago* species, goldenrods (native)

*Tagetes patula,* French marigold (annual)

*Tithonia rotundifolia,* Mexican sunflower

*Verbena* species, verbenas

*Vernonia noveboracensis,* ironweed (native)

*Vitex agnus-castus,* chaste tree

*Zinnia elegans,* zinnia

### Wildlife Plants

*Amelanchier* species, Juneberries, serviceberries (native)

*Andropogon virginicus,* broom sedge

*Aquilegia canadensis,* wild columbine (native)

*Asclepias tuberosa,* butterfly weed (native)

*Canna* x *generalis,* canna (annual)

*Cephalanthus occidentalis,* buttonbush (native)

*Cleome hassleriana,* cleome (annual)

*Cornus amomum,* swamp dogwood (native)

*Coreopsis tinctoria,* calliopsis

*Cornus florida,* flowering dogwood (native)

*Echinacea purpurea,* purple coneflower (native)

*Gaillardia pulchella,* blanketflower (native)

*Helianthus annuus,* sunflower

*Ilex decidua,* deciduous holly (native)

*Ilex* 'Nellie R. Stevens', Nellie R. Stevens holly

*Ilex opaca,* American holly (native)

*Ilex verticillata,* winterberry holly (native)

*Iris fulva,* Louisiana iris (native)

*Juniperis virginiana,* eastern red cedar (native)

*Lobelia cardinalis,* cardinal flower (native)

*Mirabilis jalapa,* four-o'clock

*Monarda didyma,* bee balm (native)

*Nicotiana alata,* flowering tobacco, red and pink varieties

*Rhus* species, sumacs (native)
*Rosa palustris,* swamp rose (native)
*Rosa rugosa,* rugosa rose
*Rudbeckia* species, rudbeckias (native)
*Salvia splendens,* scarlet sage
*Sambucus canadensis,* elderberry (native)
*Tagetes* species, hybrids, and cultivars, marigolds
*Tithonia rotundifolia,* Mexican sunflower
*Viola* species, wild violets (native)
*Zinnia elegans,* zinnia

## Subtropical Florida

The plants recommended for Subtropical Florida are appropriate for Zones 10A, 10B, and 11, unless noted as follows:

*Not for Zone 10A
**Not for Zone 11

### Butterfly Plants

*Aristolochia* species, Dutchman's-pipes, calico flowers
*Asclepias tuberosa,* butterfly weed** (native)
*Aster carolinianus,* Carolina aster (native)
*Borrichia frutescens,* sea ox-eye daisy (native)
*Centrosema virginianum,* butterfly pea (native)
*Cordia globosa,* cordia (native)
*Coreopsis leavenworthii,* tickseed (native)
*Crotalaria pumila,* rattlebox (native)
*Erigeron quercifolius,* southern fleabane (native)
*Eupatorium coelestinum,* blue mistflower** (native)
*Flaveria linearis,* yellow top (native)
*Gaillardia pulchella,* blanketflower (native)
*Hamelia patens,* firebush (native)
*Lantana* species, lantanas (native)
*Liatris* species, blazing stars** (native)
*Lippia nodiflora,* creeping charlie (native)
*Passiflora* species, passionflowers

*Passiflora suberosa,* corky-stemmed passion vine* (native)
*Pentas lanceolata,* pentas
*Pluchea* species, fleabanes (native)
*Saururus cernuus,* lizard's tail (native)
*Rudbeckia hirta,* brown-eyed Susan (native)
*Ruellia caroliniensis,* wild petunia** (native)
*Senna ligustrina* (*Cassia bahamensis*), Bahama cassia (native)
*Senna polyphylla,* desert cassia
*Solidago* species, goldenrods** (native)
*Stachytarpheta jamaicensis,* dwarf blue porter-weed (native)

### Wildlife Plants

*Ardisia escallonioides,* marlberry (native)
*Bursera simaruba,* gumbo-limbo* (native)
*Callicarpa americana,* American beautyberry (native)
*Chrysobalanus icaco,* cocoplum* (native)
*Chrysophyllum oliviforme,* satin leaf* (native)
*Coccoloba diversifolia,* pigeon plum* (native)
*Coccoloba uvifera,* sea grape* (native)
*Coccothrinax argentata,* silver palm* (native)
*Eugenia axillaris,* white stopper* (native)
*Eugenia foetida,* Spanish stopper (native)
*Ficus aurea,* strangler fig* (native)
*Lysiloma latisiliqua,* wild tamarind* (native)
*Myrcianthes fragrans* var. *simpsonii,* Simpson stopper (native)
*Myrica cerifera,* wax myrtle (native)
*Passiflora suberosa,* corky-stemmed passion-flower (native)
*Pinus elliottii* var. *densa,* slash pine (native)
*Pithecellobium keyense* (*P. guadalupense*), black-bead (native)
*Pithecellobium unguis-cati,* cat's claw (native)
*Psychotria nervosa,* wild coffee* (native)
*Sambucus canadensis* (*S. simpsonii*), southern elderberry (native)

*Sabal palmetto,* cabbage palm (native)

*Serenoa repens,* saw palmetto (native)

*Spartina patens,* saltmeadow cordgrass (native)

*Thrinax morrisii,* Key thatch palm* (native)

*Thrinax radiata,* Florida thatch* (native)

## The Midwest and Northern Great Plains

The plants are hardy to Zone 4 unless otherwise indicated.

### Butterfly Plants

*Aster novae-angliae* and other species, asters (native)

*Cleome hassleriana,* spider flower (annual)

*Echinacea purpurea* and others, purple cone-flower (native)

*Eupatorium maculatum,* Joe-Pye weed (native)

*Helianthus maximilianii* and other species, sun-flowers (native)

*Heliotropium arborescens,* common heliotrope (annual)

*Liatris aspera, L. pycnostachya,* and other species, blazing stars (native)

*Monarda fistulosa,* bergamot (native)

*Phlox maculata, P. paniculata,* phlox

*Silphium laciniatum, S. perfoliatum,* compass plant and cup plant (native)

*Tithonia rotundifolia,* Mexican sunflower (annual)

*Verbena* species, hybrids, and cultivars, verbenas (annual)

*Zizia* species, golden Alexanders (native)

*Zinnia elegans,* common zinnia (annual)

### Wildlife Plants

*Actaea pachypoda, A. rubra,* white and red baneberry (native)

*Amelanchier* species, serviceberries (native)

*Aralia racemosa,* spikenard (native)

*Aronia arbutifolia, A. melanocarpa,* red and black chokeberry (native)

*Celtis occidentalis,* hackberry (native)

*Carya ovata,* shagbark hickory (native)

*Caulophyllum thalictroides,* blue cohosh (native)

*Cornus alternifolia, C. racemosa, C. stolonifera,* pagoda, gray, and red osier dogwood (native)

*Corylus* species, hazelnuts (native)

*Echinacea purpurea* and other species, coneflowers (native)

*Helianthus maximilianii* and other species, sunflowers (native)

*Ilex verticillata,* winterberry holly (native)

*Liatris aspera, L. pychnostachya,* and other species, blazing stars (native)

*Panicum virgatum,* switchgrass (native)

*Parthenocissus quinquefolia,* Virginia creeper (native)

*Polygonatum biflorum* and other species, Solomon's seals (native)

*Quercus* species, oaks (native)

*Rhus* species, sumacs (native)

*Rudbeckia fulgida* 'Goldsturm', orange cone-flower (native)

*Rudbeckia laciniata,* green-headed coneflower (native)

*Shepherdia argentea,* silver buffalo berry (native)

*Smilacina racemosa,* Solomon's plume (native)

*Silphium laciniatum, S. perfoliatum,* compass plant and cup plant (native)

*Thermopsis villosa,* Carolina bush pea

*Viburnum acerifolium, V. dentatum, V. lentago,* maple-leaf, arrowwood, and nannyberry viburnum (native)

## Texas and the Southern Plains

Plants are appropriate for Zones 6, 7, and 8 unless otherwise noted. Plants marked (6) or (7) are only marginally adapted to those zones and may not survive in the coldest parts. Similarly, those marked (8) may not survive the hotter, drier areas of Zone 8.

## Butterfly Plants

*Acacia angustissima,* fern acacia (native) (Zones (6), 7, 8)

*Achillea millefolium,* yarrow

*Asclepias asperula,* spider antelope-horn milkweed (native)

*Asclepias tuberosa,* butterfly weed (native)

*Aster ericoides,* heath aster (native)

*Aster oblongifolius,* aromatic aster (native)

*Aster praealtus,* tall blue aster (native)

*Aster sericeus,* Christmas aster (native) (Zones 8, 9)

*Chamaecrista fasciculata,* partridge pea (native)

*Echinacea angustifolia,* black sampson (native)

*Echinacea purpurea,* purple coneflower

*Engelmannia pinnatifida,* Engelmann daisy (native)

*Eupatorium coelestinum,* wild ageratum (native)

*Hemerocallis* species, hybrids, and cultivars, daylilies

*Lantana* species, lantanas (Zones 7, 8, 9)

*Liatris mucronata* and other species, gayfeathers (native)

*Malvaviscus drummondii,* Turk's cap (native) (Zones 7, 8, 9)

*Monarda fistulosa,* bergamot, bee balm (native)

*Passiflora caerulea,* Brazilian passionflower (native) (Zones 7, 8, 9)

*Passiflora incarnata,* maypop (native) (Zones 8, 9)

*Phlox paniculata,* summer phlox, autumn phlox

*Phyla nodiflora,* frogfruit (native)

*Polytaenia nuttallii,* prairie parsley (native)

*Prunus serotina,* black cherry (native)

*Pycnanthemum tenuifolium,* narrowleaf mountain mint (native)

*Salvia coccinea,* scarlet sage (native) (annual)

*Sedum spectabile,* notably the cultivars 'Autumn Joy', 'Ruby Glow', sedum

*Solidago* species, goldenrods (native)

*Tetraneuris scaposa,* four-nerve daisy (native)

*Verbena* species, verbenas (native) (annual)

*Vernonia baldwinii,* Baldwin ironweed (native)

*Wedelia acapulcensis* var. *hispida,* zexmenia (native) (Zones 8, 9)

## Wildlife Plants

*Callicarpa americana,* American beautyberry (native) (Zones 7, 8, 9)

*Campsis radicans,* trumpet vine (native)

*Celtis reticulata,* netleaf hackberry (native)

*Chilopsis linearis,* desert willow (native) (Zones (6), 7, 8, 9)

*Cornus drummondii,* roughleaf dogwood (native)

*Crataegus* species, hawthorns (native)

*Euonymus atropurpureus,* wahoo (native) (Zones 7, 8)

*Fraxinus americana,* white ash (native)

*Fraxinus texensis,* Texas ash (native) (Zones 7, 8)

*Helianthus maximilianii,* Maximilian sunflower (native)

*Hesperaloe parviflora,* red yucca (native) (Zones 7, 8, 9)

*Ilex vomitoria,* yaupon holly (native) (Zones (7), 8, 9)

*Juniperus* species, juniper (native)

*Lonicera sempervirens,* coral honeysuckle (native)

*Malus ioensis,* prairie crabapple (native)

*Malvaviscus arboreus* var. *drummondii,* Turk's cap (native) (Zones 7, 8, 9)

*Parthenocissus quinquefolia,* Virginia creeper (native)

*Phlox paniculata,* summer phlox, autumn phlox

*Pinus edulis,* pinyon pine (native)

*Prunus angustifolia,* chickasaw plum (native)

*Prunus serotina,* black cherry (native)

*Salvia azurea* var. *grandiflora*, pitcher sage (native)

*Salvia farinacea*, mealy blue sage (native)

*Salvia lyrata*, lyreleaf sage (native)

*Salvia penstemonoides*, penstemon sage (native) (Zones (7), 8)

*Rhus aromatica*, aromatic sumac (native)

*Ribes odoratum*, buffalo currant (native) (Zones 6, 7, (8))

*Rosa setigera*, climbing prairie rose (native)

*Sambucus canadensis*, common elderberry (native)

*Ulmus* species, elm (native)

*Vitis vulpina*, winter grape (native)

*Zanthoxylum clava-herculis*, Hercules club or toothache tree (native)

## The Rocky Mountain Region

Plants are hardy to Zone 4 unless otherwise noted.

### Butterfly Plants

*Agastache cana*, wild hyssop

*Amorpha canescens*, silver leadplant (native) (Zones 2–6)

*Asclepias tuberosa*, butterfly weed (native)

*Buddleia alternifolia*, fountain butterfly bush (Zone 5)

*Caryopteris* x *clandonensis*, blue mist (Zone 5)

*Centranthus ruber*, red valerian (Zone 5)

*Chrysothamnus nauseosus*, rabbitbrush (native)

*Echinacea purpurea*, purple coneflower

*Erysimum asperum*, wallflower (native)

*Gaillardia aristata*, blanketflower (native)

*Gutierrezia sarothrae*, snakeweed (native)

*Helianthus maximilianii*, Maximilian sunflower (native)

*Heliomeris multiflora*, showy goldeneye (native)

*Ipomopsis aggregata*, scarlet gilia (native)

*Liatris punctata*, dotted gayfeather (native)

*Linum perenne* subsp. *lewisii*, blue flax (native)

*Machaeranthera tanacetifolia*, tansy aster (native)

*Monarda fistulosa*, bee balm (native)

*Ratibida columnifera*, Mexican hat coneflower

*Rudbeckia hirta*, black-eyed Susan (native)

*Salvia azurea* var. *grandiflora*, blue sage

*Senecio flaccidus*, threadleaf groundsel (native)

*Senecio spartioides*, broom groundsel (native)

*Verbena bipinnatifida*, Dakota verbena

### Wildlife Plants

*Acer glabrum*, Rocky Mountain maple (native)

*Amelanchier alnifolia*, saskatoon berry (native) (Zone 2)

*Betula fontinalis*, western river birch (native)

*Campsis radicans*, trumpet creeper

*Celtis occidentalis*, eastern hackberry (Zone 2)

*Crataegus ambigua*, Russian hawthorn

*Juniperus communis* var. *saxatilis*, common juniper (native) (Zone 2)

*Juniperus scopulorum*, Rocky Mountain juniper (native) (Zone 3)

*Lonicera involucrata*, twinberry (native) (Zone 2)

*Mahonia repens*, creeping hollygrape (native)

*Morus alba*, white mulberry (Zone 3)

*Parthenocissus tricuspidata*, Boston ivy

*Prunus americana*, American plum (native) (Zone 2)

*Prunus cerasus*, pie cherry

*Prunus virginiana* var. *melanocarpa*, chokecherry (native)

*Quercus gambelii*, gambel's oak (native)

*Rhus trilobata*, three-leaf sumac (native)

*Ribes cereum*, wax currant (native)

*Rosa woodsii*, wood's rose (native)

*Sambucus canadensis*, elderberry

*Shepherdia argentea*, silver buffaloberry (native) (Zone 2)

*Symphoricarpos albus,* snowberry (native)
*Tilia cordata,* littleleaf linden (Zone 3)
*Viburnum lentago,* nannyberry viburnum
(Zone 2)

## The Pacific Northwest

Plants are hardy to at least Zone 7 unless otherwise noted.

### Butterfly Plants

*Abelia* x *grandiflora,* glossy abelia
*Achillea millefolium,* common yarrow
*Alcea rosea,* hollyhock
*Allium schoenoprasum,* chives
*Amorpha canescens,* leadplant
*Asclepias tuberosa,* butterfly weed
*Calluna vulgaris* 'Corbett Red', heather
*Clethra alnifolia,* sweet pepperbush
*Echinacea purpurea,* purple coneflower
*Eryngium amethystinum,* sea holly
*Erysimum cheiri,* wallflower
*Helianthus* x *multiflorus,* sunflower
*Holodiscus discolor,* oceanspray (native)
*Hyssopus officinalis,* hyssop
*Lavandula angustifolia* 'Hidcote', Hidcote
lavender
*Linaria purpurea* 'Canon Went', toadflax
*Monarda fistulosa,* wild bee balm
*Salvia officinalis* 'Purpurascens', purple sage
*Scabiosa caucasica,* pincushion flower
*Sedum spectabile* 'Brilliant', sedum
*Silene armeria,* catchfly
*Thymus vulgaris,* common thyme
*Vitex agnus-castus,* chaste tree

### Wildlife Plants

*Amelanchier alnifolia,* serviceberry (native)
*Arctostaphylos uva-ursi,* kinnikinnick (native)

*Betula papyrifera,* paper birch (native)
*Chaenomeles* 'Apple Blossom', flowering quince
*Cornus nuttallii,* Pacific dogwood (native)
*Cornus stolonifera* 'Flaviramea', yellow-twig
dogwood (native)
*Fuchsia magellanica,* hardy fuchsia
*Gaultheria shallon,* salal (native)
*Larix occidentalis,* western larch (native)
*Leycesteria formosa,* Himalayan honeysuckle
*Lithocarpus densiflorus* var. *echinoides,* shrub tan
oak (native)
*Lonicera periclymenum,* Dutch honeysuckle
*Mahonia aquifolium,* Oregon grape (native)
*Malus* x 'Indian Magic', crabapple
*Myrica californica,* Pacific wax myrtle (native)
*Pinus contorta,* shore pine (native)
*Quercus kelloggii,* California black oak (native)
*Ribes sanguineum,* winter currant (native)
*Rosa nutkana,* nootka rose (native)
*Sambucus racemosa,* red elderberry (native)
*Sorbus sitchensis,* Sitka mountain ash (native)
*Symphoricarpos albus,* snowberry (native)
*Thuja plicata,* western red cedar (native)
*Vaccinium ovatum,* box blueberry (native)
*Vaccinium parvifolium,* red huckleberry (native)

## Coastal California

Plants are appropriate for the coastal regions of California from Crescent City to the border of Mexico—and east to the Coast Ranges, the western edge of Central Valley, and the southern inland valleys and southernmost Peninsular Ranges.

### Butterfly Plants

*Achillea* species, yarrows
*Alcea rosea,* hollyhock
*Aquilegia* species, columbines
*Arbutus menziesii,* madrone (native)

*Arctostaphylos* species, manzanitas (native)
*Armeria maritima,* thrift (native)
*Asclepias tuberosa,* butterfly weed
*Aster* x *frikartii* 'Monch', Frikart's aster
*Caryopteris* x *clandonensis,* blue mist
*Ceanothus thyrsiflorus,* wild lilac (native)
*Delphinium* species, delphiniums
*Echinacea purpurea,* purple coneflower
*Eriogonum latifolium* subsp. *rubescens,* red
    buckwheat (native)
*Eriogonum* species, buckwheats
*Helianthus* species, sunflowers
*Linaria purpurea,* toadflax
*Mimulus aurantiacus,* sticky monkeyflower
    (native)
*Quercus* species, oaks (native)
*Rhamnus californicus,* California coffeeberry
    (native)
*Ribes* species, currant, gooseberry (native)
*Rosmarinus officinalis,* rosemary
*Salix laevigata,* red willow (native)
*Salvia clevelandii,* Cleveland sage (native)
*Sambucus caerulea,* blue elderberry (native)
*Sidalcea malviflora,* checkerbloom (native)
*Vaccinium ovatum,* huckleberry (native)
*Verbena bonariensis,* purple top

## Wildlife Plants

*Anigozanthos flavidus,* kangaroo paw
*Arbutus menziesii,* madrone (native)
*Arctostaphylos* species, manzanitas (native)
*Ceanothus arboreus,* island ceanothus (native)
*Cercis occidentalis,* western redbud (native)
*Epilobium canum,* California fuchsia (native)
*Eriogonum giganteum,* St. Catherine's lace
    (native)
*Grevillea thelemanniana,* hummingbird
    grevillea
*Helianthus angustifolius,* no common name
*Heteromeles arbutifolia,* toyon (native)

*Mahonia aquifolium,* Oregon grape (native)
*Penstemon* 'Firebird', 'Garnet', beardtongue
*Prunus ilicifolia,* hollyleaf cherry (native)
*Quercus agrifolia,* coast live oak (native)
*Rhamnus californicus,* California coffeeberry
    (native)
*Ribes speciosum,* fuchsia-flowered gooseberry
    (native)
*Ribes sanguineum,* red flowering currant
*Rosa californica,* California rose (native)
*Rudbeckia fulgida* 'Goldsturm', black-eyed
    Susan
*Salvia clevelandii,* Cleveland sage (native)
*Salvia greggii,* autumn sage
*Trichostema lanatum,* woolly blue curls (native)
*Vaccinium ovatum,* evergreen huckleberry
    (native)
*Vitis californica,* California grape (native)
*Yucca whipplei,* Our Lord's candle (native)

## The Western Deserts

The plants are appropriate throughout the region, except those noted as follows:

\*Not cold-hardy in cold desert areas
\*\*Favor cooler/moister desert areas

## Butterfly Plants

*Achillea* species, yarrows
*Agapanthus* x 'Peter Pan', lily-of-the-Nile
*Alcea rosea,* hollyhock
*Aquilegia* species, columbines\*\* (native)
*Asclepias tuberosa,* butterfly weed (native)
*Baileya multiradiata,* desert marigold (native)
*Borago officinalis,* borage
*Buddleia marrubiifolia,* woolly butterfly bush
    (native)
*Cassia* species, sennas (native)
*Centaurea dealbata,* Persian cornflower

*Centranthus ruber,* red valerian
*Echinacea purpurea,* purple coneflower**
*Eriogonum* species, buckwheats (native)
*Eryngium amethystinum,* purple sea holly
*Foeniculum vulgare,* fennel
*Helianthus* species, sunflowers (native)
*Liatris punctata,* gayfeather (native)
*Origanum vulgare,* oregano
*Passiflora foetida,* passionflower vine*
*Ribes aureum,* golden currant** (native)
*Rosa* species, wild roses (native)
*Rosmarinus officinalis,* rosemary
*Rudbeckia hirta,* black-eyed Susan
*Sambucus mexicana,* Mexican elder (native)
*Sidalcea malviflora,* checkerbloom
*Verbena* species, verbenas (native)
*Veronica alpina,* 'Goodness Grows', Alpine
   speedwell**
*Vitex agnus-castus,* chaste tree

## Wildlife Plants

*Acacia* species, white thorns, cat-claws, and
   sweet acacias* (native)
*Agastache cana,* bubblegum mint (native)
*Amelanchier utahensis,* Utah serviceberry (native)
*Amorpha fruticosa,* false indigo (native)
*Anisacanthus thurberi,* desert honeysuckle
   (native)
*Argemone* species, prickly poppies (native)
*Atriplex canescens,* fourwing saltbush (native)
*Bouteloua curtipendula,* sideoats grama (native)
*Campsis radicans,* trumpet vine
*Celtis pallida,* desert hackberry* (native)
*Chilopsis linearis,* desert willow (native)
*Dalea purpurea,* purple prairie clover (native)
*Eriogonum fasciculatum,* pink buckwheat
   (native)
*Forestiera neomexicana,* desert olive (native)
*Helianthus maximilianii,* Maximilian sunflower
   (native)

*Hesperaloe parviflora,* red yucca (native)
*Lonicera sempervirens,* coral honeysuckle
*Mahonia haematocarpa,* algerita (native)
*Oenothera* species, evening primroses (native)
*Oryzopsis hymenoides,* Indian ricegrass (native)
*Penstemon* species, beardtongues (native)
*Pinus edulis,* pinyon pine (native)
*Quercus* species, oaks (native)
*Rhus microphylla,* littleleaf sumac (native)
*Salvia greggii,* cherry sage (native)
*Shepherdia rotundifolia,* roundleaf buffaloberry
   (native)

# Heirloom Flowers

## Heirloom Flowers for the Northeast

Plants are hardy to Zone 5, unless noted.

*Alcea rosea,* hollyhock
*Aquilegia vulgaris,* common crowsfoot
*Centaurea cineraria, C. seridis* subsp. *maritima,*
   dusty millers
*Centaurea cyanus,* bachelor's buttons
*Convallaria majalis,* lily of the valley
*Dianthus barbatus,* sweet William
*Dicentra spectabilis,* bleeding heart
*Euphorbia cyparissias,* cypress spurge
*Galium odoratum,* sweet woodruff
*Hemerocallis fulva* 'Kwanzo', double orange
   daylily
*Hemerocallis lilio-asphodelus (H. flava),* lemon
   daylily
*Hibiscus syriacus,* rose of Sharon
*Hosta lancifolia,* common plantain lily
*Hosta plantaginea,* white plantain lily
*Hosta undulata,* striped plantain lily
*Hydrangea macrophylla,* snowball hydrangea
*Iberis sempervirens,* candytuft
*Iris germanica,* bearded iris

*Lilium lancifolium,* tiger lily
*Lunaria annua,* money plant, silver dollars
*Mentha* species, mints
*Narcissus* species, hybrids, and cultivars, daffodils, narcissi
*Oenothera fruticosa* subsp. *glauca,* sundrops
*Ornithogalum umbellatum,* star of Bethlehem
*Paeonia* species, hybrids, and cultivars, peonies
*Phlox paniculata,* garden phlox
*Rosa* species, hybrids, and cultivars, roses
*Salix caprea,* pussy willow
*Sedum acre, S. hispanicum, S. sarmentosum,* sedums, live-forevers
*Sempervivum tectorum,* hens and chicks
*Spiraea prunifolia,* bridal-wreath spirea
*Syringa vulgaris,* common lilac

## Heirloom Flowers for the Southeast

Plants can be used throughout the region in Zones 6–9. Where plants are appropriate only for certain parts of the region, they are noted as follows:

US = Upper South, Zone 6
MS = Middle South, Zone 7 and parts of Zone 8 in the western edge of Mississippi, southern Arkansas, and central Texas
LS = Lower South, Zone 8 plus coastal North Carolina and parts of southern coastal Virginia
CS = Coastal South, Zone 8 in northern Florida and parts of Zone 9 in coastal Texas, Louisiana, and northeastern Florida

*Alcea rosea,* hollyhock
*Anthirrhinum majus,* snapdragon (annual)
*Belamcanda chinensis,* blackberry lily
*Canna* x *generalis,* canna (annual)
*Cephalanthus occidentalis,* buttonbush (native)
*Chaenomeles speciosa,* flowering quince

*Cosmos bipinnatus,* cosmos (annual)
*Deutzia scabra,* fuzzy deutzia
*Exochorda racemosa,* pearl bush
*Forsythia* x *intermedia,* forsythia
*Hibiscus coccineus,* Texas star hibiscus (native)
*Hibiscus syriacus,* althea
*Impatiens balsamina,* touch-me-not (annual)
*Itea virginica,* Virginia sweetspire (native)
*Jasminum nudiflorum,* winter jasmine
*Kerria japonica,* Japanese kerria
*Lathyrus odoratus,* sweetpea (annual)
*Lonicera fragrantissima,* winter honeysuckle
*Lychnis coronaria,* mullein pink
*Monarda didyma,* bee balm (native)
*Mirabilis jalapa,* four-o'clock
*Pelargonium graveolens,* rose-scented geranium
*Paeonia officinalis,* peony—US, MS, LS
*Phlox subulata,* moss pink—US, MS, LS (native)
*Prunus glandulosa,* flowering almond—US, MS, LS
*Rudbeckia fulgida,* black-eyed Susan (native)
*Saponaria officinalis,* bouncing Bet
*Sempervivum tectorum,* hens and chickens—US, MS, LS
*Solenostemon scutellarioides,* coleus (annual)
*Spiraea prunifolia,* bridal-wreath spirea
*Stachys byzantina,* lamb's ears—US, MS, LS
*Viola tricolor,* Johnny-jump-up

## Heirloom Flowers for the Midwest and Northern Great Plains

The plants are hardy to Zone 4 unless otherwise indicated.

*Alcea rosea,* hollyhock (annual)
*Amaranthus caudatus,* love-lies-bleeding (annual)
*Aquilegia vulgaris* and hybrids, columbines
*Cimicifuga racemosa,* black cohosh (native)

*Gaillardia pulchella,* blanketflower

*Helenium autumnale,* sneezeweed (native)

*Iris pallida,* sweet iris

*Lathyrus latifolius,* sweet pea

*Narcissus* species and hybrids, daffodils, narcissi

*Nigella damascena,* love-in-a-mist (annual)

*Oenothera speciosa,* Mexican primrose

*Paeonia lactiflora* hybrids, peonies

*Papaver somniferum,* opium poppy (annual)

*Phlox paniculata,* garden phlox

*Physostegia virginiana,* obedient plant (native)

*Platycodon grandiflorus,* balloonflower

*Ratibida columnifera,* Mexican hat (native)

*Rosa gallica, R. rugosa,* and other shrub roses

*Scabiosa caucasica,* pincushion flower

*Sidalcea malviflora,* checkerbloom

*Solidago* species, goldenrod (native)

*Syringa vulgaris,* common lilac

*Tanacetum parthenium,* feverfew

*Zinnia elegans,* zinnia

## Heirloom Flowers for Texas and the Southern Plains

Plants are appropriate for Zones 6, 7, and 8 unless otherwise noted. Plants marked (6) or (7) are only marginally adapted to those zones and may not survive in the coldest parts. Similarly, those marked (8) may not survive the hotter, drier areas of Zone 8.

*Catharanthus roseus,* Madagascar periwinkle (annual)

*Crinum bulbispermum,* crinum lily (Zones 7, 8, 9)

*Datura wrightii,* thorn apple (annual)

*Delphinium grandiflorum,* larkspur (annual)

*Hemerocallis fulva,* tiger lily, tawny daylily

*Hibiscus coccineus,* Texas star hibiscus (Zones 8, 9)

*Hippeastrum* x *johnsonii,* hardy red amaryllis (Zone 8)

*Ipheion uniflorum,* ipheion, blue star

*Iris pseudacorus,* yellow flag

*Iris albicans,* cemetery white flag (Zones 7, 8)

*Iris albicans* 'Early Purple', blue flag (Zones 7, 8)

*Leucojum aestivum,* summer snowflake

*Lilium regale,* regal lily

*Lycoris radiata* 'Guernsey', red spider lily (Zones 7, 8, 9)

*Lycoris squamigera,* pink lady

*Malvaviscus arboreus* var. *drummondii,* Turk's cap (native) (Zones 7, 8, 9)

*Mirabilis jalapa,* four-o'clock (Zones 7, 8, 9)

*Muscari neglectum,* grape hyacinth

*Narcissus tazetta* 'Papyraceus', paperwhite narcissus (Zones 8, 9)

*Oxalis crassipes,* pink wood sorrel

*Paeonia officinalis,* common peony (Zones 6, 7)

*Petunia* x *hybrida,* old-fashioned petunia (annual)

*Rhodophiala bifida,* schoolhouse lily (Zone 8)

*Ricinus communis,* castor bean (annual)

*Rosa* 'Cecile Brunner' and other heirloom roses

*Saponaria officinalis,* bouncing Bet

*Sternbergia lutea,* autumn crocus

*Tulipa clusiana,* lady tulip

*Viola odorata* 'Royal Robe', sweet violet

## Heirloom Flowers for the Rocky Mountain Region

Unless otherwise noted, plants are hardy to Zone 4 as long as the soil is insulated with snow or mulch during the winter.

*Althea rosea,* hollyhock

*Aquilegia vulgaris,* columbine

*Artemisia abrotanum,* southernwood (Zone 5)

*Calendula officinalis,* calendula

*Campanula medium,* canterbury bells

*Centaurea cyanus*, cornflower
*Convallaria majalis*, lily of the valley
*Dicentra spectabilis*, bleeding heart (Zone 3)
*Dianthus caryophyllus*, carnation (Zone 5)
*Hemerocallis fulva*, tawny daylily
*Hyacinthoides hispanica*, bell-flowered squill
*Iris germanica*, bearded iris
*Mertensia virginica*, Virginia bluebells
*Monarda didyma*, bee balm
*Paeonia officinalis*, peony
*Philadelphus* x *virginalis*, mock orange
*Phlox divaricata*, blue phlox
*Ribes odoratum*, clove currant
*Rosa damascena*, damask rose (Zone 5)
*Rosa* x *harisonii*, Harison rose (Zone 5)
*Salvia sclarea*, Clary sage
*Salvia officinalis*, sage
*Sambucus canadensis*, elderberry (Zones 3–9)
*Saponaria officinalis*, bouncing Bet
*Syringa vulgaris*, common lilac (Zones 3–7)
*Tanacetum parthenium*, feverfew

## Heirloom Flowers for the Pacific Northwest

Plants are hardy to at least Zone 7 unless otherwise noted.

*Aquilegia vulgaris*, columbine
*Campanula glomerata*, bellflower
*Chaenomeles speciosa*, flowering quince
*Delphinium* species, delphinium
*Forsythia suspensa*, weeping forsythia
*Galium odoratum*, sweet woodruff
*Hemerocallis lilio-asphodelus*, daylily
*Hosta plantaginea* 'Honey Bells', August lily
*Hibiscus syriacus*, rose of Sharon
*Hylotelephium spectabile* 'Autumn Glory', sedum
*Iris flavescens*, yellow flag iris
*Kolkwitzia amabilis*, beautybush
*Lilium regale*, regal lily

*Lysimachia clethroides*, gooseneck loosestrife
*Monarda didyma* 'Gardenview Scarlet', scarlet bee balm
*Mentha spicata*, spearmint
*Nigella damascena*, love-in-a-mist
*Paeonia* 'Double White', peony
*Philadelphus coronarius*, mock orange
*Physostegia virginiana*, obedient plant
*Rosa* 'Albertine', Albertine climbing rose
*Rosa* 'American Pillar', American Pillar rose
*Sempervivum tectorum*, hens and chickens
*Syringa vulgaris*, common lilac
*Weigela florida*, weigela

## Heirloom Flowers for Coastal California

Plants are appropriate for the coastal regions of California from Crescent City to the border of Mexico—and east to the Coast Ranges, the western edge of Central Valley, and the southern inland valleys and southernmost Peninsular Ranges.

*Alchemilla mollis*, lady's mantle
*Campanula medium*, Canterbury bells
*Dahlia imperialis*, tree dahlia
*Dianthus deltoides*, maiden pink
*Digitalis purpurea*, common foxglove
*Echinacea purpurea*, coneflower
*Echium wildpretii*, tower of jewels
*Gladiolus communis* subsp. *byzantinus*, sword lily
*Helleborus orientalis*, Lenten rose
*Iris germanica*, bearded iris
*Kniphofia uvaria*, red-hot poker plant
*Lavandula angustifolia*, English lavender
*Linaria purpurea*, toadflax
*Lychnis coronaria*, rose campion
*Monarda punctata*, horsemint
*Narcissus poeticus*, poet's narcissus
*Nepeta* x *faassenii*, catmint

*Rosa rugosa,* sea tomato
*Rudbeckia hirta,* black-eyed Susan
*Scabiosa caucasica,* pincushion flower
*Stachys byzantina,* lamb's ears
*Tulbaghia violacea,* society garlic
*Verbena bonariensis,* purple top
*Viola odorata,* sweet violet
*Viola tricolor,* Johnny-jump-up

## Heirloom Plants for the Western Deserts

Before modern technology made water more easily accessible, it was so precious to early settlers in the Southwest deserts that few plants were grown solely as ornamentals. To merit using such a precious commodity, a plant had to be edible or medicinal, useful as well as beautiful. Most Southwestern desert heirloom plants are vegetables, varieties of chili peppers, melons, squashes, beans, corn, and peas that could be dryland farmed or infrequently irrigated. The plants are appropriate throughout the region, except those noted as follows:

*Not cold-hardy in cold desert areas
**Favor cooler/moister desert areas

*Amaranthus caudatus,* love-lies-bleeding (annual)
*Amaranthus hypochondriacus* 'Erythrostachys', prince's plume (annual)
*Anemopsis californica,* yerba mansa (native)
*Brassica* varieties, mostaza roja, red mustard (annual)
*Capsicum annuum* (Ancho-type), Santo Domingo chocolate chili (annual)
*Helianthus annuus* 'Hopi Black Dye', sunflower (native) (annual)
*Monarda menthifolia,* bee balm, wild oregano (native)

*Phaseolus vulgaris,* Anasazi bean (annual)
*Rosa* x *damascena* var. *semperflorens,* rose of Castile
*Rosa foetida,* Persian rose
*Rosa foetida* 'Bicolor', Austrian copper rose
*Thelesperma megapotamicum,* Indian tea, cota (native) (annual or biennial)
*Vicia faba,* Espanola Valley fava bean (annual)
*Xeranthemum annuum,* immortelle (annual)

# Flowers for Cutting

## Flowers for Cutting for the Northeast

Plants are hardy to Zone 5, unless noted.

*Allium* species, especially *A. aflatunense, A. sphaerocephalum,* flowering onions
*Anaphalis margaritacea,* pearly everlasting
*Antirrhinum majus,* snapdragon (annual)
*Celosia argentea* var. *cristata,* cockscomb (annual)
*Clethra alnifolia,* sweet pepperbush (native)
*Crocosmia* 'Lucifer', montbretia
*Dahlia* species, hybrids, and cultivars, dahlias
*Dendranthema* x *grandiflorum,* garden chrysanthemum
*Echinops* species, globe thistles
*Eryngium giganteum, E. alpinum,* eryngos
*Filipendula rubra,* queen of the prairie (native)
*Forsythia* x *intermedia,* forsythia
*Gomphrena globosa,* globe amaranth (annual)
*Gypsophila paniculata,* baby's breath
*Helianthus annuus,* sunflower (native)
*Helichrysum bracteatum,* strawflower
*Heliotropium arborescens,* heliotrope
*Hyacinthoides hispanica,* Spanish bluebell
*Hydrangea arborescens* 'Annabelle', Annabelle hydrangea
*Kolkwitzia amabilis,* beautybush

*Liatris spicata,* notably the cultivar 'Kobold', blazing star (native)

*Lavandula angustifolia,* lavender

*Narcissus* species, hybrids, and cultivars, daffodils, narcissi

*Phlox paniculata,* garden phlox

*Rosa* species, hybrids, and cultivars, roses

*Salix discolor,* pussy willow

*Scabiosa* species, hybrids, and cultivars, sweet scabious

*Salvia farinacea,* mealy-cup sage

*Solidago* species, goldenrods (native)

*Syringa* species, hybrids, and cultivars, lilacs

*Tagetes erecta,* tall marigold, French marigold

*Tithonia rotundifolia,* Mexican sunflower

*Veronica* 'Sunny Border Blue', veronica

*Viburnum tomentosum,* snowball viburnum

*Zinnia elegans,* zinnia

## Flowers for Cutting for the Southeast

Plants can be used throughout the region in Zones 6–9. Where plants are appropriate only for certain parts of the region, they are noted as follows:

US = Upper South, Zone 6

MS = Middle South, Zone 7 and parts of Zone 8 in the western edge of Mississippi, southern Arkansas, and central Texas

LS = Lower South, Zone 8 plus coastal North Carolina and parts of southern coastal Virginia

CS = Coastal South, Zone 8 in northern Florida and parts of Zone 9 in coastal Texas, Louisiana, and northeastern Florida

*Achillea* species, yarrows

*Anthemis tinctoria,* golden marguerite

*Antirrhinum majus,* snapdragon (annual)

*Asclepias tuberosa,* butterfly weed (native)

*Aster* species, asters (some native)

*Baptisia australis,* wild blue indigo (native)

*Celosia argentea* var. *cristata,* cockscomb (annual)

*Centaurea cyanus,* bachelor's button

*Cosmos bipinnatus,* cosmos (annual)

*Conoclinum coelestinum,* hardy ageratum (native)

*Echinacea purpurea,* purple coneflower (native)

*Euphorbia marginata,* snow-on-the-mountain

*Helianthus annuus,* sunflower

*Heliopsis helianthoides,* heliopsis (native)

*Iris* species, irises (some native)

*Lathyrus odoratus,* sweetpea (annual)

*Liatris* species, gayfeathers (native)

*Monarda didyma,* bee balm (native)

*Rudbeckia* species, black-eyed Susans (native)

*Rudbeckia hirta* 'Gloriosa Daisy', Gloriosa daisy

*Salvia splendens,* scarlet sage

*Solenostemon scutellarioides,* coleus (annual)

*Solidago* species, goldenrods (native)

*Tagetes* species, hybrids, and cultivars, marigolds (annual)

*Tropaeolum majus,* nasturtium (annual)

*Zinnia elegans,* zinnia (annual)

## Flowers for Cutting for Subtropical Florida

The plants recommended for Subtropical Florida are appropriate for Zones 10A, 10B, and 11, unless noted as follows:

*Not for Zone 10A

**Not for Zone 11

*Alpinia purpurata,* ginger*

*Alpinia zerumbet,* shell ginger

*Anthurium* hybrids, anthuriums*

*Antirrhinum majus,* snapdragon** (annual)

*Curcuma roscoeana,* curcuma

*Dendrobium* species, orchids
*Gaillardia pulchella,* gaillardia
*Gerbera jamesonii,* gerbera daisy*
*Gladiolus* hybrids, gladioli**
*Helianthus debilis,* dune sunflower
*Heliconia bihai, H. caribaea, H. latispatha, H. psittacorum, H. rostrata, H. stricta,* heliconias*
*Lantana* species, lantanas
*Pentas lanceolata,* pentas
*Phalaenopsis* species, moth orchids
*Rosa* species, hybrids, and cultivars, roses
*Rudbeckia hirta,* brown-eyed Susan
*Salvia coccinea,* salvia
*Spathoglottis plicata,* ground orchid
*Strelitzia reginae,* bird-of-paradise
*Tagetes erecta, T. lucida,* marigolds**

## Flowers for Cutting for the Midwest and Northern Great Plains

The plants are hardy to Zone 4 unless otherwise indicated.

*Achillea filipendulina, A. millefolium,* yarrows
*Ammobium alatum,* winged everlasting (annual)
*Anthemis tinctoria,* golden marguerite
*Antirrhinum majus,* common snapdragon (annual)
*Aster novae-angliae, A. novi-belgii,* asters (native)
*Celosia argentea* var. *cristata,* cockscomb (annual)
*Consolida ambigua,* rocket larkspur (annual)
*Eustoma grandiflorum,* prairie gentian (native)
*Gladiolus* x *hortulanus,* gladiolus (annual)
*Gypsophila paniculata,* baby's breath
*Helianthus* species, sunflowers (native)
*Helichrysum bracteatum,* strawflower (annual)
*Hosta plantaginea,* sweet hosta
*Lathyrus odoratus,* sweet pea (annual)
*Leucanthemum* x *superbum,* Shasta daisy
*Limonium sinuatum,* statice (annual)
*Matthiola incana,* stock (annual)

*Paeonia lactiflora* hybrids, peonies
*Phlox paniculata,* garden phlox
*Rosa* species, hybrids, and cultivars, roses
*Solidago* species, goldenrods (native)
*Sorghastrum nutans,* Indiangrass (native)
*Syringa* species, hybrids, and cultivars, lilacs
*Tagetes erecta,* African marigold (annual)
*Zinnia elegans,* zinnia (annual)

## Flowers for Cutting for Texas and the Southern Plains

Plants are appropriate for Zones 6, 7, and 8 unless otherwise noted. Plants marked (6) or (7) are only marginally adapted to those zones and may not survive in the coldest parts. Similarly, those marked (8) may not survive the hotter, drier areas of Zone 8.

*Amorpha fruticosa,* false indigo (native)
*Andropogon glomeratus,* brushy bluestem (native)
*Aster oblongifolius,* aromatic aster (native)
*Aster praealtus,* tall blue aster (native)
*Aster sericeus* var. *microphyllus,* Christmas aster (native) (Zones 8, 9)
*Bouteloua curtipendula,* sideoats grama (native)
*Cercis canadensis* var. *texensis,* Texas redbud (native)
*Chasmanthium latifolium,* inland sea oats (native)
*Coreopsis lanceolata,* coreopsis (native)
*Cosmos sulphureus* 'Bright Lights', cosmos (native) (annual)
*Echinacea angustifolia,* black sampson (native)
*Echinacea purpurea,* purple coneflower
*Eryngium leavenworthii,* eryngo (native)
*Eustoma grandiflorum,* Texas bluebells (native)
*Forsythia* x *intermedia,* forsythia
*Gaillardia pulchella,* Indianblanket (native)
*Gomphrena globosa,* globe amaranth (native) (annual)

*Helianthus maximiliani,* Maximilian sunflower (native)

*Hydrangea* species, hydrangeas

*Iris* species, hybrids, and cultivars, irises

*Liatris mucronata* and other species, gayfeathers (native)

*Lupinus texensis,* Texas bluebonnet (native)

*Magnolia* x *soulangiana,* saucer magnolia (Zones 6, 7, (8))

*Melica nitens,* three-flower melic (native)

*Moluccella laevis,* bells of Ireland (native)

*Monarda citriodora,* lemon mint (native)

*Muhlenbergia capillaris,* Gulf muhly (native) (Zones 7, 8, 9)

*Narcissus* species, daffodils

*Phlox paniculata,* summer phlox

*Physostegia virginiana,* fall obedient plant (native)

*Pycnanthemum tenuifolium,* mountain mint (native)

*Rosa* species, hybrids, and cultivars, antique roses

*Rudbeckia hirta,* black-eyed Susan (native)

*Salvia coccinea,* scarlet sage (native) (Zones 8, 9)

*Salvia roemeriana,* cedar sage (native) (Zones (7), 8)

*Schizachyrium scoparium,* little bluestem (native)

*Solidago* species, goldenrods (native)

*Sorghastrum nutans,* Indiangrass (native)

*Stipa tenuissima,* feather grass (native)

*Tetraneuris scaposa,* four-nerve daisy (native)

*Teucrium canadense* var. *canadense,* American germander (native)

*Viburnum rufidulum,* rusty blackhaw viburnum (native)

## Flowers for Cutting for the Rocky Mountain Region

Plants are hardy to Zone 4 unless otherwise noted.

*Anaphalis margaritacea,* pearly everlasting (native)

*Asclepias tuberosa,* butterfly weed (native)

*Achillea millefolium,* yarrow (native)

*Allium aflatunense,* ornamental onion

*Briza maxima,* big quaking grass

*Calamagrostis* x *acutiflora,* feather reed grass

*Celosia argentea* var. *plumosa,* plume celosia (annual)

*Chasmanthium latifolium,* quaking oat grass

*Coix lacryma-jobi,* Job's tears (annual)

*Echinacea purpurea,* purple coneflower

*Echinops ritro,* globe thistle

*Eriogonum umbellatum,* sulfur flower (native)

*Eryngium planum,* sea holly

*Eupatorium maculatum,* Joe-Pye weed

*Gomphrena globosa,* globe amaranth (annual)

*Helichrysum bracteatum,* strawflower (annual)

*Lagurus ovatus,* hare's tail grass (annual)

*Liatris pycnostachya,* gayfeather

*Nigella damascena,* love-in-a-mist (annual)

*Penstemon digitalis* 'Husker's Red', penstemon

*Psylliostachys suworowii,* Russian statice (annual)

*Rudbeckia triloba,* brown-eyed Susan

*Saccharum ravennae,* plume grass

*Sorghastrum nutans,* Indiangrass (native)

*Statice tataricum,* tartarian statice

## Flowers for Cutting for the Pacific Northwest

Plants are hardy to at least Zone 7 unless otherwise noted.

*Agastache foeniculum,* anise hyssop

*Anemone* x *hybrida,* Japanese anemone

*Anthemis tinctoria* 'Wargrave', golden marguerite

*Astilbe* x *arendsii* 'Gloria', astilbe

*Baptisia australis,* false indigo

*Calluna vulgaris* 'H. E. Beale', heather

*Campanula persicifolia* 'Telham Beauty', bellflower

*Chaenomeles japonica* 'Cameo', cameo flowering
quince

*Cosmos bipinnatus,* cosmos (annual)

*Crocosmia* 'Lucifer', crocosmia

*Diascia rigescens,* twinspur

*Doronicum orientale,* leopard's bane

*Echinacea purpurea,* purple coneflower

*Felicia amelloides,* blue marguerite

*Helianthus* x *multiflorus,* sunflower

*Helleborus argutifolius,* Corsican hellebore

*Iris germanica,* bearded iris

*Liatris spicata,* gayfeather

*Linaria purpurea* 'Canon Went', toadflax

*Paeonia* 'Red Charm', peony

*Papaver nudicaule,* Iceland poppy

*Psylliostachys suworowii,* Russian statice

*Schizanthus pinnatus,* poor man's orchid

*Sidalcea oregana* 'Brilliant', checker mallow
(native)

*Veronicastrum virginicum,* bowman's root

## Flowers for Cutting for Coastal California

Plants are appropriate for the coastal regions of
California from Crescent City to the border of
Mexico—and east to the Coast Ranges, the
western edge of Central Valley, and the south-
ern inland valleys and southernmost Peninsular
Ranges.

*Agapanthus africanus* 'Storm Cloud', agapanthus

*Alstroemeria* hybrids, Peruvian lily

*Anemone* x *hybrida* 'Alba', Japanese anemone

*Aster* x *frikartii* 'Monch', Frikart's aster

*Centaurea cyanus,* cornflower

*Consolida ambigua,* larkspur

*Coreopsis verticillata* 'Moonbeam', threadleaf
coreopsis

*Cosmos bipinnatus,* cosmos (annual)

*Delphinium* Pacific hybrids, delphiniums

*Dianthus carthusianorum,* cluster-head pink

*Echinacea purpurea,* purple coneflower

*Gladiolus* hybrids, garden gladioli

*Helianthus annuus,* common sunflower

*Helleborus orientalis,* Lenten rose

*Lathyrus odoratus,* sweetpea (annual)

*Lavandula* species, lavenders

*Lilium lancifolium,* tiger lily

*Limonium perezii,* statice

*Rosa* species, hybrids, and cultivars, roses

*Rudbeckia fulgida* 'Goldsturm', black-eyed
Susan

*Scabiosa atropurpurea* 'Black Burgundy', pincushion flower

*Trichostema lanatum,* woolly blue curls (native)

*Trollius ledebourii,* globe flower

*Veronica spicata,* speedwell

*Zantedeschia aethiopica,* calla lily

## Flowers for Cutting for the Western Deserts

The plants are appropriate throughout the
region, except those noted as follows:

*Not cold-hardy in cold desert areas
**Favor cooler/moister desert areas

*Achillea taygetea,* yarrow

*Agastache cana,* bubblegum mint (native)

*Baileya multiradiata,* desert marigold (native)

*Centaurea cyanus,* bachelor's buttons

*Centaurea moschata,* sweet sultan

*Cosmos bipinnatus,* cosmos (annual)

*Clarkia amoena,* farewell-to-spring (native)

*Echinacea purpurea,* purple coneflower**

*Eremurus himalaicus,* foxtail lily

*Eustoma russellianum* (*E. grandiflorum*), tulip gentian (native)
*Gaillardia* x *grandiflora,* blanketflower
*Gomphrena globosa,* globe amaranth (annual)
*Gypsophila paniculata,* baby's breath
*Helianthus maximilianii,* Maximilian sunflower (native)
*Hunnemannia fumariifolia,* Mexican tulip poppy
*Iris sibirica,* Siberian iris
*Liatris punctata,* gayfeather (native)
*Limonium perezii,* statice (annual in cold deserts)
*Limonium sinuatum,* statice (annual)
*Narcissus* species, hybrids, and cultivars, daffodils, narcissi
*Perovskia atriplicifolia,* Russian sage
*Purshia mexicana,* cliffrose (native)
*Rudbeckia hirta,* Gloriosa daisy
*Scabiosa caucasica,* pincushion flower
*Trachymene coerulea,* blue lace flower (annual)

## Plants for Winter Interest

The winter garden can be a place of wonder. Instead of the kaleidoscope of color in spring and summer, the winter garden is a place for contrasts. Berries and fruits provide brilliant splashes of color against the grays and browns of bark and the white of snow. For the most part, the display of color gives way to the display of form and texture, interesting bark, and limb structure. Keep winter interest in mind when designing your garden. Think about the view of the yard from various spots inside the house, and arrange plants with winter interest accordingly. Consider also how to provide the most winter interest with the nonplant features of the garden: bricks, stones, walls, arbors, benches, and ornaments. Try to plan at least one area of the winter garden that cannot be viewed

from inside, as inducement to go outside and enjoy the garden in all seasons.

NOTE: Subtropical Florida is not included in this section, since the other lists for that region provide year-round interest.

## Plants for Winter Interest for the Northeast

Plants are hardy to Zone 5, unless noted.

### Winter Blooms

*Chimonanthus praecox,* wintersweet (Zone 7)
*Cornus mas,* cornelian cherry
*Corylopsis* species, winter hazels
*Crocus tomasinianus,* Balkan crocus
*Eranthis hyemalis,* winter aconite
*Erica carnea* 'Springwood White', heath
*Galanthus* species, snowdrops
*Hamamelis* x *intermedia,* Oriental hybrid witchhazel
*Hamamelis japonica,* Japanese witchhazel
*Hamamelis mollis,* Chinese witchhazel
*Helleborus niger,* Christmas rose
*Helleborus orientalis,* Lenten rose (Zone 6)
*Jasminum nudiflorum,* winter jasmine (Zone 6)
*Parrotia persica,* Persian parrotia, Persian ironwood
*Prunus mume* and cultivars, Japanese apricot (Zone 6)

### Interesting Stems

*Acer palmatum* 'Sangokaku', red-twig Japanese maple
*Acer pennsylvanicum,* striped maple (native)
*A. pennsylvanicum* 'Erythrocladum', red-twig striped maple (native)
*Cornus alba,* tatarian dogwood
*Cornus sanguinea,* blood-twig dogwood

*Cornus stolonifera,* red osier dogwood (native)

*Corylus avellana* 'Contorta', Harry Lauder's walking stick

*Kerria japonica,* Japanese kerria

*Rhus typhina,* staghorn sumac (native)

*Rubus cockburnianus,* ghost bramble

*Salix udensis* 'Sekka', fantail willow

*Sassafras albidum,* sassafras (native)

*Ulmus alata,* winged elm

## Interesting Bark

*Acer griseum,* paperbark maple

*Betula maximowicziana,* monarch birch

*Betula nigra* 'Heritage', heritage black birch (native)

*Betula papyrifera,* paper birch, American white birch

*Betula populifolia,* gray birch, canoe birch

*Cladrastis kentukea (C. lutea),* yellowwood

*Cornus kousa,* Japanese dogwood

*Maackia amurensis,* Amur maackia

*Maclura pomifera,* osage orange

*Parrotia persica,* Persian parrotia, Persian ironwood

*Pinus bungeana,* lacebark pine

*Pinus densiflora,* Japanese red pine

*Pinus sylvestris,* Scotch pine

*Platanus occidentalis,* American sycamore (native)

*Prunus maackii,* Manchurian cherry

*Prunus serrula,* birchbark cherry

*Rubus cockburnianus* and related species, whitecane briar, ghost bramble

*Stewartia pseudocamellia,* stewartia

*Syringa reticulata,* manchurian lilac

## Winter Fruits or Seeds

*Aronia arbutifolia,* red chokeberry (native)

*Aronia melanocarpa,* black chokeberry (native)

*Callicarpa japonica, C. dichotoma,* beautyberries

*Cotoneaster* species, cotoneasters

*Crataegus* x *lavallei,* Lavalle hybrid hawthorn

*Crataegus phaenopyrum,* Washington thorn

*Crataegus* x 'Winter King', winter king hawthorn

*Ilex serrata,* Japanese winterberry

*Ilex verticillata* cultivars, winterberry (native)

*Malus* x *zumi* 'Calocarpa', Zumi hybrid crabapple

## Evergreens

*Abies concolor,* concolor fir

*Berberis julianae,* wintergreen barberry

*Berberis* x *wisleyensis,* three-thorn barberry

*Buxus microphylla,* Japanese box, Korean box

*Buxus sempervirens* 'Variegata', variegated English box

*Cedrus atlantica* 'Glauca', blue atlas cedar

*Cephalotaxus harringtonia,* Japanese plum yew

*Chamaecyparis* species, false cypresses

*Daphne* x *burkwoodii* 'Carol Mackie', daphne

*Ilex cornuta,* Chinese holly

*Ilex* x *meserveae,* meserve hybrid hollies

*Ilex opaca,* American holly (native)

*Kalmia latifolia,* mountain laurel (native)

*Picea pungens,* blue spruce, Colorado blue spruce

*Pieris floribunda,* American andromeda, American lily-of-the-valley shrub (native)

*Pieris japonica,* Japanese andromeda, Japanese lily-of-the-valley shrub

*Pseudotsuga menziesii,* Douglas fir

*Rhododendron carolinianum,* Carolina rhododendron (Zone 6)

*Rhododendron degronianum* subsp. *heptamerum,* evergreen Japanese rhododendron

*Rhododendron* 'PJM', hybrid rhododendron

## Plants for Winter Interest for the Southeast

Plants can be used throughout the region in Zones 6–9. Where plants are appropriate only for certain parts of the region, they are noted as follows:

US = Upper South, Zone 6

MS = Middle South, Zone 7 and parts of Zone 8 in the western edge of Mississippi, southern Arkansas, and central Texas

LS = Lower South, Zone 8 plus coastal North Carolina and parts of southern coastal Virginia

CS = Coastal South, Zone 8 in northern Florida and parts of Zone 9 in coastal Texas, Louisiana, and northeastern Florida

### Winter Blooms

*Camellia japonica,* camellia—MS, LS, CS

*Camellia sasanqua,* sasanqua camellia—MS, LS, CS

*Chaenomeles speciosa,* flowering quince

*Chimonanthus praecox,* wintersweet

*Cornus mas,* cornelian cherry—US, MS

*Corylopsis glabrescens,* winter hazel—US, MS

*Crocus* species, crocuses

*Cyclamen* species, hardy cyclamens

*Eranthus hyemalis,* winter aconite

*Galanthus* species, snowdrops—US, MS

*Hamamelis* x *intermedia* 'Primavera', 'Sunburst', 'Ruby Glow', witchhazels

*Hamamelis virginiana,* witchhazel (native)

*Helleborus foetidus,* bearsfoot hellebore

*Helleborus orientalis,* Lenten rose—US, MS, LS

*Jasminum nudiflorum,* winter jasmine

*Lonicera fragrantissima,* winter honeysuckle

*Mahonia bealei,* leatherleaf mahonia—MS, LS

*Narcissus asturiensis,* daffodil

*Narcissus pseudo-narcissis* 'Ajax', daffodil

*Prunus mume,* Japanese flowering apricot

### Interesting Stems

*Chaenomeles speciosa,* flowering quince

*Cornus alba* 'Sibirica', red bark dogwood—US, MS

*Cornus stolonifera* 'Cardinal', red osier dogwood—US, MS

*Cornus stolonifera* 'Flaviramea', golden-twig dogwood—US, MS

*Corylopsis glabrescens,* winter hazel—US, MS

*Corylus avellana* 'Contorta', Harry Lauder's walkingstick—US, MS

*Hamamelis* x *intermedia* 'Primavera', 'Sunburst', 'Ruby Glow', witchhazels

*Hamamelis virginiana,* witchhazel (native)

*Jasminum nudiflorum,* winter jasmine

*Liquidambar styraciflua,* sweet gum (native)

*Lonicera fragrantissima,* winter honeysuckle

*Prunus mume,* Japanese flowering apricot

*Salix caprea,* pussy willow

*Ulmus alata,* winged elm (native)

### Interesting Bark

*Acer griseum,* paperbark maple—US, MS

*Betula nigra,* river birch (native)

*Firmiana simplex,* Chinese parasol tree—MS, LS, CS

*Lagerstroemia fauriei,* crape myrtle

*Platanus occidentalis,* sycamore (native)

*Ulmus parvifolia,* lacebark elm

### Winter Fruits or Seeds

*Andropogon glomeratus,* bushy beardgrass (native)

*Andropogon virginicus,* broomsedge (native)

*Calamagrostis* x *acutiflora* 'Stricta', feather reed grass

*Chasmanthium latifolium,* river oats (native)

*Hydrangea quercifolia,* oak-leaf hydrangea (native)

*Ilex cornuta* 'Burfordii', Burford holly (red-berried)—MS, LS, CS

*Ilex cornuta* 'D'or' and 'O'Spring', golden-berried Chinese holly—MS, LS, CS

*Ilex decidua,* deciduous holly, many cultivars (native)

*Ilex opaca,* American holly, many cultivars (native)

*Ilex verticillata,* winterberry holly, many cultivars (native)

## Evergreens

*Acorus gramineus* 'Ogon', variegated sweet flag—MS, LS, CS

*Camellia japonica,* camellia—MS, LS, CS

*Camellia sasanqua,* sasanqua camellia—MS, LS, CS

*Danae racemosa,* Alexandrian laurel—MS, LS, CS

*Daphne odora,* winter daphne—US, MS, LS

*Helleborus foetidus,* bearsfoot hellebore

*Helleborus orientalis,* Lenten rose—US, MS, LS

*Ilex cornuta* 'Burfordii', Burford holly (red-berried)—MS, LS, CS

*Ilex cornuta* 'D'or' and 'O'Spring', golden-berried Chinese holly—MS, LS, CS

*Ilex opaca,* American holly, many cultivars (native)

*Osmanthus heterophyllus,* holly-leaf osmanthus

*Polystichum acrostichoides,* Christmas fern (native)

*Rohdea japonica,* rohdea—MS, LS, CS

## Plants for Winter Interest for the Midwest and Northern Great Plains

The plants are hardy to Zone 4 unless otherwise indicated.

### Interesting Stems

*Amelanchier* species, serviceberries (native)

*Calamagrostis* x *acutiflora,* feather reed grass

*Cimicifuga racemosa,* black cohosh (native)

*Cornus alternifolia,* pagoda dogwood (native)

*Sorghastrum nutans,* Indiangrass (native)

*Spartina pectinata,* prairie cordgrass (native)

### Interesting Bark

*Acer saccharum,* sugar maple (native)

*Amelanchier* species, serviceberries (native)

*Carpinus caroliniana,* musclewood (native)

*Carya ovata,* shagbark hickory (native)

*Cornus alternifolia,* pagoda dogwood (native)

*Gymnocladus dioicus,* Kentucky coffee tree (native)

*Ilex verticillata,* winterberry holly (native)

*Prunus amurensis,* amur chokecherry

*Quercus macrocarpa,* bur oak (native)

*Syringa reticulata,* Japanese tree lilac

### Winter Fruits or Seeds

*Astilbe* species and hybrids, astilbes

*Echinacea purpurea,* purple coneflower (native)

*Eupatorium maculatum* and others, Joe-Pye weeds (native)

*Ilex verticillata,* winterberry holly (native)

*Iris sibirica,* Siberian iris

*Panicum virgatum,* switchgrass (native)

*Rudbeckia* species, black-eyed Susans (native)

*Thermopsis villosa,* Carolina bush pea

*Veronicastrum virginicum,* Culver's root (native)

## Evergreens

*Abies concolor*, concolor fir
*Chamaecyparis pisifera*, false cypress
*Juniperus chinensis*, Chinese juniper
*Juniperus communis*, common juniper (native)
*Juniperus virginiana*, eastern red cedar (native)
*Microbiota decussata*, Russian cypress
*Picea abies*, Norway spruce
*Picea glauca* 'Densata', Black Hills spruce (native)
*Pinus nigra, P. sylvestris*, Austrian pine, Scotch pine
*Pinus resinosa*, red pine (native)
*Pinus strobus*, white pine (native)
*Pseudotsuga menziesii*, Douglas fir
*Taxus* x *media*, spreading yew

## Plants for Winter Interest for Texas and the Southern Plains

Plants are appropriate for Zones 6, 7, and 8 unless otherwise noted. Plants marked (6) or (7) are only marginally adapted to those zones and may not survive in the coldest parts. Similarly, those marked (8) may not survive the hotter, drier areas of Zone 8.

### Winter Blooms

*Antirrhinum* hybrids, snapdragons (annual)
*Aster sericeus* var. *microphyllus*, Christmas aster (native) (Zones 8, 9)
*Brassica oleracea* Acephala group, flowering kale (annual)
*Gelsemium sempervirens*, Carolina jessamine (native)
*Narcissus tazetta*, narcissus (Zones 8, 9)
*Viola missouriensis*, Missouri violet (native)
*Viola* hybrids, pansies (annual)

## Interesting Stems

*Andropogon glomeratus*, brushy bluestem (native) (Zones 6, 7, 8, 9)
*Buchloe dactyloides*, buffalograss (native)
*Nolina texana*, sacahuista (native)
*Schizachyrium scoparium*, little bluestem (native)
*Stipa tenuissima*, feathergrass (native)
*Yucca glauca*, soapweed (native) (Zones 6, 7, 8, 9)

## Interesting Bark

*Crataegus viridis*, green hawthorn (native)
*Lagerstroemia indica*, crape myrtle (Zones (7), 8)
*Platanus occidentalis*, sycamore (native)
*Prunus mexicana*, Mexican plum (native)
*Sophora affinis*, Eve's necklace (native) (Zones 7, 8)

## Winter Fruits or Seeds

*Andropogon glomeratus*, brushy bluestem (native)
*Cercis reniformis* (*C. canadensis* var. *texensis* 'Oklahoma'), Texas redbud (native)
*Echinacea angustifolia*, black sampson (native)
*Ilex cornuta*, Chinese holly
*Ilex decidua*, possumhaw (native)
*Ilex vomitoria*, yaupon (native) (Zones (7), 8, 9)
*Myrica cerifera*, wax myrtle (native) (Zones 8, 9)
*Photinia serratifolia*, Chinese photinia
*Prunus caroliniana*, cherry laurel (Zones 7, 8, 9)
*Sophora affinis*, Eve's necklace (native) (Zones 7, 8)
*Symphoricarpos orbiculatus*, coralberry (native)
*Ungnadia speciosa*, Mexican buckeye (Zones (7), 8) (native)

## Evergreens

*Abelia* x *grandiflora*, glossy abelia

*Abelia* 'Edward Goucher', 'Compacta', dwarf abelia

*Antennaria neglecta*, pussytoes (native) (Zones 5, 6, 7)

*Bignonia capreolata*, crossvine (native) (Zones 7, 8, 9)

*Buxus microphylla* var. *japonica*, Japanese boxwood

*Cupressus arizonica* var. *arizonica*, Arizona cypress (native) (Zones 7, 8)

*Dasylirion texanum*, sotol (native) (Zones 7, 8)

*Elaeagnus macrophylla*, elaeagnus (Zone 8)

*Gelsemium sempervirens*, Carolina jessamine (native)

*Geum canadense*, white avens (native)

*Hypericum henryi*, St.-John's-wort (Zones (6) 7, 8)

*Ilex cornuta* 'Burfordii', Burford holly (Zones 7, 8)

*Ilex cornuta* 'Burfordii Nana', dwarf Burford holly (Zones 7, 8)

*Ilex cornuta* 'Rotunda', dwarf Chinese holly (Zones 7, 8)

*Jasminum humile*, Italian jasmine (Zones 8, 9)

*Juniperus ashei*, Ashe juniper (native)

*Juniperus virginiana*, eastern red cedar (native)

*Liriope muscari*, monkeygrass (Zones 8, 9)

*Myrica cerifera*, dwarf wax myrtle (Zones 8, 9)

*Photinia serratifolia*, Chinese photinia

*Pinus cembroides*, Mexican pinyon pine (native) (Zones 7, 8)

*Pinus edulis*, pinyon (native) (Zones 6, 7)

*Pinus mugo*, mountain pine (Zones 7, 8)

*Polystichum acrostichoides*, Christmas fern (native) (Zones 6, 7, (8))

*Prunus caroliniana*, cherry laurel (Zones 7, 8, 9)

*Quercus fusiformis*, escarpment live oak, Quartz Mountain live oak (native) (Zones 7, 8)

*Quercus virginiana*, coastal live oak (native) (Zones 8, 9)

*Ruellia brittoniana* 'Katie', Katie's ruellia (Zones 8, 9)

*Salvia lyrata*, lyreleaf sage (native)

*Senecio obovatus*, golden groundsel (native)

*Viola missouriensis*, Missouri violet (native)

*Yucca gloriosa*, soft-leaf yucca (Zones 7, 8, 9)

## Plants for Winter Interest for the Rocky Mountains

Plants are hardy to Zone 4 unless otherwise noted.

### Winter Blooms

*Acer rubrum*, red maple (Zones 3–9)

*Alnus tenuifolia*, thinleaf alder

*Corylus americana*, American filbert (Zones 4–9)

*Corylus cornuta*, hazelnut (Zones 4–7)

*Crocus* species, crocuses

*Galanthus nivalis*, snowdrop

### Interesting Stems

*Acer glabrum*, Rocky Mountain maple (native)

*Corylus avellana* 'Contorta', Harry Lauder's walking stick

*Cornus stolonifera*, red osier dogwood (native) (Zones 2–8)

*Cornus stolonifera* 'Flaviramea', yellow-twig dogwood

*Ephedra viridis*, Mormon tea

*Rhus glabra*, smooth sumac (native) (Zone 2)

*Salix exigua*, coyote willow (native) (Zone 2)

*Salix irrorata*, bluestem willow (native)

## Interesting Bark

*Acer glabrum,* Rocky Mountain maple (native)
*Alnus tenuifolia,* thinleaf alder
*Betula nigra,* eastern river birch
*Betula occidentalis* (*B. fontinalis*), western river birch (native)
*Pinus ponderosa,* ponderosa pine

## Winter Fruits or Seeds

*Achillea millefolium,* yarrow (native)
*Anaphalis margaritacea,* pearly everlasting (native) (Zone 2)
*Krascheninnikovia lanata,* winterfat (native)
*Rudbeckia triloba,* brown-eyed Susan
*Sorghastrum nutans,* Indiangrass (native)

## Evergreens

*Juniperus scopulorum,* Rocky Mountain juniper (native)
*Mahonia repens,* creeping holly grape (native)
*Picea pungens* f. *glauca,* Colorado blue spruce (native)
*Pinus aristata,* bristlecone pine (native)
*Pinus edulis,* pinyon pine
*Pinus ponderosa,* ponderosa pine
*Sempervivum species,* hens and chickens (Zone 3)

## Plants for Winter Interest for the Pacific Northwest

Plants are hardy to at least Zone 7 unless otherwise noted.

## Winter Blooms

*Chimonanthus praecox,* wintersweet
*Cornus mas,* cornelian cherry

*Corylopsis pauciflora,* winterhazel
*Erica carnea* 'Vivellii', spring heath
*Garrya elliptica* 'James Roof', silk-tassel (native) (Zone 8)
*Hamamelis mollis* 'Pallida', witchhazel
*Helleborus niger,* Christmas rose
*Jasminum nudiflorum,* winter jasmine
*Rhododendron mucronulatum,* Korean rhododendron
*Viburnum* x *bodnantense* 'Dawn', viburnum

## Interesting Stems

*Alnus sinuata,* Sitka alder (native)
*Cornus alba* 'Sibirica', Siberian dogwood
*Cornus stolonifera* 'Flaviramea', yellow-twig dogwood (native)
*Oplopanax horridus,* devil's club (native)
*Rosa glauca,* blue-leaved rose
*Spiraea thunbergii,* Thunberg spirea

## Interesting Bark

*Acer griseum,* paperbark maple
*Betula nigra,* river birch
*Clethra barbinervis,* Japanese sweet pepperbush
*Physocarpus capitatus,* ninebark (native)
*Pinus bungeana,* lacebark pine
*Prunus serrula,* paperbark cherry

## Winter Fruits or Seeds

*Arbutus unedo* 'Compacta', compact strawberry madrone
*Crataegus* x *lavallei,* Lavalle hawthorn
*Pyracantha* x 'Victory', pyracantha
*Rosa gymnocarpa,* bald-hip roses (native)
*Sorbus commixta,* Japanese mountain ash
*Symphoricarpos albus,* common snowberry (native)

## Evergreens

*Chamaecyparis pisifera* 'Filifera Aurea', gold-thread false cypress
*Picea orientalis* 'Skylands', Oriental spruce
*Pinus strobus* 'Nana', dwarf white pine
*Polystichum polyblepharum*, tassle fern
*Sciadopitys verticillata*, umbrella pine
*Taxus baccata* 'Aurea', golden English yew

# Plants for Winter Interest for Coastal California

Plants are appropriate for the coastal regions of California from Crescent City to the border of Mexico—and east to the Coast Ranges, the western edge of Central Valley, and the southern inland valleys and southernmost Peninsular Ranges.

## Winter Blooms

*Arctostaphylos* species, manzanitas (native)
*Camellia sasanqua*, sasanqua camellia
*Camellia japonica*, Japanese camellia
*Chimonanthus praecox*, wintersweet
*Garrya elliptica*, coast silk-tassel (native)
*Helleborus orientalis*, Lenten rose
*Helleborus argutifolius*, Corsican hellebore

## Interesting Stems

*Cornus stolonifera*, red osier dogwood (native)
*Dipsacus fullonum*, teasel
*Salix matsudana* 'Tortuosa', corkscrew willow

## Interesting Bark

*Arbutus* 'Marina', arbutus
*Arctostaphylos* species, manzanitas (native)
*Luma apiculata*, luma

## Winter Fruits or Seeds

*Arctostaphylos* species, manzanitas (native)
*Diospyros kaki,* persimmon
*Heteromeles arbutifolia,* toyon (native)
*Ribes sanguineum* var. *glutinosum,* flowering currant (native)
*Ribes speciosum,* fuchsia-flowering gooseberry (native)
*Rosa californica,* California rose (native)
*Sorbus aucuparia,* European mountain ash
*Viburnum tinus,* laurustinus

## Evergreens

*Abies bracteata,* Santa Lucia fir (native)
*Arctostaphylos* species, manzanitas (native)
*Camellia sasanqua,* sasanqua camellia
*Camellia japonica,* Japanese camellia
*Garrya elliptica,* coast silk-tassel (native)
*Viburnum tinus,* laurustinus

# Plants for Winter Interest for the Western Deserts

The plants are appropriate throughout the region, except those noted as follows:

*Not cold-hardy in cold desert areas
**Favor cooler/moister desert areas

## Winter Blooms

*Acacia minuta,* desert sweet acacia
*Bergenia crassifolia,* winter bergenia
*Dalea pulchra,* pea bush* (native)
*Rosmarinus officinalis,* rosemary

## Interesting Stems

*Asclepias subulata,* desert milkweed* (native)
*Carnegiea gigantea,* saguaro* (native)
*Ephedra viridis,* green joint fir (native)
*Euphorbia antisyphilitica,* candelilla* (native)
*Fouquieria splendens,* ocotillo (native)
*Opuntia bigelovii,* teddy bear cactus* (native)

## Interesting Bark

*Arbutus xalapensis,* Texas madrone (native)
*Arctostaphylos pungens,* pointleaf manzanita (native)
*Cercidium* species, palo verdes* (native)
*Eucalyptus formanii,* Forman's gum

## Interesting Fruits or Seeds

*Cotoneaster horizontalis,* rockspray
*Eragrostis trichodes,* sand lovegrass (native)
*Hylotelephium spectabile* 'Autumn Joy', 'Red Chief', sedum
*Krascheninnikovia lanata,* winterfat (native)

## Evergreens

*Agave* species, century plants* (some native)
*Artemisia tridentata,* bigleaf sage (native)
*Brahea armata,* Mexican blue palm*
*Cercocarpus ledifolius,* curly-leaf mountain mahogany (native)
*Larrea tridentata,* creosote bush (native)
*Leucophyllum candidum* 'Silver Cloud', Texas sage* (native)
*Mahonia fremontii,* algerita (native)
*Nolina microcarpa,* beargrass (native)
*Vauquelinia californica,* Arizona rosewood (native)
*Yucca* species, yuccas* (some native)

# Lawn

The front lawn has been called America's great contribution to world garden design. Unfortunately, the traditional high-maintenance approach to lawn care also contributes to weary gardeners. And more important, the wrong lawn in the wrong place contributes to environmental problems, requiring far too much water use and massive doses of chemical fertilizers and pesticides. Fortunately, lawns can prosper without overuse of water and chemicals—and without an exhausting maintenance routine. Here are some tips on how to grow a low-maintenance, good-looking lawn. (Each of these tips is covered in detail below.)

- Choose the right lawn grass for the right location.
- Break the lawn-chemical habit.
- Know when to fertilize, and use a natural fertilizer.
- Mow high, mow often, and leave the clippings on the lawn.
- Control stubborn weeds manually.
- Learn to monitor lawn pests and diseases and control them naturally.
- Revive old, worn lawns by aerating and overseeding.

## Recommended Grasses for Every Region

### Zone 1—The Humid Northeast and Upper Midwest

Kentucky blue grass: Midnight, Liberty, America, Blacksburg, Preakness, Ram I
Perennial rye grass: Yorktown III, Palmer II, Repell II, Pennfine II

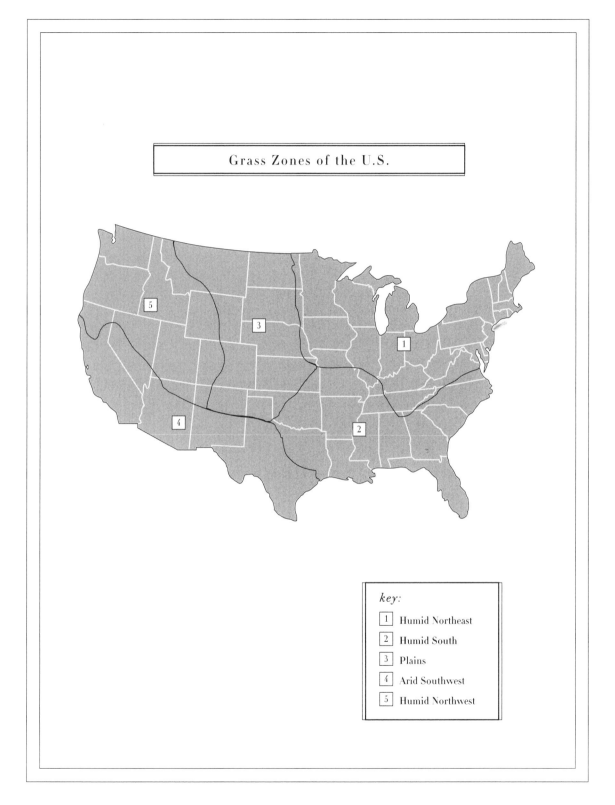

Grass Zones of the U.S.

key:
1 Humid Northeast
2 Humid South
3 Plains
4 Arid Southwest
5 Humid Northwest

Tall fescue: Mustang, Silverado, Rebel III, Rebel Jr., Rebel 3D, Olympic
Fine fescue: Spartan, Reliant, Atlanta, Jamestown II
Zoysia: Midwestern

## Zone 2—The Humid South

Bahia grass: Paraguay, Pensacola, Argentine
Bermuda grass: Tifgreen, Tifway, Vamont
Zoysia: Meyer, Emerald
Centipede grass: Oaklawn, Tennessee Hardy
St. Augustine grass: Roselawn, Floratine

## Zone 3—The Plains

Buffalo grass: Texoka, Prairie, Sharp's Improved
Kentucky blue grass: America, Dawn, Harmony, Georgetown
Fine fescue: Reliant II, Aurora, Jamestown II
Perennial rye grass: Blazer II, Palmer II, Yorktown III, Repell II
Bermuda grass: Tifway, Tifgreen

## Zone 4—The Arid Southwest

Buffalo grass: Texoka, Prairie, Sharp's Improved
Bermuda grass: Tifway II, Tifgreen, Midirion
Perennial rye grass: Palmer II, Citation II, Repell II, Yorktown III
Kentucky blue grass: Classic, Glade, Trenton, Georgetown
Fine fescue: Waldina, Scaldis
Zoysia

## Zone 5—The Humid Northwest

Kentucky blue grass: Blacksburg, Challenger, Midnight, Preakness, Ram I

Bent grass: Exeter, Putter, Prominent, Southshore
Fine fescue: Reliant II, Scaldis, Enjoy, Jamestown II
Perennial rye grass: Palmer II, Manhattan II, Repell II, Yorktown III

## Natural Lawn Care Basics

### Breaking the Lawn-Chemical Habit

In some ways, chemicals make it more difficult to grow a lawn. They destroy beneficial organisms in the soil that normally would help keep disease organisms under control, and they wipe out the beneficial insects that would control harmful ones. They weaken the grass plants by causing them to grow too fast and lush. And they do nothing to solve the cause of weed problems: compacted soil, improper watering, and mowing. As with other gardening, the key to a healthy, trouble-free lawn is healthy soil, thriving with beneficial organisms. The sooner you stop using chemical fertilizers and pesticides, the faster the soil will recover.

#### *Fertilizing*

When to fertilize, and how much, depends on where you live and the kind of grass you are growing. Remember that the more you fertilize, the more your grass will grow and the more you will have to mow.

Natural fertilizers are best. Chemical lawn fertilizers are almost always loaded with water-soluble nitrogen and require frequent applications because they have no residual action. The lawn grass will be stronger if it is fed slowly and steadily through the season with a natural fertilizer. Most natural forms of nitrogen are water-insoluble and longer lasting, allowing soil acids and microorganisms to slowly convert them to forms that plants can use. Cow manure, bloodmeal, cottonseed meal, fish emulsion, leather tankage, and mixed organic fertilizers are all good natural sources of nitrogen. Dried poultry manure is a good choice; one 25-pound bag of dried poultry manure will feed 1,000 square feet of lawn per year.

The following is a minimal fertilization schedule for the five grass zones shown on page 385. Recommendations are in pounds of nitrogen per 1,000 square feet. (To calculate the number of pounds of nitrogen in a bag of fertilizer, multiply the weight of the bag by the percentage of nitrogen in the fertilizer, represented by the first number of the nitrogen-phosphorus-potassium ratio on the fertilizer bag. For instance, the nitrogen content in a 40-pound bag of 10-3-4 fertilizer is 40 multiplied by 10 percent, or 4 pounds of nitrogen.)

**Zone 1—The Northeast and Upper Midwest:** 2 pounds in September or October or after grass stops growing.

**Zone 2—The South:** *For summer grasses,** 1 pound in June, one pound in August. *For winter grasses,** 2 pounds in September or October.

**Zone 3—The Plains:** 2 pounds in September.

**Zone 4—The Southwest:** *For summer grasses, cool-season species,** irrigated:* 1½ pounds in October or November, 1½ in May or June. *For summer grasses, warm-season species,** irrigated,* ½ pound every

*In southern regions, warm-season species such as Bermuda grass or Bahia grass are the summer grasses of choice. They are sometimes overseeded in fall with a cool season species such as Kentucky blue grass or rye grass that provides winter green after the summer grass has gone dormant.

month, May to August. *For summer grasses, warm-season species, nonirrigated:* 1 pound in April or May, 1 pound in August. *For winter grasses, cool-season species,* 2 pounds in October or November.

**Zone 5—The Northwest:** 2 pounds in October or November or after the grass stops growing.

### Mowing

Mowing is probably the most important thing you do to your lawn. When it is done properly, mowing can kill weeds, control diseases, save water, and provide fertilizer. Most people mow much too low. Mowing high is the key to a healthy lawn. It reduces stress on the grass and allows it to compete better with weeds. It also lets the grass shade the soil to inhibit germination and growth of weeds.

Leave the grass clippings on the lawn. As they break down, grass clippings contribute usable nitrogen to the lawn. Grass clippings will begin to break down within a week if the soil is alive with organisms; the process will take longer on a lawn where chemicals have been frequently applied. In that case, the smaller the clippings the better, so mow lightly and often or use a mulching mower.

### Weeding

The best defense against weeds is a thick, healthy lawn that does not allow much room for weeds. Often, the presence of abundant weeds points to an underlying problem, such as compacted soil or improper watering and mowing. Herbicides may temporarily remove the weeds, but unless the problem is corrected, the weeds will return, requiring more and more herbicides.

Even with a strong, healthy lawn, you may have to remove stubborn weeds occasionally.

## HOW LOW TO MOW

Here are the best mowing heights in inches, by species. As indicated, the mower deck should be raised in hot weather or shade, and lowered somewhat for the last mow before winter.

| Cool-Season Grasses | Cool Weather and/or Shade | Hot Weather | Last Mow |
|---|---|---|---|
| Bent grass | ⅓ | ⅔ | ⅓ |
| Kentucky blue grass | 2½ | 3 | 2 |
| Fine fescue | 1½ | 2½ | 1 |
| Tall fescue | 2½ | 4 | 2 |
| Perennial rye grass | 1½ | 2½ | 1 |
| **Warm-Season Grasses** | | | |
| Bahia grass | 2 | 3 | 1½ |
| Bermuda grass | ½ | 1 | ½ |
| Buffalo grass | 1½ | 2½ | 1 |
| Centipede grass | 1 | 2 | 1 |
| St. Augustine grass | 2 | 3 | 1½ |
| Zoysia | ½ | 1 | ½ |

The best way is without chemicals; various long-handled tools that help pull out weeds without much effort are available at garden centers or through garden-supply catalogs.

The long taproots of persistent weeds like dandelions are difficult to pull, and any root pieces left behind regenerate into new weeds. Try to remove these weeds when they are at their weakest: when they are blooming and food reserves in the roots are at their lowest. Dig out four to five inches of the root; most likely any remaining root pieces will not have enough strength to send up another stalk.

### Natural Insect and Disease Control

The first step in natural lawn-insect control is to learn what the pests look like and when to expect them. Check for insects at ground level, and pull back patches of sod to look for insects underneath. Remember that your lawn does not have to be perfectly bug-free. Take action only if damage is obvious, and then use the least toxic pesticide available. Natural pest controls, both biological and physical, are available for controlling every turf pest—such as sabadilla dust for chinch bugs, rotenone or diatomaceous earth for billbugs, and insecticidal soap or *Bt* for sod webworms. Milky spore, a good long-term control measure against Japanese beetle grubs, takes a few years to take effect. For more on managing turf pests and diseases, see "Safe Pest Control," page 538.

With a chemical-free lawn, the soil itself helps control disease problems. In healthy soil, disease pathogens are greatly outnumbered by nonpathogenic microfauna (amoebae, nematodes, and insects) and microflora (bacteria, actinomycetes, and fungi), which keep the disease-causing organisms under control. Top-dressing the lawn with manure, compost, or other organic matter can increase the disease-fighting actinomycete level in the soil. Top-dressing involves covering the lawn with a thin (⅛ to ¼ inch deep) layer of organic matter. Applications of liquid seaweed may reduce diseases such as fusarium and dollar spot.

If disease persists, consider alternatives to grass. Most disease and weed problems occur where conditions are not conducive to good grass growth. Consider substitutes in those situations, such as ground covers in shady spots or bark or gravel in pathways or heavily trafficked areas.

## Aerating and Overseeding to Revive a Worn Lawn

Old lawns often suffer from compacted soil. This is especially true for lawns that have been

---

### TIPS FOR PLANTING A NEW LAWN

The best time to completely replant a lawn is when temperatures are cool and rain is plentiful. A new lawn should have ample time to become established before summer heat and drought. Here is how to go about planting a new lawn.

**Remove all existing turf.** Dig up any existing grass or till it under. Rake up and remove the clumps. Be sure to dig deeply enough to remove the entire root of persistent, deep-rooted weeds like dandelions.

**Add organic matter, lime, and fertilizer.** Your lawn will not be healthy if soil is either too wet or too dry. Add compost or other organic matter to the existing soil to help solve soil drainage problems. Unless the problem is severe, a 4- to 6-inch layer of compost mixed into the top 8 to 10 inches of soil should be enough.

Lawn grasses do best in soil with a pH in the 6.5 to 7.0 range; essential nutrients are most available to the grass at this pH. Test your soil with a soil-test kit; if the soil pH is below 6.5, add lime to bring it up to the proper level. At the same time, add the proper amount of a complete organic fertilizer into the top 6 to 8 inches of your soil. Use a fertilizer with plenty of phosphorus. (Phosphorus is the middle number on the fertilizer bag.) For phosphorus to be effective, it has to be mixed into the soil, not just sprinkled on top.

Mix the organic matter, lime, and fertilizer into the soil by rototilling or cultivating. Rake the entire area with a wide rake to make it level. If possible, allow a few days for the ground to settle before the final raking so that you can eliminate high and low spots. Before you seed, you can add another light application of fertilizer to make sure there is adequate fertilizer near the germinating seed.

**Sow the seed and water.** If you are preparing your own seed mix, make sure that all the grass varieties are mixed thoroughly and evenly. Whether you mix your own seed or use a commercial mix, divide the grass seed in half and sow half the mixture in one direction and the other half at right angles to it. Rake lightly, just to cover the seeds with about ⅛ inch of soil—if the seeds are covered with too much soil, they may not germinate. You may want to roll the seedbed with a light roller to promote better seed-soil contact, which promotes better seed germination. Then water lightly, so that the top few inches of soil are moist; do not wash away the seeds by overwatering. After the initial watering, water lightly several times a day. Try not to walk over the newly seeded area. Mow when the grass is 3 inches high, and regularly from then on.

treated with chemicals, which slow or halt the soil-aerating activity of earthworms and microorganisms. Aerating the soil can give it a fresh start. You can either use a hand-and-foot-powered aerator with metal tines that are pushed into the ground, or rent a power aerator to do the job more quickly.

If your lawn is more than ten years old, then it is handicapped by old-fashioned grass. New varieties are tougher, more vigorous, better looking, drought-tolerant, and disease- and even insect-resistant. Find a blend that meets your requirements, then sow it at 1½ times the recommended rate, right over your current turf. If you top-dress your existing lawn first, the fresh soil will provide an ideal seedbed. If not, scratch the turf roughly with a metal rake before sowing.

## Further Reading

Roach, Margaret, ed. *The Natural Lawn and Alternatives.* Brooklyn, N.Y.: Brooklyn Botanic Garden, 1993.

Schultz, Warren. *The Chemical-Free Lawn.* Emmaus, Pa.: Rodale Press, 1989.

# Bulbs

Bulbs are a diverse category of perennial plants with underground structures that are designed to store food, allowing them to go dormant and get through hard times that they otherwise would not survive—whether extreme cold, extreme heat, or extended drought. This same storage structure allows bulbs to grow rapidly when conditions are favorable.

There are bulbs for every garden and every purpose: from shaded woodlands to sunny open slopes, from mild climates to cold ones, from areas with little rainfall to those with abundunt precipitation. Some bulbs are too tender to survive cold winters, but these can often be grown outdoors and dug up and stored over winter, or grown indoors as houseplants (see "Tender Bulbs Treated as Annuals in Temperate Climates," page 399).

Bulbs can be used in many ways in the garden—singly or in dramatic masses, sprinkled in lawns or meadows, planted among perennials, or grown in containers. There are bulbs that flower in summer, others that provide the last blooms of fall or the only color of winter. And, of course, there are the dazzling bulbs of spring.

## What Is a Bulb?

Botanists are very precise about the use of the term "bulb." A true bulb is a fleshy, underground bud. It is not a corm, rhizome, tuberous stem, or tuberous root, all of which gardeners tend to group together loosely as bulbs; these nonbulbs are actually swollen roots or stems. The botanical term for what the gardener usually calls bulb is "geophyte"—literally "earth-plant," a plant in which new growth begins below ground, not at or above ground level. In this section, however, the "bulb" will be used loosely, to include both true bulbs and other geophytes.

### Types of Bulbs

It is useful to distinguish among the different types of bulbs, since this helps determine how to plant them. One way to tell bulbs apart is to group them according to where the starches and sugars used for food are stored.

#### True Bulbs

Many of the commonly cultivated geophytes, including tulips, alliums, and lilies, are

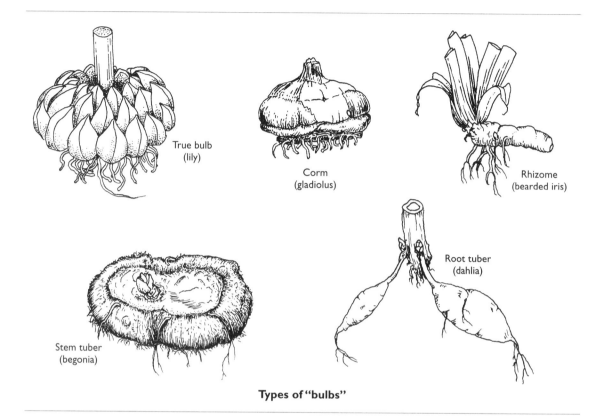

True bulb
(lily)

Corm
(gladiolus)

Rhizome
(bearded iris)

Root tuber
(dahlia)

Stem tuber
(begonia)

**Types of "bulbs"**

true bulbs. A true bulb is really just a typical shoot compressed into a shortened form. Food is stored in a number of small, fleshy "scale" *leaves.* Most true bulbs are egg-shaped, with a stem "plate" at the wider end. Attached to this stem are the storage leaves, forming concentric circles surrounding the growing tip. (If you cut a bulb in two, cross-section, you will see the concentric rings typical of an onion cut in half.) New roots form from the lower part of the stem, growing downward, so it is important to plant the bulb with this broader, root-forming end facing down.

## Corms

Gladiolus, crocus, and freesia are examples of corms. In a corm, food is stored in *stem* tissue. If you cut a corm in half you will see that it does not have the concentric rings of fleshy leaves; instead, it is one mass of homogenous stem tissue. As with bulbs, roots grow from the wider end, so the corm should also be planted with the wide side facing down. Buds poke out of the pointy end.

## Rhizomes

Irises, cannas, and lily of the valley are all rhizomes. In rhizomes, as in corms, food is stored in the stem. Indeed, "rhizome" is a general term for a stem growing more or less horizontally below ground level; thus you should plant it horizontally. Rhizomes tend to be thick, fleshy, or woody, and bear nodes with scale or foliage leaves and buds. Growth occurs at the buds on the ends of the rhizome or nearby nodes. You can distinguish rhizomes from roots by the presence of scale leaves or the scars where old leaves have fallen off.

### Stem Tubers

Some anemones and cannas produce stem tubers. It is often hard to tell a stem tuber from a rhizome; they are both swollen, horizontal, usually underground stems. But stem tubers usually form at the *ends* of a rhizome and will give rise to new rhizomes the following year. Growth starts from one or more nodes or buds, called "eyes," at the base of the older stem. Like rhizomes, stem tubers should be planted horizontally, with at least one growing eye attached to each division.

### Root Tubers

Dahlias and gloriosa lilies are examples of plants with root tubers. Root tubers are swollen roots in which food is stored. Being roots, they lack nodes, leaf scars, and buds. To be viable, they must include a portion of the stem with one or more buds. This portion of stem is usually planted facing upward.

## The Life Cycle of Bulbs

All bulbs, whether true bulbs, corms, tubers, or rhizomes, have one thing in common: a dormant period or rest period. During adverse weather—either hot and dry summers or cold and snowy winters—many bulbs shed their foliage and live off the nutrients they stored up during favorable conditions. "Dormant" is really a misnomer. Although they appear to be resting, most bulbs continue to develop, but the changes take place out of sight, underground, fueled by food stored during the previous growing season. Knowing about this

dormant period of bulbs is the key to growing them successfully, whether indoors or outdoors: Unless your climate is similar to the climate where the bulb originated, you will have to simulate those conditions, including the changes that prompt the bulb to go dormant, the conditions during dormancy, and the conditions during the bulb's active phase. This is why gardeners in cold climates dig up tender bulbs and overwinter them indoors, and it is why hardy bulbs grown indoors or outdoors in warm climates have to be chilled first.

When climatic conditions once again become more favorable for growth, the bulb is stimulated to put out roots, leaves, and flowers. Many bulbs adapted to cold respond to a rise in temperature; those adapted to hot and dry conditions respond to an increase in moisture. Bulbs are tuned finely enough that they will usually not respond to just any rise in temperature or increase in moisture such as a freak warm spell in December or a rain shower in July. This protects them from sending out vulnerable shoots that will be killed off when more typical seasonal weather again prevails.

Bulbs often start their growing season with a rush, producing flowers and leaves at the same time or sometimes producing flowers before leaves. This effort usually exhausts the bulb's store of nutrients and the plant either dies after fruiting or attempts to accumulate enough nutrients for the next flowering season. It is important not to cut off leaves right after flowering ends; they are working to build up the food stores through photosynthesis.

## Hardy or Tender

Winter-hardy bulbs can survive cold winters. Most of the winter-hardy bulbs—including daffodils, crocuses, and hyacinths—come from regions with cold winters and hot, dry summers. Other winter-hardy bulbs, including tulips and many species of lilies, come from temperate climates of Asia, while some lilies, fritillaria, anemones, and irises are native to North America. These hardy bulbs depend on a period of cool dormancy, so when they are grown indoors or in warm regions, they have to be chilled first. For more on growing bulbs indoors, see "Indoor Gardening," page 569.

From South Africa come the tender subtropical bulbs that like cool growing temperatures but cannot survive freezes, including amaryllis, clivia, freesia, gladiolus, nerine, and agapanthus. Most of these grow and bloom in fall and winter. In cold climates, they can only be grown indoors or in greenhouses; the only area in the United States where they can be grown successfully outdoors as perennials is in coastal California.

Other tender bulbs come from the tropics of Africa, Asia, and South America—including acidanthera, alocasia, alstroemeria, caladium, colocasia, crinum, dahlia, and tuberous begonias. These summer-blooming bulbs are grown outdoors as perennials in warm, wet tropical and subtropical climates such as southern Florida. In cold climates many of them can be grown successfully outdoors, dug up in the autumn after flowering is complete, and stored indoors through the winter.

## Planting and Care

Bulbs are planted in the season prior to their flowering. Plant summer-blooming bulbs such as dahlias, cannas, gladioli, and galtonias in the late spring. Plant autumn-blooming bulbs such as colchicums and autumn-blooming crocus in the late summer, and plant winter-blooming bulbs such as eranthis and galanthus and spring-flowering bulbs such as tulips, daffodils, hyacinths, lilies, scillas, and alliums in the fall. Spring-flowering bulbs need a few weeks to establish roots before the ground freezes.

### Soil Preparation

Bulbs need excellent drainage or they may rot. Mix well-rotted compost or composted manure into the planting area. Dig fairly deeply to loosen soil and allow good root penetration. You can use a hand trowel or a special bulb-planting tool with a long T-shaped handle and steel tube or cone for making the bulb hole. Since fertilizer can burn bulbs, mix it into the soil below the planting depth of the bulb. Or don't add fertilizer to the hole at all when planting; instead, top-dress with fertilizer after planting.

### Planting Depth

The general rule is to plant at a depth three times the height of the bulb. Spacing between bulbs should also be about three times the bulbs' width. Be sure to plant bulbs with the root end—usually the wider, flatter end—facing down into the ground. Cover with soil and water well. A layer of mulch over the planting area will help prevent weeds, stabilize ground temperature, and retain moisture.

### Dividing and Propagating

Many species of bulbous plants will "naturalize" or spread on their own if they are left undisturbed in the ground. Some species should be divided after a few years. Bulbs and corms often form daughter bulbs (bulblets) or daughter corms (cormels), which you can simply cut off the parent and transplant. Often rhizomes and stem tubers only need to be cut into pieces, or divisions. The most important thing to remember is that most new growth comes from buds, so you need to make sure that each division includes a bud.

## After-Bloom Care

Unless you are treating spring-blooming bulbs as annuals, do not cut back the foliage when blooming is finished. Do cut off spent blooms, but leave the foliage to mature; it needs to work to store food in the bulbs for next year's blooms. Some gardeners like to tidy up the yellowing foliage by folding it down and tying it, but this deprives the foliage of needed sunlight. Instead, the best way to camouflage bulbs' maturing foliage is to interplant bulbs with perennials that fill in as the bulb foliage begins to die back. When the bulb foliage turns yellow and flops over, it is safe to cut it back.

## Lifting and Storing Tender Bulbs

In cold climates, tender summer-blooming bulbs have to be dug up in early autumn to protect them from frost. Wait until the foliage has begun to die back, signaling that nutrients for next year's plant are stored in the bulb. Carefully dig up the bulbs, remove any remaining foliage, and brush off the loose soil. Then store the bulbs over the winter in a cool (about 50°F to 55°F) location with good air circulation. Keep the bulbs dry, but do not allow them to become totally desiccated. You can store them in cedar chips, vermiculite, or sand, and sprinkle it very lightly with water when necessary. Check the bulbs periodically and remove and discard any diseased or rotting bulbs.

# Hardy Bulbs Grown as Perennials in Temperate Climates—Spring and Summer Blooming

### Allium, Ornamental Onion
Allium plants range from 10 to more than 40 inches high; flowers are blue, pink, yellow, white, or purple, and arise from a single point in an umbel 2 to 10 inches in diameter. Bloom periods are from April to June. Plant in a sunny spot, in well-drained soil 2 to 4 inches deep.

### Anemone, Windflower
Anemones have tubers that give rise to blooms in shades of pink, red, blue, and purple very early in the spring. Soak the tuberous root in water a few hours before planting 1 to 2 inches deep in partial shade. Mulch to protect from freezing and thawing.

### Camassia, Quamash
Quamash is one of the Native American words for this native plant of the mountains and prairies. Plants are 16 to 28 inches tall, with long narrow leaves and six-petaled, blue to white star-shaped flowers in May and June. Plant in well-drained soil in full sun, 4 inches deep and spaced 8 inches apart. After a few years divide and replant in the fall.

### Chionodoxa, Glory-of-the-Snow
This little alpine gem is one of the first flowers to bloom in spring. Its flat, star-shaped flowers are held on short stems, less than 6 inches high. The flower stalk emerges from between a pair of narrow, dark green leaves, which die down shortly after flowering. Plant in a semishaded to sunny location where it is not too hot or dry in summer.

Plant 3 inches deep and replant after three years.

## Convallaria majalis, Lily of the Valley

Very fragrant, white or sometimes pink, bell-shaped flowers grow from "pips" or shoots along a rhizome. Lily of the valley produces two or three dark green leaves up to 8 inches long and 2 to 3 inches wide, and will reach a height of 10 to 12 inches. Plant in a shady area in almost any type of soil. Lily of the valley spreads, making it a good ground cover under trees and shrubs.

## Crocosmia, Crocosmia (also called Montbretia)

The name of this perennial from South Africa is derived from Greek word *krokus,* for saffron, and *osme,* for smell. When the dried flowers are placed in warm water, they produce a scent similar to saffron. The flowers are funnel-shaped and come in a wide range of colors, from yellow, orange, and copper to red, on stems up to 5 feet tall. Bloom time is late summer to early fall. The foliage is typical of the iris family: sword-shaped and reaching up to 5 feet tall, depending on the variety. Plant corms in groups of 10 to 12, about 3 to 4 inches apart and 3 inches deep in a rich, moist soil in full sun in spring. You can extend the blooming season by planting the corms in groups two weeks apart. In areas where temperatures do not drop below 0°F, they need to be heavily mulched over the winter. In colder areas, lift corms for winter storage.

## Crocus, Crocus

Crocus derives its name from the Greek word *krokos,* or saffron—also the name for the stigmas of one species, which are used as a food colorant and flavoring. More than a hundred species of crocus—a corm—exist; blooming is in spring or fall. Some species flower several weeks or months before the silver-gray streaked foliage appears. Crocus is very easy to grow; plant in a sunny, well-drained spot about 3 inches deep and 3 to 4 inches apart.

## Fritillaria, Fritillaria

More than a hundred species of fritillaria are native to North America, Europe, Asia, and North Africa, but only a handful of these interesting bulbs are cultivated; they make excellent landscape plants. Fritillaria species range in height from 10 to 36 inches. They are best grown in sun to partial shade, in well-drained soil that dries out in summer. Plant with 1 to 4 inches of soil over the top of the bulb.

## Galanthus, Snowdrop

This popular bulb welcomes spring early, in February and March. The 6- to 8-inch plants produce 1- to 1½-inch, six-petaled white flowers. Each flower has three long outer petals and three small inner petals, with green tips. Snowdrops prefer cool conditions in partial shade. Plant 5 inches deep, 4 to 6 inches apart. Clumps can be divided every few years.

## Hyacinthus, Dutch Hyacinth

The heady fragrance of hyacinth blooms is a familiar smell of spring. The plants are 8 to 10 inches tall, with bell-shaped flowers in numerous colors in March and April. Some people develop an itchy reaction when they handle hyacinth bulbs. You can prevent this by soaking the bulbs in water for a few minutes before handling, or by wearing gloves. Plant 6 inches deep in well-drained fertile soil. After a couple of years hyacinths may not bloom and should be replaced.

## Ipheion (Triteleia) uniflorum, Spring Starflower

Spring starflower, a member of the amaryllis family, is native to the eastern temperate regions of South America and is the only one of its species that is hardy. Ipheion is often listed under *Brodiaea* or *Triteleia,* but unlike these two genera, *Ipheion* is a true bulb. This onion-scented plant has a 1- to 1½-inch, star-shaped, six-petaled blue flower in April and May, which may have a slightly soapy odor. Grow in a sunny, protected spot; plant 5 inches deep and 2 inches apart. The bulbs should not be disturbed; instead, allow them to form large clumps.

## Iris, Iris

This genus consists of more than two hundred species, and is divided into rhizomatous plants such as *Iris germanica,* the German iris, and the bulbous species of iris, which are grown as cut flowers. Plants range from 4 to 20 inches tall, and flowers are white, yellow, light to dark blue, or purple. Some species bloom in February and April; others bloom in June and July. Plant 4 to 6 inches deep in a sunny to partially shaded location. For greatest impact, plant in groups of ten or more.

## Leucojum, Snowflake

The snowflake is often confused with the snow-drop because it too has white bell-shaped flowers tinged with green, but Leucojum has a hollow flower stalk and produces leaves at the base of the plant. There are spring-, sum-mer-, and fall-blooming species. Plant in partial shade or sun; leave them undisturbed in the ground.

## Lilium, Garden Lily

Lilies come in an array of flower colors and shapes ranging from trumpets to Turk's caps to flat pendants to outward-facing varieties, generally blooming from May to late June. Plants can reach 6 feet tall. Lilies need a well-drained, evenly moist, fertile soil. In certain areas, they may need to be staked to prevent breakage in the wind. Depending on the species, plant 4 to 7 inches deep; mulch to keep roots cool. Leave bulbs in the ground to multiply and then divide every three to four years. When cutting flowers, do not remove more than one-third of the total length of the stem.

## Muscari, Grape Hyacinth

Muscari is from the Greek word *moschos,* or musk, the scent of some of the species. The flowers look like clusters of grapes and are borne on stalks 4 to 8 inches tall. Plant about 2 inches deep in a sunny, well-drained spot in early fall. Many species will send out leaves in the fall that will persist through the winter. Space about 4 inches apart.

## Narcissus, Daffodil, Jonquil

The Greek myth behind the narcissus is the story of a youth of great beauty who was so entranced with his own looks that, as he gazed at his reflection in a pool, he was trans-formed by the gods into a flower. There are more than 26 species and 300 cultivars of this very popular bulb, classified in 12 groups (see the box on page 397). Flowers range from yellow and white to salmon, on stems 4 to 12 inches tall. Narcissi will natu-ralize well if planted in a sunny spot in well-drained soil. Plant 3 to 6 inches deep, depending on the cultivar.

---

## THE CLASSIFICATION OF NARCISSI

Narcissi are made up of two parts: the trumpet, technically called the *corona*, and six flat petals that compose the *perianth*. Narcissi are classified into twelve divisions based on the flower form:

- **Trumpet** daffodils have trumpets that are the same size as the other flower parts and generally have only one flower per stem. Blooming time is April and May.
- **Large-cup** daffodils have a trumpet longer than the petals and produce one flower per stalk. They bloom in April and May.
- **Short-cupped** narcissi have a trumpet shorter than the petals. Blooming time is April and May.
- **Double-flower** narcissi have flowers with many more than the usual six petals and bloom in April and May.
- **Triandrus** narcissi have two to six flowers per stalk, with trumpets almost as long as the petals, which may be curved back. Blooming time is March and April.
- **Cyclamineus** narcissi resemble cyclamen, have a narrow trumpet with backward-pointing petals, and come in both single- and multiflowered types. Blooming time is March and April.
- **Jonquils** may have two to six flowers to a stalk; the trumpet is half as long as the petals. Blooming times range from April to June.
- **Tazetta** daffodils produce four to eight single or double flowers per stem and average 6 to 14 inches tall. Paperwhites, included in this division, are used for indoor forcing. Some species in this division are not hardy outside USDA Zones 9 and 10.
- The **Poeticus** group of narcissi has a very short, red trumpet. Blooming time is April and May.
- In **split corona** narcissi, the trumpet is split at least one-third of its length.
- The next division includes the **wild** or species daffodils.
- The final division includes the various daffodils that don't fit into the other categories.

---

## Scilla, Squill

There are 80 to 90 species of scilla, which have six-petaled flowers ranging from intense violet-blue to pink to white. Blooming periods are from April to early June. Scillas like full sun and well-drained soil. Plant in groups of 10 or more, 2 to 3 inches apart. They naturalize freely if bulbs are left undisturbed in the ground.

## Triteleia (Brodiaea) laxa, Brodiaea

The genus *Brodiaea,* which has been renamed *Triteleia* by botanists, was named for Scottish botanist James Brodie. This North American corm produces an umbel of blue or white flowers in June and July on stems 14 to 16 inches tall. It is not reliably hardy outside the Pacific Northwest or the southern states (USDA Zones 7 to 8). Plant 2 to 3 inches deep and 3 to 5 inches apart in a sunny, well-drained spot. The leaves are not attractive during flowering, so brodiaea should be planted among low-growing plants. Keep dry in the summer after the foliage dies back.

## Tulipa, Tulip

During the seventeenth century, tulips were at the center of a mass hysteria that raged throughout Europe. People were so eager to own tulips that they spent as much as $300 for a single bulb. Today, the tulip is still the

## THE CLASSIFICATION OF TULIPS

Tulips are classified into more than fifteen groups based on flower size and shape as well as time of bloom, number of petals, and various crosses:

- **Single early** tulips bloom on 8- to 12-inch stems in early spring.
- **Double early** tulips are 8 to 12 inches tall, have more than six petals, and are sometimes called *peony-type tulips*.
- **Triumph** tulips are the result of crossbreeding between single early and single late tulips. They are 10 to 16 inches tall with strong stems.
- **Single late** tulips include the Darwin and Cottage tulips, 15 to 30 inches tall, with strong stems and large flowers in an array of colors.
- **Lily-flowered** tulips are tall and stately, with reflexed or lily-shaped blooms and narrow foliage.
- **Parrot** tulips have featherlike flowers that are generally streaked; the base of the petals is usually green. They are 14 to 20 inches tall and bloom in middle to late spring. Because the stems do not tend to be strong, they should be planted in protected areas.
- **Double late** tulips or peony tulips bloom late in the season and resemble peonies. They are 12 to 16 inches tall, and are not tolerant of severe weather such as wind and rain.
- **Rembrandt** tulips, which were created by introducing various viruses to Darwin tulips to achieve different color combinations, are no longer cultivated.
- **Fringed** tulips, which have slightly fringed petals, bloom late in the season on stems from 8 to 30 inches tall.
- **Kaufmannia** tulips have foliage ranging from green to striped dark brown. The stems are very short, and the flowers open almost flat in sunlight. They are early flowering and 4 to 8 inches tall.
- **Fosteriana** tulips are 10 to 20 inches tall. The plants are vigorous, with wide foliage. They bloom early, and bulbs should be left in the ground to multiply.
- **Greigii** tulips are early blooming, with brightly colored petals that open wide in the sun. They are 8 to 12 inches tall, with purple striped leaves.
- **Botanic** tulips, or species tulips, are tulips that grow in the wild. Some are so distinctive that they are also cultivated in gardens. The bulbs, which are smaller than other tulips, should be left in the ground to multiply.

most important of all commercial bulbs: Holland exports billions of them worldwide every year. Tulips are classified in 15 groups (see the box above); more than 3,000 cultivars now exist, the result of crossing cultivars and crossbreeding species tulips with *Tulipa gesneriana*. Plant from October to late November in well-drained soil about 6 to 8 inches deep. Tulips prefer full sun, but will tolerate semishade. Protect the taller varieties from wind. Tulips will not come back after about three or four years, and need to be replanted.

## Hardy Bulbs Grown as Perennials in Temperate Climates—Autumn Blooming

*Allium thunbergii*, Ornamental Onion
This dainty plant—which has no onion odor—produces umbels of lilac flowers above

grasslike foliage in October. Plant in a sunny spot, in well-drained soil 2 to 4 inches deep.

## Colchicum, Colchicum

These are the most popular of the autumn-flowering bulbs, with large, gobletlike flowers that appear in September and October. They are easily distinguished from crocuses, since they have six stamens while crocuses have only three. The flower color ranges from white to mauve-lilac. Broad, bright-green foliage appears in the spring and lasts until mid-June, when it turns yellow and droops. Purchase bulbs in August and then, the first year, enjoy them indoors; just place them on a counter or windowsill and let them bloom. After they bloom, plant about 4 inches deep in a sunny location. Leave undisturbed, and they will spread into clumps.

## Crocus Species, Autumn-Blooming Crocus
including *C. sativus, C. goulimyi, C. speciosus*

These gems can rejuvenate the fall garden, with some species blooming as early as September and others in November and even into the winter. Flower colors range from white to purple; some have the faint fragrance of violets. Deer are partial to all crocuses, so plant them in a protected spot. Different species have different-sized bulbs; plant at a depth three times the height of the bulb. The straplike foliage appears in the spring; allow it to turn yellow before cutting back.

## *Cyclamen hederifolium,* Cyclamen

This is a woodland plant with attractive silver-marked foliage from late September to May or early June. The flowers appear before the foliage, in late August or early September. Plant in rich soil that is moist but well drained, 1 or 2 inches deep, and apply a layer of mulch. The tuber grows larger and produces more flowers each year. Cyclamen produce seeds that you can gather and sow in a protected area.

# Tender Bulbs Treated as Annuals in Temperate Climates

In addition to those described in this section, the following bulbous plants can be grown as annuals in a temperate climate: caladiums, crinum-lilies, oxalis, tuberous begonias, and tulbaghia. These are covered in "Tender Bulbs Grown as Perennials in Tropical/Subtropical Climates," page 401.

## Canna, Canna

Cannas are easy-growing, enduring classics with a long season of bloom. They come in a variety of forms and in almost every flower color and color combination imaginable, with the exception of blues, purples, and greens. Many varieties are suitable for massing in beds and borders, or for planting in small groups in mixed borders. The dwarf varieties are suitable for container plantings as well. In fall, after the foliage has been blackened by frost, cut the stems to within 6 inches of the ground and discard the tops. Lift the clumps, retaining as much of the soil mass as possible. Store the clumps in flats or other containers in a dry place away from sources of heat, at about 40°F to 50°F. In the spring, remove the soil and cut the root-stocks into sections 2 to 4 inches long. Pot these rhizomes individually and start them into growth in a greenhouse or sunny window, and then plant outdoors when the soil has warmed and all danger of frost has passed.

## Dahlia, Dahlia

There are more than 20,000 cultivars of dahlias, in a huge variety of shapes, sizes, and colors. Dahlias are grouped according to their flower forms, including single, double, anemone, collerette, water lily, ball, cactus-flowered, formal, informal, mignon, and miniature. Bloom time is midsummer until frost. Plant tubers in spring after the danger of frost is past. Dig a hole 6 inches deep. Place the tuber in the hole, and cover the tuber with 1 inch of soil. As the shoot grows, continue to add soil until the hole is filled. With the exception of the dwarf varieties, dahlias should be staked. They require full sun and a soil rich with phosphorus, potash, and organic matter. Avoid nitrogen fertilizers, since nitrogen will promote more foliage and less flowering. In cold areas, lift the tubers after the first frost when the foliage has turned black. Wash off the soil and cut the stem to about an inch from where it connects to the tubers. Cut off and discard any damaged tubers before storing in sand, vermiculite, or cedar bark mulch in a cool (40°F to 50°F) location. In the spring carefully divide the tubers, leaving a piece of stem with each tuber.

## Galtonia candicans, Summer Hyacinth

Galtonia looks more like a yucca than a hyacinth. From a rosette of leaves, a 3½-foot stalk with fifteen snow-white bell-shaped flowers rises above the faded flowers of earlier perennials, lending a freshness and strong vertical accent to the late-summer border. Grow in a sunny spot in fertile, well-drained soil. Galtonias resent drought and disturbance while growing. Hardy to 5°F with perfect drainage, they must be lifted and stored like hybrid gladiolus in areas that are colder or wet in winter.

## Gladiolus Hybrids, Grandiflora Glads

The name comes from the Latin *gladius,* for sword, referring to the leaf shape. Glads are complex hybrids that derive most of their characteristics from *Gladiolus dalenii,* which grows in tropical Africa and throughout the summer-rainfall area of South Africa. These include large flowers on tall, thick spikes, and large corms that store well. Wait for mild weather to plant glads, and choose a wind-sheltered position in full sun. Excellent drainage is critical, and early staking is recommended. Avoid high-nitrogen fertilizers. Included here for cultural reasons is a commonly available species, *Gladiolus callianthus,* previously known and still sold under the name *Acidanthera bicolor.* For growing information, see Cape Gladioli on page 405.

## Polianthes, Tuberose

Grown all over the world for its fragrant, waxy white flowers, this native of Mexico requires a warm, sunny spot and rich soil. The Aztecs used the oil from the tuberose to flavor chocolate, and today it is cultivated in France for the perfume industry. Tuberose is best started indoors and planted outdoors when temperatures are in the 60s (°F). Plant the rhizomes 3 inches deep and 4 to 5 inches apart. Lift before the first frost for winter storage.

## Watsonia, Watsonias

Similar in appearance to gladioli, watsonias are less stiff and formal. Flowers are tubular and sometimes bell-shaped, usually white to pink, orange, and red. Watsonias may be deciduous or evergreen; treat the mainly winter-growing deciduous species like gladioli, and the evergreen species like agapanthus. Deciduous types benefit from lifting and dividing every few years, while evergreen varieties are best left undisturbed for many years. Plant in sandy, well-drained soil in full sun.

## Tender Bulbs Grown as Perennials in Tropical/Subtropical Climates

In addition to those described in this section, the following bulbous plants can be grown as perennials in a tropical or subtropical climate: cannas, dahlias, gladioli, and watsonias. See "Tender Bulbs Treated as Annuals in Temperate Climates," page 399, and "Tender Bulbs Treated as Perennials in Mediterranean Climates," page 404.

### Agapanthus, Lily-of-the-Nile
Lily-of-the-Nile is attractive year-round, and is easy to grow. In late spring to early summer, globular clusters of blue flowers rise to 3 feet on bare stems above handsome strap-shaped foliage. The bold clumps of evergreen leaves have pendulous tips, giving the plant a fountainlike habit. Lily-of-the-Nile prefers moist, well-drained soil in full sun, but it is not fussy. Feed with a granular or liquid balanced fertilizer during active growth, from spring into summer. Keep slightly dry in winter. It can stand considerable crowding; when dividing becomes necessary, it is easily done with a sharp spade or knife, preferably in early spring. Watch for slugs and snails. Deciduous species exist; they should be treated like daylilies.

### Alpinia zerumbet, Shell Ginger
Shell gingers are popular ornamentals worldwide in tropical gardens; the blooms are often used in leis. Typically, these plants are tall—growing to about 12 feet—leafy-stemmed, and herbaceous. In spring and summer they produce bell-shaped flowers—white on the exterior with a pale yellow interior—in nodding racemes at the tips of the gracefully arching stems. Plant rhizomes shallowly, just covered in rich soil. Shell gingers thrive with regular fertilizing.

### Begonia x tuberhybrida, Tuberous Begonia
Tuberous begonias offer spectacular flowers in a wide range of colors, plus an exceptionally long season of bloom. An outstanding feature of tuberous begonias is their ability to produce a dazzling display of colorful flowers in the shade. They have two different growth habits: upright (up to 2 feet tall) and pendulous (grown in hanging baskets). All tuberous begonias are tender and must be protected from frost. Plant tubers in early spring, but not until night temperatures are above 62°F. Pinching upright tuberous begonias encourages branching, and is recommended for mass plantings; specimen plants are often staked and kept to one or a few stems.

### Caladium bicolor, Fancy-Leaved Caladium
This popular bulb native to Brazil is popular as a bedding plant for shade—it needs less light than most tender bulbs. It is easy to grow, and its highly decorative heart- or strap-shaped leaves come in myriad patterns of pink, red, green, and white. Its flowers are typical of the arum family and are generally insignificant. Plant bulbs about 2 to 3 inches

deep. Caladiums resent temperatures below 55°F both when growing and in dormancy.

## *Chasmanthe floribunda,* Chasmanthe

Chasmanthe is among the most shade-tolerant of the South African bulbous plants; it is closely related to crocosmia, but is winter-growing and more frost tender. A fan of sword-shaped leaves gives rise to a tall spike of hot orange to red and sometimes yellow tubular flowers for a dramatic effect. Primrose-yellow *C. floribunda* var. *duckittii* is choice, and is a classic planted with agapanthus. Chasmanthe skips a flowering season if moved or disturbed; otherwise it is very easy to grow.

## Clivia, Clivia

Clivia's 16- to 20-inch-tall flower stalk supports an umbel of trumpet-shaped bright orange to nearly red flowers, sometimes with a yellow throat. Foliage is evergreen, strap-shaped, and glossy. Clivia performs well in low to moderate light and likes regular, controlled watering in summer with minimal wetting of the leaves. Take care to keep water out of the crown of the plant to avoid rotting. Cool temperatures and sparse water is the regimen in fall; water can be increased when the flower spike is initiated with renewed growth in winter. Clivia flowers better when "hungry" than when overfed; occasional light feedings high in potassium are best. Avoid harsh sun. Clivia is usually pest-free, but watch for slugs and snails.

## Crinum, Crinum-Lily, Milk-and-Wine-Lily

There are a hundred species or more of tender bulbs in the genus *Crinum.* Their flowers are usually trumpet-shaped, although many species have flowers with long, thin petals that result in a "spidery" appearance. Flowers are generally white but sometimes pink; they arise on leafless stalks from late winter into summer and fall. Some species are evergreen, some deciduous. Plant in rich soil in a sunny location, with the tapered neck of the bulb above soil level.

## *Curcuma longa,* Turmeric

*Curcuma* produces conelike flower heads made up of bracts from which the short-lived flowers arise—individual flowers last only for a matter of hours but are borne in succession. Flower color ranges from white and yellow to pink and purple. Leaves arise from thick, fleshy rhizomes, which in some species are edible. Leaves are paddle-shaped; size varies with the species. All curcumas lose their leaves in winter. They prefer high temperatures and high humidity.

## Cyrtanthus, Ifafa Lily, Vallota

This easy-to-grow South African native has graceful tubular flowers curving downward from the top of an 8- to 12-inch stem. The flowers have flaring mouths and a sweet scent and come in pastel shades of pink, yellow, and orange. *Cyrtanthus* blooms sporadically through spring and summer, with a large flush in late fall. Plant with the bulb barely covered. Allow to dry out between waterings.

## *Eucharis x grandiflora,* Amazon Lily

Unusual large, white, very fragrant flowers have a central "cup" reminiscent of narcissus, and grow several per stem above wide, deep green, glossy leaves. This evergreen bulb, native to the South American tropics, requires higher temperatures than most tender bulbs.

## *Eucrosia bicolor,* Eucrosia

The name comes from the Greek *eu,* meaning good, and *krosos,* meaning fringe, referring to the unique bloom structure. The leaves are deciduous, shaped like paddles, and 6 to 12 inches in length. The flowers, which appear before the leaves, are tubular with six petals, and have unique long, protruding stamens. Blooms are pendulous and borne on stalks from 12 to 36 inches in height. Plant with bulbs barely covered, and leave undisturbed.

## *Globba winitii,* Globba

Globbas are primarily understory plants in rich woodlands. The flowers are borne in arching or pendent racemes. At the base of the raceme, in the place of flowers, appear small bulbils, which can be used to propagate additional plants. Globbas do best in a rich, moist, well-drained soil in bright light, but will tolerate a wide range of soil types, provided there is adequate moisture. Plants go dormant in winter as evidenced by the yellowing foliage in late fall. Plant in an area that does not stay wet in winter.

## Haemanthus, Blood Lily

These are odd but charming plants. The striking flowers of the blood lilies resemble shaving- or paintbrushes. Reddish buds on spotted, leafless stems arise after heavy watering in mid to late summer. Bud "valves" open to reveal tightly clustered golden stamens atop red filaments. Fleshy, rounded leaves emerge later, persist through winter, and wither as summer approaches. The bulb most frequently available has a flower resembling a huge red dandelion seed head, and is properly known as *Scadoxus multiflorus.* The best time to plant bulbs is early summer, when the plant is inactive. Well-drained soil is best; plant the neck of the bulb level with the soil surface. Water deeply but infrequently through winter, very sparingly in late spring, and just enough through midsummer to prevent total desiccation. Resuming watering in August should initiate bloom. Feed with a fertilizer moderately low in nitrogen and high in potassium through winter into early spring. Watch for slugs and snails.

## Hedychium, Ginger-Lily

The genus name comes from the Greek *hedys,* meaning sweet, and *chion,* meaning snow, referring to the fragrant, pure white flowers of some species. Hedychiums have fleshy, rhizomatous rootstocks from which the graceful reedlike stems arise. Species vary from 1½ to 12 feet in height; potted plants are much smaller. The 2- to 4-inch flowers are borne in large clusters at the tips of the stems and are surrounded by large bracts. Flower color ranges from pure white and pink to yellow, orange, and red. Plant the rhizomatous rootstocks hortizontally and barely cover with soil.

## Hippeastrum, Amaryllis

Most gardeners know hippeastrums by the name amaryllis. The genus *Hippeastrum* includes about seventy-five species, including the large-flowered hybrids that come in a wide range of colors. Amaryllis leaves are long and strap-shaped, anywhere from several inches long to several feet. The plants shed their leaves when they go dormant in late fall; dormancy ends in mid to late winter.

## Hymenocallis, Spider Lily, Basket Flower

The approximately thirty species of tender bulbs in the genus *Hymenocallis* can be divided into two groups: evergreen and deciduous. Flower parts of the evergreen types, known as spider-lilies, are not fused together and thus have a "spidery" appearance. The deciduous types, or basket flowers, have fused staminal cups like daffodils. Leaves are strap-shaped or broadly ovate and range in length from 12 inches to several feet, depending on the species. Flowers are usually white and arise on leafless stalks directly from the bulbs. Flowering may occur anytime from late winter to summer, again depending on the species.

## Oxalis, Oxalis, Wood Sorrel

Oxalis flowers are five-petaled and open flat, with a cupped center; colors range from white through pink, red, and yellow. Leaves are usually clover- or shamrock-shaped, sometimes needlelike, and most often grow in low, neat mounds. Some oxalis are weedy. Plant shallowly.

## *Tulbaghia violacea,* Society Garlic

This South African native is a clump-forming rhizomatous plant that blooms for a prolonged period in spring and summer, with alliumlike mauve flowers high above narrow, strap-shaped leaves. The leaves emit a faint scent of garlic. Tulbaghia is very easy to grow; avoid excessively wet conditions.

## Zantedeschia, Calla Lily

The calla lily flower is the epitome of elegance: the flower spike or *spadix* is enveloped in the silken funnel formed by the *spathe*, or leaf. The arrowhead-shaped leaves are held aloft by stems that clasp the base of the plant. Calla lilies grown in tropical and subtropical climates grow 1 to 2 feet tall and bloom mid to late summer. Plant bulbs shallowly.

## *Zephyranthes grandiflora,* Fairy-Lily

Zephyranthes are sometimes also called rain lilies, because of their habit of bursting into flower when rain follows a dry period. It blooms in late summer, with crocuslike flowers. The diminutive bulbs should be massed or used in rock gardens for best effect. Plant shallowly in well-drained soil.

## *Zingiber officinale,* Ginger

*Zingiber officinale,* the common edible ginger, is the most familiar of a genus of nearly a hundred different species. Gingers have fleshy, rhizomatous rootstocks from which graceful, reedlike stems arise. Plant height varies from 1 to 12 feet, depending on the species. The flowers are borne on stalks arising directly from the soil; they are are clustered on cone-like spikes and surrounded by large bracts. Flower color ranges from pure white and pink to yellow, orange, and red. Plant the rhizomes barely covered, in rich moist soil.

## Tender Bulbs Treated as Perennials in Mediterranean Climates

The Mediterranean climate takes its name from the lands surrounding the Mediterranean Sea (such as Spain, Italy, Greece, Israel, and the Nile delta). Other areas of the world with similar climates include southern and southwestern Australia, southwestern South Africa, and coastal Chile. In the United States, only coastal California has a Mediterranean climate, which is typified by moderate temperatures and cyclical rainfall. Summers are usually long, very warm to hot, and very dry to rainless. Winters are mild and wet; an occasional frost is possible, but freezes are very rare. Winter is the primary growing season; the onset of hot, dry weather initiates dormancy in the plants adapted to this climate. The following bulbs are all winter-growing and summer-dormant. Unless otherwise noted, they should be planted in full sun in well-drained soil. Outside of coastal California, these bulbs are best suited to winter growing in a cool greenhouse.

In addition to those described in this section, the following bulbous plants can be grown in a Mediterranean climate: clivia, eucharis, galtonia, hippeastrum, hymenocallis, tulbaghia, and watsonia. See "Bulbs Grown as Perennials in Tropical/Subtropical Climates," page 401, and "Tender Bulbs Treated as Annuals in Temperate Climates," page 399.

### *Babiana stricta,* Baboon Flower

In its native southern Africa, this corm is a favorite food of grazing troops of baboons. Compact plants up to 18 inches tall sport brilliantly colored flowers, usually bright blue but varying from cream to violet and crimson. Foliage is a heavily pleated fan of finely haired, lance-shaped leaves. Plant about 3 inches deep.

### *Boophane disticha,* Boophane

Boophane is a rare genus of bulbs from Africa cultivated for their showy flowers and unusual wavy foliage. *B. disticha,* one of the two more common species, has been used to prepare poison arrows. Bulbs of this species are large—up to 1 foot across. The foliage is thick and leathery in winter, 1 to 2 feet in length, and arranged in a single plane, like a wide-spreading fan. In the summer, the foliage is dormant and flowers from deep pink to red are produced atop 12-inch stalks in a head of up to two hundred blooms. Boophane requires superb drainage; it will not tolerate any standing water. Plant in full sun

in sandy or gravelly soil, with the upper half of the bulb exposed.

### Freesia, Freesia

Once famous for their sweet to spicy scent, freesias, like roses, have undergone extensive hybridizing. Growers have selected for large or double flowers and strong, wiry stems. If you prefer fragrance over flamboyance, choose from among the species, which are native to South Africa, rather than the hybrids. Freesias come in a multitude of colors—blue, pink, yellow, red, orange-red, and white. Plant about 3 inches deep.

### Gladiolus Species, Cape Gladioli

The Cape of Good Hope in southwestern South Africa is home to the majority of the almost two hundred species in the genus *Gladiolus.* A number of these species possess a refinement and delicate fragrance that recommends them over the grandiflora gladiolus hybrids commonly grown (see page 400). However, they require a Mediterranean climate (or a greenhouse reproduction of it), and this limits their utility in North America. Simpler hybrids known as either Nanus or Butterfly types borrow traits from alpine and summer-growing species to broaden the growing range to milder parts of Zone 7, with limited tolerance to summer-wet conditions. All require superb drainage in full sun; avoid fertilizers high in nitrogen. Avoid summer irrigation even in coastal California.

### Homeria, Cape Tulp

This is a bright and colorful South African species. Typically, just one very long leaf emerges from the corm; it resembles a 2-foot blade of grass with a gently curved tip. Salmon or yellow flowers last just a few days, but are produced in such numbers that several are open at any one time, and the bloom period lasts for weeks. The flower is six-petaled and slightly cupped, not unlike some species of tulips. Plant 3 to 4 inches deep.

### Ixia, Wand Flower, Corn-Lily

Wand flower is strangely beautiful in both color and habit: a spike of clustered flowers with dark central "eyes" is carried atop tall, thin, reedy stems. Flowers remain closed on cloudy days. The foliage is narrow, upright, and stiff—contrasting with the flower stalk, which is flexible enough that it dances with the slightest breeze, giving the plant its common name, "wand flower." Plant 2 to 3 inches deep.

### *Lachenalia aloides,* Cape Cowslip

This is a spectacular plant in both leaf and flower. Its two fleshy leaves are tuliplike and heavily blotched with maroon, which also speckles the thick flower stem. The flowers are tubular, in shades of yellow to golden orange, and hang from the stem like hyacinth flowers; they are usually marked with contrasting colors and have green, red, or purple lips. Cape cowslip likes moist conditions and shade during the hottest part of the day. Plant 3 to 4 inches deep.

### Moraea, Blue Tulp

Many of the moraeas now in cultivation are the progeny of seed distributed from the Kirstenbosch National Botanical Garden in an attempt to conserve endangered species; they are often beautiful, worthy of being grown as both horticultural and genetic treasures. There are a few evergreen species of moraeas, but most are winter-growing and summer-dormant like many South African bulbous plants. Bulb sizes vary; plant at a depth three times the height of the bulb.

### *Nerine sarniensis,* Guernsey Lily

This South African species has flowers of extraordinary beauty crowded atop a leafless stem. Pink and red forms predominate, and the undulating petals glisten and sparkle in sunlight. The stamens extend well beyond the petals on long filaments, giving the flower cluster a spidery appearance. Nerine leaves are few, long, and strap-shaped, and emerge with the flower stem but elongate after flowering is complete in autumn. Plant in soil with excellent drainage, with the upper half of the bulb exposed. Avoid nitrogen fertilizers; they can suppress blooms for years.

### *Ranunculus asiaticus,* Persian Buttercup

Ranunculus is a large genus of more than four hundred species that occur throughout the temperate world. The name of the genus comes from the Latin *rana,* or frog, referring to the fact that many species grow in moist to wet soils. Flowering is in winter-spring. Plant tubers shallowly after soaking them for a couple of hours to allow them to swell.

### *Sparaxis tricolor,* Harlequin Flower, Wand Flower

Sparaxis is easy to grow and beautiful. The dramatic flowers of *Sparaxis tricolor,* which is very rare in the wild, have attracted the interest of breeders, and many forms are offered in catalogs. The boldly colored flowers are streaked with contrasting colors and patterned with black markings and a bright yellow throat. Sparaxis requires excellent drainage in full sun.

*Veltheimia bracteata,* Winter Red-Hot
Poker

The overall effect of the drooping, tubular, rosy orange, green-tipped flowers is dramatic. The handsome foliage forms a rosette at the base of the flower stem, and the nearly ever-green plants are briefly deciduous in late summer. The flower spike follows fast upon the leaves and is long-lasting, providing color from early winter well into spring. Provide some shade during the hottest part of the day. Plant with the top of the bulb just emerging from the soil.

*Zantedeschia aethiopica,* Calla Lily

Like the calla lilies grown in tropical and sub-tropical climates, the flower spike of this white calla lily is enveloped in the funnel formed by the spathe, or leaf. The arrow-head-shaped leaves are large and the stems thick. It can grow to 6 feet.

## Further Reading

Bryan, John, ed. *Royal Horticultural Society Manual of Bulbs.* Portland, Ore.: Timber Press, 1995.

Glattstein, Judy, ed. *Gardener's World of Bulbs.* Brooklyn, N.Y.: Brooklyn Botanic Garden, 1991.

Hobbs, Jack, and Terry Hatch. *Best Bulbs for Temperate Climates.* Portland, Ore.: Timber Press, 1994.

Mathew, Brian, and Philip Swindells. *The Complete Book of Bulbs, Corms, Tubers and Rhizomes.* Pleasantville, N.Y.: Reader's Digest Association, 1994.

# Easy-Care Roses

Roses, with their infinite variety of blooms and incomparable fragrance, are some of the most beloved, and coddled, plants in the garden. Traditionally, roses have been treated as the fussiest of plants—primped, pampered, and routinely sprayed with an arsenal of chemicals to ward off insects and diseases. Recently, however, there has been a movement away from this school of thought, and gardeners are becoming increasingly aware of entire classes of roses that are easier to grow and do not require an onslaught of chemicals to keep them healthy.

The key is to find the right rose for your own climate and situation. There *is* a rose for every garden—but not every rose is ideal for every garden. From miniature roses to vigorous climbers, from species roses to the popular hybrids, there are easy-care roses that can thrive without spraying; roses that can withstand the cold winters of Zone 3 and others for the warm, humid South; roses that can take the heat in the city and others that grow in containers or scramble up walls and fences.

## Rose Classification

Until recently, roses were generally grouped into the following seven categories: hybrid teas, floribundas, grandifloras, miniature roses, climbers, old-fashioned roses, and shrub roses (which included anything that did not fit into one of the other categories). Gardeners today, inspired by the escapades of the "rose rustlers," the Heritage Rose Foundation, and the many new rose nurseries specializing in unique roses, have been expanding their horizons, and the number of categories has expanded as well.

One general rule to remember is that a modern rose is a rose that belongs to a classification (such as hybrid tea or floribunda) that has evolved since 1867. That is the universally accepted date of the first hybrid tea rose. Old garden roses (also known as antique roses, heirloom roses, old-fashioned roses, old roses, or "grandma's roses") are roses that belong to a classification that existed before 1867.

### Old Garden Roses—Fifteen Classes

- **Species.** The wild roses: the source of all other rose varieties. Producing simple, very fragrant flowers once a year in spring, they are carefree, disease-resistant, and hardy.
- **Gallicas.** Descendants of *R. gallica,* probably the oldest cultivated rose in existence in the West, these are low shrubs, suckering (producing new shoots along the roots), with large, fragrant flowers borne singly or in clusters.
- **Damasks.** Closely related to gallicas but larger and taller, damasks are the most fragrant of the old garden roses, with semidouble or double blooms. 'Autumn Damask' is the only repeat bloomer.
- **Albas.** Believed to be crosses between damask or gallica roses and *R. canina,* the albas are upright, tall, and vigorous, with sparse prickles, tough leaves, and mostly fully double blooms.
- **Centifolias.** Known as cabbage roses for their globelike flowers, centifolias may be a cross between 'Autumn Damask' and an alba. They are taller than gallicas, with drooping leaves, prickly stems, and fragrant, nodding flowers.
- **Moss roses.** "Sported" (genetically mutated) from centifolias or damasks, moss roses have drooping foliage and sepals, hips, and flower stalks covered with mossy growth that gives off a pine or resin scent when rubbed.
- **Chinas.** Ever-blooming roses first discovered in China, they were brought in the late eighteenth century to Europe, where many new cultivars were created. These are the ever-blooming ancestors of all modern, repeat-blooming roses. Some Chinas are low-growing; some have tall canes and can be treated as climbers. Their small flowers usually change from light to dark; they are borne on short stems and have a distinct, light fragrance.
- **Teas.** Tea roses are very fragrant forms of the China class, with dainty leaves and stems. The first teas were crosses between *R. chinensis* and *R. gigantea.*
- **Noisettes.** The original noisettes were a cross between a China rose and European rose, and are not very cold-hardy.
- **Bourbons.** The original Bourbon was an accidental hybrid of Chinas and 'Autumn Damask', a repeat bloomer with larger, fragrant flowers.
- **Hybrid Chinas.** First generation of crosses between Chinas and other rose varieties, developed for larger flowers.
- **Hybrid Bourbons.** First generation of crosses between Bourbons and other rose varieties, developed for larger flowers and more vigorous plants.
- **Hybrid noisettes.** First generation of crosses between noisettes and other rose varieties, developed for larger flowers.
- **Portlands.** Popular in the early nineteenth century because of their repeat-blooming flowers.
- **Hybrid perpetuals.** Hybrids of Portland roses, hybrid Chinas, gallicas, and Bourbons, these were very popular in the nineteenth century. They are very hardy, ranging from sprawling to upright in habit, with fragrant, many-petaled flowers on short stems.

### Modern Roses—Ten Classes

- **Hybrid Teas.** Very popular modern roses with large flowers on long stems. Hybrid teas bloom often, in a wide range of colors; many are fragrant.

• **Polyanthas.** Low-growing shrubs with large clusters of small flowers ("polyantha" means "many-flowered"). They grow to about 2 feet, are extremely hardy, and bloom continuously, though generally with little fragrance.

• **Floribundas.** Originally hybrids between polyanthas and hybrid teas. Floribundas (the name means "cluster-flowered") are hardy, large, shrubby bushes that bloom continuously all summer.

• **Grandifloras.** Originally crosses between hybrid teas and floribundas, with clustered flowers like the floribundas but larger, and with the long stems of hybrid teas. Grandifloras are tall, often over 6 feet, with masses of color.

• **Miniatures.** Except for the miniature cascading and climbing roses, these grow to just 10 to 18 inches, with proportionately small leaves, stems, and flowers. They are very hardy, and unlike many modern roses, most grow on their own rootstocks.

• **Climbing roses.** No roses have tendrils or other means for climbing on their own, but the climbers have tall canes that with support can be trained to grow upright. Some are everblooming; others bloom just once at the beginning of the season. Ramblers are climbing roses with very pliable canes.

• **Shrub roses.** A catchall category including robust, spreading roses that bloom fairly constantly, some with single flowers, others double.

• **Hybrid musks.** Shrub roses only distantly related to the musk rose. Can tolerate poor growing conditions, such as poor soil and shade. Many set good hips (fruits). Some hybrid musks can be trained as climbers.

• **Eglantine hybrids.** Crosses between the species eglantine rose and hybrid perpetuals, Bourbons, or other roses, these are large, arching shrubs that can reach 10 to 12 feet. They produce early leaves with a spicy apple scent, fragrant blooms borne either singly or in clusters, and bright-red hips in autumn.

• **Rugosa hybrids.** Hybrids of hybrid teas and *R. rugosa.* Some of the hardiest roses, these are very easy-care, disease-resistant roses.

## Basic Rose Care

The adage "an ounce of prevention is worth a pound of cure" holds especially true for roses. The best offense against rose pests and pathogens is defense. Buy healthy, disease-resistant roses and be diligent about hygiene and preventive maintenance. Also, learn to accept some imperfections in your roses; if you demand total perfection, your roses will be very demanding, too. Here are some basic tips for growing healthy, beautiful roses with bountiful blooms.

### The Right Rose for the Right Spot

When choosing a rose, make sure that the one you fall in love with is not particularly prone to blackspot, powdery mildew, rust, or another disease that is a problem in your area. Seek out disease-resistant varieties and regionally adapted roses that are suited to your climate and conditions. If yours is a cold climate, make sure you choose hardy roses, and plant borderline-hardy roses in a protected spot. Later in this section are lists of some of the best roses for various regions.

After making your selection, give your rose the basics it needs: sun, air circulation, and good soil. Most roses need plenty of direct sun; without it they will languish, or at least will not bloom to their full potential. Good air circulation is important, too, since it helps deter

## NINE TOP ROSE PESTS AND PATHOGENS—AND CHEMICAL-FREE TECHNIQUES FOR CONTROLLING THEM

- **Aphids.** Tiny ($\frac{1}{16}$ to $\frac{5}{16}$ inch in length), pear-shaped, typically yellow-green insects that suck sap from the stems, leaves, or roots of host plants. Clusters of feeding aphids cause stunting and deformation of leaves and stems and produce copious amounts of honeydew, a sticky, sugary liquid. Aphids are eaten by lady beetles, lacewings, and many other predators. You can knock them off your plants with jets of water. Insecticidal soaps are also effective.

- **Blackspot.** Probably the most widely distributed and serious rose disease, blackspot is a fungal disease named for the black spots that develop on upper leaf surfaces. Leaf tissue surrounding the spots turns yellow, expanding until the leaf drops. Good air circulation keeps blackspot spores from germinating. Avoid excessive watering during cloudy and humid weather. Look for resistant rose varieties. Practicing good hygiene is critical. Remove affected leaves and branches to reduce overwintering of the pathogen. You can spray susceptible plants twice a month with horticultural oil during the dormant period, or every five days with a neem oil or sulfur solution.

- **Borers.** Larvae of rose-stem girdler, rose-stem sawfly, and carpenter bees bore holes in canes, causing new growth to wilt. Control borers by cutting off the infected canes below the end of the hole and coating the cut with white craft glue.

- **Downy Mildew.** A fungal disease with many of the same symptoms as blackspot, but usually starting at the top of the bush rather than the bottom. Downy mildew attacks young leaves and stems of flowers. Infected leaves develop irregular, purple-red spots. Leaflets may turn yellow, and leaf drop can be severe. Preventive measures are the same as with blackspot. To avoid excessive moisture on the leaves (especially in cool weather), allow plenty of space among plants for good air circulation. Some gardeners are also experimenting with warm water sprays. And in cold climates, you can help control downy mildew by spraying with neem oil early in the spring when you prune your roses.

- **Japanese Beetles.** Oval-shaped, $\frac{1}{2}$-inch-long, metallic green beetles with copper-colored wings. The larva, or grub, is grayish white and $\frac{1}{2}$ to 1 inch long. The adult beetles rapidly skeletonize foliage and disfigure flowers. Handpicking is the most effective way to keep beetles off your roses. (Traps often do more harm than good by attracting large numbers of beetles to your yard.) You can keep future beetle populations in check by controlling large infestations of larvae (grubs) in your lawn with parasitic nematodes and milky spore (*Bacillus popilliae*), a bacterium that causes a lethal disease specific to Japanese beetle grubs. Neem oil spray can also be effective.

- **Powdery Mildew.** A fungus that appears as powdery white growth on the surfaces of young leaves, which become twisted and distorted. Older leaves may not be distorted, but areas may be covered with the growth of the mildew fungus. Planting resistant rose cultivars can help. Spraying with a baking soda solution (1 tablespoon of baking soda and a few drops of horticultural oil or Ivory soap to 1 gallon of water) prevents and controls powdery mildew. Prune and destroy all infected parts. In regions where winters are severe, rake fallen leaves from around the bushes at the end of the season and destroy them.

- **Rose Midges.** Very tiny white maggots that hatch from eggs laid by adult insects on new growth and under the sepals of flower buds. The maggots feed on new growth, causing deformed, blackened buds and leaves. Crisp, burned-looking foliage tips are the first sign of midge infestation; you can help control midges by examining your roses daily in the early spring and early fall, and pruning and destroying all damaged parts. Pyrethrins and beneficial nematodes can also be effective controls.

- **Spider Mites.** So small ($\frac{1}{64}$ to $\frac{1}{32}$ inch long) that they are difficult to detect without a hand lens, spider mites puncture plant tissue and feed on the sap, causing severe yellowing of leaves and premature leaf death. Prune heavily infested branches to slow the spread of these pests. Spider mites and their webbing can be washed off with jets of water. They are parasitized by commercially available predatory mites. Horticultural oils and insecticidal soaps provide some control.
- **Thrips.** Extremely tiny ($\frac{1}{50}$ to $\frac{1}{25}$ inch long) insects that creep into the flower buds and begin feeding on them. The buds may brown out and refuse to open; if they do open, the flowers may have brown edges. Thrips are eaten by lacewings, minute pirate bugs, predatory mites, and insect-eating nematodes. Populations can be monitored and in some cases controlled with sticky traps. These pests do not like wet conditions and can be drowned easily, so water sprays will keep populations down. Insecticidal soap or pyrethrins may help with serious infestations.

blackspot and other fungal diseases. Diversify your plantings as well; by planting only roses together in a location, you are inviting the pests that love roses. Instead, trying planting your roses among other plants that are less appealing to pests.

### Soil Preparation and Planting

Roses like well-drained, slightly acid soil rich in organic matter. Plant your rose in a large hole—2 feet across by 2 feet deep. Add manure in the bottom of the hole to a depth of about 6 inches, and refill the hole with a mixture of half existing soil and half compost. One way to ensure good drainage is to grow roses in raised beds at least 6 inches high.

The best time to plant roses is in the fall. In cold climates, if there is not time to plant in the fall, planting in the spring is acceptable, but in hot climates with short springs, fall-planted roses often do better than spring-planted ones, which have to struggle to catch up. When planting grafted roses in cold climates, be sure to protect the graft union (the bulge where the rootstock and graft are joined) by setting it 2 to 3 inches below the ground surface.

### Recognizing Pests and Diseases

Get to know the pests and diseases that can plague roses. If you learn to recognize the problem signs early on, you will be able to control pests and diseases with the least effort—and the fewest chemicals. The box on pages 410–11 details roses' worst enemies and how to control them.

### Good Gardening Hygiene

You can fend off many problems simply by destroying diseased foliage and flowers and cleaning up around your rosebushes in the fall. In cold climates, late fall is also the time to protect roses from harsh winters. Some roses need no special protection other than a shovelful or two of shredded leaves or bark mulch on the crown of each. With a good snow cover, hardy roses will leaf out in spring with little or no winter damage. In the coldest climates, you can wrap cold-tender roses with burlap.

## Feeding and Watering

One good feeding regime is to work in about 4 to 6 inches of compost and a generous helping of composted manure in spring, around the base of each plant. A continuous supply of small amounts of nutrients from well-dug-in compost and weak solutions of fish emulsion is better than monthly jolts of high-strength fertilizers. Applying mulch or a layer of compost in June or early July can help conserve moisture, keep the roots cool, and keep down weeds as well as provide nutrients. In cold climates especially, do not feed roses after July.

Watering roses with a drip irrigation system is a good way to help avoid fungal diseases. Barring that, avoid watering in the middle of the day, when watering is least efficient anyway. Instead, water only in the early morning so that the foliage dries before nightfall, when most fungi grow and prosper.

## Pruning Roses

All roses, with the exception of species roses and the nonrepeating old garden roses, should be pruned at the beginning of the growing season. Rosebushes that are left unpruned will be less productive and more prone to insects and diseases. The best time to prune your roses is in the early spring. This is when the buds are just about to burst open and the stems are all still clearly visible. Always use the sharpest and cleanest pruning shears that you can.

• Look for weak, small growth that will not support bloom. Such growth is often where disease begins, and so it should be removed. Healthy growth is rarely infested initially, unless it is near the weaker stems.

• As roses mature, they become crowded with dead wood; cutting out such branches constitutes the majority of pruning that you will do. Dead wood can be distinguished by an absence of buds.

• Roses need air circulation. Open up the center of the plant by removing cluttered canes. Cut out any canes that cross each other.

• As canes get older, they will get leggy and produce fewer and fewer flowers. You will recognize these canes by their discolored and cracked bark at the base. Prune them to the ground.

• The lower you prune modern shrub-type roses such as floribundas, grandifloras, polyanthas, and hybrid teas, the stronger the new growth will be. Modern shrub types that are heavily pruned will develop good basal breaks, the strong canes from the base of the plant that produce the best flowers.

• Make cuts at a 45-degree angle, about ¼ inch above swelling or newly breaking buds.

• At any time of year, you may notice that a branch suddenly dies back and all of the leaves remaining on the stem turn brown and withered, or yellow and splotchy. In other cases, you might see abnormalities in the stem called galls, formed when an insect lays its eggs within the bark. To keep the problem from spreading, cut these sections out with clean pruners, wiping the blade with disinfectant after each cut.

• Deadheading faded flowers is another important part of pruning. Cut spent blooms to just above the node of a leaf composed of five leaflets.

## Easy-Care Roses for the Northeast and Lower Midwest

(Zones 5 to 8)

'Autumn Sunset'
Shrub. Sport of 'Westerland'. Tall-growing, reaching 6 to 7 feet, with spreading habit. Repeat blooming. Bears clusters of 2-inch blooms, blends of yellow, orange, and pink. Very fragrant.

'Viking Queen'
Large-flowered climber. Lax canes, spreading habit, reaching 8 to 10 feet. Repeat bloomer. Fragrant, pink blooms with high centers are good for cutting.

'Roundelay'
Grandiflora. Upright growing, reaching 6 to 7 feet. Repeat blooming. Very fragrant dark crimson flowers open from a high pointed bud to a quartered form (as if cut into quarters) with tightly packed petals. Makes an excellent cut flower.

'Ma Perkins'
Floribunda. Bushy growth, reaching 4 to 5 feet. Repeat blooming. Clusters of salmon-pink flowers open immediately to a loose form, exposing the stamens. Light fragrance attracts honeybees.

'Cadenza'
Large-flowered climber. Stiff, upright habit, reaching 8 to 10 feet. Repeat bloomer. Bears long-stemmed clusters of velvety red flowers with light fragrance.

'Peace'
Hybrid tea. Upright growing, reaching 4 to 5 feet. Repeat-blooming flowers are yellow with hints of pink (in cooler weather, the pinker shades are more prominent). Flowers tend to be globular with densely packed petals, fragrant, on long stems.

'Compassion'
Large-flowered climber. Lax canes, spreading habit, reaching 12 to 15 feet. Repeat bloomer. Apricot-pink, high-centered blooms are fragrant and good for cutting. Produces large, orange hips.

'Fashion'
Floribunda. Bushy growth reaching 4 to 5 feet. Repeat blooming. Large, loose-petaled coral blooms in clusters. Light fragrance.

'America'
Large-flowered climber. Stiff, arching habit reaching 8 to 10 feet. Repeat bloomer. Long-stemmed, high-centered blooms are bright salmon, with strong fragrance.

'Blaze'
Large-flowered climber. Stiff, arching habit, reaching 8 to 10 feet. Repeat bloomer. Clusters of cup-shaped, lightly fragrant red blooms.

'Golden Showers'
Large-flowered climber. Lax, arching habit, reaching 8 to 10 feet. Repeat bloomer. Clusters of golden-yellow, loosely petaled blooms are very fragrant. Produces large orange hips.

'Sombreuil'
Climbing tea. Spreading, arching habit, reaching 12 to 15 feet. Repeat bloomer. Very fragrant white flowers with hints of pink and apricot. Large, globular buds open to flat, tightly petaled blooms on long stems.

'Tropicana'

Hybrid tea. Upright growth reaching 6 to 7 feet. Repeat blooming. Large, orange-salmon blooms on long stems. Strong fragrance.

'Independence'

Floribunda. Height 4 to 5 feet; bushy growth. Repeat blooming. Tight, cup-shaped orange-red blooms in clusters. Fragrant.

'Hawkeye Belle'

Shrub. Upright, stiff growth reaching 6 to 7 feet. Repeat blooming. Pale pink blooms on long stems have a slight fragrance. Good for cutting.

## Easy-Care Roses for Cold Climates

(Zones 3 to 5)

'Hansa'

Hybrid rugosa. Upright, spreading habit, medium height. Freely suckering. Repeat blooming. Very fragrant magenta blooms on short stems, often in clusters.

Dog Rose (*R. canina*)

Species. Stiff and arching habit, reaching 8 to 10 feet. Nonrepeating. Pink, five-petaled blooms are borne on short stems. Blooms are 1 to 2 inches across, with light fragrance. Produces bright orange hips.

'Rose des Peintres'

Centifolia. Spreading, lax growth reaching 3 to 4 feet high. Nonrepeating bloomer. Produces large, globular, pink blooms with tightly packed petals. The weight of the blooms pulls the canes down. Very fragrant.

*R. spinosissima altaica*

Species. Moderate height, upright habit, suckering. Nonrepeating. Very fragrant white blooms are 2 to 3 inches across; very short stems.

'Old Pink Moss'

Moss. Medium height, spreading habit, freely suckering. Pink, very double blooms are about 3 inches across. Has dense, mossy glands along pedicel. Very fragrant.

'Autumn Damask'

Damask. Medium-height shrub (to about 4 feet) with a spreading habit. Bloom repeats in the autumn. Clusters of very fragrant pink flowers with 8 to 12 petals loosely formed. One of the oldest known cultivated roses.

'Rose d'Amour'

Species hybrid. Medium height (to 4 feet), freely suckering. Nonrepeating. Pink, double-petaled blooms are fragrant. Possibly a naturally occurring hybrid of the native species, *Rosa virginiana*.

Eglantine Rose (*R. rubiginosa*)

Species. Large-growing (to 10 to 12 feet), with arching canes. Nonrepeating. Pink, five-petaled blooms on short stems. Although the bloom has little fragrance, the foliage has a strong apple scent. Produces bright orange hips.

'Carefree Beauty'

Shrub. Tall-growing, spreading habit, to 5 to 6 feet tall. Repeat bloomer. Large, lightly fragrant pink blooms are loosely formed with many petals. Produces orange hips.

### 'Rose de Rescht'

Portland. Medium height, spreading, freely suckering. Repeat blooming. Magenta, very double blooms, some in clusters, more often single stemmed. Very fragrant.

### 'Alba Maxima'

Alba. Stiff, upright habit, reaching 7 to 8 feet. Nonrepeating bloomer. Produces creamy white, flat-shaped blooms 3 to 4 inches across, with wavy petals. Very fragrant.

### 'Complicata'

Species hybrid. Rambling habit; often grows up into trees. Nonrepeating. Large, single-petaled, pink blooms are 3 to 4 inches across and have little fragrance. Produces large orange hips.

### 'Champlain'

Shrub. Medium height, spreading habit. Freely suckering. Repeat blooming. Clusters of lightly fragrant red blooms 2 to 3 inches across.

### 'Harison's Yellow'

Species hybrid. Large, spreading, and freely suckering shrub. Nonrepeating. Double, yellow blooms (1 inch across) on very short stems have a mild, unusual fragrance.

### Apothecary's Rose (R. gallica 'Officinalis')

Gallica. Moderate height, spreading growth, freely suckering. Nonrepeating. Very fragrant, red-pink, semidouble blooms are often borne in clusters. One of the oldest known cultivated roses. A striped sport of Apothecary's Rose is 'Rosa mundi' (R. gallica versicolor).

## Easy-Care Roses for the South

### (Zones 7 to 9)

### 'Tausendschön'

Rambler. Large, sprawling shrub with lax, thornless canes reaching to 15 feet. Non-repeat bloomer. Produces large clusters of wavy-petaled blooms in various shades of pink to white. No fragrance.

### 'Mutabilis'

China. Large, spreading shrub grows to 5 to 6 feet. Repeat bloomer. Single-petaled, lightly fragrant blooms are about 2 inches across and change from straw yellow to vivid scarlet before dropping off the plant.

### 'Baronne Henriette de Snoy'

Tea. Large, spreading shrub. Repeat bloomer. Fragrant, large, pointed buds open to salmon-pink with flushes of red-pink.

### 'Maman Cochet'

Tea. Medium height (to about 4 feet). Repeat blooming. Large, pointed, red-tinged buds open to porcelain pink blooms that are very full and double, with a sweet fragrance.

### 'The Fairy'

Polyantha. Spreading habit; grows to 4 feet high and wide. Repeat blooming. Produces clusters of small, multiple-petaled pink blossoms with no fragrance.

### 'Dorothy Perkins'

Rambler. Sprawling habit, 15 to 20 feet high. Nonrepeating. Produces large clusters of small, light- to medium-pink flowers with no fragrance.

**'Monsieur Tillier'**

Tea. Medium to tall, averaging about 5 feet. Repeat blooming. Densely petaled blooms are combinations of red, pink, and shades of orange. Fragrant.

**'Clotilde Soupert'**

Polyantha. Low to medium height (2 to 5 feet), with spreading habit. Repeat blooming. Very fragrant, tightly packed petals are pale pink fading to white and tend to have a cupped shape. Flowers may ball up and fail to open.

**'Cl. Mrs. Herbert Stevens'**

Climbing hybrid tea. Sprawling, vigorous plant. Repeat bloomer. Long, pointed buds open to white, high-centered, multipetaled blooms. Flowers tend to nod from weight. Fragrant.

**'Vanity'**

Hybrid musk. Large, sprawling shrub, with some canes reaching up to 15 feet. Repeat bloomer. Produces clusters of large, five-petaled red-pink blooms. Light fragrance.

**'Alister Stella Gray'**

Noisette. Large, sprawling plant. Repeat blooming. Large, multipetaled yellow flowers fade to white. Clusters of fragrant flowers.

**'Bon Silène'**

Tea. Large, spreading shrub, 4 to 5 feet high. Repeat bloomer. Fragrant, bright pink, loosely double blooms.

**'Belinda'**

Hybrid musk. Large, sprawling shrub grows to 8 to 10 feet. Repeat blooming. Produces large clusters of small, five-petaled pink blooms. No fragrance.

**'Safrano'**

Tea. Reaches 8 feet tall and wide if left unpruned. Repeat bloomer. Loose, fragrant, apricot-buff flowers.

**'Marie Van Houtte'**

Tea. Large, spreading shrub grows to 4 to 5 feet. Repeat bloomer. Large, fragrant, cream-yellow blooms are flushed with pink in cool weather.

## Easy-Care Roses for Texas and the Southwest

(Zones 7 and warmer; a few will work in Zone 6)

**'Old Blush'**

China. Medium-sized shrub (to 4 to 6 feet high). Repeat bloomer. Loose-shaped blooms are pink with darker tones, lightly fragrant.

**'Mrs. B. R. Cant'**

Tea. Grows to 8 feet; can be trained into tree form. Repeat blooming. Fragrant, deeply quartered blooms are reddish pink and silvery pink.

**'Duchesse de Brabant'**

Tea. Large, spreading shrub (to 5 to 7 feet high). Repeat blooming. Tulip-shaped pink blooms have a strong fragrance. A white sport, 'Mrs. Joseph Schwartz', is equally impressive.

**'Mrs. Dudley Cross'**

Tea. Large, spreading shrub (to 5 to 7 feet high). Repeat blooming. Fragrant blooms are a distinctive, muted yellow-pink. No thorns.

### 'Céline Forestier'

Noisette. Tall growing, with an upright habit, reaching up to 15 feet. Repeat blooming. Fragrant, quartered blooms are yellow with faint shades of apricot.

### 'Cherokee'

Species. Very vigorous, spreading, mounding shrub, reaching over 15 feet. Nonrepeat bloomer. Fragrant, large, single-petaled white flowers.

### 'Archduke Charles'

Tea. Medium-sized shrub (4 to 5 feet high). Repeat blooming. Large, high-centered blooms are rich crimson with distinct shades of pink. Fragrant.

### 'Louis Philippe'

China. Medium-sized shrub (5 to 6 feet high). Repeat blooming. Full, crimson-rose, globular blooms average 3 inches across. Light, fruity fragrance.

### 'Madame Alfred Carrière'

Noisette. Tall-growing, more upright than sprawling, reaching over 15 feet. Repeat blooming. Large, cupped blooms are creamy white with hints of pink flushes. Strong fragrance. Has been known to bloom in the winter.

### 'Lamarque'

Noisette. Tall-growing, sprawling shrub, reaching as high as 15 feet. Repeat blooming. Fragrant, ivory blooms are flat and multipetaled.

### 'Jaune Desprez'

Noisette. Tall-growing, sprawling shrub, reaching over 15 feet. Repeat blooming. Large, cupped blossoms of pink have strong flushes of yellow. Fragrant.

### 'Fortuniana'

Species hybrid. Vigorous, spreading plant with long canes reaching over 20 feet. Nonrepeat bloomer. Two-inch-wide, white, multipetaled flowers have a light fragrance.

### 'Lady Banks' Rose' *(Rosa banksiae banksiae)*

Species. Very vigorous, tall-growing, and spreading shrub reaching well over 20 feet. Nonrepeat bloomer. Small, white, multipetaled flowers. Fragrant.

### 'Mermaid'

Species hybrid. Very vigorous, sprawling, easily reaching over 20 feet with long, arching canes. Repeat blooming. Large, single-petaled yellow flowers, 4 to 5 inches across. Fruity fragrance.

### 'Souvenir de la Malmaison'

Bourbon. Medium-sized, spreading shrub, reaching 3 to 4 feet high. Repeat blooming. Light pink, very double flowers, often with a button eye or a classic quartered shape. Very fragrant.

## Easy-Care Roses for the Northwest

### (Zones 6 to 8)

### 'Constance Spry'

Shrub. Large, arching canes, reaching 7 feet high. Nonrepeat bloomer. Large, double, cupped blooms are clear pink. Strong fragrance.

### 'Cécile Brünner'

Polyantha. Reaches 2 feet tall. Repeat blooming. Small, delicate pink, double blooms have light fragrance.

'Royal Blush'

Shrub. Tall-growing, up to 6 feet. Nonrepeat bloomer. Fully double, quartered blooms of soft pink. Very fragrant. New cultivar from Germany.

'Oranges and Lemons'

Shrub. Upright, spreading habit, reaching up to 6 feet. Fully double blooms of bright orange and yellow stripes. Fragrant.

'Altissimo'

Large-flowered climber. Stiff, upright growth, reaching 6 to 9 feet. Repeat blooming. Large, five-petaled, single blooms are a rich, velvety bloodred. Light fragrance.

'Westerland'

Shrub. Tall-growing, spreading habit, reaching 6 to 8 feet high. Repeat bloomer. Ruffled blooms of apricot-copper and orange blends. Fragrant.

'L. D. Braithwaite'

Shrub. Spreading, upright growth, reaching 5 feet. Repeat bloomer. Fragrant, fully double blooms are rich crimson red.

'Sally Holmes'

Shrub. Vigorous, upright growth, reaching 8 to 10 feet. Repeat bloomer. Huge trusses of soft-apricot buds open to white single blooms. Light fragrance.

'Jeanne Lajoie'

Climbing miniature. Spreading growth with canes reaching 5 to 7 feet. Repeat blooming. A profusion of small, perfectly formed hybrid-tea-shaped blooms of marshmallow pink. No fragrance.

'Queen Margrethe'

Shrub. Medium-sized with spreading growth, reaching 3 feet high. Repeat bloomer. Fully double 3-inch blooms are pink and very fragrant.

'Charles Albanel'

Hybrid rugosa. Low, spreading growth, averaging 2 feet high. Repeat bloomer. Very fragrant, red-purple, semidouble blooms.

'Dapple Dawn'

Shrub. Reaches 5 feet tall. Repeat blooming. Large, gossamer-pink, single blooms. Fragrant.

'Thérèse Bugnet'

Hybrid rugosa. Tall, upright shrub, reaching over 7 feet. Repeat blooming. Ruffled double blooms are soft lilac-pink and fragrant.

'Dortmund'

Large-flowered climber. Reaches 7 to 10 feet tall. Repeat bloomer. Medium-sized, semidouble blooms are bright scarlet red with white centers. No fragrance. Produces beautiful display of orange hips in the fall.

'Alba Semi-plena'

Alba. Upright growth to 6 or 7 feet. Nonrepeat bloomer. Semidouble, pure white blooms with golden centers. Fragrant. Produces scarlet hips.

## Easy-Care Roses for California

### (Zones 6 to 9)

'Coquette des Blanches'

Bourbon. Medium to tall growth, upright and spreading. Repeat bloomer. White, loosely cupped blooms are flushed with pink. Fragrant.

### 'Étoile de Lyon'

Tea. Medium-sized, with spreading growth. Repeat bloomer. Large, full, quartered yellow flowers. Fragrant.

### 'Nouveau Vulcain'

Gallica. Medium height, with spreading habit. Nonrepeat bloomer. Sumptuous, maroon-purple blooms are very fragrant.

### 'Adam Messerich'

Bourbon. Large, upright plant. Repeat bloomer. Clusters of loosely petaled carmine-rose flowers. Fragrant.

### 'Blanche de Belgique'

Alba. Vigorous, upright growth, reaching to 6 feet. Nonrepeat bloomer. Full, globular, pure white flowers have a strong fragrance.

### 'Blairii No. 2'

Hybrid China. Very vigorous growth, with spreading habit. Long canes reach 8 to 10 feet. Nonrepeat bloomer. Two-toned pink, cupped, multipetaled flowers. Fragrant.

### 'Spice'

Tea. Large, spreading habit. Repeat bloomer. Flowers are very pale pink, nearly white, loosely petaled with a spicy, grapefruitlike fragrance. Discovered and named by old-rose enthusiasts in Bermuda.

### 'Clytemnestra'

Hybrid musk. Very vigorous, spreading shrub. Repeat bloomer. Small, loosely petaled apricot-pink flowers. Fragrant.

### 'Granny Grimmetts'

Hybrid perpetual. Medium-growth habit, bushy. Repeat bloomer. Crimson-mauve, fully petaled, cupped flowers, strong fragrance.

### 'Comtesse du Cayla'

China. Medium-sized, upright shrub. Repeat bloomer. Nasturtium-colored, loosely formed flowers. Fragrant.

### 'Maréchal Niel'

Noisette. Tall, vigorous climber, reaching to 15 feet. Repeat bloomer. Golden yellow, bell-shaped flowers are intensely fragrant.

### 'La Rubanée'

Gallica. Medium height, with spreading growth. Nonrepeat bloomer. Large, cupped blooms have crimson-purple tones on blush white. Very fragrant. Also known as 'Village Maid'.

### 'Marchesa Boccella'

Hybrid perpetual. Medium to tall, spreading shrub. Repeat bloomer. Tightly packed magenta-pink flowers, often with a button eye. Fragrant. Has long masqueraded as 'Jacques Cartier'.

### 'Mousseline'

Moss. Medium height, spreading habit. Repeat bloomer. White, loosely petaled blooms tinged with pink. Fragrant. Often sold as 'Alfred de Dalmas'.

### 'Blush Noisette'

Noisette. Medium to tall shrub, sometimes a climber. Soft pink, multipetaled flowers in large clusters. Fragrant.

## Easy-Care Roses for the Inner City

(Zones 6 to 9)

'Cardinal de Richelieu'
Gallica. Medium-height, spreading shrub. Nonrepeat bloomer. Unique chocolate-purple flowers, lightly fragrant.

'Comte de Chambord'
Portland. Medium-growth habit, reaches to 3 feet. Spreading shrub can be pegged for compactness. Repeat bloomer. Very fragrant, large, quartered flowers packed with deep lilac-pink petals. Color stands up well to heat.

'Mrs. Herbert Stevens'
Hybrid tea. Medium height, with bushy growth habit. Repeat bloomer. Unusual nodding, white flowers look something like pinwheels. Light fragrance.

'Rose du Roi'
Portland. Medium height, upright and spreading habit. Repeat bloomer. Fully petaled blooms have wine-red centers and slate purple outer petals. Strong fragrance.

'Gloire de Dijon'
Tea. Tall, climbing habit. Repeat bloomer. Large, globular flowers are apricot to soft yellow. Strong fragrance.

'Merveille de Lyon'
Hybrid perpetual. Medium to tall habit, with long canes reaching to 5 feet. Once-bloomer with sparse repeat. Large, cupped, white flowers. Light fragrance.

'Belle de Crécy'
Gallica. Medium-height, spreading shrub. Nonrepeat bloomer. Flat, tightly petaled, quartered flowers are deep pink tarnishing to indigo, very fragrant. Holds color well in heat. Tolerant of half-day shade.

'The Reeve'
Shrub. Upright, large-growing shrub. Repeat bloomer. Large, globular, fully petaled pink flowers. Strong fragrance.

'Vershuren'
Hybrid tea. Medium, upright growth. Repeat bloomer. Globular, multipetaled, clear pink blooms. Strong fragrance. Unique, variegated foliage.

'The Yeoman'
Shrub. Medium height, upright habit. Repeat bloomer. Loosely cupped, flat, translucent yellow-orange petals. Strong myrrh fragrance.

'Boule de Neige'
Bourbon. Graceful, spreading habit. Repeat bloomer. Fully petaled, globular, white flowers. Strong fragrance.

'Lavender Pinocchio'
Floribunda. Low height, spreading habit. Repeat bloomer. Wavy-petaled blooms with unusual russet-lavender color. Light fragrance.

'Mme. Mélanie Willermoz'
Tea. Medium height, compact, graceful habit. Repeat bloomer. Small, nodding, fully petaled, ruffled white flowers with tinges of pink. Strong, fruity fragrance.

### 'Félicité Parmentier'

Alba. Low, upright, spreading habit. Shade tolerant. Nonrepeat bloomer. Flat, multipetaled, cream-white flowers. Strong fragrance.

### 'Mme. Legras de St. Germain'

Alba. Spreading, vigorous habit, medium height. Long canes with no prickles. Shade tolerant. Nonrepeat bloomer. Very double, flat, white flowers. Strong fragrance.

## Further Reading

Dobson, Beverly R., and Peter Schneider, eds. *Combined Rose List* (annual publication). Privately published; available from Peter Schneider, P.O. Box 677, Mantua, OH 44255.

Druitt, Liz. *The Organic Rose Garden.* Dallas: Taylor Publishing, 1996.

Scanniello, Stephen, and Tania Bayard. *Climbing Roses.* New York: Prentice Hall, 1994.

Scanniello, Stephen, ed. *Easy Care Roses.* Brooklyn, N.Y.: Brooklyn Botanic Garden, 1995.

Scanniello, Stephen. *A Year of Roses.* New York: Henry Holt and Company, 1997.

Stump, D. S., ed. *Roses.* Brooklyn, N.Y.: Brooklyn Botanic Garden, 1990.

## Plants for the Water Garden

Mention water gardening and most of us automatically think of water lilies. They are fine water plants, of course—but only if the water garden in question is in a sunny location and has year-round water approximately 1 to 2 feet deep. The fact is, water lilies are not the only plants to grow in open, standing water, nor is this the only category of water in the landscape.

To create an interesting, diverse water feature in your garden, you will need to understand the spectrum of waterscapes and the different plants that inhabit them. If you are enhancing a naturally occurring waterscape, it is important to determine what you are dealing with. First, is the site sunny or shaded? Next, is the water a year-round situation, one where the water level remains fairly constant, or does it fluctuate? What appears as a pond in spring after snow melt and heavy rain might be just a muddy, marshy spot in summer. If the water is a permanent condition, what is its depth? The water depth will influence your choice of plants. Is the spot really just poorly drained, wet soil? This might be due to an impervious layer of clay or hardpan beneath the surface, or it could be the result of a hollow or swale that collects runoff from the surrounding area. Is the water still or moving? Only after these different parameters—sun or shade; deep water, shallow water, or wet soil; standing or moving water—are determined can you begin the process of plant selection.

If water is not a natural feature in your landscape, you can create it. Most water gardeners start with one pond, then add more. The commonest complaint is that the first pond was too small, never that it was too big. Most first-time pond builders focus on water lilies. But don't ignore the other plants that grow in and around ponds. When you create a water feature in your garden, include as many options as you can conveniently construct. Try to design your pond to include some shallow areas along the margin, and adjacent zones with damp soil, too.

For information on creating a natural water garden, see "Natural Gardening," page 194. For information on native wetlands, see "Ecology for Gardeners," page 159.

## Constructing a Simple Water Garden

Even if you are a novice, do-it-yourself gardener, you can have a water garden, if you know how to use a shovel. If all you want is a simple water garden on your terrace or patio, you just need a container and hose to fill it—forget the shovel.

The simplest option is an aboveground water-garden tub. Start with the familiar half whiskey barrel. If yours has drainage holes, either caulk these with aquarium-grade caulking or purchase an appropriately sized liner from a special water-garden nursery. If the barrel has no drainage holes, you can still use a liner, or prepare the barrel for direct use. Scrub the inside thoroughly with a stiff brush and plain water. Rinse well three or four times, then fill and allow the staves to swell until watertight. Remember that water is heavy, so place the container on a sturdy, level surface before filling. Empty it using a length of hose as a siphon, then fill again.

Another option is to sink the half-barrel into the ground, leaving a couple of inches protruding as a decorative edge that also helps keep litter from blowing in. Remember that the container will last longer set on a terrace or patio than sunk into soil, where the staves will decay in a few years. Either of these setups is suitable for growing water lilies and emergent wetland plants.

You can also use the half-barrel as a container for marsh, wet-meadow, or swamp plants. Caulk any bottom holes and instead drill a couple of drainage holes about halfway down the side of the container, through the widest staves. Fill with a suitably retentive soil mix.

A slightly more complicated method for creating a water garden involves the use of a pre-formed, rigid fiberglass pool. These are available in a range of shapes, from round, rectangular, or kidney-shaped to more irregular configurations, and in sizes ranging from 65 gallons to more than 500 gallons. The smaller sizes are generally 11 inches deep, and the larger ones range from 15 to 17 inches deep—all adequate depths for growing water lilies.

Choose a good location, preferably where the water garden can be easily viewed from your terrace or patio and from the living room or other important rooms in the house. Site it at the toe of a slope rather than the top, since water runs downhill and a hilltop pond looks out of place. You will need a sunny location if you intend to grow water lilies.

Basically, all you need to do to install a fiberglass pool is lay the unit on the ground, trace around it, and then dig a hole only slightly larger than is needed to hold the unit. Plan in advance where you will put the soil that you dig up, because there is going to be a lot of it. Remove any rocks or tree roots, and if possible excavate deeper than necessary in order to finish off the bottom of the hole with a layer of sand. This helps cushion the pool and makes it easier to install the pool level—which is necessary for it to look right. It is easier to push sand around to level the hole than it is to try to level soil. The pool should be installed at ground level or slightly higher to keep debris from washing in, but never below the level of the surrounding soil.

After setting the pool into the hole, use a board and level to check both lengthwise and crosswise to make sure the pool is level. Once it is in place and completely level, begin to fill it with water while backfilling around the sides with some of the stockpiled soil. Where the edge of the pool shows, it will look artificial. You can use rocks around the edges to hide the pool, but make sure they are stable enough to stand on because someone inevitably will. You can also use plants to conceal the edges. A combination of techniques looks the most natural.

Still another way to create a water garden is by excavating a hole and lining it with a flexible plastic membrane. This method is more complicated than those described above but has the advantage of allowing you to create a water garden in almost any size and shape imaginable. For complete instructions, consult one of the books listed in "Further Reading," page 429.

Once your pond is constructed, you are ready to plant it. There are several different types of water plants to choose from.

## True Aquatics

True aquatics are those plants that grow with standing water above the crown, or growing point where shoots go up and roots go down into the muck of the pond bottom. These sun-lovers include water lilies and lotus. Water lilies may be hardy, able to survive northern winters—or tender, needing mild winter temperatures. Tropical water lilies are easy to grow as spectacular annual plants. All hardy water lilies are day-blooming. They are available with white, yellow, pink, or red flowers. Tropical water lilies may be day- or night-blooming, depending on the specific cultivar. There are blue-flowered tropical water lilies, as well as white-, yellow-, pink- or red-flowered ones. Consider your specific growing conditions: All water lilies want still, warm water with at least 6 hours of direct sunlight. Some are vigorous, spreading plants that need a large pond in order to have enough room to grow well. Others are dainty enough to thrive in a half whiskey barrel full of water.

### Hardy Water Lilies

Hardy water lilies should be planted in spring or early summer, up until the beginning of August. Wait until mid-May in Zone 4, late April in Zone 5, and mid-April in Zone 6. In Zone 7 you can plant from April through August; in Zone 8, April through September. In Zone 9 you can start a month earlier, in March; in Zone 10 any time is fine. Just make sure the water temperature has reached 60°F or warmer.

Small-growing water lilies cover 1 to 6 square feet of the water's surface, moderate growers spread 6 to 12 square feet, and large, vigorous water lilies cover more than 12 square feet. All hardy water lilies will be more vigorous and cover more of the water's surface when they are planted directly in the earth of a pond bottom. Their growth will be more restrained when they are grown in submerged containers. Plant hardy water lilies in a 3½-gallon container, except for the very smallest ones, such as 'Helvola', which will do fine in a 2-gallon pot.

Water lilies want a heavy, rather mucky, clay-loam soil. Avoid manure. Plant so that the growing point is at the soil surface, and the end of the tuber is at the side of the container. Top the container with gravel to keep things tidy (otherwise, disturbance by fish will muddy the water and increase algae growth). Do not use limestone, which will affect the pH balance of the water. Use gravel that is ½ to ¾ inches in diameter; aquarium gravel is too fine. Crushed traprock or bluestone is very suitable. Be sure to rinse the gravel before using, to remove dust.

Remember that the tubers must be kept from freezing in winter. Hardy water lilies will survive under ice, provided that the water at the bottom of the pond, around the container itself, does not freeze. This can be accomplished by sinking the pot to the bottom of the pool when plants are dormant. Then, in spring when growth begins, use supports such as cement blocks or bricks so that the plants have no more than 6 to 18 inches of water above the top of the pot.

*Nymphaea odorata* is the common white-flowered water lily you might see growing wild in a natural pond. There are selections more suitable for the garden, such as *N. odorata* 'Minor', with a more refined habit of growth. Other good, white-flowered cultivars that are readily available include *N.* 'Marliac Albida' and *N. pygmaea* 'Alba', which are most suitable for container cultivation. If you prefer a hardy yellow-flowered water lily, then look for *N.* 'Marliac Chromatella', or tiny *N. pygmaea* 'Helvola'. Good red-flowered cultivars include the moderate-growing *N.* 'Marliacea Carnea', dwarf *N. pygmaea* 'Rubra', and somewhat more shade-tolerant *N.* 'James Brydon'. *N.* 'Rose Arey' is a fine, moderate-sized cultivar with pink flowers. *N.* 'Solfatare' is a smaller-growing water lily with changeable flowers, opening a lovely apricot and aging to dark coppery orange, then red-orange on the third day.

## Tropical Water Lilies

Tropical water lilies need water temperatures of 75°F or warmer. Add a month to six weeks to the times suggested for planting hardy water lilies in your zone. They are hardy year-round only in Zones 10 and 11. Place the tuber in the center of the container, fanning the roots out around it. Cover with soil, firm gently, and top with gravel. Use a 2-gallon container for tropical water lilies that will be treated as annuals. There should be no more than 6 to 18 inches of water over the container.

Day-blooming tropical water lilies open their flowers midmorning, and usually close by late afternoon. These include wisteria-blue *Nymphaea colorata*, *N.* 'Dauben' (tolerant of lower light levels), and periwinkle blue *N.* 'Charles Thomas'. 'Director George T. Moore' is a very dark blue, almost purple. *N.* 'Marian Strawn' is a small to moderately spreading, white-flowered, day-blooming water lily. 'St. Louis Gold' has numerous yellow flowers, and the moderate- to large-growing 'Yellow Dazzler' has rich yellow flowers that remain open until evening.

Night-blooming water lilies, many of which are fragrant, flower from dusk until midmorning of the following day. They are invaluable for gardeners who have day jobs. These are moderate to wide-spreading cultivars. Rose-red *N.* 'Emily Grant Hutchings' is very free flowering; 'Texas Shell Pink' is a softer, light pink.

## Lotus (Nelumbo)

Though tropical in appearance, lotus are hardy aquatics. They need full sun and several weeks of 80°F or warmer weather. Given the proper conditions, lotus are in bloom for two months in midsummer. Once established (which takes a full year), they are vigorous, even aggressive plants and can be invasive when planted directly in the soil at the bottom of a pond. Growing them in containers, with 2 to 4 inches of water over the soil, will keep them in check. Because lotus are vigorous growers, they need larger containers than water lilies. Choose a pot 12 inches in diameter for dwarf cultivars, and 16 inches or greater for the larger ones. There are several small-growing cultivars especially suitable for tub cultivation, including dwarf white *Nelumbo nucifera* 'Shirokunshi' and 'Baby Doll', pink and cream 'Chawan Basu', and double-flowered rose-pink 'Momo Botan'.

## Submerged Oxygenating Plants

This is another group of aquatic plants that also root in the soil beneath the surface. Their function is practical rather than aesthetic; these plants do not necessarily reach the surface of the water, nor do they have showy flowers. Like the plants commonly grown in aquariums, submerged oxygenating plants are important for the overall health of your pond or container water garden. They take up carbon dioxide and provide oxygen, and their uptake of nutrients dissolved in the water helps reduce the growth of algae. In addition, submerged oxygenating plants provide a spawning place where fishes lay their eggs and where young fish can hide from predators.

Plant choice should be based on the size of your pond. Plant in smaller pots than necessary for water lilies, about a gallon in size. Use the same heavy loam and top with gravel. Use smaller stone than for water lilies or lotus—¼ inch is fine. Place the pots directly on the bottom of your pool. Submergent plants can have from 6 to 30 inches of water over the container. Most submergent plants are easy to propagate, either by separating naturally occurring offsets or potting stem sections.

*Egeria* (*Elodea*) *densa* is commonly called anacharis, water weed, or water thyme. It has multibranched stems densely covered with whorls of inch-long, dark green, curved leaves. The brittle stems are easily broken, and the fragments form floating, unrooted mats. These pieces readily root if more plants are needed. A close relative, *Elodea canadensis* or Canadian pond weed, has been somewhat invasive where introduced in Europe. Both of these vigorous plants are better in cooler regions where water temperature is unlikely to exceed 73°F.

Fanwort, *Cabomba caroliniana,* is a subtropical plant native to the southeastern United States. The slender branched stems are thickly covered with whorls of bright green, fanlike, finely dissected leaves. Popular for aquarium use, fanwort needs mild winters to thrive. There are look-alike relatives, one of which, *C. aquatica,* has become a rampant pest prohibited in certain areas. Thus it is best to confine their use to container water gardens.

*Myriophyllum heterophyllum* is called milfoil or parrot's feather for the plumelike appearance of its long stems densely covered with finely divided leaves. This hardy species develops longer leaves in cooler water (below 70°F). It can be invasive, and should be grown only where it cannot escape into the wild. Also called parrot's feather, *M. aquaticum* is a somewhat tender, look-alike relative. This species will even root in the muddy soil at the water's edge. Hardy winters can result in damage.

Arrowhead, swamp potato, and dwarf sagittaria are all common names for *Sagittaria natans.* This native North American species is found from Maine to Florida. The dark green, grasslike leaves make an attractive contrast to the plumes of parrot's feather. It multiplies from offsets, the young plants appearing on short runners from the parent plant. Its tolerance of brackish conditions makes it suitable for natural ponds with poor water quality.

Eelgrass or tape grass is the descriptive common name given to *Vallisneria spiralis.* This easy-to-cultivate species has ribbonlike leaves with rounded tips. A tropical plant native to North Africa and southern Europe, this species of eel grass is hardy only in Zones 10 and 11.

Curly pondweed, *Potamogeton crispus,* is an excellent oxygenating plant for large ponds. The stems can grow over 12 feet long. The narrow, rather transparent, wavy-edged leaves are attached directly to the stem and are quite decorative. It is naturalized over much of the United States, growing in polluted streams and muddy ponds as readily as in clean water. A vigorous plant, it will crowd out less robust neighbors. Use it only in contained water gardens.

## Floating Plants

The leaves of floating plants appear above the surface of the water. They flourish with their roots just dangling in the water, and need no soil. Their roots act as spawning mats and nurseries for fish. Because they absorb nutrients from the water, floating plants reduce the levels available to algae. Until the water lilies are well established and have leaves to serve this purpose, floating plants help shade the surface of the water, which also reduces algae growth. Most floating plants are tropical in origin, and will need to be replaced annually. Some are invasive plants prohibited in certain areas.

Water hyacinth, *Eichhornia crassipes,* is a beautiful plant with spikes of soft blue to lilac flowers, each with a showy yellow eye. The long purple-black roots are a potential problem. In Florida, where water hyacinth is hardy, its explosively rapid vegetative growth creates tangled masses that literally clog the inland waterways and snarl boat propellers. In fact, the plant is banned from interstate sale for this reason. It is not a problem in colder regions where the plants cannot survive the winters.

Water lettuce, *Pistia stratiotes,* is another potentially pestiferous plant in Zones 10 and 11. The velvety leaves are a pale apple green above, even paler on the underside. The clustered leaves make beautiful rosettes, which multiply into large masses as new plantlets form on short stolons. Again, although this tender plant can be a nuisance in tropical and subtropical areas, it will die in regions with cold winters.

Frogbit, *Hydrocharis morsus-ranae,* looks rather like a small water lily. Shiny green, kidney-shaped leaves make a rosette that floats on the water's surface. In summer, plants bear small, yellow-centered white flowers. In autumn the plants form small tuberlike structures that drop to the bottom of the pond. They overwinter in this fashion, then rise to the surface in spring to begin the growth cycle once again.

Water soldier or water aloe, *Stratiotes aloides,* has the same curious habit. In the summer the plant, which looks like succulent aloe, sails on the water's surface. After flowering it sinks below the surface and produces numerous new shoots. These rise to the surface later in the summer, form tuberlike resting structures, and sink to the pond bottom for the winter. It is prohibited in some regions.

Duckweed, *Lemna minor,* is a very small plant with light green leaves about the size and shape of the cutout made by a paper punch. The tiny size belies their fecundity. If you have ever seen a flat green mat over a pond, odds are it is a carpet of duckweed. Plants can spread by getting attached to ducks' breast feathers or birds' feet. Duckweed is offered for sale in every water garden catalog, but be cautious about adding it to your water garden.

## Emergent Plants

Emergents or marginal plants grow in shallow water no more than 2 to 6 inches deep. Many of these plants have wide-spreading roots. In nature they serve to stabilize the banks of a pond. This can be a problem in the confines of an ornamental pool or container water garden, so it is helpful if their roots are restricted in a container. These plants help integrate a pool into the landscape, providing a more natural appearance. Use a minimum 1-gallon pot size, larger as necessary depending on the vigor of the specific plant. Remember that these plants grow in shallow water. Either create a shelf along the margin of the pool to accommodate them, or use cement blocks or bricks to raise the pots to within 3 to 6 inches of the surface.

Emergent plants may be cold-tolerant and winter-hardy. It is safest to sink their pots to the bottom of the pool for the winter. Others are tender tropical plants, hardy only in Zone 9 or warmer; these need indoor storage in order to carry them over from year to year.

There is more diversity in the appearance of emergent plants than of water lilies and lotus. Thus you can make your selections with leaf and flower form in mind. Cattails, sweet flag, and iris all have grassy or swordlike leaves. Cannas have a blocky leaf shape, while ferns have a lacy pattern. Astilbe also has a lacy pattern. Ferns never flower, while astilbes have nice plumelike flower spikes in summer when the iris have finished flowering.

## Hardy Emergent Plants

Cattails, *Typha* species, are as much a plant of water as water lilies. Most, such as cattail, *T. latifolia,* and narrow-leaved cattail, *T. angustifolia,* are vigorous plants best suited to large natural areas rather than the confines of a small artificial pond or container water garden. There is a dwarf species from Europe, *T. minima,* which grows no more than 12 to 18 inches tall, with narrow leaves, a miniaturized version of

the velvety brown cattails of its larger relatives with a dainty habit that is suitable for the smallest water garden.

Sweet flag, *Acorus calamus,* has a long, narrow leaf that looks like that of a cattail. It grows 2 to 3 feet tall, and is easier to keep within bounds than cattails, making it a better choice for limited space. Flowers are inconspicuous, small, green, and clustered in a spikelike structure that emerges near the base of the leaf. 'Variegata' has foliage with attractive, creamy ivory markings—very handsome when reflected in shallow water.

Yellow flag, *Iris pseudacorus,* is native to Eurasia and naturalized in the United States where it grows wild in ditches, swales, and other wet places—so it is best used in contained water gardens, where it is less likely to escape into the wild. The bluish green, swordlike leaves grow 3 feet tall. Plants grow at the edges of ponds, in sites with saturated soil or even under more typical garden conditions of moist but well-drained soil. In late spring or early summer the plants have attractive yellow flowers. There are several cultivars: 'Bastardii' has paler, creamy yellow flowers and is not so vigorous; 'Flore Plena' is also less vigorous and has double yellow flowers; and 'Variegata' has leaves that are variegated only in spring, gradually turning all green as summer arrives.

Blue flag, *Iris versicolor,* is an American native with leaves 2 feet tall and slate-blue flowers marked with a cream-and-yellow blotch at the base of the lower petals. Plants grow in anything from permanently moist soil to up to 4 inches of water.

*Iris laevigata* is native to Japan and eastern Siberia. Plants grow 2 to 3 feet tall, with smooth, green, swordlike leaves. Tolerant of shallow water 3 to 4 inches deep, this iris will also grow in permanently wet soil, but dry conditions are harmful. Blue flowers appear in early summer. There are a number of superb cultivars, with flowers from white, white streaked with purplish red, and white mottled with dark blue, to deep violet or cobalt blue. One of the most elegant varieties is 'Variegata', which has soft lavender-blue flowers and attractive cream, white, and green variegated foliage.

Consider true grasses, sedges, and rushes such as manna grass, *Glyceria maxima* var. *variegata;* sedge, *Carex pendula;* fringed sedge, *Carex crinita;* tussock sedge, *Carex stricta;* rush, *Luzula sylvatica;* and variegated rush, *Scirpus tabernaemontanus* 'Zebrinus'.

Ferns have attractive leaves. They do not grow in the water. Rather, plants are on a raised mound or tussock that keeps the crown (the growing point) of the plant out of the water but allows the roots access to constant moisture. Hardy ferns to consider for your water garden include lady fern, *Athyrium filix-femina;* ostrich fern, *Matteuccia struthiopteris;* sensitive fern, *Onoclea sensibilis;* cinnamon fern, *Osmunda cinnamomea;* interrupted fern, *Osmunda claytoniana;* royal fern, *Osmunda regalis;* and the somewhat tender Virginia chain fern, *Woodwardia virginica.*

Showy, hardy flowering plants for the water's edge include marsh marigold, *Caltha palustris;* water forget-me-not, *Myosotis palustris;* golden club or never-wet, *Orontium aquaticum;* arrow arum, *Peltandra virginica;* pickerel rush, *Pontederia cordata;* and arrowhead, *Sagittaria latifolia.*

### Tender Emergent Plants

These plants need mild winters in order to survive. Their lush summer growth adds a note of tropical exuberance to the water garden. Along with summer heat and rich soil, an adequately large container is necessary to support their luxuriant growth. The ones that go dormant in winter, such as canna or elephant ear, are relatively easy to store. Others, such as papyrus, remain in growth. They require warmth, light, and moisture if they are to survive. Consider canna, *Canna* cultivars; water canna, *Thalia dealbata;* dwarf cypress, elephant ear, *Colocasia esculenta;* violet-stemmed taro, *Colocasia esculenta* var. *fontanesii;* or variegated taro, *Alocasia amazonica* 'Hilo Beauty' for the special interest they can provide alone.

### Plants for Moist Soil

Up on the bank around the edges of the pond, the soil is constantly moist but there is no standing water over the crown of the plants. Think about using hardy plants that prefer these conditions, such as goat's beard, *Aruncus dioicus;* swamp milkweed, *Asclepias incarnata;* astilbe, *Astilbe* cultivars; pink turtlehead, *Chelone lyonii;* white turtlehead, *Chelone glabra;* Joe-Pye weed, *Eupatorium purpureum;* queen of the meadow, *Filipendula ulmaria;* swamp rose mallow, *Hibiscus moscheutos;* hosta, *Hosta* cultivars; *Houttuynia cordata; Ligularia* 'Desdemona', 'Othello', 'The Rocket'; cardinal flower, *Lobelia cardinalis;* blue lobelia, *Lobelia siphilitica;* gooseneck loosestrife, *Lysimachia clethroides;* bee balm, *Monarda didyma;* Japanese primrose, *Primula japonica;* ornamental rhubarb, *Rheum palmatum; Rodgersia aesculifolia;* and New York ironweed, *Vernonia noveboracensis.*

The one plant you should not use is purple loosestrife, *Lythrum salicaria.* This aggressively invasive nonnative plant crowds out native species, is hard to eradicate, and is prohibited from cultivation in many states.

## Woody Plants for Wet Places

Water gardeners are not limited to herbaceous plants. There are trees and shrubs that grow at the water's edge, in sites that are periodically flooded or else have constantly moist soils. Site woody plants so that they do not shade the water's surface; after all, water lilies need full sun if they are to flower well. Anticipating the work of cleaning leaves from a pool in autumn may also influence your selection.

Some choice trees to consider are red maple, *Acer rubrum,* with good fall color; shadblow, *Amelanchier canadensis,* with spring flowers, summer fruit attractive to birds, and good fall color; river birch, *Betula nigra,* with its handsome peeling bark; the unusual deciduous conifer, larch, or tamarack, *Larix laricina,* whose needles turn a rich foxy red before dropping in autumn; sweet gum, *Liquidambar styraciflua,* with superb fall color; sweetbay magnolia, *Magnolia virginiana,* with deliciously fragrant flowers; black gum, *Nyssa sylvatica,* with good fall color; and the familiar pin oak, *Quercus palustris.*

Among the outstanding shrubs for moist soils are red chokeberry, *Aronia arbutifolia,* especially the excellent cultivar 'Brilliantissima' with its intense fall color and attractive fruits; shade-tolerant, fragrant, summer-blooming summersweet, *Clethra alnifolia;* blue-berried silky dogwood, *Cornus amomum,* and red osier dogwood, *C. stolonifera,* with its handsome red twigs in winter; shade-tolerant, evergreen inkberry, *Ilex glabra,* and winterberry holly, *I. verticillata,* with its brilliant red berries; summer-blooming, fragrant-flowered, shade-tolerant swamp azalea, *Rhododendron viscosum,* or the tall, shade-tolerant, evergreen *Rhododendron maximum;* the familiar pussy willow, *Salix discolor;* and blue-berried arrowwood viburnum, *Viburnum dentatum,* and cranberry bush viburnum, *Viburnum trilobum,* with its red fruit, both attractive to birds.

## Further Reading

Burrell, C. Colston, ed. *The Natural Water Garden.* Brooklyn, N.Y.: Brooklyn Botanic Garden, 1997.

Glattstein, Judy. *Waterscaping: Plants and Ideas for Natural and Created Water Gardens.* Pownal, Vt.: Storey Communications, 1994.

Schmidlin, Wilfred V., ed. *Water Gardening.* Brooklyn, N.Y.: Brooklyn Botanic Garden, 1983.

Skinner, Archie, and David Arscott. *The Stream Garden.* London: Ward Lock, 1994. (Distributed in the U.S. by Sterling Publishing Company.)

Slocum, Perry D., and Peter Robinson with Frances Perry. *Water Gardening, Water Lilies and Lotuses.* Portland, Ore.: Timber Press, 1996.

Swindell, Philip, and David Mason. *The Complete Book of the Water Garden.* Woodstock, N.Y.: The Overlook Press, 1990.

Thunhorst, Gwendolyn A. *Wetland Planting Guide for the Northeastern United States.* Environmental Concerns (P.O. Box P, 210 West Chew Avenue, St. Michaels, MD 21663), 1993.

# GARDENING TECHNIQUES

## Soil

Animal, vegetable, and mineral—soil is all three. Soil is composed of mineral particles, organic matter, water, and air. This mix is home to a dynamic collection of animal and plant organisms and microorganisms. When you scoop up a fistful of healthy soil, you hold billions of these microscopic organisms in your hand.

Soil mechanically supports plant roots and provides them with access to necessary nutrients, water, and oxygen. Soil's texture and structure essentially are responsible for how readily water (which carries dissolved nutrients) and air move through it. Its chemical properties, including pH, determine the availability of those nutrients to plant roots.

Soil exists in the upper portion of the Earth's crust. Here, boulders, rocks, stones, pebbles, sand, silt, and clay are in a constant state of flux with organic matter. The mineral nutrition provided by soil depends on what kind of rock it derives from. At the top of this crust is topsoil—where solid rock has been refined by millennia of freezing, thawing, and eroding weather coupled with the actions of unfathomable numbers of soil organisms and microorganisms on both the rock and once-living matter. Below this is the subsoil, less affected by climate and microorganisms and not nearly as hospitable to plant roots. Supporting the subsoil is bedrock (see the soil profile on page 431).

The depth of topsoil is important because it sets limits on how deep most plant roots can penetrate. The depth of topsoil varies considerably across the United States but generally is at least 6 inches. In a forested valley floor or on a floodplain, it can be much thicker. Heavy wind and water erosion can scrape this layer thin at exposed high elevations. And irresponsible development can do the same damage, or worse. On some new home sites, for example, the topsoil is removed (and sold) or the subsoil is dug out from foundations and carelessly spread atop the topsoil. Heavy equipment contributes to soil compaction.

Soils vary to a great extent regionally and locally—even across just one small backyard (see "Gardener's Atlas," page 14). There are plants that are adapted to and thrive in almost every type of soil. Of course, sun, shade, temperature, precipitation, and the topography and drainage of a garden are other variables that will affect the health and well-being of the plants. An understanding of what your soil offers and how plants respond to the various other conditions on your property will enable you to select specimens that grow successfully in your garden and meet your needs.

## The Components of Soil

About half the volume of an "ideal" soil is rock-based, another 5 percent or so is organic matter, and roughly one-quarter is made up of water and another one-quarter of air. The composition of soil never remains static. At any given time, temperatures and wind and water erosion are shaping the mineral content; the quantity of water and air may be higher or lower depending on levels of precipitation; and the amount of organic matter, renewed continuously as living organisms work to decompose dead plants and animals, is in flux.

## Minerals

Mineral particles, about half of an "ideal" soil, include sand, the largest and most visible particles; silt, finer and dustlike; and clay—the smallest particles, so small they are microscopic. Very sandy soils feel gritty; silty soils feel smooth; and clayey soils tend to be sticky.

## Organic Matter

Only about 5 percent or less of most soils is organic matter. *Organic matter* is a broad term that includes living and once-living plants and animals in varying states of decomposition. It is vital to a soil's makeup and well-being. Organic matter is fuel for the macro- and microorganisms that inhabit soil. Worms, beetles, and other macroorganisms digest tiny portions of organic matter (leaves, stems, and roots as well as composts and manures added by gardeners). Microorganisms, including bacteria and fungi, further decompose the residues. In the process, nutrients are steadily released in a form that can be absorbed by the roots of growing plants. Eventually, organic matter is chemically transformed into a dark brown or black amorphous substance, called *humus*; cool or warm temperatures as well as moisture and aeration affect the speed of decay. Humus replenishes nutrients and helps bond soil particles so that soggy soils become less clogged and sandy soils retain more water.

In woodlands and other natural habitats where the activities of plants and animals are undisturbed, organic matter in soils is renewed naturally. If garden soil is to remain in good condition, it, too, must have renewed supplies

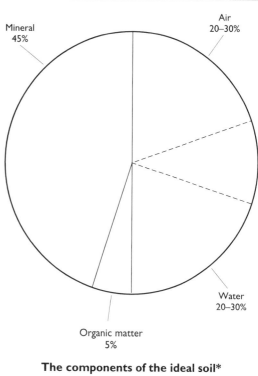

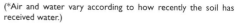

**The components of the ideal soil***

(*Air and water vary according to how recently the soil has received water.)

of organic matter. Leaf mold and compost are two excellent sources of organic matter.

## Water

Plants are composed of nearly 90 percent water. Ideally, about one-quarter of soil is water. All the mineral nutrients plants derive from soil come through their roots. In order to be absorbed, these nutrients must be suspended in solution.

Water affects soil temperature. A poorly draining soil does not warm as quickly as one that is well drained—an important consideration for spring planting.

## RENEWING THE SOIL AROUND ESTABLISHED PLANTINGS

The easiest time to add organic matter to the soil is when you are creating a new garden or planting bed. However, it is possible—and important—to ensure that established plantings receive a steady supply of organic material that can be converted into humus. Here are a few suggestions to accomplish this while disturbing the plants as little as possible.

• If possible, create zones of natural habitats in your garden—a pocket woodland, for example, or meadow border. Allow the annual accumulation of fallen leaves to remain around the plants, forming a naturally renewed mulch. (Remove only diseased plant debris.)

• In lawn areas, allow nitrogen-rich grass clippings to decompose where they fall.

• Cover the soil around shrubs and trees with an organic mulch. Over time, rainfall and the actions of soil organisms will incorporate the organic matter into the soil as it decomposes. Use finished compost for a more natural-looking mulch.

## Air

The oxygen in air is essential to plants and must be absorbed through plant roots. A healthy soil contains about as much air as it does water—roughly one-quarter. A well-aerated soil is an ideal environment for the microorganisms that break down organic matter and release nutrients back into the soil.

The ratio of water to air in a healthy soil varies each time it rains or the soil is watered. In a water-saturated soil, oxygen is unavailable to plant roots.

## Organisms

An abundance of soil microorganisms—too tiny to see without magnification—is necessary for a healthy soil. Fungi and bacteria, by far the most numerous, are vital to the decomposition of dead matter in soil: they convert organic matter into humus. However, healthy soils also contain many larger organisms at work. Earthworms, in addition to converting organic matter into food for microorganisms, tunnel up, down, and sideways through soil, aerating and loosening it. The number of earthworms is used by many gardeners to determine soil fertility: the more the better. Burrowing insects, such as pillbugs and ants, also create tunnels that increase air and water penetration.

## Soil Texture

The mix of sand, silt, and clay particles in your soil determines its texture. A soil that contains roughly equal portions of sand, silt, and clay is called a *loam*. This is considered the gardener's "ideal." It feels rich and crumbly. It also is generally rich in humus, giving it good water and nutrient retention. It has good tilth (workability) and is friable (crumbles easily); in other words, it is good for cultivation.

There are three major soil textures: sand, loam, and clay. However, these are extremes; a multitude of variations exist in between.

Sand particles, easily visible, run from fine to coarse. Soils with a high sand content feel gritty, tend to be dry, and generally are light in color. Drainage is not a problem but water retention is. When water drains through soil too quickly, it leaches valuable nutrients. Moderate proportions of sand are advantageous—they provide excellent drainage and good aeration, and increase the soil's capacity to warm up quickly in spring.

## THE TEXTURE OF VARIOUS TYPES OF SOILS

The following types of soil are listed according to texture, from the coarsest down to the finest:

### COARSE

Sandy soil
Loamy sand

### MODERATELY COARSE

Sandy loam
Fine sandy loam

### MEDIUM

Very fine loam
Silty loam

### MODERATELY FINE

Sandy clay loam
Silty clay loam
Clay loam

### FINE

Sandy clay
Silty clay
Clay soil

Clay soil is dense and heavy. The particles are so microscopic that there is usually little space between them for good water and air circulation; plant roots can literally drown or suffocate; and the surfeit of water makes clay slow to warm in spring. Clay, often red, gray, or dark brown in color, feels slippery. It is easily molded when wet, but it can dry to a concretelike hardness. The good qualities of clay (in moderation) are its ability to retain water and minerals.

Loam combines the advantageous characteristics of sand and clay soils; it drains well and has an excellent capacity for holding water and nutrients.

## Soil Structure

In a soil with good structure, air and water can move freely and plant roots can penetrate easily. The way soil particles—clay, silt, and sand as well as organic matter—bind together, or aggregate, determines structure.

When soil has been compacted by too much foot traffic or other surface pressure, the soil structure is damaged. The most effective way to improve the structure of a soil is by adding organic matter. When added to clay soils, it aids drainage by binding microscopic clay particles together to form larger, stable aggregates so that the soil becomes more porous and drains better. When added to sandy soils, humus—the end product of the decomposition of organic matter, which holds from two to four times its weight in water—enables the soil to retain more water.

## Soil pH

Soil pH, the measure of its acidity or alkalinity, determines the availability of nutrients to plants and the degree of biological activity of fungi, bacteria, and other soil microorganisms.

The term pH stands for potential hydrogen and measures the amount and type of hydrogen ions in the soil solution—the soil water and everything in it. The pH scale runs from 0 to 14; 7 is neutral; numbers below this indicate an acid soil and those above indicate an alkaline soil. Generally, soil pH ranges between a quite acidic measure of 4 and a strongly alkaline measure of 9. The majority of ornamental garden

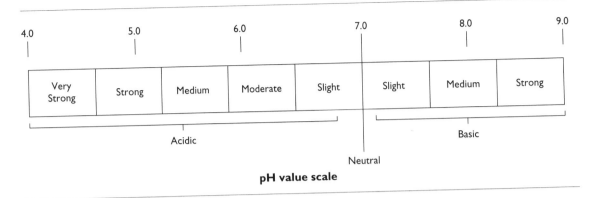

**pH value scale**

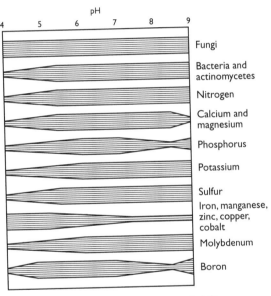

**pH effect on nutrient availability
and microorganism activity**

*Shaded areas represent zones of nutrient availability and microorganism activity. The majority of nutrients are available between a pH of 5.5 and 6.5.*

plants fit comfortably in a pH somewhere between 6.0 and 7.0.

Soil tends to be more acidic in regions like the eastern United States with high levels of precipitation. Arid regions in the western United States tend to have more alkaline soils

(see "Gardener's Atlas," page 14). In addition to natural factors, human actions can affect pH. Lime leaching from buried demolition debris or from an old building foundation is a common cause of alkaline soil. Certain fertilizers, especially those containing ammonium as the nitrogen source (ammonium sulfate, ammonium nitrate, urea, and ammonium phosphate), on the other hand, increase the acidity of soils.

## Changing Soil pH

Always test the soil before you decide to make any changes in pH. Choosing plants—nonnative as well as native—that fit the soil's environmental profile and pH will make gardening not only less disruptive ecologically but also easier. Areas with low-pH, acidic soil may be ideal for collections of heaths and heathers, blueberries, rhododendrons, or other acid-loving plants. However, if you plan to grow vegetables, a typical perennial border, or a lawn—which require a sweeter, less acidic pH—in such a soil, you will need to bring up the pH level. Have your soil tested professionally and follow the recommended amounts when adjusting pH.

Raising or lowering soil pH is a complicated process and can take several years to take effect.

Keep in mind that changing just one point on the scale is equivalent to a tenfold change in the actual acidity or alkalinity of the soil. What is more, every particle in soil has sites where hydrogen and other chemical ions can be attached, detached, or exchanged. The size of soil particles affects the quantity of soil conditioner you will need to effectively alter pH. Generally, more is required to change a clay soil (dense with many microscopic particles) than a sandy one (with fewer, larger particles).

### To Raise pH

Lime and wood ashes both raise pH. The most widely recommended forms of lime are ground limestone (calcium carbonate) and dolomitic limestone (which also adds magnesium to the soil). Both are relatively inexpensive and easy and safe to use with some precautions. The smaller the particles of the lime you apply, the more quickly they will react and speed pH changes; wear a mask so as not to inhale the fine powdery dust of pulverized limestone. Oyster-shell limestone is available in some regions as an alternative to rock-based limestones. Like lime, oyster-shell limestone is high in calcium carbonate (over 90 percent) and also provides other nutrients and micronutrients; in addition, its variable particle size provides both immediate and long-term effects. Wood ashes (which can contain up to 70 percent calcium carbonate) raise pH; they are also a good source of potassium. Hardwood ash tends to be higher in both than softwood. Ash can be quite fast acting due to its small particle size. Add small amounts (no more than 2½ pounds per 100 square feet), and test yearly.

### To Lower pH

Elemental sulfur, sometimes called flowers of sulfur, is the best form of sulfur for lowering pH. Aluminum sulfate also lowers pH, but can cause aluminum toxicity in plants. Other plant-derived conditioners, such as composted oak leaves or pine needles, will reduce soil pH, with a slower, but more long lasting effect.

### How to Apply Soil Conditioners

You can sprinkle lime or sulfur on the soil surface around existing plants—but not in direct contact with stems or leaves. Both are dusty and hence should not be applied in windy or wet weather; wear a mask to protect your lungs from the fine particles. Lime and sulfur may continue to alter pH for one or more seasons when applied in this manner. Working them into the soil will speed their reaction, but is not otherwise necessary. Test yearly to verify the results of your efforts to modify soil pH.

## Soil Analysis

To determine which plants are most appropriate for your garden, you will need to know not only what the pH of your soil is, but also its nutrient content and structure. Some plants, such as vegetables and roses, require rich, fertile soils, and you may have to amend your soils accordingly. A soil test will tell you which amendments are necessary and in what amounts. You can do this yourself, but if you intend to change the pH or add many conditioners, testing by a professional lab is recommended. Be sure to supply accurate information to the lab about the kinds of plants you intend to grow.

### Some Simple Ways to Test the Soil Yourself

The following are a few quick and easy ways to learn more about your soil:

## The soil triangle

*The soil triangle is designed to help you determine the textural class of your soil. Locate the percentages of sand, silt, and clay in your soil on the appropriate sides of the triangle. Draw a line inward from each of the three points, making each line parallel to the triangle side adjacent in a counterclockwise direction. The textural class of the soil is identified where the three lines intersect.*

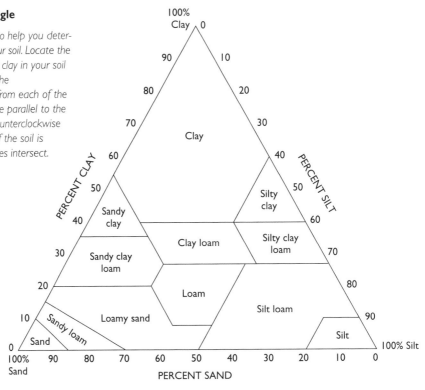

• Do a "squeeze" test. Squeeze a handful of soil. If it easily forms a ball, holds its shape, and feels slippery, the texture is mostly clay. If it is crumbly and loose, it is loam. If it does not hold together at all, even when damp, and feels gritty, it is sandy.

• Test for texture. With a trowel, take samples of soil from the surface down to about 6 inches. Put two cups of soil in a clear glass quart jar with straight sides; fill with water until almost full, then shake vigorously. Wait 24 hours for the soil to separate into layers, revealing the soil profile: sand (the largest and heaviest soil particles) will settle at the bottom. The middle layer will be silt, followed by clay, the smallest particles. What is floating on the surface is the organic matter.

You can calculate roughly the percentage of each type of particle by measuring the height of the layer and dividing by the total height of all three and then multiplying by 100; or you can simply eyeball it. Use the soil triangle, above, to help determine your soil's texture.

• Do an earthworm inventory. Some leading authorities on earthworms recommend counting the number of earthworms to determine the degree of organic matter in the soil. On a warm, humid day, select a square foot of soil where the plants or weeds are growing well. Dig out about 6 or 7 inches and carefully sift through the soil, counting the earthworms. If there are ten or more, your soil probably contains sufficient organic matter.

• Do a do-it-yourself soil profile. Dig a narrow pit several inches deep; take a slice with a spade from an undisturbed wall of the hole. Shake it off gently to shatter the soil structure. If it breaks apart into rounded crumblike pieces, it has a good structure and most likely drains well. If you end up with blocklike clods or lumpy pieces, the soil structure is poor. Dig deeper and observe the soil profile. You will see where the topsoil ends and the subsoil begins. With this information, you will know how far to dig for a professional soil test, and how deeply plant roots will be able to penetrate before encountering subsoil.

• Test the soil's drainage. Dig a hole about a foot deep. Fill the hole with water and let it drain. If it has not drained completely after 6 hours, you probably have a permanent wet spot—a prime location for a bog garden or a site for plants that appreciate "wet feet." If the soil appears sandy, it may drain too quickly. Try digging down about 6 inches two days after a soaking rain. If the soil is bone dry, consider creating a garden with drought-tolerant plants.

• Measure the soil's pH. Two simple ways to test pH at home are pH test paper kits and portable pH meters. Most garden centers, garden supply catalogs, and many Cooperative Extension offices sell easy-to-use kits that are considered accurate within half a pH point. When pH papers are immersed in a soil solution, they react by turning a color. Kits come with a color chart with which to compare shades to gauge the pH. Portable meters, also easy to use, are metal probes that, when inserted into moist soil, display an approximate pH value.

## Home Soil Tests

More comprehensive home soil test kits are also available. With these tests, you can analyze lev-

els of nitrogen, phosphorus, and potassium as well as pH. However, they are only as accurate as the tester and the kits allow. As with most products, the more you pay, the more accurate your results will probably be. The kits are often expensive with a short shelf life because of the chemicals necessary for testing. Have results confirmed by a professional lab if they reveal major imbalances in the soil. The only reliably accurate tests are those completed by professional soil-testing laboratories.

## Professional Soil Tests

State universities (see the list on page 438 often test soil for home gardeners for a nominal fee and recommend corrective measures, as do independent professional laboratories; check the yellow pages or consult your county Cooperative Extension agent or garden center for recommendations.

Many gardeners begin with a professional test and then, if only minor imbalances are found in their soil, rely on home testing for regular checkups thereafter. Equally important as the accuracy of the results from the professionals are the recommendations that come with the analysis.

To have your soil tested professionally, you will have to provide a lab with soil samples. How you take these samples will affect the accuracy of the test results. Most labs supply information on collecting procedure, often providing boxes or bags for the samples, as well as mailing directions.

A few hints on proper collection:
• First, clean all the tools and containers that will be used to collect the soil.
• Never package soil samples in metal containers; the results may be contaminated.
• Collect soil separately from vegetable gar-

# SOIL-TESTING LABORATORIES IN THE UNITED STATES AND CANADA

The Cooperative Extension Service in most states offers soil testing for home gardeners in U.S. Department of Agriculture laboratories; those that do not often will recommend private laboratories. Check in the telephone directory for the number of your county Cooperative Extension agent. The following is a list of USDA soil testing laboratories by state:

**Alabama**
Soil Testing Laboratory
Auburn University
118 Funchess Hall
Auburn, AL 36849
(334) 844-3958

**Alaska**
Soil Testing Laboratory
Agricultural Experiment Station
University of Alaska
533 E. Fireweed
Palmer, AK 99645
(907) 746-9499

**Arizona**
No soil testing is offered by a
   public agency.

**Arkansas**
Soil Testing Laboratory
University of Arkansas
273 Altheimer Drive
Fayetteville, AR 72703
(501) 575-3909

**California**
No soil testing is offered by a
   public agency.

**Colorado**
Soil, Water, and Plant Testing
   Laboratory
Colorado State University
A319 Natural and Environmen-
   tal Sciences Building
Fort Collins, CO 80523
(970) 491-5061

**Connecticut**
Soil Testing Laboratory
Plant Science Department
University of Connecticut
2019 Hillside Rd.
Storrs, CT 06269
(860) 486-4274

**Delaware**
Soil Testing
New Castle County Cooperative Extension
910 S. College Ave.
Newark, DE 19716
(302) 831-2506

**District of Columbia**
Refer to listing under Maryland.

**Florida**
Soil Testing Laboratory
University of Florida
Box 110740

Gainesville, FL 32611-0740
(352) 392-1950

**Georgia**
Soil Testing and Plant Analysis
   Laboratory
2400 College Station Rd.
Athens, GA 30602-9105
(706) 542-5353

**Hawaii**
Agricultural Diagnostic Service
   Center
University of Hawaii
1910 East-West Rd.
Sherman Laboratory, Room
   126
Honolulu, HI 96822
(808) 956-6706

**Idaho**
Analytical Sciences Laboratory
University of Idaho
Holm Research Center
West 6th St. Extension
Moscow, ID 83844-2203
(208) 885-7081

**Illinois**
No soil testing service for
   home gardeners is offered
   by a public agency.

## Indiana

No soil testing service for home gardeners is offered by a public agency.

## Iowa

Soil Testing Laboratory
Iowa State University
G501 Agronomy Hall
Ames, IA 50011
(515) 294-3076

## Kansas

Soil Testing Laboratory
Kansas State University
2308 Throckmorton Hall
Manhattan, KS 66506-5503
(913) 532-7897

## Kentucky

Soil Testing Laboratory
University of Kentucky College of Agriculture
Regulatory Services Building
Lexington, KY 40546-0275
(606) 257-2827

## Louisana

Soil Testing Laboratory
Louisiana State University
M. B. Sturgis Hall, Room 128
Baton Rouge, LA 70803
(504) 388-1261

## Maine

Soil Testing Service and Analytical Laboratory
University of Maine
5722 Deering Hall
Orono, ME 04469-5722
(207) 581-2917

## Maryland

Soil Testing Laboratory
University of Maryland
Department of Natural Resources and Landscape Architecture
2102 Plant Sciences Building
College Park, MD 20742-5821
(301) 405-1349

## Massachusetts

Soil Testing Laboratory
University of Massachusetts
West Experiment Station
Amherst, MA 01003-8020
(413) 545-2311

## Michigan

Soil and Plant Nutrient Laboratory
Michigan State University
Plant and Soil Sciences Building, Room A81
East Lansing, MI 48824
(517) 355-0218

## Minnesota

Soil Testing Laboratory
University of Minnesota
135 Crops Research Building
1903 Hendon Ave.
St. Paul, MN 55108
(612) 625-3101

## Mississippi

Soil Testing Laboratory
Box 9610
Mississippi State, MS 39762
(601) 325-3313

## Missouri

Soil Testing Laboratory
University of Missouri
23 Mumford Hall
Columbia, MO 65211
(573) 882-0623

## Montana

Soil Testing Laboratory
Montana State University
Plant Soil and Environmental Science Department
Bozeman, MT 59717-3120
(406) 994-5074

## Nebraska

Soil Plant and Analytical Laboratory
University of Nebraska
139 Keim Hall
Lincoln, NB 68583-0916
(402) 472-1571

## Nevada

Washoe County Cooperative Extension
Box 1130
Reno, NV 89520
(702) 784-4848

## New Hampshire

Analytical Services Laboratory
University of New Hampshire
Spaulding Hall
38 College Rd.
Durham, NH 03824-3544
(603) 862-3210

## New Jersey

Rutgers Soil Testing Laboratory
P.O. Box 902
Milltown, NJ 08850
(732) 932-9295

*(continued on next page)*

**New Mexico**
Soil and Water Testing Labora-
tory
New Mexico State University
Box 30003/Department 3Q
Las Cruces, NM 88003
(505) 646-4422

**New York**
Cornell Nutrient Analysis Labo-
ratory
Department of Soil, Crop, and
Atmospheric Sciences
Cornell University
804 Bradfield Hall
Ithaca, NY 14853
(607) 255-4540

**North Carolina**
Soil Testing Laboratory
Agronomic Division
North Carolina Department of
Agriculture
4300 Reedy Creek Rd.
Raleigh, NC 27607-6465
(919) 733-2655

**North Dakota**
Soil Testing Laboratory
North Dakota State University
103 Waldron Hall
P. O. Box 5575
Fargo, ND 58105
(701) 231-8942

**Ohio**
OARDC/REAL Laboratory
Ohio State University
1680 Madison Ave.
Wooster, OH 44691-4096
(330) 263-3760

**Oklahoma**
Soil Testing Laboratory
Oklahoma State University
051 AG Hall
Stillwater, OK 74078-0507
(405) 744-6414

**Oregon**
No soil testing service for
home gardeners is offered
by a public agency.

**Pennsylvania**
Agricultural Analytical Services
Laboratory
Pennsylvania State University
University Park, PA 16802
(814) 863-0841

**Rhode Island**
Refer to listing under Massachu-
setts for soil testing.
pH testing only at
Cooperative Extension Educa-
tion Center
University of Rhode Island
East Alumni Ave.
Kingston, RI 02881
(401) 874-5866

**South Carolina**
Agricultural Services Labora-
tory
Clemson University
Old Cherry Rd.
Clemson, SC 29634
(864) 656-2068

**South Dakota**
Soil Testing Laboratory
South Dakota State University

Agricultural Hall, Room 07
P.O. Box 2201
Brookings, SD 57007
(605) 688-4766

**Tennessee**
Soil and Forage Laboratory
University of Tennessee Agricultural Extension Service
5201 Marchant Dr.
Nashville, TN 37211-5112
(615) 832-5850

**Texas**
Extension Soil, Water, and For-
age Testing Laboratory
Texas A & M University
Soil and Crop Sciences Building,
Room 345
College Station, TX 77843-
2474
(409) 845-4816

**Utah**
USU Analytical Laboratory
Utah State University
Logan, UT 84322-4803
(801) 797-2217

**Vermont**
Agricultural Testing Laboratory
University of Vermont
219 Hills Building
Burlington, VT 05405-0082
(802) 656-3030

**Virginia**
Soil Testing Laboratory
Virginia Tech
145 Smyth Hall
Blacksburg, VA 24061-0465
(540) 231-6893

| Washington | Wisconsin | Wyoming |
|---|---|---|
| Refer to listing under Idaho | UWEX Soil and Plant Analysis Laboratory | Soil Testing Laboratory College of Agriculture |
| **West Virginia** | University of Wisconsin | University of Wyoming |
| Soil Testing Laboratory | 5711 Mineral Point Rd. | Box 3354 |
| West Virginia University | Madison, WI 53705-4453 | Laramie, WY 82071-3354 |
| 401 Brooks Hall | (608) 262-4364 | (307) 766-2135 |
| P.O. Box 6057 | | |
| Morgantown, WV 26506-6057 | | |
| (304) 293-3911 | | |

dens, rose gardens, bogs, and meadows; never mix soil from different planting areas.

• Collect samples of topsoil 6 to 10 inches deep with a clean shovel or trowel.

• If you use a shovel, dig a hole to the proper depth; slice off a ½-inch-thick layer of soil down one side of the hole. With the trowel, cut a 1-inch-wide strip down the middle of the slice on the shovel; push off the soil on both sides and keep the vertical strip.

• Take samples from ten or more diggings in each area, and mix them together.

## Further Reading

Bowles, John Paul, ed. *Soils.* Brooklyn, N.Y.: Brooklyn Botanic Garden, 1990.

Campbell, Stu. *Improving Your Soil.* Pownal, Vt.: Storey Publishing Bulletin A-20, Storey Communications, 1978.

Gershuny, Grace. *Start with the Soil.* Emmaus, Pa.: Rodale Press, 1993.

## Composting

Composting is simply a speeded-up version of nature's own process of recycling. Dead vegetation is decomposing constantly all over the world; this process of decay renews the soil by resupplying it with nutrients removed by growing plants and maintains a healthy soil structure by keeping up levels of organic matter. Research suggests that some fungal diseases may be suppressed by all this microbial activity in the soil, thus boosting plant health.

The U.S. Environmental Protection Agency calculates that yard trimmings account for nearly one-fifth of what goes into landfills annually; the New York City Department of Sanitation estimates that the average city household daily discards 2 pounds of organic waste—a staggering amount of raw material that could be composted. In fact, more and more municipalities are recycling yard wastes into compost, then making it available to parks, community gardens, and homeowners for free or at little cost. More and more gardeners are using compost as a replacement for peat moss, which is extracted from natural bogs at a rate faster than it can be replaced naturally and therefore is considered a nonrenewable resource.

Backyard composting is one of the most economical ways for gardeners to maintain a continuous source of nutrient-rich organic matter for soil improvement. Having space helps, but compost can be made in a small garbage can, even indoors with worms. Making compost outdoors can be as simple as collecting garden trimmings and kitchen scraps into a pile or bin, turning it a few times if possible, and waiting for it to decompose. When the compost is finished, in three months to two years, depending on the particular method employed, you will have a crumbly, dark-brown to black organic substance with a distinctive earthy smell.

## The Composting Process

To compost successfully, it is important to understand a bit about the decomposition process and the organisms responsible for it. In reality, any pile of organic matter will rot sooner or later, with or without help from humans, as microorganisms such as bacteria and fungi and larger soil creatures such as earthworms ingest and digest it. However, if you leave compost to decompose completely on its own, you may be more likely to have a dry pile that decomposes extremely slowly or may risk a wet one that produces an offensive odor. A rule of thumb for creating a trouble-free pile is to combine half wet, nitrogen-rich materials (kitchen scraps and fresh prunings) and half dry, carbon-rich ones (fall leaves, sawdust, woody prunings, and shredded paper). Ideally, you should also add enough water to keep the materials as moist as a wrung-out sponge.

This combination of ingredients, air, and moisture is necessary for odorless composting. However, should you add too many wet or dry ingredients, midcourse correction is easy. When a pile is too wet, it will decompose anaerobically and become slimy and swampy-smelling—it needs air. You can supply the pile with air by simply turning—or aerating—it, or you can add dry leaves or paper to correct the

imbalance in ingredients. Turning, although not a requisite for good compost, also helps speed the decomposition process. When a pile is too dry, it needs a sprinkle of water or more wet ingredients. It is a good idea to moisten the pile when it does not rain, and to cover it during particularly rainy weather so that it does not become too wet.

To reduce the chance of odors and the pile's appeal to animals, mix food scraps deep into the pile. In cold climates, some gardeners cover the pile with black plastic to collect solar heat to extend the composting season or surround it with some form of insulation such as hay bales; a frozen pile will not decompose, but the process will resume when the weather warms.

## Hot Composting

People who want large amounts of compost quickly take steps to make their piles run "hot." With the proper ratio of ingredients, moisture, and air, a pile can heat up to 130°F, or higher from all the microbial activity. To run a pile hot, gardeners stop adding material while the pile "cooks," which means running more than one pile so that one can cook while another is forming. Heat is a by-product of the decomposition by bacteria, and that heat in turn encourages even faster composting, which is believed to kill pathogens and many weed seeds. To promote hot composting, it is helpful to have a big pile at least 3 feet in each dimension, or 1 cubic yard (27 cubic feet). Smaller piles will decompose; they simply do not hold the heat to encourage speedy composting, and so the decay process takes longer.

Keep in mind that for a backyard-scale pile, adding heavy amounts of wet, nitrogen-rich materials, such as manure and grass clippings, will fire up microbial activity, generating heat

## MATERIALS TO COMPOST

Fresh waste is generally higher in nitrogen than dried materials, which have more carbon. Adding a couple of shovels of finished compost or manure can help get a new pile off to a good start. Likewise, chopping and shredding materials before adding them to the pile will speed their decay, especially dry, carbon-rich materials.

**CARBON-RICH MATERIALS**

*(Usually dry and brown)*

Dried leaves and plants
Straw or hay
Pine needles
Dried flowers
Small twigs
Shredded newspaper (to avoid packing, apply in thin layers)
Eggshells
Wood chips
Ground corncobs
Fireplace ashes (wood only!)
Sawdust
Old potting soil

**NITROGEN-RICH MATERIALS**

*(Usually wet and green)*

Fresh leaves or plants
Green grass
Seaweed

Weeds
Flowers
Coffee grounds, tea bags
Freshly pruned trimmings
Feathers
Vegetable peelings
Peanut hulls
Overripe produce
Manure and bedding (from farm animals and small pets such as hamsters and rabbits)
Sod

**MATERIALS THAT SHOULD NOT BE COMPOSTED**

Weeds gone to seed and extremely aggressive ones, like bindweed and quackgrass
Meat
Fish
Cheese

Large branches (unless chopped or shredded)
Diseased plants
Dog or cat wastes or litter
Poisons, insecticides, or pesticides
Pressure-treated, painted, or preserved lumber
Dead animals
Bones
Mud (but add old potting soil)
Gravel
Coal or charcoal
Sand
Sludge
Grease, fat, or oil
Magazines
Colored paper
Dishwater
Plastics
Glass
Rubber
Aluminum

and speeding decay. With long-stemmed compost thermometers, sold at garden centers, you can monitor the temperature of your pile, or touch it with your hand to gauge the heat. Hot compost piles should be turned when the temperature reaches 100°F or higher to speed the process and ensure that all materials get a chance to cook near the core or center of the pile. Turn the pile about once a week. Temperatures will rise generally between the second and fourth week of the process and cool slightly once the bulk of the decomposition is completed. As with all composting, keep a hot pile watered so that it is moist but not soggy. Expect finished compost in about three months.

## When Is It Done?

Any time the compost becomes dark in color and looks crumbly like the texture of soil, it is done. It will not have any odor other than a pleasant, earthy smell. How fine the texture should be is a matter of personal choice. Some gardeners incorporate the organic matter, lumps and all, into the soil or use it as mulch; others sift out larger particles to return to the pile for further decomposing.

## Composting Techniques

Make your own bin, try one of the numerous composting devices on the market, or create binless piles. If you have the space, it is advantageous to have two piles working at once. While one is decomposing, you can be adding new ingredients to the other.

### Binless Piles

It is not necessary to have a bin, a box, or any special container. As long as you have room, you can start a compost pile anywhere, on soil or not—although contact with the soil and soil microorganisms is preferable. For best results, start the pile with a bottom layer of dry materials, like branches and twigs, to encourage good air flow. As materials become available, add them to the top of the pile. Keep building, but stop before it reaches 4 or 5 feet as air will have a harder time reaching into the bottom layers and the pile will become compacted from too much weight. Punch holes with a garden fork or crowbar or build perforated plastic pipes into the pile, laid horizontally with the ends extended, to create avenues for air. If you turn the pile and mix the outer dry materials into

the core where the fastest decomposing occurs, you will help speed the process.

### Underground Composting

You can bury kitchen wastes in trenches or pits in the garden, covering additions with about a foot or more of soil. The smaller the pieces, the faster they will decompose. This is ideal for preparing a new garden bed for future use. Allow at least four months for decomposition before digging, either to harvest the decomposed material or to plant in it.

### Sheet Composting

Dig or till yard waste and leaves directly into a planting bed in fall or a few months before planting. By spring, the soil will be enriched with the rotted material, and the bed will be ready for planting.

### Bins

Purchase bins in garden centers or through mail-order catalogs, or build them yourself. Some are made of wood, some wire, and others plastic. Make sure the bin you choose is easy to open, load, and unload finished compost from. If rodents are a problem in your area, look for bins with rodent screens on the bottom or add your own screen cut from ¼- to ½-inch wire mesh or hardware cloth. Some bins come attached, with two or three side by side. Attached bins are convenient because it is easy to fill up the first, turn the pile into the second, and begin to refill the first. A third can be used for final curing.

Wood bins will eventually decay due to the activity of the same microorganisms that are at work on the compost. They can also warp due to dampness. Never used pressure-treated wood to build the bins or treat untreated wood with toxic preservatives, which can leach into the compost and get into your garden. Use a naturally rot-resistant wood, or simply replace rotted pieces periodically. Plastic bins do not rot and are lightweight; some are made from recycled material. Wire bins are made of galvanized metal mesh or chicken wire; some are sturdier than others, and turning and unloading may be relatively difficult, but all are comparatively inexpensive.

Many do-it-yourselfers construct their own bins from scrap lumber, old wooden shipping pallets, or chicken wire. Lumberyards and factories sometimes discard pallets, often made of slow-to-decay hardwoods. Many gardeners use one for the bottom of a pile, three others for the sides, and the fourth as the "door." To create a pallet bin, screw or wire the pallets together, or sink four vertical posts in the ground for corner supports and fasten the pallets to them.

## Rotating/Tumbling Composters

These are supposed to make turning compost easier. Some do, but others do not. Be sure the composter you choose is convenient to load and unload, and extremely easy to turn because wet compost is heavy. Some of these composters are surprisingly difficult to turn, especially when full.

## Trash Cans

Use plastic or metal garbage cans—10 gallons or larger. Punch or drill holes around the sides and in the bottom of the can for good air circulation; use a ¼- to ½-inch drill bit or a similar

size nail to punch the holes. If animals are a concern, make sure the lid is tight fitting. This is an especially good method for composting food scraps, but be sure to add some dry yard materials for balance. Composting in a trash can takes longer than in a large pile—from six months to a year or more.

## Worm Composting

Worm castings, also called vermicompost, are a rich source of plant nutrients—often twice as rich as regular compost. Use castings as a top-dressing for houseplants and plants outdoors or as an ingredient in potting soil mixes.

With the right kind of worms—red worms (*Eisenia foetida*), not ordinary, albeit hardworking garden worms—and a relatively small container, vermicomposting can be done indoors or out. Create a bin using a shallow plastic, wood, or metal box about 12 inches high, preferably with a lid. Punch holes in the lid and in a line around the top of the four sides. Commercial worm bins and red worms are readily available through most garden catalogs. Place the bin outdoors in mild weather, or in any room in the house, or in a heated garage or basement. Protect worm bins from extreme temperatures; 55°F to 75°F is best.

### Setting Up a Vermicomposter

Remember to use only red worms. Set up a bin with about 2 square feet of container space. You will need roughly 2 pounds of worms for every 1 pound of food waste you produce daily.

Prepare bedding from shredded newspapers, leaves, sawdust, or some combination of these plus a sprinkle of soil and enough water to moisten the material but not make it soggy. Layer the bottom of the bin with about 8 inches

## HOW MUCH COMPOST TO USE IN THE GARDEN

New lawns—1"–2" mixed into top 4"–6" of soil

Reseeded lawns—1" mixed into top 2"–3" of soil

Topdressing for existing lawns—⅛" spread uniformly

Topdressing for vegetables, flowers, shrubs—1"–2" spread uniformly; if spread 3"–4" deep, check for sowbugs

Ground cover and annual planting beds—1"–2" spread uniformly; if spread 3"–4" deep, check for sowbugs

Garden soil—1"–3" mixed into top 6"–8" of soil

Around shrubs—3" mixed into top 6" of soil

Potting mix—25%–30% by volume

Mulch for deciduous trees, rose beds—3"–4" spread uniformly

Mulch for vegetables, annual and perennial planting beds—2"–3" spread uniformly

Mulch for exposed slopes—2"–4" of coarse (¾"–1½") compost spread uniformly

NOTE: The application rates in this table represent ranges reported in the published literature on compost. Approximately 1,000 pounds of compost is equivalent to one cubic yard of compost. One inch of compost spread over 1 acre is equivalent to approximately 65 tons of compost at a 40 percent moisture content. Where appropriate, these rates represent annual applications.

## HOW COMPOST IMPROVES SOIL

- Improves soil structure; breaks up clay soil and improves the water retention of sandy soil.
- Reduces soil erosion and compaction.
- Increases earthworm populations.
- Increases the soil microbial activity that fosters plant growth.
- Increases soil aeration and workability.
- Moderates soil temperature.
- Provides for the slow release of nutrients.
- Increases nutrient availability; less is leached through soil, and so fertilizer needs are reduced.
- Improves drought tolerance.
- Helps suppress some plant diseases.
- Works effectively as a mulch.

lettuce leaves, beet greens, celery and carrot tops, plate scrapings, coffee grounds, citrus rinds, and grains. Do not add meat, dairy, or oily foods.

Continue to bury kitchen wastes as often as every day to once a week. If the container accumulates excess moisture, add dry bedding. Watch for signs of overfeeding: no morsel of food should remain distinguishable for more than two to three weeks.

After three to six months, push the bedding mixture, including the worms, over to one side of the bin. Add fresh bedding to the vacated portion and bury more garbage, but only in this new material. In time, most worms will find their way to the fresh food and bedding. After one more month, remove the vermicompost from the "stabilized" side. Pick out straggler worms in the finished compost, return them to the bin, add fresh bedding, and begin the cycle again.

of this loose mixture. Gently lay clumps of worms on top of the bedding; they will work their way away from the light into the mixture. Once they disappear, cover the bin; use black plastic if there is no cover. Bury organic waste under the wad of bedding. Feed the worms fruits and vegetable trimmings, such as apple peelings,

## Further Reading

Appelhof, Mary. *Worms Eat My Garbage,* 2nd ed. Kalamazoo, Mich.: Flower Press, 1997.

Campbell, Stu. *Let It Rot!* Pownal, Vt.: Storey Communications, 1990.

Hanson, Beth, ed. *Easy Compost: The Secret to Great Soil and Spectacular Plants.* Brooklyn, N.Y.: Brooklyn Botanic Garden, 1997.

Martin, Deborah L., and Grace Gershuny, eds. *The Rodale Book of Composting.* Emmaus, Pa.: Rodale Press, 1992.

## Planting and Transplanting

At one time, it was standard horticultural procedure to select plants and then try to change the site to suit their needs. As the ecological sophistication of gardeners has grown, it has become apparent that this not only is rough on plants and the natural environment, but also creates a lot of unnecessary work. Ecological gardeners select the plants that are best suited to the region and the property's various microclimates.

Gardens are made up of microenvironments defined by temperature, sun, soil, and topography. Different plants are adapted to these different habitats. Plants that grow naturally in swamps tend to wither on dry, south-facing slopes. Plants from arid regions often rot in the humus-rich soil in which woodland wildflowers thrive. Before deciding what to plant, study the site to discover how much sun it receives, how well the soil drains, and what the pH is. Are freezing or drying winds a problem? In northern gardens, low-lying areas will probably be the last to warm in the spring and the first to freeze in fall. After studying the site, choose plants adapted to the underlying conditions. Little tampering with the soil will be necessary and the plants will thrive.

Some traditional cultivated plants require what were once considered "perfect" garden conditions: full sun or close to it, rich, well-drained soils, and ample moisture. If you grow such nutrient-hungry plants as vegetables or roses, be prepared to amend the soil or top-dress annually and perhaps fertilize one or more times during the growing season. First, have your soil tested professionally (see "Soil," page 430); inform the lab of what you intend to grow so that proper recommendations can be made.

### Preparing a Planting Bed

If you are in the mood for a spirited debate, ask a crowd of gardeners about the merits of digging or, even better, double digging. The need for intensive cultivation of garden soil once was taken for granted but is now hotly contested. According to the new way of thinking, there are times when it is advantageous to cultivate the soil, and there are times when it is definitely not. Digging is not a panacea for difficult soils.

Cultivating aerates soil, which improves drainage somewhat and makes the soil more friable and hospitable to plant roots. However, introducing more air into the soil also causes microorganisms to decompose or burn up beneficial organic matter at a faster rate. What is more, it brings dormant weed seeds to the surface, where they will germinate.

Knowing when and how much to dig is important. Cultivating at the wrong time or too strenuously can actually harm soil by ruining its structure. Clay soils are most apt to be harmed by improper digging.

To avoid working the soil at the wrong time, examine it closely. Scoop up a fistful and squeeze. If it sticks together, it is too wet and needs more time to dry. When it crumbles easily, it is ready. Soil can be not only too wet to work but also too dry; when it is obviously dry and dusty, it is also difficult to work. With just the right amount of moisture, soil is most malleable. Properly tilled soil is coarse grained—never pulverized. If you use a rototiller, take care not to overtill.

## A Simple Way to Prepare a Bed

One quick, easy way to create a new bed is to requisition a portion of lawn. Smother the sod (or weeds) under layers of newspaper, 8 or 10 sheets deep and overlapped, covered with compost. In a few months or over the winter, all the vegetation will be brown and dead, and the layers of decomposing materials can be turned under by digging into the soil to the depth of a spading fork. Allow a few months for soil microorganisms to further decompose the organic matter before you plant.

## Double Digging

This is hard work, but some gardeners insist that it is the only way to start a new garden or bed. Done properly, double digging will make the soil vigorous, friable, and fertile—particularly important for vegetables and other heavy feeders. What is more, the effects of double digging last for years.

To begin, remove anything growing in the area of the new bed; weeds are most easily pulled after a soaking rain. Select a day for digging when the soil is moist but not soggy. Mark off the plot and then separate it into foot-wide sections using posts and string or lines of sand, or simply do it by eye.

Dig out a foot-wide trench across one end of the plot to the depth of a spade, about 1 foot. Store the topsoil from this trench in a wheelbarrow or on a ground cloth. Loosen the subsoil exposed at the bottom of the trench by inserting the tines of a spading fork and rocking the handle back and forth. Cover the exposed, loosened subsoil with a layer of compost.

Begin digging the topsoil out of the next trench and place it in the first. After the first trench is half filled, add and work into the soil a layer of compost or composted manure. Finish moving the soil from the second trench into the first; then break up the subsoil and layer it with compost. Topsoil from the third trench goes into the second, and so on until the end is reached.

Fill the last trench with the soil saved from the first. Rake the entire surface of the bed smooth. The double-dug soil will be a few inches higher than the surrounding, uncultivated soil.

## Raised Beds

Raised-bed gardening can solve a number of problems, such as a poorly drained or compacted soil or one that does not suit the needs of the plants you wish to grow. Additionally, raised beds require less bending and therefore can make gardening easier for those with limited mobility.

You can build the walls of the raised beds out of rocks, bricks, wooden planks, or 4×4s. The higher and longer the frame, the sturdier the material needs to be. If aggressive weeds that spread by rhizomes and stolons are a problem, consider laying a weed-suppressing cloth across the ground. Fill the bed with compost-enriched soil from your own garden. The result is a root zone with friable soil that will never be walked upon and compacted.

## Planting Seeds Outdoors

Before planting seeds outdoors, prepare the planting bed and rake it level and smooth. You can sow seeds by broadcasting (popular for lawns and meadows), or by planting in rows or in drills (individual holes). Sometimes, gardeners mound soil into hills about 6 inches high and plant sprawling cucumbers, squash, or melons in a ring around the top.

Plant seeds as deeply as the packet suggests. When in doubt, plant to a depth of roughly two times the seed's diameter. Water newly planted seeds well with a very fine spray; a blast from the hose will wash away the seeds and compact the soil. Outdoor germination can be hastened by hotcaps, plastic cloches, or other homemade or commercial covers. Once seeds germinate, the seedlings must be thinned out, leaving the sturdiest to grow on (see "Propagation by Seed," page 475).

## Planting Herbaceous Perennials

Herbaceous plants are generally available in containers or bare root. Container-grown perennials can be purchased and planted when it is convenient—almost any time the ground is not frozen. Dig a hole at least twice as wide as the container or root ball, but no deeper. Fill the hole with water and let it drain. Turn the pot on its side and tap the bottom; gently pull out the perennial by its stem. If the roots are growing in a circle, make four vertical, 1-inch-deep cuts with a sharp knife around the outside of the ball and gently "butterfly" or spread out the roots; breaking up the soil mass will encourage the roots to grow out into the new soil. (If you have a flat of plants with entangled roots, use a sharp knife and spatula to cut and remove each plant with a section of soil.) Set the crown of the

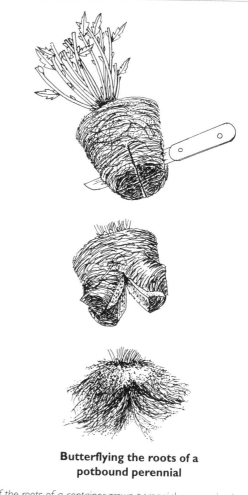

**Butterflying the roots of a potbound perennial**

*If the roots of a container-grown perennial are growing in a circle, make four vertical, 1"-deep cuts with a sharp knife around the outside of the ball and gently "butterfly" or spread out the roots to encourage them to grow out into the new soil.*

perennial at the same level in the garden as it grew in the pot. Refill the hole with soil, and firm it lightly. Water and mulch around new plantings, especially in fall. Water regularly until the new plants are established.

Perennials shipped by nurseries often arrive bare root; bare-root perennials are also sold at some garden centers. They must be planted immediately. If that is not possible, unwrap and keep the roots damp in moist soil, wood chips, or other organic matter; otherwise they will dry out and die. Dig a hole twice as large as the spread of the roots and do not bury the crown. Water before and after planting. Mulch.

## Planting Bulbs

The term "bulb," as used by gardeners, includes corms (crocus, gladiolus, freesia), rhizomes (iris, canna, lily of the valley), and root tubers (dahlia, tuberous begonia) as well as true bulbs (hyacinth, tulip). All "bulbs" come with their own store of food. Although not overly fussy about soil pH or nutrient content, bulbs will rot quickly in poorly draining soil.

Plant spring-flowering varieties as early in the fall as possible. Proper planting depth varies with the size of the bulb; the width of the hole should be slightly larger than the bulb's diameter. Bulbs ordered from catalogs come with planting instructions; when in doubt, plant at a depth three times the bulb's height—slightly deeper in sandy soil. Set bulbs with the pointed side up. When planting many together, dig up a large area, place bulbs, and then refill. Some spring-flowering bulbs, such as daffodils, crocuses, snowdrops, wood hyacinths, and grape hyacinths, make lovely naturalized plantings in woodland and meadow gardens, or even lawns. For these more permanent bulb plantings, mix a handful of bonemeal into the soil at the bottom of each planting hole. Once the ground freezes, cover bulb plantings with a winter mulch, about 3 inches, of hay, pine needles, or bark chips. Pull it away gradually when green shoots appear in spring.

Plant most summer-blooming bulbs, those of tropical and subtropical origin, in spring after

all danger of frost is past. Wait until the ground is thoroughly warm before planting especially tender varieties like tuberous begonias and caladiums, which generally do better if started earlier indoors. In most regions in the United States, summer-flowering bulbs are not winter-hardy and must be dug up and replanted yearly.

## Planting Trees and Shrubs

Trees and shrubs should be planted in spring, before hot temperatures set in and while the weather is still generally cool and rainy—excellent conditions for rapid root growth—or in fall. In autumn, even after the air temperature drops, the ground stays warm, and tree roots continue to grow until soil temperatures drop below 40°F. A few difficult-to-plant varieties, like magnolias, oaks, dogwoods, and birches, are best planted in spring, when their roots will have a longer time to become established.

The day you plant is more critical than the season for most trees. Cloudy weather is ideal; be sure to avoid the hot midday sun.

### The Planting Hole

Dig a planting hole two to three times larger than the diameter of the root ball but the same depth. Do not enrich the soil in the hole; if it is very poor soil, add small amounts of compost so that the amended soil differs only slightly from the surrounding soil. Research has shown that the traditional practice of enriching soil is not necessary and can make it more difficult for roots to adjust to the new planting site.

Prune only diseased and dead branches and damaged or dead roots—no other root pruning is necessary at planting time. If there are crossing branches, prune one or two at planting time; remove any others after the tree is established. Set the plant so that the surface roots are

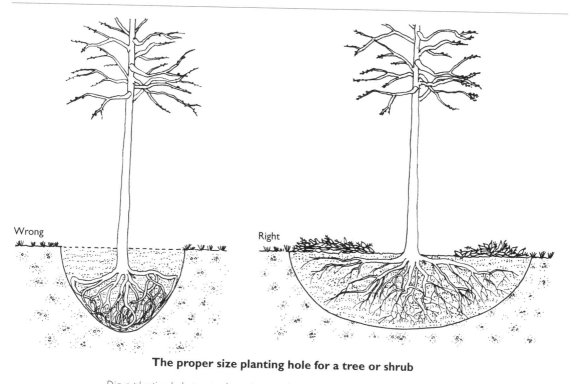

**The proper size planting hole for a tree or shrub**

*Dig a planting hole two to three times wider—but no deeper—than the root ball.*

level with the surrounding soil or slightly higher in poorly drained soil—up 1 to 2 inches. Cultivation practices in the nursery row may result in soil buildup over the roots, especially in the case of balled and burlapped trees, leaving the top of the root ball higher than the surface roots. Consequently, it is sometimes necessary to remove the soil around the stem before planting to be sure that you are setting the plant at the proper depth.

Fill in with soil around the new plant, gently pushing soil between the roots of bare-root specimens. Gently firm the surface of the soil with your hands. Some gardeners create a soil ridge, about 2 inches high, around the circumference of the planting hole to help catch rain and make watering easier. Be sure to remove the ridge after one growing season to avoid damaging delicate roots that may grow into it. Water well and mulch. Water again thoroughly several hours after planting. Until it is established, make sure the tree receives at least an inch of water weekly.

### Aftercare

Fertilize after one season. Staking is not necessary for shrubs and most trees. Where high winds are a factor, stakes can provide necessary anchorage until new roots become established. For bare-root and large trees, drive two stakes beyond the root area; tie burlap strips or soft organic cord around the trunk in a figure eight and secure the trunk to the stakes. Allow some give so the tree can sway in the wind. Remove stakes and cords within the first growing season to avoid chafing and girdling. It is no longer considered necessary to wrap young tree trunks to protect them from sunscald; research has shown that wrapping can harm trees by holding excess moisture close to the bark. If a newly planted tree is at risk from harsh sun, create a temporary shelter during peak hours with lath or burlap.

### Container-Grown Woody Plants

The majority of plants sold today are container-grown. When you select trees or shrubs in leaf, you can readily judge their health. The disadvantage of buying container-grown plants is that they are sometimes root-bound, with roots overflowing or circling the pot. Avoid these specimens. Planting root-bound trees and shrubs is risky; if set in the ground as is, the roots will have little interaction with the surrounding soil, and the plant probably will not get enough water from the soilless container medium, no matter how much you water it. Therefore, the roots of pot-bound specimens must be cut and butterflied or spread out before planting, which stresses the plant.

Remove the plant from the container by applying pressure gently to separate the soil from the sides of the pot. Turn the container on its side and ease the plant out by the trunk. Remove excess growing medium from the outside of the roots and "tease" some of the roots out of the ball to encourage them to grow out into the surrounding soil.

### Balled and Burlapped Plants

Larger trees and shrubs as well as slow-growing varieties such as yew, box, and witch-hazel often come balled and burlapped, meaning they are grown in the field, dug out with a quantity of soil around the roots, and

**Teasing out the roots of a
container-grown tree or shrub**

*After easing the plant out of the container by its trunk, remove excess growing medium from the outside of the roots and "tease" some of the roots out of the ball to encourage them to grow out into the surrounding soil.*

wrapped for shipping. Most are no longer wrapped in natural, biodegradable burlap, so it is important to slide out the covering once the tree is in the planting hole. If the root ball is very heavy, cut back what material cannot be removed. Once the root ball is in place, carefully mix as much soil as possible between the roots. Work quickly so that the plant will suffer a minimum of stress from water loss.

### Bare-Root Plants

Bare-root woody plants, dug up while dormant, are available in spring and fall; nurseries ship at the time appropriate for each region. Unwrap these upon receipt; do not allow deli-

## TREE-PLANTING TIPS

- Choose plants suited to your soil and site conditions.
- Prune diseased and dead branches and only withered or damaged roots.
- Dig a hole two to three times wider than the diameter of the root ball.
- Set the plant at the same height it was growing—or slightly higher in dense, clay soils.
- Refill the hole with unamended, or just slightly amended, soil.
- Water; if it does not rain, continue watering weekly until the new plant is established.
- Stake only in high-wind areas.
- Mulch.
- Observe the tree for any signs of stress.

cate, fibrous roots to dry out. Soak overnight in water or a slurry of mud to rehydrate the tissues. Prune any broken or dead roots. Prepare a mound at the bottom of the planting hole. Gently spread the roots around the mound, incorporating soil around them. Plant bare-root trees and shrubs before they break dormancy.

## Transplanting

It is not easy to move a tree or large shrub, and moving is also hard on the plant. Large specimens, especially those with soil-covered root balls, can be astonishingly heavy, and when a plant is dug, a large portion of its root system is severed and left behind. Understanding roots and how they function can make moving a plant a little less traumatic.

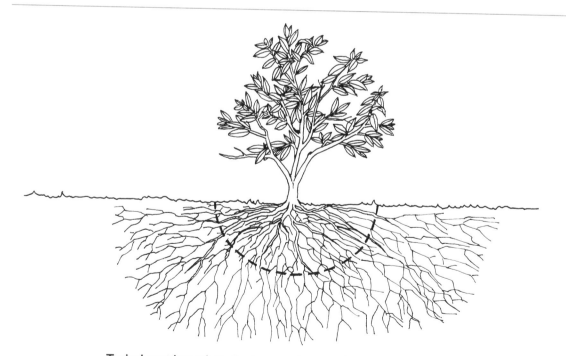

**Typical root loss when digging up a tree or shrub for transplanting**

Roots extend out one to three times the circumference of the tree or shrub canopy (called the *dripline*), anchoring the plant. They supply all aboveground parts with water and dissolved nutrients pulled from the soil—substantial amounts during the active growing season, which is why moving a large plant when it is dormant tends to be less stressful. Keep the roots moist during transplanting and work quickly; the shorter the time the roots are exposed, the less the plant will suffer.

The easiest way to transplant young deciduous trees is bare-root, so long as you work in spring or fall when the tree is dormant (for instructions, see below). Soil is very heavy; a ball of earth just 18 inches across and 12 inches deep weighs about 150 pounds (see the chart in "Weights, Measures, and Conversions," page 737, for approximate weights of the root ball needed for various size shrubs, small trees, and large trees). However, large shade trees and flowering varieties will not tolerate bare-root transplanting, and because evergreens never really go dormant, they too are generally balled and burlapped and moved with soil intact in spring.

## Preparing the Hole

As with any planting, choose an overcast day and work early in the morning or evening when temperatures are cool to lessen the stress on the tree—and on you. First, determine how large the root ball must be; for every inch of trunk diameter (calculated 12 inches up from the ground), there should be 12 inches in diameter of root ball, even more for bare-root specimens.

First, prepare the hole. It should be two to three times wider than the calculated root mass and dug to a depth of about two-thirds the diameter of the root ball.

When the hole is ready, go back to the plant and dig a foot-wide trench just outside the circumference of the calculated root ball. Dig all around to a depth of about two-thirds the root-ball diameter. When moving multistemmed evergreens, gently push up and tie branches to expose the plant base and protect the branches before you begin digging.

## Bare-Root Transplants

If you will be transplanting bare-root, take a spading fork and gently "comb" the soil out from between the plant roots into the trench. Start at the surface and scrape away a few inches of soil. Continue scraping a few inches at a time until most of the roots are exposed. Prune back cleanly any damaged or withered roots. Shake off most of the soil and mist the exposed roots with a fine spray of water. Wrap the roots in a plastic trash bag and carry the tree to the hole you have already dug. Plant immediately.

Create a mound at the bottom of the hole and gently spread the roots around it. Make sure the tree is set at the same planting depth as it was at its original site. Refill with soil, easing it in between the roots with your hands; water to settle any air pockets.

## Balled and Burlapped Transplants

Transplant evergreen trees, large shade trees, or flowering varieties with an undisturbed ball of earth. Prune any roots damaged or severed from digging back to healthy tissue. Wrap the top and sides of the exposed root ball with burlap or old canvas, and hold it in place with ropes. Undercut the root ball with a spade or shovel; use another piece of burlap to secure the bottom. Lift the tree out of the hole, or slide it up along a board.

Tie up the branches to protect them and expose the base of the plant to make it easier to work (a).

Dig a trench around the base of the plant (b).

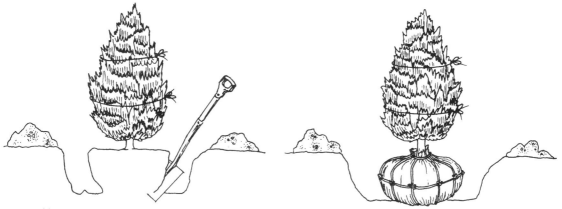

Using a spade, sever the bottom roots (c).

Reinforce the rootball by encircling it with burlap secured with rope (d).

Remove a large plant by sliding it up a board placed at an angle in the hole (e).

**Transplanting a balled and burlapped tree or shrub**

## Preliminary Root Pruning

Pruning roots one year before transplanting may increase a woody plant's chances of survival. First, determine the proper root-ball size and excavate a trench about 12 inches wide and 18 inches deep slightly inside the root-ball circumference. Prune large roots back 3 to 6 inches to the trench wall, taking care not to damage the fine, fibrous roots. Refill the trench with a mix of compost or sand and soil. After a year, when you are ready to transplant, new fibrous roots will have grown that will help the plant reestablish itself in a new location. Take care not to damage new root growth during transplanting; if necessary, increase the size of the root ball.

## Further Reading

Ellis, Barbara W., ed. *Rodale's Illustrated Encyclopedia of Gardening and Landscaping Techniques.* Emmaus, Pa.: Rodale Press, 1990.

Hyland, Bob, ed. *Shrubs: The New Glamour Plants.* Brooklyn, N.Y.: Brooklyn Botanic Garden, 1994.

Zuk, Judith D., ed. *Trees: A Gardener's Guide.* Brooklyn, N.Y.: Brooklyn Botanic Garden, 1992.

# Fertilizing

Nutrients help plants grow, flower, and fruit. Plants absorb the nutrients in the soil water through their roots. These nutrients come from several sources. Some come from the minerals present in rocks and soil particles. Rain carries nutrients such as nitrogen from the atmosphere, and microorganisms release nutrients in the process of decomposing fallen leaves and other organic matter. Finally, gardeners can add nutrients to the soil by using various fertilizers and other soil conditioners.

If you garden with native species and other specimens whose needs match your soil conditions, your plants may already have all the nutrients they need to flourish. However, many crop plants and some fussy ornamentals require quantities of nutrients that are not likely to be available naturally. Some vegetables have especially large nutrient requirements; to grow them, you will need to amend the soil with compost and in some cases fertilizer or other soil conditioners. And if you are gardening on a site where the topsoil has been removed, you will need to add generous amounts of organic matter and a balanced ration of nutrients for a few years in order to create a soil that is hospitable to your plants.

Generally, however, designing a planting that is suited to the existing natural conditions on a site is the simplest and least ecologically disruptive way to garden. For example, if your soil is naturally lean and dry, you should grow black-eyed Susan, threadleaf coreopsis, and other plants found in the wild in poor soils rather than amending the soil wholesale to support cardinal flower, turtlehead, and other species that prefer richer, wetter soils. By the same token, plantings should be designed to allow natural nutrient cycles to unfold. For example, various woody and herbaceous plants can be grouped together in woodland plantings in which the annual accumulation of leaf litter is not cleared away but rather left on the ground so that nutrients can be returned to the soil. (For more information on restoring natural nutrient cycles in the garden, see "Ecology for Gardeners," page 174.) It also makes sense to group together in special beds where the soil has been appropriately amended vegetables as well as roses and other prized ornamental plants that require large infusions of nutrients and perhaps modifications to the soil pH. For more information on meeting the needs of different types of plants, see "Fertilization Needs of Various Types of Plants," page 461.

## The Primary and Secondary Nutrients

Plants require sixteen basic elements for proper development. Too much or too little of one can affect a plant's growth or hamper the release of other nutrients by upsetting the nutrient balance in the soil solution. Three of these elements—carbon, hydrogen, and oxygen—are found in the atmosphere and are also supplied to plants via the water and air moving through the soil. To some extent, gardeners can control their availability to plants by irrigating, improving drainage, and modifying the soil structure. The other elements are obtained from minerals in soil rocks and from organic matter through the activity of microorganisms. The *primary nutrients*—the ones depleted from the soil most rapidly by plants and therefore generally of most concern to gardeners—are nitrogen, phosphorus, and potassium. Plants need smaller but still substantial amounts of calcium, magnesium, and sulfur, called *secondary nutrients*. They also require trace amounts of manganese, copper, zinc, molybdenum, boron, chlorine, and iron. Fertilizers and other soil conditioners contain various combinations and amounts of these nutrients, and can be chosen accordingly to correct a particular nutrient imbalance in the soil.

### Nitrogen, Phosphorus, and Potassium (NPK)

Nitrogen gives plant leaves their dark-green color. It is an important component of plant proteins and chlorophyll, the plant pigment essential for photosynthesis. Nitrogen pro-

motes aboveground growth; too little results in yellowed leaves and stunted growth, but too much can delay flowering and fruiting. Soil microorganisms require substantial amounts of nitrogen in the process of decomposing organic matter. Some nitrogen soil conditioners from organic sources include cow manure, cottonseed meal, fish meal, and blood meal.

Phosphorus is essential for good root development, especially in young plants (and is an excellent pick-me-up for transplants). It promotes flowering, aiding and speeding crop maturity, and can affect the number and size of developing seeds. A phosphorus deficiency can cause flowers and fruits to drop prematurely. Some organic sources of phosphorus are bonemeal, poultry manure, and the mineral rock phosphate.

Potassium promotes strong stem and root development, especially important for tuber and root crops. It promotes plant hardiness and disease resistance. Leaf scorching and spotted or curled leaves are often signs of potassium deficiency. Many vegetables and fruit trees require substantial amounts of potassium. Organic sources of potassium include wood ashes, marine-based greensand, and the commercially mined mineral sulfate of potash-magnesia.

## Types of Fertilizer

Fertilizers can be divided roughly into two categories: organic fertilizers, those derived from plant, animal, and mineral residues, and synthetic fertilizers, those that are chemically manufactured.

Commercial fertilizers are often called organic, natural, processed, synthetic, or even chemical. What these words mean is somewhat subjective. Technically, anything organic is derived only from dead or live plants and animals. In a more practical sense, "organic fertilizers" include those derived from plants, animals, and minerals. Thus, mineral-based rock phosphate can be considered organic. Organic farmers are held to strict standards that specify the use of only certain natural fertilizers and pesticides.

More to the point, however, the word "organic" has come to represent a renewed recognition that the health of the soil and its associated microorganisms is paramount—that to nurture a healthy garden, it is necessary first and foremost to nourish and maintain healthy soil; plants will not thrive in an ailing soil. The way to keep soil healthy is not to add megadoses of nitrogen or other nutrients that may upset the soil's ecological balance (and create polluting runoff and its associated environmental impacts), but rather to ensure that there is a steady, adequate supply of organic matter and nutrients to support the soil flora and fauna that are continually making nutrients available to the plants in the forms and at the rate that they need them. While it used to be necessary for organic gardeners to hand-mix several types of natural fertilizers, complete and balanced formulations of natural fertilizers now are commercially available. See "Organic vs. Synthetic Fertilizers," page 459, for a more detailed comparison of the advantages and disadvantages of so-called organic and synthetic products.

The following is a brief introduction to the different forms of fertilizer.

## Compost

Although compost is not generally classified as a fertilizer, it is used by many gardeners to fertilize their gardens. It not only provides small amounts of nutrients (see "Approximate Nutrient Values of Various Fertilizers," page 462) but, because it contains substantial amounts of organic matter, conditions the soil as well. Compost is one of the easiest organic soil amendments for gardeners to obtain; you can make it in your own backyard or even on a terrace. Dried and dehydrated forms of compost are readily available at garden centers and are relatively inexpensive. Some municipalities make compost available free or for a small charge. For more on the benefits and uses of compost, see page 441.

### Other Organic Fertilizers

#### Dry.

Dehydrated or composted cow manure, bonemeal, cottonseed meal, and rock phosphate are examples of dry organic fertilizers made from plant, animal, and mineral residues. Some organic fertilizers offer one nutrient; others are so-called "complete" fertilizers with all three primary nutrients. Organic fertilizers tend to be bulky, supplying valuable organic matter in addition to specific nutrients.

#### Liquid.

Some organic fertilizers, such as seaweed and fish emulsion, are applied in liquid form. Some gardeners make their own manure or compost "tea" by tying a few shovelsful of compost or manure, either fresh or dehydrated, in a porous cloth, such as burlap, to make a "tea bag," then submerging it in a bucket, garbage can, or barrel of water and letting it steep for a few hours to a week. The resulting liquid should be diluted to the color of weak tea, and used to water plants.

### Green Manures.

Green manures are living plants used to improve soil fertility and structure. An age-old practice, green manuring is regaining popularity as a low-cost method for improving soil in garden beds—and as an exceptionally good solution for new home sites where soil has been compacted by heavy equipment or much or all of the topsoil has been removed. Green manures are usually a mix of grasses, which provide sheer fibrous bulk and have extensive root systems that help loosen soil, and legumes, which have the ability to "fix" atmospheric nitrogen gas and therefore fertilize the soil. The soil for all green manures should be tilled first. Seeds are sown, and eventually the plants are tilled into the ground. The best time to till under a green manure crop for maximum nitrogen is just prior to bloom or before 20 percent of the blossoms open. In vegetable gardens, green manures are typically planted as an overwintering crop and tilled under in spring.

Legumes that are good candidates for green manures include alfalfa, crimson clover, and purple vetch. Nonleguminous candidates include oats, annual rye, buckwheat, and mustard. Consult your county Cooperative Extension office for recommendations on green manure crops for your region.

## Synthetic Fertilizers

### Dry Granulated.

This is the most common form of processed fertilizer. Most often it is fast-release, meaning that the nutrients are available quickly and all at once. Sometimes the granular fertilizers are plastic-encapsulated or sulfur-coated to slow the release of nutrients; the rate of release is controlled by the thickness of the coating.

---

## ORGANIC VS. SYNTHETIC FERTILIZERS

### ORGANIC FERTILIZERS

- Are less likely to burn plant tissue.
- Improve soil structure.
- Encourage more diverse communities of soil bacteria and fungi.
- Applications are easily tailored for specific nutrient deficiencies.
- Release nutrients slowly and therefore last longer, with relatively little leaching and water pollution.
- Often include trace nutrients.
- Nitrogen release, primarily based on microbial decomposition, slows in cool or dry months when plants are less active.
- If not completely decomposed (such as sawdust), may tie up nitrogen temporarily.
- Tend to be bulky, requiring larger applications.
- Fresh manures—not dried or composted—may have an odor and can burn plant tissue.

### SYNTHETIC FERTILIZERS

- Are water-soluble and quickly absorbed by plant roots for fast results.
- Coated slow-release fertilizers provide steady release of nutrients.
- Have generally higher levels of nitrogen, phosphorus, and potassium.
- Do not improve soil structure.
- Nutrients are more likely to be leached through soil before plants can absorb them, leading to water pollution and other environmental problems.
- Can burn plant tissue, especially if applied in high concentrations.
- Can kill soil-dwelling organisms.

Slow-release fertilizers lessen the need for repeat applications and the likelihood of leaching and subsequent pollution problems.

### Spikes and Pellets.

These are usually formulated for a specific purpose, such as for use around trees and shrubs, and are highly concentrated. They also can be used for boosting nutrient levels in container plantings.

### Liquid.

Both liquid concentrates and dry materials that must be diluted or dissolved before application, these can quickly fix a nutrient deficiency. To avoid burning plants, it is important to follow directions and dilute properly.

## Complete, Balanced, and Single-Nutrient Fertilizers

The fertilizer industry uses percentages of the three primary plant nutrients—nitrogen (N), phosphorus (P), and potassium (K)—to grade packaged fertilizers. The grade is expressed in a series of three numbers (called NPK; always in that order), such as 5-10-5 or 1-1-1 or 0-20-0. Several terms are used to describe the kind of NPK ratio. *Complete* fertilizers contain all three primary nutrients (in a sense, "complete" is a misnomer; these fertilizers do provide the three major nutrients, but gardeners may have to add other nutrients to the soil as well to correct deficiencies and imbalances). *Balanced* fertilizers provide equal percentages of the three major nutrients. *Single-nutrient* fertilizers supply just one of the three. Fertilizer manufacturers often print recommended uses for their product on the package. See "Calculating How Much Fertilizer to Apply," in "Weights, Measures, and Conversions," page 737, for tips on how to use the NPK ratio printed on fertilizer labels to determine how much of any particular product should be applied.

In addition to adding nutrients, some fertilizers affect soil pH; often this information is also printed on the label. If you intend to make more than one application of a fertilizer, it is a good idea to consider its effect on your soil's acidity or alkalinity.

## How to Apply Fertilizer

A certain amount of common sense is necessary when it comes to applying fertilizers. Here are a few general guidelines:

- Do not apply fertilizer on windy or rainy days, or when leaves are wet and fertilizer will stick to them.
- Never let dry processed fertilizer granules remain on plant leaves. Improper or excessive applications of fertilizer burn plants, causing leaves to wither and die.
- Use dehydrated or composted manures. If you do use fresh, apply it sparingly, because it, too, can burn plant tissue.
- Dilute liquid fertilizers according to the manufacturer's recommendations, or more.
- Apply granular fertilizer when the soil is moist, not wet or dry. Various techniques can be used for applying fertilizer.

### Broadcasting

Broadcasting is by far the easiest and most popular method of distributing dry fertilizer, both organic and synthetic. Broadcasting can be done by hand or with a drop or rotary spreader for large areas. Broadcast before you plant vegetable or flower beds and around established plantings. For best results, broadcast just before a rain, or water after applying if no rain is forecast. Do not fertilize when the soil is very dry as you can create an overabundance of nutrient ions in the soil solution, leading to the burning of plant tissues.

## Top-Dressing

Top-dressing involves applying dry fertilizer by hand around individual plants. Make a ring of fertilizer that extends out from the stem or trunk as far as the roots grow. Rain and irrigation will bring the fertilizer to plant roots. Or you can gently work it into the soil, taking care not to harm any shallow roots.

## Side-Dressing

This is similar to top-dressing, except that the fertilizer is applied in strips beside rows of plants, such as vegetables or flowers.

## Liquid Feeding

A hose attachment or watering can is used to apply diluted liquid fertilizer to the soil around plants as they are watered.

## Foliar Feeding

Water-soluble solutions of nitrogen, phosphorus, potassium, and some trace elements can be quickly absorbed by many plants through their leaves. Foliar feeding is a fast, easy, and effective quick fix, especially when a specific nutrient deficiency has been detected.

## Fertilization Needs of Various Types of Plants

Most new gardeners overdo the fertilizer. All plants benefit from regular applications of com-post, whether worked into the soil or applied on the surface as a mulch, topdressing, or side-dressing. Additional applications of fertilizer may or may not be necessary, depending on the soil and type of plant. The following are some tips on meeting the nutrient needs of vegetables, herbs, perennials, flowering annuals, trees and shrubs, roses, and lawns.

## Vegetables

An easy, efficient way to give a vegetable garden an annual nutrient boost is to plant a green manure (preferably a legume) in fall and till it under the following early spring (see page 459). Add compost and dried manure to garden plots in early spring, or processed fertilizer at the rate of 2 pounds of nitrogen per 1,000 square feet. With each new sowing of crops throughout the season, work in more compost. If particular crops show signs of nutrient deficiency, a second round of fertilizing may be necessary. Regular soil testing for vegetable plots is recommended.

## Herbs

Generally easy to grow, herbs usually require few additional nutrients beyond those supplied by an annual application of compost.

## Herbaceous Perennials

A light application of a complete, balanced, natural or slow-release synthetic fertilizer in early spring may be beneficial. Many herbaceous plants require little or no fertilizer. Achilleas, for example, tend to produce fewer flowers and more foliage if the soil is too rich. Delphiniums, on the other hand, are hungry feeders and may need two or more applications of

# APPROXIMATE NUTRIENT VALUES OF VARIOUS FERTILIZERS

| Substance | Nutrient | Additional Nutrients and Comments |
|---|---|---|
| **NATURAL, ORGANIC SOURCES** | | |
| **Nitrogen Sources** | | |
| Alfalfa meal | 5-1-2 | |
| Blood meal | 15-2-1 | |
| Dried blood | 12-3-0 | |
| Cottonseed meal | 6-2-1 | |
| Fish emulsion | 5-2-2 | |
| Fish meal | 10-4-0 | |
| Soybean meal | 7-1-2 | |
| **Phosphorus Sources** | | |
| Bonemeal (steamed) | 2-11-0 | 22% calcium |
| Colloidal phosphate (soft rock phosphate) | 0-2-0 | 20% total phosphate, 27% calcium |
| Rock phosphate | 0-3-0 | 32% total phosphate, 32% calcium |
| **Potassium Sources** | | |
| Azomite rock dust | 0-0-2.55 | many trace minerals |
| Granite meal or dust | 0-0-5 | many trace minerals |
| Greensand | 0-1-7 | 3% magnesium plus minerals |
| Sulfate of potash-magnesia | 0-0-22 | 22% magnesium, 11% sulfur |
| Wood ashes | 0-2-7 | raises pH |
| **Calcium (Ca), Magnesium (Mg), and Sulfur (S) Sources** | | |
| Eggshells | 1.2-.4-.1 | plus calcium |
| Epsom salts (magnesium sulfate) | | 10% magnesium, 13% sulfur |
| Flowers of sulfur or granulated sulfur | | 100% sulfur, lowers pH |
| Gypsum (calcium sulfate) | | 22% calcium, 17% sulfur |
| Limestone, calcitic | | 38% calcium, raises pH |
| Limestone, dolomitic | | 11% Mg, 25% calcium, raises pH |
| Lime, oystershell | | raises pH |
| Sulfate of potash-magnesia | 0-0-22 | 19% sulfur, 10% magnesium |

| Substance | Nutrient | Additional Nutrients and Comments |
|---|---|---|
| **Other Natural Nutrient Sources** | | |
| Compost (dry commercial) | 1-1-1 | |
| Compost (homemade) | .5-.5-.5 to 4-4-4 | highly variable |
| Compost (mushroom) | .7-.3-.3 | highly variable |
| Guano, bat | 10-4-2 | |
| Kelp meal/liquid seaweed | 1-1-3 | plus minerals |
| Manure, dried cow | 2-2-2 | |
| Manure, composted, horse | .7-.3-.6 | |
| Sludge, municipal sewage | 2-2-.4 | highly variable |
| Worm castings | .5-.5-.3 | |
| **Bulky Raw Materials** | | |
| Brewery wastes | 1-.5-.1 | |
| Cocoa shells/meal | 2.5-1.5-2.5 | |
| Coffee grounds (dried) | 2-.4-.7 | |
| Grass clippings | .5-.2-.5 | |
| Fish scrap | 5-3-0 | |
| Hay (legume) | 2.5-.5-2 | |
| Hay (nonleguminous) | 1-.2-2 | |
| Manures, fresh | | |
|    Cow | .5-.2-.5 | |
|    Sheep | .9-.5-.8 | |
|    Horse | .6-.3-.5 | |
| Nutshells | 2.5-0-0 | |
| Oak leaves | .8-.4-.2 | |
| Peanut shells | 3.6-.2-.5 | |
| Pine needles | .5-.1-0 | |
| Sawdust | .2-0-.2 | |
| Seaweed (dried) | 1.5-1-5 (.4-0-0 if fresh) | |
| Straw | .6-.2-1 | |

### INORGANIC OR SYNTHETIC SOURCES

| Substance | Nutrient | |
|---|---|---|
| Ammonium nitrate | 33-0-0 | |
| Ammonium sulfate | 21-0-0 | |
| Superphosphate | 0-20-0 | |
| Triple phosphate | 0-46-0 | |
| Sulfate of potash | 0-0-50 | |
| Potassium nitrate | 13-0-44 | |
| Urea | 45-0-0 | |

fertilizer in a growing season. Applications of fish emulsion to plants that are clearly in need of extra nitrogen can make poorly growing specimens lush and healthy.

## Flowering Annuals

Feed these when you transplant them with a water-soluble fertilizer. Top-dress new plantings with a balanced fertilizer or combination of organic fertilizers. If maximum display from these seasonal plants is what you are looking for, fertilize again two or three times during the growing season with a balanced, water-soluble fertilizer, such as 20-20-20.

## Trees and Shrubs

Test the soil around established plantings to see if any deficiencies exist and use a single-nutrient fertilizer to correct any problems. Adding compost or an organic mulch every year should provide enough nutrients for most established woody plants. Fertilizing many trees and shrubs when not necessary, especially with nitrogen, can be detrimental, producing excess soft growth that can attract sucking pests such as aphids.

## Roses

Roses benefit from soil rich in organic matter. Nurture soil organisms with regular applications of compost, decomposed leaves, mulches, and natural fertilizers, such as manures, bonemeal, cottonseed meal, and rock phosphate. Roses perform best in a soil pH from 5.6 to 6.6. If the roses are growing in raised beds, prepare a mix of one part existing topsoil, one part sand, and one part organic material. Fertilize monthly during the growing season. Choose a

fertilizer based on recommendations from a soil test. Applications of manure tea are a time-honored practice in the rose garden.

## Lawn

Lawns benefit from a topdressing of ⅛-inch compost annually. If you do this in spring or fall, you can reseed at the same time. Broadcast seed in any bare spots before you layer the compost. See "Natural Lawn Care Basics," page 386, for information on how much and when to fertilize your lawn. Lawns require a soil pH range from 6.2 to 6.8. If the soil tests below 6.2, apply 50 pounds of lime per 1,000 square feet, and retest the following year.

## Further Reading

*Cover Crop Gardening: Soil Enrichment with Green Manures.* Storey Publishing Bulletin A-5. Pownal, Vt.: Storey Communications, 1977.

Parnes, Robert. *Fertile Soil: A Grower's Guide to Organic and Inorganic Fertilizers.* Davis, Calif.: agAccess, 1990. [technical, but a good resource]

Siegchrist, Charles. *Fertilizers for Free.* Storey Publishing Bulletin A-44. Pownal, Vt.: Storey Communications, 1980.

# Mulching

When you cover the soil of a garden bed—or mulch—you imitate nature. Nature constantly insulates the natural landscape with falling leaves and dead vegetation and, in winter, snow. For gardeners, there are basically two kinds of mulch: organic mulch made from plant material, which decomposes over time, and inorganic mulch from mineral or synthetic sources, which is more or less permanent.

## The Benefits of Mulch

Mulching has a number of beneficial effects on the garden. It also benefits the environment by, for example, conserving water and discouraging soil erosion. Here are some of the reasons why mulching should be an important part of any gardener's routine:

- Mulching conserves moisture in the soil, making plants less susceptible to stress during periods of drought. Covering the soil slows the capillary movement of water to the surface.
- Mulch inhibits germination of weed seeds and weed growth by preventing light from reaching the soil surface, and it makes removing any weeds that do manage to grow easier. Without weeds, which are often fierce competitors, more water and nutrients are available to garden plants.
- Mulch moderates soil temperatures, helping to cool plant roots in summer and warm them in winter—especially valuable in areas where alternate periods of freezing and thawing can cause frost heave and expose plant roots.
- Mulch helps control erosion caused by wind and water.
- Mulching reduces soil compaction.
- Mulched soil stays warmer longer in fall, thus extending the period of root growth for trees and shrubs and soil microorganism activity.
- Mulch around tree trunks helps protect them from mechanical injury by lawnmowers.
- Organic mulches slowly release beneficial nutrients as they decompose.
- Many mulches are attractive.

## When and How to Apply Mulch

The following guidelines will help you make the most of the benefits of mulching.

- Apply mulch in spring after the ground warms and in fall, preferably after it cools.
- Do not apply mulch to very wet or dry soil.
- Pull back winter mulches (those on plantings, such as spring bulbs and perennials, added specifically to prevent frost heave) in early spring a little at a time, starting before new growth begins.
- Mulch can affect soil pH. Oak leaves and pine needles increase acidity; marble chips cause soil to become more alkaline.

### USING MULCH TO SOLVE COMPACTION PROBLEMS

Too much foot or heavy machinery traffic can make the soil around trees and shrubs as hard and impregnable as cement. In time, compacted soil will compromise the health of the plant. To loosen it, layer ½ inch of compost on top of compacted soil as far as the plant's top growth extends, and then mulch with 2 to 3 inches of shredded or whole leaves, preferably from the tree, or wood chips. Allow a 6-inch ring of bare soil around the base of the trunk to keep damp mulch from touching bark. (If possible, rope off the entire area to prevent further compaction.) Maintain the thick mulch, adding to it at least once a year. Microorganisms and larger soil creatures eventually will work their way into the dense soil below and start to loosen it.

For very serious compaction around woody plants, consult a professional. Arborists often drill deep, narrow holes into the hard soil and sometimes fill them with a mineral-based soil conditioner, such as sand, calcined clay, or shale. Sometimes, pressurized water is pumped into the ground to relieve the compaction. Deep-rooted trees fare better with this sort of treatment.

## RECOMMENDED MULCHES

### ORGANIC

**Buckwheat hulls.** Provide some nutrients to the soil. May cake on the surface and become moldy, but mixing with sawdust in a 2-1 ratio often alleviates the problem. Rich, dark color; excellent for formal plantings.

**Cocoa shells.** Layer loosely; can become moldy, but mixing with sawdust will help. May have a strong odor of chocolate when first applied. Rich in potassium.

**Wood chips.** Coarse or fine. Can be created from garden prunings (healthy branches only!) with a wood chipper. Apply a layer of compost first to compensate for any nitrogen loss caused by the action of soil microorganisms.

**Bark chips.** Attractive appearance. Best used around acid-loving plants. Available commercially in different grades, from large nuggets to shredded and finely ground. Often made from pine, hemlock, cedar, fir, and spruce. Apply a layer of compost first to compensate for any nitrogen loss caused by the action of soil microorganisms.

**Straw.** Breaks down quickly, in a year or less. Excellent for vegetable and cutting gardens. Often used for animal bedding and therefore available in feed stores. Straw, the stems of grain crops after they are harvested, is similar to hay, which consists of cut and partially dried grass, clover, or alfalfa; the advantage of straw is that it lacks the weed seeds that could germinate in the garden.

**Pine needles.** Decompose slowly. Attractive and mildly fragrant. Increase soil acidity. Can be a fire hazard during drought conditions.

**Pine boughs.** Readily available during the winter holidays; provide an insulating effect in winter for many plantings such as roses, spring-flowering bulbs, and perennials. Also excellent for covering and insulating container plantings.

**Compost.** If too fine, may allow weeds to germinate, but loose, crumbly compost—not fully rotted—may work well. Weed seeds may sprout from compost that has been allowed to rot on its own; compost that has "cooked" should be weed-free.

**Leaves.** Whole leaves have a tendency to pack or mat, inhibiting water penetration, and they blow around. Shredded leaves are less messy. Good for naturalistic garden settings.

**Leaf mold.** A low-cost mulch if you compost leaves yourself or your local municipality offers it free or at a discount to residents. Sprouting weeds could be a problem if seeds were collected with the leaves.

**Newspaper.** A cheap, readily accessible organic mulch. Layers of newspaper or corrugated cardboard must be weighted down. Covering newspaper with compost, manure, or bark chips hides its unsightly appearance. Use only black and white pages, not colored-inked ones, unless you know the ink is soy-based and contains no toxic dyes.

**Black kraft paper.** Warms soil by trapping the sun's heat; blocks light and suppresses weed seed germination. Porous, with crepe-paperlike flexibility, allowing water and nutrients to pass through. Available through organic farm supply catalogs.

**Locally available mulches.** Check around your area for possible locally available materials, ideal for mulching, such as hops, spent grains, nut shells, cranberry clippings, peanut hulls, seaweed, ground corncobs, cornstalks, and tobacco stems.

---

### INORGANIC

**Black plastic.** Warms soil by trapping the sun's heat; blocks light and suppresses weed seed germination. Tends to tatter and look unattractive. Can inhibit water penetration (causing either too wet or dry conditions) unless holes are punched. Best used in the vegetable garden to hasten crop maturity; water under the plastic.

**Landscape fabric.** Woven or nonwoven, also called geotextile; made from petroleum by-products. Good for erosion control. Porous, allowing water and nutrients to pass through. Cover with a thin layer of attractive mulch around ornamentals; some fabrics are sensitive to light, and mulch helps reduce disintegration from ultraviolet exposure.

**Landscaping stone.** Effective as a moisture retainer, but is a poor weed inhibitor. Available in many colors and can be arranged into patterns.

**Turkey grit.** Small, speckled granite pebbles, fine to coarse in grade. Good for alpine plantings, Japanese dry gardens, pathways. Light-colored surface reflects sunlight, which in full sun could burn the undersides of delicate leaves.

**Gravel.** Available from building contractors and lumberyards. Coarse to fine in grade. Good for alpines and in pathways.

**Calcined clay.** Stabilized baked clay; attractive white or pinkish color. Decorative around alpines and in formal knot gardens.

**Marble chips.** Good for alpines. Darker hues absorb heat and can elevate the soil temperature. Not recommended for acid-loving plants.

Saltmarsh hay and peat moss are not recommended because the former is taken from saltmarshes and the latter from northern bogs, both important wetland environments.

---

• Organic mulch that is applied too thickly may not dry out properly after rain or watering; damp mulch can prevent air from reaching plant roots, encourage rot, and attract slugs and rodents.

• The lighter the mulch, the thicker it can be applied. Two to 3 inches of heavy organic mulches like wood chips and bark is recommended; 4 to 6 inches of lighter mulches like pine needles and straw.

• Apply inorganic mulches thickly enough to cover the soil surface.

• Apply a layer of compost underneath wood chips and bark mulches; it will compensate for any nitrogen depletion caused by the soil microorganisms that require nitrogen for decomposing fresh organic mulches. Or let these mulches begin to decompose in a compost pile before applying.

## Mulching Trees and Shrubs

Mulch newly planted trees and shrubs to prevent competition from weeds, maintain soil moisture, and keep the soil warm so roots have an extended growing period in the fall. Keep the mulch at least 6 inches from the trunk, and for maximum results, extend the mulch about a foot beyond the tree's dripline. If you mulch annually with organic matter, you probably will not need to apply any other fertilizer once the plant is established. New layers can be added on top of decomposing mulches, or the old mulch can be lightly worked into the soil (taking care not to disturb delicate roots) before the new one is applied.

Some suggested mulches: wood chips, shredded bark or bark chips, leaf mold or shredded leaves, compost.

## Mulching Perennials and Bulbs

Winter mulch protects these plants against frost heave that results from alternating freezing and thawing temperatures in northern climates. Apply a thick winter mulch, up to 6 inches, after the ground is completely frozen and the foliage of perennials has died back. Starting in early spring before new growth begins, remove a little at a time to allow the soil to warm properly.

Some suggested winter mulches: pine boughs, straw, wood chips.

Apply summer mulch in late spring only after the ground has thoroughly warmed. Leave a little bare soil around flower stems; wet mulch can cause fungal problems if it is in direct contact with perennials.

Some suggested summer mulches: compost, manure, cocoa shells, shredded bark, wood chips, bark chips, shredded leaves, compost.

## Mulching the Vegetable Garden

Organic mulches conserve moisture, help eliminate weeds, and benefit the soil of vegetable gardens as they decompose. Apply them only after the soil has warmed and the crops are in; if you apply them too early, you risk delaying soil warming and therefore getting the garden off to a slow start. Use only organic materials that break down quickly; apply a layer of compost first to avoid nitrogen depletion. Some garden-

---

### HOW MUCH MULCH?

Use 1 cubic yard of organic matter to mulch a 100-square-foot area to a depth of 3 inches. One cubic yard equals 27 cubic feet; mulch is often available in 2- or 3-cubic-foot bags.

---

ers use black plastic and landscape fabric; both warm the soil by trapping sunlight but have the tendency to deteriorate and look tattered. Recycled black kraft paper has the same warming ability, and decomposes in the first year or two to become part of the soil.

Some suggested mulches: compost, cocoa shells, buckwheat hulls, shredded leaves, dried grass clippings (or, if fresh, a thin layer), straw, black kraft paper.

## Mulching the Rose Garden

Summer organic mulches conserve moisture, help eliminate weeds, and supply some nutrients. Some suggested summer mulches: compost, buckwheat hulls, bark chips, cocoa shells.

Many gardeners protect delicate roses in winter with a deep mulch—12 inches or more high and wide—of dry organic matter. Damp mulch may invite fungal problems. Suggested winter mulches: dry shredded leaves, pine boughs, straw, wood chips.

## Mulching Pathways

Inorganic mineral mulches provide an aesthetically pleasing, more or less permanent surface for pathways. When using crushed rock or pebbles, be sure to add edging to contain the loose stones. For vegetable garden pathways, use an organic mulch like straw, which will decompose and can be added to beds when no longer viable as a mulch. Layers of newspaper (use only black-and-white sheets unless you know the colored ink used is soy-based) or corrugated cardboard under an organic mulch will provide additional organic matter while at the same time discouraging the growth of weeds.

Some suggested mulches: marble chips, construction gravel, turkey grit, landscaping stone, newspaper, wood chips, straw, shredded leaves.

## Further Reading

Campbell, Stu. *The Mulch Book: A Complete Guide for Gardeners.* Pownal, Vt.: Storey Communications, 1991.

# Watering

Your soil can be the best loam there is, friable and fertile, and you can have the most viable seed in the world; but without water, there will be no garden. Seeds need water to germinate and plants need it to grow.

Plant cells are composed mainly of water. Without enough water, cells cannot grow properly. Plants draw water from the soil through their roots; when the soil is dry, plant roots have difficulty getting adequate water, and the plants can wilt. Plants can also wilt in hot, dry weather. Much of the water taken up by plant roots evaporates from the leaves and stems in a process called *transpiration*. Transpiration occurs naturally during the day because the pores, or stomates, found mostly on the undersides of leaves must be open to allow the plant to take in carbon dioxide. On extremely hot, sunny, dry days, plants sometimes cannot take up water quickly enough to replace what is lost through transpiration, and the stomates close.

When the flow of carbon dioxide is thus inhibited, photosynthesis slows and the growth and health of the plant can be threatened.

The structure and texture of the soil, or how soil particles aggregate, affects how much water is available to plants. In general, plants take in most of their water from the top 1 to 2 feet in the average soil where the majority of the roots are concentrated. Soils need adequate levels of organic matter in this upper foot or so to retain water.

## Water-Conserving Gardening

Gardeners no longer have the luxury of taking water for granted. Wasteful water use, poor land management, and pollution have taken their toll on this once pristine and plentiful resource.

Water-conserving landscaping, sometimes called *xeriscaping*, helps preserve water supplies and is good horticultural common sense. The following guidelines will help you create a water-conserving garden.

• Group together plants with similar water needs. Evaluate the site and choose plants appropriate for particular microclimates—the plants adapted to a moist depression, for example, are different from those adapted to a dry, sunny slope or a windy, exposed area.

Place the thirstier plants close to the house in beds designed to capture water runoff from downspouts, patios, driveways, and decks. (For more on the benefits of capturing water runoff, see "Ecology for Gardeners," page 142.)

Raised beds and terraces can help channel water and control runoff. A hedge can act as a windbreak and lessen the effects of drying winds.

• Limit turf areas. Consider replacing some lawn areas with a more water-efficient and low-

## SELECTED DROUGHT-TOLERANT PLANTS

The following is a starter list of plants that are adapted to low-moisture conditions. Hardiness zones for each plant refer to the USDA Hardiness Zone Map (see "Gardener's Atlas," page 30). For the best plants for your area, consult native plant societies and your county Cooperative Extension office.

### TREES AND SHRUBS

*Atriplex canescens,* saltbush, Zones 4–10

*Buddleia alternifolia,* fountain butterfly bush, Zones 6–8

*Caragana arborescens,* Siberian pea tree, Zones 2–7

*Caryopteris* x *clandonensis,* bluebeard, Zones 6–9

*Ceanothus americanus,* New Jersey tea, Zones 4–8

*Ceanothus thyrsiflorus,* California lilac, Zones 8–9

*Celtis* species, hackberries, Zones 4–8

*Cotoneaster horizontalis,* rockspray, Zones 4–9

*Crataegus crus-galli,* hawthorn, Zones 5–9

*Dodonaea viscosa* 'Purpurea', purple hop bush, Zones 8–9

*Feijoa sellowiana,* pineapple guava, Zone 8

*Gleditsia triacanthos,* locust, Zones 5–9

*Hibiscus syriacus,* rose of Sharon, Zones 5–8

*Hypericum frondosum* 'Sunburst', golden St.-John's-wort, Zones 5–8

*Ilex vomitoria,* yaupon holly, Zones 7–10

*Juniperus* species, junipers, Zones 3–9

*Kerria japonica,* Japanese kerria, Zones 4–9

*Koelreuteria paniculata,* goldenrain tree, Zones 5–8

*Morus alba,* white mulberry, Zones 5–9

*Picea glauca,* white spruce, Zones 3–6

*Picea engelmannii,* Engelmann spruce, Zones 2–5

*Pinus mugo,* dwarf mountain pine, Zones 2–7

*Pinus thunbergii,* black pine, Zones 4–8

*Potentilla fruticosa,* bush cinquefoil, Zones 2–7

*Rosa foetida* 'Bicolor', Austrian copper rose, Zones 5–10

*Rosa rugosa,* rugosa rose, Zones 3–10

*Viburnum lentago,* sheepberry, Zones 2–8

### PERENNIALS

*Achillea ptarmica,* yarrow, Zones 4–10

*A. millefolium* hybrids and cultivars, common yarrows, Zones 4–10

*Artemisia* species, artemisias, Zones 4–9

*Asclepias tuberosa,* butterfly weed, Zone 3–8

*Baptisia* species, false indigos, Zones 3–9

*Belamcanda chinensis,* blackberry lily, Zones 5–10

*Callirhoë involucrata,* poppy mallow, Zones 4–8

*Coreopsis verticillata,* tickseed, Zones 3–9

*Dianthus* species, garden pinks, Zones 4–10

*Echinacea* species, purple coneflowers, Zones 3–10

*Eryngium maritimum,* sea holly, Zones 5–10

*Hemerocallis* species, hybrids, and cultivars, daylilies, Zones 3–10

*Iris* x *germanica,* German bearded iris, Zones 2–7

*Kniphofia* species, torch lilies, red-hot pokers, Zones 5–10

*Lavandula angustifolia* 'Hidcote' and *L.* 'Quasti', dwarf lavenders, Zones 8–9

*Liatris scariosa,* tall gayfeather, Zones 2–9

*Liatris spicata,* spike gayfeather, Zones 3–9

*Limonium* species, statice, Zones 4–10

*Linum* species, flax, Zones 5–10

*Papaver orientale,* Oriental poppy, Zones 4–9

*Penstemon* species, penstemons, beardtongues, Zones 8–9

*Perovskia atriplicifolia,* Russian sage, Zones 3–8

*Salvia sclarea,* Clary sage, Zones 5–10

*Salvia* x *superba* 'East Friesland', sage, Zones 5–10

*Santolina virens,* green lavender-cotton, Zones 6–8

*Solidago* hybrids, goldenrods, Zones 3–10

*Stachys byzantina,* lamb's-ears, Zones 4–8

*Yucca glauca,* soapweed, Zones 5–10

---

**GROUND COVERS**

*Arctostaphylos uva-ursi,* kinnikinnick, Zones 3–7

*Laurentia fluviatilis,* blue star creeper, Zones 7–10

*Myoporum parvifolium,* prostrate myoporum, Zones 8–10

*Rosmarinus officinalis* 'Prostratus', rosemary, Zone 7

*Sedum* species, stonecrops, Zones 3–8

*Thymus pseudolanuginosus,* woolly thyme, Zones 4–10

**GRASSES**

*Arrhenatherum elatius* var. *bulbosum,* bulbous oat grass, Zones 5–8

*Bouteloua gracilis,* blue grama grass, Zones 6–8

*Briza media,* quaking grass, Zones 6–8

**ANNUALS**

*Centaurea cyanus,* blue cornflower

*Cosmos* species, cosmos

*Euphorbia marginata,* snow-on-the-mountain

*Gazania* species, gazania

*Gomphrena globosa,* globe amaranth

*Perilla frutescens,* perilla

*Senecio cineraria,* dusty miller

*Trachymene coerulea,* blue lace flower

*Tropaeolum majus,* nasturtium

*Verbena* species, verbenas

---

maintenance ground cover or other drought-tolerant plantings. Seed remaining lawn areas with drought-resistant varieties such as buffalo grass (*Buchloë dactyloides*). Be aware that tall fescue, one oft-recommended variety, has become an invasive weed, threatening remnant prairies in the Midwest, eastern Plains, and north Texas, and should not be planted in these areas. During hot weather, allow whatever grass you grow to become slightly taller, about 3 inches, to shade the soil and reduce evaporation.

• Improve the soil. Water leaches quickly through porous, sandy soils. Amending the soil with organic matter will improve its water retention. Home composting is one of the best ways to guarantee that there is a ready and inexpensive source of organic matter for soil improvement (see "Composting," page 441).

• Grow water-efficient plants adapted to your climate and the particular microclimates in your garden. No matter where you garden, these will include a range of beautiful trees, shrubs, flowering perennials, ground covers,

and grasses. No one list of plants can cover all regions and all conditions. A starter list of water-conserving plants is provided on page 470; consult native plant societies and your county Cooperative Extension office for lists of species best adapted to the conditions in your area. Remember that even drought-tolerant plants require deep, regular waterings until they become established, usually within a year.

• Irrigate efficiently and conservatively. In the kitchen garden and other areas that require regular supplemental irrigation, use the most water-efficient technologies possible. Sprinkler systems, with evaporation rates as high as 70 percent on dry, windy days, are wasteful; water evaporates before it hits the ground. What is more, their target area is imprecise, with the result that pavement and pathways often receive as much of the water as plantings do. In contrast, with a drip irrigation system it is possible to specifically meet the water needs of each planting. You can direct moisture where it is needed and in the proper amounts. Soaker hoses, less expensive than an elaborate drip irrigation system and simpler to install, are a good alternative. For more on these water-conserving technologies, see below.

- Use water-conserving mulches. In summer, mulches cool the soil and minimize soil evaporation, helping to maintain soil moisture. A mulch can prevent weeds, which compete with garden plants for moisture, from gaining a foothold in the soil. For mulch comparisons and recommendations, see "Mulching," page 464.

## When to Water

If you use a drip irrigation system, the time of day is not significant. If you do not, water when it is cool, preferably early in the morning, to reduce evaporation. Do not water regularly at night if your method of watering wets plant leaves; wet foliage, when it is not dried in a few hours by the sun, invites fungal or mildew problems.

During cool seasons, less watering will be necessary because there is less evaporation. However, even dormant plants may need to be watered during long periods of above-freezing temperatures, or during particularly dry winters, when there is little snow cover.

## How Much to Water

Aim for watering to the depth of a plant's root system to encourage deep, vigorous root growth. The roots of most herbaceous plants (those of perennials, annuals, ground covers, and vegetables) range from 6 to 18 inches deep. The more deeply rooted plants are, the less water they require. In a good loamy garden soil, about an inch of water penetrates to a depth of 6 inches (less in clay and more in sandy soils). Never water to the point of puddling; your soil

will become waterlogged and the plants will suffer.

## Drip Irrigation

Drip irrigation is so called because water actually "drips" into the soil, one drop at a time, through specially spaced emitters. It is this slow, gentle, carefully aimed delivery of water to a plant's root zone over an extended period of time that makes this technology unsurpassed at both saving water and promoting optimal plant growth. If the system is properly designed and managed, the soil never dries out or becomes waterlogged, and little water is lost to either evaporation or runoff. Plants get water when they need it and their foliage remains dry. Weeds or any other plants not specifically selected to receive water do not get irrigated.

Studies show that drip irrigation can conserve 50 percent or more water than conventional watering methods such as sprinkling.

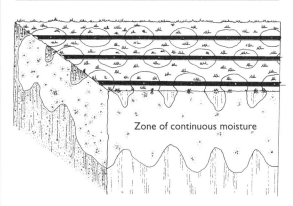

**Drip irrigation zones of moisture**

*The wet spots beneath each in-line emitter merge to form one continuous zone of moisture. The soil for the entire length of the in-line tubing is moist some 4"–6" beneath the surface, depending on the soil type.*

Drip systems can be permanent or semipermanent, and easily removed when regular cultivation is necessary, as in vegetable gardens. The method is also excellent for trees and shrubs in the landscape, flower beds, even containers. With an attractive mulch, it is possible to disguise the tubing. The main disadvantage of drip irrigation is that the tubes occasionally become clogged.

### Drip Irrigation Components

A well-designed system includes a backflow preventer, pressure regulator, filter, tubing, emitters, and, if you wish, a timer to save you the trouble of turning the system on and off.

Before you set up a system, observe how water drips into your soil—how deep and wide it spreads. Generally, the wet spot formed by the dripping water will be carrot-shaped in sandy soil and beet-shaped in clay soil. Make sure the entire root zone of any plant is adequately saturated by placing emitters accordingly.

A backflow preventer is important to protect the household water supply from possible contamination. Filters are vital to a smooth-running system; the best kinds are easily disassembled for regular cleaning. Since household water pressure ranges from 40 to 60 pounds per square inch and most drip systems can handle only 10 to 25 psi, you will need a pressure regulator.

Choose tubing with evenly prespaced emitters to deliver water along rows of vegetables. Tubing without preset emitters, which allows you to choose exactly where the water is delivered, may be better for the shrubs and trees in your landscape. Companies that sell drip irrigation equipment will generally help you design a system and supply you with instructions on setting it up. Many also sell predesigned systems.

## Soaker Hoses

Soaker hoses can be components of drip irrigation systems, or they can be used on their own. They are easily set up and dismantled. Also called porous hoses, they release water along their full length as spray or seepage through tiny holes. One drawback is they tend to be uneven; the flow of water is strongest closest to the water source, especially if the hose is set on a slope.

Soaker hoses conserve water, reduce evaporation, and, when properly laid with the spray aimed toward the ground, do not wet foliage.

## Hand Watering

Some gardeners prefer watering by hand—whether with a hose, bucket, or watering can. For them, watering is often relaxing and the time to carefully examine plants for signs of disease or insects or to observe their growth. Trigger-type nozzles that blast water are not recommended; the heavy flow compacts soil, causes erosion, and is difficult to control. A mister will provide a gentle, easily aimed stream of water.

## Further Reading

Kourik, Robert. *Drip Irrigation for Every Landscape and All Climates.* Santa Rosa, Calif.: Metamorphic Press, 1992.

Marinelli, Janet, ed. *The Environmental Gardener.* Brooklyn, N.Y.: Brooklyn Botanic Garden, 1992.

*Taylor's Guide to Water-saving Gardening.* Boston: Houghton Mifflin, 1990.

## For More Information

The National Xeriscape Council, Inc., P.O. Box 767936, Roswell, GA 30076-7936.

# Propagation

If you have ever cut branches of pussy willow or forsythia to enjoy indoors in a jar of water, you may have discovered roots when you discarded the faded display. Some woody and many herbaceous plants produce roots in water—probably the simplest way to propagate, or make one plant from another.

Plants can be propagated either sexually or asexually. When female plant parts are fertilized by male ones, sexual reproduction occurs and seeds are produced. Sexually propagated plants reflect the characteristics of the parent plants, but each new plant is genetically unique. Plants propagated asexually, or by vegetative propagation, are created from vegetative parts such as leaves and roots. Asexually propagated plants are clones, meaning that they are genetically identical to the parent.

Sexual reproduction, or propagation by seed, generally is ecologically preferable because it helps ensure the health and diversity of a species' gene pool. However, hybrids and cultivars generally do not come true from seed; propagating them by seed will result in an assortment of seedlings, some of which resemble the parent plants and others that do not. Whenever it is important to duplicate the characteristics of the parent, such as for the many cultivars bred for disease, insect, or other resistance, asexual or vegetative propagation is necessary. For more on the advantages and disadvantages of sexual and asexual propagation, see "Plant Reproduction," page 94, and "Ecology for Gardeners," page 142.

## Propagation Equipment

Propagating can require as little in the way of equipment as a glass of water or as much as is found in a laboratory outfitted for microtissue propagation. Much can be accomplished with minimal equipment. This section focuses on the many propagation techniques that can be used successfully with standard gardening tools.

### Medium

A soilless mix is generally the medium of choice for propagation. The medium must be clean, free of disease pathogens and weed seeds, and retain water yet drain well. Additionally, it must be able to hold seeds and cuttings in place during germination and rooting. Getting seeds to germinate and cuttings to root is likely to be more successful in a sterile environment. Using ordinary garden soil is not advisable, because generally it is neither porous nor clean enough. Never reuse the medium; compost it or recycle it in container plantings. Propagating media are sold at garden centers and nurseries, or you can mix your own. The following are common ingredients. (Specific recipes are given below with the various propagation techniques.)

**Builder's sand.** Aerates and provides support for cuttings. Beach sand should never be substituted.

**Grit.** Aquarium gravel; aerates and promotes drainage. Good for supporting large cuttings.

**Calcined clay.** Holds water and helps protect young leaves from drying out; a similar material is used for kitty litter and soaking up oil in garage spills.

**Perlite.** Sterile, white volcanic substance; provides good aeration.

**Vermiculite.** Expanded mica; holds water well but tends to compact over time.

**Sphagnum moss.** Holds water, drains well, and has built-in antifungal properties. Available as milled—generally used in cutting and seed media—and long-fibered, used for layering. (Sprinkle a thin layer of milled spaghnum moss over seeds if you do not include it in the propagating mix.)

**Peat moss.** Retains water very well; slightly acidic. Many gardeners are using alternatives such as hot compost, because peat moss is extracted from northern wetland habitats.

**Styrofoam.** Spongy; provides aeration. Reuse packaging materials, but shred them first.

**Compost.** Some research indicates that compost has antifungal and bacterial properties and therefore has important advantages for propagation; however, some gardeners maintain that compost is too risky to use in seed-starting and cutting medium because it is not sterile. Hot compost—made at temperatures high enough to kill disease organisms—is less likely to harbor pathogens.

### Containers

Special pots and flats, mostly plastic, are on the market for propagating, even some disposable ones, like paper fiber and peat pots. You can also recycle containers from home: milk or juice

cartons, yogurt containers, egg cartons, or anything else you can punch drainage holes in. Especially serviceable are containers with clear plastic tops, such as those for take-out food.

Or start seeds and cuttings without pots or trays. Peat pellets expand in water. Soil blocks are an alternative to pellets, which can be expensive and are made of peat moss. However, working with soil block molds is time-consuming and requires practice.

## Propagation by Seed

Starting seeds indoors or out enlarges exponentially the choice of plants for the garden. Every year, new varieties as well as rediscovered heirlooms and native species become available to gardeners, but only as seed. Nurseries and garden centers sell only a selection of popular varieties as seedlings.

### Obtaining Seed

Garden catalogs offer an immense choice of seed selections, and many include instructions on where and how to start seeds. Suggested seed-starting times are based on the date of the average last frost in each region. If you do not know this date for your area, consult your local Cooperative Extension office. Many vegetables require a longer growing season than most climates in the United States allow; so unless you live in the Deep South or Southwest, you will probably have to give some seeds a head start indoors.

Seeds of unusual varieties can be hard to find. It is often possible to obtain these seeds from botanical gardens and plant societies; for a listing, see "Essential Resources," page 697.

### Collecting Seed

Collect seed from vegetables, flowers, and woody plants as soon as it ripens. Ripe fruit tends to be darker in color than unripe fruit. Choose fruit from vigorous plants. Clean the seed thoroughly, dry, and store in well-labeled, airtight containers.

Dry capsules, like the fruits of rhododendrons and many perennials or the cones of conifers, are the easiest to process. Simply hang the capsules upside down in a paper bag; seeds fall out into the bag. For fleshy fruits, like those of tomato, dogwood, and rose, soak in water for a few days and then rub off the fermenting flesh with your fingers. Add more water. The pulp and nonviable seeds tend to float and the viable seeds to sink. Dry the seeds thoroughly on paper towels before storing; separate drying seeds so they do not stick together.

### Pretreating Seeds to Aid Germination

All seeds need moisture and warmth to germinate. Some require light; others, darkness.

To speed germination of many seeds, soak them in warm water—smaller seeds for a few hours, larger ones overnight.

Some seeds will germinate only when additional conditions are met. These seeds have an internal survival mechanism, called *dormancy*, that protects them from germinating at the wrong time—when the ground is parched or frozen, and they would certainly die. Seeds of most woody plants require special treatment prior to germination; seeds of some herbaceous plants also benefit from these procedures. There are two basic methods of pretreating seeds to break dormancy: scarification and stratification.

### Scarification

Some seeds have extra thick seed coats impervious to water. These are said to exhibit seed-coat dormancy. In nature, soil bacteria and fungi decompose the thick coats. Scarification is the propagator's way to break this external dormancy.

Scarify seeds mechanically with a file or sandpaper. Roll a sheet of sandpaper with the rough side facing in and insert it into a tall quart jar. Drop in small quantities of hard-coated seeds; cap the jar and shake vigorously until the seed coats are worn thin. Or immerse the seeds in boiling water: Remove the water from the heat, add the seeds, and allow them to steep overnight. Many members of the Leguminosae or pea family respond to scarification and will germinate immediately thereafter.

### Stratification

Stratification is a technique used to break a kind of internal dormancy controlled by temperature. Stratification involves exposing seed to cold or warm temperatures—sometimes a combination of both—plus moisture. The most common is cold stratification. Some seeds require warm stratification, but this is generally followed by a cold treatment.

For cold stratification, combine seeds in Zip-loc bags with a premoistened sterile medium made from equal parts of sand and milled sphagnum moss; one part seeds to three parts medium by volume. Temperatures can range from 32°F to 50°F (most refrigerators operate at 41°F); the time that the seeds of various plants need to be exposed to the cold varies with different species but ranges from 30 to 120 days. A good rule of thumb is 90 days at 41°F. Check the seeds weekly to ensure they are moist with no sign of fungal attack. Label bags with contents, date of stratification, and, most important, date when the seeds should be removed.

Seeds with immature embryos benefit from warm stratification (prepare as for cold stratification) at temperatures from 65°F to 80°F—room temperature for most homes or the temperature on top of the refrigerator—for 90 to 120 days. When in doubt about which process the seed of a woody plant requires, start with cold stratification for 4 to 6 weeks. If the seed does not germinate, continue with a warm treatment followed by a second cold period.

## Starting Seeds

The easiest and probably the cheapest medium to use for germinating seeds indoors is a commercial fine-grade soilless seed-starting medium, available at garden supply centers. Should you want to mix your own, combine equal parts finely ground vermiculite and sphagnum moss.

Fill a tray or pot nearly to the top with medium and moisten with water. Take a handful and squeeze—the medium should clump together loosely. If water can be squeezed out, it is too wet. Broadcast seeds carefully; overcrowding results in weak, spindly stems. Seed

### SOME PLANTS REQUIRING SCARIFICATION

*Camellia* species, camellias
*Cercis canadensis,* redbud
*Cladrastis lutea,* yellowwood
*Cornus florida,* flowering dogwood
*Gleditsia triacanthos,* honey locust
*Koelreuteria paniculata,* goldenrain tree
*Paeonia suffruticosa,* tree peony
*Rosa blanda,* meadow rose

### SOME PLANTS REQUIRING COLD STRATIFICATION

*Acer* species, maples, except *A. rubrum* (Red maple) and *A. saccharinum* (Silver maple)
*Aesculus* species, horse chesnuts, buckeyes
*Amelanchier* species, shadbushes, serviceberries
*Cornus* species, dogwoods
*Iris* species, irises
*Magnolia* species, magnolias
*Pinus* species, pines
*Rosa* species, species roses
*Thalictrum* species, meadow rues

### SOME PLANTS REQUIRING WARM AND COLD STRATIFICATION

*Cornus alternifolia,* pagoda dogwood
*Crataegus* species, hawthorns
*Davidia involucrata,* dove tree
*Halesia carolina,* Carolina silverbell
*Lilium* species and hybrids, lilies
*Sorbus* species, mountain ashes
*Stewartia* species, stewartias
*Tilia* species, lindens
*Viburnum* species, viburnums

## A FEW VEGETABLES AND FLOWERS THAT REQUIRE LIGHT TO GERMINATE

*Artemisia annua*, wormwood
*Aster* species, asters
*Aurinia saxatilis*, basket-of-gold
*Echinops ritro*, globe thistle
*Gaillardia aristata*, blanketflower
*Lactuca sativa*, lettuce
*Petunia* x *hybrida*, garden petunia
*Phlox paniculata*, garden phlox
*Portulaca grandiflora*, rose moss
*Salvia farinacea*, farinacea salvia
*Sedum* species, stonecrops
*Veronica* species, speedwells

packets list optimum planting depth; a good rule of thumb is to sow to a depth of about 1½ times the diameter of the seed. Cover and use a fine mist to water the planted seeds.

Cover the container. Use a clear plastic wrap or encase the whole tray or pot in a clear plastic bag, and seal tightly. Set the tray in bright light but not direct sun. If droplets appear on the plastic, tap them back into the medium; if too much water builds up, open briefly. About 70°F is a good temperature for germination of most seeds. Some seeds, including those of many herbaceous and most woody plants, do not require light to germinate; for these, it is possible to speed germination by placing the tray of seeds on top of the refrigerator, where the seeds will benefit from the additional warmth.

### Light

Once seedlings sprout, remove the covering—at this point, good ventilation is vital to prevent damping off, a condition in which fungi kill seeds before or soon after they break through the soil. A south-facing window will generally provide sufficient light. Turn the flats often to even out growth, as plants naturally stretch toward the sun. Maintain daytime temperatures around 60°F to 70°F, slightly cooler at night; protect seedlings near windows from cold drafts. Supplementing light with grow lamps generally results in sturdier plants.

If you are relying mainly on artificial light, seedlings may require up to 16 hours a day to keep from becoming weak and spindly. Place young seedlings close to grow lights or fluorescent tubes—start 3 inches away and move to about 6 as the plants grow.

### Water

Watering is critical to successful propagation. Let the medium dry out slightly between waterings, but never allow seedlings to droop from lack of moisture. Press your finger into the medium; when it feels dry, set the pots in a tray of shallow water and allow the water to soak up through the bottom. Remove them only after the soil surface feels wet. On warm, bright days, plantings may have to be watered two or three times, and on dark, damp days not at all.

### Pricking Out

The first leaves to emerge on new seedlings are the cotyledons, or seed leaves. The true leaves, resembling those of the mature plant, follow. When the first set of true leaves appears, transplant the young seedlings. Prepare a new medium by mixing two parts compost with one part each of peat moss (or an alternative) and perlite, by volume. Fill containers with the medium and moisten with warm water; let the water soak in.

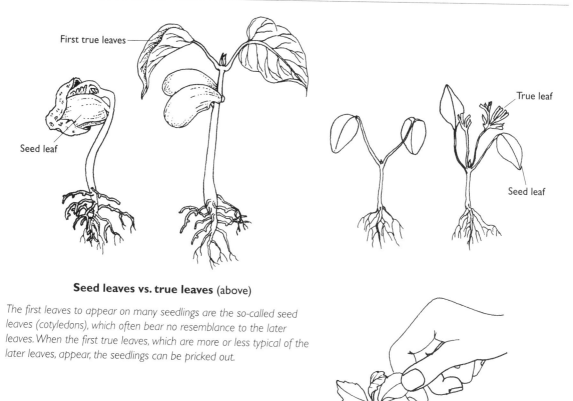

**Seed leaves vs. true leaves** (above)

*The first leaves to appear on many seedlings are the so-called seed leaves (cotyledons), which often bear no resemblance to the later leaves. When the first true leaves, which are more or less typical of the later leaves, appear, the seedlings can be pricked out.*

**Pricking out a seedling** (right)

*To prick out a seedling, grasp it by a leaf, as shown, not by the stem.*

Carefully lift or prick out tiny seedlings with a spoon or butter knife. Expose the roots to the air as little as possible. Protect roots and stems by holding the seedlings gently by a leaf, never the stem. Set the seedlings to the same depth in the new containers as they were in the germination medium; space fast-growing plants, like marigolds and tomatoes, at least 2 inches apart, or in individual pots. Gently firm the medium around the transplanted plants. Allow only the strongest seedlings to grow on. If you use individual pots, place them together in a tray or shallow pan to make watering easier.

## Fertilizing

Feed the seedlings with quarter-strength liquid fertilizer after transplanting and every two weeks thereafter until they are transplanted outdoors. Use a low-nitrogen fertilizer; too much fertilizer produces soft, leggy plants.

## Hardening Off

When all danger of frost is past, move the seedlings outdoors during the day into a shaded, sheltered location to harden them off before planting in the garden. Start with an hour or so and increase the exposure daily; after a few days, leave them out overnight. Plant in early evening or on a cloudy day; water well before and after. As with any transplant, dig a hole two times larger than the roots and set the plant to the same depth it was in the container.

## Vegetative Propagation

When it is necessary to eliminate genetic variation to ensure that characteristics of the parent plant—a certain color leaf, for example, or disease resistance—are preserved, one of the many techniques of vegetative or asexual propagation should be employed.

### Division

The crowns, clumps of suckers, tubers, corms, or bulbs of many plants are easily divided.

#### Herbaceous Perennials

In general, divide fall-blooming perennials in spring, and spring-blooming specimens after they bloom. Whether you do this annually or less often depends on the plant species. Plants that need dividing are crowded and show reduced vigor.

Choose a cloudy day. Lift out the plant with a spading fork. Break apart clumps with a spade or shovel. Pry tough clumps apart with two forks, back to back, for leverage, or chop straight through with a hatchet. Replant as quickly as possible and always to the same depth. Water thoroughly, and mulch in fall.

#### Bulbous Perennials

Perennials with bulbs or corms, like lilies or crocosmia, can be propagated from the small bulblets or cormels that form at the bulb base.

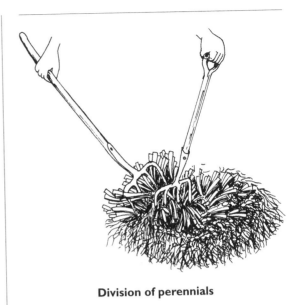

**Division of perennials**

*Break apart clumps with a spade or shovel. Pry tough clumps apart with two forks, back-to-back, for leverage, or chop straight through with a hatchet. Replant as quickly as possible.*

Some lilies can also be propagated from the bulbils that form on the stems in the axils of the leaves, or from scales on the bulbs that, when detached and placed in propagating medium, will produce bulblets. Rhizomatous perennials, such as bearded iris, are propagated by cutting the fleshy rhizome into sections.

#### Ferns

The simplest way to propagate ferns vegetatively is to divide branching rhizomes. Many divisions are possible from a modest clump of any fern with creeping rhizomes. Cut with a clean, sharp knife or pruners, or tease apart the tangled rhizomes. Make sure each division has growing tips. See "Plant Reproduction," page 100, for tips on propagating ferns from spores.

### Shrubs

Shrubs that form clumps and crowns are easily divided. Propagate in spring when they are still dormant, or in fall where winters are mild. Use a spade to chop off segments with rooted stems or dig up the entire plant and split it into sections with shears or a pruning saw. Replant immediately.

## Cuttings

Taking a cutting from a plant and rooting it is one of the easiest techniques used for vegetative propagation. Typically, the cutting is from the stem, but root and leaf cuttings are also used.

A good, sharp pair of pruning shears is essential for taking cuttings. Plastic tags and a waterproof pen are invaluable for labeling the cuttings. A grafting knife, although not essential for the beginning propagator, is useful for collecting and preparing cuttings.

### Cutting Medium

To create a good all-purpose rooting medium for cuttings, mix equal parts, by volume, of the following materials:

- Sand
- Grit
- Calcined clay
- Shredded styrofoam
- Milled spaghnum moss
- Perlite

### Sweat Box

To ensure high humidity around your cuttings, insert the tray of cuttings inside a clear plastic bag. Use twist ties to seal in moisture. Position blunt-ended stakes at the corners of the tray, or bend a hanger to form a framework to keep the plastic from touching the leaves.

---

## SOME SHRUBS WITH DIVISIBLE CROWNS OR CLUMPS

*Aesculus parviflora*, bottlebrush buckeye
*Aralia spinosa*, devil's walkingstick
*Aronia arbutifolia*, red chokeberry
*Clethra alnifolia*, summersweet
*Cornus* species, shrubby dogwoods
*Deutzia* species, deutzias
*Gaultheria procumbens*, wintergreen
*Hydrangea* species, hydrangeas
*Hypericum calycinum*, St.-John's-wort
*Indigofera* species, indigos
*Itea virginica*, Virginia sweetspire
*Kerria japonica*, Japanese kerria
*Lespedeza* species, bush clovers
*Leucothoe* species, fetterbushes
*Mahonia aquifolium*, Oregon grape holly
*Neviusia alabamensis*, snow-wreath
*Paxistima* species, paxistimas
*Potentilla fruticosa*, bush cinquefoil
*Rhododendron* species, some azaleas
*Rhus aromatica*, fragrant sumac
*Rosa* species, shrubby roses
*Rubus* species, bramble fruits
*Syringa vulgaris*, common lilac
*Vaccinium* species, blueberry, cranberry

---

Maintain even moisture and a clean environment inside the sweat box. Keep in bright light but never direct sun. Open once a week to check moisture and allow new air to circulate inside. Remove all dead leaves to avoid fungal attacks. All stem cuttings, but particularly evergreen cuttings, benefit from the addition of bottom heat. Once the roots form, open the plastic and remove it a day or so later. Plant when a strong root system is in place; keep new plants well watered and mulched.

## TIPS ON TAKING STEM CUTTINGS

- Choose healthy, vigorous plants, and water well for two days prior to taking cuttings.
- Cuttings from young plants tend to root faster and with a higher success rate than those from older ones.
- Cuttings from vertical stems, especially those of evergreens, tend to grow into upright plants; low side shoots are more apt to develop spreading habits.
- Collect cuttings early in the morning or on a cloudy day, in above-freezing temperatures.
- Select shoot tips from the current season's growth with two to three nodes or buds.
- Make cuttings uniform in length so they will not shade one another in propagating trays.
- For difficult-to-root plants, take cuttings with a "heel." Pull a side shoot down from the main branch so that some of the older wood stays attached, forming the heel.
- Do not allow cuttings to dry out; plunge the ends in a bucket of water or in plastic bags while you work.
- Root-promoting hormones can promote better rooting of cuttings and help prevent fungal attacks. Choose a powdered form and keep it clean. Never dip the cutting directly into, or return used powder to, the package. The more woody or the more difficult a plant is to root, the greater the concentration of hormone needed.
- Wounding helps some difficult plants to root. Before dipping in rooting hormone, cut away a narrow strip of bark at the cutting base no more than ¼ inch long.
- Remove the bottom set of leaves and insert cuttings up to one-half their length into a tray or pot filled with moistened propagation medium.
- To save space, trim back the individual leaves of large-leaved plants, like rhododendrons, by up to one-half.

### Propagating from stem cuttings

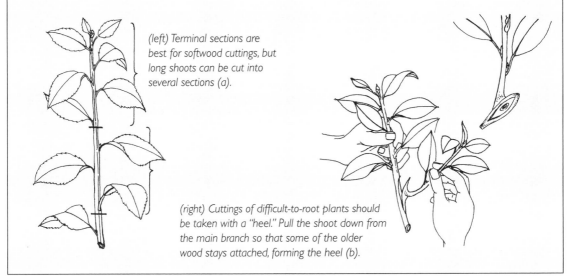

*(left) Terminal sections are best for softwood cuttings, but long shoots can be cut into several sections (a).*

*(right) Cuttings of difficult-to-root plants should be taken with a "heel." Pull the shoot down from the main branch so that some of the older wood stays attached, forming the heel (b).*

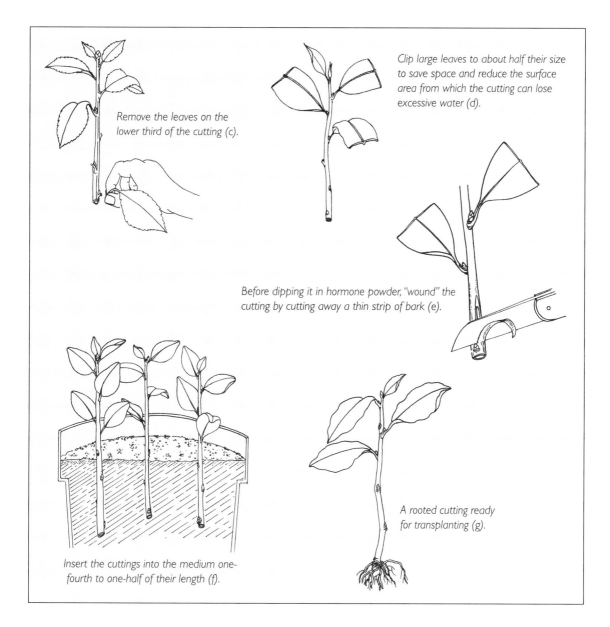

Remove the leaves on the lower third of the cutting (c).

Clip large leaves to about half their size to save space and reduce the surface area from which the cutting can lose excessive water (d).

Before dipping it in hormone powder, "wound" the cutting by cutting away a thin strip of bark (e).

A rooted cutting ready for transplanting (g).

Insert the cuttings into the medium one-fourth to one-half of their length (f).

## Stem Cuttings

Taking stem cuttings is one of the easiest ways to propagate woody and herbaceous plants. There are three basic types of stem cuttings: softwood, hardwood, and semihardwood. Follow the tips in the box for best success at rooting stem cuttings.

## Softwood Cuttings

Taken from young, flexible growth, softwood cuttings tend to root easily in high humidity. Collect from herbaceous plants in spring and summer. Take softwood cuttings from deciduous trees when the foliage is nearly mature in late spring and early summer, and

## SOME PLANTS THAT CAN BE PROPAGATED BY SOFTWOOD CUTTINGS

*Abelia* species, abelias
*Acer* species, maples
*Callicarpa* species, beautyberries
*Caryopteris* × *clandonensis*, bluebeard
*Clematis* species, clematis
*Clerodendron* species, glorybowers
*Clethra alnifolia*, summersweet
*Cornus* species, dogwoods
*Deutzia* species, deutzias
*Forsythia* species and hybrids, forsythias
*Fothergilla* species, fothergillas
*Gardenia jasminoides*, Cape jasmine
*Ginkgo biloba*, maidenhair tree
*Halesia carolina*, Carolina silverbell
*Hibiscus syriacus*, shrub althea, rose of Sharon
*Hibiscus rosa-sinensis*, Chinese hibiscus
*Hydrangea* species, hydrangeas
*Hypericum prolificum*, shrubby St.-John's-wort
*Ilex* species, deciduous hollies
*Itea virginica*, Virginia sweetspire
*Kerria japonica*, Japanese kerria

*Lagerstroemia indica*, crape myrtle
*Lavandula officinalis*, lavender
*Magnolia* species, magnolias
*Malus* species, apple, crabapple, some species and varieties
*Metasequoia glyptostroboides*, dawn redwood
*Parthenocissus tricuspidata*, Boston ivy
*Prunus* species, plum, cherry, flowering almond, cherry laurel
*Pyracantha coccinea*, scarlet firethorn
*Rhododendron* species, deciduous rhododendrons and azaleas
*Rhus aromatica*, fragrant sumac
*Rosa* species, roses
*Salix* species, willows
*Styrax* species, snowbells
*Syringa* species and hybrids, lilacs
*Ulmus* species, elms
*Viburnum* species, viburnums
*Vitex agnus-castus*, chaste tree
*Wisteria* species, wisterias

from broad-leaved evergreens in late summer. Shoots should snap when bent. For maples, magnolias, rhododendrons, and deciduous azaleas, wounding the base of the cutting will encourage rooting. Apply rooting hormone if desired.

Seal in a sweat box outdoors, or place under a mist system in a greenhouse. Plant and mulch in fall if roots are well developed. If not, overwinter by setting the container in the ground and mulching heavily or storing it indoors in temperatures below 45°F but above freezing.

### Hardwood Cuttings

Take hardwood cuttings after plants become dormant until early winter. Place cuttings in a prepared bed deep enough so that the top bud is just above the soil surface; mulch well to prevent frost heaving. Keep well watered. Or maintain the cuttings in a sweat box indoors at temperatures from 40°F to 50°F. Indoor cuttings should root by spring. Harden off and plant outdoors when all danger of frost is past.

### Semihardwood Cuttings

Collect cuttings from broadleaf evergreens in autumn and from needled evergreens in winter

## SOME PLANTS THAT CAN BE PROPAGATED BY HARDWOOD CUTTINGS

*Akebia quinata,* five-leaf akebia

*Alnus* species, alders

*Campsis radicans,* trumpet vine

*Caryopteris* × *clandonensis,* bluebeard

*Deutzia* species, deutzias

*Forsythia* species and hybrids, forsythias

*Morus* species, mulberries

*Parthenocissus* species, Boston ivy, Virginia
  creeper

*Ribes* species, currants

*Rosa* species, roses, some climbers and ramblers

*Salix* species, willows

*Vitis* species, grapes

## SOME PLANTS THAT CAN BE PROPAGATED FROM SEMIHARDWOOD CUTTINGS

### BROADLEAF EVERGREENS

*Andromeda polifolia,* bog-rosemary

*Arctostaphylos uva-ursi,* bearberry

*Buxus* species, boxes

*Calluna vulgaris,* heather

*Erica* species, heaths

*Ilex* species, hollies

*Kalmia latifolia,* mountain laurel

*Paxistima* species, paxistimas

*Pieris* species, pieris, andromedas

*Rhododendron* species, evergreen rhododendrons and azaleas

*Teucrium chamaedrys,* germander

### NEEDLED EVERGREENS

*Abies* species, firs

*Cephalotaxus harringtonia,* plum-yew

*Chamecyparis* species, false-cypresses

*Cryptomeria japonica,* cryptomeria

*Juniperus* species, junipers

*Picea* species, spruces

*Pinus* species, pines

*Sciadopitys verticillata,* Japanese umbrella-pine

*Taxus* species, yews

*Thuja* species, arborvitaes

*Tsuga* species, hemlocks

---

after at least one hard freeze; some varieties root better with a "heel" (see illustration page 482). Remove any flower buds as well as the bottom third of the leaves and insert in a sweat box. Keep cuttings indoors at temperatures between 60°F and 70°F, or in a greenhouse (misting is not recommended for needled evergreens). Cuttings also can be rooted outdoors in a cold frame. If rooted indoors, harden off and plant in spring once all danger of frost is past; plant outdoor-rooted cuttings in fall.

### Leaf Cuttings

This method is used extensively for propagating houseplants. The thick leaves of many plants, such as African violets, umbrella sedge, and snake plants (*Sansevieria* species), root easily any time of year. Water well the day before collecting. Take young, healthy leaves with 1 or 2 inches of petiole (leaf stem) attached; cut long snake plant leaves into 2-inch cross-sections. Use a sweat box; insert the petiole of full leaves up to the blade, which should rest on the surface of the medium. Push in snake plant leaf sections. New roots can take as long as 8 weeks.

### Root Cuttings

The optimum time to cut pieces of root is when plants are dormant; during the growing season, dig carefully to disturb the plant as lit-

## SOME PLANTS THAT CAN BE PROPAGATED BY ROOT CUTTINGS

### HERBACEOUS PLANTS

*Acanthus mollis*, bear's-breech
*Anchusa* species, buglosses
*Asclepias tuberosa*, butterfly weed
*Ceratostigma plumbaginoides*, leadwort
*Dicentra eximia*, bleeding heart
*Echinops* species, globe thistles
*Oenothera* species, evening primroses
*Papaver orientale*, Oriental poppy
*Pelargonium* species, geraniums
*Phlox* species, phlox
*Primula* species, primroses
*Saxifraga* species, saxifrages
*Verbascum* species, mulleins
*Yucca filamentosa*, Adam's needle

### WOODY PLANTS

*Acacia* species, acacias, some species
*Aesculus* species, buckeyes, horse chestnuts
*Aralia* species, aralias
*Asimina triloba*, pawpaw
*Calycanthus floridus*, Carolina allspice
*Clerodendron* species, glorybowers
*Fothergilla* species, fothergillas
*Gymnocladus dioicus*, Kentucky coffee tree
*Hypericum* species, St.-John's-worts
*Phellodendron amurense*, amur corktree
*Rhus* species, sumacs, some species
*Rosa* species, species roses
*Rubus* species, blackberry, raspberry
*Sassafras albidum*, sassafras
*Xanthorhiza simplicissima*, yellowroot
*Zanthoxylum americanum*, prickly ash

### Propagating from root cuttings

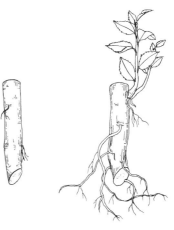

*Sturdy roots can be placed upright. Cut the top square and the bottom at an angle for quick differentiation when placing the cuttings in the propagation medium.*

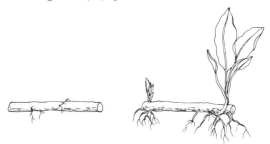

*Thin and/or flexible roots are more easily placed horizontally and covered with ¼"–½" of medium.*

tle as possible. As a rule, make 1- to 4-inch-long, ¼- to ½-inch-diameter cuttings with fine feeder roots. Variegated-leaved plants do not always come true with this method. Set root pieces—either vertically or horizontally—an inch deep or less in a prepared bed outdoors, inside in a sweat box at temperatures from 40°F to 50°F, or outdoors in a cold frame. New plants should appear by spring. Harden off and plant outdoors when all danger of frost is past.

## Layering

Layering encourages shoots still attached to the parent plant to develop roots, then the new plants are detached. Rooting time varies with the kind of plant, the age of the shoot, and the weather. There are three types of layering: simple layering, tip layering, and air layering. Which technique to use depends on the type of plant and the time of year.

### General Layering Technique

Water the parent plant well the day before you work.

To wound a shoot, make a diagonal knife cut about halfway through the stem and insert a toothpick to hold the flap open, or remove a ring of bark about half an inch wide around the portion of the shoot where roots will form.

For in-ground layering, prepare a shallow planting hole about 4 inches deep and amend the soil with compost.

Use U-shaped pieces of heavy wire to pin the shoot to keep the wound in contact with the soil.

### Simple Layering

Simple layering, which gives best results in early spring, works with many woody plants; those with low, flexible branches are best suited to this technique. Some easy-to-root plants may be ready by fall; however, where winters are severe, it is best to wait until spring before detaching the new plant. Magnolias and most evergreens can take up to two years to produce roots large enough to support a new plant.

Bend a long, supple shoot to the ground. At the spot where it touches the ground, 5 to 10 inches before the tip, dig and prepare a shallow planting hole. Wound the stem on the under-

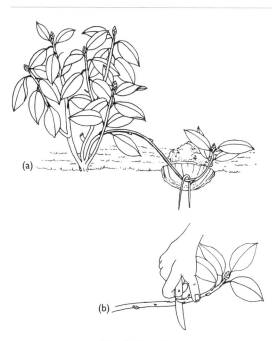

**Simple layering**

*Bend a long, supple shoot to the ground. At the spot 5"–10" before the tip, dig a shallow planting hole (a). Wound the stem on the underside (b) and pin it in place in the hole. Refill the hole, and keep well watered. When a good root system forms, separate the new plant from its parent and transplant.*

side and pin it in place in the hole. Refill the hole; stake the shoot tip if it does not stand straight. Keep well watered. When a good root system forms, separate the new plant from its parent and transplant.

Some fern species can also be propagated by simple layering. Buds growing on the fronds of these ferns can be manipulated to produce new plants. Anchor bud-bearing fronds to the ground or a pot of soil while they are still attached to the parent plant. If you must remove the fronds, keep them in high humidity, such as in a covered plastic container, while the plantlets develop.

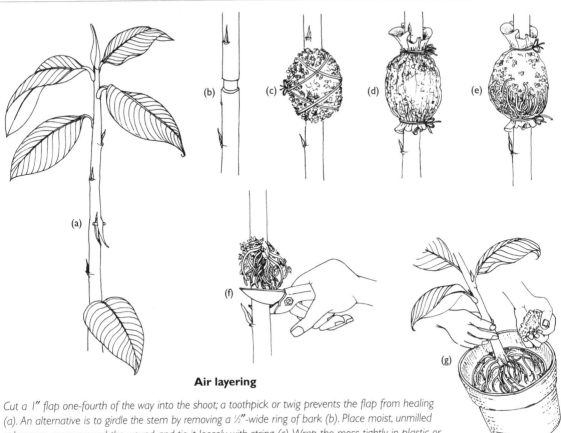

**Air layering**

*Cut a 1" flap one-fourth of the way into the shoot; a toothpick or twig prevents the flap from healing (a). An alternative is to girdle the stem by removing a ½"-wide ring of bark (b). Place moist, unmilled sphagnum moss around the wound and tie it loosely with string (c). Wrap the moss tightly in plastic or foil (d), sealing the top and bottom to conserve moisture. Roots will begin growing through the layer of sphagnum moss (e). When a healthy root system has formed, cut the air-layered stem just below the moss (f). Remove the plastic, and pot up the new plant (g).*

### Tip Layering

Tip layering is even simpler than simple layering. Toward the end of the summer, select a stem of current season growth and insert the tip in the ground. Prepare the hole, anchor the tip, and cover it with soil. Keep well watered. A new plant should poke out by autumn; when it does, cut back the cane connecting it with the parent plant at soil level. Move the new plant or leave it in place until the following spring. This method works well with bramble fruits.

### Air Layering

Some woody stems produce roots from a restricted, wounded section a few inches behind the growing tip. This procedure is most commonly performed on houseplants.

Soak long-fibered sphagnum moss in water. Select a stem from the current season's growth at any time of year for indoor plants. Trim off all the leaves and side shoots on a section 6 inches from the tip extending back to 12 inches. Wound the shoot roughly 9 inches from the tip. Use rooting hormone, if desired. Squeeze excess water from the sphagnum moss and place it around the wound. Cover with clear plastic and tie both ends with raffia. Plants in direct sun should be wrapped again in foil; clear plastic traps solar heat. Keep the moss moist. Once roots form, cut the air-layered stem just below the moss. Remove the plastic and pot up the new plant, moss and all.

Outdoors, pines are occasionally air-layered. Choose a stem in spring on wood from the previous season's growth, or in late summer from current-season growth. Use foil to shade the plastic and protect the wound from heat buildup.

## Grafting and Budding

More complicated than layering, grafting and budding are used to unite parts of two different plants. These techniques are often used to improve the disease or drought tolerance or affect the size or shape of plants. They involve attaching a scion (or bud) to an understock. The scion is the plant being propagated; the understock may be a seedling, rooted cutting, or even a mature tree.

Compatibility is key, both in terms of size and of botanical relationship: the more closely related the plants, the higher the chance of success. The scion and understock must fit together snugly so that the cambium of each comes into direct contact and grafts together; cambium is the thin, actively growing layer of tissue between the bark and the inner tissue of stems through which water and nutrients move in woody plants. Dry cambium tissue will not unite, and so speed is imperative if these forms of propagation are to be successful.

Garden supply companies offer all sorts of grafting paraphernalia, including grafting knives, special grafting tape, grafting rubbers, raffia, and wax.

**Scions.** Scions, ideally 4- to 6-inch-long stem tips ⅛ to ¼ inch in diameter, are collected from the previous season's growth in midwinter. When working with deciduous trees, select well-budded branches—with pointed leaf buds, not the rounder, fatter flower buds. Bundle the scions together and stand them straight up in about 6 inches of well-drained soil in a protected site outdoors. Or store them in moist paper towels or damp, unmilled sphagnum moss in a plastic bag in the refrigerator. Scions should be grafted in spring while still dormant; emerging leaves take too much energy from the plant and siphon off moisture.

**Understocks.** Select understock from one to three years old and the same diameter as, or larger than, the scion.

### Side-Veneer Grafting

This technique, which works well on deciduous and evergreen trees, requires well-lighted, warm interior space, or preferably a greenhouse. In autumn, pot up a young, two- to three-year-old seedling or cutting for use as understock; bring it indoors at least a month before grafting. In midwinter, collect scions with slightly smaller diameters than those of the understock.

Select a strong scion and make two sloping cuts at one end to create a blunt-edged wedge, exposing as much cambium as possible. On the stem of the understock about 2 inches above the soil, strip off a few inches of leaves and make a shallow, slightly curved cut into the wood, nearly parallel with the bark, about 1½ inches long. Gently bend the understock away from the cut and insert the scion wedge in the exposed opening. Match the cambium layers

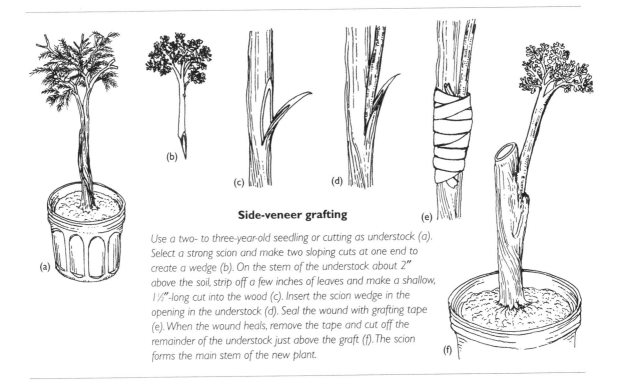

**Side-veneer grafting**

*Use a two- to three-year-old seedling or cutting as understock (a). Select a strong scion and make two sloping cuts at one end to create a wedge (b). On the stem of the understock about 2" above the soil, strip off a few inches of leaves and make a shallow, 1½"-long cut into the wood (c). Insert the scion wedge in the opening in the understock (d). Seal the wound with grafting tape (e). When the wound heals, remove the tape and cut off the remainder of the understock just above the graft (f). The scion forms the main stem of the new plant.*

and seal the wound with grafting tape. Wrap the plant in plastic to maintain high humidity and keep in temperatures between 55°F and 65°F. In a greenhouse, the graft should take in 6 to 8 weeks, slightly longer in other indoor areas.

When the wound heals, remove the tape and cut back half the understock. Two weeks later, cut off the remainder of the understock just above the graft. The scion forms the main stem of the new plant. Harden off gradually outdoors when all danger of frost is past. For best success, keep the plant in a container for one year; sink the container in the ground and mulch well during the first winter. The graft will be fragile and require protection for the first year.

### Whip-and-Tongue Grafting

This method is used mostly on fruit and ornamental deciduous trees. It requires consid-erable skill and should be performed outdoors in early spring. Scion and understock must be similar in size and cut at identical angles with matching tongue cuts for maximum cambium contact. The scion is grafted to the trunk of the understock, which is truncated to a few inches above the ground; the tongue cut and grafting tape keep the two in place until the graft heals, in from one to several months.

### Cleft-and-Saddle Grafting

This technique is performed outdoors, often on fruit trees—using either young understock or a mature tree. When performed on a mature tree, it is called *top grafting*. Young understock with a diameter of an inch or more or similar-size branches on a mature tree are truncated in early spring. The understock trunk or branch is split vertically, and the ends of two ¼-inch-

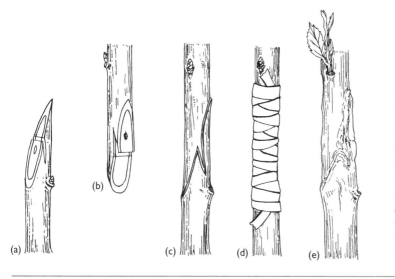

### Whip-and-tongue grafting

*This technique maximizes the amount of exposed cambium, increasing chances of success: Cut similar-size understock (a) and scion (b) at identical angles. Make longitudinal splits about one-third of the way down the length of both pieces. Fit scion to understock (c), aligning cambium layers as closely as possible. Seal the two together with grafting tape (d). When the wound heals, remove the tape and cut off the remainder of the understock just above the graft (e).*

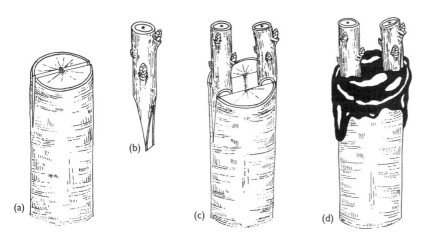

### Top or cleft-and-saddle grafting

*Truncate and then split a branch or trunk with a diameter of an inch or more (a). Select two scions each about ¹/₂″ in diameter and 3″ long, with two or three buds (b); make two sloping cuts at one end to create a wedge. Fit the two scions into the split (c), aiming for maximum cambium contact between understock and scions. Cover all exposed tissue with grafting wax (d) and cover the graft with plastic (e) to conserve moisture.*

## Budding

*Collect pencil-thin "bud sticks" (a) from the current season's growth; remove the leaf blades, but keep the petioles in place (b). Slice out single buds (c), starting from just above and making a gentle curve behind the bud; use the leaf petiole to grasp the tiny buds. Side (d), front (e), and rear (f) views of the bud are shown. On the understock a few inches above the soil, make a shallow T-cut, 2" long and 1" across (g). Loosen the bark and gently insert a bud, right side up (h). Bud is shown partially (h) and fully (i) in place. Tape the wound, being careful to leave the bud uncovered (j). Remove the tape and cut the remaining understock above when the bud takes, usually in about three weeks (k).*

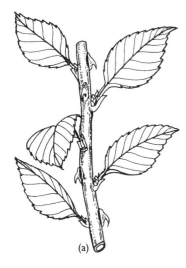

(a)

(b)

(c)

(d)

(e)

(f)

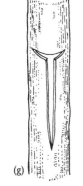

(g)

(h)

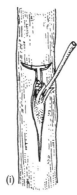

(i)

(j)

(k)

diameter scions with wedge-cut ends are inserted and arranged for maximum cambium contact. Grafting wax and a plastic covering help maintain moisture around the wound. If both scions graft successfully, only one is allowed to grow on the next season.

### Budding

Best for roses, fruit trees, and some shade trees, this technique can be accomplished only when the cambium tissue is actively growing in late summer—when the bark slips or separates easily from the wood. Bud grafts tend to heal quickly and remain dormant until spring.

Select understock at least ½ inch in diameter. Collect pencil-thin "bud sticks" from the current season's growth. Remove the leaf blades, but keep the petioles in place. (If you do not use the bud sticks immediately, wrap them in damp paper towels in plastic bags and store in the refrigerator.) Choose pointed leaf buds, not the fatter flower buds. Slice out single buds; start just above and make a gentle curve behind the bud. Use the leaf petiole to grasp tiny buds. Keep them moist and work quickly.

On the understock a few inches above the soil, make a shallow T-cut, 2 inches vertically and 1 inch across. Loosen the bark and gently insert a bud, right side up. Tape the wound, but never cover the bud. Be sure to remove the wrapping as soon as the bud takes, in about three weeks. Cut the top of the understock once the bud opens and you are sure that the graft has succeeded.

## Further Reading

Browse, Philip McMillan. *Plant Propagation.* Published in cooperation with the Royal Horticultural Society. New York: Simon & Schuster, 1988.

Dirr, Michael A. *Manual of Woody Landscape Plants: Their Identification, Ornamental Characteristics, Culture, Propagation and Uses.* Champaign, Ill.: Stipes Publishing, 1990.

Phillips, Harry R. *Growing and Propagating Wildflowers.* Chapel Hill: The University of North Carolina Press, 1990.

## Gardening in Containers

Containers can embellish a garden—or be its heart and soul. The key to successful potted plantings is recognizing that the container environment differs in some important respects from conditions in the ground. The following are a few considerations unique to container gardening.

* A container is by definition a constricted environment for plant roots. Select plants with compact root systems and those bred especially for growing in containers.

* Choose containers at least 18 inches in diameter or square for outdoor plantings; anything smaller cramps roots and makes watering an all-too-frequent chore.

* Plants in containers generally need to be watered more frequently than those in the ground.

* Container plantings also require more fertilizer than in-ground plantings because the regular waterings leach away soil nutrients.

* Roots of container specimens are more easily harmed by extreme temperatures than those of in-ground plants. Choose perennial plants that are hardy to one or two zones colder than your in-ground zone, or provide plantings in cold climates with winter protection. For plantings in full sun, select plants native to drier regions that will be more drought-tolerant.

• If you garden on a balcony or rooftop, or plan to move containers often, consider the size of the container and the weight of the medium.

• Always firmly secure with brackets or bolts any aboveground containers, such as window boxes, that could slip off ledges or balconies and injure persons below. Check with local officials to see if any regulations apply.

## Choosing Containers

Drainage holes are essential in a container, but the choice of size, style, and container material is limited only by a gardener's imagination. Select containers judiciously; a mix of types can be attractive, but too many different styles create disharmony.

### Clay or Terra Cotta

Glazed or unglazed, plain or ornate with designs raised on the surface, clay pots can be expensive and heavy, but they are the pot of choice for many gardeners. Unglazed pots, which are extremely porous, require extra watering in hot weather; however, the loss of water through evaporation cools the soil and the plant's roots, and water loss can be reduced by sealing the inside of clay containers below the soil line with the black tar paint sold for coating cut tree limbs. Some gardeners use decorative clay pots to disguise the less porous plastic ones set inside them.

In climates with freezing winter temperatures, clay pots must be covered or emptied and turned upside down to protect them from freezing and thawing, and resulting breakage.

### Plastic

Many lightweight plastic pots mimic the look of terra cotta. They tend to be a bit shiny and lack clay's ability to develop an attractive, weathered patina, but they require less watering and less overwinter care. Excellent for rooftops and window boxes where weight is an important consideration, they must be secured where heavy winds in an exposed area could blow them over.

### Wood

Planters and window boxes come in a variety of woods. Wood is sturdy and attractive but will eventually rot. Half whiskey barrel planters are a favorite of many gardeners. These are heavy and sturdy, and their thick walls provide some insulation; however, moving a planted barrel requires herculean strength.

Today, half whiskey barrels are made especially for plants. It is sometimes possible to find and recycle one that previously was used for making wine or whiskey; if necessary, drill drainage holes.

Many do-it-yourself wooden planter kits are on the market, or you can design and make your own. Do not use pressure-treated wood, which can harm plants. Use a rot-resistant wood such as redwood, teak, or cypress that has been deemed sustainably produced by a reputable certification organization; many of these species have been overexploited or grow in sensitive habitats. Apply paint or a low-toxicity borate preservative and water-resistant coating to retard decay on containers for decorative plants, but not those for edible plants.

### Concrete and Stone

Durable ornamental cast-concrete containers come in a vast array of shapes and textural finishes. These are very heavy but long-lasting. Drill drainage holes if none exists. Cast-concrete can chip, so it is a good idea to use this kind of container only if it will be placed in a permanent position. It can also suffer damage from freezing weather; like clay pots, cast-concrete ones must be protected in winter. Less expensive and lighter copies of ornate stone planters are available, some of them made from fiberglass.

## Metal

Because metal heats up quickly and holds heat, these containers are best lined with plastic—either another container or a heavy-duty plastic garbage bag. Imitation cast-iron planters, made of lighter, less expensive metals like aluminum, are available. Any number of metal household containers can be recycled to make planters, from colorful olive oil tins to old-fashioned tubs. If you are unsure about whether the metal poses a danger to your plants or want to protect the container from corrosion, line the inside.

## Planting Medium

Almost any mix that drains well and retains water will do—unadulterated soil from the garden will gradually become cementlike in a container. Soil-based media are heavier than soilless ones, which are excellent for rooftop gardens where weight can be a limiting factor, although they may dry out quicker and require more fertilizing. Before you add a growing medium to any container, cover the drainage holes with a piece of window screen or a layer or two of newspaper.

When mixing a soil-based or a soilless medium, add small amounts of organic sources of nitrogen (such as blood meal or soybean meal), phosphorus (like bonemeal or rock phosphate), and potash (such as wood ashes, greensand, or rock potash), a complete organic fertilizer, or a slow-release synthetic fertilizer such as 5-10-5 or 5-10-10.

Many gardeners have favorite recipes. Two reliable mixtures are listed in the box.

---

### PLANTING MIXES FOR CONTAINERS

#### Soil-Based Mix
(measured by volume)

2 parts compost
1 part shredded bark
1 part builder's sand
1 part perlite

If you do not make your own compost, you can purchase a commercial compost at the local garden center. The compost or other organic matter in the medium, especially in containers with perennials or trees and shrubs, will help keep soil microorganisms active and the soil healthy.

#### Soilless Mix
(measured by volume)

½ part peat moss or alternative*
½ part perlite
1 part finely shredded pine bark
1 part builder's sand

Wet with warm water to make mixing the peat moss, shredded bark, or coco peat easier. A commercially prepared mix of peat moss and perlite is sold in most garden centers.

If you are growing moisture-loving plants, substitute vermiculite for perlite in either medium.

*Peat moss is extracted from northern bogs. Many gardeners have begun experimenting with alternatives such as compost, shredded bark, and coco peat. Like compost and shredded bark, coco peat—a waste product of cutting and sifting coconuts for fiber production—is a recycled material.

---

# WINDOW BOXES

Almost any kind of plant can grow in a window box: flower and foliage plants, favorite herbs for cooking, small salad greens and other diminutive vegetables, miniature roses, little bulbs, and even small evergreens. Window boxes have great charm when they are planted with the same attention to design as a garden bed or border. Choose plants in a gradation of heights to create the illusion of depth and space. Put the tallest plants in the back; medium-sized plants next; and low ones and trailing vines along the front and sides of the box.

The best soil mix for window boxes is the same light, porous, well-drained but water-retentive medium recommended for other types of containers.

## A SAMPLING OF PLANTS FOR WINDOW BOXES

### Full Sun

*Antirrhinum majus*, snapdragon
*Arctotis stoechadifolia*, African daisy
*Calendula officinalis*, pot marigold
*Callistephus chinensis*, China aster
*Celosia plumosa*, woolflower
*Centaurea cyanus*, bachelor's button
*Cheiranthus* species, wallflowers
*Chrysanthemum* species, garden mums
*Cineraria maritima*, dusty miller
*Crocus* species, crocuses
*Dahlia* species, dahlias
*Dianthus* species, garden pinks, sweet William
*\*Dimorphotheca sinuata*, Cape marigold
*\*Eschscholzia californica*, California poppy
*\*Gazania* species, treasure flowers
*Gomphrena globosa*, globe amaranth
*Iberis umbellata*, globe candytuft
*Impatiens* species, impatiens
*\*Mesembryanthemum crystallinum*, ice plant
*Ocimum basilicum*, sweet basil
*Origanum majorana*, sweet marjoram
*Origanum vulgare* subsp. *hirtum*, Greek oregano
*Pelargonium* species, zonal geraniums, ivy-leaved geraniums, scented-leaved geraniums
*Petunia* x *hybrid*, hybrid petunias
*Phlox drummondii*, Drummond phlox, annual phlox

*\*Portulaca grandiflora*, rose moss
*Salvia* species, sages
*Tagetes* species, marigolds
*Tropaeolum* species, nasturtiums
*Verbena* x *hybrida*, garden verbenas
*Zinnia* species, zinnias

\*Indicates plants especially tolerant of hot, dry conditions

### Sun or Partial Shade

*Allium* species, chives
*Browallia speciosa*, browallia
*Buxus* species, boxwoods
*Catharanthus roseus*, Madagascar periwinkle
*Chamaecyparis* species, false cypresses
*Chionodoxa* species, glory-of-the-snow
*Hedera helix*, English ivy
*Hosta* species, small hostas
*Hyacinthus orientalis*, hyacinth
*Lobelia erinus*, lobelia
*Lobularia maritima*, sweet alyssum
*Muscari* species, grape hyacinths
*Narcissus* species, daffodils, narcissi
*Petroselinum* species, parsleys
Salad greens
*Scilla siberica*, siberian squill
*Solenostemon scutellarioides*, coleus
*Torenia fournieri*, wishbone flower

*Vinca minor,* periwinkle
*Viola* species, pansies, violas, violets

**Partial and Light Shade**

*Aucuba japonica,* gold dust tree
*Begonia* species, wax and tuberous begonias
*Caladium* species, caladiums

*Chlorophytum comosum,* spider plant
*Cordyline terminalis,* ti plant
*Dracaena marginata,* dracaena
*Fatsia japonica,* Japanese fatsia
*Galanthus* species, snowdrops
*Impatiens* species, bedding impatiens
*Primula* species, primroses
*Viola cornuta,* horned violet

In general, herbaceous plantings require about 15 to 18 inches of soil for good root development; some annual bedding plants can thrive in as little as 12 inches. Trees and shrubs require deeper quarters.

On rooftops where weight is critical, deep planters with a lot of soil or even soilless medium can be too heavy. Consequently, some gardeners fill the bottom of containers used for annual plantings with a lightweight organic or even inorganic substance such as pine cones, branches and twigs, or styrofoam packing material.

## Caring for Container Plantings

Elevate containers so that the drainage holes are not flush with the ground or rooftop and can drain freely; use bricks, boards, or other materials to raise them a few inches or more. In addition to allowing water to drain better, raising planters promotes good air circulation.

### Watering

Watering is critical for container plantings. Water-stressed plants are more vulnerable to pests and disease pathogens. Water thoroughly as soon as the soil in containers feels dry to the touch, and do not stop until after the water seeps out the bottom drainage holes. Mulch container plantings to aid moisture retention.

### THE BOTTOM OF THE POT

Some research has shown that the once-favored technique of lining pot bottoms with broken pot chards or gravel not only does not increase drainage but may actually reduce it. Water settles at the bottom of a pot, and the layer of shards reduces the overall depth of soil, which can be detrimental in shallow pots. Cover drainage holes with pieces of window screen or a layer or two of newspaper.

Inspect the plants for insect pests while you water. Use a strong water spray from the hose to blast away any aphids or spider mites; when spotted early enough, they are relatively easy to dislodge.

### Fertilizing

Feed perennial plantings annually with organic fertilizer or slow-release synthetic granular fertilizer, such as 5-10-5 or 5-10-10. For bedding plants and other annuals, fertilize every other week during the growing season with a liquid fertilizer. Foliar feedings of diluted manure, compost tea, or fish emulsion will give any planting a quick pick-me-up.

Check the pH of your container soil from

## SELECTED ANNUALS TO GROW IN CONTAINERS

*Agastache* species, agastaches
*Anethum graveolens,* dill
*Antirrhinum majus,* snapdragon
*Begonia* species, begonias
*Browallia speciosa,* browallia
*Calendula officinalis,* pot marigold
*Callistephus chinensis,* China aster
*Catharanthus roseus,* Madagascar periwinkle
*Cobaea scandens,* cup and saucer vine
*Datura inoxia,* angel's trumpet
*Dolichos lablab,* hyacinth bean
*Fuchsia* species, fuchsias
*Gomphrena globosa,* globe amaranth
*Heliotropium arborescens,* pie cherry
*Ipomoea alba,* moon vine
*Ipomoea purpurea,* morning glory
*Lantana* species, lantanas
*Lathyrus odoratus,* sweetpea
*Limonium sinuatum,* statice
*Lobelia erinus,* lobelia
*Lobularia maritima,* sweet alyssum
*Mirabilis jalapa,* four-o'clock
*Nicotiana* species, flowering tobaccos
*Ocimum basilicum,* basil
*Pelargonium* species, geraniums
*Perilla frutescens,* perilla
*Petroselinum crispum,* parsley
*Petunia* × *hybrida,* petunia
*Portulaca* species, portulacas
*Salvia splendens,* scarlet sage
*Senecio cineraria,* dusty miller
*Tagetes* species, marigolds
*Thunbergia alata,* black-eyed Susan
*Tropaeolum majus,* nasturtium
*Verbena* × *hybrida,* garden verbenas

## SELECTED PERENNIALS TO GROW IN CONTAINERS

*Achillea filipendulina,* yarrow, Zones 3–10
*Astilbe* species, astilbes, Zones 4–8
*Baptisia australis,* false indigo, Zones 3–10
*Bergenia cordifolia,* bergenia, Zones 3–10
*Dicentra eximia,* bleeding heart, Zones 3–10
*Echinacea purpurea,* purple coneflower, Zones 3–10
*Eupatorium purpureum,* Joe-Pye weed, Zones 3–10
*Hemerocallis* × *hybrida,* hybrid daylilies, Zones 3–10
*Hosta* species and hybrids, hostas, Zones 3–9
*Liatris spicata,* gayfeather, Zones 3–10
*Lychnis chalcedonica,* Maltese cross, Zones 3–10
*Monarda didyma,* bee balm, Zones 4–10
*Oenothera speciosa,* evening primrose, Zones 5–10
*Paeonia lactiflora,* garden peony, Zones 2–10
*Phlox carolina,* wedding phlox, Zones 4–9
*Rudbeckia fulgida,* orange coneflower, Zones 3–10
*Rudbeckia laciniata,* cutleaf coneflower, Zones 3–10
*Sedum spectabile,* stonecrop, Zones 4–10
*Solidago* hybrids, goldenrods, Zones 3–10
*Tanacetum vulgare,* tansy, Zones 3–9
*Thermopsis villosa,* Carolina lupine, Zones 3–10
*Veronica spicata,* speedwell, Zones 3–10

time to time, especially if you grow plants that require extremes of acidity or alkalinity, such as acid-loving rhododendrons and azaleas.

### Rejuvenation

For containers filled with annual plantings in a soil-based medium, it is not necessary to

## SELECTED VEGETABLES TO GROW IN CONTAINERS

**Basil**
'Ball Basic'
'Dwarf Italian'
'Greek Minia-
ture'
'Green Bush'
'Spicy Globe'

**Bok-Choy**

'Ching Chiang'
'Mei Qing Choy'

**Broccoli**
'Atlantic'
'Dandy Early'
'Green Comet'

**Cabbage**
'Earliana'
'Fast Ball'
'Harbinger'
'Minicole'

**Carrot**
'Amstel'
'Baby Spike'
'Golden Ball'
'Little Finger'
'Minicor'
'Mokum'

'Orbit'
'Parmex'
'Planet'
'Thumbelina'

**Cauliflower**
'Garant'
'Predominant'
'Snowbaby'

**Cress**
'Cresson'
'Moss Curled'
'Upland'

**Cucumber**
'Bush Cham-
pion'
'Bush Crop'
'Fanfare'
'Mincu'
'Pot Luck'
'Salad Bush'
'Spacemaster'

**Dill**
'Fernleaf'

**Endive**
'Fine
Maraichere'
'Galia'

'Moss Curled'

**Kale**
'Dwarf Green
Curled'
'Showbor'

**Lettuce**
'Baby Oak'
'Biondo Lisce'
'Dapple'
'Green Ice'
'Green
Mignonette'
'Little Gem'
'Lollo Biondo'
'Lollo Rossa'
'Morgana'
'Red Lep-
rechaun'
'Rougette du
Midi'
'Salina'
'Tom Thumb'
'Valeria'

**Parsley**
'Curlina'
'Extra Curled'
'Extra Curled
Dwarf'

**Pea**
'Early Patio'

**Pepper**
'Gypsy'

**Radicchio**
'Red Verona'
'Scilla'

**Radish**
'Cherry Belle'
'Comet'
'Easter Egg'
'Fluo'
'Sparkler'

**Scallion/Green
Onion**
'Red Bunching'
'Tokyo Bunch-
ing'

**Sweet Pepper**
'Albino'
'Jingle Bells'

**Swiss Chard**
'Compacta Slow
Bolting'

**Tomato**
'Better Bush
Improved'
'Gem State'
'Husky Gold'
'Northern
Exposure'
'Patio'
'Patio Prize'
'Pixie Hybrid'
'Red Robin'
'Small Fry'
'Super Bush'
'Tiny Tim'
'Toy Boy'
'Tumbler'
'Whippersnap-
per'
'Yellow Canary'

**Turnip**
'Market Express'

**Zucchini
Squash**
'Burpee Hybrid'
'Golden Rocky'

change the soil yearly. Work in some fresh compost before adding the new season's plantings. However, if the soil becomes infected with pathogens from a diseased plant, then it is necessary to remove all the soil and scrub the inside of the container thoroughly before refilling with fresh medium. Soilless mediums break down more readily, and it is a good idea to change each spring the soilless mixes in which annuals are planted to ensure proper drainage.

After three to five years, the soil in containers with permanent plantings, such as trees and

## CHOICE SHRUBS FOR POT CULTURE

All zones refer to the USDA Hardiness Zone Map (see page 30).

*Abutilon* × *hybridum,* flowering maple, Zones 9–10

*Agapetes serpens,* agapetes, Zones 9–10

*Brugmansia versicolor,* angel's trumpet, Zone 4

*Camellia sasanqua,* sasanqua camellia, Zone 8

*Cestrum elegans* 'Smithii', red cestrum, Zone 10

*Choisya ternata,* Mexican orange, Zone 7

*Cistus* × *purpureus,* orchid rockrose, Zone 7

*Cornus alba* 'Sibirica', tartarian dogwood, Zones 2–8

*Corylus avellana* 'Contorta', Harry Lauder's walking-stick, Zones 4–8

*Cotoneaster congestus* 'Likiang', cotoneaster, Zone 6

*Daphne* × *burkwoodii,* burkwood daphne, Zone 5

*Daphne cneorum,* garland daphne, Zone 4

*Enkianthus campanulatus,* enkianthus, Zone 4

*Escallonia rubra,* red escallonia, Zone 8

*Euonymus japonicus* 'Microphyllus', box-leaf euonymus, Zones 7–9

*Euonymus japonicus* 'Albo-marginatus', variegated euonymus, Zones 7–9

*Fothergilla gardenii,* dwarf fothergilla, Zones 5–8

*Gardenia augusta* (*G. jasminoides*), gardenia, Zone 8

*Hibiscus rosa-sinensis,* Hawaiian hibiscus, Zone 10

*Hydrangea macrophylla,* big-leaf hydrangea, Zone 6

*Hydrangea quercifolia,* oak-leaf hydrangea, Zone 5

*Ilex cornuta* 'Dazzler', Chinese holly, Zone 7

*Kalmia latifolia,* mountain laurel, Zones 4–9

*Leptospermum scoparium,* New Zealand tea, Zones 9–10

*Loropetalum chinense,* loropetalum, Zones 7–9

*Mahonia lomariifolia,* mahonia, Zone 7

*Melaleuca nesophylla,* pink melaleuca, Zones 9–10

*Melianthus major,* honeybush, Zones 9–10

*Myrtus communis,* Greek myrtle, Zone 8

*Nerium oleander,* oleander, Zones 7–8

*Osmanthus delavayi,* delavayi osmanthus, Zone 7

*Osmanthus heterophyllus* 'Variegatus', variegated holly-leaf osmanthus, Zone 7

*Photinia* × *fraseri,* photinia, Zones 7–9

*Pieris japonica,* mountain andromeda, Zones 5–8

*Pittosporum tobira,* pittosporum, Zone 8

*Prunus laurocerasus,* cherry laurel, Zone 6

*Rhaphiolepis indica,* Indian hawthorn, Zone 8

*Rosmarinus officinalis,* rosemary, Zone 6

*Sambucus canadensis* 'Variegata', variegated American elderberry, Zones 3–9

*Skimmia japonica,* Japanese skimmia, Zones 7–9

*Syringa microphylla* 'Superba', lilac, Zones 4–8

*Viburnum plicatum* f. *tomentosum* 'Mariesii', Japanese snowball, Zones 5–8

*Weigela florida* 'Variegata', variegated weigela, Zones 5–8

## CHOICE TREES FOR POT CULTURE

*Acer palmatum,* Japanese maple, Zones 5–8

*Amelanchier arborea,* shadblow, serviceberry, Juneberry, Zones 4–9

*Betula nigra,* river birch, Zones 4–9

*Callistemon citrinus,* bottlebrush, Zone 9

*Cercis canadensis,* redbud, Zones 4–9

*Chamaecyparis obtusa,* Hinoki cypress, Hinoki false cypress, Zones 4–8

*Chionanthus virginicus,* white fringetree, Zones 3–9

*Cornus kousa,* Japanese dogwood, Zones 4–8

*Cotinus obovatus,* American smoke tree, Zones 4–8

*Crataegus crus-galli,* cockspur hawthorn, Zones 3–7

*Crataegus viridis* 'Winter King', hawthorn, Zone 4

*Ginkgo biloba,* ginkgo, Zones 3–8

*Gleditsia triacanthos,* honey locust, Zones 3–9

*Halesia carolina,* Carolina silverbell, Zones 4–8

*Hamamelis mollis,* Chinese witchhazel, Zones 5–8

*Hibiscus syriacus,* rose of Sharon, Zones 5–8

*Ilex opaca,* American holly, Zones 5–9

*Juniperus chinensis,* Chinese juniper, Zones 3–9, depending on cultivar

*Juniperus scopulorum,* Rocky Mountain juniper, Colorado red cedar, Zones 3–7

*Juniperus virginiana,* eastern red cedar, Zones 2–9

*Lagerstroemia indica,* common crape myrtle, Zones 7–9 (will become a herbaceous perennial in temperatures below 5° to −10°F)

*Maackia amurensis,* amur maackia, Zones 3–7

*Magnolia tomentosa (M. stellata),* star magnolia, Zones 3–8

*Malus floribunda,* Japanese flowering crabapple, Zones 5–8

*Malus sargentii,* Sargent crabapple, Zones 4–8

*Oxydendrum arboreum,* sourwood, sorrel tree, Zones 4–9

*Picea glauca* var. *albertiana,* Alberta spruce, Zones 2–6

*Pinus thunbergii,* Japanese black pine, Zones 5–7

*Prunus cerasifera,* flowering plum, Zones 3–8

*Prunus* × 'Okame', Okame flowering cherry, Zones 5–8

*Prunus serrulata* and cultivars, Japanese flowering cherries, Zones 5–8, depending on cultivar

*Prunus subhirtella,* higan cherry, Zones 4–8

*Syringa reticulata,* Japanese tree lilac, Zones 4–7

*Thuja occidentalis,* arborvitae, Zones 2–8

shrubs, may need rejuvenation. Scratch out the top 2 to 3 inches of soil, taking care not to injure surface roots. Refill with fresh compost or a soilless medium. Fertilize and water.

After many years, some container plantings begin to decline. When this happens, slide the plant with root ball intact from the container. Loosen the soil and tease out roots along the sides of the ball; making clean cuts, prune roots back by an inch or more. Return the root ball to the container and fill in with fresh compost or soilless medium. If the plant is too large or heavy to remove from the container, use a sharp knife to slice a few inches of soil and roots back from the sides of the container. Refill, water, and fertilize.

## Overwintering

Water well throughout autumn to prepare the plant for the coming season, and remember to check to see if it needs water during warm, dry spells in winter. If possible, cluster trees and shrubs together in climates with severe winters and move them if necessary to a protected area away from desiccating winds. Mulch heavily.

## Plant Selection

Container-grown plants are more exposed to the elements than garden-grown ones. If you overwinter container plantings in regions with freezing temperatures, choose varieties hardy to one or even two USDA hardiness zones colder than your in-ground zone. If the planters are in full sun, select plants that grow naturally in arid, open fields, prairies, and meadows, and those native to drier regions around the world, such as the Mediterranean or warm temperate climates. Silver- and white-leaved plants generally come from warm temperate climates; tiny fuzzy grayish hairs on the foliage trap moisture.

Plant herbaceous and woody plants in containers at the same growing height that you would set them in the ground. Maintain the soil level below the container rim to allow for watering.

## Annuals

Annuals, the traditional choice for containers, can provide a splash of color anywhere you need it. Almost any annual does well in a pot, and you do not have to worry about overwintering. You can purchase annuals at your local garden center, or start them from seed indoors.

## Perennials

Growing perennials in containers, at least in cold climates, is a little more complicated than dealing with annuals because they must be overwintered. However, once you discover which ones survive for you, you will have container plantings that come back year after year.

## Bulbs

Spring- and summer-blooming bulbs are spectacular in containers. Set them in planters at the same depth recommended for ground planting, and allow the foliage of spring-flowering bulbs to die back naturally if you want them to bloom the following season. Unless winters are very mild, dig up summer bulbs and overwinter them in a sheltered location.

If you keep bulbs in the container, plant annuals as soon as flowering is finished to camouflage the yellowing foliage. Bulbs make excellent underplantings for trees and shrubs and are good companions for perennials.

## Vegetables

Vegetables in containers require the same nutrients as those grown in the ground. Most small vegetables will thrive in about 8 inches of soil; larger ones require 12 inches or more. You can cultivate almost any vegetable in a container, but those with dwarf and bushy habits are particularly appropriate; seed companies have hybridized many such varieties of broccoli, cabbage, carrot, cauliflower, cucumber, kale, lettuce, pea, pepper, radicchio, radish, scallion and onion, swiss chard, squash, tomato, and turnip.

The varieties listed in the chart (see page 499) are especially suited for tubs and pots because of their small size or compact growth habits.

## Trees and Shrubs

The mortality rate for trees in containers is high, especially in regions with severe winters. Winter is the season planters are most often neglected. Sometimes too little water, wind burn, and desiccation are the cause of the plant's demise; other times, the rapid freezes and thaws expose and damage roots.

Container size is important. The larger the container, the better the chance that the tree or shrub will survive in both winter and summer; roots stop growing at 90°F, and small containers heat up rapidly in full sun. Choose containers that can accommodate the size of the root ball and allow for two to three years' growth. Evergreens in particular do not take well to annual transplanting.

## Further Reading

Hillier, Malcolm. *The Book of Container Gardening.* New York: Simon and Schuster, 1991.

Holmes, Roger, ed. *Taylor's Guide to Container Gardening.* Boston: Houghton Mifflin Co., 1995.

Schultz, Warren. *For Your Garden: Pots and Containers.* New York: Friedman/Fairfax, 1996.

Yang, Linda. *The City Gardener's Handbook: From Balcony to Backyard.* New York: Random House, 1995.

# Pruning

Proper pruning requires an understanding of a plant's natural habit. Pruning a naturally spreading or tall tree or shrub to fit into a small space can be self-defeating. It is easier on the plant and a more practical use of your time to grow a plant whose habit and size are appropriate for the landscape and the specific site. Every action has a reaction, and with pruning this can mean intense, vigorous regrowth—exactly what you did *not* intend.

## Why Prune?

There are five good reasons to prune woody plants. (Pruning herbaceous plants is addressed at the end of this section.)

• Prune for the health of the plant. Remove dead, damaged, crossing, and diseased limbs. Prune back to healthy tissue. Most disease pathogens enter through wounds; proper pruning cuts enable the plant to better protect itself from them. Sometimes, exterior branches and foliage form an impenetrable mass, preventing sun and air from reaching interior or lower branches and resulting in weak, spindly branches that are susceptible to disease pathogens and pests. Prune branches to allow light and air to penetrate to a shrub's or tree's interior.

It is not always necessary to remove dead limbs or even trees. In a woodland or meadow garden, dead limbs—so long as they do not endanger human visitors—can become a haven for wildlife, providing shelter for nesting birds and insects for their nourishment.

• Prune for safety. Often, it becomes necessary to prune limbs that overhang power lines (call in a professional when electrical lines are involved). Sometimes, branches rub against a building, restrict a walkway, or block an entrance. Other times, limbs are thinned to reduce a security risk or enhance a view.

• Prune to maintain a plant's character. Remove aberrant branches, such as an upright branch on a weeping plant. Young, newly transplanted specimens sometimes require special pruning during the first few years to help them establish a strong, well-shaped framework. Older shrubs often can be rejuvenated by severe pruning.

• Prune for decorative effect. Flowering shrubs can be invigorated with pruning; proper pruning requires a knowledge of when and where flower buds form, or you risk destroying a year's bloom. The roots of fruit trees and wisteria vines in decline or just reluctant to flower are sometimes pruned to encourage flowering. Certain species of dogwood and willow produce brightly colored bark on new shoots; these species are pruned to ensure a preponderance of the colorful new growth. Some fruit trees are pruned to enhance fruit production.

• Prune for special effect. Trees and shrubs are often trained and pruned into special shapes for a formal look or to fit in limited space. Techniques include training a formal hedge, pleaching, espalier, topiary, and bonsai (see "Training and Sculpting Plants," page 512, and "Bonsai," page 524).

## Basic Principles

To prune with competence and confidence, you must understand the principles, basic cuts, and techniques of pruning. Pruning typically stimulates the following reactions in plants:

• Pruning stimulates growth. In most cases, pruning a healthy plant hard will result in much new growth; pruning the same plant lightly results in less regrowth.

• Pruning the tips of branches tends to encourage dense side growth below the cut. For many plants, the terminal bud (at the tip) is dominant, and the lateral buds (along the sides of the shoot) tend to be slow to develop. When the tip is pruned, the terminal dominance is broken and, although the topmost bud will grow strongest, others will develop as well.

• Pruning early in the season when plants are still dormant encourages more vigorous growth than later pruning does. When you want to control size, it is advantageous to prune later. Summer pruning will reduce suckering—the production of fast-growing, mostly upright branches that generate in response to wounding or stress. Suckers generally are poorly attached to the tree or shrub and can become a hazard. Some experts believe that pruning too late in summer in temperate climates can cause problems as well, leaving late-season growth susceptible to cold damage and new tissue covering pruning cuts prone to desiccation.

• When pruning back to a bud, consider its direction. For plants with congested branches, choose outward-facing buds.

## The Basic Cuts

There are three basic types of pruning cuts: thinning, heading, and pinching.

### Thinning Cuts

Thinning cuts open up a plant to light and air without stimulating vigorous new growth or changing the tree's or shrub's natural shape or height. Prune the branches back to their point of origin, to a branch union or to the ground.

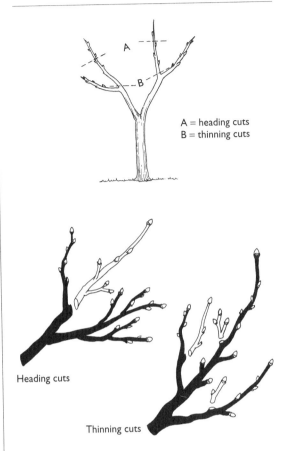

A = heading cuts
B = thinning cuts

Heading cuts

Thinning cuts

**Heading and thinning cuts**

*Heading cuts are made at the ends of branches to control the height and overall size of plants. Prune back to a point directly above a bud or side branch that faces the direction you want new growth to take.*

*Thinning cuts open up a plant to light and air. Prune each selected branch back to its point of origin.*

### Heading Cuts

These cuts are made at the ends of branches, generally to control the height and overall size of plants. Prune back to just above a bud or shoot. Sometimes, heading cuts encourage branching of young trees, create new bearing wood on fruit trees, or rejuvenate weak stems. Often, when used for grooming hedges, espaliers, and other formally pruned plants, heading cuts are made without proper attention to where the branch is cut. This nonjudicious use of these cuts can stress the tree or shrub and render it susceptible to disease and decay, vigorous regrowth, and even dieback, if too much weak growth results.

## Pinching and Candling

Most often associated with herbaceous plants, this technique for removing the growing tip or terminal bud also is appropriate for managing pines, when one-half to two-thirds of the new growth is removed by hand in a practice called *candling*. *Pinching* is best done with sharp pruning shears or a knife, or by hand when the tip is nearing maturity and snaps off crisply (see "When to Prune Needled Evergreens," page 509).

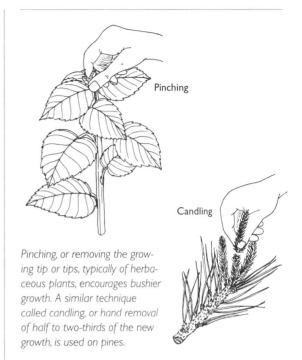

Pinching, or removing the growing tip or tips, typically of herbaceous plants, encourages bushier growth. A similar technique called candling, or hand removal of half to two-thirds of the new growth, is used on pines.

**Pinching and candling**

---

### STOP TOPPING

Never top trees. Topping, or cutting back the main branches to a uniform height, results in an unsightly tree and weakly attached suckering regrowth, which can become a safety hazard. New growth exacerbates the size problem and truncated limbs often die back—an invitation to insect pests and diseases. Consider the mature height of a tree before planting. Do not confuse topping with pollarding, a practice that uses proper pruning techniques to maintain a tree at a designated height (see "Pollarding," page 519).

---

# Guidelines for Pruning Whole Branches

Improper cuts interfere with a plant's natural defense system. Before you can prune properly, you must know what and where the branch bark collar and the branch bark ridge are. More distinct on some trees than others, the branch bark collar is the bulging ring at the base of a branch, where it joins the trunk. The branch bark ridge is the dark, raised ridge of bark at the intersection of the trunk and branch that defines the start of the branch.

To remove a limb, cut it off just outside the branch bark collar. When there is enough room between the branch and the trunk, cut from the top; to remove branches attached at tight

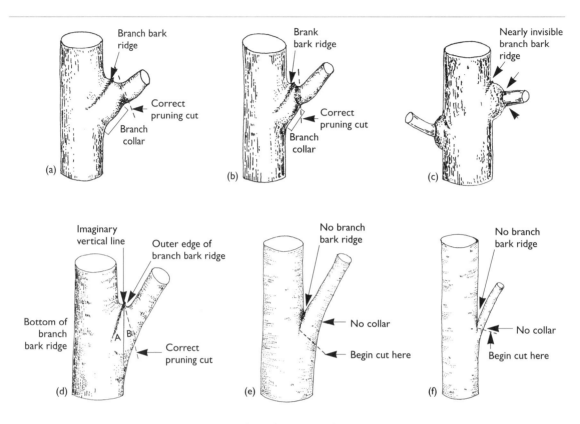

**Pruning whole branches**

*To remove a limb, cut it off just outside the branch bark collar. Branch collars and branch bark ridges vary according to tree species and age. On some trees, the branch collar is obvious (a and b); the dashed line indicates the correct pruning cut. Trunks form large collars around the base of low, horizontal branches on older trees (c), typically indicating a weak or dying limb on some species; the pruning cut should be made between the two arrows. When the bottom of the branch collar is hard to see (d), estimate angle A by drawing an imaginary vertical line parallel with the trunk. Beginning on top of the branch at the outer edge of the branch bark ridge, make a pruning cut so angle B is the same as angle A; the cut often ends even with the bottom of the branch bark ridge. Cut a branch forming a weak, V-shaped crotch with no collar or branch bark ridge (e and f) along the dashed line. The cut should end in the crotch at the point where the branch and trunk tissue meet; this may be several inches (young trees) or feet (older trees) down into the crotch. The cut may have to be finished with a chisel to prevent injury of trunk tissue.*

angles, you will have to start from the bottom. The resulting wound usually will be at an angle to the trunk and approximately circular. If the collar is not immediately recognizable—and on some trees it is not prominent—cut at an angle equal to but opposite the branch bark ridge.

Consider calling in a professional arborist for any branch over 3 or 4 inches in diameter. Special preliminary cuts are necessary to remove large branches properly. Even some smaller ones that you can comfortably cut with a handsaw may require preliminary cuts.

Without these cuts, the weight of the branch is liable to rip it from the tree while you are cutting. You risk tearing the bark and damaging the branch bark collar as well as possibly hurting yourself. Begin 6 to 12 inches from the trunk and cut about halfway through the underside of the branch. Make a second cut from above about 3 inches farther out on the branch. The branch will fall away, leaving a stub. Then prune the stub, taking care not to damage the branch bark collar.

If the branch could harm lower limbs or objects on the ground when it falls, tie it securely before cutting. Once it is cut, lower it gently to the ground. (Branches large enough to require ropes are generally best left to the professionals.)

Never paint pruning cuts. It does not aid healing and may even encourage fungal infections.

## PRUNING DISEASED WOOD

Pruning diseased wood requires some special precautions to avoid spreading the infection.

Prune diseased wood back to healthy tissue; from 6 to 12 inches beyond signs of disease is a good general rule. For fire blight, 12 inches is recommended; however, for Dutch elm disease, 10 to 15 feet is considered a safe margin.

Sterilize pruning tools after each cut.

While healthy prunings should be composted, diseased prunings should only be composted if the pile decomposes at very high temperatures—over 130°F for three days—and is turned often to ensure that everything is evenly "cooked."

## PRUNING TOOLS

The right tools will make pruning simpler for you, and safer for the plant. All tools should be kept sharp.

- **Pruning shears.** Start with a pair of good pruning shears—clean, sharp, and in excellent working order. Some have two cutting blades that work like scissors. Others have only one sharp blade that cuts against a broad, grooved plate or anvil. Anvil pruners are fine for softwood and small branches, but most serious arborists prefer scissors-type pruners, which are less likely to crush and damage delicate plant tissue. Hand pruners can cut branches up to about $\frac{1}{2}$ inch in diameter; generally, the wider the blade, the thicker the branch it can cut. Handles coated with vinyl are more comfortable and easier to grip.

- **Loppers.** Useful for pruning shrubs, a pair of loppers with long handles will help you reach between congested branches and cut branches up to $1\frac{1}{2}$ inches in diameter. For trees and shrubs with open branching, a handsaw is preferable.

- **Pruning saws.** Pruning saws with curved blades cut still larger branches; the longer the blade, the larger the branch you can manage.

- **Pole pruners.** Pole pruners aid in overhead work. A combination pole clipper (for snipping off small branches quickly) and pole saw (for larger branches) is generally useful for home pruning. When using these tools, never stand under the branch you are pruning or prune near electrical wires.

- **Hedge shearers.** Hedge shearers are essential for maintaining hedges or other formally pruned plants. Hedge shearers have long, flat blades and relatively short handles; some come with a shock-absorbing device.

For more on pruning tools, see "Garden Tools," page 614.

## DEALING WITH ACCIDENTAL WOUNDS

Proper pruning can help stem the damage caused by storms or mechanical injury. If a branch is ripped off in a storm or through an act of vandalism, cut it back to the branch collar, taking care to keep the collar intact.

Sometimes, cars, trucks, or even lawnmowers gouge out portions of bark from hapless trees. Usually, the best solution is simply to leave them alone if the bark at the edges of the wound is not loose. However, if the damaged bark is loose, cut away the injured bark and any loose wood, making rounded margins, taking care not to increase the size of the wound or point the top and bottom—a practice no longer considered good for the health of the tree. Make the cuts as shallow as possible. If there is serious damage, call in an arborist.

### Aftercare

Pruning, particularly hard pruning, can be a shock to a plant. Always check pruned trees after a few months; the way the tree responds may help you determine how to prune in the future.

If you must deal with rampant suckering—the aftermath of overpruning—first remove any crossing or rubbing branches and any that are a physical danger to persons or property. Unless it is an unacceptable eyesore, allow half or more of the new growth to grow on for a year or two before cutting, and be sure to make proper pruning cuts when you do. Remember, the harder you prune, the more you can expect the tree to respond with congested suckering.

## Pruning to Train Young Trees and Shrubs

The pruning recommended for most young trees and shrubs during the first two or three years following transplanting is very different from that for established specimens. In the case of young trees, it is important to select a framework of strong scaffold branches—those that will form the structure of the tree's canopy. This means simply working with the tree's natural growth pattern by making corrections if branches cross, grow at weak, inappropriate angles from the main trunk, become lopsided, or grow too close together. The trunks of young trees can be strengthened and the circumference enlarged by allowing low branches (that do not fit into the desired habit) to grow for two to three years before being pruned. Cut them before they grow any larger than 2 inches in diameter, however, or they will become difficult to remove.

In the case of shrubs, vigorous growth from the base of the plant provides the best framework for all future growth. Try to make only thinning cuts to maintain the natural habit of the shrub. A strong, open framework helps protect plants from damage from heavy snowfalls and from being compromised by lack of sunlight or air circulation in the plant's interior.

## Rejuvenation

Many overly large shrubs seemingly past their prime can be renewed with severe pruning called *rejuvenation*—either in one season or over a three-year period. Rejuvenate most deciduous plants when they are dormant in late winter or early spring and broad-leaved evergreens from early to late spring. To preserve blossoms, spring- and early-summer-blooming shrubs

## SOME PLANTS THAT CAN BE REJUVENATED BY CUTTING BACK TO THE GROUND

(Spring-flowering plants may not flower for two to three years when rejuvenated in early spring.)

*Abelia* species, abelias
*Chaenomeles* species, flowering quinces
*Clematis* × *jackmanii*, Jackman clematis
*Forsythia* species and hybrids, forsythias
*Hibiscus syriacus*, rose of Sharon
*Philadelphus* species, sweet mock oranges
*Polygonum aubertii*, silver fleece vine
*Syringa* species and hybrids, lilacs
*Weigela florida*, weigela
*Wisteria* species, wisterias

must be rejuvenated immediately after they flower.

Cut back all the branches (or one-third if you have opted for a less radical, three-year rejuvenation) to ground level or just above. Rampant regrowth will follow. During the first winter, thin out crowded stems, allowing a few sturdy ones to form a strong framework. Suckering will continue for a season or more; remove suckers that compete.

## When to Prune

Do not prune in bad weather; freezing temperatures or biting winds will desiccate delicate tissue. Some scientists believe pruning in wet weather spreads diseases. Pruning when the ground is soggy risks compacting the soil around the plant.

In general, try not to prune during budbreak and leaf fall. More specifically, when to prune depends on the type of plant.

### Deciduous Trees

The best time to make thinning cuts to open up plants for good light and air penetration is in early summer, after new shoots have finished growing and the wood is ripening; however, these cuts can be made in almost any season. When birch, elm, and maple are pruned in early spring, sap will ooze from the wounds; although harmless to the plant, some gardeners find it aesthetically unacceptable.

### Needled Evergreens

At maturity, conifers need minimal pruning. In fact, some, like pines, put out only one growth flush each year. Prune them in spring when new shoots, called *candles*, are from 2 to 3 inches long, by pinching back one-half to one-third of the new growth. Using pruning shears risks cutting the needles, which will cause them to brown at the tips. Pinching the candles encourages latent buds to break, creating more branching and bushier plants. Spruces and firs can also be pinched to promote denser growth. Some evergreens can be pruned almost any time as necessary. Just bear in mind that arborvitaes, junipers, chamaecyparis, and cedars will not regrow from nonactive growth (branches that are bare of needles). Prune these conifers only within the needled sections of branches. Yews, on the other hand, have latent buds in nonneedled portions that will regenerate new growth.

Occasionally, heavy snow or wind can damage conifer leaders. If this happens, correct in spring when branches are most flexible. Prune out the damaged leader and choose one of the topmost side branches to replace it. Splint it with a straight wooden stake and tie it in place with a soft material, such as a nylon stocking. Remove the support after a year.

## SOME SPRING-FLOWERING SHRUBS

Spring-flowering shrubs should be pruned immediately after flowering. Flower buds develop on the previous summer's growth. If pruned before flowering in the spring, flower buds will be removed and no flowers or fruits will be available during the current season.

*Amelanchier* species, serviceberries
*Calycanthus* species, sweet shrubs
*Cercis* species, redbuds
*Chaenomeles* species, flowering quinces
*Cornus florida,* flowering dogwood
*Cornus kousa,* Japanese dogwood
*Cornus mas,* cornelian cherry
*Deutzia* species, deutzias
*Forsythia* species and hybrids, forsythias
*Hydrangea macrophylla,* house hydrangea
*Kolkwitzia amabilis,* beautybush
*Magnolia* species, magnolias
*Malus* species, crabapples
*Philadelphus* species, mock oranges
*Prunus* species, flowering cherry, plum
*Rhododendron* species, rhododendrons, azaleas
*Rhodotypos scandens,* black jetbead
*Rosa* species, climbers and shrub roses
*Spiraea thunbergii,* Thunberg spirea
*Styrax japonicus,* Japanese snowbell
*Syringa* species, common, Chinese, and French lilacs
*Viburnum* x *burkwoodii,* Burkwood viburnum
*Viburnum carlesii,* Korean spice viburnum
*Viburnum lantana,* wayfaring tree
*Viburnum plicatum* f. *tomentosum,* doublefile viburnum

## Ornamental Shrubs

Not all shrubs require pruning for vigorous floral display. Many will bloom with no assistance from gardeners. Rampant growers like hydrangea and forsythia are more often pruned for size maintenance. Perhaps the best rule of thumb is if a shrub continues to bloom and is in scale with the rest of the garden, no pruning is necessary. When pruning a flowering shrub is necessary, however, it is vital to know when flower buds set.

### Spring- and Early-Summer-Flowering Shrubs

These shrubs bloom on wood produced the previous season; to promote flowering, prune stems with spent flowers as soon as possible after blooming. Cut these back to older wood to encourage bushy, compact shrubs and prolific flowering.

### Summer- and Early-Autumn-Flowering Shrubs

These shrubs bloom on the current season's growth and are pruned when they are dormant—ideally, in early spring when buds swell but before the leaves unfold. Prune back the previous season's wood—which will display the old, spent flowers—hard to within one or two buds from the base of each stem.

### Shrubs Grown for the Decorative Effect of Young Stems

Some dogwoods, willows, and brambles produce brightly colored bark on new stems that is most welcome in the winter landscape. To maximize production of new stems, prune these shrubs almost to ground level in early spring before they break dormancy (see "Coppicing and Pollarding," page 519).

## SOME SUMMER-BLOOMING SHRUBS

Summer-blooming shrubs develop flower buds after stem growth has started. Pruning from early to late spring before leaf buds break or just after is recommended.

*Acanthopanax* species, aralias
*Callicarpa* species, beautyberries
*Clematis* species, clematis
*Hibiscus syriacus,* rose of Sharon
*Hydrangea paniculata* 'Grandiflora', peegee hydrangea
*Hydrangea quercifolia,* oak-leaf hydrangea
*Rosa* species, species and hybrid tea roses

### Broad-Leaved Evergreens

Major pruning on broad-leaved evergreens is best done in early spring, right before new growth begins. Light pruning can be done year-round. However, where flowers and resulting fruit are the desired effect, such as with rhodo-dendron, holly, and pieris, pruning schedules vary with flowering time.

## Pruning Herbaceous Plants

Pruning—or removing unwanted plant parts—can enhance the life and beauty of herbaceous plants. Four basic techniques are used to prune herbaceous specimens: pinching, deadheading, disbudding, and cutting back.

### Pinching

Many herbaceous plants become bushier and more compact—and produce more flowers—when the growing tip is removed with a single pinch just above a leaf or pair of leaves. Garden-

## FORCING FOR INDOOR BLOOM

You can create floral arrangements in midwinter by pruning selected branches of dormant decid-uous trees and shrubs, after they endure about 6 weeks of outdoor freezing. When brought indoors, they can be forced to bloom ahead of schedule.

On a mild day, cut relatively long, heavily bud-ded branches from your favorite shrub. Make proper pruning cuts; for maximum flowering, seek out branches with rounder flower buds, not the more pointed leaf buds. Recut the ends of the stems before placing the branches in water indoors and remove any buds below the water-line. Weekly, recut the stems, change the water, and mist.

Until the buds swell, branches can be kept in the dark; then they need light but not direct sun. Ideal temperatures for forcing are between 60°F and 70°F; higher temperatures speed flowering but diminish color, size, and length of bloom time. For a succession of flowers, cut fresh branches every week or so.

Some of the best woody plants for forcing flowers and catkins are alder, apple, Cornelian cherry, deutzia, flowering almond, flowering cherry, flowering dogwood, flowering quince, for-sythia, Japanese maple, mountain laurel, peach, pieris, pussy willow, redbud, spicebush, and witch-hazel.

ers often pinch annuals and perennials at trans-planting; some plants, which tend to grow tall and weak stems, benefit from more regular pinching. For example, chrysanthemums bene-fit from weekly pinching until early summer when there is still time for flower buds to set for fall blooms. Pinching can channel extra energy into leaf production; remove the flowers before they form on coleus and some herbs, such as basil and oregano, for brighter, fuller leaves.

### Deadheading

Deadheading, or removing spent flowers from plants before they begin to form seeds, allows the plant to direct more energy toward flower, foliage, and root formation. For many annuals and perennials, such as pansies and petunias, the process results in more new flower buds. Removing spent flowers also discourages prolific self-sowers. Deadheading is not recommended for plants that produce attractive ornamental seed heads, such as those of teasel, poppy, and love-in-a-mist. Deadhead spring-flowering bulbs to conserve energy for the next season's flowers. Prune bare flower stalks, like those of most bulbs, off at their base; cut back leafy stalks to the leaves or above any flower buds once the leaves have turned yellow.

### Disbudding

Disbudding, or removing some flower buds, encourages the remaining ones to develop differently. Plants like peonies, dahlias, carnations, and chrysanthemums grow many buds along one stem. Disbudding all but the end bud—long before bloom—will result in a single but larger and more spectacular flower. Leaving the side shoot buds and taking out the end one results in more, but smaller, flowers. Disbudding is often practiced to produce show-caliber flowers.

### Cutting Back

This technique is often used to revive plants in midseason. By midsummer some annuals, such as petunias and impatiens, become unkempt

and overgrown; cut them back by a third or more to give them a second wind. Pruning back vigorous-growing perennials by a third or more after flowering will keep them in bounds. Some plants, such as bee balm and delphinium, produce new growth at ground level in late summer; once this appears, all the older stalks can be pruned back. In fall, most perennials should be trimmed back after frost blackens their foliage; cut them to the ground to reduce the risk of insects and diseases overwintering on dead leaves and compost the trimmings.

### Further Reading

Brickell, Christopher, and David Joyce. *The American Horticultural Society Pruning and Training.* New York: Dorling Kindersly, 1996.

*Caring for Young Trees from Nurseries to Landscapes* (leaflet). Shigo and Trees Associates, P.O. Box 769, Durham, NH 03824.

Cook, Allan D. *Pruning Techniques.* Brooklyn, N.Y.: Brooklyn Botanic Garden, 1991.

Hill, Lewis. *Pruning Made Easy.* Pownal, Vt.: Storey Communications, 1998.

Reich, Lee. *The Pruning Book.* Newtown, Ct.: Taunton Press, 1997.

## Training and Sculpting Plants

Many techniques for training and sculpting plants have practical as well as aesthetic applications. A hedge, whether flat, curved, geometric, or natural-looking, is designed to delineate a space as well as please the eye. Trained against a wall or fence, an espaliered tree is a natural work of art—highlighting leaf patterns, flowers, or fruit—but on a single, space-saving plane.

To be done well, the horticultural arts outlined in this section demand a knowledge of proper pruning, a steady hand, and an artistic eye. In addition, maintaining a formal hedge and topiary requires a rather drastic form of pruning called shearing. For these two techniques, all standard pruning rules must be discarded. The lines of formal pruning are crisp, sometimes straight, sometimes curved and even angled; to attain such lines, plants are cut back to whatever point necessary. Not all plants can withstand shearing or some of the other labor-intensive procedures required to create the special effects of pleaching, pollarding, or espalier. Be sure the plant you choose is appropriate not only for your site but also for the horticultural art you intend to create.

## Hedges

A hedge can be a naturalistic screen or a crisp demarcation with formal, rigid lines—depending on what you want and how you shape the plants. Hedges define space, screen out people

and animals, provide a backdrop for the rest of the garden, and block wind. The plants for high-maintenance formal hedges should be selected mostly for the quality of their foliage. Informal hedges, less maintenance-intense, are often created with flowering plants. The flowers, fruit, and dense cover of many informal hedges are appealing to wildlife.

Select plants to suit your choice of hedge style and the site conditions. Learn whether they prefer sun or shade and other conditions in the native environments to which they are adapted, how tall and how wide they become at maturity, their leaf size, and when they flower, if they do. Slow-growing plants with small leaves are excellent choices for formal hedges—be sure the plants you select can accept the intense shearing that maintaining this look demands.

### Training Formal Hedges

Mature formal hedges require shearing a minimum of twice a year to preserve the clean lines

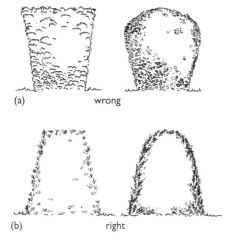

*Formal, sheared hedges should be wider at the bottom and narrower at the top to allow sunlight to reach lower branches (b), which otherwise would become bare and unsightly (a). In regions with heavy snowfall, hedges with broad, flat tops (c, left) may be damaged by the weight of excessive snow accumulation. Hedges clipped in straight lines (c, center) require frequent trimming. Rounded forms (c, right) hinder snow accumulation and require less trimming.*

(a)   wrong

(b)   right                                                                    (c)

**The proper shape for a formal hedge**

## RECOMMENDED HEDGE PLANTS

### SOME SHRUBS FOR FORMAL TRAINING

*Abelia* x *grandifora*, glossy abelia
*Buxus microphylla*, littleleaf box
*Buxus sempervirens*, common box
*Cephalotaxus* species, plum yews
*Ilex* species, hollies
*Juniperus* species, junipers
*Pinus mugo* 'Compacta', globe mugho pine
*Podocarpus* species, podocarpus
*Rhododendron* species, azaleas
*Taxus* species, yews
*Viburnum* species, viburnums

### TREES FOR FORMAL TRAINING

*Abies concolor*, white fir
*Acer campestre*, hedge maple
*Chamaecyparis* species, false cypresses
*Cryptomeria japonica*, cryptomeria
X *Cupressocyparis leylandii*, Leyland cypress
*Cupressus* species, Cypresses
*Fagus americana*, American beech
*Ilex opaca*, American holly
*Maclura pomifera*, Osage orange
*Pinus parviflora*, Japanese white pine
*Pseudotsuga menziesi*, Douglas fir
*Thuja* species, arborvitaes
*Tsuga* species, hemlocks

### HEDGE PLANTS THAT DO BEST WITH AT LEAST SEVEN HOURS OF SUN

The following plants for full or part sun include some plants appropriate for formal hedges and others that make good informal hedges.

*Carpinus caroliniana*, hornbeam
*Chamaecyparis pisifera*, false cypress
*Juniperus virginiana* 'Skyrocket', skyrocket juniper
*Poncirus trifoliata*, trifoliate orange
*Salix matsudana* 'Tortuosa', corkscrew willow
*Syringa* species and hybrids, lilacs
*Thuja* species, arborvitaes

### HEDGE PLANTS THAT TOLERATE A MINIMUM OF FOUR HOURS OF SUN

*Forsythia* species, forsythias
*Hibiscus syriacus*. rose of Sharon
*Hydrangea paniculata* 'Grandiflora', peegee hydrangea
*Ilex* species, hollies
*Ilex glabra*, inkberry
*Malus* species, crabapples
*Pyracantha coccinea*, scarlet firethorn
*Phyllostachys* species, bamboos
*Rhododendron* species, rhododendrons, azaleas
*Taxus baccata*, English yew
*Tsuga canadensis*, Canadian hemlock

and all-important hedge shape—wider at the bottom and narrower at the top to allow sunlight to reach the lower leaves; without sun, the lower branches become bare and unsightly. In regions with heavy snowfall, rounding the hedge top or creating a sloping-roof effect avoids excessive snow accumulation, which may result in damaged and broken limbs.

The training period for a formal hedge is from two to three years. Start with young plants; set them evenly along a planting trench—about 6 to 8 inches apart for smaller plants like dwarf box, or 18 to 30 inches for larger-sized plants such as yew. Give deciduous plants a month or so to establish a good root system, then cut them back hard by about a third, making heading cuts to just above a bud (see "Pruning," page 501). This initial pruning promotes dense branching critical to the overall shape of the hedge. Keep the tapered-at-the-top contour in mind when you prune side branches. Unless the plants are naturally compact, they will require severe pruning again the second year. Fast-growing plants may even require monthly pruning to establish proper branch density, at least in the first few years. In subsequent years, prune no more than one-half the new growth and allow the plants to reach the desired hedge height.

Needled evergreens should be pruned less severely. Remove any overly long shoots and prune to promote the proper side contours. Do not prune the central leader until the plants reach the desired height.

How often to prune an established formal hedge is dictated by the growth characteristics of the plants and the hedge shape. Generally, pruning twice a year is enough—less often with needled evergreens. A pair of manual hedge shears will probably do the trick; if you have a particularly large hedge, consider a power trimmer.

## Informal Hedges

Select your favorite shrub—almost any shrub will do—for an informal hedge. To create an informal hedge, space plants according to their size at maturity. During the first year, prune to bring them into scale with one another and encourage compact growth. In the second and following years, prune only when necessary to eliminate overly exuberant growth and to promote side growth, in keeping with the plant's natural form or habit. Be sure to prune flowering varieties at the proper time to avoid chopping off flowers and fruits (see "Pruning," page 501).

## Espalier

Decorative and space-saving, espaliered trees and shrubs are trained against a wall or fence—sometimes freestanding—but always in one plane. Traditionally, fruit trees were the primary subjects for espalier, and were trained in symmetrical, geometric patterns. Today, many different kinds of plants are trained into traditional and also more free-form designs. Creating espalier requires a substantial commitment of time, especially during the training phase, and constant attention after the form has been established.

Flowering and fruiting varieties are popular candidates for espalier. Evergreens offer year-round interest. Select plants adapted to the conditions of the site. Depending on the particular plant, an espalier can benefit or suffer from the reflection of light and heat from a wall. In northern climates, the heat reflected from a south-facing wall may be much appreciated by sun-loving and fruit-bearing plants, but in a warmer southern climate, the same plants may become overheated. Some recommended plants for espalier include forsythia, flowering dogwood, witchhazel, climbing rose, firethorn, hawthorn, yew, American holly, flowering quince, viburnum, and fruit trees.

Pretrained espaliers are a popular item in garden centers. They offer a head start, but without regular, skilled pruning, any espalier will soon become overgrown.

Most espaliers need to be supported against a wall or trellis. If you are working with a masonry wall, drill holes and cement in rust-proof hooks or eyes. A trellis works best against a wooden wall, fence, or other structure that requires regular maintenance. Allow a minimum of 6 inches between the trellis and the wall for good air circulation and ease of prun-

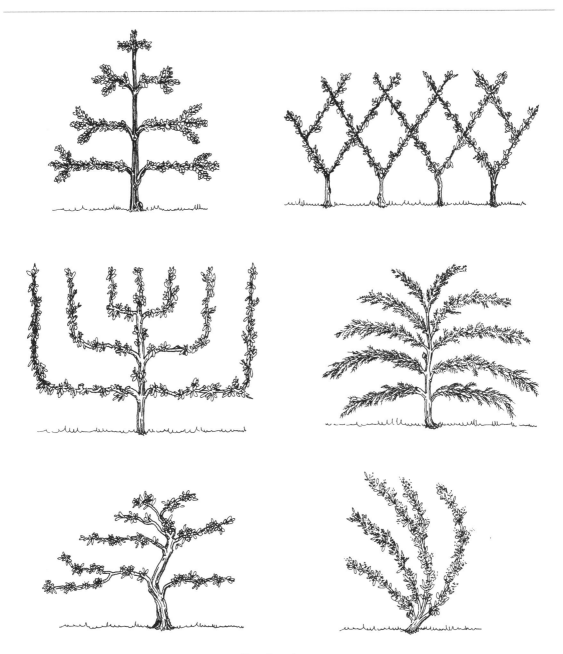

**Espalier shapes**

*Traditionally, trees and shrubs were trained in symmetrical, geometric patterns (top and center). Today, more free-form designs are common (bottom). Although space-saving and elegant, espalier requires a substantial commitment of time, especially during the training phase, and regular attention after the form has been established.*

ing. You can make a framework for espalier with two vertical wooden posts; string three or more heavy-gauge wires between them for horizontal support.

### Training an Espalier

Select a design and start with a small plant. Only flexible, young plants are able to withstand the requisite arduous pruning. Prune all the branches from the sparsest side in early spring while the plant is still dormant. Plant the specimen, flat side toward the trellis or wall, leaving at least 6 inches from the support to accommodate the trunk size at maturity.

Consider the procedure used to create the formal tree-of-life pattern; the specific instructions for other patterns will differ but the basic principles remain the same. Cut the main trunk back to just above two alternate-side buds for the first branching. When these grow, train the branches horizontally. Take care when bending branches not to snap the wood; spring is when it will be most flexible. Anchor the branches in place with natural twine or other soft ties; check all attachments at least twice a year to make sure they are not constricting growth; retie if necessary.

When a new main shoot develops, allow it to grow 15 inches (or to whatever vertical spacing you desire), then cut off the tip above another set of buds. When the next set of branches grows, tie them horizontally to the wall or trellis. Allow side shoots from the selected sets of branches to reach about 12 inches before cutting them back; side shoots, 4 to 6 inches long with at least three sets of leaves, will give the espalier a tidy appearance and provide enough leaves for photosynthesis. Do not prune the tips of branches that are part of the pattern until they reach their desired length.

When training plants for informal espalier, be creative. Sometimes plants twisted by the vagaries of weather suggest their own patterns; simply elaborate on and accentuate the plant's natural growth by guiding the branches as they grow.

The best time to prune an established espalier is early spring, while the plant is still dormant. Throughout the growing season, prune as needed to keep the pattern neat and tidy. Flowering and fruiting espalier require a specific pruning schedule (see "Pruning," page 509).

## Pleaching

On a grander scale than espalier, pleaching is the art of interweaving tree branches. The process entails pruning and bending branches and interlacing and sometimes tying them to those of the next tree. Often, a line of trees is trained to form a wall with a flattened hedge contour; sometimes tree branches are trained into an arch.

Plants with tough, flexible wood are best for pleaching. Many, like hornbeam, beech, and linden, take years to become established. Gardenias, goldenchain trees, horse chestnuts, pears, apples, and crabapples are also pleached.

### How to Pleach

Select young trees with straight, clear stems about 6 feet high to create a hedgelike wall. Plant them in a straight row spaced about 8 feet apart. Create a framework by setting vertical posts at each tree plus two posts outside the row, one at either end to accommodate the branches of the first and last trees. Attach horizontal wires or wooden supports to the posts, spaced about 2 feet apart and starting at the

(a)

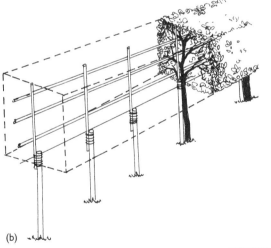

(b)

### Pleaching

*To create a hedge-like wall of pleaches, or interwoven trees, plant young specimens with straight, clear stems about 8' apart. Create a framework by setting hardwood stakes or other vertical posts at each tree, plus one at either end of the row. Attach horizontal wire or bamboo to the posts, spaced about 2' apart, starting at the height you want the foliage to begin—generally about 6' (a). Tie the main growing tip of each tree to the vertical support and side branches to the wire or bamboo with natural twine or other soft material. Cut back to the main trunk any branches that cannot be easily tied to a horizontal support. The perspective view (b) shows a well-clipped, continuous hedge clear of the ground.*

height you want the foliage to begin (about 6 feet generally allows easy access underneath the trees).

While the trees are still dormant, coax the side branches to the horizontal supports and anchor them in place with natural twine or other soft material; check ties at least twice yearly to avoid constricted branches. Tie the main growing tip of each tree to its vertical

post, and once the tip reaches the top cross support, bend and tie it horizontally. Cut back to the main trunk any branches that grow below the framework and any that cannot be easily tied to a horizontal support.

In the second year, in early spring while the tree is still dormant, prune the long side shoots growing from horizontal branches back to two or three buds to encourage branching. Continue tying branches to horizontal supports. Throughout the season, prune shoots that cannot be easily intertwined into the framework. Create the flattened hedge line—front, back, and at each end—during the third spring; prune branches by making heading cuts back to a bud (see "Pruning," page 501).

To create a pleached arch, it is necessary to erect an arch framework between two trees or between each pair of trees for a tunnel effect. Starting with trees about 6 feet tall, tie the central leader lightly to the arch frame. When the trees reach about 8 to 10 feet, the height where the frame begins to bend, begin tying the topmost horizontal branches next to the arch to the framework; prune out any lower side branches next to the arch that do not fit into the design. Prune upright shoots along the horizontal branches that cannot be tied easily to the arch. As soon as the branches from the trees meet, interweave them; ultimately they will graft together naturally to form a graceful arched ceiling.

Once the branches of the trees are thoroughly entwined and the pleached effect is complete, the framework can be dismantled. In subsequent years, continue to intertwine branches as they meet and prune to promote vigorous branching; maintain the boxed hedge shape or arch pattern.

## Coppicing and Pollarding

Coppicing is an ancient art that provided a regular supply of firewood or slender, straight branches for basket weaving or fencing. Pollarding, often practiced on trees bordering farms in Europe and along European city streets, was done to keep the trees within size bounds and to create a formal look. Both coppicing and pollarding induce vigorous tree growth. Coppicing involves cutting shrubs to ground level; for pollarding, branches are trimmed back to the trunk or a branch framework. Today, gardeners practice these severe pruning techniques for aesthetic reasons and to restrict the size of trees.

Willows are the traditional plants for coppicing. Today, this art is often practiced on deciduous shrubs with decorative young stems, such as red and yellow osier dogwoods, willows, and ornamental brambles to encourage prolific production of the brightly colored new growth.

Linden, hornbeam, London plane, ginkgo, beech, and catalpa trees are pollarded, some-times for aesthetic reasons, but usually to restrict their size.

### Training and Care

To coppice, prune back all the branches to 1 to 3 inches above the ground. Do this annually or

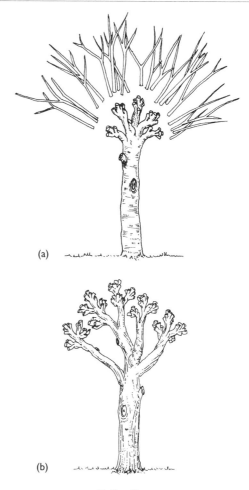

(a)

(b)

**Pollarding**

*Pollarding keeps trees within bounds and creates a formal look. Branches can be trimmed all the way back to the trunk (a) or to a branch framework (b).*

every second or third year in late winter or early spring before the plant breaks dormancy.

Pollarding, sometimes referred to as high coppicing, is the same procedure only carried out higher up—either to the main trunk stem or to a branch framework. First decide at what level you intend to pollard; some trees with upright habits such as ginkgos are better pollarded with a branch framework. Choose trees for training with trunk diameters of no more than 2 to 3 inches.

To pollard back to the main stem, select a tree with a clear stem about 6 feet high or the desired height for the pollarded head. Begin by pruning back all the branches to the main stem in late winter or early spring, taking care not to damage the branch bark collars. (For trees with many branches, the pruning can be carried out over a two- to three-year period to reduce stressing the tree.) Continue pruning out new growth every other year until a swollen head is

established, then every year or every other year thereafter. When new branch growth becomes congested, thin it out. Take care not to cut into the branch bark collars or otherwise damage the pollarded head. Do not allow any branches to develop below the pollarded head.

To create a pollard with a branch framework, choose a well-branched tree. Prune back dormant branches to from 3 to 6 feet from the trunk in late winter or early spring. Prune as described above to establish pollarded heads at each branch tip.

## Topiary

Topiary is living sculpture for the garden, and for indoors. This horticultural art dates back to ancient Rome. Plants are trained and sheared into various shapes—ranging from traditional formal architectural and geometric to informal novelty forms.

The best plants for training as topiary are fine-leaved, compact, and fast-growing. Traditional shrub favorites for outdoor topiary include box, arborvitae, juniper, and yew. When selecting a design for topiary—whether geometric or free-form—consider first the form of the plant, spreading or upright, and then the growth pattern of each individual plant.

Indoor gardeners have an even greater range of plant choices. Creeping fig (*Ficus pumila*) and English ivy (*Hedera helix*) are popular choices for creating easy, quick-growing topiaries trained on metal frames. A variety of forms and trellises are available for training plants into traditional classic and contemporary free-form topiaries.

---

### SOME PLANTS FOR OUTDOOR TOPIARY

*Buxus microphylla* var. *koreana*, Korean box
*Buxus sempervirens*, common box
*Buxus sempervirens* 'Suffruticosa', dwarf box
*Juniperus* species, junipers
*Ilex crenata*, Japanese holly
*Ilex vomitoria*, yaupon holly
*Lonicera nitida*, box honeysuckle
*Picea glauca* var. *albertiana*, Alberta spruce
*Pyracantha coccinea*, scarlet firethorn
*Rhododendron* species, evergreen azaleas
*Syzygium paniculatum*, eugenia
*Taxus baccata*, English yew
*Taxus* × *media*, intermediate yew
*Thuja* species, arborvitaes
*Tsuga canadensis*, Canadian hemlock

---

### Training and Care

Some of the easiest topiary shapes to create are simple pyramids, globes, and cones. Topiary

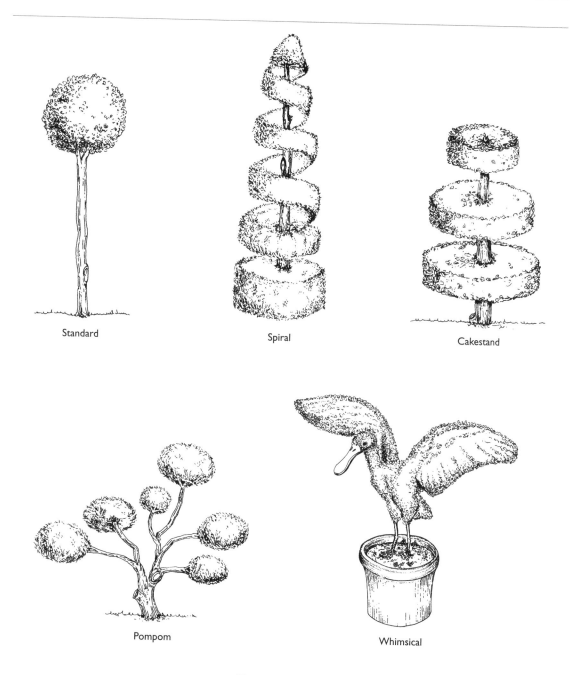

Standard

Spiral

Cakestand

Pompom

Whimsical

**Topiary shapes**

*Topiary is living sculpture for the garden. Plants are trained and clipped into various shapes, ranging from traditional, formal, architectural, and geometric to informal and whimsical.*

forms can be created freehand with stakes or cords for guides, but it is far easier to establish a form with a frame as a guideline. Selections of frames for topiary are sold in garden centers; some gardeners design their own out of rust-resistant heavy-gauge wire.

Place the frame over a young plant and, if necessary, anchor any branches that need training with natural twine or other soft ties; check the ties often to avoid damaging the bark as the plant grows. Begin by pruning only the shoot tips to encourage compact, bushy growth. Once the plant completely fills the frame, prune for form. Prune first to a rough outline; young plants will recover quickly. The best time to prune varies with plant choice; box requires trimming in late winter or early spring prior to new growth, while yew is best cut in summer. In regions with heavy snow, keep topiary free of accumulations, which can ruin their shape and break delicate branches.

Established topiary generally require at least one annual close shearing and occasional touch-ups to correct straggly growth. To maintain a topiary at the same size, prune it back annually to the previous year's cuts.

Container-grown topiary is easy to move and allows gardeners in cold climates more versatility in selecting plant varieties, as these specimens can be overwintered indoors or outside in a sheltered location.

## Standards

One of the more popular topiary shapes and often grown in containers, a tree-form standard is a plant with a single stem. Plant varieties with upright growth make the best standards; sometimes plants with more prostrate and spreading habits are grafted onto the tall stem

## SOME PLANTS FOR TRAINING AS STANDARDS

*Abutilon* × *hybridum*, flowering maple
*Argyranthemum* (*Chrysanthemum*) *frutescens*, marguerite
*Bougainvillea* × *buttiana*, bougainvillea
*Camellia* species, camellias
*Clerodendrum thomsoniae*, glorybower
*Cytisus racemosus*, florists' genista
*Eugenia uniflora*, Surinam cherry
*Euryops pectinatus*, euryops
*Fuchsia* species, fuchsias
*Gardenia* species, gardenias
*Hedera helix* hybrids, English ivies
*Heliotropium arborescens*, heliotrope
*Hydrangea paniculata* 'Grandiflora', peegee hydrangea
*Lantana camara*, common lantana
*Laurus nobilis*, bay laurel
*Leptospermum scoparium*, New Zealand tea tree
*Myrtus communis*, myrtle
*Pelargonium* species, geraniums
*Rhododendron* species, azaleas
*Rosmarinus officinalis*, rosemary
*Serissa foetida*, serissa
*Solenostemon* species, coleus
*Westringia rosmariniformis*, Victorian rosemary

of another plant in the same plant family. Some suggested candidates for potted standards include herbs (rosemary, myrtle, sweet bay, lemon verbena) and flowering plants (lantana, fuchsia, flowering maple, serissa, angel's trumpet [brugmansia], heliotrope).

Select a young plant with a single, straight stem that has never been pinched. Remove most of the side branches below the tip, but not the main stem leaves; the plant needs as many green leaves as possible for photosynthesis.

## UNSHEARING SHRUBS

Shearing can shock plants—especially if done improperly or in the wrong season. Not all plants are suited to this kind of severe pruning, and those that cannot handle the stress begin to look tired and worn. However, it is possible to "unshear" shrubs or reverse the process of shearing. The process is relatively simple.

Some reasons to unshear a shrub:

- Shearing is a lot of work.
- Flowers and berries often get sacrificed for neatness.
- Some shrubs develop dead spots from so much cutting.
- The dense canopy created by shearing eventually weakens the shrub's interior, shading it and blocking air circulation.

To unshear, you will need a sharp pruning tool and gloves (the interior of a sheared shrub is scratchy).

Cane-growing shrubs renew themselves readily from the base. Some tough cane-growers, such as forsythia, mock orange, deutzia, kolkwitzia, and potentilla, may even tolerate rejuvenation—probably the fastest and easiest way to unshear (for directions, see "Pruning" page 508). Otherwise, thin selectively, no more than one-third of the canopy in one year, especially on younger plants, to avoid rampant suckering.

Multibranched shrubs require more work. In the first year, prune out the thickest branch clumps, thin branches, and trim the stubs left by shearing. In the second year, continue to open up the shrub canopy by cutting back old branches to a branch union and thinning new growth. Continue in the third year to thin old and new growth until the shrub's natural, open form emerges.

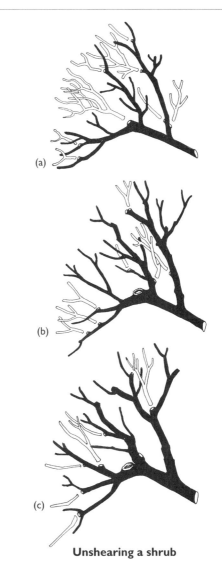

(a)

(b)

(c)

**Unshearing a shrub**

*Not all plants are suited to shearing, a severe form of pruning, and begin to look tired and worn, but it is possible to "unshear" shrubs over the course of a few years. First year (a): Remove the thickest clumps by cutting back to side branches. Thin shoots and trim stubs left by shearing. Second year (b): Continue to open the shrub canopy by cutting back old branches to side branches and thinning new growth. Third year (c): The shrub is regaining its natural open form. Continue to thin old and new growth.*

Stake the plant; insert a slender stake, equal in length to the height of the trunk you want the tree to have, plus extra inches for inserting into the soil. Use twist ties or raffia to secure the stem to the stake. Feed often and lightly with a complete fertilizer to encourage growth. Repot and restake as necessary to accommodate growth. Remove side branches as they appear; allow primary leaves along the stem (trunk) to remain until they mature and drop. When the trunk reaches the top of the stake, allow a few top side shoots to grow out, and pinch the main stem tip. As side branches develop, tip prune or pinch them once they become a few inches long. Repeat this procedure on subsequent new growth until each becomes branched and compact; the new growth forms the round, bushy head of the standard. Remove any leaves still clinging to the trunk.

---

## SOME PLANTS FOR TRAINING AS WREATHS

*Ceropegia woodii*, rosary vine
*Cissus antarctica*, kangaroo vine
*Cissus rhombifolia*, grape ivy
*Clytostoma callistegioides*, Argentine trumpet vine
*Ficus pumila*, creeping fig
*Hedera helix* hybrids, English ivies
*Hydrangea petiolaris*, climbing hydrangea
*Jasminum* species, jasmines
*Manettia inflata*, firecracker vine
*Pelargonium* species, scented geraniums
*Rosa* species and hybrids, dwarf climbing roses
*Rosmarinus officinalis* 'Prostratus', prostrate rosemary
*Scindapsus pictus* 'Argyraeus', velvet-leaf pothos
*Thunbergia alata*, black-eyed Susan vine

### Wreath or Circle Topiaries

To create a wreath topiary, the plant is flattened on a frame so that it has height and width but little depth. A simple wreath or circle can be shaped from a wire clothes hanger, grapevines, or almost anything that can be formed into a circle. Anchor this frame in a vertical position, centered in a pot. The easiest plants to train are those with a creeping habit, such as English ivy or prostrate rosemary. Coax the stems up and around the circle. Little tying is necessary because the long stems can be wound and tucked so as to hold themselves in place. The system also works for woodier growth such as that of lemon geranium, but such stems do need tying every couple of inches.

### Further Reading

Brickell, Christopher, and David Joyce. *The American Horticultural Society Pruning and Training.* London; New York: DK Publishing, 1996.

Gallup, Barbara, and Deborah Reich. *The Complete Book of Topiary.* New York: Workman Publishing, 1987.

Hammer, Patricia Riley. *The New Topiary: Imaginative Techniques from Longwood Gardens.* Northian, East Sussex: Garden Art Press, 1991.

Medic, Kris. *Rodale's Successful Organic Gardening Pruning.* Emmaus, Pa.: Rodale Press, 1995.

## Bonsai

Bonsai are dwarfed potted trees and shrubs created through meticulous pruning and shaping. This ancient art was first developed in China and then adopted and refined by the Japanese. Bonsai are living sculpture that suggest an idealized natural setting. Often, an entire miniaturized landscape is evoked, whether a tree or an entire forest struggling to exist atop a rocky cliff or on a windswept plateau.

The biggest pitfall for beginning bonsai growers is the failure to realize that there are bonsai plants for outdoors and others for indoors. Outdoor bonsai require a cold dormant period. Indoor bonsai do well inside on windowsills or with supplemental lighting. The kinds of plants appropriate for each come from radically different geographical locations. In general, temperate plants, such as pine, juniper, maple, beech, crabapple, and sweet gum, make excellent outdoor specimens, while pomegranate, bougainvillea, ficus, jasmine, and tea tree, mostly from tropical and subtropical regions, are commonly trained as indoor bonsai.

## Important Bonsai Basics

• How trunks are shaped is significant. The choice of training style for a plant is usually based on the growth patterns of the trunk; a straight trunk lends itself to the formal upright style, while a gnarled trunk might suggest a cascading form. Trunks must taper and the bottom third should be exposed, with no branches.

• The position of the trunk in the container is important. It should never be centered, but rather always slightly off-center.

• The main branches should be arranged in a pleasing pattern to the left, right, and rear of the trunk with balanced spacing between limbs; none should cross.

• Small-leaved, compact plants able to withstand severe pruning are best for bonsai. The size of trunks and branches can be encouraged or reduced by selective pruning, but leaves, flowers, and fruits are not readily altered.

• Surface roots must fan out from the base of the trunk in a graceful pattern; none should cross or appear unnatural. Thick roots are desirable because they suggest age.

• No marks should ever be visible from pruning or wiring.

• The bonsai container is second in importance to the plant itself. The shape and color of the container should complement the style of the tree.

## Bonsai Styles

The art of bonsai is subjective and open to interpretation. The classical styles of bonsai, which are based on trees in nature, offer guidelines for training specimens. The angle of the trunk is most important and helps determine style. Negative space—that is, space with no branches—is equal in importance to the arrangement of branches and trunk.

Understanding seven basic styles makes it easier to assess potential trees and train them appropriately. You need not imitate a style exactly, but as with any art it is always wise to understand what is considered ideal before venturing too far from tradition.

### Formal Upright (*Chokkan*)

A well-proportioned, tapered trunk rises straight up with asymmetrical but well-balanced branches that may slant up or down. This style suggests a tree growing in ideal landscape and weather conditions.

### Informal Upright (*Moyogi*)

This most popular style allows more latitude for creativity. The trunk curves slightly, seemingly in response to environmental conditions;

Formal upright
(*Chokkan*)

Informal upright
(*Moyogi*)

Slanting
(*Shakan*)

Cascade
(*Kengai*)

Windswept
(*Fukinagashi*)

Rock-clinging

Forest
(*Yose-Uye*)

**The seven basic bonsai styles**

innumerable examples of this style are found in nature. Although the trunk bends, the top of the tree is turned upward; limbs, angled gently down, branch from the outsides of the trunk curves.

## Slanting (*Shakan*)

The trunk slants as if buffeted by strong winds. As it would in nature, the tree develops a more pronounced root system to support the lean. Balance is created by tilting the top of the tree in the opposite direction from the slant and with the placement of the first branch. The angle of the slant is generally not greater than 45 degrees.

## Cascade (*Kengai*)

This style suggests a tree perched on a mountainside or cliff, struggling for survival. The trunk rises and then drops down in a fluid sweep at an angle of about 45 degrees to a point even with the bottom of the pot or below. Often the tree's highest point is the first branch, which angles up. Deep pots balance the tree's sweeping angles; the trunk is set in the middle or toward the back of the pot. In a variation of this style, semicascade (*Han-Kengai*), the trunk drops less dramatically to a point above the bottom of the pot.

## Windswept (*Fukinagashi*)

Branches are key for this style, which features a slanted, or even straight or gently bending trunk with exaggerated, windswept branches—typically shown blowing to one side. Sometimes, branches cross over the trunk, a feature not accepted for other styles. The trunk sits in the pot on the side opposite the direction of the windswept branches.

## Rock-Clinging (*Ishizuke*)

Symbolizing a mountain with steep cliffs and ravines or a rugged seashore, the rock—its shape, texture, and color—is the focal point of this style. The tree, generally low growing, suggesting a struggle with heavy snows and buffeting winds, sits atop the stone with exposed heavy and gnarled roots growing down and into the soil.

## Forest (*Yose-Uye*)

Odd numbers of trees are generally best for a forest or group planting as well as within each cluster in the design. Balance but never symmetry is strived for. Group plantings are often created from one species of nonflowering tree. Trees can all grow from one trunk placed horizontally, or on separate roots. If separate, try to select trees propagated from the same parent plant; their growth habits and needs will be similar, making care easier and appearance more uniform.

## Containers

Select the pot to harmonize with the bonsai; never choose the pot first and train the tree to fit it. As with all arts, the best advice is to study other bonsai to understand the aesthetic. Stoneware bonsai pots—traditionally round, oval, and rectangular—are shallow, except for those for cascade-style specimens, which are deep to balance the sweeping lines of the trunk. The majority of bonsai pots are earth-toned, but some are more colorful; tiny "feet" are pleasing to the overall design and key to drainage, as are holes in the pot bottom.

Pots can be glazed or unglazed outside, but are always unglazed inside; for outdoor bonsai, the pot must be frostproof. To test whether a pot is frostproof, sprinkle it with water. If the water dissipates in less than a minute, you can be fairly confident that the pot will survive outdoors in freezing temperatures.

A rule of thumb for pot depth is that it should be ½ to 2½ times the thickness of the trunk base. In general, curved lines go with informal, twisted, and bent trunks, while straight lines complement upright trunks. More ornate pots demand strong bonsai with obvious character. Colorful pots are most often used with fruiting or flowering trees and shrubs or those with fall color; select the pot color to complement the plant's most dramatic seasonal phase.

## Tools

Three basic bonsai tools are pruning shears, a concave branch cutter, and wire cutters. Special bonsai trimming shears are sold, but a good pair of scissors-type pruners is fine for most jobs. It must be sharp.

An ordinary chopstick is helpful for untangling roots and gently packing medium around them. Copper or aluminum wire in various gauges is used to anchor plants in the pot and for some kinds of training. Annealed copper wire is sold for bonsai training, although standard copper wire, heated to a cherry red color in a flame and then cooled gradually, can be just as effective. Special bonsai sieves aid in the preparation of the planting medium, but many gardeners simply use three gauges of screening from any hardware store: regular window screen, ⅛ to ¼ inch size, and ¼ to ½ inch size.

## Medium

Drainage is crucial; a light, airy medium is critical to the well-being of bonsai. Every bonsai enthusiast has his or her own favorite medium. A good basic soilless mix consists of one part builder's sand, one part calcined clay, and one part finely shredded pine bark. As with all soilless media, regular fertilizing is essential.

Combine sand, calcined clay, and finely shredded pine bark in equal parts. Use the three sizes of screening to prepare a large-particled layer of medium for the bottom layer in the pot and slightly smaller particles for the top layer. First, separate out the finest particles that fall through the finest mesh screen. Too-fine particles impede drainage, so save these for some other project. Sift the medium again using the ¼- to ½-inch screen; line the bottom of the container with the larger particles remaining on top. Sift the rest of the medium one more time through ⅛- to ¼-inch screening. Use the larger particles remaining on the screen to make the top layer of soil around the plant's roots; what goes through this screen can become a decorative layer on the soil surface.

For most bonsai a pH of from 6 to 7 is optimum. You can use a soil pH meter or pH strips to test the soil for plants, like rhododendrons and azaleas, that prefer a lower pH. For these, one of the acidifying liquid fertilizers on the market may suffice to bring the pH down to the proper range.

## Selecting a Tree

Choose evergreen trees with small needles and small-leaved deciduous trees. Select a three- to five-year-old plant—either one you propagate yourself or one from a commercial nursery. Sometimes the best trees for bonsai have been overlooked in nurseries due to their twisted trunks or odd branch structure; make sure the tree you pick is pest-free, with sturdy branches and healthy leaves.

## Pruning for Basic Form

Begin to train bonsai in spring; remove all but the key branches, which will become the skeleton of the bonsai. All new leaves and shoots will develop from these branches. Pinch developing new shoots to encourage branching and small leaves.

The tree in illustration (a), below, is being trained in the informal upright style. Only one branch is allowed to remain at each level. This avoids the overly symmetrical effect of opposite branches, creates a feeling of openness between branches, and accentuates the diminutive trunk.

The tree in illustration (b)—a distorted specimen, such as is occasionally found in a nursery—is being trained in a modified version of the informal upright style. It has been pruned mainly to simplify the branch structure and emphasize the asymmetrical trunk.

The two trees in illustration (c), being trained together in the forest style, are rare finds: specimens with interesting branch patterns, which, when selectively pruned, are immediately attractive as bonsai.

Before planting, bonsai require some root pruning—just enough so that the roots will fit into a shallow pot. Because of the heavy initial branch pruning, the roots should not be pruned severely at this time. They should be pruned harder when the plant is repotted at a later date.

### Pruning bonsai for basic form

*In training bonsai from nursery-grown trees, it is important to remove all but the key branches, which will form the simplified skeleton of the bonsai-to-be; foliage masses can be created around each branch if new shoots are pinched back as they develop. In tree (a), only one branch is allowed to remain at each level to avoid the oversymmetrical effect of opposite branches, create a feeling of openness between branches, and accentuate the trunk. Tree (b), the kind of distorted specimen that can occasionally be found in a nursery or growing wild, is pruned mainly to simplify the branch structure and emphasize its asymmetrical trunk. The trees in example (c) already have interesting branching patterns and with selective pruning are immediately attractive as bonsai.*

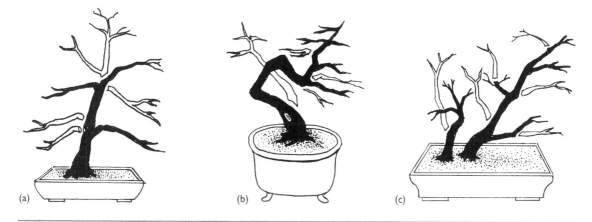

(a)　(b)　(c)

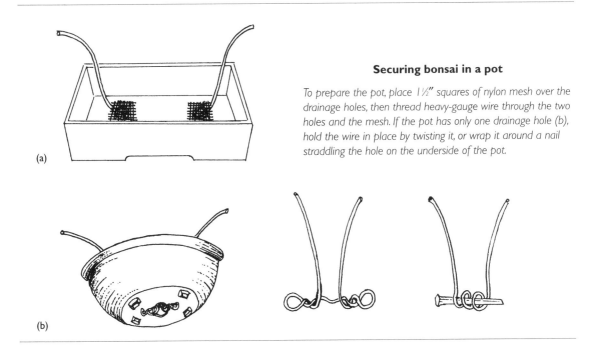

(a)

**Securing bonsai in a pot**

*To prepare the pot, place 1½″ squares of nylon mesh over the drainage holes, then thread heavy-gauge wire through the two holes and the mesh. If the pot has only one drainage hole (b), hold the wire in place by twisting it, or wrap it around a nail straddling the hole on the underside of the pot.*

(b)

## Potting and Repotting

To prepare the pot, place 1½-inch squares of nylon mesh, such as needlepoint screen, over the drainage holes. Thread heavy-gauge wire, used here to secure the bonsai in the pot, through the two drainage holes and the mesh (if the pot has only one drainage hole, hold the wire in place by twisting or wrapping it around a nail straddling the hole on the underside of the pot). Pull the ends of the wire up and over the pot rim.

Working with dry medium after it has been sifted and separated into two parts with different-sized particles, line the bottom of the container with medium with the largest-sized particles, making a layer deep enough so that the roots rest on it and the trunk base will be at eye level in the container—even with the rim. Anchor the root ball by pulling the ends of the wire across or through it and twisting the ends together. Fill in around the roots with the medium with slightly smaller-size particles; gently push it between the plant roots with a chopstick. Bend the wire and bury it in the soil. Water thoroughly with a fine spray or immerse the container underwater until bubbles stop percolating to the water surface.

Repotting is an essential part of training and maintaining bonsai. Root growth is pruned severely at this time; otherwise the tree could not survive in the same-size pot. Remove the tree from its pot, and trim off about two-thirds of the roots and two-thirds of the top growth. Thoroughly clean the pot. Replace the anchor wire and mesh, and add fresh medium. Repot deciduous bonsai every one to two years, evergreens every two to three years, pines every four to five years, and indoor bonsai every two to three years. Spring is the best time to repot outdoor bonsai—during dormancy for deciduous trees and before active growth for evergreens. Indoor bonsai can be repotted anytime.

## Root Pruning

Root pruning is done during repotting. When the bonsai is out of the pot, use a chopstick to gently untangle roots and loosen the soil ball. Cut away a taproot if one has formed, any girdling roots, and excessively large ones. Trim the rest of the roots back by approximately two-thirds; make certain the portions remaining have smaller feeder roots branching from them. Use sharp pruning shears to make clean, angled cuts.

## Watering

Watering, repotting, and pruning, in that order, are the most critical aspects of caring for a bonsai. Learning to anticipate a plant's water needs takes experience. Never let the planting medium dry out so completely that the bonsai droops, but be sure the medium dries between waterings. Expect to water often on sunny and windy days, perhaps as much as several times a day. Take time while watering to observe plants carefully for any signs of pests or disease; treat immediately.

## Fertilizing

Fertilize outdoor deciduous bonsai once a month while trees are in leaf; let them rest during dormancy. Evergreens should get the same treatment: one fertilizing a month while they are actively growing. Use a liquid fertilizer such as fish emulsion. Fertilize indoor bonsai once a month during growing periods, which vary from species to species. Fish emulsion is

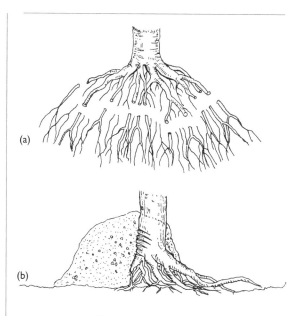

(a)

(b)

**Root pruning a bonsai**

*On a bonsai that needs more density and compactness (a), cut away a taproot if one has formed, any girdling roots, and excessively large ones. Trim back smaller roots as well. If a tree lacks roots on one side (b), take a sharp knife and scar the base of the trunk where good roots are needed, bury the tree in sand, and in a few months new roots will sprout.*

fine for these plants, but an all-purpose, water-soluble inorganic fertilizer at half the recommended strength will do as well.

## Pruning

Shape and overall appearance are critical to bonsai. Without routine top-growth pruning and root pruning, a bonsai will grow like any tree in a container. It is important to maintain a balance between roots and top-growth; when pruning roots back at repotting, prune top-growth proportionately.

What kinds of pruning cuts and when to make them depends on the plant species and

(a)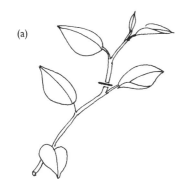

(b)

(c)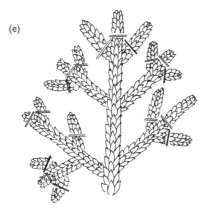

(d)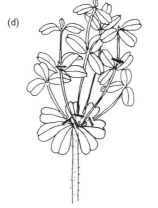

(e)

(f)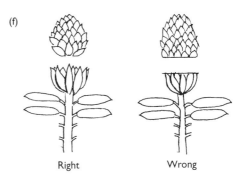

Right          Wrong

## Pinching bonsai

*Frequent pinching during active growth helps maintain the shape of the tree. In general, pinch back after as many as five new leaves develop on a young branch, to the first one or two on the top of the tree and the first three or four elsewhere (a). Pinch just above a side bud that points in the direction you want the branch to grow; for buds growing in pairs, take out one of each pair to give the plant a more asymmetrical look. Remove alternate shoots (b). All the foliage of healthy temperate deciduous species and tropical and subtropical species (never needled evergreens!) can be nipped off in early summer; a new crop of daintier leaves will form in a week or so (c). Pinch flowering and fruiting trees immediately after they bloom so that incipient flower buds will be left intact. Retain only one or two of the five new shoots that typically appear (d, left), and cut these back to two or three leaves (d, right). More or less daily, pinch off a few tips of evergreens that produce new shoots throughout the growing season while they are sending forth new growth (e). When pinching species with needled leaves (f), be careful not to cut through needles that will be left on the tree, for the remaining stumps will brown and disfigure the bonsai. In the case of pines, spruces, and firs, which produce new growth called "candles," pinch back half or more of each candle just as the individual needles begin to show (g). If the needles of a pine become too long in relation to the size of the tree, remove all buds approximately every third spring (h); this will adversely affect the plant's appearance for a season, but the new needles the following season will be much smaller.*

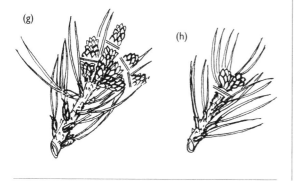

(g)

(h)

the bonsai style. There are basically two kinds of bonsai pruning: thinning and pinching. Thinning cuts are made to take whole limbs back to the trunk or partial branches back to a branch union. This severe pruning is necessary to attain the proper shape of the tree. Pinching is performed on new growth and is used to maintain the general shape of the tree.

Bear in mind that the more branches you thin, the denser the tree will be when it resprouts. Use a concave branch cutter to remove large branches; concave cuts are thought to heal faster and scar less. Pinching can be done with a sharp pair of pruning shears or your fingers if the new growth is crisp. A description of some pinching techniques follows; for more information, consult one of the references listed in "Further Reading," page 537.

Frequent pinching during active growth produces the best results (see illustration on page 532). In general, pinch back—after as many as five new leaves develop on a young branch—to the first one or two on shoots at the top of the tree, and the first three or four elsewhere.

Pinch just above a side bud that points in the direction you want a branch to grow. For buds growing in pairs, take out one of each pair to give the plant a more asymmetrical look. Remove alternate shoots.

If you are working with healthy deciduous trees of temperate species, such as maple, hornbeam, ginkgo, or zelkova, and tropical and subtropical species, such as dwarf brush cherry, serrisa, jade, and ficus, all the foliage can be nipped off in early summer; a new crop of leaves, daintier in size, develops in a week or so. This process also stimulates fall foliage color. To avoid damaging trees, snip leaves off at the base of the blade, leaving the petiole to wither and

## ADVANCING AGE

A stout, sturdy trunk is a mark of age for bonsai. You can "advance" the age of a bonsai by growing it in the ground for two to three years. Trunk diameter increases much faster in the ground than in a pot. Of course, even in the ground, the bonsai requires regular watering and fertilizing throughout the growing season, plus root pruning and top pruning. It sometimes may require a second seasonal root pruning as well.

## COMPANION PLANTS

Companion plants—dwarf forms of cultivated plants and small-leaved, low-growing specimens—should always be smaller than the bonsai. The tiny woody and herbaceous plants break the space between the container and the bonsai and carry the eye into the composition. Plants whose cultural requirements match those of the bonsai are best. Popular companion plants include grasses, mosses, dwarf bamboos, dwarf sedges, and horsetails.

## MINIATURE BONSAI

Most bonsai are trained to be from 6 inches to 2 feet tall; measurements include plant and pot. Truly miniature bonsai, called *mame*, are 6 inches or less, with correspondingly tiny pots. The biggest challenge of growing these extra-tiny bonsai is watering, which may be required many times a day during hot, dry weather—making them much more time-consuming than other bonsai.

fall off. Never strip all the leaves from needled evergreens.

Pinch flowering and fruiting trees immediately after they bloom so that incipient flower buds will be left intact. Pinch azaleas, for example, severely just after flowering. Of the five new shoots that usually appear, only one or two should be retained, and these should be cut back to two or three leaves. Later in the growing season, pinch them more sparingly to allow some flower buds to form.

If you are working with evergreens that produce new shoots throughout the growing season, pinch off a few tips more or less daily while the tree is sending forth new growth. For species such as scale-leaved juniper, remove tips. Needle-leaved species demand special attention; never cut through the needles—the remaining stumps will brown and disfigure the tree.

In the case of pines, spruces, and firs, which produce new growth resembling "candles," pinch back half or more of each candle just as the individual needles begin to show. If the needles of a pine become too long in relation to the size of the tree, remove all buds approximately every third spring. This will adversely affect the plant's appearance for a season, but the new needles the following season will be much smaller.

## Wiring

Sometimes, bonsai need to be trained with wires to attain the desired shape. Winter and early spring are the best seasons to do this. Reduce watering for two to three days before wiring so that the bonsai will become more pliable. Select wire that is roughly one-third the diameter of the branch you are training; double

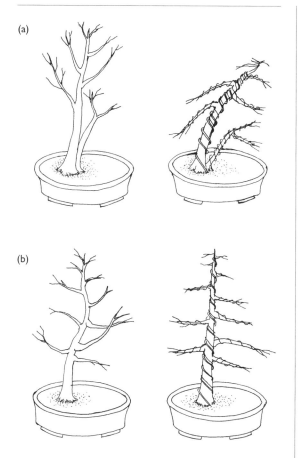

**Wiring a bonsai**

*Branches growing upward can be trained to slope downward or outward, suggesting the form of an aged tree (a). Wind wire clockwise for training a branch to the right, and counter-clockwise for training it to the left (b). Wire should be just large and stiff enough to hold the newly bent branch in position.*

the wire for thick branches. Wrap the wire at a 45-degree angle around the branch and follow the natural curves of branches when bending. Water the bonsai well after the procedure and keep it in a shaded, sheltered location without fertilizer for two to three weeks. Pay close attention to the branches so that the wires do not constrict and scar new growth; remove wires in six month to a year, depending on the species.

## Overwintering Outdoor Bonsai

Although outdoor bonsai require a period of cold dormancy to remain healthy, vigorous plants, it is unwise to leave them outdoors unprotected—especially where temperatures drop consistently below freezing. It is far better to find a protected site outdoors or a cool, well-lit indoor location.

A sunporch where night temperatures never drop below 36°F makes an ideal indoor site for overwintering bonsai. Outdoors, a deep insulated cold frame, with a plastic-covered, snugly fitting top, works well. If it is not in the shade, protect the plant from sun scorch with a lath house or shading cloth. The soil in pots thus protected should not freeze so long as night-time temperatures do not fall below 0°F. Even in this shelter, bonsai require attention. Water as needed, and remove the protective covering to give the plants some air on warmer, non-freezing winter days. Be sure to replace the cover before sunset.

## Special Requirements for Indoor Bonsai

In general, the best location for indoor bonsai is in sunlight with good air circulation. Most indoor locations are less than ideal. Often, sunlight must be supplemented with cool, white fluorescent light or special indoor gardening lamps. In order for plants to properly benefit from supplemental lighting, the tops of the bonsai plants should be within 6 to 10 inches of the bulbs. Where window light is sufficient, plants require regular turning for uniform growth.

Humidity inside most homes often is not high enough to support many tropical and subtropical species. Humidifiers are one solution. Some gardeners set bonsai pots on a tray of pebbles and water; the evaporating water raises humidity. Regularly sprinkling the leaves also will increase the moisture level around the plants.

Understanding a plant's native habitat helps gauge its requirements for light and humidity. Tropical rain-forest plants, crowded together naturally, sometimes shade one another. In gen-

eral, tropical species, such as *Ficus* and *Schefflera*, will accept low light and often relatively low humidity in homes. Bear in mind, however, that although these plants may not require bright light, they are accustomed to 12 hours of daylight and probably will need more hours of light than the natural conditions allow. Subtropical plants, such as *Serissa* and citrus, generally grow less close together and require higher light levels and a minimum of 50 percent humidity. Plants from warm temperate regions, such as *Myrtus, Cistus, Callistemon,* and *Schinus,* require a south-facing window or supplemental lighting during winter. Succulents from subtropical arid regions, including *Crassula* and *Adenium,* need very bright light and drier conditions—overwatering is the danger for these species.

---

## RECOMMENDED PLANTS FOR INDOOR BONSAI

*Bougainvillea glabra*, bougainvillea
*Callistemon linearis*, bottlebrush
*Crassula argentea*, dwarf jade
*Cycas revoluta*, sago palm
*Ficus benjamina*, Benjamin fig
*Ficus microcarpa* 'Golden Gate', Golden Gate fig
*Ilex crenata* 'Okinawa', Okinawa holly
*Jasminum fruticans*, jasmine
*Leptospermum scoparium* 'Snow White', Snow White tea tree
*Myrcaria cauliflora*, jaboticaba
*Nolina recurvata*, ponytail palm
*Ochna serrulata*, bird's-eye bush
*Punica granatum* 'Nana', dwarf pomegranate
*Sageretia thea*, Chinese sweet plum
*Schefflera arboricola*, Hawaiian umbrella tree
*Serissa foetida*, serissa
*Syzygium paniculatum*, Australian brush cherry

---

## SOME RECOMMENDED PLANTS FOR OUTDOOR BONSAI

*Acer buergerianum*, trident maple
*Acer palmatum*, Japanese maple
*Cydonia sinensis*, Chinese quince
*Fagus crenata*, Japanese beech
*Juniperus chinensis* 'Shimpaku', Shimpaku juniper
*Juniperus rigida*, needle juniper
*Lagerstroemia indica*, miniature crape myrtle
*Liquidambar orientalis*, Oriental sweetgum
*Malus baccata*, Siberian crabapple
*Malus* x *micromalus*, kaido crabapple
*Pinus densiflora*, Japanese red pine
*Pinus parviflora*, Japanese white pine
*Pinus thunbergii*, Japanese black pine
*Prunus mume*, Japanese flowering apricot
*Rhododendron indicum* 'Satsuki', Satsuki azalea
*Salix babylonica*, weeping willow
*Tsuga canadensis*, Canadian hemlock
*Ulmus parvifolia*, Chinese elm
*Zelkova serrata*, zelkova

# Further Reading

*Bonsai Today,* a bimonthly journal published by Stone Lantern Publishing Company, P.O. Box 816, Sudbury, MA 01776.

Dreilinger, Sigmund, ed. *Indoor Bonsai.* Brooklyn, N.Y.: Brooklyn Botanic Garden, 1990.

Naka, John Yoshio. *Bonsai Techniques.* Santa Monica, Calif.: Published for the Bonsai Institute of California by Dennis-Landman Publishers, 1976.

Tomlinson, Harry. *The Complete Book of Bonsai: A Practical Guide to Its Art and Cultivation.* New York: Abbeville Press, 1990.

Yashiroda, Kan, ed. *Bonsai: Special Techniques.* Brooklyn, N.Y.: Brooklyn Botanic Garden, 1966, 1990.

Yashiroda, Kan, ed. *Dwarfed Potted Trees: The Bonsai of Japan.* Brooklyn, N.Y.: Brooklyn Botanic Garden, 1953, 1991.

# 9

# SAFE PEST
# CONTROL

Many of the pest-control strategies outlined in this section have proved their effectiveness over hundreds— or thousands—of years, and were eclipsed only recently with the advent of synthetic, petro-chemical-based pesticides in the early 1940s. The new chemical pesticides flooded the market. In the rush to embrace synthetics, many reliable natural controls were dropped, and research into nonchemical approaches halted at universities across the country. The use of so-called biological controls such as predators and parasites slowed to a crawl because the heavy use of the new broad-spectrum pesticides killed beneficial insects as well as pests. Yet synthetic chemical sprays and dusts have not won the "war" against pests. In fact, crop losses due to insects have increased over the past fifty years, in part because many insects have developed resistances to commonly used pesticides.

Over that same period, the dangers of synthetic pesticides—to the people who work with them and to the environment—have become evident. They damage soils, poison wildlife and waterways, kill insects that would naturally keep pest populations in check, and can sicken or even kill farmworkers. Home gardeners need not turn to these synthetic chemicals, because with a little extra care and a heightened aware-ness of what is happening among the plants, most pests and the damage they cause can be kept at tolerable levels with less toxic controls.

One of the fundamentals of safe pest control is that the gardener must come to terms with and learn to tolerate some level of plant dam-age—a few blemishes on the apple harvest, for example, a few less tomatoes per plant, or a lawn that may include a mix of plants, includ-ing some weeds. These are the trade-offs for a healthier garden, which contributes to a healthi-er overall environment.

To succeed with safe pest-control techniques, you must become tuned in to the nuances of the garden: which pests appear and when, and at which stage of their life cycle; where certain plants thrive in the garden and where they languish; and the condition of the garden soil, to name a few. The payoff is not simply a beautiful and bountiful garden achieved without the use of potentially hazardous poisons; by spending time observing the spectrum of life unfold in the garden, you will in all likelihood find gardening even more enjoyable.

This section lays out many of the basic principles of integrated pest management and organic pest control, and should be helpful in determining when to employ specific nontoxic techniques against specific garden pests. Techniques are covered from the least to most likely to cause ecological damage, because it makes sense to try physical controls before stepping up to biological controls, and to try biological controls before deploying chemical controls, which will have a greater impact on the garden and the larger landscape.

The section concludes with an encyclopedia of many specific garden pests: insects, pathogens, and other pests. The entry for each pest in the encyclopedia covers the types of plants it prefers, the signs of infestation or infection, and the most effective and ecologically benign methods of control. Finally, commonsense weed management is discussed.

# Integrated and Organic Pest Management

Integrated pest management (IPM) is a pest-control approach first developed for commercial agriculture. Its goal is to maintain acceptable harvest levels while lowering synthetic pesticide use and environmental damage. IPM aims to reduce pest populations to tolerable levels rather than to totally eradicate them—an undesirable and unrealistic goal in part because in the absence of one pest, others may move in and do even more harm. IPM employs monitoring and a combination of management techniques—biological controls, physical controls, horticultural controls, and, as a last resort, synthetic pesticides—and relies on the farmer's awareness of the status of pest populations and plant health.

On a smaller scale—and with the omission of the synthetic pesticides—this pest-control approach makes sense in the home garden. Because synthetic controls are omitted, IPM practiced at the garden scale is sometimes called organic pest management (OPM).

The foundation of OPM, like that of IPM, is the gardener's close observation and monitoring of plant health and pest presence in the garden. These tasks are made easier by a field guide and a magnifying glass to aid in the identification of pests. Keeping a written record of your observations also will prove its usefulness over time. Look for the following as you make your regular rounds in the garden:

• Plant condition. Plants stressed by excessive sun, water, shade, fertilizer, or the lack of these, or from poor soil or mechanical damage from garden tools are vulnerable to pest attack.

• Pest presence. Pests can live in the garden without causing damage to plants. If the plants begin to show signs of damage by pests, identify the organism involved, note where and to what extent the desirable parts of plants have been affected, and try to get a fix on the size of the pest population.

• Beneficial organisms. Determine which natural enemies of garden pests are present, and

539

in what numbers, and learn the signs of pests under attack by their predators and parasites.

• Climate and microclimate. Some areas of the garden, such as damp places or those where the air circulates poorly, may be more welcoming to pests than others.

It is worth repeating that learning to tolerate a certain level of pest damage is essential to the success of IPM and OPM. You must decide how much damage you can live with, and on which plants and which parts of plants. You must then determine the point at which the pest population grows large enough to inflict that level of damage (the number of aphids per leaf, for example). Finally, you must find a level of control and combination of control methods that keeps pest damage at the level you can live with.

There is a broad range of natural or least-toxic controls to choose from, and these techniques can complement and even enhance each other when combined or integrated. The following is a list of the most ecologically sensible pest controls:

• Pest-resistant plants. Using plants bred to be resistant to attack allows you to reduce the use of other control techniques.

• Garden design. Site plants in parts of the garden where they will thrive: shade-loving plants in shady spots, water-lovers in moist areas, and so on. Rotate related plants from spot to spot in the vegetable garden to avoid pest and disease problems that can arise when the same plants are grown in the same location from year to year. Mix species together in plantings to prevent the rapid spread of pests through the garden.

• Cultural controls. Till the soil in the fall to expose pests to the elements. Clean up the garden to get rid of potential habitats where pests can find shelter over the winter. Prune infected plant parts and remove them from the garden to reduce the spread of insects and pathogens.

• Physical controls. Traps, barriers such as row covers, and flamers all can be effective in combating pests—and monitoring pest levels—if used at the right times and in the right places.

• Biological controls. Natural predators of many pests can be lured to the garden with proper shelter, food, and water, and in some cases they can be purchased at nurseries or from mail-order suppliers.

• Least-toxic chemical controls. These include, among others, insecticidal soaps, horticultural oils, diatomaceous earth, silica aerogel, growth regulators, and botanical (plant-derived) pesticides. As with all controls, these should be deployed only against the appropriate pest at the appropriate period in its life cycle.

## Designing Gardens for Pest Resistance

Gardens can be planned from the start with pest resistance as a goal. It is possible to improve the ability of even established, permanent plantings to resist pests. Existing trees, shrubs, and perennials can be incorporated into a design that includes a variety of new perennials, annuals, and vegetables chosen and sited for pest resistance. Here are some factors to consider when drawing up a garden plan.

• Know your garden. Effective garden design starts with a careful inventory of plants and conditions in the entire yard. It should include existing plants and structures and should indicate what parts of the garden they shade and when. It should note where the sun hits during the day and over the entire growing season, and for how many hours a day. It should also note areas with moist soil, frost pockets, and any other conditions that affect plant growth and health. With a detailed garden plan in hand, you can determine where best to locate specific plants and beds to ensure plant health and deter pests.

• Create diversity. The healthiest gardens tend to be those that most closely resemble nature in all of its colorful diversity—that include the greatest variety of species, and that welcome a multitude of animals and insects by providing them with food, water, and shelter. Nature keeps most pests from overrunning an ecosystem through a system of checks and balances: Plants, animals, insects, and microorganisms each have their own set of preferred food sources and are themselves food for other species. The population of each species is kept within bounds by its natural enemies. Even diverse gardens include a certain number of "pest" species but in all likelihood are home to "beneficial" species that prey on them.

• Diversify your plantings. In accordance with the same general principle that a garden should be as diverse as possible, each planting area or bed should also be diverse. Plant pathogens spread rapidly among related plants, as do many insect pests. Break up vegetable beds with flowers or unrelated vegetables to slow the growth of pest populations, being careful to group plants appropriately so that sun-loving species are not shaded out. Mingle food plants for beneficial insects—those with exposed sources of pollen and nectar—among the vegetables. Plants with easy access to pollen include members of the daisy (Compositae), carrot (Umbelliferae), and mint (Labiatae) families. Favorites of many beneficials are dill, lovage, thyme, and mints.

• Choose plants wisely. Plants grow best in

the environmental conditions—levels of rainfall, daily and annual sunlight, and temperature, soil makeup and pH, as well as associations of other plants and animals—in which they have evolved. For this reason, if located in a suitable microclimate, native plants are often dependable performers in the garden. Choose nonnatives that will also perform well under the same conditions.

Plant breeders have created varieties of many plants that are able to resist specific pathogens. These will not only ward off disease, but are less likely to be susceptible to attack by insect pests than plants that are weakened by disease. Lists of pathogens and insect pests common in regions throughout the country are available from county Cooperative Extension offices. Look for plants that resist pathogens common to your region. Plant tags or descriptions in nursery catalogs often include this information.

Healthy plants are better able to fend off attack by both insects and pathogens, and an important opportunity to ensure a plant's health is at the time of purchase. Buy plants early in the growing season, when the selection is best. Look for the healthiest individuals, those with plentiful, disease-free roots that are not "root-bound," or matted or coiled tightly in a ball. Choose plants with leaves that are consistent in color, without browning, yellowing, or blotching, and that are free of any sign of disease or insect infestation. Neither the leaves nor the stems should show signs of tearing or bruising.

• Take advantage of the site. Every garden has its own microclimates—areas that are more or less exposed to sun and wind. Many gardens are affected by other factors as well, such as proximity to a road, which will expose plants to salt, exhaust, and other pollutants. There may also be sites, especially against the house, where the soil pH changes, or sites, such as beneath drainspouts, that receive a lot of water. Learn about the different microclimates on your property and place plants where they will thrive, or at least where they will tolerate difficult conditions. A garden designed to optimize plant health will take all these nuances into consideration.

• Locate plants where air can circulate freely around them and the soil drains well. Follow seed packet and planting instructions on how far apart to space specimens. Plants grown too closely together are more likely to pass pathogens and insect infestations along to one another.

• Rotate plants. Over time, pathogens and insects infest the soil in which their host plants are grown with eggs and spores. By shifting plants (and their close relatives) from location to location in the garden each growing season, you will help deter these pests. Avoid planting where plants in the same family have been growing in the past two years. Related plants include the brassicas (cabbage, cauliflower, broccoli, and Brussels sprouts); the cucurbits (cucumbers, melons, pumpkins, and squash); and tomatoes, potatoes, peppers, eggplants, and other members of the nightshade family.

## Cultural Controls

Cultural controls cover a range of good gardening practices that should be a part of every gardener's routine. The cultural practices outlined below, if carried out regularly, will make the garden less vulnerable to pest attack and healthier overall.

• Keep your soil healthy. Healthy soil equals healthy plants. Plants grown in healthy, biologically active soil are stronger and less appealing to pathogens and insect pests. Well-drained soil that contains all the minerals and micronutrients plants need will better promote the health of plant roots, and make them more resistant to the harmful strains of nematodes. Healthy roots are better at supplying plants with micronutrients and water, both important in making plants pest resistant. Soil can be analyzed for its micronutrient content, pH, and other characteristics by a soil-testing laboratory or with kits available at garden supply centers (see "Soil," page 430).

Ensure that soil receives a slow, steady supply of nitrogen and other nutrients by amending it annually with a fall application of compost. Spread a 2-inch-thick layer on the soil and work it in. Plants supplied with excessive amounts of typical, highly soluble nitrate fertilizers are more attractive to aphids and other types of pests, which are drawn to the nitrogen-rich foliage.

Till the soil in the fall to expose insect eggs and pupae to the elements, and to eliminate spots where pests might find shelter over the winter.

Use the power of the sun to control soil-borne wilts and nematodes. Solarize soil during midsummer or any stretch of hot, clear weather by watering beds thoroughly, covering them with clear plastic 1 to 4 millimeters thick with the edges tucked into a trench around the outside of the bed, then removing the plastic after four to six weeks. Mulch if you do not plan to plant right away.

• Time planting wisely. Pests are most problematic to their target plants at specific times in pest life cycles—when insects are in the caterpillar stage, for example, and need large amounts of plant material to mature. Avoid pests when they are at their hungriest by planting when they are not active. Find out what pests prey on specific vegetables, then plant them as early or late as possible to avoid the worst infestations. For example, potatoes planted early in the season will get a good foothold and become strong enough before Colorado potato beetle populations peak to be able to withstand a moderate infestation and still produce a respectable harvest.

• Pay attention to sanitation when gardening. Gardeners can unwittingly contaminate uninfected plants with insect eggs and fungal spores by using unclean tools, and can track eggs and spores through the garden on shoes, gardening clothing, and hands. Both insects and pathogens spread readily through a garden in this fashion. Clean tools thoroughly and disinfect them with alcohol or a solution containing 1 part bleach and 9 parts water after working with diseased plants. After visiting a site of potential infection, clean shoes with a bleach solution. Wash hands and gardening clothes. Fungal spores require a film of moisture to spread from plant to plant. Minimize the chance of spreading disease by working in the garden when it is not wet.

Many insects and pathogens find shelter over the winter in the debris of their host plants. Prune infected parts during the season and destroy them by putting them on a compost pile that heats up enough to kill pests (160°F degrees for the most virulent bacteria and viruses; 180°F for weed seeds). Gather up and compost the plants and stalks of uninfected vegetables, flowers, and weeds. Compost mulch from annual and vegetable beds and spread a fresh mulch to keep winter precipitation from compacting the soil.

• Plant a cover crop. A fall cover crop is an ideal way to not only increase soil fertility but also eliminate many pests in the process of preparing the soil for planting. Tilling the soil for the cover crop will kill some wintering insects, and expose others to winter weather, hungry birds, and other predators. In lieu of a cover crop, apply a fresh mulch, which will leave the soil ready for planting with minimal preparation in spring.

## Physical Controls

Farmers and gardeners have devised a number of practical, often simple methods of eliminating or containing pest outbreaks. These range from fooling pests with fruit decoys to blasting them off leaves with a jet of water. The following physical or mechanical controls can be quite effective against a mild infestation or infection.

• Handpicking. The most straightforward method of pest control is to pick the pest right off the plant. This works best with large, slow, visible pests—slugs, snails, caterpillars, some adult insects, or even egg masses. Pests should not be confused with beneficial creatures, which may look very similar. A comprehensive insect or wildlife guide can help you distinguish the good organisms from the bad. Drop captured pests into soapy water or a mild alcohol solution. Shaking plants onto a sheet spread beneath plants also can be effective when pests are sluggish—when it is cool out, for example.

• Pruning. Plant parts heavily infested with pests, pest eggs, or disease can be cut away. Use only sharp tools to make clean cuts. On woody plants, cut back to a healthy bud or close to a main limb. Dispose of infected parts in hot compost piles or sealed containers, and disinfect tools before using them again on healthy plants.

• Water sprays. A forceful spray of water can knock small, soft-bodied pests right off plants. Spray in early morning, and avoid spraying in wet weather when the water can aid in the spread of pathogens from plant to plant.

• Baits, traps, and lures. There are many ingenious ways to lure and trap garden pests. Shallow pans filled with beer and set into the soil will lure slugs and snails into the fermented liquid, where they will drown. Upside-down clay pots draw snails during hot summer days; rolls of newspaper are hiding places for earwigs; lengths of board laid between garden rows will draw slugs, snails, cutworms, and grubs, as will lettuce and cabbage leaves. Pests captured by these means can be gathered up and destroyed. Trap apple maggots with apple-sized red spheres coated with a sticky substance such as Tanglefoot. Bright yellow boards coated with a sticky substance and placed near target plants attract and can control many insect pests, including cucumber beetles, whiteflies, cabbageworms, and thrips.

• Barriers. Copper strips will keep slugs and snails out of flower and vegetable beds when placed around the perimeter. A "collar" or ring of tar paper or cardboard or a tin can with both ends removed, when pushed into the soil about an inch deep around a seedling, will deter cutworms and slugs. When seedlings have outgrown these collars, they are no longer appetizing to these pests. Floating row covers let the sunlight through and are light enough to rest atop the foliage of growing plants, yet protect plants from a number of pests, including aphids, flea beetles, and leafhoppers. Spunbonded fabrics work best to repel pests. Covers made of heavier fabric can protect plants from cold to a certain extent and extend the growing season. Bands of fabric coated with a sticky substance and wrapped around the trunk of a tree can keep crawlers such as gypsy moth caterpillars, leaf beetles, and cutworms from reaching tender foliage in the spring. Newspapers laid atop garden soil will keep some species of thrips from reaching the soil to pupate. After thinning, enclose young apples and pears in paper bags tied securely to the limb to protect them from codling moths. Take the bags off just before you harvest.

## Biological Controls

Almost every insect (and many disease microorganisms) has its own set of natural enemies—other species that will eat it, or use its body or eggs as a place to lay their own eggs. These so-called beneficial organisms include everything from birds to insects to bacteria. Make the garden inviting for beneficials so they will arrive on their own (see "How to Entice Beneficial Insects to Your Garden," page 545). Some beneficial organisms are also available through garden suppliers, but be sure to introduce them when their prey is present; otherwise they will perish or go elsewhere. The following are a few of the common garden beneficials.

• Lady beetles. Lady beetles (ladybugs) eat a wide range of soft-bodied pests, including aphids, scales, Colorado potato beetles, mealybugs, and spider mites. If purchased and released, lady beetles may follow their instinct to migrate in order to burn off stored body fat. You can purchase insectary-reared beetles that are hungry when released and therefore are more likely to remain in your garden. They will be more likely to stay and lay eggs that hatch into hungry larvae if there is something to eat; they prefer aphids but will consume pollen and nectar of blooming herbs and flowers as well.

## HOW TO ENTICE BENEFICIAL INSECTS TO YOUR GARDEN

There are many beneficial organisms that are not for sale in mail-order catalogs, even though they are some of the most effective against garden pests. Big-eyed bugs, for example, can eat up to twelve small caterpillars or leafhoppers per day; damsel bug nymphs eat aphids, thrips, and other pests; and minute pirate bug nymphs eat many insects, including thrips, spider mites, small caterpillars, leafhopper nymphs, corn earworms, and the eggs of many insects.

In fact, it may not be necessary to buy beneficial insects at all. Naturally occurring beneficials will do a good job of managing the pests in your garden if you make it insect-friendly. Here is how to create an enticing habitat for beneficial insects.

• Grow plants that will provide nectar and pollen for beneficial insects. This will attract them and give them something to eat while they wait for the pest insects to arrive or to hatch. Many common herbs such as dill, caraway, fennel, spearmint, and lemon balm are favorites. Tansy (*Tanacetum vulgare,* the herb, not tansy ragwort, the weed) is especially attractive to lady beetles. Other plants favored by beneficial insects include white cosmos, clovers and other legumes, buckwheat, and many wildflowers. Stagger your plantings to make sure one or more of these plants is always in bloom in your garden.

• Provide a source of water, whether a small pond or a shallow dish filled with pebbles and water.

• Give beneficials some shelter from wind and rain with a hedge of tall sunflowers or perennials. A perennial border also provides food and overwintering sites. Cover crops add organic matter when you turn them into the soil, and also will provide shelter and food for beneficials.

• Avoid using pesticides. Many of them kill beneficial insects as well as pests. If you must use pesticides, use products that do not harm populations of the "good guys" in the garden.

• Lacewings. Lacewing larvae, called aphid lions, eat aphids, thrips, mealybugs, scales, moth eggs, small caterpillars, and mites. These native beneficials can be attracted to the garden with flowering weeds such as dandelions and goldenrods, or can be purchased; they will arrive in the egg stage and should be scattered around the garden—about 1,000 eggs for every 500 square feet.

• Spined soldier beetles. Spined soldier beetles or bugs are voracious predators in the nymph stage, attacking many types of caterpillars and larvae, including gypsy moth caterpillars, Colorado potato beetle larvae, and Mexican bean beetle larvae. They will be attracted to a garden that includes pollen- and nectar-rich plants. They also can be purchased commercially.

• Trichogramma wasps. Trichogramma wasps lay their own eggs inside the eggs of many garden pests, including corn earworms, cutworms, cabbage loopers, codling moths, and tomato hornworms. Their larvae, when hatched, consume the contents of the eggs. Trichogramma wasps are native to North America but can be purchased on cards that can be hung in fruit trees.

• Nematodes. Nematodes come in two forms: the nuisance species that attack plant roots, and the beneficials that attack soil-dwelling insect pests, releasing a bacterium that quickly kills them. Beneficial nematodes can provide control of many insect species, including onion maggots, Japanese beetle grubs, and wireworms. Many strains of nematodes are available commercially, and suppliers should be able to identify the most effective strain for each pest and proper application directions.

• *Bacillus thuringiensis (Bt). Bt* is a species of bacteria that produces a toxin poisonous to many common insect pests. *Bt* var. *kurstaki* controls cabbage loopers, codling moth larvae, and tomato hornworms, among other pests, while *Bt* var. *san diego* controls leaf-feeding beetles such as boll weevils and Colorado potato beetles. More than thirty-five strains of *Bt* are available to the home gardener, and a garden supplier should be able to identify the appropriate strain for a given pest problem.

• Milky spore disease. This is a bacterium that is effective in controlling Japanese beetle grubs and related insects, but it can be hard to tell when it is working properly because you won't see immediate results. Currently, there are very few suppliers of milky spore disease. One company to try is St. Gabriel Labs, 14540 John Marshall Highway, Gainesville, VA 20155, 1-800-801-0061.

• Toads and frogs. Toads and frogs are hungry insect eaters and will be drawn to gardens with cool, moist spots. Birds, bats, snakes, ducks, and geese all eat insects, as do fish in ponds or garden pools.

### Beneficials for the House and Greenhouse

Greenhouses and homes with many indoor plants can also house pests, including aphids, whiteflies, spider mites, mealybugs, and scales. Beneficials can be very effective indoors as they cannot fly away to other food sources. Among the most effective beneficials for an indoor pest

problem are lady beetles, which prey on most of the pests mentioned above; *Encarsia formosa*, tiny wasps that parasitize whiteflies by laying their eggs in whitefly larvae; predatory mites, which prey on pest mites such as spider mites, two-spotted mites, red mites, and Pacific mites; and mealybug destroyers, nonnative lady beetles whose favored food is the mealybug.

### Least-Toxic Chemical Controls

Despite your best efforts with the methods discussed above, some pest problems may fail to be contained. In these instances, use of one of the chemical controls discussed below may be appropriate. Such controls range from gentle concoctions made from herbs or baking soda to botanical pesticides, which can be quite toxic and have wide-reaching effects. Pesticide labels contain information about a particular substance's effect on the environment and human health, and should be read carefully before application. Labels also describe the active ingredients contained in the pesticide and how to mix and apply it.

• Alcohol. Rubbing alcohol (70 percent isopropyl alcohol) is an effective control for many garden pests and those afflicting houseplants with waxy foliage—particularly mealybugs, aphids, flea beetles, thrips, and whiteflies. It apparently kills the insects by drying them out, and is applied directly to the pest using a cotton swab. Many plants can tolerate a spray of equal parts water and alcohol. Test this mix on a small part of the infested plant first; if the plant shows no ill effects after a few days, spray the entire plant.

• Antitranspirants. Antitranspirants are very dilute mixtures of plastic and water. When these are sprayed on plants, they are coated with a very thin plastic film. While not registered for use as fungicides, they have proven effective against disease, including powdery mildew.

• Baking soda. Sodium bicarbonate, or baking soda, has proved to be an effective fungicide, providing control against blackspot and powdery mildew, among other fungal pathogens. Dissolve 1 teaspoon each of baking soda and dish soap into a quart of water. Spray the entire infected plant or plants, including the undersides of leaves.

• Bordeaux mix. This combination of copper sulfate and hydrated lime can be dusted onto plants or mixed with water and sprayed to control many common pathogens, such as anthracnose, bacterial leaf spots and wilts, fire blight, powdery mildew, and rust. Be aware, however, that if applied at low temperatures (below 50°F) and when humidity is high, it can burn foliage.

• Copper. Copper sulfate is available in several commercial products and is useful to protect plants against anthracnose, bacterial leaf spot, black rot, downy mildew, and Septoria leaf spot. Copper is extremely toxic to fish and is also toxic to humans and other mammals, so use it judiciously and with care. Spray the entire plant in dry weather.

• Diatomaceous earth. Diatomaceous earth (DE) is a dust made from the microscopic, fossilized shells of diatoms, a type of algae. The needlelike points covering the shells pierce insect cuticles, causing body fluids leak out. Susceptible pests include whiteflies, aphids, leafhoppers, and thrips. Beneficials are also susceptible, so apply only in problem areas. DE is applied as a dust. Use a mask to avoid lung damage.

• Garlic. When combined with mineral oil and soap, garlic is a broad-spectrum insecticide that is lethal to aphids, cabbageworms, leafhop-

pers, whiteflies, and squash bugs—as well as many beneficials, so use it on targeted areas only. It may also provide control against some fungi and nematodes.

• Insect growth regulators (IGRs). Synthetic analogs of natural growth-regulating hormones can prevent some immature insect pests from maturing. Products available provide control against fungus gnats, codling moth, Colorado potato beetle, armyworms, and whiteflies. These products are not toxic to mammals, which have different developmental processes. IGRs break down quickly in sunlight, so are most practical for shaded greenhouses. One brand, Confirm, which is produced by Rohm and Haas (100 Independence Mall West, Philadelphia, PA 19106, 215-592-3000), is labeled for use outdoors.

• Horticultural oils. Horticultural oils are refined petroleum oils that smother insects by plugging their orifices. Most of the products available today are superior oils, which are more refined than oils available in the past and therefore contain fewer impurities with potentially damaging effects on plants. These superior oils are effective against many insect pests—aphids, mealybugs, mites, and scales—and they will spare tough-bodied beneficial insects such as lady beetles. Oils may also be useful in controlling some plant pathogens. Some plants may have an adverse reaction to oils; product labels should include details on sensitive plants and on when not to spray.

• Insecticidal soaps. These dilute soap sprays penetrate insect cuticles and damage the cell membranes, causing dehydration. Insects sensitive to soap sprays include small, soft-bodied species such as aphids, mealybugs, leafhoppers, scales, and mites, and some larger insects, including Japanese beetles. They will also kill beneficials, and therefore should be applied only to problem areas. Many household soaps and liquid dishwashing detergents can be used effectively as insecticides. Mix between 1 teaspoon and a few tablespoons in a gallon of water and test the mixture's effectiveness and toxicity to pest and plant. Commercial insecticidal soaps are refined to concentrate the fatty acid molecules that are most toxic to insects, and so are most effective.

• Lime-sulfur. Lime-and-sulfur combinations penetrate leaf tissues and can kill recently germinated fungal spores. The mixture is effective against anthracnose, leaf spot, mildew, and scab as well as mites and scales. Wear protective clothing, including goggles and rubber gloves, when applying this mixture as it is extremely toxic to mammals.

• Neem. Neem is a derivative of the neem tree, an African and Indian native. Extracts of neem seeds have growth-regulating capabilities and will kill insects as they molt or hatch. Neem is useful against many leaf-chewing beetles and caterpillars, and can now be used safely on food crops, according to the federal Environmental Protection Agency.

• Pyrethrum. Extracts of the pyrethrum daisy, pyrethrins, form the basis of a number of botanical pesticides. These may also include soap or diatomaceous earth. Pyrethrins, nerve poisons to insect pests, break down rapidly in the environment. Most insects are highly susceptible, so pesticides include quite low concentrations of the active ingredient. Synthetic pyrethrins, or pyrethroids, are also used; these tend to persist longer in the environment.

• Ryania. This broad-spectrum insecticide is derived from the shrub *Ryania speciosa*, and is used mainly to control codling moth, citrus thrips, and corn earworms, but also is effective against many caterpillars, leaf beetles, and other thrips. Ryania appears to be more effective against pests than against most beneficial insects. It breaks down more slowly than other botanical insecticides. It should be applied with protective clothing. Ryania is available in combination with pyrethrins and rotenone.

• Sabadilla. This extract of the sabadilla plant, *Schoenocaulon officinale*, contains several poisonous alkaloids, and is effective against squash bugs, chinch bugs, harlequin bugs, and stink bugs as well as leaf-feeding caterpillars, Mexican bean beetles, and thrips. The formulation sold for garden use is among the least toxic of the botanicals, but the dust can be highly irritating to the respiratory tract and can cause violent allergic reactions. Wear a dust mask when applying sabadilla.

• Silica aerogel. The aerogels in this group of chemically inert substances absorb many times their weight in water and oils, and act against insect pests by absorbing the protective coating on their cuticle, causing them to dehydrate and die. Silica aerogels are effective controls against mites, beetles, and weevils as well as some beneficials, so use only where necessary.

## Encyclopedia of Common Garden Pests

The following encyclopedia of common garden pests is organized by pest type: insects, diseases, and other pests. Each pest entry in the encyclopedia includes a description of the pest, tips on how to recognize the signs of infestation, and a list of effective natural controls from least to most intensive. For information on controlling weeds, see page 565.

## Insects

Only a tiny fraction of the Earth's enormous population of insects are crop and garden pests. But if a pest population grows out of control, it can devastate a season's growth of squash or cucumbers or destroy a prized ornamental. Gardeners should work toward establishing the natural balance between populations of pests and beneficial insects rather than toward the total eradication of pests.

Pests often are more damaging to plants at a certain stage in their life cycle. Similarly, they are often most vulnerable to various controls at a particular point in their development. For this reason, it is important for gardeners to understand insect life cycles (see "The Life Cycles of Insects," below).

Botanical pesticides are not included in the list of recommended controls in each encyclopedia entry, but they may be effective against the pests below. Check the product labels for information on which pests they control and how to use them safely.

### Aphids

Aphids, tiny pear-shaped insects, suck sap from the stems, leaves, or roots of host plants, including many herbaceous plants, vegetables, trees, and shrubs. Aphids can stunt and deform leaves and stems, and can transmit viruses to healthy plants as they feed. They

---

### THE LIFE CYCLES OF INSECTS

Insects undergo changes in form as they mature and develop into adults. Scientists call this process metamorphosis. The forms that different species take vary, but there are two basic types of metamorphosis: incomplete and complete.

Insects that undergo incomplete metamorphosis include aphids, leafhoppers, earwigs, thrips, and scales. After hatching, the immature stages of these insects, called nymphs, periodically shed their skins, or molt. During their final molt, they develop into the adult stage. Nymphs and adults resemble each other and have similar feeding habits.

Cabbageworms, beetles, flies, and lacewings are some of the insects that undergo complete metamorphosis. After they emerge from the egg, they enter the larval stage, and molt repeatedly. As larvae, these insects often do the most injury to plants. Once larvae are fully developed, they become pupae. Insects in the pupal stage do not feed but undergo dramatic changes and finally molt for the last time and become adults. Larvae and adults usually look very different and have very different feeding habits.

Gardeners need to be able to recognize the various stages of the common insect pests in their area. Different pests do the most damage to particular plants during specific phases of their life cycles. For example, Japanese beetle grubs devour turfgrass roots, while the adult beetles feed on more than 200 different species of plants, rapidly skeletonizing foliage and disfiguring flowers. By the same token, different pests are most vulnerable to controls at different developmental stages, and the controls must be applied at the appropriate time. In order for *Bacillus thuringiensis* to be effective against the European corn borer, for example, it must be applied at the insect's larval stage, before the larvae tunnel into the stalks.

produce copious amounts of honeydew, a sticky, sugary liquid. Sooty mold grows readily on honeydew deposits, reducing the photosynthetic efficiency of the plant.

HOW TO CONTROL: Spray plants with jets of water, wipe with rubbing alcohol on a cotton swab, or a mild solution of dishwashing detergent and water. Attract natural enemies with flowering plants.

## Apple Maggot

The apple maggot attacks apple, crabapple, hawthorn, apricot, nectarine, plum, pear, and cherry trees, especially in the Northeast. The adult fly is about 1/5 inch long, with dark markings on the wings. The larva is a pale, legless maggot without a distinct head, also about 1/5 inch long. Young maggots hatch inside the fruit and feed on it for three or four weeks from mid-June until fruits drop. Infected apples, dark brown and dimpled, infect soil as the larvae crawl out and burrow into the ground.

HOW TO CONTROL: Hang red sticky spheres from mid-June until harvest; a few traps per tree placed in direct sunlight may be enough to control the pest population. Remove fruit from the ground as soon as it drops.

## Billbugs

The billbug, a type of weevil, is common throughout the United States. Adults have a long snout ending in mandibles. Larvae are voracious and damaging feeders on lawn grasses. Gray or brown adults overwinter in soil and in late spring lay eggs on grass stems. Small white larvae soon emerge to feed on stem tissue. Shoots brown and die. Grubs then burrow and feed on grass roots. Infested lawns are brown and drought-stressed in midsummer.

HOW TO CONTROL: Aerate lawns, water deeply, and top-dress with organic matter. Plant resistant varieties.

## Bronze Birch Borer

The bronze birch borer lives throughout the Northeast and central United States, attacking white-barked birches, especially stressed trees. Yellow-white, flat-headed larvae feed on plant tissues, often killing the trees. Yellowing leaves and dieback of stems are common signs of infestation.

HOW TO CONTROL: Prevent stressing of trees, especially mechanical damage to bark from lawn mowers; remove dying or dead stems. Replace susceptible plants with resistant species, such as *Betula lenta* (black birch) and *B. nigra* (river birch).

## Cabbage Looper

Cabbage looper caterpillars have a U-shaped crawling habit, hence the name "looper." Cabbage loopers prefer older leaves of cabbage, lettuce, spinach, potatoes, tomatoes, or celery, and chew holes, leaving greenish brown waste pellets on the undersides of the leaves. The light green caterpillars emerge in early summer, and in some warm areas, year-round activity is possible.

HOW TO CONTROL: Handpick and destroy the caterpillars. Plant resistant varieties. Dispose of crop remnants in fall. Cover plants with synthetic row covers. Parasitic trichogramma wasps may be effective. *Bt* is also effective when caterpillars first hatch.

## Cabbage Maggot

This northern root maggot attacks members of the brassica family—cabbage, cauliflower, radish, broccoli, brussels sprouts, and turnip—in the northern half of the country and southern Canada. The adult is a ¼ inch long fly. White larvae, which prefer cool, wet weather, feed on roots, weakening them and causing lower leaves to yellow and the plant to wilt and die. In feeding scars, pathogens such as black rot often develop.

HOW TO CONTROL: Protect transplants in spring and fall with floating row covers or tar-paper collars at the base of plants. Sprinkle diatomaceous earth around transplants; repeated applications may be needed as diatomaceous earth becomes ineffective as soon as the soil becomes wet.

## Cabbageworm

Cabbageworms prefer brassicas, including broccoli, cabbage, brussels sprouts, and cauliflower. Caterpillars are the color of cabbage leaves, with a yellow stripe along the back. They chew through leaves, leaving messy, dark-green waste behind. The adult stage of the cabbageworm is the bright white butterfly with black wing spots that is among the first to appear in spring. Cabbageworms hibernate under old stalks and weeds during cold weather.

HOW TO CONTROL: Handpick and destroy caterpillars. Clean up after harvest. Plant resistant varieties. Protect young plants with floating row covers. Trichogramma wasps parasitize eggs. Attract beneficials by growing herbs and flowers. *Bt* and insecticidal soaps are also effective.

## Carrot Rust Fly

The rust fly attacks carrots and related plants—celery, dill, parsnip, parsley, coriander, and fennel—and is a problem in the northern United States and southern Canada. Adult flies overwinter on plant debris. Yellowish white larvae tunnel into roots, leaving behind

rust-red-colored excrement. After a month they pupate, then start another generation in fall; this second generation is most damaging to roots. Carrot tops sometimes yellow.

HOW TO CONTROL: Remove carrot-family plant debris, including that of Queen Anne's lace, in fall. Cover crops with floating row covers. Till the soil in fall to expose any overwintering pupae to winter weather and predators.

## Chinch Bug

The chinch bug is a common turf pest across North America. Chinch bugs have an offensive odor, and a severely infested lawn will smell bad. Adults are about ⅕ inch long, with a black body. The wings lie folded over each other on the abdomen, and are marked by a small black triangle on the outer margins. Younger bugs are yellow or red, becoming darker as they mature. Chinch bugs hibernate under plant debris in winter; bright red nymphs smaller than a pinhead hatch in spring. These feed on stems and leaves, turning grass yellow and eventually killing patches. The chinch bug prefers Kentucky bluegrass, fine fescues, bentgrass, St. Augustine grass, and zoysia.

HOW TO CONTROL: Aerate and irrigate the lawn well. Reduce use of nitrogen fertilizer. Plant resistant lawn varieties.

## Codling Moth

Codling moth is the insect most destructive of apples and pears in most of the United States. Larvae of the codling moth are usually the worm in a wormy apple. Caterpillars of a spring generation feed on leaves, then fruit as it becomes available. These mature and in July produce a second, very damaging generation of caterpillars that tunnel into maturing fruits and feed on the developing seeds. Crumbly brown excrement is visible at the entry point.

HOW TO CONTROL: Pick up fallen fruits. Remove loose bark or in late winter create a spot favorable for pupation such as a trunk band of corrugated cardboard or burlap; collect and destroy pupae, and change these traps weekly. Thin developing fruits so they do not touch each other. Trichogramma wasps parasitize the eggs. *Bt* can be effective against the caterpillars. Use pheromone traps to determine when moths are most active.

## Colorado Potato Beetle

Colorado potato beetles are about ⅜ inch long, with black and yellow lengthwise stripes on their wing covers and black dots just behind their heads. Eggs are yellowish orange and laid in clusters on the undersides of leaves. Larvae are plump and red but have black heads and legs; older larvae are orange with two rows of black dots down each side of their bodies. These beetles attack potatoes, tomatoes, eggplants, and peppers. Chewed leaves are lacelike, and in severe cases, plants can be defoliated. Adult beetles overwinter in woody areas and in early spring move into gardens to feed. Up to three generations can be produced each year.

HOW TO CONTROL: Apply a thick mulch around plants. Handpick adults, larvae, and eggs. *Bt* var. *san diego* is effective against the larval stage. Lady beetles and spined soldier bugs feed on the larvae; attract them with pollen and nectar plants. Cover susceptible plants with row covers until the middle of the growing season.

## Corn Earworm

Corn earworm larvae attack corn, tomatoes, potatoes, beans, peas, peppers, and squash throughout North America. Green, white, or light yellow larvae feed on corn silks, leaves, and fruits, then pupate in the soil. Earworm can inhibit pollination and invite molds and other pathogens.

HOW TO CONTROL: Time plantings to avoid peaks of feeding. Choose varieties with long, tight husks that extend beyond the tips of the ears. Handpick after the silks have turned brown. Remove garden debris and till soil in the fall. Attract beneficials with herbs and flowering plants. Apply *Bt* before larvae burrow into the ear or fruit. Apply 20 drops of mineral oil (about ¼ teaspoon per plant) to corn silks at the tip of each ear; apply for 3–7 days after silk first appears.

## Cucumber Beetles

Cucumber beetles may be either spotted or striped. The former species is ¼ inch long, yellowish green with twelve black spots and a black head. The latter is ⅕ inch long, and yellowish orange with three black stripes down its back. These beetles attack cucumbers, melons, squash, and other cucurbits; corn, potatoes, tomatoes, eggplant, beans, peas, beets, asparagus, cabbage, and lettuce; and peaches and other soft fruits throughout North America. Both species overwinter in weedy areas and move into gardens as plants grow in spring. Adults and larvae damage stems and leaves; adults also chew on blossoms and fruit.

HOW TO CONTROL: Plant cucurbits resistant to cucumber mosaic virus and bacterial wilt, pathogens spread by the beetles. Cover plants with row covers, lifting them for several hours daily when the plants are in flower. Attract beneficials with pollen and nectar plants, including dill. Drench soil at root zone with a solution containing parasitic nematodes to kill the larvae.

## Cutworms

About 3,000 species of cutworms—large fleshy brown, gray, or black caterpillars, often with spots or stripes—attack vegetables, flowers, vines, and trees throughout North America. Cutworm infestations are especially severe in gardens recently converted from lawn or field. Larvae feed at night from spring through early summer.

HOW TO CONTROL: Remove weeds and crop residues in late summer. Till soil to expose the overwintering larvae. Protect seedlings with cutworm collars. Handpick cutworms at night. Trichogramma wasps parasitize the eggs; beneficial nematodes parasitize the larvae. Attract beneficials with herbs and flowering plants. Apply *Bt* when cutworm larvae are active.

## European Corn Borer

The European corn borer inhabits the northern and central United States and southern Canada, and consumes corn, tomatoes, eggplant, potatoes, peppers, beans, and various flowers. Tiny, creamy white, dark-headed larvae chew on leaves, whorls, and tassels, and finally stalks and ears. Shotlike holes in the upper foliage or holes in stalks or ears signal the presence of borers.

HOW TO CONTROL: Plant resistant varieties. Avoid very early or very late plantings to avoid peak periods of infestation. Till, chop, or mow affected crops close to soil to prevent overwintering. Apply *Bt* before larvae tunnel into stalks. Lure beneficials with herbs and flowering plants.

## Evergreen Bagworm

This East Coast pest feeds mainly on arborvitae but also on elms, maples, and buckeyes. The sluglike adult female spends her life inside a twig- or leaf-covered case, mates in fall, and lays eggs. Larvae hatch in spring and spend several months feeding on needles or leaves.

HOW TO CONTROL: Handpick or prune out cases. Spray with *Bt berliner* strains.

## Fall Armyworm

This southern pest migrates to the northern United States and Canada in late summer and fall, often traveling in large groups. The larvae consume sweet corn, grasses, cotton, alfalfa, peanuts, and tobacco, as well as garden crops. Larvae, green to brown with a prominent Y- or V-shaped white marking on the head, bore into corn stalks and ears, and feed on the leaves, buds, and fruit of other hosts. Freezing temperatures kill all life stages.

HOW TO CONTROL: Clean up garden debris. Protect early crops with floating row covers. Handpick larvae. Spray *Bt* every week as necessary. Encourage natural enemies with clover, alfalfa, and flowering herbs. A new insect growth regulator, Mimic, may control armyworms and other caterpillars.

## Flea Beetles

The numerous species of flea beetles live throughout North America, feeding on vegetables, especially brassicas, eggplants, potatoes, and tomatoes; leaf damage looks like tiny bullet holes. Flea beetles are all only about 1/10 inch long, but range from black to brown-black with faint stripes or markings, and jump quickly, like fleas. Thin, white larvae are up to ¾ inch long. White eggs are nearly microscopic. Adults overwinter in soil and feed on sprouting plants in spring, then lay eggs at the base of plants. Larvae burrow and feed on roots. There are two to four generations each year.

HOW TO CONTROL: Plant only large, sturdy specimens and protect young plants with row covers. Water the garden around noon; flea beetles feed at the height of the day, and do not like getting wet. Plant susceptible crops next to tall crops that will shade them at midday. Mix up plants to confuse the beetles. Cultivate the soil frequently to destroy eggs and larvae in the soil. Attract beneficial native braconid wasps and tachinid flies with pollen and nectar plants. Apply commercially available beneficial nematodes several times throughout the summer.

## Fungus Gnats

Both benign and harmful species of fungus gnats infest greenhouses and potted houseplants, preferring ferns and poinsettias. The larvae of nuisance species, transparent with a dark head, feed on the roots or root hairs of cultivated plants, introducing harmful bacterial or fungal rots. Infestation causes leaves and stems to wilt.

HOW TO CONTROL: Place yellow sticky cards at ground level around infested plants. Remove organic debris to reduce food sources. Repot, using only sterile potting soil. Destroy larvae, rotten roots, leaves, and stems, and discard soil removed from the root ball during repotting. The beneficial nematode *Steinernema feltiae* is an excellent control. Insect growth regulators are effective in indoor plantings.

## Gypsy Moth

Gypsy moth larvae feed on oaks and other tree species, mainly throughout the mid-Atlantic states and southern New England. Leaves are consumed to the midrib, and entire trees may be defoliated. In the spring, bristly larvae, distinctively patterned with five pairs of blue dots then six pairs of red, feed for seven weeks before pupating. Egg masses are conspicuous on trees and buildings.

HOW TO CONTROL: Use pheromone traps to determine population levels. Band trees with sticky tape or burlap bands; check these daily and renew the glue on sticky tapes often. Spray *Bt berliner* strains.

## Hemlock Woolly Adelgid

The hemlock woolly adelgid is common throughout the Northeast on eastern hemlock trees. These tiny sapsuckers leave white, fuzzy-looking egg sacs at the base of almost every needle. The needles discolor, dry out, and fall off. Infested limbs can die in the first summer, and trees succumb within one to four years.

HOW TO CONTROL: Spray trunk and branches with horticultural oil in early spring. Spray again with insecticidal soap in June and October.

## Japanese Beetle

The Japanese beetle is one of the most destructive pests of lawns and gardens east of the Mississippi. The metallic green adult with copper-colored wings attacks the foliage and flowers of more than 200 plant species while the gray-white larvae eat grass roots. These overwinter in the soil, emerging as winged adults in spring.

HOW TO CONTROL: Handpick adults. Neem is effective against adults. Control larvae with parasitic nematodes and the milky spore bacteria. Use floating row covers and garlic repellents.

## Lace Bugs

Lace bugs, sapsucking insects, infest a variety of ornamental shrubs and shade trees, especially azaleas, rhododendrons, and andromedas. Lace bugs get their name from the lacy appearance of the adults' dorsal surface, including the head, body, and wings. Adults are about ⅛ inch long. Lace bugs overwinter as eggs on the undersides of leaves, and adults and nymphs feed there in clusters. A lace bug infestation is signaled by brown, sticky spots and black excrement on leaves. Host plants lose vigor and may die.

HOW TO CONTROL: Apply insecticidal soaps, neem, or horticultural oil directly onto pests.

## Leafhoppers

There are many types of leafhopper, each associated with a different host, including fruit trees, grasses, ornamentals, and field and garden crops. Potato leafhoppers, which feed on beans, potatoes, and alfalfa in the eastern part of the continent, are, along with beet leafhoppers, the most troublesome. These are found in hot, dry areas of the West feeding on beets, tomatoes, spinach, squash, melons, and many ornamental plants. Beet leafhoppers, about ⅛ inch long and greenish, yellow, or brown, can transmit curly top virus disease, which deforms and kills plants. Potato leafhoppers, about ⅛ inch long and greenish, cause leaves to curl and turn darker green and plants to become stunted and nonproductive.

HOW TO CONTROL: Grow resistant varieties; potato leafhoppers, for example, avoid beans with fuzzy leaves. Cover plants with floating row covers. Grow pollen and nectar plants to attract beneficials. Spray insects with an insecticidal soap or horticultural oil.

## Leafminers

Leafminers, small, white grubs, are the larvae of more than 700 species of small flies, beetles,

and moths. Among the most troublesome are the tiny spinach leafminer, which eats threadlike tunnels through leaves, making them unsightly and inedible. Leaves with circular or snakelike trails are evidence of leafminer damage. They are most harmful to seedlings, and can interfere with nutrient uptake in mature plants.

HOW TO CONTROL: Till deeply to destroy maggots. Remove affected leaves. Keep the garden free of leaf litter and weeds to prevent reinfestation. In greenhouses, insect growth regulators are effective.

## Mealybugs

These small, white, wingless insects with a "mealy" white waxy covering on their exoskeleton suck sap from the leaves, stems, roots, and flowers of a range of plants, including citrus, orchids, cacti, African violets, palms, chrysanthemums, and ferns. They are most common in warm and humid weather. Like other sap-feeders, they exude honeydew, food for sooty mold. Heavy infestation causes leaves to yellow, stunted growth, and reduced flower and fruit size.

HOW TO CONTROL: Remove and kill mealybugs and waxy egg sacs with 70-percent rubbing alcohol. Lady beetles, particularly *Cryptolaemus montrouzieri,* are very effective. Spray with insecticidal soap or horticultural oil.

## Nematodes

These microscopic, wormlike creatures feed on the roots, leaves, and stems of more than 2,000 vegetables, fruits, and ornamental plants. The common root-knot nematode causes galls to develop on roots as it feeds. Pests overwinter as eggs in the soil. Symptoms include stunting and yellowing of leaves, and wilting of the plants during hot periods. Nematodes spread readily by water and garden tools.

HOW TO CONTROL: Remove infested plants entirely. Send soil samples to your local Cooperative Extension office for nematode identification. Solarize soil. Amend soil with organic fertilizers and amendments containing seaweed and humic acids. Grow resistant plant varieties.

## Peach Tree Borer

This pest is extremely damaging to peach, cherry, plum, and other trees in the genus *Prunus* in much of North America. Caterpillars overwinter at the base of the tree or in silken coverings, then begin feeding on bark, cambium, and large roots in spring.

HOW TO CONTROL: Band the base of trees before egg laying with burlap or heavy paper coated with a sticky substance such as Tanglefoot. Destroy individual larvae with a knife or wire. Attract borer parasites with herbs and flowering plants. Commercially available parasitic nematodes can be effective in ornamental cherry.

## Plum Curculio

The plum curculio, a native American weevil, lives east of the Rocky Mountains and feeds on most tree fruits, including peach, apricot, cherry, apple, pear, and plum. Adult curculios have light-colored patches on the back and four small humps. Adults overwinter in protective debris in and around infested trees, then feed on developing fruit in spring. Females lay eggs under fruit skin; hatched larvae—plump and legless—feed on the flesh and developing seeds. When full-grown, they cut their way out of the fruit and burrow 1 inches to 2 inches into the soil to pupate; adults emerge in August and feed

on fruit for a short time, before scattering to winter shelters. Signs of infestation are crescent-shaped scars on fruit, sunken corky areas, and small areas of rot under the skin.

HOW TO CONTROL: Shake branches to dislodge adults, collecting them on sheets spread under the tree; repeat several times over the season. Collect fruit that drops prematurely. Natural enemies include a braconid wasp, an ichneumonid wasp, and the fungus *Metarhizium anisopline.* Attract beneficials with flowering plants.

## Rose Chafer

The rose chafer, a pest of roses, peonies, hollyhocks, grapes, blackberries, and many other species of ornamental plants and fruit crops, prefers light, sandy soil and is most prevalent in the northeastern United States and eastern Canada. Rose chafers overwinter as larvae (white, ¾ inch grubs with brown heads) in the soil. In spring the larvae pupate and emerge as adults (slender tan beetle with spiny legs) in late spring. They often appear suddenly, in large swarms, feeding for four to six weeks before females lay their eggs in sandy soil. Eggs hatch within two weeks; young grubs feed on grass roots until cold temperatures force them deeper into the soil. There is a single generation per year.

HOW TO CONTROL: Handpick adults. Control grubs with commercially available parasitic nematodes.

## Scales

There are more than 200 species of scales, sap-feeding insects that attack a wide range of plants, including fruits, ornamental shrubs, and trees. Host plants turn yellow and lose leaves, and may develop sooty mold as scales excrete honeydew. Plants weaken and may die. Adult females are usually covered with a waxy shell, making them hard to treat with chemical sprays. Males go through a pupa-like stage, then become small winged adults.

HOW TO CONTROL: Remove with a soft-bristled toothbrush dipped in rubbing alcohol or soapy water. Beneficials that prey on scales prefer specific species, so proper identification is important. *Lindorus lophanthae,* a small beetle, preys on several scale species. Many small wasp species parasitize scale and are available from mail-order suppliers. Horticultural oils can be very effective. Place sticky bands on trees to keep ants away; otherwise they will protect scale from the parasitoids.

## Snails and Slugs

Both snails and slugs consume seedlings and soft-tissued parts of vegetables, fruits, and ornamental plants. Both feed at night and on cloudy, damp days. Both leave shiny slime trails. Slugs eat giant holes in plants, sometimes defoliating them. Snails create irregular holes in the middle or at the edges of leaves.

HOW TO CONTROL: Remove hiding spots. Handpick daily, then weekly when numbers drop. Snails and sometimes slugs congregate, and can be collected, under homemade traps, such as boards raised on low edges. Sink shallow pans filled with beer, keeping the lip of the pan flush with ground; empty daily. Diatomaceous earth is effective against slugs.

## Sowbugs and Pillbugs

Pillbugs and sowbugs feed mainly on decaying organic matter, but may eat seedlings, new roots, and, less often, lower leaves and fruits. Pillbugs often curl up into balls. Both

require a moist environment and spend days in dark, moist places.

HOW TO CONTROL: Water early in the day. Trap under boards and destroy. Drain wet areas. Use traps baited with diatomaceous earth.

## Spider Mites

Spider mites puncture plants and feed on sap. Outdoors, they infest a variety of ornamentals; indoors, they prefer impatiens, orchids, geraniums, and palms. They are difficult to detect without a hand lens. Infestation may cause leaves to become yellowish or silvery, and severe yellowing and rusty spots follow. Fine silk webbing may also cover leaves and stems.

HOW TO CONTROL: Wash plants with a mild detergent and follow with a water rinse. Prune heavily infested branches and isolate infested plants. Many species of predacious mites control two-spotted spider mites. A combination of two or more predator species provides optimum control. Horticultural oils and insecticidal soaps provide some control.

## Squash Vine Borer

The squash vine borer is a nuisance east of the Rocky Mountains, where it attacks squash and pumpkins, causing wilting of the vine runners in midsummer and producing yellow, sawdustlike waste that protrudes from stem holes; in sufficient numbers, borers can kill host plants. Borers overwinter in soil in tough black cocoons near crops. When plants begin producing runners, borer moths emerge; they have shiny copper-green front wings, transparent hind wings, and an orange and black abdomen and fly swiftly in a zigzag pattern around plants during the day. Females lay 200 pinhead-sized brown eggs on plant stems, leaf stalks, and fruits. Wrinkled, fat white caterpillars emerge in a week and bore into stems and fruit.

HOW TO CONTROL: Prevention is the key; once borers get inside the stem they are difficult to control. Cultivate the soil deeply. Grow resistant squash varieties. Move your squash beds every year. Plant early, because mature plants fend off damage better than young ones do. Use row covers to prevent infestation. Remove all dead vines quickly.

## Tarnished Plant Bug

The tarnished plant bug is found throughout North America, especially on the West Coast, and feeds on the sap of flowers, fruits, and vegetables, preferring the tender shoots, growth points, and flower buds. Attacked strawberries have hard, seedy ends; apples are cat-faced, small and shrunken; the flowers of ornamentals are poorly developed. The adult, ¼ inch long and light brown to black with a triangle pattern on the thorax, overwinters in garden debris, and emerges when flowers are in bud to feed and mate.

HOW TO CONTROL: Clean up in fall and keep the garden free of weeds. Cover row crops such as strawberries with a floating row cover very early in the season before bloom. Bugs can be vacuumed from plants with handheld vacuums. Grow herbs and flowers to attract beneficials.

## Tent Caterpillars

These caterpillars are common, destructive pests of cherry, apple, and other trees of the rose family. The eastern tent caterpillar and forest tent caterpillar range throughout southern Canada and the eastern United States. The larvae of both species form silken nests from which they emerge to feed on dry, sunny days. Leaves are consumed from the edges inward, and whole branches and sometimes trees may be defoliated.

HOW TO CONTROL: Prune away and destroy egg masses and the tents of the eastern tent caterpillar. Spray with *Bt berliner* strains when caterpillars are inside tents; they leave tents during the day to feed and return at night.

## Thrips

Thrips are tiny insects, $\frac{1}{50}$ inch to $\frac{1}{25}$ inch long, with two pairs of bristlelike wings. They feed on flowers, especially roses, peonies, and light-colored flowers. Flower thrips crawl into buds and feed; the buds may brown out and refuse to open. Thrips are also major onion pests; they feed on the leaves, making long, thin cuts, and the whole plant takes on a streaked, dull, grayish cast called "silvering." Onion thrips are pale yellow tinged with black; flower thrips are brown to black. Thrip eggs overwinter below the leaf surface.

HOW TO CONTROL: Clean up onions and other host plants after the first frost. Use sticky yellow traps. Spray plants often with water or, in severe cases, insecticidal soap.

## Tomato Hornworm

The dark green tomato hornworm is often perfectly camouflaged in tomato vines, where it chews on leaves and sometimes fruit, leaving black, buckshot-sized droppings at its base. The worm has white stripes down its sides, and a stout horn grows from the tip of the abdomen. The adult moth is brown with orange spots on its abdomen.

HOW TO CONTROL: Handpick larvae. Leave worms with small white cocoons on their backs alone; they are being parasitized by the beneficial braconid wasp. *Bt* may be effective against small hornworms. Cultivate soil deeply in the fall to destroy pupae.

## Weevils

Weevils, pests of plants and stored grains, have an elongated snout with jaws at the tip. Among the most destructive weevils are the black vine weevil, bean weevil, and cotton boll weevil. Larvae, generally pale, legless, and grublike, overwinter in soil or stored seed. Adults, which vary in color, shape, and size, may overwinter under garden debris. Females lay eggs near the base of susceptible plants, or shallowly deposited in plant tissue. Weevil larvae can kill plants by destroying feeder roots and girdling stems. Adult black vine weevils feed on the foliage of numerous plants, especially yews and broadleaf evergreens such as rhododendrons and euonymus, cutting holes all around the leaf margin or devouring entire leaves, except the midrib and large veins.

HOW TO CONTROL: Remove garden debris, rotate crops, and dust with diatomaceous earth. Commercially available parasitic nematodes are a useful deterrent for root-feeding larvae.

## Whiteflies

Most whitefly species are native to the tropics, and are greenhouse and houseplant pests in the Northern Hemisphere, although some species feed on vegetables, fruits, and ornamental plants outdoors. They attack fuchsias, hibiscus, begonias, geraniums, cucumbers, citrus, tomatoes, potatoes, and coleus, feeding on the undersides of leaves. Host plants are wilted and often coated with sooty molds; they lose vitality and may eventually die. Adult whiteflies are small, 1/16 inch flying insects with two pairs of opaque white wings. They have sucking mouthparts and feed heavily on plant sap. Hatchling nymphs are very active; later life stages are scalelike and cause extensive damage.

HOW TO CONTROL: Lower growing temperatures in greenhouses to decrease whitefly activity. Use yellow sticky traps to capture adults. *Encarsia formosa,* a whitefly predator, is effective. Soaps or oils applied to the undersides of leaves are effective against the scalelike stage.

## Wireworms

Wireworms are common in the West, but live throughout the United States and are most active in warm, moist soil. The worms are white or yellow; adults are brown to black beetles, which overwinter in soil. Wireworms consume potatoes, beans, beets, carrots, corn, lettuce, onions, sweet potatoes, grasses, asters, gladioli, dahlias, and other plants, chewing narrow tunnels into roots and tubers, which can be a point of entry for decay.

HOW TO CONTROL: Avoid planting where turf has grown in the past year. Handpick all stages. Till the soil several times during the growing season. Bury roots of a susceptible crop, such as carrots or potatoes, as lures, then dig and discard them with the worms. Apply commercially available beneficial nematodes to the soil.

# Diseases

Garden pathogens have a number of causal agents; fungi are the most prevalent, but disease is also caused by bacteria, viruses, and a range of cultural conditions such as micronutrient deficiencies and plant injury (see "Pathogen or Cultural Problem?" page 564). Microorganisms that cause disease are carried to a host plant on a film of water, the wind, contaminated tools, or soles of shoes, by insects, or by a number of other means, and if the conditions are right, will enter and infect plant cells. The pathogens, whether fungi, bacteria, or viruses, then feed on the plant and increase in size and number, and eventually are spread to other plants via one of the means described above.

The most effective treatment for most pathogens is to prevent them from getting a foothold in the garden in the first place. The following are some general practices that will deter pathogens from invading gardens.

- Choose plants that are suited to the site and those that have been bred to resist pathogens.
- Keep plants healthy with soil amendments.
- Rotate plants to avoid the problems that arise when the same type of plant is grown in the same, and possibly infected, soil each year.
- Keep disease-carrying insects away from plants with barriers.
- Ensure a good air flow around plants, because many pathogens thrive in a moist environment.
- Disinfect tools after using them.
- Remove and destroy infected plant parts.

The following encyclopedia of garden pathogens is by no means complete, but includes the most common pathogens across the continent, their symptoms, and the most effective controls for each.

## Anthracnose

Anthracnose is a group of a fungal pathogens that attacks woody plants, especially dog-

woods, maples, and sycamores, as well as some herbaceous plants and vegetables. Symptoms include circular brown spots on foliage, which sometimes surround holes in the tissue where dead cells have fallen out, and sunken spots on fruit. These spots may give rise to masses of pink spores in wet weather. Infection in trees can also affect the tips of young twigs before the tree leafs out.

HOW TO CONTROL: For vegetables: buy resistant varieties; plant in well-drained soil; do not garden in wet conditions; and destroy infected plants. Copper-based fungicides also may have some effect. For trees: plant resistant varieties; prune out and destroy diseased and dead wood; mulch root zone; apply a dormant spray of bordeaux mix or lime-sulfur.

## Apple Scab

This fungal disease attacks apple and crabapple, causing spots on leaves—olive-green at first, then black. Leaves may drop. Fruits develop green or brown spots that become raised and corky.

HOW TO CONTROL: Plant resistant varieties. Remove diseased fruits and leaves. Spray with copper, sulfur, or lime-sulfur in spring as leaves and fruits develop. Spray from bud break until 3–4 weeks after petal fall.

## Bacterial Canker

Fruits, shrubs, and vegetables are susceptible to this disease, especially stone fruits, lilac, oleander, rose, and sweet pea. Gummy cankers appear on branches, and these give off a foul odor. Lilac leaves and shoots develop brown spots; oleander develops oozing galls on all parts.

HOW TO CONTROL: Destroy infected parts. Thin plants to promote air circulation.

## Bacterial Leaf Spot

Host plants of bacterial leaf spot exhibit round or elongated brown spots surrounded by a yellow halo. Initially tiny, these spots can grow to cover entire leaves. Damaged tissue may drop out, leaving a hole. The disease can also cause sunken or scabby spots to develop on fruits. Plants susceptible to bacterial leaf spot include begonia, English ivy, geranium, gladiolus, and California laurel. Pathogens overwinter in soil or on contaminated tools and pots.

HOW TO CONTROL: Practice proper garden sanitation to reduce spread of the disease. Plant resistant varieties. Destroy infected plant parts. Spray copper. Cucumber beetles are a vector for the pathogen; protect plants from the beetles with floating row covers; hand-pollinate if using the row covers.

## Black Knot

Black knot is a fungal disease that attacks members of the genus *Prunus,* including cherries, plums, peaches, apricots, and flowering almond, throughout the United States. Symptoms include black swellings on branches. These may first appear as olive-green masses bursting through the bark, then turn black. Trees fail to grow and bear fruit. Black knot spores spread on the wind in the spring.

HOW TO CONTROL: In late winter, prune infected limbs well below the knots (4 to 6 inches) and destroy infected parts. Disinfect pruning shears between cuts. Remove nearby wild plum and cherry trees that may harbor pathogens. Apply two lime-sulfur sprays one week apart before buds appear in spring.

## Blackspot

This fungal disease of roses causes circular black spots to appear on foliage; these are often surrounded by yellow rings. Defoliation may follow. Purple or black blisters may also appear on young canes. Blackspot spreads from plant to plant on films of water. Plants with yellow and gold flowers are especially susceptible.

HOW TO CONTROL: Clean up and destroy infected plant parts. Spray with a baking soda solution, 3 tablespoons per gallon, weekly after rain.

## Botrytis Blight

This fungal disease attacks cabbage, onions, peonies, strawberries, and a number of other woody and herbaceous plants. It appears first on flowers as a white or gray fluffy growth, then spreads to fruits, causing stalks to weaken. Botrytis spreads on splashing water and wind.

HOW TO CONTROL: Destroy infected plant parts. Promote air circulation around plants.

## Cedar-Apple Rust

This rust is a fungal disease that requires the presence of both eastern red cedar and apple trees, as the fungus spends part of its life cycle in each host plant. Infected apples and related plants exhibit spotted leaves and may lose their leaves. Infected cedar trees have kidney-shaped galls, which develop bright orange, spore-producing growths in the spring.

HOW TO CONTROL: Eliminate one of the hosts. Plant resistant varieties.

## Cercospora Leaf Blight

This fungal disease is caused by a large group of related species that prey on the leaves and shoots of arborvitae, azalea, cypress, dahlia, geranium, and mountain laurel, to name just a few. Foliage of infected plants develops spots, which become larger and cause leaves to die. The spots may have a purple border. Gray mold may develop on infected tissues. Fungi overwinter in seeds, leaves, or needles.

HOW TO CONTROL: Prune and destroy infected plant parts. Spray with bordeaux mixture.

## Crown Gall

This bacterial disease causes callous growths to form on infected plants, which are often landscape ornamentals such as roses, crabapples, willows, poplars, and euonymus species. Young plants may succumb quickly while mature trees may decline gradually. Bacteria can persist in the soil and enter plants through wounds.

HOW TO CONTROL: Prune galls as they appear. Improve plant vigor through proper care. Purchase healthy, nonsusceptible plants.

## Cytospora Canker

Cytospora canker attacks spruce trees, particularly blue and Norway spruce. Symptoms include a browning out of branches, first those nearest the ground, then upper branches. Cankers can enlarge and girdle the branches. Resin may ooze from infected areas. Fungi overwinter in infected plant parts.

HOW TO CONTROL: Prune and destroy diseased branches and twigs. Improve plant vigor by fertilizing, and water well during dry spells.

## Damping Off

A fungal disease that mainly attacks seedlings, and can cripple them before they ever emerge from the soil. Inch-tall seedlings can topple overnight as the fungus eats through the stem at the soil line. Container-grown seedlings are most susceptible.

HOW TO CONTROL: Outdoors, plant in well-drained soil; do not crowd plants; and sprinkle a layer of sand, perlite, or sphagnum moss on the soil surface. Use sterile potting soil indoors or pasteurize soil.

## Downy Mildew

Downy mildew is a fungal disease that causes white to purple downy growth along stems and on the undersides of leaves, with corresponding yellow spots above. Plants may succumb rapidly to the disease, which is a serious problem in grapes but also attacks a number of other woody and herbaceous plants, including Boston ivy, pansy, viburnum, and sunflower.

HOW TO CONTROL: Promote air circulation by pruning and proper spacing of plants. Destroy infected plant parts. Grow resistant varieties. Spray bordeaux mix or a copper or sulfur fungicide.

## Fire Blight

Early signs of this bacterial disease are dead flowers or fruit spikes, and cankers on stems of host plants, which include members of the rose family such as apple, pear, cotoneaster, hawthorn, spirea, and mountain ash. Leaves often blacken and remain on the tree, giving the disease its name. Pathogens are spread from plant to plant by feeding insects such as bees and splashing water, and enter the plant through wounds or flowers.

HOW TO CONTROL: Spray copper sulfate or bordeaux mix at bud openings when tree is dormant. Prune infected parts 1 foot below cankers. Disinfect tool after each cut. Plant resistant varieties.

## Fusarium Wilt

Common hosts of this fungal disease include tomatoes, peas, peppers, melons, and dahlias.

It causes leaves to yellow then brown and eventually drop, and stems to droop, and it often kills the host plant. Stems may have brown streaking inside.

HOW TO CONTROL: Like those of verticillium wilt, fusarium pathogens can persist in the soil for many years. Plant resistant varieties. Remove and destroy infected plant parts. Solarize the soil.

## Mosaic

This is a viral disease that affects a number of woody and herbaceous plants, causing leaves to become mottled with dark or light spots. Fruits may exhibit the same symptoms. Mosaic is spread from plant to plant via insects such as aphids and leafhoppers.

HOW TO CONTROL: Plant resistant cultivars. Cover susceptible plants with floating row covers to prevent insect attack. Destroy infected plants.

## Phytopthora Root Rot

This soil-borne fungus attacks a wide variety of plants, including azalea, camellia, oak, pine, rhododendron, rose, snapdragon, and yew. Infected plants fail to produce new shoots, their leaves may wilt, and branches die. Infected wood at the base of the stem becomes light brown roots become limp and rotted.

HOW TO CONTROL: Destroy infected plants. Plant resistant varieties. Improve soil drainage.

## Powdery Mildew

Powdery mildew is a group of fungi that attack lilac, rose, euonymus, azalea, phlox, and other woody and herbaceous plants. White to grayish powdery growth appears on the upper sides of leaves, and new leaves become distorted. Plants may exhibit poor overall growth and low yields. Unlike most fungal pathogens, this one thrives in hot weather.

HOW TO CONTROL: Plant resistant varieties. Make sure air circulates freely around plants. Spray with sulfur, lime-sulfur, horticultural oil, a weak baking soda solution, antitranspirants, or fungicidal soap (soap and sulfur).

## Rust

Rust is caused by 4,000 or so related fungi that infect a wide range of plants such as crabapple, rose, red cedar, spruce, and white pine. Infection is signaled by yellow or white spots on upper leaf surfaces and orange or yellow crusty bumps on the undersides, which are the spore-producing structures. Infected plants weaken and become stunted.

HOW TO CONTROL: Promote air circulation. Destroy infected plant parts. Dust plants with sulfur periodically, beginning early in the season to prevent infection. Use fungicidal soaps (soap and sulfur).

## Sooty Mold

This disease is caused by a variety of fungi that feed on the honeydew left on plant foliage by sapsucking insects such as aphids. The black film can cover leaves, reducing their ability to photosynthesize. It may appear on a range of woody and herbaceous plants.

HOW TO CONTROL: Wipe soot off the leaves of smaller plants or spray with soap to clean them off. Control the insect infestation that is causing honeydew to accrete.

## Verticillium Wilt

Verticillium is a fungal disease that affects a number of woody and herbaceous plants, especially azaleas, tomatoes, peppers, strawberries, maples, and cherries. It is common in cool weather in the temperate parts of the

## PATHOGEN OR CULTURAL PROBLEM?

In addition to disease pathogens, plants may suffer from cultural problems caused by mineral deficiencies, severe weather, or overwatering, among other things. Plants that are poorly sited, exposed to pollution from streets, or damaged by wind, improperly used tools, and improper pruning may fail to thrive and exhibit symptoms that could be confused with those of many diseases caused by pathogens.

Cultural problems include cold injury, which causes stunting, yellowing, and bud or leaf drop; heat injury, which results in sunscald of fruits, leaves, or trunk on the side exposed to the most sun, as well as discoloration or blistering; and decline, a general malaise that can result from a variety of stresses and causes yellowing and wilting of leaves, stunting and distortion of growth, and dieback.

A variety of nutrient deficiencies also can cause diseaselike symptoms. Blossom-end rot, which results from a calcium deficiency at the blossom end of the fruit, causes the fruit to darken and become leathery. Deficiencies of iron, magnesium, nitrogen, and potassium can occur when the soil lacks these micronutrients, or when plants are unable to absorb them because the soil is too alkaline, for example. Deficiencies generally lead to stunting, poor yields, and increased susceptibility to pathogens.

borne pathogen can survive in the soil for up to 20 years.

HOW TO CONTROL: Plant resistant varieties. Solarize the soil.

## Other Pests

Some garden pests are not insects or fungi or weeds, but rather mammals or birds that can be enjoyable in another context. As with any pest, the best way to deter these garden visitors is to prevent them from coming into the garden in the first place. Planting species that are unappetizing to pests, fencing the garden, eliminating food, water, and brush piles, stands of weeds, boggy areas, or wood piles—shelter for these pests—can all be effective. Below are some common garden pests that are neither insects nor pathogens nor weeds.

### Birds

Bird damage can vary from a few holes poked in fruits and vegetables to a bramble or blueberry denuded of its fruit.

HOW TO CONTROL: Protect crops with row covers or stiff plastic netting. "Scare-eye" balloons that look like owls frighten birds away, as do scarecrows and likenesses of cats and snakes. These should be moved around the garden frequently so that birds do not get used to them.

### Deer

Deer can move rapidly through a garden and leave it naked behind them—they are voracious consumers of the foliage of trees and shrubs, and also perennials and vegetables. As their natural habitat and predators have disappeared, they have been frequenting more and more gardens and yards in the East, where the white-tailed deer is com-

continent. The foliage of plants infected with the disease yellow and droop, then brown and die, and symptoms appear first on the lower and outer leaves. Woody plants develop cankers, produce large numbers of seeds, and show vascular discoloration from olive-green to brown to black. This soil-

mon, and in the West, where the mule deer is native.

HOW TO CONTROL: Erect a tall fence, at least 8 feet tall, around the garden early in the season before deer become accustomed to visiting.

## Gophers

Gophers eat roots, seeds, bulbs, and grasses, and dig extensive underground networks of tunnels as they create their burrows.

HOW TO CONTROL: Mesh fencing buried 24 inches deep around the perimeter of raised beds, small flower beds, and lawns may be effective. Gopher burrows can be flooded and the gopher killed as it emerges. Gopher traps are also effective.

## Moles

Moles burrow underground searching for food—insects, slugs, and grubs—and may disturb roots and create ridges in the soil above their extensive tunnels. Mole presence is signaled by molehills—small cones of loose soil at the openings of their burrows. Moles consume huge numbers of pests such as cutworms and white grubs, and should be tolerated, if possible.

HOW TO CONTROL: Reduce the number of grubs, one of the mole's preferred foods, through the controls described in the section on insects. Flood mole tunnels in spring by poking a hose into a tunnel; this will kill young, nesting moles. Lethal traps—harpoon, scissor-jaw, or choker-loop traps—set above mole tunnels in early spring or early fall kill quickly and are very effective. Bury the mole where you catch it. Other moles will sense its presence and will stay away from that part of the garden.

## Rabbits

Jackrabbits and snowshoe hares are destructive garden pests, consuming flowers, foliage, and tender shoots.

HOW TO CONTROL: A 2-foot high fence will keep rabbits out; it should be buried at least 3 inches below ground. Repellents such as ammonium soaps, lime-sulfur, and copper carbonate can be effective.

# Weeds

The term "weed" is subjective, as it is used to describe plants that grow where they are not wanted. From a biological point of view, the plants we call weeds are highly successful, having evolved strategies that enable them to thrive in conditions where other plants might fail. As with insect and pathogen pests, the most sensible approach to managing weed populations includes learning to tolerate some. While it makes sense to work toward keeping weeds in check, total eradication of all weeds is not only unrealistic, but deprives gardeners of the positive roles that weeds can play in the garden.

Weeds perform a variety of beneficial services. They provide food and shelter for beneficial insects and birds. Deeply rooted weeds such as nightshades, pigweeds, and thistles create openings in the soil for water and bring up minerals from the subsoil; these minerals are incorporated into the upper soil layers when the plant dies. Weeds that grow on the perimeter of the garden attract pests that might otherwise be drawn to the garden's ornamentals and vegetables.

The first step toward keeping weed populations in check is developing an understanding of the plants' life cycles. Most weeds in the garden—80 percent—are annuals, which means they reproduce yearly from seed. Some of the most widespread annual weeds are ragweeds, pigweeds, smartweeds, purslane, chickweed, knotweed, and lamb's-quarter. Biennial weeds—Queen Anne's lace, mullein, burdock, and teasel, among others—live for two years, producing just leaves the first year and flowers and seeds the second. Perennial weeds reproduce both from seed and vegetatively—that is, via their rootstock. Common perennial weeds include goldenrods, dandelion, chicory, bindweed, and plantain. Woody perennials have tougher stems and include Japanese honeysuckle, poison ivy, kudzu, and multiflora rose. Weedy grasses, including quackgrass, Johnson grass, crabgrass, and yellow foxtail, can spread rapidly throughout a garden. A weed identification guide is an important tool for determining which plants are invading your garden.

Gardeners have been responsible, for the most part unwittingly, for the introduction and proliferation of a new class of invasive weeds that are degrading natural habitat throughout North America. Scores of prized ornamental plants—from purple loosestrife to princess tree to tamarisk—have jumped the garden gate and are now overruning native species and habitats (see page 136). Gardeners should avoid planting these species and remove any already on their properties that pose a threat to nearby natural areas.

## Weed Management

Weeds can be managed through a number of techniques; these are most effective when used in combination.

- To keep weeds from sprouting up between cracks and through gravel in paths, patios, and driveways, and around fence posts and rails, eliminate weed habitat by layering heavy building or roofing paper under paving materials or under and adjacent to the fence. The latter can be covered with mulch or rock and is called a mow strip.
- Raised vegetable and flower beds filled with compost-enriched soil allow desired plants to grow quickly and thereby shade out weeds. Plant vegetables and ornamentals close to each other in the rich soil to inhibit weed seeds from germinating. Mulch the beds with plastic during the off season to keep weed seeds out.
- Apply water directly to the roots of garden plants through drip irrigation systems or porous hose buried below garden plants; these will limit the amount of water that weeds get.
- By mulching at the right time—just when weed seeds need light to germinate—gardeners can suppress many annual weeds. Apply the mulch right after cultivating the soil or any other activity that could expose buried weed seeds. Mulch with organic plant residue, gravel, plastic, or newspaper.
- Alternate rows of ornamentals, vegetables, and trees with rows of sod. These will create a barrier that weeds will have difficulty crossing.
- Heavily seed newly dug beds for shrubs or ground covers with fast-growing annual flowers to eliminate potential weed habitat.
- Select plants that will grow rapidly and shade out weeds.
- Smother weeds by planting another vigorously growing crop such as alfalfa, which when turned over into the soil will also enrich it with nitrogen.
- Border lawns with good competitors such as liriope that will keep weeds from crossing into the lawn.
- Use the power of certain plants to deter the growth of others—a phenomenon called allelopathy—to suppress weeds. Allelopathic

# COMMON PESTS OF GARDEN PLANTS

Below are some of the most common garden pests categorized by host-plant type: tree, shrub, perennial, annual, vegetable, rose, and so on. These lists are by no means comprehensive, but are intended to be a general guide to the most common pests for particular types of plants.

**COMMON PESTS OF TREES, SHRUBS, AND VINES**

Anthracnose
Aphids
Bagworms
Borers
Canker
Crown gall
Gypsy moth
Japanese beetle
Leaf spots
Leafminers
Nematodes
Powdery mildew
Root rot
Rots
Sawflies
Scales
Sooty mold
Spider mites
Tent caterpillars
Webworm

**COMMON PESTS OF HERBACEOUS PERENNIALS**

Aphids
Cutworms
Flea beetles
Japanese beetle
Lace bug

Powdery mildew
Rose chafer
Slugs and snails
Sooty mold
Tarnished plant bug

**COMMON ROSE PESTS**

Aphids
Blackspot
Borers
Downy mildew
Japanese beetle
Powdery mildew
Rose midges
Spider mites
Thrips

**COMMON PESTS OF ANNUALS**

Aphids
Aster yellows
Cutworms
Damping off
Leaf rollers
Leaf spots
Mealybugs
Plant bugs
Powdery mildew
Slugs and snails
Sooty mold

Spider mites
Whiteflies

**COMMON VEGETABLE PESTS**

Aphids
Bacterial rot
Caterpillars
Cutworms
Damping off
Flea beetles
Fungal rot
Fusarium wilt
Gray mold
Leafminers
Mites
Nematodes
Powdery mildew
Snails and slugs
Verticillium wilt

**COMMON FRUIT PESTS**

Anthracnose
Aphids
Apple maggot
Apple scab
Bacterial spot
Botrytis spot
Cedar rust
Codling moth
Crown gall
Downy mildew

Fire blight grubs
Leaf curl
Peach tree borer
Phylloxera
Phytophthora root rot
Plant bug
Plum curculio
Powdery mildew
Scales
Verticillium wilt
Weevil larvae

**COMMON LAWN PESTS**

Billbug
Brown patch
Chinch bug
Dollar spot
Fusarium
Japanese beetle grubs
Powdery mildew
Sod webworms

**COMMON PESTS OF INDOOR PLANTS**

Aphids
Botrytis blight
Mealybug
Powdery mildew
Scales

Sooty mold
Spider mites

**COMMON GARDEN WEEDS**

Bindweed
Burdock
Chickweed
Chicory
Crabgrass
Dandelion
Goldenrod
Japanese honeysuckle
Johnson grass
Knotweed
Kudzu
Lamb's-quarters
Mullein
Multiflora rose
Pigweed
Plantain
Poison ivy
Purslane
Quackgrass
Queen Anne's lace
Ragweed
Smartweed
Teasel
Yellow foxtail

plants produce substances that are toxic to other plants. Sage leaves, for example, emit substances called terpenes that land on the soil, where they inhibit the germination of grasses and herbs.

- Pull up perennial weeds as soon as you spot them.
- Plant seeds, then cultivate the area as soon as weeds emerge; the desirable seeds will survive as long as you do not cultivate as deeply as they were planted.
- Hoe with a sharp tool; remove deeply rooted plants with a pointed shovel or digging fork.
- Mow annual and perennial weeds just before they set seed, when they have almost completed their life cycles.
- Use flamers, gas- or oil-fueled torches, to demolish weed seedlings.

## Further Reading

Michalak, Patricia. *Rodale's Successful Organic Gardening: Controlling Pests and Diseases.* Emmaus, Pa.: Rodale Press, 1994.

Olkowski, William, Helga Olkowski, and Sheila Daar. *Commonsense Pest Control.* Newtown, Ct.: Taunton Press, 1991.

Schultz, Warren. *Natural Insect Control: The Ecological Gardener's Guide to Foiling Pests.* Brooklyn, N.Y.: Brooklyn Botanic Garden, 1994.

Smith, Miranda, and Anna Carr. *Rodale's Garden Insect, Disease, and Weed Identification Guide.* Emmaus, Pa.: Rodale Press, 1988.

Troetschler, Ruth, Alison Woodworth, Sonja Wilcomer, Janet Hoffmann, and Mary Allen. *Rebugging Your Home and Garden.* Los Altos, Calif.: PTF Press, 1996.

# 10

# INDOOR
# GARDENING

Although the indoor environment is less forgiving than the outdoor garden, the key to success is the same: selecting the right plant for each location. Choose plants with cultural requirements that suit your indoor sites, whether you use the site as is or provide supplemental lighting and adjust temperature and humidity.

## Light

Light is essential for the well-being of plants. During winter, reduced day length can jeopardize the health of some plants. The intensity and duration of light are the two most common limiting factors for maintaining indoor plants. However, it is relatively simple to use lights to supplement daylight or to create an indoor light garden.

When you consider adding houseplants to a space, first determine the intensity and duration of light found there. North, east, west, and south exposures provide incrementally more light. North windows limit the choice of plants to those few requiring low light. A southern exposure offers maximum possibilities for sun-loving plants. The closer to windows, the higher the intensity of light; moving a plant back from or to the side of a window adjusts the amount of light—thus a plant several feet back from a south-facing window could receive roughly the equivalent of one in an eastern exposure. Morning light tends to be cooler than afternoon light; an east exposure is ideal for thin-leaved plants such as angel-wing begonia, and a west window offers the hotter light in which cacti and thicker-leaved succulents thrive. Light intensity can be further enhanced by using mirrors to reflect sunlight back onto plants. If your windowsills are too narrow for

## TEN TIPS FOR SUCCESS WITH HOUSEPLANTS

• Know the light requirements of any plant before you buy it. If you have time, research ahead of buying and make a list of potential candidates for specific sites in your home. Most plants come with labels detailing light, temperature, and moisture requirements.

• Select plant species that are not overly prone to pests and diseases.

• Prevention is the best strategy—buy only pest-free plants. Examine new plants closely. If possible, keep them quarantined for two to three weeks before locating them near other houseplants.

• Allow new plants a period of adjustment to your conditions. The shock of lower humidity and reduced light causes many a plant to lose some leaves at first.

• Make sure that the plant's container has drainage holes in the bottom (and a saucer or other water-tight tray to protect your furniture and floors). Water until water seeps out the bottom. Do not allow most plants to sit in water; within a half hour empty any remaining liquid.

• Cleanliness is important. Promptly remove dead leaves and spent flowers, as well as any stems that may have died back. Periodically clean your gardening tools.

• Water according to the needs of the plant. Keep in mind that watering extremes are the main causes of demise for houseplants. Avoid bone dryness and soggy wetness.

• Improve the vigor of plants by improving root health. If the soil is compacted, loosen it and add a bit of fresh medium, or repot.

• Treat pest problems immediately. First, hose or spray off as many as possible with water. When using horticultural oil, insecticidal soap, and other nontoxic treatments, read and follow labels carefully. Repeat applications will probably be necessary to control new hatchlings.

• Isolate any moderately or heavily infested plants. Quarantine or dispose of them. Sanitize all nearby surfaces after affected plants have been removed. Prune infested branches. Keep the plants quarantined for one month after the last treatments. Inspect them frequently and carefully for hidden infestations and be sure to check the roots.

holding plants, consider one of the numerous products for enlarging sills (gardening supply catalogs sell them), or add braces to support a larger wood, metal, or plate-glass sill. Where window light is sufficient to be the sole source of light for a particular houseplant, rotate the plant regularly to encourage uniform growth.

Unless you have chosen a particularly dark corner, it is possible to find a plant with light requirements to match the site as is, without supplemental lighting. There are even a few plants suited to low-light situations—an inte-

rior wall or hallway, sites more than 8 to 10 feet from windows—and others can accommodate them for a week or two if they are moved periodically to higher-light conditions. Many foliage plants indigenous to rain forests, where the dense tree canopy blocks most light, thrive in low-light situations.

## Artificial Lighting

Where window light will not suffice for a particular plant or plants, supplement the light-

## NATURAL POLLUTION CONTROL

Formaldehyde is a common household pollutant, mainly owing to solvents in wood products such as furniture. Research, which began at the National Space Technology Laboratories in Mississippi, indicates that some houseplants, especially the spider plant (*Chlorophytum comosum*), can remove formaldehyde pollution from indoor air. Further research has revealed that houseplants are also effective at removing other kinds of air pollutants such as carbon monoxide and nitrogen oxides, both of which are by-products of combustion. Other plants that have demonstrated the ability to remove indoor air pollutants include golden pothos (*Epipremnum aureum*) and potted oleander (*Nerium oleander*).

## ALFRESCO

Inevitably, houseplants perk up when moved outdoors in summer. A few months, or even weeks, of refreshing rains, fresh air, humidity, and generally more light can help houseplants thrive the rest of the year indoors. Here are some things to keep in mind.

• Wait until all danger of frost is well past before moving houseplants outdoors.

• Set the plants in filtered light for the first two weeks so the foliage will not burn. Protect them from winds and rain. Then, gradually move the sun-lovers to brighter spots.

• Do not forget to water outdoors; you cannot assume that rain is all the water your plants will need.

• Maintain vigilance for pests and diseases.

• If your plant requires fertilizer, apply it in spring and summer.

• Be sure to bring plants indoors well before cold weather. Allow them at least a few weeks to readjust to the home environment before you turn on the heat.

• Check for insects before bringing plants back inside. Bathe each plant; use a relatively strong spray of water to clean the undersides of leaves as well as the tops.

ing. Fluorescents are the cheapest and most efficient source of supplemental lighting. A 50:50 ratio of generic cool white and warm white tubes provides excellent supplemental lighting and can serve as the sole source of light for all types of growth—seedlings, flowering plants, and foliage plants. Plants can be placed as close as 6 inches from the tubes. Household incandescent bulbs produce too much heat to be a good source of light for indoor growing.

Light carts designed specifically for plants are a convenience. Or hang fluorescent fixtures from the ceiling and create instant growing areas. Keep in mind that the light intensity of fluorescents is strongest at the center of the tube. You can arrange plants to utilize the intensity along the length of the tube to the maximum—highlight-loving plants toward the center and low-light-tolerant plants toward the ends—or simply move plants around to even out the light

level each receives. Because of the drop-off of light intensity at the ends of tubes, use the longest bulb possible rather than two smaller lamps end to end. A good rule of thumb is to replace tubes after 12 months of use.

To increase light levels, you can use commercial shop light reflectors or paint flat white the wood from which the fixture is hung. The easiest way to time light-garden hours is with an automatic timer to turn fixtures on and off

## PLANTS FOR LOW LIGHT

The following plants tolerate low-light situations, such as a north exposure, although many would benefit from supplemental artificial lighting:

Aglaonemas, Chinese evergreens, *Aglaonema* species
Cast-iron plant, *Aspidistra elatior*
Coral berry, *Ardisia crispa*
Cornstalk plant, *Dracaena fragrans*
Dumb canes, *Dieffenbachia* species
Golden pothos, Devil's ivy, *Epipremnum aureum*
Grape ivy, *Cissus rhombifolia*
Marlberry, *Ardisia japonica*
Monstera, Swiss-cheese plant, *Monstera deliciosa*
Peperomias, *Peperomia* species
Philodendrons, *Philodendron* species
Piggyback plant, *Tolmiea menziesii*
Prayer plant, *Maranta leuconeura*
Rabbit's foot fern, *Davallia fejeensis*
Mother-in-law tongue, *Sansevieria trifasciata*

Spathiphyllums, *Spathiphyllum* species
Spider plant, *Chlorophytum comosum*
Syngonium, Arrowhead vine, *Syngonium podophyllum*

### SOME PLANTS THAT GROW WELL UNDER ARTIFICIAL LIGHT

African violet, *Saintpaulia ionantha*
Cape primroses, *Streptocarpus* species
Dwarf kangaroo vine, *Cissus antarctica* 'Minima'
Emerald ripple peperomia, *Peperomia caperata*
False heather, elfin herb, *Cuphea hyssopifolia*
Flame violet, *Episcia cupreata*
Goldfish plants, *Columnea* species
Miniature grape ivy, *Cissus striata*
Miniature gloxinia, *Sinningia pusilla*
Prayer plant, *Maranta leuconeura*
Wax plant, *Hoya carnosa*

## GROWING UNDER GLASS

You do not need a huge new structure with water, air, and a heating system to have greenhouse conditions. Window greenhouses are an option for gardeners with limited space or limited budgets. These extensions replace standard home windows. A simple 17-inch-deep model made from aluminum and featuring double-insulated glass is available for installation by do-it-yourselfers. Check local zoning restrictions before making any addition to your home.

Hobby greenhouses are manufactured in many sizes and dimensions. If you are considering one, a good source of information is the Hobby Greenhouse Association, 8 Glen Terrace, Bedford, MA 01730-2048; or on the World Wide Web at www.hortsoft.com/HGA.

according to a predetermined schedule, usually 14 to 16 hours on, 8 to 10 off. In too much light, plants grow compactly but may have a sickly yellow appearance; with too little light, they become spindly and elongated and either lack color or turn very dark green.

## Temperature and Humidity

Most houseplants grow well in daytime temperatures from 60°F to 75°F with a drop of 5° to 10° at night. However, maintaining those temperatures with heating and air-conditioning systems often causes a severe decrease in humidity, as low as 5 to 10 percent—a level unhealthy for plants, people, and fine wood furniture.

There are many ways to increase humidity.

Room humidifiers, especially cool-vapor humidifiers, are an option. Misting plants with water is a time-honored and easy method. It works for most plants; however, misting gesneriads and other hairy-leaved plants is not recommended.

Group plants for added humidity. More humidity can be furnished by growing plants on pebble trays to which water is added. Always keep the water level slightly below the pots; waterlogged plant roots can lead to problems. Some gardeners place plants on a wooden, plastic, or wire grid set on top of an inch or more of water. The normal evaporation of the water furnishes the extra humidity.

Temperature and humidity vary from room to room. Take advantage of microclimates that exist even within indoor growing areas—find the cold and hot spots. If too much or too little heat is a problem, a small circulating fan may be able to rectify the problem.

## Water

As with outdoor plants, understanding the water needs of houseplants takes time and experience. The simplest way to look at watering is to think in terms of three basic conditions: dry, evenly moist, and wet.

- Plants said to prefer dry conditions should be watered well, and then not again until the top ½ inch of soil feels dry to the touch. Any plant in the dry category will suffer from having its pot stand in a saucer of excess water; empty immediately.

- Most plants prefer evenly moist soil. Water them well. Pour off any water remaining in the saucer within a half hour or so. When the surface soil feels barely damp—but before it becomes really dry—water well again.

- Few plants prefer to be wet constantly. Chinese evergreen (*Aglaonema modestum*) does not mind wet soil, but does just as well in evenly moist conditions. Sedges, such as the umbrella plant (*Cyperus alternifolius*), require extremely wet conditions, as do all aquatics.

Requirements for each plant differ, and environmental factors also influence watering. Plants growing actively in good light and warm temperatures will require more water than those growing in poor light or coolness. Those under an automated regimen receiving a fixed light intensity and duration day to day tend to require more water—and fertilizer—than those dependent solely on the vagaries of weather and window light.

All houseplants respond best to water that is room temperature or slightly warmer.

## Growing Media

Inside the home, soil is one of the easiest to alter of all the factors affecting plant health. The important thing about potting mixes is that they drain well while providing the plant roots with plenty of water, air, and nutrients.

Using ordinary garden soil, no matter how well it proves itself outdoors, is never recommended. Garden soil in a pot tends to harden like cement. However, when mixed with other ingredients, a quantity of healthy garden soil can provide nutrients not available in a soilless mix. A good all-purpose soil-based medium for containers can be made by combining one-third each of the following:

- Good garden soil (or packaged all-purpose potting soil)
- Well-rotted compost
- Clean builder's sand

For tropical foliage plants, indigenous to soils rich in organic matter, the amount of compost in the mix is often doubled. And for cacti and other drought-tolerant desert dwellers, add a fourth equal component of grit or aquarium gravel, or double the quantity of sand. Orchids and African violets also benefit from special mixes (see below).

If mixing soil does not appeal to you, you can find packaged potting soil and soilless potting mixes for sale in nursery and garden centers.

## Fertilizing

There are essentially two types of fertilizers for houseplants on the market: those that are organic, such as fish emulsion and liquid sea-weed, and those that are petrochemically derived. All are clearly labeled as to suitability for foliage or flowering plants or both. Some are formulated and labeled specifically for orchids and African violets. Follow label directions. Do not overdo fertilizing in an effort to compensate for lack of light or dry air. Fertilizing a little regularly—mixing the fertilizer at one-fourth the rate for applying every two weeks—can give superb results, but only during the season of active growth. During the cooler, darker days of late fall and early winter, until about Valentine's Day, houseplants need little or no fertilizing. The exception is a fluorescent-light garden where the duration and quality of light is constant in all seasons and where temperatures and humidity are maintained to foster active growth and flowering.

---

### SOILLESS POTTING MIXES

Soilless potting mixes, based on a recipe known as the Cornell Peat-Lite—developed at Cornell University and comprising primarily sphagnum peat moss, perlite, and vermiculite—are widely used by commercial growers. They are notably free of pathogens that could hinder growth or even cause death of the plant. They are also lightweight, uniform in wicking moisture and holding it without being soggy, and well aerated. More-over, young roots quickly penetrate the medium. The disadvantage of soilless mixes is that plants growing in them require thoughtful and regular fertilizing, usually a little with every watering. Once the mix dries out, remoistening is tricky as peat moss, once dry, literally sheds water like a duck's back.

Seasonal flowering plants (such as cyclamen, fairy and German primrose, cineraria, and poinsettia) grow-ing in soilless mix and purchased in bloom are usually enjoyed more or less as cut flowers and added to the compost pile when the show ends. Gesneriads in general and African violets in particular are especially well suited to growing on in a soilless mix. Orchids that are intermediate between terrestrial and epiphytic, such as cymbidiums and paphiopedilums, can be grown in a mix of about two parts fine to medium fir bark to one of soilless mix. The use of timed-released fertilizer pellets, such as 14-14-14, obviates the need to apply liquid fertilizer with every watering. Otherwise, when it is time to repot a plant that began life in a soilless mix, most gardeners prefer to move it to a larger pot using a loam-based potting mix, such as equal parts packaged all-purpose potting soil, clean, sharp sand, and well-aged compost.

## Containers

The type of pot used for a particular plant not only determines how much watering will be necessary (plants in clay pots will need to be watered three to four times more frequently than those in plastic ones), it also can affect whether the plant becomes top-heavy (more likely in lightweight plastic) and whether its roots may rot from overwatering (more likely in nonporous plastic than clay).

In addition, the choice of container dramatically alters the aesthetics of plants. Today, numerous decorative pots are on the market, both domestic and imported. Plainer containers tend to complement flowering plants, while those with ornamentation better suit green or lightly variegated foliage plants.

A plant can be grown directly in a pot that has one or more drain holes. Decorative containers without drain holes are best used as "slipcovers" to hide the utilitarian pot in which the plant is growing. Use them as saucers and pour off within a half hour or so any water remaining in the bottom after watering.

Seasonal flowering and gift plants often arrive with foil covers. These are best removed immediately, as they trap water in the bottom and keep air and light from reaching the lowermost leaves. European-style dish and basket gardens are also popular as gifts and must be watered carefully so as not to drown part of the planting while permitting the rest to die for lack of moisture.

## Repotting

Repot when roots fill the pot or the plant has become top-heavy. Transfer to a container that is a size or two larger; use a chopstick to gently tease some of the roots free of the old root ball to help them get established. If, however, the roots are coiled around the root ball, prune them—it is a common practice to remove a fourth to a third of the roots. Add fresh soil mix as necessary to fill the pot.

Topdressing is one way to rejuvenate a plant without completely repotting. This technique works especially well for specimen trees or shrubs in large, heavy containers. Ideally, it should be done in late winter or spring. Moisten the soil a day or two in advance. Loosen and remove the top 2 to 3 inches of old soil; take out more of the old soil around the edges, between the root ball and the wall of the container. Refill with new potting mix.

## Housekeeping

Pinching houseplants, or removing the growing tip with a single pinch just above a leaf or pair of leaves, has the same effect as pinching outdoor plants. It produces compact, denser growth and encourages single-stemmed plants to branch out, allowing some control over the plant's shape. Large plants with woody stems may require some pruning with a pair of pruning shears.

Dust plants with a feather duster or give them an occasional shower to clean the leaves and perk them up. Remove dead, yellowed leaves and spent flowers from the plant and soil surface. In addition to being unsightly, dead plant parts can cause unsanitary and potentially unhealthy conditions.

## Types of Houseplants

### Trees for Indoors

Most ficus (excepting the creeping species) will adapt to a place indoors where they receive bright light and some direct sun. They will lose many leaves at first when placed in a site with reduced light—unless they were conditioned previously by the grower. Weeping fig (*Ficus benjamina*) and Indian laurel (*Ficus microcarpa*) are excellent choices, as well as banana fig (*Ficus alii* or *F. longifolia*), which has willow-shaped leaves. Of the palms suitable for indoors, kentia palm (*Howeia forsterana*) and lady palm (*Rhapis excelsa* and *R. humilis*) are the best all-around performers. The most widely distributed areca palm (*Chrysalidocarpus lutescens*) is next to impossible to grow for more than a season or two indoors. Tree-size specimens of yucca, pleomele, and dracaena or corn plant that will tolerate less light than ficus and palms are also available.

### Orchids

If you understand the basic needs of tropical orchids, you can grow some kinds in your home in a bright window, and many others in a greenhouse or sunroom. *Paphiopedilum* or lady slipper orchids and *Phalaenopsis* or moth orchids are two types that can be grown on windowsills or under lights. If you are new to orchid growing, start with mature, established plants.

### Habitat

Some orchids are terrestrial or ground-dwelling. Many are epiphytes, meaning they grow on another plant, but not as a parasite, merely perching on the trunk or branches of a tree or mossy rocks. An orchid's form can help you determine its culture. Orchids with thickened stems (pseudobulbs that function as water-storing organs) and fleshy, waxy leaves are indigenous to brightly lit habitats with relatively low rainfall, at least during certain seasons. Orchids with broad, thin leaves and pseudobulbs that are undeveloped or lacking are native to habitats that are shady with a uniformly high level of moisture.

### Temperature

Temperature is a major factor in orchid success. A dip of from 5°F to 10°F from day to night temperatures and a summer to winter differential of about 20°F are important. Generally, orchids perform well in one of three temperature ranges (see "Temperature Ranges for Selected Orchids," page 577). Occasional dips in temperature generally do not prove fatal. Different species in the same genus may have different requirements; some orchids may straddle two ranges, tolerating either one. Hybrids are generally more adaptable to environmental differences than species.

### Water and Humidity

Paphiopedilums and phalaenopsis, both good beginner choices, require regular watering throughout the year. Cattleyas need fewer, but still more or less consistent, waterings, while catasetums, calanthes, and some dendrobiums require copious waterings part of the year and none for the few months that they are dormant.

Clear plastic and special clay pots with extra side drainage holes are recommended for growing orchids. With clear plastic pots, you can actually see the roots, a boon for knowing when to water: White roots are dry, wet roots are green or gray. Another method for determining whether it is time to water is to tap the sides of clay pots with a fingernail or a ring. A thudding sound suggests the medium is still moist; water when the sound is hollow. Some gardeners water according to the weight of the orchid and pot. To compare moist and dry weights, first lift the pot when the medium is dry and then again right after watering. With experience, you will be able to feel when the medium is dry.

Growing mediums respond to watering differently. Finer grades, like those for terrestrial orchids, hold moisture longer than coarser ones. Watering is also affected by humidity, light intensity, air circulation, and the growth stage of the orchid. Orchids with pseudobulbs even provide not-so-subtle cues to watering. When it is time to soak the roots, the pseudobulbs just behind the active growth begin to shrink and develop grooves.

Epiphytic orchids mounted on slabs of cork

---

## TEMPERATURE RANGES FOR SELECTED ORCHIDS

The following is a list of the preferred temperature ranges of various orchid genera. Some species tolerate more than one range and are listed accordingly.

### WARM

Day temperatures from 75°F to 85°F and night around 65°F.

Angraecum
X Ascocenda
Calanthe
Doritis
Phalaenopsis
Vanda
Vanilla

### INTERMEDIATE

Day temperatures from 65°F to 75°F and night around 60°F.

X Ascocenda
Brassavola

Calanthe
Catasetum
Cattleya
Dendrobium
Epidendrum
Paphiopedilum (mottled-leaved)
Vanda

### COOL

Day temperatures from 60°F to 70°F and night at 55°F.

Anguloa
Cymbidium
Dendrobium (Nobile hybrids)
Lycaste
Masdevallia
Miltonia
Odontoglossum
Paphiopedilum (green-leaved)

## TEN TIPS FOR GROWING ORCHIDS SUCCESSFULLY

- Complete drainage after each watering is the key to growing orchids.
- Adjust watering, giving less as the potting medium ages and breaks down.
- If overwatering is suspected, cut down on frequency, not the amount of water.
- To avoid rot, do not let water remain between new foliage on soft-leaved orchids, especially catasetums, lycastes, anguloas, and calanthes.
- When repotting, clean out the old medium completely before adding the new mix.
- Carve off old bulbs and objectionable growths when repotting.
- Stake orchids after repotting to assist reestablishment.
- A temperature drop at night of at least 8°F to 10°F is important for bud formation.
- The most common cause for nonblooming but otherwise healthy-looking orchids is too little light.
- Too much nitrogen can lead to excessive foliage at the expense of flowers. Feed orchids in active growth with a soluble orchid fertilizer as recommended on the label.

## LADY SLIPPER ORCHIDS

Many gardeners find that paphiopedilums, or lady slipper orchids, grow happily in the same temperature ranges humans are comfortable in, with somewhat more humidity. Because many are native to shady rain-forest habitats, they adapt well in homes, requiring generally less light than do most other orchids. Some species—such as *Paphiopedilum philippinense, P. lowii, P. stonei,* and *P. rothschildianum*—will need supplemental lighting in northern latitudes in order to flower.

Paphiopedilums can produce flowers that last for more than a month, bloom every six months, or produce consecutively flowering stems, and they are seldom bothered by insects. Some with mottled foliage are attractive even when not in bloom.

An excellent, easy-to-mix medium for terrestrial paphiopedilum orchids is made with fir bark, builder's sand, and chopped sphagnum moss, approximately 8:2:1 by volume. Another recipe uses two parts fine or medium fir bark to one of a soilless mix.

bark or tree fern require more water more often—perhaps even daily—and very high humidity.

In general, give orchids at least 50 percent relative humidity. Moist gravel-lined trays under pots will help boost humidity, as will placing the pots on a wooden, plastic, or metal grid over water-filled containers. Surrounding orchids with foliage plants and other tropicals such as bromeliads also helps increase humidity. You can always supplement with a humidifier. Keep the air moving with a small fan aimed at a nearby wall or ceiling.

### Orchid Media and Repotting

Orchids are grown in specialty media—first and foremost well draining. Ask for recommendations when you buy plants. Epiphytic orchids, such as cattleyas and vandas, generally thrive in mixtures of tree fern or fir bark with charcoal, coarse perlite, and similar ingredients. Cymbidiums, paphiopedilums, and other more terrestrial orchids require a finer mix that drains well. Before adding the medium, layer

## NOCTURNAL BLOOMERS

Some cacti produce nocturnal white flowers with a delicious perfume designed to attract the moths that pollinate them. Many of these plants, known by the common name night-blooming cereus, are quite tough plants and can be grown as houseplants. These include *Epiphyllum oxypetalum, Hylocereus undatus, Peniocereus greggii, Selenicereus grandiflorus,* and *S. macdonaldiae.* Getting them to bloom requires an abundance of warmth, water, light, nutrients, and moist air in spring and summer and leaner conditions in fall and winter: coolness but never freezing, no fertilizer, and much less water.

Night-blooming cereus need room to grow in a sunny to half-sunny window or near one that receives full sun. Ideally, they should spend the summer outdoors, where rains and hosing down assure the moisture and humidity conducive to strong new growth, on which the next season's flowers will be borne. Individual intensely fragrant flowers last one night only.

An excellent growing medium consists of two parts well-rotted leaf mold to one each of garden loam, well-rotted manure, and coarse gravel. Fertilize regularly in spring and summer, but not at all in fall and winter.

## LIVING STONES

*Lithops,* or living stones, are South African plants that grow in the desert beside small rocks to which they bear a striking resemblance—hence the common name. The camouflage protects them from feeding animals. The tiny plants bear two leaves—flattened, rounded, and intricately patterned—fused together; a single daisylike flower grows from between the leaves. After the bloom, the leaves begin to die slowly and a new pair forms.

Somewhat difficult to grow, lithops require direct sun and do well in low humidity with no fertilizer. The rule of thumb is to water lightly and only when the leaves show signs of shriveling. However, in winter emerging new leaves derive all their needed moisture from the old leaves, which undergo a natural and complete shriveling. Do not water until the following spring.

## Cacti and Succulents

Few of us live where it is mild enough to grow succulents outdoors. However, some succulents, which include the group called cacti, grow rather well in the hot, dry rooms of many homes. These plants have survived by adapting to drought. Their Achilles' heel is *over*watering. Succulents often have strange, grotesque-looking swollen trunks, stems, and leaves, developed to enhance water storage.

The limiting factor for growing succulents indoors is usually light. Most will do well with a minimum of four or more hours of direct sun. Supplement with artificial light, if necessary. As with any rule, there are exceptions. Most notable is the remarkably low light tolerance of a number of *Sansevieria* species, the snake plants.

the bottom of the pot with an inch or two of coarse gravel, hardwood charcoal, corks from wine bottles, or plastic foam pellets to increase drainage and air circulation.

Repot orchids when they outgrow their containers or as soon as the medium shows signs that it is beginning to decompose, preferably after flowering or just before or as new growth develops. Do not disturb the roots of blooming or dormant orchids.

## HERBS FROM SEEDS

Many herbs can be started from seed indoors. Add even the first thinnings to the cooking pot.

Two quick and easy herbs for indoor culture are cress and black mustard. On a sunny windowsill, place a pot or flat filled with a well-draining friable potting soil at least 3 inches deep. Sow seeds thickly and press them into the soil. Cover the container with plastic wrap or glass until germination takes place. Thin. In 10 to 14 days, the leaves should be big enough for judicious snipping. The seeds germinate under quite cool conditions, around 55°F, and can be grown throughout winter on a windowsill.

To grow other herbs from seed, check seed packets for germination temperatures and conditions. Dwarf bush basils such as 'Spicy Globe' do better indoors than large and purple-leaved varieties. Dill, fennel, parsley, and cilantro do not transplant well; to grow them indoors, sow seeds where they are to grow in a medium to large pot, 6 to 10 inches in diameter.

## HERBS FOR INDOORS

*Allium schoenoprasum,* chives
*Anethum graveolens,* dill*
*Anthriscus cerefolium,* chervil*
*Brassica nigra,* black mustard*
*Coriandrum sativum,* coriander, cilantro*
*Foeniculum vulgare,* sweet fennel*
*Laurus nobilis,* sweet bay
*Lepidium sativum,* cress, peppercress*
*Melissa officinalis,* lemon balm
*Mentha* species, mints
*Ocimum basilicum,* basil
*Origanum vulgare,* marjoram
*Petroselinum crispum,* parsley*
*Rosmarinus officinalis,* rosemary
*Salvia officinalis,* sage
*Satureja montana,* winter savory
*Thymus vulgaris,* thyme*
*Tropaeolum majus,* nasturtium*

*easy to grow from seed

The greatest challenge with succulents, especially cacti, can be getting them to flower; you must be conscientious about giving the plants a period of dry plus cold that mimics their natural habitats.

Water succulents well while they are actively growing, then allow them to dry until the soil is barely damp before watering again. Most require a dry, dormant period in winter with little or no water. During dormancy, plants do not absorb water, and soggy soil can promote rot. Fertilize only during active growth; use a water-soluble complete fertilizer at one-quarter strength. Repotting is best done in spring following the dry, dormant winter; prune any roots that have died and withhold watering for

a week or so after repotting. Spider mites are the most common pest problem for succulents.

## Growing Herbs Indoors

In order to be truly tasty, most herbs need fresh air and baking sun, not readily available indoors, especially during the short winter days in many regions. Some herbs will perform better indoors than others. Some, such as rosemary and bay, are prized as sweet-smelling topiary.

Choose an intensely sunny spot, such as a large window or a standard or window greenhouse. Group pots together on trays of moist pebbles, and spray the leaves with water to refresh them. Indoor herbs may be prone to spider mites, whiteflies, and aphids; wash with mild soap and water in the sink and if any pests persist, spray with insecticidal soap or a 50:50 mixture of denatured alcohol and water. (Rinse well in tepid water any herb parts you cut as seasonings.)

Bringing potted herbs indoors after a summer outdoors stresses them. Many perennials, wanting a rest and unhappy about the low indoor humidity, drop leaves and stop growing actively. When this happens, decrease watering. Annual herbs should be cut back and fertilized lightly to foster new growth.

## Hardy Bulbs for Indoors

"Forcing" a pot of winter-blooming hardy bulbs is one of the simplest ways to raise spirits in that often-dreary season. Hardy bulbs provide almost foolproof blooms without the constant attention most flowering houseplants require. The one thing they do demand is a period of cold—to mimic that of their native habitat.

### Choosing Bulbs

Select large, healthy bulbs that are firm, clean, and unbruised. The tunic or outer paperlike covering on tulips and hyacinths should be intact. The best bulbs for forcing are the early-season bloomers with not overly tall stems that might easily flop.

Many bulbs can be purchased precooled. Look for pots of bulbs, ready to burst into bloom, in late winter at local retailers.

### Containers and Growing Mediums

Choose containers about 6 inches deep and 6 to 8 inches across, and with bottom drain holes. A 6-inch pot will hold five tulips, four hyacinths, three to five daffodils, or ten to twelve crocuses.

Clay pots necessitate more watering than plastic. The medium must be well drained, yet able to hold enough moisture for root production and to support the flowering bulbs. Equal parts of loam, sand, and compost work well for hardy bulbs.

### The Cold Treatment

Each type of bulb is different, but in general hardy bulbs require a 13- to 15-week cold treatment below 48°F. Pay attention to instructions that come with the bulbs; some tulip and narcissus cultivars require an average of 17 weeks of cold. Plant most bulbs with the pointed tops just above the soil level in the pot, or to about two-thirds of their depth. For

---

**INDOOR BULB TIPS**

- For simultaneous blooming, plant one kind of bulb.
- Plant bulbs pointed side up.
- For a specific bloom date, calculate the number of weeks required for the cold treatment plus two to four weeks for indoor growing.
- Bring pots of hardy bulbs indoors a few at a time for an extended indoor display.
- Tulip bulbs, roughly half-circle shaped, have a curved and flat side. Set the flat side toward the pot's perimeter so that the bulb's first leaf will unfurl gracefully outward.
- Cover crocus and grape hyacinth bulbs with an inch of soil or less.
- Do not give hardy bulbs a cold treatment longer than two weeks beyond the maximum recommended.
- Do not remove bulbs before they receive at least the minimum cold treatment.

## RECOMMENDED HARDY BULBS FOR INDOOR CULTURE

### EASY

Crocus (*Crocus*; Dutch hybrid cultivars perform best), 15-week cold treatment
    *Crocus chrysanthus*—creamy yellow
    *C. chrysanthus* 'Blue Pearl'—pearly blue
    *C. x luteus* 'Yellow Mammoth'—yellow
    *C. vernus* 'Joan of Arc'—white
    *C. vernus* 'Remembrance'—purple

Daffodil, Jonquil (*Narcissus*), 16–17-week cold treatment
    Cyclamineus daffodil, 'February Gold'—yellow
    Cyclamineus daffodil, 'Jack Snipe'—white with a yellow trumpet
    Cyclamineus daffodil, 'Tête-à-Tête'—yellow
    Large-cup daffodil, 'Ice Follies'—white
    Large-cup daffodil, 'Carlton'—canary yellow with gold-yellow cup
    Short-cup daffodil, 'Barrett Browning'—white with bright orange cup
    Trumpet daffodil, 'Dutch Master'—yellow
    Trumpet daffodil, 'Mount Hood'—white

Dutch Hyacinth (*Hyacinthus orientalis*; all cultivars force nicely; the more graceful Roman hyacinths are ideal for forcing but not always available), 12–15-week cold treatment
    'Delft Blue'—soft blue
    'Ostara'—deep violet-blue
    'Pink Pearl'—deep pink with pale edges
    'L'Innocence'—white
    'City of Haarlem'—yellow
    'Hollyhock'—double pink

Paperwhites (*Narcissus tazetta*; not winter-hardy, these bulbs require no cold treatment)
    'Albus'—pure white
    'Grand Soleil d'Or'—golden yellow with an orange cup
    'Cragford'—white petals with a vermilion-red cup
    'Ziva'—white petals with a yellow cup

Tulip (*Tulipa*), 15–16-week cold treatment
    Double early tulip, 'Baby Doll'—yellow
    Double early tulip, 'Stockholm'—bright red
    Double late tulip, 'Angelique'—pink with white edge
    Single early tulip, 'Apricot Beauty'—apricot
    Single early tulip, 'Christmas Marvel'—rose or red
    Species tulip, *Tulipa bakeri* 'Lilac Wonder'—small lilac-pink flowers with an orange-yellow heart and white edge
    Triumph tulip, 'Attila'—purple with a white edge
    Triumph tulip, 'Hibernia'—white
    Triumph tulip, 'Paul Richter'—red

### MORE CHALLENGING

Glory-of-the-Snow (*Chionodoxa*), 15-week cold treatment
    *Chionodoxa forbesii*—lavender-blue with white eyes
    *C. gigantea*—pale blue with white eyes
    *C. luciliae*—light blue with white eyes

Fritillaria (*Fritillaria*), 13–15-week cold treatment
    *Fritillaria meleagris*—pink-purple checkered
    *F. meleagris* 'Aphrodite'—pure white

Grape Hyacinth (*Muscari*), 15-week cold treatment
    *Muscari armeniacum*—blue edged with white
    *M. armeniacum* 'Heavenly Blue'—vivid blue
    *M. armeniacum* 'Blue Spike'—soft blue
    *M. botryoides* 'Album'—white
    *M. comosum* 'Plumosum'—double mauve-lilac

Iris (*Iris*), 15-week cold treatment
    *Iris reticulata* 'Cantab'—sky blue
    *I. reticulata* 'Joyce'—deep violet-blue
    *I. danfordiae*—yellow

Ornamental Onion (*Allium*), 21-week cold treatment
  
  *Allium karataviense*—pink-lilac
  
  *A. moly*—yellow

Quamash (*Camassia*), 15–17-week cold treatment
  
  *Camassia cusickii*—light blue
  
  *C. quamash*—deep blue
  
  *C. leichtlinii* 'Flore Plena'—double sulfur yellow
  
  *C. leichtlinii* 'Blue Danube'—dark blue
  
  *C. leichtlinii* 'Alba'—white
  
  *C. leichtlinii* 'Semiplena'—creamy white

Squill (*Hyacinthoides, Scilla*), 15-week cold treatment
  
  *Hyacinthoides hispanica* 'Blue Giant'—deep blue
  
  *H. hispanica* 'Blue Queen'—bright blue
  
  *H. hispanica* 'Rose Queen'—bright pink
  
  *Scilla siberica* 'Spring Beauty'—bright blue
  
  *S. siberica* 'Alba'—white

Snowdrop (*Galanthus*), 15-week cold treatment
  
  *Galanthus elwesii*—white
  
  *G. nivalis*—white
  
  *G. nivalis* 'Flore Pleno'—double white

Snowflake (*Leucojum*), 15-week cold treatment
  
  *Leucojum aestivum*—tiny, bell-shaped; white petals tinged with green
  
  *L. vernum*—bell-shaped; white petals tinged with green

Spring Star Flower (*Ipheion*), 10–12-week cold treatment
  
  *Ipheion uniflorum* 'Rolf Fiedler'—dark blue
  
  *I. uniflorum* 'Wisley Blue'—violet-blue

Windflower (*Anemone*), 15-week cold treatment
  
  *Anemone apennina*—blue
  
  *A. blanda* 'Blue Shades'—deep blue
  
  *A. blanda* 'White Splendour'—white with pink exterior

smaller ones, like crocus, snowdrop, anemone, and *Iris reticulata,* completely cover the bulb. Water well and label each pot with the name of the cultivar, planting date, and the date it should come into the house. No fertilizer is needed for hardy bulbs.

Store pots for the recommended time in a cold frame, or cold garage, basement, or unheated closet. Refrigerators work well; pots dry out more quickly in frost-free models. Keep the soil evenly moist. Outdoors in northern climates, bulbs will get adequate cold. In a controlled environment, like a refrigerator or greenhouse, keep temperatures around 45°F to 48°F until the bulbs root (search for roots at the hole in the bottom of the pot). Once bulbs root, lower the temperature to 38°F to 42°F for good shoot development. Once they are well rooted and have leaves about 1 to 2 inches high, they are ready for forcing. If bulbs achieve this height before meeting the minimum cold requirement, put them in a very cold spot (33°F to 35°F) for the remainder of the cold treatment.

When they are ready for forcing, bring the pots indoors to a sunny windowsill. Give them at least eight hours of light and cool temperatures, 60°F or less; under 55°F temperatures ensure longer-lasting flowers. Maintain night temperatures within 5°F to 10°F of day temperatures. Water adequately. Flowers open in two to four weeks, depending on the cultivar.

It is seldom possible to force the same pot of hardy bulbs again the following year. Most gardeners compost the bulbs after they bloom or transplant them into the garden in spring.

## Tender Bulbs for Indoors

Growing many of these exotics is no more difficult than caring for the average houseplant. All

## GROWING BULBS HYDROPONICALLY

Some of the easiest hardy bulbs to force in water are hyacinth, miniature narcissus, paperwhite narcissus, and crocus. Use glass hyacinth or crocus jars designed for the procedure, or any glass jar with a small enough neck to support one bulb. Or layer an inch of pebbles to hold several bulbs in a shallow bowl. Fill the containers with water to within ⅛ inch of the base of the bulbs—do not let the water touch the bulbs or they may rot. Paperwhites (and other bulbs that have been precooled) do not need a cold treatment; place them directly in a sunny window. For other daffodils, crocuses, and hyacinths, set the bulbs in the growing medium and follow the same prescribed cold treatment as you would for soil plantings of these hardy bulbs. Keep temperatures around 50°F to 55°F after the bulb sprouts to extend flowering time.

they need is sufficient light, moderate amounts of water, a good rich soil, and fertilizer during the growing season, as well as a period of dormancy or rest. Tender bulbs can be summer- or winter-blooming, depending mainly on their native habitat—most are native to South Africa, and a few to South America or Asia. Some are deciduous and lose their leaves—a sure sign they are dormant; others are evergreen and may require slightly less watering when not actively growing. Some tender bulbs must be helped into dormancy with sunlight and water deprivation; without this needed rest, they probably will not rebloom. When you order bulbs from gardening catalogs, instructions typically come with them.

### Containers and Soil Mixes

Tender bulbs, many of which are susceptible to overwatering, are best grown in tight quarters. Larger ones, like veltheimia, do best planted one to a container with a circumference about an inch larger than the bulb itself. Lachenalias, oxalis, cyrtanthus, tulbaghias, and other smaller bulbs need to be crowded several to a container. Clay pots, aside from being aesthetically pleasing, are heavy enough to support bulbs that could become top-heavy.

Since most of these tender plants prefer to be under- rather than overwatered, the planting medium needs to be porous. One such quick-draining mix is made with two parts compost, one part shredded bark, one part builder's sand, and one part perlite.

### Planting and Maintenance

In general, plant winter-flowering bulbs from late summer to autumn and summer bloomers in late winter or early spring. As with all bulbs, plant with the growing tip facing up. It is notoriously difficult to tell the top of tuberous begonias from the bottom; round, craterlike markings identify the top where a stem once sprouted. Plant most tender bulbs an inch below the soil. Exceptions are tuberous begonias, which should be only half buried, and tulbaghias, crinums, amaryllis, and veltheimias, which should be positioned so that most of the bulb is exposed.

Before they begin to sprout, tender bulbs can be kept in indirect sunlight. Water lightly when the soil is dry to the touch. During their growing and blooming cycles, most prefer a sunny south-facing windowsill. Exceptions are sinningias and clivias, which prefer slightly lower light levels. Summer-blooming achimenes and fancy-leaf caladiums do best out of hot sun, and zingibers will tolerate shade.

Because of their evolutionary makeup, most bulbs go dormant and need a rest. After they finish their growth cycle, oxalis, tuberous begonias, caladiums, and achimenes begin to brown and drop their leaves—a signal they are going dormant. Gradually stop watering. When the foliage is completely dried with no sign of growth, remove the bulbs from the soil and store them in a paper bag—or leave them in the pot, but resist the urge to water no matter how parched the soil looks. When new growth appears, repot immediately, or water and move the pot back into sunlight.

Other tender bulbs—agapanthus, eucharis, clivias, cyrtanthus, tulbaghias, and zingibers—maintain their leaves while resting and benefit from reduced waterings. Though they retain their leaves during dormancy, these bulbs will nonetheless, when the time is right, send out shoots and resume active growth.

Watering with liquid manure tea at the outset of the new growing season is a time-honored way to boost bloom and nurture roots without repotting (see page 458 for details on how to make manure tea). During active growth, tender bulbs benefit from regular light applications of fertilizer formulated for flowering plants or, for convenience, timed-release pellets applied once at the beginning of the season.

## Tender Bulbs for Indoors

### Achimenes, *Achimenes longiflora*
DECIDUOUS OR EVERGREEN: Deciduous
PLANTING TIME: February–May
BLOOMING PERIOD: Summer/early fall
DORMANCY: Fall–winter

NOTES: Flower color is typically purple but can range from white, pink, and blue to orange and orange-red. Prefers rich, moist, and well-drained soil in bright light shaded from hot afternoon sun. When blooming is finished, gradually dry off the rhizomes by withholding water.
CULTIVARS AND RELATED SPECIES:
Cultivars with white flowers include 'Ambroise Verschaffelt', 'Dainty Queen', and 'Margarita'.
Pink flowers: 'Adele Delahoute', 'Little Beauty', and 'Peach Blossom'.
Blue flowers: 'Galatea' and 'Valse Bleu'.
Orange/red flowers: 'Burnt Orange', 'Crimson Glory', and 'Master Ingram'.

### Agapanthus, Lily-of-the-Nile, *Agapanthus praecox*
DECIDUOUS OR EVERGREEN: Evergreen
PLANTING TIME: When received
BLOOMING PERIOD: Summer
DORMANCY: Winter
NOTES: An easy-to-grow plant with clusters of blue flowers and handsome strap-shaped foliage. Prefers moist, well-drained soil in full sun, but is not fussy. Keep plants slightly dry in winter.
CULTIVARS AND RELATED SPECIES:
*A. praecox* 'Alba'—white-flowered.
*A. praecox* 'Peter Pan'—dwarf, blue-flowered.
*A. praecox* 'Rancho Dwarf'—dwarf, white-flowered.

### Amaryllis, *Hippeastrum* species and hybrids
DECIDUOUS OR EVERGREEN: Mostly deciduous; some are more evergreen
PLANTING TIME: Fall–spring
BLOOMING PERIOD: Winter–spring

DORMANCY: Fall

NOTES: Small to large, single or double, showy flowers can range in color from pale pink to nearly black-red with some pale yellow and greenish cultivars and some with vivid stripes or variegation on a white background. Flowers appear a few weeks after potting; remove stalks when blooms are spent. In fall if leaves fail to wither, initiate dormancy (unless an evergreen type) by gradually reducing watering. Store bulbs dry in their pots; top-dress with fresh soil after 8 to 12 weeks and resume watering. Plants tolerate being uprooted but prefer to become established and left alone.

CULTIVARS AND RELATED SPECIES:

Numerous cultivars, including miniatures, are on the market. Recommended hybrids include 'Apple Blossom' (large pink or white flowers), 'Charm' (miniature with orange flowers), 'Cinderella' (large red blooms with white stripes), 'Red Lion' (large, bright red), 'Lady Jane' (large, double pink), 'Scarlet Baby' (miniature with red flowers), and 'White Christmas' (large pure white flowers).

## Amazon Lily, *Eucharis* x *grandiflora*

DECIDUOUS OR EVERGREEN: Evergreen

PLANTING TIME: When received

BLOOMING PERIOD: Fall, sporadically year-round

DORMANCY: Winter

NOTES: Sweetly scented white flowers. Use a rich, moisture-retentive soil. Requires higher temperatures than other tender bulbs and is recommended for warmer homes—with night temperatures above 60°F. Once plants are established, feed moderately and do not let them dry out. Reduce watering during fall and winter. Watch for mealybugs.

CULTIVARS AND RELATED SPECIES:

*E.* x *grandiflora* var. *fragrans*—especially fragrant.

*E. candida*—slightly larger, summer-blooming.

## Blood Lily, *Haemanthus coccineus*

DECIDUOUS OR EVERGREEN: Briefly deciduous

PLANTING TIME: Early summer

BLOOMING PERIOD: Fall

DORMANCY: Spring–summer

NOTES: Red filaments surround tight clusters of yellow stamens and resemble shaving brushes. Grow in full sun. Water deeply but infrequently in winter, very sparingly in late spring, and just enough to prevent total desiccation through midsummer. Resume watering in August to initiate bloom.

CULTIVARS AND RELATED SPECIES:

*H. albiflos*—evergreen with greenish white blooms; requires even watering year-round and protection from full sun in midsummer.

## Calla Lily, *Zantedeschia aethiopica*

DECIDUOUS OR EVERGREEN: Briefly deciduous

PLANTING TIME: Spring or summer

BLOOMING PERIOD: Winter

DORMANCY: Summer

NOTES: Flower spike or spadix is enveloped in a funnel formed by the spathe. Moisture is key for this native of South African marshes. Use a rich potting mix. Grows in sun or partial shade in warm or cool temperatures. It may go briefly dormant in summer if allowed to dry. Watch for bacterial rots and remove any affected plant parts.

CULTIVARS AND RELATED SPECIES:

*Z. albomaculata*—compact at 2 feet, with greenish white spathe with crimson blotches; summer dormant.

*Z. elliotiana*—yellow spathe and spotted leaves; blooms in summer, dormant in winter.

*Z. rehmannii*—shades of pink; blooms in summer.

## Clivia, *Clivia miniata*

DECIDUOUS OR EVERGREEN: Evergreen

PLANTING TIME: When received

BLOOMING PERIOD: Late winter/spring

DORMANCY: Fall/winter

NOTES: Bright orange to nearly red flowers. For best flowering, pot tightly and allow to remain in the container without repotting for years. Requires excellent drainage and tends to be top-heavy so best grown in terra cotta pots. Keep water out of the crown to avoid rot. Give regular controlled waterings in summer; cool, 50°F to 65°F temperatures and sparse water are best for fall; increase water when flower spike is initiated. Keep out of harsh sunlight.

CULTIVARS AND RELATED SPECIES:

*C. miniata* var. *citrina*—a much sought-after, rare yellow form.

*C. nobilis*—pendulous tubular flowers are orange with green tips.

## Crinum-Lily, Milk-and-Wine-Lily, *Crinum* species

DECIDUOUS OR EVERGREEN: Deciduous or evergreen, depending on species

PLANTING TIME: When received

BLOOMING PERIOD: Summer/fall

DORMANCY: Winter/spring

NOTES: White, pink, rose, or burgundy flowers are usually trumpet-shaped but many species bear flowers with long, thin petals. Water freely during the growing season. After flowering in fall, cut back on watering, but do not let plants dry completely. Divide and repot only when necessary. Keep in bright light shaded from hot sun.

CULTIVARS AND RELATED SPECIES:

*C. asiaticum*—evergreen; fragrant, spidery white and occasionally pink flowers.

*C. bulbispermum*—deciduous; bell-shaped flowers are white to pink with rose-pink stripe on each petal.

*C. moorei*—deciduous; fragrant pale to dark pink and occasionally white flowers.

## Fairy-Lily, *Zephyranthes grandiflora*

DECIDUOUS OR EVERGREEN: Semievergreen

PLANTING TIME: When received

BLOOMING PERIOD: Late summer

DORMANCY: Fall/winter

NOTES: Perfect for windowsills, this dwarf bulb produces lilylike pink flowers. Also called rain lilies for their habit of bursting into bloom when rain follows a dry period. To maintain as evergreen, water less in winter.

CULTIVARS AND RELATED SPECIES:

*Z. candida*—evergreen with crocuslike white flowers in fall.

*Z. flavissima*—yellow flowers peak in late summer; keep very moist summer through fall.

*Z. rosea*—lovely pink funnel-shaped flowers.

## Fancy-Leaved Caladium, *Caladium bicolor* (*C.* x *hortulanum*)

DECIDUOUS OR EVERGREEN: Deciduous

PLANTING TIME: Spring

BLOOMING PERIOD: Grown for foliage, not flowers

DORMANCY: Winter

NOTES: Easy to grow with highly decorative heart- or strap-shaped, patterned leaves and inconspicuous flowers. A bedding plant for sun to shade. In fall when the foliage begins to decline, withhold water. Lift and place completely dormant bulbs in barely moist peat moss or coarse vermiculite.

CULTIVARS AND RELATED SPECIES:

Many cultivars are available; dwarf types and those with strap-shaped leaves are best suited to pot culture.

## Florist's Gloxinia, *Sinningia speciosa*

DECIDUOUS OR EVERGREEN: Deciduous

PLANTING TIME: Late winter–spring

BLOOMING PERIOD: Summer

DORMANCY: Fall through early winter

NOTES: Bell-shaped, vibrantly colored blooms. Remove all sprouts from tubers before planting. Water sparingly until growth is strong, then water lightly and keep evenly moist. After foliage ripens, withhold water; resume watering when there are signs of renewed growth in spring. To produce larger flowers, remove all but one shoot. Grow plants in normal room temperatures in bright light.

CULTIVARS AND RELATED SPECIES:

*S. pusilla*—dwarf, thimble-size species, evergreen and free-blooming requiring near-terrarium conditions (See "Miniatures," page 596).

## Ginger, *Zingiber officinale*

DECIDUOUS OR EVERGREEN: Deciduous

PLANTING TIME: Spring

BLOOMING PERIOD: Spring/summer

DORMANCY: Late fall

NOTES: Flower color of ginger species ranges from pure white and pink to yellow, orange, and red. Cultivation of gingers is relatively easy: water freely throughout the growing season, then gradually reduce to initiate dormancy, and resume watering again in spring. Plants tolerate a number of light exposures but need protection from hot afternoon sun.

CULTIVARS AND RELATED SPECIES:

*Z. spectabile*—largest species with yellow flowers surrounded by yellow to scarlet bracts.

*Z. zerumbet*—white to yellow flowers and red bracts; cultivar 'Darceyi' has variegated foliage.

## Ginger-Lily, *Hedychium* species and cultivars

DECIDUOUS OR EVERGREEN: Mostly evergreen

PLANTING TIME: Spring

BLOOMING PERIOD: Summer/fall

DORMANCY: Midwinter

NOTES: Flower color ranges from pure white and pink to yellow, orange, and red. Relatively simple to cultivate; water freely throughout the growing season. Tolerates a number of exposures, but flowering increases with greater light. Plants benefit from a short forced dormancy in midwinter; to initiate, gradually reduce watering until foliage withers and then start up again in 6 to 8 weeks.

CULTIVARS AND RELATED SPECIES:

*H. coccineum*—bright red flowers with pink stamens.

*H. coronarium*—pure white, intensely fragrant flowers.

*H. flavescens*—fragrant creamy yellow flowers.

*H. gardnerianum*—called Kahili ginger-lily; pale yellow flowers with red stamens.

## Ifafa Lily, Vallota, *Cyrtanthus mackenii*

DECIDUOUS OR EVERGREEN: Evergreen

PLANTING TIME: When received

BLOOMING PERIOD: Spring/fall

DORMANCY: Winter

NOTES: Graceful tubular, scented flowers that typically are white but also pink or cream, and bloom sporadically through spring and summer with a flush in late fall. Easy to grow. Plant bulbs just below soil surface. Give plants adequate moisture at all times but slightly less during dormancy. Will not bloom unless potbound.

CULTIVARS AND RELATED SPECIES:

*C. mackenii* var. *cooperi*—yellow flowers.

*C. elatus*—trumpet-shaped scarlet flowers; often sold as *Vallota speciosa*.

*C. obliquus*—uncommon, but striking with red flowers flaring to yellow; plant with top half of bulb exposed.

## Oxalis, Wood Sorrel, *Oxalis* species and cultivars

DECIDUOUS OR EVERGREEN: Varies with species

PLANTING TIME: Varies with species

BLOOMING PERIOD: Varies with species

DORMANCY: Varies with species

NOTES: Flower color ranges from white through pink, red, and yellow. Although considered by some to be weedy, a few species of oxalis make well-behaved, charming potted bulbs. Plant bulbs about an inch deep, several per pot. Prefers cool temperatures but is otherwise undemanding. Pests and diseases are uncommon. Stop watering deciduous species during dormancy.

CULTIVARS AND RELATED SPECIES:

*O. tetraphylla* 'Iron Cross'—cross-shaped brown blotches on leaves.

*O. massoniana*—dwarf, with soft-orange flowers and delicate foliage.

*O. purpurea*—usually pink flowers with a yellow eye, but white and yellow forms exist.

*O. regnellii*—pale pink to white flowers with green foliage suffused with purple above and more vivid purple beneath.

## Shell Ginger, *Alpinia zerumbet*

DECIDUOUS OR EVERGREEN: Varies

PLANTING TIME: Spring

BLOOMS: Spring/summer

DORMANCY: Winter

NOTES: Bell-shaped white flowers with pale yellow interior. Easy to grow. Plants prefer fertile, moist soil, high humidity, and bright light. Remains evergreen with adequate moisture.

CULTIVARS AND RELATED SPECIES:

*A. tricolor*—smaller species with brightly variegated foliage.

## Society Garlic, *Tulbaghia violacea*

DECIDUOUS OR EVERGREEN: Varies

PLANTING TIME: When received

BLOOMING PERIOD: Summer

DORMANCY: Fall/winter

NOTES: Alliumlike mauve flowers and slightly garlic-scented leaves. Very easy to grow in a sunny spot; keep soil moist but not wet. In summer, allow plants to go a bit dry. Repot or divide, when necessary, in spring. Stays evergreen indoors. No serious pests.

CULTIVARS AND RELATED SPECIES:

*T. fragrans*—pink-flowered, scented at night; blooms in spring, sometimes again in fall.

## Spider Lily, Basket Flower, *Hymenocallis* species and cultivars

DECIDUOUS OR EVERGREEN: Evergreen and deciduous species

PLANTING TIME: Varies with species

BLOOMING PERIOD: Varies with species

DORMANCY: Varies with species

NOTES: Evergreen varieties are called spider lilies and deciduous varieties called basket flowers have fused cups. All flowers are white, except one yellow variety. Evergreens do best in bright light shaded from hot sun; deciduous prefer full sun. Water freely throughout the growing season. Repot evergreen species only when necessary.

CULTIVARS AND RELATED SPECIES:

*H. caribaea*—evergreen, clusters of 8 to 12 flowers per stalk in late winter.

*H. littoralis*—large evergreen, from tropical America.

*H. narcissiflora*—deciduous, with daffodil-like flowers.

*H. speciosa*—evergreen, up to 12 flowers per stalk in winter and early spring.

*H. 'Sulfur Queen'*—*H. narcissiflora* hybrid with yellow flowers.

## Tuberous Begonia, *Begonia* x *tuberhybrida*

DECIDUOUS OR EVERGREEN: Deciduous

PLANTING TIME: Early spring

BLOOMING PERIOD: Summer

DORMANCY: Autumn

NOTES: Long flowering in many different colors, begonias have two growth habits: upright and pendulous. Grow in indirect but bright light. Plant tubers shallowly, and water with caution until growth begins. Transplant to greater depth when shoots are 3 inches to 4 inches tall. To avoid rot, do not allow water to pool in hollow of tubers. In fall as temperatures drop, dormancy begins; quickly reduce watering and then withhold altogether; store dry tubers at moderate temperatures in coarse sawdust or vermiculite until replanting in early spring.

CULTIVARS AND RELATED SPECIES:

Beyond the basic choice between upright or pendulous, numerous types are available. Upright 'Nonstop' cultivars are reliable standbys with early and late bloom.

## Turmeric, *Curcuma longa*

DECIDUOUS OR EVERGREEN: Deciduous

PLANTING TIME: Spring

BLOOMING PERIOD: Summer

DORMANCY: Winter

NOTES: Conelike flower heads range in color from white and yellow to pink and purple for turmeric species—*C. longa* with pale yellow flowers is the most commonly grown. Cultivation of all species is fairly simple. Prefer high temperatures and high humidity. In fall when plants are about to go dormant, foliage yellows. Keep plants nearly dry during dormancy and resume watering with new growth.

CULTIVARS AND RELATED SPECIES:

*C. petiolata*—yellow flowers with purplish brown and green bracts.

*C. roscoeana*—yellow-orange bracts.

## Winter Red-Hot Poker, *Veltheimia bracteata*

DECIDUOUS OR EVERGREEN: Briefly deciduous

PLANTING TIME: Early spring

BLOOMS: Winter

DORMANCY: Summer

NOTES: Flowers are rosy orange and green tipped. Easy, large bulb produces offsets and is best grown in a container large enough to accommodate its clumping for a few seasons. Keep plants evenly moist except during short summer dormancy. Grow in bright light but avoid hot sun.

CULTIVARS AND RELATED SPECIES:

*V. capensis*—purplish pink flowers appear earlier than *V. bracteata;* requires more sun; has a longer dormancy.

## Fragrant Plants

With minimal care, moderate-to-strong light, and common sense, you can grow many fragrant plants indoors. Humidity is very important. Set plants on pebbles in water-filled trays. During winter when constant heating dries the atmosphere the most, it helps to mist plants once or twice daily—except those with hairy leaves.

When shopping for plants, remember that *fragrans, odorata,* or *-osme* in the plant's name usually indicates that a specimen is fragrant. Flowers are the usual source of fragrance, but do not overlook plants, such as scented geraniums, rosemary, and pineapple sage, whose leaves release a delicious fragrance when lightly bruised.

## Some Fragrant Plants for Indoors

### African Gardenia, *Mitriostigma axillare*
LIGHT: South, east, or west exposure
NOTES: A relative of the true gardenia with a similar fragrance, this plant is much more easily grown in the house. Blooms frequently through the year on new growth. Fertilize freely with an acid-type fertilizer to keep the leaves dark green.

### Fragrant Olive, *Osmanthus fragrans*
LIGHT: South or east exposure
NOTES: Creamy white flowers appear late fall into spring on this easy-to-grow shrub.

### Gardenia, *Gardenia jasminoides*
LIGHT: Very sunny south exposure
NOTES: White flowers. Difficult to grow without a greenhouse, this plant loves high humidity and acid soil. Water occasionally with leftover tea or top-dress with coffee grounds.

### Glory-Bower, *Clerodendrum philippinum*
LIGHT: South or east exposure
NOTES: White and pink double flowers smell of Cashmere Bouquet soap. Pinch new growth, and cut back drastically in midwinter. Blossoms form on new growth.

### Jasmine, *Jasminum sambac*
LIGHT: South exposure
NOTES: Can bloom almost continuously from spring through fall. White flowers. Grows well in a warm, sunny spot. Fertilize regularly. Prune when stringy. Cultivars include the deliciously fragrant 'Grand Duke of Tuscany' and 'Maid of Orleans', which produces fully double intensely fragrant flowers and tolerates an east exposure.

### Lemon, Orange, Lime, Grapefruit, *Citrus* species
LIGHT: South exposure
NOTES: Grows well in cool homes; dwarf varieties perform best as houseplants. *Citrus* x *limona,* grown indoors since the nineteenth century, blooms in spring, summer, and fall and may produce ornamental oranges.

### Madagascar Jasmine, *Stephanotis floribunda*
LIGHT: South exposure
NOTES: This vine bears creamy white clusters of waxy flowers from late spring into fall. Often needs pruning. Watch out for mealybugs and, if found, treat by removing with a cotton swab dipped in denatured alcohol.

### Night-Blooming Cereus, *Epiphyllum oxypetalum*
LIGHT: South, east, or west exposure
NOTES: Dinner-plate-size white flowers open at night; see page 579 for growing tips.

### Oleander, *Nerium oleander*
LIGHT: South exposure
NOTES: All parts of this plant are poisonous. Fertilize it well during the warm months. Keep cool but frost-free and quite dry during winter.

Orange Jasmine, *Murraya paniculata*

LIGHT: South, east, or west exposure

NOTES: Waxy white flowers smell of orange blossoms. Plant responds well to pruning and makes a wonderful tree-form standard between 15 and 18 inches tall.

Scented Geraniums, *Pelargonium* species

LIGHT: South or east exposure

NOTES: See page 593 for growing tips.

## Gesneriads

The gesneriad family includes the ever-popular African violet (*Saintpaulia*) and ubiquitous florist's gloxinia (*Sinningia*). Gesneriads in general and the African violet in particular bloom over and over again indoors, where it is not difficult to approximate the conditions in which they have evolved as understory plants in tropical forests with few seasonal changes in temperature and rainfall. With moderate light, some attention to the plant's natural growing cycle, and warm temperatures, most will thrive.

### African Violets

*Saintpaulia* species are native to eastern Africa, where they grow wild, typically with violet-shaped, five-lobed blue flowers. Today, in culture through mutation and breeding, these African violets bloom in shades from white to pink to red, pale blue to deep purple, even yellow and green and in forms from single to semi-double to double to ruffled. Even the foliage varies from all green to marbled in white, pink, or tan. Plants can be miniature or up to a foot across, but all have a rosette habit.

Light is critical for flowering—at least 8 hours a day of medium light in an east- or west-facing window. Too much light produces excessively compact plants and scorched leaves; too little causes long, weak, pale leaves. If necessary, supplement with fluorescent lights. These adaptable plants grow readily under lights; give them from 15 to 18 hours of simulated daylight with two 40-watt fluorescent tubes. Set the plants about 12 inches beneath the tubes. Three months of blooming followed by a month's rest is a reasonable goal.

Pot African violets in a light, well-draining mix, and keep it evenly moist. It is best to water from the top with tepid water, but avoid wetting the fuzzy leaves, which can cause spotting. Do not leave the pots standing in water longer than a half hour or so. However, setting pots on a pebble tray half filled with water sustains humidity immediately around the plants and boosts bloom. A violet plant that dries out too much between watering will survive, even appear to thrive, but instead of flower buds, small new growths that become new plants will occur at the base of each main leaf: these are called "suckers." Growers who specialize in African violets often grow them in self-watering pots, a practice that reduces time spent watering and assures evenly moist soil and constant flowering. Repot when roots fill the pot; relatively shallow containers promote faster drainage, minimizing the chance of rot. For maximum blooming, fertilize regularly with a product labeled specifically for African violets. These plants are easily propagated by leaf cuttings, or by division when there are two or more crowns.

### Cape Primrose

Another gesneriad, trailing only *Saintpaulia* in popularity as an all-year houseplant, is the Cape primrose (*Streptocarpus*). Some hybrids are almost everblooming; others flower cyclically like African violets. Their culture is similar.

## Geraniums

Botanists originally thought the South African native genus *Pelargonium* was closely related to hardy geraniums indigenous to the Northern Hemisphere. Although this was proven wrong, the plants in the genus are still commonly called geraniums. Perhaps most often thought of as obedient-blooming outdoor bedding plants, thousands of cultivars offer unique and varied attributes, including the fancy leaves of zonale geraniums (*P.* x *hortorum*) with a dark horseshoe marking each leaf, scented-leafed geraniums, miniature varieties, trailing geraniums with ivy-shaped leaves (*P. peltatum*), and the spectacular azalealike blooms of the Regal or Martha Washington geraniums (*P.* x *domesticum*).

Indoors, geraniums grow well in a south- or east-facing window so long as blooms are not a priority. Pot in a well-draining medium such as a mix of equal parts loam, compost, and sand or perlite. Drying out too much between waterings causes older leaves to yellow and wither prematurely. Watering too much and permitting the plants to stand in water causes root rot that will travel up the stems, turning them black and killing the plant; cuttings of tip growth not yet affected can sometimes be used to salvage a favorite specimen. Allow plants to approach dryness, then water well. Good sanitation is important; remove dead and yellowing leaves and promptly remove spent flowers as well as any petals that fall on the leaves.

In order for geraniums to flower, they need a sunny window, the sunnier the better. Martha

---

### THE MOST FRAGRANT AND BEST GROWING GERANIUMS

Scented-leaf pelargoniums are ideal for growing indoors because the leaves smell delicious even when the plants may be a bit light-starved in the dead of winter. The flowers of most varieties are inconspicuous. However, the leaves of the many diverse fragrant species and cultivars are favorite potpourri ingredients; many contribute pungent flavoring to cakes, teas, punch, salads, and salad dressings. Scented geraniums are fun to train as tree-form standards, or they can be flattened espalier-style on a simply constructed trellis made from bamboo canes.

*Pelargonium* x *citriodorum*—orange-scented

*P.* x 'Clorinda'—pungent, eucalyptus-scented

*P. crispum* 'Lemon Crispum'—called the finger-bowl geranium

*P. crispum* 'Prince Rupert'—a fine variegated, lemon-scented geranium

*P.* x *fragrans* 'Logeei'—spice-scented

*P.* x *fragrans* 'Variegatum'—nutmeg-scented

*P. graveolens*—rose-scented

*P. graveolens* 'Variegatum'—rose-scented with pink, white, and green leaves

*P.* x *limoneum*—cinnamon-scented

*P.* 'Mabel Grey'—lemon verbena fragrance, holds its scent when dried

*P. nervosum*—lime-scented

*P. odoratissimum*—apple-scented

*P. quercifolium* 'Fair Ellen'—oak leaf, pungent scent

*P.* 'Spring Park'—lemon-strawberry scented

*P. tomentosum*—peppermint-scented

*P.* x 'Toronto'—ginger-scented

Washington geraniums need night temperatures between 50°F and 55°F to set buds and usually require a greenhouse or cool sunroom. Many gardeners grow these flowering plants outdoors in warm weather and then either discard or overwinter them by taking cuttings for the indoor garden.

## Something Different for the Indoor Garden

Breeders are ever tempting us with new introductions. Sometimes it is a new dwarf form of a long-grown plant that captures the enthusiasm of indoor gardeners, other times a uniquely colored blossom, variegated leaf, or a new genus for indoors like the sweetly fragrant *Plumeria,* or frangipani, that has recently come into vogue. Following are some unusual plants for the indoor garden.

Angel's Trumpet, *Brugmansia* species and
hybrids
LIGHT: Sunny south, east, or west exposure.
NOTES: Spectacular hanging trumpet flowers are fragrant at night and come in white, yellow, apricot, or pink. Large leaves are prone to whitefly attack, yet worth some extra spraying with insecticidal soap to maintain healthy plants.

Blue Daze, *Evolvulus glomeratus*
LIGHT: Sunny south, east, or west exposure.
NOTES: Clear blue, morning-glory-like flowers are the size of a quarter. Plants will cascade nicely from the sides of a pot or hanging basket. Also blooms well under fluorescent lights.

Boophane, *Boophane disticha*
LIGHT: Sunny south exposure.

NOTES: Deciduous bulb; plant in spring in rich, well-drained soil. Deep pink to red showy flowers appear in summer on 12-inch stalks; thick, leathery foliage is wavy. Keep the soil evenly moist during the growing season. When the foliage withers, marking the onset of dormancy, withhold water until the following spring. Repot only when necessary every few years. Another similar species, *B. haemanthoides,* blooms with yellow flowers.

Calathea, *Calathea* species and hybrids
LIGHT: North or east exposure, no direct sun; ideal in fluorescent-light garden.
NOTES: Related to maranta or prayer plant, these glorious foliage plants are more durable with a waxy coating on their leaves. Give them warmth and moderate to high humidity. Mist twice daily for luxuriant foliage. *Calathea crocata* sends up showy torches of orange bracts.

Chinese Hibiscus, *Hibiscus rosa-sinensis*
LIGHT: South exposure.
NOTES: Breeders have developed plants with single and double flowers—blue, brown, yellow, gold, orange, red, or pink, with many exhibiting three or more colors in a single blossom—almost otherworldly. Some flowers last 2 to 3 days. Heavy feeders, they require a fertilizer low in phosphorus and high in potassium. Cultivars include *H.* 'All Aglow' with bright orange, yellow, and reddish tone flowers and *H.* 'Tylene' with dark brownish purple flowers with bright orange pistils.

Clivia, *Clivia miniata* var. *citrina*
LIGHT: East exposure; not direct sun.
NOTES: Much sought-after yellow form of *Clivia;* rare and expensive. See "Tender Bulbs for Indoors," page 587, for growing information.

## Dancing Lady Ginger, *Globba winitii*

LIGHT: East exposure; not direct sun.

NOTES: This dwarf ginger blooms in summer and fall. Golden yellow flowers are lined with showy purple bracts. Easy cultivation. Grows best in rich, moist, well-drained soil in bright light, but will tolerate a wide range of soils provided there is adequate moisture. Let the plants dry out during winter dormancy; resume watering in spring to commence new growth. Few insect or disease problems.

## Dwarf Ginger, *Kaempferia galanga*

LIGHT: East exposure; not direct sun.

NOTES: The violet-shaped flowers are sparkling white with a royal purple spot on the lip. Plants rarely grow more than 6 inches high. Few insect or pest problems. Use any fertilizer labeled for African violets.

## Eucrosia, *Eucrosia bicolor*

LIGHT: East or west exposure, shaded from hot sun.

NOTES: Eucrosia is a genus of tropical deciduous bulbs native to Peru and Ecuador. Clusters of flowers, orange with greenish stamens, appear on 12- to 15-inch stems in spring. Leaves drop in late fall and reappear in spring after flowering occurs. Culture is similar to that of amaryllis (see page 585).

## Flowering Maple, *Abutilon* x *hybridum*

LIGHT: Sunny south, east, or west exposure.

NOTES: Related to Chinese hibiscus, flowering maples bloom on new growth in shades of white, red, yellow, and orange. Maintain night temperatures at least 10° cooler than day for vigorous flowering. Trains well as a tree-form standard.

## Frangipani, *Plumeria* species and hybrids

LIGHT: Strong south exposure, sunrooms, greenhouses.

NOTES: Produces clusters of blossoms in a vast array of colors and scents: lemon, rose, jasmine, spice, coconut. Can bloom from mid-spring through fall. Fertilize during the growing season. Requires much sun and warm temperatures. Thrives outdoors in warm weather. Varieties include *P.* 'Dean Conklin' (rose-colored blossoms with orange tints), *P.* 'Loretta' (creamy flowers with pinkish yellow tones), *P. obtusa* 'Singapore' (white with a hint of yellow), and *P.* 'Tomlinson' (pinkish-lavender with white and yellow tones).

## Mandevilla, *Mandevilla* species and hybrids

LIGHT: Sunny south exposure or greenhouse.

NOTES: These small, flowering vines perform best in warm, sunny conditions and can become profuse bloomers. Feed with high-phosphorus fertilizer. Varieties include *M.* x *amabilis* 'Alice du Pont' with large rose-pink flowers, *M. boliviensis* with white trumpet-shaped, yellow-throated flowers and glossy dark green leaves, *M. sanderi* 'Red Riding Hood', a compact plant with glossy, bronzy green leaves and rose-red flowers, and *M. s.* 'Rosea' with clear rose-pink, yellow-throated flowers.

## Night Jessamine, *Cestrum nocturnum*

LIGHT: Sunny south, east, or west exposure.

NOTES: *C. nocturnum* has greenish white flowers in clusters that give off an intensely sweet perfume at night. Needs a warm, sunny window.

## Resurrection Lily, *Kaempferia rotunda*

LIGHT: East exposure; not direct sun.

A rare form of peacock ginger with pale silvery lavender markings on the leaves. Purple-tinged white flowers with lilac-colored lips bloom in spring before leaves emerge. This dwarf ginger can be brought to flower in a 6-inch pot year after year. Few insect or disease problems.

## Miniatures

Horticulture in miniature is a concept rife with possibilities. Some miniatures are ideally suited to growing in individual small pots, from the size of a thimble up to an inch or two, while others may succeed better if set in a larger container. The pitfall is that tiny pots can dry out in no time at all. Individual plant specimens can be variously trained as trees, shrubs, vines, or ground covers. Some are suited to becoming miniature tree-form standards or other shape topiaries or espaliers. High-humidity miniatures are naturals for terrariums.

### Miniature Gems

Dwarf Bougainvillea, *Bougainvillea* 'Pink Pixie'

LIGHT: South or west exposure; full sun.

NOTES: Twelve inches high. Inflorescences, with shell-pink bracts and pink flowers, are borne all along stems between the tiny leaves.

Miniature Begonias, *Begonia*

LIGHT: East exposure.

NOTES: A miniature angel-wing type, 'Tiny Gem', is almost everblooming—an excellent terrarium plant. Miniature rex begonias also grow well in the humid conditions of terrariums. A particularly outstanding ever-bloomer for terrariums is the tiny rhizomatous begonia, *B.* x *prismatocarpa*.

Miniature Gloxinia, *Sinningia pusilla*

LIGHT: North or east exposure with no hot, direct sun, or under fluorescent lights.

NOTES: Thimble-sized gesneriad about 1½ to 2 inches high with trumpet-shaped flowers available in a wide range of colors. Evergreen and free-blooming. Requires very high humidity. One of the all-time best flowering plants for terrariums. Plants rarely go dormant. 'Tinkerbells' produces rosy purple flowers with dark-spotted white throats.

Miniature Goldfish Plant, *Nematanthus wettsteinii*

LIGHT: East exposure without hot, direct sun, or under fluorescent lights.

NOTES: This small gesneriad produces waxy leaves and orange pouch flowers in profusion. Can be accommodated in a 3-inch hanging basket with stems cascading 6 inches down or trained into a 4- or 5-inch topiary wreath.

Porphyry Plant, *Porphyrocoma pohliana*

LIGHT: East exposure.

NOTES: Miniature member of the acanthus family from South America. Persistent foliage is silver with burgundy underneath. Long-lasting ruby bracts hold purplish flowers.

Rosary Vine, *Ceropegia woodii*

LIGHT: Any exposure.

NOTES: Ideal for a 6-inch topiary wreath set upright in a 3-inch clay pot; can also be trained on an arbor or pergola in a miniature landscape.

Snow Rose, *Serissa foetida* 'Flore-pleno'

LIGHT: South or east exposure, or under fluorescent lights.

NOTES: Gardenia relative with tiny leaves like

## TERRARIUMS

Terrariums are enclosed or partially enclosed glass or plastic homes for indoor plants. Native woodland plants or tropical plants that are slow-growing and do not like direct sunlight are recommended for terrariums.

Old aquarium tanks, restaurant-size glass jars, and cut-down plastic soft drink bottles make excellent terrariums; seal them with covers, a piece of glass, or plastic wrap. Line the bottom first with coarse aquarium gravel for drainage, followed by a ½ inch layer of charcoal chips, sold in florist and hobby shops, then top with clean potting soil.

Combine plants of different shapes and textures—some bushy, some creeping—but always with similar moisture and light requirements. Add small rocks and pieces of gnarled wood for interest. Some houseplants that do well in terrariums are small ferns, miniature begonias, Venus's-flytrap (*Dionaea muscipula*), miniature African violets (*Saintpaulia*), miniature gloxinia (*Sinningia*), and miniature selections of streptocarpus, peperomia, and episcia.

Put plants in sparsely to allow room for them to grow. After planting, water with a fine spray until you can see by looking through the glass that the mixture is moist (not wet) to the bottom. There is little need to fertilize plants in terrariums. Pinch as necessary to keep plants compact. Sealed terrariums often require almost no watering. However, if the glass fogs, water pools in the bottom, or mold begins to form on plants or soil, the moisture level is too high, and you will need to remove the cover and ventilate the terrarium. Keep terrariums out of strong sunlight, which can cook the plants.

---

boxwood and double white flowers. Easily trained as tree-form standard or as a small bonsai. Several cultivars available, some with variegated leaves, some with single or pinkish flowers.

**Variegated Prostrate Gardenia,** *Gardenia jasminoides* 'Prostrata Variegata'
LIGHT: South or east exposure.
NOTES: Tiny leaves have creamy white margins; appropriately small fragrant flowers open intermittently all year. Needs high humidity.

## Further Reading

Chicago Botanic Garden. *Indoor Gardening.* New York: Pantheon Books, 1995.

Fitch, Charles Marden, ed. *Orchids for the Home and Greenhouse.* Brooklyn, N.Y.: Brooklyn Botanic Garden, 1997.

Hays, Robert M., and Janet Marinelli, eds. *Bulbs for Indoors.* Brooklyn, N.Y.: Brooklyn Botanic Garden, 1996.

McDonald, Elvin. *The New Houseplant: Bringing the Garden Indoors.* New York: Macmillan Publishers, 1993.

Martin, Tovah. *The Essence of Paradise: Fragrant Plants for Indoor Gardens.* Boston: Little, Brown and Co., 1991.

Martin, Tovah, ed. *A New Look at Houseplants.* Brooklyn, N.Y.: Brooklyn Botanic Garden, 1993.

Martin, Tovah, ed. *Greenhouses & Garden Rooms.* Brooklyn, N.Y.: Brooklyn Botanic Garden, 1990.

For information on how to contact various plant societies, see "Essential Resources," page 697.

# CITY
# GARDENING

Worldwide population patterns have changed dramatically over the last hundred years. In the past century more and more people have moved to urban areas, a trend that shows no signs of decelerating. Whereas in 1900 only 16 cities were home to more than a million people, today 400 cities around the globe have populations exceeding a million, and some are home to tens of millions of people.

City dwellers must adapt to landscapes composed mainly of asphalt, concrete, brick, glass, and metal, but urban life need not be a sentence to a gardenless life. Some city residences have access to a front or back garden, balcony, or rooftop, while others have a doorway or windowsill. All of these can be spruced up with a few choice potted plants.

City gardens bring with them their own set of challenges. Urban yards often have compacted, acidic, and contaminated soil with poor drainage. City soil can also sometimes be alkaline because it contains concrete in construction rubble. Many city gardens receive little sunlight and are subject to poor air circulation because they are surrounded by tall buildings or fences. Balconies, rooftops, and windowsills pose their own logistical problems. Apartment dwellers may have to haul bags and bags of soil up and down elevators or through carefully furnished living areas, and haul cans of water through the same obstacle courses. There is an additional challenge: city gardens of any type are likely to be small to extremely small in size.

With a little ingenuity and effort, however, these conditions can be overcome—and in some cases turned into assets—and an urban garden transformed into a fertile refuge from the pressures of modern life.

# The Urban Environment

As cities grow up and outward, they become ecosystems unto themselves, with an interplay of forces different from those in nearby areas. Asphalt and concrete absorb heat; vehicles emit chemicals and particulates into the air; and open areas become scattered, isolating populations of wildlife and plants. What follows is an outline of some of the conditions that are of greatest concern to the city gardener.

## Urban Soil

### Soil Compaction

City dwellers often inherit gardens with soil that has become quite compacted over time from the pressures of the human foot (one of the most efficient soil compactors) and vehicle traffic, and even from the vibrations caused by street traffic, construction, and mass transit. Soils closest to the source of the vibration—along the sides of roads and above subway tunnels, for example—become extremely compacted over time. The most compacted soils develop a hydrophobic crust, which is relatively impermeable; water is shed off the surface of this crust at a high rate, so little is absorbed for plants.

Those who construct tall buildings work intentionally to make the soil compacted, because it must support the weight of the massive structures. Using heavy machinery, construction crews compress city soil until it reaches a compaction value (usually 95 percent) that will hold great weight but usually not support plant growth. Roots may not be able to penetrate through this soil to seek out sources of nutrients.

Compacted soils have fewer pores between particles, and so can hold less air than healthy, aerated soils. This, too, is detrimental to plant roots, which need to draw in oxygen from the soil. Compacted soil also conducts heat better than uncompacted soil, another disadvantage for the roots of many plants. In addition, there are few earthworms and other organisms in compacted soil. Because these are the natural agents that loosen soil and increase its fertility, without human intervention the soil is likely to remain compacted.

### Soil Contamination

Urban soils are also likely to be chemically and physically contaminated. Chemical pollutants get into city soils when manufacturing by-products or trash are dumped onto vacant lots or other areas; through polluted air and rain; as pesticides are applied to the soil; and as de-icing salts spread on streets and sidewalks wash onto the soil.

Chemical contaminants found in urban areas often include heavy metals, which are generally very persistent in soil. Lead is the most common heavy metal in urban soils, followed by arsenic. Cadmium, chromium, copper, mercury, nickel, and zinc are also commonly found. Concentrations of heavy metals are highest along roadsides, where gasoline, motor oil, and other vehicle-related pollutants accumulate. Heavy metals get into soil through a number of other routes as well—electroplating activities and discarded batteries, for example.

Roadsides are also where a huge quantity of de-icing substances, commonly salts such as sodium chloride and calcium chloride, end up. These are spread on roads and sidewalks in increasing amounts each year—as much as 88 million tons are applied annually nationwide. These salts are harmful to plants for a number of reasons. They replace other cations (positively charged chemical elements) on negatively charged sites on the surface of soil particles where nutrients are held. Plants exchange positively charged hydrogen ions, a waste product, at these sites for other positively charged substances, including the important nutrients calcium, magnesium, and potassium. Because salts change soil chemistry and pH, they can also stimulate the release of heavy metals if these are chemically bound to soil particles. These toxic substances are then free to be absorbed by plants or to be picked up as water moves through the soil. Salts also decrease soil's osmotic potential—water tends to move from plant roots to the saltier soil environment—so less water is available to plants. They contaminate waterways where they can be toxic to aquatic life. And when they are sprayed from de-icing trucks and are kicked up by automobile and truck tires, splashing onto vegetation, salts cause plants to develop witches' brooms, an abnormal growth of shoots from one point on a branch.

Sewage sludge is sometimes applied to soils as an amendment, but it can contain heavy metals flushed into treatment systems by small industries. Many treatment plants use lime to stabilize the sludge, which makes it extremely alkaline and which can cause nutrient imbalances when soil becomes alkaline following application.

Pesticides are sprayed in large quantities in urban areas. Along the East Coast, urban soils contain concentrations of persistent organochlorine pesticides higher even than those on nearby agricultural land.

Construction debris, including brick, concrete, asphalt, building stone, glass, plastic, iron, steel, and aluminum, is also common in city soils. Some of these materials can eventually break down in the soil, while others, such as glass, are much slower to disintegrate. Rubble can obstruct root growth and make soils highly permeable and therefore unable to retain water.

## The Urban Climate

### The Heat-Island Effect

The physical reality of the city—the large proportion of paved area; the dearth of respiring plants releasing cooling moisture into the air; the many huge, heat-generating buildings and heat-generating cars and machines; the heavy concentrations of heat-trapping air pollutants—creates an effect called a "heat island." Urban areas tend to be warmer, usually by 2°F to 8°F, than the surrounding areas. This effect is most obvious during the hot summer months, when buildings, paving, and concrete absorb a great deal of solar radiation and release the stored energy during the night.

The intensity of the heat island is linked to the size of the city. In very large cities, the effect is more exaggerated; New York City can be as much as 10°F warmer than its suburbs. In tropical areas this temperature difference can be even more extreme: Mexico City is sometimes 18°F hotter than outlying areas.

The heat-island effect is linked to other peculiarities of the urban climate. The higher temperatures lead to an increase of 5 to 15 percent in precipitation over cities. Wind speeds can be reduced by as much as 30 percent by the physical structures of cities, and consequently heat that would otherwise be blown away by breezes hovers over urban areas. Only when wind speeds reach 12 miles per hour does the heat island begin to dissipate.

The practical effect of the higher temperatures prevalent in cities is that the soil thaws earlier in the spring, and gardeners have extended frost-free seasons. It is possible to plant annuals earlier in the city than in surrounding areas. In central London, for example, the active growing season is about three weeks longer than it is in open areas near the city; the frost-free period is 10 weeks longer. In the United States, magnolias grow in Boston, far north of their natural range.

## Reduced Exposure to Sunlight

Plants in urban areas tend to have less access to sunlight. Many city gardens must make do with the shade cast by neighboring buildings. Gardens to the north of tall buildings get the least sunlight. In addition, air pollution can limit the amount of solar radiation that reaches the ground (see below). The overall reduced level of sunlight has a major impact on the sorts of plants that will grow in city gardens.

# Air Pollution

Because people are concentrated in cities, cars, trucks, buses, and industrial activities tend to be concentrated there as well, and levels of air pollutants are consequently higher. Automobile and industrial emissions with relatively well understood impacts on plants include sulfur dioxide ($SO_2$), nitrogen oxides ($NO_x$), the photochemicals ozone and peroxyacetyl nitrate, fluorides, and chlorine compounds. Suspended particulates from emissions can reduce the amount of sunlight that reaches the earth and hence plants.

While studies of the effects of air pollutants on plants are somewhat scarce and have focused mostly on agricultural crops, plants are known to absorb air pollutants, many of which are damaging to them. Lichens are very vulnerable to air pollutants, and are rarely found in urban areas. In fact, cities often are called "lichen deserts." Mosses are also sensitive, and found less frequently in cities.

Trees that are especially susceptible to damage by air pollutants include Douglas fir, eastern white pine, larch, Norway spruce, ponderosa pine, and Scots pine. Ornamental plants and vegetables known to be vulnerable include coleus, petunias, gladioli, beans, potatoes, and tomatoes.

# Plant Life

In cities, populations of native plants are greatly reduced, while many introduced species thrive in the disturbed urban environment. Cities historically have been the point at which people arrived from distant lands, bringing with them, either accidentally or intentionally, nonnative seeds and plants. Researchers in Brooklyn Botanic Garden's New York Metropolitan Flora project have found that once native bearberry (*Arctostaphylos urva-ursi*) and native orchids including *Arethusa bulbosa* have most likely disappeared from the city while nonnatives such as ailanthus have flourished.

A study published in the *Bulletin of the Torrey Botanical Club* analyzed the interaction of native and nonnative species in the wake of urban development. In it, three biologists at Rutgers University found that since 1879 the native flora of Staten Island, a 70-square-mile borough of New York City, has been drastically reduced: more than 40 percent of the native species are now missing. Nonindigenous species, meanwhile, are becoming an increasingly dominant part of the island's plant life, increasing from 19 to 33 percent of the flora.

## Coping with City Conditions

Against all the odds described above, cities are dotted with individual and community gardens. City-dwellers, like people everywhere, need and enjoy the feel and smell of good soil, the satisfaction of creating a spot where something can grow, and the chance to eat something they have nurtured themselves. Below, some solutions to the challenges facing the urban gardener are outlined.

### Improving Urban Soil

One of the first steps toward making city soil fertile is to understand it. Have the soil tested to determine its pH and other characteristics and whether it should be improved with various amendments. The addition of lime, for example, will make acidic soil more hospitable for vegetables and ornamental plants. Compost or rotted manure are especially important additions to most city soils, which tend to be bereft of organic matter; they help soil retain moisture, improve its structure, and provide slowly released nutrients for plants. (For more information on amending garden soil, see page 430.) Soil can take up heavy metals as they are released into the air from car and truck exhaust, from paint that flakes off old city buildings, and from industrial activity. Lead in particular is a concern in urban neighborhoods because it was used in paints and gasoline for many years. Children can suffer developmental problems from exposure to lead and, for the same reason, pregnant women should be cautious about their exposure to it.

If possible, choose a site for your garden that is not near a heavily trafficked highway or street. You can also erect a fence or plant a hedge to shield vegetables from lead particles that may be moving through the air from a roadway. If your vegetable garden is on the site of a demolished pre–World War II building, lead-contaminated paint chips may be in the soil. In this case, and if you must plant your vegetables close to a busy roadway, it may be a good idea to test the soil for lead. If you find that your soil contains high levels of lead, wear gloves while gardening, wash hands afterward and before eating, and make sure that children do not have a chance to ingest the soil directly from the garden. Airborne lead can be washed off vegetables with a solution of 1 part vinegar to 99 parts water and 0.5 percent dishwashing liquid (1 tablespoon of vinegar and ½ tablespoon of dishwashing liquid in 1½ quarts of water). Then rinse with clear water. If you are growing root vegetables such as beets, carrots, turnips, and carrots, peel off the outer layer before eating, as whatever lead is absorbed will become concentrated there and in the leaves. Vegetables that produce edible fruits, including tomatoes, peppers, cucumbers, squash, etc., will not concentrate lead in the fruits and so are considered safe to eat when grown in soil that contains lead. You can also concentrate on growing ornamental rather than edible plants if heavy metals are likely to be a problem in your yard.

If your garden consists of a shallow layer of earth sitting on top of rubble-filled soil or impenetrable clay, consider building raised beds, 18 to 24 inches high. The base of the raised beds should be lined with a layer of gravel or broken brick to provide proper drainage. This should be topped with garden soil mixed with compost, sand to create adequate drainage, and bonemeal, which contains phosphorous and stimulates root formation; bonemeal is good for bulbs, fruit trees, and perennials. Or you can dig out this poor soil to a depth of 18 to 24 inches and fill the hole with improved soil along the lines of that suggested above. Soils that cannot be improved to this depth can still support hardy ground covers, and other plants can be grown in containers. If your soil can be worked but is compacted, poorly drained, and acidic, add lime.

Small gardens are likely to be cultivated intensively and consequently should be fed well. Organic liquid fertilizers are available and are especially suited to small spaces. Mulching with straw or other organic mulches will help the soil retain moisture and continue to improve the soil's fertility over time. (See page 464 for more information on mulching.)

## Working with Shade

Another important first step in city gardening is determining the amount of sunlight that reaches the garden, during which parts of the day, and for how long. Over the course of the year, the light will change as the sun moves to its height in summer and closer to the horizon in winter, and as surrounding deciduous trees gain and lose their foliage. If your garden is oriented toward the south, you will probably receive a good deal of sun, while those facing north receive the least. West-facing gardens get the warm afternoon sun and so can welcome sun-loving plants, but the cool shade in east-facing gardens can allow many beautiful shade plants to thrive.

Once you have determined the maximum amount of light in your garden, start looking for plants that will thrive there. Plants designated by nurseries and catalogs as those that will do well in partial shade can stand from 4 to 6 hours of direct sun. If you don't get that much light, look for plants that can tolerate shade.

In some situations it is possible to increase the amount of sunlight reaching the garden by

selectively pruning tree limbs. If the limbs of a neighbor's tree spread over the garden, it is legal in most localities to remove any or all of the overhanging branches. In many cases, however, the obstructions are tall buildings or trees that are out of reach, and there is not much that can be done other than painting surrounding walls or fences white to reflect light onto plants, or strategically hanging mirrors in the landscape for the same purpose.

While there are fewer flowering plants that love shade than that love light, there are plenty of choices for the shaded garden. Woodland plants are especially suited to shady areas. Shade cast by city trees and structures creates a forestlike setting to which many woodland plants, especially understory trees, shrubs, wildflowers, and ferns that grow naturally in the shelter of tall canopy trees, are adapted. In natural forests, the soil generally is moist and airy—that is, filled with organic matter—and the roots of the plants that live in these habitats run freely through it. Adjust soil characteristics to meet the needs of shade-loving species, and mulch the plantings liberally. Nature renews the mulch in woodlands each autumn as the plants lose their leaves. Shady gardens likewise benefit from mulching.

### Plants for Shade

See "Woodland Gardens," pages 184–192, and "Plants for Every Purpose and Every Region," pages 297–384, for extensive lists of shade-loving plants organized by region.

## Small Plants for Small Spaces

Dwarf and compact plants are often the ideal solution for the small city garden. These include dwarf evergreen trees and shrubs,

## DWARF AND COMPACT AND ROCK-GARDEN PLANTS

*Aethionema* 'Warley Rose', persian candytuft
*Anemone patens* (*Pulsatilla vulgaris*), pasque flower
*Aquilegia bertolonii* and *A. saximontana*, columbine
*Arenaria montana*, mountain sandwort
*Aster alpinus*, aster
*Astilbe chinensis* 'Pumila', astilbe
*Campanula barbata*, *C. carpatica*, and *C. garganica*, campanula
*Chrysanthemum weyrichii*, chrysanthemum
*Cotoneaster apiculatus* 'Tom Thumb', cotoneaster
*Cyclamen coum* and *C. hederifolium*, cyclamen
*Daphne arbuscula* and *D. cneorum pygmaea* 'Alba', daphne
*Dianthus* 'Tiny Rubies' and 'Little Joe' and *D. microlepsis* and *D. simulans*, dianthus
*Edraianthus pumilio*, bellflower
*Erigeron alpinus*, Alpine fleabane
*Erinus alpinus* 'Alba', fairy foxglove
*Gentiana scabra*, *G. septemfida* and *G. verna*, gentian
*Geranium dalmaticum* and *G. renardii*, geranium

*Iris cristata* and *I. tectorum*, iris
*Penstemon davidsonii*, *P. rupicola*, and *P. hirsutus* 'Pygmaeus', penstemon
*Phlox subulata* and *P. bifida*, phlox
*Primula auricula*, primula
*Saxifraga* 'Peter Pan', rock-foil

### MINIATURE ROSES

'Cinderella'
'Dresden Doll'
'Green Ice'
'Little Artist'
'Mountie'
'Rise 'n Shine'
'Rouletii'
'Sachet'
'Si'
'Teddy Bear'

alpines, heathers, miniature bulbs, dwarf fruit trees, miniature roses, and small-scale annuals and vegetables. These can be grown in the ground or in containers. For specific plant recommendations, see the regional lists of trees for small spaces beginning on page 288; the lists of choice trees, shrubs, perennials, annuals, and vegetables for growing in containers beginning on page 497; and the list of fruits suited to pot culture on page 283.

## Hedges, Fences, and Arbors

City gardens often are exposed to the gaze of neighbors to the sides, the rear, and above. By adding hedges, fences, and/or arbors, gardeners can increase their privacy and perhaps reduce noise to some extent. Keep in mind, however, that if these structures are tall, they may create a tunnel effect in a long yard, and they also add shade, something many city gardens already have in abundance. Many cities require permits for the installation of fences, and most have limits on the height of the fence that can be installed—generally 6 or 7 feet.

Different fencing materials make sense in different garden settings. Chain-link fences are not necessarily attractive but allow sun and air to circulate through the garden and can be obscured with attractive climbers. Solid fences painted white or a pale shade maximize reflected light. Woven and bamboo fences make handsome natural backgrounds for many plants, and picket fences can add a classic touch to a traditional or heirloom garden.

Hedges are another option for enclosing a yard and can be clipped for a formal look or allowed to grow loosely, depending on the plant and the garden's mood. Flowering quince makes an unusual hedge for a rooftop garden, while Lombardy poplars will provide a tall hedge. Evergreen hedges can be created with upright yews or hollies. The classic box and some dwarf shrubs make good, low hedges for small city yards. For a list of recommended hedge plants, see page 514.

By adding an arbor or pergola to a yard, the gardener can extend the house into the garden and create a shaded outdoor room. These structures provide support for plants such as grapes, kiwis, and other vines with edible fruits as well as many flowering climbers. Plant the vines at least 9 inches away from the wall or fence, as the adjacent soil tends to remain dry.

## Types of City Gardens

### Rooftop Gardens

A rooftop is often one of the few very sunny places to garden in an urban setting. But a rooftop garden has its own set of challenges. Its exposed position makes a rooftop vulnerable to high winds and extreme temperatures, and it can be difficult to get soil and other gardening materials and water up to the garden.

One of the most important things to consider when planning a rooftop landscape is whether the roof itself is strong enough to support the weight of a garden. Another major consideration is to avoid the problems that can

occur when containers or structures compress the roofing material in one spot, creating a hollow where water can collect and cause further damage. The soundest way to ensure that a garden and its containers can be supported by the roof and that they will not damage it is to build a raised wooden platform whose main supporting elements rest on the building's load-bearing walls. This structural frame can hold a surface of removable decking panels. Avoid surfacing the roof using heavy paving materials, which can put too much stress on the structure.

You can also garden on the rooftop in containers, but carefully monitor the state of the roofing material below the containers over time. Most roofs are designed to hold 30 to 40 pounds per square foot; containers with 12 inches of soil usually meet these weight requirements. Move them around the roof frequently to avoid compressing the roof in any one spot and situate most of the containers around the edge of the roof to distribute the weight on load-bearing walls. This will also create a sense of open space at the center of the garden. Lead- or bituminous-clad roofs attached to a wooden frame can hold less weight than other types of roofs—20 to 30 pounds per square foot—and may not be appropriate for gardening. Rooftop garden plans should always be checked by a structural engineer to ensure that the building can support the added weight.

It can be difficult getting water up to the rooftop, and this consideration should also be factored into the garden design. Installing a faucet at roof level—ideally, hooked up to an automated and water-conserving drip irrigation system—will eliminate water waste as well as the need for carrying heavy buckets of water up and down.

## Lightweight Soil

The first rooftop gardeners used to dump the soil right on the roof and plant. Years of experience have shown that plantings should always be in containers. What is more, the containers should always be filled with lightweight soil. A good recipe for lightweight soil is 1 part topsoil, 5 parts perlite or vermiculite (lighteners), and 5 parts compost. This mix contains enough humus to support the microorganisms that make soil healthy and enough lighteners to lessen the load on your rooftop. For more information on growing plants in pots, see "Container Gardens," below, and "Gardening in Containers," pages 493–503.

## Windbreaks

Conditions on a roof are likely to be much windier and colder than they would be at ground level. One solution is a framework of wind- and cold-tolerant shrubs that will shelter more vulnerable annuals and perennials. Trellises covered with climbers also can create privacy and break the intensity of the wind. Be sure to secure trellises and other structures, as exposed rooftops are prone to high winds.

## Hardy Plants

The best solution to the extreme conditions on rooftops is to choose only plants that grow in similar situations in the wild: arid, open fields, prairies, and meadows. Plants adapted to these habitats will tolerate harsh rooftop conditions: in the summer, bright sun, high temperatures, drying winds—and little water, and in the winter, biting winds and bitter cold. See pages 206–209 for an extensive listing of prairie plants.

Gardeners have discovered that the growing season often is considerably shorter on the roof than on the ground; trees can leaf out weeks later and show fall color weeks earlier than trees just several stories down. What is more, the roots of container-grown plants are subject to freezing from the sides, up from the bottom, or down from the top. Rooftop plants must be hardy. In general, it is a good idea to choose plants that would survive in at least one USDA hardiness zone colder than the official ground-level zone for the area. Drought tolerance is another essential consideration when choosing rooftop plants. Watering can involve a staggering amount of time and effort, particularly in late summer when the plants have filled the containers with roots below and transpiring foliage above.

## Balcony Gardens

City dwellers often have a balcony off one or more of their rooms. As with rooftop gardens, weight is an important consideration on a balcony. Most can hold 30 to 40 pounds per square foot, and therefore containers 12 to 15 inches deep. Most balconies open off of a room and should be treated as an extension of this room. Therefore, unlike window boxes, which are typically viewed from the outside, balconies should be planted with specimens that face inward and can be admired from indoors. Adjustable awnings can shade very exposed balconies, and foliage plants will flourish on very shady balconies.

## Container Gardens

Growing plants in containers is a practical solution for many of the problems confronting city gardeners. The amount of soil needed for a respectable container garden is a fraction of that needed for an entire yard. Containers can be moved to follow the sun, and they can be used to create lush gardens on rooftops, balconies, and other confined spaces. Hanging baskets offer small, movable, and vertical gardens.

Just about any container can be used as a planter as long as water can drain out through a hole in the bottom. Include 2 inches of porous material in the bottom of large containers—gravel or potsherds, for example—for drainage. The minimum soil depth needed by most large plants is 12 to 18 inches, while trees and large shrubs need even more.

A rule of thumb for containers used on decks or balconies is that the container plus plant and soil should not be heavier than the average gardener can lift. Containers made of wood should have walls at least 2 inches thick so that they'll withstand a lot of wear and tear and should have air space at the bottom and holes for water drainage. Terra cotta pots will lose moisture to the air more readily than wood or plastic and crack when the soil freezes and thaws. A coat of silicone sealer or varnish will help terra cotta retain moisture.

For more information on gardening in containers, see page 493. Containers on rooftops and balconies require lightweight soil, which is discussed in "Rooftop Gardens," above.

All containers, especially hanging baskets and small pots and those on exposed balconies and rooftops, will dry out quickly in hot, dry weather and should be watered deeply every day during July and August, and whenever there is little rain. Soil in containers that is allowed to dry out will shrink away from the sides of the pot, and the water will run through this gap rather than through the soil, leaving plants high and dry. Gently break up the surface of the soil to create openings for the water to penetrate.

## Window Boxes

Almost any window, whether shaded or sunny, can accommodate a window box. These should be as large as possible so that plants have room to expand. They should be well secured with brackets to the side of the building, and within easy reach of the window so that they can be watered and maintained easily. Boxes are available in many materials including wood, plastic, ceramic, and concrete. Wood boxes should be placed a bit away from the side of the building so that air can circulate freely around the entire box to deter rot.

Before planting a new window box, clean it thoroughly. Water plants fully before planting in moist soil. Add compost each year to an established box, and feed periodically during the growing season. Window boxes need to be tended carefully and watered daily, especially in the dry summer months, as the soil will dry out quickly.

Window boxes look best if planted closely. To ensure color in early spring, plant with bulbs the preceding fall. Remove the bulbs before planting for summer. Remove spent flowers to encourage further bloom. Plant with herbs or small vegetable plants for color and an edible harvest. Window boxes will absorb heat from the side of the building, so plants bloom earlier and survive later into the season.

For more on gardening in window boxes, including recommended plants, see page 502.

## Fruit and Vegetable Gardens

Vegetables and fruits tend to be harder to grow in city gardens than in larger, sunnier spots, as most require 6 or 8 hours of sunlight a day to bear fruit, as well as space to spread out and expand. But many varieties are avail-

## SURVIVOR STREET TREES

Trees make city life more bearable—and not just aesthetically. Besides beautifying the city and providing necessary habitat for birds and wildlife, they also help purify the air, replenish groundwater supplies, and reduce storm-water runoff. They help reduce urban noise and glare, and conserve energy by blocking wind and providing much-needed shade. But street trees are in a constant struggle to survive. Four urban trees die for each one planted; the average downtown street tree may have a life expectancy of just seven years. Severely restricted root space, poor soils and poor drainage, salts used for winter de-icing, and extreme heat and low humidity all contribute to stress for street trees. If you're planting a street tree, here are a few steps to help ensure that it will survive:

• Site it properly. Avoid sites with nearby buildings and underground structures that will restrict the tree's canopy and root growth. Most trees need full sun; if the site is partially shaded, select a tree that will tolerate some shade.

• Check out the soil. Street trees need good drainage. To test drainage at the site you're considering, dig a hole as deep as the tree's root ball, fill the hole with water, and time how long it takes to drain. Adequate drainage is at least 1 inch per hour. Avoid areas where de-icing salt will be a problem, or select a tree that will tolerate salt.

• Select the right tree and plant it properly. Some trees that can tolerate environmental stress are listed below. For additional recommendations, contact your county Cooperative Extension office. Follow the steps outlined on pages 450–453 for proper tree planting. Mulching is particularly important for urban trees.

## MORE TIPS FOR CITY GARDENERS

• Deemphasize awkward spaces. If the garden is surrounded by high walls, add trellises for climbers. Break up long, narrow city plots into smaller, less linear gardens with hedges, small trees, or large shrubs and connect them with paths—angled for formal gardens or meandering for informal gardens. Use raised decking to add changes of level.

• Add a water element. The soothing sound of water recirculated through a small wall fountain can make a city garden more inviting.

• Be creative when choosing plants. White flowered plants will show up well in a shady garden, and add a glow to gardens enjoyed mostly after dark. A few magnificent specimens, such as a clipped topiary or small weeping tree, add living sculpture to the small city garden. Lush hardy ferns can show off in densely shaded spots.

• Consider lawn alternatives. Turfgrass wastes precious planting space in small gardens, and in any case struggles in the shade of most city landscapes. If an open area is required, substitute a patio. In sunny areas, a creeping ground cover such as chamomile or thyme can be a fragrant lawn substitute.

• Try terracing. In the right spot, a stepped garden composed of a series of containers or walls can enlarge the garden area and add visual interest. As with all containers, these should be sturdy, resist rot, and be deep enough to hold a proper amount of soil. Plant densely with ground covers.

• Add window boxes, wall pots, and half baskets to garden walls to increase the planting area.

able that will grow in less-than-optimal city conditions.

Compact or miniature forms of many plants are available, including tomatoes, corn, carrots, and some vining vegetables such as squash, cucumbers, and melons are produced with shorter internodes between the fruiting stems for a higher yield per plant. The harvest from a dwarf fruit tree can be quite abundant.

Small carrots, radishes, onions, and lettuces adapt well to window boxes, while tomatoes, squash, cucumbers, eggplants, and peppers adapt well to large tubs and containers. Planting in containers, which can be moved from spot to spot to follow the sun during the day, can also make the most of sunlight. See "Container Gardening," pages 493–503, and "Growing Fruits in Containers," page 283, for more information on growing fruits and vegetables in containers, including recommended varieties.

Many plants can be trained vertically to maximize growing space. Espalier is one particularly useful space-saving technique adaptable to city gardens; see page 515.

See the discussion on page 601 on lead and other heavy metals as they affect vegetable gardening in the city.

## Street Trees

City dwellers may not think of the sidewalk and its plantings as a part of the garden, but by planting a tree, especially in the front of a building, gardeners can make their street more inviting while contributing to the cooling of the city by providing shade and moisture from transpiring leaves.

City trees reduce some of the effects of the heat island, buffer noise, and can remove a certain amount of air pollutants—up to 75 per-

---

### STREET TREES FOR DRY SOILS

*Celtis occidentalis*, common hackberry
*Crataegus* species, hawthorns
*Eucommia ulmoides*, hardy rubber tree
*Ginkgo biloba*, ginkgo
*Koelreuteria paniculata*, goldenrain tree
*Quercus muehlenbergii*, chinkapin oak
*Sophora japonica*, Japanese pagoda tree—also tolerates salt

### STREET TREES FOR WET SOILS WITH POOR DRAINAGE

*Alnus glutinosa*, European alder
*Betula nigra*, river birch
*Fraxinus pennsylvanica*, green ash
*Nyssa sylvatica*, tupelo
*Platanus × acerifolia*, London plane
*Quercus bicolor*, swamp white oak
*Taxodium distichum*, bald cypress

### STREET TREES THAT TOLERATE SALT

*Acer campestre*, hedge maple
*Acer pseudoplatanus*, sycamore maple
*Caragana arborescens*, Siberian pea-shrub
*Robinia pseudoacacia*, black locust
*Sophora japonica*, Japanese pagoda tree

---

cent of the coarser particles—from the air, besides making city streets visually pleasing. However, conditions in the city are very tough on trees. Their average lifespan is just a few years, and for each tree planted in urban areas around the country, four are removed.

The roots of trees planted in sidewalk "pits" are often crowded by physical barriers, and must cope with salt-laden, generally inhospitable soil. Their stunted roots cannot draw enough water and other important nutrients from the soil. City trees are also subject to relatively higher temperatures and often relatively little sunlight.

City gardeners can improve a street tree's chances by watering it often and deeply. Small trees require 10 gallons of water every 5 days during dry, hot spells. To protect street trees against salt pollution, plant them in raised beds, which puts them above street level and increases the soil rooting volume.

## Further Reading

Craul, Phillip J. *Urban Soil in Landscape Design.* New York: John Wiley & Sons, Inc., 1992.

Davis, Becke. *Small Gardens: Inspired Plantings for Diminutive Spaces.* New York: Friedman/Fairfax, 1997.

Fawcett, Brian. *The Compact Garden: Discovering the Pleasures of Planting in Small Spaces.* East Camden, Ont.: Camden House, 1992.

Yang, Linda. *The City Gardener's Handbook: From Balcony to Backyard.* New York: Random House, 1990.

Yang, Linda, ed. *The Town and City Gardener.* Brooklyn, N.Y. Brooklyn Botanic Garden, 1992.

# 12

# GARDEN TOOLS

arden tools have evolved over eons from the rudimentary instruments our ancestors used to cultivate their crops to the incredible range of items now available—from left-handed pruners to stainless steel widgers. You will need at least several basic tools (see the box on page 619); the rest of your selection depends on the nature of your soil, the plants you choose, the size of your garden, and the size of your tool budget. Whatever tools you decide to buy, make sure that each is made of the most durable materials, with the strongest joints—where metal and wood meet, for example. Below is a description of many of the garden tools available today at garden centers and hardware stores and from gardening catalogs.

## Tools for Digging

### Bulb Planter

This metal cylinder is pushed into the soil and brings up a plug of soil, leaving behind a hole for a bulb, plug of grass, or sod. The dibble, a pointed tool, is also used for making holes for bulbs, but because of its small pointed tip can also be used to transplant seedlings and other small plants.

### Edger

This long-handled tool with a semicircular flat metal blade is used to neaten the edges of a lawn along beds, walkways, and buildings. (It is also called an edging knife, half-moon edger, lawn edge trimmer, and hand edger.) The rotary edger has a wheel on one end with sharp cutting teeth. The teeth do the edging as the wheel is rolled along the ground.

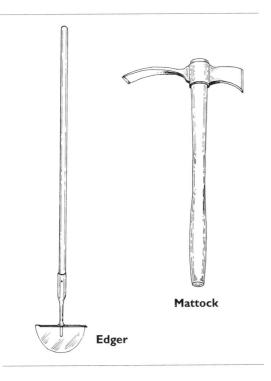

**Mattock**

**Edger**

## Fork

Several types of long-handled forks are used in the garden. The garden fork (also called a digging or English garden fork) has a head 7 to 8 inches wide with four flat or squared tines. This is a good all-purpose fork used to loosen and mix soil, lift plants, and dig root vegetables. The manure fork (also known as a stable fork and apple picker) has more tines, up to sixteen, which are round and pointed and finer than those of the garden fork; this tool is designed for lifting manure and other fine material. The spading fork (also called a turning or border fork) has four flat tines and is lighter and smaller than a garden fork. This is useful for working heavy clay soil, lifting plants, and harvesting root vegetables. The pitchfork (also known as a farm, hay, and Kansas header fork) has three to five round tapered tines and is used

to lift straw, hay, and leaf mold. A spiking fork is similar to a garden fork but has shorter tines and is used to aerate lawns.

## Mattock

This chopping tool is a hybrid of a hoe and an ax, and is useful for cutting through heavy roots, digging up tree stumps, and breaking up hard ground. Mattocks usually have an ax or pick on one end of the head and a hoe on the other.

## Posthole Digger

As the name suggests, this tool is designed to dig holes for fence posts and supports for garden structures, and also to dig holes for pit composting. The clamshell digger, two digging blades hinged together on two long handles, is the most common type of posthole digger. The user thrusts the blades into the ground, and pulls the handles apart, tightening the blades together like two halves of a clamshell around the plug of soil, which is then pulled from the ground.

## Shovel

Shovels comes in a range of designs for a variety of uses. Pointed shovels (also known by the names round-nose, dirt, and American-pattern shovels) with long handles are useful, general-purpose tools for the excavation of beds and holes for trees and shrubs, and for working compost into the soil. A shovel is a must-have tool for the garden. Shovels with narrow blades are useful for digging small trenches. Square point shovels have square blades that make lifting sand easy. Scoop shovels have broad rectangular blades that are useful for moving light materials like leaves.

## Spade

Like the shovel, the spade has a metal blade and wooden handle, but the handle is shorter and the blade is always rectangular and practically flat. Spades are used for digging holes and ditches, cutting edges, and myriad other chores. The garden or digging spade is the most common type, with a long, usually 12-inch blade and footrests at the top of the blade. The border spade is a smaller, easy-to-use spade useful for transplanting and for children and older gardeners. The tree-planting spade has a very long blade and wide footrest and, as its name suggests, is designed to make it easy to dig deep holes for trees and shrubs.

## Trowel

The trowel is a hand tool with a handle and small, shovel-like blade or scoop used for planting, transplanting, and moving soil in garden beds and containers. Trowels made in one piece from steel or aluminum or other alloys are very durable as there is no chance of the handle coming apart from the blade. V-shaped and narrow blades are excellent for planting bulbs and digging out weeds. Buy a brightly colored trowel or put bright tape around the handle to make it more visible and less likely to be lost among the plants in the garden.

# Tools for Cultivating, Weeding, and Raking

## Hoes

The hoe is a very useful all-around tool, and it has many variations. Gardeners use it for weeding, cultivating soil, and digging rows for seeds. Hoes generally have a long handle and a metal blade at something like a right angle to the handle. The basic garden hoe has a rectangular 6-inch by 4-inch blade and is used for working around delicate plants and in small pots. The eye hoe has a shorter handle and deeper, heavier blade and is designed for cutting roots and breaking up dense soil. The onion hoe has a wider, shallower blade—about 7 inches wide and 2 inches deep—with a sharpened edge. It is useful for eliminating small weeds. The scuffle hoe has a wide range of blade shapes—curved, triangular, rectangular, diamond-shaped—and is sharp on several sides of the blade so that it can be worked with a push-pull motion. It is useful for cutting weeds at the roots. The blade of the prong hoe, which can have a short or long handle, has two ends; one is basically a small garden hoe and the other has from two to four prongs. Gardeners use the pronged end to get in close to plants to pry out weeds.

## Hand Fork

This tool is similar to a table fork—it has three or four straight, flat tines—but unlike the table fork it has a short wooden or plastic handle. The hand fork is useful for cultivating the soil in small gardens and spots where it is awkward to work with bigger tools.

## Rotary Tiller

The rotary tiller (also called rototiller and power tiller) has a series of tined wheels that are spun by a gas or electric motor; as they spin, they cultivate the soil and work organic matter into the soil's upper 4 to 8 inches. Gardeners use the labor-saving rotary tiller in the spring to prepare beds or in the fall to turn crops or compost into the soil. Two types of rotary tillers are available: rear-tined and front-tined. Those with tines in the rear are heavier and designed for harder gardening jobs such as breaking ground that has not been cultivated before or working dense clay or rocky soils. Front-tined machines are designed for sandy or loamy soils and smaller jobs.

## Wheeled Cultivator

Like a rotary tiller, the wheeled cultivator is used to break up and aerate soil, and mix in amendments such as compost. This tool, also called a spiked-wheel cultivator, rotary cultivator, and star harrow, is usually a long-handled tool that ends in from two to sixteen revolving wheels with tines. As the cultivator is pushed along the ground, the wheels rotate and the tines break up the soil. It is best used for opening new garden sites and creating long garden rows.

## Asparagus Knife

This basic weeder, also called a fishtail weeder, has a long metal shaft that ends in a flat V-shaped head, attached to a handle. It is used for targeted weeding: the head is pushed into the soil under a weed such as a dandelion, to get at its long root without disturbing nearby plants and surrounding soil.

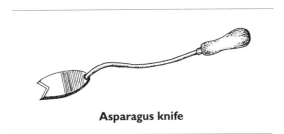

**Asparagus knife**

## Rakes

The lawn rake, also called a broom rake, leaf rake, and spring lawn rake, is a lightweight, fan-shaped rake with a long handle and bamboo, stainless steel, or plastic tines; it is very handy for gathering leaves, twigs, grass clippings, and other light materials from the lawn and garden. Soak bamboo rakes in soapy water at the beginning of the season so that they regain their flexibility. The bowhead rake has a row of short, stainless steel tines and is used for leveling a lawn, breaking up soil, and gathering debris. The back of the rake head is flat, so it is useful for smoothing uneven patches in the soil. The leveling rake has a very long head—up to 2½ feet—with sharpened wooden dowels or aluminum or magnesium teeth as tines. This rake is useful for leveling the ground for seeding a lawn or seed bed and for gathering grass clippings, leaves, and hay.

# Tools for Pruning, Cutting, and Trimming

## Pruning Shears

Pruning shears, also called secateurs and pruning snips, resemble pliers or scissors and are designed to trim small branches and twigs from trees and shrubs, as well as flowering plants. The most versatile type of pruning shears are curved bypass shears; these have a curved lower blade that hooks around the branch to stabilize it, and a curved upper blade that closes down on and cuts through the branch when the shears are closed. Straight bypass shears (also known as thinning shears, grape shears, and mini shears) look more like scissors, with straight blades, and are appropriate for lighter tasks. Anvil shears have one cutting blade and a flat-faced "anvil," on which the cutting blade closes when the handles are squeezed together. Ratchet anvil pruners allow the gardener to apply extra force to the cut; they are designed for use on tough woody plants, and the blade is less likely to bend under stress than the blade on bypass shears. The blades on all pruners should be kept sharpened, and the spring and pivot should be oiled often.

## Lopping Shears

These pruning tools, also called two-handed pruning shears, are very similar to pruning shears, but are long-handled, allowing the gardener greater leverage for cutting branches as thick as 1½ inches. Like pruning shears, loppers are designed with both anvil and bypass action (see page 614). The bypass loppers make cleaner, closer cuts.

## Hedge and Grass Shears

Hedge shears have long blades designed to cut through many tender stems of hedge plants at the same time. Most also have a notch below the point where the blades are pivoted together for cutting larger branches. For bigger jobs, power hedge shears, which run on gasoline or electricity, may be appropriate. The long blade of the power shears has many sharp sets of teeth that slide past each other, cutting through the hedge. Grass shears are either manual or powered by batteries, and are useful for cutting grass that grows next to trees, fences, and other structures where a lawn mower cannot go. Manual grass shears have handles that squeeze together vertically with a pump action, causing the blades to cut horizontally. Battery-powered shears have two sets of teeth that slide past each other, and make sense for light trimming jobs.

## Trimmers

Several types of trimmers are available. Like some types of shears, they are designed to cut unruly plants that other types of tools, such as lawn mowers, cannot reach. String trimmers (also called line trimmers), either gas- or battery-powered, are equipped with a nylon cord that spins at a high speed, whipping off the tops of grass or weeds, and cutting an 8- to 17-inch-diameter swath. Wear protective goggles when using a string trimmer.

## Saws

The smallest gardening saw is a folding pruning saw, which has a blade that folds into the handle. The edge tends to last longer than that of other saws, as it is protected inside the handle. Most pruning saws have long teeth that are designed to cut on the pull stroke; some models have teeth on the top and bottom of the saw, with coarse teeth on one side and fine teeth on the other. The long-reach pole saw and lopper allows the gardener to prune without climbing into the tree. The saw and lopping tool are mounted on the end of a long pole and are controlled by a lever attached to a cord. Chain saws, powered by gas or electricity, are used for cutting very large branches and small trees, but can be very dangerous and should be used only by gardeners with training or experience. Always wear protective goggles and earplugs when using this equipment.

## Folding Pruning Knife

This resembles a pocketknife but is 4 to 5 inches long; its curved blade is designed to trim twigs and small shoots from trees and shrubs.

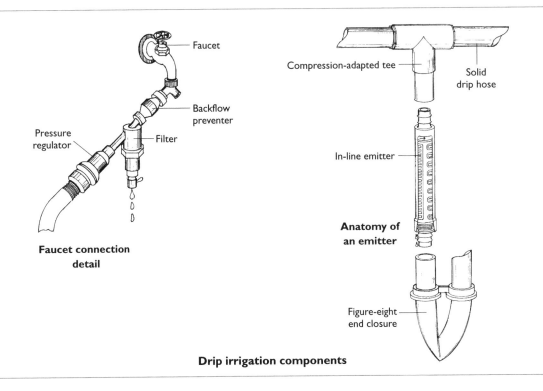

**Faucet connection detail**

- Faucet
- Backflow preventer
- Filter
- Pressure regulator

- Compression-adapted tee
- Solid drip hose
- In-line emitter
- **Anatomy of an emitter**
- Figure-eight end closure

**Drip irrigation components**

## Tools for Watering

### Drip Irrigation

In a drip irrigation system, water "drips" into the soil a drop at a time, through specially spaced emitters attached to a series of hoses. This technology is unsurpassed at saving water—50 percent or more water over conventional watering methods—and promoting optimal plant growth because water is delivered directly to a plant's root zone. If the system is properly designed and managed, the soil never dries out or becomes waterlogged, and little water is lost to evaporation or runoff. Plants get water when they need it and their foliage remains dry. Weeds or any other plants not specifically selected to receive water do not get irrigated.

Drip systems can be permanent or semipermanent, and are easily removed when regular cultivation is necessary. With an attractive mulch, it is possible to disguise the tubing. The main disadvantage of drip irrigation is that the tubes occasionally become clogged.

### Drip Irrigation Components

A well-designed system includes a backflow preventer, pressure regulator, filter, tubing, emitters, and, if you wish, a timer to turn the system on and off.

A backflow preventer is important to protect the household water supply from possible contamination. Filters are vital to a smooth-running system; the best kind are easily disassembled for regular cleaning. Since household water pressure ranges from 40 to 60 pounds per square inch and most drip systems can handle only 10 to 25 psi, you will need a pressure regulator.

Choose tubing with evenly prespaced emitters to deliver water along rows of vegetables. Tubing without preset emitters allows you to choose exactly where the water is delivered and may be better for the shrubs and trees in your landscape. Companies that sell drip irrigation equipment will generally help you design a system and supply you with instructions on setting it up. Many also sell predesigned systems.

Start small and experiment with the proper system for your garden; then expand your system as you determine what works best for you.

## Garden Hose

This all-important tool can bring water to all parts of the garden—if the hose is long enough. Hoses are usually made of several plies of material—nylon, flexible vinyl, or rubber, and often a reinforcing mesh layer. Hoses are ½ to ¾ inches in diameter and up to 100 feet long. Hoses can also be flat, expanding when filled with water; these take up less space when reeled or rolled up. Most hoses are equipped with brass or plastic couplings at both ends that attach to the water source at one end and a sprayer, sprinkler, another hose, or other attachment at the other. Soaker hoses are made of foam, vinyl, rubber, or canvas and are porous or perforated so that water slowly leaks out and soaks the ground around them. They are designed to be buried in the ground up to 14 inches deep to get water right to the roots of the plant, and can be left underground over the winter. They can be up to 500 feet long. Hoses should not be left lying in the sun when not in use; sunlight will speed the deterioration of the hose material. Drain the hose before storing it

for the winter, and coil it onto a reel or mounted hose holder.

### Hose Attachments and Accessories

Dozens of attachments for specialized jobs are made for hoses. They include the following:

• Bubbler. A nozzle designed to mix air with water and to be left on the ground for long waterings at the base of trees and large plants.

• Double hose shutoff. Also known as a Y-connector, this provides control of two hoses from one faucet. It screws onto a male-threaded faucet, and has attachments for two female hose couplings, with shutoffs for each of the two valves.

• Fan head sprayer. This triangular-shaped nozzle has a wide spray head that provides a gentle spray of lots of water; it is designed for seedlings and seeds.

• Hose hanger and reel. Two ways to store hoses when not in use. The hanger is attached to a wall and has a curved wide support over which the hose is coiled. The reel is like a large spool on which the hose is wound.

• Nozzles. Myriad kinds of nozzles are available to attach to the hose; each has a specific purpose. The pistol-grip nozzle (spray gun nozzle) is controlled by squeezing and releasing its trigger. The fogger nozzle creates a very fine mist. The seedling nozzle is designed for watering small seedlings.

• Root waterer. This long metal tube about a yard long has holes in one end and is attached to the hose with the other; it is plunged into the ground next to a shrub or tree, and is especially beneficial in compacted soil, as water will not soak into the soil on its own.

• Sprinklers. As with nozzles, there are many kinds of sprinklers for many watering jobs. The arm of the impulse sprinkler moves back and forth as it shoots out a stream of water, so that the stream is broken up; it can cover up to 5,000 square feet. The oscillating sprinkler has a curved metal tube for a sprayhead, which slowly swings back and forth; this can cover up to 3,600 square feet. The whirling sprinkler has two or four arms with nozzles on the end; these spin, releasing streams of water. This sprinkler can cover a circle 50 feet in diameter. Because sprinklers spread water over large areas, much of that water is lost through evaporation, so in many cases drip irrigation is preferable.

## Watering Can

Watering cans are essentially cans with a spout that allow the gardener to transport a certain amount of water (2 pints to 2 gallons) from the spigot to the plant. These are usually made of plastic or metal, and are available with a variety of heads or "roses." Oval-shaped roses that face upward release a fine spray and are designed for watering seedlings. Round roses that face down are appropriate for all-purpose watering. Some cans have very long spouts, up to 36 inches, and are called long-reach watering cans; these are designed so that the weight is well balanced between the spout and reservoir and are easy to handle. Dry metal cans before storing as they are likely to corrode.

## Hand Sprayer

This small bottle with a trigger spray head is also called a utility sprayer and mister. It is useful for misting tropical plants, and for spraying mixtures containing fertilizers or pesticides in small amounts and at targeted spots.

## Tools for Composting

### Compost Aerator Tool

This tool, with a long metal shaft and T-shaped handle, has a pointed tip and hinged paddles that are closed against the shaft when the tool is thrust into the pile. When the aerator is pulled from the pile, the paddles open out, stirring the pile and opening up pockets of air, which are essential for a quickly decomposing pile.

### Compost Bins

Bins for containing compost while it breaks down are available in a range of materials and styles. Whether made of wood, metal, plastic, or wire, compost bins should be vented to allow air to circulate through the pile, and lidded, so that moisture can be either kept in or out, depending on conditions inside and outside the bin. Some

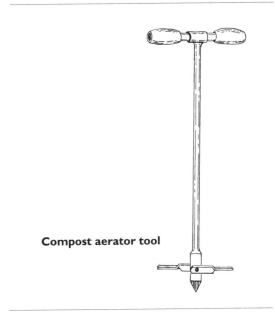

**Compost aerator tool**

bins are mounted on a metal frame and can be turned; when constructed properly, these "tumblers" make it easy to turn the compost.

## Garden Sieve

Also called a riddle, this is a metal screen stretched over a round metal, plastic, or wood frame. Soil or compost is screened through the sieve to separate the fine particles from the coarse. Larger models can be built onto legs.

## Shredders and Chippers

Also called mulchers and grinders, these machines are powered by gasoline or electricity, and turn brush and branches into homogenous chips good for mulching or smaller pieces appropriate for the compost pile. A shredder is designed to break up leaves, twigs, and other light plant material, which are dropped into the shredder's chute and pass by a spinning drum, which has a number of flails (nylon lines) attached to it. Chippers are similar but have one or more blades instead of flails, and can cut larger branches and brush. Shredder/chippers can both shred and chip. Wear protective goggles and earplugs when using this equipment.

## Tools for Lawn Care

## Aerator

Lawn aerators are long-handled tools equipped with a flat bar studded with two or four spikes. These are worked into the lawn in areas where the soil has become compacted. The gardener steps on the tool's bar, leaving behind tiny holes.

---

### BASIC TOOLS

| | |
|---|---|
| Spading fork | Flexible rake |
| Spade | Asparagus knife |
| Long-handled shovel | Hose and nozzle |
| Trowel | Watering can |
| Weeding hoe | Bypass pruning shears |
| Bowhead rake | Pruning saw |

### TAKING CARE OF YOUR TOOLS

Your tools will serve you best if you keep them in good condition. Make sure that you clean all the soil that has collected on them when you are done gardening each day. Dry, hardened soil is much more difficult to clean off than fresh soil. Keep your tools in a dry storage area where you will have no difficulty locating each tool when you need it. At the end of the season, clean any rust off the metal parts of tools with steel wool, then wipe with an oiled cloth or apply a coating of floor wax to protect the metal. Sharpen your tools regularly and sharpen them before storing over the winter so that they will be ready when the gardening season begins again in spring.

## Leaf Blower

This electric or gas-powered tool resembles an electric hair dryer—it blows out a powerful stream of air through a long tube. The operator uses the blower to blow leaves and other debris into piles. Blowers can be quite loud, so wear ear protection and also goggles when using this equipment. Due to the noise and the need for electricity or other fuel, these should be used only when necessary on very large properties.

## Lawn Sweeper

A sweeper, a bristle-covered drum that throws leaves and grass clippings up into a canvas hopper as it is run over the lawn, sweeps the grass clean, and is a quiet and energy-efficient alternative to a blower.

## Lawn Mower

The reel or push mower has five to eight curved blades attached to a reel that spins as the wheels turn. As the mower is pushed, the blades pass over the top of the grass, cutting them to the height determined by the gardener. Manual mowers are quiet and work well for small lawns and those that are mowed regularly—they are hard to push in tall grass. The blades should be kept sharp and clean. Rotary mowers are powered by gas or electricity, and have a propeller-like blade that is spun by the motor; the motor also drives the wheels of some mowers, so that they are self-propelled. Mulching mowers are preferable because they cut grass clippings into very fine pieces, which fall back onto the lawn and quickly decompose, becoming a source of natural fertilizer. Some rotary mowers can be equipped with leaf-shredding attachments. Walk-behind mowers are pushed from the rear. Riding mowers (lawn tractors) are self-propelled mowers that, like tractors, have a seat and are driven by a rider. These make sense for very large lawns.

## Further Reading

Ettlinger, Steve. *The Complete Illustrated Guide to Everything Sold in Garden Centers.* New York: Macmillan Publishing Company, 1990.

Logan, William Bryant. *The Tool Book.* New York: Workman Publishing, 1997.

# 13

# THE HORTICULTURAL TRAVELER

Once bitten by the horticultural bug, many gardeners range far beyond their own properties, traveling far and wide to sample the pleasures of—and glean ideas from—other landscapes. Below are brief sketches of some of the world's most memorable public gardens and largest flower shows. For plant enthusiasts interested in venturing beyond the cultivated comforts of the garden, ecotourism destinations featuring some of Earth's most remarkable floras are described as well. Any garden tourist interested in bringing plants back into the United States should consult "Importing Plants" on page 639.

## Public Gardens in the United States and Canada

The following are among the most beautiful public gardens in North America. For addresses and phone numbers, see "Essential Resources," page 697.

### Alabama

Birmingham Botanical Gardens, Birmingham

67 acres. Conservatory with cactus and orchid collections. Specialized gardens: herb, Japanese with Kazunori Tago–designed teahouse. Noteworthy collections: roses, camellias, rhododendrons, irises, ferns, daylilies, and orchids.

### Arizona

Desert Botanical Garden, Phoenix

145 acres. Two conservatories, one for Mexican and South American cacti and the other for southern African and Madagascan succu-

lents. This garden specializes in native Sonoran Desert plants, and features sixty interactive educational exhibits. Specialized gardens: a 30-acre core garden with desert collections from Africa, Australia, Central and South America, Mexico, and the United States; wildflower collections from the Sonoran Desert, Australia, and Africa; mesquite forest; and saguaro forest. Blooming season: early February to March for wildflowers, April to May for day-blooming cacti, summer for night-blooming cacti.

## California

### Filoli, Woodside

653 acres. Georgian Revival house and a formal, 16-acre manicured garden, garden rooms enclosed by hedging, sunken garden, bowling green, walled garden, upper and lower lawn terraces, rose garden (550 plants), knot garden, and perennial border. Noteworthy collections: fruit trees, camellias (*C. reticulata* and *C. japonica*), oriental magnolias, rhododendrons and azaleas, tree peonies, and wisteria.

### Huntington Botanical Gardens, San Marino

150 acres. Conservatory with desert plants. Originally the estate garden of railroad magnate Henry Huntington, the estate home now houses the Huntington Gallery Art Museum. Specialized gardens: desert (12 acres), Japanese, palm (200 species), rose (1,500 cultivars, including medieval varieties), Shakespeare, and jungle (gingers, bromeliads, and bamboos). Noteworthy collections: camellias (1,200 cultivars), Australian plants (150 eucalyptus species and numerous flowering plants), cycads, and acacias.

### Santa Barbara Botanic Garden, Santa Barbara

65 acres. Established at the site of a historic Franciscan-built dam (circa 1806), the garden has more than 1,000 native California species. Specialized gardens: wildflower meadow, oak woodland, redwood grove, chaparral, Channel Islands, desert, and home demonstration garden of drought-tolerant plants. Noteworthy collections: manzanita (more than 30 species), California lilacs, and irises.

### Strybing Arboretum & Botanical Gardens, San Francisco

75 acres. Specialized gardens: California native, New World cloud forest, South African, eastern Australian, southwestern Australian, Chilean, biblical, fragrance, and succulents. Noteworthy collections: magnolias.

## Colorado

### Denver Botanic Gardens, Denver

23 acres. Conservatory with a tropical rainforest collection. An extensive collection of regional plants from the Rocky Mountains and adjacent Plains, and one of the world's best collections of alpine plants, with more 4,000 taxa from around the world. Specialized gardens: Japanese, endangered species, and xeriscape with indigenous and waterthrifty plants from around the world.

## Delaware

### Winterthur Museum, Garden, and Library, Winterthur

A 983-acre former Du Pont estate, with a mansion (now a museum of American decorative arts) and a 60-acre garden designed by

Henry Francis Du Pont and Maryanne Coffin. Specialized gardens: azalea woods (8 acres of azaleas, rhododendrons, and wildflowers); March bank (a hillside planted with thousands of aconites, adonises, chionodoxas, scillas, and daffodils); quarry garden (irises, hostas, lobelias, 13 species of *Primula*); and 5-acre pinetum.

## District of Columbia

Dumbarton Oaks, Washington, D.C.

16 acres. A classic Italian garden above Rock Creek Park given an American interpretation by Beatrix Ferrand, an admirer of the work of English landscape designer Gertrude Jekyll, between 1921 and 1947. Designed as series of garden rooms, incorporating sculpture, fountains, and pools. Noteworthy collections: roses, magnolias, and cherries.

United States National Arboretum, Washington, D.C.

444 acres. Created as a research institute by an act of Congress in 1927 and opened to the public in 1946. Specialized gardens: an extensive collection of bonsai and penjing, Japanese stroll garden, native plant (ferns, prairie, Southeastern Coastal Plain) garden, and 2½-acre herb garden subdivided into ten specialty gardens (including culinary, medicinal, fragrance, colonial, dye, Native American, and beverage), a knot garden, and a garden of historical roses. Noteworthy collections: Asian (Japanese, Korean, and Chinese flora), azaleas, dwarf and slow-growing conifers (the largest in the country), magnolias, hollies, boxwoods, dogwoods, and daylilies.

## Florida

Fairchild Tropical Garden, Miami

83 acres. Conservatory. Specialized gardens: endangered species, Mayan fruit, rain forest, fern, sunken, and eleven lakes, each with its own special collection. Noteworthy collections: palms (889 taxa), cycads (149 taxa), tropical flowering trees from around the world (740 species), and flowering vines.

Marie Selby Botanical Gardens, Sarasota

8½ acres. Greenhouse. Scenically located on a peninsula along the Sarasota Bay, Selby specializes in tropical and subtropical epiphytes. twenty distinct gardens. Noteworthy collections: orchids (one of the country's largest collections), aroids, bromeliads, and ferns.

## Georgia

Atlanta Botanical Garden, Atlanta

30 acres, including 15 acres of display gardens. Conservatory with collections including poison-dart frogs, Old World palms, orchids, insectivorous plants, Madagascan succulents, and epiphytes. Specialized gardens: rose, ornamental vegetable, Japanese, herb and English knot, woodland, rock, conifer (dwarf and unusual varieties), and bog with native carnivorous plants.

Callaway Gardens, Pine Mountain

2,500 acres. Greenhouse. In addition to the garden, Callaway includes golf courses, a hotel, tennis courts, bicycle paths, and walking trails, a circa 1830 cabin, and the Day Butterfly Center, North America's largest glass-enclosed tropical butterfly conservatory, with 1,000 butterflies from more than

50 species. Specialized gardens: vegetable demonstration (one of the country's largest) and woodland. Noteworthy collections: hybrid azaleas (700 varieties), rhododendrons, hollies, and wildflowers.

## Hawaii

### National Tropical Botanical Garden, Kauai and Maui, Hawaii

Includes three gardens on Kauai and one on Maui. The 100-acre Allerton Garden on Kauai, former estate of John Allerton, features a series of garden rooms incorporating streams, ponds, and fountains, a bougainvillea-covered cliff, a cutting garden of tropical flowering plants (notably gingers and heliconias), and beaches. The 352-acre Lawai Garden contains a scientific collection of palms and heliconias. The 1,000-acre Limahuli garden and preserve features native Hawaiian flora and archaeologically important taro terraces. The 122-acre Kahanu Garden on Maui is known for its collection of breadfruit.

## Illinois

### Chicago Botanic Garden, Chicago

385 acres. Three greenhouses with cacti, topiary, succulents, and economic plants. Twenty-one specialty gardens, including rose, waterfall, English walled, bulb, Japanese, and fruit and vegetable, plus prairies and lagoons.

### The Morton Arboretum, Lisle

1,700 acres. Former country estate of Joy Morton, founder of Morton salt, the arboretum has 50 acres of formal plantings and gardens; 900 acres of natural woods, meadows, lakes, and streams; and one of the largest and old-

est restored prairies in the Midwest. Specialized gardens: hedge, old-growth woodland, Northeast Asian, ground-cover, four-season, fragrance, and daffodil glade. Noteworthy collections: trees from all over the world, including extensive crabapple and elm collections.

## Iowa

### Des Moines Botanical Center, Des Moines

14 acres. Conservatory with 150 species and cultivars of tropical and subtropical plants, cacti, and bonsai. Specialized gardens: herb, cottage, butterfly, annual and perennial, hardy cactus and succulent.

## Maryland

### Brookside Gardens, Wheaton

50 acres. Two conservatories with changing displays. Eleven specialized gardens including fragrance, formal, rose, and Japanese with a teahouse and ponds. Noteworthy collections: azaleas and large specimen trees.

## Massachusetts

### Arnold Arboretum, Jamaica Plain

265 acres. The country's first public arboretum, this National Historic Landmark was designed with the help of Frederick Law Olmsted and contains 4,000 kinds of trees, shrubs, and woody vines grouped together by plant family. Noteworthy collections: bonsai (some of the country's oldest), lilacs (250 varieties), roses, cherries, crabapples and other rosaceous plants, and century-old Asiatic shrubs and trees. In spring, a rhododendron-lined path that winds along a

brook, past two waterfalls, and through a ravine is particularly delightful.

## New England Wild Flower Society Garden in the Woods, Framingham

45 acres. Located in a glacially sculpted setting of eskers and kettle ponds, this garden contains the Northeast's largest landscaped collection of temperate North American wildflowers, displaying more than 1,600 kinds of plants in naturalistic settings. Specialized gardens: woodland, wetland (lily pond and sunny bog), pine barrens, Western, three rock gardens, meadow, and garden featuring endangered New England plants. Noteworthy collections: native rhododendrons and azaleas.

## Tower Hill Botanic Garden, Boylston

132 acres. Orangery. Located on what was an old farm, Tower Hill features a farmhouse that dates back to 1742 and an orchard with 119 varieties of pre-nineteenth-century apples. Specialized gardens: lawn, secret, English cottage, wildlife, and systematic garden arranged according to plant families.

## Minnesota

## Minnesota Landscape Arboretum, Chanhassen

935 acres. Conservatory featuring tropical plants, cacti, and succulents. In addition to trail-accessible natural areas with prairie, bog, woodland, and wetland habitats, the arboretum has fourteen specialty gardens, including rose, rock, perennial, hosta, demonstration, Japanese, and sensory. Noteworthy collections: crabapples, lilacs, azaleas, specimen trees (lindens, oaks, willows), hedges, and ornamental grasses.

## Mississippi

## Crosby Arboretum, Picayune

1,500 acres. Devoted to the preservation of regional native habitats, Crosby has no formal gardens but instead has savannahs, woodlands, ponds, and bogs. Noteworthy collections: pitcher plants, Louisiana irises, native azaleas, magnolias, asters, sunflowers, and other wildflowers.

## Missouri

## Missouri Botanical Garden, St. Louis

73 acres. three conservatories: the Climatron, a geodesic dome with a simulated tropical rain forest, a temperate-zone conservatory, and a camellia house. One of the country's oldest botanic gardens (established in 1859), the Missouri Botanical Garden features a historic section that includes the founder's nineteenth-century home, Victorian herb and flower gardens, and a yew hedge maze with a Victorian observation tower. Specialized gardens: 14-acre Japanese stroll garden, Chinese garden, twenty-three residential-size demonstration gardens, English woodland garden, boxwood garden, and two rose gardens.

## Powell Gardens, Kingsville

835 acres. Conservatory. Specialized gardens: perennial, rock and waterfall, wildflower meadow, formal gardens, woodland nature trail.

## New Jersey

## Frelinghuysen Arboretum, Morristown, and Willowwood Arboretum, Chester

These two arboreta are run by the Morris County Parks Commission. Frelinghuysen is a 127-acre former summer estate with a circa 1891 Colonial Revival–style mansion furnished with period antiques. Specialized gardens: texture and fragrance, fern, rose, annuals, and blue. Noteworthy collections: rhododendrons, azaleas, and flowering trees. Willowwood, the 130-acre former estate of Henry and Robert Tubbs, features a 1908 house furnished with period antiques. Specialized gardens: Japanese. Noteworthy collections: lilacs, cherries, hollies, and conifers, including a 90-foot-tall dawn redwood.

## New York

### Brooklyn Botanic Garden, Brooklyn

52 acres. Conservatory. The large greenhouse complex features pavilions that realistically simulate various habitats (tropical, warm temperate, desert, aquatic) as well as the Trail of Evolution, which traces the evolution of plant life on Earth, and the country's oldest and largest collection of bonsai. Specialized gardens: rose, Japanese hill-and-pond, rock, fragrance, herb including an Elizabethan knot garden, native plant, Shakespeare, Italianate, systematic garden arranged by plant family. Noteworthy collections: flowering cherries, magnolias, water lilies, lilacs, and ericaceous plants. Discovery Garden and indoor Discovery Center for children.

### The New York Botanical Garden, Bronx

250 acres. Conservatory, a rambling, ornate Victorian structure that contains sections that simulate Latin American rain forest, subtropical Australian shrubland, and African and American desert habitats. One of the oldest public gardens in the United States, this National Historic Landmark features dramatic rock outcroppings, wetlands, ponds, a river gorge, a cascading waterfall, and a 40-acre tract of virgin forest in the heart of New York City. 27 specialty gardens, including rose, rock, native plant, daylily, and herb. Noteworthy collections: orchids, peonies, lilacs, rhododendrons, azaleas, cherries, and crabapples.

### Old Westbury Gardens, Old Westbury, Long Island

88 acres. This former estate of the Phipps family features historic gardens designed by George Crowly and a Charles II–style mansion with the original furnishings. Specialized gardens: 2½-acre walled garden, formal rose garden, thatched cottage with cottage garden, boxwood gardens, demonstration garden (gray and vegetable), Japanese garden, rose testing garden, and lakeside wildflower walk. Noteworthy collections: linden and beech allées, rhododendrons, lilacs, and 100 species of trees.

### Planting Fields Arboretum State Historic Park, Oyster Bay, Long Island

409 acres. Two greenhouses, one featuring an extensive orchid collection and the other, the largest camellia collection in the Northeast. The former estate of William B. Coe, Planting Fields features a 1920s Tudor Revival mansion surrounded by some of the region's largest specimen trees. Specialized gardens: dwarf conifer, rose, systematic garden of shrubs and trees arranged by family. Noteworthy collections: azaleas, rhododendrons, magnolias, and hollies.

### Wave Hill, Bronx

28 acres. Greenhouses with alpine, tropical, and desert collections. In addition to being

the site of four historic buildings, including Greek Revival and Georgian Revival homes, Wave Hill offers striking views of the Hudson River and the Palisades. Specialized gardens: early-twentieth-century flower, wild garden of native plants, aquatic, monocot, dry, and herb.

## Ohio

The Holden Arboretum, Kirtland
3,100 acres, including a 2,500-acre nature preserve with woodland trails, a river gorge, meadows, ponds, and lakes. Specialized gardens: butterfly, display, rock, valley (featuring primroses), and hosta. Noteworthy collections: lilacs, viburnums, flowering crabapples, conifers, native plants (woodland, bog, prairie), maples, rhododendrons, and azaleas.

Kingwood Center, Mansfield
47 acres. Greenhouse. Specialized gardens: perennial, rose, shade, herb, and pink (Williamsburg-style). Noteworthy collections: daylilies, irises, and peonies.

## Pennsylvania

Longwood Gardens, Kennett Square
1,050 acres. Conservatory, a four-acre complex with a 10,010-pipe organ and twenty indoor displays, including an orangery. The former estate of Pierre S. Du Pont, Longwood was intended to recall the great pleasure gardens of Europe, combining horticulture, architecture, open-air theater, and music. With three fountain-and-statuary gardens and an Italian water garden, water is a dominant motif. twenty specialized gardens, including children's, silver, palm, cascades, Mediterranean, water lily, topiary, and an artistic woodland garden.

Morris Arboretum of the University of Pennsylvania, Philadelphia
92 acres. Greenhouse featuring a Victorian-era tropical fernery. The former summer estate of John and Lydia Morris, the arboretum features a large collection of mature Asian trees and a swan pond. Specialized gardens: a variety of naturalistic gardens, as well as English park, Italianate, and sculpture gardens. Noteworthy collections: roses and medicinal plants.

## Rhode Island

Blithewold Mansion & Gardens, Bristol
33 acres. In keeping with its grand views of Narragansett Bay and its impressive seventeenth-century English-style mansion, Blithewold features many stately trees. Many of the 2,000 trees (mostly Asian) and shrubs date back to the turn of the century. Other venerable specimens include 11 giant sequoias, a 100-year-old *Rosa roxburghii*, a 12-foot-tall chestnut rose, and a grove of yellow-grooved bamboo. Specialized gardens: rose (old-fashioned climbing roses), cutting, Japanese-style water, and rock.

## South Carolina

Brookgreen Gardens, Murrells Inlet
9,100 acres including 350 acres of gardens. Originally a colonial rice plantation, Brookgreen retains an allée of 250-year-old live oaks and the original plantation kitchen. It is especially renowned for its collection of sculpture (580 bronze and marble pieces). Specialized gardens: palmetto, plantation

kitchen. Noteworthy collections: magnolias, native azaleas, and dogwoods. Brookgreen also runs the Indigenous Wildlife Park for injured wild animals and offers history-and-nature creek excursions on a 48-foot motorized pontoon boat.

## Tennessee

### Cheekwood Botanical Gardens, Nashville

55 acres. four greenhouses, including two orchid houses, cool and warm, a camellia house, and a cloud forest house. Originally the estate of Leslie and Mabel Cheek, the 1930s Georgian-style home now houses an art museum. Specialized gardens: Japanese, herb, daylily, wildflower, perennial, daffodil, rose, water, and color. Noteworthy collections: dogwoods (two dozen varieties) and boxwoods.

## Texas

### Dallas Arboretum and Botanical Garden, Dallas

66 acres. In addition to its 1940 Spanish Revival sixteen-room mansion and antique-rose arbor, this garden stands out for its Dallas Blooms festival in March, with 150,000 tulips and daffodils, thousands of Iceland poppies, and 60,000 annuals. Specialized gardens: color, fern (100 species), sunken, ornamental, and woman's garden with reflecting pools and fountains. Noteworthy collections: 20,000 azaleas (including 2,000 different varieties, said to be the country's largest private azalea collection).

## Utah

### Red Butte Garden and Arboretum, Salt Lake City

400 acres, including 30 acres of display gardens and four miles of nature trails. Nestled at the mouth of Red Butte Canyon, this garden scenically overlooks the city. Specialized gardens: wildflower meadow, herb, children's, waterfall-and-water, and dwarf conifer. Noteworthy collections: ornamental grasses and daylilies.

## Virginia

### Lewis Ginter Botanical Garden, Richmond

80 acres, including 15 under cultivation. Greenhouse. Specialized gardens: Asian valley, perennial, wetland, Victorian, and children's. Noteworthy collections: daylilies, daffodils, ivies, dwarf conifers, and rhododendrons.

### Monticello, Charlottesville

5,000 acres. Designed by Thomas Jefferson himself, the gardens and house are restored according to his original plans, often with the same species and antique varieties of vegetables, flowers, and fruits. The gardens include orchards with many types of apples, peaches, cherries, and plums; squares planted with currants, gooseberries, and raspberries; twenty-four vegetable plots; and a collection of eighteenth-century roses.

## Washington

### The Bloedel Reserve, Bainbridge

160 acres, with 2½ miles of trails that connect a series of gardens, including moss gardens,

reflecting pool, woods walk, meadow, bird marsh, trestle bridge across a ravine, boardwalk through a bog, rhododendron glen, Japanese garden, and forest of red cedar, Douglas fir, and red alder. French country-style estate home overlooks Puget Sound.

## Washington Park Arboretum, Seattle

200 acres. Established in 1936, the arboretum includes 5,000 varieties of woody plants from 100 different countries—a collection that rivals the Arnold Arboretum's in quantity. Specialized gardens: winter, Mediterranean, and Japanese. Noteworthy collections: Japanese maples (110 cultivars), magnolias, camellias, and rhododendrons (one of the country's top five).

# Canada

## British Columbia

## Butchart Gardens, Victoria

56 acres. A former limestone quarry, Butchart Gardens was started in the early 1900s by Jenny Butchart, who dangled by rope over precipices to plant ivy into crevices in the towering, once-bare stone walls. Still owned by the Butcharts, it includes six specialized gardens, including sunken, Japanese, Italian, and rose.

## University of British Columbia Botanical Garden, Vancouver

70 acres. Situated on Point Grey overlooking the Pacific, the garden includes 12,000 plant taxa from around the world. Specialized gardens: Asian, alpine (2½ acres), food, British Columbia native plant, and physic (European medicinal plants from the Renaissance

era). The garden's Nitobe Memorial Garden, a 2-acre Japanese stroll garden, is located 2 miles from the main site. Noteworthy collections: espaliered fruit trees, perennials, Asian magnolias and rhododendrons, and one of the world's largest collections of vines.

## VanDusen Botanical Gardens, Vancouver

55 acres, formerly a golf course and now an open-forested garden. Specialized gardens: Sino-Himalayan, Canadian Heritage (Canadian cultivars and plants from a variety of Canadian ecosystems), heather, woodland, and perennial. Noteworthy collections: rhododendron hybrids and species, magnolias, and Eastern woodland wildflowers. Other features include an Elizabethan hedge maze of Eastern cedar, a series of manmade lakes, and a collection of modern sculpture.

## Ontario

## Royal Botanical Gardens, Hamilton

2,700 acres. Greenhouse with Mediterranean plants. Specialized gardens: scented, medicinal, Mediterranean, perennials, and 125,000-bulb rock garden. Noteworthy collections: roses, irises (250,000 individual plants), and one of the largest lilac collections in the world (800 varieties). Thirty miles of nature trails wind through wetlands and woodlands.

## Quebec

## Montreal Botanical Garden, Montreal

175 acres. Conservatory, ten interconnected greenhouses with major collections that include penjing, orchids, bromeliads, aroids, cacti and succulents, African violets, ferns,

and begonias. Thirty specialized gardens, including rose, marsh and bog, alpine, Chinese, and 5-acre Japanese garden.

## International Public Gardens

The following include some of the oldest and finest botanical gardens outside of North America, as well as landscapes that are milestones in the history of the garden. Addresses are listed; for phone numbers and additional information, consult national tourist offices.

## Europe

### Austria

**University Botanic Garden,** Vienna

Botanischer Garten der Universitat Wien, Rennweg 14, A-1030 Wien, Austria

20 acres. Noteworthy collections: tropical woody plants, welwitschia, cycads, and orchids. Specialized gardens: rock and pharmaceutical.

### Belgium

**Kalmthout Arboretum,** Kalmthout

Arboretum Kalmthout, Heuvel 2, B-2920 Kalmthout, Belgium

25 acres. Noteworthy collections: rhododendrons, conifers, witchhazels, daylilies, and roses.

### France

**Lyon Botanic Garden,** Lyon

Jardin Botanique de la Ville de Lyon, Parc de la Tête d'Or, F-69459 Lyon Cedex 06, France

17 acres. Noteworthy collections: alpines, ferns, roses, camellias, conifers, and cycads.

**University Botanic Garden,** Montpellier

Jardins des Plantes de l'Université, 163 rue Auguste-Broussonet, F-34000 Montpellier, France

12 acres. Noteworthy collections: Mediterranean trees and plants, succulents.

**Château de Versailles,** Versailles

78000 Versailles, France

The magnificent formal garden surrounding the Palace of Versailles, designed for Louis XIV by André Le Nôtre, features radiating avenues, carefully manicured parterres, great works of sculpture, and an elaborate system of fountains and reflecting pools that required feats of hydraulic engineering unmatched in the seventeenth century.

**Château de Vaux-le-Vicomte,** Maincy

Domaine de Vaux-le-Vicomte, 77950 Maincy, France

Considered by some to be one of the great garden masterpieces, the epitome of the monumental French seventeenth-century garden, featuring symmetry on a grand scale. Designed by André Le Nôtre for the château of Louis XIV's superintendent of finances, Nicolas Fouquet. Among the attractions are statuary, parterres, terraces, canals, fountains, and pools.

**Claude Monet's Garden,** Giverny

Rue Claude Monet, 27620 Giverny, France

The home where French Impressionist painter Claude Monet lived from 1883 until his death in 1926. Monet's garden slopes gently to the banks of the River Epte. It comprises a walled garden planted according to Monet's own design and a Japanese-inspired water garden, featuring Japanese-style bridges over a water-lily pond, a great weeping willow tree, and bamboos and rhododendrons at the waterside.

## Germany

### Berlin Botanic Garden, Berlin

Botanischer Garten und Botanisches Museum Berlin-Dahlem, Koenigin-Luise-Strasse 6-8, D-14191 Berlin, Germany

106 acres. Noteworthy collections: cacti and succulents, begonias, ferns, welwitschia, and bromeliads. Specialized gardens: historical herb, kitchen, and garden for the blind.

### Munich Botanic Garden, Munich

Botanischer Garten Munchen, Menzingerstrasse 61, D-80638 Munchen, Germany

54 acres. Noteworthy collections: alpines, insectivorous plants, cacti, African succulents, and staghorn ferns.

## Great Britain

There are more than 3,000 public and private British gardens open to the public—no secret to many North American gardeners, who in recent years have flocked to the often unparalleled landscapes. To describe all of these gardens would require a book of its own, and in fact, several good references are available. Bodnant Garden, Barnsley House, Exbury Gardens, Great Dixter, Hidcote Manor Garden, Knightshayes Court, Pitmedden, Rosemoor, Savill Gardens, Sissinghurst Castle, Stourhead, and Tresco Abbey are just a few that are more than worth the visit. To find out about these and other gardens, refer to the books listed in "Further Reading," page 640.

### Royal Botanic Gardens, Edinburgh

Royal Botanic Garden, Inverleith Row, Edinburgh EH3 5LR, U.K.

60 acres. Noteworthy collections: rhododendrons, heathers, primulas, meconopses, and plants in the lily family.

### Royal Botanic Gardens, Kew

Royal Botanic Gardens, Kew, Richmond, Surrey TW9 3AB, U.K.

300 acres. Conservatories, including the huge palm house designed by Decimus Burton and built in 1844–1848. Noteworthy collections include orchids, cycads, palms, heathers, ferns, insectivorous plants, economic plants, succulent plants, Australian species, and marine plants. Specialized gardens include alpine, grass, and herb.

### The Royal Horticultural Society's Garden, Wisley

The Royal Horticultural Society's Garden, Wisley, Woking, Surrey GU23 6QB, U.K.

240 acres. Noteworthy collections: rhododendrons, rock-garden plants, conifers, heathers, colchicums, hostas, Mediterranean and Near East bulbs, and apples.

## Ireland

### National Botanic Gardens, Glasnevin

National Botanic Gardens, Glasnevin, Dublin 9, Ireland

47 acres. Noteworthy collections: orchids and dwarf conifers.

## Italy

### University of Padua Botanic Garden, Padua

Orto Botanico di Padova, Via Orto Botanico 15, 35123 Padova, Italy

4.9 acres. One of the first modern botanical gardens, founded in 1545 on the instigation of the medical botanist Francesco Bonafede. Noteworthy collections: medicinal plants, orchids, insectivorous plants, succulents, grasses, asters, legumes, and plants in the lily family.

## Ninfa Gardens, Sermoneta

Giardino di Ninfa, Doganella di Ninfa, Sermoneta (Latina), Italy

This garden was built on the site of the city of Ninfa, which was abandoned in the sixteenth century, and the ruins of the medieval city are still visible in the grounds. The gardens contain over 10,000 plants from around the world. Noteworthy collections: sweet gums, Japanese maples, and loquats. Specialized gardens: walled lemon garden.

## Villa d'Este, Tivoli

Piazza Trento, 00019 Tivoli, Italy

Begun in 1550 for the Cardinal Ippolito d'Este on the edge of the hill town of Tivoli, at the summit of the steep hill with magnificent views of the Campagna and the dim outlines of Rome in the distance. Water in every conceivable manifestation—especially a magnificent system of fountains—is a primary element of the sixteenth-century garden.

## Netherlands

## Leiden University Botanic Garden, Leiden

Leiden University Botanic Garden, Nonnensteeg 3, 2311 VJ Leiden, The Netherlands

5 acres. Conservatory. Founded in 1587, this is one of Europe's first botanical gardens. Planting was begun when the famous botanist Carolus Clusius was appointed professor at the university. Some of the trees at the garden are extremely old and noteworthy. Other noteworthy collections: cycads, ferns, Southeast Asian orchids.

## Agricultural University Botanic Garden, Wageningen

Botanical Gardens, Agricultural University, P.O. Box 2010, 6700 ED Wageningen, The Netherlands

69 acres. Noteworthy collections: irises, lily family, roses, tropical African plants, beeches, and elms.

## Portugal

## University Botanic Garden, Coimbra

Jardim Botânico da Universidade, Departamento de Botânica, Faculdate de Ciencias e Tecnologia, Caáada Martim de Freitas (Arcos do Jardim), 3049 Coimbra, Portugal

35 acres. Noteworthy collections: tropical plants, narcissi, ornithogalums, succulents, and conifers.

## Spain

## Alhambra, Granada

Real de la Alhambra, s/n, 18009 Granada, Spain

The city of Granada was the last Moorish foothold in Europe. The Alhambra, a Moorish castle and royal residence dating back to the mid-thirteenth century though now partially destroyed, is one of only two gardens in Europe that have survived with any Islamic character, such as the pervasive presence of water in courtyard pools and the intimacy of spaces. The celebrated Court of the Lions includes a renowned massive gray fountain.

## Generalife, Granada

Real de la Alhambra, s/n, 18009 Granada, Spain

The other garden in which traces of Islamic influence have survived. The summer palace of the kings of Granada, built in the thirteenth and fourteenth centuries on the slopes of the Cerro del Sol overlooking the city and the Alhambra. Among the attractions is the Camino de las Cascadas, a water stairway dating from Moorish times.

## Switzerland

### Geneva Botanic Garden, Geneva

Conservatoire et Jardin Botaniques, Case Postale 60, CH-1292 Geneve, Switzerland

44 acres. Conservatory. Among the noteworthy collections are alpine plants.

### Isole di Brissago Botanic Garden, Brissago

Parco Botanico del Cantone Ticino (Lago Maggiore), Isole di Brissago, CH-6614, Switzerland

7 acres. Founded in 1890 by the Baroness of St. Légeer. Noteworthy collections: subtropical and Mediterranean plants.

### University of Zurich Botanic Garden

Garten zur Katze, Zollikerstrasse 107, 8008 Zurich, Switzerland

17 acres. Noteworthy collections: orchids, ferns, insectivorous plants.

# Africa

## South Africa

### National Botanical Institute of South Africa, Kirstenbosch

Includes the main garden, Kirstenbosch National Botanical Garden, National Botanical Institute, Private Bag X7, Claremont 7735, South Africa, which features an array of South African native flora, plus the following seven satellite gardens:

**Harold Porter National Botanical Garden,** Clarence Drive, Betty's Bay, Cape, P.O. Box 35, Betty's Bay, 7141, RSA. Specializes in coastal Cape flora.

**Karoo National Botanical Garden,** Roux Way, Van Riebeeck Park, Off National Road, P.O. Box 152, Worcester, 6850, Cape, RSA. Specializes in native desert flora.

**Lowveld National Botanical Garden,** Off White River Road (Opposite Sabie intersection), P.O. Box 1024, Nelspruit, 1200, RSA. Specializes in low-veld flora.

**Natal National Botanical Garden,** Mayor's Walk, Pietermaritzburg, P.O. Box 11448, Dorpspruit, 3206, RSA. Specializes in Natal flora.

**Orange Free State National Botanical Garden,** Rayton Road, off Dan Pienaar Drive, P.O. Box 1536, Bloemfontein, 9300, RSA. Specializes in the flora of Orange Free State.

**Pretoria National Botanical Garden,** 2 Cussonia Avenue, Brummeria, Pretoria, Private Bag X101, Pretoria, 0001, RSA. Specializes in Northern Transvaal flora.

**Witwatersrand National Botanical Garden,** Malcolm Road, Poortview, Roodepoort, P.O. Box 2194, Wilropark, 1731, RSA. Specializes in Southern Transvaal flora.

### Botanical Garden, University of Stellenbosch

Botanical Garden, University of Stellenbosch, Stellenbosch 7599, South Africa

7 acres. Noteworthy collections: welwitschia, succulents, xerophytes, pelargoniums.

## Zimbabwe

### National Botanic Garden, Harare

University of Zimbabwe Botanic Garden, P.O. Box MP 167, Harare, Zimbabwe

168 acres. Noteworthy collections: woody flora of Zimbabwe and nearby areas. Specialized gardens: succulents, replicas of indigenous rain forest and other indigenous habitats, and African alpine garden.

### Vumba Botanical Garden, Mutare

Vumba Botanical Garden, P/Bag V 7472, Mutare, Zimbabwe

393 acres. Noteworthy collections: wide range of temperate and subtropical species. Specialized gardens: herb.

## Australia and Southwest Pacific Islands

### Botanic Garden of Adelaide, Adelaide

Botanic Garden of Adelaide, North Terrace, Adelaide, South Australia 5000, Australia

101 acres. Noteworthy collections: subtropical and arid-region plants, orchids, and native flora. Specialized gardens: rose, herb, and a simulated tropical rain forest in the conservatory.

### Australian National Botanic Gardens, Canberra

Australian National Botanic Gardens, G.P.O. Box 1777, Canberra, A.C.T. 2601, Australia

220 acres. Noteworthy collections: Australian and related flora.

### Royal Botanic Gardens, Melbourne

Royal Botanic Gardens, Melbourne, Birdwood Avenue, South Yarra, Victoria 3141, Australia

90 acres. Noteworthy collections: Australian rain-forest plants, rhododendrons, camellias, succulents, bromeliads, and orchids.

### Royal Botanic Gardens, Sydney

Royal Botanic Gardens, Mrs. Macquarie's Road, Sydney, New South Wales 2000, Australia

75 acres. Noteworthy collections: orchids, myrtles, palms, cacti, cycads, bromeliads, and proteas. Specialized gardens: rose, palm, and rain forest.

### Kings Park and Botanic Garden, West Perth

Kings Park and Botanic Gardens, West Perth, Western Australia 6005, Australia

110 acres. Noteworthy collections: Western Australian native flora. Specialized gardens: rare and endangered species, native taxa suitable for gardening, and fragrance.

## New Zealand

### Auckland Botanic Garden, Auckland

Botanic Garden, University of Auckland, Grounds Department, Private Bag, Auckland, New Zealand

35 acres. Noteworthy collections: North American, Mediterranean, Sino-Japanese, Australian, and Maori cultural and economic plants. Specialized gardens: medicinal herb.

### Christchurch Botanic Gardens

Christchurch Botanic Gardens, City Council, Parks and Recreation Department, P.O. Box 237, Christchurch, New Zealand

74 acres. Noteworthy collections: New Zealand flora, cacti and succulents, tropical plants, and rock and alpine plants.

## Dunedin Botanic Garden

Dunedin Botanic Garden, City Council, Parks and Recreation Department, P.O. Box 5045, Dunedin, New Zealand

67 acres. Noteworthy collections: rhododendrons, New Zealand, Australian, Mexican, Himalayan, North Asian, North American, and South American plants.

## Pukeiti Rhododendron Trust, New Plymouth

Pukeiti Rhododendron Trust Inc., R.D.4, Carrington Road, New Plymouth, Taranaki, New Zealand

790 acres. Noteworthy collections: New Zealand trees, rhododendrons, camellias, conifers, primulas, plants in the lily family, hostas, magnolias, and hydrangeas.

## Otari Native Plant Museum, Wellington

Otari Native Botanic Garden, Wilton, P.O. Box 2199, Wellington N5, New Zealand.

198 acres. Noteworthy collections: New Zealand flora.

# Asia

## China

### Nanjing Botanic Garden, Nanjing

Nanjing Botanic Garden Mem. Sun Yat-Sen, P.O. Box 1435, Nanjing 210014, Jiangsu Province, China

460 acres. Noteworthy collections: subtropical Chinese trees and shrubs, woody oil plants, and medicinal plants.

### Shanghai Botanic Garden, Shanghai

Shanghai Botanic Garden, Long Wu Lu, Shanghai, Shanghai 201102, China

200 acres. Noteworthy collections: azaleas, camellias, Chinese orchids. Specialized gardens: penjing and medicinal plants.

## Indonesia

### Botanic Gardens of Indonesia, Bogor

UPT Balai Pengembangan Kebun Raya-LIPI, Jalan Ir. H. Juanda No. 13, P.O. Box 309, BOGOR, 16003 Java, Indonesia

215 acres. Noteworthy collections: palms, orchids, and tropical fruits.

## Israel

### Jerusalem and University Botanical Gardens

Jerusalem and University Botanical Gardens, the Hebrew University of Jerusalem, Jerusalem, 91904 Israel

50 acres. Noteworthy collections: Mediterranean and Central Asian plants.

## Singapore

### Singapore Botanic Gardens, Singapore

Singapore Botanic Gardens, National Parks Board, Cluny Road, Singapore 1025, Singapore

115 acres. Noteworthy collections: orchids, palms, and bamboos.

## South Korea

### Chollipo Arboretum, Chungchong Namdo

Chollipo Arboretum, San 185, Uihangni 1-gu, Sowon Myon, Sosan Gun, Chungchong Namdo, 352-33, South Korea

175 acres. Noteworthy collections: ornamental woody plants, including hollies, magnolias, barberries, conifers, mahonias, lindens, and maples.

### Sri Lanka

Royal Botanic Gardens Peradeniya

Royal Botanic Gardens, Peradeniya, Sri Lanka
150 acres. Noteworthy collections: orchids, palms, gymnosperms, flowering trees, and endangered tropical rain-forest plants. Specialized gardens: medicinal plants and fernery.

## South America

### Brazil

Botanic Garden of Rio de Janeiro

Jardim Botânico do Rio de Janeiro, Rua Pacheco Leao 915, 22460-030 Rio de Janeiro, Brazil
340 acres. Noteworthy collections: cacti, succulents, orchids, bromeliads, insectivorous plants, and medicinal plants.

# Flower Shows

There are scores of local and regional flowers shows throughout the country and around the world. For an extensive listing of local U.S. flower shows, consult *The Garden Tourist* (see "Further Reading," page 640). Here are the six biggest.

## United States

New England Spring Flower Show
Boston, Massachusetts
Mid-March
Sponsored by the Massachusetts Horticultural Society, the New England Spring Flower Show is the third largest flower show (5½ acres) in the world and features over sixty major exhibits and fifty life-sized gardens. First held in 1829, this annual event, now nine days long and usually held in the Bayside Exposition Center, includes educational programs for children and adults, demonstrations, competitions, and a large gardener's market. For more information, contact the Massachusetts Horticultural Society, 300 Massachusetts Ave., Boston, MA 02115; 617-536-9280.

Northwest Flower and Garden Show
Seattle, Washington
Mid-February
This five-day show has developed into the third largest flower show in North America. Its five acres of exhibition space feature 30 designed gardens, 200 commercial exhibitors, nonstop lectures and demonstrations, and orchid shows by the Northwest and Baker Orchid Societies. It is held at the Washington State Convention and Trade Center, 9th and Pike Streets in Seattle. For more information, contact: Northwest Flower and Garden Show, 1515 NW 51st Street, Seattle, WA 98107; 206-789-5333.

Philadelphia Flower Show
Philadelphia, Pennsylvania
Early March
The country's oldest flower show is held in downtown Philadelphia at the Pennsylvania Convention Center. Said to be the world's largest indoor flower show (10 acres of exhibition space), it includes sixty gardens demonstrating the latest in garden design and the newest plant species and cultivars to come on the market. Elsewhere during the weeklong show, you can find lectures, seminars, and more than one hundred horticultural demonstrations; a large gardener's

market (nearly 150 vendors selling plants, bulbs, tools, and more); and a 2,000-entry competition of rare or new plants. For more information, contact the Pennsylvania Horticultural Society, 100 North 20th Street, Philadelphia, PA 19103; 215-988-8800.

## International

### Chelsea Flower Show
London, England
Third week of May
Held on the grounds of the Royal Hospital, in Chelsea, London, this is considered by many to be the ultimate gardening event. For more information, contact the Royal Horticultural Society, 80 Vincent Square, London SW1P 2PE, U.K.; tel: 011 44 171 821 3000, fax: 011 44 171 828 2304.

### Hampton Court Palace Flower Show
East Molesey, Surrey, England
Early July
Noted for its displays of summer-flowering plants, especially roses, this flower show has become the world's largest. It is held at the Hampton Court Palace, in East Molesey, Surrey. For more information, contact the Royal Horticultural Society, 80 Vincent Square, London SW1P 2PE, U.K.; tel: 011 44 171 821 3000, fax: 011 44 171 828 2304.

### Journées des Plantes de Courson
Courson Monteloup, France
Mid-May
A large plant show and sale held on the grounds of the Château de Courson, near Paris. Two hundred exhibitors display the newest and worthiest plants, which are judged by a jury of noted horticulturists. For more informa-tion, contact Domaine de Courson, 91680 Courson Monteloup, France; tel: 011 33 64 58 90 12.

## Botanically Noteworthy Ecotourism Sites

The following countries or regions are known for their unique plant life. For more information, consult tour operators (including the many botanical gardens that sponsor tours to these areas) and national tourist offices.

## United States

### Hawaii

This island group is the most isolated and remote of all the floristic regions of the world. Nearly all of Hawaii's indigenous species, many with striking flowers, are found nowhere else on Earth. The Hawaiian flora is threatened with extinction by introduced plants.

### Olympic Peninsula

This peninsula in northwest Washington State, which encompasses the Olympic National Forest and National Park, contains one of the most pristine ecosystems in the contiguous United States, from lush temperate rain forest to rocky alpine zone. Some the nation's biggest trees—Western cedars as wide as 20 feet and Douglas firs as high as 300 feet—grow here, as do more than 100 species of wildflowers, nine of which are endemic.

### Sonoran Desert

A large, botanically rich desert extending from central Arizona to northwestern Mexico. In

Arizona, the plant community is particularly rich, with numerous small trees and cacti of many types, including the towering saguaros. Blooming season is early February to March (wildflowers) and April to May (cacti).

## International

### Australia

In addition to its unique mammals and birds, this isolated continent possesses a rich endemic flora, particularly along the eastern and southwestern coasts. Some of the more dramatic flowering plants and trees include eucalyptus, acacias, proteaceous plants—especially banksias—and orchids.

### Brazil

The Amazon River basin's diversity and abundance of plants—more than 25,000 species, especially orchids—and animals—nearly a third of the world's bird species are found here—exceeds that of any other place. And nowhere else in the world do tropical rain forests occupy so vast an area.

### China

Szechuan and Hunan provinces have a rich diversity of endemic plants, including numerous camellias and primulas, and some 650 species of rhododendrons.

### Costa Rica

Because of its large variety of ecosystems, including dry deciduous forests, lowland rain forests, and high-altitude cloud forests, Costa Rica has more than 9,000 species of higher plants—including over a thousand different orchids—205 mammal species, rich insect life, and more bird and butterfly species than the entire United States.

### Ecuador

Because it has so many types of habitats, including cloud and rain forests, Ecuador is blessed with 20,000 plant species—more than 30 heliconias and 150 orchids alone—as well as many bird species. A trip to Ecuador is usually combined with a visit to the Galapagos Islands, which has many of its own endemic plants, from prickly pears to passionflowers, and animals.

### Greece

In spring, the Grecian hillsides are abloom with many wildflower species, including anemones, crocuses, grape hyacinths, stars-of-Bethlehem, and striking terrestrial orchids.

### Japan

Japan's numerous endemics include a multitude of flowering trees, with a number of magnolia and rhododendron species. Admired for their fall color, temperate deciduous trees grow at the higher elevations and include beech, maple, oak, and the katsura tree, intermixed with conifers like larch, false cypress, and pine. Natural stands of the flowering cherry can still be found in the mountains.

### Madagascar

This large island off Africa's east coast has a rich diversity of endemic plants, especially orchids—at least 900 species—euphorbias, aloes, and many other woody succulents, and the flowering royal poinciana tree (*Delonix regia*).

## Madeira and Porto Santo

Noted for its misty laurel forests, these eastern Atlantic islands can boast more than 750 species (from 112 plant families), of which at least 120 are endemic, including the striking Madeira orchid, geranium, chrysanthemum, and scilla.

## Nepal

Starting in early April to early June, the forested mountainsides teem with masses of red rhododendrons, purple primulas, and ornate *Arisaema* species beneath hemlocks and firs, while in the valleys, epiphytic orchids show their blooms.

## New Zealand

This island nation is rich in flowering plants and trees, including forests of podocarpus, an abundance of epiphytes, small ferns, and tree ferns, as well as lichens and mosses and unusual birds.

## Peru

The Peruvian Amazon rain forest, like that of Brazil, harbors diverse plant life, including many bromeliads, staghorn ferns, anthuriums, and philodendrons.

## South Africa

The Cape region of South Africa is floristically rich, with more than 6,000 endemic species, including proteas, heaths, lilies, irises, orchids,

and amaryllids. The area is best visited in early spring: September and October.

## Sri Lanka

Though better known for its gardens, Sri Lanka is rich in wild flora, with more than 800 endemic plant species and nearly 170 orchids, including the endemic daffodil orchid.

## Turkey

This country is the home of many beautiful bulbous plants, a number of which have been cultivated in European and American gardens for centuries. The best time to visit is spring, when the mountains and hillsides blossom with wild hyacinths, chionodoxas, fritillarias, bearded and nonbearded irises, tulips, and scillas, to name a few.

# Importing Plants

If you are leaving the U.S. mainland and plan on bringing plants back home with you, be aware that government regulations place restrictions on what you can import. For example, you may not bring any soil or sand into the country, because of the threat of soil-borne organisms and pathogens. Therefore, any plants entering the mainland must be free of all soil. For more information on restrictions and requirements (including a detailed listing of acceptable plants), write to the Animal and Plant Health Inspection Service of the U.S. Department of Agriculture (USDA APHIS, Plant Protection and Quarantine, P.O. Box 96464, Washington, DC 20090-6464, Attn: Port Operations). You can also phone (look in your phone book for the nearest office or call the central office at 301-734-8645) or visit the APHIS's web site (www.aphis.usda.gov).

The Convention on International Trade in Endangered Species of Wild Fauna and Flora (CITES) regulates international trade of plants and animals deemed to be threatened or likely to be threatened by commercial exploitation. To bring back any plant species listed under CITES, you will need permits from the country of origin as well as from the U.S. Department of Interior's Fish and Wildlife Service (FWS), which regulates the import of wild and endangered plants and animals. For more information, refer to two FWS publications: *Facts about Federal Wildlife Laws* (available on-line, http://www.fws.gov/laws/facts.html) and "Buyer Beware Guide." Or contact the Federal Wildlife Permit Office, U.S. Department of the Interior, Fish and Wildlife Service, Washington, DC 20240. For more information on CITES, see "Vanishing Plants," page 134.

## Further Reading

Gapper, Frances, Patience Gapper, and Sally Drury. *Blue Guide: Gardens of England*. New York: W. W. Norton, 1991.

Pearson, Robert, Susanne Mitchell, and Candida Hunt, eds. *The Ordnance Survey Guide to Gardens in Britain*. London: W. W. Norton, 1986.

Rose, Grapham. *Good Gardens Guide*. London: Vermilion, 1997.

Rosenfeld, Lois G. *The Garden Tourist*. New York: The Garden Tourist Press, 1997.

# 14

# POISONOUS PLANTS

Contact between people and plants is on the increase. Gardening ranks at the very top of the list of favorite leisure activities; family jaunts into the countryside as well as vacations at national parks and hikes along rural trails are more popular than ever; potted plants in the home and office will always have their place. Plants are clearly vital to our physical health and psychological well-being. As the popularity of plants increases, however, it is important to understand that some species are poisonous and can cause distress, or even death.

This section includes an encyclopedia of forty plants (including several fungi) that are the most common causes of documented cases of poisoning. Some of these species are widely cultivated, while others are found in the wild. The encyclopedia entry for each species includes a drawing and description of the plant to aid in identification, as well as the symptoms of poisoning. In addition to providing detailed information about specific poisonous species, this section explains how to recognize the signs of plant poisoning—and what to do about it. It also offers some commonsense suggestions on how to avoid plant poisonings in the first place. At the end of the section is a list of the telephone numbers of official Poison Control Centers throughout the United States to call in an emergency. It is a good idea to keep the number of the nearest Poison Control Center by your telephone.

## How Poisonous Plants Can Affect the Body

Depending upon its particular toxic property or properties, a poisonous plant can affect the human body in several ways:

- Internal poisoning from eating.
- Irritation to the skin, eyes, or other external organs from contact with the plant.
- Photosensitization, or the appearance of a rash after contact with the plant and subsequent exposure to sunlight.
- Allergic reaction, mostly from breathing in fungal spores or pollen grains.

# Common Poisonous Substances Found in Poisonous Plants

Plants are storehouses of chemical compounds. Some of the poisonous compounds, whether by scent, bitter taste, or toxicity, deter animals from eating the plants that contain them. Most of the remaining poisons have no readily apparent purpose.

The following categories of poisonous compounds are some of the most often encountered and best investigated. According to 1991 statistics of the American Association of Poison Control Centers, 5 to 10 percent of all calls to poison control centers involved plants. While most of these did not result in any serious health damage, it is important to be aware that plants do contain a range of toxic agents that can harm humans.

## Alkaloids

Alkaloids are nitrogen-containing compounds with a bitter taste. All have a powerful pharmacological action on animals, including humans, commonly causing marked effects on the nervous system. The same alkaloid may be found in related species or in different genera. One example of an alkaloid is the nicotine found in tobacco (*Nicotiana*). Vincristine and vinblastine, alkaloids used as anticancer drugs, are found in rosy periwinkle (*Catharanthus*).

## Glycosides

Glycosides are substances in which a sugar is attached to some other type of molecule. There are various types of glycosides:

### Cyanogenic Glycosides

When they interact with certain enzymes in the body, these produce cyanide, which inhibits the uptake of oxygen by the cells, resulting in their death. The amygdalin in seeds of many members of the rose family (Rosaceae) such as apple (*Malus*) and cherry (*Prunus*) is an example of a cyanogenic glycoside.

### Cardiac Glycosides

These glycosides can increase the contraction of the heart muscle. Examples of plants that contain cardiac glycosides are lily of the valley (*Convallaria*), oleander (*Nerium*), and foxglove (*Digitalis*). Indiscriminate use of the latter as an herbal remedy has resulted in disruption of the heart rhythm, ending in death.

### Saponin Glycosides

These form a soapy foam with water. When they are ingested and get into the bloodstream, they injure the lining of the digestive tract and destroy red blood cells. Pokeweed (*Phytolacca*) is an example of a plant that contains saponin glycosides.

## Oxalates

These substances can occur in plants either as soluble sodium or potassium salts or as insoluble calcium oxalate in the form of needlelike crystals that penetrate the delicate tissue of the mouth and throat, causing a burning sensation and swelling. They are most commonly encountered in dumbcane (*Dieffenbachia*), the leafy parts (less so in the edible leaf stalks) of rhubarb (*Rheum*), and oxalis (*Oxalis*).

## Resins

Resins are complex chemical substances that are insoluble in water. Depending upon the plants involved, they can cause blistering of the skin or irritation of the gastrointestinal tract, or affect the central nervous system. These substances are found in milkweed (*Asclepias*), marijuana (*Cannabis*), some members of the heath family (Ericaceae), and poison ivy (*Toxicodendron*).

## Phytotoxins

Phytotoxins have the largest protein molecules of all toxins, which contributes to their highly reactive nature. Most of these compounds inhibit the action of enzymes, disrupting the synthesis of proteins. The most poisonous phytotoxins known come from the seeds of the precatory bean (*Abrus*) and castor-oil (*Ricinus*) plants.

## Skin Irritants

### Stinging or Irritant Hairs

The hairs of the stinging nettle (*Urtica*) are the classical example of this phenomenon. Chemicals in the glandular base of hairs found on the leaves and stems are injected under the skin when the pointy tips pierce the skin. Spines of some cacti (*Opuntia,* for example) can also irritate as their tips break off and remain embedded under the skin.

### Irritant Sap

Sap containing toxic substances, including resins, can irritate the skin. One example of an irritant plant sap is the clear or milky latex produced by some members of the spurge family (Euphorbiaceae).

### Photosensitizing Agents

These substances cause an abnormal sensitivity to light after contact with a plant, and typically result in a rash. Some examples of plants that contain photosensitizing agents are the sap of leaves and stems of giant hogweed (*Heracleum*) and rue (*Ruta*) and the rind of lime (*Citrus*).

### Substances That Cause Allergic Dermatitis

There are a host of substances that cause dermatitis upon contact with the skin. They are most commonly encountered in the skin of the fruit as well as the leaves and stems of the mango (*Mangifera*), in all parts of poison ivy (*Toxicodendron*) and some parts of other members of the cashew family (Anacardiaceae), and in the fruits of chili pepper (*Capsicum*).

## Poisonous Fungi, Including Mushrooms

A number of mushrooms and other fungi are deadly to humans. Among these, the amanitas

On more than a few occasions, it has occurred to people that the solution to the problem of poisonous plants is simple: eradicate them. This is obviously not the answer. Plants have not evolved to plague us. The very plants we have grown to despise, such as poison ivy, play important roles in nature. We humans are often the intruders in their environments, and we must find the most constructive way to coexist with them.

Here are some steps to take to reduce the likelihood of a plant poisoning:

• Know the identification of the plants growing in your garden and in your home. Find out which ones can be toxic if touched or ingested.

• Locate poisonous plants such as mountain laurel (*Kalmia latifolia*) toward the very back of a border to put them beyond the reach of young children and therefore out of harm's way.

• Locate houseplants beyond the reach of young children; well-placed furniture can be an effective barricade.

• Do not pick and chew on plants in the garden or in the wild—or even from potted herbs on the kitchen windowsill—in front of small children. This invites them to do the same with plants at random.

• Establish a strict code that distinguishes all plants meant for consumption from those used purely for decoration. For example, it should be a rule that only after plants have passed through the kitchen—where they are sorted, cleaned, bagged for refrigeration, and so on—are they "approved" for eating. This helps not only to avoid potential poisonings but also to prevent a child from associating all plants with toxicity, even those important in his or her diet.

• Discourage children from brewing "tea" using leaves collected in the garden, from using hollow stems as peashooters, and from sucking nectar from flowers, especially tube-shaped ones.

• Teach children to avoid certain plants, such as poison ivy, by pointing out the species' essential features. Devising games or rhymes around, say, leaf characteristics can be educational and a lot of fun. For example, one traditional rhyme about poison ivy, which has compound leaves composed of three leaflets, is "Leaves of three, let it be!"

• Do not assume that plants, fruits, and seeds that are safe for animals to eat are safe for human consumption. Animals often have enzyme systems to neutralize various substances in plants, which are not found in the human body.

• Do not assume that cooking or drying will destroy dangerous substances in plants.

• Keep all gardening items such as fertilizers, herbicides, insecticides, bulbs, and seeds in a safe place, beyond the reach of children and pets. It is important not to store bulbs in the kitchen, because they can be confused with onions.

• Disregard all supposed fail-safe tests for distinguishing between edible or poisonous plants. The many tests for separating "toadstools" from mushrooms, for example, are legend—and all useless.

• Do not eat plants collected from the wild unless you are sure of their identity or are with someone with proven expertise in the correct identification of plants.

• Using plants from the wild or from your garden for self-medication can be very dangerous. While the plant you choose may be similar to—for example, in the same genus as—one listed in a reference book or on herbal packaging, the particular species to which you have access may be dangerous.

• Avoid chewing or sucking on jewelry made from plant parts. Some of these, especially fruits and seeds, can be toxic. The precatory bean (*Abrus*), castor bean (*Ricinus*), and cashew nut (*Anacardium*)—all of which have poisonous parts—are often made into necklaces and bangles and sold in Caribbean markets.

(*Amanita*) are most often implicated in fatal poisonings. They affect the central nervous system or cause severe damage to the kidneys and liver.

## How to Recognize Poisoning by Plants

While the effects of some poisonous substances manifest themselves days, weeks, or even months after exposure, most of the commonest plant poisons act rapidly. The severity of the reaction depends on a number of factors, including the individual's sensitivity to the poison, his or her health, and his or her size; for this reason, the symptoms are usually more severe in children than in adults. In fact, most poisonings in which plants have been implicated involve small children; their innate curiosity leads them to collect interesting or eye-catching objects and put them in their mouths.

In many suspected poisonings, especially where young children are involved, it is necessary first of all to determine whether or not a plant is the cause. Here are some things to look for.

• In cases of irritation to the skin or to sensitive parts such as the eyes, it is logical to suspect plants with spines, thorns, or irritant hairs, or those with sap (clear or milky) known to be corrosive or allergenic.

• Stains around the mouth are a good indication that a fruit or fruits have been ingested.

• The child may be clutching a bunch of berries or other potentially poisonous plant part in his or her hands.

• Any plant parts vomited by the child or in his or her stools are another good indication that a plant has caused the reaction.

Collect any evidence in a plastic bag and keep it on hand for further reference if necessary. It not only may help identify the plant(s) suspected of causing the distress but may also be essential in determining the type of treatment to employ (this is particularly true in cases in which mushrooms are involved). If you suspect that the sap of the plant may have caused irritation to the skin, drape your hand in a plastic bag when collecting the specimen. You may be asked to describe the features of the plant in order to help establish its identity. If possible, determine what parts of the plant were eaten, the amount eaten, and the time of ingestion. Be prepared as well to describe the symptoms.

## What to Do If You Suspect a Plant Poisoning

• **CALL YOUR PHYSICIAN.** He or she will be able to provide instructions on how to proceed.

• If you cannot reach your physician and you are not sure whether a plant is involved or about the identity of the plant(s), **CALL THE NEAREST POISON CONTROL CENTER.** See page 665 for a listing of telephone numbers for Poison Control Centers across the United States.

• Poison Control will be able to tell you what to do in an emergency situation. In extreme cases, they may advise that you call 911 for emergency assistance or that you bring the patient to the nearest emergency room.

• Be sure to take the sample of the plant(s) suspected of causing the poisoning with you to the physician's office or hospital.

## PLANT POISONING IN DOGS AND CATS

It is not always possible to equate the symptoms that humans exhibit as a result of contact or ingestion of toxic plants with those in animals. Dogs and cats are not herbivorous by nature, although they are known, on occasion, to seek out plants, especially grass, to eat. Puppies and, less frequently, kittens tend to chew on almost anything they come across, and the chances that they might accidentally ingest plants harmful to them is higher at that young age. Dogs of all ages, particularly when confined alone for long hours, may resort to abnormal behavior and chew on plants to relieve their boredom.

It is good sense to suspect that any plant known to be toxic to humans may be dangerous to pets. Be especially careful about houseplants containing poisonous compounds. Because it is difficult, if not impossible, to prevent a cat from getting access to these plants, it may be necessary to remove the plants from the room or restrict the pets to areas in the house where the plants have been removed. This is particularly important when pets are left alone for any length of time. Some houseplants that can be toxic to pets are oleander; daffodils and most other plants with bulbs; castor bean plant; holiday plants such as the Jerusalem cherry (*Solanum pseudocapsicum*), chili plants, poinsettia, and mistletoe; dumbcane and all related aroids; and lantana.

Often, spiny plant parts, such as those found in weedy thistle seeds in parks and open lots, can be a problem. These become attached to the fur of pets, and when they start chewing or licking to remove them, some may be swallowed and can irritate the delicate tissue of the mouth and throat. Obvious signs, including coughing or salivating, are signs of this condition. When it is possible to do so, removing the offending spiny plant parts may rectify the problem; but in this and all other situations where an animal is suspected of ingesting toxic or irritant plant parts, it is wise to seek professional help from a veterinarian.

Just as it is important to keep the number of your physician and poison control center near your telephone, it is also a good idea to do the same with the number of your veterinarian and nearest animal 24-hour emergency facility if you have a pet.

---

Advice from Poison Control often includes the following:

- If a poisonous plant has been eaten, have the patient **DRINK WATER TO DILUTE THE TOXIN.**

- If the poison swallowed was not a plant but rather a strong acid, alkali, or petroleum distillate, **DO NOT INDUCE VOMITING.**

- **DO NOT INDUCE VOMITING** if the patient is unconscious, is convulsing, or has already vomited.

- When irritation to the skin is apparent, especially due to contact with sap or latex, **WASH AFFECTED PARTS OF THE SKIN WITH COLD RUNNING WATER.**

# Encyclopedia of Poisonous Plants

The poisonous plants in the following encyclopedia are listed in alphabetical order by botanical name (the name that is italicized and in parentheses). See the index, beginning on page 761, for an alphabetical listing by common name. Poisonous mushrooms and other fungi are covered separately, beginning on page 662.

## How to Use This Encyclopedia

This encyclopedia is intended to help with the identification of poisonous plants. Once the plant has been identified, treatment will depend on the person's reaction, his or her age, and other factors. Your physician or the nearest Poison Control Center is best qualified to suggest treatment.

If you are fairly certain that a particular plant is the cause of a poisoning but know only its common name, refer to the index beginning on page 761 for its scientific name. If you do not know the name of the plant, referring to the illustrations and descriptions of the plants that follow may help in identification. Please be aware that this encyclopedia includes only the plants and fungi that are the most frequently implicated in reported poisonings. It behooves all parents to know the names of the plants in their gardens and homes and to have other references at hand to complement this list.

*Abrus precatorius,* Rosary Pea, Precatory Bean
Pea family (Fabaceae)
DESCRIPTION: A twining perennial vine. Leaves are alternate (borne singly at each node on a

stem), with eight to fifteen pairs of leaflets. Flowers are in clusters, and red to purple. Seeds are shiny, red and black, and in a pod.
RANGE: Native to the tropics. Has escaped into the wild in Florida.
TOXIC PARTS: Seeds.
TOXICITY: Seeds contain abrin, a phytotoxin. Very toxic when seeds are chewed and swallowed.
SYMPTOMS: Severe stomach pain with nausea, vomiting, and diarrhea. In extreme cases, kidney failure, circulatory collapse, and death.

*Aconitum napellus* and other species,
Monkshood, Aconite
Buttercup family (Ranunculaceae)
DESCRIPTION: A perennial herb. Leaves are alternate (borne singly at each node on a stem), with three to nine lobes or segments. Flowers are terminal (at the tip of a stalk), usually blue but also can be white or yellow. Top of flower (upper sepal) is hoodlike, hence the common same. Roots are tuberous and black.
RANGE: *A. napellus* is native to Europe but com-

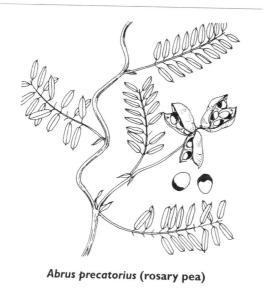

**Abrus precatorius (rosary pea)**

**Aconitum napellus (monkshood)**

monly cultivated in North America. Other species are native to North America.

TOXIC PARTS: All parts, especially the roots and seeds.

TOXICITY: All parts contain the alkaloid aconitine.

SYMPTOMS: Symptoms are intense: tingling in mouth and skin, nausea, vomiting, diarrhea, respiratory paralysis, and convulsions.

*Aesculus hippocastanum* and other species, Horse Chestnut, Buckeye
Buckeye family (Hippocastanaceae)

DESCRIPTION: Trees and shrubs. Leaves are opposite (borne opposite from one another at the same node) and deciduous, with five to seven leaflets. Flowers are red, white, or yellow, in clusters at branch tips. Fruits have a leathery shell, prickly in *Aesculus hippocastanum,* and contain one or more shiny brown seeds that can be mistaken for edible chestnuts.

RANGE: Native to southeastern Europe. This and many North American species are cultivated.

TOXIC PARTS: Leaves, flowers, fruits.

TOXICITY: Contain the glycosidic saponin aesculin.

SYMPTOMS: Loss of coordination and twitching of muscles, vomiting, diarrhea, and paralysis.

*Arisaema triphyllum,* Jack-in-the-Pulpit
Arum family (Araceae)

DESCRIPTION: A perennial herb with a swollen underground stem (corm). Leaves have three leaflets. Flowers are ensheathed by a purple spathe. Fruit is a head of red berries, each containing one to three seeds.

RANGE: Native to woodlands throughout North America. Also cultivated.

TOXIC PARTS: All parts.

TOXICITY: Contain needlelike crystals of calcium oxalate and other toxins.

SYMPTOMS: When chewed, calcium oxalate crystals become embedded in mucous membranes, causing burning and irritation of mouth and throat, vomiting, and diarrhea. Sap causes dermatitis.

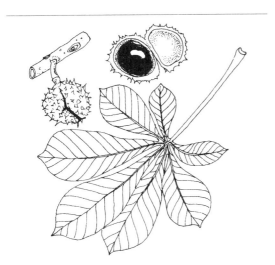

**Aesculus hippocastanum (horse chestnut)**

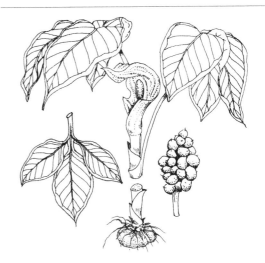

**Arisaema triphyllum (jack-in-the-pulpit)**

**Asclepias syriaca (milkweed)**

**Atropa belladonna (belladonna)**

*Asclepias syriaca* and other species, Milkweed
Milkweed family (Asclepiadaceae)

DESCRIPTION: A perennial herb. Leaves are opposite (borne opposite from one another at the
same node). Flowers are axillary (borne
between the stem and leaf) and terminal (at
the end of a stalk), and rose to purple, rarely
white. Fruit is a soft-spiny follicle with
numerous seeds, each with a tuft of silky
hairs. The orange-flowered butterfly weed is
*A. tuberosa.*

RANGE: Native to meadows in the eastern and
midwestern United States. Also cultivated.

TOXIC PARTS: All parts.

TOXICITY: Contain cardiac glycosides.

SYMPTOMS: Vomiting, stupor, weakness when
eaten. Milky sap may cause dermatitis.

*Atropa belladonna,* Belladonna, Deadly
Nightshade
Nightshade family (Solanaceae)

DESCRIPTION: A perennial herb. Leaves are alternate (borne singly on each node of a stem).

Flowers are tubular and purple. Fruit is a
purplish black berry.

RANGE: Native to Europe. Has escaped into the
wild in North America. Found in weed lots.

TOXIC PARTS: All parts, especially the berries.

TOXICITY: Contain the alkaloids hyoscyamine,
scopolamine, and atropine.

SYMPTOMS: Fever, flushed skin (hot and dry),
dilation of pupils, weak and rapid pulse,
confusion.

*Capsicum annuum* and other species, Chili
Pepper
Nightshade family (Solanaceae)

DESCRIPTION: Annual or perennial herbs. Leaves
are alternate (borne singly at each node on a
stem). Flowers are solitary. Fruits vary in
shape, size, and color.

RANGE: North America and northern South
America.

TOXIC PARTS: Mainly the fruits, especially the
soft tissue attaching the seeds to the fruit
wall.

**Capsicum annuum (chili pepper)**

TOXICITY: Contain the alkaloid capsaicin.

SYMPTOMS: Intense burning when eyes and other sensitive parts are touched after raw chilies have been handled. NOTE: Wear rubber gloves when working with chilies.

*Cicuta maculata,* Water Hemlock

Carrot family (Apiaceae)

DESCRIPTION: A perennial herb. Leaves are alternate (borne singly at each node on a stem), and divided into toothed leaflets. Stem is hollow, except at the base where horizontal membranes divide it into chambers. Roots are tuberous. Flowers are tiny and greenish white, in terminal umbels (flat-topped clusters occurring at the tip of a stalk).

RANGE: Native to eastern North America in marshy habitats.

TOXIC PARTS: All parts, especially the roots.

TOXICITY: Contain cicutoxin, an alcohol that acts on the central nervous system in about 30 minutes. Roots have been mistaken for parsnips. Very toxic.

SYMPTOMS: Salivation, convulsions, dilation of pupils, severe stomach pain, diarrhea.

*Colchicum autumnale,* Autumn Crocus, Meadow Saffron

Lily family (Liliaceae)

DESCRIPTION: An herb with a bulblike underground structure called a corm. Leaves die back before flowers appear in the fall. Flowers are white to purple. Fruit is a capsule.

RANGE: Native to the Mediterranean region. Cultivated widely in North America.

TOXIC PARTS: All parts, especially the corms and seeds.

TOXICITY: Contain the alkaloid colchicine. Most concentrated in the corm.

SYMPTOMS: Burning pain in the mouth after the

**Cicuta maculata (water hemlock)**

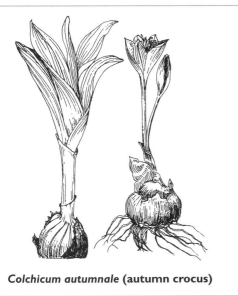

**Colchicum autumnale (autumn crocus)**

**Conium maculatum (poison hemlock)**

**Convallaria majalis (lily of the valley)**

plant is chewed. Abdominal pain and diarrhea, followed by labored breathing and kidney failure.

*Conium maculatum,* Poison Hemlock
Carrot family (Apiaceae)

DESCRIPTION: A biennial herb. Leaves are finely dissected. Stems are hollow. Taproot is turnip-like and solid.

RANGE: Native to Eurasia. Has escaped into the wild in North America and is often seen in roadside ditches.

TOXIC PARTS: All parts, especially the roots and seeds.

TOXICITY: Contain the alkaloid coniine and others. Plant has an unpleasant odor and taste, but leaves have been mistaken for parsley, roots for parsnips, and seeds for anise.

SYMPTOMS: Nausea, vomiting, diarrhea, loss of coordination, muscle weakness, slowed heartbeat, coldness in extremities, convulsions.

*Convallaria majalis,* Lily of the Valley
Lily family (Liliaceae)

DESCRIPTION: An herbaceous perennial. Leaves arise from running roots. Flowers are white, bell-shaped, fragrant, formed on a long stalk, and all face in one direction. Fruits are red berries.

RANGE: Native to Eurasia. Cultivated and naturalized in North America.

TOXIC PARTS: All parts.

TOXICITY: Contain the cardiac glycosides convallarin, convallamarin, and convallatoxin.

SYMPTOMS: Abdominal pain, nausea and vomiting, irregular heartbeat, decreased pulse, clammy skin, circulatory failure. NOTE: Compare symptoms with those of foxglove (*Digitalis*) and oleander (*Nerium*).

*Datura stramonium,* Jimsonweed, Thornapple

Nightshade family (Solanaceae)

DESCRIPTION: An annual herb. Leaves are alternate (borne singly at each node on a stem). Flowers are funnel-shaped and white to lavender. Fruit is a dry capsule armed with sharp prickles and contains many dark seeds.

RANGE: Native to North America, where it is a common weed.

TOXIC PARTS: All parts, especially the leaves and seeds.

TOXICITY: Contain the alkaloids hyoscyamine, atropine, and scopolamine. It is dangerous to brew "tea" from leaves or seeds or suck nectar from flowers. Overinhalation of flower fragrance can lead to headache and dizziness.

SYMPTOMS: Thirst, dilation of pupils, flushed skin, delirium, rise in blood pressure, hallucinations, convulsions. Sap can cause dermatitis.

*Dieffenbachia maculata,* Dumbcane

Arum family (Araceae)

DESCRIPTION: A perennial herb with a fleshy stem. Leaves are large, often streaked or spotted with white or yellow-green.

RANGE: Native to tropical America. Widely cultivated as a houseplant or grown outdoors in subtropical areas.

TOXIC PARTS: All parts.

TOXICITY: Contain calcium oxalate in needle-

**Datura stramonium (jimsonweed)**

**Dieffenbachia maculata (dumbcane)**

like crystals plus other toxins, including enzymes.

SYMPTOMS: Chewing on leaves and stems leads to severe irritation of the mouth and throat. Resulting swelling can lead to choking. Sap may cause dermatitis. NOTE: Symptoms are similar to those of *Alocasia, Caladium, Xanthosoma,* and other aroids.

## *Digitalis purpurea,* Foxglove
Snapdragon family (Scrophulariaceae)

DESCRIPTION: A biennial herb. Leaves are alternate (borne singly at each node on a stem). Flowers are tubular, terminal (grow at the tip of a stalk), and purple, pink, rose, or white, often with spots inside tube. Fruit is a dry capsule.

RANGE: Native to Europe. Widely cultivated and used medicinally.

TOXIC PARTS: Flowers, leaves, seeds.

TOXICITY: Contain the cardiac glycosides digitalin, digitoxin, and others.

SYMPTOMS: Nausea, diarrhea, headache, irregular heartbeat and pulse, convulsions. Poisoning often results when adults try to use the plant to medicate themselves.

## *Hyoscyamus niger,* Henbane
Nightshade family (Solanaceae)

DESCRIPTION: An annual or perennial herb. Leaves are alternate (borne singly at each node on a stem). Flowers grow in leaf axils (where the leaf meets the stem). Flowers are tubular, and yellowish with purple veins. Fruit is a capsule with small lobes surrounded by a prominent calyx (the outermost bractlike part of the flower).

RANGE: Native to Britain and Europe. Has escaped into the wild in southern Canada and the United States, and is seen often in very disturbed areas.

TOXIC PARTS: All parts.

TOXICITY: Contain the alkaloids hyoscyamine, atropine, and scopolamine.

SYMPTOMS: Salivation (not a symptom of *Atropa* and *Datura* poisoning), rapid pulse, increased blood pressure, convulsions.

**Digitalis purpurea (foxglove)**

**Hyoscyamus niger (henbane)**

653

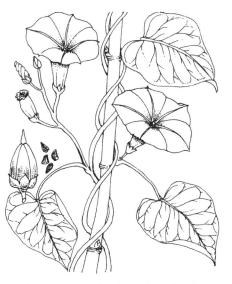

**Ipomoea tricolor (morning glory)**

**Jatropha multifida (physic nut)**

*Ipomoea tricolor,* Morning Glory
Morning glory family (Convolvulaceae)
DESCRIPTION: A perennial twining vine. Leaves are alternate (borne singly at each node on a stem). Flowers are funnellike and blue, white, rose-lavender, or striped. Cultivated varieties include 'Heavenly Blue', 'Pearly Gates', 'Blue Star', 'Flying Saucers', 'Summer Skies', and 'Wedding Bells'.
RANGE: Native to tropical America. Widely cultivated.
TOXIC PARTS: Seeds.
TOXICITY: Contain lysergic acid amides and other alkaloids. Similar to but less concentrated in effect than LSD.
SYMPTOMS: Hallucination. Side effects include nausea, vomiting, diarrhea, tenseness of muscles.

*Jatropha multifida,* Physic Nut, Coral Plant
Spurge family (Euphorbiaceae)
DESCRIPTION: A shrub or tree. Leaves are alter-

nate (borne singly at each node on a stem) and deeply divided into seven to eleven lobes. Flowers are scarlet. Fruits are yellow.
RANGE: Native to tropical America. Cultivated outdoors in warm areas, indoors elsewhere as a houseplant. Most poisonings are reported from south Florida and the Southwest.
TOXIC PARTS: All parts, especially the seeds.
TOXICITY: Contain the phytotoxin curcin. Overdoses of jatropha oil, used as a purgative, do occur.
SYMPTOMS: When eaten by children, fruits and seeds have caused nausea, violent vomiting, stomach cramps, bloody diarrhea, dehydration, dizziness. Some of the other species provide useful medicines.

*Kalmia latifolia,* Mountain Laurel
Heath family (Ericaceae)
DESCRIPTION: A broad-leaved evergreen shrub. Leaves are alternate (borne singly at each node on a stem). Flower clusters are terminal

**_Kalmia latifolia_ (mountain laurel)**

**_Lantana camara_ (yellow sage)**

(grow at the tip of a stalk) and white to rose. Fruit is a dry capsule.

RANGE: Native to eastern North America, where it is found in the understory of moist woodlands. Also cultivated.

TOXIC PARTS: All parts, including pollen.

TOXICITY: Contain the toxic resinoid andromedotoxin.

SYMPTOMS: Watering of mouth, nose, and eyes, followed by nausea, vomiting, abdominal pain, low blood pressure, weakness, paralysis of limbs. Honey from the nectar is poisonous but also very bitter. NOTE: The same toxic compound is found in rhododendrons and azaleas (_Rhododendron_ species).

_Lantana camara,_ Yellow Sage
Vervain family (Verbenaceae)

DESCRIPTION: A shrub. Stems are square, prickly. Leaves are opposite (borne opposite each other at each node on a stem) and rough. Flowers are tubular, white, yellow, and

orange to red, and occur in flat clusters. Fruits are bluish black and berrylike.

RANGE: Native to tropical America. Widely cultivated for its ornamental value, typically in hanging baskets.

TOXIC PARTS: All parts, especially the unripe berries.

TOXICITY: Contain the photosensitizing alkaloid lantanine.

SYMPTOMS: Muscle weakness, vomiting, bloody diarrhea, labored breathing, circulatory collapse.

_Melia azedarach,_ Chinaberry
Mahogany family (Meliaceae)

DESCRIPTION: A deciduous tree. Leaves are alternate (borne singly at each node on a stem), and compound, with many leaflets. Flowers are terminal panicles (clusters that grow at the tip of a stalk) and lilac in color. Fruit is a berrylike drupe, cream in color, and persists all winter.

**Melia azedarach (Chinaberry)**

**Narcissus species (narcissus, daffodil, jonquil)**

RANGE: Native to Asia. Is cultivated and has escaped into the wild and become invasive in warmer areas, especially the southern United States.

TOXIC PARTS: Fruits (ripe ones are more toxic than unripe ones), leaves.

TOXICITY: Contain neurotoxins and unidentified resins that can lead to the degeneration of the kidneys and liver.

SYMPTOMS: "Tea" brewed from leaves causes a burning sensation in the mouth. Fruit poisoning causes nausea, abdominal pain, vomiting, bloody diarrhea, thirst, irregular breathing, convulsions.

*Narcissus* species, Narcissus, Daffodil, Jonquil
Amaryllis family (Amaryllidaceae)

DESCRIPTION: Perennial herbs with a prominent underground bulb. Leaves are long and linear. Flowers can be solitary or in groups. Typically, flowers have a short tube- or ring-like formation of the petals called a corona.

RANGE: Native to Europe. Cultivated widely.

TOXIC PARTS: Bulbs cause most poisonings; they are often mistaken for onions.

TOXICITY: Contain the alkaloids galanthamine, lycorine, tazettine, haemanthamine, and others. Bulbs may contain calcium oxalate crystals.

SYMPTOMS: Nausea, vomiting, diarrhea, convulsions. Sap may cause dermatitis.

*Nerium oleander,* Oleander
Dogbane family (Apocynaceae)

DESCRIPTION: A shrub or small tree. Leaves are opposite (borne opposite from one another at the same node) or whorled. Flowers are in clusters at branch tips, and are white or pink to deep red, single or double.

RANGE: Native to southern Europe. Widely cultivated outdoors in the subtropics and often used as a decorative container plant in homes and offices.

TOXIC PARTS: All parts.

TOXICITY: Contain the cardiac glycosides neriin and oleandrin. Sucking nectar from flowers

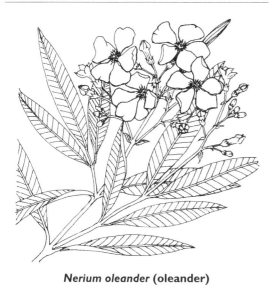

**Nerium oleander (oleander)**

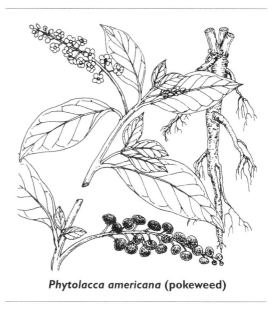

**Phytolacca americana (pokeweed)**

**Podophyllum peltatum (mayapple)**

or using branches as skewers for barbecuing is dangerous.

SYMPTOMS: Dizziness, vomiting, irregular heart-beat, convulsions, loss of consciousness. Leaf sap may cause dermatitis.

*Phytolacca americana,* Pokeweed, Pokeberry
Pokeweed family (Phytolaccaceae)

DESCRIPTION: A shrubby herb. Leaves are alternate (borne singly at each node on a stem). Flowers are in erect or drooping clusters at the ends of shoots. Fruits are drooping clusters of berries, shiny black when ripe.

RANGE: Native to the eastern United States and Canada. Common in disturbed areas.

TOXIC PARTS: All parts, especially the rootstock.

TOXICITY: Contain the saponins phytolaccin, phytolaccatoxin, and phytolaccigenin and salts of phytolaccic acid. Sap contains mitogens, which can cause blood cell abnormalities. NOTE: Wear gloves when handling the plant.

SYMPTOMS: Nausea, vomiting, diarrhea, labored breathing, respiratory failure, convulsions.

*Podophyllum peltatum,* Mayapple
Barberry family (Berberidaceae)

DESCRIPTION: A perennial herb. Two leaves per plant, each with five to nine lobes or segments. Flowers are solitary and white. Fruit is a yellow berry.

RANGE: A North American native found in dense woodland colonies.

TOXIC PARTS: All parts, especially the roots and unripe fruits.

TOXICITY: Contain the resins podophyllin and podophyllotoxin. Both exhibit antitumor properties.

SYMPTOMS: Misuse of mayapple as an herbal medicine can be very dangerous. Symptoms include diarrhea and vomiting. Powdered root can cause inflammation of the cornea and conjunctivitis if accidentally introduced into the eyes, and dermatitis if it comes into contact with the skin.

*Prunus serotina* and other species, Wild Cherry, Black Cherry

Rose family (Rosaceae)

DESCRIPTION: Shrubs and trees. Leaves are alternate (borne singly at each node on a stem). Flowers are white or pink. Fruits are fleshy and dark purple, with a hard pit.

RANGE: Native to the eastern United States. Common in woods and fields.

TOXIC PARTS: Seeds, leaves, bark (the fleshy part of the fruit is edible).

TOXICITY: The cyanogenic glycoside amygdalin in the leaves, bark, and especially the seeds leads to the formation of hydrocyanic acid in the body, which can result in cyanide poisoning. Seeds chewed and eaten in quantity or "tea" brewed from the leaves are dangerous.

SYMPTOMS: Cyanide poisoning results in difficulty in breathing, twitching, and an acetone odor on the breath. NOTE: Exert similar caution with seeds, leaves, and bark of plum, apricot, bitter almond, peach, cherry laurel, apple, crabapple.

*Rheum* x *cultorum (R. rhabarbarum)*, Rhubarb

Buckwheat family (Polygonaceae)

DESCRIPTION: An herbaceous perennial. Leaves consist of a large, flat blade and long, red or green stalk.

**Prunus serotina (wild cherry)**

**Rheum x cultorum (rhubarb)**

RANGE: Native to northwestern China. Widely cultivated for eating.

TOXIC PARTS: The flat leaf blade (the stalk is edible).

TOXICITY: Contains soluble oxalates and oxalic acid, which cause corrosion of mouth and intestinal tract, and insoluble calcium oxalate, which causes kidney damage.

SYMPTOMS: Nausea, burning of mouth and throat, kidney damage, stomach cramps, internal bleeding.

*Ricinus communis,* Castor-Oil Plant, Castor Bean

Spurge family (Euphorbiaceae)

DESCRIPTION: A shrubby herb; an annual in cool climates. Leaves are alternate (borne singly at each node on a stem) with five to eleven long lobes or segments. Fruits grow in clusters on stalks. Seeds are mottled with black, brown, or white markings.

RANGE: Native to tropical Africa. Has escaped into the wild in other warm parts of the world.

TOXIC PARTS: The entire plant, especially the seeds.

TOXICITY: Contains the phytotoxin ricin, especially the seeds, an extremely toxic substance.

SYMPTOMS: Chewing the seeds causes burning sensation in mouth and throat, vomiting, bloody diarrhea, liver and kidney damage, convulsions. Sap from leaves can cause dermatitis or irritation to eyes.

*Sambucus canadensis,* Elderberry

Honeysuckle family (Caprifoliaceae)

DESCRIPTION: A shrub. Stems have long spaces between successive leaf joints. Leaves are opposite (borne opposite from one another at each node on a stem), with five to eleven leaflets. Flowers are white and in umbels (flat-topped clusters). Fruit is berrylike and red or black.

**Ricinus communis (castor-oil plant)**

**Sambucus canadensis (elderberry)**

RANGE: Eastern Canada south to Florida and Texas.

TOXIC PARTS: All parts, except the berries, which are edible.

TOXICITY: Contain alkaloids and cyanogenic glycosides that release hydrocyanic acid (cyanide). Using stems as peashooters is dangerous.

SYMPTOMS: Nausea, vomiting, diarrhea. NOTE: compare the symptoms of *Prunus*.

*Solanum dulcamara,* European Bittersweet
Nightshade family (Solanaceae)

DESCRIPTION: A woody vine often found growing on fences. Leaves are alternate (borne singly at each node on a stem) with lobes or segments at the base. Flower clusters arise opposite the leaves, and are deep purple-blue. Fruits are drooping, oval berries, green changing to red.

RANGE: Native to Eurasia. Has escaped into the wild in areas around the world.

TOXIC PARTS: All parts, especially unripened fruits.

TOXICITY: Contain the alkaloid solanine and dulcamarine, a glycoside that produces effects similar to those of atropine (see *Atropa belladonna*).

SYMPTOMS: Headache, stomach pain, subnormal temperature, dilated pupils, vomiting, diarrhea, circulatory and respiratory depression. NOTE: Black nightshade, *Solanum nigrum,* is also a common weed. This annual herb's black fruit, which can be attractive to children, can also cause poisoning. In addition, household potatoes that have turned green from exposure to sunlight and any that have sprouted should be discarded because they, too, contain solanine.

*Taxus baccata,* as well as other *Taxus* species such as Japanese and native North American yews, Yew
Yew family (Taxaceae)

DESCRIPTION: A coniferous evergreen shrub or small tree. Leaves are alternate (borne singly at each node on a stem) and narrow. Fruit is

**Solanum dulcamara (European bittersweet)**

**Taxus baccata (English yew)**

a fleshy, scarlet, berrylike aril that surrounds a single seed.

RANGE: English and other yews are widely cultivated.

TOXIC PARTS: All parts, except the red aril around the seed; the seed must be chewed to release the toxin.

TOXICITY: Contain the alkaloid taxine.

SYMPTOMS: Slow heartbeat, difficulty breathing, diarrhea, vomiting, dilation of pupils, convulsions.

*Toxicodendron radicans,* Poison Ivy
Sumac family (Anacardiaceae)

DESCRIPTION: A climbing or trailing vine. Leaves are alternate (borne singly at each node on a stem), with three leaflets. Flowers are in axillary clusters (grow between the leaf and stem), and white to yellowish. Fruits are green to white. (The related poison sumac, *Toxicodendron vernix,* a small tree native to the eastern United States and found mostly in swampy areas, has leaves with seven to thirteen leaflets.)

RANGE: Native to eastern and central North America. Common at edges of woods, near fences, and on beaches.

TOXIC PARTS: All parts.

TOXICITY: Contain an oleoresin urushiol that causes allergic contact dermatitis. Do not burn the plant, because the urushiol is carried in the smoke and can be deposited on the skin or inhaled and irritate the lungs.

SYMPTOMS: Severe itching some hours after contact with bruised or broken plant tissue. Swelling and blistering follow. Scratching leads to secondary infections. NOTE: Other members of the sumac family capable of causing an allergic reaction include the skin of the fruit and leaves of the mango (*Mangifera*) and the shell enclosing the cashew nut (*Anacardium*), as well as the leaves of the plant.

*Urtica dioica,* Stinging Nettle
Nettle family (Urticaceae)

DESCRIPTION: A perennial herb. Leaves are opposite (borne opposite from one another at each

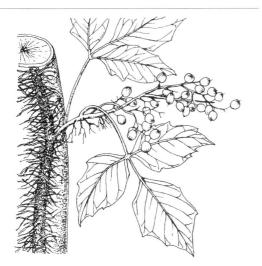

**Toxicodendron radicans (poison ivy)**

**Urtica dioica (stinging nettle)**

node on a stem). Flowers grow in clusters in leaf axils (where the leaf meets the stem). Leaves and stems are covered with stinging hairs.

RANGE: Native to Europe and Asia. Has escaped widely into the wild.

TOXIC PARTS: Leaves, stems

TOXICITY: The bulbous base of the stinging hairs contains various compounds, including acetylcholine, histamine, and 5-hydroxy-tryptamine.

SYMPTOMS: Stinging sensation of the skin on contact with plant. The stinging sensation on contact lasts less than 60 minutes due to alleviation by the lecithin in the plant's own sap.

## Mushrooms and Other Fungi

While fungi, including mushrooms, are now assigned to their own kingdom, separate from the plants with which they were previously grouped, they are included here for several reasons. First and foremost, fungi grow in the same habitats as plants and share a close biological relationship with them. The chance of encountering fungi during plant-related activities is high. The chance of encountering a poisonous species is likewise high.

A wide range of fungi are known to be toxic. Covered here are the relatively few species that have caused most reported poisonings, as well as those that the average gardener and outdoors enthusiast are likely to come across in the garden or the woods.

NEVER COLLECT FUNGI FROM THE WILD FOR EATING UNLESS YOU ARE ABSOLUTELY CONFIDENT IN YOUR ABILITY TO IDENTIFY THEM CORRECTLY. Many poisonous and nonpoisonous species are "look-alikes," and some of the dead-

liest ones may end up on your plate. The loss of a life or the need for a liver transplant is too high a price to pay for the adventure of collecting and eating mushrooms from the wild.

*Amanita* species, Amanita mushrooms

These are the species most often reported in poisonings:

a. Death cap (*Amanita phalloides*)

b. Destroying angel (*Amanita virosa*)

c. Spring destroying angel (*Amanita verna*)

d. Fly agaric (*Amanita muscaria,* discussed in greater detail in the next entry)

DESCRIPTION: Species (a) to (c) are the deadliest of the amanitas. They have the typical mushroom form, with an oval cap, which is greenish to yellowish in *A. phalloides* and pure white in *A. virosa* and *A. verna.* Gills are white but can be yellowish in *A. phalloides.* A skirt (veil) around the stipe (stalk) toward the cap is often evident. In all four species the stalks have a swelling, which may be cup-shaped, at their base. This swelling, called a volva, is usually just below ground. IMPORTANT: Always check for the presence of a volva when collecting mushrooms because this, especially in the case of the amanitas, is a key feature in identification. Never collect mushrooms by cutting the stalk at ground level.

RANGE: Mixed woodlands with coniferous and deciduous trees throughout North America.

SEASON: Spring through autumn.

TOXICITY: Contain amatoxins, especially amanitin.

SYMPTOMS: Generally, there is a symptomless period of 8 to 12—or even 24—hours after ingestion. This is followed by violent vomiting and diarrhea lasting about a day. The patient often feels quite well thereafter. However, severe damage to the liver and kid-

**Left: *Amanita virosa* (destroying angel)**
**Right: *Amanita muscaria* (fly agaric)**

neys may be well underway, a process that commences immediately after ingestion. IMPORTANT: Suspect amanita poisoning if there is a delay in symptoms after ingestion. Samples of the specimens eaten, even fragments from the vomit, should be collected to aid in identification.

*Amanita muscaria,* Fly Agaric

DESCRIPTION: Cap is bloodred to orange-red and flecked with patches of white warts. Other details are similar to those of (a) to (c) above.

RANGE: Mixed coniferous and deciduous woodlands.

SEASON: Summer into autumn.

TOXICITY: Contains muscarine, muscimol, ibotenic acid, and other related compounds.

SYMPTOMS: Slowing of the heart, dilation of blood vessels, delirium, deep sleep. NOTE: A similar mushroom depicted with a bright red cap with marshmallowy flecks is often seen in children's books. Be alert to the fact that a young child who comes across the fly agaric in the wild may associate it with the mushroom in storybooks and be tempted to handle or even sample a specimen.

*Conocybe filaris,* Deadly Conocybe

DESCRIPTION: Cap is ¼ inch to 1 inch in diameter and yellow-brown. Gills are rusty brown. Stipe (stalk) is yellow to yellow-orange with a veil (skirt).

RANGE: North America, in grass or on wood chips.

SEASON: Summer to autumn.

TOXICITY: Contains amanitin.

SYMPTOMS: See *Amanita.*

*Galerina autumnalis,* Deadly Galerina

DESCRIPTION: Cap is 1 inch to 2½ inches in diameter and dark brown, with a slight bump, called an umbo, at the top. Gills are yellow to rusty brown. Lower part of the brown stalk has prominent white fungal threads.

RANGE: North America, on conifer and hardwood stumps.

SEASON: Spring to autumn.

TOXICITY: Contains amanitin.

SYMPTOMS: See *Amanita.*

*Conocybe filaris* (deadly conocybe)

**Galerina autumnalis (deadly galerina)**

**Coprinus atramentarius (inky cap)**

**Omphalotus illudens (jack-o'-lantern)**

*Omphalotus illudens,* Jack-o'-Lantern
DESCRIPTION: Cap is 2 inches to 8 inches in diameter, convex to funnel-shaped, and orange-
yellow. Gills are also orange-yellow. Stalk is
2 inches to 8 inches long. When fresh, gills
emit a greenish yellow glow in the dark.
RANGE: North America, on base of stumps or

buried roots of oaks and other deciduous
trees. Common in gardens and on lawns.
SEASON: All summer.
TOXICITY: Toxins are not well known.
SYMPTOMS: Nausea, vomiting, diarrhea.

*Coprinus atramentarius,* Inky Cap, Tippler's Bane
DESCRIPTION: Cap is 1¼ inches to 2¾ inches in
diameter, conical, and gray-brown. Gills are
white, turning gray then black. Stalk is 2¾
inches to 6½ inches long, white, and hollow,
with remnants of a veil (skirt).
RANGE: North America, on rotting wood or
roots buried underground.
SEASON: Spring to early winter.
TOXICITY: Toxins are not well known.
SYMPTOMS: While this mushroom is edible, it
should not be eaten with or followed by alcohol. Causes flushing in the face and neck,
nausea, palpitations.

*Gyromitra esculenta,* False Morel
DESCRIPTION: Cap is 1¼ inches to 4½ inches in

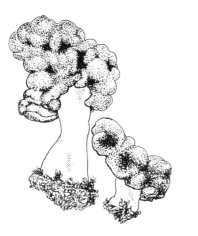

**Gyromitra esculenta (false morel)**

diameter, brainlike, and reddish brown. Stalk is ½ inch to 2½ inches long. This fungus is in a group different from that of those mentioned above and does not have gills.

OCCURRENCE: North America, in coniferous and hardwood forests.

SEASON: Early spring.

TOXICITY: Contains the toxin monomethylhydrazine and others.

SYMPTOMS: Symptoms may be delayed some 5 to 6 hours after eating. They include a bloated sensation, cramps, vomiting, diarrhea, and convulsions.

## Certified Poison Control Centers

The following are regional poison control centers that are certified by the American Association of Poison Control Centers. They are listed by state, but some centers serve several states. They are open 24 hours a day.

## Alabama

**Alabama Poison Center,** Tuscaloosa
408-A Paul Bryant Drive
Tuscaloosa, AL 35401
Emergency Phone:
(800) 462-0800 (AL only)
(205) 345-0600

**Regional Poison Control Center**
The Children's Hospital of Alabama
1600 Seventh Avenue South
Birmingham, AL 35233-1711
Emergency Phone:
(205) 939-9201
(800) 292-6678 (AL only)
(205) 933-4050

## Arizona

**Arizona Poison and Drug Information Center**
Arizona Health Sciences Center, Room #1156
1501 North Campbell Avenue
Tucson, AZ 85724
Emergency Phone:
(800) 362-0101 (AZ only)
(520) 626-6016

**Samaritan Regional Poison Center**
Good Samaritan Regional Medical Center,
    Ancillary-1
1111 East McDowell Road
Phoenix, AZ 85006
Emergency Phone:
(602) 253-3334

## California

**Central California Regional Poison Control Center**
**Valley Children's Hospital**
3151 North Millbrook, IN31
Fresno, CA 93703
Emergency Phone:
(800) 346-5922 (Central CA only)
(209) 445-1222

**San Diego Regional Poison Center**
UCSD Medical Center
200 West Arbor Drive
San Diego, CA 92103-8925
Emergency Phone:
(619) 543-6000
(800) 876-4766 (in 619 area code only)

**University of California, Davis, Medical Center**
Regional Poison Control Center
2315 Stockton Boulevard
Sacramento, CA 95817
Emergency Phone:
(916) 734-3692
(800) 342-9293 (Northern CA only)

## Colorado

**Rocky Mountain Poison and Drug Center**
8802 East Ninth Avenue
Denver, CO 80220-6800
Emergency Phone:
(303) 629-1123

## Connecticut

**Connecticut Regional Poison Center**
University of Connecticut Health Center
263 Farmington Avenue
Farmington, CT 06030
Emergency Phone:
(800) 343-2722 (CT only)
(203) 679-3056

## District of Columbia

**National Capital Poison Center**
3201 New Mexico Avenue N.W., Suite 310
Washington, DC 20016
Emergency Phone:
(202) 625-3333,
(202) 362-8563 (TTY)

## Florida

**Florida Poison Information Center—Miami**
University of Miami School of Medicine
Department of Pediatrics
P.O. Box 016960 (R-131)
Miami, FL 33101
Emergency Phone:
(800) 282-3171 (FL only)

**Florida Poison Information Center—Jacksonville**
University Medical Center
University of Florida Health Science Center—
   Jacksonville
655 West 8th Street
Jacksonville, FL 32209
Emergency Phone:
(904) 549-4480
(800) 282-3171 (FL only)

**The Florida Poison Information and Toxicology
   Resource Center**
Tampa General Hospital
P.O. Box 1289
Tampa, FL 33601
Emergency Phone:
(813) 253-4444 (Tampa)
(800) 282-3171 (Florida)

## Georgia

**Georgia Poison Center**
Grady Memorial Hospital
80 Butler Street S.E.
P.O. Box 26066
Atlanta, GA 30335-3801
Emergency Phone:
(800) 282-5846 (GA only)
(404) 616-9000

## Indiana

**Indiana Poison Center**
Methodist Hospital of Indiana
1701 North Senate Boulevard
P.O. Box 1367
Indianapolis, IN 46206-1367
Emergency Phone:
(800) 382-9097 (IN only)
(317) 929-2323

## Kentucky

Kentucky Regional Poison Center of
Kosair's Children's Hospital
Medical Towers South, Suite 572
P. O. Box 35070
Louisville, KY 40232-5070
Emergency Phone:
(502) 629-7275
(800) 722-5725 (KY only)

## Louisiana

Louisiana Drug and Poison Information Center
Northeast Louisiana University
Sugar Hall
Monroe, LA 71209-6430
Emergency Phone:
(800) 256-9822
(318) 362-5393

## Maryland

Maryland Poison Center
20 North Pine Street
Baltimore, MD 21201
Emergency Phone:
(410) 528-7701
(800) 492-2414 (MD only)

National Capital Poison Center
(D.C. suburbs only)
3201 New Mexico Avenue N.W., Suite 310
Washington, DC 20016
Emergency Phone:
(202) 625-3333
(202) 362-8563

## Massachusetts

Massachusetts Poison Control System
300 Longwood Avenue
Boston, MA 02115
Emergency Phone:
(617) 232-2120
(800) 682-9211

## Michigan

Poison Control Center
Children's Hospital of Michigan
4160 John Rd., Suite 425
Detroit, MI 48201
Emergency Phone:
(313) 745-5711

## Minnesota

Hennepin Regional Poison Center
Hennepin County Medical Center
701 Park Avenue
Minneapolis, MN 55415
Emergency Phone:
(612) 347-3141
Petline: (612) 337-7387

Minnesota Regional Poison Center
8100 34th Avenue South
P.O. Box 1309
Minneapolis, MN 55440-1309
Emergency Phone:
(612) 221-2113

## Missouri

Cardinal Glennon Children's Hospital
Regional Poison Center
1465 South Grand Boulevard
St. Louis, MO 63104
Emergency Phone:
(314) 772-5200
(800) 366-8888

## Montana

Rocky Mountain Poison and Drug Center
8802 East Ninth Avenue
Denver, CO 80220
Emergency Phone:
(303) 629-1123

# Nebraska

**The Poison Center**
8301 Dodge Street
Omaha, NE 68114
Emergency Phone:
(402) 390-5555 (Omaha)
(800) 955-9119 (NE & WY)

# New Jersey

**New Jersey Poison Information and Education**
   **System**
201 Lyons Avenue
Newark, NJ 07112
Emergency Phone:
(800) 962-1253

# New Mexico

**New Mexico Poison and Drug Information**
   **Center**
University of New Mexico
Health Sciences Library, Room 125
Albuquerque, NM 87131-1076
Emergency Phone:
(505) 843-2551
(800) 432-6866 (NM only)

# New York

**Central New York Poison Control Center**
SUNY Health Science Center
750 East Adams Street
Syracuse, NY 13203
Emergency Phone:
(315) 476-4766
(800) 252-5655 (NY only)

**Finger Lakes Regional Poison Center**
University of Rochester Medical Center
601 Elmwood Avenue
Box 321, Room G-3275
Rochester, NY 14642
Emergency Phone:
(800) 333-0542
(716) 275-5151

**Hudson Valley Regional Poison Center**
Phelps Memorial Hospital Center
701 North Broadway
North Tarrytown, NY 10591
Emergency Phone:
(800) 336-6997
(914) 366-3030

**Long Island Regional Poison Control Center**
Winthrop University Hospital
259 First Street
Mineola, NY 11501
Emergency Phone:
(516) 542-2323, 542-2324,
(516) 542-2325, 542-3813

**New York City Poison Control Center**
N.Y.C. Department of Health
455 First Avenue, Room 123
New York, NY 10016
Emergency Phone:
(212) 340-4494
(212) P-O-I-S-O-N-S

# North Carolina

**Carolinas Poison Center**
1012 South Kings Drive, Suite 206
P.O. Box 32861
Charlotte, NC 28232-2861
Emergency Phone:
(704) 355-4000
(800) 84-TOXIN
(800) 848-6946

# Ohio

**Central Ohio Poison Center**
700 Children's Drive
Columbus, OH 43205-2696
Emergency Phone:
(614) 228-1323
(800) 682-7625
(614) 228-2272 (TTY)
(614) 461-2012

Cincinnati Drug & Poison Information Center
and
Regional Poison Control System
P.O. Box 670144
Cincinnati, OH 45267-0144
Emergency Phone:
(513) 558-5111
(800) 872-5111 (OH only)

## Oregon

Oregon Poison Center
Oregon Health Sciences University
3181 S.W. Sam Jackson Park Road, CB550
Portland, OR 97201
Emergency Room:
(503) 494-8968
(800) 452-7165 (OR only)

## Pennsylvania

Central Pennsylvania Poison Center
University Hospital
Milton S. Hershey Medical Center
Hershey, PA 17033
Emergency Phone:
(800) 521-6110

The Poison Control Center
3600 Sciences Center, Suite 220
Philadelphia, PA 19104-2641
Emergency Phone:
(215) 386-2100

Pittsburgh Poison Center
3705 Fifth Avenue
Pittsburgh, PA 15213
Emergency Phone:
(412) 681-6669

## Rhode Island

Rhode Island Poison Center
593 Eddy Street
Providence, RI 02903
Emergency Phone:
(401) 444-5727

## Tennessee

Middle Tennessee Poison Center
The Center for Clinical Toxicology
Vanderbilt University Medical Center
1161 21st Avenue South
501 Oxford House
Nashville, TN 37232-4632
Emergency Phone:
(800) 288-9999
(615) 936-2034

## Texas

Central Texas Poison Center
Scott & White Memorial Hospital
2401 South 31st Street
Temple, TX 76508
Emergency Phone:
(800) 764-7661

North Texas Poison Center
5201 Harry Hines Boulevard
P.O. Box 35926
Dallas, TX 75235
Emergency Phone:
(800) 764-7661
Texas Watts (800) 441-0040

Southeast Texas Poison Center
The University of Texas Medical Branch
301 University Avenue
Galveston, TX 77550-2780
Emergency Phone:
(409) 765-1420 (Galveston)
(713) 654-1701 (Houston)
(800) 764-7661

## Utah

Utah Poison Control Center
410 Chipeta Way, Suite 230
Salt Lake City, UT 84108
Emergency Phone:
(801) 581-2151
(800) 456-7707 (UT only)

## Virginia

**Blue Ridge Poison Center**
P.O. Box 67, Blue Ridge
University of Virginia Medical Center
Charlottesville, VA 22901
Emergency Phone:
(804) 924-5543
(800) 451-1428

**National Capital Poison Center (Northern VA only)**
3201 New Mexico Avenue N.W., Suite 310
Washington, DC 20016
Emergency Phone:
(202) 625-3333

## Washington

**Washington Poison Center**
155 N.E. 100th Street, Suite 400
Seattle, WA 98125
Emergency Phone:
(206) 526-2121
(800) 732-6985
(800) 572-0638 (TDD only)
(206) 517-2394

## West Virginia

**West Virginia Poison Center**
3110 MacCorkle Avenue S.E.
Charleston, WV 25304
Emergency Phone:
(800) 642-3625 (WV only)
(304) 348-4211

## Wyoming

**The Poison Center**
8301 Dodge Street
Omaha, NE 68114
Emergency Phone:
(402) 390-5555 (Omaha)
(800) 955-9119 (NE and WY)

# Further Reading

Blackwell, W. H. *Poisonous and Medicinal Plants.* Englewood Cliffs, N.J.: Prentice Hall, 1990.

Hardin, J. W., and J. M. Arena. *Human Poisoning from Native and Cultivated Plants.* Durham, N.C.: Duke University Press, 1974.

Kinghorn, A. D., ed. *Toxic Plants.* New York: Columbia University Press, 1979.

Lewis, W. H., and M. P. F. Elvin-Lewis. *Medical Botany: Plants Affecting Man's Health.* New York: John Wiley and Sons, 1977.

Phillips, R. *Mushrooms of North America.* Boston: Little, Brown and Co., 1991.

Turner, N. J., and A.F. Szczawinski. *Common Poisonous Plants and Mushrooms of North America.* Portland, Ore.: Timber Press, 1991.

# 15

# PLANTS IN LITERATURE AND LORE

Plants have loomed large in the literature and lore of human cultures around the globe. Myths and legends sprang up in ancient times to explain the origin of some of the more beautiful, fragrant, or otherwise fascinating flowers. Trees and shrubs with unusual attributes were ascribed symbolic powers. An elaborate system of flowers as symbols for sentiments and values, called "the language of flowers," seized the fancy of much of the Western world in the nineteenth century. Thus, a gift of violets indicated loyalty and faithfulness, and one of honeysuckle suggested being united in love. In 1830, Aimé Martin, best known as the author of *Lettres à Sophie,* compiled *Langage des Fleurs* and another, similar book on the subject under the pseudonym Madame Charlotte de la Tour. Translations of these French works, as well as others, appeared in a number of European languages. The origins of this symbolic communication are fuzzy—some believe it to have evolved in the Orient while others suggest that it simply arose in Europe and spread to the United States.

Following is an encyclopedia of some of the plants that have figured most prominently in Western cultures and influenced cultures worldwide.

## Almond

According to Greek mythology, Princess Phyllis of Thrace fell in love with a youth who was shipwrecked in her father's kingdom. The youth departed with promises of matrimony and everlasting love, but the princess waited in vain for his return and wasted away. The gods honored her constant love by turning her into an almond tree (*Amygdalus communis*), where she stood vigil by the sea with arms outstretched. The youth, having long ago forgotten his promise, did eventually return and learn of Phyllis's fate. Consumed by guilt, he weepingly embraced the almond tree, his tears watering its roots. Happy at last, the tree burst into bloom. Interestingly, the almond tree represented indiscretion and promise in the language of flowers.

Christians identify the almond as one of the many flowers of the Virgin Mary. In Hebraic tradition, Aaron, the brother of Moses, carried a rod made from almond wood, which miraculously budded and bore ripe almonds overnight: "And it came to pass, that on the morrow Moses went into the tabernacle of witness; and behold, the rod of Aaron for the house of Levi was budded, and brought forth buds, and bloomed blossoms, and yielded almonds."—Numbers 17:23.

## Apple

Despite the prevailing misconception, the apple (*Malus*) was never identified in the Bible as the forbidden fruit from the Tree of Knowledge of Good and Evil that tempted Eve.

From Greece came the legend of the judgment of Paris, son of the king of Troy, explaining what provoked the Trojan War. Paris was called upon by the god of the heavens, Zeus, to award a golden apple to the fairest goddess—a difficult task considering that the three rivals each offered him bribes. Hera, wife of Zeus, offered power and wealth. Athena, goddess of the hunt, offered glory in war. But it was the goddess of love, Aphrodite, whose gift of the most beautiful mortal woman in the world Paris accepted. That mortal was Helen, wife of the king of Sparta, and it is her liaison with Paris that is credited with sparking the Trojan War.

Throughout his plays, Shakespeare mentions apples, the different varieties, and even grafting

with apple trees in a rather straightforward manner. In *The Merchant of Venice,* I.3, Antonio sees Shylock and comments:

> An evil soul producing holy witness,
> Is like a villain with a smiling cheek,
> A goodly apple rotten at the heart.

Also memorable are the words of the American poet Robert Frost in "Mending Wall":

> My apple trees will never get across
> And eat the cones under his pines, I tell
>    him.
> He only says, "Good fences make good
>    neighbors."

## Ash

Ash (*Fraxinus*) is the legendary tree of life in Norse mythology, called Yggdrasil. This sacred tree, rooted in the netherworld, grew through earth to spread its branches into Paradise, where its leaves became clouds and its fruit the stars. To the Romans, ash was the sacred tree of Mars, god of war. Achilles was said to carry a spear made from an ash tree, and Cupid fashioned arrows from it. "May your footfall be by an ash's root" is an old English saying, wishing good luck. The Algonquian Indians believed that the Creator pierced the heart of an ash tree, and the first humans emerged.

## Aspen

The aspen tree (*Populus tremula*) has leaves with silver undersides that move at the least stirring of air and appear to shimmer or tremble. According to a Christian legend, the aspen was the wood used to construct the cross of Jesus; hence the tree shivers with shame and remorse at its history. Chaucer invokes the trembling aspen to describe Criseyde in the arms of Troilus (*Troilus and Criseyde* III.1200): "Right as an aspes leef she gan to quake." Shakespeare makes reference to agitated anger in *Henry IV, Part Two,* II.4, "Feel, masters, how I shake. . . . Yea, in very truth do I, an 'twere an aspen leaf I cannot abide swaggerers."

## Cedar

The cedar of Lebanon (*Cedrus libani*), referred to in the Bible as "the glory of Lebanon" (Isaiah 35:2), was once abundant in forests of Lebanon, with some trees over a thousand years old. Ancient people revered the trees for their strength and longevity. The Egyptians built ships, thrones, and buildings with the wood and used the tree's resin in the elaborate process of mummification. The Bible records the negotiations of King Solomon for the cedar wood required to build his palace and temple in Jerusalem.

Shakespeare refers to cedar to suggest ancient and notable ancestry (*Richard III* I.3):

But I was born so high,
Our aerie buildeth in the cedar's top,
And dallies with the wind and scorns the
    sun.

## Cherry

In the Orient, viewing flowers, especially flowering cherries (*Prunus*), has been a popular spring ritual for thousands of years. An ancient Japanese legend surrounds an unusual autumn-blooming cherry variety, *Prunus subhirtella* 'Autumnalis'. One November afternoon in A.D. 408, an emperor was hunting with his men at his palace near Kyoto when he beheld a cherry petal floating into his cup of sake. He wondered whether he had drunk too much? He dispatched his men to search for—and continue searching until they discovered and brought back—the mysterious tree from which petals fell in autumn.

Shakespeare uses cherry fruit and its bright color for imagery in his plays. In *A Midsummer Night's Dream,* his descriptions include "my cherry lips," "this cherry nose," and a comparison of friendship with a double cherry in *A Midsummer Night's Dream* III.2:

So we grow together
Like to a double cherry, seeming parted;
But yet a union in partition—
Two lovely berries molded on one stem.

## Chestnut

In Christian lore, the chestnut tree (*Castanea sativa*) is an emblem of virtue and chastity—a sharp-prickled outer covering encases each of the sweet chestnuts. The ancient Greeks dedicated chestnuts to Zeus, god of the heavens, but it is the Romans who are credited with spreading the chestnut throughout Europe. Roasting chestnuts over a fire is an old European winter custom, popular in Shakespeare's time. Unless properly lanced, roasting chestnuts rupture with explosive force, as Shakespeare denotes in *The Taming of the Shrew* I.2:

And do you tell me of a woman's tongue,
That gives not half so great a blow to
    hear
As will a chestnut in a farmer's fire?

## Fig

Long in cultivation, the fig (*Ficus carica*) is represented in ancient Egyptian tomb and temple art. In Roman mythology, the fig became sacred as the tree under which the cradle of the founders of Rome, Romulus and Remus, was found. References to the fig, a staple of the biblical diet, are ample throughout the Bible. Fig trees are perhaps best remembered from the story of Adam and Eve in Genesis 3:7: "Then the eyes of both were opened, and they knew that they were naked; and they sewed fig leaves together and made themselves aprons."

Two other species of fig, both native to Asia—the bo tree or peepul (*F. religiosa*) and the banyan (*F. benghalensis*)—are sacred in Eastern lore. The founder of Buddhism attained wisdom meditating under the bo tree, and the Hindu god Vishnu was believed to have been born under the same species. The banyan is revered by Hindus as the tree into which the god Brahma was transformed.

## Forget-Me-Not

The name of the forget-me-not (*Myosotis arvensis*) expresses its meaning in the language of flowers. According to European lore, a chivalrous lover noted his beloved's admiration for a dainty blue flower and set out to pluck a bouquet for her. The flowers grew on the other side of a lake, and the young man swam across to pick a bouquet. Alas, with his prized bouquet in hand, he tired while swimming back. With his last bit of strength, he hurled the flowers onto the bank at his beloved's feet and cried out, "Forget me not," just before he sank to a watery grave.

In Christian lore, after creating the Garden of Eden, God set about naming all the plants, counseling them to remember their names. One tiny flower, overlooked by God, timidly asked for a name. Struck by this oversight and the flower's loveliness, God chose to call the flower "forget-me-not."

## Frankincense

Frankincense—the resin from shrub species in the genus *Boswellia,* used in ancient times as an ingredient in incenses and perfumes—was widely traded by the ancients. Several references in the Bible evidence its prized standing; perhaps most famous is the gift of the wise men to the baby Jesus Christ in Matthew 2:11: ". . . they presented unto him gifts; gold, and frankincense, and myrrh."

## Garlic

Since ancient times, garlic (*Allium sativum*) was recommended for almost everything that ails humans. The pyramid builders in Egypt were reputed to have eaten the herb to build strength, Roman soldiers believed it heightened courage, and the Greeks that it stimulated athletes. In Homer's *Odyssey,* garlic is the charm recommended to Ulysses to safeguard him from the sorceress Circe, capable of transforming men into swine. In the Bible, Numbers 11:5, garlic is one of the remembered foods left behind by the Children of Israel seeking the Promised Land.

## Hemlock

This herb (*Conium maculatum*), poisonous to plants and animals, is linked to the ancient

Greek philosopher Socrates, who, as a condemned man accused of corrupting the youth of Athens, was purported to have died after drinking a cup of the herb. In Greek and Roman times, hemlock was administered by the state to political offenders.

Shakespeare capitalized on the fearsome properties of hemlock in *Macbeth* IV.1 in the famous ("Double, double toil and trouble, / Fire burn and caldron bubble") witch scene. The third witch contributes to the brew:

> Scale of dragon, tooth of wolf;
> Witches' mummy; maw, and gulf
> Of the ravined salt-sea shark,
> Root of hemlock, digged i' the dark. . . .

## Holly

The tradition of using holly (*Ilex*) as a festive winter decoration dates to Roman times when gifts of holly branches were tokens of goodwill at the celebration of the god Saturn. Holly was considered a plant of good fortune because of its habit of staying green all winter and its bright-colored berries; branches of the tree itself were believed to bring good luck to a home. Later, Druids adorned their altars with the plant. Today, Christians often decorate their homes with holly for the joyous Christmas season. Some legends associate the prickly leaves of some hollies and their bloodred berries with the crown of thorns and the crucifixion of Jesus Christ.

## Honeysuckle

In the language of flowers, honeysuckle (*Lonicera*) means united in love—a reference to its twisting, twining habit. Shakespeare evoked this meaning when he characterized a lover's embrace in *A Midsummer Night's Dream* IV.1: "So doth the woodbine and the sweet honeysuckle / Gently entwist."

## Horse Chestnut

Some say that the common name horse chestnut (*Aesculus hippocastanum*) comes from the fact that when the leaves of the tree fall, the scars on the young branches resemble horse's hooves. Others say that it comes from the ancient Greeks or Turks, who used the fruits to cure ailments in horses. The almost mahogany-colored, shiny fruits, called conkers, are poisonous if eaten raw. Henry Wadsworth Longfellow's most famous description in "The Village Blacksmith"—"Under the spreading chestnut tree / The village smithy stands"—is said to immortalize a horse chestnut tree that once grew in Cambridge, Massachusetts.

## Hyacinth

This flower gets its name from a Greek myth. Both Apollo, the sun god, and Zephyr, the wind, loved a beautiful youth named Hyacinthus. While Apollo and Hyacinthus were playing the ancient game of quoits, the jealous Zephyr caused a discus thrown by Apollo to veer off the mark and strike Hyacinthus in the head, killing him. Grief-stricken, Apollo changed the drops of blood from Hyacinthus' head into the hyacinth flower (*Hyacinthus*). Associated with remembrance, the hyacinth has long been carved into tombstones.

## Iris

The iris (*Iris*) flower, an ancient symbol of royalty, adorns Egyptian wall paintings in the Valley of the Kings and was carved in the stone walls of the temple of Karnak. The plant genus was named for Iris, the Greek goddess of the rainbow, Hera and Zeus's special messenger to mortals. The Greeks often planted irises on the graves of women in recognition of the goddess's role of ushering souls to the next world along a rainbow bridge. Muslims customarily planted white irises, reflecting the color for mourning, at grave sites. Christians claim the three-petaled iris, which for them symbolically reflects the Trinity, as the Virgin Mary's flower.

The iris became the symbolic flower of France, called the fleur-de-lis. In one legend, the sixth-century King Clovis outwitted the Goths through simple horticultural deduction. The King's beleaguered army was backed against the river Lys, bordering Flanders, when he noticed flag irises growing out into the river. Knowing that these irises could survive only in shallow water, Clovis forded the river to safety. The grateful King adopted the iris as his emblem, and it became known as Fleur-de-Lys. In another legend, King Clovis prayed to the Christian God of his wife Clotilde for victory. Following his success in battle, he converted to Christianity and replaced the three toad emblems on his banner with three irises, the flowers of the Virgin Mary. During the twelfth-century crusades, King Louis VII carried the iris banner, which became known as Fleur de Louis, eventually evolving to fleur-de-lis.

To complicate matters further, the iris or fleur-de-lis ("flower-de-luce" as it was known in Shakespeare's era) was thought to be a lily. In *The Winter's Tale* IV.4, Perdita talks of "lilies of all kinds, / The flower-de-luce being one!"

## Ivy

Sacred to the Greek and Roman wine gods—Bacchus or Dionysus—ivy (*Hedera helix*) was often pictured encircling the divine heads in leafy crowns as it was believed to be an antidote to inebriation. The Bible, in II Maccabees 6:7, describes a festival to the wine god: "And when the feast of Dionysus came, they were compelled to walk in the procession in honor of Dionysus, wearing wreaths of ivy." Out of ivy's association with wine probably grew the European custom of hanging a wreath, branch, or shrub of evergreens, usually ivy—called a "bush"—to indicate the entrance of a tavern or seller of wine. An English proverb recounted by Shakespeare in the epilogue of *As You Like It* suggests that good wine needs no recommendation: "If it be true that good wine needs no bush, 'tis true that a good play needs no epilogue." In *A Midsummer Night's Dream* IV.1, the playwright uses the clinging habit of ivy as a simile for embracing: "the female ivy so enrings the barky fingers of the elm."

## Lily

"Lily" usually refers to a plant in the *Lilium* genus, but not always (see "Iris," above). Biblical scholars suggest that many flowers—including lilies, irises, anemones, and even wildflowers in general—may be the famous "lilies of the field" in the New Testament, Matthew 6:28–29—"Consider the lilies of the field, how they grow; they toil not, neither do they spin: And yet I say unto you, That even Solomon in all his glory was not arrayed like one of these."

The capitals of columns in ancient Egypt were dressed with stone images of the white lily (*Lilium candidum*). To the Greeks, the white lily was the flower of Hera, goddess of motherhood, marriage, and the sky. The Romans made it the emblem of Juno, goddess of the heaven and protector of women. In one Roman legend, the lily sprang from a drop of milk that the baby Hercules spilled while suckling at his mother Juno's divine breast; another drop streaked the heavens and can be seen as the Milky Way. In Christian lore, the white lily sprang from the tears of Eve after she was expelled from the Garden of Eden.

Throughout the Renaissance, the white lily was regularly featured in religious paintings depicting the Archangel Gabriel's announcement to the Virgin Mary that she was to become the mother of the savior of the world. The white lily also came to be commonly called the Madonna lily, symbolizing purity, virtue, and innocence for Christians.

Shakespeare capitalized on the rich imagery of the lily as an emblem of beauty and chastity in *Love's Labour Lost,* when he called a maiden's honor "as pure as the unsullied lily." Conversely, in *Macbeth,* the phrase, "Thou lily-liver'd boy," suggests cowardly behavior when Macbeth berates a terrified servant.

## Lily of the Valley

In Sussex, England, the lilies of the valley (*Convallaria majalis*) growing in abundance in the woods were said to have sprung from the blood of St. Leonard, a local hero who fought the frightful dragon, Temptation. For three days St. Leonard struggled mightily with the beast and finally was victorious. The flowers identify spots where drops of St. Leonard's blood, drawn by the dragon's fierce claws, fell. In another tradition, the flowers are said to be the tears of the Virgin Mary—sometimes called Our Lady's

tears. In Norse legend, lilies of the valley belong to Ostara, the goddess of spring, and their blooming heralds her arrival.

## Lotus

The lotus (*Nelumbo nucifera*) is well represented in cultures of the early Mediterranean, the East, and the Americas. Ancient peoples attached great significance to the plant's habit of rising from the mucky bottoms of ponds, lakes, and rivers to bloom unsullied by muddy waters; it symbolized purity and beauty.

To the Egyptians, the lotus was sacred to Horus, deity of the sun, who issued forth from its blossom. Similar is the Hindu story of the birth of Brahma, who also arose from a sacred lotus. In India, Buddhists believe that the lotus sprang up to proclaim the birth of Buddha. In Mayan art, the lotus flower is often a symbol for Earth.

## Mandrake

Throughout history, the oddly humanlike shape of the mandrake root (*Mandragora officinarum*), in addition to the plant's narcotic properties, have captured the imagination. In Genesis 30:14–15, Rachel calls for mandrakes to help her conceive: "And Reuben went in the days of wheat harvest, and found mandrakes in the field, and brought them unto his mother Leah. Then Rachel said to Leah, Give me, I pray thee, of thy son's mandrakes." The Greeks attributed aphrodisiac properties to the plant, calling it the love apple; mandrake became identified with the sorceress Circe, who concocted magical potions capable of turning men into swine.

In medieval times, pulling a mandrake root out of the ground was said to cause an excruciatingly unbearable sound, capable of inciting insanity if not certain death. Shakespeare related this lore in *Romeo and Juliet* IV.3:

> And shrieks like mandrakes' torn out of
> the earth,
> That living mortals hearing them run
> mad.

He also referred to the narcotic properties of the plant in *Antony and Cleopatra* I.5. In this play, Cleopatra desires a draft of mandragora, the old Greek name for mandrake, upon her separation from Antony—"That I might sleep out this great gap of time / My Antony is away." Shakespeare's contemporary John Donne wrote the following in "Song":

> Go and catch a falling star,
> Get with child a mandrake root,
> Tell me where all past years are,
> Or who cleft the devil's foot.

## Marigold

Known in Roman times, and the longest cultivated of all the flowers loosely referred to as marigold, is the yellow pot marigold or calendula (*Calendula officinalis*), which opens and closes with the sun. A Greek myth recounts the story of Caltha, a young maid, who so loved the sun god Apollo that she remained in the fields all night to catch the first glimpse of his rising. Consumed by love, she lost herself in the sun's rays, and a solitary marigold grew in her stead. Shakespeare elaborates on the flower's association with the sun in *The Winter's Tale* IV.4: "The marigold, that goes to bed wi' the sun / And

with him rises weeping." Christians claim the golden marigold as the Virgin Mary's flower, believing she wore the flowers, Mary-golds, on her breast. The flowers were widely used in medieval church festivals.

The commonly misnamed African marigold (*Tagetes erecta*) arrived in Europe from Mexico, where it is known as the flower of the dead—long used in ceremonies to honor the deceased on All Souls' Day. Equally misnamed, the French marigold (*Tagetes patula*) is native to Mexico. Legend identifies the orange-red flecks on the flowers of French marigolds as the blood of Aztecs slaughtered by Spanish conquistadors in their quest for gold.

## Medlar

A native European fruit relatively unknown today, medlar (*Mespilus germanica*) was a favorite during the Middle Ages in spite of its unappetizing-looking fruits that are rock hard when harvested and require more ripening before they are edible. Because of the odd-looking brown fruit with the tip flared wide, Chaucer called medlar the "open-arse" fruit. Some suggest that in *Romeo and Juliet* II.1, Shakespeare wrote "open et cetera" to avoid using Chaucer's term:

> If love be blind, love cannot hit the
> mark.
> Now will he sit under a medlar tree,
> And wish his mistress were that kind of
> fruit
> As maids call medlars when they laugh
> alone.
> Oh, Romeo, that she were, Oh, that she
> were
> An open et cetera, thou a poperin pear!

## Mistletoe

The mistletoe of legend is the European species (*Viscum album*). The Druids venerated this evergreen plant, bringing it into their homes to ward off evil spirits. Partially parasitic and growing high up in trees, mistletoe symbolized the spirits and its twin berries suggested fertility—perhaps reflected in our modern-day habit of kissing under the mistletoe. According to an old Christian tradition, the mistletoe, once a large tree, became the wood for the cross of Jesus Christ, after which it was reduced to a tiny parasite. In Scandinavian lore, the god of light, Baldur, was felled by a spear made of mistletoe. The gods brought him back to life but in order to prevent the mistletoe from doing any further harm, they decided the plant could never touch the earth again.

## Myrrh

As far back as ancient Egypt, myrrh was a precious resin used in holy ointments, incense, and cosmetics, even in medicine and embalming. Perhaps the most universally known story about myrrh is the arrival of "the wise men" at the birth of Jesus Christ (see "Frankincense," page 674). At Christ's death, Nicodemus, as recounted in John 19:39, "brought a mixture of myrrh and aloes, about an hundred pound weight" for embalming the body.

Myrrh resin flows naturally from openings in the bark of flowering shrubs in the genus *Commiphora*. According to legend, the resin is the tears of Myrrha, daughter of the king of Cyprus, who at first loved her father incestuously but then fled his drunken pursuits. In pity, the gods turned her into the myrrh shrub, which sheds her bitter tears.

## Myrtle

Myrtle (*Myrtus communis*), with fragrant flowers and evergreen leaves suggesting immortality, captured the admiration of all the peoples in the ancient Mediterranean world. Egyptians dedicated the plant to Hathor, goddess of love and happiness. The Greek and Roman goddesses of love, Aphrodite and Venus, continued the sacred association with myrtle—according to some legends, each goddess arose from the sea preceded by sea nymphs bearing garlands of myrtle. In the Bible, myrtle is a symbol for divine generosity. From Isaiah 55:13: "Instead of the thorn shall come up the fir tree, and instead of the brier shall come up the myrtle tree: and it shall be to the Lord for a name, for an everlasting sign that shall not be cut off." Shakespeare uses the myrtle shrub, so popular in England, as descriptive imagery in *Antony and Cleopatra* III.12:

> I was of late as petty to his ends
> As is the morn dew on the myrtle leaf
> To his grand sea.

## Narcissus

*Narcissus* is the Latin name for many species of bulbs, including daffodils. Until recently, narcissus flowers with a strong fragrance were associated with death. In fact, in the Victorian era, the fragrance was thought capable of inducing a coma if inhaled for too long or too deeply. In one Greek myth, Pluto, god of the underworld, used narcissus flowers to entice Persephone or so dull her senses that he could abduct her to his subterranean realm.

The most famous myth is the story of Narcissus—the son of the river god Cephissus and the forest nymph Liriope—beloved by the mountain nymph Echo. The attractive youth did not return Echo's love. Despairing, she wasted away, until she was just a voice. Narcissus, the personification of self-love, was so enchanted by his own reflection in a clear pool that he had to possess it. He slipped in and drowned, or, in another version, wasted away, turning into the sweet-smelling poet's narcissus often found growing along streams and rivers. In the language of flowers, narcissus stands for egotism and conceit.

Both Shakespeare and William Wordsworth delighted in yellow daffodils (*Narcissus pseudo-narcissus*). In *The Winter's Tale* IV.3, Perdita expresses her enchantment: "Daffodils, / That come before the swallow dares, and take / The winds of March with beauty." In his 1804 poem, "I Wandered Lonely as a Cloud," Wordsworth lamented:

> I wandered lonely as a cloud
> That floats on high o'er vales and hills,
> When all at once I saw a crowd,
> A host, of golden daffodils.

## Nettle

In Isaiah 34:13, the nettle suggests destruction and decay: "And thorns shall come up in her palaces, nettles and brambles in the fortresses thereof." The nettle of the Bible is generally thought to be the Roman nettle (*Urtica*) carried by Julius Caesar's soldiers on their campaigns to Britain. Coming from warmer climates, the Romans, some suggest, rubbed their skin with nettle, inflaming it with the plant's sharp hairs to counteract the miserably cold, damp English climate.

In Shakespeare's play *Richard II*, III.2, the king begs for his English soil to "yield stinging nettles to mine enemies." In the language of flowers, nettle represents cruelty and spite.

## Oak

In the language of flowers, an oak tree represents stability and hospitality. The many species of oak (*Quercus*) worldwide are synonymous with strength, steadfastness, and great achievement. "Tall oaks from little acorns grow," is an old saying still commonly heard today. Shakespeare's metaphors about oak trees capitalize on the tree's reputation for strength. "But when the splitting wind / Makes flexible the knees of knotted oaks" evokes the force of nature in *Troilus and Cressida* I.3.

The oak was a sacred tree in both Greek and Roman mythology. The Roman god Jupiter was said to aim his thunderbolts at the mighty oak, which was strong enough to withstand them. In other cultures, the tree was widely believed to be sacred. One example appears in the Bible in Ezekiel 6:13:

> Then shall ye know that I am the Lord,
> when their slain men shall be among
> their idols round about their altars . . .
> and under every thick oak, the place
> where they did offer sweet savour to all
> their idols.

The Druids planted groves of oak and enacted mystic rites underneath the trees. In Flushing, New York, an oak served as a meeting house for Quaker missionary George Fox, and one in Natick, Massachusetts, was revered by Native Americans as a peace tree.

## Olive

The olive (*Olea europaea*) is so firmly established as a symbol of peace that reference to it can be found throughout recorded history. In the Bible, in Genesis 8:11, Noah sees the olive as a sign of the receding floodwaters: "And the dove came back to him in the evening; and, lo, in her mouth was an olive leaf pluckt off: so Noah knew that the waters were abated from off the earth." Shakespeare used the olive as a symbol of peace in *Antony and Cleopatra* IV.6, when Octavius Caesar declares:

> The time of universal peace is near.
> Prove this a prosperous day, the three-
>    nook'd world
> Shall bear the olive freely.

Today, the United Nations identifies itself with the olive branch.

Greek legend links the olive tree to the goddess Athena. In a contest with the god Poseidon for possession of a newly founded city, the two deities vied to give the gift that would most benefit humankind. As her offering, Athena created the olive tree. Poseidon's gift of the horse, symbolic of war, was deemed less worthy, and the city of Athens took the goddess's name.

## Pomegranate

The pomegranate is associated with Persephone—daughter of Zeus and Demeter, the goddess of agriculture, in Greek mythology. When Zeus gave Persephone in marriage to the god Hades, she was taken by him to live in his netherworld. Her mother was so distraught at the loss of her daughter that she left heaven to live on Earth among humankind where she blessed all she felt deserved her kindness and cursed those who did not. Such was the turmoil she created that Zeus instructed Hades to return his bride. The clever Hades, upon releasing Persephone, gave her a pomegranate and persuaded her to eat it. In so doing, she granted him power to keep her with him. Persephone could only rejoin her mother for half the year, but during that time her mother rejoiced. This myth is said to explain the change of seasons—spring and fertility bloom when Persephone returns to her mother following the barren winter when she resides in the underworld.

In the Bible, the pomegranate is one of the fruits of the promised land awaiting the Jews wandering in the desert (Deuteronomy 8:8). The fruit is a simile for beauty in the Song of Songs 4:3: "Your lips are like a scarlet thread, and your mouth is lovely. Your cheeks are like halves of a pomegranate behind your veil." Shakespeare uses the image of the pomegranate with its honeycomb of many seeds in *All's Well That Ends Well* II.3: "Go to sir. You were beaten in Italy for picking a kernel out of a pomegranate. You are a vagabond, and no true traveller."

## Rose

The rose's (*Rosa*) beauty, fragrance, and medicinal uses have been recognized since earliest times, making it one of the oldest of cultivated flowers. Greek mythology credits Chloris, goddess of flowers, with creating the rose. Chloris appealed to the gods to transform the lifeless body of a beautiful wood nymph into a flower to surpass all others. Aphrodite, the goddess of love, gave the rose beauty; the three Graces supplied brightness, joy, and charm; and the wine god Dionysus lent the flower nectar and fragrance for its lovely perfume. The west wind Zephyr scattered the clouds, allowing the sun's rays to touch the new flower so that it could bloom. In the language of flowers, the red rose symbolizes love and desire, and the white rose charm and innocence.

In an ancient Persian legend, a nightingale's spilled blood stained the rose's petals from white to red. When the rose first bloomed, the nightingale sang lovingly to it. By dawn, impassioned and overcome with the rose's intoxicating perfume, the weary bird flew to the rosebush, where one of the sharp thorns pierced its breast.

Ancient Roman pleasure-seekers found the rose irresistible. Cleopatra celebrated the visit of Antony with banquet halls knee-deep in rose petals, and it is said that one emperor accidentally smothered guests under a flood of rose petals. Early Christians adopted the rose; the red rose became a symbol of Christian martyrs' blood and the crown of thorns, and the white rose of the Virgin Mary's innocence, virginity, and purity.

Shakespeare made countless references to the rose. Perhaps best-known are the words of Juliet in *Romeo and Juliet* II.2: "What's in a name? That which we call a rose / By any other name would smell as sweet." In the seventeenth century, poet Robert Herrick wrote "To the Virgins, to Make Much of Time," beginning with the famous lines:

Gather ye rosebuds while ye may,
Old Time is still a-flying;
And this same flower that smiles today,
Tomorrow will be dying.

The twentieth century's primary contribution to the language of roses is Gertrude Stein's reference in "Sacred Emily": "Rose is a rose is a rose is a rose."

In 1986, the American government made the rose its official flower. Five hundred years earlier, at the end of the War of the Roses, the rose became England's royal emblem. The war from 1455 to 1485 climaxed the struggle for the English throne between the houses of Lancaster and York, often represented by the red and the white rose respectively.

## Rosemary

Rosemary, used in mummification, was found in the tombs of the ancient Egyptians. The Latin name for this perennial Mediterranean herb, *Rosmarinus,* means "sea dew" and refers to the plant's preference for coastal regions. Rosemary is a sacred symbol of the Roman love goddess Venus, who arose from the sea. In the language of flowers, rosemary signifies love and faithfulness. Shakespeare evokes this symbolic association in *Hamlet* IV.5, when Ophelia says, "There's rosemary, that's for remembrance—pray you, love, remember."

## Samphire

Native to the European Atlantic seaboard, samphire (*Crithmum maritimum*) is an ancient salad herb, which—loaded with vitamin C, mineral salts, and iodine—is credited with having cured Caesar's soldiers of scurvy. According to the sixteenth-century herbalist John Gerard, the English collected and cultivated samphire in their gardens. Found along the coast on rocks, sometimes at dizzying heights, the herb has been immortalized along with its cliff-hanging collectors by Shakespeare in *King Lear*

IV.6: "Halfway down / Hangs one that gathers samphire, dreadful trade!"

## Scarlet Pimpernel

Because of this flower's practice of closing before rain, or not opening at all on dark days, the scarlet pimpernel (*Anagallis arvensis*) is often called poor man's weather glass. The English appreciate its steadfastness on fine days—opening in early morning and closing in midafternoon. This flower was the symbol chosen by the aristocratic but humbly disguised main character in the French Revolution–era novel *The Scarlet Pimpernel* by Baroness Orczy.

## Shamrock

In the fifth century, St. Patrick set out on his missionary journey to convert the Irish to Christianity. According to legend, while attempting to explain the Holy Trinity, Saint Patrick plucked a shamrock or trefoil and with the tiny three-leaved plant was able to reveal the mysteries of the three-in-one concept of the Trinity. Many plants are claimed to be the true shamrock, but no clear evidence documents St. Patrick's choice. Some plants commonly called Irish shamrock are *Oxalis acetosella, Trifolium procumbens,* and *Trifolium repens* f. *minus.*

## Sunflower

The sunflower (*Helianthus annuus*), native to the Americas, figures in indigenous cultures of the Western Hemisphere. To the Incas of Peru, the flower symbolized the god of the sun, and images of the flower appear in stone on ancient

---

### SOME BIBLICAL PLANTS

| | |
|---|---|
| Almond | Mandrake |
| Cedar | Myrrh |
| Fig | Myrtle |
| Frankincense | Nettle |
| Garlic | Oak |
| Ivy | Olive |
| Lily | Pomegranate |

---

ruins and in gold religious icons. The North American Plains Indians set bowls of sunflower seeds at the burial sites of their dead; the sacred seeds were intended to sustain the departed on the difficult pilgrimage to the next life.

An ancient Greek myth recounts the origin of the "sunflower," assumed to be another but probably similar-appearing flower. The beautiful nymph Clytie fell desperately in love with Helios, the sun god. Helios did not return her love and Clytie wasted away, becoming the sunflower, rooted in the ground in the image of her lover.

## Thyme

Thyme (*Thymus vulgaris*) was well known to the Greeks. According to one legend, it sprang from the tears of Helen of Troy. Aromatic sprigs of thyme were made into incense, and its scent permeated Greek sacred sites. In the Middle Ages, ladies presented their Crusades-bound knights with thyme or scarves embroidered with a sprig of the herb for added bravery. In the language of flowers, thyme stands for courage and activity. In *A Midsummer Night's Dream* II.1, Shakespeare writes of wild thyme (*T. serphyllum*), a creeping form, equally fragrant:

I know a bank where the wild thyme
  blows,
Where oxlips and the nodding violet
  grows;
Quite overcanopied with luscious woodbine,
With sweet musk roses, and with eglantine.

## Tree of Heaven

Native to western China, the tree of heaven
(*Ailanthus altissima*) is today considered an
invasive weed in much of temperate North
America. Betty Smith, identifying the tree
with tenements, made it an emblem for struggle in *A Tree Grows in Brooklyn:* "No matter
where its seed fell, it made a tree which struggled to reach the sky."

## Violet

In the language of flowers, the violet represents
faithfulness and loyalty. Strong scented, the
purple flowers of the sweet violet (*Viola odorata*)
appear in spring in woodlands and forests. A
Greek myth credits the god Zeus with creating
violets for his young mistress, Io. In order to
protect her from the jealous wrath of his wife
Hera, Zeus turned the young girl into a white
heifer and set her in a field of violets. Hera was
suspicious of the lovely contented animal
munching on the violets and demanded Zeus
give the animal to her. Not daring to confess,
Zeus gave his wife the heifer, whereupon Hera
began torturing Io until she leaped desparately
into the sea. Only when Zeus agreed never to
look upon his young mistress again did Hera
turn Io back into a girl.
    According to Christian lore, the violet droops

| SOME FLOWERS FAVORED BY SHAKESPEARE | |
| --- | --- |
| Apple | Marigold |
| Aspen | Medlar |
| Cedar | Myrtle |
| Cherry | Nettle |
| Chestnut | Oak |
| Daffodil | Olive |
| Fleur-de-lis (Iris) | Pomegranate |
| Hemlock | Rose |
| Honeysuckle | Rosemary |
| Ivy | Samphire |
| Lily | Thyme |
| Mandrake | Violet |

in sorrow because the shadow of the cross passed
over it on the day of cruxifixion. Shakespeare
was fond of the violet as a symbol of faithfulness
in love and also of humility. In *Hamlet* V.1,
commemorating the death of Ophelia, Shakespeare wrote "Lay her i' the earth, / And from her
fair and unpolluted flesh, / May violets spring!"
Perhaps better known is the line from *Henry V,*
IV.1—"I think the king is but a man, as I am.
The violet smells to him as it doth to me."

## Further Reading

de Bray, Lys. *Fantastic Garlands.* Poole, Dorset: Bland-
ford Books, 1982.

Dent, Alan. *World of Shakespeare: Plants.* New York:
Taplinger Publishing, 1971.

Martin, Laura C. *Garden Flower Folklore.* Chester, Ct.:
Globe Pequot Press, 1987.

Seaton, Beverly. *The Language of Flowers.* Charlottesville: University Press of Virginia, 1995.

Shewell-Cooper, W. E. *Plants, Flowers, and Herbs of the
Bible.* New Canaan, Conn.: Keats Publishing, 1977.

# 16

# PLANT TRIVIA

## The Old and the Ancient

The Great Basin bristlecone pine (*Pinus longaeva*) holds the record for the oldest living tree. A few of these trees growing high in the eastern California mountains are more than 4,600 years old; one bristlecone pine in Nevada is said to be 4,900 years old. The growing conditions—cold winters and arid summers—are so severe that the tallest specimens of bristlecone pines are only 30 feet high.

Some of the world's oldest living trees are the coastal redwoods (*Sequoia sempervirens*) found on the coasts of northern California and southern Oregon. Among these trees are specimens that are 2,000 years old. The giant sequoias of central California (*Sequoiadendron giganteum*) are even older—with some specimens more than 3,000 years old. Giant sequoias are 100 years old before they begin producing cones.

Another tree of ancient origin is the ginkgo, commonly used as a street tree because of its resistance to disease and insects and its ability to withstand harsh urban conditions. The genus *Ginkgo* dates back at least 165 million years. The modern ginkgo, *Ginkgo biloba,* known in the United States as the "stinkbomb" tree because of the unpleasant odor of its fruit, is prized in China because of its fruit's nutrients and the medicinal powers of its leaves, used to counter dizziness and short-term memory loss.

Apart from trees, plants with the longest life span include the yuccas (*Yucca* species), which can live 200 to 300 years.

Some of the earliest photosynthesizing plants were algae, appearing some 600 million years ago. Nearly 200 million years later came the mosses and liverworts, the first plants to have distinct leaf- and stemlike appendages. These were followed by ferns, club mosses, and horsetails. The early club mosses and horsetails were giants compared to the ones that exist today; club mosses, for example, grew to more than 90 feet tall, whereas modern forms grow to about 8 inches tall. These plants flourished during the Carboniferous period and are now petrified in the coal seams that provide today's fossil fuels.

Ancestors of today's conifers flourished after the Permian Ice Age 230 to 280 million years ago; flowering plants were not fully established until about 50 million years ago.

## Fast- and Slow-Growing Plants

One of the fastest-growing plants in the world may be the giant water lily (*Victoria amazonica*) in the Amazon, which can grow from seed to full size—with circular leaves 6 feet wide—in just 7 months. The British were so impressed with the first specimen that was brought to England, in 1837, that it was named after Queen Victoria. The architect of the first glass houses in England, including the Crystal Palace in London, used the ribs of the water lily as the model for these structures.

*Bambusa vulgaris* can grow 40 feet in 40 days. Each species of bamboo flowers just once in its life; and in a phenomenon known as synchrony, every plant in the same bamboo species in the world flowers at the same time, then goes to seed and dies.

The saguaro cactus (*Carnegiea gigantea*) grows slowly. At 8 years, a saguaro may be just 4 inches tall, and at 20 years, just 10 inches high.

Eventually, it can reach 50 feet tall—taller than many trees.

Orchids can be very slow to flower: Some species of *Cypripedium* (lady slipper) take 15 years to flower. Orchids are the largest family of flowering plants, with some 20,000 species—one-tenth of all flowering plants.

## The Largest Plants and Largest Flowers

California's giant sequoia (*Sequoiadendron giganteum*), which can grow to 250 feet tall and 110 feet in diameter at the base of the trunk, are the largest living organisms on Earth. It has been estimated that a single giant sequoia could provide the lumber for 150 homes. California's coastal redwoods (*Sequoia sempervirens*) are among the largest living organisms in the world; these evergreens reach a height of 300 feet, and measure up to 30 feet in diameter at the base.

Palms are also among the tallest plants—some reach 200 feet high—and are among the most ancient of all flowering plants.

The largest single flower in the world is produced by a parasitic plant, *Rafflesia arnoldii,* that attaches to the roots or underground stems of a vine in the rain forests of Sumatra and Borneo. When fully opened, the flower can be 3 feet in diameter; its petals are about 1 inch thick and are a deep flesh color, with cream-colored specks. The nectar-holding bowl of the flower is large enough to hold 6 quarts of water.

Found growing in the same rain forests is a giant relative of the jack-in-the-pulpit, the titan arum (*Amorphophallus titanum*). This rare plant has a flowering structure, or inflorescence, that can rise 10 feet from the ground and weigh more than 100 pounds. The bloom lasts about 2 days and emits a powerful stench described as a cross between rotting fish and burnt sugar. It is pollinated by small bees that feed on the sweat of mammals and are attracted by the strong smell.

## More Noteworthy Blooms

Rhododendron flowers are so poisonous that even the honey made by bees that collect their nectar is toxic.

The flower of the sacred lotus can regulate its own temperature, the way warm-blooded animals do. Lotus flowers can maintain a temperature of more than 90°F, even when the air temperature is much cooler—possibly in order to lure pollinators.

Part of the flower—the stigma—of a particular crocus, *Crocus sativus,* is used to make saffron; around 4,000 stigmas are needed to make a single ounce.

During the "tulip mania" craze in Europe in the sixteenth century, some tulip bulbs sold for the equivalent of hundreds and even thousands of today's dollars.

## Plant Survival Tactics

Because both bald cypresses (*Taxodium distichum*) and mangroves (*Rhizophora mangle*) have roots that grow under water or in swampy conditions where they cannot get enough oxygen, the roots have porous, breathing "knees," called pneumatophores, that project above the surface of the water.

Birches (*Betula* species) have evolved as the main deciduous trees in many northern evergreen forests. While evergreens are able to shed snow easily because of their needles, birches have adapted to the snow and cold by bending instead of breaking. But the problem for trees in cold climates is not just the cold but the sun's heat. Dark bark absorbs heat from the sun during the day, and the sudden drop in temperature at night can cause smooth bark to crack. Many trees adapt to this with furrows in their bark that can expand and contract with temperature extremes. Instead of furrows, birches have white bark that reflects heat during the day rather than absorbing it. The reason birches peel so easily may be to keep from accumulating lichen and moss that would darken the bark.

Some desert plants have deep root systems for tapping into any underground water reservoirs. Others live off the air, absorbing any moisture it contains. Cacti often fill out with this stored water; their leaves have evolved into spines to protect against animals seeking out the moisture. One saguaro can hold several tons of water. The century plant (*Agave americana*) has succulent leaves with sunken pores to reduce water evaporation.

Many desert plants are ephemeral, appearing only when rainfall creates the right conditions. Since these conditions are short-lived, the plants work quickly—growing, budding, flowering, seeding, and then dying all in a matter of days. They disappear until the next downpour, when the seeds sprout and the abbreviated life cycle commences again.

Window-plants (*Fenestraria* species) grow in southwest Africa where the air is very dry. The bulk of the plant grows underground, with only the leaf tips appearing above ground. These leaves are completely transparent, without chlorophyll, and look as if they are made of glass. They serve to prevent leakage of moisture into the air, and reflect sunlight to the buried leaf parts where photosynthesis takes place.

The seedlings of the strangler fig (*Ficus aurea*) may start life high up in the forest canopy, in soil created by leaf mold on a tree branch. Eventually, it drops roots down to the forest floor, along the trunk of the host tree. When the roots hit the ground and draw in more nutrients, the fig's growth becomes more vigorous and it creates more and more roots. The host tree gradually dies, either literally by strangulation—since its trunk cannot expand—or by losing the competition for light above or nutrients from the soil below.

*Mimosa pudica,* or sensitive plant, has spread-out, leathery green leaves that are inviting to insects. But when would-be diners land on the leaves, electric currents cause the leaves to suddenly contract into unappealing "stems."

## Plant Deception

The pebble plant (*Lithops* species) has rounded leaves that are close to the ground and bloated with moisture—which would make the plant irresistible to animals if they could find it. The leaves' mottled color exactly matches the gravel stones in the African desert around them, creating an effective camouflage.

The pointed leaves of the vicious stinging nettle (*Urtica dioica*) are very distinctive, and easily recognized by rabbits and other animals that shun the plant to avoid the toxin contained in its needlelike hairs. The harmless deadnettle (*Lamium album*), which has no such toxin, has evolved leaves that are almost indistinguishable from the stinging nettle's—so animals avoid it as well.

Many plants use deception to lure pollinators. Orchids in the genus *Ophrys* have coloring, form, and a velvety surface that makes them look like a female bee, plus a fragrance that mimics the female bee's scent. In a process known as pseudocopulation, male bees repeatedly land on the orchids and try to mate with them—in the process pollinating the flowers.

## Pollination Machinations

To ensure their survival, many plants have developed elaborate techniques for attracting insects to help carry their pollen to other flowers to fertilize them. Although some plants rely on a large variety of insects and birds for pollination, many have developed very specialized forms, colors, and scents to attract particular pollinators. (This helps ensure that the insects will visit other flowers of the same species, completing the pollination process.) Since bees are attracted to sweet odors, for instance, flowers that rely on bees for pollination are usually fragrant; they often have a strong lower petal for bees to land on, and hold their nectar in places where it is inaccessible to other insects. Because bees fly only during the day, many flowers that attract them close at night. Flowers that rely on moths and butterflies for pollination do not have thick petals since butterflies and moths do not rest on flowers the way bees do.

It has been estimated that without bees to help pollinate them, some 100,000 plant species would disappear from the planet.

The Madagascar orchid, *Angraecum sesquipedale,* has white, star-shaped flowers with waxy petals about 6 inches across, and a long tube—usually a foot long—with nectar at the bottom. The unusual moth that pollinates it has a coiled tongue that straightens out to about 1 foot long.

The flower of the bucket orchid, *Coryanthes macrantha,* produces a heavily scented liquid that collects in its bucket-shaped lips. Male bees are attracted to the flower, become intoxicated by the scent, and slip into the bucket. The only escape is through a narrow tunnel that is covered with pollen, which collects on the bee as it escapes. A final obstruction in the flower's form holds the bee long enough for the bee to become sober. The flower then releases it to fly away, find another flower, and repeat the process—this time leaving pollen behind.

When a bee loses its footing on the slippery lip of the *Gangora grossa* orchid, it slides along a curved column covered with pollen—and deposits this pollen when it slips on the next blossom.

When a moth-fly slides down the slippery cowl of the cuckoopint (*Arum maculatum*), a ring of hairs traps it in an area of female stigmas. After a few days the hairs relax; as the fly leaves, it is showered with pollen to take to the next flower.

When an insect is drawn to the nectar of the mosquito plant (*Cynanchum acuminatifolium*), it gets caught by a cliplike mechanism that fastens to its leg. The more the insect struggles, the more the clip tightens. When the insect finally gets away, the clip is still attached. At the next mosquito plant the insect visits, the clip—and the pollen on it—fits exactly into the flower and breaks away to free the insect.

The stamens of the mountain laurel (*Kalmia latifolia*) have pouches at the ends that are filled with pollen. At the slightest touch of an insect, a springlike mechanism straightens out the stamens and the pollen is released toward the middle, onto the insect.

To attract the carrion flies that pollinate them, the African succulent stapelia (*Stapelia* species) has the texture and scent of rotting meat, complete with flickering hairs that give the impression of a mass of flies feeding on them.

The female yucca moth lays eggs in the flower of the yucca plant (*Yucca* species) in the spring. The moth then collects pollen from other yucca flowers and deposits it near the eggs for the young caterpillars to feed on when they hatch. The insects do not consume all the pollen—but instead leave enough to pollinate the flower.

## Traveling Seeds

Often if seeds simply fall to the ground below the parent plant, the resulting seedlings will not survive, since they will have to compete with their parent for sunlight, water, and nutrients from the soil. Consequently, plants have developed various methods for effectively dispersing their seeds—some by forcibly ejecting them, others by releasing them gently to float away on the wind or water.

Most plants rely on sheer quantity of seed production to ensure that at least some will germinate. An oak tree can produce as many as 90,000 acorns in one growing season. Squirrels are the unwitting partners of oaks when they gather the acorns, carry them away, and bury them in the ground for later consumption— and then forget where many are buried.

In one season, a mature female tree of heaven (*Ailanthus altissima*) produces as many as a million winged seeds that are spread effectively by the wind. Ashes, elms, birches, sycamores, and maples all have seeds with leafy attachments that act like aerodynamic wings; many of these seeds, including those of the sycamore, swirl to the ground and then partially bury themselves to aid germination. In the tropical forests of Asia, alsomitras (*Alsomitra* species) have seeds with delicate, paper-thin wings about 6 inches long that are so aerodynamically perfect that the seeds can be carried by the slightest breeze as far as 100 yards.

Seeds of many other plants, including dandelions (*Taraxacum officinale*), have fine hairlike tufts that help them travel long distances in the air, parachute fashion.

Other plants have seeds that hitch a ride on animal (or human) passersby. Agrimony (*Agrimonia* species), herb bennet (*Geum urbanum*), wood avens (*Geum rivale*), and goosegrass (*Eleusine indica*) have hooks on their seeds that catch easily onto animals' fur or people's clothing. The fine hooks on the burrs of burdock (*Arctium* species) provided the inspiration for Velcro fasteners.

Poppies (*Papaver* species) and columbines (*Aquilegia* species) both have small, lightweight seeds that travel in the wind after being shaken from the seed head, pepper-shaker fashion, by the wind or a passing animal.

Violets (*Viola* species) have seeds with an extra piece called an aril that is appetizing to ants. Ants carry the seeds off, take them underground, and then eat just the aril, leaving the seed itself to germinate.

Some plants' seed pods explode with force to disperse their seeds. Tension in the outer covering of the pods of peas (*Pisum* species) and honesty (*Lunaria* species) cause the pods to suddenly burst open and expel the seeds. In some cases the sun's heat triggers a seed pod to burst; in others, insects or animals brush up against the pod and cause it to explode.

In the Mediterranean squirting cucumber (*Ecballium elaterium*), the pressure within the fruit increases when the fruit wall contracts, causing the seeds to shoot out through an opening at the base of the fruit in a powerful stream of liquid as far as 20 feet.

The water of streams, rivers, and even oceans is an efficient conveyor for many types of seeds. Pussy willows (*Salix caprea*) growing at the edges of ponds and streams have seeds with fine, silky hairs that are blown onto the surface of the water and carried downstream, where some of them germinate when they are washed ashore.

Between the seed and the hard woody shell of the coconut (*Cocos nucifera*) are spongy fibers filled with air that make the fruit light enough to float. Coconuts can travel long distances on ocean currents, and if seawater does not soak through the outer coverings, the seeds can germinate on shores far away from the parent plants.

Water-lily seeds are encased in spongy capsules that drift downstream. When they become waterlogged, they sink and settle into the bottom soil, where they germinate.

Many plants rely on birds or other animals to disperse their seeds: They eat the ripe, tasty fruit and then spit out or excrete the seeds. In Southeast Asian forests, the fruit of the durian tree (*Durio zibethinus*) has a scent so powerful that it can be detected half a mile away. The custardlike fruit around the seeds is extremely appetizing to a variety of animals, from mouse deer to squirrels to orangutan. Although some of these animals eat the fruit and dispose of the seed under the parent plant, others obligingly swallow the seed with the fruit and then transport it some distance before excreting it. Humans find the fruit either nauseating or delightful. It has been banned from hotels and airline flights due to its penetrating and distinctive odor.

The bird-cage plant (*Oenothera deltoides*) in western deserts of the United States grows on sand dunes in a place where there is at least some shade and moisture. When the sands shift and the resulting intense sunlight kills the plant, its stems curl up and form a hollow lattice ball that gets caught by the wind and carried away, sometimes for days and miles, until it is blown against another sand dune—where the seeds inside the dead plant have a sheltered spot to grow.

## Economic Plants

Most of the telephone poles, dock pilings, and log cabins in the eastern United States are made of Norway pine (*Pinus resinosa*).

Douglas fir (*Pseudotsuga menziesii*) was used in building thousands of miles of railroad tracks, as well as telegraph and telephone poles, in the West. For many people, it is also the Christmas tree of choice.

Ash (*Fraxinus americana*) provides the shock-resistant wood for baseball bats, oars, and paddles.

Black alder (*Alnus glutinosa*), with its natural rot resistance, was used for making wooden shoes in the Netherlands. Dogwood (*Cornus* species) is a hardwood often used in making golf club heads.

Lightweight aspen (*Populus tremuloides*) wood is often used for making cheese containers.

Basketball court floors are often made from the wood of the river birch, *Betula nigra.* Native Americas used river birch for birch bark canoes; the frames were northern white cedar (*Thuja occidentalis*), caulking was pine or balsam resin, and the fibers for sewing the canoes were made from tamarack (*Larix laricina*) roots.

The American beech, *Fagus grandifolia,* is called the lightning tree because people believed that planting it near a house would protect the house from lightning; indeed, records show that lightning does not strike beeches as often as other trees.

In China, bamboo (*Phyllostachys* species) is used as food, as thatch for housing, for ship masts, in sleeping mats, umbrellas, walking sticks, drinking cups, scaffolding for high-rises, and chopsticks. Thomas Edison used bamboo filament in making his early incandescent light-bulbs. (It was later replaced by thin metal wires.)

The most abundant crop in the world is rice, *Oryza sativa.*

Bread, which historically has provided more than half of the diet in the Western world, is made from a variety of grains in the grass family. Wheat grain, *Triticum aestivum,* is best for leavening, with rye, *Secale cereale,* second best.

Of the world's three main cereal crops, wheat, rice, and corn, only corn (*Zea mays*) is native to America.

Another main staple crop for the world, the potato (*Solanum tuberosum*) is closely related to deadly nightshade, henbane, and nicotiana, which contain some of the most potent poisons known.

Tea leaves come from a bush in the camellia family, *Thea sinensis,* which has been grown in China since prehistoric times.

The apple (*Malus* species), a native of western Asia, is one of the oldest cultivated fruits in the world.

*Cinnamomum zeylanicum,* a tree closely related to the camphor tree, provides the bark that is dried and ground into cinnamon powder.

## Carnivorous Plants

To obtain nitrogen and other nutrients that are not available to them through the soil, various plants have developed forms or mechanisms for trapping and digesting small animals—mostly insects. The Latin name for Venus's-flytrap (*Dionaea muscipula*) means "mousetrap of Venus," although its largest victims are flies and other insects. The plant has sensitive triggers on the surface of its leaves. To keep the plant from reacting to a "false alarm" such as a breeze, the trapping mechanism is finely tuned to react only if an insect touches one of the triggers twice, or two triggers in rapid succession. Then the triggers react like electrical switches, causing water to suddenly flow out of the cells along the leaf's midrib, so that the leaf snaps shut, trapping the insect.

The leaves of sundews (*Drosera* species) have many hairs with tiny drops of liquid at the ends, which look like dew in the sun. Insects are drawn to the "dew" and to the plant's sweet fragrance. When they land on the leaf, they get stuck in the sticky liquid, and the plant's hairs act like tentacles to fold over the insect, trapping it. Digestive enzymes are then given off, enabling the plant to extract the nutrients.

Pitcher plants (*Sarracenia* species) are common in swampy regions in eastern North America. It is their tubular shape, rather than a mechanical device, that helps them trap insects. Insects are drawn to the abundant sweet nectar at the lip of the plant and slip deep into the pitcher, where they are digested. Animals have learned to take advantage of the trumpet pitcher's insect-trapping abilities. Small green frogs sometimes sit inside them, waiting to catch insects that are attracted to the plant; similarly, spiders spin almost invisible webs over the pitcher opening to catch insects before the plant does, and birds often split open the pitchers to get to the trapped insects.

The water-trap plant, *Aldrovanda versiculosa,* found in freshwater ponds in Europe, India, and Australia, has trigger hairs similar to those of Venus's-flytrap that allow it to catch water beetles and even small crustaceans.

The bladderwort, *Utricularia vulgaris,* has bubblelike chambers with protruding triggers. When an insect touches the triggers, the plant's chamber opens, sucks in the insect, and shuts tight.

## Hallucinogens, Aphrodisiacs, and More

In the eighteenth century, hemp (*Cannabis sativa*) was one of the most important agricultural crops in the southern United States. George Washington grew it on his estate at Mount Vernon. The stems are used to make strong waterproof fibers; the female flower heads provide the resin known as hashish. Marijuana comes from the flowering head and leaves of the plant.

Mescal buttons have been used as a hallucinogen since the time of the Aztec empire. They come from peyote (*Lophophora williamsii*), a cactus that grows in Texas, the Rio Grande valley, and northern and central Mexico. Ololiuqui is another hallucinogen used in Native American rites since prehistoric times. It is produced by grinding the seeds of the vine *Turbina corymbosa,* soaking them in water, and filtering the liquid.

The leaves of coca, *Erythroxylum coca,* which is native to the Andes and the Amazon, are the source of cocaine—which is second only to morphine in its addictive powers.

The betel nut, a widely used stimulant in India and many other parts of the world, comes from the palm *Areca catechu.* Over time, chewing the betel nut can cause teeth to be discolored brown or black—a sign of high social status on some Pacific islands where the tree grows.

Ayahuasca is a hallucinogen and purported aphrodisiac derived from the bark of *Banisteriopsis caapi,* a climbing plant native to Latin American rain forests.

Cocoa is produced by shelling, roasting, and grinding the beans of the cacao tree, *Theobroma cacao.* In Europe, cocoa was considered an aphrodisiac when the Spanish brought it back from Central America in the sixteenth century.

Fly agaric, *Amanita muscaria,* is a hallucinogenic mushroom with a bright red cap flecked with white—the dancing mushrooms in the Disney film *Fantasia.*

Opium is derived from the latex obtained from the unripe seed capsules—not the seeds themselves—of the opium poppy, *Papaver somnifera.*

## Plants, Light, and Color

Botanists characterize plants in terms of their need for sunlight: short-day plants like poinsettias (*Euphorbia pulcherrima*) and Christmas cactus (*Schlumbergera bridgesii*) require less than 12 hours of light a day to bloom, while long-day plants such as asters (*Aster* species) may not bloom unless they get 12 to 16 hours of light. Some plants also require a minimum number of hours of continuous dark—morning glories (*Ipomoea purpurea*) may not bloom properly if they grow near the artificial light of a streetlight.

Plants are green because of chlorophyll, a green pigment in plant leaves that interacts with sunlight to convert unusable sugars into usable starch. Oxygen is the by-product of this process, called photosynthesis. In the fall, with cooler weather and fewer hours of sunlight in which to work, leaves stop photosynthesizing. Colorful fall foliage results when trees withdraw the chlorophyll from their leaves, and the yellow/orange pigment carotene that is also present shows through. Some plants, such as sugar maple (*Acer saccharum*) and tupelo (*Nyssa sylvatica*), have bright red anthocyanin pigment.

Flowers probably would not be brightly colored if they did not rely on insects for pollination. Bees prefer blues, purples, and yellows, so flowers that are pollinated by bees often have those colors. In addition, bees are able to detect ultraviolet patterns in flowers, patterns that are invisible to humans, but that point directly to the nectar—and pollen. Moths and butterflies can see reds, so flowers pollinated by them are often red and orange.

*Asclepias* species, or milkweeds, produce a toxic chemical that can cause mild to severe poisoning in cattle or insects that eat them. Because monarch butterflies are immune to the plants' poisons, they have almost exclusive access to them. Monarchs then store the chemical in their own tissues, so that the butterflies themselves are poisonous to any would-be predators. Birds learn to recognize and avoid monarchs because of their distinctive orange and black coloring—they also avoid viceroys and other harmless butterflies that have developed similar coloring.

## Diverse Rain Forest

One small area of the Brazilian rain forest northeast of Rio de Janeiro has been found to include 476 tree species, more than any area of a similar size ever studied. A similar 2½-half-acre patch of typical North American temperate forest typically would contain less than twenty tree species.

## State Trees

Alabama—southern pine: *Pinus caribaea,* slash pine; *P. palustris,* longleaf pine; *P. taeda,* Loblolly pine
Alaska—*Picea sitchensis,* sitka spruce
Arizona—*Cercidium* species, palo verde
Arkansas—*Pinus* species, pines
California—*Sequoia sempervirens,* redwood
Colorado—*Picea pungens* f. *glauca,* Colorado blue spruce
Connecticut—*Quercus alba,* white oak
Delaware—*Ilex opaca,* American holly
District of Columbia—*Quercus coccinea,* scarlet oak

Florida—*Sabal palmetto*, cabbage palmetto
Georgia—*Quercus virginiana*, live oak
Hawaii—*Aleurites moluccana*, kuki, candlenut
Idaho—*Pinus monticola*, western white pine
Illinois—*Quercus* species, oaks
Indiana—*Liriodendron tulipifera*, tulip tree
Iowa—*Quercus* species, oaks
Kansas—*Populus deltoides*, cottonwood
Kentucky—*Liriodendron tulipifera*, tulip tree
Louisiana—*Taxodium distichum*, bald cypress
Maine—*Pinus strobus*, white pine
Maryland—*Quercus alba*, white oak
Massachusetts—*Ulmus americana*, American elm
Michigan—*Pinus strobus*, white pine
Minnesota—*Pinus resinosa*, red pine
Mississippi—*Magnolia grandiflora*, southern magnolia
Missouri—*Cornus florida*, flowering dogwood
Montana—*Pinus ponderosa*, western yellow pine
Nebraska—*Ulmus americana*, American elm
Nevada—*Pinus cembroides* var. *monophylla*, singleleaf pine
New Hampshire—*Betula papyrifera*, canoe birch
New Jersey—*Quercus rubra*, red oak
New Mexico—*Pinus edulis*, pinyon, nut pine
New York—*Acer saccharum*, sugar maple
North Carolina—*Pinus* species, pines
North Dakota—*Ulmus americana*, American elm
Ohio—*Aesculus glabra*, Ohio buckeye
Oklahoma—*Cercis canadensis*, redbud
Oregon—*Pseudotsuga menziesii*, Douglas fir
Pennsylvania—*Tsuga canadensis*, Canada hemlock
Rhode Island—*Acer rubrum*, red maple
South Carolina—*Sabal palmetto*, cabbage palmetto
South Dakota—*Picea glauca* 'Densata', Black Hills spruce

Tennessee—*Liriodendron tulipifera*, tulip tree
Texas—*Carya illinoensis*, pecan
Utah—*Picea pungens* f. *glauca*, Colorado blue spruce
Vermont—*Acer saccharum*, sugar maple
Virginia—*Cornus florida*, flowering dogwood
Washington—*Tsuga heterophylla*, western hemlock
West Virginia—*Acer saccharum*, sugar maple
Wisconsin—*Acer saccharum*, sugar maple
Wyoming—*Populus sargentii*, plains cottonwood

## State Flowers

Alabama—*Solidago serotina*, goldenrod
Alaska—*Myosotis alpestris*, forget-me-not
Arizona—*Carnegiea gigantea*, saguaro cactus
Arkansas—*Malus sylvestris*, apple blossom
California—*Eschscholzia californica*, California poppy
Colorado—*Aquilegia caerulea*, blue columbine
Connecticut—*Kalmia latifolia*, mountain laurel
Delaware—*Prunus persica*, peach blossom
District of Columbia—*Rosa* 'American Beauty', American Beauty rose
Florida—*Citrus sinensis*, orange blossom
Georgia—*Rosa laevigata*, Cherokee rose
Hawaii—*Hibiscus rosa-sinensis*, hibiscus
Idaho—*Philadelphus lewisii*, mock orange
Illinois—*Viola* species, native violet
Indiana—*Zinnia elegans*, zinnia
Iowa—*Rosa suffulta*, wild rose
Kansas—*Helianthus annuus*, sunflower
Kentucky—*Solidago serotina*, goldenrod
Louisiana—*Magnolia grandiflora*, magnolia
Maine—*Pinus strobus*, Pinecone and tassel
Maryland—*Rudbeckia hirta*, black-eyed Susan
Massachusetts—*Epigaea repens*, trailing arbutus

Michigan—*Malus sylvestris,* apple blossom

Minnesota—*Cypripedium reginae,* showy lady slipper

Mississippi—*Magnolia grandiflora,* magnolia

Missouri—*Crataegus mollis,* red hawthorn

Montana—*Lewisia rediviva,* bitterroot

Nebraska—*Solidago serotina,* goldenrod

Nevada—*Artemisia tridentata,* sagebrush

New Hampshire—*Syringa vulgaris,* purple lilac

New Jersey—*Viola* species, violet

New Mexico—*Yucca* species, yucca

New York—*Rosa* species, wild rose

North Carolina—*Cornus florida,* flowering dogwood

North Dakota—*Rosa arkansana,* wild prairie rose

Ohio—*Dianthus caryophyllus,* scarlet carnation

Oklahoma—*Phoradendron flavescens,* mistletoe

Oregon—*Mahonia aquifolium,* Oregon grape

Pennsylvania—*Kalmia latifolia,* mountain laurel

Rhode Island—*Viola* species, violet

South Carolina—*Gelsemium sempervirens,* yellow jessamine

South Dakota—*Anemone patens,* pasqueflower

Tennessee—*Iris* species, iris

Texas—*Lupinus subcarnosus,* bluebonnet

Utah—*Calochortus nuttallii,* sego lily

Vermont—*Trifolium pratense,* red clover

Virginia—*Cornus florida,* flowering dogwood

Washington—*Rhododendron macrophyllum,* rhododendron

West Virginia—*Rhododendron maximum,* big rhododendron

Wisconsin—*Viola* species, wood violet

Wyoming—*Castilleja lineariaefolia,* Indian paintbrush

## Birth Flowers

January—*Galanthus nivalis,* snowdrop

February—*Primula vulgaris,* primrose

March—*Viola* species, violet

April—*Chrysanthemum* species, daisy

May—*Crataegus* species, hawthorn

June—*Rosa* species, rose

July—*Nymphaea* species, water lily

August—*Papaper* species, poppy

September—*Ipomoea* species, morning glory

October—*Humulus lupulus,* hops

November—*Chrysanthemum* species, chrysanthemum

December—*Ilex* species, holly

## Further Reading

Attenborough, David. *The Private Life of Plants.* Princeton, N.J.: Princeton University Press, 1995.

Behme, Robert Lee. *Incredible Plants: Oddities, Curiosities, and Eccentricities.* New York: Sterling Publishing Co., 1992.

Emboden, William A. *Bizarre Plants: Magical, Monstrous, Mythical.* New York: Macmillan Publishing Co., 1974.

Lehane, Brendan. *The Power of Plants.* Maidenhead, England: McGraw-Hill Book Co. (UK) Ltd., 1977.

Martin, Laura C. *The Folklore of Trees and Shrubs.* Chester, Conn.: The Globe Pequot Press, 1992.

# ESSENTIAL RESOURCES

Botanical gardens, arboreta, and other public gardens, especially those in your area, are often the best sources of information on plants and gardening techniques most suited to local conditions. They are certainly the best places to see plants you may be considering for your garden, or to find others you may not even be aware of. Many botanical gardens have other resources as well, including libraries open to the public, courses and workshops, and plant information hot lines. And when you're out of town, public gardens are great places to visit. Check the following list of public gardens in the United States and Canada, organized by state or province, for those nearest you. See "The Horticultural Traveler," page 621, for descriptions of some of the most remarkable public gardens in North America and around the world. Plant societies are excellent sources of information on particular groups of plants. A list of plant societies and other plant-related organizations begins on page 723.

## Botanical Gardens, Arboreta, and Other Public Gardens

### United States

#### Alabama

**Auburn University Arboretum**
Dept. of Botany & Microbiology
Auburn, AL 36849
(334) 844-1625, fax (334) 844-1645

**Bellingrath Gardens and Home**
12401 Bellingrath Gardens Rd.
Theodore, AL 36582
(334) 973-2217, fax (334) 973-0540

**Birmingham Botanical Gardens**
2612 Lane Park Rd.
Birmingham, AL 35223
(205) 879-1227, fax (205) 879-3751

**Dismals Canyon**
Rte. 3
Box 281
Phil Campbell, AL 35581
(800) 808-7998

**Huntsville–Madison County Botanical Garden**
4747 Bob Wallace Ave.
Huntsville, AL 35805
(205) 830-4447, fax (205) 533-4275

**Mobile Botanical Gardens**
South Alabama Botanical & Horticultural Society
Langan Park
Pat Ryan Dr.
P.O. Box 8382
Mobile, AL 36608
(334) 342-0555, fax (334) 342-3149

**University of Alabama Arboretum**
Pelham Loop Rd.
Box 870334
Tuscaloosa, AL 35487
(205) 553-3278

**University of Alabama in Huntsville**
Facilities & Operations Building
Huntsville, AL 35899
(205) 895-6482, fax (205) 895-6838

## Alaska

**Alaska Botanical Garden**
P.O. Box 202202
Anchorage, AK 99520
(907) 278-2814

**Governor's Mansion**
9th St. & Calhoun Ave.
Juneau, AK 99801
(907) 586-2201

**The Gardens at the Museum of Alaska Transportation**
P.O. Box 909
Palmer, AK 99645
(907) 745-4493

## Arizona

**Arboretum at Arizona State University**
Facilities Management/Department Grounds
Tempe, AZ 85287
(602) 965-9498, fax (602) 965-8121

**Arizona–Sonora Desert Museum**
2021 N. Kinney Rd.
Tucson, AZ 85743
(520) 883-1380, fax (520) 883-2500

**Boyce Thompson Southwestern Arboretum**
37615 U.S. Rte. 60
Superior, AZ 85273
(520) 689-2723, fax (520) 689-5858

**Desert Botanical Garden**
1201 N. Galvin Pkwy.
Phoenix, AZ 85008
(602) 941-1225, fax (602) 481-8124

**The Arboretum at Flagstaff**
S. Woody Mountain Rd.
P.O. Box 670
Flagstaff, AZ 86002
(520) 774-1442, fax (520) 774-1441

**Sharlot Hall Historical Society**
415 W. Gurley St.
Prescott, AZ 86301
(520) 445-3122, fax (520) 776-9053

**Tohono Chul Park**
7366 N. Paseo del Norte
Tucson, AZ 85704
(520) 742-6455, fax (520) 797-1213

**Tucson Botanical Gardens**
2150 N. Alvernon Way
Tucson, AZ 85712
(520) 326-9686, fax (520) 324-0166

## Arkansas

**Arkansas State Capitol Rose Garden**
State Capitol
Little Rock, AR 72201
(501) 371-5164

**Botanical Garden Society of the Ozarks, Inc.**
P.O. Box 3079
Fayetteville, AR 72702
(501) 839-2301

**Eureka Springs Gardens**
Rte. 6., Box 362
Hwy. 62 W.
Eureka Springs, AR 72632
(501) 253-9244

**Northwest Arkansas Zoological Society**
P.O. Box 6907
Springdale, AR 72766
(501) 750-4404

## California

**All-American Gladiolus Selections**
11734 Rd. 33 1/2
Madera, CA 93638
(209) 645-5329

**Balboa Park**
Laurel St. & 6th Ave.
San Diego, CA 92101
(619) 236-5984

**The Ruth Bancroft Garden**
1815D Ygnacio Valley Rd.
Walnut Creek, CA 94598
(510) 210-9663

**Berkeley Rose Garden**
Euclid Ave. & Bayview Place
Berkeley, CA 94720
(415) 644-6530

**Blake Garden**
University of California
70 Rincon Rd.
Kensington, CA 94707
(510) 524-2449

**California State University**
Fresno Arboretum
2351 E. Barstow Ave.
Fresno, CA 93740
(209) 278-6930, fax (209) 278-7698

**Chapman University**
Facilities Management
333 N. Glassell
Orange, CA 92666
(714) 997-6658, fax (714) 997-6500

**Clovis Botanical Garden**
1909 Harvard Ave.
Clovis, CA 93612
(209) 299-0392

**Conservatory of Flowers**
Golden Gate Park
Fell & Stanyan Sts.
San Francisco, CA 94117
(415) 666-7106

**Daffodil Hill**
18510 Ram's Horn Grade
Volcano, CA 95689
(209) 296-7048

**Davis Arboretum**
University of California
Davis, CA 95616
(916) 752-2498, fax (916) 752-5796

**Descanso Gardens (LASCA)**
1418 Descanso Dr.
La Canada Flintridge, CA 91011
(818) 952-4401, fax (818) 790-3291

**Dunsmuir House and Gardens**
2960 Peralta Oaks Ct.
Oakland, CA 94605
(510) 562-0328

**The Eddy Arboretum**
Institute of Forest Genetics
2480 Carson Rd.
Placerville, CA 95667
(916) 622-1225

**Exposition Park Rose Garden**
701 State Dr.
Los Angeles, CA 90012
(213) 748-4772

**Fairhaven Memorial Park and
Mortuary**
1702 E. Fairhaven Ave.
Santa Ana, CA 92701
(714) 633-1442, fax (714) 633-5471

**Fioli Center**
Canada Rd.
Woodside, CA 94062
(415) 366-2880, fax (415) 366-7836

**Fullerton Arboretum**
California State University
Yorba Linda Blvd. & Associated Rd.
Fullerton, CA 96234
(714) 773-3579, fax (714) 449-7066

**Elizabeth F. Gamble Garden
   Center**
1431 Waverley St.
Palo Alto, CA 94301
(415) 329-1356, fax (415) 329-1688

**Ganna Walska Lotusland**
695 Ashley Rd.
Santa Barbara, CA 93108
(805) 969-3767, fax (805) 969-4423

**J. Paul Getty Museum**
17985 Pacific Coast Hwy.
Malibu, CA 90265
(310) 459-7611, fax (310) 454-6633

**Green Gulch Farm**
1601 Shoreline Hwy.
Sausalito, CA 94965
(415) 383-3134

**Greystone Park**
905 Lomas Vista Dr.
Beverly Hills, CA 90210
(310) 285-2537

**Hakone Gardens**
21000 Big Basin Way
Saratoga, CA 95070
(408) 867-3438

**Hearst San Simeon State Historical
   Monument**
750 Hearst Castle Rd.
San Simeon, CA 93452
(805) 927-2020, fax (805) 927-2031

**Humboldt Botanical Gardens**
P.O. Box 6181
Eureka, CA 95502
(707) 839-0500, fax (707) 839-0500

**Huntington Botanical Gardens**
1151 Oxford Rd.
San Marino, CA 91108
(818) 405-2160, fax (818) 405-2260

**Japanese Tea Garden**
Golden Gate Park
Hagiwara Tea Garden Dr. at South Dr.
San Francisco, CA 94117
(415) 666-7107

**Japanese Tea Garden at Central
   Park**
50 E. Fifth Ave.
San Mateo, CA 94403
(415) 377-3345

**Kruse Rhododendron State
   Reserve**
Pacific Coast Hwy.
Fort Ross, CA
(mailing address):
Dept. of State Parks
25050 Coast Hwy. 1
Jenner, CA 95450
(707) 847-3221

**Lakeside Park Garden Center**
666 Bellevue Ave.
Oakland, CA 94612
(510) 273-2199

**The Living Desert**
47-900 Portola Ave.
Palm Desert, CA 92260
(619) 346-5694

**The Arboretum of Los Angeles
   County**
301 N. Baldwin Ave.
Arcadia, CA 91007
(818) 821-3222, fax (818) 447-3763

**Marin Art and Garden Center**
Sir Francis Drake Blvd. & Laurel
   Grove Ave.
P.O. Box 437
Ross, CA 94957
(415) 454-5597

**Markham Arboretum**
P.O. Box 21672
Casa Correo Station
Concord, CA 94521
(510) 486-1550, fax (510) 486-1550

**Mildred E. Mathias Botanical Garden (UCLA)**
405 Hilgard Ave.
Los Angeles, CA 90024
(310) 835-3620, fax (310) 206-3987

**Mendocino Coast Botanical Gardens**
18220 N. Hwy. 1
Fort Bragg, CA 95437
(707) 964-4352, fax (707) 964-3114

**Hortense Miller Garden**
3035 Bert Dr.
Laguna Beach, CA 92651
(714) 497-0716

**Moorten Botanic Garden**
1701 South Palm Canyon Dr.
Palm Springs, CA 92264
(619) 327-6555

**Morcom Amphitheater of Roses**
1520 Lakeside Dr.
Oakland, CA 94612
(415) 273-3090

**Mourning Cloak Ranch**
22101 Old Town Rd.
Tehachapi, CA 93561
(805) 822-1661, fax (805) 822-8422

**Muir Woods National Monument**
Mill Valley, CA 94941
(415) 388-2596

**Museum of Creativity Project**
1250 Fourth St. #280
Santa Monica, CA 90401
(310) 998-3010, fax (310) 998-3013

**Niguel Botanical Preserve**
29751 Crown Valley Pkwy.
Laguna Niguel, CA 92677
(714) 493-6274

**The Oakland Museum and Gardens**
1000 Oak St.
Oakland, CA 94607
(510) 273-3401

**Overfelt Gardens**
McKee Rd. & Educational Park Dr.
San Jose, CA 95133
(415) 251-3323

**Pacific Horticultural Foundation**
1914 Napa Ave.
Berkeley, CA 94707
(510) 526-2853, fax (510) 524-1914

**Pageant of Roses Garden**
3900 S. Workman Mill Rd.
Whittier, CA 90608
(213) 699-0921

**Theodore Payne Foundation**
10459 Tuxford St.
Sun Valley, CA 91352
(818) 768-1802

**Pitzer College Arboretum**
1050 N. Mills Ave.
Claremont, CA 91711
(909) 607-3608, fax (909) 621-8481

**Quail Botanical Gardens**
230 Quail Gardens Dr.
P.O. Box 230005
Encinitas, CA 92023
(619) 436-3036, fax (619) 632-0917

**Quarryhill Botanical Garden**
P.O. Box 232
Glen Ellen, CA 95422
(707) 996-3166, fax (707) 996-3198

**Rancho Los Alamitos Historic Site and Gardens**
6400 Bixby Hill Rd.
Long Beach, CA 90815
(310) 431-3541, fax (310) 430-9695

**Rancho Santa Ana Botanic Garden**
1500 N. College Ave.
Claremont, CA 91711
(909) 625-8767, fax (909) 625-3489

**Redding Arboretum by the River**
P.O. Box 990185
Redding, CA 96099
(916) 243-5457, fax (916) 243-5533

**Regional Parks Botanic Garden**
Tilden Regional Park
Berkeley, CA 94708
(510) 841-8732

**Virginia Robinson Gardens**
1008 Elden Way
Beverly Hills, CA 90210
(310) 276-4823

**San Diego Wild Animal Park**
15500 San Pasqual Valley Rd.
P.O. Box 551
Escondido, CA 92027
(619) 738-5018, fax (619) 746-7081

**San Diego Zoo**
Balboa Park
2920 Zoo Dr.
Box 551
San Diego, CA 92112
(619) 231-1515

**San Luis Obispo Botanical Garden**
P.O. Box 4957
San Luis Obispo, CA 93403
(805) 546-3501, fax (805) 563-0352

**San Mateo Japanese Garden**
Central Park
Laurel & Fifth Aves.
San Mateo, CA 94403
(415) 377-4700

**Santa Barbara Botanic Garden**
1212 Mission Canyon Rd.
Santa Barbara, CA 93105
(805) 682-4726, fax (805) 563-0352

**Sherman Library and Gardens**
2647 East Coast Hwy.
Corona del Mar, CA 92625
(714) 673-2261, fax (714) 675-5458

**Soka University of America**
26800 W. Mulholland Hwy.
Calabasas, CA 91302
(818) 880-6400, fax (818) 878-3795

S E S S E N T I A L   R E S O U R C E S

Sonoma Horticultural Nursery
3970 Azalea Ave.
Sebastopol, CA 95472
(707) 823-6832

South Coast Botanic Garden
(LASCA)
26300 Crenshaw Blvd.
Palos Verdes Peninsula, CA 90274
(310) 772-5813

Strybing Arboretum & Botanical
Gardens
Golden Gate Park
9th Ave. & Lincoln Way
San Francisco, CA 94122
(415) 753-7089, fax (415) 661-7427

Sunset Gardens
80 Willow Rd.
Menlo Park, CA 94025
(415) 321-3600

UCLA Botanical Gardens
405 Hilgard Ave.
Los Angeles, CA 90095
(310) 825-3620, fax (310) 206-3987

UCLA Hannah Carter Japanese
Garden
10619 Bellagio Rd.
Los Angeles, CA 90024
(213) 825-3620

The University of California,
Berkeley, Botanical Garden
200 Centennial Dr.
Berkeley, CA 94720
(510) 642-0840, fax (510) 642-5045

The University of California,
Davis, Arboretum
Environmental Design Department
Arboretum
Putah Creek
Davis, CA 95616
(916) 752-2498, fax (916) 752-5796

The University of California,
Irvine, Arboretum
School of Biological Sciences
Irvine, CA 92717
(714) 824-5833, fax (714) 824-8511

The University of California,
Riverside, Botanic Garden
Riverside, CA 92521
(909) 787-4650, fax (909) 787-8511

The University of California, Santa
Cruz, Arboretum
Empire Grade
Santa Cruz, CA 95064
(408) 427-2998

Villa Montalvo Arboretum
15400 Montalvo Rd.
P.O. Box 158
Saratoga, CA 95071
(408) 741-3421

Western Hills Nursery
16250 Coleman Valley Rd.
Occidental, CA 95465
(707) 974-3731

Wrigley Memorial Garden
P.O. Box 88
Avalon, CA 90704
(310) 510-2288, fax (310) 510-2354

Yerba Buena Nursery
19500 Skyline Blvd.
Woodside, CA 94062
(415) 851-1668, fax (415) 851-5565

M. Young Botanic Garden
14178 W. Kearney
Kerman, CA 93630
(209) 846-7881, fax (209) 846-9567

## Colorado

Denver Botanic Gardens
909 York St.
Denver, CO 80206
(303) 331-4000, fax (303) 370-4013

Betty Ford Alpine Gardens
183 Gore Creek Dr.
Vail, CO 81657
(970) 476-0103, fax (970) 476-8702

Hudson Gardens
2888 W. Maplewood Ave.
Littleton, CO 80120
(303) 797-8565, fax (303) 797-3650

Montrose Botanic Gardens
P.O. Box 0323
Montrose, CO 81402
(970) 249-9055, fax (970) 249-2229

## Connecticut

Audubon Fairchild Garden of the
National Audubon Society
613 Riversville Rd.
Greenwich, CT 06831
(203) 869-5272, fax (203) 869-4437

Bartlett Arboretum
University of Connecticut
151 Brookdale Rd.
Stamford, CT 06903
(203) 322-6971, fax (203) 595-9168

Bartlett Tree Experts
P.O. Box 3067
Stamford, CT 06905
(203) 323-1131, fax (203) 323-1129

Beardsley Zoological Gardens
1875 Noble Ave.
Bridgeport, CT 06610
(203) 576-7534, fax (203) 576-7534

The Connecticut College
Arboretum
5625 Connecticut College
270 Mohegan Ave.
New London, CT 06320
(203) 439-5020, fax (203) 439-2519

Dinosaur State Park
400 West St.
Rocky Hill, CT 06067
(860) 257-7601, fax (860) 257-1405

Elizabeth Park
25 Stonington St.
Hartford, CT 06106
(203) 722-6541

Harkness Memorial State Park
275 State Park Rd.
P.O. Box 10
Waterford, CT 06385
(860) 443-5725, fax (860) 443-5725

701

**Highstead Arboretum**
P.O. Box 1097
Redding, CT 06875
(203) 938-8809, fax (203) 938-0343

**Hubbard Park**
W. Main St.
Meriden, CT 06450
(203) 630-4259

**The University of Connecticut**
189 Auditorium Rd.
Storrs, CT 06269
(860) 486-2306

**White Flower Farm**
Rte. 63
P.O. Box 50
Litchfield, CT 06759
(860) 567-8789

## Delaware

**Delaware Center for Horticulture**
1810 N. Dupont St.
Wilmington, DE 19806
(302) 658-6262, fax (302) 658-6267

**Eleutherian Mills**
Hagley Museum & Library
Rte. 141
P.O. Box 3630
Wilmington, DE 19807
(302) 658-2400

**The Homestead**
Rehoboth Art League
Henlopen Acres
12 Dodds Lane
Rehoboth Beach, DE 19971
(302) 227-8408

**Mt. Cuba Center**
P.O. Box 3570
Greenville, DE 19807
(302) 239-4244

**Nemours Mansion and Gardens**
1600 Rockland Rd.
Wilmington, DE 19899
(302) 651-6912

**The George Read II House and
    Garden**
42 The Strand
New Castle, DE 19720
(302) 322-8411

**Rockwood Museum**
610 Shipley Rd.
Wilmington, DE 19809
(302) 761-4340, fax (302) 764-4570

**The Henry Francis DuPont
    Winterthur Museum**
Rte. 54
Winterthur, DE 19735
(302) 888-4880, fax (302) 888-4907

## District of Columbia

**Dumbarton Oaks**
1703 32nd St. N.W.
Washington, DC 20007
(202) 342-3290, fax (202) 339-6450

**Hillwood Museum**
4155 Linnean Ave. N.W.
Washington, DC 20008
(202) 686-8500, fax (202) 966-7846

**Kenilworth Aquatic Gardens**
National Park Service
Anacostia Ave. & Douglas St. N.E.
Washington, DC 20019
(202) 426-6905, fax (202) 690-0892

**Smithsonian Institution**
Horticultural Services Div.
900 Jefferson Dr. S.W.
Arts & Industries Bldg. #2282
Washington, DC 20560
(202) 357-1926, fax (202) 786-2026

**U.S. Botanic Garden**
245 First St. S.W.
Washington, DC 20024
(202) 225-8333, fax (202) 225-1561

**United States National Arboretum**
3501 New York Ave. N.E.
Washington, DC 20002
(202) 245-3875, fax (202) 245-4575

**White House Gardens**
1600 Pennsylvania Ave.
Washington, DC 20500
(202) 426-6700

## Florida

**American Bat Conservation
    Society**
P.O. Box 181725
Casselberry, FL 32718
(301) 309-6610, fax (301) 424-3938

**American Orchid Society**
6000 S. Olive Ave.
West Palm Beach, FL 33405
(407) 585-8666, fax (407) 585-0654

**The Arboretum**
University of Central Florida
Orlando, FL 32816
(407) 823-2978

**Audubon House & Tropical
    Gardens**
205 Whitehead St.
Key West, FL 33040
(305) 294-2116, fax (305) 294-4513

**Bok Tower Gardens**
1151 Tower Blvd.
Lake Wales, FL 33853
(941) 676-1408, fax (941) 676-6770

**The Botanical Garden, Inc.**
3584 Exchange Ave. #A
Naples, FL 33942
(941) 643-7275, fax (941) 649-7306

**Coral Gables Merrick House**
907 Coral Way
Coral Gables, FL 33134
(305) 460-5361, fax (941) 460-5371

**Edison Botanical Gardens**
Edison Winter Home & Museum
2350 McGregor Blvd.
Fort Myers, FL 33901
(813) 334-3614, fax (813) 332-6684

**Fairchild Tropical Garden**
10901 Old Cutler Rd.
Miami, FL 33156
(305) 667-1651, fax (305) 661-8953

**Flamingo Gardens**
3750 Flamingo Rd.
Fort Lauderdale, FL 33330
(954) 473-2955, fax (954) 473-1738

**Florida Cypress Gardens**
State Rte. 540
Cypress Gardens, FL 33880
(813) 324-2111

**Nancy Forrester's Secret Garden**
One Free School Lane
Key West, FL 33040
(305) 294-0015

**Four Arts Garden**
Society of the Four Arts
2 Four Arts Plaza
Palm Beach, FL 33480
(407) 655-7227, fax (407) 655-7233

**Gemini Botanical Garden**
2000 S. Ocean Blvd.
Manalapan, FL 33462
(407) 533-0611, fax (407) 533-0815

**Heathcote Botanical Gardens**
210 Savannah Rd.
Fort Pierce, FL 34982
(407) 464-4672, fax (407) 464-4672

**Indian River Land Trust**
4871 North A1A
Vero Beach, FL 32963
(407) 234-3288, fax (407) 231-4166

**The Kampong of the National**
    **Tropic Botanical Garden**
4013 Douglas Rd.
Coconut Grove, FL 33133
(305) 442-7169, fax (305) 442-2925

**Harry P. Leu Gardens**
1920 N. Forest Ave.
Orlando, FL 32803
(407) 426-2620, fax (407) 426-2849

**Lowry Park Zoo**
7530 North Blvd.
Tampa, FL 33604
(813) 935-8552, fax (813) 935-9486

**The Montgomery Foundation**
11901 Old Cutler Rd.
Miami, FL 33156
(305) 667-3800, fax (305) 661-5984

**Mounts Botanical Garden**
531 Military Trail
West Palm Beach, FL 33415
(407) 233-1749, fax (407) 233-1768

**Orchid Jungle**
Fennell Orchid Co.
26715 S.W. 157th Ave.
Homestead, FL 33031
(954) 247-4824

**Marie Selby Botanical Gardens**
811 S. Palm Ave.
Sarasota, FL 34236
(941) 366-5730, fax (941) 366-9807

**Sunken Gardens**
1825 4th St. N.
St. Petersburg, FL 33704
(813) 896-3186

**The University of West Florida**
Botanical Garden and Arboretum
11000 University Pkwy.
Pensacola, FL 32514
(904) 474-2940, fax (904) 474-3166

**Vizcaya Museum & Gardens**
3521 S. Miami Ave.
Miami, FL 33129
(305) 250-9133, fax (305) 285-2004

**Walt Disney World**
P.O. Box 10000
Lake Buena Vista, FL 32830
(407) 824-6429, fax (407) 824-7353

**Wilmot Memorial Garden**
University of Florida
Gainesville, FL 32611
(904) 392-1830

**A World of Orchids**
2501 Old Lake Wilson Rd.
Kissimmee, FL 34747
(407) 396-1887, fax (407) 396-4177

## Georgia

**Atlanta Botanical Garden**
1345 Auburn Ave. N.E.
P.O. Box 77426
Atlanta, GA 30357
(404) 876-5859, fax (404) 876-7472

**Atlanta History Garden**
130 W. Paces Ferry Rd. N.W.
Atlanta, GA 30305
(404) 814-4000, fax (404) 814-2041

**Callaway Gardens**
U.S. Hwy. 27
P.O. Box 2000
Pine Mountain, GA 31822
(706) 663-5150, fax (706) 663-5004

**Fernbank Science Center**
156 Heaton Park Dr. N.E.
Atlanta, GA 30307
(404) 378-4311, fax (404) 370-1336

**Georgia Southern Botanical**
    **Garden**
Georgia Southern University
LB 8039—The Botanic Garden
Statesboro, GA 30460
(912) 871-1114, fax (912) 871-1779

**Lockerly Arboretum**
1534 Irwinton Rd.
Milledgeville, GA 31061
(912) 452-2112

**Massee Lane Gardens**
American Camellia Society
    Headquarters
1 Massee Lane
Fort Valley, GA 31030
(912) 967-2358, fax (912) 967-2083

Oak Hill and the Martha Berry
    Museum
189 Mount Berry Station
Mount Berry, GA 30149
(706) 232-5374, fax (706) 802-0902

The State Botanical Garden of
    Georgia
University of Georgia
2450 S. Milledge Ave.
Athens, GA 30605
(706) 542-1244, fax (706) 542-3091

Vines Botanical Gardens
3500 Oak Grove Rd.
Loganville, GA 30239
(404) 466-7532, fax (404) 466-7854

Zoo Atlanta
800 Cherokee Ave. S.E.
Atlanta, GA 30315
(404) 624-5620, fax (404) 627-7514

## Hawaii

Amy B. H. Greenwell
    Ethnobotanical Garden
    (Hawaii)
P.O. Box 1053
Captain Cook, HI 96704
(808) 323-3318, fax (808) 323-2394

Hawaii Tropical Botanic Garden
    (Hawaii)
248 Kahoa Rd.
Hilo, HI 96720
(808) 964-5233, fax (808) 964-1338

Liliuokalani Gardens (Hawaii)
Rtes. 200 & 11
Hilo, HI 96720
(808) 961-8311

Nani Mau Gardens (Hawaii)
421 Makalika St.
Hilo, HI 96720
(808) 959-3541

Moir's Gardens (Kauai)
Poipu Beach
RR 1, Box 73
Koloa, HI 96756
(808) 742-6411

National Tropical Botanical
    Garden (Kauai)
P.O. Box 340
Halima Rd.
Lawai, HI 96765
(808) 332-7324, fax (808) 332-9765

The National Tropical Botanical Garden includes the following four gardens:

Allerton Garden (Kauai)
c/o National Tropical Botanical
    Garden (see above)
(808) 742-2623

Lawai Garden (Kauai)
c/o National Tropical Botanical
    Garden (see above)
(808) 742-2623

Limahuli Garden (Kauai)
P.O. Box 808
Hanalei, HI 96714
(808) 826-1053

Kahanu Garden (Maui)
P.O. Box 95
Hana, HI 96714
(808) 248-8912

Olu Pua Botanical Garden and
    Plantation (Kauai)
Hwy. 50
Box 518
Kalaheo, HI 96741
(808) 332-8182

Kula Botanical Gardens (Maui)
Kekaulike Rd.
RR 2
Box 288
Kula, HI 96790
(808) 878-1715

Foster Botanical Garden (Oahu)
50 N. Vineyard Blvd.
Honolulu, HI 96817
(808) 522-7066

Honolulu Botanic Gardens (Oahu)
50 N. Vineyard Blvd.
Honolulu, HI 96817
(808) 533-3406

Ho'omaluhia Botanical Garden
    (Oahu)
45-680 Luluku Rd.
Kanehoe, HI 96744
(808) 233-7323

Harold L. Lyon Arboretum (Oahu)
3860 Manoa Rd.
Honolulu, HI 96822
(808) 988-3177, fax (808) 988-4231

Moanalua Gardens (Oahu)
1352 Pineapple Place
Honolulu, HI 96819
(808) 839-5334

Queen Emma Summer Palace
    (Oahu)
2913 Pali Hwy.
Honolulu, HI 96819
(808) 595-6291

Wahiawa Botanical Garden (Oahu)
1396 California Ave.
Wahiawa, HI 96786
(808) 621-7321

Waimea Falls Park Arboretum &
    Botanic Garden (Oahu)
59-864 Kamehameha Hwy.
Haleiwa, HI 96712
(808) 638-8655

## Idaho

Idaho Botanical Gardens
2355 Old Penitentiary Rd.
P.O. Box 2140
Boise, ID 83701
(208) 343-8649, fax (208) 343-8649

**Charles Huston Shattuck
  Arboretum**
University of Idaho Arboretum &
  Botanical Garden
205 C.E.B.
Moscow, ID 83844
(208) 885-6250, fax (208) 885-4040

## Illinois

**Robert Allerton Park &
  Conference Center**
University of Illinois
515 Old Timber Rd.
Monticello, IL 61856
(217) 244-1035, fax (217) 244-9982

**Chicago Botanic Garden**
1000 Lake Cook Rd.
P.O. Box 400
Glencoe, IL 60022
(847) 835-5440, fax (847) 835-4484

**College of DuPage**
425 22nd St.
Glen Ellyn, IL 60137
(708) 942-3806, fax (708) 942-3789

**Early American Museum &
  Gardens**
State Rte. 47
P.O. Box 1040
Mahomet, IL 61853
(217) 586-2612, fax (217) 586-5020

**Fell Arboretum at Illinois State
  University**
Campus Box 3200
Normal, IL 61790
(309) 438-7681, fax (309) 438-5748

**Garfield Park Conservatory**
800 N. Central Park Blvd.
Chicago, IL 60605
(312) 746-5100, fax (312) 922-7481

**Grant Park**
Chicago Park District
700 S. Columbus Dr.
Chicago, IL 60605
(312) 294-2286

**Illinois Central College**
Horticulture Dept.
East Peoria, IL 61635
(309) 694-5415, fax (309) 694-5799

**Illinois Wesleyan University**
P.O. Box 2900
Bloomington, IL 61702
(309) 556-3066, fax (309) 556-3154

**Lilacia Park—Lombard Park
  District**
150 S. Park
Lombard, IL 60148
(708) 627-1281, fax (708) 627-1286

**Lincoln Memorial Garden and
  Nature Center**
2301 East Lake Dr.
Springfield, IL 62707
(217) 529-1111

**Lincoln Park Conservatory**
2400 N. Stockton Dr.
Chicago, IL 60614
(312) 742-7736

**George L. Luthy Memorial
  Botanical Garden**
2218 N. Prospect Ave.
Peoria, IL 61603
(309) 686-3362, fax (309) 685-6240

**The Morton Arboretum**
Rte. 53
Lisle, IL 60532
(708) 986-0074, fax (708) 719-2450

**Northern Illinois Botanical Society**
1220 Rock St.
Rockford, IL 61101
(815) 965-8146, fax (815) 968-6830

**The Oak Park Conservatory**
615 Garfield St.
Oak Park, IL 60304
(708) 386-4700

**Southern Illinois University at
  Edwardsville Arboretum**
Edwardsville, IL 62026
(618) 692-3311, fax (618) 692-3174

**The University of Illinois
  Arboretum**
406 Mumford Hall
1301 W. Gregory Dr.
Urbana, IL 61801
(217) 333-9355, fax (217) 333-6479

**Washington Park Botanical
  Garden**
Springfield Park District
Fayette & Chatham Rds.
P.O. Box 5052
Springfield, IL 62705
(217) 753-6228, fax (217) 544-1811

**Winnebago County Forest Pres.
  District**
5500 Northrock Dr.
Rockford, IL 61103
(815) 877-6100, fax (815) 877-6124

## Indiana

**Christie Woods of Ball State
  University**
200 W. University Ave.
Muncie, IN 47306
(317) 285-8838

**Foellinger-Freimann Botanical
  Conservatory**
1100 S. Calhoun St.
Fort Wayne, IN 46802
(219) 427-6440, fax (219) 427-6450

**Garfield Park Conservatory**
2450 S. Shelby St.
Indianapolis, IN 46201
(317) 327-7184

**Hayes Regional Arboretum**
801 Elks Rd.
Richmond, IN 47274
(317) 962-3745, fax (317) 966-1931

**International Friendship Garden**
Michigan City, IN 46360
(219) 874-3664

Eli Lilly Botanical Garden
Indianapolis Museum of Art
1200 W. 38th St.
Indianapolis, IN 46208
(317) 923-1331, fax (317) 923-8931

Minnetrista Cultural Center
Oakhurst Gardens
1200 N. Minnetrista Pkwy.
P.O. Box 1527
Muncie, IN 47308
(317) 282-4848, fax (317) 741-5110

## Iowa

Bickelhaupt Arboretum
340 S. 14th St.
Clinton, IA 52732
(319) 242-4771

Arie den Boer Arboretum
Des Moines Water Works Park
408 Fleur Dr.
Des Moines, IA 50321
(515) 283-8791

Brucemore
2160 Linden Dr. S.E.
Cedar Rapids, IA 52402
(319) 362-7375, fax (319) 362-9481

Des Moines Botanical Center
909 E. River Dr.
Des Moines, IA 50316
(515) 242-2934, fax (515) 242-2797

Dubuque Arboretum & Botanical
 Gardens
3800 Arboretum Dr.
Dubuque, IA 52001
(319) 556-2100

Ewing Park Lilac Arboretum
3226 University
Des Moines, IA 50311
(515) 271-4700

Iowa Arboretum
1875 Peach Ave.
Madrid, IA 50156
(515) 795-3216, fax (515) 795-3216

Reiman Gardens
Iowa State University
Ames, IA 50011
(515) 294-0028, fax (515) 294-4817

Stampe Lilac Garden
2816 Eastern Ave.
Davenport, IA 52803
(319) 326-7812

University of Northern Iowa
 Gardens
Cedar Falls, IA 50613
(319) 273-2456

VanderVeer Park Botanical Center
 & Park
215 W. Central Park Ave.
Davenport, IA 52803
(319) 326-7818

## Kansas

Bartlett Arboretum
301 North Line
Belle Plaine, KS 67013
(316) 488-3541

Botanica, The Wichita Gardens
701 N. Amidon
Wichita, KS 67203
(316) 264-0448, fax (316) 264-0587

Dyck Arboretum of the Plains
Hesston College
Box 3000
Hesston, KS 67062
(316) 327-8127, fax (316) 327-8300

Meade Park Botanic Gardens
124 N. Fillmore
Topeka, KS 66606
(913) 232-5493

Overland Park Arboretum &
 Botanical Garden
8500 Santa Fe
Overland Park, KS 66212
(913) 685-3604, fax (913) 685-3098

E. F. A. Reinisch Rose and Test
 Gardens
Gage Park
4320 W. 10th St.
Topeka, KS 66604
(913) 272-6150

## Kentucky

Bernheim Arboretum and
 Research Forest
Hwy. 245
Clermont, KY 40110
(502) 955-8512, fax (502) 543-2331

Cave Hill Cemetery
701 Baxter Ave.
Louisville, KY 40204
(502) 451-5630, fax (502) 451-5655

Commonwealth Arboretum
University of Kentucky
N324 ASCN
Lexington, KY 40546
(606) 628-2583, fax (606) 257-2859

The Lexington Cemetery
833 W. Main St.
Lexington, KY 40508
(606) 255-5522, fax (606) 258-2774

## Louisiana

American Rose Society Garden
8877 Jefferson Paige Rd.
Box 3000
Shreveport, LA 71130
(318) 938-5402

Hilltop Arboretum
P.O. Box 82608
Baton Rouge, LA 70884
(504) 767-6916, fax (504) 768-7740

Hodges Garden
Hwy. 171 S.
P.O. Box 921
Many, LA 71449
(318) 586-3523

**Jungle Gardens**
Avery Island, LA 70513
(318) 365-8173, fax (318) 369-6326

**Live Oak Gardens**
5505 Rip Van Winkle Rd.
New Iberia, LA 70560
(318) 367-3485, fax (318) 365-3354

**Longue Vue House and Gardens**
7 Bamboo Rd.
New Orleans, LA 70124
(504) 488-5488, fax (504) 486-7015

**Metairie Cemetery**
5100 Ponchartrain Blvd.
New Orleans, LA 70124
(504) 486-6331

**New Orleans Botanical Garden**
City Park
1 Palm St.
New Orleans, LA 70124
(504) 483-9386, fax (504) 483-9485

**Rosedown Plantation**
12501 State Hwy. 10
Saint Francisville, LA 70775
(504) 635-3332

**Zemurray Gardens**
Rte. 1, Box 201
Loranger, LA 70446
(504) 878-6731

## Maine

**Asticou Azalea Garden**
Asticou Way
Northeast Harbor, ME 04662
(207) 276-5456

**Bath Marine Museum and Garden**
963 Washington St.
Bath, ME 04530
(207) 443-1316

**Coastal Maine Botanical Garden**
P.O. Box 244
Wiscosset, ME 04578
(207) 882-4232, fax (207) 882-4232

**Deering Oaks Rose Circle**
Deering Oaks Park
55 Portland St.
Portland, ME 04101
(207) 874-8871

**Hamilton House**
Vaughan's Lane
South Berwick, ME 03908
(207) 384-5269

**Merryspring**
Conway Rd.
Box 893
Camden, ME 04843
(207) 236-9046

**Pine Tree State Arboretum**
P.O. Box 344
Augusta, ME 04332
(207) 621-0031

**Thuya Gardens**
P.O. Box 1120
Northeast Harbor, ME 04662
(207) 276-5130

**Wild Gardens of Acadia**
Acadia National Park
Sieur de Monts Spring
Mount Desert Island
Bar Harbor, ME 04609
(207) 228-3338

## Maryland

**The Adkins Arboretum**
P.O. Box 147
Hillsboro, MD 21641
(410) 634-2847, fax (410) 634-2878

**Baltimore Conservatory**
Druid Hill Park
Gwynns Falls Pkwy. and
    McCulloh St.
Baltimore, MD 21217
(410) 396-0180

**Brookside Gardens**
1500 Glenallan Ave.
Wheaton, MD 20902
(301) 929-6509, fax (301) 949-0571

**Cylburn Garden Center**
4915 Greenspring Ave.
Baltimore, MD 21209
(410) 367-2217

**Ladew Topiary Gardens**
3535 Jarretsville Pike
Monkton, MD 21111
(410) 557-9570

**London Town House & Gardens**
London Town Foundation, Inc.
839 Londontown Rd.
Edgewater, MD 21037
(410) 222-1919, fax (410) 222-1918

**William Paca Garden**
1 Martin St.
Annapolis, MD 21401
(410) 267-7619, fax (410) 267-6189

**Salisbury State University**
1101 Camden Ave.
Salisbury, MD 21801
(410) 543-6200, fax (410) 543-6068

**Surreybrooke**
8537 Hollow Rd.
Middletown, MD 21769
(301) 371-7466

## Massachusetts

**Arnold Arboretum**
Harvard University
125 Arborway
Jamaica Plain, MA 02130
(617) 524-1718, fax (617) 524-1418

**Ashumet Holly Reservation**
Massachusetts Audubon Society
286 Ashumet Rd.
East Falmouth, MA 02536
(508) 563-6390

**Barnard's Inn Farm**
RFD 1, Box 538
Vineyard Haven, MA 02568
(508) 693-0925

**Berkshire Botanical Garden**
Rte. 102 & Rte. 183
P.O. Box 826
Stockbridge, MA 01262
(413) 298-3926, fax (413) 298-5355

**The Botanic Garden of Smith
 College**
Lyman Plant House
College Lane
Northampton, MA 01063
(413) 585-2740, fax (413) 585-2744

**Codman House, The Grange**
Codman Rd.
Lincoln, MA 01773
(781) 259-8843

**Isabella Stewart Gardner Museum**
280 The Fenway
Boston, MA 02115
(617) 566-1401

**Heritage Plantation of Sandwich**
Grove & Pine Sts.
Sandwich, MA 02563
(508) 888-3300

**Jeremiah Lee Mansion**
161 Washington St.
P.O. Box 1048
Marblehead, MA 01945
(781) 631-1069

**Long Hill Reservation, Sedgwick
 Gardens**
572 Essex St.
Beverly, MA 01915
(978) 921-1944, fax (978) 921-1948

**Longfellow National Historic Site**
105 Brattle St.
Cambridge, MA 02138
(617) 566-1689

**The Lyman Estate**
185 Lyman St.
Waltham, MA 02154
(781) 893-7232, fax (781) 277-9204

**Massachusetts Horticultural
 Society**
Horticultural Hall
300 Massachusetts Ave.
Boston, MA 02115
(617) 536-9280, fax (617) 262-8780

**Mount Auburn Cemetery**
580 Mount Auburn St.
Cambridge, MA 02138
(617) 547-7105, fax (617) 876-4405

**Mount Holyoke College Botanic
 Garden**
Mount Holyoke College
South Hadley, MA 01075
(413) 538-2199, fax (413) 538-2144

**Naumkeag**
Prospect Hill Rd.
P.O. Box 792
Stockbridge, MA 01262
(413) 298-3239

**New England Wild Flower Society**
Garden in the Woods
180 Hemenway Rd.
Framingham, MA 01701
(508) 877-7360, fax (508) 877-3658

**Newbury Perennial Gardens**
65 Orchard St.
Byfield, MA 01922
(978) 462-1144

**Old Sturbridge Village**
1 Old Sturbridge Village Rd.
Sturbridge, MA 01566
(508) 347-3362, fax (508) 347-5375

**Ropes Mansion**
318 Essex St.
Salem, MA 01970
(978) 744-3390

**Sedgwick Gardens**
The Trustees of Reservations
572 Essex St.
Beverly, MA 01915
(978) 921-1944, fax (978) 921-1948

**Stanley Park**
Western & Kensington Aves.
P.O. Box 1191
Westfield, MA 01086
(413) 568-9312

**Tower Hill Botanic Garden**
11 French Dr.
P.O. Box 598
Boylston, MA 01505
(508) 869-6111, fax (508) 869-0314

**Wellesley College**
106 Central St.
Wellesley, MA 02181
(781) 283-3074, fax (781) 283-3642

**Williams College**
P.O. Box 626
Williamstown, MA 01267
(413) 597-3304, fax (413) 597-4013

## Michigan

**Andrews University Campus
 Arboretum**
Alumni House
Andrews University
Berrien Springs, MI 49104
(616) 471-3344, fax (616) 471-9751

**W. J. Beal Botanical Garden**
West Circle Dr.
412 Olds Hall—MSU
East Lansing, MI 48824
(517) 355-9582, fax (517) 336-1090

**Cranbrook House and Gardens**
380 Lone Pine Rd.
Bloomfield Hills, MI 48013
(810) 645-3149

**Detroit Zoological Institute**
8450 W. 10 Mile Rd.
Royal Oak, MI 48068
(810) 398-0903, fax (810) 398-0504

**The Dow Gardens**
1018 W. Main St.
Midland, MI 48640
(517) 631-2677, fax (800) 631-0675

**Fernwood Nature Center**
13988 Range Line Rd.
Niles, MI 49120
(616) 695-6491, fax (616) 695-6688

**For-Mar Nature Preserve and Arboretum**
Genesee County Parks & Recreation
5045 E. Stanley Rd.
Flint, MI 48506
(810) 742-6132, fax (810) 736-7220

**Grand Hotel**
Mackinac Island, MI 49757
(906) 847-3331

**Hidden Lake Gardens**
Michigan State University
Rte. M-50
6280 W. Munger Rd.
Tipton, MI 49287
(517) 431-2060, fax (517) 431-9148

**Leila Arboretum Society**
928 W. Michigan Ave.
Battle Creek, MI 49017
(616) 969-0270, fax (616) 969-0616

**Matthaei Botanical Gardens**
University of Michigan
1800 N. Dixboro Rd.
Ann Arbor, MI 48105
(313) 998-7061, fax (313) 998-6205

**Frederik Meijer Gardens**
3411 Bradford N.E.
Grand Rapids, MI 49546
(616) 957-1580, fax (616) 957-5792

**Nichols Arboretum**
University of Michigan
Dana Bldg.
430 E. University
Ann Arbor, MI 48109
(313) 763-6632, fax (313) 936-2195

**Slayton Arboretum of Hillsdale College**
Dept. of Biology
Hillsdale, MI 49242
(517) 437-7341, fax (517) 437-3923

**Anna Scripps Whitcomb Conservatory**
Belle Isle Park
Conservatory Dr.
Detroit, MI 48207
(313) 267-7133, fax (313) 224-1743

## Minnesota

**Eloise Butler Wildflower Garden and Bird Sanctuary**
Theodore Wirth Blvd. and
Glenwood Ave.
Minneapolis, MN 55409
(612) 348-5702, fax (612) 348-9354

**Como Park Conservatory**
1325 Aida Place
St. Paul, MN 55103
(612) 487-0608, fax (612) 487-8960

**Dodge Nature Center**
1795 Charlton St.
W. St. Paul, MN 55118
(612) 455-8559, fax (612) 455-2575

**Linnaeus Arboretum & Sculpture Garden**
Gustavus Adolphus College
St. Peter, MN 56082
(507) 933-7324, fax (507) 933-7041

**Minnesota Landscape Arboretum**
University of Minnesota
3675 Arboretum Dr., Box 39
Chanhassen, MN 55317
(612) 443-2460, fax (612) 392-4979

**Northland Arboretum**
Paul Bunyan Conservation Area
P.O. Box 375
Brainerd, MN 56401
(218) 829-8770, fax (218) 829-1221

**Schell Mansion and Gardens**
Jefferson St. S.
New Ulm, MN 56073
(507) 354-5528

## Mississippi

**Beauvoir**
2244 Beach Blvd.
Biloxi, MS 39531
(601) 388-1313

**Crosby Arboretum**
1986 Ridge Blvd.
P.O. Box 190
Picayune, MS 39466
(601) 799-2311, fax (601) 799-2372

**Wister Henry Garden**
Rte. 3
P.O. Box 237
Belzoni, MS 39038
(601) 247-3025

**Mynelle Gardens**
City of Jackson
4736 Clinton Blvd.
Jackson, MS 39209
(601) 960-1894

## Missouri

**Center for Plant Conservation**
Missouri Botanical Garden
P.O. Box 299
St. Louis, MO 63166
(314) 577-9450, fax (314) 577-9465

**Horticulture and Agro Forestry Research**
10 Research Center Rd.
New Franklin, MO 65274
(816) 848-2268, fax (816) 848-2144

**Missouri Botanical Garden**
4344 Shaw Blvd.
P.O. Box 299
St. Louis, MO 63166
(314) 577-5100, fax (314) 577-9595

**Powell Gardens**
1609 N.W. U.S. Hwy. 50
Kingsville, MO 64061
(816) 697-2600, fax (816) 697-2619

**Shaw Arboretum**
State Hwy. 100
Box 38
Gray Summit, MO 63039
(314) 742-3512

**Laura Conyers Smith Municipal**
**Rose Garden**
5605 E. 63rd St.
Kansas City, MO 64130
(816) 561-9710

## Montana

**Memorial Rose Garden**
700 Brook St.
Missoula, MT 59801
(406) 721-7275

**The University of Montana**
**Zoological Museum &**
**Herbarium**
Facilities Services Dept.
Physical Plant Bldg.
Campus Dr.
Missoula, MT 59812
(406) 243-5599, fax (406) 243-2335

## Nebraska

**Arbor Lodge State Historical Park**
RR 2, Centennial Ave.
P.O. Box 15
Nebraska City, NE 68410
(402) 873-7222

**Folsom Children's Zoo &**
**Botanical Garden**
1222 S. 27th St.
Lincoln, NE 68502
(402) 475-6741, fax (402) 475-6742

**General Crook House Museum**
30th & Fort St.
P.O. Box 11398
Fort Omaha
Omaha, NE 68111
(402) 455-9990

**Nebraska Statewide Arboretum**
P.O. Box 830715
University of Nebraska
Lincoln, NE 68583
(402) 472-2971, fax (402) 472-8095

**Omaha Botanical Center**
1605 S. 113th Plaza
Omaha, NE 68144
(402) 333-2359, fax (402) 397-4633

**State Fair Park Arboretum**
Nebraska State Board of Agriculture
P.O. Box 81223
Lincoln, NE 68501
(402) 474-5371, fax (402) 473-4114

**The University of Nebraska**
Lincoln Botanical Garden &
Arboretum
1340 N. 17th St.
Lincoln, NE 68588
(402) 472-2679, fax (402) 472-9615

## Nevada

**Wilbur D. May Arboretum and**
**Botanical Garden**
1502 Washington St.
Reno, NV 89503
(702) 785-4153, fax (702) 785-4707

**The University of Nevada—Las**
**Vegas**
4505 Maryland Pkwy.
Las Vegas, NV 89154
(702) 895-3392, fax (702) 895-4173

## New Hampshire

**Fuller Gardens**
10 Willow Ave.
North Hampton, NH 03862
(603) 964-5414

**Moffatt-Ladd House and Garden**
154 Market St.
Portsmouth, NH 03801
(603) 436-8221

**Rhododendron State Park**
Rtes. 12 & 119
Fitzwilliam, NH 03447
(mailing address) P.O. Box 856
Concord, NH 03301
(603) 271-3254

**Saint-Gaudens National Historical**
**Site**
RR 2, Box 73
Cornish, NH 03745
(603) 675-2175

**Strawberry Banke Museum**
Horticulture Dept.
454 Court St.
P.O. Box 300
Portsmouth, NH 03802
(603) 433-1100, fax (603) 433-1115

## New Jersey

**Leonard J. Buck Gardens**
Somerset County Park Commission
11 Layton Rd.
Far Hills, NJ 07931
(908) 234-2677

**Sr. Mary Grace Burns Arboretum**
Georgian Court College
900 Lakewood Ave.
Lakewood, NJ 08701
(908) 364-2200, fax (908) 905-8571

**Colonial Park**
Rudolf W. van der Groot Rose
Garden
RD 1, Box 49B
Mettler's Rd.
Somerset, NJ 08873
(732) 873-2459

**Duke Gardens**
State Rte. 206 S.
P.O. Box 2000
Somerville, NJ 08876
(908) 722-3700

**George Griswold Freylinghuysen Arboretum**
53 E. Hanover Ave.
P.O. Box 1295
Morristown, NJ 07962
(973) 326-7600

**Cora Hartshorn Arboretum and Bird Sanctuary**
324 Forest Dr. S.
Short Hills, NJ 07078
(973) 376-3587

**Leaming's Run Gardens**
1845 Rte. 9 N.
Cape May Courthouse, NJ 08210
(609) 884-2736

**James A. McFaul Environmental Center**
Crescent Ave.
Wyckoff, NJ 07481
(201) 891-5571, fax (201) 891-5583

**Medford Leas**
Rte. 70
Medford, NJ 08055
(609) 654-3000, fax (609) 654-7894

**Monmouth County Shade Tree Commission**
Holmdel Arboretum
P.O. Box 1255
Freehold, NJ 07728
(908) 431-7903, fax (908) 409-4820

**Morris County Park Commission**
P.O. Box 1295
Morristown, NJ 07962
(973) 326-7600, fax (973) 644-2726

**Presby Memorial Iris Garden**
474 Upper Mountain Ave.
Upper Montclair, NJ 07043
(973) 783-5974

**Reeves-Reed Arboretum**
165 Hobart Ave.
Summit, NJ 07901
(908) 273-8787

**The Rutgers Gardens**
Ryders Lane at U.S. Rte. 1
Log Cabin Rd.
P.O. Box 231
Cook College
New Brunswick, NJ 08903
(908) 932-8451, fax (908) 932-7060

**Skylands Association**
New Jersey State Botanical Garden
Morris Rd.
P.O. Box 302
Ringwood, NJ 07456
(973) 962-7527, fax (973) 962-9534

**Somerset County Park Commission**
11 Layton Rd.
Far Hills, NJ 07931
(908) 234-2677, fax (908) 234-9409

**Wetlands Institute**
1075 Stone Harbor Blvd.
Stone Harbor, NJ 08247
(609) 368-1211, fax (609) 368-3871

**Willowwood Arboretum**
Portersville Rd. Rte. 512
Chester, NJ 07624
(mailing address):
Morris County Parks Commission
P.O. Box 1295
Morristown, NJ 07962
(201) 326-7600

## New Mexico

**Living Desert State Park Zoo & Gardens**
1504 Miehls Dr.
P.O. Box 100
Carlsbad, NM 88221
(505) 887-5516, fax (505) 885-4478

**Rio Grande Botanic Garden**
903 10th St. S.W.
Albuquerque, NM 87102
(505) 764-6200, fax (505) 764-6281

**Santa Fe Botanical Garden**
P.O. Box 23343
Santa Fe, NM 87502

**The University of New Mexico**
1841 Lomas Blvd. N.E.
Albuquerque, NM 87131
(505) 277-2236, fax (505) 277-2238

## New York

**Bailey Arboretum**
Bayville Rd. and Feeks Lane
Lattingtown, NY 11560
(516) 676-4497

**Battery Park City Parks**
2 South End Ave.
New York, NY 10280
(212) 267-9700, fax (212) 267-9707

**Bayard Cutting Arboretum**
Montauk Hwy.
P.O. Box 466
Oakdale, NY 11769
(516) 581-1002, fax (516) 581-1031

**Boscobel Restoration**
Rte. 9D
Garrison-on-Hudson, NY 10524
(914) 265-3638, fax (914) 265-4405

**Brooklyn Botanic Garden**
1000 Washington Ave.
Brooklyn, NY 11225
(718) 622-4433, fax (718) 857-2430

**Buffalo & Erie County Botanical Gardens**
2655 S. Park Ave.
Buffalo, NY 14218
(716) 696-3555, fax (716) 828-0091

**Buffalo Zoological Garden**
300 Parkside Ave.
Buffalo, NY 14214
(716) 837-3900, fax (716) 837-0738

**Mary Flagler Cary Arboretum**
Institute of Ecosystem Studies
Rte. 44A
Millbrook, NY 12545
(914) 677-5343, fax (914) 677-5976

Clark Garden
193 I.U. Willets Rd.
Albertson, NY 11507
(516) 484-8600

The Cloisters
Fort Tryon Park
New York, NY 10040
(212) 923-3700, fax (212) 795-3640

The Conservatory Garden
5th Ave. at 105th St.
Central Park Conservatory
839 Fifth Ave.
New York, NY 10021
(212) 860-1330, fax (212) 360-2754

Cornell Plantations
One Plantations Rd.
Cornell University
Ithaca, NY 14850
(607) 255-3020, fax (607) 255-2404

George Eastman House
900 East Ave.
Rochester, NY 14607
(716) 271-3361, fax (716) 271-3970

Highland Botanical Park
180 Reservoir Ave.
Rochester, NY 14620
(716) 256-4967, fax (716) 256-4968

Hofstra University Arboretum
Hempstead, NY 11550
(516) 560-5320

The Horticultural Society of New
    York
128 W. 58th St.
New York, NY 10019
(212) 757-0915, fax (212) 246-1207

The John P. Humes Stroll Garden
Dogwood Lane
Mill Neck, NY
(mailing address) P.O. Box 671
Locust Valley, NY 11560
(516) 676-4486

Innisfree Gardens
Innisfree Foundation
Tyrrel Rd.
Millbrook, NY 12545
(914) 677-8000

International Bonsai Arboretum
1070 Reservoir Ave.
Rochester, NY 14620
(716) 244-8079

Donald M. Kendall Sculpture
    Gardens
Pepsico World Headquarters
Purchase, NY 10577
(914) 253-2890, fax (914) 253-2070

George Landis Arboretum
Lape Rd.
P.O. Box 186
Esperance, NY 12066
(518) 875-12066

Locust Grove
Samuel F. B. Morse Historic House
    and Grounds
370 South Rd., Rte. 9
P.O. Box 1649
Poughkeepsie, NY 12601
(914) 454-4500, fax (914) 485-7122

Lyndhurst
635 S. Broadway
Tarrytown, NY 10591
(914) 631-4481

The Madoo Conservancy
P.O. Box 362
Sagaponack, NY 11962
(516) 537-0802

Marist College Arboretum
Division of Science
Marist College
Poughkeepsie, NY 12601
(914) 575-3000, fax (914) 471-6213

Mohonk Mountain House
Lake Mohonk
New Paltz, NY 12561
(914) 255-1000

Montgomery Place
River Rd.
P.O. Box 32
Annandale-on-Hudson, NY 12504
(914) 758-5461

New York Botanical Garden
200th St. & Southern Blvd.
Bronx, NY 10458
(718) 817-8700, fax (718) 220-6504

Oceanside School Six Memorial
    Botanical Garden & Arboretum
Brower and Skillman Aves.
Oceanside, NY 11572
(516) 678-1200, fax (516) 678-1224

Old Westbury Gardens
71 Old Westbury Rd.
P.O. Box 430
Old Westbury, NY 11568
(516) 333-0048, fax (516) 333-6807

Pace University Garden &
    Arboretum
Biology Dept.
Bedford Rd.
Pleasantville, NY 10570
(914) 773-3563, fax (914) 773-3441

Howard Phipps Estate
55 Post Rd.
P.O. Box 531
Westbury, NY 11590
(516) 333-0287, fax (516) 997-1098

Planting Fields Arboretum State
    Historic Park
Planting Fields Rd.
P.O. Box 58
Oyster Bay, NY 11771
(516) 922-9200, fax (516) 922-7603

Quaker Hill Native Plant Garden
P.O. Box 667
Pawling, NY 12564
(914) 855-1531, fax (914) 855-1357

Queens Botanical Garden
43-50 Main St.
Flushing, NY 11355
(718) 886-3800, fax (718) 463-0263

**Rockefeller Center Management Corp.**
1230 Avenue of the Americas
New York, NY 10020
(212) 698-8973, fax (212) 698-8549

**Sonnenberg Gardens**
151 Charlotte St.
P.O. Box 496
Canandaigua, NY 14424
(716) 394-4922, fax (716) 394-2192

**State University of New York**
College of Environmental Science and
    Forestry
1 Forestry Dr.
Syracuse, NY 13210
(315) 470-6784, fax (315) 470-6934

**Staten Island Botanical Garden**
1000 Richmond Terrace
Staten Island, NY 10301
(718) 273-8200, fax (718) 442-3645

**Stonecrop Gardens**
RR 2, Box 371
Cold Spring, NY 10516
(914) 265-2000, fax (914) 265-2047

**Three Village Garden Club Arboretum**
P.O. Box 2083
Setauket, NY 11733
(516) 941-9252

**Vanderbilt Mansion National Historic Site**
Rte. 9
P.O. Box 329
Hyde Park, NY 12538
(914) 229-7770

**Wave Hill**
675 W. 252nd St.
Bronx, NY 10471
(718) 549-3200, fax (718) 884-8952

**Yonkers Parks, Recreation & Cons.**
Subdivision of Shade Trees
285 Nepperhan Ave.
Yonkers, NY 10701
(914) 377-6425, fax (914) 377-6428

## North Carolina

**Alpina Research & Montane Garden**
Rte. 2, Box 265B
Asheville, NC 28805
(704) 288-4751

**The Biltmore Estate**
One North Pack Square
Asheville, NC 28801
(704) 255-1776, fax (704) 255-1111

**The Botanical Gardens at Asheville**
151 W. T. Weaver Blvd.
Asheville, NC 28804
(704) 252-5190

**Cape Fear Botanical Garden**
536 N. Eastern Blvd.
P.O. Box 53485
Fayetteville, NC 28305
(910) 486-0221, fax (910) 486-4209

**Charlotte Botanical Garden**
P.O. Box 31395
Charlotte, NC 28231
(704) 331-5566, fax (704) 342-1531

**Coker Arboretum**
University of North Carolina
Raleigh St. & Cameron Ave.
Chapel Hill, NC 27514
(919) 962-0522, fax (919) 962-3531

**Davidson College Arboretum**
P.O. Box 1748
Davidson, NC 28036
(704) 892-2119, fax (704) 892-2586

**Sarah P. Duke Gardens**
Duke University
Box 90341
Durham, NC 27708
(919) 684-3698, fax (919) 684-5412

**Elizabethan Gardens**
Manteo, NC 27954
(919) 473-3234

**Haywood Community Gardens**
Campus Arboretum Dept.
Freedlander Dr.
Clyde, NC 28721
(704) 627-2821, fax (704) 627-3606

**The North Carolina Arboretum**
P.O. Box 6617
Asheville, NC 28816
(704) 665-2492, fax (704) 665-2371

**North Carolina Botanical Garden**
CB Box 3375, Totten Center
University of North Carolina
Chapel Hill, NC 27599
(919) 962-0522, fax (919) 962-3531

**North Carolina State University Arboretum**
Box 7609
Dept. of Horticultural Sciences
Raleigh, NC 27695
(919) 515-3132, fax (919) 515-7747

**North Carolina Zoological Park**
4401 Zoo Pkwy.
Asheboro, NC 27203
(910) 879-7400, fax (910) 879-2891

**Orton Plantation Gardens**
Hwy. NC 133
RFD
Winnabow, NC 28479
(910) 371-6851

**Reynolda Gardens**
Wake Forest University
100 Reynolda Village
Winston-Salem, NC 27106
(910) 759-5593

**Sandhills Horticultural Gardens**
Sandhill Community College
2200 Airport Rd.
Pinehurst, NC 28374
(919) 692-6185

**Daniel Stowe Botanical Garden**
P.O. Box 1047
Belmont, NC 28012
(704) 825-4490, fax (704) 825-4492

**Tryon Palace Restoration**
610 Pollock St.
New Bern, NC 28563
(919) 514-4900, fax (919) 514-4876

**The University of North Carolina**
601 S. College Rd.
Wilmington, NC 28403
(910) 395-3030, fax (910) 350-4050

**UNC Charlotte Botanical Gardens**
UNC Campus
Mary Alexander & Craven Rds.
Charlotte, NC 28223
(704) 547-4055

**Wing Haven Gardens & Bird
  Sanctuary**
248 Ridgewood Ave.
Charlotte, NC 28209
(704) 331-0664, fax (704) 331-9368

## North Dakota

**International Peace Garden**
Hwy. 281
RR 1, Box 116
Dunseith, ND 58329
(701) 263-4390, fax (701) 263-3169

## Ohio

**Cincinnati Board of Parks
  Commission**
Mount Airy Forest & Arboretum
Irwin M. Krohn Conservatory
950 Eden Park Dr.
Cincinnati, OH 45202
(513) 352-4080, fax (513) 352-4096

**Cincinnati Zoo and Botanical
  Garden**
3400 Vine St.
Cincinnati, OH 45220
(513) 559-7721, fax (513) 559-7790

**Cleveland Botanical Garden**
11030 East Blvd.
Cleveland, OH 44106
(216) 721-1600, fax (216) 721-2056

**Cleveland Metroparks Zoo**
3900 Brookside Dr.
Cleveland, OH 44109
(216) 661-6500, fax (216) 661-3312

**Columbus Park of Roses**
Whetstone Park
3923 N. High St.
Columbus, OH 43214
(614) 645-3343, fax (614) 645-8839

**Columbus Zoological Gardens**
9990 Riverside Dr.
P.O. Box 400
Powell, OH 43065
(614) 645-3400, fax (614) 645-3465

**Cox Arboretum—Five River
  MetroParks**
Dayton–Montgomery County
6733 Springboro Pike
Dayton, OH 45449
(513) 434-9005, fax (513) 438-0601

**The Dawes Arboretum**
7770 Jacksontown Rd. S.E.
Newark, OH 43056
(614) 323-2355, fax (614) 323-4058

**Falconskeape Gardens**
7359 Branch Rd.
Medina, OH 44256
(216) 723-4966

**Fellows Riverside Gardens**
Mill Creek Metropolitan Park
  District
816 Greenwood Ave.
Youngstown, OH 44502
(330) 740-7116, fax (330) 740-7132

**Franklin Park Conservatory and
  Botanical Garden**
1777 E. Broad St.
Columbus, OH 43203
(614) 645-3000, fax (614) 645-5921

**Garden Center of Greater
  Cleveland**
11030 East Blvd.
Cleveland, OH 44106
(216) 721-1600

**The Holden Arboretum**
9500 Sperry Rd.
Kirtland, OH 44094
(216) 256-1110, fax (216) 256-1655

**Stan Hywet Hall and Gardens**
714 N. Portage Path
Akron, OH 44303
(216) 836-5533, fax (216) 836-2680

**Inniswood Metro Gardens**
940 Hempstead Rd.
Westerville, OH 43081
(614) 895-6216

**Kent State University Botanical
  Gardens**
Kent, OH 44242
(330) 672-3613

**Kingwood Center**
900 Park Ave. W.
Mansfield, OH 44906
(419) 522-0211

**Irwin M. Krohn Conservatory**
950 Eden Park Dr.
Cincinnati, OH 45202
(513) 421-4086, fax (513) 352-4096

**Mount Airy Arboretum**
5083 Colerain Ave.
Cincinnati, OH 45223
(513) 352-4080, fax (513) 352-4096

**The Ohio State University
  Chadwick Arboretum**
2001 Fyffe Ct.
Columbus, OH 43210
(614) 292-4678

**Rockefeller Park Greenhouse**
750 E. 88th St.
Cleveland, OH 44108
(216) 664-3103

**Schoepfle Garden**
12882 Diagonal Rd.
La Grange, OH 44050
(216) 965-7237, fax (216) 458-8924

Secrest Arboretum
Ag Research & Development Center
Ohio State University
1680 Madison Ave.
Wooster, OH 44691
(330) 263-3761, fax (330) 263-3767

Stranahan Arboretum
Dept. of Biology
The University of Toledo
Toledo, OH 43606
(419) 882-6806, fax (419) 537-7737

Toledo Botanical Garden
5403 Elmer Dr.
Toledo, OH 43615
(419) 936-2986, fax (419) 936-2987

Toledo Zoological Society
2700 Broadway
P.O. Box 4010
Toledo, OH 43609
(419) 385-5721, fax (419) 385-6935

Woodland Arboretum
118 Woodland Ave.
Dayton, OH 45415
(513) 228-3221, fax (513) 222-7259

## Oklahoma

Muskogee Parks
641 Park Dr.
Muskogee, OK 74403
(918) 684-6302

Myriad Botanical Gardens
100 Myriad Gardens
Oklahoma City, OK 73102
(405) 297-3995, fax (405) 297-3620

Oklahoma Botanical Garden &
    Arboretum
Oklahoma State University
Horticulture & Landscape
    Architecture
360 Agriculture Hall
Stillwater, OK 74078
(405) 744-5414, fax (405) 744-9693

Oklahoma City Zoological Park
2101 N.E. 50th St.
Oklahoma City, OK 73111
(405) 425-3344, fax (405) 425-0207

Philbrook Museum of Art
2727 S. Rockford Rd.
Tulsa, OK 74114
(918) 748-5321, fax (918) 743-4230

Will Rogers Horticultural Gardens
3500 N.W. 36th St.
Oklahoma City, OK 73102
(405) 943-0827

Tulsa Garden Center
2435 S. Peoria Ave.
Tulsa, OK 74114
(918) 746-5125, fax (918) 746-5128

## Oregon

Azalea Park
16330 Lower Harbor Rd.
P.O. Box 940
Brookings, OR 97415
(541) 469-3181

The Berry Botanic Garden
11505 S.W. Summerville Ave.
Portland, OR 97219
(503) 636-4112, fax (503) 636-7496

The Catlin Gabel School
8825 S.W. Barnes Rd.
Portland, OR 97225
(503) 203-5100, fax (503) 297-0139

Crystal Springs Rhododendron
    Garden
S.E. 28th Ave. by Woodstock Blvd.
Portland, OR 97202
(503) 823-3640

Greer Gardens
1280 Goodpasture Rd.
Eugene, OR 97401
(503) 686-8266

The Grotto
Sandy Blvd. & N.E. 85th Ave.
P.O. Box 20002
Portland, OR 97220
(503) 254-7371

Hendricks Park Rhododendron
    Garden
1800 Skyline Dr.
Eugene, OR 97403
(800) 551-6949

Hoyt Arboretum
Bureau of Parks
4000 S.W. Fairview Blvd.
Portland, OR 97221
(503) 228-8733, fax (503) 823-4213

John Innskeep Environmental
    Learning Center
19600 S. Molalla Ave.
Oregon City, OR 97236
(503) 657-6958

International Rose Test Garden
Washington Park
400 S.W. Kingston Ave.
Portland, OR 97201
(503) 248-4302

The Japanese Garden at
    Washington Park
Kingston Blvd.
Portland, OR 97201
(503) 223-1321

Jenkins Estate
S.W. 209th & Farmington Rd.
Tualatin Hills Park & Recreation
    District
P.O. Box 5868
Aloha, OR 97006
(503) 642-3855

Leach Botanical Garden
6704 S.E. 122nd Ave.
Portland, OR 97236
(503) 761-9503

**Mount Pisgah Arboretum**
34901 Frank Parish Rd.
P.O. Box 5621
Eugene, OR 97405
(503) 747-3817, fax (503) 747-3817

**Owen Rose Garden**
Summit Ave.
Parks Services Division
210 Cheshire St.
Eugene, OR 97401
(503) 687-5333

**Peavy Arboretum**
College of Forestry
Oregon State University
8692 Peavy Arboretum Rd.
Corvallis, OR 97331
(541) 754-2608

**Shore Acres State Park Garden**
13030 Cape Arago Hwy.
P.O. Box 1172
Coos Bay, OR 97420
(503) 888-3732

**Cecil and Molly Smith Garden**
5065 Ray Bell Rd.
Saint Paul, OR 97137
(503) 246-3710

## Pennsylvania

**The American College**
270 S. Bryn Mawr Ave.
Bryn Mawr, PA 19010
(610) 526-1228, fax (610) 526-1224

**The Barnes Foundation
Arboretum**
300 N. Latch's Lane
P.O. Box 128
Merion Station, PA 19066
(610) 667-0290, fax (610) 667-1566

**Historic Bartram's Garden**
54th St. & Lindbergh Blvd.
Philadelphia, PA 19143
(215) 729-5281, fax (215) 729-1047

**Bowman's Hill Wildflower
Preserve**
Washington Crossing Historic Park
P.O. Box 103
Washington Crossing, PA 18977
(215) 493-4076, fax (215) 493-4820

**Brandywine Conservancy**
Brandywine River Museum
U.S. Rte. 1
P.O. Box 141
Chadds Ford, PA 19317
(610) 388-2700, fax (610) 388-1197

**Bryn Mawr College**
101 N. Merion Ave.
Bryn Mawr, PA 19010
(610) 526-7930, fax (610) 526-7940

**Cedar Crest College**
100 College Dr.
Allentown, PA 18104
(610) 740-3792, fax (610) 606-4616

**Chanticleer**
786 Church Rd.
Wayne, PA 19087
(610) 687-6894, fax (610) 293-0149

**Chatham College**
Woodland Rd.
Pittsburgh, PA 15232
(412) 365-1157, fax (412) 365-1502

**The Coover Arboretum**
Rte. 3, Box 23
Dillsburg, PA 17019
(717) 766-6681

**Crozer Arboretum**
1 Medical Center Blvd.
Upland, PA 19018
(610) 447-2281, fax (610) 447-2234

**Erie Zoological Society**
423 W. 38th St.
P.O. Box 3268
Erie, PA 16508
(814) 864-4091

**Friends Hospital**
4641 Roosevelt Blvd.
Philadelphia, PA 19124
(215) 831-4781

**Harrisburg Area Community
College**
1 HACC Dr.
Harrisburg, PA 17110
(717) 780-2611, fax (717) 780-2670

**Haverford College Arboretum**
370 Lancaster Ave.
Haverford, PA 19041
(610) 896-1101, fax (610) 896-1095

**Henry Foundation for Botanical
Research**
801 Stony Lane
P.O. Box 7
Gladwyne, PA 19035
(610) 525-3252, fax (610) 525-4024

**Hershey Rose Gardens and
Arboretum**
170 Hotel Rd.
P.O. Box 416
Hershey, PA 17033
(717) 534-3492

**Horticultural Society of Western
Pennsylvania**
P.O. Box 5126
Pittsburgh, PA 15206
(412) 361-8677, fax (412) 362-8192

**The Horticulture Center**
West Fairmount Park
N. Horticulture Dr. and
Montgomery Ave.
P.O. Box 21601
Philadelphia, PA 19131
(215) 685-0096, fax (215) 879-4062

**Jenkins Arboretum**
631 Berwyn-Baptist Rd.
Devon, PA 19333
(610) 647-8870, fax (610) 647-6664

**Longwood Gardens**
Rte. 1
P.O. Box 501
Kennett Square, PA 19348
(610) 388-6741, fax (610) 388-2079

**Masonic Homes Arboretum**
One Masonic Dr.
Elizabethtown, PA 17022
(717) 367-1121, fax (717) 367-6768

**Meadowbrook Farm**
1633 Washington Lane
Meadowbrook, PA 19046
(610) 887-5900

**Meadows Arboretum**
Arco Chemical Co.
375 S. Flowers Mill Rd.
Langhorne, PA 19047
(610) 859-0901, fax (610) 859-0906

**Morris Arboretum of University of Pennsylvania**
100 Northwestern Ave.
Philadelphia, PA 19118
(215) 247-5777, fax (215) 248-4439

**Muhlenberg College**
Biology Dept.
2400 Chew St.
Allentown, PA 18104
(610) 821-2358, fax (610) 821-3234

**Pennsbury Manor**
400 Pennsbury Memorial Rd.
Morrisville, PA 19067
(215) 946-0400, fax (215) 295-2936

**The Pennsylvania Horticultural Society**
325 Walnut St.
Philadelphia, PA 19106
(215) 625-8250

**Phipps Conservatory**
One Schenley Park
Pittsburgh, PA 15213
(412) 622-6915, (412) 622-7363

**The Pittsburgh Civic Garden Center**
Mellon Park
1059 Shady Ave.
Pittsburgh, PA 15232
(412) 441-4442, fax (412) 665-2368

**Pittsburgh Zoo**
One Hill Rd.
Pittsburgh, PA 15206
(412) 665-3639, fax (412) 665-3661

**Rodef Shalom Biblical Botanical Garden**
4905 Fifth Ave.
Pittsburgh, PA 15213
(412) 621-6566, fax (412) 621-5475

**Henry Schmieder Arboretum**
Delaware Valley College
700 E. Butler Ave.
Doylestown, PA 18901
(215) 345-1500, fax (215) 345-5277

**Scott Arboretum of Swarthmore College**
500 College Ave.
Swarthmore, PA 19081
(610) 328-8025, fax (610) 328-8673

**Swiss Pines**
Charlestown Rd.
Malvern, PA 19355
(215) 933-6916

**Taylor Memorial Arboretum**
10 Ridley Dr.
Wallingford, PA 19086
(610) 876-2649, fax (610) 353-0517

**Temple University**
Landscape Architecture/Horticulture
580 Meeting House Rd.
Ambler, PA 19002
(215) 283-1292, fax (215) 283-1497

**Tyler Arboretum**
515 Painter Rd.
Media, PA 19063
(610) 566-5431, fax (610) 891-1490

**Villanova University**
800 Lancaster Ave.
Villanova, PA 19085
(610) 519-4426, fax (610) 519-6903

**Wyck**
6026 Germantown Ave.
Philadelphia, PA 19144
(215) 848-1690

## Rhode Island

**Blithewold Mansion & Gardens**
101 Ferry Rd. Rte. 116
P.O. Box 716
Bristol, RI 02809
(401) 253-2707, fax (401) 253-0412

**Green Animals Topiary Gardens**
380 Cory's Lane
Portsmouth, RI 02871
(401) 683-1267

**Meadowbrook Herb Garden**
93 Kingstown Rd. Rte. 138
Wyoming, RI 02898
(401) 539-7603

**Shakespeare's Head**
21 Meeting St.
Providence, RI 02903
(401) 831-7440

**Wilcox Park**
71½ High St.
Westerly, RI 02891
(401) 596-8590

**Roger Williams Park Greenhouse and Gardens**
Broad St.
Providence, RI 02905
(401) 785-9450

## South Carolina

**Brookgreen Gardens**
1931 Brookgreen Gardens Dr.
Murrells Inlet, SC 29576
(803) 237-4218, fax (803) 237-1014

**Cypress Gardens**
Hampton Park
Charleston, SC 29403
(803) 553-0515

**Edisto Memorial Garden**
P.O. Box 316
Orangeburg, SC 29116
(803) 534-6821

**Kalmia Gardens of Coker College**
1624 W. Carolina Ave.
Hartsville, SC 29550
(803) 383-8081, fax (803) 383-8095

**Magnolia Plantation & Gardens**
Rte. 4
Charleston, SC 29414
(803) 571-1266, fax (803) 571-5346

**Middleton Place**
Ashley River Rd.
Charleston, SC 29414
(803) 556-6020

**Riverbanks Zoo and Botanical Garden**
500 Wildlife Pkwy.
P.O. Box 1060
Columbia, SC 29202
(803) 779-8717, fax (803) 256-6463

**South Carolina Botanical Garden**
Clemson University
1 Perimeter Rd.
Clemson, SC 29634
(803) 656-3405, fax (803) 656-4960

**Swan Lake Iris Garden**
W. Liberty St.
Sumter, SC 29150
(803) 775-5811

## South Dakota

**Great Plains Garden**
Great Plains Native Plant Society
P.O. Box 461
Hot Springs, SD 57747
(605) 745-3397, fax (605) 745-3397

**McCrory Gardens**
South Dakota State University
6th & 27th Sts.
Brookings, SD 57007
(605) 688-5136

## Tennessee

**The Arboretum at Interstate Packaging**
Hwy. 47 N.
P.O. Box 789
White Bluff, TN 37187
(615) 797-9000, fax (615) 797-9411

**Cheekwood Botanical Gardens**
Tennessee Botanical Gardens and Museum of Art
1200 Forrest Park Dr.
Nashville, TN 37205
(615) 353-2148, fax (615) 353-2156

**The Dixon Gallery and Gardens**
4339 Park Ave.
Memphis, TN 38117
(901) 761-5250, fax (901) 682-0943

**The Hermitage: Home of Andrew Jackson**
4580 Rachel's Lane
Hermitage, TN 37076
(615) 889-2941, fax (615) 889-2989

**Memphis Botanic Garden**
750 Cherry Rd.
Memphis, TN 38117
(901) 685-1566, fax (901) 682-1561

**Reflection Riding**
Chattanooga Nature Center
400 Garden Rd.
Chattanooga, TN 37419
(423) 821-9582, fax (423) 821-9582

**Southwestern Arboretum**
Southwestern College of Memphis
200 North Pkwy.
Memphis, TN 38112
(901) 458-0964

**Tennessee Aquarium**
P.O. Box 11048
Chattanooga, TN 37401
(423) 265-0695, fax (423) 267-3561

**The University of Tennessee Arboretum**
901 Kerr Hollow Rd.
Oak Ridge, TN 37830
(423) 483-3571, fax (423) 483-3572

**Vanderbilt University**
Campus Planning & Development
130 Bryan Bldg.
Nashville, TN 37240
(615) 322-2715, fax (615) 343-4830

## Texas

**Bayou Bend Collection and Gardens**
1 Westcott
P.O. Box 6826
Houston, TX 77625
(713) 639-7750, fax (713) 639-7770

**Beaumont Botanical Gardens**
Tyrell Park
P.O. Box 7962
Beaumont, TX 77726
(409) 842-3135

**Botanical Research Institute of Texas**
509 Pecan St.
Fort Worth, TX 76102
(817) 332-4441, fax (817) 332-4112

**Chihuahuan Desert Research Institute**
Hwy. 118
P.O. Box 1334
Alpine TX 79831
(915) 837-8370, fax (915) 837-8370

**Corpus Christi Botanical Gardens**
8510 S. Staples
Corpus Christi, TX 78413
(512) 852-2100, fax (512) 852-7875

**Dallas Arboretum & Botanical Garden**
8525 Garland Rd.
Dallas, TX 75218
(214) 327-8263, fax (214) 324-9801

**Dallas Civic Garden Center**
Fair Park
P.O. Box 152537
3601 Martin Luther King Blvd.
Dallas, TX 75315
(214) 428-7476, fax (214) 428-5538

**Fort Worth Botanic Garden**
3220 Botanic Garden Blvd.
Fort Worth, TX 76107
(817) 871-7686, fax (817) 871-7638

**Greenwood & Mount Olivet Cemeteries**
P.O. Box 9450
Fort Worth, TX 76147
(817) 335-0584, fax (817) 335-6409

**Heard Natural Science Museum & Wildlife Sanctuary**
One Nature Place
McKinney, TX 75069
(214) 562-5566

**Houston Arboretum & Nature Center**
4501 Woodway
Houston, TX 77024
(713) 681-8433

**McMurry College Iris Garden**
Sayles Blvd. & S. 16th St.
Abilene, TX 79605
(915) 692-3938

**Mercer Arboretum & Botanic Gardens**
22306 Aldine-Westfield Rd.
Humble, TX 77338
(713) 443-8731, fax (713) 443-6078

**Moody Gardens**
One Hope Blvd.
Galveston, TX 77554
(409) 744-1745, fax (409) 740-2616

**The National Wildflower Research Center**
4801 LaCrosse Ave.
Austin, TX 78739
(512) 292-4200, fax (512) 292-4627

**San Antonio Botanical Garden**
555 Funston Pl.
San Antonio, TX 78209
(210) 821-5143, fax (210) 820-3528

**Texas Botanical Garden**
P.O. Box 5642
Austin, TX 78763
(512) 478-0010

**Tyler Municipal Rose Garden**
420 S. Rose Park Dr.
Tyler, TX 75710
(214) 531-1212

**Zilker Botanical Gardens**
2220 Barton Springs Rd.
Austin, TX 78746
(512) 477-8672

## Utah

**Red Butte Garden and Arboretum**
University of Utah
300 Wakara Way
Salt Lake City, UT 84108
(801) 581-5322, fax (801) 585-9663

**Utah Botanical Garden**
Utah State University
1817 N. Main
Farmington, UT 84025
(801) 451-3204

## Vermont

**The Horticulture Farm**
P.O. Box 64788
Burlington, VT 05406
(802) 864-3073, fax (802) 656-4656

**The Park-McCullough House**
West St.
P.O. Box 366
N. Bennington, VT 05257
(802) 442-5441

**Shelburne Museum**
U.S. Rte. 7
P.O. Box 10
Shelburne, VT 05482
(802) 985-3346

**University of Vermont Agricultural Experiment Station**
Pearl St., Rte. 7
Burlington, VT 05405
(802) 656-2980

## Virgin Islands

**Estate Saint Peter Greathouse Botanical Garden**
Main Post Office
P.O. 11711
Charlotte Amalie
Saint Thomas, VI 00801
(809) 774-4999

**Saint George Village Botanical Garden**
Box 3011
Kingshill
Saint Croix, VI 00851
(809) 772-3874, fax (809) 692-2874

## Virginia

**American Horticultural Society**
7931 E. Boulevard Dr.
Alexandria, VA 22308
(703) 768-5700, fax (703) 765-6032

**Ash Lawn–Highland**
James Monroe Pkwy.
Charlottesville, VA 22902
(804) 293-9539, fax (804) 293-8000

**Bryan Park Azalea Gardens**
900 E. Broad St.
Richmond, VA 23219
(804) 780-8785

**Lewis Ginter Botanical Society**
1800 Lakeside Ave.
Richmond, VA 23228
(804) 262-9887, fax (804) 262-9934

**Green Spring Gardens Park**
4603 Green Spring Rd.
Alexandria, VA 22312
(703) 642-5173, fax (703) 642-8095

**Gunston Hall Plantation**
10709 Gunston Rd.
Mason Neck
Lorton, VA 22079
(703) 550-9220, fax (703) 550-9480

**Hampden-Sydney College**
Box 104
Hampden-Sydney, VA 23943
(804) 223-6320, fax (804) 223-6344

**Heritage Gardens**
303 Ramsey Ave.
Hopewell, VA 23860
(804) 458-1892

**James Madison University
   Arboretum**
Biology Dept.
James Madison University
Harrisonburg, VA 22807
(540) 568-6340, fax (540) 568-7873

**Maymount Foundation**
1700 Hampton St.
Richmond, VA 23220
(804) 358-7166, fax (804) 358-9994

**Monticello**
Rte. 58
Gardens & Grounds Dept.
P.O. Box 316
Charlottesville, VA 22901
(804) 984-9808, fax (804) 977-7757

**Mount Vernon**
George Washington Pkwy. S.
Mount Vernon, VA 22121
(703) 780-2000, fax (703) 777-4427

**Norfolk Botanical Garden**
Azalea Garden Rd.
Norfolk, VA 23518
(804) 441-5830, fax (804) 853-8294

**Oatlands Plantation**
Rte. 15
Box 352
Leesburg, VA 22075
(703) 777-3174, fax (703) 777-4427

**Virginia Polytechnic Institute
   Arboretum**
Blacksburg, VA 24061
(703) 961-5609

**Virginia Zoological Park**
3500 Granby St.
Norfolk, VA 23504
(804) 441-2374, fax (804) 441-5408

**Orland E. White Arboretum**
State Arboretum of Virginia
U.S. Rte. 50
P.O. Box 175
Boyce, VA 22620
(540) 837-1758, fax (540) 837-1523

**Colonial Williamsburg**
134 N. Henry St.
Williamsburg, VA 23187
(804) 229-1000, fax (804) 220-7727

**The Winkler Botanical Preserve**
4900 Seminary Rd.
Alexandria, VA 22311
(703) 578-7888, fax (703) 578-9320

**Woodlawn Plantation**
9000 Richmond Hwy.
Alexandria, VA 22309
(703) 780-4000, fax (703) 780-8509

## Washington

**Bellevue Botanical Garden**
12001 Main St.
P.O. Box 40536
Bellevue, WA 98015
(206) 451-3755, fax (206) 454-7603

**The Bloedel Reserve**
7571 N.E. Dolphin Dr.
Bainbridge, WA 98110
(206) 842-7631, fax (206) 842-8970

**Carl S. English, Jr., Gardens**
Hiram M. Chittenden Locks
3015 N.W. 54th St.
Seattle, WA 98107
(206) 783-7059

**The Herbfarm**
32804 Issaquah–Fall City Rd.
Fall City, WA 98024
(206) 784-2222

**Japanese Garden of Washington
   Park Arboretum**
Washington Park
Seattle, WA 98112
(206) 684-4725

**Lakewold Gardens**
12317 Gravelly Lake Dr. S.W.
P.O. Box 98092
Tacoma, WA 98498
(206) 584-4106, fax (206) 584-3021

**Manito Park Conservatory and
   Gardens**
Grand Blvd.
Spokane Parks Dept.
4 W. 21st Ave.
Spokane, WA 99203
(509) 456-4331

**Ohme Gardens**
3327 Ohme Rd.
Wenatchee, WA 98801
(509) 662-5785

**Point Defiance Park**
5600 N. Pearl St.
Tacoma, WA 98405
(206) 591-5328

**Rhododendron Species Botanical
   Garden and Pacific Rim Bonsai
   Collection**
Weyerhauser Corporate Headquarters
2525 S. 336th St.
P.O. Box 3798
Federal Way, WA 98063
(206) 838-4646, fax (206) 838-4686

**W. W. Seymour Botanical
Conservatory**
316 S. G St.
Tacoma, WA 98405
(206) 591-5330

**State Capitol Conservatory**
West Capitol Campus
11th & Water Sts.
Olympia, WA 98504
(360) 586-8687

**Washington Park Arboretum**
2300 Arboretum Dr. E.
University of Washington
Box 358010
Seattle, WA 98195
(206) 543-8800, fax (206) 325-8893

**Woodland Park Zoological
Gardens**
5500 Phinney Ave. N.
Seattle, WA 98103
(206) 684-4800

**Yakima Area Arboretum**
1401 Arboretum Dr.
Yakima, WA 98901
(509) 248-7337, fax (509) 248-8197

## West Virginia

**Core Arboretum**
WVU Evansdale Campus
Monongahela Blvd., Rte. 7
Morgantown, WV 26506
(304) 293-5201, fax (304) 293-6363

**Sunrise Museum**
746 Myrtle St.
Charleston, WV 25314
(304) 344-8035, fax (304) 344-8038

**Sunshine Farm & Gardens**
Rte. 5GT
Renick, WV 24966
(304) 497-3163

## Wisconsin

**Boerner Botanical Gardens**
Whitnall Park
Milwaukee County Parks
5879 S. 92nd St.
Hales Corners, WI 53130
(414) 425-1132, fax (414) 425-8679

**Cofrin Arboretum**
University of Wisconsin—Green Bay
2420 Nicolet Dr.
Green Bay, WI 54311
(414) 465-2277

**Green Bay Botanical Garden**
2600 Larsed Rd.
Green Bay, WI 54307
(414) 490-9457

**Memorial Park Arboretum and
Gardens**
P.O. Box 5022
Appleton, WI 54913
(414) 734-5721x4400, fax (414)
730-4781

**Mitchell Park Conservatory**
524 S. Layton Blvd.
Milwaukee, WI 53215
(414) 649-9830, fax (414) 649-8616

**Olbrich Botanical Gardens**
3330 Atwood Ave.
Madison, WI 53704
(608) 246-4550, fax (608) 246-4719

**Paine Art Center and Arboretum**
1410 Algoma Blvd.
Oshkosh, WI 54901
(414) 235-6903, fax (414) 235-6303

**Rotary Gardens**
1455 Palmer Dr.
Janesville, WI 53545
(608) 752-3885, fax (608) 752-3853

**The University of Wisconsin—
Madison Arboretum**
1207 Seminole Hwy.
Madison, WI 53711
(608) 263-7888, fax (608) 262-5209

## Wyoming

**Cheyenne Botanic Garden**
710 S. Lions Park Dr.
Cheyenne, WY 82001
(307) 637-6458, fax (307) 637-6454

# Canada

## Alberta

**Calgary Zoo Botanical Gardens**
Botanical Operations
P.O. Box 3036, Station B
Saint George's Island
Calgary, AB T2M 4R8
(403) 232-9372, fax (403) 237-7582

**Muttart Conservatory**
Edmonton Parks & Recreation
9626-96 A St.
P.O. Box 2359
Edmonton, AB T5J 2R7
(403) 496-8755

**The University of Alberta
Devonian Botanic Garden**
Hwy. 60
Edmonton, AB T6G 2E9
(403) 987-3054, fax (403) 987-4141

## British Columbia

**Bloedel Conservatory**
Queen Elizabeth Park
Cambie St. and 33rd Ave.
Vancouver, BC V5X 1C5
(604) 257-8570

**The Butchart Gardens**
800 Benvento Ave.
P.O. Box 4010
Brentwood Bay
Victoria, BC V8M 1J8

**Government House**
1401 Rockland Ave.
Victoria, BC V8S 1V9
(604) 387-2080

**Minter Gardens**
52892 Bunker Rd.
Rosedale, BC V2P 1X0
(604) 794-7191
(mailing address):
P.O. Box 40
Chilliwack, BC V2P 6H7

**Park & Tilford Gardens**
Low Level Rd. & Brooksbank Ave.
BCE Development Corp.
440-333 Brooksbank Ave.
North Vancouver, BC V7J 4E5
(604) 984-8200

**Richmond Nature Park**
11851 Westminster Hwy.
and No. 5 Rd.
Richmond, BC V6X 1B4
(604) 273-7015

**Stanley Park**
W. Georgia St.
Vancouver Board of Parks and
Recreation
2099 Beach Ave.
Vancouver, BC V6G 1Z4
(604) 872-5513

**Dr. Sun Yat-Sen Classical Chinese
Garden**
578 Carrall St.
Vancouver, BC V6B 2J8
(604) 689-7133

**The University of British
Columbia Botanical Garden**
6804 S.W. Marine Dr.
Vancouver, BC V6T 1Z4
(604) 822-9666, fax (604) 822-2016

**VanDusen Botanical Gardens**
5251 Oak St.
Vancouver, BC V6M 4H1
(604) 878-9274, fax (604) 263-1777

## New Brunswick

**Kingsbrae Horticultural Garden**
220 King St.
St. Andrew, NB E0G 2X0
(506) 529-3335

**The New Brunswick Botanical
Garden**
C.P./P.O. Box 599
Saint Jacques, NB E0L 1K0
(506) 739-6335, fax (506) 735-3074

## Newfoundland

**Memorial University of
Newfoundland Botanical
Garden**
Pippy Park
306 Mount Scio Rd.
Saint Johns, NF A1C 5S7
(709) 737-8590, fax (709) 737-8596

## Nova Scotia

**Annapolis Royal Historic Gardens**
441 Saint George St.
Box 278
Annapolis Royal, NS B0S 1A0
(902) 532-4681, fax (902) 532-7445

**Halifax Public Gardens**
Spring Garden Rd. & S. Park St.
Halifax, NS
(mailing address):
City of Halifax
Parks & Grounds Div.
P.O. Box 812
Armdale, Halifax, NS B3L 4K5
(902) 421-6551

## Ontario

**Allan Gardens**
19 Horticultural Ave.
Toronto, ON M5A 2P2
(416) 392-7288

**Appleby College**
Oakville, ON L6K 3P1
(905) 845-4681, fax (905) 845-9828

**Cullen Gardens and Miniature
Village**
300 Taunton Rd. W.
Whitby, ON L1N 5R5
(905) 668-6606

**Dominion Arboretum**
Agriculture Canada Bldg. 50
Central Experimental Farm
Ottawa, ON K1A 0C6
(613) 995-3700

**Dundurn Castle**
Dundurn Park
610 York Blvd.
Hamilton, ON L8R 3H1
(416) 522-5313

**Edwards Gardens**
777 Lawrence Ave. E.
North York, ON M3C 1P2
(905) 445-1552

**Floral Clock and Lilac Gardens**
River Rd.
Niagara Falls, ON L2E 6T2
(416) 356-2241

**Gage Park**
Department of Public Works
71 Main St.
Hamilton, ON L8N 3T4

**The Arboretum, University of
Guelph**
Guelph, ON N1G 2W1
(519) 842-4120, fax (519) 763-9598

**Lakehead University Arboretum**
School of Forestry
Lakehead University
Thunder Bay, ON P7B 5E1
(807) 345-2121

**Laurentian University Arboretum**
Ramsey Lake Rd.
Sudbury, ON P3E 2C6
(705) 675-1151

**Metro Toronto Zoo**
361A Old Finch Ave.
Scarborough, ON M1B 5K7
(416) 392-5973, fax (416) 392-4979

**City of Mississauga Community Services**
Planning, Research & Development
300 City Centre Dr.
Mississauga, ON L5B 3C1
(905) 896-5373, fax (905) 615-3469

**Niagara Botanical Gardens**
Niagara Parks Commission
P.O. Box 150
Niagara Falls, ON L2E 6T2
(905) 354-1721

**Royal Botanical Gardens**
680 Plains Rd. W.
P.O. Box 399
Hamilton, ON L8N 3H8
(416) 527-1158

**Sherwood Fox Arboretum**
Biological & Geological Bldg.
University of Western Ontario
London, ON N6A 5B7
(519) 679-2111, fax (519) 661-3935

**City of Toronto Dept. of Parks & Recreation**
City Hall
100 Queens St. W.
Toronto, ON M5H 2N2
(416) 392-0724, fax (416) 392-0916

**Whitehern**
41 Jackson St. W.
Hamilton, ON L8P 1L3
(614) 522-5664

## Quebec

**Les Jardins de Metis**
Grand-Metis, PQ
C.P. 242
Mont-Joli, PQ G5H 3L1
(418) 775-2221

**Montreal Botanical Garden**
4101 E. Sherbrooke St.
Montreal, PQ H1X 2B2
(514) 872-1400, fax (514) 872-3765

**Morgan Arboretum**
P.O. Box 500
MacDonald College
Ste. Anne de Bellevue, PQ H9X 1C0
(514) 398-7811, fax (514) 398-7959

## Saskatchewan

**Indian Head Tree Nursery**
Indian Head, SK S0G 2K0
(306) 695-2284

# Plant Societies and Other Organizations

Listed below, by state, are the phone numbers and addresses of horticultural societies and other plant-related groups, along with the name of the organization's publication, if any. A listing of national organizations begins on page 724. For information on plant societies, see page 726.

## State Organizations

### California

**California Botanical Society**
Herbarium, Life Sciences Bldg.
University of California
Berkeley, CA 94720
*Madrono: A Western American Journal of Botany*

**California Horticultural Society**
California Academy of Sciences
Golden Gate Park
San Francisco, CA 94118

**Pacific Horticulture Foundation**
P.O. Box 22609
San Francisco, CA 94122
*Pacific Horticulture*

**San Diego Floral Association**
Casa del Prado Room 105
Balboa Park
2125 Park Blvd.
San Diego, CA 92101
(619) 232-5762
*California Garden*

**Southern California Botanists**
Dept. of Biology
Fullerton State University
Fullerton, CA 92634
(714) 449-7034

**Southern California Horticultural Society**
P.O. Box 41080
Los Angeles, CA 90041
*Newsletter*

**Western Horticultural Society**
P.O. Box 60507
Palo Alto, CA 94306

### Connecticut

**Connecticut Botanical Society**
Osborn Memorial Laboratory
167 Prospect St.
New Haven, CT 06511
(203) 388-6148

### District of Columbia

**Botanical Society of Washington**
Dept. of Botany, NHB/166
Smithsonian Institution
Washington, DC 20560

### Florida

**The Florida Academy of Sciences**
P.O. Box 033012
Indiatlantic, FL 32903
*Florida Scientist*

### Maryland

**Chesapeake Audubon Society**
Rare Plant Committee
P.O. Box 3173
Baltimore, MD 21228

## Massachusetts

**Massachusetts Audubon Society**
South Great Rd.
Lincoln, MA 01773
(781) 259-9500
*Sanctuary*

**Massachusetts Horticultural**
**Society**
Horticulture Hall
300 Massachusetts Ave.
Boston, MA 02115
(617) 536-9280, fax (617) 262-8780
*Leaflet*
*Journal of the New England Garden*
*History Society*

**New England Botanical Club**
22 Divinity Ave.
Cambridge, MA 02138
*Rhodora*

**Worcester County Horticultural**
**Society**
Tower Hill Botanic Garden
11 French Dr.
Boylston, MA 01505
(508) 869-6111, fax (508) 869-0314

## Michigan

**Michigan Botanical Club**
University of Michigan Herbarium
2001 N. University Bldg.
1205 N. University Ave.
(313) 764-2407
*Michigan Botanist*

## Minnesota

**Minnesota State Horticultural**
**Society**
1755 Prior Ave. N.
Falcon Heights, MN 55113
(612) 643-3601
*Minnesota Horticulturist*

## New York

**The Horticultural Society of New**
**York**
128 W. 58th St.
New York, NY 10019
(212) 757-0915, fax (212) 246-1207
*Newsletter*

**Long Island Botanical Society**
Muttontown Preserve
Muttontown Lane
East Norwich, NY 11737
*L.I. Botanical Society Newsletter*

**New York City Audubon Society**
71 W. 23rd St.
New York, NY 10010
(212) 691-7483
*The Urban Audubon*

**New York Flora Association**
New York State Museum Institute
3140 CEC
Albany, NY 12230
*NYFA Newsletter*

## Ohio

**Ohio Association of Garden Clubs**
2215 ECR 181
Green Spring, OH 44836
*Garden Path*

## Pennsylvania

**Pennsylvania Horticultural Society**
100 N. 20th St.
Philadelphia, PA 19103
(215) 988-8800
*The Green Scene*
*PHS News*

**Philadelphia Botanical Club**
Academy of Natural Sciences of
Philadelphia
1900 Benjamin Franklin Pkwy.
Philadelphia, PA 19103
(215) 299-1000
*Bartonia*

## South Carolina

**Southern Appalachian Botanical**
**Club**
Dept. of Biological Sciences
University of South Carolina
Columbia, SC 29208

## South Dakota

**Great Plains Botanical Society**
P.O. Box 461
Hot Springs, SD 57747
(605) 745-3397

## Washington

**Northwest Horticultural Society**
University of Washington
Isaacson Hall GF-15
Seattle, WA 98195

# National Organizations

**Alliance for Historic Landscape**
**Preservation**
82 Wall St., Ste. 1105
New York, NY 10005
*Newsletter*

**American Association of Botanical**
**Gardens and Arboreta**
**(AABGA)**
351 Longwood Rd.
Kennett Square, PA 19348
(610) 925-2500, fax (610) 925-2700
*AABGA Newsletter*
*Public Garden*

**American Community Gardening**
**Association**
325 Walnut St.
Philadelphia, PA 19106
(215) 625-8280
*Community Greening Review*

**American Forestry Association**
P.O. Box 2000
Washington, DC 20013-2000
(202) 667-3300, fax (202) 667-7751
*American Forests*
*Urban Forests*

**American Horticultural Society**
7931 E. Boulevard Dr.
Alexandria, VA 22308
(703) 768-5700, fax (703) 765-6032
*American Gardener*

**American Horticultural Therapy Association**
362A Christopher Ave.
Gaithersburg, MD 20879
(301) 948-3010, fax (301) 869-2397
*Journal of Therapeutic Horticulture*

**American Institute of Biological Sciences**
1444 Eye St. N.W., Ste. 200
Washington, DC 20005
(202) 628-1500, fax (202) 628-1509
*BioScience*

**American Littoral Society**
Sandy Hook
Highlands, NJ 07732
(908) 291-0055
*Littorally Speaking*
*Coastal Reporter*

**American Nature Study Society**
Pocono Environmental Education Center
RD 2, Box 1010
Dingmans Ferry, PA 18328
*Nature Study*
*ANSS Newsletter*

**American Society for Horticultural Science**
600 Cameron St.
Alexandria, VA 22314
(703) 836-4606, fax (703) 836-2024
*Journal of the American Society for Horticultural Science*

**Bio-Integral Resource Center**
P.O. Box 7414
Berkeley, CA 94707
(510) 524-2567
*Common Sense Pest Control Quarterly*
*IPM (Integrated Pest Management) Practitioner*

**Botanical Society of America**
1735 Neil Ave.
Columbus, OH 43210
(614) 292-3519, fax (614) 292-3519
*American Journal of Botany*
*Plant Science Bulletin*

**Cenozic Society**
P.O. Box 455
Richmond, VT 05477
(802) 434-4077
*Wild Earth*

**Center for Plant Conservation**
Missouri Botanical Garden
P.O. Box 299
St. Louis, MO 63166
(314) 577-9450
*Plant Conservation*

**Dynamics International Gardening Association**
Drawer 1165
Asheboro, NC 27204
(919) 625-4790
*Garden News Today*

**Garden Club of America**
598 Madison Ave.
New York, NY 10022
(212) 753-8287, fax (212) 753-0134
*Garden Club of America Bulletin*

**Garden Writers Association of America**
10210 Leatherleaf Ct.
Manassas, VA 22111
(703) 257-1032, fax (703) 257-0213
*Quill & Trowel Newsletter*

**The Gardeners of America**
5560 Merle Hay Rd.
P.O. Box 241
Johnston, IA 50131
(515) 278-0295, fax (515) 278-6245
*Gardener*
*MGCA Newsletter*

**Hobby Greenhouse Association**
8 Glen Terrace
Bedford, MA 01730
(617) 275-0377, fax (617) 275-5693
*HGA News*
*Hobby Greenhouse*

**Hunt Institute for Botanical Documentation**
Carnegie Mellon University
5000 Forbes Ave.
Pittsburgh, PA 15213
(412) 268-2434, fax (412) 268-5677
*Huntia*
*Bulletin*

**Hydroponic Society of America**
Box 3075
San Ramon, CA 94583
(510) 743-9605, fax (510) 743-9302
*Soilless Grower*

**Indoor Gardening Society of America**
944 S. Munroe Rd.
Tallmadge, OH 44278
(216) 666-5522
*House Plant Magazine: IGSA Column*

**International Plant Propagators Society**
University of Washington
Center for Urban Horticulture
Seattle, WA 98195
(206) 543-8602
*Proceedings*

**International Society of Arboriculture**
P.O. Box GG
Savoy, IL 61874
(217) 355-9681
*Arborist News*

**National Audubon Society**
700 Broadway
New York, NY 10003
(212) 979-3000, fax (212) 353-0377
*Audubon*
*Audubon Activist*
*Audubon Adventures*
*Field Notes*

National Council of State Garden
  Clubs
4401 Magnolia Ave.
St. Louis, MO 63110
(314) 776-7574, fax (314) 776-5108
*National Gardener*

National Gardening Association
180 Flynn Ave.
Burlington, VT 05401
(802) 863-1308, fax (802) 863-5962
*Growing Ideas*
*National Gardening*

National Junior Horticultural
  Association
1424 N. 8th Ave.
Durant, OK 74701
(405) 924-0771
*Going and Growing*

The Nature Conservancy
1815 N. Lynn St.
Arlington, VA 22209
(703) 841-5300
*Nature Conservancy*

Perennial Plant Association
3383 Schirtzinger Rd.
Hilliard, OH 43026
(614) 771-8431, fax (614) 876-5238
*PPA Newsletter*
*Symposium Proceedings*

Seed Savers Exchange
9823 E. Michigan Ave.
Galesburg, MI 49053
(616) 665-7500
*Fruit, Berry and Nut Inventory*
*The Garden Seed Inventory*

Society for Ecological Restoration
University of Wisconsin—Madison
  Arboretum
1207 Seminole Hwy.
Madison, WI 53711
(608) 262-9547
*Restoration & Management Notes*

Southern Garden History Society
Drawer F. Salem Station
Winston-Salem, NC 27108
(910) 724-3125, fax (910) 721-7335
*Magnolia*

Terrarium Association
P.O. Box 276
Newfane, VT 05345
(802) 365-4721

Torrey Botanical Club
H. H. Lehman College, CUNY
Bronx, NY 10468
*Journal of the Torrey Botanical Society*
*Memoirs of the Torrey Botanical Society*

The Wilderness Society
900 17th St. N.W.
Washington, DC 20002
(202) 833-2300
*Wilderness*
*Wilderness America*

# Plant Societies

## African Violet

African Violet Society of America
2375 North
Beaumont, TX 77702
(409) 839-4725, fax (409) 839-4329
*African Violet Magazine*

Saintpaulia International
8011 Conarroe Rd.
Indianapolis, IN 46278
(317) 872-5931
*Saintpaulia International News*

## Aril

Aril Society International
3262-B Walnut
Los Alamos, NM 85744
(505) 662-6840
*Aril Society International Newsletter*
*Aril Society International Yearbook*

## Aroid

International Aroid Society
P.O. Box 43-1853
South Miami, FL 33143
(305) 221-3251
*Aroideana*
*International Aroid Society Newsletter*

## Azalea

Azalea Society of America
P.O. Box 34536
Bethesda, MD 20827
(301) 855-5269
*The Azalean*

## Bamboo

American Bamboo Society
750 Krumkill Rd.
Albany, NY 12203
(518) 458-7618, fax (518) 458-7625
*Newsletter; Journal*

## Begonia

American Begonia Society
157 Monument Rd.
Rio Dell, CA 95562
(707) 764-5407
*The Begonian*
*Begonia Culture Bulletin*

## Bonsai

American Bonsai Society
Box 358
Keene, NH 03431
(603) 352-9034
*Bonsai Journal*

Bonsai and Orchid Association
26 Pine St.
Dover, DE 19901
(302) 736-6781, fax (302) 736-6763
*Green World News*

**Bonsai Clubs International**
2636 W. Mission Rd. #277
Tallahassee, FL 32304
*Bonsai Magazine*
*Bonsai Source List*

**Bonsai Society of Greater New York**
P.O. Box 565
Glen Oaks, NY 11004
(516) 293-9246
*Bonsai Bulletin*

**Potomac Bonsai Association**
U.S. National Arboretum
3501 New York Ave. N.E.
Washington, DC 20002
(202) 226-4082
*PBA Clippings*

## Boxwood

**American Boxwood Society**
Box 85
Boyce, VA 22620
(703) 939-4646
*The Boxwood Bulletin*

## Bromeliad

**Bromeliad Society**
720 Millertown Rd.
Auburn, CA 95603
(916) 885-0201, fax (916) 885-0201
*Bromeliad Society Journal*
*Bromeliad Society Affiliates Newsletter*

## Cactus and Succulent

**Cactus and Succulent Society of America**
1535 Reeves St.
Los Angeles, CA 90035
(310) 556-1923, fax (310) 286-9629
*Cactus and Succulent Journal*

## Camellia

**American Camellia Society**
Massee Lane Gardens
1 Massee Lane
Fort Valley, GA 31030
(912) 967-2358, fax (912) 967-2083
*Camellia Journal*
*American Camellia Yearbook*

**International Camellia Society**
P.O. Box 750
Brookhaven, MS 39601
(601) 833-2718
*International Camellia Journal*

## Carnivorous Plants

**International Carnivorous Plant Society**
California State University
Fullerton Arboretum
Fullerton, CA 92634
(714) 773-2766, fax (714) 773-3426
*Carnivorous Plant Newsletter*

## Chrysanthemum

**National Chrysanthemum Society**
10107 Homar Pond Dr.
Fairfax Station, VA 22039
(703) 978-7981
*The Chrysanthemum*

## Conifers

**American Conifer Society**
P.O. Box 360
Keswick, VA 22947
(804) 984-3660, fax (804) 984-3660
*Bulletin; Newsletter; Seed List*

## Crabapple

**International Ornamental Crabapple Society**
Agriculture Dept.
Western Illinois University
Macomb, IL 61455
(309) 298-1160
*Malus*

## Cryptanthus

**The Cryptanthus Society**
2355 Rusk
Beaumont, TX 77702
(409) 835-0644, fax (409) 835-5265
*Journal*

## Cycads

**Cycad Society**
1161 Phyllis Ct.
Mountain View, CA 94040
*Cycad Society Newsletter*

## Cymbidium

**Cymbidium Society of America**
P.O. Box 2244
Orange, CA 92669
(714) 532-4719, fax (714) 532-3611
*Orchid Advocate*

## Daffodil

**American Daffodil Society**
1686 Grey Fox Trails
Milford, OH 45150
(513) 248-9137, fax (513) 248-0898
*Daffodil Journal*
*Daffodil Data Bank*

## Dahlia

**American Dahlia Society**
16816 County Rd. 10, Rte. 2
Bristol, IN 46507
(219) 848-4888
*American Dahlia Society Bulletin*

**Puget Sound Dahlia Association**
Box 5602
Bellevue, WA 98006
*Dahlias of Today*

## Dianthus

**The American Dianthus Society**
P.O. Box 22232
Santa FE, NM 87502
(505) 438-7038
*The Gilliflower Times*

## Epiphyllum

**Epiphyllum Society of America**
P.O. Box 1395
Monrovia, CA 91017
(818) 447-9688
*Epiphyllum Bulletin*
*Epiphyllum Society of America*

## Ferns

**American Fern Society**
326 West St. N.W.
Vienna, VA 22180
*American Fern Journal*
*Memoirs*
*Fiddlehead Forum*

**Los Angeles International Fern Society**
11258 Ringwood Ave.
Santa Fe Springs, CA 90670
(310) 803-6887
*LAIFS Fern Journal*

## Fruit

**American Pomological Society**
102 Tyson Building
University Park, PA 16802
*Fruit Varieties Journal*

**Home Orchard Society**
Box 230192
Tigard, OR 97281
(503) 630-3392
*Pome News*

**North American Fruit Explorers**
RR 2, Box 167
Bloomington, IL 61704
*Pomona*

## Fuchsia

**American Fuchsia Society**
San Francisco County Fair Bldg.
9th Ave. & Lincoln Way
San Francisco, CA 94122
(408) 257-0752
*American Fuchsia Society Bulletin*

**National Fuchsia Society**
11507 E. 187th St.
St. Louis, MO 63110
*Fuchsia Fan*

## Gardenia

**Gardenia Society of America**
P.O. Box 879
Atwater, CA 95301
(209) 358-2231
*Growing Gardenias*

## Geranium

**International Geranium Society**
P.O. Box 92734
Pasadena, CA 91109
(818) 727-0309, fax (818) 908-8867
*Geraniums Around the World*

## Gesneriad

**American Gloxinia and Gesneriad Society**
290 Federal St.
Belchertown, MA 01007
(413) 323-6661
*The Gloxinian*

**Gesneriad Hybridizers Association**
69-28 Loubet St.
Forest Hills, NY 11375
(718) 793-9583
*CrossWords*

**Gesneriad Society International**
11510 124th Terrace N.
Largo, FL 33778
(813) 559-7772
*Gesneriad Journal*

## Gladiolus

**All-America Gladiolus Selections**
11734 Rd. 33½
Madera, CA 93638
(209) 645-5329, fax (209) 645-1300

**North American Gladiolus Council**
4335 Noal Dr.
Salt Lake City, UT 84124
(801) 277-9576
*North American Gladiolus Council Bulletin*
*Gladiograms*

## Gloxinia

**American Gloxinia and Gesneriad Society**
290 Federal St.
Belchertown, MA 01007
(413) 323-6661
*The Gloxinian*

## Gourds

**American Gourd Society**
P.O. Box 274
Mount Gilead, OH 43338
(419) 362-6446, fax (419) 362-6446
*American Gourd Society Bulletin*
*The Gourd*

## Heather

**North American Heather Society**
E. 502 Haskel Hill Rd.
Shelton, WA 98584
(360) 427-5318, fax (360) 427-5318
*Heather News*

**Northeast Heather Society**
Highland View
P.O. Box 101
Alstead, NH 03602
*Heather Notes*

## Heliconia

**Heliconia Society International**
Fairchild Tropical Gardens
10901 Old Cutler Rd.
Miami, FL 33156
(305) 667-1651, fax (305) 661-8953
*Bulletin*

## Herbs

**Herb Research Foundation**
American Botanical Council
P.O. Box 201660
Austin, TX 78720
(512) 331-8868, fax (512) 331-1924
*HerbalGram*

**Herb Society of America**
9019 Kirtland Chardon Rd.
Kirtland, OH 44095
(216) 252-0514, fax (216) 252-0541
*Herb Society of America Newsletter*
*The Herbarist*

## Hemerocallis

**American Hemerocallis Society**
1454 Rebel Dr.
Jackson, MS 39211
(601) 366-4362
*Daylily Journal*
*Checklist of Registered Cultivars*

## Hibiscus

**American Hibiscus Society**
P.O. Drawer 321540
Cocoa Beach, FL 32932
(407) 783-2576, fax (407) 783-2576
*The Seed Pod*
*Hibiscus Handbook*

## Holly

**Holly Society of America**
11318 W. Murdock
Wichita, KS 67212
*Holly Society Journal*

## Hosta

**American Hosta Society**
9448 Mayfield Rd.
Chesterland, OH 44026
(216) 729-9838
*Journal of the American Hosta Society*

## Hoya

**International Hoya Society**
1444 E. Taylor St.
Vista, CA 92084
(619) 758-4290, fax (619) 945-8934
*Fraterna*

## Iris

**American Iris Society**
8426 Vinevalley Dr.
Sun Valley, CA 91352
(818) 767-5512, fax (818) 767-8513
*Bulletin of the American Iris Society*

**Dwarf Iris Society of America**
3167 E. U.S. Rte. 224
Ossian, IN 46777
(219) 597-7403
*Dwarf Iris Newsletter*

**Median Iris Society**
682 Huntley Heights Dr.
Ballwin, MO 63021
*Medianite*
*Checklist of Median Iris Registrations*

**Reblooming Iris Society**
1146 W. Rialto
Fresno, CA 93705
(209) 229-6434
*The Reblooming Iris Recorder*

**Society for Japanese Irises**
9823 E. Michigan Ave.
Galesburg, MI 49053
(616) 665-7500
*The Japanese Iris*
*The Review*

**Society for Louisiana Irises**
University of Southwestern Louisiana
Box 40175
Lafayette, LA 70504
(318) 856-5859
*The Louisiana Iris*

## Society for Pacific Coast Native Irises

**Society for Pacific Coast Native Irises**
4333 Oak Hill Rd.
Oakland, CA 94605
(510) 638-0658
*Almanac: Society for Pacific Coast Irises*

**Society for Siberian Irises**
802 Camellia Dr.
Anderson, SC 29625
(803) 224-6966
*Siberian Iris*

**Species Iris Group of North America**
486 Skiff St.
North Haven, CT 06473
(203) 789-7238
*SIGNA*

**Spuria Iris Society**
Rte. 2, Box 328
Buckholts, TX 76518

## Ivy

**American Ivy Society**
P.O. Box 2123
Naples, FL 33939
*Between the Vines*
*Ivy Journal*

## Lilac

**International Lilac Society**
9500 Sperry Rd.
Kirtland, OH 44094
(216) 946-4400, fax (216) 256-1655
*Corrigenda to the Register*
*Lilac Study*
*New Lilac Culture*
*Lilacs*

## Lilies

**North American Lily Society**
P.O. Box 272
Owatonna, MN 55060
(507) 451-2170
*North American Lily Society Quarterly Bulletin*
*North American Lily Society Yearbook*

## Magnolia

**The Magnolia Society**
6616 81st St.
Cabin John, MD 20818
(301) 320-4296
*Magnolia: Journal of the Magnolia Society*
*Magnolia Magazine*

## Marigold

**Marigold Society of America**
P.O. Box 5112
New Britain, PA 18901
(916) 756-8099
*Amerigold Newsletter*

## Native Plants
## (see Wildflowers and
## Native Plants)

## Nuts

**Northern Nut Growers Assn.**
9870 S. Palmer Rd.
New Carlisle, OH 45344
*The Nutshell*
*Annual Report*

## Oaks

**International Oak Society**
P.O. Box 310
Pen Argyl, PA 18072
(610) 588-1037, fax (610) 599-0968
*Journal of International Oak Society*

## Oleander

**International Oleander Society**
P.O. Box 3431
Galveston, TX 77552
(409) 762-9334
*Nerium News*

## Orchid

**American Orchid Society**
6000 S. Olive Ave.
West Palm Beach, FL 33405
(561) 585-8666, fax (561) 585-0654
*Orchids; AQ Awards Quarterly*
*Lindleyana*

**Bonsai and Orchid Association**
26 Pine St.
Dover, DE 19901
(302) 736-6781, fax (302) 736-6763
*Green World News*

**Cymbidium Society of America**
P.O. Box 2244
Orange, CA 92669
(714) 532-4719, fax (714) 532-3611
*Orchid Advocate*

**North American Native Orchid
Alliance**
84 Etna St.
Brighton, MA 02135
*North American Native Orchid Journal*

**Pacific Orchid Society of Hawaii**
1778 Hoolana St.
Pearl City, Oahu, HI 96782
(808) 259-9629
*Hawaii Orchid Journal*

## Palm

**International Palm Society**
P.O. Box 1897
Lawrence, KS 66044
*Principes*

## Penstemon

**American Penstemon Society**
1569 S. Holland Ct.
Lakewood, CO 80232
(303) 986-8096
*American Penstemon Society Bulletin*

## Peony

**American Peony Society**
250 Interlachen Rd.
Hopkins, MN 55343
(612) 938-4706
*American Peony Society Bulletin*

## Peperomia

**Peperomia and Exotic Plant
Society**
100 Neil St.
New Orleans, LA 70131
(504) 394-4146
*The Gazette*

## Plumeria

**Plumeria Society of America**
P.O. Box 22791
Houston, TX 77227
(713) 780-8326
*Plumeria Potpourri*

## Primrose

**American Primrose, Primula and
Auricula Society**
White Horse Village
535 Gradyville Rd., Ste. G153
Newtown Square, PA 19073
*Primroses*

## Pumpkin

**World Pumpkin Confederation**
14050 Rte. 62
Collins, NY 14034
fax (716) 532-5690
*World Pumpkin Confederation Journal*

## Rhododendron

**American Rhododendron Society**
P.O. Box 1380
Gloucester, VA 23061
(804) 693-4433
*American Rhododendron Society Journal*

**Rhododendron Species Foundation**
P.O. Box 3798
Federal Way, WA 98063
(206) 838-4646, fax (206) 838-4686
*Rhododendron Notes & Records*
*Rhododendron Species Foundation
  Newsletter*

## Rock Gardening

**North American Rock Garden Society**
P.O. Box 67
Millwood, NY 10546
(914) 762-2948
*Rock Garden Quarterly*

## Rose

**All-America Rose Selections**
221 N. LaSalle St., Ste. 3900
Chicago, IL 60601
(312) 372-7090, fax (312) 372-6160
*Rose Report*

**American Rose Society**
P.O. Box 30000
Shreveport, LA 71130
(318) 938-5402, fax (318) 938-5405
*American Rose Magazine*
*American Rose Annual*
*Handbook for Selecting Roses*
*Miniature Rose Growers Bulletin*

**Heritage Rose Foundation**
1512 Gorman St.
Raleigh, NC 27606
(919) 834-2591
*Heritage Rose Foundation News*

**Heritage Roses Group**
RD 1, Box 299
Clinton Corners, NY 12514
(914) 266-3562
*Rose Letter*

**Rose Hybridizers Association**
21 S. Wheaton Rd.
Horseheads, NY 14845
(607) 562-8592
*Rose Hybridizers Association Newsletter*

## Saintpaulia

**Saintpaulia International**
8011 Conarroe Rd.
Indianapolis, IN 46278
(317) 872-5931
*Saintpaulia International News*

## Water Gardening

**National Pond Society**
286 Village Pkwy.
Marietta, GA 30067
(770) 859-9282, fax (770) 859-0864
*Pondscapes*

## Water Lily

**International Water Lily Society**
c/o Santa Barbara Botanic Garden
1212 Mission Canyon Rd.
Santa Barbara, CA 93105
(805) 682-4726, fax (805) 563-0352
*Water Garden Journal*

## Wildflowers and Native Plants

**Eastern Native Plant Alliance**
P.O. Box 6101
McLean, VA 22106

**National Wildflower Research Center**
4801 La Crosse Ave.
Austin, TX 78739
(512) 292-4200, fax (512) 292-4627
*Wildflower*

**New England Wild Flower Society**
Garden in the Woods
180 Hemenway Rd.
Framingham, MA 01701
(508) 237-4924
*New England Wildflower Society Bulletin*

**Prairie/Plains Resource Institute**
1307 L St.
Aurora, NE 68818
(402) 694-5535

**Save the Tallgrass Prairie, Inc.**
4101 West 54th Terrace
Shawnee Mission, KS 66025

**Canadian Wildflower Society**
35 Bauer Crescent
Unionville, ON L3R 4H3

**Alabama Wildflower Society**
c/o George Wood
11120 Ben Clements Rd.
Northport, AL 35476

**Alaska Native Plant Society**
Box 141613
Anchorage, AK 99514
(907) 333-8212
*Borealis*

**Arizona Native Plant Society**
P.O. Box 41206
Tucson, AZ 85717

**Arkansas Native Plant Society**
P.O. Box 250250
Little Rock, AR 72225

**California Native Plant Society**
1755 J St., Ste. 17
Sacramento, CA 95814
(916) 447-2677
*Fremontia*
*California Native Plant Society Journal*

**Colorado Native Plant Society**
P.O. Box 200
Fort Collins, CO 80522

**Florida Native Plant Society**
P.O. Box 6116
Spring Hill, FL 34611
(813) 856-8202
*The Palmetto*

**Idaho Native Plant Society**
Box 9451
Boise, ID 83707
*Sage Notes*

**Illinois Native Plant Society**
Forest Glen Preserve
RR1, Box 495A
Westville, IL 61883
(217) 662-2142

**Southern Illinois Native Plant Society**
Botany Department
Southern Illinois University
Carbondale, IL 52901

ANVIL (Association for the Use of
Native Vegetation in the
Landscape)
871 Shawnee Ave.
Lafayette, IN 47905

Kansas Wildflower Society
Mulvane Arts Center
Washburn University
Topeka, KS 66621
(913) 231-1010, fax (913) 233-2780
*Kansas Wildflower Society Newsletter*

Kentucky Native Plant Society
Eastern Kentucky University
Richmond, KY 40475

Louisiana Native Plant Society
Rte. 1, Box 151
Saline, LA 71070

Louisiana Project Wildflower
c/o Lafayette Natural History
    Museum
637 Girard Park Dr.
Lafayette, LA 70503
(318) 261-8350

Maryland Native Plant Society
14720 Claude Lane
Silver Spring, MD 20904
(301) 236-4124
*Newsletter*

Minnesota Native Plant Society
University of Minnesota
220 Biological Science Center
1445 Gortner Ave.
St. Paul, MN 55108

Mississippi Native Plant Society
Mississippi Museum of Natural
    Science
111 N. Jefferson St.
Jackson, MS 39202
(601) 354-7303
*Mississippi Native Plants*

Missouri Native Plant Society
Department of Natural Resources
P.O. Box 176
Jefferson City, MO 63102

Montana Native Plant Society
P.O. Box 992
Bozeman, MT 59771
(406) 587-0120

Native Plant Society of New
    Mexico
Box 5917
Santa Fe, NM 87502
*Newsletter*

New Jersey Native Plant Society
Cook College
P.O. Box 231
New Brunswick, NJ 08903
*Newsletter*

North Carolina Wildflower
    Preservation Society
UNC-CH
Totten Center 457-A
Chapel Hill, NC 27514

Northern Nevada Native Plant
    Society
Box 8965
Reno, NV 89507
(702) 829-1645
*Newsletter*

Ohio Native Plant Society
6 Louise Dr.
Chagrin Falls, OH 44022

Oklahoma Native Plant Society
2435 S. Peoria Ave.
Tulsa, OK 74114
(918) 749-6401

Native Plant Society of Oregon
2584 N.W. Savier St.
Portland, OR 97210

Pennsylvania Native Plant Society
1806 Commonwealth Bldg.
316 Fourth Ave.
Pittsburgh, PA 15222

Rhode Island Wild Plant Society
12 Sanderson Rd.
Smithfield, RI 02917

Wildflower Alliance of South
    Carolina
P.O. Box 12181
Columbia, SC 29211
(803) 799-6889

Tennessee Native Plant Society
Dept. of Botany
University of Tennessee
Knoxville, TN 37916
(615) 974-2256

Texas Native Plant Society
Box 891
Georgetown, TX 78627
(512) 863-9685, fax (512) 869-0393
*Texas Native Plant Society News*

Utah Native Plant Society
3631 South Carolyn St.
Salt Lake City, UT 84106

Virginia Native Plant Society
Box 844
Annandale, VA 22003
(703) 332-7850, fax (703) 332-9989
*Bulletin*

Washington Native Plant Society
University of Washington
Department of Botany
Box 351330
Seattle, WA 98195
(206) 543-1942
*Occasional Papers*

West Virginia Native Plant Society
West Virginia University
Morgantown, WV 26506

Wild Ones
9701 North Lake Dr.
Milwaukee, WI 53217
(414) 352-0734

Wyoming Native Plant Society
P.O. Box 1471
Cheyenne, WY 82003

# WEIGHTS, MEASURES, AND CONVERSIONS

## Fahrenheit/Celsius Conversion

To calculate Fahrenheit from Celsius degrees, multiply by 9, divide by 5, and then add 32, or $°C \times 9/5 + 32 = °F$

    EXAMPLE: To determine how many °F equal 30°C, multiply 30°C by 9 to get 270, divide by 5 to get 54, and then add 32 to get the answer: 86°F.

To calculate Celsius from Fahrenheit degrees, subtract 32, multiply by 5, and divide by 9, or $°F − 32 \times 5/9 = °C$

    EXAMPLE: To determine how many °C equal 50°F, subtract 32 from 50°F to get 18, multiply by 5 to get 90, and divide by 9 to get the answer: 10°C.

### Equivalent Temperatures*— Celsius and Fahrenheit

| °F | °C |
|---|---|
| −20 | −29 |
| −15 | −26 |
| −11 | −24 |
| −6 | −21 |
| −2 | −19 |
| 0 | −18 |
| 2 | −17 |
| 5 | −15 |
| 7 | −14 |
| 9 | −13 |
| 10 | −12 |
| 12 | −11 |
| 14 | −10 |
| 16 | −9 |
| 18 | −8 |
| 19 | −7 |
| 21 | −6 |
| 23 | −5 |
| 25 | −4 |
| 27 | −3 |
| 28 | −2 |
| 30 | −1 |
| 32 | 0 |
| 34 | 1 |

*Celsius temperatures have been rounded to the nearest degree.

| °F | °C |
|---|---|
| 36 | 2 |
| 37 | 3 |
| 39 | 4 |
| 41 | 5 |
| 43 | 6 |
| 45 | 7 |
| 46 | 8 |
| 48 | 9 |
| 50 | 10 |
| 52 | 11 |
| 54 | 12 |
| 55 | 13 |
| 57 | 14 |
| 59 | 15 |
| 61 | 16 |
| 63 | 17 |
| 64 | 18 |
| 66 | 19 |
| 68 | 20 |
| 70 | 21 |
| 72 | 22 |
| 73 | 23 |
| 75 | 24 |
| 77 | 25 |
| 79 | 26 |
| 81 | 27 |
| 82 | 28 |
| 84 | 29 |
| 86 | 30 |
| 88 | 31 |
| 90 | 32 |
| 91 | 33 |
| 93 | 34 |
| 95 | 35 |
| 97 | 36 |
| 99 | 37 |
| 100 | 38 |
| 102 | 39 |
| 104 | 40 |
| 106 | 41 |
| 108 | 42 |
| 212 | 100 |

# Gardener's Mathematics

## Liquid and Dry Measures

### Liquid Equivalent Measures

| 3 teaspoons (tsp) | = | 1 tablespoon (tbs) |
|---|---|---|
| 2 tablespoons | = | 1 fluid ounce (oz) |
| 8 fluid ounces | = | 1 cup |
| 2 cups | = | 1 pint (pt) |
| 2 cups | = | 1 quart (qt) |
| 4 quarts | = | 1 gallon (gal) |

### Dry Equivalent Measures

| 3 teaspoons (tsp) | = | 1 tablespoon (tbs) |
|---|---|---|
| 16 tablespoons | = | 1 cup |
| 2 cups | = | 1 pint |
| 2 cups | = | 1 quart |
| 8 quarts (2 gallons) | = | 1 peck |
| 4 pecks | = | 1 bushel |

### Conversion Equations

| Milliliter (ml) | ⟺ | teaspoon (tsp) |
|---|---|---|
| ml/5 = tsp | | tsp × 5 = ml |

| Milliliter | ⟺ | tablespoon (tbs) |
|---|---|---|
| ml/15 = tbs | | tbs × 15 = ml |

| Liter (l) | ⟺ | cup |
|---|---|---|
| l/.24 = cup | | cup × .24 = l |

| Liter | ⟺ | pint (pt) |
|---|---|---|
| l/.47 = pt | | pt × .47 = l |

| Liter | ⟺ | quart (qt) |
|---|---|---|
| l/.95 = qt | | qt × .95 = l |

| Liter | ⟺ | gallon (gal) |
|---|---|---|
| l/3.8 = gal | | gal × 3.8 = l |

# Length

## Equivalent Measures

| 12 inches (in) | = | 1 foot (ft) |
|---|---|---|
| 3 feet (ft) | = | 1 yard (yd) |

1,000 millimeters (mm)   =   1 meter (m)
10 millimeters (mm)   =   1 centimeter (cm)
100 centimeters (cm)   =   1 meter (m)
1,000 meters (m)   =   1 kilometer (km)

## Conversion Equations

| Millimeters (mm) | $\Leftrightarrow$ | inches (in) |
|---|---|---|
| mm/25.4 = in | | in $\times$ 25.4 = mm |

| Centimeters (cm) | $\Leftrightarrow$ | inches |
|---|---|---|
| cm/2.54 = in | | in $\times$ 2.54 = cm |

| Millimeters | $\Leftrightarrow$ | feet (ft) |
|---|---|---|
| mm/303 = ft | | ft $\times$ 303 = mm |

| Centimeters | $\Leftrightarrow$ | feet |
|---|---|---|
| cm/30 = ft | | ft $\times$ 30 = cm |

| Meter (m) | $\Leftrightarrow$ | feet |
|---|---|---|
| m/.303 = ft | | ft $\times$ .303 = m |

| Meter | $\Leftrightarrow$ | yards (yd) |
|---|---|---|
| m/.91 = yd | | yd $\times$ .91 = m |

| Kilometers (km) | $\Leftrightarrow$ | mile |
|---|---|---|
| km/1.6 = miles | | miles $\times$ 1.6 = km |

## Area and Volume

### Area Formulas

Use the following formulas to determine the area (A) of a

| Rectangle: | A = bh | *or* base times height |
|---|---|---|
| Square: | A = s$^2$ | *or* side squared |
| Triangle: | A = bh/2 | *or* base times height divided by 2 |
| Circle: | A = $\pi$ r$^2$ | *or* $\pi$ times the radius squared; $\pi$ = 3.14 |

### Equivalent Measures

| 1 square foot (ft$^2$) | = | 144 square inches (in$^2$) |
|---|---|---|
| 1 square yard (yd$^2$) | = | 9 square feet (ft$^2$) |
| 1 acre (a) | = | 4,840 square yards (yd$^2$) |

## Conversion Equations

| Square centimeters (cm$^2$) | $\Leftrightarrow$ | square inches (in$^2$) |
|---|---|---|
| cm$^2$/6.45 = in$^2$ | | in$^2$ $\times$ 6.45 = cm$^2$ |

| Square meters (m$^2$) | $\Leftrightarrow$ | square feet (ft$^2$) |
|---|---|---|
| m$^2$/.09 = ft$^2$ | | ft$^2$ $\times$ .09 = m$^2$ |

| Square meters (m$^2$) | $\Leftrightarrow$ | square yards (yd$^2$) |
|---|---|---|
| m$^2$/.8 = yd$^2$ | | yd$^2$ $\times$ .8 = m$^2$ |

| Square feet (ft$^2$) | $\Leftrightarrow$ | acres (a) |
|---|---|---|
| ft$^2$/43,560 = a | | A $\times$ 43,560 = ft$^2$ |

| Hectares (ha) | $\Leftrightarrow$ | acres (a) |
|---|---|---|
| ha/.4 = a | | a $\times$ .4 = ha |

### Volume Formulas

Use the following formulas to determine the volume (V) of a

| Cube: | V = s$^3$ | *or* one of the dimensions cubed |
|---|---|---|
| Rectangle: | V = lwh | *or* length times width times height |
| Pyramid: | V = Ah | *or* the area of the base times height |
| Cylinder: | V = $\pi$ r$^2$h | *or* $\pi$ times the radius of the base squared times height; $\pi$ = 3.14 |

### Equivalent Measures

| 1 cubic foot (ft$^3$) | = | 1,728 cubic inches (in$^3$) |
|---|---|---|
| 1 cubic yard (yd$^3$) | = | 27 cubic feet (ft$^3$) |

# How Much Potting Soil Do You Need to Fill a Pot?

Potting soil is usually sold in quantities measured in quarts or cubic feet. The volume of soil needed for some popular sizes of standard pots is calculated below in cubic inches. The volume for these standard (slightly sloping) pots is calculated using the formula for a cylinder (V = π r²h), with an average radius.

EXAMPLE: If you have an 8-inch standard pot, first calculate the average diameter by averaging the diameter of the top, measuring 8 inches, and that of the bottom, 5½ inches; that average diameter is roughly 6¾ inches, or 6.75 inches. The radius is half the diameter or 3.38 inches, rounded off. Figuring that you want the soil to fill the pot to roughly 1 inch below the top, then the height of the soil is 7½ inches or 7.5 (1 inch below total pot height of 8½ inches).

Using the formula* for a cylinder: $V = \pi\, r^2 h$

$V = 3.14 \times (3.38)^2 \times 7.5$
$V = 3.14 \times 11.42 \times 7.5$
$V = 268.9$ or 269 cubic inches for a standard 8-inch pot
*$\pi = 3.14$

The figures in the chart below indicate the number of pots that each volume of soil (or bag weight) is capable of filling.

| Pot Diameter | Soil Volume | | |
|---|---|---|---|
| | *1 Quart* *(67.2 cu in)* | *1 Gallon (4 Quarts) (231 cu in)* | *1 Cubic Foot (1,728 cu in)* |
| 4 inches (34 cu in) | 2 | 6.9 | 51.3 |
| 5 inches (72 cu in) | — | 3.2 | 24.1 |
| 6 inches (98 cu in) | — | 2.4 | 17.6 |
| 8 inches (269 cu in) | — | — | 6.4 |
| 10 inches (573 cu in) | — | — | 3 |
| 12 inches (1,045 cu in) | — | — | 1.7 |
| 14 inches (1,726 cu in) | — | — | 1 |

The volume of soil required for rectangular and square planters is far easier to figure. Calculate the total cubic inches with the formula for a rectangle or a cube, and then use the equivalent measures below to determine how much soil you will need. Remember to subtract 1 inch from the container height so that the soil will not be level with the top.

## Equivalent Measures

| | | |
|---|---|---|
| 1 cubic foot | = | 1,728 cubic inches |
| 1 quart | = | 67.2 cubic inches |
| 1 cup | = | 14.4375 cubic inches |

# Dilution Rates

Liquid fertilizers require diluting before they can be applied. Some gardeners apply these liquid fertilizers, such as fish emulsion and seaweed emulsion, to container plantings at half or one-quarter the recommended dosage at shorter intervals—giving the plants the recommended dose but on a different timetable. One of the issues with container plantings is that plant nutrients can leach out with each watering. By applying fertilizers at reduced dosages and more often, this problem can be minimized. Usually these dosages are given per gallon of water and it is easy to halve or quarter the amount of fertilizer before adding.

Occasionally liquid fertilizer dilution rates are given in quantities that home gardeners may never use. The chart below gives equivalent quantities for different amounts of water. For example, if the package reads add 8 fluid ounces of emulsion to 25 gallons of water and you want to fertilize just a few plants and need only a small amount mixed, you can tell at a glance from the chart that the equivalent quantity for 1 gallon of water would be 2 teaspoons.

| Water | 1 Gallon | 5 Gallons | 25 Gallons | 100 Gallons |
|---|---|---|---|---|
| Amount of Emulsion | ½ tsp | 1 tbs | 2 fl oz | ½ pint |
| | 1 tsp | 1 fl oz | 4 fl oz | 1 pint |
| | 2 tsp | 2 fl oz | 8 fl oz | 2 pints |
| | 3 tsp | 2½ fl oz | 12 fl oz | 3 pints |
| | 4 tsp | 3 fl oz | 1 pint | 4 pints |
| | 5 tsp | 4 fl oz | 1¼ pint | 5 pints |

Horticultural oils are usually mixed with water in a 1 to 3 percent solution. A 1 percent solution means that the oil is mixed 1 part oil to 100 parts water. The chart below provides some dilution rates for mixing quantities up to 15 gallons.

| Dilution Rate | 1% 1 to 100 | 2% 2 to 100 | 3% 3 to 100 |
|---|---|---|---|
| Quantities of Water | | | |
| 1 gallon | 2 tbs + 2 tsp | ¼ cup + 4 tsp | ½ cup |
| 3 gallons | ½ cup | 1 cup | 1½ cups |
| 5 gallons | ¾ cup + 5 tsp | 1½ cup + 3 tbs + 1 tsp | 2½ cup + 1 tbs |
| 15 gallons | 1 cup + 3 tbs | 2¼ cup + 2 tbs | 3½ cups + 1 tbs |

## How Much Does a Root Ball Weigh?

### Shrubs and Small Trees

| Plant Height (in feet) | Diameter of Root Ball (in inches) | Weight (in pounds) |
|---|---|---|
| 1½–2 | 11 | 35 |
| 2–3 | 12 | 45 |
| 3–4 | 14 | 65 |
| 4–5 | 16 | 80 |
| 5–6 | 18 | 150 |

## Large Trees

| Tree Diameter in Inches (measured 12″ above ground) | Diameter of Root Ball (in inches) | Weight (in pounds) |
|---|---|---|
| 1¼–1½ | 18 | 150 |
| 1½–1¾ | 20 | 190 |
| 1¾–2 | 22 | 225 |
| 2–2½ | 24 | 300 |
| 2½–3 | 28 | 600 |

# Calculating How Much Fertilizer to Apply

Consider the following example: a soil test has recommended that you apply 2 pounds of nitrogen per 1,000 square feet in your vegetable garden, and you have decided to use 18-5-9 on the 20-by-75-foot plot.

Application-rate recommendations are usually in pounds of nitrogen (N) per 1,000 square feet. The numbers in the ratios on fertilizer labels, such as 18 in 18-5-9 (NPK), refer to pounds of nutrient (in this case nitrogen) per 100 pounds of fertilizer. Here is how to calculate how that translates into an actual amount to apply to your garden:

1. First figure the pounds of 18-5-9 fertilizer that contain 1 pound of actual nitrogen by dividing 100 by 18. In other words, 5.55 pounds of this particular fertilizer product contain 1 pound of actual nitrogen.
2. Since the recommendation is 2 pounds of actual nitrogen per 1,000 square feet, multiply 5.55 pounds of fertilizer by 2. This tells you that 11.1 pounds of fertilizer give you 2 pounds of nitrogen.
3. Calculate the square footage of your vegetable plot by multiplying 20 feet by 75 feet, which comes to 1,500 square feet.
4. If 11.1 pounds of fertilizer are necessary for a 1,000-square-foot garden, then use the following equation with x representing the unknown

amount of fertilizer to figure out how much is needed for your 1,500 square feet:

$$11.1/1,000 = x/1,500 \text{ or}$$
$$1,000x = 16,650$$
$$x = 16.6$$

That is, 16.6 pounds of fertilizer will give you 2 pounds of actual nitrogen for your 1,500 square foot vegetable plot.

## How Much Mulch?

Use one cubic yard of organic matter to mulch a 100-square-foot area to a depth of three inches. One cubic yard equals 27 cubic feet; mulch is often available in 2- or 3-cubic-foot bags.

# GLOSSARY

Many terms used commonly in everyday life have very specific botanical or horticultural meanings. In the following glossary, only the specific definitions are listed. For example, to a botanist, the word "inferior" does not mean "poorer," but rather is used to describe the location of the ovary when it is found below the other flower parts.

**Achene:** A simple, one-seeded fruit in which the pericarp (fruit wall) is attached to the seed.

**Actinomorphic:** Radially symmetrical. When looking down on an actinomorphic corolla or calyx, you can see an infinite number of bisecting lines or planes that can cut the flower in equal halves.

**Acuminate:** Of a leaf, having a sharp apex with less than a 90-degree angle and concave sides.

**Acute:** Of a leaf, tapering to a sharp point at the base or apex with straight to convex sides.

**Adventitious root:** A root occurring in other than the usual location, as from stem or leaf tissue.

**Aerial roots:** Roots formed and remaining above ground.

**Aerobic:** Requiring oxygen to live and grow.

**Air layering:** A propagation method that involves wounding, enclosing, and blocking light from a section on a woody stem a few inches behind the growing tip until roots form and the new plant can be potted.

**Alfisols:** A soil classification, whose members typically exhibit a humus content restricted to the upper soil surface. Formed by podzolization, these gray-brown soils are found in wooded areas.

**Alternate:** Arranged singly on different sides and heights of the main stem or axis, as with branches or leaves.

**Alternation of generations:** A component of the life cycle of sexually reproducing plants featuring the alternation from the gametophyte generation to the sporophyte generation. The gametophyte generation is usually derived from the sporophyte generation as a result of meiosis, and the change from gametophyte back to sporophyte is usually the result of syngamy. In vascular plants, what we recognize as "the plant" is the sporophyte generation.

**Anaerobic:** Living and growing in the absence of oxygen.

**Androecium:** All the stamens, the male parts, of the flower.

**Anemochory:** Dispersal by wind.

**Anemophily:** Pollination by wind.

**Angiosperm:** A plant characterized by the production of seeds that are enclosed in a fruit.

**Annual:** A plant that produces its flowers and fruits within a single year and then dies. Also known as a therophyte in Raunkiaer's plant classification system.

**Annulus:** A ringlike layer of cells found in the capsules of mosses or in the sporangium walls of ferns.

**Anthecium:** A grass fruit in which a single spikelet with fertile florets breaks apart above the glumes (the bracts at the base of the spikelet).

**Anther:** The apical (top) part of a stamen composed of microsporangia and in which pollen grains are produced.

**Antheridium (*pl.* antheridia):** In bryophytes and pteridophytes, the multicellular structure where sperm are produced.

**Anthocarp:** A fruit formed from the ovary and attached floral parts that have undergone marked development after fertilization in order to aid in the dissemination of the seeds.

**Antitranspirant:** A dilute mixture of plastic and water that, when sprayed on foliage, decreases water loss through microscopic openings in the leaves. While not registered for use as a fungicide, antitranspirants have proven to be effective against disease, including powdery mildew.

**Apetalous:** Said of a flower lacking petals. Common in wind-pollinated plants.

**Apical:** At the tip; pertaining to the apex.

**Apiculate:** Of a leaf, terminating in a sharp, flexible point that includes tissue from the midvein and the lamina.

**Apomixis:** The development of a plant without fusion of gametes (without syngamy), sometimes referred to as vegetative reproduction.

**Appressed:** Pressed flat or nearly flat against another organ, such as hairs on a leaf.

**Archegonium (*pl.* archegonia):** In bryophytes and pteridophytes, the multicellular structure where eggs are produced.

**Aridisols:** A soil classification whose members are characteristically dry for extended periods, low in humus, and displaying some calcification. These are typically desert soils.

**Aristate:** Of a leaf, awned, ending in a hard, straight tip.

**Asexual:** Without sex; without syngamy.

**Asexual propagation:** See **vegetative propagation.**

**Auriculate:** Having a base with rounded projections that have a concave inner margin, as on some leaves and petals.

**Autochory:** Dispersal by physical expulsion, often explosively.

**Autotrophic:** Capable of self-nourishment. Autotrophic plants produce their own nourishment via photosynthesis.

**Awn:** A slender, bristlelike appendage.

**Awned:** Having awns.

**Axis (*pl.* axes):** Any line of development of a plant from which various organs or parts grow, as stems or branches. The main axis of a plant usually includes the stem and primary root.

**Bacca:** A simple, fleshy fruit that does not dehisce; also called "berry."

***Bacillus thuringiensis (Bt):*** A species of bacterium that produces a toxin poisonous to many common insect pests.

**Balanced:** Said of fertilizers that provide equal percentages of the three primary plant nutrients: nitrogen, phosphorus, and potassium. Compare **complete** and **single-nutrient.**

**Balled and burlapped:** Term for plants sold with a quantity of soil around their roots and wrapped in burlap, or often today in nonbiodegradable materials.

**Banner:** Topmost petal of the flowers of some plants in the pea family.

**Bare-root:** Term for plants sold without a quantity of soil around their roots. Bare-root woody plants should be planted before they break dormancy.

**Bark:** The external layer of a woody stem.

**Basal:** Arising at the base.

**Beard:** A sepal or petal with a dense cluster or line of hairs.

**Biennial:** A plant that takes two years to produce flowers and fruits before dying. See also **hemicryptophyte.**

**Bilabiate:** Of flowers, with two lips composed of fused petals.

**Binomial:** A plant's species name. It is made up of two words: the genus and the specific epithet; for example, *Malus coronaria,* which is the Latin name for what is commonly called American crabapple.

**Biodiversity:** A healthy mixture of ecosystems, plant communities within the ecosystems, species within the communities, populations within the species, and individuals within the population.

**Biological controls:** Pest-management strategies utilizing pests' natural predators, either lured to the garden with proper shelter, food, and water, or in some cases purchased at nurseries or from mail-order suppliers.

**Biomass:** The sum of all the living biological material within a specific habitat or population—the total mass of all the plants and animals.

**Bisexual:** Said of flowers with both stamens and pistils.

**Bog:** A wetland fed by groundwater and characterized by highly acidic soils, poor drainage, spaghnum mosses, and peat. Bogs are nutrient-poor and generally form in basins with no inlet or outlet for surface water.

**Bonsai:** The ancient Japanese art of creating dwarfed potted trees and shrubs through meticulous pruning and shaping.

**Bordeaux mix:** A combination of copper sulfate and hydrated lime dusted on plants or mixed with water to make a spray used to control many common pathogens, such as anthracnose, wilt, and powdery mildew.

**Boreal forest:** A vegetation type characterized by mostly coniferous trees, just south of the tundra in the Northern Hemisphere. Also known as northern coniferous forest and taiga.

**Botanical pesticide:** A substance that is extracted from plants such as pyrethrum, ryania, and sabadilla and used to control or kill pest organisms.

**Bowhead rake:** A rake with a row of short, stainless steel tines used for leveling a seed bed, breaking up soil, and gathering debris.

**Bract:** A reduced leaf or leaflike organ associated with flowers.

**Bracteole:** A small bract found on the pedicel of a flower.

**Bramble:** A shrub or vine of the genus *Rubus.* The name usually refers to blackberry or raspberry, but more broadly to any thorny or prickly woody plant.

**Branch bark collar:** The bulging ring at the base of a branch, where it joins the trunk.

**Branch bark ridge:** The dark, raised ridge of bark at the intersection of the trunk and branch that defines the start of the branch.

**Broadcasting:** The practice of scattering seed or dry fertilizer freely by hand or with a mechanical spreader.

**Broadleaf evergreen:** A plant with broad, flat leaves as opposed to needle-shaped ones, that maintains its foliage year-round.

**Bryophyte:** A photosynthetic plant that lacks xylem and phloem; commonly known as mosses, hornworts, and liverworts.

***Bt:*** See ***Bacillus thuringiensis.***

**Bud:** Small shoot with scalelike leaves—containing an embryonic leaf, leaf cluster, or flower—that, when given the proper conditions, bursts out in growth.

**Budding:** A grafting method, often performed on roses and fruit trees, in which single leaf buds are inserted under the bark of other compatible trees or shrubs.

**Bulb:** An underground swollen bud, serving as a food storage organ.

**Bulbil:** See **bulblet.**

**Bulblet:** A small bulb or bulblike structure that forms usually at the base of some bulbs and from which new plants can be propagated. Sometimes called a bulbil.

**Calcification:** A soil-forming process occurring in semiarid to arid regions where evaporation from the soil exceeds precipitation and characterized by the accumulation of calcium carbonate. Calcified soils usually are neutral to slightly alkaline. Plains, prairies, and desert regions are typically areas where calcification occurs.

**Calcined clay:** Stabilized baked clay, often applied as an inorganic mulch.

**Calyx:** All the sepals of a flower.

**Cambium:** The thin, actively growing layer of tissue between the bark and the inner tissue of stems and on roots through which water and nutrients move in woody plants.

**Campanulate:** Bell-shaped; as some corollas.

**Candles:** New spring shoots, with immature needles packed tightly and resembling candles, that emerge from the branch tips of pines.

**Candling:** A pruning technique to manage new "candles" on pines. In spring, one-half to one-third of a candle can be pinched by hand.

**Canopy:** The top level of a forest's or wooded environment's vertical structure consisting of the leaves and branches of the tallest trees.

**Cantharophily:** Pollination by beetles.

**Capitulum:** An inflorescence in which the flowers are found on a flattened surface called a receptacle, as in the sunflower family (Asteraceae).

**Capsule:** (1) A dehiscent fruit formed from more than one carpel; (2) a structure where spores are produced.

**Carnivore:** An organism that eats the flesh of animals, including insectivorous plants.

**Carpel:** The unit of an ovary formed from one highly modified leaf. Simple pistils have a single carpel. Compound pistils have several to many carpels (often three or five) fused together.

**Carr:** A shrub swamp.

**Catkin:** A pendulous, dense spike of reduced flowers. Catkins are adapted to wind pollination.

**Caudate:** Of a leaf, very acuminate, with a long and thin tip.

**Caulifory:** A inflorescence found on the stem of a tree. Inflorescences on the American redbud tree (*Cercis canadensis*) are examples.

**Chamaephyte:** A woody or herbaceous evergreen perennial from 10 to 20 inches tall or whose shoots die back periodically. The term comes from Raunkiaer's plant classification system.

**Chaparral:** A vegetation type characterized by shrubs and small, shrubby trees, as found in California; herbaceous vegetation is generally absent, except after fires, which occur frequently.

**Chartaceous:** Thin and papery; deciduous leaves are sometimes chartaceous.

**Chimera:** A structure or tissue that is formed from two genetically different sources.

**Chiropterogamy:** Pollination by bats.

**Chlorophyll:** A green pigment involved in photosynthesis.

**Chloroplast:** A chlorophyll-containing structure found in the cells of most photosynthetic organisms.

**Ciliate:** With hairs along the margin, as on some leaves.

**Circinate:** Of a leaf, with the tip curling down toward the base. Many ferns exhibit circinate vernation in their "fiddleheads."

**Cladistics:** A method of classification that portrays the evolutionary history of living organisms as branching trees, using derived characteristics.

**Cladogram:** The result of a cladistic study—a branching diagram formed by grouping together species with similar characteristics and showing evolutionary relationships.

**Claw:** A very narrow, stalklike base of a sepal or petal.

**Clay:** A rock-derived component of soil with tiny microscopic particles. The clay content in a soil helps determine its texture. Soils with high proportions of clay are dense and heavy.

**Cleft:** Of a leaf, with the margin cut in toward the midvein.

**Cleft-and-saddle grafting:** A grafting technique in which two wedge-cut scions are inserted into a vertical split at the top of the truncated understock. Compare **top grafting**.

**Cleistogamy:** Self-pollination within a closed flower.

**Cloche:** Derived from the bell-shaped glass caps used by French vegetable growers (*cloche* means bell in French). Refers to similar hot caps, commercial or homemade, used by gardeners to protect tender plants from excessively cool temperatures.

**Clone:** An organism that is genetically identical to the parent.

**Coevolution:** Any situation where two or more non-interbreeding populations act as selective agents for one another. Many flowering plants have benefited from coevolution with their animal pollinators.

**Cold frame:** Simple four-sided structure, usually made of wood with a sloping top of a transparent material to allow in sunlight and capture warmth.

**Collar:** A circle of paper, tar paper, or other material placed around a plant stem to protect against damage from cutworms, slugs, or other pests.

**Complete:** (1) Said of flowers that have all four floral whorls (that is, calyx, corolla, stamens, and pistils). (2) Fertilizers containing all three primary nutrients: nitrogen, phosphorus, and potassium. Compare **balanced** and **single-nutrient.**

**Compound leaf:** A leaf with two or more lamina (called leaflets). In general, compound leaves can be recognized as distinct from simple leaves by the absence of a bud at the base of the leaflet.

**Cool-season crop:** A heat-sensitive crop that tends to go to seed in summer heat. Cool-season crops can be planted or set out before the last expected spring frost.

**Conifers:** Cone-bearing trees; the most economically important class of the gymnosperms. Most conifers are evergreen, but deciduous conifers include the larches and dawn redwood.

**Coppicing:** The regular pruning of branches to ground level to promote vigorous new growth. Coppicing used to be performed to provide a regular supply of firewood; more often today, its practice encourages the growth of vividly colored branches on osier dogwoods and other deciduous shrubs with decorative young stems.

**Cordate:** Heart-shaped at the base, as on some leaves. The base has a notch similar to that at the top of a heart. Compare **obcordate.**

**Coriaceous:** Thick and leathery; evergreen leaves are usually coriaceous.

**Corm:** An underground, vertical stem that is swollen. Gladioli, crocuses, and freesias grow from corms.

**Cormel:** Tiny corm or cormlike structure produced at the base of some corms from which new plants can be propagated.

**Corolla:** All the petals of a single flower.

**Cortex:** The layer of cells surrounding the vascular tissue in plant stems; the inner bark of woody plants.

**Corymb:** An inflorescence that is a flat-topped raceme; the lower branches of the raceme are long and the upper branches are short so that the overall shape is flat.

**Cotyledon:** The food-storage leaf in seeds, often the first to unfurl after germination, which differs from the plant's true leaves that follow. Commonly known as the seed leaf.

**Cover crop:** A crop planted, often in the dormant season, to protect soil against erosion and that when plowed under contributes organic matter to the soil.

**Crenate:** With low, rounded teeth along the margin that have no point, as on some leaves.

**Crop rotation:** Strategy of agriculture in which different crops are sown in successive years on the same plot to reduce the loss of nutrients from the soil and decrease potential disease and pest problems.

**Cross-fertilization:** The union of sperm and egg from different plants or flowers.

**Crossing-over:** In meiosis, the exchange of genetic material that results in recombination between homologous chromosomes.

**Cross-pollination:** In angiosperms, the transfer of pollen from one plant to a stigma on a different plant, but of the same species.

**Crozier:** The tightly coiled, young or developing leaf or frond in ferns.

**Cruciform:** Cross-shaped. Said of a corolla that, when viewed from above, appears cross-shaped.

**Cultivar:** A cultivated variety. Written as a non-Latin, nonitalicized name set off by single quotation marks. *Clematis alpina* 'Ruby' is a selection of *Clematis alpina* with rosy-red flowers. *Magnolia* x 'Elizabeth' is a magnolia hybrid resulting from the crossing of at least two *Magnolia* species.

**Cultural controls:** Pest management techniques that promote healthy soil or capitalize on pest life cycles. Good garden sanitation is an important cultural control.

**Cuneate:** Tapering to a sharp point at the base, as on some leaves and petals. Similar to acute but with straight, not convex, sides.

**Cusp:** A rigid, abrupt, sharp tip.

**Cuspidate:** Of a leaf, tapering gradually to a sharp point (cusp) at the apex.

**Cutting:** A part of a plant such as a portion of stem, root, or leaf removed to be propagated vegetatively into a new plant.

**Cutting back:** Revitalizing plants by pruning drastically to promote new growth. In midsummer some annuals, such as petunias and impatiens, are cut back by a third or more to give them a "second wind."

**Cyme:** An inflorescence that terminates in a flower, and lateral branches arising below this flower also terminate in flowers.

**Cypsela:** A fruit with wings or bristles at its tip, such as that on dandelion (*Taraxacum officinale*).

**Cytokinesis:** The stage of cell division in which the cytoplasm and the two daughter nuclei separate into new cells.

**Cytoplasm:** The protoplasm within a cell excluding its nucleus.

**Damping off:** A condition in which fungi kill seedlings before or soon after they break through the soil.

**Deadheading:** Removing spent flowers from plants before they begin to form seeds.

**Deciduous:** Used to describe plants that deliberately drop their leaves at the onset of a difficult season—winter in temperate and boreal areas and the dry season in desert areas of the world. Compare **evergreen.**

**Dehisce:** To split open, as a seed pod, along a definite line.

**Dehiscent:** Said of fruits that split open, allowing the seeds to fall out and be dispersed.

**Deltoid (deltate):** Like the Greek letter delta. Shaped like a triangle in which all sides are the same length, as some leaves.

**Dendrogram:** A branching diagram, created through either phenetic or phylogenetic research, which can be used to create a classification.

**Dentate:** With teeth along the margin that are pointed outward from the margin, as on some leaves.

**Determinate:** Having an inflorescence where the main or terminal flower opens first, thereby halting further lengthening of the main axis.

**Diatomaceous earth:** A dust—made from the microscopic, fossilized shells of diatoms, a type of alga—used to control insect populations; kills nonselectively and should be applied only to problem areas.

**Dichotomous:** Characterized by a type of branching in which the stem tip divides into two equal parts.

**Dicot:** A shortened or abbreviated term for dicotyledon.

**Dicotyledon:** A plant whose seeds have two cotyledons or seed leaves.

**Dioecious:** Said of species having male and female plants (that is, only male flowers on some plants and only female flowers on different plants).

**Dioecy:** The condition of being dioecious.

**Diploid:** Cells having two sets of chromosomes; also, the chromosome number indicative of the sporophyte generation.

**Disbudding:** Removing some flower buds to encourage the remaining ones to develop differently.

**Disjunct:** A species or population geographically isolated from other related species or populations.

**Disturbance:** An event—for example, fire, flooding, damage by insects and diseases, or windstorm—that alters local habitats, maintaining them in different stages of vegetation development, thus ensuring the presence of a diverse mix of plants and animals that characterize each phase of the change.

**Division:** The process of making more than one plant out of a large crown, clump of suckers, tubers, corms, or bulbs by separating out sections, and replanting.

**Dolomitic lime:** A soil conditioner made from dolomite, a rock consisting mostly of calcium and magnesium carbonate. Dolomitic lime or limestone adds magnesium to a soil as well as the calcium carbonate of ground limestone.

**Dominance:** Within a plant community, the condition of one or more species most influencing the life and character of the community.

**Dormancy:** The condition of reduced or suspended physiological activity in organisms. Dormancy protects plant seeds from germinating at the wrong time, such as when the ground is parched or frozen.

**Double digging:** A process of cultivation involving successive trenches in which the top layer of soil from the first trench is dug out, the subsoil loosened, and amended soil from the top of the second trench is used to refill the first; soil from the first trench refills the last. Done properly, double digging will make a soil vigorous, friable, and fertile.

**Double fertilization:** A feature primarily associated with angiosperms requiring two male nuclei for fertilization, involving the union of one sperm with an egg to make the embryo and the other sperm with two polar nuclei or a secondary nucleus forming a unit that results in the production of endosperm, a nutritive tissue.

**Double serrate:** With serrate teeth along the margins of other, larger serrate teeth, as on some leaves.

**Drip irrigation:** The technique of watering in which water, carefully aimed toward a plant's root system and applied over an extended period of time, actually "drips" into the soil. With a properly designed drip irrigation system, soil never dries out or becomes waterlogged and little water is lost to runoff or evaporation.

**Drupe:** A simple, fleshy, indehiscent fruit with three layers of fruit wall: thin external layer; thicker, more or less fleshy layer; and hard, stony internal layer (the pit)—such as a peach or mango.

**Ecology:** The study of organisms in terms of their interrelationships and their environment, including light, temperature, soil, disturbance, and water; a branch of biology.

**Ecosystem:** A functioning natural system that combines biological communities and the environments with which they interact.

**Ecotone:** The transitional region between two plant communities, including species from both communities and often unique species as well, resulting in usually the most diverse ecosystems. In the Midwest, the eastern deciduous forest grades into the prairie in an ecotone called oak savannah.

**Edaphic:** Soil-related.

**Egg:** The female gamete.

**Elliptic:** One and a half to two times longer than wide. Shaped like a narrow oval, as some leaves.

**Emarginate:** Broadly notched at the apex, as some leaves and petals.

**Endemic:** Native to, and confined to, a specific region.

**Endemism:** The quality or condition of being endemic.

**Endocarp:** The inner layer of the pericarp (fruit wall).

**Endosperm:** A nutritive tissue consumed by the developing embryo in angiosperms.

**Endozoochory:** Dispersal through animal ingestion and excretion.

**Entire:** Without any indentations or teeth along the margin, as some leaves.

**Entisols:** A soil classification, with members characterized by erosion and little or no distinct soil horizons. They are commonly found on floodplains.

**Entomophily:** Pollination by insects.

**Ephemeral:** (1) Short-lived; (2) a plant that completes all or part of its life cycle in a very short time, such as days or weeks. Dutchman's-breeches, a spring ephemeral, relies on tubers to provide the energy needed for rapid leaf and flower development.

**Epiascidiate leaves:** Container leaves, such as those of pitcher plants (*Sarracenia* species) in which insects are caught.

**Epicarp (Exocarp):** The outer layer of the pericarp (fruit wall).

**Epidermis:** The outermost, protective layer of living cells for many plant organs; this layer is replaced by bark on the stems of woody plants.

**Epigynous:** The perianth (sepals and petals) and the androecium (male parts) are attached above the base of the ovary; the ovary is said to be inferior or half-inferior.

**Epiphyte:** Plant that germinates and roots on other plants, never coming in contact with the soil, such as many orchids and bromeliads. Not usually parasitic.

**Epizoochory:** Dispersal by attachment to fur or feathers.

**Equitant:** Overlapping one another into two vertical rows or ranks, forming a fan, as the leaves of irises.

**Errant vascular hydrophyte:** Free-moving water plant or floating aquatic plants. The term comes from Raunkiaer's plant classification system.

**Espalier:** The art of training a tree or shrub in a single plane, usually against a wall or fence. Traditionally, fruit trees were trained in symmetrical, geometric patterns; today many different kinds of plants are trained into traditional and also free-form designs.

**Evapotranspiration:** A natural process characterized by water loss into the atmosphere from plants through transpiration and from the soil through evaporation.

**Evenness:** Said of species diversity, the measure of the number of individuals of each species within a specific area.

**Evergreen:** Used to describe plants that retain their leaves for more than one year. Compare **deciduous.**

**Exotic species:** A plant introduced from another country. Also called a nonnative plant. Compare **native species.**

**Fascicle:** A dense cluster of leaves, flowers, stems, or other organ.

**Fascicled:** Clustered, as the needles of most species of pine.

**Fasciation:** A stem, root, or other plant part that is abnormally flattened or sometimes develops into a hollow tube (ring fasciation).

**Fern:** An herb that produces no flowers and reproduces by spores.

**Fertilization:** Syngamy; the fusion of two gametes, resulting in the formation of a new individual cell.

**Fibrous bark:** With threadlike strands.

**Fibrous roots:** Adventitious, threadlike, numerous roots, such as those of many grasses.

**Fiddlehead:** See **crozier.**

**Filament:** The stalklike part of the stamen that supports the anther.

**Flamer:** Specialized torch, powered by gasoline or oil, used to sear the tops of young weeds.

**Flora:** All the plants growing in a particular area, climate, or era; also a comprehensive book that includes all the plants of a particular area. The flora of a region is an enumeration and description of each of the various kinds (taxa) of plants growing there with the emphasis on the species. Compare **vegetation.**

**Floret:** The smallest unit of an inflorescence; a tiny flower. In grasses, the floret comprises the flower and two bracts called the palea and lemma.

**Floristic province:** A rank in a classification system used by botanists involved in the comparative study of the vegetation around the world. The highest rank is the floristic kingdom or realm, characterized by endemic families and by very high rates of generic and species endemism. Kingdoms are subdivided into regions (with high rates of species and generic endemism), which are subdivided into provinces (with some endemic genera), which are subdivided into districts (characterized mainly by endemism at the subspecies level).

**Flower:** The collective term for the reproductive structure in angiosperms (i.e., the calyx, corolla, stamens, and pistils).

**Foliar feeding:** The practice of applying liquid fertilizer in spray form to plant leaves, which absorb the nutrients.

**Follicle:** A dry, dehiscent fruit that develops from one carpel and opens through only one slit. Milkweed pods are follicles.

**Foot:** The nutrient-absorbing portion of the embryonic sporophyte in bryophytes and pteridophytes.

**Forb:** A broad-leaved herbaceous plant.

**Fork:** A long-handled garden tool. There are several types. The all-purpose *garden fork* has a head 7 to 8 inches wide with four flat or squared tines. The *manure fork* has more tines, up to sixteen, which are round and pointed and finer than those of the garden fork. The *spading fork* has four flat tines and is lighter and smaller than the garden fork. The *pitchfork* has three to five round tapered tines. The *spiking fork* is similar to the garden fork but has shorter tines and is used to aerate lawns.

**Form:** Officially written forma (*pl.* formae). A subdivision of a species designating a minor variation within a species. For example, albino forms of species are often designated a forma *alba.*

**Formation:** The principal vegetation of a region, for example, prairie, eastern deciduous forest, or desert in North America.

**Friability:** The condition of a soil, gauged by how easily it crumbles.

**Frond:** A fern leaf; also refers to large divided leaves, such as those of palms.

**Frost heave:** A process that occurs when water in the soil freezes and expands, pushing plants out of the ground and exposing the roots to sun or drying winds.

**Fruit:** The mature ovary or ovaries of one or more flowers; the seed-bearing organ.

**Fruitlet:** The part of a fruit that becomes dispersed in schizocarpic fruits.

**Funnelform:** Funnel-shaped, as some corollas.

**Furrowed bark:** With longitudinal grooves.

**Galeate:** With a helmet-shaped appendage, as the corollas of monkshood.

**Gall:** A structure formed in response to insect, nematode, mite, or fungal infestations.

**Gametes:** Sex cells (that is, egg and sperm).

**Gametophyte:** The haploid phase of the plant reproductive cycle that produces gametes.

**Genetic diversity:** The measure of the genetic variation among populations of individual species.

**Genus (*pl.* genera):** A group of closely related plants sharing common characteristics and including one or more species. The rank in plant classification between family and species. For example, *Malus* is the genus for apples in the family Rosaceae; *Malus coronaria* is the binomial, or genus and species name, for the American crabapple.

**Geophyte:** Perennial (or biennial) herbaceous plant in which the stems die back to a remnant shoot system with storage organs that are embedded in the soil, such as corms, rhizomes, tubers, and true bulbs. The term comes from Raunkiaer's plant classification system.

**Geotropic:** Growing toward gravity.

**Germination:** The initiation or resumption of growth in structures such as seeds and buds.

**Girdling roots:** Roots of container-grown plants that coil tightly, encircling the plant like a "girdle." Plants with girdling roots do not transplant well.

**Glabrescent:** Becoming glabrous over time.

**Glabrous:** Without any hair or other surface covering.

**Glans:** A fruit in which the receptacle, pedicel, or peduncle is enlarged, such as an acorn.

**Gleyization:** A soil-forming process—occurring in areas of standing water or where drainage is poor—producing waterlogged soils low in oxygen. The breakdown of organic matter is incomplete, and so it may accumulate as peat. Gleyization occurs in coastal wetlands and in the permafrost region of northern tundra areas.

**Glume:** A small bract at the base of a grass spikelet.

**Grafting:** A vegetative propagation method in which a scion of one plant is grafted onto an understock of a compatible tree or shrub. Grafting techniques are often used to improve disease or drought tolerance or affect size or shape of plants.

**Graminoid:** A grasslike herb with very narrow leaves.

**Green manure:** Living plants grown and then plowed under to improve soil fertility and structure. Legumes such as alfalfa, clover, and vetch are popular green manures.

**Ground layer:** The lower level in a forest's or wooded environment's vertical structure, consisting of wildflowers, ferns, and mosses.

**Gymnosperm:** A plant characterized by the production of naked seeds (that is, seeds that are not enclosed in an ovary during development).

**Gynoecium:** All the pistils of a flower; the female parts.

**Habit:** The overall appearance of a plant, defined by the way it grows: upright, weeping, spreading, etc.

**Half-inferior:** The ovary is surrounded by, or embedded in, the receptacle (the region at the top of either the peduncle or pedicel where floral appendages are attached).

**Hammock:** A fertile region, found in the southern United States, typically with hardwood vegetation and often impenetrable.

**Handpicking:** A method of pest control in which gardeners manually remove large, slow, visible pests, such as slugs, caterpillars, some adult insects, and even egg masses.

**Haploid:** Cells having one set of chromosomes (half the normal number); also, the chromosome number indicative of the gametophyte generation.

**Hardening off:** The process of gradually exposing windowsill- or greenhouse-raised seedlings to cooler temperatures and direct sun to ready them for planting outdoors.

**Hardiness:** Refers to a plant's ability to survive throughout the winter.

**Hardwood cutting:** A stem cutting taken from woody trees and shrubs when the plants are dormant in order to propagate the plant vegetatively.

**Hastate:** Having a base with outwardly pointed lobes, as some leaves.

**Haustorium (*pl.* haustoria):** The specialized area of a parasitic plant that attaches to its host, through which the parasite absorbs nutrients.

**Hay:** Cut and partially dried grass, clover, or alfalfa. Compare **straw.**

**Heading cut:** A pruning cut, made at the ends of branches, that takes the branch back to just above a bud or shoot. Heading cuts generally are made to control the height and overall size of plants. Compare **thinning cut.**

**Hemicryptophyte:** Perennial (or biennial) herbaceous plant in which the stems die back to a remnant shoot system that lies on the ground, such as herbaceous plants with runners. The term comes from Raunkiaer's plant classification system.

**Hemiepiphyte:** Plant that germinates on other plants and then establishes soil contact, such as the strangler fig; or plant that germinates on the ground but later loses contact with the soil. The term comes from Raunkiaer's plant classification system.

**Herb:** A nonwoody plant. There are several types of herbs, including forbs, graminoids, ferns, and herbaceous vines.

**Herbaceous:** Term used to describe nonwoody plants.

**Herbaceous vine:** A nonwoody plant that climbs on other plants.

**Herbivore:** An animal that eats plants.

**Herbivory:** An interaction in which an animal consumes a plant or plant part.

**Hesperidium:** A fleshy, berrylike fruit with a tough rind, such as orange, lemon, and other citrus.

**Heterosporous:** Capable of producing two different kinds of spores: microspores and megaspores.

**Heterotrophic:** Obtaining nourishment from other organisms. Heterotrophic plants, such as vascular parasites, depend on other organisms for nourishment. Vascular semiparasites depend to some extent on other organisms but also photosynthesize.

**Hirsute:** With rough, coarse hairs.

**Hispid:** With stout, stiff hairs.

**Histosols:** A soil classification, with members characterized by high organic content. Usually formed by gleyization, they are commonly found in bogs.

**Homologous:** Identical.

**Homosporous:** Capable of producing only one kind of spore.

**Honey guides:** Special patterns or markings on the perianth of a flower that "guide" visiting insects to the nectar within.

**Hoop house:** A minigreenhouse, constructed with hoops or arch-shaped supports, often set up over a garden bed to protect crops from harsh weather conditions.

**Horizontal structure:** Within a plant community, the pattern of growth of the dominant species based on response to environmental and edaphic, or soil-related, factors. Within the horizontal structure of an eastern North American deciduous forest, oaks are found on the drier sites while maples and basswood grow in the moister soil on east and north slopes.

**Horticultural oil:** A refined petroleum oil that smothers insects by plugging their orifices; effective against many pests such as aphids, mealybugs, mites, and scales while sparing tough-bodied beneficial insects such as lady beetles.

**Hot composting:** The process of decomposition of vegetable matter and animal manures in a compost pile at an accelerated rate at temperatures as high as 130°F due to the intense microbial activity. Hot composting is believed to kill pathogens and many weed seeds.

**Humus:** A dark brown or black amorphous substance, the organic content of soil. Humus replenishes nutrients that plants need and helps bond soil particles.

**Hydric:** Wet; characterized by abundant moisture. Compare **mesic** and **xeric.**

**Hydrochory:** Dispersal by water.

**Hydrophily:** Pollination by water.

**Hypanthium:** The cup formed from the receptacle and/or perianth that has fused with the androecium; sometimes referred to as the floral cup. Not all flowers have a hypanthium.

**Hyphae:** Long, thin threads that form the structural basis of fungi.

**Hypocotyl:** The portion of the embryo below the cotyledons.

**Hypogynous:** The perianth (sepals and petals) and androecium (male parts) are attached below the ovary; the ovary is superior.

**Imbricate:** Overlapping one another. The leaves of Norfolk Island pine (*Araucaria heterophylla*) are imbricate.

**Imperfect:** Said of flowers lacking either stamens or pistils.

**Inceptisols:** A soil classification, with members formed by podzolization and substantial erosion, making them typically shallow.

**Incised:** Of a leaf, cut sharply and deeply, into usually regularly shaped lobes.

**Incomplete:** Said of flowers lacking one or more of the four floral whorls (calyx, corolla, stamens, or pistils).

**Indehiscent:** Said of fruits that do not split open, such as berries.

**Indeterminate:** Having an inflorescence on which the first flower's blooming does not arrest the continued growth of the main stem.

**Indumentum:** A coating or covering, especially of hairs.

**Indusium (*pl.* indusia):** A membranous structure covering the sorus in some ferns.

**Inferior:** The ovary sits primarily below the attach-ment point of the perianth (sepals and petals) and androecium (male parts).

**Inflorescence:** The flowering part of the plant; a flower cluster with from one to many blossoms.

**Insect growth regulators (IGRs):** Synthethic analogs of natural growth-regulating hormones that can prevent some immature insect pests from maturing.

**Insecticidal soap:** A dilute soap spray that penetrates insect cuticles and damages cell membranes, causing dehydration; kills nonselectively and should be applied only to problem areas.

**Integrated pest management (IPM):** A pest-control approach first developed for commercial agriculture. The aim of IPM is to maintain acceptable harvest levels while lowering synthetic pesticide use and environmental damage by reducing pest populations to tolerable levels rather than trying to eradicate them totally. IPM employs monitoring and a combination of management techniques: biological controls, physical controls, horticultural controls, and, as a last resort, synthetic pesticides. Compare **organic pest management (OPM).**

**Integument:** In seed plants, the outermost tissue layer covering an ovule. Gymnosperms usually have one integument while angiosperms usually have two.

**Invertization:** A soil-forming process—occurring in regions with distinct wet seasons followed by periods of evaporation and drying and in soils with a high clay content near the surface—characterized by surface cracking during prolonged dry periods that allows the upper and lower soil layers to mix. Invertization occurs in prairie and other grassland regions.

**Keel:** The two united lowermost petals of the flowers of some plants in the pea family. See also **banner** and **wing.**

**Key:** A device used to identify plants. Typically there are several sets of keys—to identify first plant families, then genera, and finally species.

**Lacerate:** Of a leaf, irregularly lobed with deep incisions that look as if they were torn.

**Laciniate:** Of a leaf or petal, slashed; similar to incised, but the cuts are sharply angled.

**Lamina:** The flat portion of a leaf, also called the leaf blade.

**Lanceolate:** Three to six times longer than wide. Shaped like the tip of a lance, as some leaves. Leaf margins are symmetrically curved, and the leaf is widest below the middle.

**Larva (*pl.* larvae):** The stage of development—between egg and pupa—for certain insects, including cabbageworms, beetles, flies, and lacewings. These insects do the most injury to plants as larvae.

**Laterization:** Also called oxisolation; a soil-forming process that occurs in warm, moist climates, during which nutrients like calcium, magnesium, and potassium leach down through the soil away from plant roots and into the groundwater, leaving an abundance of hydrogen ions behind that make the soil very acidic. Typical vegetation is subtropical and tropical forests.

**Layering:** A method of vegetative propagation in which new plants develop roots from shoots still attached to the parent plant. See **simple layering, tip layering,** and **air layering.**

**Leaf cutting:** A leaf or leaf portion that can be rooted to develop a new plant. Thick-leaved African violets are readily propagated from leaf cuttings.

**Leaf mold:** Decayed or composted leaves.

**Legume:** (1) A dry, dehiscent fruit formed from a single carpel, which usually opens along two sides; (2) a member of the Leguminosae, or pea or bean family.

**Liana:** A woody plant that germinates on the ground and maintains soil contact while using another plant for support via tendrils, hooks, pads, aerial roots, or other mechanisms. Grapevines are an example.

**Limb:** (1) A main branch on a tree or shrub; (2) in fused corollas, any extension of the petal beyond its fused base.

**Linear:** More than twelve times longer than wide, as some leaves. Long and narrow with more or less parallel leaf margins.

**Loam:** The gardener's "ideal" soil, friable and generally rich in humus, making it fertile and good for cultivation.

**Lobe:** Any distinct segment of a divided organ, such as a leaf, sepal, or petal.

**Locule:** A chamber within the anther, ovary, or fruit.

**Long-day plant:** A species that requires exposure to long periods of light followed by relatively short periods of darkness to stimulate it to flower; for example, wheat and cabbage.

**Malacophily:** Pollination by slugs or snails.

**Marsh:** A usually open, sunny, and shallow wetland with standing water for all or part of the year dominated by herbaceous plants, such as sedges, grasses, and water-tolerant forbs.

**Mattock:** A chopping tool used for cutting through heavy roots, digging up tree stumps, and breaking up hard ground. It usually has an ax or pick on one end of the head and a hoe on the other.

**Meadow:** A vegetation type characterized primarily by grass and formed naturally or through cultivation on land either too wet or too dry to support woody vegetation. Meadows are a temporary stage in the evolution of a forest.

**Megasporangium (*pl.* megasporangia):** A sporangium producing only megaspores.

**Megaspore:** A spore that develops into a female gametophyte.

**Megaspore mother cell:** See **megasporocyte.**

**Megasporocyte:** A diploid cell that produces megaspores following meiosis; also called the megaspore mother cell.

**Megasporophyll:** A leaf or leaflike structure bearing one or more megasporangia.

**Megastrobilus (*pl.* megastrobili):** A megaspore-producing strobilus; a female cone.

**Meiocyte:** See **sporocyte.**

**Meiosis:** The process of cell division during which the chromosome complement or number is reduced from the diploid condition to the haploid condition.

**Meiospore:** A spore that develops immediately after meiosis.

**Melittophily:** Pollination by bees.

**Membranaceous:** Thin and flexible; deciduous leaves are often membranaceous.

**Mesic:** Moist; characterized by a moderate amount of moisture. Compare **hydric** and **xeric.**

**Mesocarp:** The middle layer of the pericarp (fruit wall).

**Mesophytic:** Capable of tolerating moderately moist growing conditions.

**Metamorphosis:** The process of significant changes in form that some insects and other animals undergo as they mature and develop.

**Microclimate:** A small part of the overall climate that differs from it, often defined by topography.

**Micropyle:** The passageway through the integument of an ovule.

**Microsporangium:** A sporangium producing only microspores.

**Microspore:** A spore that develops into a male gametophyte.

**Microspore mother cell:** See **microsporocyte**.

**Microsporocyte:** A diploid cell that produces microspores following meiosis; also called the microspore mother cell.

**Microsporophyll:** A leaf or leaflike structure bearing one or more microsporangia.

**Microstrobilus** (*pl.* **microstrobili**): A microspore-producing strobilus; a male cone.

**Mollisols:** A soil classification, with members typically dark and rich in nutrients and found in semi-humid prairie areas. These soils result from podzolization and some calcification.

**Monocot:** A shortened term for monocotyledon.

**Monocotyledon:** A plant whose seeds have only one cotyledon or seed leaf.

**Monoculture:** In farming, the cultivation of a single crop. Invasive plants often form monocultures by crowding out other species.

**Monoecious:** Said of species with both sexes on the same plant; however, the male and female structures are in separate, unisexual flowers.

**Morphology:** The study of form and structure; a branch of biology.

**Mucro:** A short, abrupt, sharp tip or spur.

**Mucronate:** Of a leaf, having a sharp point (mucro) formed by a continuation of the midvein.

**Mulch:** A covering applied on top of the soil around plants to conserve moisture, moderate soil temperature, inhibit weed growth, and reduce erosion or soil compaction. Popular mulches are bulky organic substances, such as wood chips, bark chips, compost, and leaf mold, that supply nutrients to the soil as they decompose. Inorganic substances, such as gravel, marble chips, and black plastic, can also be used as mulch.

**Muskeg:** A sphagnum bog in the boreal forest.

**Mutualism:** An obligate interaction between organisms that requires contributions from both organisms and in which both benefit.

**Mycorrhizae:** Fungi connected to a plant via haustoria. Mycorrhizae efficiently absorb nutrients from the soil, channeling some to the host plant.

**Myophily:** Pollination by flies.

**Myrmecochory:** Dispersal by ants.

**Myrmecophily:** Pollination by ants.

**Native species:** An indigenous plant; a plant meeting certain criteria of location and time. A North American native species is generally defined as one found growing on a particular site under a given set of environmental conditions, approximately 150 to 200 years ago, before plants were massively displaced or introduced by European immigrants. Compare **exotic species**.

**Neck canal:** The liquid-filled passageway of the archegonia of certain bryophytes.

**Nitrogen fixation:** The conversion of inorganic, atmospheric nitrogen into an organic form usable by plants. Nitrogen fixation, occurring in the roots of leguminous plants, is made possible by bacteria that live symbiotically in nodules on the roots and absorb nitrogen gas and convert it directly to a form usable by plants.

**Nodule:** A small swelling, as on the roots of members of the bean family, that acts as a connection between the plant and either bacteria or fungi.

**Nonnative species:** See **exotic species**.

**Northern coniferous forest:** See **boreal forest**.

**NPK:** Refers to the three primary plant nutrients—nitrogen (N), phosphorus (P), and potassium (K). The NPK ratio is used by the fertilizer industry to grade packaged fertilizers.

**Nutrient cycle:** The movement of carbon, oxygen, hydrogen, and nitrogen and other chemicals, in which plants convert energy of the sun and atmospheric carbon into biomass through photosynthesis.

**Nymph:** The immature stage of certain insects, including aphids, leafhoppers, earwigs, thrips, and scales. Nymphs and adult insects resemble each other and have similar feeding habits.

**Obcordate:** Heart-shaped; notched at the apex (tip) like the top of a heart, as some leaves. Compare **cordate.**

**Oblique:** Having a base that is not symmetrical on both sides, as some leaves.

**Oblong:** One and a half to two times longer than wide, as some leaves. Similar to elliptic but leaf margins are parallel, not curved.

**Obtuse:** Tapering to a blunt point at the base (bottom) or apex (tip), as some leaves and petals.

**Old field:** A stage in a sequence of ecological communities from farmland (that was once forest) back to forest. Succeeding a meadow, an old field is an extremely rich, floriferous blend of trees, shrubs, and herbaceous species particularly favored by wildlife.

**Opposite:** Borne across from one another at the same node; paired. Maples have opposite leaves.

**Organic:** Derived from live or dead plants and animals.

**Organic fertilizer:** Generally accepted as any fertilizer derived from plants, animals, or minerals.

**Organic matter:** Living and once-living plants and animals in varying states of decomposition.

**Organic pest management (OPM):** The name given to integrated pest management (IPM) when the use of synthetic pesticides is omitted. See **integrated pest management (IPM).**

**Ornithogamy:** Pollination by birds.

**Orthotropic:** Characterized by vertical growth.

**Ovary:** The typically enlarged basal portion of the pistil that encloses the ovule(s).

**Ovate:** One and a half to two times longer than wide. Shaped like an egg, as some leaves. Leaf margins are symmetrically curved, and the leaf is widest below the middle.

**Ovule:** The egg-containing structure within the ovary that develops, after fertilization, into the seed.

**Ovuliferous scale:** An ovule-bearing appendage on a megastrobilus.

**Oxisols:** A soil classification, with members typically highly weathered and often red, yellow, or gray. Resulting from laterization, these soils are found in tropical and subtropical regions.

**Palmate:** Like the spread fingers of a hand radiating out from a common point. Palmate leaves are compound with three or more leaflets.

**Parthenocarpy:** The formation of fruit without fertilization.

**Pathogen:** Any organism capable of causing disease.

**Pectinate:** Of a leaf, with close, regularly spaced lobes like the teeth of a comb. The same as pinnatifid but with more numerous, straighter, and narrower lobes.

**Pedate:** Of a leaf, similar to palmate, but the lateral lobes are further dissected.

**Pedicel:** The portion of "stalk" that supports a single flower in an inflorescence made up of more than one flower.

**Peduncle:** The "stalk" that supports a solitary flower or an inflorescence.

**Peltate:** Of a leaf, borne on a stalk attached to the lower surface rather than to the base or margin of the leaf.

**Perennial:** A plant that persists for a number of growing seasons. See also **hemicryptophyte.**

**Perfect:** Said of flowers having both stamens and pistils.

**Perfoliate:** With the bases of two opposite leaves fused around the stem, so that the stem appears to pass through the leaf.

**Perianth:** The collective term for all the sepals and petals surrounding the stamens and pistils in a flower (that is, the calyx and corolla) in angiosperms.

**Pericarp:** The fruit wall, often composed of three layers: epicarp, mesocarp, and endocarp.

**Pericarpium:** A fruit formed solely from the ovary, such as a drupe, capsule, or samara.

**Perigynous:** With the perianth (sepals and petals) and androecium (male parts) fused at the base so that the sepals, petals, and stamens appear to arise from the rim of a floral cup (the hypanthium).

**Perlite:** Sterile, white volcanic substance added to some growing media to aid aeration.

**Petal:** A frequently conspicuously colored component of the corolla in a flower.

**Petiole:** The stalk of a leaf.

**pH:** Potential hydrogen, which measures the amount and type of hydrogen ions in a soil solution. For gardeners, the pH number on a scale from 0 to 14 indicates the degree of acidity or alkalinity in the soil; pH 7 is neutral with numbers below measuring degrees of acidity and those above measuring alkalinity.

**Phalaenophily:** Pollination by moths.

**Phanerophyte:** A woody or herbaceous evergreen perennial, taller than 20 inches, whose shoots do not die back, such as trees and shrubs. The term comes from Raunkiaer's plant classification system.

**Phloem:** The living, thin-walled cells in a plant's vascular system that transport food to the roots and the stem.

**Photoperiodism:** The effect on the growth and flowering of a plant of the relative lengths of alternating periods of lightness and darkness.

**Photosynthesis:** A process in which energy from sunlight is converted in chlorophyll-containing cells of green plants into chemical energy and used to produce carbohydrates.

**Phototropic:** Growing toward light.

**Phylloclade:** A flattened, green stem with small, scalelike leaves that looks and even functions as a leaf.

**Phyllode:** A broadened, leaflike petiole with no true lamina or leaf blade.

**Phylogeny:** the study of the evolution of organisms and how they are related to each other through evolution.

**Physical controls:** Gardening techniques such as the use of traps, barriers like row covers and collars, and selective pruning, used to combat pests and monitor pest levels.

**Pinching:** Removing the growing tip or terminal bud with a single pinch just above a leaf or pair of leaves, most often performed on herbaceous plants to encourage a bushy, compact habit. Pinching is also a technique for managing new growth, called candles, on pines. Compare **candling.**

**Pinnate:** Aligned in pairs along opposite sides of a central axis. Pinnately compound leaves have leaflets set along both sides of a single stalk, or rachis; bipinnately compound leaves are pinnately divided again; and leaves that are tripinnate are pinnately compound a third time.

**Pinnatifid:** Of a leaf, pinnately lobed half the distance or more to the midrib, but not all the way to the midrib.

**Pistil:** A single female reproductive "unit"; a carpel, typically with a stigma, style, and ovary.

**Pistillate:** Said of female flowers; bearing one or more pistils, but without stamens.

**Pit:** The stony endocarp of a peach or other drupe.

**Pith:** A region of spongy, undifferentiated cells in the center of stems and branches of most angiosperms.

**Plagiotropic:** Characterized by horizontal growth.

**Plant community:** All the plant species that grow within a specific habitat or region.

**Plant community ecology:** The science that explores the processes that form and influence plant communities and the patterns of distribution within them.

**Plated bark:** With shallow, circular depressions.

**Pleaching:** The art of interweaving tree branches to form a wall with a flattened hedge contour or an arched canopy.

**Pneumatophores:** Almost hollow roots; found on plants in swampy areas in which there is not enough oxygen in the water for the root to survive—growing toward the water surface and then bending over to form a knob above the water, such as the knees of cypress (*Taxodium distichum*).

**Pocosin:** A swamp or marsh.

**Podzolization:** Also called spodsolization; a soil-forming process occurring in moist climates with variation in seasonal temperatures, during which winter temperatures slow the decomposition of organic matter in the upper soil layers. Typical vegetation is deciduous and coniferous forest.

**Pollarding:** The regular pruning of woody branches to keep trees within size bounds and to create a formal look.

**Pollen:** The spores or grains borne by the anther (in angiosperms) and the microsporangium (in gymnosperms) containing the male gametes.

**Pollen chamber:** The area where pollen grains are deposited, located at the apex of the megasporangium.

**Pollen grain:** The structure derived from a microspore that becomes a male gametophyte.

**Pollination:** The transfer of pollen grains to the stigma in angiosperms or the micropyle in gymnosperms.

**Pollination droplet:** A droplet of fluid involved in pollination, located at the micropyle.

**Pollinator:** Any agent responsible for, or assisting in, the transfer of pollen from the microsporangium to the micropyle in gymnosperms or the stigma in angiosperms.

**Pollinium:** A specialized cluster of pollen grains commonly encountered in milkweeds (Asclepiadaceae or the milkweed family) and orchids (Orchidaceae or the orchid family).

**Polyembryony:** Having more than one embryo in a seed.

**Polygamo-dioecious:** Polygamous, but primarily dioecious.

**Polygamo-monoecious:** Polygamous, but primarily monoecious.

**Polygamous:** Said of species having both imperfect (pistillate and/or staminate) flowers and perfect flowers on the same plants.

**Pome:** A fruit in which the hypanthium (a cup formed by the fusion of the sepals, petals, and stamens) becomes enlarged and fleshy, such as an apple.

**Prairie:** A type of grassland vegetation influenced by excessive summer heat, persistent winds, and low precipitation, such as found in the midcontinental United States. Typically flat or rolling land, prairies are covered with a mix of grasses with some native wildflowers.

**Predator:** An animal that preys on other animals and devours them for food.

**Pricking out:** The process of transplanting young seedlings to larger pots, trays, or flats to give them space to grow on.

**Prickle:** A sharp, spiny structure formed on the surface of a leaf or stem; similar to a spine, which is a modified stem, leaf, or root.

**Primary nutrients:** Term for the three nutrients that are depleted most rapidly from the soil by plants—nitrogen (N), phosphorus (P), and potassium (K). See **NPK.**

**Primary producer:** An organism able to manufacture its own food through photosynthesis or other chemical process. Plants are the primary producers in the nutrient cycle.

**Propagation:** The method of producing one plant from another, either with seed or vegetatively—that is, sexually or asexually.

**Prop roots:** Roots, generally adventitious, that act as support for a plant.

**Prophyll:** A modified leaf found at the first node of a shoot or at the base of a flower.

**Prothallus or prothallium (*pl.* prothalli):** The gametophyte plant of ferns.

**Protonema:** The threadlike or platelike precursor to the "leafy" gametophyte in bryophytes; the product of spore germination.

**Protoplasm:** The entire contents of a cell (that is, cytoplasm and nucleus).

**Psychophily:** Pollination by butterflies.

**Pteridophytes:** Ferns and fern allies: vascular, non-seedbearing plants.

**Ptyxis:** The folding of mature leaves.

**Pubescent:** Downy; with short, soft hairs.

**Pulvinus:** A swollen area at the base of a leaf petiole.

**Pupa (*pl.* pupae):** The stage of development between larva and adult of certain insects. Insects in the pupal stage do not feed but undergo dramatic changes, finally molting for the last time to become adults.

**Raceme:** An unbranched, elongated shoot with lateral flowers that mature from the bottom upward.

**Rachis:** The central stalk of a structure, as of a compound leaf or an inflorescence.

**Raised bed:** A planting bed elevated above ground level, surrounded and contained by walls of stone, brick, timber, cement block, etc. Raised beds can solve a number of problems, including poor drainage and compacted soil, and make gardening easier for persons with limited mobility.

**Ray:** The outermost flowers of a composite inflorescence. The rays often look like petals of a flower.

**Receptacle:** (1) The typically enlarged apex (tip) of the peduncle or pedicel where the various floral whorls are attached (that is, calyx, corolla, stamens, pistils); (2) the fertile regions on fern fronds that bear sporangia.

**Rejuvenation:** Revitalizing a tree or shrub through severe pruning in which the main branches are cut back to force new growth.

**Retuse:** Slightly notched at the apex (tip), as some leaves and petals.

**Revolute:** Of a leaf, when the margins are curled under toward the underside.

**Rhexocarpic:** Said of a fruit that splits open to shed the seeds (for example, a capsule); a dehiscent fruit.

**Rhizoid:** A rootlike structure lacking xylem and phloem.

**Rhizomatous:** Having a rhizome.

**Rhizome:** A horizontal stem found underground. Rhizomes are distinguished from roots by the presence of nodes.

**Richness:** Said of species diversity, the measure of the number of different species in a specific area.

**Ridged bark:** With prominent, longitudinal ribs.

**Root-bound:** Said of container-grown plants with roots that completely fill the pot, circling around and through the soil. Root-bound plants do not transplant well.

**Root cutting:** A portion of root that can be propagated into a new plant. The optimum time to take root cuttings is when a plant is dormant.

**Root hairs:** Small, hairlike projections from the epidermis or outermost layer of a root. Most absorption of water and nutrients occurs via root hairs.

**Roots:** Plant parts that can bear other roots and stems but never leaves. Roots anchor a plant to a site, absorb water and nutrients from the soil, store nutrients, and support bacteria or fungal hyphae, which work with the root to the benefit of both organisms.

**Rosette:** A dense configuration of leaves radiating from a crown, usually at or close to ground level.

**Rosulate:** Arranged in a basal rosette, with little or no stem.

**Rotate:** Wheel-shaped.

**Row cover:** A protection, created from lightweight synthetic fabric either resting directly on rows of plants or supported on thin wire hoops, that allows enough air, light, and water to reach crops but also traps warmth and keeps insects out.

**Runner:** A thin, horizontal stem found above ground with a rosette of leaves at the end. Compare **stolon.**

**Runoff:** Precipitation that flows over the soil surface into streams.

**Saccate:** With an enlarged, pouchlike appendage.

**Sagittate:** With a downwardly pointed lobe on each side of the base, as some leaves. Arrowhead-shaped.

**Saltmarsh:** A nutrient-rich coastal wetland, found in estuaries and backwaters, behind barrier beaches, and along bays and inlets, subjected to twice-daily tidal water-level fluctuations and dominated by grasses.

**Salverform:** Trumpet-shaped.

**Samara:** A simple, dry, indehiscent fruit with wings.

**Sand:** A rock-derived component of soil with easily visible particles that run from fine to coarse. The sand content in a soil helps determine its texture. Moderate proportions of sand in a soil provide excellent drainage and good aeration.

**Sarcocarp:** Any internal fleshy layer of a fruit.

**Savannah:** A vegetation type characterized by grassland and scattered trees found in areas with long periods of drought, such as the oak savannahs of the Midwest. During the extended drought cycles, wildfire typically burns away the woody vegetation, and during wet cycles, the trees regrow and reseed.

**Scape:** A leafless stem arising at ground level and ending at the inflorescence. The term is equivalent to peduncle but only for plants with basal leaves.

**Scarification:** Method used to help break the dormancy of some seeds with extra thick seed coats, involving scratching or wearing down the thick covering.

**Schizocarp:** A dry, dehiscent fruit that forms from one ovary but breaks into two or more fruitlets, each containing seeds.

**Schizocarpic:** Said of dry, dehiscent fruits, called schizocarps.

**Scion:** The portion of stem or bud cut from trees or shrubs to be used for grafting.

**Sclerophyll:** A tough, stiff and usually evergreen leaf that has adapted to arid conditions and is often found on species growing in warm, comparatively dry climates.

**Secondary nutrients:** Term for calcium, magnesium, and sulfur, which are vital to plant health but not as quickly depleted from the soil as the primary nutrients.

**Seed:** Mature ovule composed of a seed coat, endosperm (starch or oil used to nourish the developing embryo), and embryo.

**Segment:** A division or portion of a leaf, petal, calyx, corolla, perianth, or fruit.

**Self-fertilization:** The union of sperm and egg from the same plant or flower.

**Self-fruitful:** Plants capable of producing fruit when pollinated with their own pollen.

**Self-pollination:** In angiosperms, the transfer of pollen from an anther to a stigma in the same flower or to a flower on the same plant.

**Self-sterile:** Fruit trees that need pollen from a different variety of the same kind of fruit in order to bear.

**Semihardwood cutting:** A stem cutting taken from some broadleaf and needled evergreens in autumn or early winter in order to propagate the plant vegetatively.

**Sepal:** A typically green, photosynthetic component of the calyx in a flower in angiosperms.

**Septum (*pl.* septa):** A partition; the region where two carpels are fused together.

**Sere:** The entire progression of seral stages, from the first one to colonize bare ground to the climax community; or, one stage in the progression.

**Serrate:** With teeth along the margin that are pointed upward toward the tip, as some leaves.

**Seta:** The stalklike structure between the foot and capsule in bryophytes.

**Sex cells:** See **gametes.**

**Sexual propagation:** The method of creating plants by seed. Sexually propagated plants reflect the characteristics of the parent plants, but each new plant is genetically unique.

**Sexual spore:** See **meiospore.**

**Shade cloth:** Synthetic fabric, usually providing from 30 to 90 percent protection from sunlight, used to protect heat-sensitive plants.

**Sheath:** A broadened petiole base that surrounds the stem, as the leaf base of grass.

**Short-day plant:** A species that requires exposure to short periods of light followed by relatively long periods of darkness to stimulate it to flower; for example, violets and strawberries.

**Shrub:** A woody plant that branches near the base and therefore has several trunks.

**Shrubland:** A vegetation type characterized by plant communities of shrubs and small, shrubby trees, as in the chaparral that covers large areas of California and the shrubby pinyon-juniper woodland of the Southwest and Great Basin.

**Shrub layer:** The level in a forest's or wooded environment's vertical structure situated between the under story and the ground layer, consisting of shrubs.

**Side-dressing:** The practice of applying dry fertilizer to the soil surface in strips beside rows of plants.

**Side-veneer grafting:** A grafting technique in which a scion is inserted into an opening in the side of the main stem of an understock, which is truncated once the graft takes.

**Simple layering:** A propagation method in which a flexible woody branch is bent to the ground, wounded a few inches behind the tip, and buried in a shallow hole until roots form and a new plant can be separated and transplanted.

**Simple leaf:** A leaf with only one lamina, or leaf blade.

**Single-nutrient:** A fertilizer that supplies only one of the three primary plant nutrients: nitrogen, phosphorus, or potassium. Compare **complete** and **balanced.**

**Slow release:** A fertilizer formulated to release its nutrients into the soil over an extended period of time.

**Smooth bark:** Without hair, glands, or roughness.

**Soaker hose:** Any hose designed to release water along its full length as spray or seepage through tiny holes; also called porous hoses.

**Softwood cutting:** A stem cutting taken from certain herbaceous plants, deciduous trees, and shrubs, and broadleaf evergreens when the stem is young, green, and flexible in order to propagate the plant vegetatively.

**Soil compaction:** Soil with structure damaged due to too much foot or heavy machinery traffic. Compacted soils are hard and impermeable.

**Soiless mix:** A sterile growing medium without soil.

**Sorus (*pl.* sori):** A group of sporangia in ferns.

**Spade:** A garden tool used for digging holes and ditches, cutting edges, and other chores. Like the shovel, the spade has a metal blade and wooden handle, but its handle is shorter and the blade is always rectangular and practically flat.

**Spadix (*pl.* spadices):** A spike with small flowers on a fleshy stem characteristic of jack-in-the-pulpit and other members of the Arum family.

**Spathe:** A large bract or leaf below and enclosing the inflorescence.

**Species (*pl.* species):** The basic category in plant classification, consisting of plants that share distinctive characteristics and are capable of breeding with each other.

**Species diversity:** The number and relative abundance of different species in a given area.

**Sperm:** A male gamete.

**Spermatogenous:** Sperm-producing.

**Sphagnum moss:** A kind of peat moss found in bogs in the Northern Hemisphere that holds water, drains well, and has certain antifungal properties. Sphagnum moss is available milled, generally used in cutting and seed media, and long-fibered, used for layering.

**Spike:** A raceme with unstalked flowers maturing from the bottom upward.

**Spine:** A modified stem (or leaf stipule, or root) that is sharp. *Opuntia* and other cacti have spines. The term "thorn" is a synonym.

**Spodosols:** A soil classification, with members typically light gray in color and common in eastern North America. These soils are the result of podzolization.

**Sporangium (*pl.* sporangia):** A structure in which spores are produced; also called a capsule.

**Spore:** A simple reproductive structure that is the product of cell meiosis in a sporangium; the first cell of the gametophyte generation.

**Spore mother cell:** See **sporocyte**.

**Sporocyte:** A diploid cell that undergoes meiosis to form four haploid spores or nuclei.

**Sporophyte:** The diploid phase of the plant reproductive cycle that produces spores.

**Spur:** Any hollow protuberance from a sepal or petal.

**Stamen:** The male reproductive structure of a flower made up of an anther and a filament.

**Staminate:** Said of male flowers; bearing stamens, but without pistils.

**Staminode:** A whorl of modified leaves just outside the stamens; a modified sterile stamen.

**Standard:** A plant with a single, vertical stem below a head of branches.

**Stellate:** With hairs that branch and look like small stars.

**Stem:** The portion of the plant, usually above ground, that bears leaves and flowers.

**Stem cutting:** A stem or portion of stem that can be rooted to develop a new plant. Many shrubs and trees can be propagated from softwood stem cuttings taken in spring or summer.

**Stigma:** Typically the apical (top) portion of a pistil receptive to pollen.

**Stipule:** A usually small growth, typically found in pairs, at the base of the leaf stalk, characteristic of a number of species. Often leaflike, but may be papery or even spinelike.

**Stolon:** A horizontally growing stem at ground level with leaves along its length (not just a rosette at the end, as in a runner) and adventitious roots that form at the nodes.

**Stoma (*pl.* stomata):** A minute opening or pore found in the epidermis of plant leaves and stems through which gases are exchanged.

**Stone:** The hardened endocarp of a peach or other drupe.

**Stratification:** Method used to help break the dormancy of some seeds controlled by temperature involving exposing the seed to cold or warm temperatures—sometimes a combination of both—plus moisture.

**Straw:** The stems of grain crops after they have been harvested. Compare **hay**.

**Strigose:** With long, stiff, flattened hairs.

**Strobilus** (*pl.* **strobili**): A cone; the reproductive structure of pines and other gymnosperms.

**Style:** The region of a pistil between the stigma and ovary; typically long and thin.

**Subsoil:** The layer of soil just below the topsoil and not nearly as hospitable to plant roots.

**Subspecies** (*pl.* **subspecies**): A subdivision of a species with characteristics that distinguish it from the species—usually geographically distinct and usually approaching species status.

**Subtending:** Situated below and close to a flower, as a bract, particularly when the bract is prominent.

**Succession:** The gradual changes in the composition of a plant community in a given area over time.

**Succulent:** Juicy and fleshy. The term is usually applied to plants with thick, swollen leaves or stems that enable them to survive in arid climates.

**Sucker:** (1) A shoot growing directly from the root or from the ground near the base of the plant; (2) a fast-growing upright branch generated in response to poor pruning and wounding.

**Superior:** With an ovary that sits primarily above the attachment point of the perianth (sepals and petals) and androecium (male parts).

**Swamp:** A wetland dominated by flood-tolerant woody vegetation, with soil that is inundated for all or part of the year. There are three main categories: shrub swamps, deciduous swamps, and coniferous swamps.

**Sweat box:** An enclosed greenhouselike environment made with clear plastic draped over a framework, designed to maintain high humidity for propagating some cuttings.

**Symbiotically:** Characterized by a long-running association of two or more dissimilar organisms, almost exclusively indicating a relationship that is mutually beneficial.

**Syngamy:** The fusion of gametes (egg and sperm).

**Synthetic:** Produced by a laboratory process; made artificially and not extracted from living organisms, as synthetic fertilizers. Compare **organic fertilizer.**

**Taiga:** See **boreal forest.**

**Taproot:** A primary root that has more or less enlarged and grown downward, like that of a carrot.

**Taxon** (*pl.* **taxa**): Any taxonomic entity, regardless of rank, including family, genus, and species.

**Taxonomy:** The science of classification of living organisms.

**Tendril:** A modified stem or leaf—found, for example, on vines—that grasps other plants and acts like a grappling hook.

**Tepal:** The term used for any single "unit" of the perianth when sepals and petals are morphologically similar.

**Ternate:** In threes; ternate leaves have three leaflets, and the terminal leaf is not stalked. Biternate leaves are doubly ternate with ternate divisions again ternately divided.

**Terrarium** (*pl.* **terraria**): A transparent, enclosed container, usually made of glass, used for growing and displaying moisture-loving plants.

**Therophyte:** Annual; or plant that dies after seed production and completes its entire life cycle within one year. The term comes from Raunkiaer's plant classification system.

**Thinning cut:** A pruning cut that takes branches back to their point of origin, to a branch union, or to the ground. Thinning cuts generally are made to open a plant to light and air without changing its natural shape or height. Compare **heading cut.**

**Throat:** The opening at the top of the tube in fused corollas.

**Tilth:** The condition of being workable or tilled.

**Tip layering:** A propagation method in which the current-season growth from bramble fruits and some other woody plants is bent to the ground and the branch tip buried; when a new plant grows it can be separated and transplanted.

**Tomentose:** Woolly; with long, soft, matted hairs.

**Top-dressing:** The practice of applying dry fertilizer or compost to surface soil around individual plants and allowing rain and irrigation to bring it to plant roots.

**Top grafting:** The cleft-and-saddle grafting technique performed on mature trees. Top-grafted apple trees can produce different varieties of apples on the same tree.

**Topiary:** The art of training and shearing plants into various shapes—ranging from traditional formal architectural and geometric to informal novelty forms.

**Topping:** Cutting back the main branches of a tree to a uniform height, a practice detrimental to a tree's health. Topping destroys a tree's beauty and shortens its life.

**Topsoil:** The uppermost layer of soil, which is relatively rich in organic matter and generally at least 6 inches or more deep, above the subsoil. The depth of topsoil is important as it sets limits on how deep most plant roots can penetrate.

**Transpiration:** The process by which a portion of the water absorbed by the roots of plants is returned to the atmosphere—released as water vapor through the stomata, the gas-exchange pores found in plant leaves and stems.

**Tree:** A woody plant with a single or few trunks near the base.

**Trichome:** A hair or bristle growing from a plant's epidermis.

**Trifoliate:** Leaves with three leaflets and in which the terminal leaflet is stalked.

**Trowel:** A garden tool with a handle and small, shovellike blade or scoop, used for planting, transplanting, and moving soil in garden beds and containers.

**Truncate:** Having a base that is squared off at the ends, as if cut off, as on some leaves.

**Tube:** The tubelike structure where the petals are united at the bottom of fused corollas.

**Tuber:** An underground, swollen stem, such as the potato.

**Tuberous root:** A swollen root in which nutrients (usually starch) are stored for the parent plant, such as those of dahlias and yams (*Dioscorea*).

**Tubular:** Cylindrical, as some corollas.

**Tundra:** Land where the ground stays frozen year-round, except for a thin layer at the surface—with too hostile a climate for trees to grow.

**Turkey grit:** Small, speckled granite pebbles, often applied as an inorganic mulch.

**Umbel:** A flat-topped inflorescence in which the pedicels all originate from a single point, much like the struts of an umbrella.

**Understock:** The plant base onto which a scion is grafted. Dwarf fruit trees are created when a scion is grafted to an understock with a dwarf habit. Sometimes called rootstock.

**Understory:** The second highest level in a forest's or wooded environment's vertical structure, consisting of the leaves and branches of the lower trees; under the canopy.

**Undulate:** With a wavy margin, as on some leaves and petals.

**Unisexual:** Strictly male or female plants or flowers; if an entire plant has flowers of only one sex, another related term is dioecious; if a flower is unisexual, it is also imperfect and incomplete.

**Upland:** Situated on high land, above flood level.

**Urceolate:** Urn-shaped, as some corollas.

**Utisols:** A soil classification, with members characterized by intense leaching and weathering and containing a large proportion of clay. Formed by podzolization, these soils are found in warm climates of the southeastern United States.

**Valve:** One of the parts of a pericarp (fruit wall) that is separated by dehiscence and splits at maturity.

**Variegated:** Having diversified coloration on leaves, often in stripes, along margins, or mottled.

**Variety:** A subdivision of a species with similar, common characteristics, traditionally used to denote taxa that are approaching species but have not yet reached species status. Variety and subspecies are often used interchangeably.

**Vascular parasite:** Nongreen plant growing on living, green plants, such as Indian pipe (*Monotropa uniflora*). The term comes from Raunkiaer's plant classification system.

**Vascular semiparasite:** Green plant growing attached to other living, green plants. Many plants, such as the eastern North American native gerardia (*Agalinis purpurea*), photosynthesize but also supplement their nutrients by parasitizing other plants. The term comes from Raunkiaer's plant classification system.

**Vascular tissue:** The ring or series of bundles surrounding the pith that contains the cells (xylem and phloem) that transport fluids and nutrients in plant stems.

**Vegetation:** All the plants growing in an area, particularly the mosaic of plant communities that covers the region, emphasizing the kinds of forest, grasslands, deserts, etc. Compare **flora.**

**Vegetation association:** A more or less distinct vegetation subtype within a formation, such as the tallgrass, shortgrass, and mixed-grass prairies of the Midwest and Plains states.

**Vegetative propagation:** Asexual propagation, most often by cuttings or division, not by seed. New plants created through vegetative propagation are genetically identical to the parent.

**Vegetative reproduction:** Asexual reproduction without syngamy, the fusion of gametes (egg and sperm). Plants created through vegetative reproduction are genetically identical to the parent.

**Vermicomposting:** A process of composting in which worms are the agents of decomposition, generally of organic kitchen scraps.

**Vermiculite:** Expanded mica added to some growing media to promote water retention.

**Vernalization:** The process of shortening the growth period of a plant, usually by exposing it to cold. The young plants of some species—biennials, for example—require a period of exposure to cold in order to flower. Gardeners must mimic the cold winters of hardy bulbs' native habitats by exposing them to cold temperatures in order to force them to bloom indoors.

**Vernation:** The disposition of leaves in the leaf bud.

**Vertical structure:** Within a plant community, the pattern of growth based on the size and growth pattern of the dominant species. The vertical structure of a forest consists of the canopy, understory, shrub layer, and ground layer. Also called vertical layering.

**Vertisols:** A soil classification, with members typically exhibiting deep, wide cracks when dry. These dark clay soils are formed by invertization and found, for example, in Texas.

**Villous:** Shaggy; with long, soft, unmatted hairs.

**Viscid:** Sticky.

**Warm-season crop:** A cold-sensitive crop. Warm-season crops cannot be safely sown or transplanted without protection until the risk of frost has passed.

**Water cycle:** The movement of water through the environment, involving condensation, precipitation, runoff, transpiration, and evaporation.

**Watershed:** The catchment basin or total land area from which a body of water receives drainage and thus collects water.

**Wetlands:** Regions of very wet soils that support special vegetation types, most commonly marshes, bogs, swamps, and saltmarshes. Wetlands take up excess water unleashed by storms and release it slowly, thereby reducing or eliminating flooding, and they filter and break down pollutants and replenish aquifers.

**Wet meadow:** The zone where wetland grades into upland, which is characterized by periods of wet and dry and may be dominated by either herbaceous plants or shrubs and trees.

**Whip-and-tongue grafting:** A grafting technique in which the scion and the truncated understock are joined by aligning matching-angled tongue cuts.

**Whorl:** A ring of three or more leaves, flowers, or other organs arising from a common node or point.

**Whorled:** With three or more leaves at the same node; arranged in whorls.

**Wings:** One of two lateral petals of the flower of some plants in the pea family.

**Xeric:** Dry; low in or without available moisture for the support of plants. Compare **mesic** and **hydric.**

**Xeriscaping:** Water-conserving landscaping that involves growing drought-tolerant plants, installing low-volume irrigation systems, and designing gardens zoned according to water needs; evolved in the desert Southwest.

**Xylem:** Specialized tissue in the plant's vascular system for conducting water and dissolved nutrients upward from the roots to the leaves.

**Zoophily:** Pollination by animals.

**Zygomorphic:** Bilaterally symmetrical. When looking down on a zygomorphic corolla or calyx, you can see only one bisecting line that can cut the flower in equal halves.

**Zygote:** The diploid cell resulting from syngamy, the fusion of an egg and sperm.

# INDEX

*Abelia,* 484, 509
    *chinensis,* 310
    'Edward Goucher', 316
    x *grandiflora,* 360, 365, 381,
        514; 'Compacta', 381
abelias (*Abelia*), 484, 509
*Abelmoschus esculentus,* 244,
    354
*Abies,* 485
    *amabilis,* 190
    *balsamea,* 166, 334
    *bracteata,* 305, 383
    *concolor,* 304, 377, 380, 514;
        'Candicans', 304
    *fraseri,* 7
    *lasiocarpa,* 170
abnormal growth, forms of,
    69
*Abronia,* 209; *macrocarpa,* 126
*Abrus precatorius,* 647
absinthe (*Artemisia absinthium*),
    137
*Abutilon:*
    *eremitopetalum,* 128
    *menziesii,* 128
    x *hybridum,* 317, 500, 522,
        595; 'Little Imp', 317;
        'White Parasol', 317
*Acacia,* 45, 82, 367, 486;
    *angustissima,* 343, 363; *auri-*
        *culiformis,* 152; *constricta,* 307;
    *farnesiana,* 307; *melanoxylon,*
    137; *minuta,* 383; *redolens:*
    'Desert Carpet', 345; *salicina,*
    307; *smallii,* 307; *stenophylla,*
    307; *wrightii,* 303, 337
acacias (*Acacia*), 486
*Acaena exigua,* 131

*Acalypha wilkensiana,* 336, 337
*Acanthomintha duttonii,* 126
*Acanthus: mollis,* 486; *spinosa,*
    329
*Acatea,* 189
*Acer,* 477, 484
    *barbatum,* 302
    *buergerianum,* 298, 536
    *campestre,* 304, 514, 609
    *carpinifolium,* 298; 'Esveld',
        298
    *circinatum,* 190, 191, 201,
        202, 305, 306
    *ginnala,* 137, 304
    *glabrum,* 190, 202, 304, 364,
        381, 382
    *glabrum* subsp. *douglasii,* 190
    *grandidentatum,* 302, 304
    *griseum,* 13, 298, 305, 377,
        378, 382
    *japonicum,* 305; 'Aconiti-
        folium', 305
    *leucoderme,* 299
    *macrophyllum,* 202
    *negundo,* 108, 220, 221, 224,
        225, 226; 'Flamingo', 338
    *palmatum,* 13, 298, 299, 305,
        306, 315, 500, 536;
        'Atropurpureum', 315;
        'Bloodgood', 298; 'Crimson
        Queen', 334; 'Dissectum',
        334; 'Ever Red', 334; 'Fili-
        gree', 334; 'Garnet', 315,
        334; 'Hessei', 298; 'Red
        Filigree Lace', 334; 'San-
        gokaku', 298, 376; 'Seiryu',
        305; 'Shigitatsu Sawa',
        298; 'Waterfall', 315

    *pensylvanicum,* 298, 376;
        'Erythrocladum', 376
    *platanoides,* 137, 186
    *pseudoplatanus,* 609
    *rubrum,* 13, 161, 167, 168,
        200, 201, 297, 299, 301,
        304, 381, 477; 'Red Sun-
        set', 304; *trilobum,* 199; var.
        *trilobum,* 300
    *saccharinum,* 167, 200, 477;
        'Wieri', 338
    *saccharum,* 166, 167, 187,
        189, 297, 379, 391; subsp.
        *leucoderme,* 188
    *shirasawanum* 'Aureum', 333,
        338
    *spicatum,* 301, 308
    *tataricum,* 304
    *triflorum,* 305
acerola (*Malpighia glabra*),
    284
*Acerphyllum rossii,* 329
achene, 91, 92
*Achillea,* 321, 322, 330, 359,
    365, 366, 372
    *clypeolata,* 329; 'Moonshine',
        329
    'Coronation Gold', 322
    *filipendulina,* 324, 325, 373,
        498
    'King George', 330
    *millefolium,* 108, 220, 221,
        224, 225, 228, 229, 265,
        324, 327, 328, 330, 331,
        356, 363, 365, 373, 374,
        382, 470; 'Summer Pas-
        tels', 356
    'Moonshine', 330

    *ptarmica,* 470
    *taygetea,* 332, 375; 'Moon-
        shine', 332
achimenes (*Achimenes longiflora*),
    585
*Achimenes longiflora,* 585
*Achyranthes tollensis,* 131
acidanthera (*Acidanthera bicolor*),
    321
*Acidanthera bicolor,* 321
*Acoelorraphe wrightii,* 199, 301
aconite (*Aconitum napellus*),
    647–48
*Aconitum,* 324; *napellus,* 647–
    48
*Acorus: calamus,* 197, 200, 201,
    264, 336; *gramineus* 'Ogon',
    379
*Acrostichum danaeifolium,* 335
*Actaea: alba,* 187, 188; *pachy-*
    *poda,* 187, 188, 362; *rubra,*
    190, 191, 362
*Actinidia,* 13, 270, 282, 283;
    *arguta,* 349; *chinensis,* 347;
    *deliciosa,* 352; *kolomikta,* 333,
    346, 347, 348, 349, 351
actinidia vine (*Actinidia
    kolomikta*), 351
acuminate leaf apex, 81
acute leaf apex, 81
acute leaf base, 77, 78
Adam's needle (*Yucca filamen-
    tosa*), 216, 321, 486
Adanson, Michel, 3
*Adenostoma fasciculatum,* 170,
    215
*Adiantum:*
    *capillus-veneris,* 188, 336

*Adiantum (cont'd)*:
  *pedatum*, 187, 189, 191, 202,
    203, 325, 329, 339; var.
    *aleuticum*, 190
*Adonophorus periens*, 128
*Aechmea*, 324, 342; *mexicana*,
  335
*Aegopodium podagraria*, 341, 344;
  'Variegata', 341
aerator, 619
aerial roots, 69–70
*Aesculus*, 477, 486; *arguta*, 303;
  *californica*, 216, 305, 307;
  *glabra*, 225, 226, 304; *hippocastanum*, 13, 648, 675;
  *octandra*, 303; *parviflora*, 188,
  315, 481; *pavia*, 108, 187,
  188, 189, 220, 222, 225,
  299; x *carnea*, 304
*Aethionema* 'Warley Rose', 604
Africa: climatic conditions in,
  24; public gardens in, 633–34
African bush daisy (*Gamolepis
  chrysanthemoides*), 342
African daisy (*Arctotis*), 358
African daisy (*Arctotis stoechadifolia*), 357, 496
African daisy (*Arctotis venusta*),
  354
African daisy (*Dimorphotheca sinuata*), 358
African gardenia (*Mitriostigma
  axillare*), 591
African marigold (*Tagetes erecta*),
  355, 356, 373
African sumac (*Rhus lancea*),
  306
African violet (*Saintpaulia ionantha*), 572, 592
*Agalinis acuta*, 126; *calycina*,
  131
*Agapanthus*, 331, 401
  *africanus*, 323; 'Storm Cloud',
    375
  *praecox*, 585
  x 'Peter Pan', 366
agapanthus (*Agapanthus praecox*),
  585
agapetes (*Agapetes serpens*), 500
*Agapetes serpens*, 500
*Agarista (Leucothoe) populifolia*,
  188, 197, 309
agarito (*Mahonia trifoliata*), 313
*Agastache*, 340, 498; *cana*, 333,
  364, 367, 375; *foeniculum*,
  253, 336, 374; *rupestris*, 332
agastaches (*Agastache*), 498
*Agave*, 169, 339, 384; *americana*,
  339; *attenuata*, 323; *deserti*,
  169; *lechuguilla*, 169
Agaves (*Agave*), 169
ageratum (*Ageratum
  houstonianum*), 354, 355
*Ageratum houstonianum*, 354, 355

*Aglaonemas*, 572
*Agloanema modestum*, 323
*Agropyron*, 169; *smithii*, 169,
  208; *spicatum*, 208
*Agrostemma githago*, 357
*Ailanthus altissima*, 137, 684
air layering, 488–89
*Ajuga reptans*, 341, 342, 343,
  344; 'Catlin's Giant', 345
*Akebia*: *quinata*, 281, 282, 347,
  351, 484; *trifoliata*, 347
akebia (*Akebia trifoliata*), 347
akebia (*Akebia quinata*), 281,
  282, 347
Alabama, 438, 621, 665, 694,
  695, 697–98
Alabama leather-flower (*Clematis
  socialis*), 126
alani (*Melicope paniculata*), 132
Alaska, 438, 694, 695, 698
Alberta spruce (*Picea glauca* var.
  *albertiana*), 501, 520
*Albizia julibrissin*, 10
*Alcea rosea*, 365, 366, 367, 368,
  369
*Alchemilla mollis*, 258, 328, 370
alcohol for pest control, 546
alder buckthorn (*Rhamnus frangula*), 138
alders (*Alnus*), 161, 484
alecost (*Tanacetum balsamita*),
  256
Aleppo pine (*Pinus halepensis*),
  307
*Aletris*: *farinosa*, 198; *lutea*, 199
Aleutian maidenhair fern (*Adiantum pedatum* var. *aleuticum*),
  190
Alexandrian laurel (*Danae racemosa*), 310, 379
alfalfa (*Medicago sativa*), 70–71,
  359
algerita (*Mahonia fremontii*), 384
algerita (*Mahonia haematocarpa*),
  318, 367
algerita (*Mahonia trifoliata*), 313
*Alisma plantago-aquatica*, 200,
  201
Alismatidae, 59
alkaloids, 642
alkanet (*Brunnera macrophylla*),
  328
*Allamanda*: *cathartica*, 311; *neriifolia*, 310; *schottii*, 310
allamanda (*Allamanda cathartica*), 311
allamanda (*Allamanda schottii*),
  310
Allegheny pachysandra
  (*Pachysandra procumbens*), 188
Allegheny serviceberry (*Amelanchier laevis*), 304, 305
Allegheny spurge (*Pachysandra
  procumbens*), 341, 342, 343

alligator-bark juniper (*Juniperus
  deppeana*), 215
alligator flag (*Thalia geniculata*),
  200
alligator lily (*Hymenocallis
  palmeri*), 199
alligator weed (*Alternanthera
  philoxeroides*), 137
Allion speedwell (*Veronica
  allionii*), 344
*Allium*, 359, 371, 394, 496,
  583; *aflatunense*, 320, 371,
  374; *cepa*, 240–41; *cernuum*,
  207; *moly*, 320; *porrum*, 240;
  *sativum*, 239, 257, 674;
  *schoenoprasum*, 255, 365, 580;
  *sphaerocephalum*, 320, 371; *stellatum*, 326; *thunbergii*,
  398–99; *tuberosum*, 345
allspice (*Pimenta dioica*), 300
almond (*Amygdalus communis*),
  671–72
*Alnus*, 161, 484; *glutinosa*, 609;
  *incana* subsp. *rugosa*, 200;
  *rhombifolia*, 202; *rubra*, 190;
  *sinuata*, 382; *tenuifolia*, 304,
  381, 382
*Alocasia* x *amazonica*, 323
*Aloe*, 45, 324
aloe (*Aloe*), 45, 324
*Aloysia*: *gratissima*, 108, 227; *triphylla*, 259, 339
Alpine currant (*Ribes alpinum*),
  315
Alpine fleabane (*Erigeron alpinus*), 604
alpine tundra, 145, 166
*Alpinia*:
  *purpurata*, 372
  *zerumbet*, 323, 335, 372, 401,
    589; 'Variegata', 336
*Alsinidendron*: *obovatum*, 128;
  *trinerve*, 128
*Alstroemeria*, 375; *aurea*, 330
*Alternanthera philoxeroides*, 137
alternate leaf arrangement, 82,
  83
alternation of generations, sexual
  reproduction by, 96
althea (*Hibiscus syriacus*), 368
aluminum plant (*Pilea cadierei*),
  342
alum root (*Heuchera micrantha*),
  203, 331
alum root (*Heuchera richardsonii*),
  207
*Alygyne huegelii*, 317; 'Mood
  Indigo', 317
*Alyssum saxatile*, 330, 340
*Amanita*, 662–63; *muscaria*, 663
amanita mushrooms (*Amanita*),
  662–63
*Amaranthus*: *canadensis*, 357; *caudatus*, 368, 371; *hypochondria-*

*cus* 'Erythrostachys', 371; *tricolor*, 355
Amargosa niterwort (*Nitrophila
  mohavensis*), 127
amaryllis (*Hippeastrum*), 403,
  585–86
Amazon elephant's ear (*Alocasia
  x amazonica*), 323
Amazon lily (*Eucharis* x *grandiflora*), 402, 586
*Ambrosia*, 169; *eriocentra*, 169
*Amelanchier*, 45, 187, 189, 190,
  281, 282, 283, 284, 360,
  362, 379, 477, 510
  *alnifolia*, 190, 312, 314, 364,
    365; 'Regent', 312
  *arborea*, 298, 500
  *canadensis*, 315
  *laevis*, 196, 302, 304, 305
  *stolonifera*, 189, 314
  *utahensis*, 367
  x *grandiflora*, 299; 'Autumn
    Brilliance', 299
American andromeda (*Pieris
  floribunda*), 377
American arborvitae (*Thuja occidentalis*), 298
American ash (*Fraxinus americana*), 305
American beautyberry (*Callicarpa americana*), 310, 311,
  312, 313, 361, 363
American beech (*Fagus
  americana*), 514
American beech (*Fagus grandifolia*), 167, 299
American bittersweet (*Celastrus
  scandens*), 346, 349, 351, 359
American chestnut (*Castanea
  dentata*), 124, 146, 167
American columbine (*Aquilegia
  canadensis*), 319
American cranberry bush (*Viburnum opulus* var. *americanum*),
  314, 315
American cranberry bush (*Viburnum trilobum*), 190, 196
American dogwood (*Cornus
  stolonifera*), 202
American elderberry (*Sambucus
  canadensis*), 196, 315
American elm (*Ulmus americana*),
  72, 148, 303
American filbert (*Corylus americana*), 381
American germander (*Teucrium
  canadense*), 327
American germander (*Teucrium
  canadense* var. *canadense*), 374
American ginseng (*Panax quinquefolius*), 124
American holly (*Ilex opaca*), 187,
  189, 299, 360, 377, 379,
  501, 514

American hornbeam (*Carpinus caroliniana*), 189

American Horticultural Society, 135

American lily-of-the-valley shrub (*Pieris floribunda*), 377

American linden (*Tilia americana*), 304

American lotus (*Nelumbo lutea*), 197, 198, 201

American mountain ash (*Sorbus americana*), 302, 304

American pennyroyal (*Hedeoma pulegioides*), 261

American plum (*Prunus americana*), 189, 302, 314, 364

American pussy willow (*Salix discolor*), 359

American smoke tree (*Cotinus obovatus*), 189, 298, 301, 302, 303, 500

American sweetgum (*Liquidambar styraciflua*), 305

American sycamore (*Platanus occidentalis*), 377

American white birch (*Betula papyrifera*), 377

American wisteria (*Wisteria frutescens*), 346, 347, 348, 350, 351

American wisteria (*Wisteria macrostachya*), 346

amethyst flower (*Browallia speciosa*), 357

*Ammobium alatum*, 373

*Ammophila breviligulata*, 168, 216

*Amomum compactum*, 323

*Amorpha*: *canescens*, 207, 208, 226, 314, 364, 365; *fruticosa*, 313, 367, 373

*Amorphophallus*, 324

*Ampelopsis*: *arborea*, 199; *brevipedunculata*, 137

*Amsinckia grandiflora*, 126

*Amsonia*: *ciliata*, 326; *hubrechtii*, 335; *kearneyana*, 126; *tabernaemontana*, 320, 322, 325

amsonia (*Amsonia tabernaemontana*), 320

amur chokeberry (*Prunus amurensis*), 379

amur chokeberry (*Prunus maackii*), 302, 304

amur cork tree (*Phellodendron amurense*), 302, 486

amur maackia (*Maackia amurensis*), 298, 377, 501

amur maple (*Acer ginnala*), 137, 304

amur peatree (*Maackia amurensis*), 298

amur silver grass (*Miscanthus sacchariflorus*), 138

amur silver grass (*Miscanthus sinensis*), 138

*Amygdalus communis*, 671–72

*Anagallis arvensis*, 683

*Ananas comosus*, 284

*Anaphalis margaritacea*, 328, 371, 374, 382

*Anchusa*, 486; *capensis*, 357

anchusa (*Anchusa capensis*), 357

androecium, 86, 104, 106

*Andromeda*, 45 *glaucophylla*, 201 *polifolia*, 312, 485; 'Nana', 312; var. *glaucophylla*, 200

andromeda (*Leucothoe populifolia*), 197

andromedas (*Pieris*), 485

*Andropogon*, 337; *gerardii*, 168, 169, 206, 207; *glomeratus*, 198, 326, 373, 378, 380; *virginicus*, 206, 216, 360, 378

*Anemone*, 135, 394, 583 *canadensis*, 189, 190, 371 *hupehensis*, 7 *hybrida*, 329, 330; 'September Charm', 329 *japonica*, 319 *lancifolia*, 188 *nemorosa*, 325, 329 *patens*, 190, 208, 604 *pulsatilla*, 329 *ranunculoides*, 325 x *hybrida*, 322, 374; 'Alba', 375

*Anemonella thalictroides, see Thalictrum thalictroides*

anemones (*Anemone*), 135

*Anemopsis californica*, 203, 345

*Anethum graveolens*, 256, 334, 360, 498, 580

*Angelica*: *archangelica*, 252; *venenosa*, 188

angelica (*Angelica archangelica*), 252

angelita daisy (*Hymenoxys acaulis*), 333

angel's trumpet (*Brugmansia*), 316, 594

angel's trumpet (*Brugmansia versicolor*), 311, 500

angel's trumpet (*Brugmansia x candida*), 311

angel's trumpet (*Datura inoxia*), 487

angel's wand (*Dierama pulcherrimum*), 330

angiosperms: about, 104 propagating, 110 sexual reproduction of, 104–10; the flower, 104–106; the fruit and, 110; pollination, 106–109

*Anigozanthos flavidus*, 330, 366

Animalia kingdom, 51

animals, 176–79; gardening for wildlife, 217–31, 358–67; herbivore-plant relationships, 176–77; as pests, 564–65; pollination by, 107–109, 177–78; seed dispersal by, 93, 178. *see also specific animals*

*Anisacanthus*: *quadrifidus* var. *wrightii*, 313; *thurberi*, 109, 228, 367

anise (*Myrrhis odorata*), 334

anise (*Pimpinella anisum*), 252

anise hyssop (*Agastache foeniculum*), 253, 374

*Anisodontea* x *hypomandarum*, 317

*Annona glabra*, 199

annual lobelia (*Lobelia erinus*), 356

annual phlox (*Phlox drummondii*), 496

annuals, 67, 104, 353–58; for coastal California, 358; for container plantings, 498, 502; drought-resistant, 471; fertilizing of, 464; half-hardy, 353; hardy, 353; for the Midwest and Northern Great Plains, 355–56; for the Northeast, 354; for the Pacific Northwest, 357; planting and care of, 354; the the Rocky Mountain region, 356–57; for the Southeast, 355; for Subtropical Florida, 355; tender, 353; for Texas and the Southern Plains, 356; use in the garden, 353–54; for western deserts, 358

annual tobacco (*Nicotiana sylvestris*), 354

*Antennaria*, 342; *dioica*, 345; *neglecta*, 343, 381; *parvifolia*, 190; *plantaginifolia*, 206; *rosea*, 328

anthecium, 92, 93

*Anthemis*: *nobilis*, 255 *tinctoria*, 372, 373; 'Wargrave', 374

anther, 86, 106

anthracnose, 560

*Anthriscus cereifolium*, 255, 580

*Anthurium*, 323, 324, 372; *clarinervium*, 336; *hookeri*, 35, 324; *magnificum*, 336, 368; *salviniae*, 324, 335

anthurium (*Anthurium clarinervium*), 336

anthurium (*Anthurium magnificum*), 336

anthuriums (*Anthurium*), 323, 372

*Antigonon leptopus*, 352, 353

*Antirrhinum*, 355, 380; *majus*, 354, 356, 358, 371, 372, 373, 496, 498

antitranspirants, 546–47

antplants (*Acacia*), 82

Apache plume (*Fallugia paradoxa*), 213, 312, 313, 318

Apalachicola rosemary (*Conradina glabra*), 126

*Aphelandra*, 323

aphids, 410, 549–50

aphrodisiacs, 693

Apiaceae, 56

apiculate leaf apex, 81

*Apios tuberosa*, 347

*Apocynum androsaemifolium*, 108, 220, 222, 224, 225, 226

apomixis, 95

apothecary's rose (*Rosa gallica officinalis*), 415

apple-blossom cassia (*Cassia javanica*), 300

Applegate's milk-vetch (*Astragalus applegatei*), 126

apple maggot, 550

apples (*Malus*), 270, 271–73, 283, 484, 672; pests of, 284

apple scab, 560

apricot mallow (*Sphaeralcea ambigua*), 109, 228

apricots, 270, 274; pests of, 285–86

*Aptenia cordifolia*, 345

*Aquilegia*, 324, 365, 366; *bertolonii*, 604; *caerulea*, 190, 227, 319, 328, 331; *canadensis*, 187, 189, 206, 220, 221, 222, 225, 226, 319, 322, 327, 335, 360; *chrysantha*, 327, 328, 332; *formosa*, 109, 192, 201, 202, 229, 329, 331; *saximontana*, 604; *vulgaris*, 319, 367, 368, 369, 370

*Arabidopsis thaliana*, 68

*Arabis hastatula*, 131

Araceae, 45, 59, 85

*Aralia*, 486; *californica*, 191, 201, 202; *racemosa*, 187, 189, 336, 362; *spinosa*, 360, 481

aralias (*Aralia*), 486

*Araucaria heterophylla*, 83

arboreta, botanical gardens, and other public gardens, listing by state and province, 697–723

arbors for city gardens, 604–605

arborvitae (*Thuja occidentalis*), 302, 501

arborvitaes (*Thuja*), 485, 514, 520

*Arbutus*: 'Marina', 306, 383 *menziesii*, 170, 191, 365, 366

*Arbutus* (*cont'd*):
*texana,* 307
*unedo,* 282, 306; 'Compacta',
315, 382
*xalapensis,* 384
arbutus (*Arbutus*), 306
archangel deadnettle (*Lamias-
trum galeobdolon*), 344
archangel plant (*Lamium galeobdolon*), 321, 341
Arctic tundra, 144–45, 166
*Arctomecon humilis,* 126
*Arctostaphylos,* 191, 215, 366, 383
'Emerald Carpet', 345
*manzanita,* 306; 'St. Helena',
306
'Pacific Mist', 345
*pajaroensis,* 316; 'Paradise', 316
*patula,* 170
*pungens,* 318, 384
*uva-ursi,* 190, 216, 281, 282,
318, 342, 344, 365, 471,
485; 'Massachusetts', 344
*Arctotis,* 358; *stoechadifolia,* 357,
496; *venusta,* 354
*Ardisia: crispa,* 572; *elliptica,*
137; *escallonioides,* 311, 361;
*japonica,* 572
Arecaceae, 59
Arecidae, 59
*Arenaria: montana,* 604; *paludicola,* 126
*Argemone,* 367
Argentine trumpet vine
(*Clytostoma callistegioides*),
524
*Argyroxiphium kauense,* 128
*Arisaema: dracontium,* 188, 196;
*triphyllum,* 187, 188, 196,
320, 648
aristate leaf apex, 81
*Aristida,* 170; *stricta,* 167
*Aristolochia,* 361; *californica,* 202,
352; *durior,* 346, 349, 351;
*grandiflora,* 348; *macrophylla,*
346, 349, 351
Arizona, 438, 621–22, 665,
694, 695, 698
Arizona cypress (*Cupressus arizon-
ica* var. *arizonica*), 381
Arizona penstemon (*Penstemon
pseudospectabilis*), 109, 228
Arizona rainbow cactus
(*Echinocereus pectinatus*), 215
Arizona rosewood (*Vauquelinia
californica*), 318, 384
Arizona walnut (*Juglans major*),
307
Arkansas, 438, 694, 695, 698
Arkansas bluestar (*Amsonia
hubrechtii*), 335
*Armeria:
maritima,* 328, 330, 331, 366;
var. *californica,* 216

*Armoracia rusticana,* 258
aromatic aster (*Aster oblongifolius*), 326, 327, 363, 373
aromatic sumac (*Rhus aromatica*),
313, 314, 337, 364
*Aronia,* 359
*arbutifolia,* 187, 189, 201,
312, 362, 377, 481; 'Brilliantissima', 312
*melanocarpa,* 281, 282, 315,
362, 377; var. *elata,* 312
*Arrhenatherum elatius,* 137; var.
*bulbosum,* 471
arrow arum (*Peltandra virginica*),
197, 198, 200, 333
arrowhead (*Sagittaria lancifolia*),
200
arrowhead vine (*Syngonium
podophyllum*), 572
arrow-leaf (*Peltandra virginica*),
198
arrow leaf balsam root (*Balsamorhiza sagittata*), 208
arrowwood (*Viburnum dentatum*),
188, 196, 200, 312, 314,
362
*Artemisia,* 169, 208, 253, 316,
338, 470
*abrotanum,* 335, 338, 369
*absinthium,* 137
*annua,* 478
*californica,* 170, 216
*cana,* 314
*dracunculus,* 265, 334
*filifolia,* 318, 338
*frigida,* 338
*ludoviciana,* 336, 337, 343;
'Silver King', 335
'Powis Castle', 316, 339
*pycnocephala,* 216, 339;
'David's Choice', 330
*tridentata,* 169, 215, 314,
318, 384
*vulgaris,* 137
x 'Powis Castle', 340
artemisias (*Artemisia*), 253, 338,
470
artichoke thistle (*Cynara cardunculus*), 137
artillery plant (*Pilea microphylla*),
323, 342
arugula (*Eruca sativa*), 237
arugula (*Eruca vesicaria* subsp.
*sativa*), 237
arum (*Arum italicum* subsp.
*italicum*), 337
arum family, 59
*Arum italicum,* 322, 335; subsp.
*italicum,* 333, 337
*Aruncus dioicus,* 191, 201, 320,
329; 'Kneiffii', 320, 334
*Arundo donax,* 137
*Asarum,* 187; *arifolium,* 325;
*canadense,* 325, 342; *cauda-*

*tum,* 191, 192, 345;
*europaeum,* 325, 343, 344;
*shuttleworthii,* 189; *virginicum,*
189
*Asclepias,* 169, 206, 207, 208,
224, 360; *asperula,* 363; *incarnata,* 196, 359; *subulata,* 108,
227, 384; *syriaca,* 219, 359,
649; *tuberosa,* 207, 208, 220,
221, 222, 224, 225, 226,
227, 321, 322, 326, 332,
333, 359, 360, 361, 363,
364, 365, 366, 372, 374,
470, 486
*Ascocenda,* 324
asexual plant propagation, *see*
vegetative propagation
asexual plant reproduction, 94,
95
ash (*Fraxinus*), 672
ash (*Fraxinus oxycarpa*), 306
Ashe juniper (*Juniperus ashei*),
302, 381
ashy dogwood (*Thymophylla
tephroleuca*), 127
Asia: climatic conditions in,
23–24; public gardens in,
634–35
Asian jasmine (*Trachelospermum
asiaticum*), 343
Asiatic sweetleaf (*Symplocos paniculata*), 359
*Asimina: tetramera,* 126; *triloba,*
187, 188, 189, 196, 200,
281, 282, 283, 284, 360,
486
*Asocentrum,* 324
*Asparagus: densiflorus,* 323; *officinalis,* 237, 320, 334
asparagus (*Asparagus officinalis*),
237, 320, 334
asparagus fern (*Asparagus densiflorus*), 323
asparagus knife, 614
aspen (*Populus tremula*),
672–73
*Asperula odorata, see Galium odor-
atum*
*Aspidistra elatior,* 342, 572
*Asplenium: leucostegioides,* 131;
*nidus,* 324; *rhomboideum,* 128
aster (*Aster*), 169, 206, 207,
208, 355, 362, 372, 478
*Aster,* 169, 206, 207, 208, 355,
372, 478
*alpinus,* 604
*carolinianus,* 199, 361
*divaricatus,* 187, 325
*dumosus,* 220, 222
*ericoides,* 326, 363
'Esther', 326
*frikartii,* 330; 'Monch', 330
*laevis,* 205
*lanceolatus* var. *lanceolatus,*
200
*macrophyllus,* 189, 343

*novae-angliae,* 321, 324, 325,
359, 360, 362, 373
*novi-belgii,* 324, 373
*oblongifolius,* 326, 327, 363,
373
*praealtus,* 326, 363, 373
*pratensis,* 327, 337, 363
*puniceus,* 200
*sericeus,* 363; var. *microphyllus,*
373, 380
*spinosus,* 209
*subspicatus,* 329
x *frikartii,* 320, 330, 331,
359; 'Monch', 331, 366,
375
aster (*Aster alpinus*), 604
aster (*Aster novae-angliae*), 324,
373
aster (*Aster novi-belgii*), 324, 373
aster (*Aster spinosus*), 209
aster (*Aster x frikartii*), 331
Asteraceae, 57–58, 84
aster family, 57–58
Asteridae, 57–59
*Asteriscus maritimus,* 330
asters (*Aster*), 169, 206, 207,
208, 355, 362, 372, 478
*Astilbe,* 322, 325, 379, 498
*arendsii,* 329; 'Fanal', 329
*biternata,* 201
*chinensis,* 319, 320; 'Pumila',
319, 320, 328, 344, 604
*taquetii,* 325; 'Superba', 325
*thunbergii,* 319, 320
x *arendsii,* 319, 320; 'Gloria',
374
astilbe (*Astilbe arendsii*), 329
astilbe (*Astilbe chinensis* 'Pumila'),
604
astilbe (*Astilbe taquetii*), 325
astilbes (*Astilbe*), 319, 320, 322,
325, 379, 498
*Astilboides tabularis,* 338
*Astragalus,* 208; *albens,* 126;
*applegatei,* 126; *bibullatus,* 126;
*canadensis,* 207; *coccineus,* 109,
228; *humillimus,* 126; *osterhoutii,* 126
astrantia (*Astrantia major*), 330
*Astrantia major,* 330; 'Hadspen
Blood', 330
*Astrophytum asterias,* 126
*Athyrium:
asplenioides,* 188
*filix-femina,* 197, 202, 320,
322, 325, 328, 334; var.
*cyclosorum,* 203
*goeringianum,* 341
*nipponicum,* 320, 341; 'Pictum', 320, 325, 333, 341,
342; var. *pictum,* 335
*pycnocarpon,* 197, 320
Atlantic golden aster (*Pityopsis
falcata*), 206

Atlantic white cedar (*Chamaecyparis thyoides*), 168
atlas cedar (*Cedrus atlantica*), 297
*Atriplex,* 169; *californica,* 216; *canescens,* 367, 470; *parryi,* 169
*Atropa belladonna,* 649
*Aucuba japonica,* 310, 497
auricula (*Primula auricula*), 355
*Aurinia saxatilis,* 330, 340, 478
Australia, 638; climatic conditions in, 24; public gardens in, 634
Australian blackwood (*Acacia melanoxylon*), 137
Australian brush cherry (*Syzygium paniculatum*), 536
Australian fuchsia (*Correa*), 317
Australian pine (*Casuarina equisetifolia*), 137, 152
Australian tea tree (*Leptospermum laevigatum*), 306
Australian willow (*Geijera parviflora*), 306
Austria, 630
Austrian copper rose (*Rosa foetida*), 318
Austrian pine (*Pinus nigra*), 304, 307, 380
autochory, 93
autotrophic plants, 67
autumn anemone (*Anemone japonica*), 319
autumn crocus (*Colchicum autumnale*), 320, 650–51
autumn crocus (*Crocus sativus*), 256
autumn crocus (*Sternbergia lutea*), 369
autumn olive (*Elaeagnus umbellata*), 137
autumn phlox (*Phlox paniculata*), 326, 363
autumn sage (*Salvia greggii*), 213, 313, 366
autumn sneezeweed (*Helenium autumnale*), 329
*Averrhoa carambola,* 300
*Avicennia: germinans,* 197; *nitida,* 168
Avon Park harebells (*Crotalaria avonensis*), 126
awn grasses (*Aristida*), 170
*Azalea* 'Everest', 316
azaleas (*Rhododendron*), 187, 188, 189, 191, 481, 510, 514, 522
*Azara microphylla,* 317

*Babiana stricta,* 405
baboon flower (*Babiana stricta*), 405
baby blue eyes (*Nemophila menziesii*), 209, 358

baby cyclamen (*Cyclamen hederifolium*), 331
baby's breath (*Gypsophila paniculata*), 138, 331, 371, 373, 376
baby snapdragon (*Linaria marrocana*), 358
bacca, 91, 92
*Baccharis: angustifolia,* 197; *halimifolia,* 168, 216, 309; *pilularis,* 215, 216; x 'Centennial', 318, 345
bachelor's button (*Centaurea cyanus*), 372, 375, 496
bachelor's buttons (*Centaurea cyanus*), 367
*Bacillus thuringiensis,* 546
*Bacopa caroliniana,* 198
bacterial canker, 560
bacterial leaf spot, 561
Bahama cassia (*Senna ligustrina*), 311, 361
Bahama strongwood (*Bourreria ovata*), 224
Bailey, Liberty Hyde, Jr., 3–4
*Baileya multiradiata,* 169, 209, 358, 366, 375
Baja red fairyduster (*Calliandra californica*), 318
Baja ruellia (*Ruellia peninsularis*), 318
baking soda, 547
balcony gardens, 606
bald cypress (*Taxodium distichum*), 161, 168, 188, 198, 303, 609
bald-hip roses (*Rosa gymnocarpa*), 382
Baldwin ironweed (*Vernonia baldwinii*), 326, 327, 363
Balkan crocus (*Crocus tomasinianus*), 376
balled and burlapped trees and shrubs: planting, 452; transplanting, 454–55
balloon flower (*Platycodon grandiflorus*), 7, 320, 325, 369
balsam fir (*Abies balsamea*), 166, 334
*Balsamorhiza sagittata,* 208
Baltic rush ( *Juncus balticus*), 203
bamboo (*Sasa palmata*), 333
bamboo muhly (*Muhlenbergia dumosa*), 340
bamboos (*Phyllostachys*), 514
banana (*Musa acuminata*), 284
banana (*Musa x paradisiaca*), 323
banana yucca (*Yucca baccata*), 215
baneberries (*Actaea*), 189
baneberry (*Actaea rubra*), 191
Banks, Joseph, 4
*Baptisia,* 206, 207, 470; *alba,* 321; *arachnifera,* 126; *australis,* 320, 325, 326, 372,

374, 498; *leucantha,* 321, 325; *pendula,* 321
barberry (*Berberis*), 281, 282
barberry cotoneaster (*Cotoneaster dammeri*), 341
Barbour, Michael G., 17
bare-root plants:
perennials, 449–50
trees and shrubs: planting, 452–53; transplanting, 454
bark, 71–72
Barneby reed-mustard (*Schoenocrambe barnebyi*), 127
Barneby ridge-cress (*Lepidium barnebyanum*), 127
barrel cactus (*Ferocactus acanthodes*), 169
barren strawberry (*Waldsteinia fragarioides*), 343, 344
barrenwort (*Epimedium grandiflora*), 325
barrenwort (*Epimedium rubrum*), 328
barrenwort (*Epimedium x youngianum*), 325, 336
Barton, Benjamin Smith, 4
Bartram, John, 4
Bartram, William, 4
basal leaf arrangement, 82, 83
basil (*Ocimum basilicum*), 334, 498, 580
basket flower (*Centaurea americana*), 357
basket flower (*Hymenocallis*), 403–404, 589–90
basket of gold (*Aurinia saxatilis*), 330, 340, 478
*Bassia scoparia,* 137
basswood (*Tilia americana*), 167, 221, 225, 301
bat flowers (*Tacca*), 323
bats, flower pollination by, 107, 109, 177–78
*Bauhinia x blakeana,* 300
bay (*Laurus nobilis*), 253
bayberry (*Myrica pensylvanica*), 187, 216, 308, 334, 359
bay laurel (*Laurus nobilis*), 522
beach berry (*Scaevola sericea* var. *taccada*), 139
beach evening primrose (*Camissonia cheiranthifolia*), 216
beach grass (*Ammophila breviligulata*), 168, 216
beach heather (*Hudsonia tomentosa*), 216
beach jacquemontia ( *Jacquemontia reclinata*), 127
beach layia (*Layia carnosa*), 127
beach pea (*Lathyrus japonicus*), 216
beach peanut (*Okenia hypogaea*), 342

beach plum (*Prunus maritima*), 216, 359
beach sunflower (*Helianthemum debilis*), 323
beach verbena (*Verbena maritima*), 342
bearberry (*Arctostaphylos uvaursi*), 190, 281, 282, 342, 485
bearberry honeysuckle (*Lonicera involucrata*), 221, 229, 230
bearded allocarya (*Plagiobothrys hystriculus*), 132
bearded iris (*Iris germanica*), 319, 321, 324, 326, 332, 367, 370, 375
beardtongue (*Penstemon digitalis*), 206, 221, 222, 223, 225, 226
beardtongue (*Penstemon smallii*), 206
beardtongues (*Penstemon*), 190, 208, 213, 367, 470
beargrass (*Nolina microcarpa*), 339, 384
bear's-breech (*Acanthus mollis*), 486
bearsfoot hellebore (*Helleborus foetidus*), 378, 379
beautiful pawpaw (*Deeringothamnus pulchellus*), 126
beautyberries (*Callicarpa*), 308, 484
beautyberry (*Callicarpa americana*), 187, 308, 309
beautyberry (*Callicarpa dichotoma*), 308, 377
beautyberry (*Callicarpa japonica*), 308, 377
beautybush (*Kolkwitzia amabilis*), 13, 370, 371, 510
beavertail cactus (*Opuntia basilaris*), 169
*Bebbia juncea,* 108, 227
bedding impatiens (*Impatiens*), 497
bee balm (*Monarda didyma*), 206, 221, 253–54, 359, 360, 368, 370, 372, 498
bee balm (*Monarda fistulosa*), 326, 359, 363, 364
bee balm (*Monarda menthifolia*), 371
bee bush (*Aloysia gratissima*), 108, 227
beech (*Fagus*), 72
beech (*Fagus grandifolia*), 359
bee plant (*Scrophularia californica*), 216
bees: flower pollination by, 107, 108, 177; gardening to attract, 219, 220–30
beetles, flower pollination by, 107, 108
beets (*Beta vulgaris*), 237–38

*Begonia,* 45, 323, 356, 497, 498, 596
  *coccinea,* 355
  *grandis,* 322
  *semperflorens,* 354, 355, 358; 'Ambassador', 358; 'Cocktail', 358
  x *semperflorens-cultorum,* 355
  x *tuberhybrida,* 354, 401, 590
begonia (*Begonia coccinea*), 355
begonia (*Begonia semperflorens*), 355
begonias (*Begonia*), 323, 356, 498
*Belamcanda chinensis,* 321, 322, 368, 470
Belgium, 630
belladonna (*Atropa belladonna*), 649
bellflower (*Campanula carpatica*), 328
bellflower (*Campanula glomerata*), 370
bellflower (*Campanula rotundifolia*), 331
bellflower (*Edraianthus pumilio*), 604
bell-flowered squill (*Hyacinthoides hispanica*), 370
bellflowers (*Campanula*), 324
bells of Ireland (*Moluccella laevis*), 356, 374
bellwort (*Uvularia grandiflora*), 146
bellworts (*Uvularia*), 189
Benjamin fig (*Ficus benjamina*), 536
Bentham, George, 8
*Berberis,* 281, 282; *haematocarpa,* 318; *julianae,* 377; *koreana,* 314; *reptans,* 343; *thungergii,* 137; *verruculosa,* 315
bergamot (*Monarda fistulosa*), 198, 206, 207, 326, 337, 362, 363
*Bergenia: cordifolia,* 325, 328, 330, 332, 336, 337, 498; *crassifolia,* 383
bergenia (*Bergenia cordifolia*), 328, 336, 498
Berkeley sedge (*Carex tumulicola*), 203
*Berlandiera texana,* 326
*Beta vulgaris,* 237–38
*Betula,* 359
  *fontinalis,* 190, 314, 364, 382
  *lenta,* 301
  *maximowicziana,* 377
  *nigra,* 167, 187, 189, 196, 197, 201, 297, 299, 301, 303, 378, 381, 500, 609; 'Heritage', 297, 303, 377
  *occidentalis,* 202, 314, 382
  *papyrifera,* 166, 187, 189, 201, 365, 377

*pendula,* 298; 'Gracilis', 298, 334
*platyphylla* var. *japonica,* 301; 'Whitespire', 301
*populifolia,* 187, 298, 377
*utilis* var. *jacquemontii,* 304
Betulaceae, 54, 109
Bible leaf (*Tanacetum balsamita*), 256
*Bidens: cernua,* 200; *wiebkei,* 128
biennials, 67, 104
big bluestem (*Andropogon gerardii*), 168, 169, 205, 207
Bigelow oak (*Quercus sinuata* var. *breviloba*), 302
bigleaf aster (*Aster macrophyllus*), 189, 343
big-leaf hydrangea (*Hydrangea macrophylla*), 327, 500
bigleaf magnolia (*Magnolia macrophylla*), 299
bigleaf maple (*Acer macrophyllum*), 202
bigleaf mountain mahogany (*Cercocarpus betuloides*), 170
bigleaf sage (*Artemisia tridentata*), 318, 384
bigleaf scurfpea (*Orbexilum macrophyllum*), 132
*Bignonia: capreolata,* 347, 348, 350, 353, 381; *violacea,* 353
big quaking grass (*Briza maxima*), 374
bigroot geranium (*Geranium macrorrhizum*), 336
big sagebrush (*Artemisia tridentata*), 215, 314
big-toothed sunflower (*Helianthus grosseserratus*), 200
bigtooth maple (*Acer grandidentatum*), 302, 304
*Billbergia pyramidalis,* 324, 342
billbugs, 550
Billings, W. D., 17
bins for composting, 444–45, 618–19
biodiversity, 165–71; basic levels of, 112–13; benefits of, 171; defined, 112
biogeochemical cycle, 173
biological structure of plant communities, 165–71
bipinnate, 75, 76
birchbark cherry (*Prunus serrula*), 377
birches (*Betula*), 359
birch family, 54
bird-of-paradise (*Caesalpinia gilliesii*), 313, 318
bird-of-paradise (*Strelitzia reginae*), 323, 332, 373
birds, 230; fending off, from fruit plants, 286, 564; flower pollination by, 107, 109, 177,

178; gardening for, 218–19, 220–30
bird's-eye bush (*Ochna serrulata*), 536
bird's foot trefoil (*Lotus corniculatus*), 138
bird's-nest anthurium (*Anthurium hookeri*), 324, 335
bird's-nest anthurium (*Anthurium salviniae*), 324, 335
bird's-nest fern (*Asplenium nidus*), 324
birth flowers, 696
*Bischofia javanica,* 137, 152
bishop pine (*Pinus muricata*), 216
bishop's cap (*Mitella breweri*), 191
bishop's cap (*Mitella diphylla*), 190
bishop's cap (*Mitella ovalis*), 203
bishop's hat (*Epimedium perralderianum*), 344
bishop's weed (*Aegopodium podagraria*), 344
bishopwood (*Bischofia javanica*), 137, 152
bishopwort (*Aegopodium podagraria*), 341
*Bismarckia nobilis,* 301
Bismarck palm (*Bismarckia nobilis*), 301
bistorts (*Polygonum*), 166
biternate, 75, 76
bitterroot (*Lewisia rediviva*), 190
bittersweet (*Celastrus orbiculatus*), 137
black ash (*Fraxinus nigra*), 161, 196, 200
blackbead (*Pithecellobium guadalupense*), 108, 223, 361
blackbead (*Pithecellobium keyense*), 310
blackberries (*Rubus*), 270, 277, 278–79, 284, 486; pests of, 286
blackberry lily (*Belamcanda chinensis*), 321, 322, 368, 470
black cherry (*Prunus serotina*), 303, 359, 363, 658
black chokeberry (*Aronia melanocarpa*), 315, 362, 377
black cohosh (*Cimicifuga racemosa*), 187, 188, 319, 325, 368, 379
black dalea (*Dalea frutescens*), 313, 318
black-eyed Susan (*Rudbeckia fulgida* var. *sullivantii*), 322, 379
black-eyed Susan (*Rudbeckia hirta*), 199, 206, 207, 208, 328, 356, 364, 367, 371, 374
black-eyed Susans (*Rudbeckia*), 372

black-eyed Susan vine (*Thunbergia alata*), 347, 349, 352, 357, 498, 524
Blackfoot daisy (*Melampodium leucanthum*), 208, 213, 332, 333, 356
black grama (*Bouteloua eriopoda*), 209
black gum (*Nyssa sylvatica*), 196, 298, 299
black haw viburnum (*Viburnum prunifolium*), 281, 282, 308
Black Hills spruce (*Picea glauca*), 304
blackjack oak (*Quercus marilandica*), 167, 216
black jetbead (*Rhodotypos scandens*), 510
black knot, 561
black locust (*Robinia pseudoacacia*), 139, 222, 223, 609
black mangrove (*Avicennia germinans*), 197
black mangrove (*Avicennia nitida*), 168
black mondo grass (*Ophiopogon planiscapus*), 341
black mustard (*Brassica nigra*), 580
black oak, California (*Quercus kelloggii*), 170
black oak (*Quercus velutina*), 167, 168
black olive (*Bucida buceras*), 300
black pine (*Pinus thunbergii*), 470, 536
black plum (*Prunus nigra*), 302
black raspberry (*Rubus occidentalis*), 284
black rush (*Schoenus nigricans*), 199
black sampson (*Echinacea angustifolia*), 326, 363, 373, 380
black snakeroot (*Cimicifuga racemosa*), 187, 188, 319
black-spored quillwort (*Isoetes melanospora*), 127
blackspot, 410, 561
black spruce (*Picea mariana*), 166, 196, 200
black tupelo (*Nyssa sylvatica*), 305
black walnut (*Juglans nigra*), 282, 301, 302
black willow (*Salix nigra*), 200, 303
bladdernuts (*Staphylea*), 308
bladderpod (*Isomeris arborea*), 230
bladderwort (*Utricularia foliosa*), 199
bladderworts (*Utricularia*), 82, 160

blanco crabapple (*Malus ioensis*), 303

blanketflower (*Gaillardia aristata*), 208, 328, 329, 364, 369, 478

blanketflower (*Gaillardia pulchella*), 206, 208, 223, 342, 355, 360, 361

blanketflower (*Gaillardia* x *grandiflora*), 376

blazing star (*Liatris punctata*), 215, 319, 321

blazing star (*Liatris spicata*), 372

blazing star (*Mentzelia lindleyi*), 358

blazing stars (*Liatris*), 153, 169, 206, 207, 223, 359, 361, 362

*Blechnum: penna-marina,* 345; *serrulatum,* 342; *spicant,* 191, 192, 202, 203, 339

blechnum (*Blechnum penna-marina*), 345

bleeding heart (*Clerodendrum tromsoniae*), 311

bleeding heart (*Dicentra eximia*), 335

bleeding heart (*Dicentra spectabilis*), 7, 322, 328, 367, 370, 498

bletilla (*Bletilla striata*), 329

*Bletilla striata,* 329

blood lily (*Haemanthus coccineus*), 586

blood lily (*Haemanthus*), 403

bloodred trumpet vine (*Distictis buccinatoria*), 352

bloodroot (*Lachnanthes caroliniana*), 199

bloodroot (*Sanguinaria canadensis*), 147, 188, 320, 325

blood-twig dogwood (*Cornus sanguinea*), 376

bloody cranesbill (*Geranium sanguineum*), 324, 344

blue atlas cedar (*Cedrus atlantica*), 306

blue avena (*Helictotrichon sempervirens*), 328, 329

bluebeard (*Caryopteris* x *clandonensis*), 309, 316, 470, 484, 485

bluebeards (*Caryopteris*), 359

blue beech (*Carpinus caroliniana*), 189, 301

bluebell (*Campanula rotundifolia*), 190

bluebell (*Mertensia lanceolata*), 190

blueberries (*Vaccinium*), 270, 276–77, 282, 284, 481; pests of, 286

blueblossom (*Ceanothus thyrsiflorus*), 170, 316

bluebunch wheatgrass (*Agropyron spicatum*), 208

blue chicory (*Cichorium intybus*), 180

blue clerodendron (*Clerodendrum ugandense*), 311

blue cohosh (*Caulophyllum thalictroides*), 362

blue columbine (*Aquilegia caerulea*), 319

blue cornflower (*Centaurea cyanus*), 471

blue cupflower (*Nierembergia hippomanica* var. *violacea*), 354

blue daze (*Evolvulus glomeratus*), 323, 342, 594

blue elderberry (*Sambucus caerulea*), 366

blue-eyed grass (*Sisyrinchium angustifolium*), 196, 206

blue-eyed grass (*Sisyrinchium bellum*), 203

blue-eyed grasses (*Sisyrinchium*), 324

blue false indigo (*Baptisia australis*), 326

blue fescue (*Festuca glauca*), 345

blue fescue (*Festuca ovina* var. *glauca*), 341

blue flag (*Iris virginica* var. *shrevei*), 207

blue flag iris (*Iris versicolor*), 197, 200, 201

blue flax (*Linum lewisii* var. *lewisii*), 328

blue flax (*Linum perenne* subsp. *lewisii*), 364

blue flax (*Linum perenne*), 332

blue grama grass (*Bouteloua gracilis*), 471

bluegrass (*Poa scabrella*), 170

blue gum (*Eucalyptus globulus*), 137

blue hibiscus (*Alyogyne huegelii*), 317

bluejack oak (*Quercus incana*), 167

blue lace flower (*Trachymene coerulea*), 376, 471

blue-leaved rose (*Rosa glauca*), 382

blue lobelia (*Lobelia syphilitica*), 196, 319

blue marguerite (*Felicia amelloides*), 375

blue mist (*Caryopteris* x *clandonensis*), 316, 317, 318, 364, 366

blue mistflower (*Eupatorium coelestinum*), 198, 199, 361

blue oak (*Quercus douglasii*), 170

blue oat grass (*Helictotrichon sempervirens*), 319, 338

blue palo verde (*Parkinsonia florida*), 307

blue passionflower (*Passiflora caerulea*), 348, 349

blue phlox (*Osmunda divaricata*), 320, 370

blue phlox (*Phlox divaricata*), 189, 190

blue porterweed (*Stachytarpheta jamaicensis*), 223

blue rug juniper (*Juniperus horizontalis*), 340

blue sage (*Salvia azurea* var. *grandiflora*), 326, 332, 364

bluesage (*Eranthemum pulchellum*), 311

blue sedge (*Carex glauca*), 339

blue southern iris (*Iris hexagona*), 198

blue spurge (*Euphorbia myrsinites*), 332

bluestar (*Amsonia tabernaemontana*), 320, 322, 325

blue star (*Ipheion uniflorum*), 369

blue star creeper (*Laurentia fluviatilis*), 471

bluestem willow (*Salix irrorata*), 314, 381

bluet (*Centaurea montana*), 320

blue taro (*Xanthosoma violaceum*), 333

bluets (*Houstonia caerulea*), 189

blue tulp (*Moraea*), 406

blue vervain (*Verbena hastata*), 200

blue water hyssop (*Bacopa caroliniana*), 198

blue water lily (*Nymphaea elegans*), 198

blue yucca (*Yucca baccata*), 169

blunt-lobe cyanea (*Cyanea obtusa*), 131

bog bean (*Menyanthes trifoliata*), 196, 198, 201, 202, 203

bog-buttons (*Lachnocaulon anceps*), 199

bog rosemary (*Andromeda polifolia* var. *glaucophylla*), 200, 201

bog rosemary (*Andromeda polifolia*), 312, 485

bogs, 160, 192, 194

boltonia (*Boltonia asteroides*), 322

*Boltonia asteroides,* 322; 'Snowbank', 322

boneset (*Eupatorium perfoliatum*), 200, 206, 207

bonsai, 524–37
  "advancing" the age of, 534
  basics, 525
  companion plants, 534
  containers, 527–28

fertilizing, 531
indoor, special requirements for, 535–36
medium for, 528
miniature (mame), 534
overwintering outdor, 535
potting and repotting, 530–31
pruning, 531–34; for basic form, 529; of roots, 531
selecting a tree, 528–29
styles of, 525–27
tools, 528
watering, 531
wiring, 534–35

boophane (*Boophane disticha*), 405, 594

*Boophane disticha,* 405, 594

borage (*Borago officinalis*), 254, 366

*Borago officinalis,* 254, 366

bordeaux mix, 547

boreal forest, *see* Northern coniferous forest

borers, roses and, 410

*Borrichia frutescens,* 342, 361

Bosenberg, Henry F., 4

Boston fern (*Nephrolepis exaltata*), 342

Boston ivy (*Parthenocissus*), 485

Boston ivy (*Parthenocissus tricuspidata*), 346, 347, 349, 350, 352, 353, 364, 484

botanical resources, arboreta, and other public gardens, listing by state and province, 697–723

*Bothriochloa barbinodis,* 339

*Botrychium subbifoliatum,* 131

botrytis blight, 561

bottlebrush (*Callistemon citrinus*), 500

bottlebrush (*Callistemon linearis*), 536

bottlebrush buckeye (*Aesculus parviflora*), 188, 315, 481

bottle gentian (*Gentiana andrewsii*), 207

bottle gentian (*Gentiana clausa*), 187

bottle sedge (*Carex comosa*), 201

bottle tree (*Brachychiton populneus*), 306

*Bougainvillea,* 45, 311, 348, 349; *glabra,* 310, 536; 'Pink Pixie', 597; 'San Diego Red', 352; *spectabilis,* 352, 353; x *buttiana,* 522

bougainvillea (*Bougainvillea glabra*), 310, 536

bougainvillea (*Bougainvillea spectabilis*), 352, 353

bougainvillea (*Bougainvillea* x *buttiana*), 522
bougainvilleas (*Bougainvillea*), 311, 348, 349
Boulder raspberry (*Rubus deliciosa*), 315
bouncing Bet (*Saponaria officinalis*), 368, 369, 370
*Bourreria ovata,* 224
*Bouteloua,* 169, 208, 213; *chondroisiodes,* 209; *curtipendula,* 206, 326, 327, 367, 373; *eriopoda,* 209; *filiformis,* 209; *gracilis,* 471
bowman's root (*Gillenia trifoliata*), 187
bowman's root (*Veronicastrum virginicum*), 375
box (*Buxus*), 485
box blueberry (*Vaccinum ovatum*), 365
box elder (*Acer negundo*), 108, 220, 221, 224, 225, 226
box honeysuckle (*Lonicera nitida*), 520
boxleaf azara (*Azara microphylla*), 317
boxwoods (*Buxus*), 496
*Brachychiton populneus,* 306
*Brachycome iberidifolia,* 355, 357; 'Amethyst', 357
*Brachypodium sylvaticum,* 137
bracken fern (*Pteridium aquilinum*), 343
bracteoles, 82
bracts, 82
*Brahea armata,* 384
bramble fruits (*Rubus*), 481
branched Solomon's seal (*Smilacina racemosa*), 203
*Brassia,* 324
*Brassica,* 359, 371; *juncea,* 260; *nigra,* 580; *oleracea,* 238, 239–40, 357, 380; *rapa,* 242
Brassicaceae, 55
*Braya pilosa,* 131
Brazil, 636, 638
Brazilian passionflower (*Passiflora caerulea*), 350, 363
Brazilian pepper tree (*Schinus terebinthifolius*), 139, 152
*Breynia: disticha,* 336; *nivosa,* 310
briar (*Rubus*), 359
bridal bouquet (*Stephanotis floribunda*), 348, 349
bridal-wreath (*Spiraea x vanhouttei*), 84, 311
bridal-wreath spirea (*Spiraea prunifolia*), 309, 368
bridal-wreath spirea (*Spiraea veitchii*), 13, 313, 314
Bridgeman, Thomas, 4

*Brighamia: insignis,* 128; *rockii,* 128
Brisbane box (*Tristania conferta*), 306
bristlecone pine, Rocky Mountains (*Pinus aristata*), 304, 307, 382
bristlecone pines (*Pinus longaeva*), 68
Britton, Nathaniel Lord, 4
broadcasting of fertilizer, 460–61
broad-leaved cotton grass (*Eriophorum latifolium*), 197
broad-leaved nodding-caps (*Triphora latifolia*), 132
broccoli (*Brassica*), 359
broccoli (*Brassica oleracea*), 238
*Brodiaea: elegans,* 209; *laxa, see Triteleia laxa*
brodiaea (*Triteleia laxa*), 397
*Bromeliaceae,* 45
bromeliads (*Aechmea*), 324, 342
bromeliads (*Billbergia pyramidalis*), 324, 342
bromeliads (*Billbergia*), 342
bromeliads (*Cryptanthus*), 342
bromeliads (*Guzmania*), 324
bromeliads (*Neoregelia*), 324, 342
bromeliads (*Tillandsia*), 324
bromeliads (*Vriesea*), 342
bronze birch borer, 550
Brooksville bellflower (*Campanula robinsiae*), 126
broom groundsel (*Senecio spartioides*), 364
broom sedge (*Andropogon virginicus*), 206, 216, 360
broomsedge (*Andropogon virginicus*), 378
browallia (*Browallia speciosa*), 354, 355, 356, 496, 498
*Browallia speciosa,* 354, 355, 356, 357, 496, 498; 'Blue Bells Improved', 357
Brown, Lancelot "Capability," 4–5
brown-eyed Susan (*Rudbeckia hirta*), 361, 373
brown-eyed Susan (*Rudbeckia triloba*), 374, 382
brownspire prickly pear (*Opuntia phaeacantha*), 337
*Bruckenthalia,* 45
*Brugmansia,* 316, 594; 'Betty Marshall', 316; *versicolor,* 311, 500; x *candida,* 311
*Brunfelsia: americana,* 310, 311; *grandiflora,* 310, 311; *pauciflora,* 310, 311
*Brunnera macrophylla,* 325, 328
brushy bluestem (*Andropogon glomeratus*), 326, 373, 380
Brussels sprouts (*Brassica*), 359

Brussels sprouts (*Brassica oleracea*), 238
Bryan's haplostachys (*Haplostachys bryanii*), 131
Bryophyta, 51–52; sexual reproduction of, 96–98
bubblegum mint (*Agastache*), 340
bubblegum mint (*Agastache cana*), 333, 367, 375
*Buchloe dactyloides,* 169, 208, 343, 380
*Bucida buceras,* 300
buckbrush (*Ceanothus fendleri*), 190
buckbrush (*Symphoricarpos orbiculatus*), 343
buckeye (*Aesculus californica*), 216, 648
buckeyes (*Aesculus*), 477, 486
buckthorn (*Rhamnus cathartica*), 138
buckwheat (*Eriogonum fasciculatum*), 332
buckwheat (*Eriogonum latifolium* subsp. *grande*), 216
buckwheat (*Eriogonum*), 366
buckwheats (*Eriogonum*), 215, 367
Budding, Edwin B., 5
budding, propagation by, 489, 492, 493
*Buddleia: alternifolia,* 364, 470; *davidii,* 137 *fallowiana,* 317; 'Lochinch', 317 *marrubiifolia,* 366
buds, 74
buffalo berry (*Shepherdia argentea*), 281, 282
buffalo currant (*Ribes odoratum*), 108, 224, 225, 226, 313, 364
buffalo gourd (*Cucurbita foetidissima*), 337
buffalo grass (*Buchloe dactyloides*), 169, 208, 343, 380
bugbane (*Cimicifuga japonica* var. *acerina*), 325
bugbane (*Cimicifuga laciniata*), 201
bugbane (*Cimicifuga simplex*), 325
bugleweed (*Ajuga reptans*), 341, 342, 343
buglosses (*Anchusa*), 486
builder's sand, 474
Bullbay magnolia (*Magnolia grandiflora*), 167
bulbous oat grass (*Arrhenatherum elatius* var. *bulbosum*), 471
bulb planter, 611
bulbs, 82
after-bloom care, 394
for container plantings, 502

defined, 390
dividing and propagating, 393–94, 480
growing hydroponically, 584
hardy, 392–93; grown as perennials, autumn blooming, 398–99; grown as perennials, spring and summer blooming, 394–98
as indoor plants, 581–90
life cycle of, 392
mulching of, 468
planting and care of, 393, 450
soil preparation for, 393–94
storing and lifting of tender, 394
tender, 393; grown as perennials in tropical/subtropical climates, 401–404; treated as annuals in temperate climates, 399–401; treated as perennials in Mediterranean climates, 404–407
trade in, 134–35
types of, 390–92
bull thistle (*Cirsium vulgare*), 137
*Bulnesia arborea,* 300
bulrush (*Scirpus tabernaemontani*), 197
bulrushes (*Scirpus*), 201, 202
bumald spirea (*Spirea* x *bumalda*), 312, 316
bunchberry (*Cornus canadensis*), 146, 187, 191, 344
bunched arrowhead (*Sagittaria fasciculata*), 127
bunchflower (*Melanthium virginicum*), 189
Burbank, Luther, 5
Burke's goldfields (*Lasthenia burkei*), 127
Burkwood daphne (*Daphne* x *burkwoodii*), 500
Burkwood viburnum (*Viburnum* x *burkwoodii*), 308, 318, 510
bur oak (*Quercus macrocarpa*), 167, 168, 169, 189, 205, 301, 302, 304, 379
bur reeds (*Sparganium*), 201
bur sages (*Ambrosia*), 169
*Bursera simaruba,* 168, 300, 361
bush anemone (*Carpenteria californica*), 191, 215, 317
bush beans (*Phaseolus vulgaris*), 242–43
bush cinquefoil (*Potentilla fruticosa*), 470, 481
bush clover (*Lespedeza thunbergii*), 309
bush clovers (*Lespedeza*), 481
bush germander (*Teucrium fruticans*), 317

bush honeysuckle (*Diervilla lonicera*), 189, 312
bush honeysuckle (*Lonicera involucrata*), 191
bush honeysuckles (*Lonicera*), 138
bush lupine (*Lupinus arboreus*), 138
bush morning glory (*Convolvulus cneorum*), 318
bush muhly (*Muhlenbergia porteri*), 209
bushy beardgrass (*Andropogon glomeratus*), 378
bushy bluestem grass (*Andropogon glomeratus*), 198
bushy rockrose (*Helianthemum dumosum*), 206
*Butea monosperma,* 300
butter & eggs(*Linaria vulgaris*), 138
butterbur (*Petasites japonica*), 333
buttercup (*Ranunculus flabellaris*), 201
buttercup family, 53
butterflies: flower pollination by, 107, 108–109, 177; gardening for, 219, 220–30, 358–67
butterfly bush (*Buddleia davidii*), 137
butterfly bush (*Buddleia fallowiana*), 317
butterfly pea (*Centrosema virginianum*), 361
butterfly sage (*Cordia globosa*), 223, 224
butterfly weed (*Asclepias tuberosa*), 206, 207, 208, 220, 221, 224, 225, 226, 227, 321, 322, 326, 332, 333, 360, 361, 363, 364, 365, 366, 372, 374, 470, 486
butternut ( *Juglans cinerea*), 282
buttonbush (*Cephalanthus occidentalis*), 196, 197, 199, 201, 221, 222, 309, 359, 360, 368
buttonwood (*Conocarpus erectus*), 168, 300
*Buxus,* 46, 485, 496
    *microphylla,* 377, 514; var. *japonica,* 313, 381; var. *koreana,* 312
    *sempervirens,* 514, 520; 'Suffruticosa', 520; 'Variegata', 377
*Byrsonima lucida,* 310

cabada palm (*Chrysalidocarpus cabadae*), 301
cabbage (*Brassica oleracea*), 238
cabbage looper, 550
cabbage maggot, 550–51
cabbage palmetto (*Sabal palmetto*), 168, 197, 199, 301, 362

cabbages (*Brassica*), 359
cabbageworm, 551
Cactaceae, 54
cactus family, 54, 133, 134, 169; as indoor plants, 579–80; photosynthesis by, 156; water collection and storage by, 156
caesalpina (*Caesalpinia mexicana*), 300
*Caesalpinia: gilliesii,* 137, 313, 318; *kavaiensis,* 128; *mexicana,* 300; *pulcherrima,* 318
*Caladium,* 333, 356, 497; *bicolor,* 336, 354, 355, 401–402, 587–88
caladium (*Caladium bicolor*), 336, 355
caladiums (*Caladium*), 333, 356, 497
*Calamagrostis* x *acutiflora,* 319, 374, 379; 'Stricta', 319, 379
calamint (*Calamintha nepeta*), 254
*Calamintha nepeta,* 254
*Calathea,* 323, 594
calathea (*Calathea*), 323, 594
calcification process, 37
calcined clay, 474–75
calendula (*Calendula officinalis*), 254, 369
*Calendula officinalis,* 254, 358, 369, 496, 498, 678
calico flower (*Aristolochia*), 361
California, 438, 622, 665–66, 694, 695, 698–702, 723
California bay (*Umbellularia californica*), 202, 339
California bell (*Phacelia minor*), 230
California black oak (*Quercus kelloggii*), 191, 305, 306, 365
California bluebells (*Phacelia campanularia*), 35
California blue-eyed grass (*Sisyrinchium bellum*), 192, 216
California buckeye (*Aesculus californica*), 305, 307
California chaparral, 158, 159, 170, 172, 213, 215
California coffeeberry (*Rhamnus californicus*), 366
California dissanthelium (*Dissanthelium californicum*), 131
California fan palm (*Washingtonia filifera*), 202
California fescue (*Festuca californica*), 209
California fuchsia (*Zauschneria californica*), 215, 331, 366
California goldenrod (*Solidago californica*), 192
California grape (*Vitis californica*), 352, 366

California huckleberry (*Vaccinium ovatum*), 202
California incense cedar (*Calocedrus decurrens*), 305
California Indian pink (*Silene californica*), 230
California jewelflower (*Stanfordia californica*), 127
California juniper ( *Juniperus californica*), 170, 215
California lilac (*Ceanothus thyrsiflorus*), 470
California lilacs (*Ceanothus*), 215
California live oak (*Quercus agrifolia*), 191
California oatgrass (*Danthonia californica*), 209
California pipevine (*Aristolochia californica*), 202, 215
California polypody (*Polypodium californicum*), 203
California poppy (*Eschscholzia californica*), 108, 209, 216, 227, 357, 358, 496
California Province, 158–59, 170; California grassland, 158, 170; chaparral, 158, 159, 170; oak woodland, 158–59, 170
California rhododendron (*Rhododendron macrophyllum*), 202
California rose (*Rosa californica*), 366, 383
California sagebrush (*Artemisia californica*), 170, 216
California scrub oak (*Quercus cumosa*), 215
California seablite (*Suaeda californica*), 127
California snowdrop bush (*Styrax officinalis*), 202
California sycamore (*Platanus racemosa*), 170
California wax myrtle (*Myrica californica*), 216
California wild rose (*Rosa californica*), 202
calla lily (*Zantedeschia*), 404
calla lily (*Zantedeschia aethiopica*), 375, 407, 586–87
*Calla palustris,* 196, 197, 201, 220
Callery pear (*Pyrus calleryana*), 305
*Calliandra: eriophylla,* 108, 109, 227, 228, 318; *haematocephala,* 300
*Calliandra californica,* 318
*Callicarpa,* 484; *americana,* 187, 188, 308, 309, 310, 311, 312, 313, 361, 363; *bodinieri* 'Profusion', 315; *dichotoma,* 308, 377; *japonica,* 308, 377

calliopsis (*Coreopsis tinctoria*), 358, 360
*Callirhoe: involucrata,* 326, 327, 332, 333, 470; *triangulata,* 207
*Callistemon: citrinus,* 500; *linearis,* 536
*Callistephus,* 46; *chinensis,* 496, 498
*Callitriche hamulata,* 109
*Calluna,* 46
    *vulgaris,* 344, 485; 'Corbett Red', 365; 'H. E. Beale', 375; 'J. H. Hamilton', 344
*Calocedrus decurrens,* 170, 190, 305, 306
*Calochortus,* 208; *indecorus,* 130; *monanthus,* 131
calophytum rhododendron (*Rhododendron calophytum*), 305
*Caltha: leptosepala,* 166, 202; *palustris,* 108, 146, 161, 196, 201, 224
*Calycanthus,* 108, 510; *floridus,* 187, 188, 310, 338, 486; *occidentalis,* 202
calylophus (*Calylophus hartwegii*), 326
*Calylophus hartwegii,* 326, 332, 333
*Calyptocarpus vialis,* 343
*Calyptranthes pallens,* 310
calyx, 86, 104, 105–106
camas (*Camassia*), 208
camas (*Cammasia quamash*), 201
*Camassia,* 208, 394, 583; *cusickii,* 196; *leichtlinii,* 320; *quamash,* 190, 201; *scilloides,* 326
camassia (*Camassia cusickii*), 196
cambium, 71
*Camellia,* 46, 477, 522
    *japonica,* 10, 310, 378, 379, 383
    *sasanqua,* 310, 315, 378, 379, 383, 500; 'Yuletide', 315
    x *williamsii,* 316; 'Donation', 316; 'J. C. Williams', 316
camellia (*Camellia japonica*), 10, 310, 378, 379
camellia (*Camellia* x *williamsii*), 316
camellias (*Camellia*), 477, 522
Camerarius, Rudolph Jacob, 5
*Camissonia cheiranthifolia,* 216
camosh (*Camassia leichtlinii*), 320
*Campanula:*
    *barbata,* 604
    *carpatica,* 324, 325, 328, 604
    *garganica,* 604
    *glomerata,* 324, 331, 370; 'Joan Elliot', 331
    *lactiflora,* 324
    *medium,* 369, 370

*Campanula* (cont'd):
persicifolia 'Telham Beauty',
375
*portenschlagiana, 344*
*poscharskyana, 343, 345*
*robinsiae, 126*
*rotundifolia,* 190, 207, 331
campanula (*Campanula barbata*),
604
campanula (*Campanula carpatica*),
604
campanula (*Campanula
garganica*), 604
*Campsis:*
*radicans,* 222, 223, 346, 347,
348, 349, 350, 351, 352,
353, 359, 363, 364, 367,
484; 'Flava', 348, 351
x *tagliabuana* 'Madame
Galen', 351
Canada: public gardens in,
629–30, 721–23. *see also*
North America
Canada anemone (*Anemone
canadensis*), 189, 190
Canada columbine (*Aquilegia
canadensis*), 221, 222, 225, 226
Canada dick trefoil (*Desmodium
canadense*), 207
Canada hemlock (*Tsuga canadensis*), 167
Canada lily (*Lilium canadense*),
196, 206
Canada milk vetch (*Astragalus
canadensis*), 207
Canada thistle (*Cirsium arvense*),
137
Canada violet (*Viola canadensis*),
190
Canadian hemlock (*Tsuga
canadensis*), 316, 520, 536
Canadian mayflower (*Maianthemum canadense*), 320
Canadian moonseed (*Menispermum canadense*), 346
*Canaga odorata,* 300
*Canavalia molokaiensis,* 128
candelilla (*Euphorbia antisyphilitica*), 384
candlebush (*Senna alata*), 311
candlestick plant (*Senna alata*),
337, 356
candling, 505
Candolle, Augustin Pyramus de,
5–6
candytuft (*Iberis sempervirens*),
321, 332, 367
cane bluestem (*Bothriochloa
barbinodis*), 339
cane cactus (*Opuntia imbricata*),
215
*Canna,* 399; *flaccida,* 198, 199;
*indica,* 333; x *generalis,* 321,
355, 360, 368

canna (*Canna*), 399
canna (*Canna* x *generalis*), 321,
355, 360, 368
cannas (*Canna indica*), 333
canoe birch (*Betula populifolia*),
298, 377
canopy, 163, 184
canteloupe (*Cucumis melo*), 244
Canterbury bells (*Campanula
medium*), 369, 370
canyon live oak (*Quercus chrysolepsis*), 170
canyon penstemon (*Penstemon
pseudospectabilis*), 332
canyon phlox (*Phlox nana*), 215
Cape cowslip (*Lachenalia aloides*),
406
Cape gladioli (*Gladiolus* species),
405
Cape jasmine (*Gardenia jasminoides*), 484
Cape mallow (*Anisodontea* x *hypomandarum*), 317
Cape marigold (*Dimorphotheca
sinuata*), 358, 496
Cape primroses (*Streptocarpus*),
572, 592–93
caper-fruited tropidocarpum
(*Tropidocarpum capparideum*),
132
Cape tulp (*Homeria*), 405–406
capitulum, 84, 85
*Capparis cynophallophora,* 300
*Capsicum annuum,* 244–45, 371,
649–50
capsule, 91, 92
*Caragana:*
*arborescens,* 470, 609
*frutex,* 314; 'Globosa', 314
carambola (*Averrhoa carambola*),
300
caraway (*Carum carvi*), 254
caraway thyme (*Thymus herbabarona*), 345
*Cardamine: micranthera,* 126;
*pratensis,* 201
cardboard palm (*Zamia pumila*),
335
cardinal climber (*Ipomoea* x *multifida*), 347
cardinal flower (*Lobelia
cardinalis*), 198, 200, 203,
206, 207, 221, 223, 225,
226, 319, 322, 332, 359, 360
cardinal larkspur (*Delphinium
cardinale*), 109, 230
cardamom (*Elettaria
cardamomum*), 323
cardoon (*Cynara cardunculus*),
338
*Carduus nutans,* 137
*Carex,* 161, 162, 166, 322; *aboriginum,* 130; *comosa,* 201; *elegantissima* 'Variegata', 339;

*glauca,* 336, 339; *morrowii*
'Aureo-variegata', 329; *muskingumensis,* 197, 201; *nigra,*
336; *obnupta,* 202; *paniculata,*
197; *pendula,* 197, 201;
*planostachys,* 343; *siderosticha*
'Variegata', 336; *stipata,* 197;
*tumulicola,* 203
*Carissa:*
*grandiflora,* 284
*macrocarpa,* 310; 'Horizontalis', 342
carnation (*Dianthus caryophyllus*),
370
*Carnegiea gigantea,* 124, 169, 384
carnivores, 174
carnivorous plants, 692–93
carob (*Ceratonia siliqua*), 306
Carolina allspice (*Calycanthus
floridus*), 187, 188, 338, 486
Carolina aster (*Aster carolinianus*),
361
Carolina basswood (*Tilia caroliniana*), 303
Carolina buckthorn (*Frangula
caroliniana*), 302, 303
Carolina buckthorn (*Rhamnus
caroliniana*), 188
Carolina bush pea (*Thermopsis
villosa*), 362, 379
Carolina jessamine (*Gelsemium
sempervirens*), 350, 352, 353,
380, 381
Carolina linden (*Tilia
caroliniana*), 303
Carolina lupine (*Thermopsis caroliniana*), 322
Carolina lupine (*Thermopsis villosa*), 498
Carolina rhododendron (*Rhododendron carolinianum*), 308,
309, 377
Carolina silverbell (*Halesia carolina*), 187, 188, 300, 305,
477, 484, 500
Caroline jessamine (*Gelsemium
sempervirens*), 197
Carpathian bellflower (*Campanula carpatica*), 325
carpel, 86, 90
carpenter bees, 410
*Carpenteria californica,* 191, 215,
317; 'Elizabeth', 317
carpet bugle (*Ajuga reptans*),
344
carpet geranium (*Geranium
incanum*), 345
carpet juniper (*Juniperus horizontalis*), 308
*Carpinus:*
*betulus,* 301; 'Fastigiata', 301
*caroliniana,* 189, 299, 301,
379, 514
*cordata,* 305

*Carpobrotus: chilensis,* 137; *edulis,*
137
carrot family, 56
carrot rust fly, 551
carrots (*Daucus carota*), 238–39
carrotwood (*Cupaniopsis anacardiodes*), 137
Carson, Rachel, 142
*Carum carvi,* 254
*Carya,* 167, 282, 359; *aquatica,*
168; *ovata,* 189, 301, 362, 379
Caryophyllaceae, 55
Caryophyllidae, 54–55
*Caryopteris,* 359
x *clandonensis,* 309, 314, 316,
317, 318, 364, 366, 470,
484; 'Dark Knight', 316
cascade's grape (*Mahonia nervosa*),
345
Cascades Oregon grape (*Mahonia
nervosa* var. *nervosa*), 191
cascara sagrada (*Rhamnus purshiana*), 202
*Cassia,* 366; *alata,* 337; *fistula,*
300; *javanica,* 300; *nemophila,*
318
*Cassiope,* 166
*Castanea,* 282, 673; *dentata,* 124,
146, 167; *mollissima,* 305
caster-oil plant (*Ricinus communis*), 333
*Castilleja,* 208; *angustifolia,* 109;
*californica,* 209; *chromosa,* 226,
227, 228; *coccinea,* 208, 220,
221, 222; *cruenta,* 130; *indivisa,* 356; *integra,* 215, 226,
227; *miniata,* 226, 227, 228;
*purpurea,* 326; *sessiliflora,* 109,
225, 226, 227, 229
cast-iron plant (*Aspidistra elatior*), 342, 572
castor bean (*Ricinus communis*),
337, 355, 356, 369, 659
castor-oil plant (*Ricinus
communis*), 659
*Casuarina equisetifolia,* 137, 152
Catalina currant (*Ribes viburnifolium*), 215
catalpa (*Catalpa speciosa*), 337
*Catalpa speciosa,* 302, 303, 337
*Catasetum,* 324
catawba rhododendron (*Rhododendron catawbiense*), 308, 309
catbriar (*Smilax laurifolia*), 199
catchfly (*Silene armeria*), 365
cat-claws (*Acacia*), 367
*Catharanthus,* 46; *roseus,* 137,
323, 324, 354, 355, 358,
369, 487, 496
catkin, 84, 85
catmint (*Nepeta mussinii*),
254–55, 325
catmint (*Nepeta racemosa*),
254–55

catmint (*Nepeta sibirica*), 325

catmint (*Nepeta x faassenii*), 254–55, 331, 332, 370

catmint (*Nepeta x mussinii*), 319

catnip (*Nepeta cataria*), 255

cats and poisonous plants, 646

cat's claw (*Caesalpinia gilliesii*), 137

cat's claw (*Pithecellobium unguis-cati*), 361

cat's claw vine (*Macfadyena unguis-cati*), 352, 353

catseye (*Cryptantha aperta*), 131

cattail (*Typha angustifolia*), 198

cattail (*Typha domingensis*), 203

cattails (*Typha*), 195

*Cattleya,* 324

caudate leaf apex, 81

cauliflory, 84, 85

*Caulophyllum thalictroides,* 362

*Ceanothus,* 215, 317; *americanus,* 108, 187, 206, 207, 220, 221, 222, 224, 225, 226, 359, 470; *arboreus,* 306, 366; *fendleri,* 190; *ferrisae,* 126; 'Frosty Blue', 317; *integerrimus,* 170; 'Julia Phelps', 317; *maritimus:* 'Pt. Sierra', 345; 'Ray Hartman', 306; *thyrsiflorus,* 170, 216, 316, 366, 470

ceanothus (*Ceanothus*), 306

cedar-apple rust, 561

cedar elm (*Ulmus crassifolia*), 188, 303

cedar of Lebanon (*Cedrus libani*), 673

cedar sage (*Salvia roemeriana*), 327, 337, 374

cedar sedge (*Carex planostachys*), 343

*Cedrus:*
    *atlantica,* 297, 306; 'Glauca', 297, 377;
    *deodara,* 305, 306
    *libani,* 673

celandine poppy (*Stylophorum diphyllum*), 188

*Celastrus: orbiculatus,* 137; *scandens,* 346, 349, 351, 359

*Celosia,* 355, 356
    *argentea,* 69; var. *cristata,* 371, 372, 373; var. *plumosa,* 374
    *cristata,* 69
    *plumosa,* 496

celosias (*Celosia*), 355

*Celtis,* 470; *occidentalis,* 281, 282, 301, 303, 359, 362, 364, 609; *pallida,* 108, 227, 367; *reticulata,* 304, 306, 363

cemetery white flag (*Iris albicans*), 369

cenizo (*Leucophyllum frutescens*), 312, 337

*Centaurea: americana,* 357; *cineraria,* 367; *cyanus,* 367, 370, 372, 375, 471, 496; *dealbata,* 366; *montana,* 320; *moschata,* 375; *seridis* subsp. *maritima,* 367

*Centaurium sebaeoides,* 128

Center for Plant Conservation (CPC), 124–25, 129

Central prairies and plains, 152–54, 168–69; mixed-grass prairie, 154, 169; oak savannah, 153–54, 168; shortgrass prairie, 154, 169; tallgrass prairie, 154, 169

*Centranthus ruber,* 319, 321, 328, 330, 332, 333, 360, 364, 367

*Centres of Plant Diversity: A Guide and Strategy for Their Conservation,* 114

*Centrosema virginianum,* 361

century plant (*Agave americana*), 339

century plants (*Agave*), 339, 384

*Cephalanthus occidentalis,* 196, 197, 199, 201, 221, 222, 309, 359, 360, 368

*Cephalotaxus,* 514
    *harringtonia,* 308, 377, 485; 'Nana', 341

*Cerastium tomentosum,* 328, 331, 342, 344, 345

*Ceratonia siliqua,* 306

*Ceratophyllum,* 109

*Ceratostigma plumbaginoides,* 320, 345, 486

*Cercidiphyllum: japonicum,* 297, 305; x 'Desert Museum', 307

*Cercidium,* 169, 384; *floridum,* 169

*Cercis,* 510
    *canadensis,* 84, 187, 189, 222, 298, 299, 302, 305, 477, 500; 'Forest Pansy', 305; var. *texensis,* 302, 303, 307, 373; var. *texensis* 'Oklahoma', 299, 302, 303, 380
    *occidentalis,* 306, 307, 317, 366
    *reniformis,* 303, 380

*Cercocarpus,* 215; *betuloides,* 170; *ledifolius,* 318, 384; *montanus* var. *argentus,* 303

cercospora leaf blight, 561–62

*Ceropegia woodii,* 524, 596

*Cestrum: elegans* 'Smithii', 500; *nocturnum,* 595

*Chaenomeles,* 46, 509, 510 'Apple Blossom', 365; *japonica,* 310; 'Cameo', 375 *speciosa,* 313, 368, 370, 378

chain fern (*Woodwardia fimbriata*), 202, 203

chalice vine (*Solandra guttata*), 348, 349

chalk lettuce (*Dudleya pulverulenta*), 216

chalk maple (*Acer leucoderme*), 299

chalk maple (*Acer saccharum* subsp. *leucoderme*), 188

*Chamaebatiaria millefolium,* 318, 338

*Chamaecrista fasciculata,* 356, 363

*Chamaecyparis,* 377, 496, 514
    *obtusa,* 298, 500; 'Aurea', 338
    *pisifera,* 380, 514; 'Filifera Aurea', 383
    *thyoides,* 161, 168

*Chamaedaphne calyculata,* 166, 200

*Chamaedorea elegans,* 301

*Chamaelirium luteum,* 188

*Chamaemelum nobile,* 255

*Chamaesyce: deppeana,* 128; *halemanui,* 128; *kuwaleana,* 128

*Chamaecyparis,* 485

chamisa (*Chrysothamnus nauseosus*), 213, 313

chamise (*Adenostoma fasciculatum*), 170, 215

chaparral, 158, 159, 170, 172, 213, 215

chaparral sage (*Salvia clevelandii*), 318

Chapman rhododendron (*Rhododendron chapmanii*), 127

chartaceous leaves, 76

chasmanthe (*Chasmanthe floribunda*), 402

*Chasmanthe floribunda,* 402

*Chasmanthium latifolium,* 198, 216, 320, 322, 327, 328, 343, 373, 374, 379

chaste tree (*Vitex agnus-castus*), 300, 307, 309, 318, 359, 360, 365, 367, 484

che (*Cudrania tricuspidata*), 281

checkbloom (*Sidalcea malviflora*), 366

checkerberry (*Gaultheria procumbens*), 282

checkerbloom (*Sidalcea malviflora*), 209, 367, 369

*Cheiranthus,* 496

*Chelone glabra,* 196, 207, 221, 223

Chenault coralberry (*Symphoricarpos* x *chenaultii*), 315

cherries, 270–71, 283; pests of, 285–86

cherry laurel (*Prunus caroliniana*), 188, 314, 381

cherry laurel (*Prunus carolinianaa*), 380

cherry laurel (*Prunus laurocerasus*), 500

cherry plum (*Prunus cerasifera*), 304

cherry sage (*Salvia greggii*), 318, 367

chervil (*Anthriscus cereifolium*), 255, 580

chestnut (*Castanea*), 282, 673

chestnut oak (*Quercus muehlenbergii*), 72

chia (*Salvia columbariae*), 209

chicksaw plum (*Prunus angustifolia*), 363

chicory (*Cichorium intybus*), 255

Chihuahuan Desert, 156, 169–70

Chihuahuan sage (*Leucophyllum laevigatum*), 318

Chihuahua scurfpea (*Pediomelum pentaphyllum*), 132

Chilean gunnera (*Gunnera tinctoria*), 338

Chilean myrtle (*Luma apiculata*), 306

chili pepper (*Capsicum annuum*), 649–50

*Chilopsis linearis,* 109, 202, 213, 228, 302, 303, 306, 307, 337, 363, 367

*Chimaphila maculata,* 188

chimera, 69

*Chimonanthus praecox,* 309, 376, 378, 382, 383

China, 635, 638

China aster (*Callistephus chinensis*), 496, 498

chinaberry (*Melia azedarach*), 138, 655–56

China fir (*Cunninghamia lanceolata*), 299

China pink (*Dianthus chinensis*), 354

chinch bug, 551

Chinese abelia (*Abelia chinensis*), 310

Chinese anemone (*Anemone hupehensis*), 7

Chinese astilbe (*Astilbe chinensis*), 328

Chinese chestnut (*Castanea mollissima*), 305

Chinese date (*Zizyphus jujuba*), 307

Chinese elm (*Ulmus parvifolia*), 536

Chinese evergreen (*Aglaonema modestum*), 323

Chinese evergreens (*Aglaonemas*), 572

Chinese fan palm (*Livistona chinensis*), 301

Chinese flame tree (*Koelreuteria bipinnata*), 306

Chinese fringe tree (*Chionanthus retusus*), 305

Chinese hibiscus (*Hibiscus rosa-sinensis*), 484, 594

Chinese holly (*Ilex cornuta*), 377, 380

Chinese holly grape (*Mahonia lomariifolia*), 339

Chinese houses (*Collinsia heterophylla*), 209

Chinese juniper (*Juniperus chinensis*), 308, 380, 501

Chinese lilac (*Syringa chinensis*), 312, 315

Chinese lilacs (*Syringa*), 318, 510

Chinese parasol tree (*Firmiana simplex*), 299, 378

Chinese photinia (*Photinia serratifolia*), 380, 381

Chinese pistache (*Pistacia chinensis*), 299, 307

Chinese quince (*Cydonia sinensis*), 536

Chinese sweet plum (*Sageretia thea*), 536

Chinese tallow tree (*Sapium sebiferum*), 139

Chinese wisteria (*Wisteria sinensis*), 139, 346, 350, 351, 352

Chinese witchhazel (*Hamamelis mollis*), 298, 376, 501

chinkapin oak (*Quercus muehlenbergii*), 302, 609

*Chionanthus: retusus*, 305; *virginicus*, 187, 188, 299, 302, 500

*Chionodoxa*, 394–95, 496, 582

chipmunks, 230

chippers, 619

chitalpa (x *Chitalpa tashkentensis*), 307

chives (*Allium schoenoprasum*), 255, 365, 580

chives (*Allium*), 359, 496

*Chloris*, 337

*Chlorophytum comosum*, 323, 342, 497, 571, 572

chocolate vine (*Akebia quinata*), 351

*Choisya ternata*, 500

chokeberries (*Aronia*), 359

chokeberry (*Aronia melanocarpa*), 281, 282

chokecherry (*Prunus virginiana* var. *melanocarpa*), 364

chokecherry (*Prunus virginiana*), 359

cholla (*Opuntia imbricata*), 337

*Chorisia speciosa*, 300

*Chorizanthe: howellii*, 126; *valida*, 126

Christmas aster (*Aster pratensis*), 327, 337, 363

Christmas aster (*Aster sericeus* var. *microphyllus*), 373, 380

Christmas fern (*Polystichum acrostichoides*), 188, 198, 320, 322, 343, 379, 381

Christmas rose (*Helleborus niger*), 330, 376, 382

*Chrysalidocarpus cabadae*, 301

*Chrysanthemum*, 496; *balsamita*, 256; *frutescens*, 522; *maximum*, 320; *parthenium, see Tanacetum parthenium; weyrichii*, 604

chrysanthemum (*Chrysanthemum weyrichii*), 604

chrysanthemum (*Dendranthema* x *grandiflorum*), 321, 324

*Chrysobalanus icaco*, 310, 361

*Chrysogonum virginianum*, 187, 188, 322

*Chrysophyllum oliviforme*, 168, 300, 361

*Chrysopsis floridana*, 126

*Chrysothamnus*, 169; *nauseosus*, 213, 215, 313, 364

Chuckwalla's delight (*Bebbia juncea*), 108, 227

chuparosa (*Justica californica*), 109, 228

Church, Thomas Dolliver, 6

*Cibotium*, 324

*Cichorium intybus*, 180, 255

cilantro (*Coriandrum sativum*), 580

ciliate leaf margin, 79

*Cimicifuga: japonica* var. *acerina*, 325

*laciniata*, 201, 329

*racemosa*, 187, 188, 319, 325, 368, 379; 'Atropurpurea', 319

*simplex*, 325

*Cineraria maritima*, 496

cinnamon clethra (*Clethra acuminata*), 187

cinnamon fern (*Osmunda cinnamomea*), 190, 198, 201, 320, 335

cinnamon vine (*Dioscorea battatas*), 346

cinquefoils (*Potentilla*), 166

circinate leaf folding, 82

*Circuta maculata*, 650

*Cirsium: arvense*, 137; *vulgare*, 137

*Cissus: antarctica*, 524; 'Minima', 572

*rhombifolia*, 524, 572

*striata*, 572

*Cistus:* x *corbariensis*, 316; x *purpureus*, 500; x *skanbergii*, 317

CITES, 134, 640

*Citrullus lanatus*, 244

*Citrus*, 284, 300, 301, 306, 591; *latifolia*, 300

citruses (*Citrus*), 284, 300, 301, 306, 591

city gardening, 598–610; air pollution and, 601; balcony gardens, 606; climate and, 600–601; container gardens, 606–607; coping with conditions of, 602–605; dwarf and compact plants for, 603–604; fruit and vegetable gardens, 607–609; hedges, fences, and arbors, 604–605; native and nonindigenous plants, 601; rooftop gardens, 605–606; soil and, 599–600, 602–603; trees, street, 608, 609–10; window boxes, 607

cladistics, 62–63

*Cladium jamaicensis*, 168

cladograms, 62–63

*Cladrastis kentukea (C. lutea)*, 10, 188, 298, 306, 377, 477

claret ash (*Fraxinus augustifolia*), 307

claret cup (*Echinocereus triglochidiatus*), 215

*Clarkia*, 215; *amoena*, 209, 375; *concinna*, 358; *franciscana*, 126

clarkias (*Clarkia*), 215

Clary sage (*Salvia sclarea*), 263, 339, 370, 470

classification of plants, *see* plant classification

clay soil, 433

*Claytonia virginica*, 147

clear-cutting, 124

cleft-and-saddle grafting, 490–93

*Clematis*, 46, 484

*armandii*, 347, 348, 352

*davidiana*, 309

*dioscoreifolia*, 347, 350

'Jackmanii', 351

*ligusticifolia*, 202, 351

*montana:* 'Grandiflora', 347; var. *rubens*, 351, 353

*morefieldii*, 126

'Niobe', 351

*orientalis*, 351

*paniculata*, 347, 349, 351

*pitcheri*, 350

*rehderiana*, 351

*socialis*, 126

*stans*, 309

*tangutica*, 349

*terniflora*, 137, 347, 350, 351

*texensis*, 347, 348, 353

*virginiana*, 349

*vitalba*, 351

*viticella*, 349, 351; 'Rubra', 351

x *henryi*, 348

x *jackmanii*, 347, 352, 509

clematis (*Clematis armandii*), 347, 348, 352

clematis (*Clematis montana* var. *rubens*), 351

clematis (*Clematis rehderiana*), 351

clematis (*Clematis viticella*), 349, 351

clematis (*Clematis* x *henryi*), 348

clematis (*Clematis* x *jackmanii*), 347, 352

clematis (*Clematis* x *terniflora*), 347

clematis (*Clematis*), 484

Clements, Frederic E., 6

cleome (*Cleome hassleriana*), 355, 360

*Cleome hassleriana*, 355, 356, 357, 358, 360, 362

*Clermontia: lindseyana*, 128; *multiflora*, 131; *peleana*, 128; *pyrularia*, 128

clerodendron (*Clerodendrum thomsoniae*), 348, 349

*Clerodendrum*, 484, 486; *philippinum*, 591; *thomsoniae*, 311, 348, 349, 522; *trichotomum*, 299, 305; *ugandense*, 311; *wallichii*, 310, 311

*Clethra: acuminata*, 187; *alnifolia*, 108, 187, 188, 201, 220, 222, 225, 226, 309, 310, 312, 360, 365, 371, 481, 484; *barbinervis*, 308, 382

Cleveland sage (*Salvia clevelandii*), 317, 366

cliff penstemon (*Penstemon rupicola*), 229

cliffrose (*Cowania mexicana*), 318

cliffrose (*Purshia mexicana*), 376

climate, 21–33; conditions by continent, 23–24; evaporation, 31–33; frost and freezing, 29, 32–33; precipitation, 29–31, 34–35, 36; regions of the U.S., 21–23; temperatures, high and low, 24–29

climbing aster (*Aster carolinianus*), 199

climbing hempweed (*Mikania scandens*), 199

climbing hydrangea (*Hydrangea anomala*), 346, 347, 348, 351, 352

climbing hydrangea (*Hydrangea petiolaris*), 349, 351, 524

climbing jasmine (*Jasminum officinale*), 351, 352

climbing prairie rose (*Rosa setigera*), 364

*Clintonia andrewsiana*, 192

*Clivia*, 402
  *miniata*, 587; var. *citrina*, 594
clivia (*Clivia*), 402
clivia (*Clivia miniata*), 587
clivia (*Clivia miniata* var. *citrina*), 594
cloches (hot caps), 234
clove currant (*Ribes odoratum*), 281, 282, 283, 370
clove pink (*Dianthus caryophyllus*), 262
clovers (*Trifolium*), 359
clustered bellflower (*Campanula glomerata*), 331
cluster-head pink (*Dianthus carthusianorum*), 375
*Clytostoma callistegioides*, 352, 353, 524
coastal buckwheat (*Eriogonum fasciculatum*), 108, 229, 230
coastal California region, 294–95; annuals for, 358; butterflies and wildlife, plants to attract, 365–66; flowers for cutting, 375; foliage plants for, 339; ground covers for, 345; heirloom flowers, 370–71; perennials for, 330–32; shrubs for, 316–17; trees for, 305–306; vines for, 352; winter interest, plants for, 383
coastal live oak (*Quercus virginiana*), 381
Coastal Plain, 20, 149–51; bottomland forest, 150, 168; maritime communities, 150–51, 168; mesic pine forest, 149–50, 167; Northern Pine Barrens, 149, 167; savannah and pocosin, 150, 167–68; upland hardwood forest, 149, 167; xeric pine forest, 149, 167
coastal plains willow (*Salix caroliniana*), 199
coastal strawberry (*Fragaria chiloensis*), 216
coastal wallflower (*Erysimum concinnum*), 216
coastal wallflower (*Erysimum suffrutescens*), 216
coast live oak (*Quercus agrifolia*), 170, 216, 306, 366
coast redwood (*Sequoia sempervirens*), 66, 170, 306
coast silk-tassel (*Garrya elliptica*), 306, 317, 383
*Cobaea scandens*, 348, 487
*Coccoloba: diversifolia*, 168, 300, 361; *uvifera*, 108, 223, 361
*Coccothrinax*, 301; *argentata*, 301, 361
coccothrinax palms (*Coccothrinax*), 301

*Cocculus laurifolius*, 310
cockscomb (*Celosia argentea* var. *cristata*), 371, 372, 373
cockscomb (*Celosia cristata*), 69
cockscombs (*Celosia*), 356
cockspur hawthorn (*Crataegus crus-galli*), 303, 307, 500
Coco-de-mer palm (*Lodoicea maldivica*), 110
coconut palm (*Cocos nucifera*), 301
cocoplum (*Chrysobalanus icaco*), 310, 361
*Cocos nucifera*, 301
*Codiaeum*, 310; *variegatum*: var. *pictum*, 336
codling moth, 551–52
codominants, 165
*Coelorachis rugosa*, 199
coevolution, 104, 107, 176
coffeeberry (*Rhamnus californica*), 191, 215, 216
Coffey, George Nelson, 37–38
*Coix lacryma-jobi*, 374
*Colchicum*, 399; *autumnale*, 320, 650–51
colchicum (*Colchicum*), 399
Colden, Jane, 6
cold frames, 234–35
*Coleus, see Selenostemon; amboinicus, see Plectranthus amboinicus*
coleus (*Solenostemon*), 522
coleus (*Solenostemon scutellaroides*), 354, 355, 357, 368, 372, 496
colic root (*Canna flaccida*), 199
collection, plants threatened by, 123, 133–35
*Collinsia*, 215; *heterophylla*, 209, 358
collinsias (*Collinsia*), 215
*Colocasia esculenta*, 333
Colorado, 438, 622, 666, 694, 695
Colorado blue spruce (*Picea pungens*), 304, 305, 315, 377
Colorado blue spruce (*Picea pungens* f. *glauca*), 382
Colorado columbine (*Aquilegia caerulea*), 227
Colorado four-o'clock (*Mirabilis multiflora*), 209
Colorado male ern (*Dryopteris filix-mas*), 328
Colorado pinyon (*Pinus edulis*), 215
Colorado potato beetles, 552
Colorado red cedar (*Juniperus scopulorum*), 501
coltsfoot (*Maianthemum dilatatum*), 345
coltsfoot (*Petasites frigidus*), 191, 200

*Colubrina oppositifolia*, 128
columbine (*Aquilegia bertolonii*), 604
columbine (*Aquilegia canadensis*), 322, 335
columbine (*Aquilegia formosa*), 201
columbine (*Aquilegia saximontana*), 604
columbine (*Aquilegia vulgaris*), 370
columbine meadow rue (*Thalictrum aquilegiifolium*), 335
columbines (*Aquilegia*), 324, 365, 366
columbines (*Aquilegia vulgaris*), 368, 369
*Columnea*, 572
Comb speedwell (*Veronica pectinata*), 344
comfrey (*Symphytum officinale*), 256
Commelinidae, 59–61
common box (*Buxus sempervirens*), 514, 520
common camas (*Camassia quamash*), 190
common cherries (*Prunus domestica*), 85
common crape myrtle (*Lagerstroemia indica*), 501
common crowsfoot (*Aquilegia vulgaris*), 367
common elderberry (*Sambucus canadensis*), 364
common evening primrose (*Oenothera biennis*), 108, 220, 222, 224, 225
common fennel (*Foeniculum vulgare*), 360
common fig (*Ficus carica*), 333
common foxglove (*Digitalis purpurea*), 370
common guava (*Psidium guajava*), 138
common hackberry (*Celtis occidentalis*), 303, 609
common heliotrope (*Heliotropium arborescens*), 355, 362
common horehound (*Marrubium vulgare*), 138
common ironweed (*Vernonia noveboracensis*), 197
common juniper (*Juniperus communis*), 190, 380
common juniper (*Juniperus communis* var. *saxatilis*), 344, 364
common lantana (*Lantana camara*), 522
common lilac (*Syringa vulgaris*), 311, 313, 315, 368, 369, 370, 481
common lilacs (*Syringa*), 510

common moonseed (*Menispermum canadense*), 349
common ninebark (*Physocarpus opulifolius*), 314
common oleander (*Nerium oleander*), 138
common owl's clover (*Orthocarpus purpurascens*), 209
common plantain lily (*Hosta lancifolia*), 367, 369
common reed (*Phragmites communis*), 162
common snowberry (*Symphoricarpos albus*), 382
common St-John's wort (*Hypericum perforatum*), 138
common sunflower (*Helianthus annuus*), 208, 215, 375
common tarweed (*Madia elegans*), 209
common teasel (*Dipsacus fullonum*), 137
common thyme (*Thymus vulgaris*), 265, 338, 365, 580, 683
common toadflax (*Linaria vulgaris*), 138
common winter hazel (*Corylopsis spicata*), 309
common yarrow (*Achillea millefolium*), 331, 365
common zinnia (*Zinnia elegans*), 356, 362
communities, plant, *see* plant communities
compass plant (*Silphium laciniatum*), 207, 362
composites, 169
composting, 441–47; amount to use, 446; benefits of, 446; done, knowing when it is, 444; as fertilizing method, 458; hot, 442–43; materials suitable for, 443; the process of, 442; propagation medium, compost as, 475; rule of thumb for, 442; techniques for, 444–46; tools for, 618–19
compound leaves, 74–76
*Comptonia peregrina*, 216, 334
concolor fir (*Abies concolor*), 377, 380
coneflower (*Echinacea purpurea*), 370
coneflower (*Rudbeckia californica*), 203
coneflower (*Rudbeckia fulgida*), 321
coneflowers (*Echinacea*), 153, 207, 362
Confederate jasmine (*Trachelospermum jasminoides*), 347, 348

*Congea tomentosa,* 348, 349
Congressional Office of Technology, 136
conifers (Pinophyta), 46, 52; propagating, 103
*Conium maculatum,* 650–51, 674–75
Connecticut, 438, 666, 694, 695, 723
*Conocarpus erectus,* 168, 300
*Conoclinium coelestinum,* 372
*Conocybe filaris,* 663
*Conradina:* etonia, 126; *glabra,* 126
conservation, *see* plant diversity; vanishing plants
*Consolida:* ajacis, 358; *ambigua,* 373, 375
Consultative Group on International Agricultural Research (CGIAR), 122
container gardening, 493–501; annuals for, 498; bulbs for, 498; for city gardeners, 606–607; container selection, 493, 494–95; covering drainage holes, 495, 497; fertilizing, 493, 497–98; for fruits, 283–84; for herbs, 249–50; overwintering, 501; perennials for, 498; planting medium, 236, 495–96; plant selection, 501–502; rejuvenation, 498–401; shrubs for, 500, 501; trees for, 500–501; unique considerations for, 493; for vegetables, 235–36, 498–99; watering, 493, 497
*Convallaria majalis,* 320, 343, 344, 367, 370, 395, 651–52, 677
Convention on Biological Diversity, 112
Convention on International Trade in Endangered Species of Wild Fauna and Flora (CITES), 134, 640
conversions, weights, and measures, 733–37
*Convolvulus:* cneorum, 318; *sabatius,* 345; *tricolor,* 347
cooba (*Acacia salicina*), 307
Cook, Captain James, 4
Cooley's meadowrue (*Thalictrum cooleyi*), 127
coolibah (*Eucalyptus microtheca*), 306
coontie (*Zamia integrifolia*), 342
coontie (*Zamia pumila*), 168
Cooperative Extension Service, 233, 438
*Cooperia pedunculata,* 326, 327
copper, 547
copperleaf (*Acalypha wilkensiana*), 336, 337

copperpod (*Peltophorum pterocarpum*), 301
coppicing, 519
*Coprinus atramentarius,* 664
*Coprosma,* 46
*Coptis,* 161; *laciniata,* 191, 344; *trifolia* subsp. *groenlandica,* 196
coral bean (*Erythrina herbacea*), 222, 223, 224
coral bells (*Heuchera americana*), 187, 328, 332
coral bells (*Heuchera maxima*), 331
coral bells (*Heuchera sanguinea*), 190, 322, 329
coral berry (*Ardisia crispa*), 572
coralberry (*Symphoricarpos orbiculatus*), 221, 225, 226, 312, 343, 380
coral honeysuckle (*Lonicera heckrottii*), 353
coral honeysuckle (*Lonicera sempervirens*), 197, 347, 348, 349, 350, 353, 363, 367
coral plant (*Jatropha multifida*), 311, 654
coral vine (*Antigonon leptopus*), 352, 353
cordate leaf base, 78, 79
*Cordia:* boissieri, 318; *globosa,* 223, 224, 361; *sebestena,* 224, 300
cordia (*Cordia globosa*), 361
*Cordylanthus palmatus,* 126
*Cordyline terminalis,* 336, 497
*Coreopsis,* 207
*auriculata,* 221; 'Nana', 345
*grandiflora,* 324, 357; 'Early Sunrise', 357
*lanceolata,* 208, 326, 327, 328, 330, 373; 'Goldfink', 330
*leavenworthii,* 199, 223, 361
*tinctoria,* 356, 358, 360
*verticillata,* 319, 321, 322, 324, 325, 329, 330, 334, 335, 470; 'Moonbeam', 319, 329, 330, 375
coreopsis (*Coreopsis*), 207
coreopsis (*Coreopsis grandiflora*), 324, 357
coreopsis (*Coreopsis lanceolata*), 326, 327, 328, 373
coreopsis (*Coreopsis verticillata*), 319, 324, 330, 334
*Coreopsis tinctoria,* 360
coriaceous leaves, 76
coriander (*Coriandrum sativum*), 580
coriander (*Tanacetum balsamita*), 256
*Coriandrum sativum,* 580
cork oak (*Quercus suber*), 306, 307

corky-stemmed passion vine (*Passiflora suberosa*), 361
corms, 72, 73, 391. *see also* bulbs
corn, sweet (*Zea mays*), 243
corn cockle (*Agrostemma githago*), 357
corn earworm, 552
cornelian cherry (*Cornus mas*), 281, 282, 283, 376, 378, 510
cornflower (*Centaurea cyanus*), 370, 375
corn lily (*Veratrum californicum*), 203
corn-lily (*Ixia*), 406
cornstalk plant (*Dracaena fragrans*), 572
*Cornus,* 46, 161, 477, 481, 484
*alba,* 201, 312, 376; 'Argenteo-marginata', 338; 'Elegantissima', 16; 'Sibirica', 378, 382, 500
*alternifolia,* 189, 201, 302, 304, 362, 379, 477
*amomum,* 196, 360
*canadensis,* 146, 187, 191, 344
*drummondii,* 303, 313, 363
'Eddie's White Wonder', 306
*florida,* 10, 108, 187, 188, 189, 218, 220, 221, 225, 298, 299, 360, 477, 510
*kousa,* 298, 300, 305, 316, 377, 500, 510; 'Lustgarten Weeping', 316; 'Rosabella', 305
*mas,* 281, 282, 283, 376, 378, 382, 510
*nuttallii,* 10, 190, 191, 305, 365
*racemosa,* 201, 312, 314, 362
*sanguinea,* 376
*stolonifera,* 190, 196, 201, 202, 311, 314, 362, 377, 381, 383; 'Cardinal', 378; 'Flaviramea', 314, 365, 378, 381, 382; 'Isanti', 314, 315; 'Silver and Gold', 308, 334
corolla, 86, 106; parts of, 89; shapes of, 89–90
corona, 86
*Coronilla varia,* 137
*Correa,* 317; 'Ivory Bells', 317
Corsican hellebore (*Helleborus argutifolius*), 375, 383
*Cortaderia:* jubata, 137; *selloana,* 137
cortex of the stem, 71
corydalis (*Corydalis scouleri*), 201
*Corydalis scouleri,* 201, 338
*Corylopsis,* 376; *glabrescens,* 378; *pauciflora,* 308, 382; *spicata,* 309

*Corylus,* 282, 362
*americana,* 359, 381
*avellana,* 359, 500; 'Contorta', 377, 378, 381; *cornuta,* 381; var. *californica,* 191, 306
corymb, 84, 85
corymb deutzia (*Deutzia corymbosa*), 312
*Coryphantha vivipara,* 215
*Cosmos,* 471
*bipinnatus,* 334, 358, 368, 372, 375
*sulphureus,* 356, 357, 360; 'Bright Lights', 356, 357, 373; 'Sunny Gold', 357
cosmos (*Cosmos*), 471
cosmos (*Cosmos bipinnatus*), 334, 368, 372, 375
cosmos (*Cosmos sulphureus*), 356, 357
Costa Rica, 638
costmary (*Tanacetum balsamita*), 256
*Costus speciosus,* 323
cota (*Thelesperma megapotamicum*), 371
*Cotinus:*
coggygria, 299, 311, 317; 'Royal Purple', 317, 339
obovatus, 189, 298, 301, 302, 303, 500
*Cotoneaster,* 46, 377
*acutifolia,* 314
*apiculatus,* 308; 'Tom Thumb', 604
*buxifolius,* 318
*congestus* 'Likiang', 500
*dammeri,* 341
*divaricata,* 314
*horizontalis,* 308, 384, 470
*lacteus,* 137
*microphyllus,* 137, 345
*multiflorus,* 314
*pannosus,* 137
cotoneaster (*Cotoneaster lacteus*), 137
cotoneaster (*Cotoneaster microphyllus*), 137
cotoneaster (*Cotoneaster pannosus*), 137
cotoneasters (*Cotoneaster*), 377
cottage garden style, 248
cottage pink (*Dianthus plumarius*), 321
cottongrass (*Eriophorum vaginatum* var. *spissum*), 201
cottongrass (*Eriophorum viridicarinatum*), 202
cottongrasses (*Eriophorum*), 166
cottonwood (*Populus deltoides*), 167
*Cowania mexicana,* 318

cow parsnip (*Heracleum lanatum*), 202, 203

coyote bush (*Baccharis pilularis*), 215, 216

coyote ceanothus (*Ceanothus ferrisae*), 126

coyote willow (*Salix exigua*), 381

crabapple (*Malus*), 270, 273, 282, 304, 484, 510, 514

cranberry (*Vaccinium*), 481

cranberry (*Vaccinium macrocarpon*), 281, 282, 284

cranberry bush (*Viburnum opulus*), 139

cranberry cotoneaster (*Cotoneaster apiculatus*), 308

cranesbill (*Geranium endressii*), 329

cranesbill (*Geranium maculatum*), 187, 188, 189, 202

crape jasmine (*Tabernaemontana divaricata*), 311

crape myrtle (*Lagerstroemia fauriei*), 378

crape myrtle (*Lagerstroemia indica*), 10, 303, 306, 307, 311, 380, 484

*Crassula argentea*, 536

*Crataegus*, 218, 282, 283, 284, 359, 363, 477, 609
    *apiifolia*, 188, 299
    *crus-galli*, 302, 303, 304, 307, 470, 500; 'Inermis', 302, 304
    *douglasii*, 191
    *lavallei*, 305
    *marshallii*, 188, 299
    *mollis*, 304
    *monogyna*, 137
    *phaenopyrum*, 305, 307
    *viridis*, 187, 303, 380; 'Winter King', 500
    x *lavallei*, 298, 377, 382
    x *mordenensis* 'Snowbird', 302
    x 'Winter King', 377

creek dogwood (*Cornus stolonifera*), 201

creeping baby's breath (*Gypsophila repens*), 332, 333

creeping barberry (*Berberis reptans*), 343

creeping Charlie (*Lippia nodiflora*), 342, 361

creeping cinquefoil (*Potentilla neumanniana*), 344

creeping fern (*Lygodium palmatum*), 198

creeping fig (*Ficus pumila*), 348, 524

creeping fig (*Ficus repens*), 348, 349

creeping hollygrape (*Mahonia repens*), 364, 382

creeping juniper ( *Juniperus horizontalis*), 216, 311, 343, 344

creeping lilyturf (*Liriope spicata*), 341

creeping Oregon grape (*Mahonia repens*), 191, 312, 318, 344

creeping phlox (*Phlox stolonifera*), 320, 325

creeping phlox (*Phlox subulata*), 343

creeping St.-John's wort (*Hypericum calycinum*), 341

creeping veronica (*Veronica repens*), 343

creeping wintergreen (*Gaultheria procumbens*), 282

creeping zinnia (*Sanvitalia procumbens*), 354, 356, 358

crenate leaf margin, 79

creosote bush (*Larrea tridentata*), 169, 213, 318, 340, 384

crepe ginger (*Costus speciosus*), 323

*Crescentia alata*, 300

cress (*Lepidium sativum*), 580

crested iris (*Iris cristata*), 187

crested wood fern (*Dryopteris cristata*), 201

crimson glory vine (*Vitis coignetiae*), 351

*Crinum*, 402, 587; *americanum*, 198, 199, 323, 324; *asiaticum*, 323; *bulbispermum*, 369; x *amabile*, 323

crinum lily (*Crinum bulbispermum*), 369

crinum-lily (*Crinum*), 402, 587

*Crithmum maritimum*, 682–83

*Crocosmia*, 331, 395; 'Lucifer', 331, 371, 375

crocosmia (*Crocosmia*), 331, 395

*Crocus*, 378, 381, 395, 399, 496
    *chrysanthus*, 582; 'Blue Pearl', 582
    *goulimyi*, 399
    *sativus*, 256, 399
    *speciosus*, 399
    *tomasinianus*, 376
    *vernus*, 582; 'Joan of Arc', 582; 'Remembrance', 582
    x *luteus* 'Yellow Mammoth', 582

crocus (*Crocus sativus*), 256

crocuses (*Crocus*), 378, 381, 395, 399, 496, 582

Cronquist, Arthur, 17, 144

crop plant diversity, 119–22; threats to, 139–41

crossandra (*Crossandra infundibuliformis*), 355

*Crossandra infundibuliformis*, 355

cross-bearing pelea (*Melicope cruciata*), 132

cross-leaved heath (*Erica tetralix*), 108

*Crossopetalum ilicifolium*, 342

cross-pollination, 106

cross vine (*Bignonia capreolata*), 347, 348, 350, 353, 381

*Crotalaria: avonensis*, 126; *pumila*, 361

croton (*Codiaeum variegatum* var. *pictum*), 336

crotons (*Codiaeum*), 310

crown gall, 562

crown of thorns (*Euphorbia milii*), 324, 342

crown pink (*Lychnis coronaria*), 331

crown vetch (*Coronilla varia*), 137

*Cryptantha: aperta*, 131; *crassipes*, 126

*Cryptanthus*, 342

*Cryptomeria: japonica*, 299, 485, 514; 'Elegans', 299, 315

cryptomeria (*Cryptomeria japonica*), 485, 514

*Cryptostegia madagascariensis*, 348

*Crysothamnus nauseosus*, 215

*Ctenitis squamigera*, 128

cucumber beetles, 552

cucumber family, 55–56

cucumbers (*Cucumis sativus*), 243

*Cucumis: melo*, 244; *sativus*, 243

*Cucurbita: foetidissima*, 337; *pepo*, 110, 245

cucurbitaceae, 55–56

*Cudrania tricuspidata*, 281

cultivated plants, naming of, 41; registration authorities for, 44, 45–50; system of rules for, 43–44

Culver's root (*Veronicastrum virginicum*), 197, 207, 325, 379

*Cunila origanoides*, 206

*Cunninghamia lanceolata*, 299

cup and saucer vine (*Cobaea scandens*), 348, 487

*Cupaniopsis anacarioides*, 137

cupflower (*Nierembergia hippomanica*), 332, 357

*Cuphea hyssopifolia*, 342, 572

cup plant (*Silphium perfoliatum*), 196, 207, 362

*Cupressus*, 514; *abramsiana*, 126; *arizonica* var. *arizonica*, 381; *macrocarpa*, 137, 216

*Curcubita*, 245–46

*Curcuma: longa*, 402, 590; *roscoeana*, 323, 372

curcuma (*Curcuma roscoeana*), 372

curly-leaf mountain mahogany (*Cercocarpus ledifolius*), 318, 384

currants (*Ribes*), 270, 366, 485

curry plant (*Helichrysum italicum*), 340

Curtis, William, 6

*Cuscuta*, 70

Cushenbury milk-vetch (*Astragalus albens*), 126

cushions and buns, 145

cuspidate leaf apex, 81

cut-leaf coneflower (*Rudbeckia laciniata*), 196, 498

cut-leaf delissea (*Delissea laciniata*), 131

cutleaf goldthread (*Coptis laciniata*), 344

cutleaf stephanandra (*Stephanandra incisa*), 312

cut-leaved bugbane (*Cimicifuga laciniata*), 329

cut-leaved sumac (*Rhus typhina*), 299

cutting back herbaceous plants, 512

cuttings: flowers for cutting, 371–76; propagation from, *see* vegetative propagation, from cuttings

cutworms, 553

*Cyanea: arborea*, 131; *asarifolia*, 128; *asplenifolia*, 131; *comata*, 131; *giffardii*, 131; *lobata*, 131; *longissima*, 131; *mannii*, 128; *marksii*, 131; *mceldowneyi*, 128; *obtusa*, 131, 283; *pinnatifida*, 128; *pohaku*, 131; *procera*, 128; *profuga*, 131; *pycnocarpa*, 131; *quercifolia*, 131; *shipmanii*, 131; *stictophylla*, 128; *superba*, 128; *truncata*, 128; *undulata*, 128

*Cyathea cooperi*, 324

Cycadophyta, 52

Cycads (Cycadophyta), 52

*Cycas revoluta*, 536

*Cyclamen*, 134, 378; *coum*, 604; *hederifolium*, 135, 331, 344, 399, 604

cyclamen (*Cyclamen coum*), 604

cyclamen (*Cyclamen hederifolium*), 344, 399, 604

cyclamens (*Cyclamen*), 134

*Cydonia: oblonga*, 282; *sinensis*, 536

*Cymbidium*, 324

*Cymbopogon citratus*, 259, 336

cyme, 84, 85

*Cynara cardunculus*, 137, 338

*Cynoglossum grande*, 109, 229

Cyperaceae, 46, 109

*Cyperus: auriculatus*, 131; *fauriei*, 128; *kunthianus*, 131; *papyrus*, 323; *pennatiformis*, 128; *rockii*, 131; *tetragonus*, 199

cyperus (*Cyperus tetragonus*), 199
cypress (*Taxodium*), 168
cypresses (*Cupressus*), 514
cypress spruge (*Euphorbia cyparissias*), 367
cypress vine (*Ipomoea quamoclit*), 347, 350
*Cypripedium:*
*acaule,* 179
*calceolus,* 179; var. *pubescens,* 187
cypsela, 92, 93
*Cyrilla racemiflora,* 161, 168, 197, 299
*Cyrtandra: crenata,* 131; *filipes,* 131; *giffardii,* 128; *gracilis,* 131; *kohalae,* 131; *lydgatei,* 131; *munroi,* 128; *olona,* 131; *polyantha,* 128; *pruinosa,* 131; *rivularis,* 131; *tintinnabula,* 131; *waiolani,* 131
*Cyrtanthus,* 402; *mackenii,* 588–89
*Cyrtomium falcatum,* 342
*Cytisus: racemosus,* 522; *scoparius,* 137
cytokinesis, 97
cytospora canker, 562

*Daboecia,* 46
*Dactylorhiza maculata,* 201
daffodil (*Narcissus*), 369, 374, 376, 396, 496, 582, 656; classification of narcissi, 397
daffodil (*Narcissus asturiensis*), 378
Dahlberg daisy (*Thymophylla tenuiloba*), 356, 358
*Dahlia,* 46, 354, 371, 400, 496; *imperialis,* 370
dahlia (*Dahlia*), 354, 400, 496
dahlias (*Dahlia*), 371
Dahoon holly (*Ilex cassine*), 188, 197, 198, 300
Dakota verbena (*Verbena bipinnatifida*), 364
*Dalea,* 169
*candidum,* 207
*formosa,* 312, 313, 318
*frutescens,* 108, 227, 313
*greggii,* 108, 213, 228, 345
*pulchra,* 383
*purpurea,* 207, 367; var. *purpurea,* 208
Dalmation bellflower (*Campanula portenschlagiana*), 344
damask rose (*Rosa damascena*), 370
damping off, 562
*Danae racemosa,* 310, 379
dancing lady ginger (*Globba winitii*), 595
*Danthonia: californica,* 209; *spicata,* 206

*Daphne:*
*arbuscula,* 604
*burkwoodii,* 316; 'Carol Mackie', 316
*cneorum,* 500
*cneorum pygmaea* 'Alba', 604
*odora,* 309, 317, 379; 'Leucanthe', 317
x *burkwoodii,* 308, 311, 500; 'Carol Mackie', 308, 311, 377
daphne (*Daphne arbuscula*), 604
daphne (*Daphne* x *burkwoodii*), 308, 311, 316
*Darlingtonia californica,* 202, 203
darmera (*Darmera peltata*), 338
*Darmera peltata,* 202, 203, 336, 338, 339
*Dasylirion: texanum,* 337, 381; *wheeleri,* 169, 339
date (*Phoenix dactylifera*), 284
*Datura: inoxia,* 487; *stramonium,* 359, 652; *wrightii,* 332, 369
*Daucus carota,* 85, 137, 180, 238–39
*Davallia fejeensis,* 324, 336, 572
*Davidia involucrata,* 298, 300, 477
David's bush clematis (*Clematis davidiana*), 309
Davidson bushmallow (*Malacothamnus davidsonii*), 132
David viburnum (*Viburnum davidii*), 315
dawn redwood (*Metasequoia glyptostroboides*), 298, 305, 484
daylilies (*Hemerocallis*), 319, 321, 322, 323, 324, 325, 326, 327, 329, 341, 363, 470
daylily (*Hemerocallis fulva*), 138
daylily (*Hemerocallis lilio-asphodelus*), 370
deadheading, 512
deadly conocybe (*Conocybe filaris*), 663
deadly galerina (*Galerina autumnalis*), 663–64
deadly nightshade (*Atropa belladonna*), 649
deadnettle (*Lamium maculatum*), 336
death camas (*Zigadenus elegans*), 200
deciduous azaleas (*Rhododendron*), 484
deciduous hollies (*Ilex*), 360, 484
deciduous holly (*Ilex decidua*), 379
deciduous plants, 76, 297; when to prune, 509
deciduous rhododendrons (*Rhododendron*), 484

deciduous wild ginger (*Asarum canadense*), 342
decumaria (*Decumaria sinensis*), 352
*Decumaria sinensis,* 352
deer, 230, 564–65
deer brush (*Ceanothus integerrimus*), 170
deer fern (*Blechnum spicant*), 191, 192, 202, 203, 339
deergrass (*Muhlenbergia rigens*), 170, 209, 339
*Deeringothamnus pulchellus,* 126
deerweed (*Lotus scoparius*), 108, 229
Degener's catchfly (*Silene degeneri*), 132
Degener's pelea (*Melicope degeneri*), 132
Degener's peperomia (*Peperomia degeneri*), 132
dehiscent, 90
delavayi osmanthus (*Osmanthus delavayi*), 317, 500
Delaware, 438, 622–23, 694, 695, 702
*Delissea: fallax,* 131; *laciniata,* 131; *lauliiana,* 131; *parviflora,* 131; *rhytidosperma,* 128; *sinuata,* 131
*Delonix regia,* 300
*Delosperma: cooperi,* 345; *nubigenum,* 345
*Delphinium,* 46, 324, 329, 366, 370, 375; *cardinale,* 109, 230; 'Cliveden Beauty', 329; *glaucum,* 203; *grandiflorum,* 369; *nudicaule,* 109, 230
delphinium (*Delphinium*), 329
delphiniums (*Delphinium*), 324, 366, 370, 375
Delta duck potato (*Sagittaria latifolia*), 198
deltoid (deltate) leaves, 77
*Dendranthema* x *grandiflorum,* 321, 324, 371
*Dendrobium,* 324, 373
dendrogram, 62
*Dendromecon: harfordii,* 306; *rigida* subsp. *harfordii,* 216
*Dennstaedtia punctilobula,* 320, 334, 341
dentate leaf margin, 79
deodar cedar (*Cedrus deodara*), 305, 306
*Deparia kaalaana,* 131
*Deschampsia caespitosa,* 203, 209
desert bell (*Phacelia campanularia*), 109, 228
desert cassia (*Senna nemophila*), 318
desert cassia (*Senna polyphylla*), 361

desert gardens, 210–13; maintaining, 213; planting, 211–13; plants for, 212–13; preparing, 211
desert hackberry (*Celtis pallida*), 108, 227, 367
desert honeysuckle (*Anisacanthus thurberi*), 109, 228, 367
desert lavender (*Hyptis emoryi*), 108
desert lavender (*Lycium andersonii*), 227, 228
desert marigold (*Baileya multiradiata*), 169, 209, 358, 366, 375
desert milkweed (*Asclepias subulata*), 108, 227, 384
desert olive (*Forestiera neomexicana*), 307, 367
desert paintbrush (*Castilleja angustifolia*), 109
desert paintbrush (*Castilleja chromosa*), 226, 227, 228
desert penstemon (*Penstemon pseudospectabilis*), 209
desert plume (*Stanleya pinnata*), 208, 209
deserts, 154–55; gardens, *see* desert gardens; western, *see* western deserts; western deserts region
desert senna (*Senna covesii*), 109, 227
desert spoon (*Dasilirion wheeleri*), 339
desert sunflower (*Geraea canescens*), 108, 227
desert sweet acacia (*Acacia minuta*), 383
desert willow (*Chilopsis linearis*), 109, 202, 213, 228, 302, 303, 306, 307, 337, 363, 367
desert zinnia (*Zinnia grandiflora*), 209, 213, 215, 333
*Desmodium canadense,* 207
*Deutzia,* 481, 484, 485, 510
*corymbosa,* 312
*gracilis,* 312, 316; 'Nikko', 312, 316
*scabra,* 368
deutzias (*Deutzia*), 481, 484, 485, 510
devil's club (*Oplopanax horridus*), 202, 382
Devil's ivy (*Epipremnum aureum*), 572
devil's walkingstick (*Aralia spinosa*), 360, 481
dewberry (*Rubus ursinus*), 191
*Dianthus,* 46, 355, 470, 496; *barbatus,* 367; *carthusianorum,* 375; *caryophyllus,* 262, 370; *chinensis,* 354; *deltoides,* 328, 370; 'Little Joe', 604; *microlep-*

*sis, 604; plumarius, 321, 324; simulans,* 604; 'Tiny Rubies', 604
dianthus (*Dianthus*), 355
dianthus (*Dianthus microlepsis*), 604
dianthus (*Dianthus simulans*), 604
*Diascia rigescens,* 375
diatomaceous earth, 547
*Dicentra: canadensis,* 187; *chrysantha,* 109, 230; *cucullaria,* 147, 187; *eximia,* 188, 221, 223, 322, 325, 328, 329, 330, 335, 336, 486, 498; *formosa,* 191, 192, 203, 325, 331, 338, 344; *spectabilis,* 7, 322, 325, 328, 367, 370
*Dicerandra: christmanii,* 126; *cornutissima,* 126; *frutescens,* 126; *immaculata,* 126
dichotomous plants, 68
*Dicksonia antarctica,* 339
dicots, 53–59
*Dictamnus albus,* 328, 330; 'Ruber', 329
*Dictyosperma album,* 301
*Dieffenbachia,* 323, 572; *maculata,* 336, 652–53
*Diellia: erecta,* 128; *falcata,* 128; *laciniata,* 128; *mannii,* 131; *unisora,* 128
*Dierama pulcherrimum,* 330, 331
*Diervilla lonicera,* 189, 312
*Dietes vegeta,* 323
digger pine (*Pinus sabiniana*), 170
digging tools, 611–13
*Digitalis,* 324; *grandiflora,* 331; *lutea,* 320; *mertonensis,* 328; *purpurea,* 320, 321, 355, 370, 653
dill (*Anethum graveolens*), 256, 334, 360, 498, 580
Dilleniidae, 55–56
*Dimorphotheca sinuata,* 358, 496
dioecy, 106
*Dionaea muscipula,* 82, 134, 170
*Dioscorea,* 71; *battatas,* 346
Dioscorides, Pedanius, 6
*Diospyros,* 282, 283; *kaki,* 306, 383; *virginiana,* 284, 302, 303
*Diphylleia cymosa,* 336
*Diplazium molokaiense,* 128
*Dipsacus fullonum,* 137, 383
*Dirca palustris,* 189, 196
disbudding, 512
diseases, plant, 559–64; encyclopedia of, 560–64. *see also* pests; *specific diseases*
dishcloth gourds (*Luffa*), 346
*Disporum: hookeri,* 191; *sessile:* 'Variegatum', 334, 341; *smithii,* 330

*Dissanthelium californicum,* 131
*Distictis buccinatoria,* 352
District of Columbia, 438, 623, 666, 694, 695, 702, 723
disturbance, 172, 173
dittany (*Cunila origanoides*), 206
diversity, plant, *see* plant diversity
division, propagation by, 393–94, 480–81
divisions in plant classification, 51–52
Dodder (*Cuscuta*), 70
*Dodecahema leptoceras,* 126
*Dodecatheon,* 192; *clevelandii,* 215; *dentatum,* 203; *hendersonii,* 215; *meadia,* 187, 189, 196, 205, 206, 207
*Dodonaea:* procumbens, 345
viscosa, 310; 'Purpurea', 470
*Dodonata viscosa,* 318
doghobble (*Leucothoe fontanesiana*), 187
dog rose (*Rosa canina*), 414
dogs and poisonous plants, 646
dogtooth violet (*Erythronium oregonum*), 191
dogtooth violet (*Erythronium revolutum*), 191
dogwoods (*Cornus*), 161, 306, 477, 484
Dokuchaiev, V. V., 37
*Dolichos lablab,* 346, 347, 349, 350, 487
doll's eyes (*Actaea pachypoda*), 187
*Dombeya,* 311
dominance, species, 165
*Doronicum orientale,* 375
dotted gayfeather (*Liatris punctata*), 328, 364
dotted mint (*Monarda punctata*), 206, 207, 208
double digging, 448
double fertilization, 52, 104
doublefile viburnum (*Viburnum plicatum*), 7, 510
double serrate leaf margin, 79
Douglas' aster (*Aster subspicatus*), 329
Douglas fir (*Pseudotsuga menziesii*), 66, 170, 190, 191, 304, 305, 377, 380, 514
Douglas hawthorn (*Crataegus douglasii*), 191
Douglas iris (*Iris douglasiana*), 192, 209, 215, 216, 331
Douglas maple (*Acer glabrum douglasii*), 190
dove tree (*Davidia involucrata*), 298, 300, 477
Downing, Andrew Jackson, 6–7, 13

downy hawthorn (*Crataegus mollis*), 304
downy mildew, 410, 562
downy paintbrush (*Castilleja sessiliflora*), 109, 225, 226, 227, 229
downy phlox (*Phlox pilosa*), 189, 207
*Dracaena: fragrans,* 572; *marginata,* 497
dracaena (*Dracaena marginata*), 497
drip irrigation, 472–73, 616–17
drooping leucothoe (*Leucothoe catesbaei*), 316
drooping leucothoe (*Leucothoe fontanesiana*), 187, 308, 310
drooping sedge (*Carex pendula*), 197, 201
*Drosera,* 82, 160; *rotunifolia,* 203
drought-resistant plants, 470–71
Drummond phlox (*Phlox drummondii*), 356, 496
drupe, 91–93
*Dryopteris,* 187; *campyloptera,* 330; *cristata,* 201; *erythrosorus,* 320; *filix-mas,* 190, 325, 328; *goldiana,* 197, 325; *ludoviciana,* 322; *marginalis,* 320, 325, 343; *setiferum,* 325
*Dubautia: herbstobatae,* 128; *latifolia,* 128; *pauciflorula,* 128
*Duchesnea indica,* 344
duck potato (*Sagittaria latifolia*), 196, 197, 198, 200, 201
duckweed (*Lemna*), 195
duckweed (*Wolffia*), 110
*Dudleya: pulverulenta,* 216; *traskiae,* 127
dumbcane (*Dieffenbachia maculata*), 336, 652–53
dumbcanes (*Dieffenbachia*), 323, 572
dune broomgrass (*Schizachyrium scoparium* ssp. *littorale*), 216
dunecaps (*Orostachys furusei*), 340
dune sunflower (*Helianthus debilis*), 373
*Duranta repens,* 311
dusty miller (*Centaurea cineraria*), 367
dusty miller (*Centaurea seridis* subsp. *maritima*), 367
dusty miller (*Cineraria maritima*), 496
dusty miller (*Senecio cineraria*), 331, 471, 498
Dutch honeysuckle (*Lonicera periclymenum*), 365
Dutch hyacinth (*Hyacinthus*), 395–96, 582

Dutchman's-breeches (*Dicentra cucullaria*), 147, 187
Dutchman's-pipe (*Aristolochia macrophylla*), 346, 349, 351
Dutchman's-pipes (*Aristolochia*), 361
Dutchman's-pipe vine (*Aristolochia californica*), 352
dwarf bear-poppy (*Arctomecon humilis*), 126
dwarf blanket flower (*Gaillardia* x *grandiflora*), 322
dwarf blue porterweed (*Stachytarpheta jamaicensis*), 361
dwarf bush germander (*Teucrium fruticans*), 317
dwarf cinquefoil (*Potentilla canadensis*), 206
dwarf crested iris (*Iris cristata*), 343
dwarf elm (*Ulmus pumila*), 139
dwarf fothergilla (*Fothergilla gardenii*), 187, 310, 316, 500
dwarf French marigold (*Tagetes patula*), 355
dwarf ginger (*Kaempferia galanga*), 595
dwarf ginseng (*Panax trifolius*), 189
dwarf jade (*Crassula argentea*), 536
dwarf Korean lilac (*Syringa meyeri*), 311, 315
dwarf lantana (*Lantana depressa*), 323
dwarf morning glory (*Convolvulus tricolor*), 347
dwarf mountain pine (*Pinus mugo*), 308, 311, 470
dwarf palmetto (*Sabal minor*), 337
dwarf plumbago (*Ceratostigma plumbaginoides*), 345
dwarf schefflera (*Schefflera arboricola*), 311, 336
dwarf smooth sumac (*Rhus glabra* var. *cismontana*), 314
dwarf wax myrtle (*Myrica cerifera*), 309
dwarf wax myrtle (*Myrica pusilla*), 381
dwarf winter hazel (*Corylopsis pauciflora*), 308
Dyman, Donald, 30
*Dypsis decaryi,* 301
dyssodia (*Thymophylla pentachaeta* var. *pentachaeta*), 109, 227
*Dyssodia tenuiloba,* 358

eared flatsedge (*Cyperus auriculatus*), 131

earleaf acacia (*Acacia auriculiformis*), 152
early Japanese flowering cherry (*Prunus subhirtella*), 298
earthworms, 432
eastern arborvitae (*Thuja occidentalis*), 196
Eastern bluebells (*Mertensia virginica*), 109, 221
Eastern deciduous forest, 17–20, 146–48, 166–67; beech/maple forest, 148, 167; floodplain forest, 148, 167; maple-basswood forest, 148, 167; mesophytic forest, 147, 167; oak/chestnut forest, 146–47, 167; oak/hickory forest, 148, 167
eastern flowering dogwood (*Cornus florida*), 10, 187, 188, 189
eastern larch (*Larix laricina*), 196
eastern persimmon (*Diospyros virginiana*), 302, 303
eastern redbud (*Cercis canadensis*), 187, 189
eastern red cedar ( *Juniperus virginiana*), 187, 188, 189, 216, 298, 302, 308, 334, 359, 360, 380, 381, 501
eastern river birch (*Betula nigra*), 382
eastern white cedar (*Thuja occidentalis*), 166, 196
Eaton's beardtongue (*Penstemon eatonii*), 109, 226, 227, 228
*Echinacea,* 153, 207, 470; *angustifolia,* 326, 363, 373, 380; *pallida,* 208; *purpurea,* 108, 206, 222, 224, 225, 319, 320, 321, 322, 324, 325, 326, 327, 328, 360, 362, 363, 364, 365, 366, 367, 370, 372, 373, 374, 375, 379, 498
*Echinocereus: fendleri,* 215; *pectinatus,* 215; *triglochidiatus,* 215; *viridiflorus,* 215
*Echinops,* 359, 371, 486; *nivalis,* 331; *ritro,* 319, 320, 374, 478
*Echium wildpretii,* 331, 370
*ecology* for gardeners, 142–79; biological structure of plant communities, 165–71; definition of ecology, 142; functions of plant communities, 171–79; plant community ecology, 162–65; vegetative associations, *see* vegetative associations (habitat types); wetland ecosystems, 159–62, 193
economic plants, 691–92
ecosystem: defined, 142, 165; diversity, 112, 113, 165
ecotones, 164
ecotourism sites, botanically noteworthy, 637–39
Ecuador, 638
edger, 611
edging lobelia (*Lobelia erinum*), 354, 355
edible fig (*Ficus carica*), 138, 307
*Edraianthus pumilio,* 604
eggleaf skullcap (*Scutellaria ovata*), 326, 327
eggplant (*Solanum melongena*), 243–44
*Eichhornia crassipes,* 137, 152
*Elaeagnus: angustifolia,* 137; *macrophylla,* 313, 337, 381; *multiflora,* 281, 282; *pungens,* 318; *umbellata,* 137
elaeagnus (*Elaeagnus macrophylla*), 313, 337, 381
elderberry (*Sambucus canadensis*), 189, 199, 281, 282, 283, 310, 361, 370, 659–60
elegant brodiaea (*Brodiaea elegans*), 209
*Eleocharis: acicularis,* 202; *cellulosa,* 200
*Eletarria cardamomum,* 323
elfin herb (*Cuphea hyssopifolia*), 572
elk clover (*Aralia californica*), 191, 201, 202
elkhorn fern (*Polypodium grandiceps*), 335
elliptic leaves, 77
elm (*Ulmus*), 364, 484
elmleaf goldenrod (*Solidago ulmifolia*), 327
*Elodea: canadensis,* 197, 201; *schweinitzii,* 131
*Elymus,* 170; *canadensis,* 205; *virginicus,* 205, 343
emarginate leaf apex, 81
emerald ripple peperomia (*Peperomia caperata*), 572
emergence, leaf, 82
*Emilia: coccinea,* 354; *javanica,* 354
Emory oak (*Quercus emoryi*), 307
*Encarsia formosa,* 546
endangered species, 124. *see also* threatened species
Endangered Species Act, 125–27
endemism, 114–19
endocarp, 90
endosperm, 104
endozoochory, 93
Engelmann daisy (*Engelmannia pinnatifida*), 326, 363
*Engelmannia pinnatifida,* 326, 363
Engelmann oak (*Quercus engelmanii*), 170
Engelmann's ivy (*Parthenocissus quinquefolia* var. *engelmannii*), 351
Engelmann spruce (*Picea engelmannii*), 170, 470
English bluebells (*Hyacinthoides hispanica*), 320
English hawthorn (*Crataegus monogyna*), 137
English holly (*Ilex aquifolium*), 138
English ivy (*Hedera helix*), 138, 496, 520, 522, 524
English lavender (*Lavandula angustifolia*), 318, 370
English oak (*Quercus robur*), 304, 305
English yew (*Taxus baccata*), 514, 520, 660–61
*Enkianthus: campanulatus,* 308, 315, 500; *perulatus,* 308
enkianthus (*Enkianthus campanulatus*), 308, 500
enkianthus (*Enkianthus perulatus*), 308
entire leaf margin, 79
Environmental Protection Agency, 441
*Ephedra,* 169; *viridis,* 381, 384
epiascidiate leaves, 82
epicarp, 90
epidermis of the stem, 71
*Epilobium: angustifolium,* 190, 207; *canum,* 331, 332, 366
*Epimedium,* 320, 341 *grandiflora,* 325 *perralderianum,* 344 *rubrum,* 328 *versicolor,* 328; 'Sulphureum', 328 x *rubrum,* 343 x *youngianum,* 325, 336
epimediums (*Epimedium*), 320, 341
*Epipactis gigantea,* 203
*Epiphyllum,* 324, 591
epiphytes, 324. *see also* specific epiphytes, e.g. bromeliads; orchid family
*Epipremnum aureum,* 571, 572
*Episcia cupreata,* 572
epizoochory, 93
*Equisetum,* 201, 202; *hyemale,* 198, 202, 203
equitant leaf arrangement, 83
*Eragrostis,* 199; *deflexa,* 131; *hosakai,* 131; *mauiensis,* 131; *trichodes,* 213, 384
*Eranthemum pulchellum,* 311
*Eranthus hyemalis,* 376, 378
*Eremurus himalaicus,* 375
*Erianthus: giganteus,* 199; *ravennae,* 328

*Erica,* 46, 485
*carnea,* 308, 340; 'Springwood White', 308, 340, 376; 'Vivellii', 382
*cinerea* 'Atrorubens', 344
*tetralix,* 108
x *darleyensis,* 344; 'Furzey', 344
Ericaceae, 56
*Ericameria laricifolia,* 318
*Erigeron: alpinus,* 604; *compositus,* 328, 329; *divergens,* 209; *glaucus,* 216, 329; *mariposanus,* 131; *quercifolius,* 361; x 'Moerheimii', 331
*Erinus alpinus* 'Alba', 604
*Eriobotrya japonica,* 307
*Eriocaulon decangulare,* 199
*Eriogonum,* 209, 215, 366, 367 *arborescens,* 216 *crocatum,* 317 *fasciculatum,* 108, 229, 230, 332, 367 *giganteum,* 216, 317, 366 *latifolium:* subsp. *grande,* 216; subsp. *rubescens,* 216, 366 *truncatum,* 131 *umbellatum,* 328, 329, 374
*Eriophorum,* 166 *angustifolium,* 197 *gracile,* 203 *latifolium,* 197; var. *viridicarinatum,* 202 *vaginatum* var. *spissum,* 201 *viridicarinatum,* 202
*Eriophyllum: latilobum,* 127; *stoechadifolium,* 216
*Erodium,* 46
*Eruca: sativa,* 237; *vesicaria* subsp. *sativa,* 237
*Eryngium: alpinum,* 371; *amethystinum,* 365, 367; *cuneifolium,* 127; *giganteum,* 371; *leavenworthii,* 356, 373; *maritimum,* 470; *planum,* 374; *yuccifolium,* 207
eryngo (*Eryngium leavenworthii*), 356, 373
eryngos (*Eryngium alpinum*), 371
eryngos (*Eryngium giganteum*), 371
*Erysimum:* *asperum,* 169, 328, 364 *capitatum,* 109, 230 *cheiri,* 365 *concinnum,* 216 *linifolium,* 329, 331, 332, 333; 'Bowles Mauve', 329, 331, 332, 333 *suffrutescens,* 216
*Erythrina herbacea,* 222, 223, 224
*Erythronium: americanum,* 187, 188; *oregonum,* 191; *propullans,* 127; *revolutum,* 191

*Escallonia,* 47; *rubra,* 500
escarpment live oak (*Quercus fusiformis*), 307, 381
*Eschscholzia: californica,* 108, 209, 215, 216, 227, 357, 358, 496; *mexicana,* 209
*Escobaria minima,* 127
espalier, 515–17
Espanola Valley fava bean (*Vicia faba*), 371
Etonia rosemary (*Conradina etonia*), 126
*Eucalyptus: formanii,* 384; *globulus,* 137; *microtheca,* 306; *pauciflora* subsp. *niphophila,* 305; *regnans,* 66
*Eucharis* x *grandiflora,* 402, 586
*Eucommia ulmoides,* 609
eucrosia (*Eucrosia bicolor*), 403, 595
*Eucrosia bicolor,* 403, 595
*Eugenia: axillaris,* 300, 361; *confusa,* 300; *foetida,* 361; *koolauensis,* 128; *uniflora,* 522
eugenia (*Syzygium paniculatum*), 520
eulalia (*Miscanthus sinensis*), 328
*Euonymus:*
    *alatus,* 137
    *americanus,* 188, 189, 309
    *atropurpureus,* 313, 363
    *fortunei,* 137
    *japonicus:* 'Albo-marginatus', 500; 'Microphyllus', 500
    *occidentalis,* 191, 202
*Eupatorium,* 359; *coelestinum,* 198, 199, 319, 321, 327, 360, 361, 363; *corollata,* 207, 208; *droserolepis,* 131; *hyssopifolium,* 206; *maculatum,* 83, 196, 206, 207, 319, 321, 362, 374, 379; *odoratum,* 224; *perfoliatum,* 200, 206, 207; *purpureum,* 319, 321, 324, 329, 360, 498
*Euphorbia:*
    *amygdaloides:* 'Purpurea', 344; var. *robbiae,* 344
    *antisyphilitica,* 384
    *characias* subsp. *wulfenii,* 329, 331
    *cyparissias,* 367
    *leucocephala,* 311
    *marginata,* 372, 471
    *milii,* 324, 342
    *myrsinites,* 332
    *rigida,* 339
Euphorbiaceae, 56
Eureka dune grass (*Swallenia alexandrae*), 127
Europe: climatic conditions in, 23; flower shows, 637; public gardens in, 630–33
European alder (*Alnus glutinosa*), 609

European beech (*Fagus sylvatica*), 305
European bittersweet (*Solanum dulcamara*), 660
European corn borer, 553
European crowfoot (*Aquilegia vulgaris*), 319
European dogwood (*Cornus alba*), 312
European hornbeam (*Carpinus betulus*), 301
European larch (*Larix decidua*), 304
European mountain ash (*Sorbus aucuparia*), 306, 383
European white birch (*Betula pendula*), 298
European wild ginger (*Asarum europaeum*), 343, 344
euryops (*Euryops pectinatus*), 522
*Euryops pectinatus,* 522
*Eustachys glauca,* 199
*Eustoma: grandiflorum,* 208, 356, 358, 373, 376; *russellianum,* 376
evaporation, 31–33, 175
evapotranspiration, 173
evening primrose (*Oenothera*), 486
evening primrose (*Oenothera biennis*), 206
evening primrose (*Oenothera macrocarpa*), 331
evening primrose (*Oenothera speciosa*), 498
evening primroses (*Oenothera*), 367
everblooming bleeding heart (*Dicentra eximia*), 325
everblooming bleeding heart (*Dicentra formosa*), 325
Everglades daisy (*Helenium pinnatifidum*), 199
Everglades morning glory (*Ipomoea sagittata*), 199
Everglades palm (*Acoelorraphe wrightii*), 301
evergreen azaleas (*Rhododendron*), 485, 520
evergreen bagworm, 553
evergreen currant (*Ribes viburnifolium*), 317
evergreen huckleberry (*Vaccinium ovatum*), 191, 192, 316, 317, 366
evergreen Japanese rhododendron (*Rhododendron degronianum* subsp. *heptamerum*), 377
evergreen plants, 76, 297; when to prune, 509, 510
evergreen rhododendrons (*Rhododendron*), 485
evergreen sumac (*Rhus virens*), 313

evergreen sweetbay (*Magnolia virginiana* var. *australis*), 197
evergreen vancouveria (*Vancouveria planipetala*), 191
evergreen wisteria (*Millettia reticulata*), 353
Eve's date (*Yucca baccata*), 284
Eve's necklace (*Sophora affinis*), 337, 380
*Evolvulus glomeratus,* 323, 342, 594
exocarp, 90
*Exocarpos luteolus,* 128
*Exochorda racemosa,* 368
exotic plants, 152, 180–81. see *also* invasive species
extinct plants, 130–33

Fabaceae, 56–57
Fagaceae, 54, 109
*Fagus,* 47, 72
    *americana,* 514
    *crenata,* 536
    *grandifolia,* 167, 299, 359
    *sylvatica,* 305; 'Atropunicea', 334; 'Purple Rivers', 305
fairybells (*Disporum hookeri*), 191
fairyduster (*Calliandra eriophylla*), 108, 109, 227, 228
fairy lanterns (*Disporum smithii*), 330
fairy-lily (*Zephyranthes grandiflora*), 404, 587
fairy trumpet (*Gilia aggregata*), 215
fairy wand (*Chamaelirium luteum*), 188
fairy wand (*Dierama pulcherrimum*), 331
Fakahatchee grass (*Tripsacum dactyloides*), 199
fall armyworm, 553
fall-blooming obedient plant (*Physostegia virginiana*), 198
fall obedient plant (*Physostegia virginiana*), 326, 374
fall phlox (*Phlox paniculata*), 108, 220, 222, 224
*Fallugia paradoxa,* 213, 312, 313, 318
false cypress (*Chamaecyparis pisifera*), 380, 514
false cypresses (*Chamaecyparis*), 377, 485, 496, 514
false goatsbeard (*Astilbe biternata*), 201
false health (*Cuphea hyssopifolia*), 572
false hellebore (*Veratrum californicum*), 202
false hellebore (*Veratrum viride*), 200
false indigo (*Amorpha fruticosa*), 313, 367, 373

false indigo (*Baptisia australis*), 320, 325, 374
false indigo (*Baptisia eucantha*), 325
false indigos (*Baptisia*), 207, 470, 498
false lily-of-the-valley (*Maianthemum dilatatum*), 202, 203
false morel (*Gyromitra esculenta*), 664–65
false oat (*Arrhenatherum elatius*), 137
false rue-anemone (*Isopyrum biternatum*), 189
false Solomon's seal (*Smilacina racemosa*), 188, 189, 191, 192, 320, 330, 331
false willow (*Baccharis angustifolia*), 197
families in plant classification: most diverse, 60; rarest family, 62; summary of, 51–62
fancy-leaved caladium (*Caladium bicolor*), 354, 401–402, 587–88
farewell-to-spring (*Clarkia amoena*), 209, 375
*Fargesia dracocephala,* 338
farinacea salvia (*Salvia farinacea*), 478
Farrand, Beatrix Jones, 7
fasciation, 69
fascicle, 85
fascicled leaf arrangement, 83
fast plants, 68, 686
*Fatsia japonica,* 338, 497
fawn lily (*Erythronium oregonum*), 191
fawn lily (*Erythronium revolutum*), 191
feather dalea (*Dalea formosa*), 312, 313
feather grass (*Stipa gigantea*), 329
feathergrass (*Stipa tenuissima*), 326, 374, 380
feather reed grass (*Calamagrostis* x *acutiflora*), 319, 374, 379
*Feijoa* (*Feijoa sellowiana*), 284
*Feijoa sellowiana,* 284, 306, 470
*Felicia amelloides,* 375
fences for city gardens, 604–605
*Fendlera rupicola,* 215
Fendler's bush (*Fendlera rupicola*), 215
fennel (*Foeniculum vulgare*), 138, 256, 334, 367
fern acacia (*Acacia angustissima*), 343, 363
Fernald, Merritt Lyndon, 7
fernbush (*Chamaebatiaria millefolium*), 318, 338
fernleaf Catalina ironwood (*Lyonothamnus floribundus* subsp. *asplenifolius*), 306

fernleaf full moon maple (*Acer japonicum*), 305

fernleaf yarrow (*Achillea filipendulina*), 325, 328

fern-leaved peony (*Paeonia tenuifolia*), 338

ferns (Polypodiophyta), 52, 161

ferns (pteridophytes): propagating, 100, 480; sexual reproduction of, 98–101

*Ferocactus acanthodes,* 169

fertilizers/fertilizing, 456–64
  of annuals, 464
  application methods, 460–61
  balanced, 460
  of bonsai, 531
  of bulbs, 393
  calculating how much to apply, 737–38
  complete, 460
  container plantings, 493, 497–98
  dilution rates, 736–37
  general advice, 456–57
  of herbs, 461
  of houseplants, 574
  of lawns, 386–87, 464
  NPK ratio, 457, 460
  nutrient values of, chart of, 462–63
  organic, 457–59
  of perennials, 461–64
  primary and secondary nutrients, 457; nutrient values of various fertilizers, chart of, 462–63
  for roses, 412, 464
  seedlings, 479
  of shrubs, 464
  single-nutrient, 460
  synthetic, 457, 459–60
  of trees, 464
  types of, 457–59
  of vegetables, 461; container gardening, 236

*Festuca:*
  *arundinacea,* 138
  *californica,* 209
  *glauca,* 208
  *idahoensis,* 208
  *ovina,* 138; var. *glauca,* 341

fetterbushes (*Leucothoe*), 481

feverfew (*Tanacetum parthenium*), 257, 331, 369, 370

fibrous roots, 70

*Ficus,* 152, 576, 674
  *altissima,* 138
  *aurea,* 168, 198, 361
  *benghalensis,* 138
  *benjamina,* 536
  *carica,* 138, 284, 307, 333; 'Brown Turkey', 307, 333; 'Texas Everbearing', 307
  *citrifolia,* 300

*microcarpa,* 138; 'Golden Gate', 536
  *pumila,* 348, 524
  *repens,* 348, 349

field mint (*Mentha arvensis*), 334

figs (*Ficus*), 138, 152, 280–81, 284, 576, 674

figwort family, 58

filament, 86, 106

filbert (*Corylus*), 282

*Filipendula: rubra,* 207, 320, 371; *ulmaria,* 320

fire, 172; prairies and, 154

fire blight, 562

firebush (*Hamelia patens*), 223, 311, 361

firecracker (*Penstemon eatonii*), 209

firecracker vine (*Manettia inflata*), 524

fire pink (*Silene virginica*), 221

firethorn (*Pyracantha angustifolia*), 318

firethorn (*Pyracantha coccinea*), 309

fireweed (*Epilobium angustifolium*), 190, 207

*Firmiana simplex,* 299, 378

firs (*Abies*), 485

five-finger fern (*Adiantum pedatum*), 203, 339

five-leaf akebia (*Akebia*), 351, 484

five-spot nemophila (*Nemophila maculata*), 357

flag actinidia (*Actinidia kolomikta*), 333, 346

flame acanthus (*Anisacanthus quadrifidus* var. *wrightii*), 313

flame azalea (*Rhododendron calendulaceum*), 308, 309

flame creeper (*Tropaeolum speciosum*), 351

flame-of-the-forest (*Butea monosperma*), 300

flame vine (*Pyrostegia venusta*), 349

flame violet (*Episcia cupreata*), 572

flannel bush (*Fremontodendron californicum*), 215

flannel bush (*Fremontodendron mexicanum*), 317

flannel-leaved mullein (*Verbascum thapsus*), 139

*Flaveria linearis,* 361

flax (*Linum*), 470

fleabane (*Erigeron compositus*), 328, 329

fleabanes (*Pluchea*), 361

flea beetles, 553–54

floating heart (*Nymphoides aquatica*), 198, 199

flooding, 175–76

*Flora of North America, The,* 136

Flora's paintbrush (*Emilia coccinea*), 354

floret, 84

Florida, 438, 623, 666, 695, 702–703, 723; Subtropical Florida (vegetative association), 151–52, 168; Subtropical region, *see* Subtropical Florida region

Florida anise (*Illicium floridanum*), 188, 310

Florida azalea (*Rhododendron austrinum*), 197, 310

Florida Everglades, 152

Florida golden aster (*Chrysopsis floridana*), 126

Florida leucothoe (*Agarista populifolia*), 188, 309

Florida maple (*Acer barbatum*), 302

Florida royal palm (*Roystonea regia*), 301

Florida shield fern (*Dryopteris ludoviciana*), 322

Florida thatch (*Thrinax radiata*), 362

Florida torreya (*Torreya taxifolia*), 127

Florida violet (*Viola floridana*), 323

Florida ziziphus (*Ziziphus celata*), 127

floristic provinces, 14–21, 181
  of North America, 17–21, 144; vegetative associations of, 143–69, 166–70

florists' genista (*Cytisus racemosus*), 522

florist's gloxinia (*Sinningia*), 592

florist's gloxinia (*Sinningia speciosa*), 588

floss-silk (*Chorisia speciosa*), 300

*Flourensia cernua,* 169

flowering almond (*Prunus glandulosa*), 368

flowering cherry (*Prunus*), 510, 673

flowering cotoneaster (*Cotoneaster multiflorus*), 314

flowering crabapple (*Malus floribunda*), 306

flowering crabapples (*Malus* hybrids), 300

flowering currant (*Ribes sanguineum* var. *glutinosum*), 383

flowering dogwood (*Cornus florida*), 108, 218, 220, 221, 225, 298, 299, 360, 477, 510

flowering kale (*Brassica oleracea*), 380

flowering maple (*Abutilon* x *hybridum*), 317, 500, 522, 595

flowering onions (*Allium*), 371

flowering plants (Magnoliophyta), 52–62; smallest and largest, 110

flowering plum (*Prunus cerasifera*), 501

flowering quince (*Chaenomeles speciosa*), 368, 370, 378

flowering quinces (*Chaenomeles*), 509, 510

flowering spurge (*Eupatorium corollata*), 207, 208

flowering tobacco (*Nicotiana alata*), 355, 360

flowering tobacco (*Nicotiana sylvestris*), 354

flowering tobaccos (*Nicotiana*), 498

flowers, 68, 85–90; birth flowers, 696; corolla parts, 89; corolla shapes, 89–90; flower sexuality, 87; number of parts, 87; parts of, 86–87, 104–106; perianth terminology, 88–89; plant sexuality, 87; position of parts, 88; state, 695–96

flower shows, 636–37

*Flueggea neowawraea,* 128

fly agaric (*Amanita muscaria*), 663

fly honeysuckle (*Lonicera canadensis*), 221, 222, 223

foamflower (*Tiarella cordifolia*), 188, 189, 190, 322, 323, 328

foamflower (*Tiarella trifoliata*), 191

*Foeniculum vulgare,* 138, 256, 334, 360, 367, 580

foliage plants, 333–40; for coastal California, 339; for the Midwest and Northern Great Plains, 336; for the Northeast, 333–34; for the Pacific Northwest, 338–39; for the Rocky Mountain region, 337–38; for the Southeast, 334–35; for Subtropical Florida, 335–36; for Texas and the Southern Plains, 336–37; for western deserts, 339–40

follicle, 92, 93

food bodies, leaf, 82

foothill pine (*Pinus sabiniana*), 306

Forbes' loosestrife (*Lysimachia forbesii*), 132

forcing bulbs, 581–83, 584

forcing woody plants for indoor bloom, 511

*Forestiera neomexicana,* 307, 367
forest lousewort (*Pedicularis canadensis*), 221, 222, 223, 226
forest phlox (*Phlox divaricata*), 221, 222, 223
forget-me-not (*Myosotis arvensis*), 674
forget-me-nots (*Myosotis*), 355
fork, 612
form, naming of a, 40, 41
Forman's gum (*Eucalyptus formanii*), 384
*Forsythia,* 47, 484, 485, 509, 510, 514
    *suspensa,* 370; var. *sieboldii,* 13
    x *intermedia,* 309, 310, 312, 313, 368, 371, 373;
        'Spring Glory', 309
forsythia (*Forsythia* x *intermedia*), 309, 310, 312, 313, 368, 371, 373
forsythias (*Forsythia*), 484, 485, 509, 510, 514
Fortune, Robert, 7
fortune's osmanthus (*Osmanthus fortunei*), 309
*Fothergilla,* 308, 484, 486
    *gardenii,* 187, 310, 316, 500;
        'Blue Mist', 316
    *major,* 310
fothergilla (*Fothergilla major*), 310
fothergillas (*Fothergilla*), 308, 484, 486
fountain butterfly bush (*Buddleia alternifolia*), 364, 470
fountain grass (*Pennisetum alopecuroides*), 319, 329
fountain grass (*Pennisetum setaceum*), 138
fountain grasses (*Pennisetum*), 341
*Fouquieria splendens,* 109, 169, 213, 228, 384
four-nerve daisy (*Tetraneuris scaposa*), 326, 363, 374
four-o'clock (*Mirabilis jalapa*), 355, 357, 360, 368, 369, 498
four-petal pawpaw (*Asimina tetramera*), 126
fourwing saltbush (*Atriplex canescens*), 367
fowl meadow grass (*Poa palustris*), 197
foxglove (*Digitalis lutea*), 320
foxglove (*Digitalis mertonensis*), 328
foxglove (*Digitalis purpurea*), 320, 321, 355, 653
foxgloves (*Digitalis*), 324
foxtail (*Setaria parviflora*), 199
foxtail lily (*Eremurus himalaicus*), 375

*Fragaria,* 72; *chiloensis,* 216; *moschata,* 281, 282
fragrant goldenrod (*Solidago odora*), 327, 337
fragrant herbs, 268
fragrant hyssop (*Agastache foeniculum*), 336
fragrant mimosa (*Mimosa borealis*), 313
fragrant sarcococca (*Sarcococca ruscifolia*), 315
fragrant snowbell (*Styrax obassia*), 305
fragrant sumac (*Rhus aromatica*), 308, 311, 334, 341, 481, 484
France, 630–31, 637
*Francoa sonchifolia,* 331
frangipani (*Plumeria*), 595
*Frangula caroliniana,* 188, 302, 303
frankincense, 674
*Franklinia* (*Franklinia alatamaha*), 299
*Franklinia alatamaha,* 188, 299
Franklin tree (*Franklinia alatamaha*), 188
Fraser, John, 7
Fraser fir (*Abies fraseri*), 7
Fraser magnolia (*Magnolia fraseri*), 7
*Fraxinus,* 672
    *americana,* 297, 301, 303, 363; 'Autumn Blaze', 301; 'Autumn Purple', 303, 305
    *augustifolia,* 307
    *caroliniana,* 198
    *nigra,* 161, 196, 200
    *oxycarpa,* 306, 307; 'Raywood', 306
    *pennsylvanica,* 167, 301, 303, 609; 'Summit', 303
    *texensis,* 302, 363
    *velutina,* 216
*Freesia,* 405
freesia (*Freesia*), 405
freezing and frost, 29, 32–33
Fremont cottonwood (*Populus fremontii*), 170, 202
Fremont geranium (*Geranium fremontii*), 190
*Fremontodendron:*
    *californicum,* 215
    *mexicanum,* 317; 'Pacific Sunset', 317
French hydrangea (*Hydrangea macrophylla*), 313
French lilacs (*Syringa*), 510
French marigold (*Tagetes erecta*), 372
French marigold (*Tagetes patula*), 356, 360
French mulberry (*Callicarpa americana*), 188

French parsley (*Anthriscus cereifolium*), 255
French sorrel (*Rumex scutatus*), 264
French tarragon (*Artemisia dracunculus*), 265
freycinetia (*Freycinetia arborea*), 324
*Freycinetia arborea,* 324
Frikart's aster (*Aster* x *frikartii*), 319, 330, 359
fringecups (*Tellima grandiflora*), 190
fringed bleeding heart (*Dicentra eximia*), 328, 329
fringed sage (*Artemisia frigida*), 338
fringeleaf ruellia (*Ruellia humilis*), 327
fringe tree (*Chionanthus virginicus*), 187, 188, 299, 302
*Fritillaria,* 395, 582
fritillaria (*Fritillaria*), 395, 582
frogbit (*Elodea canadensis*), 197, 201
frogfruit (*Phyla nodiflora*), 343, 363
frogs, 546
frost and freezing, 29, 32–33
fruit, 69, 86, 90–94, 104; dispersal of seed and, means of, 93–94; general types of, 91–92; growing, *see* fruit growing; parthenocarpic, 110; smallest and largest, 110; terms for describing, 90–91
fruit growing, 269–86; blueberries, 276–77; brambles, 277–79; by city gardeners, 607–609; in containers, 283–84; in dry regions, 284; edible landscaping, 281–83; figs, 280–81; general tips on, 269; getting started, 269; grapes, 279–80; native American fruits, 284; pests and, 269, 284–86, 567; pollination and, 269–71; pome fruits, 271–73; stone fruits, 273–74; strawberries, 274–76; unusual fruits, 281
fruitlet, 90–91
*Fuchsia,* 47, 487, 522; *magellanica,* 365
fuchsia-flowering gooseberry (*Ribes speciosum*), 383
fuchsias (*Fuchsia*), 487, 522
fungi, poisonous, 643–45, 662–64
fungi kingdom, 51
fungus gnats, 554
fusarium wilt, 526–63
fuschia-flavored goosebery (*Ribes speciosum*), 366

fuzzy deutzia (*Deutzia scabra*), 368

*Gahnia lanaiensis,* 128
*Gaillardia:*
    *aristata,* 208, 328, 364, 478
    *pulchella,* 206, 208, 223, 225, 226, 342, 355, 356, 360, 361, 369, 373
    x *grandiflora,* 322, 376; 'Goblin', 322
gaillardia (*Gaillardia pulchella*), 373
*Galanthus,* 134, 135, 376, 378, 395, 497, 583; *elwesii,* 135, 325; *nivalis,* 325, 381
galberry (*Ilex glabra*), 199
*Galerina autumnalis,* 663–64
*Galium: odoratum,* 264, 338, 341, 343, 344, 367, 370; *verum,* 258
galls, 69
*Galphimia gracilis,* 311
*Galtonia candicans,* 400
gambel oak (*Quercus gambelii*), 190, 304
Gambel's watercress (*Rorippa gambellii*), 127
gameophyte stage of plant reproduction, 96
*Gamolepis chrysanthemoides,* 342
gaping panicum (*Panicum hians*), 199
gap phase succession, 172
garden ageratum (*Ageratum houstonianum*), 355
garden asparagus (*Asparagus officinalis*), 334
garden chrysanthemum (*Dendranthema* x *grandiflorum*), 371
Garden Club of America, 135
gardener's atlas, *see* plant geography
garden gladioli (*Gladiolus*), 375
garden heliotrope (*Valeriana officinalis*), 265
*Gardenia:*
    *augusta,* 500
    *brighamii,* 128
    *jasminoides,* 309, 311, 484, 500, 591; 'Prostrata Variegata', 597
    *thungergia, see Gardenia jasminoides*
gardenia (*Gardenia augusta*), 500
gardenia (*Gardenia jasminoides*), 309, 311, 591
gardenias (*Gardenia*), 522
garden lily (*Lilium*), 396
garden mums (*Chrysanthemum*), 496
garden peony (*Paeonia lactiflora*), 498

garden petunia (*Petunia* x *hybrida*), 478

garden phlox (*Phlox paniculata*), 325, 368, 369, 372, 373, 478

garden pinks (*Dianthus*), 470, 496

garden sage (*Salvia officinalis*), 332

garden sieve, 619

garden verbenas (*Verbena* x *hybrida*), 496, 498

garland daphne (*Daphne cneorum*), 500

garlic (*Allium sativum*), 239, 257, 674; for pest control, 547

garlic chives (*Allium tuberosum*), 345

garlics (*Allium*), 359

Garrett's mint (*Dicerandra christmanii*), 126

*Garrya elliptica,* 215, 306, 317, 383; 'Evie', 317; 'James Roof', 382

gas plant (*Dictamnus albus*), 328, 329, 330

*Gaultheria: procumbens,* 188, 282, 334, 481; *shallon,* 191, 201, 281, 282, 317, 344, 365

gaura (*Gaura lindheimeri*), 319, 321, 326, 331, 332

*Gaura lindheimeri,* 319, 321, 326, 331, 332

gayfeather (*Liatris punctata*), 332, 333, 367, 376

gayfeather (*Liatris pycnostachya*), 321, 374

gayfeather (*Liatris spicata*), 321, 375, 498

gayfeathers (*Liatris*), 226, 360, 363, 372, 374

*Gaylussacia,* 281, 282, 284

*Gazania,* 358, 471, 496; *rigens* 'Sungold', 345

gazanias (*Gazania*), 358, 471

geiger tree (*Cordia sebestena*), 224, 300

*Geijera parviflora,* 306

*Gelsemium sempervirens,* 197, 341, 347, 348, 350, 352, 353, 380, 381

genetic diversity, 112, 171

gentian (*Gentiana scabra*), 604

gentian (*Gentiana septemfida*), 604

gentian (*Gentiana verna*), 604

*Gentiana,* 47; *andrewsii,* 207; *clausa,* 187; *scabra,* 604; *septemfida,* 604; *verna,* 604

geography, plant, *see* plant geography

Georgia, 438, 623–24, 666, 695, 703–704

geotropic plants, 68

*Geraea canescens,* 108, 227

*Geranium,* 47
    *arboreum,* 128
    *dalmaticum,* 604
    *endressii,* 329; 'Wargrave Pink', 329
    *fremontii,* 190
    *incanum,* 345
    'Johnson's Blue', 324, 330, 331
    *macrorrhizum,* 336
    *maculatum,* 147, 187, 188, 189, 202
    *renardii,* 604
    *sanguineum,* 324, 328, 329, 332, 344
    x *cantabrigiense* 'Biokovo', 343

geranium (*Geranium dalmaticum*), 604

geranium (*Geranium renardii*), 604

geranium (*Pelargonium* x *hortorum*), 355

geraniums (*Pelargonium*), 332, 355, 486, 498, 522, 593–94

gerbera daisy (*Gerbera jamesonii*), 355, 373

*Gerbera jamesonii,* 355, 373

German bearded irs (*Iris* x *germanica*), 470

germander (*Teucrium canadense*), 344

germander (*Teucrium chamaedrys*), 257, 485

German iris (*Iris germanica*), 319

Germany, 631

gesneriad family, 58, 592

Gesnericeae, 47, 58

*Geum: canadense,* 343, 381; *radiatum,* 127; *rivale,* 108, 220, 224; *triflorum,* 207, 208, 343

ghost bramble (*Rubus cockburnianus*), 377

giant blue hyssop (*Agastache foeniculum*), 253

giant chain fern (*Woodwardia fimbriata*), 339

giant coneflower (*Rudbeckia maxima*), 198

giant four-o-clock (*Mirabilis multiflora*), 332, 333, 345

giant Louisiana iris (*Iris giganticaerulea*), 198

giant red paintbrush (*Castilleja miniata*), 226, 227, 229

giant reed (*Arundo donax*), 137

giant reed (*Phragmites australis*), 195

giant snowdrop (*Galanthus elwesii*), 135

giant spider lily (*Crinum* x *amabile*), 323

Giffard's cyanea (*Cyanea giffardii*), 131

*Gilia aggregata,* 215, 364

*Gillenia trifoliata,* 187

ginger (*Alpinia purpurata*), 372

ginger (*Zingiber officinale*), 72, 404, 588

ginger-lily (*Hedychium*), 403, 588

ginkgo (*Ginkgo biloba*), 282, 298, 299, 301, 302, 306, 500, 609

Ginkgo (Ginkgophyta), 52

*Ginkgo biloba,* 10, 282, 298, 299, 301, 302, 305, 306, 484, 500, 609; 'Autumn Gold', 305

Ginkgophyta, 52

ginseng (*Panax quinquefolius*), 134

glabrescent plant surfaces, 94

glabrous plant surfaces, 94

glade fern (*Athyrium pycnocarpon*), 197

glades lobelia (*Lobelia glandulosa*), 199

gladioli (*Gladiolus*), 373

*Gladiolus,* 47, 373, 375; *communis* subsp. *byzantinus,* 370; hybrids, 400; species, 405; x *hortulanus,* 373

gladiolus (*Gladiolus* x *hortulans*), 373

*Glandularia gooddingii,* 108, 227

glans, 92, 93

glasswort (*Salicornia*), 162

*Glaucium oxylobum,* 339

*Glaucocarpum suffrutescens,* 127

Gleason, Henry, 17, 144

*Glechoma hederacea,* 138, 344

*Gleditsia,* 47
    *triacanthos,* 298, 301, 303–304, 470, 477, 500; 'Imperial', 304; 'Inermis', 303–304; 'Moraine', 304; 'Shademaster', 304

gleyization process, 37

global warming, 122–23

globba (*Globba winitii*), 403

*Globba winitii,* 403, 595

globe amaranth (*Gomphrena globosa*), 354, 355, 356, 358, 360, 371, 373, 374, 376, 471, 487, 496

globe candytuft (*Iberis umbellata*), 496

globe flower (*Trollius ledebourii*), 375

globe thistle (*Echinops nivalis*), 331

globe thistle (*Echinops ritro*), 319, 320, 374, 478

globe thistles (*Echinops*), 359, 371, 486

gloriosa daisy (*Rudbeckia hirta*), 355, 357, 376

glory-bower (*Clerodendrum philippinum*), 591

glory-bower (*Clerodendrum thomsoniae*), 522

glorybowers (*Clerodendron*), 484, 486

glory-of-the-snow (*Chionodoxa*), 394–85, 496, 582

glossary, 739–60

glossy abelia (*Abelia grandiflora*), 365

glossy abelia (*Abelia* x *grandiflora*), 360, 514

glossy black chokeberry (*Aronia melanocarpa* var. *elata*), 312

glycosides, 642

*Glycyrrhiza glabra,* 259

goatsbeard (*Aruncus dioicus*), 191, 201, 320, 329

goatweed (*Aegopodium podagraria*), 341

Goethe, Johann Wolfgang von, 7

gold chip (*Asteriscus maritimus*), 330

gold dust tree (*Aucuba japonica*), 497

golden alexander (*Zizia aurea*), 197, 205, 207

golden alexanders (*Zizia*), 362

goldenball leadtree (*Leucaena retusa*), 307

golden banner (*Thermopsis rhombifolia* var. *montana*), 208, 215, 328

golden-beard penstemon (*Penstemon barbatus*), 227

golden chain tree (*Laburnum* x *watereri*), 306

golden clematis (*Clematis tangutica*), 349

golden club (*Orontium aquaticum*), 196, 197, 198, 200, 201, 202

golden columbine (*Aquilegia chrysantha*), 328

golden currant (*Ribes aureum*), 190, 315, 367

golden dewdrop (*Duranta repens*), 311

golden eardrops (*Dicentra chrysantha*), 109, 230

golden-eyed grass (*Sisyrinchium californica*), 192

golden fleece (*Thymophylla tenuiloba*), 358

golden groundsel (*Senecio obovatus*), 327, 343, 381

golden iris (*Iris innominata*), 192

golden larch (*Pseudolarix kaempferi*), 298

golden leaf leadtree (*Leucaena retusa*), 213
golden marguerite (*Anthemis tinctoria*), 372, 373
golden pothos (*Epipremnum aureum*), 571, 572
golden ragwort (*Senecio aureus*), 196, 200
goldenrain tree (*Koelreuteria paniculata*), 300, 306, 307, 470, 477, 609
goldenrods (*Solidago*), 108, 109, 169, 200, 206, 207, 208, 220, 222, 223, 224, 225, 226, 229, 321, 322, 323, 359, 360, 361, 369, 372, 373, 374, 470, 498
golden shower (*Cassia fistula*), 300
golden shrimp plant (*Pachystachys lutea*), 311
golden trumpet tree (*Tabebuia chrysotricha*), 306
golden variegated Japanese sedge (*Carex morrowii* 'Aureo-variegata'), 329
goldenwave (*Coreopsis tinctoria*), 356
goldfields (*Lasthenia chrysostoma*), 209
goldfish plants (*Columnea*), 572
Goldie's wood fern (*Dryopteris goldiana*), 197
gold poppy (*Eschscholzia mexicana*), 209
goldspur columbine (*Aquilegia chrysantha*), 332
goldthread (*Coptis laciniata*), 191
goldthread (*Coptis trifolia* subsp. *groenlandica*), 196
goldthreads (*Coptis*), 161
*Gomphrena globosa*, 354, 355, 356, 358, 360, 371, 373, 374, 376, 471, 487, 496
*Good Bulb Guide, The*, 135
gooseberry (*Ribes*), 270, 366
gooseneck loosestrife (*Lysimachia clethroides*), 319, 324, 370
gopher plant (*Euphorbia rigida*), 339
gophers, 565
*Gordonia lasianthus*, 161, 197
*Gouania: hillebrandii*, 128; *meyenii*, 128; *vitifolia*, 128
grafting, 489–93
grafting knife, 481
*Grama*, 337
grama grasses (*Bouteloua*), 169, 208, 213
grandiflora glads (*Gladiolus* hybrids), 400
grape (*Vitis labrusca*), 352

grape hyacinth (*Muscari botryoides*), 321
grape hyacinth (*Muscari racemosum*), 369
grape hyacinths (*Muscari*), 396, 496, 582
grape ivy (*Cissus rhombifolia*), 524, 572
grapes (*Vitis*), 270, 279–80, 284, 359, 485; pests of, 286
grapevine (*Vitis vulpina*), 351
grasses, 337; drought-resistant, 471; lawn, *see* lawn
grass family, 60–61
grassland gardens, 203–10
maintaining, 210
planting, 205–10
plants for, 206–209; desert grasslands, 208–209; Eastern meadows, 206; Intermountain Grassland, 208; Midwest, 206–207; Shortgrass Prairie, 207–208
preparing, 204–205
grass-of-Parnassus (*Parnassia californica*), 203
grass-of-Parnassus (*Parnassia glauca*), 200
grass shears, 615
Gray, Asa, 7–8, 13
gray birch (*Betula populifolia*), 298, 377
gray dogwood (*Cornus racemosa*), 312, 314, 362
gray goldenrod (*Solidago nemoralis*), 208, 326
grayleaf cotoneaster (*Cotoneaster buxifolius*), 318
Gray's phyllostegia (*Phyllostegia brevidens*), 132
gray stenogyne (*Stenogyne cinerea*), 132
Great Basin, 155, 169
great blue lobelia (*Lobelia siphilitica*), 206, 207, 322
Great Britain, 631, 637
great coneflower (*Rudbeckia maxima*), 320
great hedge nettle (*Stachys cooleyae*), 229
great merry bells (*Uvularia grandiflora*), 325
Great Plains yucca (*Yucca glauca*), 215
Great Solomon's seal (*Polygonatum commutatum*), 188, 189
Greece, 638
greek germander (*Teucrium aroanum*), 340, 345
Greek myrtle (*Myrtus communis*), 500
greek oregano (*Origanum heracleoticum*), 496

green-and-gold (*Chrysogonum virginianum*), 187, 188, 322
green arum (*Peltandra virginica*), 199
green ash (*Fraxinus pennsylvanica*), 167, 301, 303, 609
green dragon (*Arisaema dracontium*), 188, 196
green-flowered hedgehog (*Echinocereus viridiflorus*), 215
green-flowering tobacco (*Nicotiana langsdorffii*), 354
green hawthorn (*Crataegus viridis*), 303, 380
green-headed coneflower (*Rudbeckia laciniata*), 362
green hellebore (*Helleborus foetidus*), 341
greenhouses, 572; beneficial insects for, 546
green joint fir (*Ephedra viridis*), 384
green lavender-cotton (*Santolina virens*), 470
green-leafed wax begonia (*Begonia* x *semperflorens-cultorum*), 355
greenleaf manzanita (*Arctostaphylos patula*), 170
green manures, 459
green stenogyne (*Stenogyne viridis*), 132
*Grevillea*, 317; *robusta*, 138; 'Robyn Gordon', 317; *thelemanniana*, 366
grevillea (*Grevillea*), 317
ground covers, 340–45; drought-resistant, 471; herbs for, 250
ground ivy (*Glechoma hederacea*), 138, 344
ground layer, 163, 184
ground morning glory (*Convolvulus sabatius*), 345
groundnut (*Apios tuberosa*), 347
ground orchid (*Spathoglottis plicata*), 373
groundsel bush (*Baccharis halimifolia*), 168, 216
growing regions of the United States, 288–96. *see also* individual regions
growth, architecture, and branching structure, grouping of plants by, 68
*Guaiacum: officinale*, 300; *sanctum*, 300, 223
Guam, 108, 223
guernsey lily (*Nerine sarniensis*), 406
Gulf coast penstemon (*Penstemon tenuis*), 198
Gulf muhly (*Muhlenbergia capillaris*), 198, 326, 374

gumbo-limbo (*Bursera simaruba*), 168, 300, 361
gumi (*Elaeagnus multiflora*), 281, 282
*Gunnera tinctoria*, 338
*Guzmania*, 324
*Gymnocarpium dryopteris*, 190
*Gymnocarpium robertianum*, 190
*Gymnocladus dioicus*, 301, 302, 304, 307, 337, 379, 486
gymnosperms: about, 101; propagating, especially conifers, 103; sexual reproduction of, 101–104
gynoecium, 86, 104, 106
*Gypsophila: paniculata*, 138, 331, 371, 373, 376; *repens*, 332, 333
gypsy moth, 554
*Gyromitra esculenta*, 664–65

habitat types, *see* vegetative associations (habitat types)
habits of plants, grouping by, 65
hackberries (*Celtis*), 470
hackberry (*Celtis occidentalis*), 281, 282, 301, 359, 362
*Haemanthus*, 403; *coccineus*, 586
hairgrass (*Deschampsia cespitosa*), 203
hairless allocarya (*Plagiobothrys glaber*), 132
hairy puccoon (*Lithospermum caroliniense*), 207
hairy rattleweed (*Baptisia arachnifera*), 126
hairy rockcress (*Braya pilosa*), 131
hairy wikstoemia (*Wikstroemia villosa*), 132
*Hakonechloa macra*, 320; 'Alboaurea', 334; 'Aureola', 320
*Haleakala* stenogyne (*Stenogyne haliakalae*), 132
Hales, Stephen, 8
*Halesia: carolina*, 187, 188, 298, 300, 305, 477, 484, 500; *tetraptera*, 298
Hall, George Rogers, 8
*Halophila*, 109
Hamamelidae, 53–54
*Hamamelis: japonica*, 376
*mollis*, 298, 376, 501; 'Pallida', 382
*virginiana*, 108, 187, 189, 220, 222, 312, 378
x *intermedia*, 298, 376; 'Primavera', 378; 'Ruby Glow', 378; 'Sunburst', 378
*Hamelia patens*, 223, 224, 311, 361
hand fork, 613

handicrafts, herbs used in making, 267–68
handkerchief tree (*Davidia involucrata*), 298, 300
hand sprayer, 618
hand watering, 473
*Haplostachys: bryanii,* 131; *haplostachya,* 128; *linearifolia,* 131; *munroi,* 131; *truncata,* 131
*Hardenbergia: comptoniana,* 352; *violacea,* 352, 353
hardening off seedlings, 479
hardhack (*Spirea douglasii*), 201
hardhack (*Spirea tomentosa*), 200
hardiness of plants, 24
  growing regions of the United States, 288–96. *see also individual regions*
  hardiness zone maps, 30–31, 288
hardy ageratum (*Conoclinum coelestinum*), 372
hardy ageratum (*Eupatorium coelestinum*), 360
hardy begonia (*Begonia grandis*), 322
hardy cyclamen (*Cyclamen hederifolium*), 135
hardy cyclamens (*Cyclamen*), 378
hardy dragon bamboo (*Fargesia dracocephala*), 338
hardy fuchsia (*Fuchsia magellanica*), 365
hardy kiwi (*Actinidia*), 282, 283
hardy kiwi (*Actinidia arguta*), 349
hardy red amaryllis (*Hippeastrum x johnsonii*), 369
hardy rubber tree (*Eucommia ulmoides*), 609
hardy verbena (*Verbena rigida*), 356
harebell (*Campanula rotundifolia*), 207
hare's tail grass (*Lagurus ovatus*), 374
Harison rose (*Rosa x harisonii*), 370
harlequin flower (*Sparaxis tricolor*), 406
harlequin glorybower (*Clerodendrum trichotomum*), 299, 305
*Harmful Non-Indigenous Species in the United States,* 136
*Harperocallis flava,* 127
Harper's beauty (*Harperocallis flava*), 127
hastate leaf base, 78, 79
haustoria, 70
Hawaii, 438, 624, 637, 695, 704; endemics in, 119; most imperiled plants of, 128–29
Hawaiian catchfly (*Silene cryptopetala*), 132

Hawaiian hibiscus (*Hibiscus rosa-sinensis*), 500
Hawaiian umbrella tree (*Schefflera arboricola*), 536
*Haworthia fasciata,* 323
hawthorn (*Crataegus*), 282, 283, 284
hawthorn (*Crataegus crus-galli*), 470
hawthorn (*Crataegus viridis*), 187
hawthorn (*Crataegus x mordenensis*), 302
hawthorns (*Crataegus*), 218, 359, 363, 477, 609
hay-scented fern (*Dennstaedtia punctilobula*), 320, 334, 341
hazelnut (*Corylus americana*), 359
hazelnut (*Corylus avellana*), 359
hazelnut (*Corylus cornuta*), 381
hazelnuts (*Corylus*), 362
heartleaf bergenia (*Bergenia cordifolia*), 325, 330, 337
heartleaf golden alexander (*Zizia laptera*), 207
heartleaf harebells (*Bergenia cordifolia*), 332
heartleaf hornbeam (*Carpinus cordata*), 305
hearts-a-bustin'(*Euonymus americanus*), 188, 189
hearts and flowers (*Aptenia cordifolia*), 345
heath (*Erica carnea*), 308, 340
heath (*Erica x darleyensis*), 344
heath aster (*Aster ericoides*), 326, 363
heather (*Calluna vulgaris*), 344, 485
heath family, 56
heaths (*Erica*), 485
*Hebe,* 47
Heckrott hybrid honeysuckle (*Lonicera x heckrotti*), 347
*Hedeoma: pilosa,* 131; *pulegioides,* 261
*Hedera,* 47; *helix,* 138, 496, 520, 522, 524, 676
hedgehog cactus (*Echinocereus fendleri*), 215
hedge maple (*Acer campestre*), 304, 514, 609
hedge nettle (*Stachys bullata*), 230
hedges, 513–15; for city gardens, 604–605; informal, 515; recommended plants, 514; training formal, 513–15
hedge shears, 507, 615
*Hedychium,* 403, 588; *gardnerianum,* 138
*Hedyotis: cookiana,* 128; *coriacea,* 128; *degeneri,* 128; *foliosa,* 131; *manni,* 128; *nigricans,* 326; *parvula,* 128; *st.-johnii,* 128

heirloom flowers, 367–71
Heirloom Seed Project, 40
*Helenium: autumnale,* 200, 206, 321, 329, 369; *pinnatifidum,* 199
*Helianthemum,* 345; *debilis,* 323, 373; *dumosum,* 206
*Helianthus,* 153, 169, 207, 366, 367, 373
  *angustifolius,* 196, 198, 206, 331, 360, 366
  *annuus,* 206, 208, 215, 355, 357, 358, 371, 372, 375, 683; 'Colour Fashion', 357; 'Hopi Black Dye', 371
  *grosseserratus,* 200
  *maximiliani,* 326, 362, 363, 364, 367, 374, 376
  *multiflora,* 365
  *occidentalis,* 208
  *salicifolius,* 337
  *tuberosus,* 206
  x *multiflorus,* 375
*Helichrysum:*
  *angustifolium,* 340
  *bracteatum,* 371, 373, 374
  *italicum,* 340
  *petiolare,* 331, 356; 'Limelight', 331, 354
*Heliconia,* 323
  *caribaea,* 335, 373
  *latispatha,* 373
  *psittacorum,* 373
  *rostrata,* 373
  *stricta,* 373; 'Carli's Sharonii', 336
heliconia (*Heliconia caribaea*), 335
heliconias (*Heliconia*), 323, 373
*Helictotrichon sempervirens,* 319, 328, 329, 338
*Heliomeris multiflora,* 364
heliopsis (*Heliopsis helianthoides*), 372
*Heliopsis helianthoides,* 207, 321, 324, 372
heliotrope (*Heliotropium arborescens*), 358, 371, 522
*Heliotropium arborescens,* 257, 352, 355, 358, 371, 487, 522
hellebore (*Helleborus argustifolius*), 331
hellebores (*Helleborus*), 320, 335
*Helleborus,* 320, 335; *argustifolius,* 331, 375, 383; *foetidus,* 341, 378, 379; *niger,* 330, 376, 382; *orientalis,* 322, 342, 370, 375, 376, 378, 379, 383
*Hemerocallis,* 47, 319, 321, 322, 323, 324, 325, 326, 327, 329, 341, 363, 470; 'Ed Murray', 319; *flava,* 367; *fulva,* 138,

369, 370; 'Kwanzo' 319, 367; *lilio-asphodelus,* 330, 367, 370; 'Tender Love', 329; x *hybrida,* 498
hemlock (*Conium maculatum*), 674–75
hemlocks (*Tsuga*), 485
hemlock woolly adelgid, 554
henbane (*Hyoscyamus niger*), 653
hens and chickens (*Sempervivum*), 382
hens and chickens (*Sempervivum tectorum*), 368, 370
*Hepatica,* 146; *acutiloba,* 187, 188; *americana,* 188, 189
hepaticas (*Hepatica*), 146
*Heracleum lanatum,* 202, 203
herb gardens:
  designs for, 247–50; container gardens, 249–50; cottage garden, 248; knot gardens, 247–48; raised beds, 248
  edges and hedges, 250–51
  ground covers, 250
  shady areas, 250
  *see also herbs*
herbivores, 174; -plant relationships, 176–77
herbs, 252–68
  for culinary and confectionary use, 266; harvesting and preserving, 251–52
  defined, 247
  for dyeing and crafts, 267–68
  for edges and hedges, 250–51
  encyclopedia of, 252–65
  fertilizing of, 461
  for fragrance, 268
  for ground covers, 250
  growing, 251
  herb gardens, *see herb gardens*
  as indoor plants, 580–81
  medicinal, 267
  for shady areas, 250
  for tea and other beverages, 266–67
  *see also specific herbs*
Hercules club (*Zanthoxylum clava-herculis*), 364
herperidium, 92, 93
*Hesperaloe parviflora,* 312, 318, 337, 339, 363, 367
*Hesperomannia: arborescens,* 128; *arbuscula,* 128; *lydgatei,* 128
*Heteromeles arbutifolia,* 191, 215, 317, 366, 383
heterotrophic plants, 67
*Heuchera:*
  *americana,* 187
  *maxima,* 192, 331
  *micrantha,* 203, 330, 331; 'Chocolate Ruffles', 338; 'Palace Purple', 331, 335, 338; 'Plum Pudding', 338

*richardsonii,* 207
*sanguinea,* 190, 322, 328, 329, 332
*Hexastylis: shuttleworthii,* 189; *virginicum,* 189
*Hibiscadelphus: bombycinus,* 131; *distans,* 128; *wilderianus,* 132
*Hibiscus,* 319
*brackenridgei,* 128
*clayi,* 128
*coccineus,* 198, 368, 369
*laevis,* 198
*militaris,* 198
*moscheutos,* 321; subsp. *lasiocarpos,* 200
*palustris,* 196
*rosa-sinensis,* 47, 484, 500, 594
'Southern Belle', 319
*syriacus,* 138, 303, 310, 315, 367, 368, 370, 470, 484, 501, 509, 514
hibiscus (*Hibiscus*), 319
hickory (*Carya*), 167, 282, 359
Higan cherry (*Prunus subhirtella*), 298, 501
highbush blueberry (*Vaccinium corymbosum*), 308, 309
highbush cranberry (*Viburnum trilobum*), 281, 282, 284, 311
*Hilaria mutica,* 209
hill country rain lily (*Cooperia pedunculata*), 326, 327
Hillebrand bur-cucumber (*Sicyos hillebrandi*), 132
Hillebrand's phyllostegia (*Phyllostegia hillebrandii*), 132
Himalayan honeysuckle (*Leycesteria formosa*), 365
Himalayan white birch (*Betula utilis* var. *jacquemontii*), 304
Hinoki cypress (*Chamaecyparis obtusa*), 500
Hinoki false cypress (*Chamaecyparis obtusa*), 298, 500
*Hippeastrum,* 403, 585–86; x *johnsonii,* 369
*Hippophae rhamnoides,* 314, 338
hirsute plant surfaces, 94
hispid plant surfaces, 94
hoary vervain (*Verbena stricta*), 207
hobblebush (*Leucothoe fontanesiana*), 308
hoes, 613
*Hoffmannseggia tenella,* 127
Hogg, Thomas, 8
holboellia (*Holboellia coriacea*), 351
*Holboellia coriacea,* 351
holei (*Ochrosia kilaueaensis*), 132
holiday cacti (*Schlumbergera*), 324
hollies (*Ilex*), 161, 187, 299, 359, 485, 514

holly fern (*Cyrtomium falcatum*), 342
holly grape (*Mahonia repens*), 190
holly grapes (*Mahonia*), 191
hollyhock (*Alcea rosea*), 365, 366, 367, 368, 369
hollyleaf cherry (*Prunus ilicifolia*), 366
holly-leaf osmanthus (*Osmanthus heterophyllus*), 379
holly-leaved cherry (*Prunus ilicifolia*), 215
*Holodiscus: discolor,* 365; *dumosus,* 315
Holy Ghost ipomopsis (*Ipomopsis sancti-spiritus*), 127
*Homeria,* 405–406
honesty (*Lunaria annua*), 354
honeybush (*Melianthus major*), 339, 500
honeycreepers, flower pollination by, 178
honey locust (*Gleditsia triacanthos*), 298, 301, 303, 477, 500
honey mesquite (*Prosopis glandulosa*), 169, 302, 337
honeysuckle (*Lonicera caerulea* var. *edulis*), 281, 282
honeysuckle (*Lonicera flava*), 347
honeysuckle (*Lonicera hispidula* var. *vacillans*), 202
honeysuckles (*Lonicera*), 675
Hong Kong orchid (*Bauhinia* x *blakeana*), 300
Hooke, Robert, 8
Hooker, Joseph Dalton, 8
Hooker, William Jackson, 8
Hooker's evening primrose (*Oenothera hookeri*), 208, 209
hoop houses, 235
hopbush (*Dodonaea viscosa*), 318
hop hornbeam (*Ostrya virginiana*), 189
hops (*Humulus lupulus*), 349
hop tree (*Ptelea trifoliata*), 190, 303, 312, 338
horehound (*Marrubium vulgare*), 257–58
horizon, soil, 35
horizontal structure of plant communities, 164
hornbeam (*Carpinus caroliniana*), 514
hornbeam maple (*Acer carpinifolium*), 298
horned bladderwort (*Utricularia cornuta*), 199
horned poppy (*Glaucium oxylobum*), 339
horned violet (*Viola cornuta*), 497
hornwort (*Ceratophyllum*), 109

hornworts, *see* mosses, liverworts, and hornworts
horse chestnut (*Aesculus hippocastanum*), 13, 648, 675
horse chestnuts (*Aesculus*), 477, 486
horseherb (*Calyptocarpus vialis*), 343
horsemint (*Monarda citriodora*), 322, 356, 370
horseradish (*Armoracia rusticana*), 258
horsetail (*Equisetum hyemale*), 198, 202, 203
horsetails (*Equisetum*), 201, 202
horticultural oils, 547
Hosack, David, 8–9
Hosaka love grass (*Eragrostis hosakai*), 131
hose, garden, 617–18
*Hosta,* 47, 320, 321, 322, 325, 328, 336, 342, 496, 498
*clausa,* 341
'Frances Williams', 334
'Gold Standard', 338
*lancifolia,* 344, 367
*plantaginea,* 367, 373; 'Honey Bells', 370
*sieboldiana,* 330, 333, 337; 'Elegans', 335; 'Frances Williams', 330
*undulata,* 367; 'Albomarginata', 335
*ventricosa:* 'Albo-marginata', 334
hosta (*Hosta sieboldiana*), 333, 337
hostas (*Hosta*), 320, 321, 322, 328, 336, 342, 498
hot caps (cloches), 234
Hottentot fig (*Carpobrotus edulis*), 137
hound's-tongue (*Cynoglossum grande*), 109, 229
house hydrangea (*Hydrangea macrophylla*), 510
houseplants, *see* indoor gardening
*Houstonia caerulea,* 189
*Houttuynia:* *cordata,* 340; 'Chameleon', 340; 'Plena', 340
houttuynia (*Houttuynia cordata*), 340
*Hovenia dulcis,* 281, 282
*Howeia forsteriana,* 301
Howell's spineflower (*Chorizanthe howellii*), 126
*Hoya,* 349; *carnosa,* 572
huckleberry (*Gaylussacia*), 281, 282, 284
huckleberry (*Vaccinum ovatum*), 366
*Hudsonia tomentosa,* 216

hummingbird (*Grevillea thelemanniana*), 366
hummingbirds: flower pollination by, 109, 177, 178; gardening for, 219, 220–30
hummingbird trumpet (*Epilobium canum*), 332
*Humulus lupulus,* 349
humus, 174, 433
*Hunnemannia fumariifolia,* 354, 376
hurricane palm (*Dictyosperma album*), 301
hyacinth (*Hyacinthus*), 675
hyacinth (*Hyacinthus orientalis*), 496
hyacinth bean (*Dolichos lablab*), 346, 347, 349, 350, 487
*Hyacinthoides,* 583; *hispanica,* 320, 370, 371
*Hyacinthus,* 395–96, 675; *orientalis,* 496, 582
hybrid daylilies (*Hemerocallis* x *hybrida*), 498
hybrid fall aster (*Aster* x *frikartii*), 320
hybrid oriental witchhazel (*Hamamelis* x *intermedia*), 298
hybrid petunias (*Petunia* x *hybrid*), 496
*Hydrangea,* 47, 374, 481, 484
*anomala,* 346, 347, 348, 351, 352; subsp. *petiolaris,* 349, 351
*arborescens,* 188, 310, 312, 313; 'Annabelle', 310, 371
*macrophylla,* 310, 313, 317, 327, 367, 500, 510; 'Mariesii', 310, 317
*paniculata:* 'Grandiflora', 13, 310, 514, 522; 'Pee Gee', 311; 'Tardiva', 311
*petiolaris,* 349, 351, 524
*quercifolia,* 187, 188, 308, 310, 312, 313, 316, 335, 337, 338, 379, 500; 'Snowflake', 316
*sargentiana,* 315
hydrangea (*Hydrangea macrophylla*), 317
hydrangeas (*Hydrangea*), 374, 481, 484
hydrochory, 93
*Hydrolea corymbosa,* 199
*Hydrophyllum virginianum,* 189
*Hylotelephium spectabile* 'Autumn Glory', 370; 'Autumn Joy', 384; 'Red Chief', 384
*Hymenocallis,* 403–404, 589–90; *caroliniana,* 200; *liriosome,* 198; *palmeri,* 199
hymenoxys (*Tetraneuris scaposa*), 326
*Hymenoxys acaulis,* 333

*Hyoscyamus niger,* 653
hypanthium, 86
*Hypaxis hirsuta,* 206
*Hypericum,* 486
　　*calycinum,* 341, 344, 481
　　*cistifolium,* 199
　　*frondosum* 'Sunburst', 470
　　*henryi,* 313, 381
　　*patulum,* 321; 'Hidcote', 321
　　*perforatum,* 138
　　*prolificum,* 484
　　*virginicum,* 196
hypericum (*Hypericum patulum*), 321
*Hyptis emoryi,* 108, 227, 228
hyssop (*Hyssopus officinalis*), 258, 365
hyssop-leaved thoroughwort (*Eupatorium hyssopifolium*), 206
*Hyssopus officinalis,* 258, 365

*Iberis: sempervirens,* 321, 332, 367; *umbellata,* 496
Iceland poppy (*Papaver nudicaule*), 375
iceplant (*Carpobrotus edulis*), 137
ice plant (*Mesembryanthemum crystallinum*), 496
Idaho, 438, 695, 704
Idaho fescue (*Festuca idahoensis*), 208
ifafa lily (*Cyrtanthus*), 402
ifafa lily (*Cyrtanthus mackenii*), 588–89
*Ilex,* 47, 161, 187, 484, 485, 514, 675
　　*ambigua,* 359
　　*aquifolium,* 138
　　*cassine,* 188, 197, 198, 300
　　*cornuta,* 309, 377, 380; 'Burfordii', 309, 313, 379, 381; 'Burfordii Nana', 313, 381; 'Dazzler', 500; 'D'or', 379; 'O'Spring', 379; 'Rotunda', 313, 381
　　*crenata,* 308, 520; 'Okinawa', 536
　　*decidua,* 299, 302, 303, 359, 360, 379
　　*glabra,* 199, 216, 308, 514
　　'Nellie R. Stevens', 299, 360
　　*opaca,* 187, 189, 299, 359, 360, 377, 379, 501, 514
　　*serrata,* 377
　　*verticillata,* 189, 197, 218, 311, 360, 362, 377, 379
　　*vomitoria,* 188, 299, 312, 314, 318, 363, 380, 470, 520; 'Nana', 312, 314, 318, 341; 'Pendula', 312, 314; 'William Fleming', 312, 314

x *meserveae,* 308, 377
*Illicium floridanum,* 188, 310
Illinois, 438, 624, 695, 705
imbricate leaf arrangement, 83
immortelle (*Xeranthemum annuum*), 371
imparipinnate, 76
*Impatiens,* 354, 356, 496, 497; *balsamina,* 355, 368; *capensis,* 221, 223, 225; *walleriana,* 354, 355, 356, 357, 360
impatiens (*Impatiens*), 354, 356, 496
impatiens (*Impatiens balsamina*), 355
impatiens (*Impatiens walleriana*), 354, 355, 356, 357, 360
*Imperata cylindrica,* 138; 'Rubra', 339
importing plants, 639–40
incense cedar (*Calocedrus decurrens*), 170, 306
indehiscent, 91
indeterminate growth of leaves, 82
India hawthorn (*Rhaphiolepis indica*), 318
Indiana, 439, 666, 695, 705–706
Indian blanket (*Gaillardia pulchella*), 225, 226
Indian blanket flower (*Gaillardia pulchella*), 225, 226
Indian cherry (*Frangula caroliniana*), 302, 303
Indian cress (*Tropaeolum majus*), 260–61
Indiangrass (*Sorghastrum nutans*), 169, 206, 207, 208, 326, 327, 328, 337, 373, 374, 379, 382
Indian hawthorn (*Rhaphiolepis indica*), 311, 500
Indian paintbrush (*Castilleja californica*), 209
Indian paintbrush (*Castilleja coccinea*), 208, 220, 221, 222
Indian paintbrush (*Castilleja indivisa*), 356
Indian paintbrush (*Castilleja integra*), 215
Indian physic (*Gillenia trifoliata*), 187
Indian pink (*Spigelia marilandica*), 222, 223
Indian rhubarb (*Darmera peltata*), 202, 203, 339
Indian ricegrass (*Oryzopsis hymenoides*), 209, 213, 367
Indian tea (*Thelesperma megapotamicum*), 371
indigobush (*Dalea frutescens*), 108, 227

indigobush (*Dalea greggii*), 108, 228
*Indigofera,* 481
indigos (*Indigofera*), 481
Indonesia, 635
indoor gardening, 569–97; of bulbs, 581–90; cacti and succulents, 579–80; containers for, 575; fertilizing, 574; of fragrant plants, 590–92; of geraniums, 593–94; of gesneriads, 592–93; of herbs, 580–81; housekeeping, 575; lighting and, 569–72; media, growing, 573–74; miniatures for, 596–97; moving plants between outdoors and indoors, 571; orchids for, 576–79; pests and, 546, 567; pollution control with, 571; repotting, 575; temperature and humidity, 572–73; tips for, 570; trees for, 576; types of houseplants, 576–97; unusual plants for, 594–96; watering, 573
inflorescences, 83–85
inkberry (*Ilex glabra*), 308
inkberry (*Scaevola plumieri*), 311
inkberry holly (*Ilex glabra*), 216, 514
inky cap (*Coprinus atramentarius*), 664
inland sea oats (*Chasmanthium latifolium*), 198, 327, 343, 373
insect growth regulators (IGRs), 547
insecticidal soaps, 547–48
insectivorous plants, 82, 160. *see also specific plants*
insects: beneficial, 545, 546; encyclopedia of, 549–59; fruit pests, 284–86; gardening to attract, 219, 220–30; lawn, natural measures to control, 388–89; life cycles of, 549; pollination by, 107, 108–109, 177, 178; rose pests, 410–11. *see also* pests; *specific insects*
insect traps, leaf, 82
inside-out flower (*Vancouveria hexandra*), 191, 345
inside-out flower (*Vancouveria planipetala*), 192
Inter-Governmental Panel on Climate Change, 122–23
interior live oak (*Quercus wislizenii*), 170
intermediate yew (*Taxus x media*), 520
*International Code of Botanical Nomenclature,* 39, 42–43, 50
International Union for Conservation of Nature, 123

interrupted fern (*Osmunda claytoniana*), 190, 192, 197, 320
invasive species, 123, 136–39, 152, 181; wetland gardens and, 195, 203; woodland gardens, clearing from, 186
invertization process, 37
Inyo rock daisy (*Perityle inyoensis*), 132
Iowa, 439, 624, 695, 706
*Ipheion,* 583; *uniflorum,* 369, 396
ipheion (*Ipheion uniflorum*), 369
*Ipomoea,* 349, 357
　　*alba,* 347, 348, 350, 352, 498
　　'Heavenly Blue', 352
　　*microdactyla,* 224
　　*purpurea,* 348, 498
　　*quamoclit,* 347, 350
　　*sagittata,* 199
　　*tricolor,* 350, 654; 'Heavenly Blue', 353
　　x *multifida,* 347
*Ipomopsis: aggregata,* 209, 226, 227, 229; *rubra,* 222, 223, 358; *sancti-spiritus,* 127
Ireland, 631
Iridaceae, 61
*Iris,* 47, 326, 327, 329, 331, 335, 372, 374, 396, 477, 582, 676
　　*albicans,* 369; 'Early purple', 369
　　*brevicaulis,* 198
　　*cristata,* 187, 343, 604
　　*douglasiana,* 192, 209, 215, 216, 331
　　*ensata,* 319; 'Variegata', 334
　　*flavescens,* 370
　　*fulva,* 198, 360
　　*germanica,* 319, 321, 324, 326, 332, 367, 370, 375, 470
　　*giganticaerulea,* 198
　　*hexagona,* 198
　　*innominata,* 192
　　*kaempferi,* 322
　　*missouriensis,* 190, 202
　　*nelsonii,* 198
　　*pallida,* 369; 'Argentea Variegata', 338; 'Aurea Variegata', 338
　　*pallida variegata,* 329
　　*pseudacorus,* 322, 369
　　*sibirica,* 319, 321, 322, 324, 325, 376, 379
　　*tectorum,* 604; 'Alba', 330
　　*tenax,* 209
　　*versicolor,* 197, 200, 201
　　*virginica,* 198, 200, 201
　　*virginica* var. *shrevei,* 207
　　x *fulvala,* 321
iris (*Iris*), 396, 582, 676
iris (*Iris cristata*), 604

iris (*Iris tectorum*), 604

irises (*Iris*), 326, 327, 329, 331, 335, 372, 374, 477

iris family, 61

ironweed (*Vernonia fasciculata*), 207

ironweed (*Vernonia noveboracensis*), 206, 360

ironwood (*Carpinus caroliniana*), 189, 299

ironwood (*Krugiodendron ferreum*), 300

ironwood (*Ostrya virginiana*), 302

island alum root (*Heuchera maxima*), 192

island bush poppy (*Dendromecon harfordii*), 306

island bush poppy (*Dendromecon rigida* subsp. *harfordii*), 216

island ceanothus (*Ceanothus arboreus*), 306, 366

*Isodendrion: hosakae*, 128; *pyrifolium*, 128

*Isoetes: louisianensis*, 127; *melonospora*, 127; *tegetiformans*, 127

*Isomeris arborea*, 230

*Isopyrum biternatum*, 189

Israel, 635

Italian arum (*Arum italicum*), 322

Italian jasmine (*Jasminum humile*), 381

Italy, 631–32

*Itea virginica*, 187, 188, 197, 308, 313, 316, 368, 481, 484; 'Henry's Garnet', 316

Ithuriel's spear (*Triteleia laxa*), 192

*Iva microcephala*, 199

ivy (*Hedera helix*), 676

ivy geranium (*Pelargonium peltatum*), 356

ivy geraniums (*Pelargonium*), 496

*Ixia*, 406

*Ixora*, 311

ixora (*Ixora*), 311

jaboticaba (*Myrcianthes cauliflora*), 536

jacaranda (*Jacaranda mimosifolia*), 300

*Jacaranda mimosifolia*, 300

jack-in-the-pulpit (*Arisaema triphyllum*), 187, 188, 196, 320, 648

Jackman clematis (*Clematis* x *jackmanii*), 509

jack-o'-lantern (*Omphalotus illudens*), 664

Jacob's ladder (*Polemonium reptans*), 188, 330

*Jacquemontia reclinata*, 127

Jamaica caper (*Capparis cynophallophora*), 300

Jamaica dogwood (*Piscidia piscipula*), 108, 223

*Jamesia americana*, 190, 315

Japan, 638

Japanese andromeda (*Pieris japonica*), 309, 310, 377

Japanese anemone (*Anemone* x *hybrida*), 322, 330, 374

Japanese apricot (*Prunus mume*), 376

Japanese aucuba (*Aucuba japonica*), 310

Japanese autumn fern (*Dryopteris erythrosora*), 320

Japanese azalea (*Rhododendron obtusum*), 308

Japanese barberry (*Berberis thunbergii*), 137

Japanese beech (*Fagus crenata*), 536

Japanese beetles, 410, 554

Japanese black pine (*Pinus thunbergii*), 377

Japanese bleeding heart (*Dicentra spectabilis*), 330

Japanese blood grass (*Imperata cylindrica*), 138

Japanese box (*Buxus microphylla*), 377

Japanese boxwood (*Buxus microphylla* var. *japonica*), 313, 381

Japanese camellia (*Camellia japonica*), 383

Japanese cedar (*Cryptomeria japonica*), 299

Japanese clethra (*Clethra barbinervis*), 308

Japanese climbing fern (*Lygodium japonicum*), 138

Japanese crabapple (*Malus floribunda*), 13, 305, 501

Japanese crape myrtle (*Lagerstroemia fauriei*), 300

Japanese dogwood (*Cornus kousa*), 298, 377, 500, 510

Japanese elm (*Zelkova serrata*), 298

Japanese fatsia (*Fatsia japonica*), 497

Japanese flowering apricot (*Prunus mume*), 299, 378, 536

Japanese flowering cherry (*Prunus serrulata*), 298, 501

Japanese flowering quince (*Chaenomeles japonica*), 310

Japanese flowering quince (*Chaenomeles speciosa*), 313

Japanese forest grass (*Hakonechloa macra*), 320

Japanese holly (*Ilex crenata*), 308, 520

Japanese honeysuckle (*Lonicera japonica*), 8, 138

Japanese iris (*Iris ensata*), 319

Japanese iris (*Iris kaempferi*), 322

Japanese kerria (*Kerria japonica*), 310, 368, 377, 470, 481, 484

Japanese knotweed (*Polygonum cuspidatum*), 138

Japanese lily-of-the-valley shrub (*Pieris japonica*), 309, 377

Japanese maple (*Acer palmatum*), 13, 298, 299, 305, 306, 315, 500, 536

Japanese mountain ash (*Sorbus commixta*), 382

Japanese pachysandra (*Pachysandra terminalis*), 341, 342

Japanese pagoda tree (*Sophora japonica*), 298, 299, 609

Japanese painted fern (*Athyrium nipponicum*), 320, 325, 341

Japanese painted fern (*Athyrium nipponicum* var. *pictum*), 335

Japanese pieris (*Pieris japonica*), 316

Japanese plum yew (*Cephalotaxus harringtonia*), 377

Japanese pussy willow (*Salix gracilistyla*), 309

Japanese red pine (*Pinus densiflora*), 377, 536

Japanese scholar tree (*Sophora japonica*), 307

Japanese shrub clematis (*Clematis stans*), 309

Japanese skimmia (*Skimmia japonica*), 500

Japanese snowbell (*Styrax japonica*), 298, 306, 510

Japanese spiraea (*Spiraea japonica*), 139

Japanese stewartia (*Stewartia pseudocamellia*), 305

Japanese styrax (*Styrax japonica*), 305

Japanese sweet pepperbush (*Clethra barbinervis*), 308, 382

Japanese tree lilac (*Syringa reticulata*), 302, 304, 379, 501

Japanese umbrella-pine (*Sciadopitys verticillata*), 485

Japanese white birch (*Betula platyphylla* var. *japonica*), 301

Japanese white pine (*Pinus parviflora*), 514, 536

Japanese winterberry (*Ilex serrata*), 377

Japanese wisteria (*Wisteria floribunda*), 13, 346, 352

Japanese witchhazel (*Hamamelis japonica*), 376

Japanese yew (*Taxus cuspidata*), 8

Japan fatsia (*Fatsia japonica*), 338

jasmine (*Jasminum fruticans*), 536

jasmine (*Jasminum sambac*), 591

jasmines (*Jasminum*), 138, 524

*Jasminum*, 524; *dichotomum*, 138; *fluminense*, 138; *fruticans*, 536; *humile*, 381; *nudiflorum*, 310, 368, 376, 378, 382; *officinale*, 351, 352; *polyanthum*, 352; *sambac*, 591

jatropha (*Jatropha multifida*), 311

*Jatropha multifida*, 311, 654

*Jeffersonia diphylla*, 189

Jekyll, Gertrude, 9

Jensen, Jens, 9

Jerusalem artichoke (*Helianthus tuberosus*), 206

Jerusalem sage (*Phlomis fruticosa*), 331, 332

jimsonweed (*Datura stramonium*), 359, 652

Job's tears (*Coix lacryma-jobi*), 374

Joe-Pye weed (*Eupatorium maculatum*), 83, 196, 206, 319, 321, 362, 374, 379

Joe-Pye weed (*Eupatorium purpureum*), 319, 321, 324, 329, 360, 498

Joe-Pye weeds (*Eupatorium*), 359, 379

Johnny-jump-up (*Viola tricolor*), 355, 358, 368, 371

jojoba (*Simmondsia chinensis*), 318

jonquil (*Narcissus*), 396, 582, 656; classification of narcissi, 397

Joseph's coat (*Amaranthus tricolor*), 355

Joshua tree (*Yucca brevifolia*), 169, 307

jostaberry (*Ribes nidigrolaria*), 281

*Jovibarba*, 48

jubata grass (*Cortaderia jubata*), 137

Juglandaceae, 54, 109

*Juglans: cinerea*, 282; *major*, 307; *nigra*, 282, 301, 302; *regia*, 282

jujube (*Ziziphus jujuba*), 284

Juncaceae, 48, 109

*Juncus*, 202; *balticus*, 203; *megacephalus*, 199

juncus (*Juncus megacephalus*), 199

Juneberries (*Amelanchier*), 270, 281, 282, 283, 284

Juneberry (*Amelanchier alnifolia*), 312

Juneberry (*Amelanchier arborea*), 500

Junegrass (*Koeleria cristata*), 170, 208, 209

juniper (*Juniperus procumbens*), 308

junipers (*Juniperus*), 168, 363, 470, 485, 514, 520

*Juniperus*, 363, 470, 485, 514, 520
*ashei*, 302, 381
*californica*, 170, 215
*chinensis*, 308, 380, 501; 'Pfitzeriana', 308; 'Sargentii', 341; 'Shimpaku', 536
*communis*, 190, 380; var. *saxatilis*, 344, 364
*conferta* 'Blue Pacific', 341
*deppeana*, 215
*horizontalis*, 216, 311, 343, 344; 'Bar Harbor', 340; 'Blue Rug', 341; 'Wiltoni', 216, 308, 311, 340, 343
*monosperma*, 215
*osteosperma*, 215
*procumbens*, 308; 'Nana', 308, 341, 344
*rigida*, 536
*scopulorum*, 190, 304, 364, 382, 501; 'Wichita Blue', 304
*virginiana*, 168, 187, 188, 189, 216, 298, 299, 302, 308, 334, 359, 360, 380, 381, 501; 'Skyrocket', 514

*Justica: brandegeana*, 82; *californica*, 109, 228

*Kaempferia: galanga*, 595; *rotunda*, 595–96

Kahili ginger (*Hedychium gardnerianum*), 138

kaido crabapple (*Malus* x *micromalus*), 536

*Kalanchoe*, 324, 342; *blossfeldiana*, 355; *pinnata*, 323; *tomentosa*, 323

kalanchoe (*Kalanchoe blossfeldiana*), 324, 355

kalanchoes (*Kalanchoe*), 342

kale (*Brassica oleracea*), 239–40

*Kalmia*, 48, 109; *latifolia*, 187, 221, 222, 223, 308, 316, 377, 485, 500, 654–55

kangaroo paw (*Anigozanthos flavidus*), 330, 366

kangaroo vine (*Cissus antarctica*), 524

Kansas, 439, 695, 706

Katsura tree (*Cercidiphyllum japonicum*), 297, 305

Kauai sanicle (*Sanicula kauaiensis*), 132

Kawahae hibiscadelphus (*Hibiscadelphus bombycinus*), 131

Kearney's slimpod (*Amsonia kearneyana*), 126

kentia palm (*Howeia forsteriana*), 301

Kentucky, 439, 667, 695, 706

Kentucky bluegrass (*Poa pratensis*), 85

Kentucky coffee tree (*Gymnocladus dioicus*), 301, 302, 304, 307, 337, 379, 486

Kentucky yellowwood (*Cladrastis kentukea*), 188

*Kerria japonica*, 310, 368, 377, 470, 481, 484; 'Picta', 334; 'Pleniflora', 309

keys for plant identification, 63–64

Key thatch palm (*Thrinax morrisii*), 301, 362

kingdom, classification of life by, 50–51

kinnikinnick bearberry (*Arctostaphylos uva-ursi*), 216

kinnikinnick (*Arctostaphylos uva-ursi*), 190, 318, 344, 365, 471

kitchen gardening, 232–87; fruit growing, *see* fruit growing; herbs, *see* herbs; vegetables, *see* vegetable gardens

kiwi (*Actinidia*), 13, 270, 282

kiwi (*Actinidia deliciosa*), 352

kiwi fruit (*Actinidia chinensis*), 347

Klondike cosmos (*Cosmos sulphureus*), 360

knees of cypress (*Taxodium distichum*), 71

*Kniphofia*, 331, 470; 'Little Maid', 331; *uvaria*, 321, 332, 370; x 'Primrose Beauty', 329

knot gardens, 247–48

Knudsen's phyllostegia (*Phyllostegia knudsenii*), 132

kochia (*Bassia scoparia*), 137

*Koeleria: cristata*, 170, 208, 209; *macrantha*, 170

*Koelreuteria: bipinnata*, 306; *paniculata*, 300, 306, 307, 470, 477, 609

*Kokia: drynarioides*, 128; *lanceolata*, 132

*Kolkwitzia amabilis*, 13, 370, 371, 510

kolomikta vine (*Actinidia kolomikta*), 347, 348, 349

Korean azalea (*Rhododendron mucronulatum*), 308, 309

Korean barberry (*Berberis koreana*), 314

Korean box (*Buxus microphylla*), 377

Korean box (*Buxus microphylla* var. *koreana*), 520

Korean boxwood (*Buxus microphylla* var. *koreana*), 520

Korean mountain ash (*Sorbus alnifolia*), 302

Korean rhododendron (*Rhododendron mucronulatum*), 382

Korean spice viburnum (*Viburnum carlesii*), 309, 316, 510

*Kosteletzkya virginica*, 216, 322

Kousa dogwood (*Cornus kousa*), 300, 305, 316

*Krascheninnikovia lanata*, 382, 384

*Krugiodendron ferreum*, 300

kudzu vine (*Pueraria lobata*), 8

laboratories for soil testing, 438–41

*Labordia lydgatei*, 128

Labrador grape (*Vitis labrusca*), 346

Labrador tea (*Ledum groenlandicum*), 166, 196, 200, 338

Labrador tea (*Rhododendron groenlandicum*), 82

*Laburnum* x *watereri*, 306

lacebark elm (*Ulmus parvifolia*), 303, 307, 378

lacebark pine (*Pinus bungeana*), 298, 377, 382

lace bugs, 554–55

lace-cap hydrangea (*Hydrangea macrophylla*), 310

lacewings, 545

*Lachenalia aloides*, 406

*Lachnanthes caroliniana*, 199

*Lachnocaulon anceps*, 199

*Lactuca sativa*, 240, 478

ladies' tobacco (*Antennaria plantaginifolia*), 206

Lady Banks rose (*Rosa banksiae*), 347, 352

lady beetles (lady bugs), 544, 546

lady fern (*Athyrium filix-femina*), 197, 202, 203, 320, 322, 325, 328, 334

lady-of-the-night (*Brunfelsia americana*), 310, 311

lady-of-the-night (*Brunfelsia grandiflora*), 310, 311

lady-of-the-night (*Brunfelsia pauciflora*), 310, 311

lady palm (*Rhapis excelsa*), 301

lady's bedstraw (*Galium verum*), 258

lady slipper orchids (*Paphiopedilum*), 324, 576, 578

lady's mantle (*Alchemilla mollis*), 258, 328, 329, 370

lady's smock (*Cardamine pratensis*), 201

lady tulip (*Tulipa clusiana*), 369

*Lagerstroemia*, 48
*fauriei*, 300, 378; 'Fantasy', 300
*indica*, 10, 303, 306, 307, 311, 380, 484, 501, 536; 'Alba', 306
*speciosa*, 300

*Laguncularia racemosa*, 168

*Lagurus ovatus*, 374

Lakela's mint (*Dicerandra immaculata*), 126

lamb's ears (*Stachys byzantina*), 258, 328, 329, 332, 333, 335, 368, 371, 470

lamb's ears (*Stachys lanata*), 336

Lamiaceae, 58

lamina or leaf blade, 74

*Lamium*:
*galeobdolon*, 321, 341, 344; 'Variegatum', 321, 341
*maculatum*, 336, 344; 'Beacon Silver', 345

lanceleaf coreopsis (*Coreopsis lanceolata*), 208

lanceleaf cottonwood (*Populus* x *acuminata*), 304

lanceleaf plantain lily (*Hosta lancifolia*), 344

lanceolate leaves, 77

lancewood (*Nectandra coriacea*), 300

Landreth, Cuthbert, 9

Landreth, David, 9

*Lantana*, 48, 361, 363, 373, 498; *camara*, 138, 326, 356, 360, 522, 655; *depressa*, 323, 324, 342; *montevidensis*, 323, 345, 356; *urticoides*, 327

lantana (*Lantana camara*), 138, 360

lantana (*Lantana depressa*), 324

lantanaphyllum viburnum (*Viburnum* x *rhytidophylloides*), 314, 315

lantanas (*Lantana*), 361, 363, 373, 498

Lapland rose (*Rhododendron lapponicum*), 166

larches (*Larix*), 161, 166

large-flowered bellwort (*Uvularia grandiflora*), 190

large-flowered fiddleneck (*Amsinckia grandiflora*), 126

large-fruited sand verbena (*Abronia macrocarpa*), 126

largest plants and flowers, 686–87

*Larix*, 161, 166; *decidua*, 304; *laricina*, 196, 200; *occidentalis*, 190, 365

larkspur (*Consolida ajacis*), 358

larkspur (*Consolida ambigua*), 375
larkspur (*Delphinium grandiflorum*), 369
*Larrea tridentata,* 68, 169, 213, 318, 340, 384
*Lasthenia: burkei,* 127; *chrysostoma,* 209
laterization process, 37
*Lathyrus:*
　*japonicus,* 216; sub. *maritimus,* 216
　*latifolius,* 347, 369
　*odoratus,* 346, 347, 350, 368, 372, 373, 375, 498
Lauraceae, 53
laurel family, 53
laurel oak (*Quercus laurifolia*), 168, 199
"laurel" of Caesar (*Ruscus hypoglossum*), 72
*Laurentia fluviatilis,* 471
*Laurus nobilis,* 253, 522, 580
laurustinus (*Viburnum tinus*), 383
Lavalle hawthorn (*Crataegus* x *lavallei*), 298, 305, 377, 382
*Lavandula,* 258–59, 317, 375
　*angustifolia,* 318, 338, 370, 372, 470; 'Hidcote', 365, 470; 'Munstead', 318
　*officinalis,* 484
　'Quasti', 470
*Lavatera:*
　*assurgentiflora,* 216
　*thuringiaca* 'Rosea', 329
　*trimestris,* 355; 'Silver Cup', 357
lavatera (*Lavatera trimestris*), 355
lavender (*Lavandula angustifolia*), 338, 372
lavender (*Lavandula officinalis*), 484
lavender cotton (*Santolina chamaecyparissus*), 318, 328
lavender meadow-rue (*Thalictrum rochebrunianum*), 320
lavenders (*Lavendula*), 258–59, 317, 375
lavender tree (*Vitex agnus-castus*), 303, 337
lavender trumpet vine (*Clytostoma callistegioides*), 353
lawn, 384–90
　chemical habit, breaking the, 386
　fertilizing, 386–87, 464
　grass zones of the United States: map of, 385; recommended grasses, by region, 384–86
　insect and disease control, 388–89

mowing, 387, 388
natural care basics, 386–89
new, planting a, 389
old, aerating and overseeding, 389–90
pests, common, 567
tools for lawn care, 619–20
weeding, 387–88
lawn mover, 620
lawn sweeper, 620
layering, propagation by, 487–89
*Layia: carnosa,* 127; *heterotricha,* 132; *platyglossa,* 358
leadplant (*Amorpha canescens*), 207, 208, 365
lead plant (*Amorpha canescens*), 226
leads (botanical statements), 63
leadwort (*Ceratostigma plumbaginoides*), 320, 486
leaf flower, 619–20
leafhoppers, 555
leafminers, 555
leafy bluet (*Hedyotis foliosa*), 131
leather fern (*Acrostichum danaeifolium*), 335
leather flower (*Clematis pitcheri*), 350
leatherleaf (*Chamaedaphne calyculata*), 166, 200
leatherleaf mahonia (*Mahonia bealei*), 378
leatherwood (*Dirca palustris*), 189, 196
leaves, 68–69, 73–85; apex of, 80–81; arrangement of, 82–83; base of the blade, shapes of, 77–79; division, 74–76; evergreen vs. deciduous plants, 76; folding, 81–82; inflorescences, 83–85; margin of, 79; modifications, 82; parts of, 74; role of, 73–74; shapes of, 76–77; texture, 76
lechuguilla (*Agave lechuguilla*), 169
*Ledum groenlandicum,* 166, 196, 200, 338
*Leea coccinea,* 311
leeks (*Allium*), 240, 359
legumes, 92, 93, 169
*Lemna,* 195
lemon balm (*Melissa officinalis*), 259, 334, 580
lemon daylily (*Hemerocallis lilioasphodelus*), 330, 367
lemon geranium (*Pelargonium crispum*), 334
lemongrass (*Cymbopogon citratus*), 259, 336
lemon mint (*Monarda citriodora*), 356, 357, 374

lemon thyme (*Thymus citriodorus*), 344
lemon verbena (*Aloysia triphylla*), 259, 339
Le Nôtre, André, 9
Lenten rose (*Helleborus orientalis*), 322, 342, 370, 375, 376, 378, 379, 383
Leoncita false foxglove (*Agalinas calycina*), 131
leopard's base (*Doronicum orientale*), 375
*Lepidium: barnebyanum,* 127; *sativum,* 580
*Leptospermum,* 48
　*laevigatum,* 306, 317; 'Reevesii Compacta', 317
　*scoparium,* 306, 500, 522; 'Helene Strybing', 306; 'Snow White', 536
*Lespedeza,* 481; *capitata,* 207, 208; *thunbergii,* 309
*Lesquerella pallida,* 127
lettuce (*Lactuca sativa*), 240, 478
*Leucaena retusa,* 213, 307
*Leucanthemum: maximum,* 331; *vulgare,* 138, 327; x *superbum,* 321, 373
*Leucocrinum montanua,* 190
*Leucojum,* 396, 583; *aestivum,* 369
*Leucophyllum:*
　*candidum,* 318; 'Silver Cloud', 318, 384
　*frutescens,* 213, 311, 337; 'Compacta', 312; 'Green Cloud', 312; 'White Cloud', 312
　*laevigatum,* 318
*Leucothoe,* 481; *axillaris,* 316; *davisiae,* 315; *fontanesiana,* 187, 308, 310; *populifolia,* see Agarista (Leucothoe) populifolia
*Levisticum officinale,* 259
*Lewisia rediviva,* 190
Lewis monkeyflower (*Mimulus lewisii*), 329
*Leycesteria formosa,* 365
Leyland cypress (x *Cupressocyparis leylandii*), 514
*Liatris,* 153, 169, 206, 207, 223, 226, 360, 361, 372
　*aspera,* 208, 362
　*mucronata,* 326, 363, 374
　*punctata,* 215, 328, 332, 333, 364, 367, 376
　*pycnostachya,* 200, 321, 362, 374
　*scariosa,* 470
　*spicata,* 319, 321, 359, 372, 375, 470, 498; 'Kobold', 372

licorice (*Glycyrrhiza glabra*), 259
licorice mint (*Agastache*), 340
licorice mint (*Agastache foeniculum*), 253
licorice mint (*Agastache rupestris*), 332
licorice plant (*Helichrysum petiolatum*), 331, 356
*Licuala,* 301
licuala palms (*Licuala*), 301
life stages, grouping of plants by, 67–68
lignum vitae (*Guaiacum officinale*), 300
lignum vitae (*Guaiacum sanctum*), 108, 223
*Ligularia,* 319
　*dentata,* 330, 336; 'Desdemona', 330
　*stenocephala,* 336
　'The Rocket', 319
ligularia (*Ligularia*), 319
ligularia (*Ligularia dentata*), 330, 336
ligularia (*Ligularia stenocephala*), 336
*Ligustrum: japoncium,* 138; *sinense,* 138; *vulgare,* 138
lilacs (*Syringa*), 309, 372, 373, 484, 509, 514
lilac vine (*Hardenbergia comptoniana*), 352, 353
lilac vine (*Hardenbergia violacea*), 352
Liliaceae, 61
lilies (*Lilium*), 320, 324
lilies-of-the-Nile (*Agapanthus*), 331, 401
Liliidae, 61
Liliopsida, 59–62
*Lilium,* 48, 320, 324, 396, 477, 676–77; *canadense,* 196, 206; *lancifolium,* 368, 375; *occidentale,* 127; *philadelphicum,* 188; *regale,* 369, 370; *superbum,* 188, 196, 207, 221, 223
liliwai (*Acaena exigua*), 131
lily (*Lilium*), 477, 676–77
lily magnolia (*Magnolia liliflora*), 305
lily-of-the-Nile (*Agapanthus africanus*), 323
lily-of-the-Nile (*Agapanthus praecox*), 585
lily of the valley (*Convallaria majalis*), 320, 343, 344, 367, 370, 395, 651–52, 677
lily turf (*Liriope muscari*), 321, 323, 324, 344
lily turf (*Liriope spicata*), 323, 324
lime (*Citrus latifolia*), 300
limeberry (*Triphasia trifolia*), 311

limestone oak fern (*Gymnocarpium robertianum*), 190
lime-sulfur mixtures, 548
*Limnanthes douglasii,* 357
*Limonium,* 470; *perezii,* 375, 376; *sinuatum,* 358, 373, 376, 498
*Linaria: maroccana,* 358
*purpurea,* 331, 366, 370; 'Canon Went', 365, 375
*vulgaris,* 138
linden (*Tilia americana*), 189
lindens (*Tilia*), 477
*Lindera benzoin,* 218, 308, 334
Lindheimer's muhly (*Muhlenbergia lindheimeri*), 198, 326
linear-leaved haplostachys (*Haplostachys linearifolia*), 131
linear leaves, 77
lingonberry (*Vaccinium vitis-idaea*), 281, 282, 284, 345
Linneaus, Carolus, 9–10, 39, 40
*Linum,* 470
*grandiflorum* 'Rubrum', 358
*lewisii* var. *lewisii,* 328
*perenne,* 332; subsp. *lewisii,* 207, 364
*Lipochaeta: bryanii,* 132; *degeneri,* 132; *fauriei,* 128; *kamolensis,* 128; *micrantha,* 128; *perdita,* 132; *tenuifolia,* 128; *venosa,* 128; *waimeaensis,* 128
*Lippia: citriodora,* 259; *nodiflora,* 342, 361
*Liquidambar: orientalis,* 536
*styraciflua,* 167, 196, 197, 299, 305, 378; 'Rotundiloba', 299
*Liriodendron tulipifera,* 13, 167, 187, 298, 299, 305
*Liriope: muscari,* 321, 323, 324, 341, 342, 343, 344, 381; 'Variegata', 335
*spicata,* 323, 324, 341, 342
liriope (*Liriope muscari*), 323, 324, 341, 342
liriope (*Liriope spicata*), 323, 324, 341, 342
lisianthus (*Eustoma grandiflorum*), 358
*Litchi chinensis,* 301
literature and lore, plants in, 671–84
*Lithocarpus densiflorus,* 315; var. *echinoides,* 365
*Lithodora diffusa* 'Grace Ward', 331
lithops, 579
*Lithospermum caroliniense,* 207
little bluestem (*Schizachyrium scoparium*), 168, 169, 206, 208, 326, 327, 337, 374, 380
little golden zinnia (*Zinnia grandiflora*), 208, 209, 213
littleleaf box (*Buxus microphylla*), 514
littleleaf horsebrush (*Tetradymia glabrata*), 169
littleleaf linden (*Tilia cordata*), 301, 304, 365
littleleaf mock orange (*Philadelphus microphyllus*), 318, 338
littleleaf sumac (*Rhus microphylla*), 213, 318, 367
live forever (*Kalanchoe pinnata*), 323
live-forever (*Sedum acre*), 368
live-forever (*Sedum hispanicum*), 368
live-forever (*Sedum sarmentosum*), 368
live oak (*Quercus virginiana*), 167, 168, 188, 223, 299, 300
liverleaf (*Hepatica acutiloba*), 187, 188, 189
liverleaf (*Hepatica americana*), 188
liverworts, *see* mosses, liverworts, and hornworts
living stones, 579
*Livistona chinensis,* 301
lizards, 230
lizard's tail (*Saururus cernuus*), 196, 197, 198, 200, 201, 361
lizard tail (*Eriophyllum stoechadifolium*), 216
loam, 432, 433
lobed cyanea (*Cyanea lobata*), 131
*Lobelia: cardinalis,* 198, 200, 203, 206, 207, 221, 223, 225, 226, 319, 322, 332, 359, 360; *erinus,* 354, 355, 358, 496, 498; *glandulosa,* 199; *oahuensis,* 128; *remyi,* 132; *siphilitica,* 196, 206, 207, 319, 322; *spicata,* 200
lobelia (*Lobelia erinus*), 358, 496, 498
loblolly bay (*Gordonia lasianthus*), 161, 167, 197
loblolly pine (*Pinus taeda*), 167, 197, 299
*Lobularia maritima,* 355, 358, 496, 498
locoweed (*Oxytropis splendens*), 208
locoweeds (*Oxytropis*), 169
locule, 86
locust (*Gleditsia triacanthos*), 470
locust (*Robinia*), 307
locustberry (*Byrsonima lucida*), 310
lodgepole pine (*Pinus contorta*), 170, 190
*Lodoicea maldivica,* 110
lonchocarpus (*Lonchocarpus violaceus*), 301
*Lonchocarpus violaceus,* 301
London plane (*Platanus* x *acerifolia*), 609
long-day plants, 104
longevity, grouping of plants by, 67
longleaf pine (*Pinus palustris*), 167, 168, 188, 299
long-spurred mint (*Dicerandra cornutissima*), 126
long-spurred violet (*Viola rostrata*), 188
long-stalked aster (*Aster dumosus*), 220, 222
*Lonicera,* 675
*albiflora,* 312, 313, 314, 350
*caerulea* var. *edulis,* 281, 282
*canadensis,* 221, 222, 223
*caprifolium,* 347
*ciliosa,* 229
*flava,* 347
*fragrantissima,* 309, 368, 378
*heckrottii,* 353
*hispidula* var. *vacillans,* 202
*involucrata,* 191, 201, 221, 229, 230, 315, 364
*japonica,* 8, 138
*maackii,* 138
*morrowii,* 138
*nitida,* 520
*periclymenum,* 365; 'Serotina', 352
*sempervirens,* 109, 197, 221, 222, 223, 226, 347, 348, 349, 350, 351, 353, 363, 367
*tatarica,* 138
x *brownii* 'Dropmore Scarlet', 349
x *heckrotti,* 347
loosestrife (*Lysimachia punctata*), 330
lopping shears, 615
loquat (*Eriobotrya japonica*), 307
loropetalum (*Loropetalum chinense*), 310, 500
*Loropetalum chinense,* 310, 500
*Lotus: corniculatus,* 138; *scoparius,* 108, 229
lotus (*Nelumbo nucifera*), 677
Louisiana, 439, 667, 695, 706–707
Louisiana artemisia (*Artemisia ludoviciana*), 337, 343
Louisiana hybrid irises (*Iris* x *fulvala*), 321
Louisiana iris (*Iris fulva*), 360
Louisiana phlox (*Phlox divaricata*), 198
Louisiana quillwort (*Isoetes louisianensis*), 127
lovage (*Levisticum officinale*), 259
love grass (*Eragrostis*), 199
love-in-a-mist (*Nigella damascena*), 358, 369, 370, 374
love-lies-bleeding (*Amaranthus caudatus*), 357, 368, 371
lowbush blueberry (*Vaccinum angustifolium*), 282
*Luffa,* 346; *aegyptiaca,* 347, 348
luffa gourd (*Luffa aegyptiaca*), 347, 348
luma (*Luma apiculata*), 383
*Luma apiculata,* 306, 383
*Lunaria annua,* 354, 368
lungwort (*Pulmonaria saccharata*), 320
lungworts (*Pulmonaria*), 336
lupine (*Lupinus nanus*), 209, 215
lupine (*Lupinus perennis*), 208
lupines (*Lupinus*), 169
*Lupinus,* 169, 208; *arboreus,* 138; *nanus,* 209, 215, 358; *perennis,* 206, 207, 208; Russell hybrids, 329; *sublanatus,* 132; *texensis,* 208, 226, 356, 374
Lutyens, Edwin, 9
*Luzula nivea,* 328
lychee (*Litchi chinensis*), 301
*Lychnis: chalcedonica,* 332, 498; *coronaria,* 330, 331, 368, 370
*Lycium: andersonii,* 228, 272; *barbarum,* 351; *halmifolium,* 351
*Lycopersicon esculentum,* 246, 346
Lycophyta, 52
*Lycopodium nutans,* 128
*Lycoris: radiata* 'Guernsey', 369; *squamigera,* 369
Lydgate's cyrtandra (*Cyrtandra lydgatei*), 131
*Lygodium: japonicum,* 138; *palmatum,* 198
Lyonia (*Lyonia lucida*), 167
*Lyonia lucida,* 167
*Lyonothamnus floribundus* subsp. *asplenifolius,* 306
lyreleaf sage (*Salvia lyrata*), 198, 327, 343, 364, 381
*Lysichiton americanus,* 161, 202, 203, 336
*Lysiloma latisiliquum,* 223, 300, 361
*Lysimachia: clethroides,* 319, 324, 370; *filifolia,* 128; *forbesii,* 132; *lydgatei,* 128; *nummularia,* 138, 344; *punctata,* 321, 330; *terrestris,* 196

*Lythrum: salicaria,* 138, 181, 195; *virgatum,* 138

*Maackia amurensis,* 298, 377, 501
*Macfadyena unguis-cati,* 352, 353
*Machaeranthera tanacetifolia,* 364
*Macleaya cordata,* 333
*Maclura pomifera,* 138, 377
Madagascar, 638–39
Madagascar jasmine (*Stephanotis floribunda*), 348, 349, 352, 591
Madagascar periwinkle (*Catharanthus roseus*), 137, 354, 355, 358, 369, 487, 496
Madagascar rubber vine (*Cryptostegia madagascariensis*), 348
madder family, 58
Madeira and Porto Santo, 639
*Madia elegans,* 209
madrone (*Arbutus menziesii*), 365, 366
*Madura pomifera,* 514
*Magnolia,* 48, 187, 188, 477, 484, 510
   *fraseri,* 7
   *grandiflora,* 167, 299; 'Little Gem', 299
   *liliflora* 'Nigra', 305
   *macrophylla,* 299
   *sieboldii,* 305
   *stellata,* 300, 302, 501; 'Royal Star', 302
   *tormentosa,* 501
   *virginiana,* 168, 197, 198, 201, 298, 299, 301, 359; var. *australis,* 197
   x *loebneri* 'Merrill', 302
   x *soulangiana,* 298, 303, 306, 374
magnolia (*Magnolia grandiflora*), 299
magnolias (*Magnolia*), 187, 188, 477, 484, 510
Magnoliidae, 53
Magnoliophyta, 52–62
Magnoliopsida, 53–59
*Mahonia,* 191
   *aquifolium,* 191, 281, 282, 283, 310, 315, 316, 318, 365, 366, 481; 'Compacta', 315, 318, 344
   *bealei,* 378
   *fremontii,* 384
   *haematocarpa,* 318, 367
   *lomariifolia,* 339, 500
   *nervosa,* 345
   *nervosa* var. *nervosa,* 191
   *nevinii,* 191, 317
   *repens,* 190, 191, 312, 318, 344, 364, 382
   *swaseyi,* 313
   *trifoliata,* 313

mahonia (*Mahonia lomariifolia*), 500
*Maianthemum: canadense,* 188, 320; *dilatatum,* 202, 203, 345
maidencane (*Panicum hemitomon*), 199
maiden fern (*Adiantum pedatum*), 329
maiden grass (*Miscanthus sinensis*), 321
maidenhair (*Adiantum pedatum*), 325
maidenhair fern (*Adiantum capillus-veneris*), 336
maidenhair fern (*Adiantum pedatum*), 187, 189, 191, 202
maidenhair tree (*Ginkgo biloba*), 10, 305, 484
maiden pink (*Dianthus deltoides*), 370
maiden pinks (*Dianthus deltoides*), 328
maiden's wreath (*Francoa sonchifolia*), 331
Maine, 439, 695, 707
makou (*Botrychium subbifoliatum*), 131
*Malacothamnus: clementinus,* 127; *davidsonii,* 132
*Malcolmia maritima,* 357
male fern (*Dryopteris filix-mas*), 190, 320
Malheur wire-lettuce (*Stephanomeria malheurensis*), 127
mallow (*Malva alcea*), 328
mallow (*Senecio cineraria*), 331
*Malpighia: coccigera,* 311; *glabra,* 284
Maltese cross (*Lychnis chalcedonica*), 332, 498
*Malus,* 48, 282, 365, 484, 510, 514, 672; *baccata,* 536; 'Beverly', 304; 'Coralburst', 304; 'Donald Wyman', 304; *floribunda,* 13, 298, 305, 306, 501; *hupehensis,* 306; hybrids, 300; *ioensis,* 303, 363; 'Liset', 304; 'Red Spendor', 302; *sargentii,* 302, 501; x 'Indian Magic', 365; x *micromalus,* 536; x *zumi* 'Calocarpa', 377
*Malva alcea* 'Fastigiata', 328
*Malvaviscus arboreus* var. *drummondii,* 327, 363, 369
mammals, seed dispersal by, 178
Manchurian cherry (*Prunus maackii*), 377
Manchurian lilac (*Syringa reticulata*), 377
Mancos milk-vetch (*Astragalus humillimus*), 126
*Mandevilla,* 595; *sanderi,* 348; *splendens,* 348, 349

mandevilla (*Mandevilla sanderi*), 348
mandevilla (*Mandevilla*), 595
*Mandragora officinarum,* 677–78
mandrake (*Mandragora officinarum*), 677–78
*Manettia inflata,* 524
*Mangifera indica,* 48, 301
mango (*Mangifera indica*), 301
mangrove mallow (*Pavonia spicata*), 224
mangroves (*Rhizophora*), 71
*Manihot walkerae,* 127
*Manilkara: bahamensis,* 223; *zapota,* 300
man-in-the-ground (*Ipomoea microdactyla*), 224
*Manual of Cultivated Trees and Shrubs* (Rehder), 30
many-spined opuntia (*Opuntia polyacantha*), 208
manzanita (*Arctostaphylos manzanita*), 306
manzanitas (*Arctostaphylos*), 191, 215, 366, 383
Mapes, James Jay, 10
mapleleaf (*Acerphyllum rossii*), 329
maple-leaf viburnum (*Viburnum acerifolium*), 312, 362
maples (*Acer*), 477, 484
*Maranta leuconeura,* 572
marginal wood fern (*Dryopteris marginalis*), 320, 343
marguerite (*Argyranthemum frutescens*), 522
marigolds (*Tagetes*), 354, 361, 372, 373, 496, 498, 678
mariola (*Parthenium incanum*), 169
marjoram (*Origanum vulgare*), 580
Mark's cyanea (*Cyanea marksii*), 131
marlberry (*Ardisia escallonioides*), 311, 361
marlberry (*Ardisia japonica*), 572
marronbacoba (*Solanum conocarpum*), 132
*Marrubium: rotundifolium,* 345; *vulgare,* 138, 257–58
marsh aster (*Aster lanceolatus* var. *lanceolatus*), 200
marsh cinquefoil (*Potentilla palustris*), 196
marsh elder (*Iva microcephala*), 199
marshes, 159–60, 192, 194
marsh fern (*Thelypteris palustris*), 197, 199
marsh fingergrass (*Eustachys glauca*), 199
marsh fleabane (*Pluchea rosea*), 199

marsh goldenrod (*Solidago uliginosa*), 196
marsh mallow (*Hibiscus militaris*), 198
marsh mallow (*Hibiscus moscheutos*), 321
marsh mallow (*Hibiscus moscheutos* subsp. *lasiocarpos*), 200
marsh mallow (*Hibiscus palustris*), 196
marsh marigold (*Caltha leptosepala*), 166, 202
marsh marigold (*Caltha palustris*), 108, 146, 161, 196, 197, 201, 220, 224
marsh sandwort (*Arenaria paludicola*), 126
marsh sneezeweed (*Helenium pinnatifidum*), 199
marsh St.-John's-wort (*Triadenum virginicum*), 197
*Marsilea villosa,* 128
Marx, Roberto Burle, 10
Maryland, 439, 624, 667, 695, 707, 723
Maryland senna (*Senna marilandica*), 326
*Masdevallia,* 324
Massachusetts, 439, 624–25, 667, 695, 707–708, 723–24
matilija poppy (*Romneya coulteri*), 215, 331
*Matricaria recutita,* 255
matrimony vine (*Lycium barbarum*), 351
*Matteuccia: pensylvanica,* 190; *struthiopteris,* 188, 325
*Matthiola incana,* 358, 373
mattock, 612
Maui love grass (*Eragrostis mauiensis*), 131
*Maurandella antirrhiniflora,* 353
Maximilian sunflower (*Helianthus maximiliani*), 326, 363, 364, 367, 374, 376
Mayacamas popcorn-flower (*Plagiobothrys lithocaryus*), 132
mayapple (*Podophyllum peltatum*), 188, 189, 333, 341, 657–58
Mayday tree (*Prunus padus*), 304
mayflower (*Liriope spicata*), 341
maypop (*Passiflora incarnata*), 281, 282, 284, 363
meadow clematis (*Clematis stans*), 309
meadow foam (*Limnanthes douglasii*), 357
meadow rose (*Rosa blanda*), 477
meadow rue (*Thalictrum aquilegiifolium*), 330

meadow rue (*Thalictrum rochebrunianum*), 328, 330
meadow rues (*Thalictrum*), 336, 477
meadows, 148, 172, 204; wet, 192, 194
meadow saffron (*Colchicum autumnale*), 650–51
meadow sidalcea (*Sidalcea campestris*), 329
mealy sage (*Salvia farinacea*), 326, 355, 364, 372
mealybugs, 555
measures, weights, and conversions, 733–37
*Medicago sativa*, 70–71, 359
medicinal properties of plants, 123; herbs, 267
medinilla (*Medinilla magnifica*), 324
*Medinilla magnifica*, 324
Mediterranean spurge (*Euphorbia characias* subsp. *wulfenii*), 331
medium, planting: for bonsai, 528; for container gardening, 236, 495–96; for houseplants, 573–74; for orchids, 578–79; propagation, 474–75, 481
medlar (*Mespilus germanica*), 281, 282, 283, 678
meiosis, 95
*Melaleuca: nesophylla*, 500; *quinquenervia*, 138, 152
*Melampodium leucanthum*, 208, 213, 332, 333, 356
*Melanthium virginicum*, 189
Melastomataceae, 57
melastome family, 57
*Melia azedarach*, 138, 655–56
*Melianthus major*, 339, 500
*Melica*, 209; *imperfecta*, 170; *nitens*, 327, 374
Melic grasses (*Melica*), 209
*Melicope: adscendens*, 128; *balloui*, 128; *cruciata*, 132; *degeneri*, 132; *haleakalae*, 132; *haupuensis*, 128; *knudsenii*, 128; *lydgatei*, 128; *mucronulata*, 128; *munroi*, 132; *nealae*, 132; *obovata*, 132; *ovalis*, 128; *pallida*, 128; *paniculata*, 132; *quadrangularis*, 128; *reflexa*, 128; *wailauensis*, 132
*Melissa officinalis*, 259, 334, 580
melons, 244
membranaceous leaves, 76
memorial rose (*Rosa wichuraiana*), 341
*Menispermum canadense*, 346, 349
*Mentha*, 260, 321, 335, 368, 580; *arvensis*, 334; *pulegium*,

261, 334; *spicata*, 334, 370; x *piperita*, 334
*Mentzelia lindleyi*, 358
*Menyanthes trifoliata*, 196, 198, 201, 202, 203
Merced monardella (*Monardella leucocephala*), 132
Merlin's grass (*Isoetes tegetiformans*), 127
*Merremia tuberosa*, 138
*Mertensia: lanceolata*, 190; *virginica*, 109, 188, 189, 190, 196, 221, 325, 330, 370
*Mesembryanthemum crystallinum*, 496
meserve hybrid holly (*Ilex* x *meserveae*), 308, 377
mesocarp, 91
*Mespilus germanica*, 281, 282, 283, 678
mesquites (*Prosopis*), 169, 213, 307
*Metasequoia glyptostroboides*, 298, 305, 484
*Metrosideros excelsus*, 306
Mexican bluebells (*Ruellia brittoniana*), 342
Mexican blue palm (*Brahea armata*), 384
Mexican blue sage (*Salvia chamaedryoides*), 332, 333
Mexican buckeye (*Ungnadia speciosa*), 303, 380
Mexican bush marigold (*Tagetes lemmoni*), 317, 339
Mexican bush sage (*Salvia leucantha*), 326, 355
Mexican calabash (*Crescentia alata*), 300
Mexican elder (*Sambucus mexicana*), 307, 367
Mexican evening primrose (*Oenothera speciosa*), 328, 345
Mexican hat (*Ratibida columnifera*), 326, 364, 369
Mexican heather (*Cuphea hyssopifolia*), 342
Mexican orange (*Choisya ternata*), 500
Mexican palo verde (*Parkinsonia aculeata*), 306, 307
Mexican pinyon pine (*Pinus cembroides*), 215, 302, 303, 381
Mexican plum (*Prunus mexicana*), 303, 380
Mexican primrose (*Oenothera speciosa*), 369
Mexican sage (*Salvia leucantha*), 333
Mexican sunflower (*Tithonia rotundifolia*), 355, 358, 360, 361, 362, 372

Mexican tulip poppy (*Hunnemannia fumariifolia*), 354, 376
Mexican vase (*Aechmea mexicana*), 335
Mexican water lily (*Nymphaea mexicana*), 198
Michaux, André, 10
Michaux, François, 10
Michigan, 439, 667, 695, 696, 708–709, 724
*Micranthemum micranthemoides*, 132
*Microbiota decussata*, 380
microclimates, 30
Midwest and Northern Great Plains region, 291; annuals for, 355–56; butterflies and wildlife, plants to attract, 362; flowers for cutting, 373; ground covers for, 342–43; heirloom flowers, 368–69; perennials for, 324–25; shrubs for, 311–12; trees for, 301–302; vines for, 349; winter interest, plants for, 379–80
*Mikania scandens*, 199
milk-and-wine-lily (*Crinum*), 402, 587
milk vetches (*Astragalus*), 208
milkweed (*Asclepias syriaca*), 359, 649
milkweeds (*Asclepias*), 169, 206, 207, 219, 224, 359, 360
milky spore disease, 546
*Millettia reticulata*, 353
*Miltonia*, 324
mimosa (*Albizia julibrissin*), 10
*Mimosa borealis*, 313
*Mimulus*, 108, 228, 229; *aurantiacus*, 109, 215, 216, 230, 317, 366; *brandegei*, 130; *cardinalis*, 203; *guttatus*, 196, 202, 203; *hybridus*, 358; *lewisii*, 329; *longiflorus*, 216; *primuloides*, 203; *ringens*, 200; *traskiae*, 130; *whipplei*, 130
mina (*Mina lobata*), 348
*Mina lobata*, 348
miniature begonia (*Begonia*), 596
miniature crape myrtle (*Lagerstroemia indica*), 536
miniature gloxinia (*Sinningia pusilla*), 572
miniature goldfish plant (*Nematanthus wettsteinii*), 596
miniature grape ivy (*Cissus striata*), 572
Minnesota, 439, 625, 667, 695, 696, 709, 724
Minnesota trout lily (*Erythronium propullans*), 127

mint (*Mentha*), 260, 321, 335, 368, 580
mint family, 58
*Mirabilis: jalapa*, 355, 357, 360, 368, 369, 498; *longiflora*, 209; *multiflora*, 209, 213, 332, 333, 345
*Miscanthus: sacchariflorus*, 138; *sinensis*, 138, 321, 328; 'Gracillimus', 321; 'Zebrinus', 339
Mississippi, 439, 625, 695, 696, 709
Missouri, 439, 625, 667, 695, 696, 709–10
Missouri evening primrose (*Oenothera macrocarpa* subsp. *macrocarpa*), 333
Missouri violet (*Viola missouriensis*), 198, 343, 380, 381
mistletoe (*Viscum album*), 679
*Mitchella repens*, 146, 188, 189
*Mitella: breweri*, 191; *diphylla*, 190; *ovalis*, 203
miterwort (*Mitella breweri*), 191
mites, predatory, 546
*Mitriostigma axillare*, 591
*Mnium cuspidatum*, 341
mock orange (*Philadelphus coronarius*), 13, 310, 370
mock orange (*Philadelphus lewisii*), 202, 317
mock orange (*Philadelphus* x *virginalis*), 370
mock oranges (*Philadelphus*), 510
mock strawberry (*Duchesnea indica*), 344
Mogollon dock (*Rumex tomentella*), 132
Mojave Desert, 155, 169
Mojave sage (*Salvia mohavensis*), 169
Mojave yucca (*Yucca schidigera*), 169
moles, 565
*Moluccella laevis*, 356, 374
monarch birch (*Betula maximowicziana*), 377
*Monarda: citriodora*, 356, 357, 374; *didyma*, 196, 206, 221, 253–54, 322, 359, 360, 368, 370, 372, 498; 'Gardenview Scarlet', 370; *fistulosa*, 109, 198, 206, 207, 220, 221, 222, 223, 226, 227, 229, 326, 327, 337, 359, 362, 363, 364, 365; 'Claire Grace', 326; *menthifolia*, 371

*punctata*, 206, 207, 208, 322, 370
x 'Marshall's Delight', 340
*Monardella: leucocephala,* 132; *pringlei,* 130
mondo grass (*Ophiopogon japonicus*), 343
Monera kingdom, 51
money plant (*Lunaria annua*), 368
moneywort (*Lysimachia nummularia*), 138, 344
monkeyflower (*Mimulus aurantiacus*), 215
monkeyflower (*Mimulus guttatus*), 203
monkeyflower (*Mimulus hybridus*), 358
monkeyflower (*Mimulus ringens*), 200, 202
monkeyflowers (*Mimulus*), 108, 228, 229
monkeygrass (*Liriope muscari*), 343, 381
monkey musk (*Mimulus guttatus*), 196
monkshood (*Aconitum napellus*), 647–48
monkshoods (*Aconitum*), 324
monocots, 59–62
mono lupine (*Lupinus sublanatus*), 132
monstera (*Monstera deliciosa*), 572
*Monstera deliciosa,* 335, 349, 572
Montana, 439, 667, 695, 696, 710
*Montbretia, see Crocosmia*
Monterey cypress (*Cupressus macrocarpa*), 137, 216
Monterey pine (*Pinus radiata*), 216
Montezuma county beardtongue (*Penstemon parviflorus*), 132
montgomery palm (*Veitchia montgomeryana*), 301
moonflower (*Ipomoea alba*), 347, 348, 350, 352
moon vine (*Ipomoea alba*), 498
moosewood (*Acer pensylvanicum*), 298
*Moraea,* 406
Morefield's leather-flower (*Clematis morefieldii*), 126
Mormon tea (*Ephedra viridis*), 381
Mormon teas (*Ephedra*), 169
morning glories (*Ipomoea*), 349, 357
morning glory (*Ipomoea purpurea*), 348, 498
morning glory (*Ipomoea tricolor*), 350, 654

*Morus,* 281, 282, 284, 485; *alba,* 364, 470
mosaic, 563
moss (*Mnium cuspidatum*), 341
moss (*Thuidium delicatulum*), 341
mosses, liverworts, and hornworts (Bryophyta), 51–52; propagating mosses, 98; sexual reproduction of, 96–98
moss phlox (*Phlox subulata*), 320
moss pink (*Phlox subulata*), 108, 220, 221, 320, 368
moss rose (*Portulaca grandiflora*), 354
moss verbena (*Verbena tenuisecta*), 356
mostaza roja (*Brassica*), 371
mother-in-law tongue (*Sansevieria trifasciata*), 572
moth orchids (*Phalaenopsis*), 324, 373, 576
moths, flower pollination by, 107, 108–109
mountain andromeda (*Pieris japonica*), 500
mountain ash (*Sorbus sitchensis*), 191
mountain ashes (*Sorbus*), 477
mountain dogwood (*Cornus nuttallii*), 10, 190, 191
mountain heathers (*Cassiope*), 166
mountain heaths (*Phyllodoce*), 166
mountain hemlock (*Tsuga mertensiana*), 191, 305
mountain hydrangea (*Hydrangea arborescens*), 188
mountain laurel (*Kalmia latifolia*), 109, 187, 221, 222, 223, 308, 316, 377, 485, 500, 654–55
mountain mahogany (*Cercocarpus*), 215
mountain maple (*Acer spicatum*), 301, 308
mountain mint (*Pycnanthemum incanum*), 322, 335
mountain mint (*Pycnanthemum muticum*), 109, 220, 222, 334
mountain mint (*Pycnanthemum tenuifolium*), 374
mountain mint (*Pycnanthemum virginianum*), 334
mountain ninebark (*Physocarpus monogynus*), 190, 314, 315
mountain pine (*Pinus mugo*), 381
mountain rosebay (*Rhododendron catawbiense*), 7, 308, 309
mountain sage (*Salvia regla*), 313, 314
mountain sandwort (*Arenaria montana*), 604
Mt. Diablo buckwheat (*Eriogonum truncatum*), 131
mucronate leaf apex, 81

mugwart (*Artemisia vulgaris*), 137
*Muhlenbergia,* 337; *capillaris,* 198, 199, 326, 374; *dumosa,* 34; *lindheimeri,* 198, 326; *porteri,* 209; *rigens,* 170, 209, 339
muhly grass (*Muhlenbergia capillaris*), 199
mulberry (*Morus*), 281, 282, 284, 485
mulching, 464–69, 472; application, timing and amount of, 465–67, 468, 738; benefits of, 465; of bulbs, 468; compaction problems, to solve, 465; inorganic, 464, 467; organic, 464, 466; of pathways, 468–69; of perennials, 468; of roses, 468; of shrubs, 467–68; soil pH and, 465; of trees, 467–68; of vegetable gardens, 468
mule's ears (*Wyethia amplexicaulis*), 208
mule's ears (*Wyethia mollis*), 209
mullein pink (*Lychnis coronaria*), 368
mulleins (*Verbascum*), 486
multiflora rose (*Rosa multiflora*), 139, 180
*Munroidendron racemosum,* 128
Munro's haplostachys (*Haplostachys munroi*), 131
Munro's pelea (*Melicope munroi*), 132
*Murraya paniculata,* 310
*Musa: acuminata,* 284; *coccinea,* 324; x *paradisiaca,* 323; *zebrina,* 336
*Muscari,* 396, 496, 582; *botryoides,* 321; *racemosum,* 369
musclewood (*Carpinus caroliniana*), 379
mushrooms, poisonous, 643–45, 662–64
musk strawberry (*Fragaria moschata*), 281, 282
musk thistle (*Carduus nutans*), 137
mustard (*Brassica juncea*), 260
mustard family, 55
mustards (*Brassica*), 359
mutualism, 178–79
mycorrhizal fungi, 71, 178–79
Myers, Norman, 114
*Myoporum: laetum,* 138; *parvifolium,* 471
myoporum (*Myoporum laetum*), 138
*Myosotis,* 355
*Myosotis arvensis,* 674
*Myrcianthes: cauliflora,* 536

*fragrans,* 300; var. *simpsonii,* 361
*Myrica:*
*californica,* 202, 216, 306, 315, 365
*cerifera,* 168, 199, 216, 309, 311, 313, 318, 337, 361, 380; var. *pumila,* 309
*gale,* 166, 200
*pensylvanica,* 187, 216, 308, 334, 359
*pusilla,* 381
myrmecochory, 93–94
myrrh, 679
*Myrrhis odorata,* 264, 334
myrsine (*Myrsine guianensis*), 311
*Myrsine guianensis,* 311
myrtle (*Myrtus communis*), 522, 679
*Myrtus communis,* 260, 339, 500, 522, 679

naiad (*Najas*), 109
*Najas,* 109
naming of plants, 39–44
changes in names, reasons for, 44
common specific epithets, 41–42
cultivar, 41; registration authorities, 44, 45–50; system of rules for, 43–44
form, 40, 41
genus and species, 39–40
subspecies, 40–41
system of rules for, 42–43; cultivated plants, 43–44
taxon, 39
variety, 40, 41
nandina (*Nandina domestica*), 138
*Nandina domestica,* 138
Nanking cherry (*Prunus tomentosa*), 281, 282, 283, 314
nannyberry (*Viburnum lentago*), 281, 282, 365
nannyberry (*Viburnum prunifolium*), 302, 304, 308, 362
narcissi (*Narcissus*), 319, 321, 368, 369, 372, 376, 496, 656, 679–80
*Narcissus,* 48, 319, 321, 368, 369, 372, 374, 376, 396, 496, 582, 656, 679–80
*asturiensis,* 378
classification of narcissi, 397
*poeticus,* 370
*pseudo-narcissis:* 'Ajax', 378
*tazetta,* 380, 582; 'Papyraceus', 369
narcissus (*Narcissus tazetta*), 380
narrowleaf gayfeather (*Liatris mucronata*), 326
narrowleaf goldenrod (*Solidago stricta*), 199

narrowleaf mountain mint (*Pycnanthemum tenuifolium*), 363

narrow-leaf zinnia (*Zinnia angustifolia*), 356

narrow-leaved cotton grass (*Eriophorum angustifolium*), 197

*Nassella tenuissima,* 340

nasturtium (*Tropaeolum majus*), 260–61, 356, 357, 372, 471, 498, 580

nasturtiums (*Tropaeolum*), 496

natal plum (*Carissa grandiflora*), 284

natal plum (*Carissa macrocarpa*), 310

National Collection of Endangered Plants, 129–30

*National Garden Book* (Sunset Publishing), 31

National Gardening Association, 134

national organizations, 724–26

National Plant Germplasm System, 140–41

National Seed Storage Laboratory, 140

Native Seed/SEARCH, 140

native species: choosing, 181–82; defined, 143, 180; nursery-propagated, 182

natural gardening, 180–230
   basics of natural landscaping, 181–84; choosing plants and a plant community, 181–82; designing the garden, 182–83; maintaining the garden, 183–84
   desert gardens, *see* desert gardens
   grassland gardens, *see* grassland gardens
   seaside gardens, *see* seaside gardens
   shrubland gardens, *see* shrubland gardens
   wetland gardens, *see* wetland gardens
   for wildlife, 217–31
   woodland gardens, *see* woodland gardens

*Natural Geography of Plants, The* (Gleason and Cronquist), 17, 144

Nature Conservancy, The, 126, 130, 131, 133, 152

Neal pelea (*Melicope nealae*), 132

Nebraska, 439, 668, 695, 696, 710

necklace pod (*Sophora tomentosa*), 223, 224, 311

*Nectandra coriacea,* 300

nectarines, 270, 274, 283; pests of, 285–86

needle-and-thread (*Stipa comata*), 208

needlegrasses (*Stipa*), 170

needle juniper ( *Juniperus rigida*), 536

needle palm (*Rhapidophyllum hystrix*), 188, 335

Neem, 548

nehe (*Lipochaeta bryanii*), 132

nehe (*Lipochaeta degeneri*), 132

nehe (*Lipochaeta perdita*), 132

Nellie Cory cactus (*Escobaria minima*), 127

Nelson's iris (*Iris nelsonii*), 198

*Nelumbo,* 48; *lutea,* 197, 198, 201, 333; *nucifera,* 333, 677

*Nematanthus wettsteinii,* 596

nematodes, 545–46, 555–56

*Nemesia strumosa,* 358

*Nemophila: maculata,* 357; *menziesii,* 209, 358

*Neomarica,* 323

*Neoregelia,* 324, 342

Nepal, 639

*Nepeta: cataria,* 255; *mussinii,* 254–55, 325; *racemosa,* 254–55; *sibirica,* 325; x *faassenii,* 254–55, 331, 332, 370; x *mussinii,* 319

*Nephrolepis exaltata,* 342

*Neraudia: angulata,* 128; *sericea,* 128

*Nerine sarniensis,* 406

*Nerium oleander,* 138, 318, 500, 571, 591–92, 656–57

Netherlands, 632

netleaf hackberry (*Celtis reticulata*), 304, 306, 363

netted chain fern (*Woodwardia areolata*), 189, 201

nettle (*Urtica*), 680

Nevada, 439, 695, 696, 710

Nevin's Oregon grape (*Mahonia nevinii*), 191, 317

*Neviusia alabamensis,* 481

Newberry penstemon (*Penstemon newberryi*), 329

New England aster (*Aster novae-angliae*), 321, 325, 359, 360

New Hampshire, 439, 695, 696, 710

New Jersey, 439, 625–26, 668, 695, 696, 710–11

New Jersey tea (*Ceanothus americanus*), 108, 187, 206, 207, 220, 221, 222, 224, 225, 226, 359, 470

New Mexico, 440, 668, 695, 696, 711

New Mexico locust (*Robinia neomexicana*), 227, 315

newts, 231

New York, 440, 626–27, 668, 695, 696, 711–13, 724

New York ironweed (*Vernonia noveboracensis*), 359

New Zealand, 634–35, 639

New Zealand Christmas tree (*Metrosideros excelsus*), 306

New Zealand flax (*Phormium tenax*), 138, 332, 339

New Zealand tea tree (*Leptospermum scoparium*), 306, 500, 522

Nicolson, Harold, 12

*Nicotiana,* 355, 498; *alata,* 355, 357, 360; *langsdorffii,* 354; *sylvestris,* 354, 357

nicotiana (*Nicotiana alata*), 357

nicotianas (*Nicotiana*), 355

*Nierembergia hippomanica,* 332, 357; var. *violacea,* 354, 356

*Nigella damascena,* 358, 369, 370, 374

night-blooming cereus (*Epiphyllum*), 591

night jessamine (*Cestrum nocturnum*), 595

nightshade family, 58–59

ninebark (*Physocarpus capitatus*), 202, 317, 382

ninebark (*Physocarpus opulifolius*), 312

nitrogen, 457; nutrient values of various fertilizers, chart of, 462–63

nitrogen fixation, 175

*Nitrophila mohavensis,* 127

nodding bidens (*Bidens cernua*), 200

nodding pink onion (*Allium cernuum*), 207

nodules, 70–71

*Nolina: microcarpa,* 339, 384; *recurvata,* 536; *texana,* 337, 380

Nootka rose (*Rosa nutkana*), 191, 365

Norfolk Island pine (*Araucaria heterophylla*), 83

North America:
   climatic conditions in, 23
   floristic provinces of, 17–21, 144, 181; vegetative associations of, 143–69, 166–70
   plant diversity, by state and province, 117–19
   public gardens in, 621–30
   wetland ecosystems of, 159–62
   *see also* United States

North American Native Terrestrial Orchid Conference, 133

*North American Terrestrial Vegetation* (Barbour and Billings), 17

North Carolina, 440, 668, 695, 696, 713–14

North Dakota, 440, 695, 696, 714

Northeast region, 289–96; annuals for, 354; butterflies and wildlife, plants to attract, 359; flowers for cutting, 371–72; foliage plants for, 333–34; ground covers for, 340–41; heirloom flowers, 367–68; perennials for, 319–21; shrubs for, 308–309; trees for, 297–98; vines for, 346–47; winter interest, plants for, 376–77

northern beech fern (*Phegopteris connectilis*), 197

northern catalpa (*Catalpa speciosa*), 302, 303

Northern coniferous forest, 17, 145–46, 166; mixed coniferous/hardwood forest, 145–46, 166; taiga, 145, 166

Northern Great Plains region, *see* Midwest and Northern Great Plains region

Northern pin oak (*Quercus ellipsoidalis*), 167

northern red oak (*Quercus rubra*), 167, 189, 298

Northwest Coastal Forest, 156–57, 170

Norway maple (*Acer platanoides*), 137, 186

Norway spruce (*Picea abies*), 380

*Nothocestrum: breviflorum,* 128; *peltatum,* 128

*Nuphar: advena,* 197, 201; *lutea* subsp. *advena,* 200; *lutea* subsp. *variegata,* 200; *variegata,* 201

nursery-propagated plants, 182

nutrient cycling, 173–75

nutrition, grouping of plants by mode of, 67

Nuttall, Thomas, 10

Nuttall's micranthemum (*Micranthemum micranthemoides*), 132

*Nymphaea,* 48; *elegans,* 198; *mexicana,* 198; *odorata,* 196, 197, 198, 200, 201; *tetragona,* 197, 202; *tuberosa,* 197, 198, 201, 202, 203

*Nymphoides aquatica,* 198, 199

*Nyssa,* 161
   *aquatica,* 168
   *sylvatica,* 196, 298, 299, 305, 306, 609; var. *biflora,* 168

oak family, 54

oak fern (*Gymnocarpium dryopteris*), 190

oak-leaf cyanea (*Cyanea quercifolia*), 131

oak-leaf hydrangea (*Hydrangea quercifolia*), 187, 188, 308, 310, 312, 313, 316, 335, 337, 338, 379, 500

oaks (*Quercus*), 187, 359, 362, 366, 367, 680

obcordate leaf apex, 81

obedient plant (*Physostegia virginiana*), 200, 322, 330, 369, 370

oblique leaf base, 78, 79

oblong leaves, 77

obovate pelea (*Melicope obovata*), 132

obtuse leaf apex, 81

oceanspray (*Holodiscus discolor*), 365

*Ochna serrulata*, 536

*Ochrosia kilaueaensis*, 132

*Ocimum basilicum*, 253, 334, 496, 498, 580

Oconee bells (*Shortia galacifolia*), 10, 189

ocotillo (*Fouquieria splendens*), 109, 169, 213, 228, 384

*Odontoglossum*, 324

*Oemleria cerasiformis*, 191

*Oenothera*, 367, 486
  *berlandieri*, 345
  *biennis*, 108, 206, 220, 222, 224, 225
  *caepitosa*, 332
  *fruticosa* subsp. *glauca*, 368
  *hookeri*, 208, 209
  *macrocarpa*, 207, 325, 328, 329, 331; subsp. *macrocarpa*, 333
  *missouriensis*, see *Oenothera macrocarpa*
  *speciosa*, 328, 345, 369, 498; 'Siskiyou', 328
  *tetragona*, 321

Ohio, 440, 627, 668–69, 695, 696, 714–15, 724

Ohio buckeye (*Aesculus glabra*), 304

Ohio spiderwort (*Tradescantia ohiensis*), 327

*Okenia hypogaea*, 342

Oklahoma, 440, 695, 696, 715

Oklahoma redbud (*Cercis canadensis* var. *texensis*), 307

okra (*Abelmoschus esculentus*), 244

Olcott, Ralph Thrall, 10

old blue pennyroyal (*Hedeoma pilosa*), 131

oldest plants, 68

old-fashioned bleeding heart (*Dicentra spectabilis*), 325

*Olea europaea*, 284, 306, 681

oleander (*Nerium oleander*), 318, 500, 591–92, 656–57

olive (*Olea europaea*), 284, 306, 681

Olmsted, Frederick Law, 10–11, 13

*Omphalodes cappadocica*, 331

*Omphalotus illudens*, 664

*Oncidium*, 324

oniongrass (*Melica imperfecta*), 170

onions (*Allium*), 359

onions (*Allium cepa*), 240–41

*Onoclea sensibilis*, 198, 201

*Onopordum acanthium*, 138

*Ophiopogon*:
  *japonicus*, 343
  *planiscapus*, 341; 'Arabicus', 342; 'Aribicus', 334, 341; 'Black Knight', 334, 341

opium poppy (*Papaver somniferum*), 369

*Oplopanax horridus*, 202, 382

opposite leaf arrangement, 83

*Opuntia*, 72, 169, 281, 284; *basilaris*, 169; *bigelovii*, 384; *compressa*, 216; *humifusa*, 216; *imbricata*, 215, 337; *phaeacantha*, 337; *polyacantha*, 169, 208

opuntia (*Opuntia*), 284

orange bush monkeyflower (*Mimulus aurantiacus*), 109, 230

orange coneflower (*Rudbeckia fulgida*), 325, 498

orange honeysuckle (*Lonicera ciliosa*), 229

orange jasmine (*Murraya paniculata*), 310

orange larkspur (*Delphinium nudicaule*), 109, 230

*Orbexilum: macrophyllum*, 132; *stipulatum*, 130

Orchidaceae, 48, 61–62

orchid cacti (*Epiphyllum*), 324

orchid family (orchids), 61–62, 133, 134, 146, 161, 179; as indoor plants, 576–79

orchid rockrose (*Cistus* x *purpureus*), 500

orchids (*Dendrobium*), 373

oreganillo (*Eupatorium droserolepsis*), 131

oregano (*Origanum pulchellum*), 331

oregano (*Origanum vulgare*), 261, 338, 367

Oregon, 440, 669, 695, 696, 715–16

Oregon box (*Paxistima myrsinites*), 191

Oregon boxwood (*Paxistima myrtifolia*), 191

Oregon grape (*Mahonia aquifolium*), 315, 316, 365, 366

Oregon grape (*Mahonia repens*), 190

Oregon grape holly (*Mahonia aquifolium*), 191, 281, 282, 283, 310, 318, 481

Oregon grapes (*Mahonia*), 191

Oregon sidalcea (*Sidalcea oregana* sub. *spicata*), 203

Oregon white oak (*Quercus garryana*), 305

Oregon wood sorrel (*Oxalis oregana*), 191

organizations, 723–32

Oriental clematis (*Clematis orientalis*), 351

Oriental hybrid witchhazels (*Hamamelis* x *intermedia*), 376

Oriental poppy (*Papaver orientale*), 325, 329, 330, 470, 486

Oriental sweetgum (*Liquidambar orientalis*), 536

*Origanum*:
  *laevigatum*, 331; 'Hopley's', 331, 345
  *libanoticum*, 332
  *majorana*, 260, 496
  *onites*, 259–60
  *pulchellum*, 331
  *vulgare*, 261, 338, 367, 580; subsp. *hirtum*, 496

origanum (*Origanum laevigatum*), 331

ornamental cabbage (*Brassica oleracea*), 357

ornamental gardening, 288–537
  bulbs, see bulbs
  container gardening, see container gardening
  growing regions, 288–96
  lawn, see lawn
  shrubs, see shrubs
  techniques, 430–57. see also specific techniques, e.g. composting; mulching; soil
  trees, see trees
  water gardens, see water gardens

ornamental okra (*Abelmoschus esculenta*), 354

ornamental onion (*Allium aflatunense*), 374

ornamental onion (*Allium thunbergii*), 398–99

ornamental onions (*Allium*), 320, 394, 583

ornamental oregano (*Origanum libanoticum*), 332

ornamental red banana (*Musa coccinea*), 324

*Ornithogalum umbellatum*, 368

*Orontium aquaticum*, 196, 197, 198, 200, 201, 202

*Orostachys furusei*, 340

*Orthocarpus purpurascens*, 209

orthotropic plants, 68

*Oryzopsis hymenoides*, 209, 213, 367

osage orange (*Maclura pomifera*), 377, 514

*Osmanthus*:
  *delavayi*, 316, 317, 500
  *fragrans*, 10
  *heterophyllus*, 379; 'Variegatus', 500
  x *fortunei*, 309

osmanthus (*Osmanthus delavayi*), 316

*Osmunda*:
  *cinnamomea*, 190, 198, 201, 320, 335
  *claytonia*, 320
  *claytoniana*, 190, 192, 197
  *regalis*, 189, 190, 197, 201, 320, 335; var. *spectabilis*, 197, 199

osoberry (*Oemleria cerasiformis*), 191

Osterhout milk-vetch (*Astragalus osterhoutii*), 126

ostrich fern (*Matteuccia pensylvanica*), 190

ostrich fern (*Matteuccia struthiopteris*), 188, 325

*Ostrya virginiana*, 189, 302

Oswego tea (*Monarda didyma*), 196, 206, 253–54

Our Lord's candle (*Yucca whipplei*), 339, 366

oval-leafed viburnum (*Viburnum ellipticum*), 191

ovary, 86, 104, 106

ovate leaves, 77

overcup oak (*Quercus lyrata*), 168, 299

ovule, 86

oxalates, 643

*Oxalis*, 404, 589; *acetosella*, 683; *crassipes*, 369; *oregana*, 191, 203, 331, 345

oxalis (*Oxalis*), 404, 589

ox-eye (*Heliopsis helianthoides*), 207, 324

ox-eye daisy (*Leucanthemum vulgare*), 138, 327

*Oxydendrum arboreum*, 189, 298, 300, 305, 501

*Oxypetalum caeruleum*, 354

*Oxytropis*, 169; *splendens*, 208

Oyama magnolia (*Magnolia sieboldii*), 305

oyster plant (*Rhoeo spathacea*), 323

Ozark sundrops (*Oenothera macrocarpon*), 325

*Pachysandra: procumbens,* 188, 341, 342, 343; *terminalis,* 341, 342
*Pachystachys lutea,* 311
Pacific bleeding heart (*Dicentra formosa*), 203, 338, 344
Pacific coast red elderberry (*Sambucus callicarpa*), 216
Pacific dogwood (*Cornus nuttallii*), 190, 191, 305, 365
Pacific love grass (*Eragrostis deflexa*), 131
Pacific madrone (*Arbutus menziesii*), 170, 191
Pacific ninebark (*Physocarpus capitatus*), 191
Pacific Northwest region, 293–94; annuals for, 357; butterflies and wildlife, plants to attract, 365; flowers for cutting, 374–75; foliage plants for, 338–39; ground covers for, 344–45; heirloom flowers, 370; perennials for, 329–30; shrubs for, 315–16; trees for, 304–305; vines for, 351–52; winter interest, plants for, 382–83
Pacific Prairie, 204
Pacific rhododendron (*Rhododendron macrophyllum*), 316
Pacific silver fir (*Abies amabilis*), 190
Pacific wax myrtle (*Myrica californica*), 315, 365
Pacific yew (*Taxus brevifolia*), 191
*Paeonia,* 48, 108, 309, 319, 325, 368; 'Double White', 370; *lactiflora,* 325, 369, 373, 498; *officinalis,* 368, 369, 370; 'Red Charm', 375; *suffruticosa,* 477; *tenuifolia,* 338; x 'Prairie Moon', 329
pagoda dogwood (*Cornus alternifolia*), 189, 201, 302, 304, 362, 379, 477
paintbrushes (*Castilleja*), 208
painted ribbongrass (*Phalaris arundinacea*), 341
pajaro manzanita (*Arctostaphylos pajaroensis*), 316
paleleaf yucca (*Yucca pallida*), 337
pale purple coneflower (*Echinacea pallida*), 208
pale-spiked lobelia (*Lobelia spicata*), 200
pale yellow tidy-tips (*Layia heterotricha*), 132
palmate-bracted bird's-beak (*Cordylanthus palmatus*), 126

palmate compound leaves, 75, 76
Palmer's penstemon (*Penstemon palmeri*), 108, 109, 209, 227, 228
palmettos (*Sabal*), 168
palm family, 59
palm sedge (*Carex muskingumensis*), 197, 201
Palouse Prairie, 204
palo verdes (*Cercidium*), 384
palo verdes (*Cercidium floridum*), 169
pampas grass (*Cortaderia selloana*), 137
*Panax: quinquefolius,* 124, 134, 199; *trifolius,* 189
*Pandorea: jasminoides* 'Alba', 352; *pandorana,* 352
panicle, 85
panicled dogwood (*Cornus racemosa*), 201
panicled sedge (*Carex paniculata*), 197
*Panicum: hemitomon,* 199; *hians,* 199; *virgatum,* 169, 198, 205, 206, 207, 362
pansies (*Viola*), 355, 380
pansy (*Viola cornuta*), 358
pansy (*Viola wittrockiana*), 354
*Papaver:*
    *nudicaule,* 375
    *orientale,* 325, 329, 330, 470, 486; 'Karine', 329
    *rhoeas,* 357, 358
    *somniferum,* 369
paperbark maple (*Acer griseum*), 13, 298, 305, 377, 378, 382
paperbark tree (*Melaleuca quinquenervia*), 138, 152
paper birch (*Betula papyrifera*), 166, 187, 189, 201, 365, 377
paperwhites (*Narcissus tazetta*), 582
*Paphiopedilum,* 324, 576, 578
papyrus (*Cyperus papyrus*), 323
paradise tree (*Simarouba glauca*), 168, 300
paripinnate, 76
*Parkinsonia: aculeata,* 306, 307; *florida,* 307
parlor palm (*Chamaedorea elegans*), 301
*Parnassia: californica,* 203; *glauca,* 200
*Parrotia persica,* 305, 376, 377
Parry penstemon (*Penstemon parryi*), 209
Parry pinyon (*Pinus quadrifolia*), 170
Parry saltbrush (*Atriplex parryi*), 169
Parry's penstemon (*Penstemon parryi*), 332

parsley (*Petroselinum crispum*), 241, 261, 360, 498, 580
parsley hawthorn (*Crataegus apiifolia*), 188
parsley leaf hawthorn (*Crataegus marshallii*), 299
parsleys (*Petroselinum*), 496
*Parthenium: incanum,* 169; *integrifolium,* 207
parthenocarpic fruit, 110
*Parthenocissus,* 485
    *henryana,* 351
    *inserta,* 352
    *quinquefolia,* 13, 341, 346, 347, 348, 349, 350, 351, 362, 363; var. *engelmannii,* 351
    *tricuspidata,* 346, 347, 349, 350, 352, 353, 364, 484; 'Lowii', 351
partridgeberry (*Mitchella repens*), 146, 189
partridge feather (*Tanacetum densum*), 340
partridge pea (*Chamaecrista fasciculata*), 356
parts of plants, *see* plant structure and their functions, plant parts
pascuita (*Euphorbia leucocephala*), 311
pasqueflower (*Anemone patens*), 190, 208, 604
pasqueflower (*Anemone pulsatilla*), 329
*Passiflora,* 284, 361; *caerulea,* 348, 349, 350, 363; *coccinea,* 348, 349; *edulis,* 348; *foetida,* 352, 353, 367; *incarnata,* 281, 282, 284, 347, 363; 'Lavender Lady', 352; *mollissima,* 138; *suberosa,* 361
passionflower (*Passiflora foetida*), 352, 353
passionflower (*Passiflora incarnata*), 347, 367
passion flower (*Passiflora mollissima*), 138
passion flowers (*Passiflora*), 361
passionfruit (*Passiflora*), 284
passionfruit (*Passiflora edulis*), 348
pathways, mulching of, 468–69
patridgeberry (*Mitchella repens*), 188
patridge pea (*Chamaecrista fasciculata*), 363
patrinia (*Patrinia scabiosifolia*), 322
*Patrinia scabiosifolia,* 322
*Paulownia tomentosa,* 138
paurotis palm (*Acoelorraphe wrightii*), 199, 301
*Pavonia spicata,* 224
pawpaw (*Asimina triloba*), 187,

188, 189, 196, 200, 270, 281, 282, 283, 284, 360, 486
*Paxistima,* 481, 485; *canbyi,* 343; *myrsinitis,* 191; *myrtifolia,* 191
paxistima (*Paxistima canbyi*), 343
paxistimas (*Paxistima*), 481, 485
pea bush (*Dalea pulchra*), 383
peaches, 270, 274, 283; pests of, 285–86
peach tree borer, 556
pea family, 56–57
pearl bush (*Exochorda racemosa*), 368
pearly everlasting (*Anaphalis margaritacea*), 328, 371, 374, 382
pears, 270, 271, 272–73, 283; pests of, 285
peas (*Pisum sativum*), 241
peatlands, 160, 194
peat moss, 475; potting mix without, 236
pecans (*Carya*), 359
pedate checker-mallow (*Sidalcea pedata*), 127
pedicel, 84, 86
*Pediomelum pentaphyllum,* 132
*Pedicularis canadensis,* 221, 222, 223, 226
*Pediomelum pentaphyllum,* 132
peduncle, 84, 86, 105
Peking cotoneaster (*Cotoneaster acutifolia*), 314
*Pelargonium,* 48, 257, 332, 355, 486, 496, 498, 522, 524, 592; *crispum,* 334; *graveolens,* 368; *peltatum,* 356; *tomentosum,* 334; x *hortorum,* 355, 356
pelea (*Melicope wailauensis*), 132
pelican flower (*Aristolochia grandiflora*), 348
*Peltandra virginica,* 197, 198, 199, 200, 333
peltate leaf base, 78, 79
*Peltiphyllum peltatum,* 202
peltoboykinia (*Peltoboykinia tellimoides*), 330
*Peltoboykinia tellimoides,* 330
*Peltophorum pterocarpum,* 301
*Pennisetum,* 341
    *alopecuroides,* 319, 329
    *setaceum,* 138; 'Rubrum', 334
Pennsylvania, 440, 627, 669, 695, 696, 716–17, 724
pennyroyal (*Mentha pulegium*), 334
*Penstemon,* 48, 190, 208, 213, 332, 367, 470
    *ambiguus,* 332
    *barbatus,* 215, 227
    *davidsonii,* 604

*digitalis,* 206, 207, 221, 222, 223, 225, 226; 'Husker Red', 336; 'Husker's Red', 374
*eatonii,* 109, 209, 226, 227, 228
'Firebird', 366
'Garnet', 366
*hirsutus* 'Pygmaeus', 604
*newberryi,* 329
*palmeri,* 108, 109, 209, 227, 228
*parryi,* 209, 332
*parviflorus,* 132
*pinifolius,* 328, 332
*pseudospectabilis,* 109, 209, 228, 332
*rupicola,* 229, 604
*smallii,* 206
*spectabilis,* 209
*strictus,* 227
*subulatus,* 209
*tenuis,* 198
penstemon (*Penstemon davidsonii*), 604
penstemon (*Penstemon rupicola*), 604
penstemon (*Penstemon spectabilis*), 209
penstemon (*Penstemon subulatus*), 209
penstemons (*Penstemon*), 332, 470
penstemon sage (*Salvia penstemonoides*), 326, 364
pentas (*Pentas lanceolata*), 324, 355, 361, 373
*Pentas lanceolata,* 324, 355, 361, 373
peonies (*Paeonia*), 48, 108, 309, 319, 325, 368
peony (*Paeonia lactiflora*), 325, 369, 373
peony (*Paeonia officinalis*), 368, 370
people contributing to botany, horticulture, and related fields, 3–13
*Peperomia,* 323, 324, 342, 572; *caperata,* 572; *degeneri,* 132; *obtusifolia,* 324
peperomia (*Peperomia obtusifolia*), 324
peperomias (*Peperomia*), 323, 324, 342, 572
peppercress (*Lepidium sativum*), 580
peppermint (*Mentha* x *piperita*), 334
peppermint geranium (*Pelargonium tomentosum*), 334
peppers (*Capsicum annuum*), 244–45
pepper tree (*Schinus molle*), 139

peppervine (*Ampelopsis arborea*), 199
perennial forget-me-not (*Omphalodes cappadocica*), 331
perennial pea (*Lathyrus latifolius*), 347
perennials, 67, 104, 319–33; for coastal California, 330–32; for container plantings, 498, 502; drought-resistant, 470; fertilizing of, 461–64; for the Midwest and Northern Great Plains, 324–25; mulching of, 468; for the Northeast, 319–21; for the Pacific Northwest, 329–30; pests, common, 567; planting and care of, 319, 448–49; propagation by division, 393–94, 480; for the Rocky Mountain region, 327–29; for the Southeast, 321–23; for Subtropical Florida, 323–24; for Texas and the Southern Plains, 325–27; for western deserts, 332–33
perfoliate leaf base, 78, 79
perianth, 86; terminology, 88–89
pericarp, 91
pericarpium, 91
perilla (*Perilla frutescens*), 471, 498
*Perilla frutescens,* 498; 'Atropurpurea', 261–62, 471
*Perityle inyoensis,* 132
periwinkle (*Catharanthus roseus*), 323, 324
periwinkle (*Vinca major*), 139
periwinkle (*Vinca minor*), 139, 497
perlite, 475
perovskia (*Perovskia atriplicifolia*), 308
*Perovskia atriplicifolia,* 308, 317, 325, 326, 328, 333, 376, 470
*Persea borbonia,* 161, 168, 198
Persian buttercup (*Ranunculus asiaticus*), 406
Persian coneflower (*Centaurea dealbata*), 366
Persian ironwood (*Parrotia persica*), 305, 376, 377
Persian rose (*Rosa foetida*), 371
persimmon (*Diospyros kaki*), 306, 383
persimmons (*Diospyros*), 282, 283, 284
persistent trillium (*Trillium persistens*), 127
Peru, 639
Peruvian lily (*Alstroemeria*), 375
Peruvian lily (*Alstroemeria aurea*), 330

Peruvian verbena (*Verbena peruviana*), 333, 355
pesticides, 177, 219, 549
pests, 538–68
   beneficial insects, 545, 546
   biological controls, 544–48
   chemical controls, the least toxic, 546–48
   common, by plant type, 567
   cultural controls, 542–43
   designing gardens for resistance to, 540–42
   encyclopedia of common, 548–67; diseases, 560–64; insects, 549–59
   fruit growing and, 269, 284–86
   integrated pest management, 539, 540
   lawns and, 388–89
   organic pest management, 539–40
   physical controls, 543–44
   roses and, 410–11
   safe management of, 538–68
   *see also* names of specific pests
petal, 86–87, 104
*Petalostemum,* 169
*Petasites:*
   *frigidus,* 191, 200; var. *palmatus,* 203
   *japonica,* 333
petiole, 74
*Petrea volubilis,* 348, 349
*Petroselinum,* 496
*Petroselinum crispum,* 241, 261, 360, 498, 580
pets and poisonous plants, 646
*Petunia,* 49, 355; x *hybrida,* 355, 356, 369, 478, 496, 498
petunia (*Petunia* x *hybrida*), 355, 356, 369, 498
petunias (*Petunia*), 355
pH, soil, 433–35; home kits to test, 437; mulching and, 465; professional testing of, 437–41; vegetable gardens and, 233
*Phacelia: campanularia,* 109, 228, 358; *cinera,* 130; *linearis,* 209; *minor,* 230
*Phalaenopsis,* 324, 373, 576
*Phalaris arundinacea,* 138, 195, 341; 'Picta', 341; 'Variegata', 341
*Phaseolus: coccineus,* 352, 353; *vulgaris,* 242–43, 371
*Phegopteris connectilis,* 197
*Phellodendron amurense,* 302, 486
*Philadelphus,* 49, 509, 510
   *coronarius,* 13, 310, 312, 370
   *lewisii,* 202, 315, 317; 'Goose Creek', 317
   *microphyllus,* 318, 338

*texensis,* 313
x *virginalis,* 312, 370; 'Minnesota Snowflake', 312
*Philodendron,* 324, 572; *selloum,* 335
philodendron (*Philodendron selloum*), 335
philodendrons (*Philodendron*), 324, 572
phloem, 71
*Phlomis: fruticosa,* 331, 332; *russelliana,* 345
*Phlox,* 486
   *adsurgens,* 108, 229
   *bifida,* 604
   *carolina,* 498
   *divaricata,* 189, 190, 198, 221, 222, 223, 320, 322, 325, 370
   *drummondii,* 356, 496
   *maculata,* 322, 362; 'Alpha', 330; 'Miss Lingard', 322
   *nana,* 215
   *paniculata,* 108, 220, 222, 224, 319, 325, 326, 327, 362, 363, 368, 369, 372, 373, 374, 478; 'Bright Eyes', 319; 'David', 319; 'Miss Lingard', 319; 'Mr. Fuji', 326; 'Summer phlox', 319
   *pilosa,* 189, 198, 207, 326
   *stolonifera,* 325
   *subulata,* 108, 220, 221, 320, 341, 343, 368, 604
phlox (*Phlox*), 486
phlox (*Phlox adsurgens*), 108, 229
phlox (*Phlox bifida*), 604
phlox (*Phlox maculata*), 362
phlox (*Phlox paniculata*), 362
phlox (*Phlox subulata*), 604
*Phoenix: dactylifera,* 284; *roebelenii,* 301
*Phormium,* 49; 'Maori Maiden', 339; *tenax,* 138, 332, 339; 'Yellow Wave', 339
phosphorus, 457; nutrient values of various fertilizers, chart of, 462–63
*Photinia: serratifolia,* 380; *serrulata,* 381; x *fraseri,* 500
photinia (*Photinia* x *fraseri*), 500
photoperiodism, 104
photosynthesis, 73–74, 174; cacti and, 156
phototropic plants, 68
*Phragmites: australis,* 195; *communis,* 162
*Phyla nodiflora,* 343, 363
phylloclade, 72
phyllode, 74
*Phyllodoce,* 166
*Phyllostachys,* 514

*Phyllostegia: brevidens,* 132; *hille-brandii,* 132; *imminuta,* 132; *knudsenii,* 132; *mannii,* 128; *mollis,* 128; *rockii,* 132; *vari-abilis,* 132; *wawrana,* 132; *wiameae,* 132

phylogeny, 62–63

physic nut ( *Jatropha multifida*), 654

*Physocarpus: capitatus,* 191, 202, 317, 382; *monogynus,* 190, 314, 315; *opulifolius,* 312, 314

*Physostegia: angustifolia,* 198

*virginiana,* 198, 200, 322, 326, 330, 369, 370, 374; 'Vivid', 330

*Phytolacca americana,* 657

phytophthora root rot, 563

phytotoxins, 643

*Picea,* 485

*abies,* 380

*engelmannii,* 170, 470

*glauca,* 166, 302, 304, 470; 'Black Hills', 302; 'Den-sata', 304, 380; var. *alber-tiana,* 501, 520

*mariana,* 166, 196, 200

*omorika,* 298

*orientalis* 'Skylands', 383

*pungens,* 305, 315, 377; f. *glauca,* 304, 382; 'Hoopsii', 305; 'R. H. Montgomery', 315

*sitchensis,* 170

pickerel rush (*Pontederia cordata*), 196, 197, 198, 201

pickerel weed (*Pontederia lanceo-lata*), 199, 200

pie cherry (*Heliotropium arborescens*), 487

pie cherry (*Prunus cerasus*), 304, 364

*Pieris,* 49, 485

*floribunda,* 377

*japonica,* 309, 310, 316, 377, 500; 'Valley Valentine', 316

pieris (*Pieris*), 485

pigeonberry (*Rivina humilis*), 343

pigeon grape (*Vitis cinerea* var. *floridana*), 199

pigeon plum (*Coccoloba diversifo-lia*), 168, 300, 361

piggyback plant (*Tolmiea men-ziesii*), 572

*Pilea: cadierei,* 342; *microphylla,* 323, 342

pillbugs, 557

*Pimenta dioica,* 300

*Pimpinella anisum,* 252

pinching, 505, 511–12, 533–34

*Pinckneya bracteata,* 300

pincushion cactus (*Coryphantha vivipara*), 215

pincushion flower (*Scabiosa*), 320

pincushion flower (*Scabiosa atropurpurea*), 359

pincushion flower (*Scabiosa cau-casica*), 365, 369, 371, 376

pineapple (*Ananas comosus*), 284

pineapple guava (*Feijoa sell-owiana*), 306, 470

pineapple sage (*Salvia elegans*), 335

pineapple sage (*Salvia rutilans*), 263

pinecone ginger (*Zingiber zerum-bet*), 323

pineland lantana (*Lantana depressa*), 342

pineleaf penstemon (*Penstemon pinifolus*), 328, 332

pines (*Pinus*), 282, 477, 485

pink anemone clematis (*Clematis montana* var. *rubens*), 353

pink buckwheat (*Eriogonum fasci-culatum*), 367

pink fairyduster (*Calliandra erio-phpylla*), 318

pink family, 55

pink jasmine ( *Jasminum polyan-thum*), 352

pink lady (*Lycoris squamigera*), 369

pink lady slipper (*Cypripedium acaule*), 179

pink mandevilla (*Mandevilla splendens*), 348, 349

pink melaleuca (*Melaleuca neso-phylla*), 500

pink rain lily (*Zephyranthes gran-diflora*), 332

pinks (*Dianthus plumarius*), 324

pinkster flower (*Rhododendron periclymenoides*), 221, 222, 223

pink trumpet vine (*Podranea ric-asoliana*), 348, 352, 353

pink weigela (*Weigela florida*), 317

pink wood sorrel (*Oxalis cras-sipes*), 369

pinnate, 75, 76

pin oak (*Quercus palustris*), 196

Pinophyta, 52; propagating, 103

*Pinus,* 282, 477, 485

*albicaulis,* 170

*aristata,* 304, 307, 382

*bungeana,* 298, 377, 382

*cembra,* 298, 303

*cembroides,* 215, 302, 381

*contorta,* 170, 190, 305, 365

*densiflora,* 377, 536

*echinata,* 167

*edulis,* 215, 303, 307, 338, 363, 367, 381, 382

*elliottii,* 167, 168; var. *densa,* 300, 361; var. *elliotti,* 199

*halepensis,* 307

*koraiensis,* 282

*longaeva,* 68

*monophylla,* 215

*mugo,* 308, 311, 381, 470; 'Compacta', 514

*muricata,* 216

*nigra,* 304, 307, 380

*palustris,* 167, 168, 188, 299

*parviflora,* 514, 536

*pinea,* 138

*ponderosa,* 170, 190, 304, 382

*quadrifolia,* 170

*radiata,* 216

*resinosa,* 72, 302, 380

*rigida,* 167, 216

*sabiniana,* 170, 306

*serotina,* 167

*strobus,* 189, 298, 299, 302, 305, 359, 380; 'Nana', 315, 383

*sylvestris,* 304, 377, 380

*taeda,* 167, 197, 299

*thunbergii,* 470, 501, 536

*virginiana,* 299

pinxterbloom azalea (*Rhododen-dron periclymenoides*), 310

pinyon pine (*Pinus edulis*), 303, 307, 338, 363, 367, 381, 382

pipewort (*Eriocaulon decangulare*), 199

*Piscidia piscipula,* 108, 223

*Pistacia chinensis,* 299, 307

pistil, 87, 104, 106

*Pisum sativum,* 241

pit, 91

pitcher plant (*Darlingtonia cali-fornica*), 202, 203

pitcher plants (*Sarracenia*), 82, 160

pitch pine (*Pinus rigida*), 167, 216

*Pithecellobium: guadalupense,* 108, 223, 361; *keyense,* 310, 361; *unguis-cati,* 361

pith of the stem, 71

*Pittosporum,* 49; *tenuifolium,* 317; *tobira,* 500

pittosporum (*Pittosporum tenuifolium*), 317

pittosporum (*Pittosporum tobira*), 500

*Pityopsis falcata,* 206

*Plagiobothrys: glaber,* 132; *hys-triculus,* 132; *lamprocarpus,* 132; *lithocaryus,* 132

*Plagiomnium cuspidatum,* 341

plagiotropic plants, 68

plains beargrass (*Yucca glauca*), 313, 337

plains coreopsis (*Coreopsis tincto-ria*), 356

plains cottonwood (*Populus del-toides*), 302, 304

plains prickly pear (*Opuntia poly-acantha*), 169

Plantae kingdom, 51

*Plantago lhawaiensis,* 128

plantain lily (*Hosta sieboldiana*), 330

plant classification, 50–64; cladistics, 62–63; keys, 63–64; phylogeny, 62–63; the ranking system, 50; sum-mary of classification of life, particularly plants, 51–62

plant communities, 165; biolog-ical structure of, 165–71; choosing native, 181–82; ecology, 162–64; fragmenta-tion of, pollination and, 177; functions of, 171–79

plant conservation, *see* plant diversity; vanishing plants

plant diversity, 112–22; crop, 119–22; distribution of, 113–14; by ecological region, 115; endemism, 114–19; hotspots, 114; levels of biodi-versity, 112–13; species rich-ness, 114, 116, 171; by state and province of North Amer-ica, 117–19

plant geography, 14–38

factors in plant distribution, 21–38; climate, 21–33; soil, 33–38

floristic provinces, *see* floristic provinces

planting, 447–53; of annuals, 354; of bulbs, 393, 450; of desert gardens, 211–13; of grassland gardens, 205–10; of herbaceous perennials, 449–50; of lawns, 389; preparing a planting bed, 447–48; of roses, 411; of sea-side gardens, 217; of seeds outdoors, 449; selecting plants suitable for site, 447; of shrubland gardens, 214; of shrubs, 308, 450–53; of trees, 297, 450–53; of wetland gar-dens, 195; of woodland gar-dens, 186

plant names, *see* naming of plants

plant parts, *see* plant structure and their functions, plant parts

plant reproduction:

asexual, 94, 95

sexual plant life cycle, 95–96; alternation of generations, 96; of angiosperms, *see* angiosperms, reproduction by; of bryophytes, 96–98; of ferns (pteridophytes), 98–101; of gymnosperms, 101–104; meiosis, 95
see also propagation
plant societies, 726–32
plant structures and their functions, 65–94
grouping by, 65–68; growth, architecture, and branching, 68; habit, 65; life stages, 67; longevity, 67; nutrition, mode of, 67; Raunkiaer's classification system, 65–67
plant parts, 68–94; flowers, 69, 85–90; fruit, 69, 90–94; leaves, 68–69, 73–85; roots, 69–71; stem, 68, 71–73; surface features, 94
*Platanus: racemosa,* 170, 202; x *acerifolia,* 609
*Platanus occidentalis,* 167, 377, 378, 380
*Platycerium,* 324
*Platycodon grandiflorus,* 7, 320, 325, 369
pleaching, 517–19
*Plectranthus amboinicus (Coleus amboinicus),* 334
Pliny, 11
*Pluchea,* 361; *rosea,* 199
plumbago (*Plumbago auriculata*), 311
*Plumbago auriculata,* 311
plum curculio, 556
plume grass (*Saccharum giganteum*), 199
plume grass (*Saccharum ravennae*), 328, 374
plume poppy (*Macleaya cordata*), 333
*Plumeria,* 49, 595
plum-leaf azalea (*Rhododendron prunifolium*), 310
plums (*Prunus*), 270, 283, 284, 510; pests of, 285–86
plum yew (*Cephalotaxus harringtonia*), 308, 485
plum yews (*Cephalotaxus*), 514
pneumatophores, 70, 71
*Poa: manni,* 128; *palustris,* 197; *pratensis,* 85; *sandvicensis,* 128; *scabrella,* 170; *siphonoglossa,* 128
Poaceae, 49, 60–61, 109
*Podocarpus,* 514
podocarpus (*Podocarpus*), 514

*Podophyllum peltatum,* 188, 189, 333, 341, 657–58
*Podranea ricasoliana,* 348, 352, 353
podzolization process, 37
poet's narcissus (*Narcissus poeticus*), 370
poinsettia tree (*Pinckneya bracteata*), 300
pointleaf manzanita (*Arctostaphylos pungens*), 318, 384
poison hemlock (*Conium maculatum*), 650–51
poison ivy (*Toxicodendron radicans*), 70, 168, 218, 661
poisonous plants, 641–70; categories of poisonous substances found in, 642–45; dogs and cats and, 646; effects of, 641–42; encyclopedia of, 646–64; poison control centers, 665–70; preventing plant poisonings, 644; recognizing, 645; what to do if you suspect a poisoning from, 645–46
pokeweed (*Phytolacca americana*), 657
pole beans (*Phaseolus vulgaris*), 242–43
*Polemonium reptans,* 188, 330
pole pruners, 507
*Polianthes,* 400
*Polianthes tuberosa,* 323
pollarding, 519–20
pollen, 87, 106
pollination, 106–109; by animals, 107–109, 177–78; fruit growing and, 269–71; threats to pollinators, 177; by wind, 107, 109, 177
*Polygonatum: biflorum,* 188, 221, 222, 223, 322, 362; var. *commutatum,* 188, 189, 320 *odoratum,* 330, 331; 'Variegatum', 334, 336
*Polygonum,* 166; *affine* 'Border Jewell', 344; *amphibium,* 200; *aubertii,* 346, 347, 349, 350, 351, 352, 353, 509; *cuspidatum,* 138
Polypodiophyta, 52
*Polypodium,* 324; *californicum,* 203, 339; *grandiceps,* 335
polypodium (*Polypodium californicum*), 339
polypodium ferns (*Polypodium*), 324
*Polystichum: acrostichoides,* 188, 198, 320, 322, 343, 379, 381; *kwakiutlii,* 132; *munitum,* 192, 202, 203, 330, 339; *polyblepharum,* 383

*Polytaenia nuttallii,* 363
pome, 92, 93
pomegranate (*Punica granatum*), 284, 313, 318, 681
*Poncirus trifoliata,* 303, 514
pond apple (*Annona glabra*), 199
pond cypress (*Taxodium ascendens*), 168, 200
Ponderosa pine (*Pinus ponderosa*), 170, 190, 304
ponderosa pine (*Pinus ponderosa*), 382
pond pine (*Pinus serotina*), 167
pondweed (*Potamogeton illinoensis*), 199
*Pontederia: cordata,* 196, 197, 198, 200, 201; *lanceolata,* 199, 200
ponytail palm (*Nolina recurvata*), 536
poor man's orchid (*Schizanthus pinnatus*), 375
pop ash (*Fraxinus caroliniana*), 198
popcorn flower (*Plagiobothrys lamprocarpus*), 132
Popolo ku mai (*Solanum incompletum*), 132
poppy (*Papaver rhoeas*), 358
poppy mallow (*Callirhoë involucrata*), 470
poppy mallow (*Callirhoë triangulata*), 207
population, 165
*Populus,* 49
*alba,* 138
*deltoides,* 167; var. *monilifera,* 304; var. *monilifera* 'Siouxland', 304; var. *occidentalis,* 302
*fremontii,* 170, 190, 202
*tremula,* 672–73
*tremuloides,* 166, 190, 302, 359
x *acuminata,* 304
porcelain berry (*Ampelopsis brevipedunculata*), 137
porch penstemon (*Penstemon strictus*), 227
*Porphyrocoma pohliana,* 596
Portugal, 632
*Portulaca,* 355, 498; *grandiflora,* 354, 355, 356, 358, 478, 496; *oleracea,* 138, 342; *sclerocarpa,* 128
portulacas (*Portulaca*), 498
possumhaw (*Ilex decidua*), 299, 302, 303
posthole digger, 612
post oak (*Quercus stellata*), 216, 302
*Potamogeton illinoensis,* 199
potassium, 457; nutrient values

of various fertilizers, chart of, 462–63
potatoes (*Solanum tuberosum*), 241–42
*Potentilla,* 166; *canadensis,* 206; *fruticosa,* 49, 108, 200, 220, 224, 226, 311, 470, 481; *multijuga,* 130; *neumanniana,* 344; *nevadensis,* 328, 329; *palustris,* 196; *recta,* 138; *tabernaemontani,* 344
*Poterium sanguisorba,* 254
pot marigold (*Calendula officinalis*), 254, 358, 496, 498, 678
pot marigold (*Origanum onites*), 259–60
potted oleander (*Nerium oleander*), 571
poverty grass (*Danthonia spicata*), 206
powdery mildew, 410, 563
powdery thalia (*Thalia dealbata*), 198
prairie acacia (*Acacia angustissima*), 343
prairie blazing star (*Liatris pycnostachya*), 200
prairie bluets (*Hedyotis nigricans*), 326
prairie clover (*Dalea purpureum*), 207
prairie clovers (*Dalea*), 169
prairie coneflower (*Ratibida columnifera*), 328
prairie cordgrass (*Spartina pectinata*), 379
prairie crabapple (*Malus ioensis*), 303, 363
prairie dock (*Parthenium integrifolium*), 207
prairie dock (*Silphium integrifolium*), 207
prairie dock (*Silphium terebinthinaceum*), 207
prairie flameleaf sumac (*Rhus lanceolata*), 303
prairie flax (*Linum perenne* subsp. *lewisii*), 207
prairie gentian (*Eustoma grandiflorum*), 208, 373
prairie onion (*Allium stellatum*), 326
prairie parsley (*Polytaenia nuttallii*), 363
prairie phlox (*Phlox pilosa*), 189, 198, 207, 326, 327
prairie rose (*Rosa setigera*), 350, 351
prairies, 204; Central prairies, *see* Central prairies and plains; classification of, 153; fire's role in, 154

prairie sage (*Artemisia ludoviciana*), 336
prairie skullcap (*Scutellaria orientalis*), 332, 333
prairie smoke (*Geum triflorum*), 207, 208, 343
prairie verbena (*Verbena bipinnatifida*), 356
prayer plant (*Maranta leuconeura*), 572
precatory pea (*Abrus precatorius*), 647
precipitation, 29–31, 34–35, 36, 173, 175
Presidio clarkia (*Clarkia franciscana*), 126
Preston lilac (*Syringa* x *prestoniae*), 169
prickle, 72, 82
prickly ash (*Zanthoxylum americanum*), 486
prickly ashes (*Zanthoxylum*), 334
prickly pear cactus (*Opuntia compressa*), 216
prickly pears (*Opuntia*), 169, 281
prickly poppies (*Argemone*), 367
pride of Burma (*Curcuma roscoeana*), 323
primrose (*Primula japonica*), 330
primrose (*Primula obconica*), 358
primrose (*Primula vulgaris*), 325
primrose monkeyflower (*Mimulus primuloides*), 203
primroses (*Primula*), 486, 497
*Primula,* 486, 497
  *auricula,* 355, 604
  *japonica,* 330; 'Miller's Crimson', 330
  *obconica,* 358
  *vulgaris,* 325
primula (*Primula auricula*), 604
Prince, William, 11
prince's plum (*Stanleya pinnata*), 109, 225, 228
princess flower (*Tibouchina urvilleana*), 317
princess tree (*Paulownia tormentosa*), 138
*Pritchardia: lowreyana,* 132; *munroi,* 128
*Priva portoricensis,* 132
privets (*Ligustrum*), 138
propagation, 474–93; asexual, *see* vegetative propagation; equipment for, 474–75; pathogens, stopping, 475; by seed (sexual propagation), 474, 475–80. *see also* plant reproduction
prophyll, 82
prophyry plant (*Porphyrocoma pohliana*), 596
prop root, 70, 71

*Prosopis,* 169, 213, 307; *glandulosa,* 169, 302, 337; *pubescens,* 307; *velutina,* 109, 227
prostrate germander (*Teucrium chamaedrys*), 345
prostrate indigobush (*Dalea greggii*), 213
prostrate myoporum (*Myoporum parvifolium*), 471
*Proteaceae,* 49
Protista kingdom, 51
pruning, 503–12; basic cuts, 504–505; basic principles of, 503–504; of bonsai, *see* bonsai, pruning of; candling, 505; of diseased wood, 507; heading cuts, 504–505; of herbaceous plants, 511–12; painting pruning cuts, 507; pest control and, 543; pinching, 505, 511–12, 533–34; reasons for, 503; rejuvenation, 508–509; of roses, 412; thinning cuts, 504; tools for, 507, 614–15; to train young trees and shrubs, 508; transplanting, in preparation for, 456; unshearing shrubs, 523–24; when to prune, 509–11; whole branches, 505–508. *see also* training and sculpting plants
pruning knife, folding, 615
pruning saws, 507
pruning shears, 481, 507, 528, 614–15
*Prunus,* 510, 673
  *americana,* 189, 284, 302, 314, 364
  *amurensis,* 379
  *angustifolia,* 363
  *besseyi,* 315
  *caroliniana,* 188, 314, 380, 381
  *cerasifera,* 304, 501
  *cerasus,* 364; 'Montmorency', 304; 'North Star', 304
  *domestica,* 85
  *glandulosa,* 368
  *ilicifolia,* 215, 366
  *laurocerasus,* 500
  *maackii,* 302, 304, 377
  *maritima,* 216, 359
  *mexicana,* 303, 380
  *mume,* 299, 376, 378, 536
  *myrtifolia,* 300
  *nigra,* 302; 'Princess Kay', 302
  *padus,* 304
  *serotina,* 303, 359, 363, 658
  *serrula,* 377, 382
  *serrulata,* 298, 501; 'Kwanzan', 298; 'Ojochin', 298
  *subhirtella,* 298, 501
  *tenella,* 315

*tomentosa,* 281, 282, 283, 314
*virginiana,* 190, 191, 359; 'Shubert', 304; var. *melanocarpa,* 304, 364
  x 'Okame', 298, 501
*Pseudobombax ellipticum,* 301
*Pseudolarix kaempferi,* 298
*Pseudophoenix sargentii,* 301
*Pseudotsuga menziesii,* 66, 170, 190, 191, 304, 305, 377, 380, 514
*Psidium guajava,* 138
*Psilotum nudum,* 324
*Psychotria nervosa,* 223, 311, 361
*Psylliostachys suworowii,* 374, 375
*Ptelea trifoliata,* 190, 303, 312, 338
*Pteralyxia kauaiensis,* 128
pteridophytes: about, 98; reproduction of, 98–101
*Pteridum aquilinum,* 343
*Pteris lydgatei,* 128
*Ptychosperma elegans,* 301
pubescent plant surfaces, 94
public gardens: international, 630–36; in North America, 621–30, 697–723
*Pueraria lobata,* 8
*Pulmonaria,* 336
  *longifolia* 'Roy Davidson', 338
  *saccharata,* 320; 'Mrs. Moon', 320
*Pulsatilla: patens, see Anemone patens; vulgaris, see Anemone patens*
pulvinus, 74
pumpkin (*Cucurbita pepo*), 110, 245
*Punica granatum,* 284, 313, 318, 681; 'Nana', 536
purple bell vine (*Rodochiton atrosanguineum*), 357
purple bladderwort (*Utricularia purpurea*), 199
purple Chinese houses (*Collinsia heterophylla*), 358
purple coneflower (*Echinacea purpurea*), 108, 206, 222, 224, 225, 319, 320, 321, 322, 324, 325, 326, 327, 328, 360, 362, 363, 364, 365, 366, 367, 372, 373, 374, 375, 379, 498
purple coneflowers (*Echinacea*), 470
purple cupflower (*Nierembergia hippomanica* var. *violacea*), 356
purple groundcherry (*Quincula lobata*), 343
purple iceplant (*Delosperma cooperi*), 345
purple laurel (*Rhododendron catawbiense*), 222, 223

purple-leaved rollandia (*Rollandia purpurellifolia*), 132
purple-leaved weigela (*Weigela floribunda*), 316
purple loosestrife (*Lythrum salicaria*), 138, 181, 195
purple loosestrife (*Lythrum virgatum*), 138
purple mist flower (*Thalictrum rochebrunianum*), 320
purple needlegrass (*Stipa pulchra*), 209
purple osier willow (*Salix purpurea*), 314
purple paintbrush (*Castilleja purpurea*), 326
purple pitcher plant (*Sarracenia purpurea*), 200
purple prairie clover (*Dalea purpurea* var. *purpurea*), 208
purple prairie clover (*Dalea purpurea*), 367
purple queen (*Setcreasea pallida*), 323
purple sage (*Salvia leucophylla*), 216
purple sea holly (*Eryngium amethystinum*), 367
purple smoke bush (*Cotinus coggygria*), 317
purple-stemmed aster (*Aster puniceus*), 200
purple top (*Verbena bonariensis*), 366, 371
purple trailing lantana (*Lantana montevidensis*), 356
Pursh, Frederick, 11
*Purshia mexicana,* 376
purslane (*Portulaca oleracea*), 138, 342
purslanes (*Portulaca*), 355
pussy ears (*Kalanchoe tomentosa*), 323
pussytoes (*Antennaria*), 342
pussytoes (*Antennaria dioica*), 345
pussytoes (*Antennaria neglecta*), 343, 381
pussytoes (*Antennaria parvifolia*), 190
pussytoes (*Antennaria rosea*), 328
pussy willow (*Salix caprea*), 368, 378
pussy willow (*Salix discolor*), 196, 372
*Pycnanthemum: incanum,* 322, 335; *muticum,* 109, 220, 222, 334; *tenuifolium,* 363, 374; *virginianum,* 334
pygmy date palm (*Phoenix roebelenii*), 301
pygmy water lily (*Nymphaea tetragona*), 197, 202

Pyne's ground-plum (*Astragalus bibullatus*), 126
*Pyracantha*, 49
 *angustifolia*, 318; 'Gnome', 318
 *coccinea*, 309, 484, 514, 520
 x 'Victory', 382
pyrethrum, 548
*Pyrostegia venusta*, 349
*Pyrus*:
 *calleryana*, 305; 'Red Spire', 305
 *ussuriensis*: 'Mordak', 302

quadripinnate, 76
quailberry (*Crossopetalum ilicifolium*), 342
Quaker ladies (*Houstonia caerulea*), 189
quaking aspen (*Populus tremuloides*), 166, 190, 302, 359
quaking grass (*Briza media*), 471
quaking oat grass (*Chasmanthium latifolium*), 374
quamash (*Camassia*), 394, 583
quamash (*Camassia leichtlinii*), 320
Quartz Mountain live oak (*Quercus fusiformis*), 381
Queen Anne's lace (*Daucus carota*), 85, 137, 180
queen-of-the-meadow (*Filipendula ulmaria*), 320
queen of the prairie (*Filipendula rubra*), 207, 320, 371
queen's crape myrtle (*Lagerstroemia speciosa*), 300
queen's wreath (*Antigonon leptopus*), 352, 353
queen's wreath (*Petrea volubilis*), 348, 349
*Quercus*, 187, 359, 362, 366, 367, 680
 *acutissima*, 138
 *agrifolia*, 170, 191, 216, 306, 366
 *alba*, 167, 298, 299, 301, 304
 *bicolor*, 200, 301, 304, 609
 *chrysolepis*, 170
 *coccinea*, 305
 *cumosa*, 215
 *douglasii*, 170
 *dumosa*, 170
 *ellipsoidalis*, 167
 *emoryi*, 307
 *engelmanii*, 170
 *falcata*, 167
 *fusiformis*, 307, 381
 *gambelii*, 190, 304, 364
 *garryana*, 305
 *ilicifolia*, 167
 *incana*, 167

 *inopina*, 167
 *kelloggii*, 170, 191, 305, 365
 *laevis*, 167
 *laurifolia*, 168, 199
 *lobata*, 170, 191, 202, 306
 *lyrata*, 168, 299
 *macrocarpa*, 167, 168, 169, 189, 205, 301, 302, 304, 379
 *marilandica*, 167, 216
 *michauxii*, 299
 *muehlenbergii*, 72, 167, 302, 609
 *nigra*, 167, 197
 *palustris*, 196
 *phellos*, 197, 299
 *robur*, 304, 305; 'Fastigiata', 305
 *rubra*, 167, 189, 298, 301, 304
 *shumardii*, 302
 *sinuata* var. *breviloba*, 302
 *stellata*, 216, 302
 *suber*, 72, 306, 307
 *velutina*, 167, 168
 *virginiana*, 108, 167, 168, 188, 223, 299, 300, 381
 *wislizenii*, 170
quince (*Cydonia oblonga*), 282, 283
*Quincula lobata*, 343
*Quisqualis indica*, 349

rabbitbrush (*Crysothamnus nauseosus*), 215, 364
rabbitbrushes (*Chrysothamnus*), 169
rabbiteye blueberry (*Vaccinium ashei*), 309
rabbits, 230, 565
rabbit's foot fern (*Davallia fejeensis*), 324, 336, 572
raceme, 85
rachis, 84, 87
radishes (*Raphanus sativus*), 242
rafflesia (*Rafflesia arnoldii*), 110
*Rafflesia arnoldii*, 110
rain lilies (*Zephyranthes*), 323, 333, 342
rain lily (*Zephyranthes atamasco*), 189
raised beds, 448; for herbs, 248
raisin tree (*Hovenia dulcis*), 281, 282
rakes, 614
*Randia aculeata*, 311
Rangoon creeper (*Quisqualis indica*), 349
Ranunculaceae, 53
*Ranunculus: asiaticus*, 406; *flabellaris*, 200, 201
*Raphanus sativus*, 242
*Raphiolepis indica*, 311

rare plants, 124
raspberries (*Rubus*), 270, 277–78, 486; pests of, 286
*Ratibida: columnifera*, 326, 328, 364, 369; *pinnata*, 207
rattlebox (*Crotalaria pumila*), 361
rattlesnake master (*Eryngium yuccifolium*), 207
rattlesnake plant (*Calathea*), 323
Raunkiaer's classification system, 65–67
*Ravenala madagascariensis*, 335
ray, 84
Ray, John, 11
receptacle, 87, 105
red alder (*Alnus rubra*), 190
red banana (*Musa zebrina*), 336
red baneberry (*Actaea rubra*), 362
red barrenwort (*Epimedium* x *rubrum*), 343
red bay (*Persea borbonia*), 161, 168, 198
redberry stopper (*Eugenia confusa*), 300
red bird-of-paradise (*Caesalpinia pulcherrima*), 318
red buckeye (*Aesculus pavia*), 108, 187, 188, 189, 220, 222, 225, 299
red buckwheat (*Eriogonum grande* var. *rubescens*), 366
redbud (*Cercis canadensis*), 84, 298, 299, 305, 477, 500
redbuds (*Cercis*), 510
red cedar (*Juniperus virginiana*), 299
red chokeberry (*Aronia arbutifolia*), 187, 189, 201, 312, 362, 377, 481
red clintonia (*Clintonia andrewsiana*), 192
red columbine (*Aquilegia formosa*), 109, 202, 229, 329
"Red Data Books" of IUCN, 123
red elderberry (*Sambucus pubens*), 315
red elderberry (*Sambucus racemosa*), 191, 203, 365
red escallonia (*Escallonia rubra*), 500
red flowering currant (*Ribes sanguineum*), 108, 191, 192, 202, 216, 228, 229, 230, 317, 366
red horse chestnut (*Aesculus* x *carnea*), 304
red-hot poker (*Kniphofia uvaria*), 321, 370
red-hot pokers (*Kniphofia*), 470
red huckleberry (*Vaccinium parvifolium*), 191, 365
redleaf rose (*Rosa glauca*), 315
red Louisiana iris (*Iris fulva*), 198

red mangrove (*Rhizophora mangle*), 168
red maple (*Acer rubrum*), 13, 161, 167, 168, 200, 201, 297, 299, 300, 301, 304, 381, 477
red maple (*Acer rubrum* var. *trilobum*), 199
red mustard (*Brassica*), 371
red oak (*Quercus rubra*), 301, 304
red osier dogwood (*Cornus stolonifera*), 190, 196, 308, 311, 314, 362, 377, 381, 383
red passionflower (*Passiflora coccinea*), 348, 349
red pine (*Pinus resinosa*), 72, 302, 380
red powder puff (*Calliandra haematocephala*), 300
red ribbons clarkia (*Clarkia concinna*), 358
red splendor crabapple (*Malus* 'Red Spendor'), 302
red-twig dogwood (*Cornus alba*), 201
red valerian (*Centranthus ruber*), 319, 321, 328, 330, 360, 364, 367
red-vein enkianthus (*Enkianthus campanulatus*), 315
red willow (*Salix laevigata*), 202, 366
redwood (*Sequoia sempervirens*), 191
redwood sorrel (*Oxalis oregana*), 203, 331, 345
red yucca (*Hesperaloe parviflora*), 312, 318, 337, 339, 363, 367
reed canary grass (*Phalaris arundinacea*), 138, 195
Reeves skimmia (*Skimmia reevesiana*), 316
regal lily (*Lilium regale*), 369, 370
regions of the United States, growing, 288–96. *see also* individual regions
Rehder, Alfred, 30
rejuvenation, 508–509
*Remya: kauaiensis*, 128; *mauiensis*, 128; *montgomeryi*, 128
Remy's lobelia (*Lobelia remyi*), 132
reproduction of plants, *see* plant reproduction
reptiles, seed dispersal by, 178
Repton, Humphrey, 11
resins, 643
resources, 697–732; botanical gardens, arboreta, and other public gardens, 697–723; plant societies and other organizations, 723–32

resurrection lily (*Kaempferia rotunda*), 595–96
retuse leaf apex, 81
revolute leaf folding, 82
*Rhamnus: californicus,* 191, 215, 216, 366; *caroliniana, see Frangula caroliniana; cathartica,* 138; *frangula,* 138; *purshiana,* 202
*Rhaphiolepis indica,* 318, 500
*Rhapidophyllum hystrix,* 188, 335
*Rhapis excelsa,* 301
*Rheum: palmatum* 'Atrosanguineum', 338; x *cultorum,* 333, 658–59
rhizomes, 72, 73, 391–92. *see also* bulbs
*Rhizophora,* 71; *mangle,* 168
Rhode Island, 440, 627, 669, 695, 696, 717
*Rhododendron,* 49, 187, 188, 189, 191, 481, 484, 485, 510, 514, 520, 522
  *arborescens,* 196
  *austrinum,* 197, 310
  'Bow Bells', 316
  *calendulaceum,* 308, 309
  *calophytum,* 305
  *carolinianum,* 308, 309, 377
  *catawbiense,* 7, 222, 223, 308, 309
  *chapmanii,* 127
  *degronianum:* subsp. *heptamerum,* 377; subsp. *yakushimanum,* 316
  'Dora Amateis', 316
  *groenlandicum,* 82
  *indicum* 'Satsuki', 536
  *lapponicum,* 166
  *macrophyllum,* 202, 316
  *maximum,* 196, 308
  *mucronulatum,* 308, 309, 382
  'Northern Lights Series', 311
  *oblongifolium,* 197
  *obtusum,* 308
  *occidentale,* 201, 202, 316, 317
  *periclymenoides,* 221, 222, 223, 310
  'PJM', 308, 309, 312, 339, 377
  *prunifolium,* 310
  *schlippenbachii,* 308, 309, 315
  *viscosum,* 221, 223, 308, 309
rhododendrons (*Rhododendron*), 187, 188, 189, 191, 510
*Rhodophiala bifida,* 369
*Rhodotypos scandens,* 510
*Rhoeo spathacea,* 323
rhubarb (*Rheum* x *cultorum*), 333, 658–59

*Rhus,* 216, 219, 309, 361, 362, 486
  *aromatica,* 308, 311, 313, 314, 334, 337, 341, 359, 364, 481, 484
  *copalina,* 308, 359
  *glabra,* 312, 313, 359, 381; 'Laciniata', 334; var. *cismontana,* 314
  *lancea,* 306
  *lanceolata,* 303
  *microphylla,* 213, 318, 367
  *ovata,* 318
  *trilobata,* 213, 314, 364
  *typhina,* 298, 299, 312, 359, 377; 'Dissecta', 299, 335; 'Laciniata', 314, 338
  *virens,* 313
*Rhynchospora colorata,* 198, 199
*Ribes,* 366, 485
  *alpinum,* 315
  *aureum,* 190, 315, 367
  *cereum,* 314, 364
  *nidigrolaria,* 281
  *odoratum,* 108, 224, 225, 226, 281, 282, 283, 313, 364, 370
  *sanguineum,* 108, 191, 202, 216, 228, 229, 230, 316, 317, 365, 366; 'Elk River Red', 316; var. *glutinosum,* 192, 383
  *speciosum,* 366, 383
  *viburnifolium,* 215, 317
*Ricinus communis,* 333, 337, 355, 356, 369, 659
riddle, 619
riparian wetlands, 194
riverbank grape (*Vitis riparia*), 349
riverbank vervain (*Verbena riparia*), 132
river birch (*Betula nigra*), 167, 187, 189, 196, 197, 201, 299, 301, 303, 378, 382, 500, 609
river fern (*Thelypteris kunthii*), 198
river oats (*Chasmanthium latifolium*), 322, 379
*Rivina humilis,* 343
Robb's spurge (*Euphorbia amygdaloides* var. *robbiae*), 344
*Robinia: neomexicana,* 227, 315; *pseudoacacia,* 139, 222, 223, 609; x *ambigua* 'Purple Robe', 307
Robinson, William, 11–12
rocket larkspur (*Consolida ambigua*), 373
rockfoil (*Saxifraga cuneifolia*), 330
rock gardens, 604; alpine, 145
rockrose (*Cistus* x *skanbergii*), 317

Rock's phyllostegia (*Phyllostegia rockii*), 132
rock spirea (*Holodiscus dumosus*), 315
rockspray (*Cotoneaster horizontalis*), 384, 470
rockspray (*Cotoneaster microphyllus*), 345
rock spray cotoneaster (*Cotoneaster horizontalis*), 308
Rocky Mountain columbine (*Aquilegia caerulea*), 190, 328, 331
Rocky Mountain Forest, 157, 170
Rocky Mountain juniper (*Juniperus scopulorum*), 190, 304, 364, 382, 501
Rocky Mountain maple (*Acer glabrum*), 190, 304, 364, 381, 382
Rocky Mountain raspberry (*Rubus deliciosus*), 190
Rocky Mountain region, 292–93; annuals for, 356–57; butterflies and wildlife, plants to attract, 364–65; flowers for cutting, 374; foliage plants for, 337–38; ground covers for, 344; heirloom flowers, 369–70; perennials for, 327–29; shrubs for, 314–15; trees for, 303–304; vines for, 351; winter interest, plants for, 381–82
rodgersia (*Rodgersia aesculifolia*), 330
*Rodgersia aesculifolia,* 330
*Rodochiton atrosanguineum,* 357
rohdea (*Rohdea japonica*), 342, 379
*Rohdea japonica,* 342, 379
*Rollandia: crispa,* 128; *parvifolia,* 132; *purpurellifolia,* 132
*Romneya coulteri,* 215, 331
rooftop gardens, 605–606
root hairs, 71
roots, 69–71; systems, 69; types and modifications of, 69–71
ropebark (*Dirca palustris*), 189
*Rorippa: coloradensis,* 130; *gambellii,* 127
*Rosa,* 49, 262, 282, 283, 312, 313, 350, 367, 368, 372, 373, 374, 375, 477, 481, 484, 485, 486, 510, 523, 524, 681–82
  'Adam Messerich', 419
  'Alba Maxima', 415
  'Alba Semi-plena', 418
  'Albertine', 370
  'Alister Stella Gray', 416
  'Altissimo', 418
  'America', 413

'American Pillar', 370
Apothecary's Rose, 415
'Archduke Charles', 417
'Autumn Damask', 414
'Autumn Sunset', 413
*banksiae,* 347, 352; 'Lutea', 351; var. *banksiae,* 348, 417
'Baronne Henriette de Snoy', 415
'Belinda', 416
'Belle de Crécy', 420
'Blairii No. 2', 419
'Blanche de Belgique', 419
*blanda,* 477
'Blaze', 413
'Blush Noisette', 419
'Bon Silène', 416
'Boule de Neige', 420
'Cadenza', 413
*californica,* 202, 366, 383
*canina,* 282, 414
'Cardinal de Richelieu', 420
'Carefree Beauty', 414
'Cécile Brünner', 369, 417
'Céline Forestier', 417
'Champlain', 415
'Charles Albanel', 418
'Cherokee', 417
'Cinderella', 604
'Cl. Mrs. Herbert Stevens', 416
'Clotilde Soupert', 416
'Clytemnestra', 419
'Compassion', 413
'Complicata', 415
'Comte de Chambord', 420
'Comtesse du Cayla', 419
'Constance Spry', 417
'Coquette des Blanches', 418–19
*damascena,* 370
'Dapple Dawn', 418
'Dorothy Perkins', 415
'Dortmund', 418
'Dresden Doll', 604
'Duchesse de Brabant', 416
*eglanteria,* 316
Eglantine Rose, 414
'Etoile de Lyon', 419
'Explorer Series', 311
'Fashion', 413
'Félicité Parmentier', 421
*foetida,* 318, 371; 'Bicolor', 318, 371, 470
'Fortuniana', 417
*gallica,* 316, 369; 'Iceberg', 316; 'Officinalis', 415
*glauca,* 315, 382
'Gloire de Dijon', 420
'Golden Showers', 413
'Granny Grimmetts', 419
'Green Ice', 604
*gymnocarpa,* 382

'Handel', 351
'Hansa', 414
'Harison's Yellow', 415
'Hawkeye Belle', 414
'Independence', 414
'Jaune Desprez', 417
'Jeanne Lajoie', 418
'Lady Banks' Rose', 417
'Lamarque', 417
'La Rubanée', 419
'Lavender Pinocchio', 420
'L. D. Braithwaite', 418
'Little Artist', 604
'Louis Philippe', 417
'Madame Alfred Carrière', 417
'Maman Cochet', 415
'Ma Perkins', 413
'Marchesa Boccella', 419
'Maréchal Niel', 419
'Marie Van Houtte', 416
'Mermaid', 417
'Merveille de Lyon', 420
'Mme. Mélanie Willermoz', 420
'Monsieur Tillier', 416
'Mountie', 604
'Mousseline', 419
'Mrs. B. R. Cant', 416
'Mrs. Dudley Cross', 416
'Mrs. Herbert Stevens', 420
*multiflora*, 139, 180
'Mutabilis', 415
'New Dawn', 352
'Nouveau Vulcain', 419
*nutkana*, 191, 365
'Old Bush', 416
'Old Moss Pink', 414
'Oranges and Lemons', 418
*palustris*, 196, 197, 361
'Parkland Series', 311
'Peace', 413
'Queen Margrethe', 418
'Rise 'n Shine', 604
'Rose d'Amour', 414
'Rose de Rescht', 415
'Rose des Peintres', 414
'Rose du Roi', 420
'Rouletii', 604
'Roundelay', 413
'Royal Blush', 418
'Royal Sunset', 352
*rubiginosa*, 414
*rubrifolia*, see *Rosa glauca*
*rugosa*, 282, 315, 369, 470
'Sachet', 604
'Safrano', 416
'Sally Holmes', 418
*setigera*, 350, 351, 364
'Si', 604
'Sombreuil', 413
'Souvenir de la Malmaison', 417
'Spice', 419

*spinosissima altaica*, 414
'Tausendschön', 415
'Teddy Bear', 604
'The Fairy', 415
'The Reeve', 420
'Thérèse Bugnet', 418
'Tropicana', 414
'Vanity', 416
'Vershuren', 420
'Viking Queen': 413
*virginiana*, 216
'Westerland', 418
*wichuraiana*, 341, 344; 'Alba Meidiland', 341; 'Red Meidiland', 341
*woodsii*, 315, 364
x *damascena* var. *semperflorens*, 371
x *harisonii*, 370
'Yeoman', 420
Rosaceae, 57, 86
rosary pea (*Abrus precatorius*), 647
rosary vine (*Ceropegia woodii*), 523, 524, 596
rose (*Rosa gallica*), 316
rose apple (*Syzygium jambos*), 139
rosebay (*Rhododendron maximum*), 308
rosebay rhododendron (*Rhododendron maximum*), 196
rose campion (*Lychnis coronaria*), 330, 370
rose chafer, 556
rose family, 57, 86
rose lavatera (*Lavatera thuringiaca*), 329
rose mallow (*Lavatera trimestris*), 357
rosemary (*Rosmarinus officinalis*), 262, 318, 335, 366, 367, 383, 471, 500, 522, 580, 682
rosemary willow (*Salix elaeagnos*), 201
rose midges, 410–11
rose moss (*Portulaca grandiflora*), 355, 356, 358, 478, 496
rose of Castile (*Rosa* x *damascena* var. *semperflorens*), 371
rose of Sharon (*Hibiscus syriacus*), 138, 303, 310, 315, 367, 370, 470, 484, 501, 509, 514
roses (*Rosa*), 262, 282, 283, 311, 312, 313, 350, 368, 369, 372, 373, 374, 375, 407–21, 477, 484, 485, 486, 510, 523, 681–82
basic care, 409–12
for California, 418–19
classification of, 407–409; modern, 408–409; old garden, 407–408
for cold climates, 414–15
feeding and watering, 412
fertilizing of, 409, 464

for the inner city, 420–21
mulching of, 468
for Northeast and lower Midwest, 413–14
for the Northwest, 417–18
pests and pathogens, 410–11
pruning, 412
selection and siting of, 409–11
soil preparation and planting, 411
for the South, 415–16
for Texas and the Southwest, 416–17
see also *Rosa* for names of individual cultivars
Rosidae, 56–57
rosinweed (*Silphium gracile*), 326, 327
rosinweed (*Silphium integrifolium*), 207
rosinweeds (*Silphium*), 169
*Rosmarinus officinalis*, 262, 318, 335, 366, 367, 383, 500, 522, 580, 682; 'Arp', 318, 338; 'Huntington Blue', 339; 'Prostratus', 345, 471, 524
*Rosularia*, 49
rosulate leaf arrangement, 83
rosy buckwheat (*Eriogonum latifolium* subsp. *rubescens*), 216
rotary tiller, 613–14
rougeplant (*Rivina humilis*), 343
rough blazingstar (*Liatris aspera*), 208
roughleaf dogwood (*Cornus drummondii*), 303, 313, 363
rough verbena (*Verbena rigida*), 345
round cardamon (*Amomum compactum*), 323
roundheaded bush clover (*Lespedeza capitata*), 207, 208
roundleaf buffaloberry (*Shepherdia rotundifolia*), 367
roundleaf catchfly (*Silene rotundifolia*), 223
roundleaf horehound (*Marrubium rotundifolium*), 345
round-toothed cyrtandra (*Cyrtandra crenata*), 131
rowan (*Sorbus*), 281, 282
row covers, 235
royal azalea (*Rhododendron schlippenbachii*), 308, 309, 315
royal fern (*Osmunda regalis*), 189, 190, 197, 198, 199, 201, 320, 335
royal palm (*Roystonea regia*), 168
royal poinciana (*Delonix regia*), 300
*Roystonea regia*, 168, 301

rubber rabbitbrush (*Chrysothamnus nauseosus*), 313
Rubiaceae, 58
*Rubus*, 284, 359, 481, 486; *aliceae*, 132; *cockburnianus*, 377; *deliciosa*, 315; *deliciosus*, 190; *macvaughii*, 132; *maniseensis*, 132; *occidentalis*, 284; *parviflorus*, 191; *phoenicolasius*, 281; *spectabilis*, 191, 201, 202; *tygartensis*, 132; *ursinus*, 191; *uscetanus*, 132
*Rudbeckia*, 360, 361, 372, 379 *californica*, 203 *fulgida*, 321, 325, 332, 368, 498; 'Goldsturm', 320, 321, 332, 343, 359, 362, 366, 375; var. *sullivantii*, 322 *hirta*, 199, 206, 207, 208, 328, 355, 356, 361, 364, 367, 371, 373, 374, 376; 'Gloriosa Daisy', 372 *laciniata*, 196, 322, 362, 498; 'Herbstone', 322 *maxima*, 198, 320 *subtomentosa*, 207 *triloba*, 374, 382
rudbeckia (*Rudbeckia fulgida*), 332
rudbeckias (*Rudbeckia*), 360, 361
rue (*Ruta graveolens*), 262, 340
rue anemone (*Thalictrum thalictroides*), 189, 190, 325, 336
*Ruellia*: *brittoniana*, 342; 'Katie', 343, 381 *caroliniensis*, 189, 323, 361 *humilis*, 327 *nudiflora*, 327 *peninsularis*, 318
rugosa rose (*Rosa rugosa*), 315, 470
*Rumex*: *scutatus*, 264; *tomentella*, 132
running plantain lily (*Hosta clausa*), 341
running serviceberry (*Amelanchier stolonifera*), 189, 314
runoff, 175, 176
*Ruscus hypoglossum*, 72
rushes (*Juncus*), 202
Russell lupine (*Lupinus* Russell hybrids), 329
russet buffaloberry (*Shepherdia canadensis*), 216
Russian cypress (*Microbiota decussata*), 380
Russian flowering almond (*Prunus tenella*), 315
Russian hawthorn (*Crataegus ambigua*), 364
Russian olive (*Elaeagnus angustifolia*), 137

Russian peashrub (*Caragana fru-tex*), 314
Russian sage (*Perovskia atriplici-folia*), 308, 317, 325, 326, 328, 333, 376, 470
Russian statice (*Psylliostachys suworowii*), 374, 375
rust, 563
rusty blackhaw viburnum (*Viburnum rufidulum*), 303, 374
*Ruta graveolens,* 262, 340
ryania, 548

sabadilla, 548
*Sabal,* 168; *mexicana,* 197; *minor,* 337; *palmetto,* 168, 188, 197, 199, 301, 362
sabal palm (*Sabal palmetto*), 188, 199, 301
sacahuista (*Nolina texana*), 337, 380
*Saccharum: giganteum,* 199; *raven-nae,* 374
*Saccifoliaceae,* 62
*Saccifolium bandeirae,* 62
Sackville-West, Vita, 12
sacred datura (*Datura wrightii*), 332
sacred lotus (*Nelumbo lutea*), 333
sacred lotus (*Nelumbo nucifera*), 333
saffron (*Crocus sativus*), 256
saffron buckwheat (*Eriogonum crocatum*), 317
sage (*Salvia*), 496
sage (*Salvia brandegei*), 216
sage (*Salvia clevelandii*), 215
sage (*Salvia officinalis*), 262–63, 370, 580
sagebrushes (*Artemisia*), 169, 208
sage orange (*Maclura pomifera*), 138
*Sageretia thea,* 536
*Sagittaria: fasciculata,* 127; *lanci-folia,* 200; *latifolia,* 196, 197, 198, 200, 201
sagittate leaf base, 79
sago palm (*Cycas revoluta*), 536
saguaro (*Carnegiea gigantea*), 124, 133, 169, 384
St. Catherine's lace (*Eriogonum giganteum*), 216, 317, 366
St.-John's-wort (*Hypericum calycinum*), 344, 481
St.-John's-wort (*Hypericum cisti-folium*), 199
St.-John's-wort (*Hypericum henryi*), 313, 381
St.-John's-worts (*Hypericum*), 486
*Saintpaulia,* 49, 592; *ionantha,* 572

salad burnet (*Sanguisorba minor*), 254
Salad greens, 496
salal (*Gaultheria shallon*), 191, 201, 281, 282, 317, 344, 365
salamanders, 231
*Salicornia,* 162
*Salix,* 161, 166, 360, 484, 485
*babylonica,* 536
*caprea,* 368, 378
*caroliniana,* 199
*discolor,* 196, 359, 372
*elaeagnos,* 201
*exigua,* 381
*gracilistyla,* 309
*hindsiana,* 202
*irrorata,* 314, 381
*laevigata,* 202, 366
*lucida* subsp. *lasiandra,* 202
*matsudana* 'Tortuosa', 383, 514
*nigra,* 200, 303
*purpurea,* 314; 'Nana', 311, 314, 315, 339
*scouleriana,* 201
*udensis* 'Sekka', 377
salmonberry (*Rubus parviflorus*), 191, 202
salmonberry (*Rubus spectabilis*), 191, 201
saltbush (*Atriplex californica*), 216
saltbush (*Atriplex canescens*), 470
saltbushes (*Atriplex*), 169
salt cedars (*Tamarix*), 139
saltmarshes, 161–62
saltmeadow cordgrass (*Spartina patens*), 362
*Salvia,* 356, 360, 496
*apiana,* 216
*azurea* var. *grandiflora,* 326, 332, 364
*brandegei,* 216
*chamaedryoides,* 331, 332, 333
*clevelandii,* 215, 317, 318, 366; 'Allen Chickering', 317, 318
*coccinea,* 223, 224, 337, 356, 358, 363, 373, 374
*columbariae,* 209
*elegans,* 335
*farinacea,* 326, 355, 364, 372, 478; 'Victoria', 354
*greggii,* 213, 313, 318, 366, 367
*leucantha,* 326, 333, 355
*leucophylla,* 216
*lyrata,* 198, 327, 343, 364, 381
*mohavensis,* 169
*officinalis,* 262–63, 332, 370, 580; 'Purpurascens', 365
*penstemonoides,* 326
*regla,* 313, 314

*roemeriana,* 327, 337, 374
*rutilans,* 263
*sclarea,* 263, 339, 370, 470
*splendens,* 355, 361, 372, 498
x *superba* 'East Friesland', 470
salvia (*Salvia coccinea*), 373
salvias (*Salvia*), 356, 360
samara, 92, 93
*Sambucus:*
*caerulea,* 366
*callicarpa,* 216
*canadensis,* 189, 196, 199, 281, 282, 283, 310, 315, 361, 364, 370, 659–60; 'Aurea', 315; 'Laciniata', 315; 'Variegata', 500
*mexicana,* 307, 367
*nigra* 'Aurea', 338
*pubens,* 315
*racemosa,* 191, 203, 365
*simpsonii,* 361
samphire (*Crithmum maritimum*), 682–83
San Clemente Island broom (*Malacothamnus clementinus*), 127
sandbar willow (*Salix hindsiana*), 202
sand cordgrass (*Spartina bakeri*), 199
sandhill sage (*Artemisia pycno-cephala*), 216, 330
sand lily (*Leucodrinum montana*), 190
sand lovegrass (*Eragrostis trichodes*), 213, 384
sand penstemon (*Penstemon ambiguus*), 332
sandplain gerardia (*Agalinis acuta*), 126
sand sage (*Artemisia filifolia*), 318, 338
sand verbenas (*Abronia*), 209
sandy soils, 432
*Sanguinaria canadensis,* 147, 188, 320, 325
*Sanguisorba minor,* 254
*Sanicula: kauaiensis,* 132; *mariversa,* 128
San Mateo thornmint (*Acan-thomintha duttonii*), 126
San Mateo woolly-sunflower (*Eriophyllum latilobum*), 127
*Sansevieria trifasciata,* 572
Santa Barbara Island dudleya (*Dudleya traskiae*), 127
Santa Cruz cypress (*Cupressus abramsiana*), 126
Santa Cruz Island buckwheat (*Eriogonum arborescens*), 216
Santa Fe raspberry (*Rubus aliceae*), 132
Santa Lucia fir (*Abies bracteata*), 305, 383

Santo Domingo chocolate chili (*Capsicum annuum*), 371
*Santolina,* 263; *chamaecyparissus,* 318, 328; *virens,* 470
santolina (*Santolina*), 263
*Sanvitalia procumbens,* 354, 356, 358
*Sapindus drummondii,* 303, 307
*Sapium sebiferum,* 139
sapodilla (*Manilkara zapota*), 300
*Saponaria: ocymoides,* 345; *offici-nalis,* 368, 369, 370
sarcocarp, 91
*Sarcococca: hookeriana* var. *humilis,* 342, 345; *ruscifolia,* 315
sarcococca (*Sarcococca hookeriana* var. *humilis*), 342
Sargent, Charles Sprague, 12
Sargent crabapple (*Malus sargen-tii*), 302, 501
Sargent's hydrangea (*Hydrangea sargentiana*), 315
Sargent's palm (*Pseudophoenix sar-gentii*), 301
Sargent viburnum (*Viburnum sar-gentii*), 316
*Sarracenia,* 82, 160; *purpurea,* 200
sasanqua camellia (*Camellia sasanqua*), 310, 315, 378, 379, 383, 500
*Sasa palmata,* 333
Saskatoon berry (*Amelanchier alnifolia*), 364
Saskatoon serviceberry (*Ame-lanchier alnifolia*), 314
sassafras (*Sassafras albidum*), 218, 298, 360, 377, 486
*Sassafras albidum,* 218, 298, 360, 377, 486
satin leaf (*Chrysophyllum olivi-forme*), 168, 300, 361
*Satureja: hortensis,* 263; *montana,* 263–64, 580
saucer magnolia (*Magnolia* x *soulangiana*), 298, 303, 306, 374
*Saururus cernuus,* 196, 197, 198, 200, 201, 361
sawgrass (*Cladium jamaicensis*), 168
saw palmetto (*Serenoa repens*), 167, 168, 199, 223, 301, 362
saws, 615
sawtooth oak (*Quercus acutissima*), 138
*Saxifraga,* 49, 486; *cuneifolia,* 330; *pensylvanica,* 200; 'Peter Pan', 604; *stolonifera,* 335, 342
saxifrages (*Saxifraga*), 486
*Scabiosa,* 320, 372
*atropurpurea,* 359; 'Black Bur-gundy', 375

'Butterfly Blue', 320, 359
*caucasica,* 365, 369, 371, 376
*Scaevola: coriacea,* 128; 'Mauve
   Clusters', 345; *plumieri,* 311;
   *sericea* var. *taccada,* 139; *suaveolens,* 356
scaevola (*Scaevola suaveolens*),
   356
scales (insects), 556–57
scape, 84
scarification, 476, 477
scarlet bugler (*Penstemon
   barbatus*), 215
scarlet clematis (*Clematis texensis*), 353
scarlet firethorn (*Pyracantha coccinea*), 484, 514, 520
scarlet gilia (*Ipomopsis aggregata*),
   209, 364
scarlet globe mallow (*Sphaeralcea
   coccinea*), 208
scarlet honeysuckle (*Lonicera sempervirens*), 349
scarlet leather flower (*Clematis
   texensis*), 347, 348
Scarlet locoweed (*Astragalus coccineus),* 109, 228
scarlet mint (*Stachys coccinea*),
   333
scarlet monkeyflower (*Mimulus
   cardinalis*), 203
scarlet oak (*Quercus coccinea*), 305
scarlet pimpernel (*Anagallis
   arvensis*), 683
scarlet runner bean (*Phaseolus coccineus*), 352, 353
scarlet sage (*Salvia coccinea*), 223,
   224, 337, 356, 358, 361,
   363, 372, 374
scarlet sage (*Salvia splendens*),
   355, 498
scented-leaved geraniums
   (*Pelargonium*), 257, 496, 524,
   592, 593
*Schefflera: actinophylla,* 139;
   *arboricola,* 311, 336, 536
*Schiedea: adamantis,* 128;
   *apokremnos,* 128; *haleakalensis,*
   128; *implexa,* 132; *kaalae,*
   128; *lydgatei,* 128
*Schinus: molle,* 139; *terebinthifolius,* 139, 152
*Schizachyrium,* 337
   *scoparium,* 168, 169, 206, 208,
   326, 327, 337, 374, 380;
   ssp. *littorale,* 216
*Schizanthus pinnatus,* 375
schizocarp, 91
schizophragma (*Schizophragma
   hydrangeoides*), 351
*Schizophragma hydrangeoides,* 351
*Schlumbergera,* 324
*Schoenocrambe barnebyi,* 127
*Schoenus nigricans,* 199

scholar tree (*Sophora japonica*),
   298
schoolhouse lily (*Rhodophiala
   bifida*), 369
Schott's yucca (*Yucca schottii*), 215
Schweinit's waterweed (*Elodea
   schweinitzii*), 131
*Sciadopitys verticillata,* 383, 485
*Scilla,* 397, 583; *hispanica,* 320;
   *sibirica,* 496
*Scindapsus pictus* 'Argyraeus', 524
scion, 489
*Scirpus,* 201, 202; *tabernaemontani,* 197, 199, 201
*Sclerocactus wrightiae,* 127
Scotch broom (*Cytisus scoparius*),
   137
Scotch pine (*Pinus sylvestris*),
   304, 377, 380
Scotch thistle (*Onopordum acanthium*), 138
Scouler's corydalis (*Corydalis
   scouleri*), 338
scouler's willow (*Salix
   scouleriana*), 201
screwbean mesquite (*Prosopis
   pubescens*), 307
*Scrophularia californica,* 216
Scrophulariaceae, 58
scrub mint (*Dicerandra frutescens*),
   126
scrub oak, California (*Quercus
   dumosa*), 170
scrub oak (*Quercus ilicifolia*), 167
scrub oak (*Quercus inopina*), 167
sculpting, *see* training and
   sculpting plants
*Scutellaria: incana,* 188; *orientalis,*
   332, 333; *ovata,* 326, 327; *serrata,* 188
sea buckthorn (*Hippophae rhamnoides*), 314, 338
sea fig (*Carpobrotus chilensis*),
   137
seagrape (*Coccoloba uvifera*), 108,
   223, 361
sea grass (*Halophila*), 109
sea holly (*Eryngium
   amethystinum*), 365
sea holly (*Eryngium maritimum*),
   470
sea holly (*Eryngium planum*), 374
sea lavender (*Limonium sinuatum*),
   358
sea myrtle (*Baccharis halimifolia*),
   309
sea oats (*Chasmanthium
   latifolium*), 168, 216, 320
sea ox-eye daisy (*Borrichia
   frutescens*), 342, 361
sea pink (*Armeria maritima*), 328,
   331
sea pink (*Armeria maritima*
   subsp. *californica*), 216

seashore mallow (*Kosteletzkya virginica*), 216, 322
seaside daisy (*Erigeron glaucus*),
   216, 329
seaside gardens, 216–17; maintaining, 217; plants for, 216;
   preparing and planting, 217
seaside goldenrod (*Solidago sempervirens*), 216
sea thrift (*Armeria maritima*), 330
sea tomato (*Rosa rugosa*), 371
sedge (*Carex glauca*), 336
sedge (*Carex nigra*), 336
sedge (*Carex obnupta*), 202
sedges (*Carex*), 161, 162, 166,
   322
*Sedum,* 471, 478
   *acre,* 321, 368
   *hispanicum,* 321, 368
   *sarmentosum,* 321, 368
   *spathulifolium,* 329, 345; 'Cape
      Blanco', 329
   *spectabile,* 320, 321, 322, 325,
      327, 332, 333, 360, 363,
      498; 'Autumn Joy', 320,
      325, 327, 332, 333, 363;
      'Brilliant', 365; 'Herbst-
      freude', 320; 'Red Chief',
      332, 333; 'Ruby Glow',
      327, 363
   *spurium,* 343
   *telephium,* 321
   x 'Vera Jameson', 320
sedum (*Sedum spectabile*), 320,
   321, 325, 327, 332, 333,
   363
sedums (*Sedum*), 321, 368
seeds, 91, 104; dispersal, means
   of, 93–94, 178, 689–91;
   planting outdoors, 449; prop-
   agaton by, *see* propagation, by
   seed (sexual propagation);
   smallest and largest, 110
Seed Savers Exchange, 140
Seeds Blum, 140
Seeds of Change, 140
segment (of a fruit), 91
Sego lilies (*Calochortus*), 208
*Selaginella: involvens,* 342; *uncinata,* 342
selaginella (*Selaginella involvens*),
   342
selaginella (*Selaginella uncinata*),
   342
self-pollination, 106
*Sempervivens,* 382; *tectorum,* 368,
   370
*Sempervivum,* 49
*Senecio: aureus,* 196, 200;
   *cineraria,* 331, 471, 498; *flaccidus,* 364; *obovatus,* 327, 343,
   381; *spartioides,* 364
*Senna: alata,* 311, 337, 356;
   *covesii,* 109, 227; *ligustrina,*

   311, 361; *marilandica,* 326;
   *nemophila,* 318; *polyphylla,*
   361
sennas (*Cassia*), 366
sensitive fern (*Onoclea sensibilis*),
   198, 201
sepal, 87, 104
septum, 91
Sequoia (*Sequoiadendron
   giganteum*), 170
*Sequoiadendron giganteum,* 170
*Sequoia sempervirens,* 66, 170,
   191, 306
Serbian bellflower (*Campanula
   poscharskyana*), 343, 345
serbian spruce (*Picea omorika*),
   298
*Serenoa repens,* 167, 168, 199,
   223, 361, 362
serissa (*Serissa foetida*), 522, 536
*Serissa foetida,* 522, 536; 'Flore-
   pleno', 596–97
serrate leaf margin, 79
serviceberries (*Amelanchier*), 187,
   189, 190, 360, 362, 379,
   477, 510
serviceberry (*Amelanchier alnifolia*), 190, 302, 365
serviceberry (*Amelanchier
   arborea*), 298, 500
serviceberry (*Amelanchier
   canadensis*), 315
serviceberry (*Amelanchier* x *grandiflora*), 299
*Setaria parviflora,* 199
*Setcreasea pallida,* 323, 342
sexual plant life cycle, *see* plant
   reproduction, sexual plant life
   cycle
shadbush (*Amelanchier arborea*),
   298, 500
shadbush (*Amelanchier laevis*),
   196
shadbushes (*Amelanchier*), 477
shade cloth, 234
shady areas, plantings for, *see
   under type of planting and
   region,* e.g. perennials, for the
   Northeast
shagbark hickory (*Carya ovata*),
   189, 301, 362, 379
shamrock, 683
Shasta daisy (*Leucanthemum maximum*), 331
Shasta daisy (*Leucanthemum* x
   *superbum*), 321, 373
shaving brush tree (*Pseudobombax
   ellipticum*), 301
sheath, 74
sheepberry (*Viburnum lentago*),
   470
sheep's fescue (*Festuca ovina*), 138
shell ginger (*Alpinia zerumbet*),
   323, 372, 401, 589

*Shepherdia: argentea,* 215, 281, 282, 314, 362, 364; *canadensis,* 216; *rotundifolia,* 367

Sherff schiedea (*Schiedea implexa*), 132

shibataea (*Shibataea kumasaka*), 330

*Shibataea kumasaka,* 330

shieldleaf rodgersia (*Astilboides tabularis*), 338

shining coneflower (*Rudbeckia laciniata*), 322

shining sumac (*Rhus copalina*), 308

shiny-leaved spirea (*Spirea* var. *lucida*), 316

Shipman's cyanea (*Cyanea shipmanii*), 131

Shirley poppy (*Papaver rhoeas*), 357

shoebutton ardisia (*Ardisia elliptica*), 137

shoestring acacia (*Acacia stenophylla*), 307

shooting star (*Dodecatheon clevelandii*), 215

shooting star (*Dodecatheon dentatum*), 203

shooting star (*Dodecatheon hendersonii*), 215

shooting star (*Dodecatheon meadia*), 187, 189, 196, 205, 206, 207

shooting stars (*Dodecatheon*), 192

shore juniper (*Juniperus horizontalis*), 340

shore pine (*Pinus contorta*), 305, 365

short-day plants, 104

*Shortia galacifolia,* 10, 189

short-leaf fig (*Ficus citrifolia*), 300

shortleaf pine (*Pinus echinata*), 167

Short's goldenrod (*Solidago shortii*), 127

shovel, 612

shower of orchids (*Congea tomentosa*), 348, 349

showy crabapple (*Malus floribunda*), 298

showy gentian (*Eustoma grandiflora*), 356

showy goldeneye (*Heliomeris multiflora*), 364

showy sedum (*Sedum spectabile*), 322, 360

showy skullcap (*Scutellaria incana*), 188

shredders, 619

shrimp plant (*Justica brandegeana*), 82

shrub althea (*Hibiscus syriacus*), 484

shrubby cinquefoil (*Potentilla fruticosa*), 200, 311

shrubby dogwoods (*Cornus*), 481

shrubby five-fingers (*Potentilla fruticosa*), 108, 220, 224, 226

shrubby roses (*Rosa*), 481

shrubby spurge (*Euphorbia characias* subsp. *wulfenii*), 329

shrubby St.-John's-wort (*Hypericum prolificum*), 484

shrubby wallflower (*Erysimum linifolium*), 331

shrubland gardens, 213–15
maintaining, 214
planting, 214
plants for, 215; California chaparral, 215; pinyon-juniper woodland, 215
preparing, 214

shrubs, 163, 184, 307–18
for coastal California, 316–17
for containers, 500, 502
fertilizing of, 464
for the Midwest and Northern Great Plains, 311–12
mulching of, 467–68
for the Northeast, 308–309
for the Pacific Northwest, 315–16
pests, common, 567
planting and care, 308, 450–53; balled and burlapped, 452; bare-root, 452–53
propagation of: by division, 481; vegetative, *see* vegetative propagation
pruning, *see* pruning
for the Rocky Mountain region, 314–15
for the Southeast, 309–10
for Subtropical Florida, 310–11
for Texas and the Southern Plains, 312–14
transplanting, 453–56
for western deserts, 317–18

shrub tan oak (*Lithocarpus densiflorus* var. *echinoides*), 365

shumard red oak (*Quercus shumardii*), 302

Siberian bugloss (*Brunnera macrophylla*), 325

Siberian crabapple (*Malus baccata*), 536

Siberian elm (*Ulmus pumila*), 139

Siberian iris (*Iris sibirica*), 319, 321, 322, 324, 325, 376

Siberian pea-shrub (*Caragana arborescens*), 470, 609

Siberian squill (*Scilla siberica*), 496

*Sicyos hillebrandii,* 132

*Sida inflexa,* 132

*Sidalcea:*
*campestris,* 329
*malviflora,* 209, 331, 366, 367, 369
*oregana:* 'Brilliant', 375; subsp. *spicata,* 203
*pedata,* 127

side-dressing, 461

sideoats grama (*Bouteloua curtipendula*), 206, 326, 327, 367, 373

side-veneer grafting, 489–90

Siebold forsythia (*Forsythia suspensa* var. *sieboldii*), 13

Sierra maple (*Acer glabrum*), 202

Sierra Montane Forest, 157, 170

signet marigold (*Tagetes tenuifolia*), 356

*Silene: alexandri,* 128; *armeria,* 365; *californica,* 230; *caroliniana,* 84; *cryptopetala,* 132; *degeneri,* 132; *lanceolata,* 129; *perlmanii,* 129; *regia,* 223; *rotundifolia,* 223; *virginica,* 221

silicia aerogel, 548

silk-tassel bush (*Garrya elliptica*), 215, 382

silky dogwood (*Cornus amomum*), 196

silky oak (*Grevillea robusta*), 138

silky wisteria (*Wisteria venusta*), 352

*Silphium,* 169; *gracile,* 326, 327; *integrifolium,* 207; *laciniatum,* 207, 362; *perfoliatum,* 196, 207, 362; *terebinthinaceum,* 207

silverbell tree (*Halesia tetraptera*), 298

silverberry (*Elaeagnus pungens*), 318

silver buffalo berry (*Shepherdia argentea*), 215, 314, 362

silver dollars (*Lunaria annua*), 368

silver lace vine (*Polygonum aubertii*), 346, 347, 349, 350, 351, 352, 353, 509

silver leadplant (*Amorpha canescens*), 314, 364

silver linden (*Tilia tomentosa*), 298, 304

silver maple (*Acer saccharinum*), 167, 200, 477

silver mountain mahogany (*Cercocarpus montanus* var. *argentus*), 303

silver palm (*Coccothrinax argentata*), 301, 361

silver sagebrush (*Artemisia cana*), 314

silver-vein creeper (*Parthenocissus henryana*), 351

silvery glade fern (*Athyrium pycnocarpon*), 320

*Simarouba glauca,* 168, 300

*Simmondsia chinensis,* 318

simple leaf, 74, 75

Simpson's stopper (*Myrcianthes fragrans*), 300

Simpson stopper (*Myrcianthes fragrans* var. *simpsonii*), 361

Singapore, 635

Singapore holly (*Malpighia coccigera*), 311

single flower, 85

single-flowered mariposa (*Calochortus monanthus*), 131

single-needle pinyon (*Pinus monophylla*), 215

single-seed juniper (*Juniperus monosperma*), 215

*Sinningia,* 592; *pusilla,* 572; *speciosa,* 588

*Sisyrinchium,* 324; *angustifolium,* 196, 206; *bellum,* 192, 203, 216; *californicum,* 192

Sitka alder (*Alnus sinuata*), 382

Sitka mountain ash (*sorbus sitchensis*), 365

Sitka spruce (*Picea sitchensis*), 170

*Skimmia: japonica,* 500; *reevesiana,* 316

skin irritants, 643

Skottsberg's wikstroemia (*Wikstroemia skottsbergiana*), 132

skunk cabbage (*Lysichiton americanum*), 161, 203

skunk cabbage (*Symplocarpus foetidus*), 161, 197, 200, 201

skyflower (*Hydrolea corymbosa*), 199

skyrocket (*Ipomopsis aggregata*), 226, 227, 229

skyrocket (*Ipomopsis rubra*), 358

slash-and-burn farming, 124

slash pine (*Pinus elliottii*), 167, 168, 199, 300, 361

slender cotton grass (*Eriophorum gracile*), 203

slender cyrtandra (*Cyrtandra gracilis*), 131

slender deutzia (*Deutzia gracilis*), 312, 316

slender false brome (*Brachypodium sylvaticum*), 137

slender grama (*Bouteloua filiformis*), 209

slender-horned spineflower (*Dodecahema leptoceras*), 126

slender-petaled mustard (*Thelypodium stenopetalum*), 127
slender rush-pea (*Hoffmannseggia tenella*), 127
slender-stalked cyrtandra (*Cyrtandra filipes*), 131
slippery elm (*Ulmus rubra*), 303
slow-growing plants, 686
slugs, 557
small-anthered bittercress (*Cardamine micranthera*), 126
small cranberry (*Vaccinium oxycoccus*), 202
smallest plants, 66
small-flowered alumroot (*Heuchera micrantha*), 330
small-flowered delissea (*Delissea parviflora*), 131
small-flowered rollandia (*Rollandia parvifolia*), 132
small Himalayan sarcococca (*Sarcococca hookeriana* var. *humilis*), 345
small hostas (*Hosta*), 496
*Smilacina: racemosa*, 188, 189, 191, 192, 203, 320, 330, 331, 362; *stellata*, 192, 203, 330
smilax (*Smilax laurifolia*), 348
*Smilax laurifolia*, 199, 348
smoke tree (*Cotinus coggygria*), 299, 311
smooth blue aster (*Aster laevis*), 205
smooth penstemon (*Penstemon digitalis*), 207
smooth sumac (*Rhus glabra*), 313, 381
snails, 557
snailseed (*Cocculus laurifolius*), 310
snake-bark maple (*Acer pensylvanicum*), 298
snakes, 230
snapdragon (*Antirrhinum majus*), 354, 356, 358, 368, 371, 372, 373, 496, 498
snapdragons (*Antirrhinum*), 355, 380
snapdragon vine (*Maurandella antirrhiniflora*), 353
sneezeweed (*Helenium autumnale*), 200, 206, 321, 369
snowball hydrangea (*Hosta macrophylla*), 367
snowball viburnum (*Viburnum tomentosum*), 372
snowbells (*Styrax*), 484
snowberry (*Symphoricarpos albus*), 221, 225, 227, 312, 315, 365
snowberry (*Symphoricarpos albus* var. *laevigatus*), 203
snowberry (*Symphoricarpos occidentalis*), 190

snowbush (*Breynia disticha*), 336
snowbush (*Breynia nivosa*), 310
snowdrop (*Galanthus elwesii*), 325
snowdrop (*Galanthus nivalis*), 325, 381
snowdrop bush (*Styrax officinalis* var. *californicus*), 317
snowdrops (*Galanthus*), 134, 135, 376, 378, 395, 497, 583
snowflake (*Leucojum*), 396, 583
snowgum eucalyptus (*Eucalyptus pauciflora* subsp. *niphophila*), 305
snow-in-summer (*Cerastium tomentosum*), 328, 331, 342, 344, 345
snowmound spirea (*Spirea nipponica*), 312
snow-on-the-mountain (*Euphorbia marginata*), 372, 471
snow queen (*Synthyris reniformis*), 191
snow-wreath (*Neviusia alabamensis*), 481
soapberry (*Sapindus drummondii*), 307
soaptree (*Yucca elata*), 307
soapweed (*Yucca glauca*), 313, 380, 470
soapwort (*Saponaria ocymoides*), 345
society garlic (*Tulbaghia violacea*), 323, 331, 332, 339, 342, 371, 404, 589
softleaf yucca (*Yucca gloriosa*), 337, 381
soft-stem bulrush (*Scirpus tabernaemontani*), 199, 201
soil, 33–38, 430–41
  analysis, 435–51; home kits for, 437; professional, 437–41, 447; simple tests, 435–37
  bulbs, preparation for, 393–94
  city gardening and, 599–600, 602–603
  classification, 37–38
  compaction problems, mulch and, 465
  components of, 430–32
  formation of, 35–37
  mathematics, 735–36
  pH, 433–35; home kits to test, 437; mulching and, 465; professional testing, 437–41; vegetable gardens and, 233
  profiles, 35, 37, 430
  roses, preparation for, 411
  structure, 433

testing, *see* soil, analysis
texture of, 432–33, 436
triangle, 436
vegetable gardens, preparation for, 233
Solander, Daniel, 4
*Solandra guttata*, 348, 349
Solanaceae, 58–59
Solano grass (*Tuctoria mucronata*), 127
*Solanum: conocarpum*, 132; *dulcamara*, 660; *incompletum*, 132; *jasminoides*, 352; *melongena*, 243–44; *sandwicense*, 129; *tuberosum*, 241–42
*Solenostemon (Coleus)*, 522
*Solenostemon scutellarioides*, 354, 355, 357, 368, 372, 496
*Solidago*, 108, 109, 169, 206, 207, 208, 220, 222, 223, 224, 225, 226, 229, 321, 322, 323, 359, 360, 361, 369, 372, 373, 374, 470, 498; *californica*, 192; *gigantea*, 200; *nemoralis*, 208, 326; *odora*, 327, 337; *ohioensis*, 200; *riddellii*, 200; *rigida*, 208; *sempervirens*, 216; *shortii*, 127; *stricta*, 199; *uliginosa*, 196; *ulmifolia*, 327
solitaire palm (*Ptychosperma elegans*), 301
Solomon's plume (*Smilacina racemosa*), 362
Solomon's seal (*Polygonatum biflorum*), 221, 222, 223, 322, 362
Solomon's seal (*Polygonatum biflorum* var. *commutatum*), 320
Solomon's seal (*Polygonatum odoratum*), 330, 331
Sonoma spineflower (*Chorizanthe valida*), 126
Sonoran Desert, 155–56, 169–70, 637–38
sooty mold, 563
*Sophora: affinis*, 303, 337, 380; *japonica*, 298, 299, 307, 609; *secundiflora*, 307, 313, 314; *tomentosa*, 223, 224, 311
*Sorbaria sorbifolia*, 312
*Sorbus*, 281, 282, 477; *alnifolia*, 302; *americana*, 302, 304; *aucuparia*, 306, 383; *commixta*, 382; *sitchensis*, 191, 365
*Sorghastrum nutans*, 69, 206, 207, 208, 326, 327, 328, 337, 373, 374, 379, 382
sorrel tree (*Oxydendrum arboreum*), 298, 305, 501
sotol (*Dasylirion texanum*), 337, 381
sotol (*Dasylirion wheeleri*), 169
sour gum (*Nyssa sylvatica*), 196, 298

sourwood (*Oxydendrum arboreum*), 189, 298, 300, 501
South Africa, 633, 639
South America: climatic conditions in, 23; public gardens in, 636
South Carolina, 440, 627–28, 695, 696, 717–18, 724
South Dakota, 440, 695, 696, 718, 724
Southeast region, 289–90; annuals for, 355; butterflies and wildlife, plants to attract, 360–61; flowers for cutting, 372; foliage plants for, 334–35; ground covers for, 341–42; heirloom flowers, 368; perennials for, 321–23; shrubs for, 309–10; trees for, 298–300; vines for, 347–48; winter interest, plants for, 378–79
southern bush monkeyflower (*Mimulus longiflorus*), 216
southern elderberry (*Sambucus canadensis*), 361
southern fleabane (*Erigeron quercifolius*), 361
Southern lady fern (*Athyrium asplenioides*), 188
southern magnolia (*Magnolia grandiflora*), 299
Southern maidenhair fern (*Adiantum capillus-veneris*), 188
Southern Plains region, *see* Texas and Southern Plains region
Southern red oak (*Quercus falcata*), 167
southern shield fern (*Thelypteris kunthii*), 322, 335
southern wax myrtle (*Myrica cerifera*), 313, 337
southern wisteria (*Wisteria macrostachya*), 349
southernwood (*Artemisia abrotanum*), 335, 338, 369
southern wood fern (*Thelypteris kunthii*), 343
South Korea, 635
southwestern paintbrush (*Castilleja integra*), 226, 227
sowbugs, 557
spadderdock (*Nuphar lutea* subsp. *variegata*), 200
spade, 613
spadix, 85
Spain, 632–33
spangle grass (*Chasmanthium latifolium*), 320
Spanish bayonet (*Yucca aloifolia*), 335
Spanish bluebell (*Hyacinthoides hispanica*), 320, 371

Spanish broom (*Spartium junceum*), 318
Spanish cinquefoil (*Potentilla nevadensis*), 328, 329
Spanish stopper (*Eugenia foetida*), 361
Spanish thyme (*Coleus amboinicus*), 334
*Sparaxis tricolor*, 406
*Sparganium*, 201
*Spartina: bakeri*, 199; *patens*, 362; *pectinata*, 379
Spartina grasses, 162
*Spartium junceum*, 318
spathe, 84
*Spathiphyllum*, 572
spathiphyllums (*Spathiphyllum*), 572
*Spathoglottis plicata*, 373
spatterdock (*Nuphar advena*), 197, 201
spatterdock (*Nuphar lutea* subsp. *advena*), 200
spatterdock (*Nuphar lutea* subsp. *variegata*), 200, 201
spearmint (*Mentha spicata*), 334, 370
species diversity, 112, 113, 171
species dominance, 165
species richness, 114, 116, 171
speckled alder (*Alnus incana* subsp. *rugosa*), 200
speedwell (*Veronica alpina*), 332
speedwell (*Veronica spicata*), 328, 329, 330, 375, 498
speedwells (*Veronica*), 320, 478
*Spermolepis hawaiiensis*, 129
*Sphaeralcea: ambigua*, 109, 228; *coccinea*, 208
*Sphagnum*, 166
sphagnum mosses (*Sphagnum*), 166, 475
spicebush (*Lindera benzoin*), 218, 308, 334
spicewood (*Calyptranthes pallens*), 310
spider antelope-horn milkweed (*Asclepias asperula*), 363
spider flower (*Cleome hassleriana*), 355, 356, 357, 358, 362
spider lily (*Hymenocallis*), 403–404, 589–90
spider lily (*Hymenocallis caroliniana*), 200
spider lily (*Hymenocallis liriosome*), 198
spider mites, 411, 557
spider plant (*Chlorophytum comosum*), 323, 342, 497, 571, 572
spiderwort (*Tradescantia occidentalis*), 326
spiderwort (*Tradescantia ohiensis*), 322, 326

spiderwort (*Tradescantia virginiana*), 197, 206, 323, 324, 328
spiderworts (*Tradescantia*), 207, 208
*Spigelia marilandica*, 222, 223
spike, 85
spike gayfeather (*Liatris spicata*), 470
spikenard (*Aralia racemosa*), 187, 189, 336, 362
spike rush (*Eleocharis acicularis*), 202
spike rush (*Eleocharis cellulosa*), 200
spinach (*Spinacia oleracea*), 242
*Spinacia oleracea*, 242
spine, 72, 73
spined soldier beetles, 545
spineless century plant (*Agave attenuata*), 323
spineless yucca (*Yucca elephantipes*), 335
spiny-leaved acanthus (*Acanthus spinosa*), 329
*Spiraea:*
  *densiflora*, 191
  *douglasii*, 201, 203
  *japonica*, 139
  *nipponica*, 312
  *prunifolia*, 309, 313, 314, 368
  *thunbergii*, 382, 510
  *tomentosa*, 200
  *vanhouttei*, 310
  var. *lucida*, 316
  *veitchii*, 13
  *virginiana*, 200
  x *bumalda*, 312, 316;
    'Anthony Waterer', 316
  x *cinerea* 'Grefsheim', 311
  x *van houtei*, 84, 311
spirea (*Spiraea douglasii*), 203
spirea (*Spiraea virginiana*), 200
spleenwort-leaved cyanea (*Cyanea asplenifolia*), 131
sporophyte stage of plant reproduction, 96
spotted deadnettle (*Lamium maculatum*), 344
spotted ground orchid (*Dactylorhiza maculata*), 202
spotted touch-me-not (*Impatiens capensis*), 221, 223, 225
spotted wintergreen (*Chimaphila maculata*), 188
spreading avens (*Geum radiatum*), 127
spreading cotoneaster (*Cotoneaster divaricata*), 314
spreading dogbane (*Apocynum androsaemifolium*), 108, 220, 222, 224, 225, 226

spreading fleabane (*Erigeron divergens*), 209
spreading yew (*Taxus* x *media*), 380
spring beauty (*Claytonia virginica*), 147
spring-blooming obedient plant (*Physostegia angustifolia*), 198
spring starflower (*Ipheion uniflorum*), 396
spring star flower (*Ipheion*), 583
spruces (*Picea*), 485
sprucetop grama (*Bouteloua chondroisiodes*), 209
spurge family, 56
squash (*Curcubita*), 245–46
squash vine borer, 557–58
squill (*Scilla*), 397, 583
squirrel corn (*Dicentra canadensis*), 187
squirrels, 230
Sri Lanka, 636, 639
*Stachys:*
  *bullata*, 230
  *byzantina*, 258, 328, 329, 332, 333, 335, 368, 371, 470;
    'Silver Carpet', 333, 345
  *coccinea*, 333
  *cooleyae*, 229
  *lanata*, 336
*Stachytarpheta jamaicensis*, 223, 361
staghorn ferns (*Platycerium*), 324
staghorn sumac (*Rhus typhina*), 298, 377
stamen, 87
standing cypress (*Ipomopsis rubra*), 222, 223
*Stanfordia californica*, 127
*Stanleya pinnata*, 109, 208, 209, 225, 228
*Staphylea*, 308
starbush (*Illicium floridanum*), 188
star cactus (*Astrophytum asterias*), 126
starflower (*Trientalis borealis*), 188
stargrass (*Hypoxis hirsuta*), 206
star magnolia (*Magnolia stellata*), 300, 302
star of Bethlehem (*Ornithogalum umbellatum*), 368
starry false Solomon's seal (*Smilacina stellata*), 192, 203, 330
state flowers, 695–96
state trees, 694–95
statice (*Limonium*), 470
statice (*Limonium perezii*), 375, 376
statice (*Limonium sinuatum*), 373, 376, 498

*Statice tataricum*, 374
stauntonia (*Stauntonia hexaphylla*), 351
*Stauntonia hexaphylla*, 351
Steele, Fletcher, 12
stellate plant surfaces, 94
stem, 68, 71–73; functions of, 71; modifications, 72–73
*Stenogyne: bifida*, 129; *campanulata*, 129; *cinerea*, 132; *cranwelliae*, 132; *haliakalae*, 132; *kanehoana*, 129; *oxygona*, 132; *viridis*, 132
*Stephanandra incisa*, 312; 'Crispa', 312
*Stephanomeria malheurensis*, 127
*Stephanotis floribunda*, 348, 349, 352, 591
steppe mint shrub (*Perovskia atriplicifolia*), 308
*Sternbergia*, 134, 135; *lutea*, 369
*Stewartia*, 477; *pseudocamellia*, 298, 305, 377
stewartia (*Stewartia pseudocamellia*), 298, 377
stewartias (*Stewartia*), 477
sticky leaves, 82
sticky monkeyflower (*Mimulus aurantiacus*), 216, 317, 366
stiff goldenrod (*Solidago rigida*), 208
stigma, 87, 106
stinging nettle (*Urtica dioica*), 661–62
sting lily (*Crinum americanum*), 323
*Stipa*, 170, 337; *comata*, 208; *gigantea*, 329; *pulchra*, 209; *spartea*, 207; *tenuissima*, 326, 340, 374, 380
stipule, 74
Stokes' aster (*Stokesia laevis*), 206, 320
*Stokesia laevis*, 206, 320
stolon, 72, 73
stomata, 74
stone, 91
stonecrop (*Sedum spathulifolium*), 329
stonecrop (*Sedum spectabile*), 498
stonecrop (*Sedum spurium*), 343
stonecrops (*Sedum*), 471, 478
Stone pine (*Pinus pinea*), 138
Stone's pelea (*Melicope haleakalae*), 132
strangler fig (*Ficus aurea*), 168, 198, 361
stratification, 476–77
strawberries (*Fragaria*), 72, 270, 274–76; pests of, 286
strawberry begonia (*Saxifraga stolonifera*), 335, 342

strawberry bush (*Euonymus americanus*), 188, 189, 309

strawberry tree (*Arbutus unedo*), 282, 306

strawflower (*Helichrysum bracteatum*), 371, 373, 374

stream orchid (*Epipactis gigantea*), 203

*Strelitzia reginae,* 323, 332, 373

*Streptanthus niger,* 127

*Streptocarpus,* 572, 592–93

strigose plant surfaces, 94

string lily (*Crinum americanum*), 199

striped maple (*Acer pensylvanicum*), 298, 376

*Strobilanthes dyerianus* 'Persian shield', 334

structure of plant communities, 162–65; ecotones, 164; horizontal, 164; vertical, 163–64

structure of plants, *see* plant structures and their functions

style (flower part), 87, 106

*Stylophorum diphyllum,* 188

*Styrax,* 484
  *japonica,* 298, 305, 306, 510
  *obassia,* 305
  *officinalis,* 202; var. *californicus,* 317
  *texanus,* 127

*Suaeda californica,* 127

subalpine fir (*Abies lasiocarpa*), 170

subalpine spirea (*Spirea densiflora*), 191

subspecies, naming of, 40–41

Subtropical Florida (vegetative association), 151–52, 168

Subtropical Florida region, 290–91; annuals for, 355; butterflies and wildlife, plants to attract, 361–62; flowers for cutting, 372–73; foliage plants for, 335–36; ground covers for, 342; hardwood hammock, 151, 168; mangrove swamps, 152, 168; perennials for, 323–24; pinelands, 151, 168; savannah, 151, 168; shrubs for, 310–11; swamp forests, 151, 168; trees for, 300–301; vines for, 348–49

succession, 148, 172–73, 181

succulent, 82

sugarbush (*Rhus ovata*), 318

sugar maple (*Acer saccharum*), 166, 167, 187, 189, 297, 301, 379

sulfur cinquefoil (*Potentilla recta*), 138

sulfur flower (*Eriogonum umbellatum*), 328, 329, 374

sumacs (*Rhus*), 216, 219, 309, 312, 359, 361, 362, 486

summer cypress (*Bassia scoparia*), 137

summer hyacinth (*Galtonia candicans*), 400

summer phlox (*Phlox paniculata*), 326, 327, 363, 374

summer savory (*Satureja hortensis*), 263, 360

summer snowflake (*Leucojum aestivum*), 369

summersweet (*Clethra alnifolia*), 188, 201, 310, 312, 481, 484

sundew (*Drosera rotundifolia*), 203

sundews (*Drosera*), 82, 160

sundrops (*Calylophus hartwegii*), 332, 333

sundrops (*Oenothera fruticosa* subsp. *glauca*), 368

sundrops (*Oenothera macrocarpa*), 207

sundrops (*Oenothera tetragona*), 321

sunflower (*Helianthus annuus*), 206, 355, 357, 358, 360, 371, 372, 683

sunflower (*Helianthus* x *multiflorus*), 365, 375

sunflower heliopsis (*Heliopsis helianthoides*), 321

sunflowers (*Helianthus*), 153, 169, 207, 362, 366, 367, 373

sunny areas, plantings for, *see under type of planting and region,* e.g. perennials, for the Northeast

sunrose (*Helianthemum*), 345

Sunset Publishing Corporation, 31

Surinam cherry (*Eugenia uniflora*), 522

*Swallenia alexandrae,* 127

swamp azalea (*Rhododendron viscosum*), 221, 223, 308, 309

swamp candles (*Lysimachia terrestris*), 196

swamp chestnut oak (*Quercus michauxii*), 299

swamp cypress (*Taxodium distichum*), 299

swamp dogwood (*Cornus amomum*), 360

swamp fern (*Blechnum serrulatum*), 342

swamp "honeysuckle" (*Rhododendron viscosum*), 308, 309

swamp iris (*Iris virginica*), 198

swamp lily (*Crinum americanum*), 198, 199, 323, 324

swamp mallow (*Hibiscus laevis*), 198

swamp milkweed (*Asclepias incarnata*), 196

swamp rose (*Rosa palustris*), 196, 197, 361

swamps, 161, 194

swamp saxifrage (*Saxifraga pensylvanica*), 200

swamp sunflower (*Helianthus angustifolius*), 196, 198, 206

swamp tupelo (*Nyssa sylvatica* var. *biflora*), 168

swamp white oak (*Quercus bicolor*), 200, 301, 609

Swan River daisy (*Brachycome iberidifolia*), 355, 357

sweat box, 481

sweet acacia (*Acacia farnesiana*), 307

sweet acacias (*Acacia*), 367

sweet alyssum (*Lobularia maritima*), 355, 358, 496, 498

sweet autumn clematis (*Clematis paniculata*), 349, 351

sweet autumn clematis (*Clematis terniflora*), 347, 350

sweet azalea (*Rhododendron arborescens*), 196

sweet azalea (*Rhododendron oblongifolium*), 197

sweet basil (*Ocimum basilicum*), 253, 496

sweet bay (*Laurus nobilis*), 580

sweetbay (*Magnolia virginiana*), 168, 197, 198, 201, 298, 299, 301, 359

sweet birch (*Betula lenta*), 301

sweet black-eyed Susan (*Rudbeckia subtomentosa*), 207

sweetbriar rose (*Rosa eglanteria*), 316

sweet cicely (*Myrrhis odorata*), 264, 334

sweet corn (*Zea mays*), 243

sweet fennel (*Foeniculum vulgare*), 580

sweet fern (*Comptonia peregrina*), 216, 334

sweet flag (*Acorus calamus*), 197, 200, 201, 264, 336

sweet four-o'clock (*Mirabilis longiflora*), 209

sweet gale (*Myrica gale*), 166, 200

sweet gum (*Liquidambar styraciflua*), 167, 196, 197, 299, 378

sweet hosta (*Hosta plantaginea*), 373

sweet iris (*Iris pallida*), 369

sweet marjoram (*Origanum majorana*), 260, 496

sweet mock orange (*Philadelphus coronarius*), 312

sweet mock oranges (*Philadelphus*), 509

sweet myrtle (*Myrtus communis*), 260

sweet olive (*Osmanthus fragrans*), 10

sweet pea (*Lathyrus latifolius*), 369, 373

sweetpea (*Lathyrus odoratus*), 346, 347, 350, 368, 372, 375, 498

sweet pepperbush (*Clethra alnifolia*), 108, 187, 201, 220, 222, 225, 226, 309, 365, 371

sweet scabious (*Scabiosa*), 372

sweet scabious (*Scabiosa atropurpurea*), 359

sweet shrub (*Calycanthus floridus*), 187, 188, 310

sweet shrubs (*Calycanthus*), 108, 510

sweetspire (*Itea virginica*), 197, 308, 316

sweet sultan (*Centaurea moschata*), 375

sweet violet (*Viola odorata*), 265, 371

sweet William (*Dianthus*), 496

sweet William (*Dianthus barbatus*), 367

sweet woodruff (*Galium odoratum*), 338, 341, 343, 344, 367, 370

Swiss cheese plant (*Monstera deliciosa*), 335, 349, 572

Swiss stone pine (*Pinus cembra*), 298

switchgrass (*Panicum virgatum*), 169, 198, 205, 206, 207, 362, 379

Switzerland, 633

sword fern (*Polystichum munitum*), 192

sword lily (*Gladiolus communis* subsp. *byzantinus*), 370

sycamore (*Platanus occidentalis*), 167, 378, 380

sycamore maple (*Acer pseudoplatanus*), 609

*Symphoricarpos:*
  *albus,* 221, 225, 227, 312, 315, 365, 382; var. *laevigatus,* 203
  *occidentalis,* 190
  *orbiculatus,* 221, 225, 226, 312, 343, 380
  x *chenaultii,* 315; 'Hancock', 315

*Symphytum officinale,* 256

*Symplocarpus foetidus,* 161, 197, 200, 201

*Symplocos paniculata,* 359

synapomophies, 62

syngonium (*Syngonium podophyllum*), 572
*Syngonium podophyllum*, 572
*Synthyris reniformis*, 191
*Syringa*, 50, 372, 373, 484, 509, 510, 514; *meyeri*, 311, 315; *microphylla* 'Superba', 315, 500; *reticulata*, 302, 304, 306, 377, 379, 501; *vulgaris*, 309, 311, 313, 315, 368, 369, 370, 481; x *chinensis*, 309, 312, 315, 318; x *hyacinthiflora*, 309; x *prestoniae*, 311
*Syzygium*: *jambos*, 139; *paniculatum*, 520, 536

*Tabebuia*, 300, 301; *chrysotricha*, 306
tabebuias (*Tabebuia*), 300, 301
*Tabernaemontana divaricata*, 311
*Tacca*, 323
*Tagetes*, 59, 354, 361, 372, 496, 498
  *erecta*, 355, 356, 372, 373
  *lemmoni*, 317, 339
  *lucida*, 373
  *patula*, 355, 356, 360
  *tenuifolia*, 356; 'Lemon Gem', 358
taiga, 145, 166
Takhtajan, Armen, 14–17
tall blue aster (*Aster praealtus*), 326, 363, 373
tallest plants, 66
tall fescue (*Festuca arundinacea*), 138
tall gayfeather (*Liatris scariosa*), 470
tall ironweed (*Vernonia gigantea*), 200, 206, 207
tall marigold (*Tagetes erecta*), 372
tall meadow rue (*Thalictrum dasycarpum*), 327
tall meadow rue (*Thalictrum pubescens*), 196
tall tickseed (*Coreopsis auriculata*), 221
tamarack (*Larix laricina*), 196, 200
tamarind (*Tamarindus indica*), 300
*Tamarindus indica*, 300
tamarisk (*Tamarix ramosissima*), 334
tamarisks (*Tamarix*), 139
*Tamarix*: *aphylla*, 139; *parviflora*, 139; *ramosissima*, 139, 334
Tampa blackberry (*Rubus uscetanus*), 132
*Tanacetum*:
  *balsamita*, 256
  *densum*, 340

*parthenium*, 257, 331, 369, 370; 'Aureum', 331
  *vulgare*, 139, 264–65, 498
tan oak (*Lithocarpus densiflorus*), 315
tansy (*Tanacetum vulgare*), 139, 264–65, 498
tansy aster (*Machaeranthera tanacetifolia*), 364
tap root, 70, 71
tarbush (*Flourensia cernua*), 169
tarnished plant bug, 558
taro (*Colocasia esculenta*), 333
tarragon (*Artemisia dracunculus*), 334
tartarian statice (*Statice tataricum*), 374
Tasmanian tree fern (*Dicksonia antarctica*), 339
tassel-flower (*Emilia coccinea*), 354
tassle fern (*Polystichum polyblepharum*), 383
tatarian dogwood (*Cornus alba*), 376
Tatarian maple (*Acer tataricum*), 304
tawny daylily (*Hemerocallis fulva*), 369, 370
*Taxodium*, 168; *ascendens*, 168, 200; *distichum*, 71, 161, 168, 188, 198, 299, 303, 609
taxonomy, 39
*Taxus*, 485, 514
  *baccata*, 514, 520, 660–61; 'Aurea', 383; 'Repandens', 316
  *brevifolia*, 191
  *cuspidata*, 8
  x *media*, 380, 520
tea, herbs for, 266–67
tea crabapple (*Malus hupehensis*), 306
teasel (*Dipsacus fullonum*), 383
tea tree (*Leptospermum laevigatum*), 317
techniques of gardening, 430–537. *see also* specific techniques, *e.g.* composting; mulching; soil
*Tecoma stans*, 318
teddy bear cactus (*Opuntia bigelovii*), 384
*Tellima grandiflora*, 190
temperature: fahrenheit/celsius conversion, 733–34; plant distribution and, 24–29
tendril and hook, 72, 73
Tennessee, 440, 628, 669, 695, 696, 718
Tennessee yellow-eyed grass (*Xyris tennesseensis*), 127

tent caterpillars, 558
tepal
Terlingua Creek cat's eye (*Cryptantha crassipes*), 126
ternate, 75, 76
terrariums, 597
*Tetradymia glabrata*, 169
*Tetramolopium*: *arenarium*, 129; *capillare*, 129; *conyzoides*, 132; *filiforme*, 129; *remyi*, 129; *tenerrimum*, 132
*Tetraneuris scaposa*, 326, 363, 374
*Tetraplasandra gymnocarpa*, 129
*Tetrazygia bicolor*, 311
*Teucrium*:
  *aroanum*, 340, 345
  *canadense*, 199, 327, 344; var. *canadense*, 374
  *chamaedrys*, 257, 317, 345, 485
  *fruticans*, 317; 'Azureum', 317; 'Compacta', 317
Texas, 440, 628, 669, 695, 696, 718–19
Texas and Southern Plains region, 292; annuals for, 356; butterflies and wildlife, plants to attract, 362–64; flowers for cutting, 373–74; foliage plants for, 336–37; ground covers for, 343; heirloom flowers, 369; perennials for, 325–27; shrubs for, 312–14; trees for, 302–303; vines for, 349–51; winter interest, plants for, 380–81
Texas ash (*Fraxinus texensis*), 302, 363
Texas barberry (*Mahonia swaseyi*), 313
Texas bluebells (*Eustoma grandiflora*), 356
Texas bluebonnet (*Lupinus texensis*), 208, 226, 356, 374
Texas bluestar (*Amsonia ciliata*), 326
Texas buckeye (*Aesculus arguta*), 303
Texas evening primrose (*Oenothera macrocarpa*), 328, 329
Texas greeneyes (*Berlandiera texana*), 326
Texas lantana (*Lantana camara*), 326, 477
Texas lantana (*Lantana urticoides*), 327
Texas madrone (*Arbutus texana*), 307
Texas madrone (*Arbutus xalapensis*), 384
Texas mock orange (*Philadelphus texensis*), 313

Texas mountain laurel (*Sophora secundiflora*), 307, 313, 314
Texas olive (*Cordia boissieri*), 318
Texas palm (*Sabal mexicana*), 197
Texas ranger (*Leucophyllum candidum*), 318
Texas ranger (*Leucophyllum frutescens*), 213
Texas redbud (*Cercis canadensis* var. *texensis*), 302, 303, 373
Texas redbud (*Cercis reniformis*), 380
Texas silverleaf (*Leucophyllum frutescens*), 213, 311
Texas snowbells (*Styrax texanus*), 127
Texas sophora (*Sophora affinis*), 303
Texas star hibiscus (*Hibiscus coccineus*), 198, 368, 369
Texas wild-rice (*Zizania texana*), 127
thale cress (*Arabidopsis thaliana*), 68
*Thalia*: *dealbata*, 198; *geniculata*, 200
*Thalictrum*, 336, 477
  *aquilegifolium*, 330, 335
  *cooleyi*, 127
  *dasycarpum*, 327
  *minus* 'Adiantifolium', 338
  *pubescens*, 196
  *rochebrunianum*, 320, 328, 330; 'Lavender Mist', 328
  *thalictroides*, 189, 190, 325
thatch palm (*Thrinax parviflora*), 301
thatch palm (*Thrinax radiata*), 301
*Thelesperma megapotamicum*, 371
*Thelypodium stenopetalum*, 127
*Thelypteris*: *kunthii*, 198, 322, 335, 343; *palustris*, 197, 199
Theophrastus, 12
*Thermopsis*: *caroliniana*, 322; *montana*, 208, 215; *rhombifolia* var. *montana*, 328; *villosa*, 362, 379, 498
thick-leaf phlox (*Phlox maculata*), 322
thimbleberry (*Rubus parviflorus*), 191
thin-leaf alder (*Alnus tenuifolia*), 304, 381, 382
*Thismia americana*, 132
thismia (*Thismia americana*), 132
thorn, *see* spine
thorn apple (*Datura wrightii*), 369
thornless cockspur hawthorn (*Crataegus crus-galli*), 302, 304

thornless common honey locust (*Gleditsia triacanthos*), 303–304

thoroughwort (*Eupatorium odoratum*), 224

threadgrass (*Nassella tenuissima*), 340

threadleaf coreopsis (*Coreopsis verticillata*), 321, 322, 329, 335

threadleaf groundsel (*Senecio flaccidus*), 364

threadleaf phacelia (*Phacelia linearis*), 209

threadleaf sage (*Artemisia filifolia*), 318

threatened species, 123–24

three-flowered maple (*Acer triflorum*), 305

three-flower melic (*Melica nitens*), 327, 374

three-leaf sumac (*Rhus trilobata*), 213, 314, 364

thrift (*Armeria maritima*), 366

thrift (*Armeria maritima* var. *californica*), 216

thrift (*Phlox subulata*), 341

*Thrinax: morrisii,* 301, 362; *parviflora,* 301; *radiata,* 301, 362

thrips, 411, 558

thryallis (*Galphimia gracilis*), 311

*Thuidium delicatulum,* 341

*Thuja,* 485, 514, 520; *occidentalis,* 166, 196, 200, 298, 302, 501; *plicata,* 170, 365

Thunberg, Carl Pieter, 12

*Thunbergia: alata,* 347, 348, 349, 352, 357, 498, 524; *mysorensis,* 348

Thunberg spirea (*Spiraea thunbergii*), 382, 510

thunbergia (*Thunbergia mysorensis*), 348

thyme, common, *see* common thyme

thymes (*Thymus*), 336

*Thymophylla: pentachaeta* var. *pentachaeta,* 109, 227; *tenuiloba,* 356, 358; *tephroleuca,* 127

*Thymus,* 336
  *citriodorus,* 344
  *herba-barona,* 345
  *pseudolanuginosus,* 338, 340, 471
  *serpyllum* 'Minor', 345
  *vulgaris,* 265, 338, 365, 580, 683; 'Ray Williams', 339

*Tiarella:*
  *cordifolia,* 188, 189, 190, 328; var. *collina,* 322, 323, 330
  *trifoliata,* 191
  *wherryi, see T. cordifolia* var. *collina*

*Tibouchina urvilleana,* 317

Tiburon jewelflower (*Streptanthus niger*), 127

tickseed (*Coreopsis lanceolata*), 330

tickseed (*Coreopsis leavenworthii*), 199, 223, 361

tickseed (*Coreopsis verticillata*), 470

tidy tips (*Layia platyglossa*), 358

tiger lily (*Hemerocallis fulva*), 369

tiger lily (*Lilium lancifolium*), 368, 375

*Tilia,* 477
  *americana,* 167, 189, 221, 225, 301, 304; 'Redmond', 304
  *caroliniana,* 303
  *cordata,* 301, 304, 365
  *tomentosa,* 298, 304

*Tillandsia,* 324

ti plant (*Cordyline terminalis*), 336, 497

Tippler's bane (*Coprinus atramentarius*), 664

*Tithonia rotundifolia,* 355, 358, 360, 361, 362, 372

titi (*Cyrilla racemiflora*), 161, 168, 197, 299

toadflax (*Linaria purpurea*), 331, 366, 370

toad-flax cress (*Glaucocarpum suffrutescens*), 127

toad lily (*Tricyrtis hirta*), 322, 325

toad lily (*Tricyrtis latifolia*), 325

toad lily (*Tricyrtis macropoda*), 325

toads, 231, 546

tobacco (*Nicotiana sylvestris*), 357

tobosa grass (*Hilaria mutica*), 209

tolmiea (*Tolmiea menziesii*), 203

*Tolmiea menziesii,* 203, 572

tomatoes (*Lycopersicon esculentum*), 246, 346

tomato hornworm, 558–59

tomentose plant surfaces, 94

tools, gardening, 507, 611–20; caring for, 619; *see also specific tools*

toothache tree (*Zanthoxylum clava-herculis*), 364

toothache trees (*Zanthoxylum*), 334

top-dressing, 461

topiary, 520–24

topsoil, 430; *see also* soil

torch lilies (*Kniphofia*), 329, 470

torch lily (*Kniphofia uvaria*), 332

*Torenia fournieri,* 354, 356, 496

Torrey, John, 8, 13

*Torreya taxifolia,* 127

touch-me-not (*Impatiens balsamina*), 368

tough-leaved iris (*Iris tenax*), 209

tower delphinium (*Delphinium glaucum*), 203

tower of jewels (*Echium wildpretii*), 331, 370

*Toxicodendron radicans,* 70, 168, 218, 661

toyon (*Heteromeles arbutifolia*), 191, 215, 317, 383

*Trachelospermum: asiaticum,* 343; *jasminoides,* 347, 348

*Trachymene coerulea,* 376, 471

Tradescant, John, Jr., 13

Tradescant, John, Sr., 13

*Tradescantia,* 207, 208; *occidentalis,* 326, 327; *ohiensis,* 322, 326, 327; *pallida:* 'Purple Heart', 342; *virginiana,* 197, 206, 323, 324, 328

trailing indigobush (*Dalea greggii*), 213, 345

trailing lantana (*Lantana montevidensis*), 323, 345

training and sculpting plants, 512–24; coppicing, 519; espalier, 515–17; hedges, 513–15; pleaching, 517–19; pollarding, 519–20; topiary, 520–24; *see also* pruning

transpiration, 175

transplanting, 453–56

traveler's joy (*Clematis vitalba*), 351

traveler's tree (*Ravenala madagascariensis*), 335

treasure flowers (*Gazania*), 496

tree cyanea (*Cyanea arborea*), 131

tree dahlia (*Dahlia imperialis*), 370

tree fern (*Cibotium*), 324

tree fern (*Cyathea cooperi*), 324

tree lilac (*Syringa reticulata*), 306

tree lily (*Crinum asiaticum*), 323

tree mallow (*Lavatera assurgentiflora*), 216

tree of heaven (*Ailanthus altissima*), 137, 684

tree peony (*Paeonia suffruticosa*), 477

trees, 297–307
  city, 609–10
  for coastal California, 305–306
  for containers, 500–501, 502
  drought-resistant, 470
  fertilizing of, 464
  for indoors, 576
  for the Midwest and Northern Great Plains, 301–302
  mulching of, 467–68
  for the Northeast, 297–98
  for the Pacific Northwest, 304–305

pests, common, 567

planting and care for, 297, 450–53; balled and burlapped, 452; bare-root, 452–53; tips for, 453

pruning of, *see* pruning

for the Rocky Mountain region, 303–304

selection, considerations in, 297

for the Southeast, 298–300

state, 694–95

for Subtropical Florida, 300–301

for Texas and the Southern Plains, 302–303

topping, negatives of, 505

transplanting, 453–56

vegetative propagation of, *see* vegetative propagation

for western deserts, 306–307

*Triadenum virginicum,* 196

triangle palm (*Dypsis decaryi*), 301

trichogramma wasps, 545

*Trichostema lanatum,* 317, 366, 375

*Tricyrtis: hirta,* 322, 325; *latifolia,* 325; *macropoda,* 325

trident maple (*Acer buergerianum*), 298, 536

*Trientalis borealis,* 188

trifoliate, 76

trifoliate orange (*Poncirus trifoliata*), 303, 514

*Trifolium,* 359
  *repens,* 72; f. *minus,* 683

*Trillium,* 133, 147, 188, 189; *grandiflora,* 325; *ovatum,* 191, 192; *persistens,* 127

trilliums (*Trillium*), 133, 147, 188, 189

trimezia (*Trimezia martinicensis*), 323

*Trimezia martinicensis,* 323

trimmers, 615

tripannate, 75, 76

*Triphasia trifolia,* 311

*Triphora latifolia,* 132

*Tripsacum dactyloides,* 199

*Tristania conferta,* 306

*Triteleia: laxa,* 192, 397; *uniflorum, see Ipheion uniflorum*

*Triticum aestivum,* 85

trivia, plant, 685–96

*Trollius ledebourii,* 375

*Tropaeolum,* 496; *majus,* 260–61, 356, 357, 372, 471, 498, 580; *speciosum,* 351

tropical lantern (*Lantana camara*), 356

tropical rain forests, 124, 694

tropical snowballs (*Dombeya*), 311

*Tropidocarpum capparideum,* 132
trout lily (*Erythronium americanum*), 187, 188
trowel, 613
true bulbs, 390–91
true geranium (*Geranium sanguineum*), 332
true heliotrope (*Heliotropium arborescens*), 257
true laurel (*Laurus nobilis*), 253
true myrtle (*Myrtus communis*), 339
true pennyroyal (*Mentha pulegium*), 261
trumpet creeper (*Campsis radicans*), 222, 223, 346, 347, 350, 359, 364
trumpet honeysuckle (*Lonicera sempervirens*), 109, 221, 222, 223, 226, 347, 351
trumpet vine (*Campsis*), 484
trumpet vine (*Campsis radicans*), 348, 349, 350, 351, 352, 353, 363, 367
truncate haplostachys (*Haplostachys truncata*), 131
truncate leaf base, 79
*Tsuga,* 485
    *canadensis,* 167, 316, 520, 536; 'Jeddeloh', 316
    *heterophylla,* 170, 305
    *mertensiana,* 191, 305
tuberose (*Polianthes*), 400
tuberose (*Polianthes tuberosa*), 323
tuberous begonia (*Begonia* x *tuberhybrida*), 354, 401, 590
tuberous begonias (*Begonia*), 497
tubers, 72–73, 391, 392. *see also* bulbs
tuberous root, 70, 71
*Tuctoria mucronata,* 127
tufted hair grass (*Deschampsia caespitosa*), 209
*Tulbaghia violacea,* 323, 331, 332, 339, 342, 371, 404, 589; 'Silver Lace', 331
tulip (*Tulipa*), 397–98, 582; classification of, 398
*Tulipa,* 397–98, 582; classification of, 398; *clusiana,* 369
tulip gentian (*Eustoma russellianum*), 376
tulip tree (*Liriodendron tulipifera*), 13, 167, 187, 298, 299, 305
tundra, 17, 144–45, 166; alpine, 145, 166; Arctic, 144–45, 166
tupelo (*Nyssa aquatica*), 168, 306
tupelo (*Nyssa sylvatica*), 196, 298, 609
tupelos (*Nyssa*), 161
Turkey, 639
turkey oak (*Quercus laevis*), 167

Turkish speedwell (*Veronica liwanensis*), 345
Turk's cap (*Malvaviscus arboreus var. drummondii*), 327, 363, 369
Turk's cap lily (*Lilium superbum*), 188, 196, 207, 221, 223
turmeric (*Curcuma longa*), 402, 590
turnip (*Brassica rapa*), 242
turpentine bush (*Ericameria laricifolia*), 318
turtlehead (*Chelone glabra*), 207, 221, 223
tussock sedge (*Carex stipata*), 197
tweedia (*Oxypetalum caeruleum*), 354
twinberry (*Lonicera involucrata*), 201, 315, 364
twinleaf (*Jeffersonia diphylla*), 189, 190
twinspur (*Diascia rigescens*), 375
Tygart Valley blackberry (*Rubus tygartensis*), 132
*Typha,* 195; *angustifolia,* 198; *domingensis,* 203; *latifolia,* 359

Ulmaceae, 109
*Ulmus,* 50, 364, 484; *alata,* 377, 378; *americana,* 72, 148, 303; *crassifolia,* 188, 303; *parvifolia,* 303, 307, 378, 536; *pumila,* 139; *rubra,* 303
umbel, 85
*Umbellularia californica,* 202, 339
umbrella leaf (*Darmera peltata*), 336
umbrella leaf (*Diphylleia cymosa*), 336
umbrella pine (*Sciadopitys verticillata*), 383
umbrella plant (*Peltiphyllum peltatum*), 202
umbrella tree (*Schefflera lactinophylla*), 139
understock, 489
understory, 163, 184
undulate leaf margin, 79
*Ungnadia speciosa,* 303, 380
unicorn root (*Aletris farinosa*), 198
*Uniola: latifolia, see Chasmanthium latifolium; paniculata,* 168
U.N. Food and Agriculture Organization, 124
United States:
    climate in regions of, 21–23
    ecotourism sites, 637–38
    flower shows in, 636–37
    growing regions in, 288–96. *see also individual regions*

mean, monthly, and average maximum and minimum temperatures for cities in the U.S., 25–29
public gardens in, 621–30
soil testing laboratories in, 438–41
state flowers, 695–96
state trees, 694–95
vanishing plants in, 124–30, 131–32; ranked historic, 131–32
U.S. Comprehensive Soil Classification System, 38
U.S. Department of Agriculture, 140, 639–40; Hardiness Zone Map, 31, 288; soil testing laboratories, 438–41
U.S. Environmental Protection Agency, 441
U.S. Federal Trade Commission, 135
U.S. Fish and Wildlife Service, 125, 127, 134, 640
unshearing shrubs, 523–24
ural spirea (*Sorbaria sorbifolia*), 312
*Urera kaalae,* 129
*Urtica,* 680; *dioica,* 661–62
Urticaceae, 109
ussurien pear (*Pyrus ussuriensis*), 302
Utah, 440, 628, 669, 695, 696, 719
Utah juniper (*Juniperus osteosperma*), 215
Utah serviceberry (*Amelanchier utahensis*), 367
*Utricularia,* 82, 160; *cornuta,* 199; *foliosa,* 199; *purpurea,* 199
*Uvularia,* 189; *grandiflora,* 146, 190, 325; *sessilifolia* 'Variegata', 336

*Vaccinium,* 282, 359, 481; *angustifolium,* 282, 284; *ashei,* 284, 309; *corymbosum,* 284, 308, 309; *macrocarpon,* 281, 282, 284; *ovatum,* 191, 192, 202, 316, 317, 365, 366; *oxycoccus,* 202; *parvifolium,* 191, 365; *vitis-idaea,* 281, 282, 284, 345
valerian (*Centranthus ruber*), 332, 333
valerian (*Valeriana officinalis*), 265
*Valeriana officinalis,* 265
valley cottonwood (*Populus fremontii*), 190
valley oak (*Quercus lobata*), 170, 191, 202, 306
vallota (*Cyrtanthus*), 402

valves, 91
*Vancouveria: hexandra,* 191, 192, 343, 345; *planipetala,* 191, 192
Vancouveria (*Vancouveria hexandra*), 192, 343
*Vanda,* 324
Vanhoutte spirea (*Spiraea vanhouttei*), 310
vanilla orchid (*Vanilla planifolia*), 349
*Vanilla planifolia,* 349
vanishing plants, 122–41
    crop plant diversity, threats to, 139–41
    extinct plants, 130–33
    global warming and, 122–23
    invasive species and, 123, 136–39, 152, 181
    overcollection and, 123, 133–35
    in the U.S., 124–30, 131–32; ranked historic, 131–32
variable phyllostegia (*Phyllostegia variabilis*), 132
variegated iris (*Iris pallida variegata*), 329
variety, naming of a, 40, 41
varnish leaf (*Dodonaea viscosa*), 310
vascular system of the stem, 71
*Vauquelinia californica,* 318, 384
Vaux, Calvert, 13
Vavilov, Nikolai, 119
vegetable gardens, 232–47
    city, 607–609
    in containers, 235–36, 502
    encyclopedia of vegetables, 236–46; cool-season, 236, 237–42; warm-season, 236, 242–46
    extending the season for, 233–35
    fertilizing of, 461; in containers, 236
    mulching of, 468
    pests, common, 567
    siting of, 232–33
    soil preparation, 233
vegetative associations (habitat types), 143–59; globally rare, 114; of North America, 143–59, 166–70
vegetative propagation, 480–93
    by budding, 489, 492, 493
    from cuttings, 481–86; hardwood cuttings, 484, 485; leaf cuttings, 485; root cuttings, 485–86; semihardwood cuttings, 484–85; softwood cuttings, 483–84; stem cuttings, 481, 482–83

by division, 100, 393–94, 480–81
by grafting, 489–93
by layering, 487–89
vegetative reproduction, 95
*Veitchia montgomeryana,* 301
*Veltheimia bracteata,* 407, 590
velvet ash (*Fraxinus velutina*), 216
velvetbur (*Priva portoricensis*), 132
velvet mesquite (*Prosopis velutina*), 109, 227
Venus's fly-trap (*Dionaea muscipula*), 82, 134, 170
*Veratrum: californicum,* 202, 203; *viride,* 200
verawood (*Bulnesia arborea*), 300
*Verbascum,* 486; *bombyciferum* 'Arctic Summer', 355, 358; *thapsus,* 139
*Verbena,* 226, 359, 360, 362, 363, 367, 471
*bipinnatifida,* 356, 364
*bonariensis,* 331, 332, 354, 356, 366, 371
*canadensis,* 332, 333; 'Homestead Purple', 332, 333, 345
*hastata,* 200
*maritima,* 342
*patagonica,* 356
*peruviana,* 333, 355
*rigida,* 345, 356
*riparia,* 132
*stricta,* 207
*tenuisecta,* 356
x *hybrida,* 355, 496, 498
verbena (*Glandularia gooddingii*), 108, 227
verbena (*Verbena bonariensis*), 356
verbena (*Verbena canadensis*), 332, 333
verbena (*Verbena x hybrida*), 355
verbenas (*Verbena*), 226, 359, 360, 362, 363, 367, 471
vermicomposter, 445–46
vermiculite, 475
Vermont, 440, 695, 696, 719
vernalization, 104
*Vernonia:*
*altissima, see Vernonia gigantea*
*baldwinii,* 326, 327, 363
*fasciculata,* 207
*gigantea,* 206, 207; subsp. *gigantea,* 200
*noveboracensis,* 197, 206, 359, 360
*Veronica,* 320, 325, 478
*allionii,* 344
*alpina,* 332; 'Goodness Grows', 332, 367
*liwanensis,* 345
*pectinata,* 329, 344

*repens,* 343
*spicata,* 328, 329, 330, 375, 498; 'Blue Charm', 329, 330; 'Minuet', 328; 'Red Fox', 328
'Sunny Border Blue', 320, 372
veronica (*Veronica*), 320, 325
*Veronicastrum virginicum,* 197, 207, 325, 375, 379
vertical structure of plant communities, 164–65
verticillium wilt, 563–64
vervain (*Verbena rigida*), 356
vetches (*Vicia*), 359
*Viburnum,* 50, 187, 189, 218, 477, 484, 514
*acerifolium,* 312, 359, 362
*carlesii,* 309, 316, 510
*cassinoides,* 359
*davidii,* 315
*dentatum,* 188, 196, 200, 312, 314, 359, 362
*ellipticum,* 191
*lantana,* 311, 314, 510; 'Mohican', 311
*lentago,* 281, 282, 302, 304, 362, 365, 470
*opulus,* 139; var. *americanum,* 314, 315
*plicatum,* 7; f. *tomentosum,* 316, 510; f. *tomentosum* 'Mariesii', 500; f. *tomentosum* 'Pink Beauty', 316
*prunifolium,* 281, 282, 308, 359
*rhytidophyllum:* 'Allegheny', 338
*rufidulum,* 303, 374
*sargentii,* 311, 316; 'Onondaga', 311, 316
*tinus,* 383
*trilobum,* 190, 196, 281, 282, 284, 311
x *burkwoodii,* 308, 318, 510
x *rhytidophylloides,* 314, 315; 'Allegheny', 314, 315
viburnums (*Viburnum*), 187, 189, 218, 359, 477, 484, 514
*Vicia,* 359; *faba,* 371; *menziesii,* 129
vicks plant (*Coleus amboinicus*), 334
Victorian rosemary (*Westringia rosmarinformis*), 522
*Vigna owahuensis,* 129
villous plant surfaces, 94
*Vinca:*
*major,* 139
*minor,* 139, 497; 'Variegata', 69
*rosea,* 354
vine maple (*Acer circinatum*), 190, 191, 201, 202, 305, 306

vines, 346–53; for coastal California, 352; for the Midwest and Northern Great Plains, 349; for the Northeast, 346–47; for the Pacific Northwest, 351–52; for the Rocky Mountain region, 351; for the Southeast, 347–48; for Subtropical Florida, 348–49; for Texas and the Southern Plains, 349–51; for the western deserts, 352–53
*Viola,* 146, 189, 192, 206, 355, 358, 359, 361, 380, 497, 684
*canadensis,* 190
*cornuta,* 358, 497
*floridana,* 323
*glabra,* 330
*helenae,* 129
'Imperial', 358
*labradorica,* 345
*lanaiensis,* 129
*macloskeyi,* 202
*missouriensis,* 198, 343, 380, 381
*odorata,* 265, 371; 'Royal Robe', 369
*rostrata,* 188
*tricolor,* 355, 358, 368, 371
*walteri,* 198
*wittrockiana,* 354
violas (*Viola*), 497
violet (*Viola labradorica*), 345
violets (*Viola*), 146, 189, 192, 206, 359, 497, 684
violet trumpet vine (*Clytostoma callistegioides*), 352
virginal mock orange (*Philadelphus* x *virginalis*), 312
Virginia, 440, 628, 670, 695, 696, 719–20
Virginia bluebells (*Mertensia virginica*), 188, 189, 190, 196, 325, 330, 370
Virginia blue flag (*Iris virginica*), 200, 201
Virginia chain fern (*Woodwardia virginica*), 197, 199
Virginia creeper (*Parthenocissus*), 485
Virginia creeper (*Parthenocissus quinquefolia*), 13, 199, 341, 346, 347, 348, 349, 350, 351, 362, 363
Virginia pine sida (*Sida inflexa*), 132
Virginia rose (*Rosa virginiana*), 216
Virginia stock (*Malcolmia maritima*), 357
Virginia sweetspire (*Itea virginica*), 187, 188, 310, 313, 368, 481, 484

Virginia waterleaf (*Hydrophyllum virginianum*), 189
Virginia wild rye (*Elymus virginicus*), 343
Virginia willow (*Itea virginica*), 308
Virgin Islands, 719
virgin's bower (*Clematis ligusticifolia*), 202
virgin's bower (*Clematis virginiana*), 349
viscid plant surfaces, 94
*Viscum album,* 679
*Vitex agnus-castus,* 300, 303, 307, 309, 318, 337, 359, 360, 365, 367, 484
*Vitis,* 359, 485; *californica,* 352, 366; *cinerea* var. *floridana,* 199; *coignetiae,* 351; *labrusca,* 284, 346, 352; *riparia,* 349; *rotundifolia,* 284; *vinefera* 'Purpurea', 351; *vulpina,* 350, 351, 364
Von Siebold, Philipp, 13
voodoo lily (*Amorphophallus*), 324
*Vriesea,* 342

wafer ash (*Ptelea trifoliata*), 303
wahoo (*Euonymus atropurpureus*), 313, 363
wahoo (*Euonymus occidentalis*), 191
Waiolan's cyrtandra (*Cyrtandra waiolani*), 131
*Waldsteinia fragarioides,* 343, 344
Walker's manioc (*Manihot walkerae*), 127
walking irises (*Neomarica*), 323
wallflower (*Erysimum cheiri*), 365
wallflower (*Erysimum linifolium*), 329, 332, 333, 364
wallflowers (*Cheiranthus*), 496
wall germander (*Teucrium chamaedrys*), 317
walnut (*Juglans regia*), 282
walnut family, 54
Walter's violet (*Viola walteri*), 198
wand flower (*Ixia*), 406
wand flower (*Sparaxis tricolor*), 406
*Warea amplexifolia,* 127
warty barberry (*Berberis verruculosa*), 315
Washington, 441, 628–29, 670, 695, 696, 720–21, 724
Washington, D.C., *see* District of Columbia
Washington hawthorn (*Crataegus phaenopyrum*), 305, 307

*Washingtonia filifera,* 202
water/watering, 469–74; amount to water, 472; of bonsai, 531; container plantings, 493, 497; drip irrigation, 472–73; drought-resistant plants, 470–71; guidelines for water-conserving garden, 469–72; by hand, 473; houseplants, 573; of orchids, 576–78; of roses, 412; as soil component, 431; timing of, 472; tools for, 616–18; wildlife's attraction to, 218, 230
water arum (*Calla palustris*), 201
water ash (*Ptelea trifoliata*), 190
water avens (*Geum rivale*), 108, 220, 224
water birch (*Betula fontinalis*), 190
water birch (*Betula occidentalis*), 202
water buttercup (*Ranunculus flabellaris*), 200
water cycling, 173, 175–76
water gardens, 421–29; constructing simple, 422–23; emergent plants, 426–28; floating plants, 426; moist soils, plants for, 428–29; plants for, 423–29; submerged oxygenating plants, 425–26; true aquatics, 423–24. *see also* wetland ecosystems of North America; wetland gardens
water hemlock (*Cicuta maculata*), 650
water hickory (*Carya aquatica*), 168
water hyacinth (*Eichhornia crassipes*), 137, 152
watering can, 618
water meal (*Wolffia globosa*), 66
watermelon (*Citrullus lanatus*), 244
water oak (*Quercus nigra*), 167, 197
water plantain (*Alisma plantago-aquatica*), 200, 201
water smartweed (*Polygonum amphibium*), 200
water starwort (*Callitriche hamulata*), 109
*Watsonia,* 400–401
watsonias (*Watsonia*), 400–401
wavy-leaf delissea (*Delissea sinuata*), 131
wax begonia (*Begonia semperflorens*), 354, 358
wax begonias (*Begonia*), 497
wax currant (*Ribes cereum*), 314, 364

waxflower (*Jamesia americana*), 190, 315
wax myrtle (*Myrica californica*), 202, 306, 318
wax myrtle (*Myrica cerifera*), 168, 199, 216, 309, 311, 361, 380
wax plant (*Hoya carnosa*), 572
wax plants (*Hoya*), 349
wayfaring tree (*Viburnum lantana*), 314, 510
wedding phlox (*Phlox carolina*), 498
*Wedelia acapulcensis* var. *hispida,* 327, 363
wedge-leaved button-snakeroot (*Eryngium cuneifolium*), 127
weeds, 565–68
weeping forsythia (*Forsythia suspensa*), 370
weeping wattle (*Acacia salicina*), 307
weeping willow (*Salix babylonica*), 536
weevils, 559
*Weigela,* 50 *floribunda,* 316; 'Victoria', 316 *florida,* 7, 310, 312, 317, 370, 509; 'Variegata', 500
weigela (*Weigela florida*), 7, 310, 312, 509
weights, measures, and conversions, 733–37
western azalea (*Rhododendron occidentale*), 201, 202, 316, 317
western bleeding heart (*Dicentra formosa*), 191, 192, 331
western blue flag (*Iris missouriensis*), 190, 202
western buckeye (*Aesculus glabra*), 225, 226
western burning bush (*Euonymus occidentalis*), 191, 202
western chain fern (*Woodwardia fimbriata*), 330
western chokeberry (*Prunus virginiana*), 190, 191, 304
western coltsfoot (*Petasites frigidus* var. *palmatus*), 203
western columbine (*Aquilegia formosa*), 331
Western Coniferous Forest, 156–58, 170; Northwest Coastal Forest, 156–57, 170; Rocky Mountain Forest, 157, 170; Siera Montane Forest, 157, 170; subalpine forest, 157–58, 170
western deserts, 154–58, 169–70; Chihauhuan Desert, 156, 169–70; Great Basin, 155, 169; Mojave Desert, 155, 169; Sonaran Desert, 155–56, 169–70

western deserts region, 295–96; butterflies and wildlife, plants to attract, 366–67; flowers for cutting, 375–76; foliage plants for, 339; ground covers for, 345; heirloom flowers, 371; perennials for, 332–33; shrubs for, 317–18; trees for, 306–307; vines for, 352–53; winter interest, plants for, 383–84
*Western Garden Book* (Sunset Publishing), 31
western hazelnut (*Corylus cornuta* var. *californica*), 191, 306
western hemlock (*Tsuga heterophylla*), 170, 305
western larch (*Larix occidentalis*), 190, 365
western leucothoe (*Leucothoe davisiae*), 315
western lily (*Lilium occidentale*), 127
western red baneberry (*Actaea rubra*), 190
western redbud (*Cercis occidentalis*), 306, 307, 317, 366
western red cedar (*Thuja plicata*), 170, 190, 365
western river birch (*Betula fontinalis*), 364
western river birch (*Betula occidentalis*), 314, 382
western sand cherry (*Prunus besseyi*), 315
western skunk cabbage (*Lysichiton americanum*), 202, 203, 336
western soapberry (*Sapindus drummondii*), 303
western spicebush (*Calycanthus occidentalis*), 202
western spiderwort (*Tradescantia occidentalis*), 327
western sunflower (*Helianthus occidentalis*), 208
western sweet white violet (*Viola macloskeyi*), 192
western sword fern (*Polystichum munitum*), 202, 203, 330, 339
western sycamore (*Platanus racemosa*), 202
western trillium (*Trillium ovatum*), 191, 192
western virgin's bower (*Clematis ligusticifolia*), 351
western wallflower (*Erysimum asperum*), 169, 328
western wallflower (*Erysimum capitatum*), 109, 230
western wheatgrass (*Agropyron smithii*), 169, 208
western wild ginger (*Asarum caudatum*), 191, 192

West Indian cherry (*Prunus myrtifolia*), 300
West Indian holly (*Leea coccinea*), 311
West Indian lilac (*Tetrazygia bicolor*), 311
*Westringia rosmariniformis,* 522
West Virginia, 441, 670, 695, 696, 721
wetland ecosystems of North America, 159–62, 193
wetland gardens, 192–203 invasive species and, 195, 203 maintaining, 195–203 midwest and Great Plains, 200–201 planting, 195 plants for, 196–203; California, 202–203; Northeast and Mid-Atlantic, 196–97; Pacific Northwest and Rocky Mountains, 201–202; Southeast and Deep South, 197–98; South Florida, 198–200 preparing, 194 types of wetlands, 192–94
wheatgrasses (*Agropyron*), 169
wheat (*Triticum aestivum*), 85
wheeled cultivator, 614
Wherry's foamflower, *see* foamflower (*Tiarella cordifolia* var. *collina*)
whip-and-tongue grafting, 490, 491
whisk fern (*Psilotum nudum*), 324
white alder (*Alnus rhombifolia*), 202
white ash (*Fraxinus americana*), 297, 301, 303, 363
white avens (*Geum canadense*), 343, 381
white baneberry (*Actaea pachypoda*), 187, 188, 362
whitebark pine (*Pinus albicaulis*), 170
white birch (*Betula populifolia*), 187
white bladderpod (*Lesquerella pallida*), 127
whitecane briar (*Rubus cockburnianus*), 377
white cedar (*Chamaecyparis thyoides*), 161
white cedar (*Thuja occidentalis*), 200
white clerodendron (*Clerodendrum wallichii*), 310, 311
white clover (*Trifolium repens*), 72
white fir (*Abies concolor*), 304, 514
whiteflies, 559

white fragrant water lily (*Nymphaea odorata*), 196, 197, 198, 200, 201

white fringetree (*Chionanthus virginicus*), 500

white indigo berry (*Randia aculeata*), 311

white Lady Banks rose (*Rosa banksiae* var. *banksiae*), 348

white laurel (*Rhododendron maximum*), 308

white limestone honeysuckle (*Lonicera albiflora*), 312, 313, 314, 350

white mangrove (*Laguncularia racemosa*), 168

white mulberry (*Morus alba*), 364, 470

white oak (*Quercus alba*), 167, 298, 299, 301, 304

white pine (*Pinus strobus*), 189, 298, 299, 302, 305, 359, 380

white plantain lily (*Hosta plataginea*), 367

white poplar (*Populus alba*), 138

white potato vine (*Solanum jasminoides*), 352

white prairie clover (*Dalea candidum*), 207

white rockrose (*Cistus* x *corbariensis*), 316

white sage (*Salvia apiana*), 216

white spruce (*Picea glauca*), 166, 302, 470

white stopper (*Eugenia axillaris*), 300, 361

white swamp cedar (*Thuja occidentalis*), 298

whitethorn (*Acacia constricta*), 307

white thorns (*Acacia*), 367

white-topped sedge (*Rhynchospora colorata*), 198, 199

white trillium (*Trillium grandiflora*), 325

white-tufted evening primrose (*Oenothera caepitosa*), 332

white turtlehead (*Chelone glabra*), 196

white water lily (*Nymphaea tuberosa*), 197, 201, 202, 203

white wood aster (*Aster divaricatus*), 187, 325

white yarrow (*Achillea millefolium*), 327

whorled coreopsis (*Coreopsis verticillata*), 325

wide-leaf warea (*Warea amplexifolia*), 127

*Wikstroemia: hanalei,* 132; *skottsbergiana,* 132; *villosa,* 132

wild ageratum (*Eupatorium coelestinum*), 319, 321, 327, 363

wild bee balm (*Monarda fistulosa*), 365

wild bergamot (*Monarda fistulosa*), 109, 220, 221, 222, 223, 226, 227, 229

wild bleeding heart (*Dicentra eximia*), 187, 188, 221, 223, 336

wild blue indigo (*Baptisia australis*), 372

wild buckwheats (*Eriogonum*), 209

wild calla (*Calla palustris*), 196

wild chamomile (*Matricaria recutita*), 255

wild cherry (*Prunus serotina*), 658

wild coffee (*Psychotria nervosa*), 223, 311, 361

wild columbine (*Aquilegia canadensis*), 187, 189, 206, 360

wild dilly (*Manilkara bahamensis*), 223

wild four-o'clock (*Mirabilis multiflora*), 213

wild geranium (*Geranium maculatum*), 147, 188

wild ginger (*Asarum arifolium*), 325

wild ginger (*Asarum canadense*), 325

wild ginger (*Asarum caudatum*), 345

wild ginger (*Asarum europaeum*), 325

wild ginger (*Hexastylis virginicum*), 189

wild gingers (*Asarum*), 187

wild hyacinth (*Camassia scilloides*), 326

wild hydrangea (*Hydrangea arborescens*), 310, 313

wild hyssop (*Agastache cana*), 364

wild indigos (*Baptisia*), 206

wildlife, *see* animals

wild lilac (*Ceanothus*), 317

wild lilac (*Ceanothus thyrsiflorus*), 216, 366

wild lily of the valley (*Maianthemum canadense*), 320

wild lupine (*Lupinus perennis*), 206, 207

wild marjoram (*Origanum vulgare*), 261

wild mock orange (*Philadelphus lewisii*), 315

wild oats (*Chasmanthium latifolium*), 328

wild oregano (*Monarda menthifolia*), 371

wild petunia (*Ruellia caroliniensis*), 189, 323, 361

wild petunia (*Ruellia nudiflora*), 327

wild pink (*Silene caroliniana*), 84

wild pink (*Silene regia*), 223

wild pink onion (*Allium stellatum*), 326

wild quinine (*Parthenium integrifolium*), 207

wild red columbine (*Aquilegia canadensis*), 327

wild rice (*Zizania aquatica*), 201, 359

wild roses (*Rosa*), 367

wild ryes (*Elymus*), 170, 205

wild sweet William (*Osmunda divaricata*), 320

wild tamarind (*Lysiloma latisiliquum*), 223, 300, 361

wild violets (*Viola*), 361

wild white indigos (*Baptisia*), 321

*Wilkesia hobdyi,* 129

willowleaf sunflower (*Helianthus salicifolius*), 337

willow oak (*Quercus phellos*), 197, 299

willows (*Salix*), 161, 166, 360, 484, 485

Wilson, Ernest Henry "Chinese," 12, 13

wind, pollination by, 107, 109, 177

windflower (*Anemone hybrida*), 329

windflower (*Anemone lancifolia*), 188

windflower (*Anemone*), 394, 583

window boxes, 607; plants for, 496–497

wineberry (*Rubus phoenicolasius*), 281

winecup (*Callirhoe involucrata*), 326, 327, 332, 333

winecup (*Callirhoe involucrata*), 326, 327, 332, 333

winged elm (*Ulmus alata*), 377, 378

winged euonymus (*Euonymus alatus*), 137

winged everlasting (*Ammobium alatum*), 373

winter aconite (*Eranthus hyemalis*), 376, 378

winter bergenia (*Bergenia crassifolia*), 383

winterberry holly (*Ilex verticillata*), 189, 197, 218, 311, 360, 362, 377, 379

wintercreeper (*Euonymus fortunei*), 137

winter currant (*Ribes sanguineum*), 316, 365

winter daffodils (*Sternbergia*), 134, 135

winter daphne (*Daphne odora*), 309, 317, 379

winterfat (*Krascheninnikovia lanata*), 382, 384

winter grape (*Vitis vulpina*), 350, 364

wintergreen (*Gaultheria procumbens*), 188, 334, 481

wintergreen barberry (*Berberis julianae*), 377

winter hazel (*Corylopsis glabrescens*), 378, 382

winter hazels (*Corylopsis*), 376

winter honeysuckle (*Lonicera fragrantissima*), 309, 368, 378

winter interest, plants for, 376–84

winter jasmine (*Jasminum nudiflorum*), 310, 368, 376, 378, 382

winter red-hot poker (*Veltheimia bracteata*), 407, 590

winter savory (*Satureja montana*), 263–64, 580

wintersweet (*Chimonanthus praecox*), 309, 376, 378, 382, 383

wiregrass (*Aristida stricta*), 167

wireworms, 559

Wisconsin, 441, 695, 696

wishbone flower (*Torenia fournieri*), 354, 356, 496

*Wisteria,* 347, 484, 509 *floribunda,* 13, 346, 352; 'Issai Perfect', 351 *frutescens,* 346, 347, 348, 350, 351 *macrostachya,* 349 *sinensis,* 139, 346, 350, 351, 352, 353 *venusta,* 352

wisteria (*Wisteria sinensis*), 353

wisterias (*Wisteria*), 347, 484, 509

witchhazel (*Hamamelis virginiana*), 108, 187, 189, 220, 222, 312, 378

wolfberry (*Lycium andersonii*), 227, 228

wolfberry (*Lycium scopanius*), 108

wolfberry (*Symphoricarpos occidentalis*), 190

*Wolffia,* 110; *globosa,* 66

wonga-wonga vine (*Pandorea pandorana*), 352

wood anemone (*Anemone nemorosa*), 329

woodbine (*Lonicera caprifolium*), 347

woodbine (*Parthenocissus inserta*), 352

woodfern (*Dryopteris campy-loptera*), 330
wood fern (*Dryopteris filix-mas*), 325
wood fern (*Dryopteris goldiana*), 325
wood fern (*Dryopteris marginalis*), 325
wood fern (*Dryopteris setiferum*), 325
wood ferns (*Dryopteris*), 187
woodflower (*Celosia plumosa*), 496
woodland anemones (*Anemone ranunculoides*), 325
woodland angelica (*Angelica venenosa*), 188
woodland gardens, 184–92
  maintaining, 186–92
  planting, 186
  plants for, 187–92; California, 191–92; Midwest, 189–90; Northeast and Mid-Atlantic, 187–88; Pacific Northwest, 190–91; Rocky Mountains, 190; Southeast and Deep South, 188–89
  preparing, 186
  vertical layers of, 184–86
woodland hydrangea (*Hydrangea arborescens*), 312
woodland phlox (*Phlox divaricata*), 322, 325
wood lily (*Lilium philadelphicum*), 188
wood rose (*Merremia tuberosa*), 138
wood rush (*Luzula nivea*), 328
wood sage (*Teucrium canadense*), 199, 327
wood sorrel (*Oxalis*), 404, 589
wood's rose (*Rosa woodsii*), 315, 364
*Woodwardia: areolata*, 189, 201; *fimbriata*, 202, 203, 330, 339; *virginica*, 197, 199
woolly blue curls (*Trichostema lanatum*), 317, 366, 375
woolly bur sage (*Ambrosia eriocentra*), 169
woolly butterfly bush (*Buddleia marrubiifolia*), 366
woolly thyme (*Thymus pseudolanuginosus*), 338, 340, 471
woolly veronica (*Veronica pectinata*), 329
World Conservation Monitoring Centre, 114
World Conservation Union (IUCN), 123
World Health Organization, 123

World Resources Institute, 124
World Wildlife Fund, 114, 135
worm composting, 445
wormwood (*Artemisia*), 253, 316
wormwood (*Artemisia annua*), 478
wreaths, 523, 524
Wright acacia (*Acacia wrightii*), 303, 337
Wright fishhook cactus (*Sclerocactus wrightiae*), 127
wrinkled joint-tail (*Coelorachis rugosa*), 199
*Wyethia: amplexicaulis*, 208; *mollis*, 209
Wyoming, 441, 670, 695, 696

*Xanthoceras sorbifolium*, 282, 298
*Xanthorhiza simplicissima*, 187, 309, 341, 486
*Xanthosoma violaceum*, 333
x *Chitalpa tashkentensis*, 307; 'Morning Cloud', 305
x *Cupressocyparis leylandii*, 514
*Xeranthemum annuum*, 371
xylem, 71
*Xylosma crenata*, 129
*Xyris*, 200; *iridifolia*, 197; *tennesseensis*, 127

yaku rhododendron (*Rhododendron degronianum* subsp. *yakushimanum*), 316
yam-leaved clematis (*Clematis terniflora*), 137
yams (*Dioscorea*), 71
yarrow (*Achillea clypeolata*), 329
yarrow (*Achillea filipendulina*), 324, 498
yarrow (*Achillea millefolium*), 108, 220, 221, 224, 225, 228, 229, 265, 324, 327, 330, 356, 363, 374, 382, 470
yarrow (*Achillea ptarmica*), 470
yarrow (*Achillea taygetea*), 332, 375
yarrows (*Achillea*), 321, 322, 330, 360, 365, 366, 372
yaupon (*Ilex vomitoria*), 380, 470, 520
yaupon holly (*Ilex vomitoria*), 188, 299, 312, 314, 318, 363
yellow bedstraw (*Galium verum*), 258
yellow bells (*Tecoma stans*), 318
yellow buckeye (*Aesculus octandra*), 303
yellow chestnut oak (*Quercus muehlenbergii*), 167
yellow colic root (*Aletris utea*), 199

yellow columbine (*Aquilegia chrysantha*), 327
yellow coneflower (*Ratibida pinnata*), 207
yellow-eyed grass (*Xyris iridifolia*), 197
yellow-eyed grasses (*Xyris*), 200
yellow flag (*Iris pseudacorus*), 322, 369
yellow flag iris (*Iris flavescens*), 370
yellow-flowered barrenwort (*Epimedium versicolor*), 328
yellow foxglove (*Digitalis grandiflora*), 331
yellowhorn (*Xanthoceras sorbifolium*), 282, 298
yellow iceplant (*Delosperma nubigenum*), 345
yellow jessamine (*Gelsemium sempervirens*), 341, 347, 348
yellow lady slipper (*Cypripedium calceolus* var. *pubescens*), 187
yellow lady slipper (*Cypripedium calceolus*), 179
yellow loosestrife (*Lysimachia punctata*), 321
yellow lotus (*Nelumbo lutea*), 198
yellow pond lily (*Nuphar advena*), 197, 201
yellowroot (*Xanthorhiza simplicissima*), 187, 309, 341, 486
yellow sage (*Lantana camara*), 655
yellow top (*Flaveria linearis*), 361
yellow violet (*Viola glabra*), 330
yellow water crowfoot (*Ranunculus flabellaris*), 201
yellow willow tree (*Salix lucida lasiandra*), 202
yellowwood (*Cladrastis kentukea* [*C. lutea*]), 10, 298, 306, 377, 477
yerba mansa (*Anemopsis californica*), 203, 345, 371
yews (*Taxus*), 485, 514
ylang-ylang (*Cananga odorata*), 300
*Yucca*, 169, 384
  *aloifolia*, 335
  *baccata*, 169, 215, 284
  *brevifolia*, 169, 307
  *elata*, 169, 307
  *elephantipes*, 335
  *filamentosa*, 216, 321, 486; 'Golden Sword', 334
  *glauca*, 215, 313, 337, 380, 470
  *gloriosa*, 337, 381
  *pallida*, 337
  *schidigera*, 169

  *schottii*, 215
  *smalliana*: 'Bright Edge', 334
  *whipplei*, 339, 366
yuccas (*Yucca*), 169, 384
Yukon daisy (*Chrysanthemum maximum*), 320

*Zamia: furfuracea*, 335; *integrifolia*, 342; *pumila*, 168, 335
*Zantedeschia*, 404; *aethiopica*, 375, 407, 586–87
*Zanthoxylum*, 334; *americanum*, 486; *clava-herculis*, 364; *hawaiiense*, 129
*Zauschneria californica*, 215, 331, 332
*Zea mays*, 243
zebra haworthia (*Haworthia fasciata*), 323
zebra plants (*Aphelandra*), 323
zelkova (*Zelkova serrata*), 298, 536
*Zelkova serrata*, 298, 536
Zenobia (*Zenobia pulverulenta*), 168
*Zenobia pulverulenta*, 168
*Zephyranthes*, 323, 333, 342; *atamasco*, 189; *grandiflora*, 332, 404, 587; *treatiae*, 323
zephyr lily (*Zephyranthes treatiae*), 323
zexmenia (*Wedelia acapulcensis* var. *hispida*), 327, 363
*Zigadenus elegans*, 200
zig-zag iris (*Iris brevicaulis*), 198
Zimbabwe, 634
*Zingiber: officinale*, 72, 404, 588; *zerumbet*, 323
Zingiberidae, 61
*Zinnia*, 169, 359, 496; *angustifolia*, 356, 358; *elegans*, 355, 356, 360, 361, 362, 369, 372, 373; *grandiflora*, 208, 209, 213, 215, 333
zinnia (*Zinnia angustifolia*), 358
zinnia (*Zinnia elegans*), 355, 360, 361, 369, 372, 373
zinnias (*Zinnia*), 169, 359, 496
*Zizania: aquatica*, 201, 359; *texana*, 127
*Zizia*, 362; *aptera*, 207; *aurea*, 197, 205, 207
*Ziziphus: celata*, 127; *jujuba*, 284
*Zizyphus jujuba*, 307
zonal geranium (*Pelargonium hortorum*), 356
zonal geraniums (*Pelargonium*), 496
Zuccarini, J. G., 13
*Zygopetalum*, 324